Lecture Notes in Computer Science 3746

Commenced Publication in 1973
Founding and Former Series Editors:
Gerhard Goos, Juris Hartmanis, and Jan van Leeuwen

Editorial Board

David Hutchison
  Lancaster University, UK
Takeo Kanade
  Carnegie Mellon University, Pittsburgh, PA, USA
Josef Kittler
  University of Surrey, Guildford, UK
Jon M. Kleinberg
  Cornell University, Ithaca, NY, USA
Friedemann Mattern
  ETH Zurich, Switzerland
John C. Mitchell
  Stanford University, CA, USA
Moni Naor
  Weizmann Institute of Science, Rehovot, Israel
Oscar Nierstrasz
  University of Bern, Switzerland
C. Pandu Rangan
  Indian Institute of Technology, Madras, India
Bernhard Steffen
  University of Dortmund, Germany
Madhu Sudan
  Massachusetts Institute of Technology, MA, USA
Demetri Terzopoulos
  New York University, NY, USA
Doug Tygar
  University of California, Berkeley, CA, USA
Moshe Y. Vardi
  Rice University, Houston, TX, USA
Gerhard Weikum
  Max-Planck Institute of Computer Science, Saarbruecken, Germany

Panayiotis Bozanis   Elias N. Houstis (Eds.)

Advances in Informatics

10th Panhellenic Conference on Informatics, PCI 2005
Volos, Greece, November 11-13, 2005
Proceedings

 Springer

Volume Editors

Panayiotis Bozanis
Elias N. Houstis
University of Thessaly
Department of Computer and Communication Engineering
Glavani 37, 382 21 Volos, Greece
E-mail: {pbozanis,enh}@inf.uth.gr

Library of Congress Control Number: 2005934195

CR Subject Classification (1998): H.2, D.2, I.2, I.4, C.2, K.3, E.1, F.2, H.5.2-3

ISSN   0302-9743
ISBN-10   3-540-29673-5 Springer Berlin Heidelberg New York
ISBN-13   978-3-540-29673-7 Springer Berlin Heidelberg New York

This work is subject to copyright. All rights are reserved, whether the whole or part of the material is concerned, specifically the rights of translation, reprinting, re-use of illustrations, recitation, broadcasting, reproduction on microfilms or in any other way, and storage in data banks. Duplication of this publication or parts thereof is permitted only under the provisions of the German Copyright Law of September 9, 1965, in its current version, and permission for use must always be obtained from Springer. Violations are liable to prosecution under the German Copyright Law.

Springer is a part of Springer Science+Business Media

springeronline.com

© Springer-Verlag Berlin Heidelberg 2005
Printed in Germany

Typesetting: Camera-ready by author, data conversion by Scientific Publishing Services, Chennai, India
Printed on acid-free paper   SPIN: 11573036   06/3142   5 4 3 2 1 0

Preface

This volume contains a subset of the papers presented at the 10th Panhellenic Conference in Informatics (PCI 2005), which took place at the City of Volos, Greece, during November 11-13, 2005.

After an international call for papers, 252 full papers were submitted. The number of the submitted papers constitutes a record number for the conference and reveals its growing dynamics. The authors represented universities and institutes from the following countries: Algeria, Bulgaria, China, Cyprus, Czech Republic, Finland, Greece, The Netherlands, Hungary, Italy, Japan, Korea, The Kingdom of Saudi Arabia, Lebanon, Lithuania, Malaysia, Poland, Romania, Spain, Taiwan, Turkey, Ukraine, UK, and USA. Of the submitted papers, 81 were accepted for inclusion in this volume, giving an acceptance ratio of approximately 32.2%. The papers are classified into 17 thematic sections as follows:

- data bases and data mining
- algorithms and theoretical foundations
- cultural and museum information systems
- Internet-scale software/information systems
- wearable and mobile computing
- computer graphics, virtual reality and visualization
- AI, machine learning and knowledge bases
- languages, text and speech processing
- bioinformatics
- software engineering
- educational technologies
- e-business
- computer and sensor hardware and architecture
- computer security
- image and video processing
- signal processing and telecommunications
- computer and sensor networks

We would like to thank all the Program Committee members and the additional reviewers for devoting time, effort and expertise so bounteously. Athanasios Fevgas and Manos Koutsoumbelias at the University of Thessaly deserve much credit for setting up and managing the conference website and the Web-based paper reviewing system. Furthermore, Chryssa Grantza, Mary Karasimou, Eleni Tsitsigianni and Eleni Syriveli merit special thanks for their contribution towards preparing and organizing the conference. Last but not least, we would like to express our gratitude to the Rector of the University of Thessaly, Prof. Constantinos Bagiatis for hosting the conference and to our sponsors for their generous support.

November 2005   Panayiotis Bozanis, Elias Houstis

Organization

The Greek Computer Society (EPY) and the Department of Computer and Communication Engineering of the University of Thessaly organized the 10th Panhellenic Conference on Informatics (PCI 2005) at Volos, Greece, during 11–13 of November 2005.

PCI is a biennial event established by EPY. The 1st conference took place in Athens (1984), the 2nd in Thessaloniki (1988), the 3rd in Athens (1991), the 4th in Patras (1993), the 5th in Athens (1995), the 6th in Athens (1997), the 7th in Ioannina (1999), the 8th in Nicosia/Cyprus (2001), and the 9th in Thessaloniki (2003).

Program Committee

E. Houstis, University of Thessaly, Greece (Conference and Program Chair)
G. Akrivis, University of Ioannina, Greece
S. Ananiadou, University of Salford, UK
G. Antoniou, University of Crete, Greece
Y. Apostolakis, National Center of Public Administration, Greece
A. Apostolico, Purdue University, West Lafayette, Indiana, USA
M. Attalah, Purdue University, West Lafayette, Indiana, USA
N. Avouris, University of Patras, Greece
M. Bekakos, Democritean University of Thrace, Greece
K. Berberidis, University of Patras, Greece
A. Bilas, University of Crete, Greece
P. Bozanis, University of Thessaly, Greece
P. Constantopoulos, Athens University of Economics and Business, Greece
A. Dollas, Technical University of Crete, Greece
A. Ephremides, University of Maryland, College Park, Maryland, USA
A.K. Elmagarmid, Purdue University, West Lafayette, Indiana, USA
D. Fotiadis, University of Ioannina, Greece
E. Gallopoulos, University of Patras, Greece
M. Grigoriadou, University of Athens, Greece
D. Gritzalis, Athens University of Economics and Business, Greece
A. Hatzigeorgiou, University of Pennsylvania, Philadelphia, USA
Y. Ioannidis, University of Athens, Greece
G. Karayannis, Technical University of Athens, Greece
N. Karanikolas, TEI of Athens, Greece
M. Koubarakis, Technical University of Crete, Greece
S. Lalis, University of Thessaly, Greece
P. Loucopoulos, UMIST Manchester, UK

Y. Manolopoulos, Aristotle University, Greece
V. Maglaris, Technical University of Athens, Greece
K. Margaritis, University of Macedonia, Greece
D. Metaxas, Rutgers University, New Jersey, USA
J. Michopoulos, US Naval Research Lab, USA
P. Mitkas, Aristotle University, Greece
G. Moustakidis, University of Thessaly, Greece
J. Mylopoulos, University of Toronto, Ontario, Canada
C. Nikolaou, University of Crete, Greece
S. Nikolopoulos, University of Ioannina, Greece
G. Pangalos, Aristotle University, Greece
C. Papanikolas, University of Athens, Greece
Th. Papatheodorou, University of Patras, Greece
E. Pitoura, University of Ioannina, Greece
I. Pitas, Aristotle University, Greece
D. Plexousakis, University of Crete, Greece
D. Pnevmatikatos, Technical University of Crete, Greece
N. Roussopoulos, University of Maryland, College Park, Maryland, USA
T. Sellis, National Technical University of Athens, Greece
D. Serpanos, University of Patras, Greece
N. Sidiropoulos, Technical University of Crete, Greece
D. Spinellis, Athens University of Economics and Business, Greece
P. Spirakis, University of Patras, Greece
C.D. Spyropoulos, NCSR 'DEMOKRITOS', Greece
A. Stafylopatis, National Technical University of Athens, Greece
G. Stamoulis, University of Thessaly, Greece
C. Stefanidis, University of Crete, Greece
A. Symvonis, National Technical University of Athens, Greece
W. Szpankowski, Purdue University, West Lafayette, Indiana, USA
L. Tassiulas, University of Thessaly, Greece
Y. Tollis, University of Crete, Greece
P. Triantafyllou, University of Patras, Greece
A. Tsakalidis, University of Patras, Greece
P. Tsanakas, National Technical University of Athens, Greece
E. Tsoukalas, Purdue University, West Lafayette, Indiana, USA
K. Tsouros, Aristotle University, Greece
A. Vakali, Aristotle University, Greece
E. Vavalis, University of Thessaly, Greece
I. Vlahavas, Aristotle University, Greece
S. Vosniadou, University of Athens, Greece
I. Voyiatzis, University of Athens, Greece

Organizing Committee

N. Ioannidis, Chairman of EPY, Greece
P. Bozanis, University of Thessaly, Greece
Th. Fevgas, University of Thessaly, Greece
Ch. Grantza, University of Thessaly, Greece
M. Karasimou, University of Thessaly, Greece
Y. Katopodis, Treasurer of EPY, Greece
G. Stamoulis, University of Thessaly, Greece
E. Syriveli, University of Thessaly, Greece
E. Tsitsiyanni, University of Thessaly, Greece
P. Tsompanopoulou, University of Thessaly, Greece

Additional Referees

I. Aekaterinidis
S. Asteriadis
R. Athanasios
S. Androutsellis
G. Apostolopoulos
N. Bassiliades
A. Batzios
N.P. Chrisochoides
M. Comin
C. Contopoulos
P. Cotter
T. Dalamagas
S. Daskalaki
C. Dimou
G. Dimitriou
P. Dimitropoulos
S. Diplaris
N. Evmorfopoulos
M. Flouris
K. Fotis
I. Fudos
G.F. Georgakopoulos
G. Gousios
C. Houstis
J. Iliadis
G. Kahrimanis
G. Kakarontzas
V. Kandylas

V. Karakoidas
N. Karayannidis
M. Karyda
I. Karydis
A. Karypidis
D. Katsaros
P. Katsaros
A. Kayrgiannis
D. Kehagias
P. Kikiras
S. Kokolakis
D. Kontos
S. Kopsidas
Th. Korakis
F. Koravos
M. Kordaki
C. Kotropoulos
I. Kotsia
V. Koutsonikola
I. Koutsopoulos
M. Koziri
F. Kpravos
M. Krinidis
K. Kutsikos
P. Lampsas
T. Loukopoulos
M. Marazakis
M. Megraw

S.K. Moste'faoui
Z. Nemeth
N. Nikolaidis
N. Ntarmos
N. Okazaki
G. Paliouras
G. Pallis
Y. Panagis
M. Papadopouli
C. Papamanthou
K. Patroumpas
I. Petrounias
M. Pitikakis
K. Potika
V. Prevelakis
F.E. Psomopoulos
D. Raptis
K. Raptopoulou
M. Reczko
Y. Roussos
E. Sakkopoulos
G. Sigletos
C. Sintoris
D. Sirivelis
S. Skiadopoulos
V. Solachidis
S. Souldatos
V. Stamati

K. Stefanidis
G.A. Stoica
K. Stoupa
A. Symeonidis
M. Terrovitis
T. Theodosiou
C. Tjortjis
N. Tselios

A. Tsois
K. Tsoukatos
G. Tsoumakas
T. Tzouramanis
I. Varlamis
G. Vasilakis
M. Vassilakopoulos
V. Verykios

V. Vlachos
E. Voyiatzaki
D. Xinidis
T. Zamani
T. Zenonas
D. Zisiadis

Sponsoring Institutions

University of Thessaly, Volos, Greece
Department of Computer and Communication Engineering, University of Thessaly
Foundation for Research and Technology–Hellas (FORTH), Crete, Greece
Center for Research and Technology–Hellas (CERTH), Thessaloniki, Greece

Sponsors

Alpha Bank, Greece
Microsoft Hellas, Greece
Hellenic Organization of Telecommunications (OTE S.A.), Division of Thessaly
Municipality of Volos, Greece

Table of Contents

Data Bases and Data Mining

Closest Pair Queries with Spatial Constraints
*Apostolos N. Papadopoulos, Alexandros Nanopoulos,
Yannis Manolopoulos* 1

Database Support for Data Mining Patterns
Evangelos Kotsifakos, Irene Ntoutsi, Yannis Theodoridis 14

Visual Techniques for the Interpretation of Data Mining Outcomes
*Ioannis Kopanakis, Nikos Pelekis, Haralampos Karanikas,
Thomas Mavroudkis* 25

Towards In-Situ Data Storage in Sensor Databases
*D. Zeinalipour-Yazti, V. Kalogeraki, D. Gunopulos, A. Mitra,
A. Banerjee, W. Najjar* 36

Algorithms and Theoretical Foundations

A Primal-Dual Algorithm for Online Non-uniform Facility Location
Dimitris Fotakis 47

Routing and Wavelength Assignment in Generalized WDM Tree
Networks of Bounded Degree
*Stratis Ioannidis, Christos Nomikos, Aris Pagourtzis,
Stathis Zachos* 57

Maximum-Size Subgraphs of P4-Sparse Graphs Admitting a Perfect
Matching
Stavros D. Nikolopoulos, Leonidas Palios 68

Boundary Labelling of Optimal Total Leader Length
M.A. Bekos, M. Kaufmann, K. Potika, A. Symvonis 80

Successive Linear Programs for Computing All Integral Points in a
Minkowski Sum
Ioannis Z. Emiris, Kyriakos Zervoudakis 90

The Contribution of Game Theory to Complex Systems
Spyros Kontogiannis, Paul Spirakis 101

Estimated Path Selection for the Delay Constrained Least Cost Path
Moonseong Kim, Young-Cheol Bang, Hyunseung Choo 112

Finding Feasible Pathways in Metabolic Networks
Esa Pitkänen, Ari Rantanen, Juho Rousu, Esko Ukkonen 123

One-Dimensional Finger Searching in RAM Model Revisited
S. Sioutas, Y. Panagis, E. Theodoridis, A. Tsakalidis 134

How to Place Efficiently Guards and Paintings in an Art Gallery
Christodoulos Fragoudakis, Euripides Markou, Stathis Zachos 145

Cultural and Museum Information Systems

Virtual Reality Systems and Applications: The Ancient Olympic Games
A. Gaitatzes, D. Christopoulos, G. Papaioannou 155

Auction Scenarios of Cultural Products over the WWW
D.K. Koukopoulos 166

Exploring Cultural Information Interaction Design: A Case Study of a Multimedia Exhibition Based on Customizable User Interfaces
George Pehlivanides 177

Using Personal Digital Assistants (PDAs) to Enhance the Museum Visit Experience
Katy Micha, Daphne Economou 188

Trial Evaluation of Wireless Info-communication and Indoor Location-Based Services in Exhibition Shows
Adamantia G. Pateli, George M. Giaglis, Diomidis D. Spinellis 199

Internet-Scale Software/Information Systems

Epidemic Collaborative Geocast for Reliable Segmented File Sharing in Mobile Peer-to-Peer Devices
Constandinos X. Mavromoustakis, Helen D. Karatza 211

Investigating Factors Influencing the Response Time in ASP.NET Web Applications
Ágnes Bogárdi-Mészöly, Zoltán Szitás, Tihamér Levendovszky, Hassan Charaf 223

Storing and Locating Mutable Data in Structured Peer-to-Peer Overlay Networks
  Antony Chazapis, Nectarios Koziris 234

Performance Analysis of Overheads for Matrix - Vector Multiplication in Cluster Environment
  Panagiotis D. Michailidis, Vasilis Stefanidis, Konstantinos G. Margaritis 245

Wearable and Mobile Computing

Middleware for Building Ubiquitous Computing Applications Using Distributed Objects
  Nicolas Drosos, Eleni Christopoulou, Achilles Kameas 256

A Suffix Tree Based Prediction Scheme for Pervasive Computing Environments
  Dimitrios Katsaros, Yannis Manolopoulos 267

Factors That Influence the Effectiveness of Mobile Advertising: The Case of SMS
  Dimitris Drossos, George M. Giaglis 278

An Improved HCI Method and Information Input Device Using Gloves for Wearable Computers
  Jeong-Hoon Shin, Kwang-Seok Hong 286

Computer Graphics, Virtual Reality and Visualization

Efficient Parameterization of 3D Point-Sets Using Recursive Dynamic Base Surfaces
  Philip Azariadis, Nickolas Sapidis 296

Interactive Dynamics for Large Virtual Reality Applications
  Georgios Papaioannou 307

A Pictorial Human Computer Interaction to Query Geographical Data
  Fernando Ferri, Patrizia Grifoni, Maurizio Rafanelli 317

AI, Machine Learning and Knowledge Bases

Bagging Model Trees for Classification Problems
  S.B. Kotsiantis, G.E. Tsekouras, P.E. Pintelas 328

On the Utility of Incremental Feature Selection for the Classification of
Textual Data Streams
Ioannis Katakis, Grigorios Tsoumakas, Ioannis Vlahavas 338

Gossip-Based Greedy Gaussian Mixture Learning
Nikos Vlassis, Yiannis Sfakianakis, Wojtek Kowalczyk 349

A Knowledge Management Architecture for 3D Shapes
and Applications
*Marios Pitikakis, Catherine Houstis, George Vasilakis,
Manolis Vavalis* 360

Using Fuzzy Cognitive Maps as a Decision Support System for Political
Decisions: The Case of Turkey's Integration into the European Union
Athanasios K. Tsadiras, Ilias Kouskouvelis 371

Languages, Text and Speech Processing

Developing a Robust Part-of-Speech Tagger for Biomedical Text
*Yoshimasa Tsuruoka, Yuka Tateishi, Jin-Dong Kim, Tomoko Ohta,
John McNaught, Sophia Ananiadou, Jun'ichi Tsujii* 382

Weaving Aspect-Oriented Constraints into Metamodel-Based Model
Transformation Steps
László Lengyel, Tihamér Levendovszky, Hassan Charaf 393

A Graphical Rule Authoring Tool for Defeasible Reasoning in the
Semantic Web
*Nick Bassiliades, Efstratios Kontopoulos, Grigoris Antoniou,
Ioannis Vlahavas* 404

Bioinformatics

Initial Experiences Porting a Bioinformatics Application to a Graphics
Processor
Maria Charalambous, Pedro Trancoso, Alexandros Stamatakis 415

Improving the Accuracy of Classifiers for the Prediction of Translation
Initiation Sites in Genomic Sequences
*George Tzanis, Christos Berberidis, Anastasia Alexandridou,
Ioannis Vlahavas* 426

A New Test System for Stability Measurement of Marker Gene
Selection in DNA Microarray Data Analysis
  *Fei Xiong, Heng Huang, James Ford, Fillia S. Makedon,
  Justin D. Pearlman* 437

Protein Classification with Multiple Algorithms
  *Sotiris Diplaris, Grigorios Tsoumakas, Pericles A. Mitkas,
  Ioannis Vlahavas* 448

Computational Identification of Regulatory Factors Involved in
MicroRNA Transcription
  *Praveen Sethupathy, Molly Megraw, M. Inmaculada Barrasa,
  Artemis G. Hatzigeorgiou* 457

Web Service-Enabled Grid-Based Platform for Drug Resistance
Management
  *P. Gouvas, G. Magiorkinis, A. Bouras, D. Paraskevis,
  D. Alexandrou, A. Hatzakis, G. Mentzas* 469

Software Engineering

The Enhancement of Class Model Development Using Business Rules
  Tomas Skersys, Saulius Gudas 480

Scenario Networks: Specifying User Interfaces with Extended Use Cases
  Demosthenes Akoumianakis, Ioannis Pachoulakis 491

Educational Technologies

Teaching Programming with Robots: A Case Study on Greek Secondary
Education
  Maya Sartatzemi, Vassilios Dagdilelis, Katerina Kagani 502

ASPIS: An Automated Information System for Certification and
Analysis of Examination Process
  *Georgios Katsikis, Naoum Mengoudis, Alexandros Nanopoulos,
  Ioannis Samoladas, Ioannis Stamelos* 513

Bridging the Contextual Distance: The e-CASE Learning Environment
for Supporting Students' Context Awareness
  *Stavros N. Demetriadis, Pantelis M. Papadopoulos,
  Ioannis A. Tsoukalas* 523

Designing Mobile Learning Experiences
  Giasemi Vavoula, Charalampos Karagiannidis 534

E-Business

From e-Business to Business Transformation
  Christos Nikolaou, Jakka Sairamesh, Markus Stolze 545

Trust, Privacy and Security in E-Business: Requirements and Solutions
  Sokratis K. Katsikas, Javier Lopez, Günther Pernul 548

Adoption of Enterprise Resource Planning Systems in Greece
  Angeliki K. Poulymenakou, Spiros A. Borotis 559

Supply Chains of the Future and Emerging Consumer-Based Electronic Services
  Georgios Doukidis, Katerina Pramatari 571

Computer and Sensor Hardware and Architecture

A Quantum Computer Architecture Based on Semiconductor Recombination Statistics
  D. Ntalaperas, K. Theodoropoulos, A. Tsakalidis, N. Konofaos ... 582

TSIC: Thermal Scheduling Simulator for Chip Multiprocessors
  Kyriakos Stavrou, Pedro Trancoso 589

Tuning Blocked Array Layouts to Exploit Memory Hierarchy in SMT Architectures
  Evangelia Athanasaki, Kornilios Kourtis, Nikos Anastopoulos, Nectarios Koziris 600

A Tool for Calculating Energy Consumption in Wireless Sensor Networks
  G. Dimitriou, P.K. Kikiras, G.I. Stamoulis, I.N. Avaritsiotis .. 611

Hardware Support for Multithreaded Execution of Loops with Limited Parallelism
  Georgios Dimitriou, Constantine Polychronopoulos 622

A Low – Power VLSI Architecture for Intra Prediction in H.264
  Georgios Stamoulis, Maria Koziri, Ioannis Katsavounidis, Nikolaos Bellas 633

Reducing TPC-H Benchmarking Time
  Pedro Trancoso, Christodoulos Adamou, Hans Vandierendonck 641

Computer Security

CryptoPalm: A Cryptographic Library for PalmOS
  *Georgios C. Alexandridis, Artemios G. Voyiatzis,
  Dimitrios N. Serpanos* 651

On the Importance of Header Classification in HW/SW Network
Intrusion Detection Systems
  *Vassilis Dimopoulos, Giorgos Papadopoulos,
  Dionisios Pnevmatikatos* 661

NGCE - Network Graphs for Computer Epidemiologists
  *Vasileios Vlachos, Vassiliki Vouzi, Damianos Chatziantoniou,
  Diomidis Spinellis* 672

Workflow Based Security Incident Management
  Meletis A. Belsis, Alkis Simitsis, Stefanos Gritzalis 684

A Deterministic Approach to Balancedness and Run Quantification in
Pseudorandom Pattern Generators
  Amparo Fúster-Sabater, Pino Caballero-Gil 695

Image and Video Processing

Protecting Intellectual Property Rights and the JPEG2000 Coding
Standard
  B. Vassiliadis, V. Fotopoulos, A. Ilias, A.N. Skodras 705

Computationally Efficient Image Mosaicing Using Spanning Tree
Representations
  Nikos Nikolaidis, Ioannis Pitas 716

An MPEG-7 Based Description Scheme for Video Analysis Using
Anthropocentric Video Content Descriptors
  N. Vretos, V. Solachidis, I. Pitas 725

Detecting Abnormalities in Capsule Endoscopic Images by Textural
Description and Neural Networks
  V.S. Kodogiannis, E. Wadge, M. Boulougoura, K. Christou 735

Unsupervised Learning of Multiple Aspects of Moving Objects from Video
Michalis K. Titsias, Christopher K.I. Williams 746

The Feature Vector Selection for Robust Multiple Face Detection
Seung-Ik Lee, Duk-Gyoo Kim 757

Signal Processing and Telecommunications

A Low Complexity Turbo Equalizer
Dimitris Ampeliotis, Kostas Berberidis 765

Bit Error Rate Calculation for DS-CDMA Systems with WDS in the Presence of Rayleigh Fading and Power-Control Error
Ibrahim Develi, Cebrail Ciftlikli, Aytekin Bagis 776

Multivariate AR Model Order Estimation with Unknown Process Order
Stylianos Sp. Pappas, Assimakis K. Leros, Sokratis K. Katsikas 787

Cortical Lateralization Analysis by Kolmogorov Entropy of EEG
Lianyi Zhang, Chongxun Zheng 798

Computer and Sensor Networks

Source-Based Minimum Cost Multicasting: Intermediate-Node Selection with Potentially Low Cost
Gunu Jho, Moonseong Kim, Hyunseung Choo 808

Efficient Active Clustering of Mobile Ad-Hoc Networks
Damianos Gavalas, Grammati Pantziou, Charalampos Konstantopoulos, Basilis Mamalis 820

Evaluation of Audio Streaming in Secure Wireless Access Network
Binod Vaidya, JongWoo Kim, JaeYoung Pyun, JongAn Park, SeungJo Han 828

Reliable Transmission Using Intermediate Sink or Source Nodes in Sensor Networks
Bo-Hyung Lee, Hyung-Wook Yoon, Jongho Park, Min Young Chung, Tae-Jin Lee 839

A Novel Heuristic Routing Algorithm Using Simulated Annealing in Ad Hoc Networks
Lianggui Liu, Guangzeng Feng 849

Balancing HTTP Traffic Using Dynamically Updated Weights, an Implementation Approach
   A. Karakos, D. Patsas, A. Bornea, S. Kontogiannis 858

Industrial Exhibition Paper

A Review of Microsoft Products, Strategy and Technologies
   Fotis Draganidis 869

Author Index 871

Closest Pair Queries with Spatial Constraints*

Apostolos N. Papadopoulos, Alexandros Nanopoulos, and Yannis Manolopoulos

Department of Informatics, Aristotle University, GR-54124 Thessaloniki, Greece
{apostol, alex, manolopo}@delab.csd.auth.gr

Abstract. Given two datasets $\mathcal{D}_A$ and $\mathcal{D}_B$ the closest-pair query (CPQ) retrieves the pair (a,b), where $a \in \mathcal{D}_A$ and $b \in \mathcal{D}_B$, having the smallest distance between all pairs of objects. An extension to this problem is to generate the k closest pairs of objects (k-CPQ). In several cases spatial constraints are applied, and object pairs that are retrieved must also satisfy these constraints. Although the application of spatial constraints seems natural towards a more focused search, only recently they have been studied for the CPQ problem with the restriction that $\mathcal{D}_A = \mathcal{D}_B$. In this work we focus on constrained closest-pair queries (CCPQ), between two distinct datasets $\mathcal{D}_A$ and $\mathcal{D}_B$, where objects from $\mathcal{D}_A$ must be enclosed by a spatial region R. A new algorithm is proposed, which is compared with a modified closest-pair algorithm. The experimental results demonstrate that the proposed approach is superior with respect to CPU and I/O costs.

1 Introduction

Research in spatial and spatiotemporal databases is very active in the last twenty years. The literature is rich in efficient access methods, query processing techniques, cost models and query languages, providing the necessary components to build high quality systems. The majority of research efforts aiming at efficient query processing in spatial and spatiotemporal databases, concentrated in the following significant query types: range query, k nearest-neighbor query, spatial join query and closes-pair query. t is a combination of spatial join and nearest neighbor queries. Given two spatial datasets $\mathcal{D}_A$ and $\mathcal{D}_B$, the output of a k closest-pair query is composed of k pairs o_a, o_b such that $o_a \in \mathcal{D}_A$, $o_b \in \mathcal{D}_B$. These k pair-wise distances are the smallest amongst all possible object pairs.

Spatial joins and closest-pair queries require significant computation effort and many more I/O operations than simpler queries like range and nearest neighbors. Moreover, queries involving more than one datasets are very frequent in real applications, and therefore, special attention has been given by the research community [11,5,6,14,17,3].

---

* Research supported by ARCHIMEDES project 2.2.14, "Management of Moving Objects and the WWW", of the Technological Educational Institute of Thessaloniki (EPEAEK II), and by the 2003-2005 Serbian-Greek joint research and technology program.

In this study, we focus on the k-Semi-Closest-Pair Query (k-SCPQ), and more specifically, on an interesting variation which is derived by applying spatial constraints in the objects of the first dataset. We term this query k-Constrained-Semi-Closest-Pair Query (k-CSCPQ). In the k-SCPQ query we require k object pairs (o_a, o_b) with $o_a \in \mathcal{D}_A$ and $o_b \in \mathcal{D}_B$ having the smallest distances between datasets $\mathcal{D}_A$ and $\mathcal{D}_B$ such that each object o_a appears at most once in the final result. In the k-CSCPQ query, an additional spatial constraint is applied, requiring that each object $o_a \in \mathcal{D}_A$ that appears in the final result must be enclosed by a spatial region R[1]. An example is given in Figure 1, illustrating the results of the aforementioned CPQ variations for $k = 2$.

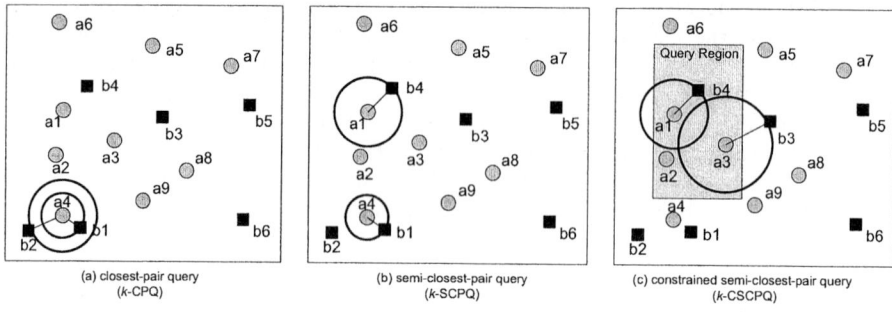

Fig. 1. Results of CPQ variations for $k=2$

Distance-based queries, such as nearest-neighbor and closest-pair, play a very important role in spatial and spatiotemporal databases. Apart from the fact that these queries compose an important family of queries on their own, they can be used as fundamental building blocks for more complex operations, such as data mining algorithms. Several data mining tasks require the combination of two datasets in order to draw conclusions. A clustering algorithm based on closest pairs has been proposed in [12]. In [2,3] the authors study applications of the k-NN join operation to knowledge discovery, which is a direct extension of the k-semi-closest-pair query. More specifically, the authors discuss the application of k-NN join to clustering, classification and sampling tasks in data mining operations, and they illustrate how these tasks can be performed more efficiently. In [19] it is reported that the k-NN join can also be used to improve the performance of LOF algorithm, which is used for outlier detection in a single dataset [4], and also to improve the performance of the Chameleon clustering algorithm [10]. The importance of dynamic closest-pair queries to hierarchical clustering has been studied in [8]. In the same paper the authors discuss the application of CPQ to other domains such as the Traveling Salesman Problem (TSP), non-hierarchical clustering, and greedy matching, to name a few.

---

[1] For the rest of the study we assume that both datasets $\mathcal{D}_A$ and $\mathcal{D}_B$ contain multi-dimensional points. The methods are also applicable for non-point objects.

Taking into consideration the significance of distance-based queries in several disciplines, in this work we focus on the semi-closest-pair query with spatial constraints and study efficient algorithms for its computation. The motivation behind the current study is the fact that in many realistic cases the user focuses on a portion of the dataspace rather than in the whole dataspace. Although this sounds natural, specifically for large dataspaces and large populations, there is limited research work towards constrained spatial query processing. Moreover, spatial constraints may be applied implicitly by the system as a result of user query. For example, consider the query: "Find the three closest parks from all hotels located at the center of the city". The hotels located at the city center are usually enclosed by a polygonal region which determines the center of the city. Finally, many complex algorithms first perform a partitioning of the dataspace into cells, and then operate in each cell separately. Therefore, our methods can be used as of-the-self components of more complex operations, in order to speed up specific algorithmic steps.

The rest of the article is organized as follows. Section 2 presents the appropriate background, the related work and the main contributions of the paper. The query processing algorithms are presented and studied in Section 3. Section 4 contains the performance evaluation results, whereas Section 5 concludes the work and motivates for further research in the area.

2 Problem Definition and Related Work

Let $\mathcal{D}_A$ and $\mathcal{D}_B$ be two datasets of multi-dimensional points, each indexed by means of a spatial access method. We assume that the R*-tree [1] is used to index each dataset, although other variations could be applied equally well. Dataset $\mathcal{D}_A$ is called the *primary dataset*, whereas dataset $\mathcal{D}_B$ is called the *reference dataset*. We are interested in determining the k objects from $\mathcal{D}_A$ that are closer to objects from the reference dataset $\mathcal{D}_B$, under the constraint that all points from $\mathcal{D}_A$ that are part of the answer must be enclosed by a spatial region R_q. If the number of objects from $\mathcal{D}_A$ contained in R is less than k, then all objects are reported, ranked by their NN distance to the reference dataset $\mathcal{D}_B$. For simplicity and clarity we assume that R_q is a rectangular region, although arbitrary query regions can be used as well.

The first method towards processing of constrained closest-pair queries has been proposed in [13], where it is assumed that $\mathcal{D}_A = \mathcal{D}_B$. Moreover, the authors assume that in order for a pair (o_1, o_2) to be part of the answer, both o_1 and o_2 must be enclosed by the query region R. In order to facilitate efficient query processing, the R-tree is used to index the dataset. The proposed method augments the R-tree nodes with auxiliary information concerning the closest pair of objects that resides in each tree branch. This information is adjusted accordingly during insertions and deletions. Performance evaluation results have shown that the proposed technique outperforms by factors existing techniques based on closest pairs. This method can not be applied in our case, since we assume that datasets $\mathcal{D}_A$ and $\mathcal{D}_B$ are distinct. This method can only be applied if for every pair of datasets we maintain a different index structure, which is not considered a feasible approach.

In [16] the authors study the processing of closest-pair queries by applying cardinality constraints on the result. For example, the query "determine objects from $\mathcal{D}_A$ such that they are close to at least 5 objects from $\mathcal{D}_B$", involves a distance join (closest-pair) and a cardinality constraint on the result. However, we are interested in applying spatial constraints on the objects of $\mathcal{D}_A$.

Research closely related to ours include the work in [20] where the All-Semi-Closest-Pair query is addressed, under the term All-Nearest-Neighbors. The authors propose a method to compute the nearest neighbor of each point in dataset $\mathcal{D}_A$, with respect to dataset $\mathcal{D}_B$. They also provide a solution in the case where there are no available indexing mechanisms for the two datasets. The fundamental characteristics of these methods is the application of batching operations, aiming at reduced processing costs. Although the proposed methods are focused on evaluating the nearest-neighbor for every object in $\mathcal{D}_A$, they can be modified towards reporting the best k answers, under spatial constraints. The details of the algorithms are given in the subsequent section.

Methods proposed for Closest-Pair queries [9,6,7] can be used in our case by applying the necessary modifications in order to: 1) process Semi-Closest-Pair queries and 2) support spatial constraints. Algorithms for Closest-Pair queries are either recursive or iterative and work by synchronized traversals of the two index structures. Performance is improved by applying plane-sweeping techniques and bidirectional node expansion [15]. The details of the Closest-Pair algorithm, which is used for comparison purposes, are given in the subsequent section.

3 Processing Techniques

3.1 The Semi Closest-Pair Algorithm (SCP)

Algorithms that process k-CPQ queries can be adapted in order to answer k-CSCPQ queries. In this study, we consider a heap-based algorithm proposed in [7], enhanced with plane-sweeping optimizations [15]. Moreover, the algorithm is enhanced with batching capabilities, towards reduced processing costs. Algorithm SCP is based on a bidirectional expansion of internal nodes which has been proposed in [15], in contrast to a unidirectional expansion [9]. A minheap data structure is used as a priority queue to keep pairs of entries of T_A and T_B, which are promising to contain relevant object pairs from the two datasets. The minheap structure stores pairs of internal nodes only, keeping the size of the minheap at reduced levels. In addition, a maxheap data structure maintains the best k distances determined so far.

Algorithm SCP continuously retrieves pairs of entries from the minheap, until the priority of the minheap top is greater than the current d_k. Let (E_A, E_B) be the next pair of entries retrieved by the minheap. We distinguish the following cases:

- Both E_A and E_B correspond to internal nodes: in this case a bidirectional expansion is applied in order to retrieve the sets of MBRs of the two nodes

pointed by E_A and E_B respectively. Then, plane-sweeping is applied in order to determine new entry pairs, which are either rejected or inserted into minheap according to their distance.
- Both E_A and E_B correspond to leaf nodes: in this case a batch operation is executed, by means of the plane-sweep technique, in order to determine object pairs (a_i, b_j) of the two datasets that may contribute to the final answer. If $dist(a_i, b_j) > d_k$ then the pair is rejected. If $dist(a_i, b_j) \leq d_k$ and object a_i does not exist in maxheap, then the pair (a_i, b_j) is inserted into maxheap. However, if a_i is already in maxheap, we check if the new distance is smaller than the already recorded one. In this case, the distance of a_i is replaced in maxheap.
- One of the two entries corresponds to an internal node, and the other entry corresponds to a leaf node: in this case a unidirectional expansion is performed only for the entry which corresponds to an internal node. New entry pairs are either rejected or inserted into minheap.

In summary, the SCP algorithm can be used for k-CSCPQ query processing, provided that:

- a node of T_A is inspected only if its MBR intersects the query region R and
- during plane-sweeping operations each object from $\mathcal{D}_A$ is considered only once.

3.2 The Proposed Approach (The Probe-and-Search Algorithm)

In this section, we present a new algorithm for answering k-CSCPQ queries, when the two datasets under consideration are indexed by means of R*-trees or similar access methods. We would like to devise an algorithm having the following properties:

- The algorithm should have reduced CPU cost, which is enabled by the use of batching operations,
- Buffer exploitation should be increased introducing as few buffer misses as possible,
- The working memory of the algorithm should be low, and
- Pruning of T_A should be enforced in order to avoid inspecting all tree nodes intersected by R.

In the sequel we present in detail the proposed algorithm, which is termed Probe-and-Search (PaS). It consists of three stages: a) searching the primary tree, b) pruning the primary tree and c) performing batching operations in the reference tree.

Searching the Primary Tree. Given the number of requested answers k and the query region R, the algorithm begins its execution by inspecting relevant nodes of the primary dataset, which is organized by T_A. Instead of using a recursive method to traverse the tree, a heap structure is used to accommodate relevant entries. The heap priority is defined by the Hilbert value of the MBR centroid of every inspected node entry, as it has been used in [20]. We call this structure *HilbertMinHeap*. When a new node of T_A is visited, we check which of its entries are intersected by the query region R. Then, the Hilbert value of each of these entries is calculated, and the pair (entry, HilbertValue) is inserted into *HilbertMinHeap*.

The use of the Hilbert value guarantees that locality of references is preserved, and therefore, nodes that are located close in the native space are likely to be accessed sequentially. The search is continued until a node is reached which resides in the level right above the leaf level.

Pruning the Primary Tree. In order to prune the primary tree T_A, the PaS algorithm should be able to determine whether a node of T_A cannot contribute to the result. Let N_A be a node examined by PaS (i.e., it has been inserted in *HilbertMinHeap*). For each N_A's entry, $N_A[i]$, PaS checks if there is an intersection of $N_A[i]$ with R. If this is true, then a 1-NN query is issued to T_B and the minimum distance *mindist* between $N_A[i].mbr$ and an object in T_B is determined. If the calculated *mindist* is larger than the current k-th best distance, then it is easy to see that the further examination of $N_A[i]$ can be pruned, because $N_A[i]$ will not contain any object whose distance from any object of T_B will be less than the currently found k-th distance. In this case, we avoid the access to the corresponding page and the examination of $N_A[i]$'s entries.

Since PaS uses the aforementioned pruning criterion, we would like to prioritize the examination of the entries of T_A according to their *mindist* distance from the entries of T_B. This way, the most promising entries of T_A are going to be examined first. Thus, the current k-th best distance will be accordingly small so as to prune many entries of T_A and the final result will be shaped more quickly. PaS performs the required prioritization by placing the examined entries of T_A into a second heap structure. An entry in this heap comprises a pair $(N_A[i], mindist)$, where *mindist* is the result of the 1-NN query issued to T_B by $N_A[i].mbr$. The entries in this heap are maintained according to their *mindist* values.

It is easy to contemplate that the closer to the root of T_A a node is, the smaller its corresponding *mindist* from T_B will be. Therefore, the nodes of the upper levels of T_A are more difficult to be pruned. Moreover, we would spend considerable cost to issue 1-NN queries for such nodes, which will not payoff. For this reason, PaS uses the prioritization scheme only for the leaves of T_A. Since the number of leaves in the R*-tree is much larger than the number of internal nodes, the expected gain is still significant. Consequently, once an internal node $N_A[i]$, which is a father of a leaf, is inspected (i.e., was previously an entry in the *HilbertMinHeap*), then for all its children (leaves) $N_A[i]$ that intersect query region R, a 1-NN query is issued against T_B. As a result, pairs of the form $(N_A[i], mindist)$ are inserted into the second priority heap, which is denoted as *LeafMinHeap*. Evidently, a leaf node never enters the *HilbertMinHeap*, thus no duplication incurs. The entries of *LeafMinHeap* are examined (in a batch mode) in the sequel, in order to find those that will contribute to the final result. This issue is considered in more detail in the following subsection.

Figure 2 illustrates a schematic description of the searching and pruning operations of the PaS algorithm. The figure also illustrates the separate parts of the tree, which populate the different heap structures that are maintained.

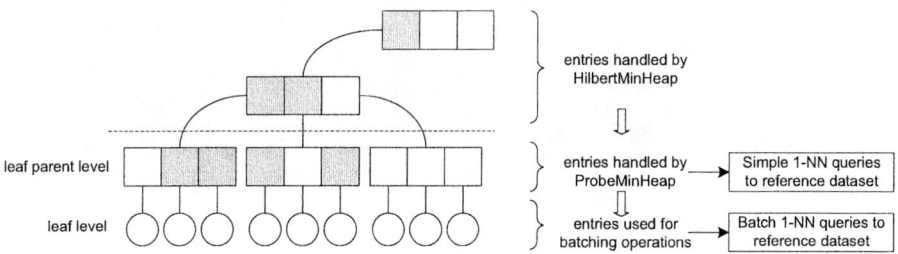

Fig. 2. Bird's eye view of the Probe-and-Search algorithm

Enhancing the Algorithm with Batching Capabilities. Pruning the primary tree is one direction towards reducing the number of distance calculations. Another direction to achieve this, is to apply batching operations during query processing. The basic idea is to perform multiple nearest-neighbor queries for a set of data objects, instead of calculating the nearest neighbor for each object separately.

The BNN algorithm which has been proposed in [20] uses batching operations in an aggressive way, in order to avoid individual 1-NN queries as much as possible. Recall that BNN focuses on All-NN queries instead of k-NN queries. Therefore, the size of each chunk can be quite large resulting in increased CPU and I/O costs. This effect is stronger when the primary dataset $\mathcal{D}_\mathcal{A}$ is dense in comparison to $\mathcal{D}_\mathcal{B}$. In this case, a large number of leaf nodes of T_A participate in the formulation of each chunk before the area criterion is violated.

Instead of relying on when the area criterion will be violated, we enforce that batching is performed for objects contained in a single leaf of T_A. The relevant leaf entries that may change the answer set are accommodated in the ProbeMinHeap structure. These entries are inspected one-by-one by removing the top of the heap. For each such entry $N_A[i]$, the following operations are applied:

- The leaf node L pointed by $N_A[i].ptr$ is read into main memory.
- The MBR of all objects in L enclosed by R is calculated.
- If the area of the MBR is less than or equal to the average leaf area of all leaf nodes of T_B, a batch query is issued to T_B.
- Otherwise, objects are distributed to several chunks, and for each chunk a separate batch query is issued.

Each batch query is executed recursively by traversing nodes of T_B with respect to the *mindist* distance between the MBR of the chunk and the MBR of each visited node entry. Each time a leaf node is reached, the pairwise distances

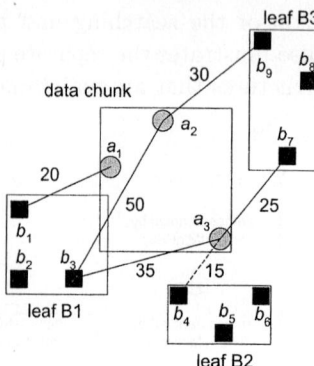

Fig. 3. Batch query processing by means of the *BatchHashTable* structure

are calculated by using a plane-sweep technique, in order to avoid checking all possible pairs of objects. A hash table is maintained, called *BatchHashTable*, which stores the currently best distance for each object in the chunk. When another leaf node of T_B is reached, a test is performed in order to determine if there is an object in the new leaf that change the best answers determined so far. Figure 3 illustrates an example of a batch query and the contents of the *BatchHashTable* structure after each leaf inspection. The best answers after each leaf process are shown shaded in the hash table.

The number of *BatchHashTable* elements is bounded by the maximum number of entries that can be accommodated in a leaf node, and therefore, its size is very small. After the completion of the batch query execution, the contents of *BatchHashTable* are merged with the globally determined k best answers, which are maintained in a heap structure, called *AnswersMaxHeap*. This structure accommodates the best k answers during the whole process.

4 Performance Study

4.1 Preliminaries

The algorithms PaS and SCP have been implemented in C++, and the experiments have been conducted on a Windows XP machine with Pentium IV at 2.8Ghz. The real datasets used for the experimentation are taken from TIGER [18]. The LA1 dataset contains 131,461 centroids of MBRs corresponding to roads in Los Angeles. Dataset LA2 contains 128,971 centroids of MBRs corresponding to rivers and railways in Los Angeles. Finally, dataset CA contains 1,300,000 centroids of road MBRs of California. These datasets are available from http://www.rtreeportal.org/spatial.html. In addition to the above datasets, we also use uniformly distributed points. All datasets are normalized to a square, where each dimension takes real values between 0 and 1023.

LA1 and LA2 are quite similar, having similar data distributions and populations. On the other hand, dataset CA shows completely different data distribution and population. The selection of these datasets have been performed in order to test the performance of the algorithms in cases where the primary and reference dataset follow the same distribution. In the sequel, we investigate the performance of the algorithms for three cases: 1) $\mathcal{D}_\mathcal{A}$=LA1 and $\mathcal{D}_\mathcal{B}$=CA, 2) $\mathcal{D}_\mathcal{A}$=CA and $\mathcal{D}_\mathcal{B}$=LA1, and 3) $\mathcal{D}_\mathcal{A}$=LA1 and $\mathcal{D}_\mathcal{B}$=LA2. The aforementioned cases correspond to the three different possibilities regarding the relative size between the primary and the reference dataset. In particular, in case (1) the primary dataset is significantly smaller than the reference dataset, in case (2) the primary dataset is significantly larger than the reference dataset, and in case (3) the primary and the reference datasets are of about the same size. In most application domains, the reference objects are much less than the objects in the primary dataset (e.g., authoritative sites are much smaller than domestic buildings) Therefore, (2) is the case of interest for the majority of application domains. Case (3) can also be possible in some applications. In contrast, one should hardly expect an application domain for case (1). Nevertheless, for purposes of comparison, we also consider this case, in order to examine the relative performance of the examined methods in all possible cases.

In each experiment, 100 square-like queries are executed following the distribution of the primary dataset $\mathcal{D}_\mathcal{A}$. CPU and I/O time correspond to average values per query. The disk page size is set to 1024 bytes for all experiments conducted. An LRU page replacement policy is assumed for the buffer operation. The capacity of the buffer is measured as a percentage of the database size. In the sequel we present the results for different parameter values, i.e., the number of answers, the area of the query region, the size of the buffer, and the population of the datasets. Moreover, a discussion of the memory requirements of all methods is performed in a separate section.

4.2 Performance vs Different Parameter Values

In this section we present representative experimental results which demonstrate the performance of each method under different settings.

We start by first testing case (1), that is, when the primary dataset is significantly smaller than the reference dataset. As mentioned, this case is only examined for purposes of comparison, since it does not constitute a case of interest for the vast majority of applications. Figure 4 illustrates the performance of the algorithms when $\mathcal{D}_\mathcal{A}$=LA1 and $\mathcal{D}_\mathcal{B}$=CA, by varying the number of answers k. Evidently, $\mathcal{D}_\mathcal{B}$ contains many more objects than $\mathcal{D}_\mathcal{A}$. The query region is set to 1% of the dataspace area, the buffer capacity is 10% of the total number of pages of both trees.

PaS manages to keep the CPU cost at low levels for all values of k. With respect to I/O cost, which is depicted in Figure 4(b), the situation is quite different.

The I/O cost of PaS is maintained at low levels, especially for k greater than 10. It is evident that PaS outperforms SCP Therefore, even for the extreme case when the reference dataset is significantly larger than the primary, the performance of PaS is reasonably good, whereas SCP is not able to maintain a good performance.

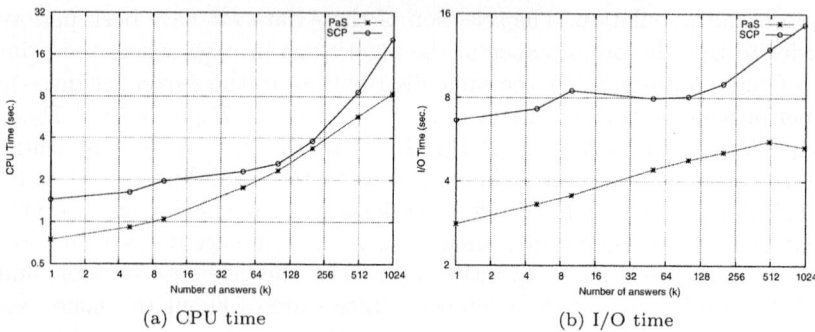

Fig. 4. CPU and I/O time vs k for $\mathcal{D}_A$=LA1 and $\mathcal{D}_B$=CA (logarithmic scales)

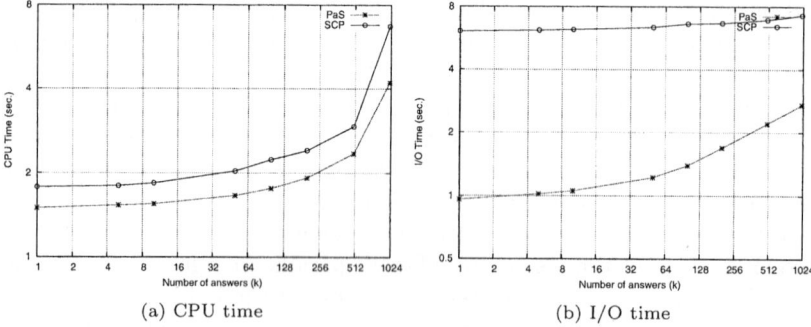

Fig. 5. CPU and I/O time vs k for $\mathcal{D}_A$=CA and $\mathcal{D}_B$=LA1 (logarithmic scales)

Figure 5 depicts the performance of the algorithms vs k when $\mathcal{D}_A$=CA and $\mathcal{D}_B$=LA1. Again, the query region is set to 1% of the dataspace area and the buffer capacity is 10% of the total number of pages of both trees. It is evident that algorithm PaS shows the best performance over the other methods. PaS is capable of pruning several nodes due to the probes performed on the reference tree. Page requests are absorbed by the buffer, resulting in significantly less I/O time with respect to SCP.

Figure 6 illustrates the performance of the algorithms under study for $\mathcal{D}_A$=LA1 and $\mathcal{D}_B$=LA2. These datasets follow similar distributions and they have similar populations. The query region is set to 1% of the dataspace area and the buffer capacity is 10% of the total number of pages of both trees. Again, PaS shows the best performance with respect to CPU time. With respect to the overall performance of the methods, PaS shows the best performance.

Figure 7 depicts the total running time of all methods, for all three dataset combinations, vs the area of the query region. The number of answers k is set to 100, whereas the buffer capacity is set to 10% of the total number of pages of both trees. Evidently, PaS shows the best performance and outperforms SCP significantly.

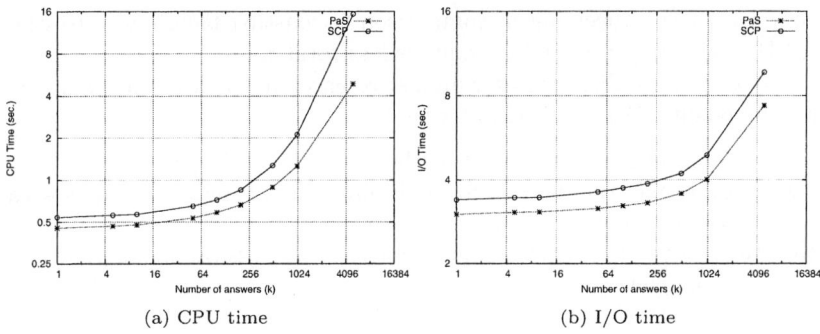

Fig. 6. CPU and I/O time vs k for $\mathcal{D}_\mathcal{A}$=LA1 and $\mathcal{D}_\mathcal{B}$=LA2 (logarithmic scales)

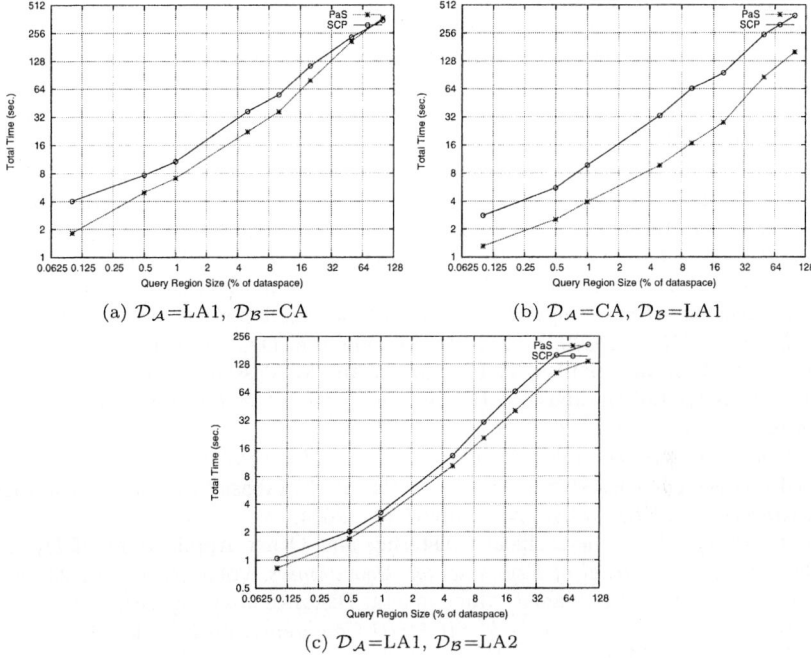

Fig. 7. Total time vs query region size (logarithmic scales)

5 Concluding Remarks and Further Research

Distance based queries are considered very important in several domains, such as spatial databases, spatiotemporal databases, data mining tasks, to name a few. An important family of distance-based queries involve the association of two or more datasets. In this paper, we focused on the k-Semi-Closest-Pair query with spatial constraints applied to the objects of the first dataset (primary dataset). We proposed a new technique which has the following benefits: a) requires less memory for query processing in comparison to existing techniques, b) requires less CPU processing time and c) requires less total running time.

There are several directions for further research in the area that may lead to interesting results. We note the following:

- the application of the proposed method for k-NN join processing,
- the adaptation of the method for high-dimensional spaces (perhaps with the aid of more efficient access methods), and
- the study of processing techniques when constraints are also applied to the reference dataset.

References

1. N. Beckmann, H.-P. Kriegel, R. Schneider, and B. Seeger: "The R*-tree: an Efficient and Robust Access Method for Points and Rectangles", *Proc. ACM SIGMOD*, pp. 322-331, Atlantic City, NJ, May 1990.
2. C. Bohm and F. Krebs: "Supporting KDD Applications by the K-Nearest Neighbor Join", *Proceedings of the 14th International Conference on Database and Expert System Applications (DEXA 2003)*, pp.504-516, Prague, Czech Republic, 2003.
3. C. Bohm and F. Krebs: "The k-Nearest Neighbor Join: Turbo Charging the KDD Process", *Knowledge and Information Systems (KAIS)*, 2004.
4. M. M. Breunig, H.-P. Kriegel, R. T. Ng, and J. Sander: "LOF: Identifying Density-Based Local Outliers", *Proceedings of the ACM International Conference on the Management of Data (SIGMOD 2000)*, pp.93-104, Dallas, TX, 2000.
5. T. Brinkhoff, H. P. Kriegel, and B. Seeger: "Efficient Processing of Spatial Joins Using R-trees", *Proceedings of the ACM International Conference on Management of Data (SIGMOD 1993)*, pp.237-246, Washington, D.C., May 1993.
6. A. Corral, Y. Manolopoulos, Y. Theodoridis and M. Vassilakopoulos: "Closest Pair Queries in Spatial Databases", *Proceedings of the ACM International Conference on the Management of Data (SIGMOD 2000)*, Dallas, TX, 2000.
7. A. Corral, Y. Manolopoulos, Y. Theodoridis and M. Vassilakopoulos: "Algorithms for Processing K-Closest-Pair Queries in Spatial Databases", *Data and Knowledge Engineering (DKE)*, Vol.49, No.1, pp.67-104, 2004.
8. D. Eppstein: "Fast Hierarchical Clustering and Other Applications of Dynamic Closest Pairs", *Journal of Experimental Algorithmics*, Vol.5, No.1, pp.1-23, 2000.
9. G.R. Hjaltason and H. Samet: "Incremental Distance Join Algorithms for Spatial Databases", *Proceedings of ACM SIGMOD Conference*, pp.237-248, 1998.
10. G. Karypis, E.-H. Han, and V. Kumar: "Chameleon: Hierarchical Clustering Using Dynamic Modeling", *Computer*, Vol.32, No.8, pp.68-75, 1999.
11. P. Mishra and M. H. Eich: "Join Processing in Relational Databases", *ACM Computing Surveys*, Vol.24, No.1, 1992.
12. A. Nanopoulos, Y. Theodoridis and Y. Manolopoulos: "C^2P: Clustering Based on Closest Pairs", *Proceedings of the 27th International Conference on Very Large Databases (VLDB 2001)*, Roma, Italy, 2001.
13. J. Shan, D. Zhang and B. Salzberg: "On Spatial-Range Closest-Pair Query", *Proceedings of the 8th International Symposium on Spatial and Temporal Databases (SSTD 2003)*, pp.252-269, Santorini, Greece, 2003.
14. K. Shim, R. Srikant and R. Agrawal: "High-Dimensional Similarity Joins", *IEEE Transactions on Knowledge and Data Engineering (TKDE)*, Vol.14, No.1, pp.156-171, 2002.

15. H. Shin, B. Moon and S. Lee: "Adaptive Multi-Stage Distance Join Processing", *Proceedings of the ACM SIGMOD Conference*, pp.343-354, 2000.
16. Y. Shou, N. Mamoulis, H. Cao, D. Papadias, and D. W. Cheung: "Evaluation of Iceberg Distance Joins", *Proceedings of the 8th International Symposium on Spatial and Temporal Databases (SSTD 2003)*, pp.270-278, Santorini, Greece, 2003.
17. Y. Tao and D. Papadias: "Time-Parameterized Queries in Spatio-Temporal Databases" *Proceedings of the ACM International Conference on the Management of Data (SIGMOD 2002)*, pp. 334-345, 2002.
18. TIGER/Line Files, 1994 Technical Documentation / prepared by the Bureau of the Census, Washington, DC, 1994.
19. C. Xia, H. Lu, B. C. Ooi and J. Hu: "GORDER: An Efficient Method for KNN Processing", *Proceedings of the 30th International Conference on Very Large Data Bases (VLDB 2004)*, pp.756-767, Toronto, Canada, 2004.
20. J. Zhang, N. Mamoulis, D. Papadias and Y. Tao: "All-Nearest-Neighbors Queries in Spatial Databases", *Proceedings of the 16th International Conference on Scientific and Statistical Databases (SSDBM 2004)*, pp.297-306, Santorini, Greece, 2004.

Database Support for Data Mining Patterns

Evangelos Kotsifakos, Irene Ntoutsi, and Yannis Theodoridis

Department of Informatics, University of Piraeus,
80 Karaoli-Dimitriou St, GR-18534 Piraeus, Greece
{ek, ntoutsi, ytheod}@unipi.gr

Abstract. The need of extracting useful knowledge from large collections of data has led to a great development of data mining systems and techniques. The results of data mining are known as patterns. Patterns can also be found in other scientific areas, such as biology, astronomy, mathematics etc. Today requirements impose the need for a system that efficiently manipulates complex and diverse patterns. In this work, we study the problem of the efficient representation and storage of patterns in a so-called pattern-base Management System. Towards this aim we examine three well known models from the database domain, the relational, the object-relational and the semi-structured (XML) model. The three alternative models are presented and compared based on criteria like generality, extensibility and querying effectiveness. The comparison shows that the semi-structure representation is more appropriate for a pattern-base.

1 Introduction

Data mining comprises a step of the knowledge discovery process and is mainly concerned with methodologies for extracting knowledge artifacts, i.e. patterns, from large data repositories. Decision trees, association rules, clusters are some well known patterns coming from the data mining area. Patterns can also be found in other areas, such as Mathematics (e.g. patterns in sequences, in numbers, in graphs, in shapes etc.), Geometry, Signal Processing etc. [11]. Nowadays, databases are huge, dynamic, come from different application domains and a lot of different and complex patterns can be extracted from those. In order for someone to be able to exploit the information these patterns represent, an efficient and global (general) Pattern Base Management System (PBMS) for handling (storing / processing / retrieving) patterns is becoming necessary for a lot scientific areas apart from data mining [8]. Scientists of every field have their special needs for pattern creation and management and a PBMS approach would be the solution to the custom-per-problem application that they have to build.

The area of pattern representation and management is recent, and there are only few efforts. PMML [7], SQL/MM [4], CWM [2], JDMAPI [5], PQL [3] are systems developed for storing data mining and statistical patterns. PMML of the data mining Group (DMG) is the most popular approach. Using XML documents it provides a quick and easy way for applications to define predictive models and share these models between PMML compliant applications. PMML defines a variety of specific mining patterns such as decision trees, association rules, neural networks etc. but does not support custom pattern types. PMML version 3.0 provides more patterns and some functions for data preprocessing [7].

The above approaches concentrate mostly on the definition of data mining and statistical models-patterns and the exchange of a set of patterns with specific characteristics between applications rather than on the creation of a general system for the representation and management of different pattern types. Pattern storage and querying techniques as well as pattern-to-data mapping are not among their capabilities.

Recently, two research projects, CINQ [1] and PANDA [10], defined the problem of pattern storage and management and proposed some solutions. CINQ aims at studying and developing query techniques for inductive databases, i.e. databases that store the raw data along with the patterns produced by these data collections [1]. On the other hand, PANDA [10] aims to the definition and design of a PBMS for the efficient representation and management of various types of patterns that arise from different application domains (not only from data mining). Patterns will reside and be managed (indexing, querying, retrieving) in the PBMS just like primitive data reside and are managed in the DBMS. Different types of patterns will be efficiently managed (generality) and new pattern types will be easily incorporated (extensibility) in the PBMS. A very critical decision regarding to the PBMS is whether it should be build from scratch or as an additional layer on top of a DBMS.

The scope of this work is to deal with the problem of pattern representation and storage following the later approach (i.e. working on top of a DBMS). Towards this aim, we examine three well known DBMS approaches: the relational, the object-relational and the semistructured (XML) model.

2 Patterns and Pattern-Bases

We adopt the PANDA project approach as it tries to incorporate all kinds of patterns. The pattern concept is the cornerstone of the PBMS. A *pattern* is a compact and rich in semantics representation of raw data. A *pattern-base* is a collection of persistently stored patterns. A *PBMS* is a system for handling patterns, defined over raw data and organized in pattern-bases, in order to efficiently support pattern matching and to exploit pattern-related operations generating nontrivial information [10]. A PBMS treats patterns just like a DBMS treats raw data.

In order to efficiently manage patterns, a PBMS should fulfill some requirements [10]:

- *Generality*: The PBMS must be able to manage different types of patterns coming from different application domains.
- *Extensibility*: The PBMS must be extensible to accommodate new kinds of patterns introduced by novel and challenging applications.
- *Exploitation of patterns special characteristics:* The PBMS should take into account the special features of patterns so as to improve several operations, like indexing and query processing.

- *Constraint implementation:* The PBMS should implement the constraints defined in the logical pattern model as well as validate patterns in line with these constraints.
- *Reusability:* PBMS must include constructs encouraging the reuse of what has already been defined.

The PANDA consortium has defined a logical model for the PBMS [8], which consists of three basic entities: pattern type, pattern and class defined as follows:

Definition 1. (Pattern Type): A pattern type is a quintuple $pt = (n, ss, ds, ms, f)$, where n is the pattern type name, ss is the structure schema that describes the structure of the pattern type (in an association rule for example the structure consists of head and body), ds is the source schema that describes the dataset from which patterns of this pattern type are constructed, ms is the measure schema that defines the quality of the source data representation achieved by patterns of this pattern type and f is the formula that describes the relationship between the source space and the pattern space.

An example of the association rule pattern type is presented below:

n: AssociationRule
ss: TUPLE(head: SET(STRING), body: SET(STRING))
ds: BAG(transaction: SET(STRING))
ms: TUPLE(confidence: REAL, support: REAL)
f: head U body $\subseteq$ transaction

Definition 2. (Pattern): A pattern p, is an instance of a pattern type pt, and has the corresponding values for each component. An example of an association rule pattern, instance of the AssociationRule pattern type defined above, is the following:

pid: 413
s: (head={'Boots'}, body={'Socks', 'Hat'})
d: 'SELECT SETOF(article) AS transaction FROM sales GROUP BY transactionId'
m: (confidence=0.75, support=0.55)
e: {transaction: {'Boots', 'Socks', 'Hat'} $\subseteq$ transaction}

Definition 3. (Class): A class c, over a pattern type pt, is defined as a triple $c = (cid, pt, pc)$ where cid is the unique identifier of the class, pt is the pattern type and pc is a collection of patterns of type pt.

A class is defined for a given pattern type and contains only patterns of that type. Each pattern must belong to at least one class. The relationships between the three basic entities of a PBMS, i.e. pattern types, patterns and classes, are shown in the figure below:

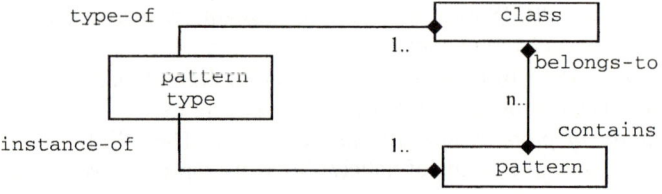

Fig. 1. Relationships between pattern types, patterns and classes

3 Physical Representation in a Pattern-Base

For the representation and storage of the contents of a pattern-base, we examine three traditional DBMS approaches: the relational, the object-relational and the semistructured (XML) model using the entities presented in the previous section.

Next, we present each approach and give some representative queries that point out the advantages and disadvantages of each one. For the implementation we have used Oracle 9i DBMS. This comparison aims to examine the applicability of the logical model in current DBMS technology and is based on qualitative rather than quantitative criteria. The primary goal is to examine whether a PBMS can be built based on the three models presented and which one is the more efficient on supporting the patterns special characteristics.

3.1 Relational Approach

Our main concern during the design and implementation of the pattern-base was to satisfy the three basic requirements of the logical model: generality, extensibility and pattern characteristics exploitation [10]. The relational schema is depicted in Fig 2:

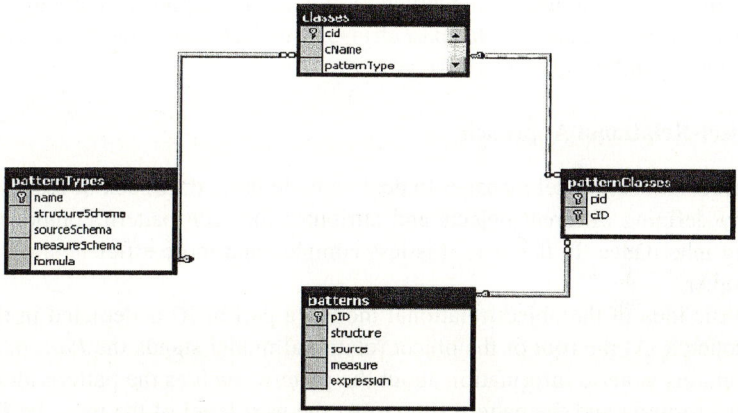

Fig. 2. The relational schema of the pattern-base

Various pattern types are stored in the table *patternTypes*, patterns are stored in the table *patterns* and pattern classes are stored in table *classes*. The table *patternClasses* relates patterns with classes (a class contains one or more patterns of the same class and every pattern belongs to at least one class).

Below we present only some representative queries due to space limitations. The queries will be first described in natural language and then in SQL-like syntax:

RQ1) *Find the structure (respectively, the source, the measure or the expression) of the association rules belonging to class Association_Rule_1.*

```
select patterns.structure from classesr
inner join patternclasses on classesr.cid = patternclasses.cid
inner join patterns on patternclasses.pid = patterns.pid
where (classesr.cname='Association_Rule_1');
```

RQ2) *Find all association rules belonging to class Association_Rule_1 whose structure contains "org" or whose coverage is greater than 0.7.*

```
select pid from classesr
inner join patternclasses on classesr.cid = patternclasses.cid
inner join patterns on patternclasses.pid = patterns.pid
where (classesr.cname='Association_Rule_1') AND
(INSTR(SUBSTR(structure,INSTR(measure,'body'),length(measure)),'ORG')
>0 OR substr(measure,10,instr(measure,'(')-10)>0.007);
```

RQ3) *Return the head and body parts of the structure of patterns that they belong to class Association_Rule_1.*

```
Select Substr(structure,1,instr(structure,'body')-2) as head,
Substr(structure,instr(structure,'body')) as body from classesr
inner join patternclasses on classesr.cid = patternclasses.cid
inner join patterns on patternclasses.pid = patterns.pid
where (classesr.cname='Association_Rule_1');
```

The relational approach is characterized by simplicity and ease of implementation. However, it has a lot of disadvantages that arise from the fact that this approach does not take into account the underlying structure of pattern components (structure, measure, etc.) and treats them as simple texts/ strings. This fact makes querying a complex, time consuming and mostly ineffective process.

3.2 Object-Relational Approach

The object-relational model manages to deal with the basic drawback of the relational model, by defining different objects and attributes for each pattern component and exploiting inheritance. In that way it is less complex and more efficient since querying is simpler.

The basic idea of the object-relational model (a part of it) is depicted in the following schema. At the root of the object relational model stands the *Pattern* entity, which contains generic information about the pattern, such as the pattern identifier, the pattern formula and the pattern source. At the next level of the tree, the *Pattern* is specialized, according to the pattern type it belongs to, for example to association rules patterns, to clusters patterns etc. These entities differ according to their structure and measure components but they also have some attributes in common, those inherited by the *Pattern* entity. For example, object *Association Rule Pattern* contains every attribute from object *Pattern* and it also has the attribute *Structure* that consists of a *head* and a *body*. This object can be further specialized based on the measure component. As it seems in Fig. 3 in the object *Association Rule Pattern 1* the *Measure* component consists of *confidence* and *support*, whereas in the object *Association Rule Pattern 2* the *Measure* component consists of *coverage*, *strength*, *lift* and *leverage*.

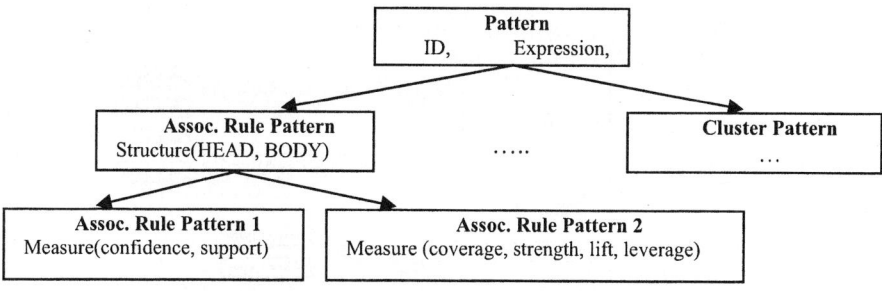

Fig. 3. The basic idea of the object-relational approach

Below we present some representative queries for the object-relational model:

OQ1) *Find the expression (respectively, the ID, the source, the measure or the structure) of patterns.*

```
select expression from hr.tbl_patterns p;
```

OQ2) *Find the body of the structure of association rule patterns*

```
select p.id, value(e) from hr.tbl_patterns p,
table(treat(value(p) as hr.assrule_pattern).structureschema.body) e ;
```

OQ3) *Find the confidence of the measure of association rule patterns.*

```
select p.id, treat(value(p) as
hr.assrule_pattern_1).measureschema.confidence as
confidence from hr.tbl_patterns p;
```

The object-relational approach overcomes some of the relational approach limitations due to the capability of modeling complex entities as objects. It also exploits the similarities among objects through inheritance. The object-relational model is more flexible and efficient from the relational model but it requires exact definition of any new object and of its components.

3.3 Semi-structured (XML) Approach

Unlike traditional databases, in an XML base the format of the data is not so rigid. This property is valuable in our case since patterns come from different application fields having thus different characteristics. For the XML implementation, we have to create an XML schema for each pattern type. Patterns of a specific pattern type will be the XML documents (instances) of the XML schema of this type.

For example, the association rules pattern type is described through the schema "association_rule.xsd" (Fig. 4), whereas the XML document "pattern-association_rules.xml" (Fig. 5) contains patterns of the association rule pattern type schema.

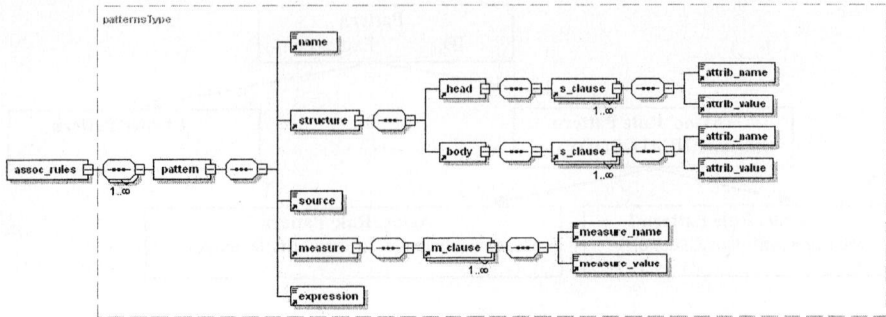

Fig. 4. association_rule.xsd

```
<assoc_rules ptype="association_rule">
    <pattern id="1"> <name>rule 1</name>
      <structure>
        <head>
          <s_clause>
            <attrib_name>buys</attrib_name>
            <attrib_value>scarf</attrib_value>
          </s_clause>
        </head>
        <body>
          <s_clause>
            <attrib_name>buys</attrib_name>
            <attrib_value>gloves</attrib_value>
          </s_clause>
        </body>
      </structure>
      <source>SELECT * FROM orders</source>
      <measure>
        <m_clause>
          <measure_name>support</measure_name>
          <measure_value>0.35</measure_value>
        </m_clause>
        <m_clause>
          <measure_name>confidence</measure_name>
          <measure_value>0.75</measure_value>
        </m_clause>
      </measure>
     <expression>
     {buys="hat",buys="cap",buys="gloves"}
     </expression>
     </pattern>
```

Fig. 5. association_rule.xml

Below we present some representative queries for the XML model in ORACLE XML-SQL syntax:

XQ1) *Find the structure (respectively, the source, the measure or the expression) of the association rule patterns belonging to class "class1".*

```
select
  extract(value(y),'//pattern[@id="'||extract(value(e),
  'pid/text()')||'"]/structure') as structures from assoc_rules y,
  classes x, TABLE(XMLsequence(extract(value(x),
  'class[@name="class1"]//pids/pid'))) e where exists-
  Node(value(y),'//pattern[@id="'||extract(value(e),'pid/text()')||'"]/
  structure') = 1
```

XQ2) *Return all patterns of a specific pattern type.*

```
select distinct extracValue(value(y),'//pattern[@id="'||
extract(value(e),'pid/text()')||'"]/name/text()') as pattern_name
from assoc_rules y, classes x,
TABLE(XMLsequence(extract(value(x),
'class[@ptype="association_rule"]//pids/pid'))) e
```

XQ3) *Find all the different measures(inside the measure component) of the association rules.*

```
select distinct extractValue(value(r),
'//m_clause/measure_name/text()') as measures from assoc_rules y,
classes x,TABLE(XMLsequence(extract(value(x),'//pids/pid'))) e,
TABLE(XMLsequence(extract(value(y),'//pattern[@id="'||
extract(value(e),'pid/text()')||'"]//m_clause'))) r;
```

XQ4) *Find patterns with the maximum value of the measure lift from patterns belonging to "class1".*

```
select extract(value(aa),'//pattern/name/text()') as pattern_names
from assoc_rules aa, (select max(extractvalue(value(val),'//text()'))
as maximum_lift from assoc_rules a,
TABLE(xmlsequence(extract(value(a),'//m_clause[measure_name="Lift"]
/measure_value'))) val) xxx
where existsNode(value(aa),
'//m_clause[measure_name="Lift"][measure_value="'||
xxx.maximum_lift||'"]') = 1
```

With XML pattern-base, the definition of a new pattern type is easy (extensibility). Furthermore, it is possible to create a proper XML schema for a pattern type, general enough to include every variation of patterns of this type (generality). The XML schema affects also the effectiveness of querying. Queries like "find all the different measures of the association rules", can be easily implemented, unlike the relational and object-relational approaches.

4 A Qualitative Comparison

In this section we present the criteria for the comparison of the three alternative representations and the conclusions we reached.

 # 1. Pattern-Base Implementation Complexity

All the three models we presented can be easily implemented. The simplest model is the relational, where both the pattern-base construction and insert operations can be performed in an easy and fast way. The object relational model is slightly more difficult since it requires the definition of different objects for each pattern type (and each of its variations). Insert operations are also more difficult as it should be different for each pattern type and its variations. Finally, the difficulty of the XML model is the fact that its success depends straightforward on the quality (generality) of the XML schema for each pattern type. However, after creating the proper schema insert operations can be easily performed. Furthermore, if this schema is general enough, variations of patterns belonging to a specific pattern type can be easily supported through this pattern type schema.

2. Constraint Implementation

The basic constraints imposed by the logical model [8] are the following: (a) every pattern is an instance of one pattern type, (b) every pattern belongs to at least one class, (c) a pattern class should contain only patterns of the same pattern type.
These constraints can be easily implemented in the relational model through the foreign key constraints. In the object relational model these constraints are supported directly by the definition of the pattern type, for example it is impossible to assign a cluster into the association rule pattern type. In the XML model, finally, the implementation of constraints are supported by the DBMS with mechanisms that associate XML documents.

3. Pattern Characteristics Exploitation

According to the logical model [8], every pattern consists of five basic components: name, structure, source, measure and formula. However, different pattern types differentiate on some of these components, e.g. in structure or measure. If we exploit the special characteristics of each pattern type we can improve operations like indexing and querying. The relational model does not exploit the underlying structure of patterns as it considers every pattern component as a string. Whereas, both object-relational and XML models take into account the special characteristics of pattern component according to the pattern type.

4. Query Effectiveness

The pattern-base does not aim only at the storage of patterns but mainly at their easy management, so the effectiveness of querying is an important criterion. From the representative queries we gave above for each implementation, it is obvious that in the relational model query construction is a complex and time consuming process (it is all about string manipulation formulas). The rest two models exploit the underlying pattern structure, thus queries are expressed more easily.

5. Extensibility

Extensibility is the ability to incorporate a new pattern type in the pattern-base; the easier this process is the more extensible the system is. The relational model is very extensible; a new pattern type is simply a new record in the table pattern types. The object-relational model requires the creation of new objects for every new pattern type and its components (the same stands also for the variations of a pattern type). That means that more than one association rule schema maybe required to incorporate the differences in the structure of each association rule. In the XML model a new schema is required for each new pattern type, but on the other hand, since this schema exists and is general enough, variations of patterns of this type can be easily incorporated without any modification.

 # 6. Pattern validation

The validity check during insert/ update operations in the pattern-base is critical. With the term validity we mean that each pattern in the pattern-base should follow its pattern type definition. The above criteria is violated in the relational model, whereas it stands for both XML and object relational models because of the XML schemas and the objects' definition respectively.

The conclusions of the evaluation are summarized in the table below:

Table 1. Comparison results

	Relational pattern-base	Object-relational pattern-base	XML pattern-base
Implementation Complexity	High	Medium	High
Constraint Implementation	Yes	Yes	Yes
Pattern characteristics exploitation	No	Yes	Yes
Query effectiveness	Low	Medium	Medium
Pattern validation	No	Yes	Yes
Extensibility	High	Medium	High

From the above table it is clear that the XML pattern-base implementation is the best among the three choices. There are however some points (e.g. query effectiveness) that it is not so efficient. This raises the question whether a special querying language designed exclusively for patterns is needed, like the one proposed in [9].

5 Conclusions and Future Work

Since patterns are compact and rich in semantics representations of raw data [10], they share some common characteristics, but also differentiate according to the type they belong to. Moreover, there are also variations between patterns of the same type.

Patterns nature requires a data-oriented approach whereas traditional databases follow a structure-oriented direction. For the pattern representation problem a semi-structured model is more appropriate than a relational or an object-relational schema. Using XML for the implementation of the pattern-base, we could achieve to build a more complete and general PBMS. There are some points however, where XML suffers such as query efficiency. To deal with efficiency problems a composite model that will be based on both XML and object-relational models should be examined or XML query methods should be developed. Although PMML is an XML-based language and tends to support more and more pattern types, a more general aspect should be adopted. Patterns should be defined per application or scientific area, so the system should be open to user extensions. Pattern querying and data-to-pattern mapping are issues that PMML is not currently taking into account, though important in order to create a more complete PBMS.

References

1. CINQ (Consortium on Discovering Knowledge with Inductive Queries). http://www.cinq-project.org.
2. CWM (Common Warehouse Model). http://www.omg.org/cwm.
3. Information Discovery Data Mining Suite. http://www.patternwarehouse.com/dmsuite.htm.
4. ISO SQL/MM Part 6. http://www.sql-99.org/SC32/WG4/Progression_Documents/FCD/fcd-datamining-2001-05.pdf, 2001.
5. Java Data Mining API, http://www.jcp.org/jsr/detail/73.prt.
6. PANDA (Patterns for Next-generarion Database Systems). http://dke.cti.gr/panda.
7. PMML (Predictive Model Markup Language). http://www.dmg.org/pmml-v3-0.html.
8. Rizzi S., Bertino E., Catania B., Golfarelli M., Halkidi M., Terrovitis M., Vassiliadis P., Vazirgiannis M., Vrahnos E.. Towards a logical model for patterns. *Proc. ER Conference*, Chicago, IL, USA, 2003.
9. Terrovitis M., Vassiliadis P., Skiadopoulos S., Bertino E., Catania B., Maddalena A. Modelling and Language Support for the Management of Pattern-Bases. *Proc. SSDBM Conference*, Santorini, Greece, 2004.
10. Theodoridis Y., Vazirgiannis M., et al. A manifesto for pattern bases. PANDA Technical Report TR-2003-03, 2003. Available at http://dke.cti.gr/panda.
11. Vazirgiannis M., Halkidi M., Tsatsaronis G., Vrachnos E., et al. A Survey on Pattern Application Domains and Pattern Management Approaches. PANDA Technical Report TR-2003-01, 2003. Available at http://dke.cti.gr/panda.

Visual Techniques for the Interpretation of Data Mining Outcomes

Ioannis Kopanakis[1], Nikos Pelekis[2], Haralampos Karanikas[3], and Thomas Mavroudkis[4]

[1] Technological Educational Institute of Crete, Heraklion Crete, Greece
i.kopanakis@emark.teicrete.gr
[2] Univ. of Piraeus, Piraeus, Greece
npelekis@unipi.gr
[3] UMIST, Manchester, UK
karanik@co.umist.ac.uk
[4] National & Kapodistrian Univ. of Athens,
Knowledge Management Lab., Athens, Hellas

Abstract. The visual senses for humans have a unique status, offering a very broadband channel for information flow. Visual approaches to analysis and mining attempt to take advantage of our abilities to perceive pattern and structure in visual form and to make sense of, or interpret, what we see. Visual Data Mining techniques have proven to be of high value in exploratory data analysis and they also have a high potential for mining large databases. In this work, we try to investigate and expand the area of visual data mining by proposing a new 3-Dimensional visual data mining technique for the representation and mining of classification outcomes and association rules.

Keywords: Visual Data Mining, Association Rules, Classification, Visual Data Mining Models.

Categories: I.2.4, I.2.6

Research Paper: Data Bases, Work Flow and Data mining

1 Introduction and Motivation

Classification is a primary method for machine learning and data mining [Frawley, 92]. It is either used as a stand-alone tool to get insight into the distribution of a data set, e.g. to focus further analysis and data processing, or as a pre-processing step for other algorithms operating on the detected clusters. The main enquiries that the knowledge engineer usually has on his/her attempt to understand the classification outcomes are: How well separated are the different classes? What classes are similar or dissimilar to each other? What kind of surface separates various classes, (i.e. are the classes linearly separable?) How coherent or well formed is a given class?

Those questions are difficult to be answered by applying the conventional statistical methods over the raw data produced by the classification algorithm. Unless the user is supported by a visual representation that will actually be his/her navigational tool in the N-dimensional classified world, concluding inferences will be a tedious task [Keim, 95]. Our main aim therefore should be to visually represent and understand the spatial relationships between various classes in order to answer questions such as the above mentioned.

Further more, mining for association rules, as a central task of data mining, has been studied extensively by many researchers. Much of the existing research, however, is focused on how to generate rules efficiently. Limited work has been done on how to help the user understand and use the discovered rules. In real-life applications though, the knowledge engineer wants first to have a good understanding over a set of rules before trusting them and use the mining outcomes [David, 01]. Investigation and comprehension of rules is a critical pre-requirement for their application. Those issues become even more tightening if we consider the "large resulting rule set", the "hard to understand" and the "rule behaviour" problem [Zhao, 01].

In this paper, the proposed visual data mining model constructs 3D graphical representations of the classification outcomes produced by common data mining processes. Furthermore, association rules are also visualized in that representation, revealing each association rule's "state" in their original N-dimensional world. Our attempt is to equip the knowledge engineer with a tool that would be utilized on his/her attempt to gain insight over the mined knowledge, presenting as much information extracted in a human perceivable way. The model proposed have distinctive advantageous characteristics, addressing the commonly tedious issues that the knowledge engineer handles during the exploitation of the classification outcomes. Furthermore, it brings us one step closer to make human part of the data mining process, in order to exploit human's unmatched abilities of perception.

In section 2 we introduce our application domain, along with the presentation of our 3D Class-Preserving Projection Technique. In section 4 we investigate the application of this model for the visualization of association rules, which is followed by two case studies in sections 5 and 6. Finally, the related work is presented in section 7 and we summarize our work in section8.

2 Visualizing Data Mining Classification Outcomes

On our attempt to graphically reveal the knowledge extracted by a classifier we have mainly based our research effort on the underlying ideas of the geometric projection techniques [Dhillon, 98]. Among the several geometric projection techniques that we have studied, the most interesting methodology was the Class-Preserving Projection Algorithm [Dhillon, 99], due to the robust behaviour that it has and its middle level of computational complexity.

The main characteristic of classified data embedded in high-dimensional Euclidean space is that proximity in R^n implies similarity. During the mapping procedures, class-preserving projection techniques preserve the properties of the classified data in the R^n space also to the projection plane in order to construct corresponding representations from which accurate inferences could be extracted. Our research study on those techniques formed a new geometric projection technique that expands the existing methods in the area of visualizing classified data. That new technique named 3D

Class-Preserving Projection technique projects from the R^n to the R^3 space along with being capable of preserving the class distances (discriminating) among a larger number of classes.

3 3D Class-Preserving Projection Technique

In this section we introduce 3D class-preserving projections of multidimensional data. The main advantage of those projections is that they maintain the high-dimensional class structure by the utilization of linear projections, which can be displayed on a computer screen. The challenge is in the choice of those planes and the associated projections. Considering the problem of visualizing high-dimensional data that have been categorized into various classes, our goal is to choose those projections that best preserve inter-class and intra-class distances in order to extract inferences regarding their relationships.

On our attempt to expand the existing projection techniques we worked on the definition of a projection scheme that would result on the construction of a 3D world. Compared to the existing 2D class-preserving projection techniques, the proposed 3D technique results on the construction of an information rich representation due to the freedom provided by the additional dimension in the projection world would. In order to project onto the 3D space we should define our orthonormal projection vectors based on four points. If we chose those four points to be the class-means of the classes of our interest, we have managed to maximize the inter-class distances among those four classes on our projection. Such an approach provides the flexibility of distinguishing among four classes instead of three, as long as being promoted into the 3D projection space.

We consider the case where the data is divided into four classes. Let $x_1, x_2, \ldots, x_n$ be all the N-dimensional data points, and m_1, m_2, m_3, m_4 denote the corresponding class-centroids. Let w_1, w_2 and w_3 be an orthonormal basis of the candidate 3D world of projection. The point x_i gets projected to $(w_1^T x_i, w_2^T x_i, w_3^T x_i)$ and consequently, the means m_j get mapped to $(w_1^T m_j, w_2^T m_j, w_3^T m_j)$ j=1,2,3,4.

One way to obtain good separation of the projected classes is to maximize the difference between the projected means. This may be achieved by choosing vectors $w_1, w_2, w_3 \in R^n$ such that the objective function

$$C(w_1, w_2, w_3) = \sum_{i=1}^{3}\left\{\left|w_i^T(m_2 - m_1)\right|^2 + \left|w_i^T(m_3 - m_1)\right|^2 + \left|w_i^T(m_4 - m_1)\right|^2 + \left|w_i^T(m_3 - m_2)\right|^2 + \left|w_i^T(m_4 - m_2)\right|^2 + \left|w_i^T(m_4 - m_3)\right|^2\right\}$$

is maximized. The above may be rewritten as

$$C(w_1, w_2, w_3) = \sum_{i=1}^{3}\left\{w_i^T\left\{(m_2 - m_1)(m_2 - m_1)^T + \ldots + (m_4 - m_3)(m_4 - m_3)^T\right\}w_i\right\}$$

$$= w_1^T S_B w_1 + w_2^T S_B w_2 + w_3^T S_B w_3 = W^T S_B W$$

Where
$$W = [w_1, w_2, w_3],\ w_i^T w_i = 1,\ w_i^T w_j = 0,\ i \neq j,\ i,j = 1,2,3 \text{ and}$$
$$S_B = (m_2 - m_1)(m_2 - m_1)^T + \ldots + (m_4 - m_3)(m_4 - m_3)^T$$

The positive semi-definite matrix S_B can be interpreted as the inter-class or between-class scatter matrix. Note that S_B has rank≤ 3, since $(m_3 - m_2) \in span\{(m_2 - m_1), (m_3 - m_1)\}$, $(m_4 - m_2) \in span\{(m_4 - m_1), (m_2 - m_1)\}$, $(m_4 - m_3) \in span\{(m_4 - m_1), (m_3 - m_1)\}$.

It is clear that the search for the maximizing w_1, w_2 and w_3 can be restricted to the column (or row) space of S_B. But as we noted above, this space is at most of dimension 3. Thus, in general, the optimal w_1, w_2 and w_3 must form an orthonormal basis spanning the space determined by the vectors $(m_2 - m_1)$, $(m_3 - m_1)$ and $(m_4 - m_1)$. This technique can be applied in any number of classes. In the constructed visual representation though it will best discriminate the four selected classes.

4 Class-Preserving Projection Techniques and Association Rules

Class-preserving projection techniques could be also applied in the area of visual mining of association rules. Even in the case of association rules, inventing new visual data mining models is actually conceiving new mapping techniques from the multidimensional space to a lower dimensional space. As each attribute participating in a rule is actually adding an additional dimension to our data space, we try to map each association rule existing in R^n to a lower dimensional space. Those notions conform to the fundamental theory of the class-preserving projection techniques.

Theoretically, each rule could be perceived as an n-dimensional surface which encloses a sub-space in the high dimensional data space. The boundaries of that area are defined by the conditions of rule's sub-expressions, which pose the limits in each dimension (i.e. the sub-expressions of the association rule IF $((L_1<x_1<U_1)$ and $(L_2<x_2<U_2)$ and ... $(L_n<x_n<U_n))$ THEN (...) set the upper and lower limits for each dimension of the n-dimensional space). The set of tuples in the data set, corresponding to points in the high-dimensional space, that have been included into the sub-space are those which satisfy rule's conditions. This is actually a different perspective that we could perceive the definition of association rules.

Following the mapping procedures of the class-preserving projection techniques, we are able to construct 2D or 3D representations of the classified high-dimensional data space, which has also been partitioned by the examined rule's sub-space. That attempt will equip us with a model capable to represent the "state" of an association rule in the high-dimensional world that it belongs. As in the case of visual mining the classified data space, the enquiries posed in this case will also be regarding coherence, discrimination, relationships etc. among the classes and the rule's sub-space. It will be like representing an association rule under the prism of the projection of the high-dimensional world.

In sections 5 and 6 we are evaluating the behavior of this model, which suggests the application of the class-preserving projection techniques for the visual mining of association rules. We are presenting two case studies, in order to examine the potential of constructing 2D and 3D representations of the classified high-dimensional world when partitioned to the sub-space defined by the association rule examined.

5 Wine Case Study

To begin with, we selected for our case study the wine data set [Blake, 98]. These data are the results of a chemical analysis of 178 wines grown in the same region in Italy but derived from three different cultivars. The analysis determined the quantities of 13 constituents found in each wine of the three cultivars. We selected to visualize the following rules:

Rule	Sup.%	Conf.%
IF ((3.82 < ColorIntensity <= 4.85)) THEN (Class=Class3)	15.73	21.43
IF ((3.82 < ColorIntensity <= 4.85)) THEN (Class=Class2)	15.73	28.57
IF ((3.82 < ColorIntensity <= 4.85)) THEN (Class=Class1)	15.73	50

This set of rules is actually providing the information regarding the categorization of the wines with color intensity in the range of (3.82 , 4.85] among the three cultivars. It would be interesting to visually examine this information and derive inferences if possible.

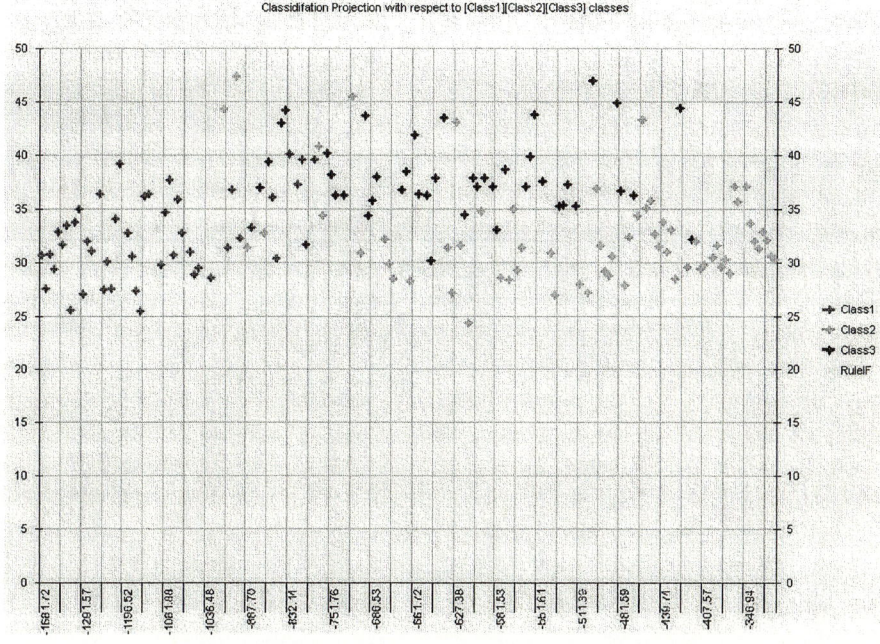

Fig. 1. 2D Class-Preserving Projection (Wine Case Study)

In Fig. 1 the sub-set of wines that has color intensity in the range of (3.82 , 4.85] has been yellow marked. As expected, the distribution of those points is among all three classes. In Fig. 2 we have visualized the first rule which provides the information regarding the third cultivar (class 3). In Fig. 3 all three rules have been visualized. The green

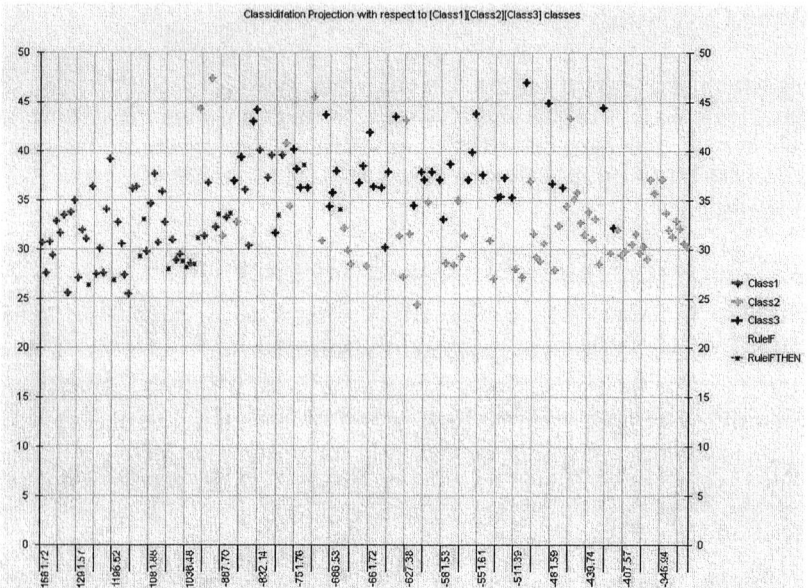

Fig. 2. 2D Class -Preserving Projection (THEN part)

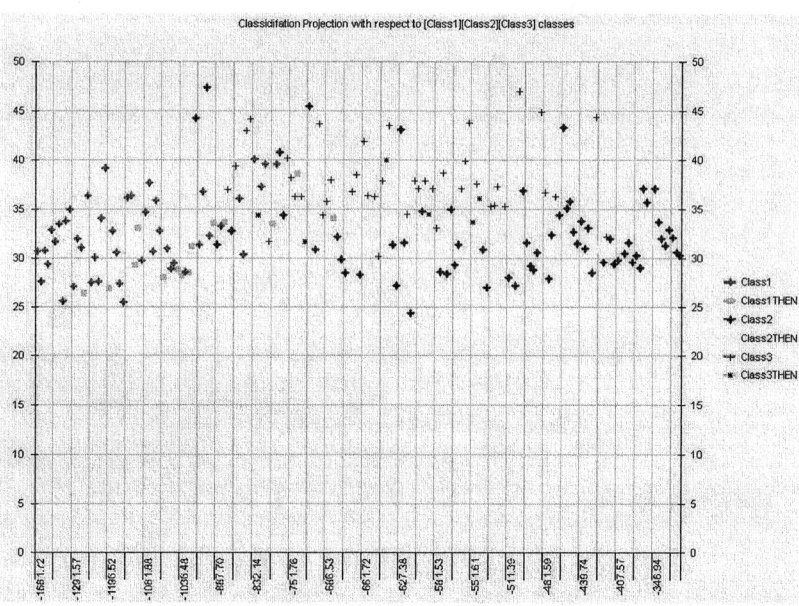

Fig. 3. 2D Class -Preserving Projection (Set of Rules)

marks correspond to the wines of the first cultivar (class 1, red marks) that have color intensity in the range examined. The yellow marks correspond to the wines of the second cultivar (class 2, blue marks) in that range. Analogously is represented the third cultivar.

Several inferences are concluded by the investigation of the alternative perspectives of the segmented high dimensional space provided by those representations. The distribution of the points in each class is quite high. In our application domain that is translated to the conclusion that each cultivar has made sure that it has a variety of types of "rose" wines. That range of middle color intensity is expected to correspond to the category of "rose" wines. Therefore, the distribution of this category to the whole class indicates the different properties of the chemical analysis that those wines have. In other words, there is a significant chemical variance among the wines of this sub-category, indicating the desirable variety of rose wines in each cultivar.

Following a reverse way of thinking, evaluating the three cultivars on respect to the variety of the wines of this type would be like comparing the distribution and the number of wines in each cultivar with color intensity in the range of (3.82 , 4.85]. Examining the corresponding representation of Fig. 3 we could urge that the first and second cultivars have a satisfactory variety and number of "rose" wines, in contradiction to the third cultivar which has a small production of wines of this type. The small variance of the third cultivar's "rose" wines in the representation indicates also the similarity among their chemical analysis factors and as a consequence the small variety among the types of wines of this category.

6 Letter Image Recognition Case Study

Having examined the application of class-preserving projection technique for the visual mining of association rules in 2D we are expecting that the advanced properties of the presented model will be enhanced even more by the additional dimension provided in the 3D space. That flexibility of our projection world is expected to represent more accurately larger volumes of information regarding the classified data and the rules' sub-spaces.

For our case study we have selected the letter image recognition data set [Blake, 98]. Character images of the 26 capital letters of the English alphabet based on 20 different fonts were converted into 16 primitive numerical attributes (statistical moments and edge counts) that formed our data set. We have chosen to visualize the instances of A, B, C and D letters for the following set of association rules.

Rule	Sup.%	Conf.%
IF ((5.50 < x2ybr <= 6.50)) THEN (lettr=C)	25	32
IF ((5.50 < x2ybr <= 6.50)) THEN (lettr=B)	25	32
IF ((5.50 < x2ybr <= 6.50)) THEN (lettr=D)	25	28

In the context of the classified world constructed, according to our projection technique, the set of tuples that satisfy rules left-hand clause has been represented in Fig. 4 by the white spheres. The instances of letters A, B, C and D have been represented by the red, green, blue and mauve spheres correspondingly. The x2ybar attribute corresponds to the x^2y statistical factor, where x and y are the mean values of the position of the "on" pixels in each character in the horizontal and vertical direction. As expected from the set of rules examined, the tuples with x2ybar within the range of (5.5 , 6.5] are among the classes B, C and D.

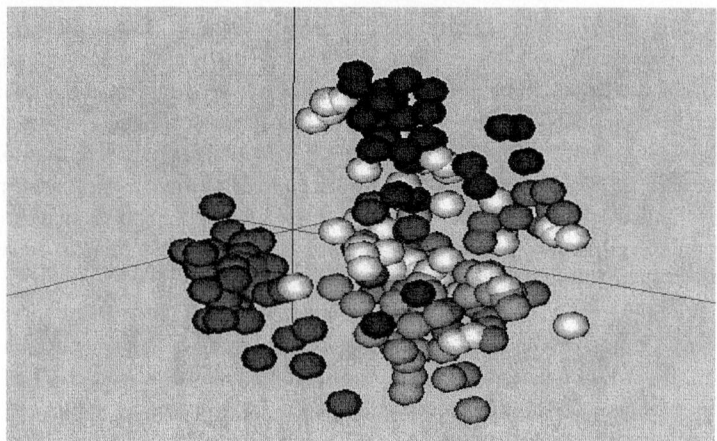

Fig. 4. 3D Class-Preserving Projection (Letter case study)

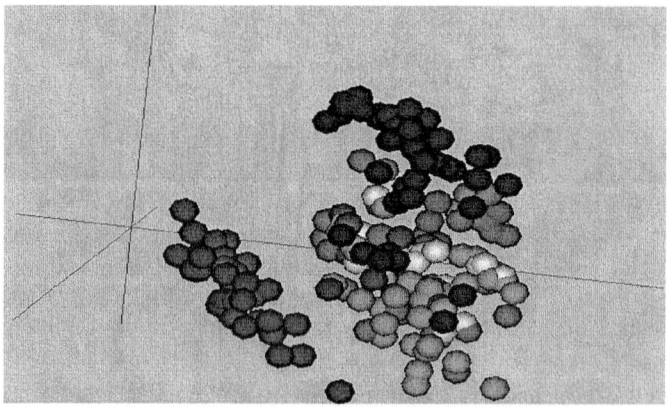

Fig. 5. 3D Class-Preserving Projection (Rule B)

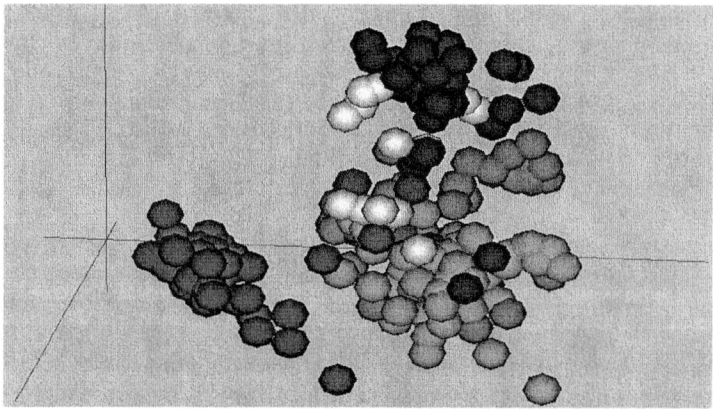

Fig. 6. 3D Class-Preserving Projection (Rule C)

In Fig. 6 and Fig. 5 we are analogously presenting each one of the rules selected to be mined, following the same coloring scheme. For their printed presentation we tried to select the best viewing angle that would give us an adequate perspective of the 3D world. The resulting image though can not be compared with the actual model developed. The ability to interact and navigate in the constructed 3D world finding visual patters, making assumptions and trying to verify them could not be presented in a single figure.

Our attempt to derive inferences regarding the properties of the statistical factor examined is quite difficult, as it is not easy to assign qualitative properties to the factor x2ybar. A combined observation which is derived when we examine each rule's representation is that they all tend to occupy space in the area among the classes B, C and D. That directed us to make the assumption that the space among the three classes is the projection space of the examined range (5.5 < x2ybar <= 6.5) in the 3D world. In other words, that hypothesis indicates that most spheres that enter in that region of the 3D world tend to be within the range of (5.5 , 6.5]. Our mapping procedure therefore, preserved the properties of the classified data, along with the sub-space of the rules examined and projected the x2ybar statistical factor with quite good properties.

7 Related Work

In the context of visualizing classified data, geometric projection techniques try to find "interesting" projections of multidimensional data sets in such a way that the structure, properties and patterns of the data set in the n-dimensional space will be revealed [Spears, 99] [Dhillon, 98] [Dhillon, 99]. Scatter Plots generate $N(N-1)/2$ pair-wise parallel projections with each one providing a general impression of the relationships among the data visualized, within the context of the pair of dimensions selected (i.e. Scatter-Plot Matrix, HyperSlice [Van, 93]). Advantages of scatter plots include ease of interpretation and robustness to the size of the data set. Major limitation though is that the high dimensionality results in decreasing the screen space provided for each projection.

The Prosection Views model indicates the application of the various projection techniques to sections of the data, in the hope that various multidimensional structures will reveal themselves in lower dimensions [Furnas, 94]. Grand Tour Technique & Projection Pursuit model [Spears, 99] smoothly rotate the 2D plane revealing unusual structures within the multidimensional data [Asimov, 85]. The quest for "interesting" projections of the data is referred to as "projection pursuit" [Friedman, 87]. Parallel Coordinates [Inselberg, 85], Radial Coordinate (RadViz) [Hoffman, 00] and GridViz [Hoffman, 99] are also well known techniques of this category.

In the commercial field, several innovative techniques have been proposed. Cluster Visualizer of SGI's MineSet tool [SGI, M] for the visualization of clustering results uses box plots arranged in rows and columns. For the visualization of association rules, IBM Intelligent Miner - Rules Graph has been based on the graph-based techniques [IBM, IMD]. The rules graph uses nodes to represent item sets and lines with arrows to represent rules. The 3D Scatter-Plots of IBM's Data Explorer [IBM, DE] have been proposed for the exploration of raw data. The SAS Enterprise Miner Scatter-Plots [SAS, EM] has utilized the scatter-plot matrix technique linked with simple bar and plot charts. According to SGI's MineSet Scatter and Splat Visualizers, [SGI, M] data points are represented in one, two, or three dimensional scatter-plots. For the visualization of classified data and association rules several techniques have been proposed. None of them though combines them both.

8 Conclusions

Conclusively, the utilization of the class-preserving projection techniques for the visual mining of association rules is expected to enhance our attempt on gaining insight into the properties of the sub-spaces defined by the examined association rules in the context of the classified high dimensional data space. As in the case studies presented, we expect that in general the deductive abilities of the human analytical mind will be capable to combine the perspectives of the high dimensional space provided by those views and analogously derive combined inferences. Interesting inferences are possible to be derived and the interaction among the visualization technique and the human is enhanced by the flexibility of the model.

That flexibility and adaptive characteristics of this visual data mining model makes us confident that further study in this research area will derive fruitful outcomes. The research focus should be mainly targeted to the visualization capabilities regarding lager volumes of data and association rules as long as its behavior and capability to reveal visual patterns in a variety of case studies and application domains.

References

[Asimov, 85] D. Asimov: "The Grand Tour: A Tool for Viewing Multidimensional Data", SIAM Journal on Scientific Computing, 6, 1985, pp.128-143.

[Blake, 98] C. L. Blake & C. J. Merz: "UCI Repository of machine learning databases" [http://www.ics.uci.edu/~mlearn/MLRepository.html]. Irvine, CA: University of California, Department of Information and Computer Science, (1998).

[David, 01] David Law & Yuh Foong: "A Visualization-Driven Approach for Strategic Knowledge Discovery", In: Information Visualization in Data Mining and Knowledge Discovery, Morgan Kaufmann 2001, pp. 182-190, (2001).

[Dhillon, 98] I. S. Dhillon, D. S. Modha & W. S. Spangler: "Visualizing Class Structure of Multidimensional Data", Proceedings of the 30th Symposium on the Interface: Computing Science and Statistics, Interface Foundation of North America, vol. 30, pages 488-493, Minneapolis, May, (1998).

[Dhillon, 99] I. S. Dhillon, D. S. Modha & W. S. Spangler: "Class Visualization of High-Dimensional Data with Application", IBM Almaden Research Center, San Jose, (1999).

[Frawley, 92] W. Frawley, G. Piatetsky-Shapiro & C. Matheus: "Knowledge Discovery in Databases: An Overview", AI Magazine, pp. 213-228, (1992).

[Friedman, 87] J. H. Friedman: "Exploratory Projection Pursuit", Journal of the American Statistical Association, Vol. 82, 1987, pp.249-266.

[Furnas ,94] G. Furnas and A. Buja: "Prosection Views: Dimensional Inference through Sections and Projections", In: Journal of Computational and Graphical Statistics, Vol. 3, No. 4, pp. 323-353, 1994.

[Hoffman, 00]	P. E. Hoffman and G. Grinstein: "Dimensional Anchors: A Graphic Primitive for Multidimensional Multivariate Information", Workshop of New Paradigms in Information Visualization and Manipulation, in conjunction with the ACM conference on Information and knowledge Management CIKM '99, to be published in 2000.
[Hoffman, 99]	P. E. Hoffman: "Table Visualizations: A Formal Model and its Applications", Doctoral Dissertation, Computer Science Department, University of Massachusetts Lowell, MA, 1999.
[IBM, DE]	IBM Open Visualization Data Explorer Project: "What is IBM Open Visualization Data Explorer?", "Documentation", "Proceedings of 1996 Data Explorer Symposium", http://www.research.ibm.com/dx/
[IBM, IMD]	IBM DB2 Intelligent Miner for Data: "Using the Intelligent Miner for Data", http://www-3.ibm.com/software/data/iminer/fordata/
[Inselberg, 85]	A. Inselberg: "The plane with Parallel Coordinates", Special Issue on Computational Geometry, The Visual Computer, Vol. 1, 1985, pp. 69-91.
[Keim, 95]	D. A. Keim & H.-P. Kriegel: "Possibilities and Limits in Visualizing Large Amounts of Multidimensional Data", In: Perceptual Issues in Visualization, Springer 1995, pp. 203-214, (1995).
[SAS, EM]	SAS Enterprise Miner: "Data Mining and Enterprise Miner Stand-alone Tutorial", http://www.sas.com/products/miner/
[SGI, M]	SGI MineSet ™ Enterprise Edition: "User's Guide for the Windows", "Tutorial for Windows", "Reference Guide", "Interface Guide", http://www.sgi.com/software/mineset.html
[SGI, M]	SGI MineSet ™ Enterprise Edition: "User's Guide for the Windows", "Tutorial for Windows", "Reference Guide", "Interface Guide", http://www.sgi.com/software/mineset.html
[Spears, 99]	W. Spears: "An Overview of Multidimensional Visualization Techniques", Visualization Workshop of GECCO'99, Genetic and Evolutionary Computation Conference, Orlando, Florida, USA, July 1999.
[Van, 93]	J. J. Van Wijk and R. Van Liere: "HyperSlice", IEEE Visualization '93, G. M. Nielson and R. D. Bergeron editors, Los Alamitos, CA, IEEE Computer Society Press, 1993, pp.119-125.
[Zhao, 01]	K. Zhao & B. Liu: "Visual Analysis of the Behavior of Discovered Rules", ACM SIGKDD Int. Conf. on Knowledge Discovery & Data Mining (KDD 2001), Proc. Workshop on Visual Data Mining, San Francisco, USA. pp. 59-64, (2001).

Towards In-Situ Data Storage in Sensor Databases

D. Zeinalipour-Yazti, V. Kalogeraki, D. Gunopulos,
A. Mitra, A. Banerjee, and W. Najjar

Department of Computer Science & Engineering,
University of California - Riverside,
Riverside CA 92521, USA
{csyiazti, vana, dg, amitra, anirban, najjar}@cs.ucr.edu

Abstract. The advances in wireless communications along with the exponential growth of transistors per integrated circuit lead to a rapid evolution of *Wireless Sensor Devices (WSDs)*, that can be used for monitoring environmental conditions at a high fidelity. Following the current trends, WSDs are soon expected to automatically and continuously collect vast amounts of temporal data. Organizing such information in centralized repositories at all times will be both impractical and expensive. In this paper we discuss the challenges from storing sensor readings *In-situ* (at the generating sensor). This creates a network of tiny databases as opposed to the prevalent model of a centralized database that collects readings from many sensors. We also discuss some of the inherent problems of such a setting, including the lack of efficient distributed query processing algorithms for handling *temporal* data and the lack of efficient access methods to locally store and retrieve large amounts of sensor data. The presented solutions are in the context of the *RISE (Riverside Sensor)* hardware platform, which is a wireless sensor platform we developed for applications that require storing in-situ many MBs of sensor readings.

1 Introduction

The improvements in hardware design along with the wide availability of economically viable embedded sensor systems enable researchers nowadays to sense environmental conditions at extremely high resolutions. Traditional approaches to monitor the physical world include passive sensing devices which transmit their readings to more powerful processing units for storage and analysis. *Wireless Sensor Devices (WSDs)* on the other hand, are tiny computers on a chip that is often as small as a coin or a credit card. These devices feature a low frequency processor ($\approx$4-58MHz) which significantly reduces power consumption, a small on-chip flash card ($\approx$32KB-512KB) which can be used as a small local storage medium, a wireless radio for communication, on-chip sensors, and an energy source such as a set of AA batteries or solar panels [9]. This multitude of features constitute *WSDs* powerful devices which can be used for in-network processing, filtering and aggregation [8,7,11]. Large-scale deployments of sensor network devices have already emerged in environmental and habitant monitoring[17,9], seismic and structural monitoring [12], factory and process automation and a large array of other applications [18,7,8,11].

Conventional approaches to monitoring have focused on dense deployed networks that either transfer the data to a central sink node or perform in-network computation and generate alerts when certain events arise. An important attribute of these applications is that the time interval between consecutive query re-evaluations (*epoch*) is small because the applications require the ability to quickly react to various alerts. For example, a query might continuously manipulate the temperature at some region in order to identify fires or other extreme situations (e.g. *"Find which sensors record a temperature>95F?"*). Therefore the querying node (*sink*) must continuously maintain an updated view of the values recorded at the sensors [11,7]. In such *short-epoch* applications, the frequency of updates and the timely delivery of information from the sensors play a vital role in the overall success of the system.

On the other hand, a class of applications that was not addressed to this date are *long-epoch* applications. In these applications the user needs an answer to his query more sparsely (e.g. weekly or monthly), although the sensor still acquires data from its surrounding environment frequently (e.g. every second). The user might then ask: *"Find the time instance on which we had the highest average temperature in the last month?"*. In order to evaluate this query using current techniques would require each sensor to report all its values for the last month. This happens because the data is fragmented across the different nodes and an answer to the query can only be obtained after accessing all distributed relations in their entirety. We call this type of *in-situ* data fragmentation *vertical partition*, because each sensor's timeseries is one dimension in the n-dimensional space of sensor readings. This makes it a challenging task to answer user queries efficiently.

Our Contribution: In this paper we study the deployment of sensor devices characterized by large external memories. This will allow each sensor node to accumulate measurements over a large window of time, avoiding the multi-hop burden of transferring everything to the sink. This creates a network of tiny databases as opposed to the prevalent model of a centralized database that collects readings from many sensors. We also address some of the inherent problems of such a distributed database setting. Specifically we propose efficient distributed query processing algorithms for efficiently answering top-k queries in a distributed environment. These queries have been extensively studied by the database community and their task is to retrieve the k highest ranked answers to a given query. An example of a top-k query might be *"Find the three moments on which we had the highest average temperature in the last month?"*.

Temporal and top-k queries are useful in a number of contexts. Our work is motivated by the requirements of the Bio-Complexity and the James Reserve Projects at the Center of Conservation Biology (CCB) at UC Riverside.[1] CCB

---
[1] http://www.ccb.ucr.edu/

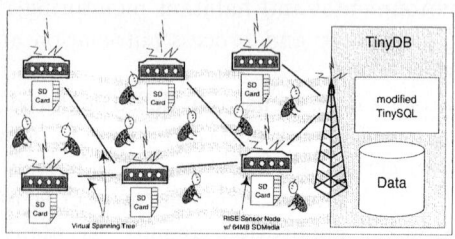 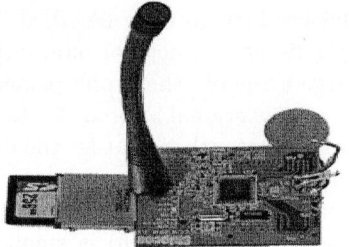

Fig. 1. a) Soil-Organism Monitoring Application: Each sensor stores locally on external flash memory the CO_2 levels in a sliding window fashion. The user might then ask: "Find the time instance on which we had the highest average CO_2 levels in the last month?". b) Our platform: The RISE (Riverside Sensor), which is the first sensor device that features a large external storage medium (an SDMedia flash card).

is working towards the conservation and restoration of species and ecosystems by collecting, evaluating scientific information (Figure 1a). The bio-complexity project is designed to develop the kinds of instruments that can monitor the soil environment directly, rather than in laboratory recreations.

We have developed the *RISE platform*, in which sensors feature a large external memory (SD flash memory). RISE sensors are able to store measurements of Carbon-dioxide levels in the soil as well as ambient sound from the surrounding environment over a large period of time. This will allow scientists to monitor the long-term behavior of certain soil micro-organisms and bird species.

We also address the efficient evaluation of top-k queries in our platform by sketching an algorithm that estimates some threshold below which tuples do not need to be fetched from the sensor nodes. Key ideas of our algorithm are to transmit only the necessary information towards the querying node and to perform the query execution in the network rather than in a centralized way.

2 The RISE Platform

The *RISE (RIverside SEnsor)* platform (see figure 1b) employs a System-on-Chip interfaced with a large external storage memory, an off-the-shelf SD (Secure Digital) media card, to develop a new paradigm of "sense and store" as opposed to the prevalent "sense and send". The RISE platform was conceived by observing the twin trends of falling flash memory prices and the need of larger memories on sensor devices for more efficient querying, processing and communication. Also, higher levels of device integration at low cost and size now provide us with single chip solutions for most of the sensor and communication needs, reducing complexity and improving performance. The RISE wireless platform is built around the Chipcon CC1010 System on Chip (SoC), which together with just a few external passive components and the required sensors constitutes a powerful, robust and versatile wireless embedded sensor system. The following is a description of the important components of the RISE platform :

1. **The MicroController Unit (MCU):** The Chipcon CC1010 SoC is a true single-chip RF transceiver with an integrated high performance 8051 microcontroller and high end features which include a 32KB flash memory, an SPI (Serial Peripheral Interface) bus, DES encryption, 26 general I/O pins and many other components constituting it appropriate for a multitude of sensor and computation needs.

2. **The SD-Card interface:** An SD-Card (Secure Digital Card) has been interfaced to the main chip using the SPI bus equipping the RISE platform with a large external storage memory (up to a 4 GB!). Data can be buffered on the 32KB flash memory for efficiently reading and writing on the SD-Card. Data is transferred to the SDCard in blocks of 512 bytes at a maximum rate of 82KBps (although the SPI interface supports up to 3MBps). We have developed tiny access method structures which are deployed directly on the sensor. These provide efficient sorted and random access to local data in the event of some query.

3. **The OS & Compilation:** To facilitate ease and modularity of programming, we have ported the most prevalent design environment, the TinyOS (version 1.1) and nesC (version 1.2alpha1), facilitating easier and modular programming, interfacing of an SD-CARD and developing the reactive methodology of query based response on large datasets stored locally on the nodes.

4. **Deployed Sensors:** The platform has a temperature sensor and is also being interfaced with a CO_2 sensor and a microphone.

Note that the energy cost of writing to flash memory is much cheaper than the RF transmission cost even in the case of a single hop. We have measured the performance of transmitting one byte over the RF radio and found that it requires 164 μJ while storing the same byte on the flash card requires 1.5 μJ. Although writing to the external flash card can only be performed on a page-to-page basis (i.e. 512 bytes), the 32KB on-chip flash memory allows us to buffer a page before it is written out. This in combination of the fact that the energy required for the transmission of one byte is roughly equivalent to executing 1120 CPU instructions, makes local storage and processing highly desirable.

3 The Query Processing Framework

In this section we expand on the class of queries we consider in the RISE platform. This class represents queries that are interesting and important in our framework that is characterized by long-epochs and large storage capacities at individual sensors. We also describe and contrast alternative frameworks that have been proposed for data acquisition in sensor networks.

3.1 Temporal and Top-k Queries in RISE

We use a query dissemination mechanism similar to the one described in [8,7], which creates a "virtual" *Query Spanning Tree (QST)* interconnecting all nodes in the network. This provides each node with the next hop towards the sink (See Figure 1). Alternatively each node could maintain multiple parents in order to achieve fault tolerance [1].

Let $G(V, E)$ denote the undirected and connected network graph that interconnects n sensors in V using the edge set E. The edges in E, represent the virtual connections (i.e. nodes are within communication radius) between the sensors in V. Also assume that each sensor has enough storage to record a window of m measurements. Each measurement has the form (ts, val), where ts denotes the timestamp on which the measurement was taken and val the recording at that particular time moment.[2] Essentially each sensor v_i has locally the following timeseries $list(v_i) = \{o_{i1}, o_{i2}, \ldots, o_{im}\}$, where o_{ij} denotes the recording of the ith sensor node at the jth time moment. Each time moment could logically be viewed as a collection of n values. A node can maintain several lists (e.g. temperature, humidity, others); for simplicity we assume that only one such time-series is being maintained. We look at two main classes of queries.

Temporal Queries: The queries we consider allow the user to find the state of the sensor network at different time intervals, but also to identify intervals that certain conditions hold. Examples of such queries are: *"Find the time intervals such that the sensor values satisfy a given condition,"* and *"Given a sequence of values, identify time intervals that show similar sequences in the values recorded by the sensor."*

Top-k Queries: An example of a top-k query is *"Find the k time instances with the highest average reading across all sensors."* More formally, consider $Q = (q_1, q_2, \ldots, q_n)$, a top-k query with n attributes. Each attribute of Q refers to the corresponding attribute of an object and the query attempts to find the k objects which have the maximum value in the following scoring function: $Score(o_i) = \sum_{j=1}^{n} w_j * sim_j(q, o_i)$, where $sim_j(q, o_i)$ is some similarity function which evaluates the jth attribute (sensor) of the query q against the jth attribute of an object o_i and returns a value in the domain $[0,1]$ (1 denotes the highest similarity). Since each sensor might have a different factor of importance, we also use a weight factor w_j ($w_j > 0$), which adjusts the significance of each attribute according to the user preferences. Note that, similarly to [4], we require the score function to be *monotone*. A function is monotone if the following property holds: if $sim_j(q, o_1) > sim_j(q, o_2)$ ($\forall j \in m$) then $Score(o_1) > Score(o_2)$. This is true when $w_j > 0$.

---
[2] Sensors are time synchronized through a lower layer mechanism (e.g. The Operating System).

4 Query Evaluation Techniques

From the sink's point of view, denoted as v', the data in this scenario is vertically fragmented across the network. Therefore answering such a query would require v' to gather the whole space of $n * m$ values. In this section we sketch the TJA algorithm which alleviates the burden of transferring everything to the sink.

4.1 A Taxonomy of Data Gathering Techniques

Below we provide a taxonomy of data gathering techniques as a function of the available storage available at each node:

1. **Sense and Send (SS):** In this naive case each sensor node propagates its generated value towards its parent every time such value becomes available. This is, according to the terminology of [1], the LIST approach.

2. **Sense, Merge and Send (SMS):** In this scheme, each node aggregates the values coming from its children before forwarding its values to its parent. This is essentially the TAG approach [8]. In this scheme, all aggregates can not be treated in the same way. For example *Distributive Aggregates (e.g. Sum, Max, Min, Count)* can locally be aggregated into one value. *Holistic Aggregates (e.g. Median)* on the other hand, can not be treated in the same way as aggregation into one value could produce a wrong result.

3. **Sense, Store, Merge and Send (SSMS):** This is the scheme deployed in our platform, RISE. Each sensor node maintains locally in the flash memory a window of m measurements. This sliding window evolves with time, and therefore, once the limit of the available storage is reached, at each new time moment the oldest measurement is deleted. We note however that given the capacities of flash cards m can be very large. Registered queries can perform some local aggregation, if the correctness of the query outcome is not violated, before values are propagated towards the parent. Note that this is not possible in current systems such as TinyDB [7].

The three gathering techniques outlined above basically represent the scale of available memory at the sensor nodes (i.e. $SSMS \supset SMS \supset SS$). We believe that although the SMS approach offers in practice the most efficient way to cope with short-epoch applications, the SSMS approach is more practical for long-epoch applications.

We note that under the SS model evaluating the kinds of queries we propose requires sending all information to the sink. Under the SMS model we can design algorithms that perform aggregation or more sophisticated computation in the network, there are however significant limitations. Due to the short-epoch emphasis of this model when information gets older than the window of interest, we have to discard this information or we have to transmit it for permanent storage to the sink (or other specially designated nodes in the network).

4.2 Providing Local Access Methods

Efficiently evaluating the queries described above requires efficient access to the data that is stored on the "external" flash memory. However, flash memory features some distinct characteristics that differentiate it from other storage media. Specifically, deleting data stored on flash memory can only be performed at a block granularity (typically 8KB-64KB) and writing can only be performed at a page granularity (typically 256B-512B), after the respective block has been deleted. Finally, each flash page has a limited life-time (10K-100K writes), after which the page wears out and can no longer be used. The problem of indexing over magnetic disks and RAM memory is well studied in the database community, however indexing on flash memory in conjunction with the low energy budget of sensor nodes introduce many new challenges. We have designed and implemented efficient access methods that provide random and sorted access to records stored on the flash medium. Our access methods serve as primitive functions for the efficient execution of a wide spectrum of queries. Pages on the flash card are organized as a *heap file*, which is naturally ordered by time. Note that a flash card can only hold up to m pages ($o_{i0}..o_{im}$) and hence the available memory is organized as a circular array, in which the newest o_{ij} pair replaces the oldest o_{ij} pair if the memory becomes full.

i) Random Access By Value: An example of such operation is to locally load the records that have a temperature of 95F. In order to fetch records by their value we have implemented a *static* hash index with a swap directory that gracefully keeps in memory the directory buckets with the highest hit ratio. We use a static index as opposed to a dynamic hashing index, such as *extendible* or *linear*, because the latter structures are considerably more power demanding (i.e. due to page splits during insertions).

ii) Sorted Access By Value: An example of such operation is to locally load the records that have a temperature between 94F-96F. An important observation is that sensor readings are numeric readings in a discrete range (for example the temperature is between -40F and 250F). In order to enable such range queries, we currently use an extension of our random-access index in which we query every discrete value in the requested range. However, we are also developing a simple B+ tree index, which is a minimalistic version of its counterpart found in a real database system. It consists of a small number of non-leaf index pages which provide pointers to the leaf pages. In our current design, we keep a small number of highly used non-leaf index pages (such as the root) in main memory.

4.3 Efficient Top-k Query Evaluation in RISE

We now sketch a *Threshold Join Algorithm* which is an efficient top-k query processing algorithm for sensor networks. In the naive case, such queries could be answered by transferring all sensor values to the sink and then find the correct result. In our algorithm, we use an additional probing and filtering phase in order to eliminate this expensive step. More specifically, we use the following phases:

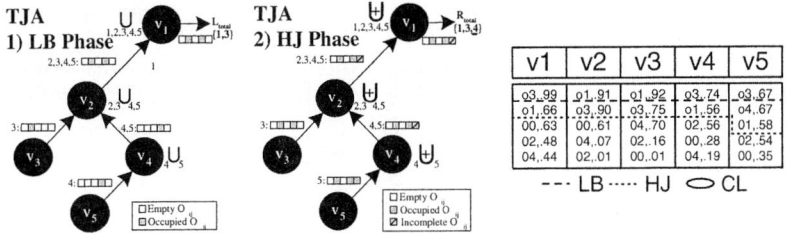

Fig. 2. The QST for two phases of the TJA Algorithm (the third phase is omitted as it does not contribute to the final result). The table on the right shows the objects qualifying in each phase.

1) the *Lower Bound* phase, in which the sink collects the union of the top-k results from all nodes in the network (denoted as $L_{sink}=\{l_1, l_2, \ldots, l_o\}$, $o \geq k$),
2) the *Hierarchical Joining* phase, in which each node uses L_{sink} for eliminating anything that has a value below the least ranked item in L_{sink},
3) the *Clean-Up* phase, in which the actual top-k results are identified.

In figure 2, we can see the execution for the two initial phases of the algorithm. In the illustration, each node $[v_1..v_5]$ is assumed to have a local rank of five objects $[o_1..o_5]$ and the nodes are interconnected in a tree topology. The illustration shows that the sink requires only to fetch the objects above the lower line, which represents the execution of the second phase of our algorithm.

5 Experimental Evaluation

We have tested our top-k algorithm in a Peer-to-Peer network using a real dataset of temperature measurements collected at 32 sites in Washington and Oregon.[3] Each site (node) maintained the average temperature on an hourly basis for 208 days between June 2003 and June 2004 (i.e. 4990 time moments), and our query was to find the 10 moments at which the average temperature was the highest. Our algorithm uses our local access methods to execute efficiently. In Figure 3a we compare our approach with the *SS* approach (sending all data over the network), and our results indicate that *SS* consumes an order of magnitude more network bytes than the *SSMS* approach. We also compare our approach with a simpler approach that computes the scores of all tuples in the network, combining partial results as data is transmitted to the sink. This approach does not use any index methods, and can be implemented in the *SMS* framework. Our preliminary results show that our approach significantly outperforms this technique.

We have also calculated the energy gains that can be achieved by using the sense and store methodology by measuring the energy consumption of storing

---

[3] http://www-k12.atmos.washington.edu/k12/grayskies/

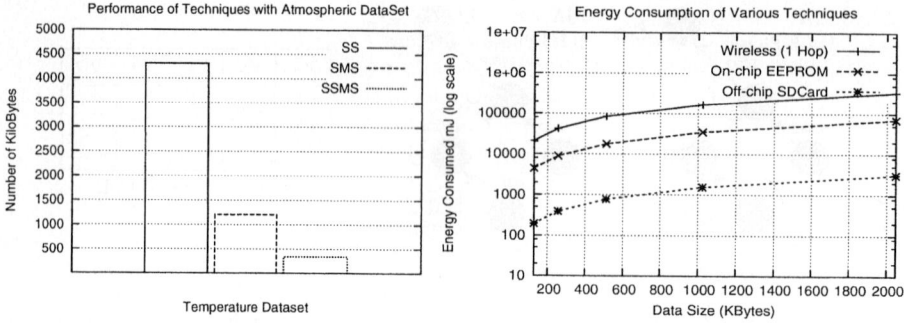

Fig. 3. a) Number of bytes transmitted in the *SS*, *SMS*, and *SSMS* models using atmospheric data. b) A comparison of the amount of energy expended to transfer data via the wireless interface vs Storing it on the on-chip EEPROM and the off-chip SD-Card.

data locally on flash card as opposed to blindly sending it over the wireless network. Specifically, we used the RISE mote to measure the cost of transmitting packages of various sizes over a 9.6Kbps radio (at 60mA) and storing the respective data locally on flash (see figure 3b). In the case of 512B (one page), we found that it takes on average $416ms$ or $82,368\mu J$. Comparing this with the $763.12\mu J$ required for writing the same amount of data to local flash, along with the fact that transmission of one byte is roughly equivalent to executing 1120 CPU instructions, makes local storage and processing highly desirable.

6 Related Work

There has been a lot of work in the area of query processing, in-network aggregation and data-centric storage in sensor networks. To our knowledge, our work is the first that addresses issues related to in-situ data storage in sensor devices with large memories.

Systems such as TinyDB[7] and Cougar[11] achieve energy reduction by pushing aggregation and selections in the network rather than processing everything at the sink. Both approaches propose a declarative approach for querying sensor networks. These systems are optimized for sensor nodes with limited storage and relatively short-epochs, while our techniques are designated for sensors with larger external flash memories and longer epochs. Note that in TinyDB users are allowed to define fixed size materialization points through the `STORAGE POINT` clause. This allows each sensor to gather locally in a buffer some readings, which cannot be utilized until the materialization point is created in its entirety. Therefore even if there was enough storage to store MBs of data, the absence of efficient access methods makes the retrieval of the desired values quite expensive.

A large number of flash-based file systems have been proposed in the last few years, including the Linux compatible Journaling Flash File System (JFFS and JFFS2)[15], the Yet Another Flash File System (YAFFS)[16] specifically designed for NAND flash with it being portable under Linux, uClinux, and Windows CE. The first file system for sensor nodes was Matchbox and this is provided as an integral part of the TinyOS [5] distribution. Recently the Efficient Log Structured Flash File System (ELF)[2] shows that it offers several advantages over Matchbox including higher read throughput and random access by timestamp. However the main job of a file system is to organize the sectors of the storage media into files and directories and to determine whether these are being used or not. Filenames are then accessible by their unique identifier (such as an inode). Therefore a filesystem does not support retrieving records by their value as we do in our approach.

An R-tree and B-Tree index structure for flash memory on portable devices, such as PDA's and cell phones, has been proposed in [13] and [14] respectively. These structures use an in-memory address translation table, which hides the details of the flash wear-leveling mechanism. However, such a structure has a very large footprint (3-4MB) which constitutes it inapplicable in our context.

In *Data Centric Routing (DCR)*, such as directed diffusion [6], low-latency paths are established between the sink and the sensors. Such an approach is supplementary to our framework. In Data Centric Storage (DCS) [10] data with the same name (e.g. humidity readings) is stored at the same node in the network, offering therefore efficient location and retrieval. However the overhead of relocating the data in the network will become huge if the network generates many MBs of GBs of data. Finally, local compression techniques, such as the one proposed in [3], would improve the efficiency of our framework and their investigation will be a topic of future research.

7 Conclusions

In this paper we discussed many of the data management issues that arise in the context of the *RISE* sensor network platform. In RISE, sensors feature a large memory which creates a new paradigm for power conservation in long epoch applications. We believe that many applications can benefit from a large local storage, as such storage can be used for local aggregation or compression before transmitting the results towards the sink. We expect that this in addition with the provisioning of efficient access methods will also provide a powerful new framework to cope with new types of queries, such as temporal or top-k, that have not been addressed adequately to this date. In the future we plan to investigate the effectiveness of our framework in field experiments which will be conducted in conjunction with the Center of Conservation Biology at UC-Riverside.

References

1. J. Considine, F. Li, G. Kollios, and J. Byers. "Approximate Aggregation Techniques for Sensor Databases", In *Proceedings of the 20th International Conference on Data Engineering*, Boston, Maryland, USA, Page 449, 2004.

2. H. Dai, M. Neufeld, R. Han, "ELF: an efficient log-structured flash file system for micro sensor nodes", In *Proceedings of the 2nd international conference on Embedded networked sensor systems* Baltimore, MD, USA, Pages 176-187, 2004.
3. A. Deligiannakis, Y. Kotidis, N. Roussopoulos, "Compressing historical information in sensor networks", In *Proceedings of the ACM SIGMOD international conference on Management of data* Paris, France, Pages 527-538, 2004.
4. R. Fagin, "Fuzzy Queries In Multimedia Database Systems", In *Proceedings of the seventeenth ACM SIGACT-SIGMOD-SIGART symposium on Principles of database systems*, Seattle, Washington, USA, Pages 1-10, 1998.
5. J. Hill, R. Szewczyk, A. Woo, S. Hollar, D. Culler, K. Pister, "System architecture directions for network sensors", In *Proceedings of the ninth international conference on Architectural support for programming languages and operating systems*, Cambridge, Massachusetts, USA, Pages 93-104, 2000.
6. C. Intanagonwiwat, R. Govindan, D. Estrin, "Directed diffusion: A scalable and robust communication paradigm for sensor networks", In *Proceedings of the 6th annual international conference on Mobile computing and networking*, Boston, Massachusetts, USA, Pages 56-67, 2000.
7. S.R. Madden, M.J. Franklin, J.M. Hellerstein, W. Hong, "The Design of an Acquisitional Query Processor for Sensor Networks", In *Proceedings of the 2003 ACM SIGMOD international conference on Management of data*, San Diego, California, USA, Pages 491-502, 2003.
8. S.R. Madden, M.J. Franklin, J.M. Hellerstein, W. Hong, "TAG: a Tiny AGgregation Service for Ad-Hoc Sensor Networks", In *Proceedings of the 5th symposium on Operating systems design and implementation* Boston, MA, pp. 131-146, 2002.
9. C. Sadler, P. Zhang, M. Martonosi, S. Lyon, "Hardware Design Experiences in ZebraNet", In *Proceedings of the 2nd international conference on Embedded networked sensor systems*, Baltimore, Maryland, USA, Pages 227-238, 2004.
10. S. Shenker, S. Ratnasamy, B. Karp, R. Govindan, D. Estrin, "Data-centric storage in sensornets", ACM SIGCOMM Computer Communication Review, Vol. 33, Iss. 1, pp. 137-142, 2003.
11. Y. Yao, J.E. Gehrke, "Query Processing in Sensor Networks", In *CIDR'03*, Asilomar, California, USA, 2003.
12. N. Xu, S. Rangwala, K. Chintalapudi, D. Ganesan, A. Broad, R. Govindan and D. Estrin, "A Wireless Sensor Network for Structural Monitoring", In *Proceedings of the 2nd international conference on Embedded networked sensor systems*, Baltimore, Maryland, USA, Pages 13-24, 2004.
13. C-H. Wu, L-P. Chang, T-W. Kuo, "An Efficient R-Tree Implementation Over Flash-Memory Storage Systems", In *Proceedings of the 11th ACM international symposium on Advances in geographic information systems*, New Orleans, Louisiana, Pages 17-24, 2003.
14. C-H. Wu, L-P. Chang, T-W. Kuo, "An Efficient B-Tree Layer for Flash Memory Storage Systems", In *RTCSA'03*, Tainan, Taiwan, 2003.
15. D. Woodhouse "JFFS : The Journalling Flash File System" Red Hat Inc., Available at: http://sources.redhat.com/jffs2/jffs2.pdf
16. Wookey "YAFFS - A filesystem designed for NAND flash", In *Linux 2004*.
17. R. Szewczyk, A. Mainwaring, J. Polastre, J. Anderson, D. Culler, "An Analysis of a Large Scale Habitat Monitoring Application", In *Proceedings of the 2nd international conference on Embedded networked sensor systems* Baltimore, Maryland, USA, Pages 214-226, 2004.
18. Crossbow Technology Inc. http://www.xbow.com/

A Primal-Dual Algorithm for Online Non-uniform Facility Location

Dimitris Fotakis

Department of Information and Communication Systems Engineering,
University of the Aegean, 83200 Karlovasi, Samos, Greece
fotakis@aegean.gr

Abstract. In the online version of Facility Location, the demand points arrive one at a time and must be irrevocably assigned to an open facility upon arrival. The objective is to minimize the sum of facility and assignment costs. We present a simple primal-dual deterministic algorithm for the general case of non-uniform facility costs. We prove that its competitive ratio is no greater than $4\log(n+1) + 2$, which is close to the lower bound of $\Omega(\frac{\log n}{\log\log n})$.

1 Introduction

In the (metric uncapacitated) Facility Location problem, we are given a metric space along with a facility cost for each point and a (multi)set of demand points, and we seek for a set of facility locations which minimize the sum of facility and assignment costs. Facility Location provides a simple and natural model for network design and data clustering problems and has been the subject of intensive research over the last decade (e.g. see [12] for a survey and [6] for approximation algorithms and applications). In addition to the offline setting, there are many practical applications where either the demand points are not known in advance or the solution must be constructed incrementally using limited (if any) information about future demands (e.g. see [11] for some examples from the areas of network design and data clustering).

The definition of *Online Facility Location* [11] is motivated by similar considerations. In Online Facility Location, the demand points arrive one at a time and must be irrevocably assigned to either an existing or a new facility upon arrival. The objective is to minimize the sum of facility and assignment costs, where the assignment cost of a demand is the distance from the facility to which the demand is assigned.

Related Work. In the offline setting, where the demand points are fully known in advance, there are constant factor approximation algorithms based on Linear Programming rounding (e.g. [13,14]), local search (e.g. [4,2]), and the primal-dual method (e.g. [9,8]). The best known polynomial-time algorithm achieves an approximation ratio of 1.52 [10], while no polynomial-time algorithm has an approximation ratio less than 1.463 unless $\mathrm{NP} \subseteq \mathrm{DTIME}(n^{O(\log\log n)})$ [7].

Meyerson [11] introduced the online version of Facility Location and presented a randomized algorithm which achieves a constant performance ratio if the demands are examined in random order. In the standard framework of competitive analysis (e.g. see [3]), where both the set of demands and their arrival order are selected by an oblivious adversary, Meyerson's algorithm achieves a competitive ratio of $O(\log n)$. Meyerson also proved a lower bound of $\omega(1)$ on the competitive ratio of any online algorithm.

In previous work [5], we improved the lower bound to $\Omega(\frac{\log n}{\log \log n})$ even for the special case that the metric space is a line segment and the facility costs are uniform. We also presented a deterministic algorithm with an (asymptotically) optimal competitive ratio of $\Theta(\frac{\log n}{\log \log n})$ for general metric spaces and non-uniform facility costs. The algorithm is rather complicated to formulate and implement. Its analysis exploits locality in a novel and highly non-trivial way and is lengthy and quite technical. Hence despite being a significant contribution towards understanding the problem from a theoretical point of view, the algorithm of [5] is of limited practical applicability.

This observation motivated a recent work by Anagnostopoulos et al. [1], who presented a simple $\Theta(2^d \log n)$-competitive deterministic algorithm for Online Facility Location in d-dimensional Euclidean spaces. The algorithm works only for the fixed-location uniform-cost model, where the facilities have the same opening cost and can be located at a fixed subset of points. For the Euclidean plane, the algorithm is quite fast and its performance in practice is comparable to the performance of the algorithms in [11,5]. Nevertheless, the approach of [1] cannot be applied to general metric spaces and the arbitrary non-uniform facility costs.

Contribution. We present a new primal-dual algorithm for Online Facility Location (e.g. see [15] for an introduction to primal-dual approximation algorithms). The algorithm is deterministic and works for every metric space and non-uniform facility costs.

The algorithm maintains the invariant that the distances of each demand to the nearest algorithm's facility constitute a feasible solution to the dual of a natural Linear Programming relaxation for Facility Location. Every time a dual constraint is violated due to the arrival of a new demand, the algorithm opens a new facility at the location corresponding to the most violated dual constraint, and the dual feasibility is restored.

We prove that the algorithm's competitive ratio is no greater than $4\log(n+1) + 2$, which is close to the lower bound of $\Omega(\frac{\log n}{\log \log n})$ [5]. The analysis is simple and gives a new insight into the behaviour of previously known algorithms for Online Facility Location and related problems.

Our algorithm is the first deterministic algorithm which works for every metric space and the general case of non-uniform facility costs, and is simple to formulate and analyze, easy to implement, and quite fast in terms of running time.

The only previously known deterministic algorithm which works for every metric space and non-uniform facility costs is the algorithm of [5]. That algorithm achieves an (asymptotically) optimal competitive ratio of $\Theta(\frac{\log n}{\log \log n})$, but is quite complicated to formulate, implement, and analyze. Moreover, since there are quite large multiplicative and additive constants involved in its competitive ratio, we expect that the algorithm presented in this paper will outperform the algorithm of [5] in practice.

The algorithm of [1] only works for Euclidean spaces of small dimension and uniform facility costs. In addition, its competitive ratio is exponential in the dimension of the metric space. Hence, our results are not comparable to the results of [1].

Problem Definition and Notation. We evaluate the performance of online algorithms using *competitive analysis* (e.g. see [3]). An online algorithm is c-competitive if for all instances, the cost incurred by the algorithm is at most c times the cost incurred by an optimal offline algorithm, which knows the demand sequence in advance.

In Online Facility Location, we are given a metric space $\mathcal{M} = (M, d)$, where M denotes the set of points and $d : M \times M \mapsto \mathbb{R}_+$ denotes the distance function which is non-negative, symmetric and satisfies the triangle inequality. For each point $w \in M$, we are also given the cost f_w of opening a facility at w. The facility costs of some points may be infinite, in which case we are not allowed to open a facility there. We slightly abuse the notation by letting the same symbol denote both a demand/facility and the corresponding point of the metric space.

The demand sequence consists of (not necessarily distinct) points $u \in M$. When a new demand u arrives, the algorithm can open some new facilities, in which case it incurs the corresponding opening cost. The decision of opening a facility at a particular location is *irrevocable*. Then, u is *irrevocably* assigned to the nearest facility. If u is assigned to a facility at w, u's assignment cost is $d(w, u)$. The objective is to minimize the sum of facility and assignment costs.

We only consider unit demands and allow multiple demands to be located at the same point. We use n to denote the total number of demands. We consider the general case of *non-uniform* facility costs, where the opening costs depend on the location and there are no restrictions on them.

A metric space $\mathcal{M} = (M, d)$ is usually identified by its point set M. For a point $u \in M$ and a subset of points $M' \subseteq M$, $d(M', u) \equiv \min_{v \in M'}\{d(v, u)\}$ denotes the distance between u and the nearest point in M'. We let $d(\emptyset, u) = \inf$. We use $\log x$ to denote the base-2 logarithm of a positive number x. For every numbers x, y, let $x \dotdiv y \equiv \max\{x - y, 0\}$. In the technical part of the paper, we repeatedly use $x \dotdiv y \geq x - y$.

Organization. In Section 2, we formulate the algorithm and discuss the intuition behind it. We also state our main result, namely that the algorithm's competitive ratio is no greater than $4 \log(n + 1) + 2$, and outline its proof. The main invariant maintained by the algorithm is formally proven in Section 3. Using this invariant, we bound the algorithm's assignment cost in Section 4 and the algorithm's facility cost in Section 5. The conclusions and some directions for further research are discussed in Section 6.

2 The Primal-Dual Algorithm

The algorithm *Simple Non-Uniform Facility Location* (SNFL, Fig. 1) maintains the *set of demands* considered so far, denoted L, its *facility configuration*, denoted F, and the *potential* of each point z, denoted $p(z)$. At any point in time, $p(z) = \sum_{v \in L} d(F, v) \dotdiv d(z, v)$ for all $z \in M$. The algorithm maintains the invariant that the potential of each point z does not exceed the cost of opening a facility at z, namely $p(z) \leq f_z$. Every time this invariant is violated, the algorithm opens a new facility at an appropriately selected location and the invariant is restored.

Initially, $L = \emptyset$, $F = \emptyset$, and $p(z) = 0$ for all $z \in M$. When a new demand arrives, the algorithm updates the potentials of all points and computes the point w of maximum $p(w) - f_w$. If $p(w) > f_w$, the algorithm opens a new facility at w and computes the potentials again according to the new facility configuration. Due to w's choice, opening a new facility at w restores the invariant $p(z) \leq f_z$ for all points z (cf. Lemma 1). If

| ```
F ← ∅; L ← ∅; initializePotentials ();
for each new demand u:
    L ← L ∪ {u};
    updatePotentials (F, u);
    w ← arg max_{z∈M} {p(z) − f_z};
    if p(w) − f_w > 0 then
        F ← F ∪ {w};
        computeNewPotentials (F, L);
    assign u to the nearest facility in F;
``` | ```
initializePotentials ()
    for all z ∈ M do
        p(z) ← 0;
updatePotentials (F, u)
    for all z ∈ M do
        p(z) ← p(z) + d(F, u) ∸ d(z, u);
computeNewPotentials (F, L)
    for all z ∈ M do
        p(z) ← ∑_{v∈L} d(F, v) ∸ d(z, v);
``` |

Fig. 1. The algorithm Simple Non-Uniform Facility Location – SNFL

$p(w) \leq f_w$, the invariant holds for all points and no new facilities open. Finally, the new demand is assigned to the nearest facility in the updated facility configuration.

Intuition. Before establishing the competitive ratio, we give an intuitive description and a primal-dual interpretation of SNFL. We regard the distance of each demand $v \in L$ to the nearest algorithm's facility, namely the distance $d(F, v)$, as a credit currently held by v. The demands contribute their credit towards opening new facilities closer to them. More specifically, when a new facility w opens, the credit of each demand v becomes $d(F \cup \{w\}, v) \leq d(F, v)$. The difference $d(F, v) - d(F \cup \{w\}, v) = d(F, v) \dotdiv d(w, v)$ is regarded as v's contribution to w's opening cost.

The potential of each point z corresponds to the total decrease in the demands' credit if a facility at z opens. The algorithm opens a new facility only if the total decrease in the demands' credit exceeds the corresponding opening cost. In simple words, a new facility opens only if the demands are willing to spend an adequate amount of credit for it. The location of the new facility is the point maximizing the difference between the credit spent for the new facility and the actual opening cost.

We formalize the intuitive description above by resorting to Linear Programming duality. The offline version of Facility Location is formulated as the following $0 - 1$ Integer Program:

$$\begin{aligned}
\min \ & \sum_{z \in M} f_z y_z + \sum_{z \in M} \sum_{v \in L} x_{zv} d(z, v) \\
\text{s.t} \ & \sum_{z \in M} x_{zv} = 1 & \forall v \in L \\
& x_{zv} \leq y_z & \forall z \in M, \forall v \in L \quad \text{(IP)} \\
& y_z \in \{0, 1\}, x_{zv} \in \{0, 1\} & \forall z \in M, \forall v \in L
\end{aligned}$$

Setting the variable y_z to 1 corresponds to opening a facility at z and setting the variable x_{zv} to 1 corresponds to assigning demand v to facility z. We obtain a Linear Programming relaxation of (IP) by replacing the $0 - 1$ constraints with $y_z \geq 0$ and $x_{zv} \geq 0$ respectively. The dual of the Linear Programming relaxation is:

$$\begin{aligned}
\max \ & \sum_{v \in L} c_v \\
\text{s.t} \ & \sum_{v \in L} [c_v \dotdiv d(z, v)] \leq f_z & \forall z \in M \quad \text{(DP)} \\
& c_v \geq 0 & \forall v \in L
\end{aligned}$$

SNFL maintains its facility configuration F so as the distances $d(F, v)$, $v \in L$, (in other words, the demand credits) to constitute a feasible solution to (DP). Every time a dual constraint is violated due to the arrival of a new demand, a new facility opens at the location corresponding to the most violated dual constraint and the dual feasibility is restored. Thus, SNFL is a primal-dual online algorithm.

The running time of SNFL is $O(n |M| |F|)$, where n is the number of demands, $|M|$ is the number of points with finite facility cost, and $|F|$ is the number of facilities opened by the algorithm. The remaining part of the paper is devoted to the proof of the algorithm's competitive ratio.

Theorem 1. *The competitive ratio of* SNFL *is no greater than* $4\log(n+1) + 2$.

2.1 Preliminaries

For an arbitrary fixed sequence of n demands, we compare the algorithm's cost with the cost of the offline optimal solution. We denote the set of optimal facilities by F^*. To avoid confusing the algorithm's facilities with the optimal facilities, we use the term *optimal center*, or simply *center*, to refer to an optimal facility in F^* and the term *facility* to refer to an algorithm's facility in F.

We let the optimal solution F^* consist of k centers $c_1, c_2, \ldots, c_k$. We use f_{c_i}, $i = 1, \ldots, k$, to denote the opening costs of the optimal centers. In the optimal solution, each demand is assigned to the nearest center in F^*. Hence, F^* partitions the demand sequence into optimal clusters $C_1, C_2, \ldots, C_k$. For each demand v, let $d_v^* \equiv d(F^*, v)$ denote the assignment cost of v in the optimal solution, let $\text{Asg}^* \equiv \sum_v d_v^*$ denote the total optimal assignment cost, and let $\text{Fac}^* \equiv \sum_{c_i \in F^*} f_{c_i}$ denote the total optimal facility cost. The total optimal cost is $\text{Fac}^* + \text{Asg}^*$. For a demand set C, let $\text{Asg}^*(C) \equiv \sum_{v \in C} d_v^*$ denote the total optimal assignment cost for the demands in C.

We usually distinguish between the arrival and the assignment time of a new demand because the algorithm's configuration may have changed in between. We use the convention that unprimed symbols refer to the algorithm's configuration just before a new demand arrives and primed symbols refer to the updated algorithm's configuration at the demand's assignment time.

2.2 Outline of the Analysis

We start by showing that SNFL maintains the invariant that $p(z) \le f_z$ for all $z \in M$ (Lemma 1). Therefore, after j demands from cluster C_i have been considered, there is a facility within a distance of $\frac{1}{j}[f_{c_i} + 2\text{Asg}^*(C_i)]$ from the optimal center c_i (Corollary 1). This implies that the algorithm's assignment cost is within a logarithmic factor of the total optimal cost (Lemma 2).

We allocate a credit of $c(u) = \min\{d(F, u), \min_{z \in M}\{f_z - p(z) + d(z, u)\}\}$ to each new demand u, where F denotes the facility configuration and $p(z)$ denotes z's potential just before u arrives. We show that the algorithm's facility cost never exceeds the total credit allocated to the demands in L (Lemma 4). Corollary 1 implies that the total credit is within a logarithmic factor of the total optimal cost (Lemma 5).

3 Basic Properties

We start by establishing the algorithm's main invariant.

Lemma 1 (Main Invariant). *Let L be the demand set, and let F be the facility configuration just before a new demand arrives. For all $z \in M$, $p(z) \leq f_z$.*

Proof. We prove the lemma by induction on the number of demands considered by the algorithm. The invariant holds before the first demand arrives because initially $p(z) = 0 \leq f_z$ for all $z \in M$. We inductively assume that the invariant holds just before a new demand u arrives and prove that the invariant holds after u's assignment.

Let F be the algorithm's facility configuration, let L be the demand set, and let $p(z) = \sum_{v \in L} d(F,v) \dotdiv d(z,v) \leq f_z$ be the potential of each point z just before u arrives. We denote by $p'(z)$ and $p''(z)$ the potential of z when w is computed and at u's assignment time respectively. We show that for all $z \in M$, $p''(z) \leq f_z$.

The new demand does not open a new facility only if $p'(z) \leq f_z$ for all $z \in M$. Then the facility configuration remains unchanged and $p''(z) = p'(z) \leq f_z$.

If a new facility opens at w, let $F' = F \cup \{w\}$ denote the facility configuration at u's assignment time. We claim that u is closer to w than to any facility in F, i.e. $d(w,u) < d(F,u)$, which implies that $d(F',u) = d(w,u)$. The claim follows from the following inequalities:

$$0 < p'(w) - f_w = d(F,u) \dotdiv d(w,u) + p(w) - f_w$$
$$\leq d(F,u) \dotdiv d(w,u) = d(F,u) - d(w,u) \quad (1)$$

The first inequality holds because a new facility at w opens. The next equality follows from $p'(w) = p(w) + d(F,u) \dotdiv d(w,u)$. The next inequality uses $p(w) - f_w \leq 0$ by the inductive hypothesis. Finally, we observe that $d(F,u) \dotdiv d(w,u) > 0$.

We also observe that for every $z \in M$,

$$p(z) = \sum_{v \in L}[d(F,v) \dotdiv d(z,v)] \geq \sum_{v \in L}[d(F',v) \dotdiv d(z,v)] \quad (2)$$

because $d(F',v) \leq d(F,v)$ for all demands $v \in L$.

For all points z with $d(z,u) \geq d(w,u)$, $d(F',u) \dotdiv d(z,u) = 0$ and

$$p''(z) = \sum_{v \in L}[d(F',v) \dotdiv d(z,v)] \leq p(z) \leq f_z$$

where the first inequality follows from (2) and the second from the inductive hypothesis.

After the potentials of all points have been updated, the algorithm selects w as the location of the new facility. Therefore for every $z \in M$, $p'(w) - f_w \geq p'(z) - f_z$ and:

$$d(F,u) - d(w,u) \geq p'(w) - f_w \geq p'(z) - f_z = d(F,u) \dotdiv d(z,u) + p(z) - f_z$$
$$\geq d(F,u) - d(z,u) + \sum_{v \in L}[d(F',v) \dotdiv d(z,v)] - f_z$$

The first inequality follows from (1). The equality follows from the definition of $p'(z)$. For the last inequality, we use $d(F,u) \dotdiv d(z,u) \geq d(F,u) - d(z,u)$ and (2). Therefore, for all points z with $d(z,u) < d(w,u)$, $d(F',u) \dotdiv d(z,u) = d(w,u) - d(z,u)$ and:

$$0 \geq d(w,u) - d(z,u) + \sum_{v \in L}[d(F',v) \dotdiv d(z,v)] - f_z = p''(z) - f_z$$

Consequently, after w opens, for every point z, $p''(z) \leq f_z$. $\square$

The invariant of Lemma 1 implies that the algorithm's facility configuration converges fast to the optimal centers as more and more demands are considered.

Corollary 1. *Let L be the demand set, and let F be the facility configuration after all demands in L have been considered. For each optimal cluster C_i with center c_i,*

$$|L \cap C_i| d(F, c_i) \le f_{c_i} + 2 \operatorname{Asg}^*(C_i)$$

Proof. We apply the invariant of Lemma 1 for the optimal center c_i:

$$f_{c_i} \ge p(c_i) = \sum_{v \in L} d(F, v) \dot{-} d(c_i, v) \ge \sum_{v \in L \cap C_i} d(F, v) \dot{-} d_v^*$$

$$\ge \sum_{v \in L \cap C_i} [(d(F, c_i) - d_v^*) - d_v^*] = |L \cap C_i| d(F, c_i) - 2 \sum_{v \in L \cap C_i} d_v^*$$

The second inequality holds because the first sum consists of non-negative terms. In addition, for all $v \in C_i$, $d(c_i, v) = d_v^*$. For the third inequality, we apply $x \dot{-} y \ge x - y$ and the triangle inequality. Finally, we observe that $\operatorname{Asg}^*(L \cap C_i) \le \operatorname{Asg}^*(C_i)$. □

4 Assignment Cost

Then we use Corollary 1 and bound the algorithm's assignment cost.

Lemma 2. *The algorithm's assignment cost is no greater than*

$$\log(n+1) \operatorname{Fac}^* + (2 \log(n+1) + 1) \operatorname{Asg}^*$$

Proof. Let C_i be an optimal cluster with center c_i, let $n_i \equiv |C_i|$ be the number of demands in C_i, and let $u_1, u_2, \ldots, u_{n_i}$ be the demands of C_i in the order considered by the algorithm. For each demand u_j, let F'_{u_j} be the facility configuration at u_j's assignment time. Hence, the algorithm's assignment cost for u_j is:

$$d(F'_{u_j}, u_j) \le d(F'_{u_j}, c_i) + d_{u_j}^* \le \tfrac{1}{j}[f_{c_i} + 2\operatorname{Asg}^*(C_i)] + d_{u_j}^* \qquad (3)$$

We first apply the triangle inequality. For the second inequality, we use Corollary 1 with $L \cap C_i = \{u_1, \ldots, u_j\}$ since the algorithm has considered the first j demands from C_i and reached the facility configuration F'_{u_j}.

Summing up (3) for all $j = 1, \ldots, n_i$, we conclude that the algorithm's assignment cost for the demands in C_i is:

$$\sum_{j=1}^{n_i} d(F'_{u_j}, u_j) \le [f_{c_i} + 2\operatorname{Asg}^*(C_i)] \sum_{j=1}^{n_i} \tfrac{1}{j} + \sum_{j=1}^{n_i} d_{u_j}^*$$

$$\le \log(n_i + 1) f_{c_i} + (2\log(n_i + 1) + 1) \operatorname{Asg}^*(C_i)$$

For the last inequality, we use $\sum_{j=1}^{n} 1/j \le \log(n+1)$ for all $n \in \mathbb{N}$. The lemma follows by summing up the inequality above over all optimal clusters. □

5 Facility Cost

We allocate a credit of $c(u) = \min\{d(F, u), \min_{z \in M}\{f_z - p(z) + d(z, u)\}\}$ to each new demand u, where F denotes the facility configuration and $p(z)$ denotes z's potential just before u arrives.

Lemma 3. *For each new demand u, $c(u) = f_w - p(w) + d(w, u)$ if u opens a new facility at w, and $c(u) = d(F, u)$ otherwise.*

Proof. Let F be the facility configuration, and let $p(z)$ be the potential of each point z just before u arrives. Let also $p'(z) = p(z) + d(F, u) - d(z, u)$ denote the updated potential of each point z.

Let the new demand u open a new facility at w. Due to the choice of w, $p'(w) - f_w \geq p'(z) - f_z$ for all points $z \in M$. Therefore,

$$p'(w) - f_w = p(w) + d(F, u) - d(w, u) - f_w$$
$$\geq p(z) + d(F, u) - d(z, u) - f_z \geq p(z) + d(F, u) - d(z, u) - f_z$$

The equality holds because u is closer to w than to any facility in F (see also (1) in the proof of Lemma 1). Hence, $f_w - p(w) + d(w, u) = \min_{z \in M}\{f_z - p(z) + d(z, u)\}$. Since a new facility opens, $p'(w) - f_w > 0$ and $d(F, u) > f_w - p(w) + d(w, u)$. Consequently, if the new demand u opens a new facility at w, u's credit is $c(u) = f_w - p(w) + d(w, u)$.

If the new demand u does not open a new facility, for all points $z \in M$,

$$f_z \geq p'(z) = p(z) + d(F, u) - d(z, u) \geq p(z) + d(F, u) - d(z, u)$$

Therefore, $d(F, u) \leq f_z - p(z) + d(z, u)$ and u's credit is $c(u) = d(F, u)$. □

Using Lemma 3, we show that the cost for the facilities in F does not exceed the total credit allocated to the demands in L.

Lemma 4. *Let L be the demand set, and let F be the facility configuration after all demands in L have been considered. Then, $\sum_{w \in F} f_w \leq \sum_{v \in L} c(v)$.*

Proof. We prove the lemma by a potential function argument. We define the potential function $\Phi = \sum_{v \in L} d(F, v)$ and calculate the change $\Delta\Phi$ in the value of the potential function when a new demand u is considered. Let L be the demand set, let F be the facility configuration, and let $p(z)$ be the potential of each point z just before u arrives.

If u does not open a new facility, then $\Delta\Phi = d(F, u) = c(u)$, by Lemma 3.

If u opens a new facility at w, let $F' = F \cup \{w\}$. By definition, $d(F, v) - d(F', v) = d(F, v) - d(w, v)$ for all demands v. Therefore,

$$\Delta\Phi = d(w, u) - \sum_{v \in L}[d(F, v) - d(F', v)]$$
$$= d(w, u) - \sum_{v \in L}[d(F, v) - d(w, v)] = d(w, u) - p(w)$$

By Lemma 3, u's credit is $c(u) = f_w - p(w) + d(w, u)$. Hence $\Delta\Phi + f_w = c(u)$.

Thus, we have shown that the credit allocated to each new demand u is equal to the change in the value of Φ plus the cost for the facility opened by u (possibly none).

Initially, $\Phi = 0$ because the demand set is empty. By definition, Φ remains non-negative throughout the execution of the algorithm. Therefore, the opening cost for the facilities in F never exceeds the total credit allocated to the demands in L. □

Finally, we use Corollary 1 and bound the total credit allocated to the demand set.

Lemma 5. *Let L be the demand set. Then,*

$$\sum_{v \in L} c(v) \leq (\log n + 1)\text{Fac}^* + (2\log n + 1)\text{Asg}^*$$

Proof. As in the proof of Lemma 2, let C_i be an optimal cluster with center c_i, let $n_i \equiv |C_i|$, and let $u_1, u_2, \ldots, u_{n_i}$ be the demands of C_i in the order considered by the algorithm. For each demand u_j, let F_{u_j} be the facility configuration just before u_j arrives.

The credit of each demand u_j is $c(u_j) \leq \min\{d(F_{u_j}, u_j), f_{c_i} + d_{u_j}^*\}$ because the potential of c_i is non-negative. For the first demand, we use $c(u_1) \leq f_{c_i} + d_{u_1}^*$. For each of the remaining demands u_j, $j = 2, \ldots, n_i$, we use

$$c(u_j) \leq d(F_{u_j}, u_j) \leq d(F_{u_j}, c_i) + d_{u_j}^* \leq \tfrac{1}{j-1}[f_{c_i} + 2\text{Asg}^*(C_i)] + d_{u_j}^*$$

For the second inequality, we use Corollary 1 with $L \cap C_i = \{u_1, \ldots, u_{j-1}\}$ since the algorithm has considered the first $j-1$ demands from C_i just before u_j arrives.

Summing up the above inequalities for all $j = 1, \ldots, n_i$, we conclude that the total credit allocated to the demands in C_i is:

$$\sum_{j=1}^{n_i} c(u_j) \leq f_{c_i} + [f_{c_i} + 2\text{Asg}^*(C_i)] \sum_{j=2}^{n_i} \tfrac{1}{j-1} + \sum_{j=1}^{n_i} d_{u_j}^*$$

$$\leq (\log n_i + 1)f_{c_i} + (2\log n_i + 1)\text{Asg}^*(C_i)$$

For the last inequality, we use $\sum_{j=1}^{n-1} 1/j \leq \log n$ for all $n \in \mathbb{N}$. The lemma follows by summing up the previous inequality for all optimal clusters. □

Lemmas 4 and 5 imply that the facility cost is no greater than $(\log n + 1)\text{Fac}^* + (2\log n + 1)\text{Asg}^*$. Combining this bound with the bound of Lemma 2, we obtain that the total algorithm's cost is no greater than

$$(2\log(n+1) + 1)\text{Fac}^* + (4\log(n+1) + 2)\text{Asg}^* \leq (4\log(n+1) + 2)(\text{Fac}^* + \text{Asg}^*)$$

This concludes the proof of Theorem 1.

6 Conclusions

We presented a simple and practical primal-dual algorithm for Online Facility Location with non-uniform facility costs. The algorithm maintains the invariant that the distances of each demand to the nearest facility constitute a feasible dual solution. Every time a dual constraint is violated due to the arrival of a new demand, a new facility opens at the location corresponding to the most violated dual constraint, and the dual feasibility is restored. We prove that the algorithm's competitive ratio is $4\log(n+1) + 2$, which is close to the lower bound of $\Omega(\frac{\log n}{\log\log n})$.

We are not aware of any examples establishing that the algorithm's competitive ratio is $\Omega(\log n)$. Thus, it remains open whether the competitive ratio of SNFL is $\Theta(\log n)$ or can be improved by a more careful analysis.

In retrospect, we observe that all known algorithms for Online Facility Location can be regarded as maintaining a similar invariant *implicitly*. More specifically, all known algorithms have the property that the distances of each demand to the nearest facility form an *approximately* feasible dual solution. In the light of this observation, it is natural to ask whether there is a generic primal-dual framework for formulating and establishing the competitive ratios of all known algorithms for Online Facility Location and related problems.

References

1. A. Anagnostopoulos, R. Bent, E. Upfal, and P. Van Hentenryck. A Simple and Deterministic Competitive Algorithm for Online Facility Location. *Information and Computation*, 194:175–202, 2004.
2. V. Arya, N. Garg, R. Khandekar, A. Meyerson, K. Munagala, and V. Pandit. Local Search Heuristics for k-Median and Facility Location Problems. *Proc. of STOC '01*, pp. 21–29, 2001.
3. A. Borodin and R. El-Yaniv. *Online Computation and Competitive Analysis*. Cambridge University Press, 1998.
4. M. Charikar and S. Guha. Improved Combinatorial Algorithms for the Facility Location and k-Median Problems. *Proc. of FOCS '99*, pp. 378–388, 1999.
5. D. Fotakis. On the Competitive Ratio for Online Facility Location. *Proc. of ICALP '03*, LNCS 2719, pp. 637–652, 2003.
6. S. Guha. *Approximation Algorithms for Facility Location Problems*. PhD thesis, Stanford University, 2000.
7. S. Guha and S. Khuller. Greedy Strikes Back: Improved Facility Location Algorithms. *Proc. of SODA '98*, pp. 649–657, 1998.
8. K. Jain, M. Mahdian, and A. Saberi. A New Greedy Approach for Facility Location Problems. *Proc. of STOC '02*, pp. 731–740, 2002.
9. K. Jain and V. Vazirani. Approximation Algorithms for Metric Facility Location and k-Median Problems Using the Primal-Dual Schema and Lagrangian Relaxation. *J. of the ACM*, 48(2):274–296, 2001.
10. M. Mahdian, Y. Ye, and J. Zhang. Improved Approximation Algorithms for Metric Facility Location Problems. *Proc. of APPROX '02*, LNCS 2462, pp. 229–242, 2002.
11. A. Meyerson. Online Facility Location. *Proc. of FOCS '01*, pp. 426–431, 2001.
12. D. Shmoys. Approximation Algorithms for Facility Location Problems. *Proc. of APPROX '00*, LNCS 1913, pp. 27–33, 2000.
13. D. Shmoys, E. Tardos, and K. Aardal. Approximation Algorithms for Facility Location Problems. *Proc. of STOC '97*, pp. 265–274, 1997.
14. M. Sviridenko. An Improved Approximation Algorithm for the Metric Uncapacitated Facility Location Problem. *Proc. of IPCO '02*, LNCS 2337, pp. 240–257, 2002.
15. V. Vazirani. *Approximation Algorithms*. Springer, 2001.

Routing and Wavelength Assignment in Generalized WDM Tree Networks of Bounded Degree[*]

Stratis Ioannidis[1], Christos Nomikos[2], Aris Pagourtzis[3], and Stathis Zachos[3,4]

[1] Department of Computer Science, University of Toronto
[2] Department of Computer Science, University of Ioannina
[3] School of Elec. & Comp. Engineering, National Technical University of Athens
[4] CIS Department, Brooklyn College, Cuny
stratis@cs.utoronto.ca
cnomikos@cs.uoi.gr
{pagour, zachos}@cs.ntua.gr

Abstract. The increasing popularity of all-optical networks has led to extensive research on the routing and wavelength assignment problem, also termed as the *Routing and Path Coloring problem* (RPC). Here we present a polynomial time algorithm that solves RPC exactly in *generalized tree networks* of bounded degree. This new topology is of practical interest since it models tree-like backbone networks connecting bounded-size LANs of any form. Tree-like backbone structure is very common in practice and bounded size LANs is a reasonable assumption, since LANs are by nature networks unable to sustain a large number of hosts.

Keywords: routing and path coloring, wavelength assignment, WDM networks, optical networking.

1 Introduction

All-Optical Networks. Optical fiber technology evolves rapidly and will eventually lead to networks consisting solely of optical connections. In such networks, which are called *all-optical*, signal multiplexing is achieved through the WDM (*wavelength division multiplexing*) technique; a different wavelength is assigned to each signal, thus enabling multiple signals to be transmitted through the same fiber.

The bottleneck in current optical connections lies in the conversion of electrical signals to optical ones and vice versa. Consequently, it appears that all-optical networks should minimize such conversions. To that purpose, messages that are routed through the network should be processed as little as possible. One way to achieve this is to maintain the same wavelength throughout the network for each signal transmitted from one host to another. In other words, when two (possibly

---

[*] Research supported in part by "Pythagoras" grant of the Ministry of Education of Greece, co-funded by the European Social Fund (75%) and National Resources (25%) — Operational Programme for Education and Initial Vocational Training (EPEAEK II).

non-adjacent) hosts communicate with each other through a connection, optical signals realizing this connection use only one wavelength.

The Routing and Path Coloring Problem. All-optical networks can be modeled as graphs and *connection requests* between two hosts can be represented by pairs of nodes. In the case of *full-duplex* communication the requests, hence also the pairs of nodes, are actually unordered. Such requests are *routed* into actual connections through appropriate paths connecting the two nodes. Each of these connections uses the same wavelength for all transmissions, so wavelength assignment can be modeled as coloring of the corresponding path. The fact that two signals can be multiplexed in a fiber only if different wavelengths are assigned to them imposes restrictions on possible colorings of the path set. If we assume that adjacent hosts are connected through a single fiber link, a coloring shall be feasible only if *overlapping* paths (i.e. sharing at least one edge) are assigned different colors.

The *Routing and Path Coloring problem* (RPC) is stated as follows: Given a graph G and a set of connection requests R (unordered pairs of nodes), find a routing of R, i.e. a set of corresponding paths P, and a feasible coloring of paths in P using the least possible number of colors. Note that the minimum number of colors among all possible routings and colorings is sought. It also makes sense to consider the problem where the routing is pre-determined and only an optimal coloring is sought; this is known as the *Path Coloring problem* (PC): Given a graph G and a set of paths P, find a feasible coloring of paths in P using the least possible number of colors.

We are interested in simple paths only, since any routing and coloring that uses non-simple paths can be transformed to one with only simple paths and at most the same cost (number of colors needed). Hence, in acyclic topologies there is a unique possible routing and RPC coincides with PC. Note also that paths are not necessarily distinct, i.e. two paths may pass through identical edges and nodes. This captures the possibility of more than one connections between two nodes, all using the same fiber links.

Related Work. Both RPC and PC have been studied for a variety of topologies, such as chains, rings, trees, trees of rings, grids, to name only a few.

As mentioned above, the two problems coincide in acyclic topologies and can be solved exactly within polynomial time in chains [31] and in bounded degree trees [26,10]. Furthermore, PC in stars is equivalent to edge coloring [14] in general multigraphs and thus is NP-hard [16] and approximable within a factor of $\frac{4}{3}$ [15,25]. The same approximation factor can be achieved in unbounded degree trees [26,10].

PC in rings, also known as the *Circular-Arc Coloring problem*, was proved to be NP hard by Garey et al. [13]; Shih and Hsu [33] presented an approximation algorithm with ratio $\frac{5}{3}$ and Karapetian [17] developed a $\frac{3}{2}$-approximation algorithm. A randomized algorithm that achieves a 1.37 asymptotic approximation factor with high probability, in instances where the optimum solution is large, was given by V. Kumar [20]. Results combining the above with approximation algorithms for PC in trees yield approximation results for trees of rings [26,24,8]. RPC in rings is also NP-hard [10,4]; simple algorithms with approximation ratio 2 were presented by Raghavan and Upfal [32] (undirected problem) and by Mihail et al. [24] (directed problem); A randomized algorithm for RPC in rings with asymptotic approximation ratio 1.38 was given by V. Kumar [19] and was later improved by Cheng [5].

PC in undirected trees can be approximated within a ratio of 1.1 (asymptotically). This is due to the fact that PC in undirected trees is equivalent to edge coloring of multigraphs via approximation preserving reductions [14]; hence the 1.1-approximation algorithm of Nishizeki and Kashiwagi [25] for edge coloring of multigraphs yields an algorithm for PC in undirected trees with the same approximation ratio. In directed trees, the best known algorithm is a 5/3-approximation (using at most $5L/3$ colors) due to Erlebach et al. [11].

S. R. Kumar et al. [18] proved that PC in trees can be solved exactly in polynomial time provided that the degree of the tree is bounded. They did this by showing that RPC in constant size graphs (with unbounded number of requests) is in P; to this end, they employed an integer programming technique. On the other hand, Nomikos [26] proved that PC is non-approximable in meshes (unless P=NP), and thus in arbitrary graphs as well. Extensive work has been done for PC and RPC in (unbounded) directed tree topologies [24,11,18,10].

A related problem is the MAXIMUM ROUTING AND PATH COLORING PROBLEM (MAXRPC), where the goal is to route and color as many requests as possible using only the available colors; the variation where the routing is pre-determined is called MAXIMUM PATH COLORING PROBLEM (MAXPC). MAXPC in chains, also known as the "k-coloring of intervals" problem, can be solved exactly [3]. Nomikos, Pagourtzis and Zachos [29] have proposed a 3/2-approximation algorithm for MAXRPC in undirected rings and a 11/7-approximation algorithm for the directed case; they have also given a 3/2-approximation algorithm for MAXPC in rings, both for the undirected and the directed case [30]. For trees, a 1.58 approximation for the undirected case was presented by Wan and Liu [34], while for the directed case a 2.22-approximation is due to Erlebach and Jansen [9].

Variants of PC and RPC, where multiple fibers are allowed, have been extensively studied in recent years [28,35,22,23,27,12]; in these papers, constant ratio approximation algorithms are presented for various basic topologies such as chains, rings, stars and trees. In [1,2] they give lower and upper bounds on the approximability of multiple-fiber problems for general topologies. Other related work includes traffic grooming; in this approach one can combine low speed traffic components onto high speed channels in order to minimize network cost. Traffic grooming in path, star and tree networks is NP-complete [7]; the same holds for ring networks [6].

Generalized Trees. A generalized tree G is constructed from a set S of connected graphs (LANs) and a tree T as follows: Every node v of T is replaced by a LAN V from S. Every edge (u,v) of T is replaced by an edge (u',v'), where u' is any node of LAN U and v' is any node of LAN V (U replaces u and V replaces

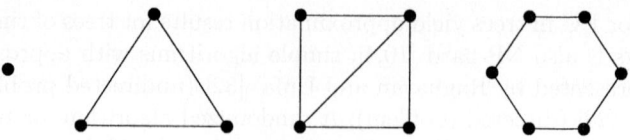

Fig. 1. A finite set of graphs (LANs)

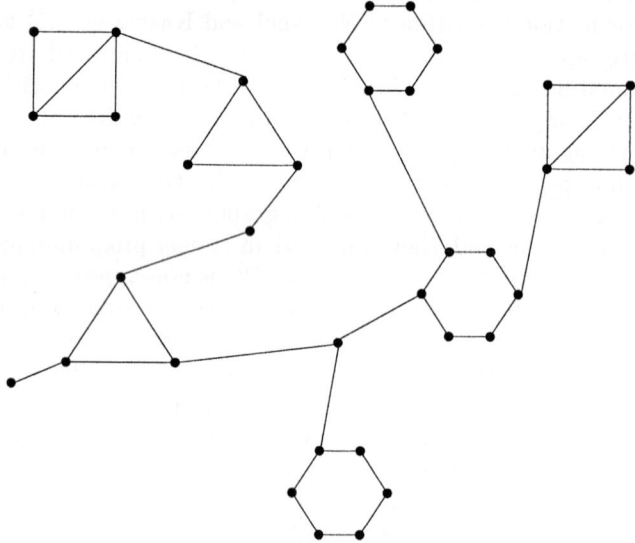

Fig. 2. A generalized tree with LANs from the set shown in Figure 1

v). We call (u', v') a *bridge*. An example of a set of LANs and a generalized tree are shown in figures 1 and 2 respectively.

We define the degree of a generalized tree to be the degree of the underlying tree T. We shall focus on generalized trees with the following two properties:

1. The degree of the generalized tree is bounded by a fixed constant D.
2. The size (number of nodes) of the LANs is bounded by a fixed constant B.

Definition 1. *We call graphs with the above properties* g-trees *of degree* $\leq D$ *and LAN size* $\leq B$, *or simply* g-trees.

The path coloring problem (PC) in generalized trees is NP-hard, since a tree is a special case of a generalized tree, and PC for trees is known to be NP-hard [14]. In contrast, we will show that PC in g-trees can be solved exactly in polynomial time. This is quite surprising, considering that PC and RPC are NP-hard in very simple topologies (e.g. in rings and in unbounded degree trees) end even non-approximable in simple topologies like meshes.

The g-tree topology is of particular practical interest because it captures a wide class of existing networks: tree-like backbone structure and bounded size LANs are reasonable assumptions, since LANs are by nature networks unable to sustain a large number of hosts; besides, the degree of the underlying tree is often small, therefore it makes sense to consider it bounded.

2 A Polynomial-Time Algorithm

Theorem 1. *For any $D, B > 0$ there exists a polynomial-time algorithm that solves PC for any given g-tree of degree $\leq D$ and LAN size $\leq B$.*

We will show the above theorem by presenting such an algorithm. The algorithm has two ingredients: a *recursive coloring* technique and a subroutine for coloring g-stars (g-trees where the underlying graph is a star).

2.1 Recursive Coloring

Let (G, P) be an instance of PC in g-trees, that is G is a g-tree and P is a set of paths on G. In the following we adapt ideas from [32] to show how to color paths in P recursively.

If G contains more than one LAN, it also has a bridge e, i.e. an edge of the underlying tree T, joining two LANs. We break G into two g-trees G_1 and G_2 as shown in Figure 3. From the set of paths P two sets of paths P_1 and P_2 are constructed:

$$P_1 = \{q \mid q = p \cap G_1,\ p \in P\}$$
$$P_2 = \{q \mid q = p \cap G_2,\ p \in P\}$$

That is, every path that passes through edge e is split into two subpaths, whereas paths not passing through e are contained either in P_1 or in P_2. Such a split is shown in Figure 4.

This partitioning gives two new instances of PC in g-trees, namely (G_1, P_1) and (G_2, P_2). Given colorings of these two instances we can produce a common coloring of the initial instance (G, P) using a number of $\max(c_1, c_2)$ colors, where c_i is the number of colors used for instance (G_i, P_i). Paths in P_1, P_2 that were created by splitting a path in P must be assigned the same color. This can be easily done in polynomial time by a color permutation. Such a permutation is feasible because all paths that pass through edge e overlap and thus all belong to different color classes in each of the colorings of (G_1, P_1) and (G_2, P_2). Obviously, the number of colors used is $\max(c_1, c_2)$. Moreover, if the colorings (G_1, P_1) and (G_2, P_2) are optimal, so is the coloring of (G, P), otherwise an optimal coloring would induce a coloring on one of the instances with fewer colors, a contradiction.

All paths in G can be colored recursively by repeated application of the above splitting technique. In order to fully define the recursion scheme, we need to be able to color the paths at the basis of the recursion, i.e. for only one LAN, with at most D additional edges (rays). We call such a graph a *g-star*.

In the following we show that a g-star can be colored optimally in polynomial time.

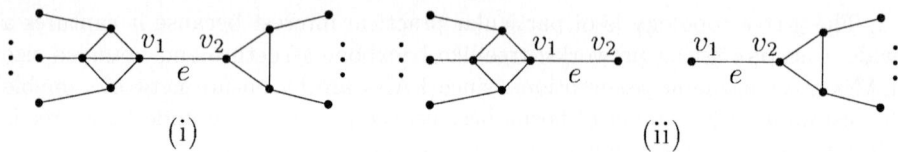

Fig. 3. Dividing a g-tree G (i) into G_1 and G_2 (ii) over bridge e

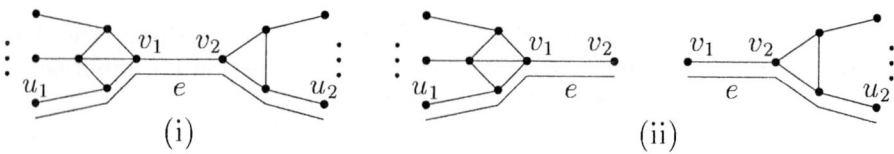

Fig. 4. Dividing a path p on G (i) into a path on G_1 and a path on G_2 (ii) over bridge e

2.2 Coloring a g-Star

Consider a g-star H consisting of a LAN V of size at most B with at most D rays. (Note: the total number of nodes is at most $B + D$.) We show that there exists an algorithm that colors a set of paths P in H in time polynomial in the size of P.

Two paths are called *distinct* if they differ in at least one edge. Since the size of H is bounded by $B + D$ (a constant), the number of (simple) distinct paths between any two nodes of H is also bounded by a constant c. A rather rough estimation for this constant is $c = (D+1)^2(B+1)!/2$ which can be shown as follows: each path on H can be seen as a permutation of the nodes of LAN V — possibly together with a starting (ending) node outside V attached to the first (resp. last) node of the permutation; there are $(B+1)!$ such permutations (we add a dummy "finishing" node in order to take into account paths that contain fewer than B nodes in V as well), and each permutation, together with its possible endpoints outside V, corresponds to at most $(D+1)^2$ paths (again using a dummy node to capture cases where paths start or end inside V); since paths are undirected they are encountered twice; dividing by two we obtain our estimation. Let Q be the set of all distinct paths in H. We denote with $Q_1, Q_2, \ldots, Q_l$ all the non-empty subsets of Q that contain *edge-disjoint* paths (i.e. paths that do not have common edges). Obviously, $l \leq 2^c$ and thus l is also a constant, independent of the size of the given input. Note that, actually, constant l is usually much smaller because most subsets of Q contain paths which are not edge-disjoint.

Consider an instance (H, P) of PC. A coloring of paths in P is merely a partitioning of P into subsets of edge-disjoint paths (color classes); therefore, each color class corresponds to a subset Q_i. As we have already pointed out, P may contain more than one "copies" of a path, i.e. two or more non-distinct paths. Two copies of the same path belong to different color classes in any coloring of P; hence it may happen that two color classes are described by the same subset Q_i. In such a case, it does not make any difference to the cardinality of the solution (i.e. the number of colors used), which copy of a path is used in which color class; an interchange between two copies in a feasible solution yields yet another feasible solution of the same cardinality. Therefore, a coloring of P can be described in general as a multiset of Q_i sets.

Assume that k_i is the multiplicity of Q_i in a solution. Note that k_i is bounded by p_i, where p_i is the minimum multiplicity of a path in P among paths contained in Q_i. Let $p = \max_{1 \le i \le l} p_i$; clearly, p is bounded by the maximum multiplicity of any path in P. An optimal solution can be found by exhaustive search: out of all possible values of $k_1, k_2, \ldots, k_l$, where $0 \le k_i \le p_i$, we choose as feasible solutions the corresponding multisets that constitute a partitioning of P. Out of these, the optimal solution is the one with the least cardinality, i.e. the one that minimizes the quantity $\sum k_i$.

Checking whether a multiset is a partitioning of P can be done in $O(|P|)$ steps, and the number of all possible multisets is $O((p+1)^l)$. Thus, for any g-star H, PC can be solved in time $O(|P|p^l)$ (also $O(|P|^{l+1})$), where l is a constant depending only on B and D and not on the size of the input.

Note that an alternative approach would be to use [18]'s idea of formulating the problem as an integer program and solving it using Lenstra's algorithm [21]. However, this does not seem to improve the time complexity, since it also involves explicit generation of all path matchings (sets of edge-disjoint paths) before solving the IP.

2.3 Complexity of the g-tree Algorithm

The number of g-stars in a g-tree $G = (V, E)$ is at most $|V|$ and at least $|V|/B$, therefore it is $\Theta(|V|)$, and the number of paths in each g-star is at most $|P|$. Hence, the complexity of coloring the g-stars is $O(|V||P|^{l+1})$. Color permutations (recoloring) can be done in $O(|V||P|)$ time in total [26]. Thus, there exists an algorithm that solves PC for g-trees of degree $\le D$ and LAN size $\le B$ in $O(|V||P|^{l+1})$, where l is a constant depending only on D and B.

3 Routing and Path Coloring

We next explain how to extend the above algorithm to an algorithm for the *Routing and Path Coloring problem (RPC)* on g-trees. An instance of RPC consists of a g-tree G and a set R of *connection requests*, i.e. pairs of nodes. A feasible solution is a routing of the connection requests into a set of paths P, and a coloring of this set so that overlapping paths are not assigned the same color. The goal is to minimize the number of colors used.

We now show how to adapt the algorithm for PC in g-trees so as to obtain a polynomial-time algorithm that solves RPC in g-trees exactly. We break G into

G_1 and G_2 as before (with bridge e) and introduce a request-splitting technique as follows: a request between a node in G_1 and a node in G_2 is split into two requests, each one containing a node from the original pair and an endpoint of bridge e. Since bridge $e = (v_1, v_2)$ is contained in any path connecting a node w_1 of G_1 with a node w_2 of G_2, any routing of a request (w_1, w_2) can be seen as a routing of a request from w_1 to bridge v_2 and a routing of a request from bridge v_1 to w_2 (see Figure 5). After color assignment, the two solutions can be combined using the permutation technique as before; optimality of the partial solutions guarantees the optimality of the combined solution.

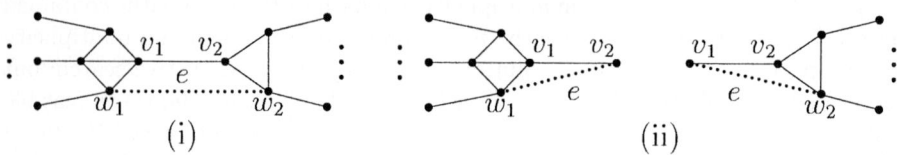

Fig. 5. Dividing a request on G (i) into a request on G_1 and a request on G_2 (ii) over bridge e

The basis of the recursion is practically the same as before: each multiset of Q_i sets is a feasible solution if it defines a set of paths P which implements a routing of requests in R. The optimal solution will be again a feasible solution of minimum cardinality. Therefore, the following is true:

Theorem 2. *For any $D, B > 0$ there exists a polynomial-time algorithm that solves RPC for any given g-tree of degree $\leq D$ and LAN size $\leq B$.*

4 Algorithm Improvement

The performance of the above algorithm can be improved substantially by reducing l, i.e. the number of Q_i sets. To this end it suffices to observe that only maximal sets of edge-disjoint paths are necessary: for any two sets Q_i, Q_j of edge-disjoint paths with $Q_i \subset Q_j$, Q_j can replace Q_i in any solution that contains Q_i, without affecting the cost of the solution. In the modified algorithm, a multiset of Q_i sets is a feasible solution if it defines a superset of P rather than P itself. This modification will ensure that the algorithm yields an optimal solution. This follows from two properties: First, for any multiset of Q_i sets which is a minimum cardinality partition of P (i.e. is an optimal solution) there exists a multiset with the same cardinality that includes only maximal Q_i sets and defines a superset of P. Second, from every multiset of maximal Q_i sets which defines a superset of P one can construct a partition of P with cardinality at most the same.

The above technique may render the algorithm practicable enough, since the number of maximal Q_i sets can be relatively small compared to the total number of Q_i sets. More specifically, for each maximal Q_i, all non-empty subsets of Q_i are present in the initial collection; all these subsets are now represented by Q_i alone.

5 Conclusions

We have studied PC in g-trees and proved that it can be solved exactly by a polynomial time algorithm. This result is of practical interest, considering the wide variety of networks that can be modeled by g-trees. We also showed how to extend this result to RPC in g-trees, that is, for the case in which the topology is not acyclic and thus routing is not trivial.

An interesting question remains, namely whether there exist similar or more generic topologies than g-trees for which PC and RPC are solvable in polynomial time. Our technique does not seem to apply immediately to the case where requests and paths are directed; however, similar topologies may exist for which a polynomial solution can be obtained for the directed case as well.

Future research may also address such questions in variations of PC such as considering weighted graphs, multi-fiber networks, as well as maximization problems and traffic grooming.

Future research may also address such questions for PC/RPC variants. For example, it would be interesting to consider PC and RPC in weighted graphs or in multifiber networks, as well as to study maximization versions of the problem and traffic grooming.

References

1. M. Andrews and L. Zhang. Wavelength Assignment in Optical Networks with Fixed Fiber Capacity. In *Proc. ICALP 2004*, pp. 134–145.
2. M. Andrews and L. Zhang. Bounds on fiber minimization in optical networks with fixed fiber capacity. In *Proc. INFOCOM 2005*.
3. M. C. Carlisle and E. L. Lloyd. On the k-coloring of intervals. *Discrete Applied Mathematics*, 59:225–235, 1995.
4. T. Carpenter, S. Cosares, and I. Saniee. Demand routing and slotting on ring networks. Technical Report 97-02, 28, 1997.
5. C. C. T. Cheng. A new approximation algorithm for the demand routing and slotting problem with unit demands on rings. In *Proceedings RANDOM-APPROX'99*, Lecture Notes in Computer Science, 1671:209–220, 1999.
6. A. L. Chiu and E. Modiano. Traffic grooming algorithms for reducing electronic multiplexing costs in WDM ring networks. *Journal of Lightwave Technology*, 18(1):2–12, 2000.
7. R. Dutta, S. Huang, and G. N. Rouskas. Traffic grooming in path, star, and tree networks: complexity, bounds, and algorithms. In *Proc. of the 2003 ACM SIGMETRICS international conference on Measurement and modeling of computer systems*, pages 298–299. ACM Press, 2003.
8. T. Erlebach. *Scheduling Connections in Fast Networks*. PhD thesis, Technische Universität München, 1999.

9. T. Erlebach and K. Jansen. Maximizing the number of connections in optical tree networks. In *Proceedings of the 9th Annual International Symposium on Algorithms and Computation (ISAAC'98)*, LNCS 1533, pages 179–188, 1998.
10. T. Erlebach and K. Jansen. The complexity of path coloring and call scheduling. *Theoretical Computer Science*, 255(1–2):33–50, 2001.
11. T. Erlebach, K. Jansen, C. Kaklamanis, M. Mihail, and P. Persiano. Optimal wavelength routing in directed fiber trees. *Theoretical Computer Science*, 221:119–137, 1999.
12. T. Erlebach, A. Pagourtzis, K. Potika, and S. Stefanakos. Resource allocation problems in multifiber WDM tree networks. In *29th Workshop on Graph Theoretic Concepts in Computer Science (WG 2003)*, Elspeet, Netherlands, June 2003.
13. M. R. Garey, D. S. Johnson, G. L. Miller, and C. Papadimitriou. The complexity of coloring circular arcs and chords. *SIAM Journal of Algorithms and Discrete Mathematics*, 1(2):216 - 227, 1980.
14. M. C. Golumbic and R. E. Jamison. The edge intersection graphs of paths in a tree. *J. Comb. Theory Series B*, 38(1):8–22, February 1985.
15. D. S. Hochbaum, T. Nishizeki, and D. B. Shmoys. A better than"best possible" algorithm to edge color multigraphs. *Journal of Algorithms*, 7:79–104, 1986
16. I. Holyer. The NP-completeness of edge coloring. *SIAM Journal on Computing*, 10(4):718–720, 1981.
17. I. A. Karapetian. On the coloring of circular arc graphs. Docladi (Reports) of the Academy of Science of the Armenian Soviet Socialist Republic, 70(5):306–311, 1980, in Russian.
18. S. R. Kumar, R. Panigrahy, A. Russel, and R. Sundaram. A note on optical routing on trees. *Information Processing Letters*, 62(6):295–300, 1997.
19. V. Kumar. *Bandwidth Allocation Algorithms for All-Optical Networks*. PhD thesis, Northwestern University, Evanston, Illinois, 1997.
20. V. Kumar. Approximating circular arc colouring and bandwidth allocation in all-optical ring networks. In *Proceedings of Approximation Algorithms for Combinatorial Optimization Problems (APPROX '98)*, Aalborg, Denmark, 1998.
21. H.W. Lenstra Jr. Integer programming with a fixed number of variables. *Math. Oper. Res.* 8 (1983), pp. 538–548.
22. G. Li and R. Simha. On the wavelength assignment problem in multifiber WDM star and ring networks. *IEEE/ACM Transactions on Networking*, 9(1):60–68, 2001.
23. L. Margara and J. Simon. Wavelength assignment problem on all-optical networks with k fibres per link. In *Proceedings of the 27th International Colloquium on Automata, Languages, and Programming (ICALP 2000)*, LNCS 1853, pages 768–779, 2000.
24. M. Mihail, C. Kaklamanis, and S. Rao. Efficient access to optical bandwidth. In *Proc. IEEE Symp. Foundations of Computer Science*, pages 548–557, Milwaukee, Wisconsin, 1995.
25. T. Nishizeki and K. Kashiwagi. On the 1.1 edge-coloring of multigraphs. *SIAM J. Disc. Math.*, 3(3):391–410, August 1990.
26. C. Nomikos. *Path Coloring in Graphs*. PhD thesis, National Technical University of Athens, Athens, 1997.
27. C. Nomikos, A. Pagourtzis, K. Potika, and S. Zachos. Fiber Cost Reduction and Wavelength Minimization in Multifiber WDM Networks. In *Proc. NETWORKING 2004*, LNCS 3042, pp. 150–161, 2004.
28. C. Nomikos, A. Pagourtzis, and S. Zachos. Routing and path multicoloring. *Information Processing Letters*, 80(5):249–256, December 2001.

29. C. Nomikos, A. Pagourtzis, and S. Zachos. Minimizing request blocking in all-optical rings. In *Proc. INFOCOM 2003*.
30. C. Nomikos, A. Pagourtzis, and S. Zachos. Satisfying a maximum number of pre-routed requests in all-optical rings. *Computer Networks: The International Journal of Computer and Telecommunications Networking*, 42(1):55–63, 2003.
31. S. Olariu. An optimal greedy heuristic to color interval graphs. *Information Processing Letters*, 37:21–25, 1991.
32. P. Raghavan and E. Upfal. Efficient routing in all-optical networks. In *Proceedings of the Annual ACM Symposium on Theory of Computing STOC '94*, pages 134–143, 1994.
33. W. K. Shih and W. L. Hsu. An approximation algorithm for coloring circular-arc graphs. In *SIAM Conference on Discrete Mathematics*, 1990.
34. P.-J. Wan and L. Liu. Maximal throughput in wavelength-routed optical networks. In *Multichannel Optical Networks: Theory and Practice*, volume 46 of *DIMACS Series in Discrete Mathematics and Theoretical Computer Science*, pages 15–26. AMS, 1998.
35. P. Winkler and L. Zhang. Wavelength assignment and generalized interval graph coloring. In *Proc. of the 14th Annual ACM-SIAM Symposium on Discrete Algorithms*, pages 830–831, Baltimore, MD, January 2003.

Maximum-Size Subgraphs of P4-Sparse Graphs Admitting a Perfect Matching

Stavros D. Nikolopoulos and Leonidas Palios

Department of Computer Science, University of Ioannina,
P.O.Box 1186, GR-45110 Ioannina, Greece
{stavros, palios}@cs.uoi.gr

Abstract. In this paper, we address the problem of computing a maximum-size subgraph of a P_4-sparse graph which admits a perfect matching; in the case where the graph has a perfect matching, the solution to the problem is the entire graph. We establish a characterization of such subgraphs, and describe an algorithm for the problem which for a P_4-sparse graph on n vertices and m edges, runs in $O(n + m)$ time and space. The above results also hold for the class of complement reducible graphs or cographs, a well-known subclass of P_4-sparse graphs.

Keywords: Perfect graphs, P_4-sparse graphs, cographs, maximum-size subgraphs, maximum matchings, perfect matching.

1 Introduction

The class of P_4-*sparse* graphs was introduced by Hoàng in his doctoral dissertation [11], as the class of graphs for which every set of five vertices induces at most one P_4 (chordless path on four vertices). Hoàng gave a number of characterizations of these graphs and showed that the P_4-sparse graphs are perfect in the sense of Berge (a graph G is perfect if for every induced subgraph H of G, the chromatic number of H equals the clique number of H), and in fact perfectly orderable in the sense of Chvátal [1,9]. The class of P_4-sparse graphs generalizes the well known class of *complement reducible* graphs, also known as *cographs* [14].

The study of P_4-sparse graphs and cographs led naturally to constructive characterizations that implied several linear-time recognition algorithms and also enabled the construction of unique, up to isomorphism, tree representations [2,4,12,13]. In addition, since P_4-sparse graphs and cographs are perfect, many interesting optimization problems in graph theory, which are NP-complete in general graphs, admit polynomial sequential solutions; their tree representations are used by many researchers to develop algorithms for such problems (see [1,9]). In particular, Jamison and Olariu [13] proposed linear-time algorithms for solving five optimization problems on the class of P_4-sparse graphs: maximum-size clique, maximum-size stable set, minimum coloring, minimum covering by cliques, and minimum fill-in. Moreover, in [12] the same authors provided efficient solutions to other classical optimization problems; that is, finding the clique number, the stable number, the chromatic number and the clique cover number of a P_4-sparse graph. Giakoumakis and Vanherpe [8] obtained linear-time algorithms for the maximum weight clique and for the maximum weight stable set problems on P_4-sparse graphs using the modular decomposition tree representation [5,15]. Yang and Yu [18] exhibited a linear time algorithm for the maximum matching problem in cographs, while Fouquet, Parfenoff, and Thuillier [7] extended this algorithm to P_4-tidy graphs, a class containing both P_4-sparse graphs and cographs.

A *matching* M of a graph G is a subset of the edge set $E(G)$ such that no two edges in M share a common endpoint; M is a *maximum matching* if it contains a maximum number of edges; M is a *perfect matching* if every vertex of G is an endpoint of an edge in M. The best known algorithm for solving the maximum matching problem in general graphs is due to Micali and Vazirani [16] and has $O(\sqrt{n}\,m)$ time complexity; recall that in P_4-sparse graphs and cographs, the same problem is solved in linear time due to the algorithm of Fouquet, Parfenoff, and Thuillier [7].

In this paper, we are interested in solving the problem of finding a maximum-size subgraph of a P_4-sparse graph which has a perfect matching. In other words, we want to find and remove the smallest number of edges so that the graph which we obtain if we ignore any isolated vertices has a perfect matching. The problem belongs to the class of problems in which we are asked to remove as few edges or vertices as possible so that the resulting subgraph has some particular properties.

We show that any maximum-size subgraph of a graph G which has a perfect matching is a subgraph induced by the vertices of a maximum matching of G. In this way, we reduce the problem to that of finding a maximum-size subgraph induced by the vertices of a maximum matching of G. Then, we establish a characterization of such subgraphs which by means of the modular decomposition tree representation of the P_4-sparse graphs enables us to obtain a linear-time solution to the problem we consider.

2 Preliminaries

We consider finite undirected graphs with no loops or multiple edges. For a graph G, we denote its vertex and edge set by $V(G)$ and $E(G)$, respectively. Let S be a subset of the vertex set of a graph G. Then, the subgraph of G induced by S is denoted by $G[S]$. Moreover, we denote by $G - S$ the graph $G[V(G) - S]$.

Modular Decomposition

A subset M of vertices of a graph G is said to be a *module* of G, if every vertex outside M is either adjacent to all vertices in M or to none of them. The emptyset, the singletons, and the vertex set $V(G)$ are *trivial* modules and whenever G has only trivial modules it is called a *prime* (or *indecomposable*) graph. A module M of G is called a *strong module* if, for any module M' of G, either $M' \cap M = \emptyset$ or one module is included into the other. Furthermore, a module in G is also a module in $\overline{G}$ (i.e., the complement of the graph G).

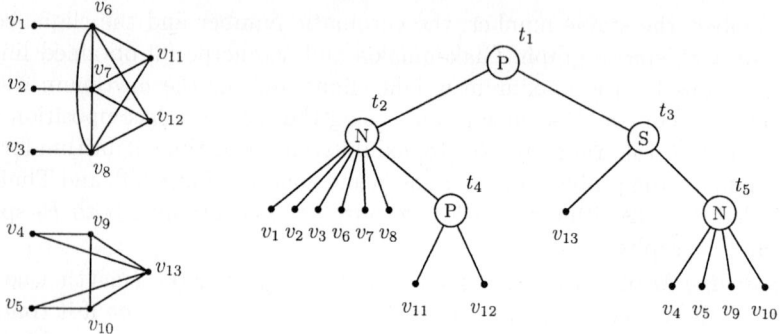

Fig. 1. A disconnected P_4-sparse graph on 13 vertices and its md-tree

The *modular decomposition* of a graph G is a linear-space representation of all the partitions of $V(G)$ where each partition class is a module. The *modular decomposition tree* $T(G)$ of the graph G (or *md-tree* for short) is a unique labeled tree associated with the modular decomposition of G in which the leaves of $T(G)$ are the vertices of G and the set of leaves associated with the subtree rooted at an internal node induces a strong module of G. Thus, the md-tree $T(G)$ represents all the strong modules of G. An internal node is labeled by either P (for *parallel* module), S (for *series* module), or N (for *neighborhood* module). It has been shown that for every graph G the md-tree $T(G)$ is unique up to isomorphism and it can be constructed in linear time; the first linear-time algorithms for the construction of the md-tree are described in [5,15], while more recent and more practical ones can be found in [6,10]. Figure 1 depicts a P_4-sparse graph G on 13 vertices and its md-tree $T(G)$.

Let t be an internal node of the md-tree $T(G)$ of a graph G. We denote by $M(t)$ the module corresponding to t which consists of the set of vertices of G associated with the subtree of $T(G)$ rooted at node t. Let $u_1, u_2, \ldots, u_p$ be the children of the node t of $T(G)$. We denote by $G(t)$ the *representative graph* of the module $M(t)$ defined as follows: $V(G(t)) = \{u_1, u_2, \ldots, u_p\}$ and $u_i u_j \in E(G(t))$ if there exists edge $v_k v_\ell \in E(G)$ such that $v_k \in M(u_i)$ and $v_\ell \in M(u_j)$; by the definition of a module, if a vertex of $M(t_i)$ is adjacent to a vertex of $M(t_j)$ then every vertex of $M(t_i)$ is adjacent to every vertex of $M(t_j)$. Thus, $G(t)$ is isomorphic to the graph induced by a subset of $M(t)$ consisting of a single vertex from each maximal strong submodule of $M(t)$ in the modular decomposition of G. For the P-, S-, and N-nodes, the following lemma holds (see also [8]):

Lemma 2.1. *Let G be a graph, $T(G)$ its modular decomposition tree, and t an internal node of $T(G)$. Then, $G(t)$ is an edgeless graph if t is a P-node, $G(t)$ is a complete graph if t is an S-node, and $G(t)$ is a prime graph if t is an N-node.*

P_4-sparse Graphs

A graph G is called a *spider* if the vertex set $V(G)$ of the graph G admits a partition into sets S, K, and R such that:

(P1) $|S| = |K| \geq 2$, the set S is an independent set, and the set K is a clique;
(P2) all the vertices in R are adjacent to all the vertices in K and to no vertex in S;
(P3) there exists a bijection $f : S \longrightarrow K$ such that exactly one of the following statements holds:
  (i) for each vertex $v \in S$, $N(v) \cap K = \{f(v)\}$;
  (ii) for each vertex $v \in S$, $N(v) \cap K = K - \{f(v)\}$.

The triple (S, K, R) is called the *spider-partition*. A graph G is a *prime spider* if G is a spider with $|R| \leq 1$. If the condition of case P3(i) holds then the spider G is called a *thin spider*, whereas if the condition of case P3(ii) holds then G is a *thick spider*; note that the complement of a thin spider is a thick spider and vice versa.

Observation 2.1 (Observation 2.8 in [12]). *If a graph G is a spider, then exactly one of the following statements holds:*

(i) for every $v \in S$ and $u \in K$, $degree(v) = 1$ and $degree(u) = |V(G)| - |S|$;
(ii) for every $v \in S$ and $u \in K$, $degree(v) = |K| - 1$ and $degree(u) = |V(G)| - 2$.

Observation 2.2 (Observation 2.9 in [12]). *If a graph G is a spider and R is nonempty, then for every choice of v, u, and r in S, K, and R, respectively, $degree(v) < degree(r) < degree(u)$.*

It is not difficult to see that a spider with $|K| = |S| = k$ contains exactly $\frac{k(k-1)}{2} + \ell$ P_4s, where ℓ is the number of P_4s in the subgraph $G[R]$. From the definition of the spider and Observations 2.1 and 2.2, it follows that if G is a spider, then S, K, and R are unique (see [12]). Finally, from the properties of a spider G, and also from the definition of the P_4-sparse graphs, it easily follows that G is P_4-sparse iff the graph $G[R]$ is P_4-sparse.

Let us now return to general P_4-sparse graphs. Then, the following result holds:

Lemma 2.2 (Theorem 1 in [12]). *For a graph G, the following conditions are equivalent:*

(i) G is a P_4-sparse graph;
(ii) for every induced subgraph H of G with at least two vertices, exactly one of the following statements is satisfied: (a) H is disconnected; (b) $\overline{H}$ is disconnected; (c) H is a spider.

Regarding the modular decomposition of P_4-sparse graphs, Giakoumakis and Vanherpe [8] showed the following result (recall that the graph $G(t)$ has vertices the children of the node t in $T(G)$):

Lemma 2.3. *Let G be a graph and let $T(G)$ be its modular decomposition tree. The graph G is P_4-sparse iff for every N-node t of $T(G)$, $G(t)$ is a prime spider with a spider-partition (S, K, R) and no vertex of $S \cup K$ is an internal node in $T(G)$.*

3 Finding a Max-size Subgraph That Has a Perfect Matching

In this section we give an optimal sequential algorithm for the problem of finding a maximum-size subgraph which has a perfect matching. It is important to note that such a subgraph is an induced subgraph; the condition that this subgraph be of maximum size requires that the subgraph be the subgraph induced by its vertex set. Below, we show that any maximum-size subgraph of a graph G, which has a perfect matching, is induced by the matched vertices in a maximum matching of G (Lemma 3.1); then, we prove the property that characterizes a maximum-size subgraph of G, among the subgraphs that are induced by the vertices of maximum matchings of G (Observation 3.1).

Lemma 3.1. *Let G be a graph and let G_1 be a maximum-size subgraph of G which has a perfect matching. Then, the subgraph G_1 is induced by the vertices participating in a maximum matching of G.*

Proof: Let M_{max} be a maximum matching of G, whose vertex set is V_{max}; if $n_{max} = |V_{max}|$ then any matching involving n_{max} matched vertices is a maximum matching of G. If $V_1 \subseteq V(G)$ is the vertex set of the subgraph G_1, then, because G_1 has a perfect matching, $|V_1| \leq n_{max}$. We will show that $|V_1| = n_{max}$, because then any perfect matching of G_1 is a maximum matching of G. It suffices to show that $|V_1| \geq n_{max}$. Suppose, for contradiction, that $|V_1| < n_{max}$. Then, we have that $V_1 \not\subseteq V_{max}$, since otherwise the vertices in V_{max} would induce a subgraph that has a perfect matching and is of size larger than that of G_1, in contradiction to the maximality of G_1. Yet, we will show that we can construct a matching of G whose vertex set has cardinality n_{max} and is a proper superset of V_1; this will yield a contradiction to the maximality of G_1.

Let M_1 be a perfect matching of G_1 (the vertices in V_1 are all matched in the matching M_1) and let us consider the graph H spanned by the non-common edges of the matchings M_1 and M_{max}. Then, the vertices in H have degree at most 2; in particular, the vertices in $V_1 - V_{max}$ have degree exactly 1 and are incident on an edge that participates in M_1. The fact that the degrees of the vertices of H do not exceed 2 implies that each connected component of H is either a path or a cycle. Additionally, edges of M_{max} and M_1 alternate on these paths and cycles.

Let us consider a vertex $x \in V_1 - V_{max}$ and let $\rho = v_0 v_1 \cdots v_t$, $t \geq 1$, be the path (connected component) of H to which x belongs; since x is an endpoint of ρ, we assume without loss of generality that $x = v_0$. Then, the length of ρ cannot be 1; otherwise, $v_1 \in V_1 - V_{max}$, which implies that the edges in M_{max} and the edge xv_1 define a matching of G larger than M_{max}, in contradiction to the optimality of M_{max}. In fact, the length of ρ cannot be odd: if $t = 2q + 1$, where $q \geq 1$, then the edges $v_{2i-1} v_{2i}$, $1 \leq i \leq q$, belong to M_{max} and the edges $v_{2i} v_{2i+1}$, $0 \leq i \leq q$, belong to M_1; thus, the vertices $v_1, v_2, \ldots, v_{t-1}$ belong to $V_1 \cap V_{max}$ and the vertices v_0, v_t belong to $V_1 - V_{max}$, which implies that we can replace all the edges $v_{2i-1} v_{2i}$, $1 \leq i \leq q$, by the remaining edges and obtain a matching of G with vertex set $V_{max} \cup \{x, v_t\}$, again in contradiction to the maximality of M_{max}. Therefore, the path ρ has even length, say, $t = 2q$ where $q \geq 1$. Then, as above, the edges $v_{2i-1}v_{2i}$, $1 \leq i \leq q$, belong to M_{max}, the edges $v_{2i}v_{2i+1}$, $0 \leq i \leq q-1$, belong to M_1, the vertices $v_1, v_2, \ldots, v_{t-1}$ belong to $V_1 \cap V_{max}$ and $v_0 \in V_1 - V_{max}$ and $v_t \in V_{max} - V_1$. Thus, if we replace all the edges $v_{2i-1}v_{2i}$, $1 \leq i \leq q$, by the remaining edges, we obtain a matching of G with vertex set $(V_{max} \cup \{v_0\}) - \{v_t\}$; this matching has n_{max} matched vertices among which we find vertex x whereas the vertex $v_t \in V_{max} - V_1$ is left unmatched.

By doing the above process for each vertex in $V_1 - V_{max}$ and by taking into account that the paths in H to which the vertices in $V_1 - V_{max}$ belong are disjoint, we obtain a matching M of G with vertex set V_M such that $|V_M| = n_{max}$ and $V_1 \subset V_M$. But then, the subgraph $G[V_M]$ has a perfect matching and is of size larger than the size of $G_1 = G[V_1]$, a contradiction to the maximality of G_1. Therefore, the number of vertices of a maximum-size subgraph of G which has a perfect matching is n_{max} and thus is induced by the vertices of a maximum matching of G. ∎

Lemma 3.1 implies that each maximum-size subgraph of a graph G which has a perfect matching is a maximum-size subgraph of G induced by the vertices of a maximum matching of G. Therefore, in the following, we will be referring to the problem of finding a maximum-size subgraph that has a perfect matching while concentrating on maximum-size subgraphs induced by maximum matchings. Then, the following observation allows us to characterize the maximum matching that will yield a maximum-size induced subgraph of G which we seek.

Observation 3.1. *Among all maximum matchings of a graph G, any one whose vertices induce a maximum-size subgraph of G exhibits the minimum sum of degrees of unmatched vertices.*

Proof: Observe that any two vertices left unmatched during the computation of a maximum matching are not adjacent; otherwise, the edge connecting them would produce a larger matching. Hence, the number of edges of the subgraph of G induced by the vertices participating in a maximum matching is equal to the total number of edges of G minus the sum of the degrees of the unmatched vertices. Thus, in order to obtain a maximum-size subgraph of G induced by the vertices of a maximum matching of G, we need to find a maximum matching of G such that the unmatched vertices have the smallest sum of degrees in G. ∎

Based on Observation 3.1, one might think that, if we know the number k of vertices left unmatched in a maximum matching of G, the maximum-size subgraph of G that we seek can be obtained by removing the k vertices of G of smallest degrees. This is not however the case: consider for example the graph H on 14 vertices $\{v, x_1, x_2, x_3, y_1, \ldots, y_5, z_1, \ldots, z_5\}$ where v is adjacent to all the remaining vertices, $H[\{x_1, x_2, x_3\}]$ is a complete graph on 3 vertices, and $H[\{y_1, \ldots, y_5\}]$ and $H[\{z_1, \ldots, z_5\}]$ are complete graphs on 5 vertices each; H has a maximum matching involving 12 vertices, yet, the subgraph induced by removing any two of the vertices $\{x_1, x_2, x_3\}$ (which exhibit the smallest degrees in H) does not have a perfect matching.

The following lemma establishes another useful property pertaining to a maximum matching.

Lemma 3.2. *Let G be a graph, M_{opt} be a maximum matching of G inducing a subgraph of G whose size is maximum (among all subgraphs induced by the vertices of a maximum matching), M be any other maximum matching of G, and U_{opt} (resp. U) be the set of vertices of G left unmatched by M_{opt} (resp. M). Then there is a bijection $f : U \to U_{opt}$ such that for each vertex $x \in U$, $degree(f(x)) \leq degree(x)$ in G, where by $degree(v)$ we denote the degree of vertex v in G.*

Our algorithm relies on the following lemma as well.

Lemma 3.3. *Let G be a spider and let (S, K, R) be its spider-partition. If a maximum-size subgraph of $G[R]$ induced by a maximum matching results after removal of the vertices in $U \subseteq R$, then*

(i) if $|U| \leq |S|$, a maximum-size subgraph of G induced by a maximum matching is $G - X$ where X is an arbitrary subset of S of cardinality $|U|$;

(ii) if $|U| > |S|$, a maximum-size subgraph of G induced by a maximum matching is $G - (S \cup Y)$ where Y is the set of the $|U| - |S|$ vertices of U of smallest degrees in G.

Our algorithm takes advantage of the modular decomposition tree $T(G)$ of the input graph G. To simplify the computations, we "binarize" the S-nodes and P-nodes of the tree $T(G)$. The algorithm processes the resulting tree $T'(G)$ as follows: in each node t of the tree, it computes a maximum matching for the subgraph $G[M(t)]$ of G corresponding to the subtree of $T'(G)$ rooted at t, while at the same time minimizing the sum of the degrees of the vertices of $G[M(t)]$ left unmatched.

Algorithm MaxSubgraph
Input: a P_4-sparse graph G.
Output: a maximum-size subgraph of G which has a perfect matching.

1. Compute the degrees of all the vertices in the graph G and store them in an array;
2. Construct the md-tree $T(G)$ of G;
   Make each S-node or P-node of $T(G)$ binary, obtaining the modified modular decomposition tree $T'(G)$;
3. Execute the subroutine *process(root)*, where *root* is the root node of the modified md-tree $T'(G)$; the sought subgraph is the subgraph $G - U$, where U is the set of vertices returned by the subroutine.

where the description of the subroutine *process( )* is as follows:

process(node t)

Input: node t of the modified md-tree $T'(G)$ of the input graph G.
Output: the set U_t of vertices whose removal leaves a maximum-size subgraph of $G[M(t)]$ which has a perfect matching.

1. if t is a leaf
   then return($\{v\}$), where v is the vertex associated with the leaf t;
2. if t is an N-node
   then compute the spider-partition (S, K, R) of $G(t)$;   {*note:* $|R| \leq 1$}
        if $R = \{t_R\}$
           then $U_R \leftarrow$ *process*(t_R);
           else $U_R \leftarrow \emptyset$;   {*note:* $R = \emptyset$}
        if $|U_R| \leq |S|$
           then $X \leftarrow$ arbitrary subset of S of cardinality $|U_R|$;
           else $Y \leftarrow$ set of $|U_R| - |S|$ vertices of U_R of smallest degrees in G;
                $X \leftarrow S \cup Y$;
        return(X);
3. {*node t is an S-node or a P-node that has a left and a right child with associated vertex subsets V_ℓ and V_r respectively*}
   $U_\ell \leftarrow$ *process*(left child of t);
   $U_r \leftarrow$ *process*(right child of t);
   suppose without loss of generality that $|U_\ell| \geq |U_r|$, otherwise swap the two children of t and the corresponding sets;
4. if t is a P-node
   then return($U_\ell \cup U_r$);
5. if t is an S-node
   then if $|U_\ell| = |V_r|$
        then return($\emptyset$);
        else if $|U_\ell| < |V_r|$
             then if $|U_\ell| - |U_r|$ is even
                  then return($\emptyset$);
                  else $v \leftarrow$ vertex in $V_\ell \cup V_r$ of smallest degree in G;
                       return($\{v\}$);
             else   {$|U_\ell| > |V_r|$}
                  $X \leftarrow$ set of $|U_\ell| - |V_r|$ vertices of U_ℓ of smallest deg. in G;
                  return(X);

For each node t of the tree $T'(G)$, subroutine process() computes a maximum matching for the subgraph $G[M(t)]$ implicitly; it can be easily modified to store and print such a matching. The correctness of Algorithm MaxSubgraph follows from Lemma 3.4.

Lemma 3.4. *When applied on a P_4-sparse graph G, Algorithm MaxSubgraph correctly computes a maximum-size subgraph of G which has a perfect matching.*

Proof: We need only prove the correctness of subroutine process(). The proof proceeds inductively on the height of the (sub)tree of the modified md-tree $T'(G)$

of the input graph G rooted at the node t that is currently processed by the subroutine. If the (sub)tree is of height 0, then t is a leaf. Hence, it corresponds to a subgraph on 1 vertex; such a graph has no matching and its single vertex is left unmatched, which is what the subroutine returns (Step 1).

For the inductive hypothesis, we assume that the subroutine process( ) correctly handles any (sub)tree of height at most $h \geq 0$; we show that it correctly handles any (sub)tree of height $h+1$. Let t be the root of such a (sub)tree; then, t is an N-node, a binarized S-node, or a binarized P-node. If t is an N-node, then the graph $G(t)$ is a prime spider (Lemma 2.3); let (S, K, R) be its spider partition (recall that $R = \emptyset$ or $R = \{t_R\}$). Lemma 3.3 certifies the correctness of the computation in Step 2 taking into account that the ordering of the vertices of $G(t)$ by their degree in $G(t)$ is identical to the ordering based on their degree in G (note that $V(G(t))$ is a module and thus each vertex in $V(G(t))$ is adjacent to the same vertices in $V(G) - V(G(t))$), and that if $R = \{t_R\}$, by the inductive hypothesis, subroutine process( ) has correctly computed a maximum-size subgraph of $G[M(t_R)]$ which has a perfect matching. Suppose now that t is a P-node or an S-node; in either case, t has two children. If V_ℓ and V_r are the vertex subsets corresponding to the leaves of the left and right child of t respectively, and U_ℓ and U_r are the sets of unmatched vertices returned by subroutine process( ) respectively, then by the inductive hypothesis, the subgraphs $G[V_\ell - U_\ell]$ and $G[V_r - U_r]$ are maximum-size subgraphs of $G[V_\ell]$ and of $G[V_r]$ which have a perfect matching.

If t is a P-node, then there are no edges of G connecting a vertex in V_ℓ to a vertex in V_r; hence, the optimal solution for the subgraph of G corresponding to t, i.e., induced by $V_\ell \cup V_r$, is the union of the optimal solutions for the subgraphs $G[V_\ell]$ and $G[V_r]$, just as the algorithm does (Step 4).

Finally consider that t is an S-node, and assume without loss of generality (as the algorithm assumes) that $|U_\ell| \geq |U_r|$. Then, if $|U_\ell| = |V_r|$, the subgraph $G[V_\ell \cup V_r]$ has a perfect matching: extend the perfect matching of $G[V_\ell - U_\ell]$ with a matching resulting from an arbitrary bijection from U_ℓ to V_r; subroutine process( ) correctly reports that no vertex remains unmatched in this case. An optimal solution is also produced if $|U_\ell| < |V_r|$: a perfect matching is obtained if the total number of vertices is even, otherwise exactly the vertex of U_r with the smallest degree in G (which has the smallest degree in $G[M(t)]$ as well because $V_\ell \cup V_r$ is a module) is left unmatched (the optimality of this solution follows from Observation 3.1), and this can be easily shown to be feasible since $|U_r| \leq |U_\ell| < |V_r|$.

Consider now the case in which $|U_\ell| > |V_r|$. In this case, the algorithm constructs the set X containing the $|U_\ell| - |V_r|$ vertices in U_ℓ of minimum degrees in G, which it returns as the set of vertices left unmatched; this is indeed a feasible solution because a perfect matching in $G[(V_\ell - X) \cup V_r]$ can be constructed from a matching of $G[V_\ell - U_\ell]$ and a matching resulting from an arbitrary bijection from $U_\ell - X$ to V_r. Suppose for contradiction that this is not an optimal solution for the subgraph $G[M(t)]$ of G corresponding to the subtree of $T'(G)$ rooted at the S-node t; let U be the set of unmatched vertices in an optimal solution for

$G[M(t)]$. Then, $|U| = |X|$: the optimality of $G[M(t)] - U$ implies that $|U| \leq |X|$, while if $|U| < |X|$ the fact that the subgraph $G[M(t)] - U$ has a perfect matching would imply that a maximum-size subgraph of $G[V_\ell]$ which has a perfect matching would leave a number of unmatched vertices at most $|U|+|V_r| < |U_\ell|$, in contradiction to the optimality of the solution for $G[V_\ell]$ which leaves unmatched the vertices in U_ℓ. The optimality of $G[M(t)] - U$ and the choice of X also imply that

$$\sum_{v \in U} \text{degree}(v) < \sum_{v \in X} \text{degree}(v) \leq \sum_{v \in A} \text{degree}(v) \qquad (1)$$

for any subset A of U_ℓ of cardinality $|U_\ell| - |V_r|$, where $degree(v)$ denotes the degree of vertex v in G.

Additionally, $U \subseteq V_\ell$; if not, then the fact that U cannot contain both a vertex in V_ℓ and V_r (for otherwise two such vertices would be matched resulting in a larger matching) would imply that $U \subseteq V_r$, which would in turn imply that $G[V_\ell]$ has a matching leaving unmatched at most $|V_r| - |U| \leq |V_r| < |U_\ell|$ vertices, a contradiction. We note however that it does not have to be the case that $U \subseteq U_\ell$; nevertheless, we will show that there exists a bijection $g : U \to W$, where $W \subseteq U_\ell$, such that for each vertex $x \in U$, $degree(g(x)) \leq degree(x)$.

Let us consider the restriction of the matching which yields the optimal solution for the graph $G[M(t)]$ (and leaves unmatched the vertices in U) to the vertex set V_ℓ; if Z is the set of vertices left unmatched by the resulting matching M', then clearly $U \subseteq Z$ and $|Z| \leq |U| + |V_r| = |U_\ell|$. Thus, since the optimal matching for this subgraph (by the inductive hypothesis) leaves unmatched the vertices in U_ℓ, $|Z| = |U_\ell|$ and the matching M' is maximum for the subgraph $G[V_\ell]$. Then, Lemma 3.2 applied on the two matchings for the graph $G[V_\ell]$, which leave unmatched the vertices in Z and U_ℓ respectively, yields that there exists a bijection $f : Z \to U_\ell$ such that for each $x \in Z$, $degree(f(x)) \leq degree(x)$. Then, the desired bijection g is the restriction of the bijection f to the domain U, and the set W is the set of images $f(x)$ of the vertices x in U. The properties of the bijection g imply that

$$\sum_{v \in W} \text{degree}(v) \leq \sum_{v \in U} \text{degree}(v),$$

which comes into contradiction with Inequality (1), since W is a subset of U_ℓ of cardinality $|U| = |U_\ell| - |V_r|$. Therefore, the solution produced by the algorithm for the case when $|U_\ell| > |V_r|$ is also optimal. ∎

Time and Space Complexity of Algorithm MaxSubgraph: Let n and m be the number of vertices and edges of the input P_4-sparse graph G. Then, the degrees of the vertices of G can be computed in $O(n+m)$ time and can be stored in $O(n)$ space, so that Step 1 of the algorithm takes $O(n+m)$ time and $O(n)$ space. The md-tree $T(G)$ can be constructed in $O(n+m)$ time and space [5,15,6,10] and has $O(n)$ size. Binarizing the S- and P-nodes takes $O(n)$ time and the resulting tree $T'(G)$ has $O(n)$ size. Thus, Step 2 takes $O(n+m)$ time and space as well.

Let us now bound the time and space needed by all the executions of subroutine process( ). The set of unmatched vertices returned by a call to process( ) is stored in an unordered linked list so that linking two such lists takes constant time. Observe that each node t of the tree $T'(G)$ is processed exactly once. If t is a leaf, then the processing of t takes constant time (Step 1). If t is an N-node, then t's processing takes $O(|S| + |U_R|)$ time (see Step 2): the set S is readily available from the md-tree; forming the set Y requires copying the vertices in U_R along with their degrees in an array, applying the linear-time selection algorithm [3] on this array to locate the value of the $(|U_R| - |S|)$-th smallest degree, and using this value to partition the vertices in U_R based on their degrees (special attention is needed for the vertices with degree equal to the partitioning value). In turn, the processing of a P-node takes constant time (thanks to the linked list representation of the set of unmatched vertices), while the processing of an S-node takes $O(|V_\ell|+|V_r|)$ time (again, forming the set X requires the application of the linear-time selection algorithm). We get a bound on the time taken for the processing of the entire tree $T'(G)$ by using the following crediting scheme: we credit each leaf and each (binary) P-node with 1 credit; we credit each N-node (corresponding to a spider with partition sets S, K, and R) with the number of edges of G connecting vertices in S and K, and additionally if $R = \{t_R\}$ with the number of edges connecting vertices in K and $M(t_R)$, which is at least equal to $|S|$ or $|S|+|K| \cdot |M(t_R)|$ respectively; we credit each (binary) S-node with 1 plus the number of edges of G connecting a vertex associated with a leaf in the left subtree of the S-node to a vertex associated with a leaf in the right subtree, that is, with $1 + |V_\ell| \cdot |V_r|$ credits. Since $|K| \geq 2$, $|V_\ell| + |V_r| \leq 1 + |V_\ell| \cdot |V_r|$, and $|U_R| \leq |M(t_R)|$ if $R = \{t_R\}$, the time taken is bounded by a constant multiple of the number of credits. Then, because each edge of G contributes at most one credit in our crediting scheme and because the size of $T'(G)$ is $O(n)$, the time required for the completion of Step 3 of Algorithm MaxSubgraph is $O(n+m)$. Clearly, the space needed by subroutine process( ) is $O(n)$.

The results of this section can be summarized in the following theorem.

Theorem 3.1. *Let G be a P_4-sparse graph on n vertices and m edges. The problem of finding a maximum-size subgraph of G admitting a perfect matching is solved in $O(n+m)$ time and space.*

4 Concluding Remarks

Motivated by this work, it would be interesting to consider the related problem where edges are added so that the resulting graph has a perfect matching while remaining in the same class of graphs, that is,

- Given a P_4-sparse graph (or cograph) G, find the minimum number of edges which need to be added to the edge set of G such that the resulting graph is a P_4-sparse graph (or cograph) and admits a perfect matching.

We expect that the structural results and the algorithmic approach used in this paper can help develop efficient algorithms for solving this problem as well.

References

1. A. Brandstädt, V.B. Le, and J.P. Spinrad, *Graph Classes: A Survey*, SIAM Monographs on Discrete Mathematics and Applications, 1999.
2. A. Bretscher, D. Corneil, M. Habib, and C. Paul, A simple linear time LexBFS cograph recognition algorithm, *Proc. 29th Int'l Workshop on Graph Theoretic Concepts in Comput. Sci. (WG'03)*, LNCS 2880 (2003) 119–130.
3. T.H. Cormen, C.E. Leiserson, R.L. Rivest, and C. Stein, *Introduction to Algorithms* (2nd edition), MIT Press, Inc., 2001.
4. D.G. Corneil, Y. Perl, and L.K. Stewart, A linear recognition algorithm for cographs, *SIAM J. Comput.* **14** (1985) 926–934.
5. A. Cournier and M. Habib, A new linear algorithm for modular decomposition, *Proc. 19th Int'l Colloquium on Trees in Algebra and Programming (CAAP'94)*, LNCS **787** (1994) 68–84.
6. E. Dahlhaus, J. Gustedt, and R.M. McConnell, Efficient and practical algorithms for sequential modular decomposition, *J. Algorithms* **41** (2001) 360–387.
7. J.L. Fouquet, I. Parfenoff, and H. Thuillier, An O(n) time algorithm for maximum matchings in P_4-tidy graphs, *Inform. Process. Lett.* **62** (1999) 281–287.
8. V. Giakoumakis and J. Vanherpe, On extended P_4-reducible and extended P_4-sparse graphs, *Theoret. Comput. Sci.* **180** (1997) 269–286.
9. M.C. Golumbic, *Algorithmic Graph Theory and Perfect Graphs*, Academic Press, Inc., 1980.
10. M. Habib, F. de Montgolfier, and C. Paul, A simple linear-time modular decomposition algorithm for graphs, using order extension, *Proc. 9th Scandinavian Workshop on Algorithm Theory (SWAT'04)*, LNCS 3111 (2004) 187–198.
11. C. Hoàng, Perfect graphs, *Ph.D. thesis*, McGill University, Montreal, Canada, 1985.
12. B. Jamison and S. Olariu, A tree representation for P_4-sparse graphs, *Discrete Appl. Math.* **35** (1992) 115–129.
13. B. Jamison and S. Olariu, Linear-time optimization algorithms for P_4-sparse graphs, *Discrete Appl. Math.* **61** (1995) 155–175.
14. H. Lerchs, On cliques and kernels, *Technical Report*, Department of Computer Science, University of Toronto, March 1971.
15. R.M. McConnell and J. Spinrad, Linear time modular decomposition and efficient transitive orientation of comparability graphs, *Proc. 5th ACM-SIAM Symp. on Discrete Algorithms (SODA'94)* (1994), 536–545.
16. S. Micali and V.V. Vazirani, An $O(\sqrt{n}\,m)$ algorithm for finding maximum matching in general graphs, *Proc. 21st Annual IEEE Symposium on Foundation of Computer Science (FOCS'80)*, (1980) 17–27.
17. K. Nakano, S. Olariu, and A.Y. Zomaya, A time-optimal solution for the path cover problem on cographs, *Theoret. Comput. Sci.* **290** (2003) 1541–1556.
18. C-H. Yang and M-S. Yu, An O(n) time algorithm for maximum matchings in cographs, *Inform. Process. Lett.* **47** (1993) 89–93.

Boundary Labelling of Optimal Total Leader Length[*]

M.A. Bekos[1], M. Kaufmann[2], K. Potika[1], and A. Symvonis[1]

[1] National Technical University of Athens,
School of Applied Mathematical & Physical Sciences, Athens, Greece
{mikebekos, symvonis}@math.ntua.gr, epotik@cs.ntua.gr
[2] University of Tübingen, Institute for Informatics, Tübingen, Germany
mk@informatik.uni-tuebingen.de

Abstract. In this paper, we consider the *leader length minimization problem* for *boundary labelling*, i.e. the problem of finding a legal leader-label placement, such that the total leader length is minimized. We present an $O(n^2 log^3 n)$ algorithm assuming *type-opo leaders* (rectilinear lines with either zero or two bends) and labels of uniform size which can be attached to all four sides of rectangle R. Our algorithm supports *fixed* and *sliding ports*, i.e., the point where each leader is connected to the label (referred to as *port*) may be fixed or may slide along a label edge.

1 Introduction

One of the most challenging tasks in map labelling is the automated visualization of the information on a map, i.e. the association of text labels with graphical features. In order to ensure readability, unambiguity and legibility, cartographers suggest that the labels should be pairwise disjoint and close to the point (also referred to as *site*) to which they belong [5,12]. Unfortunately, the majority of map labelling problems are shown to be NP-complete [1,4,6]. Due to this fact, graph drawers and computational geometers have suggested labelling approximations [1,4,10] and heuristics [11], which often try to maximize either the label size or the number of features with labels. A detailed bibliography on map labelling can be found in [9]. It is worth mentioning that the ACM Computational Geometry Task Force [3] has identified label placement as an important area of research.

Research on map labelling has been primarily focussed on labelling point-features, where the basic requirement is that the labels should be pairwise disjoint. It is clear that this is not achievable in the case of large labels (or, equivalently, large point sets). Large labels are common in technical drawings or medical atlases where certain site-features are explained with blocks of text.

---

[*] This work has partially been supported by the DFG grant Ka 512/8-3, by the German-Greek cooperation program GRC 01/048 and by the Operational Program for Educational and Vocational Training II (EPEAEK II) and particularly the Program PYTHAGORAS (co-funded by the European Social Fund (75%) and National Resources (25%)).

To address this problem, Bekos et. al. defined *boundary labelling*[2]. In boundary labelling, labels are attached on the boundary of a rectangle R which encloses all sites. The main task is to place the labels in distinct positions on the boundary of R so that they do not overlap and, to connect each site with its corresponding label by non-intersecting polygonal lines, so called *leaders*.

The basic boundary labelling problem can be formally described as follows: We are given an axis-parallel rectangle $R = [l_R, r_R] \times [b_R, t_R]$ and a set P of n sites $p_i = (x_i, y_i)$ in general position, i.e. no three sites lie on a line and no two sites have the same x or y coordinate. We denote with W and H the width and the height of R, respectively. Each site p_i lie in the interior of R (i.e. $l_R < x_i < r_R$ and $b_R < y_i < t_R$) and is associated with an axis-parallel, rectangular label l_i of width w_i and height h_i. Each label should lie outside R but touch the boundary of R. Our task is to place the labels in distinct positions on the boundary of R, so that they do not overlap and, to connect each site with its label, such that no connection (referred to as *leader*) intersect any other connection or site. Such labellings are called *legal leader-label labellings or crossing free labellings*.

The point where each leader touches its corresponding label is referred to as *port*. Ports may be fixed (e.g., at the middle of a label edge) or may slide along a label edge. Based on the type of allowed ports (*fixed* of *sliding*) one can define the corresponding variations of the boundary labelling problem. Furthermore, one can define more variations of boundary labelling problems based on the location of the labels. More specifically, labels are usually attached to one, two or all four sides of the enclosing rectangle and are either placed at predefined locations (*fixed labels*) along the sides or can slide (*sliding labels*).

The leaders connecting the sites to their corresponding labels can be of several types, each giving rise to a new boundary labelling model. Of particular interest are two types of leaders: *rectilinear* and *straight* leaders.

- **Rectilinear Leaders:** Each leader consists of a sequence of axis-parallel segments, which are either parallel (p) or orthogonal (o) to the side of R to which the associated label is attached. This suggests that a leader c of type $c_1 c_2 \ldots c_k$, where $c_i \in \{o, p\}$ consists of an x- and y-monotone connected sequence $(s_1, s_2, \ldots, s_k)$ of segments from the site to the label, where segment s_i is parallel to the side containing the label if $c_i = p$; otherwise it is orthogonal to that side. Our primary focus has been on *opo* and *po* leaders, see Figures 1 and 2, respectively. For each *opo* leader we further insist that the parallel p segment lies immediately outside R, in the so called *track routing area*. Type-*o* leaders can be considered as either type *opo* or type *po*.
- **Straight Leaders:** Each leader is drawn as a straight line segment (see Figure 3). According to the previous classification scheme, we refer to straight leaders as type s leaders.

Given a boundary labelling problem specified by a set of points inside an enclosing rectangle and a labelling model (as specified by restrictions on the type of ports, the location and type of labels, and the type of leaders), we are interested in finding a solution that is optimal with respect to some objective. We usually aim at:

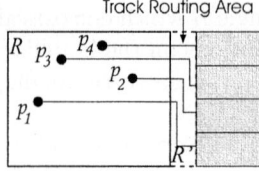 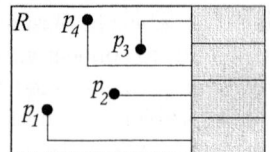 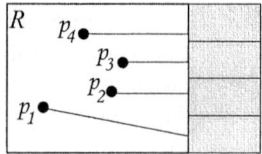

Fig. 1. Type-*opo* leaders   **Fig. 2.** Type-*po* leaders   **Fig. 3.** Type-*o* and type-*s* leaders

- **Short Leaders:** Find a legal leader-label placement, such that the total leader length is minimum. Such a labelling minimizes the average leader length.
- **Simple Layout:** Find a legal leader-label placement, such that the total number of bends in minimum. Such a labelling minimizes the average number of bend per leader.

Table 1 summarizes the results of Bekos et. al. [2] on boundary labelling. They examined a variety of models based on the type of leader, the location of the label and the size of the label and presented algorithms for legal leader-label assignments and leader-bend and leader-length minimization. These are the only published results on boundary labelling.

Table 1. Known results on boundary labelling. TLL stands for "Total Leader Length".

Model	Objective	Time complexity
opo, 1-side, variable size labels	legal	$O(n \log n)$
	#bends	$O(n^2)$
opo, 4-side, uniform square labels	legal	$O(n \log n)$
po, 1-side, uniform	legal	$O(n^2)$
opo, 2-side (opposite), uniform labels of max-size	TLL	$O(n^2)$
po, 2-side (opposite), uniform labels of max-size	TLL	$O(n^2)$
opo, 4-side, uniform square labels	TLL	$O(n^5)$
opo, 2-side (opposite), variable size labels	TLL	$O(nH^2)$
s, 1-side, uniform labels	legal	$O(n \log n)$
s, 1-side, uniform labels	TLL	$O(n^{2+\delta}), \delta > 0$
s, 4-side, uniform square labels	TLL	$O(n^{2+\delta}), \delta > 0$

One of the presented algorithms in [2] examines 4-side *opo* labelling with uniform square labels. In $O(n^5)$ time, it computes a boundary labelling of minimum total leader length. The algorithm is based on an $O(n^2 log^3 n)$ minimum cost bipartite matching algorithm for the production of a minimum total leader length solution which may have crossings, and the subsequent elimination of these crossings in $O(n^5)$ time (based on techniques used in VLSI routing). In this paper, we present a solution of $O(n^2 log^3 n)$ time complexity which is also based on minimum cost bipartite matching and an improved $O(n \log n)$ algorithm to eliminate crossings.

2 Four-Sided, Uniform Label, *opo* Boundary Labelling

We show how to compute in $O(n^2 log^3 n)$ time an *opo* boundary labelling of minimum total leader length where the labels can be placed on all four sides of the enclosing rectangle's boundary. We assume labels of uniform size and sliding ports.

We first make some observations regarding *opo*-labelling (which might contain crossings) of minimum total leader length for the case of four-sided labelling with labels of uniform size and sliding ports. Consider an *opo*-leader c which originates from point p and is connected with a label on side AB of the rectangle at port q (see Figure 4). The line containing the segment of the leader which is incident to site p (and is orthogonal to side AB) divides the plane into two half-planes. We say that leader c *is oriented towards* corner A of the rectangle if port q and corner A are on the same half-plane, otherwise, we say that leader c *is oriented away of* corner A. In the case where the *opo*-leader consists of only one segment, i.e., the port lies on the line which defines the two half-planes, we consider the leader to be oriented towards corner A (and also towards corner B).

Lemma 1. *Consider four-sided labelling with labels of uniform size and sliding ports and let L be an opo-labelling (which might contain crossings) of minimum total leader length. Let c_i and c_j be two leaders originating from sites p_i and p_j, respectively, which cross each other. Then it holds:*

(i) The labels associated with leaders c_i and c_j are located at two adjacent sides of the rectangle incident to, say, corner A.
(ii) Leaders c_i and c_j are oriented towards corner A of the rectangle.
(iii) Leaders c_i and c_j can be rerouted so that they do not cross each other and the sum of their leader lengths remains unchanged.

Proof. Showing that *"the labels associated with leaders c_i and c_j are located at two adjacent sides of the rectangle"* is easy. We simply have to show that it is not possible to have the labels located at the same side or opposite sides of the rectangle. For the sake of contradiction, assume first that the labels lie on the same side, say AB, of the rectangle. Then the segments of the leaders which are incident to the sites are parallel to each other. Since the sites have distinct X and Y coordinates, these segments do not overlap each other, and thus, the intersection of the two leaders takes place outside the rectangle (in the track routing area). This implies that, along the direction of side AB, the order of the sites is the reverse of the order of their associated labels. However, by swapping the labels, we can reduce the total leader length (and also eliminate a crossing), a contradiction since we assumed that the total leader length of the labelling is minimum (see Figure 5). Consider now the case where, for the sake of contradiction the labels lie on opposite sides of the rectangle. Then, since

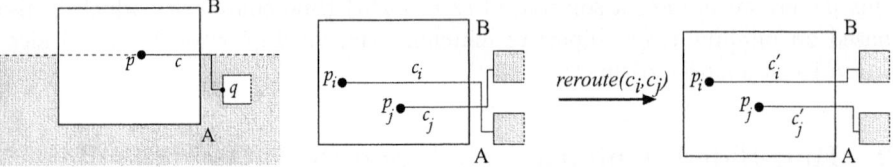

Fig. 4. Orientation of a leader with respect to a corner. Leader c is oriented *towards* corner A and *away of* corner B.

Fig. 5. Rerouting used to prove that in an *opo*-labelling (where crossings are allowed) of minimum total leader length, the labels associated with two crossing leaders do not lie on the same side of the rectangle

the leaders intersect each other, the segments of the leaders which are inside the rectangle (and incident to the sites) have to intersect. However, since these segments are parallel to each other, they have to overlap, and thus have the same X or Y coordinates, a contradiction since we assume that the sites are in general position. Having eliminated the cases that the labels lie on the same or on opposite sides of the rectangle implies that, assuming that we can identify two crossing leaders, their associated labels lie on adjacent sides of the rectangle.

Let A be the corner which is incident to the two sides of the rectangle containing the labels associated with leaders c_i and c_j. In order to show that in a labelling of minimum total leader length both *"leaders c_i and c_j are oriented towards corner A"*, it is enough to show that (in a labelling of minimum total leader length) it is impossible to have one or both leaders oriented away of corner A. We proceed to consider these two cases.

Case 1: Exactly one leaders, say c_i, is oriented away of corner A. This case is described in the left-hand side of Figure 6.a. Rerouting the leaders as described in Figure 6.a results in a reduction of the total leader length, a contradiction since we assumed that the total leader length of the labelling is minimum. Note that, in the figure we only show the sub-case where site p_j is below the horizontal line passing through port q_i. When p_j is on or above the horizontal line passing through port q_i, rerouting again results to a reduction of the total leader length. Thus, a labelling of minimum total leader length does not contain two crossing leaders where one of them is oriented away of the corner A incident to the sides containing their associated labels.

Case 2: Both leaders c_i and c_j are oriented away of corner A. When both leaders are oriented away of corner A, rerouting results in higher reduction of the total leader length, compared to Case 1 where only one leader was oriented away of corner A. The rerouting of the leaders is described in Figure 6.b. Again, only one of the four possible sub-cases based on whether site p_i (p_j) is to the right (below) the vertical (horizontal) line passing through port q_j (q_i) is shown. Given that rerouting results to reduction of the total leader length, we conclude that a labelling of minimum total leader length does not contain two crossing leaders where both of them are oriented away of the corner A incident to the sides containing their associated labels.

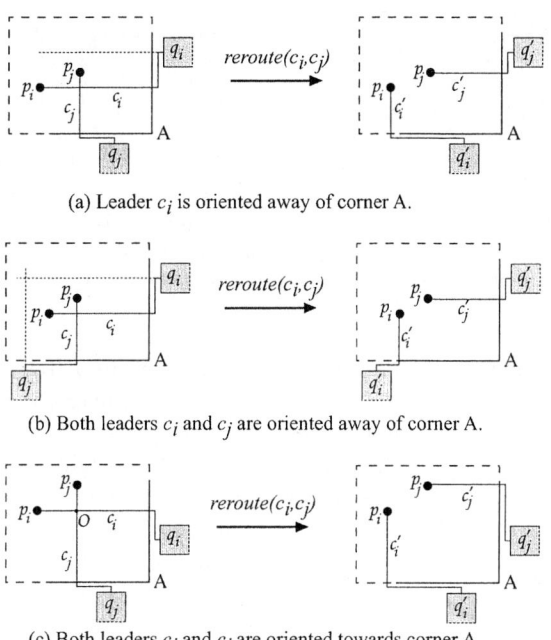

Fig. 6. Rerouting used to prove that in an *opo*-labelling (where crossings are allowed) of minimum total leader length, two crossing leaders are oriented towards the corner incident to the sides of the rectangle containing the associated labels and that their crossing can be eliminated without reducing the sum of their leader length

Having eliminated the cases where one or both crossing leaders are oriented away of corner A, implies that (assuming that we can identify two crossing leaders) they are both oriented towards corner A.

Showing that *"leaders c_i and c_j can be rerouted so that they do not cross each other and the sum of their leader lengths remains unchanged"* is easy. In the rerouting described in Figure 6.c, use the crossing point O to partition the first segment of each leader c_i and c_j into two sub-segments. Then, leaders c'_i and c'_j can be obtained by a parallel translation of the (sub)segments of leaders c_i and c_j, leaving their sum unchanged.

To complete the proof of the lemma, we note that whenever we performed a rerouting, we never changed the position of a port. So, since the used port would also be available in the case where the sliding-port model is used, the lemma applies to sliding ports, as stated. □

Theorem 1. *Consider opo-labelling of n sites with uniform labels and sliding ports where crossings are allowed. Then, given a labelling L of minimum total leader length, we can always identify a crossing-free opo-labelling L' with total leader length equal to that of L. Moreover, labelling L' can be obtained in $O(n \log n)$ time.*

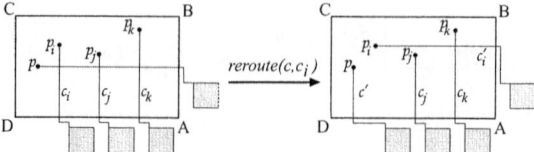

Fig. 7. Rerouting used to eliminate crossings in an *opo*-labelling of minimum total leader length. The crossings to be eliminated are identified in a left-to-right pass of the sites, followed by a right-to-left pass. See proof of Theorem 1.

Proof. We will show how to eliminate all crossings in L by rerouting the intersecting leaders. Our method performs two passes over the sites, one in the left-to-right and one in the right-to-left direction.

Consider first the left-to-right pass. In the left-to-right pass of labelling L, we consider all sites with labels on the right side of the rectangle. We examine the sites in order from left-to-right and focus only on those which are incident to crossing leaders. Let p be the leftmost such site and let c be the leader that connects it with its corresponding label on the right side of the rectangle (see Figure 7). Given that L is an *opo*-labelling of minimum total leader length, Lemma 1.(i) implies that leader c intersects only with leaders that are connected with labels on the top and bottom sides of the rectangle. Without loss of generality, assume that c is oriented towards the bottom-right corner of the rectangle, say A. Then all leaders that intersect c have their labels on the bottom of the rectangle and are also oriented towards A (Lemma 1.(ii)). Let c_i be the leftmost leader that intersects c, and let p_i be its incident site. According to Lemma 1.(iii), we can reroute leaders c and c_i so that the total leader length remains unchanged (Figure 7). Observe that the rerouting possibly eliminates more than one crossing (e.g., the crossings between leader c and leaders c_j and c_k) but, in general, it might also introduce new crossings (e.g., the crossings between leaders c'_i and c_k). However, the total number of crossings is reduced and, more importantly, the leftmost site incident to an intersecting leader connected to a label on the right side of the rectangle is located to the right of site p. Continuing in the same manner, the leftmost site which participates in a crossing (in the left-to-right pass) is pushed to the right, which guarantees that all "left-to-right" crossings are eventually eliminated.

Another important property is that it is impossible to introduce any "right-to-left" crossing during the left-to-right pass. To see this, assume that such a crossing was introduced and that it involves leader c' and the leader c_l which connects site p_l to a label on the left side of the rectangle (Figure 8). Given that the rerouting does not increase the total leader length, the labelling resulting after all rerouting is still one of minimum total leader length. Then, according to Lemma 1.(i), both leaders c' and c_l must be oriented towards corner D, a contradiction since leader c' is oriented away of corner D (and towards corner A).

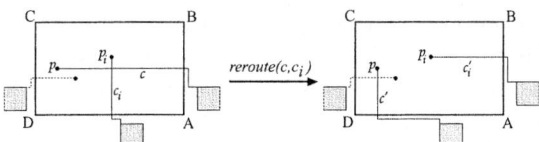

Fig. 8. It is impossible to introduce any right-to-left crossing during the left-to-right pass described in the proof of Theorem 1

From the above discussion, it follows that a left-to-right pass eliminating crossings involving leaders with their associated labels on the right side of the rectangle, followed by a similar right-to-left pass, results to a labelling L' without any crossings and of total leader length equal to that of L, that is, minimum.

To complete the proof of the theorem, it remains to explain how to obtain in $O(n \log n)$ time the new labelling L', given labelling L of minimum total leader length. Consider the left-to-right pass. The analysis for the right-to-left pass is symmetric. During the pass, we process the sites with labels on the right side of the enclosing rectangle in order of increasing X-coordinate. Sorting the sites in increasing order with respect to their X-coordinate can be done in $O(n \log n)$ time.

In order to process site $p = (x_p, y_p)$ and to eliminate the crossings (if any) involving its leader c, we have to identify the leftmost site p_i such that its corresponding leader (say c_i) intersects leader c. Of course, the intersection involves the first segment of leader c_i that is parallel to the Y-axis. The processing of the sites during the left-to-right pass can be accomplished by employing a data structure storing "vertical line segments" and supporting *visibility queries* of the form "*given a query point $p_0 = (x_0, y_0)$ return the first line segment to the right of p_0 that is intersected by line $y = y_0$*", as well as *insert* (for initialization) and *delete* operations. For the case of vertical line segments of *finite size*, the visibility query can be answered in $O(\log^2 n)$ time by employing a combination of interval trees and priority search trees [7, pp. 211]. This results to a total of $(n \log^2 n)$ time for the left-to-right pass and, consequently, for the elimination of all crossings. However, the time needed to eliminate all crossings can be further reduced to $O(n \log n)$ if we take into account the fact that all vertical segments considered during the left-to-right pass have one of their endpoints on the bottom or the top side of the enclosing rectangle.

Without loss of generality, assume that leader c is oriented towards the bottom-right corner of the enclosing rectangle. (The case where it is oriented towards the top-right corner can be handled in a symmetric manner.) Then, according to Lemma 1.(ii) all leaders intersecting leader c are also oriented towards the bottom-left corner and, thus, their associated labels are placed on the bottom side of the enclosing rectangle. So, leader c can only intersect vertical line segments which have one of their end-points on the bottom side of the enclosing rectangle.

When we have to solve a visibility query on the set of line segments having one of their end-points on the bottom side of the enclosing rectangle, we can relax the restriction that the segments are of finite size and assume that they are semi-infinite rays having their associated site as their higher endpoint. This is due to the fact that all leader intersections take place inside the enclosing rectangle. Recall that r_R denotes the Y-coordinate of the right side of the enclosing rectangle R. In the case of semi-infinite segments, the visibility query (with $p_0 = (x_0, y_0)$ as the query point) on set of vertical line segments reduces to finding the site of smallest X-coordinate in the semi-infinite vertical strip defined by $x > x_0$, $y \leq y_0$, and $x < r_R$. The *MinXinRectangle* query just described can be answered in time $O(\log n)$ by employing a dynamic priority search tree based on half-balanced trees [7, pp. 209]. Insertions and deletions are also supported in $O(\log n)$ time.

Thus, identifying the (at most n) pairs of leaders to be rerouted during the left-to-right pass takes only $O(n \log n)$ time, resulting to a total time complexity of $O(n \log n)$ for the production of the crossing free boundary labelling L'. □

Theorem 2. *Consider four-sided opo-labelling of n sites with uniform labels and sliding ports. A crossing-free solution of minimum total length can be computed in $O(n^2 \log^3 n)$ time.*

Proof. Let M be the set of the n labels around the boundary of the rectangle. We construct a complete bipartite graph $G = (P \cup M, E)$ between all the sites $p \in P$ and all the labels $m \in M$, with edge weights to be the Manhattan length of the corresponding leaders. Note that the length of each leader depends on the type of the port. For the case of sliding ports, the leader typically connects the site to one of the corners of the label. We proceed by applying the Vaidya's algorithm [8] for minimum-cost bipartite matching for points in the plane under the Manhattan metric. It runs in $O(n^2 \log^3 n)$ time and finds a matching between sites and labels that minimizes the total Manhattan distance of the matched pairs. The leaders in the produced solution might overlap. However, based on Theorem 1 we can eliminate all crossings in $O(n \log n)$ additional time. □

3 Conclusion

There are several issues that should be considered in future work on boundary labelling. Among them, we distinguish:

- **Labelling "Area Features" of Maps.** Better quality labellings can be produced by allowing a site to slide along a line segment or along the boundary of a polygon. In this case, the solution of the boundary labelling problem has to also specify the final location of each site.
- **Mixed Boundary Labellings.** Examples for type-*opo* and type-*po* leaders show advantages and also some disadvantages of both types. A practical solution might be to mix both types in order to cope with disadvantages while keeping advantages.

References

1. P. Agarwal, M. van Kreveld, and S. Suri. Label placement by maximum independent set in rectangles. Computational Geometry: Theory and Applications, 11:209–218, 1998.
2. M. Bekos, M. Kaufmann, A. Symvonis, and A. Wolff. Boundary labeling: Models and efficient algorithms for rectangular maps. In Janos Pach, editor, *Proc. 12th Int. Symposium on Graph Drawing (GD'04)*, Lecture Notes in Computer Science, New York, September 2004.
3. B. Chazelle and 36 co-authors. The computational geometry impact task force report. In B. Chazelle, J. E. Goodman, and R. Pollack, editors, *Advances in Discrete and Computational Geometry*, vol. 223, pp. 407–463. AMS, 1999.
4. M. Formann and F. Wagner. A packing problem with applications to lettering of maps. In *Proc. 7th ACM Symp. Comp. Geom. (SoCG'91)*, pages 281–288, 1991.
5. E. Imhof. Positioning Names on Maps. The American Cartographer, vol.2 (1975), 128-144.
6. C. Iturriaga and A. Lubiw. NP-hardness of some map labeling problems. Technical Report CS-97-18, University of Waterloo, 1997.
7. K. Mehlhorn. *Data Structures and Algorithms 3: Multi-dimensional Searching and Computational Geometry*, volume 3 of *EATCS Monographs on Theoretical Computer Science*. Springer-Verlag, Heidelberg, Germany, 1984.
8. P. M. Vaidya. Geometry helps in matching. *SIAM J. Comput.*, 18:1201–1225, 1989.
9. A. Wolff and T. Strijk. The Map-Labeling Bibliography. http://i11www.ira.uka.de/map-labeling/bibliography/, 1996.
10. F. Wagner. Approximate map labeling is in Omega (n log n). Technical Report B 93-18, Fachbereich Mathematik und Informatik, Freie Universitat Berlin, 1993.
11. F. Wagner and A. Wolff. Map labeling heuristics: provably good and practically useful Proceedings of the eleventh annual symposium on Computational geometry, p.109-118, 1995
12. P. Yoeli. The Logic of Automated Map Lettering. The Cartographic Journal 9, 1972, 99-108

Successive Linear Programs for Computing All Integral Points in a Minkowski Sum

Ioannis Z. Emiris and Kyriakos Zervoudakis

Dept. of Informatics and Telecommunications,
National University of Athens, Greece

Abstract. The computation of all integral points in Minkowski (or vector) sums of convex lattice polytopes of arbitrary dimension appears as a subproblem in algebraic variable elimination, parallel compiler code optimization, polyhedral combinatorics and multivariate polynomial multiplication. We use an existing approach that avoids the costly construction of the Minkowski sum by an incremental process of solving Linear Programming (LP) problems. Our main contribution is to exploit the similarities between LP problems in the tree of LP instances, using duality theory and the two-phase simplex algorithm. Our public domain implementation improves substantially upon the performance of the above mentioned approach and is faster than porta on certain input families; besides, the latter requires a description of the Minkowski sum which has high complexity. Memory consumption limits commercial or free software packages implementing multivariate polynomial multiplication, whereas ours can solve all examined data, namely of dimension up to 9, using less than 2.7 MB (before actually outputting the points) for instances yielding more than 3 million points.

Keywords: convex polytope, Minkowski sum, integral points, linear programming, duality theory, polyhedral combinatorics.

1 Introduction

Definition 1. *Let* $q_1, \ldots, q_n$ *be convex polytopes in* $\mathbb{R}^d$ *with integral vertices. The* Minkowski *sum* $q_1 + \cdots + q_n$ *is the set of points* $p = p_1 + \cdots + p_n$ *such that* $p_i \in q_i$, $\forall i$. *We shall be interested in computing all such points* $p \in \mathbb{Z}^d$.

Our main motivation comes from the theory of *toric, or sparse, elimination*, a modern method in symbolic computation and computational algebraic geometry [7,12]. Polynomials in k variables are characterized by a finite subset in $\mathbb{Z}^k$, known as their *support*, constituted of all monomial exponents corresponding to nonzero coefficients. The *Newton polytope* of a polynomial is the convex hull of its support. Hence, several operations in toric elimination rely crucially on efficiently manipulating integral points, which are in bijection with monomials, as well as Newton polytopes and their Minkowski sums. Computing the integral points inside Minkowski sums of Newton polytopes is an important operation in constructing matrix formulae for the *toric resultant*, which is a powerful tool for studying and solving algebraic systems; e.g. [7,11].

In particular, in [11] a general method for constructing Sylvester-type resultant matrices is proposed and implemented, yielding in general the smallest matrices of this type. Moreover, it generates all known optimal formulae of Sylvester type [22] as well as the multigraded formulae studied in [8,12] (cf. sect. 4). One of the bottlenecks is to compute a *subset* of the integral points inside a Minkowski sum of Newton polytopes, which can be obtained by a straightforward adaptation of the algorithm proposed below; cf. [10]. In fact, this algorithm has to solve $d+1$ integral point computation problems for all d-subsets of a given set of $d+1$ Newton polytopes. Other resultant formulations, e.g. [8,7], require all points in the strict interior of the Minkowski sum or in a small perturbation of the Minkowski sum. These are not hard to obtain with our algorithm. Integral point computation occurs as a subproblem in several other applications such as code optimization by parallel compilers [1,5], volume approximation [14] and deriving the linear description of a polytope [3, sect. 5].

Efficient software exists for computing all integral points inside a single polytope, namely porta [2]. In sect. 5 we shall see that our software improves upon the time complexity of porta for the cyclic-root input family. Moreover, generating a description of the Minkowski sum can be very costly. In fact, it is known that neither a facet nor a vertex representation of the Minkowski sum can be computed in polynomial arithmetic complexity, when n, d are parameters as in our case. If one of these parameters is fixed and we work with vertex representations, then there exists a polynomial-time algorithm [15].

A related problem is multivariate polynomial multiplication, provided we consider each given polytopes as the Newton polytope of a polynomial. The Minkowski sum points would then correspond to the support of the product and could be efficiently computed, provided that each can be obtained as a sum of some points from the input polytopes. But this is not true! Take q_1, q_2 with vertex sets $\{(0,0),(1,1)\}$ and $\{(1,0),(0,1)\}$. Their product has only four terms and misses $(1,1)$ which lies in q_1+q_2. Further examples are in sect. 4.

Our algorithm is based on the Mayan pyramid approach of [11,10], which avoids the explicit construction of the Minkowski sum. Moreover, it can use Linear Programming (LP) relaxation to avoid any integer programming as we discuss below. However, successive LPs are very related but this had not been exploited so far. For this paper, we have implemented the simplex algorithm and exploited its flexibility in order to exploit the relationship between successive LPs. A first step is to use the solution to a minimization LP as a feasible solution for the corresponding maximization LP, when the set of constraints does not change. Our main contribution is to apply duality theory in conjunction with the branch-and-bound approach of the Mayan pyramid algorithm in order to accelerate the simplex algorithm, especially by avoiding execution of its first phase, when the set of constraints is incremented.

By reducing the number of Phase I executions, we improve the runtime complexity of [10] by a factor between 4 and 5; this tends to increase slowly with the problem dimension. The implementation is publicly available and performs better than several tested approaches in terms of speed or memory consumption; cf. sect. 5. It computes more than 3 million points in a 9-dimensional Minkowski sum in less than 27 minutes while using less than 2.7 MB, since it does not have to store any intermediate points. More importantly, running time is roughly linear in the number of output points, which confirms the expected output-sensitive behavior of the algorithm. The LP problems have maximum size of about 100 variables and 20 constraints, besides the positivity constrains.

The paper is structured as follows. The next section presents the Mayan pyramid algorithm. Sect. 3 details our algorithm and estimates its time and space complexity. Sect. 4 presents the implementation and certain experimental results, and sect. 5 provides a comparison with other approaches to the problem or to the problem of multivariate polynomial multiplication.

2 Basic Algorithms

Let the vertex set of polytope q_i be $\{p_{i,1}, \ldots, p_{i,n_i}\} \subset \mathbb{Z}^d$. The Minkowski sum $q_1 + \cdots + q_n$ of def. 1 can now be expressed as the set of points p such that $p = \sum_{i=1}^{n} \sum_{j=1}^{n_i} \lambda_{i,j} p_{i,j}$, $\sum_{j=1}^{n_i} \lambda_{i,j} = 1$, $i = 1, \ldots, n$. Denote the convexity constraints by $E_i := \sum_{j=1}^{n_i} \lambda_{i,j}$, $\forall i \leq n$, and let P be the set of equations $E_1 = 1, \ldots, E_n = 1$. We also define the constraint on the k-th coordinate of the sought points to be $E_{n+k} := \sum_{i=1}^{n} \sum_{j=1}^{n_i} p_{i,j}(k)$, $1 \leq k \leq d$, where $p_{i,j}(k)$ is the k-th coordinate of $p_{i,j}$. The number of LP variables equals the total number vertices in all polytopes. The points of the Minkowski sum are given by the solutions of $E_1, \ldots, E_n$ such that $E_{n+1}, \ldots, E_{n+d}$ are integral.

To avoid the construction of the Minkowski sum, the algorithm from [10,11] (alg. 1 below) finds the minimum and maximum integral values of E_{n+k} when $E_{n+1}, \ldots, E_{n+k-1}$ have been fixed, then proceeds to examine all possible values of the k-th coordinate. In other words, the algorithm examines *orthogonal projections* of the Minkowski sum to linear subspaces. Therefore its bottleneck is computing the last coordinate given the points in the projection of dimension $d - 1$. In terms of LPs, this approach essentially splits the feasible region according to the value of each coordinate.

Minimization and maximization of z (lines 7 and 8) can be achieved with by LP relaxation. This yields the interval of the corresponding coordinate of any point in the Minkowski sum. We round the real endpoints outwards to integers in order to ensure that all integral points are accounted for, assuming that numerical error in the LP is not larger than one unit. This is always the case as we have verified experimentally; the reason is that all input quantities are integral. It is of course possible to guarantee formally that all integral points shall be found, by further enlarging the interval at line 13. In any case, if line 13 creates a range for a which is larger than optimum, this will lead to certain infeasible problems (line 4) but will not generate extraneous points. The same observations hold for the last coordinate at line 10, which ranges in $[\lfloor z_{min} \rfloor, \lceil z_{max} \rceil]$. The optimality of this interval is not tested in the flowchart of alg. 1, but it is straightforward to

Algorithm 1. Mayan pyramid algorithm

1: $b_i \leftarrow 1, i = 1, \ldots, n$
2: $allpoints \leftarrow \emptyset$
3: RECURSIVE(1)

1: DEFINE RECURSIVE(K)
2: $P_k \leftarrow \{E_1 = b_1, \ldots, E_{n+k-1} = b_{n+k-1}\}$
3: $z \leftarrow E_{n+k}$
4: **if** P_k is infeasible **then**
5:    RETURN
6: **end if**
7: Minimize z for P_k
8: Maximize z for P_k
9: **if** $k = d$ **then**
10:    $allpoints \leftarrow allpoints \cup \{(b_1, \ldots, b_{d-1}, z) \mid z = \lfloor z_{min} \rfloor, \ldots, \lceil z_{max} \rceil\}$
11:    RETURN
12: **else**
13:    **for** $a = \lfloor z_{min} \rfloor, \ldots, \lceil z_{max} \rceil$ **do**
14:       $b_k \leftarrow a$; RECURSIVE($k+1$)
15:    **end for**
16: **end if**

do it; see [10] for details. Standard references for the simplex algorithm include [4,21]. The rest of this section introduces the notation used.

An LP problem is a pair (F, c) where $F = \{x : x \in \mathbb{R}^n, Ax = b, x \geq 0\}$, $c : x \to c'x$, m, n are positive integers, $b \in \mathbb{Z}^m$, $c \in \mathbb{Z}^n$ and A an $m \times n$ matrix. By B we denote a basis. By multiplying $Ax = b$ with B^{-1} a solution $b' := B^{-1}b$ is attained. Whenever $b' \geq 0$ the solution is a *basic feasible solutions* (BFS). For any basis we define, $\bar{c} = c - c_B B^{-1} A$, $z = -c'_B b'$, where c_B expresses the coordinates of c which correspond to the basic columns. $-z$ is the value of the objective function. The $\bar{c}$ vector provides the *termination* criterion. To find one initial BFS, m "artificial" variables are introduced. The process of optimally solving the artificial problem is called Phase I. The process of minimizing the original cost variable is called Phase II. For each LP problem of the form $\min c'x : a'_i x = b_i, x_j \geq 0$, its *dual* problem is $\max \pi' b : \pi'_i A_j \leq c_j$, where the π_i variables are free and a_i, A_j the rows and columns of the original matrix respectively. We apply the dual simplex method in our approach in order to "repair" primal solutions. Our work aims at exploiting the existing solutions in order to avoid solving Phase I for the rest of the problems. The LPs in our case have obvious similarities; problems which arise from two successive calls of the function RECURSIVE in line 12 differ only by one right hand side term.

3 Improved Algorithm and Its Complexity

The solved LPs form a tree-like structure. In each node of the tree one minimization and one maximization problem is solved. The root node is the initial problem of finding the minimum and maximum values of E_1, z_{min} and z_{max}. The root's children correspond to the problems that are constructed by adding $E_1 = b$ to the initial problem where $\lfloor z_{min} \rfloor \leq b \leq \lceil z_{max} \rceil$ and optimizing E_2. The number of the problems that have to be solved is exponential with respect to the dimension of the space in which lie the polytopes. It can be observed that all LP problems in the same depth of the tree have exactly the same matrix A. The only parameters that vary between LP problems in the same level (or at the same depth) of the tree are the right-hand sides. Having solved one of the problems of any level the solution can be used in order to find a solution to any other problem of the same level.

Proposition 1. *An optimal solution to any primal minimization or maximization problem P_k of the alg. 1 is also a BFS to the dual of any other problem $P_{k'}$ if $k = k'$.*

The proposition does not guarantee that $B^{-1}b \geq 0$ for any other problem $P_{k'}$. The solution will be dually feasible, though not necessarily dually optimal.

Corollary 1. *Having solved just one primal problem at a level (depth) of the tree, Phase I can be avoided for all other LP problems at the same level.*

The new algorithm, after reusing a previously found basis B, has to examine the vector $b' = B^{-1}b$ as follows: If all coordinates are non-negative then the solution is optimal so only the objective function's value $z = c_B b$ needs updating. Otherwise, the solution is feasible but not optimal so Phase II of the dual problem has to be solved. To explain this in more detail let us focus on the process of solving a minimization problem. First, it is checked whether it is the first problem at depth k of the problem tree. If this is the case the problem is solved using the primal simplex method. The solved state of the minimization problem m_k is not altered. The basis corresponding to the solution is, of course, part of the solution; we denote with $\underline{B}_k$ the basis of the last minimizing problem solved. The algorithm applies the basis of the last minimization problem solved in depth k to the current problem, and calculates the values b' of the variables. If all values are non-negative, then the algorithm recomputes the value of the objective function. In the opposite case, the vector b' replaces the right hand side in problem m_k and the dual simplex method is applied. In an analogous manner, solved maximization LPs M_i and their corresponding basis $\overline{B}_k$ are used for solving new maximization problems. Recursion is at the end of the algorithm and can be removed, but it makes for conceptual and programming simplicity. We have experimented with the *revised simplex* algorithm, but for reasons of numerical stability we focused on the standard version described so far. In fact, we observed that values close to zero could appear as slightly negative, thus increasing the number of iterations. Let us now examine the algorithm's complexity.

Lemma 1. *If M is the amount of memory needed by an algorithm to solve an LP problem then the amount of memory needed by our algorithm is at most $2Md$.*

Memory consumption is thus increased but within reasonable limits. Storing the last optimal solution to both minimization and maximization problems is not necessary. Since the stored solutions are both feasible any of the two could serve as a starting point for the Phase II of the other. Practically, however, solutions of the one kind of optimization problems are "closer" to solutions of the same kind after minor changes of the right-hand sides like in our case. For the same reason, we do not store the first solution of each level in the problem tree but instead the last one found for each specific k since it will probably be "closer" to the next problem to be solved.

Alternatively, it is possible that instead of storing the whole solution one could only store the indices of the basis' columns. In that way memory consumption would drop to very low levels but also the algorithm would have to re-invert the basis before solving each LP.

Proposition 2. [10] *Suppose that, in alg. 1, for any $k \in [1, d]$, the number of points in the k-dimensional projection which do not give rise to any point with $k + 1$ coordinates is a constant fraction of the total number of points in that projection. Then the number of LPs is proportional to Td and the bit complexity is in $O(Td^{3.5}m^{1.5}L^2 \log L)$, where T is the number of integral points in the Minkowski sum, m bounds the number of vertices per polytope and L is the maximum bit-size of any polytope's vertex coordinates.*

For time complexity, the benefit from the proposed approach is that instead of solving both Phase I and II for each problem, only Phase II is solved (except for d initial problems which will have to be solved from scratch). For some problems even Phase II can be avoided since

Remark. We may roughly suppose that Phase I consumes on the average as much time as Phase II so we can expect that the time for our improved approach will be at most half the time needed for the original one. Intuitively, we can expect even better execution times since the dual simplex method repairs existing solutions instead of finding new ones from scratch.

We also propose and implement a heuristic rule for arranging the $E_i = 1$ lines of the problems P_k. The algorithm is modified in order to set z equal to that $E_i, i = n+k, \ldots, n+d$ for which $z_{max} - z_{min}$ is minimized. This rule effectively reduces the tree's branching factor and fewer LPs are solved.

Our approach is general in the sense that no assumption is made regarding the input polytopes q_i, except convexity. We observe, however, that if some of the input polytopes are equal a simple improvement can be made as a preprocessing step. If n polytopes $q_1, \ldots, q_n$ are the same and each with vertices $p_1, \ldots, p_m$ their Minkowski sum is simply the polytope with vertices $np_1, \ldots, np_m$. Thus, equal polytopes in the input are found in a preprocessing step and substituted by one polytope having scaled vertices. This reduces the practical complexity of our algorithm for certain input families.

4 Implementation and Practical Performance

The proposed approach, including an LP solver utilizing the necessary functions was implemented in C++. The CBLAS routines provided by the ATLAS package [23] were used for the low level matrix operations. The source code does not exceed 4000 lines and the object files are approximately 120 KB on a Sun SPARC. It is freely available at: http://www.di.uoa.gr/~quasi/intpoints/cip.tgz. The only system requirement for compilation is an ANSI C++ compiler. We used gnu g++ and version 2.95.2 or later is required. The CBLAS routines are not required. The needed functions were also implemented from scratch and are provided as an alternative. It has to be noted however that the CBLAS routines speed up execution time by about 15%.

Table 1. Problem data (dimension, # of summand polytopes, # of integral points in the sum, i # of terms in the polynomial product and # of solved LPs), simplex iterations and execution times in [10], here and relative reduction

System	d	n	#points	#terms	#probl.	[10]	here	red.	[10]	here	red.
			Problem data			simplex iterations			Execution times		
c3old	3	3	20	14	34	189	54	3.5	0.01	0	5.5
c4old	4	4	101	60	168	1353	259	5.2	0.04	0.01	4.0
c5old	5	5	622	342	1018	11663	1999	5.8	0.42	0.08	5.3
c6old	6	6	4103	1948	6484	60030	17213	3.5	3.12	0.71	4.4
c7old	7	7	32958	14394	49098	651180	168015	3.9	37.77	8.29	4.6
c8old	8	8	263045	100060	372776	6340139	1579332	4.0	430.29	91.55	4.7
c9old	9	9	2370386	826790	3199894	69473488	16926412	4.1	5333.04	1096.64	4.9
c7new	6	6	7197	7197	8908	100934	25981	3.9	5.24	1.14	4.6
c8new	7	7	50030	50030	64986	945543	228727	4.1	59.68	12.38	4.8
c9new	8	8	413395	413395	518252	9929149	2250308	4.4	694.38	136.95	5.1
c10new	9	9	3313612		4262434	103073274	22893612	4.5	8647.36	1579.80	5.5
(2,1;1,2)	4	5	2541	2541	518	1663	123	13.5	0.05	0.01	5.0
(1;2,1)	4	5	4356	4356	1718	6771	1190	5.7	0.25	0.05	5.0
(1;3,1)	4	5	9216	9216	3618	14691	2296	6.4	0.49	0.10	4.9
(1;3,2,1)	4	5	16896	16896	6178	25482	2296	11.1	0.84	0.13	6.5
(1;3,3,1)	4	5	24576	24576	8738	35675	2302	15.5	1.20	0.15	8.0

We applied several approaches to our test problems including the simple approach presented in [10]. All were variants of the algorithm presented earlier in this paper. We concluded that the best performance was obtained by the algorithm enriched with the heuristic and the preprocessing technique described earlier. In the following we present experimental results for this implementation and the simple approach of [10]. In all cases the incoming variable selection criterion is that of minimum reduced cost.

Systems of n identical polytopes are called *unmixed*, whereas those with different polytopes are *mixed*. The experiments concentrate on 3 classes of systems: multi-homogeneous unmixed systems and 2 variants of the standard algebraic benchmark of cyclic roots. The former are composed of polynomials in d variables, partitioned into r disjoint subsets, with d_k being the k-th group's number of variables such that $\sum_{k=1}^{r} d_k = d$. If, with the addition of one homogenizing variable for each group, the polynomial is homogeneous for each group, the polynomial is called *multi-homogeneous*. If the degree of the k-th group is δ_k and the system is unmixed, it is said to be multi-homogeneous of type $(d_1, \ldots, d_r; \delta_1, \ldots, \delta_r)$. Equivalently a multi-homogeneous system can be defined as an unmixed system where each Newton polytope is the Minkowski sum of r simplices lying in complementary linear subspaces of dimensions $d_1, \ldots, d_r$. The i-th simplex is the unit simplex scaled by δ_i. Such polytopes are also known as products of lower-dimensional simplices. The cyclicnold systems are defined from polynomials $f_k = \sum_{i=1}^{n} \prod_{j=i}^{i+k-1} x_j$, $k = 1, \ldots, n-1$, ($x_{n+t} \equiv x_t$), and $f_n = x_1 x_2 \ldots x_n - 1$. These are very sparse systems, in the sense that all polytopes are lower-dimensional; still, the sum of any $n-1$ among them is of full dimension. The system cyclicnnew is obtained from the system cyclicnold by setting $y_i = \frac{x_i}{x_n}$, $i = 1, \ldots, n-1$, and $y_n = 1$, thus $f_k = \sum_{i=1}^{n} \prod_{j=i}^{i+k-1} y_j$ for $k = 1, \ldots, n-1$, where $y_n = 1$ and $y_{n+t} = y_t$. This gives a problem which is algebraically equivalent but has one fewer variable and one fewer equation, i.e. is of dimension $n-1$ despite its being labeled cyclicnnew.

Table 1 summarizes the inputs and shows the output size; notice that the number of integral points in the Minkowski sum grows exponentially, as expected. Simplex iterations and execution times are also shown in tables 1 and 1 for the approach of [10], for the approach presented here and the relative reduction between them. Experiments were conducted on a 480 MHz SUN UltraSPARC-II running Solaris 8 with 2 GB of RAM. One iteration is a full simplex pivoting cycle: incoming variable selection, outgoing variable selection and pivoting.

It is interesting that the savings factor grows from 3.5 to 5.8 for the cyclic families as the problem size grows, which agrees with the intuition that the savings should be at least a constant around 2 that would grow as the tree of LPs becomes larger. This translates to a runtime speedup of between 4 and 5.5, again strictly increasing with the problem's size; the price to pay is roughly doubling the memory usage, where the output is not stored. For the multi-homogeneous family, the sample is too small for deducing a clear pattern. On this family, the preprocessing step described at the end of the previous section, exploits the fact that all polytopes are identical and has reduced runtime by a factor of 10 or more, since it has decreased the size of the LP tableaux by $n = 5$.

Memory consumption ranges from 2 to 122 MBs on the examined inputs. It has to be noted that most of the consumed space is used for storing the enumerated integer points. The algorithm itself should not consume more than 100 KB on the examined inputs. More detailed data appear in [9].

Fig. 1 depicts the relation between the output size, that is the number of computed integral points, and the execution time in the cyclic data sets. The relation seems to be linear, thus verifying prop. 2 and the remark that follows and establishing an output-sensitive behavior. Corresponding data for the multi-homogeneous data sets can be found in [9]. Fig. 2 shows the relation between runtime and the input dimension d of the cyclic families. This is again linear, despite the prediction of prop. 2. Notice, though, that the same proposition predicts a linear number of LPs, assuming the input is not very special, and this is confirmed. The super-linear power of d in prop. 2 is due to the complexity of

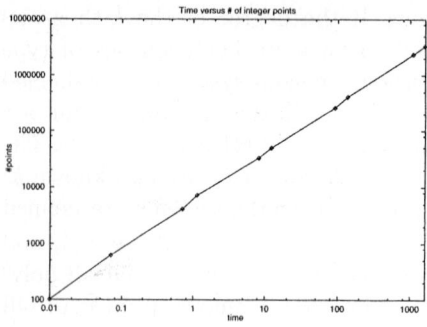 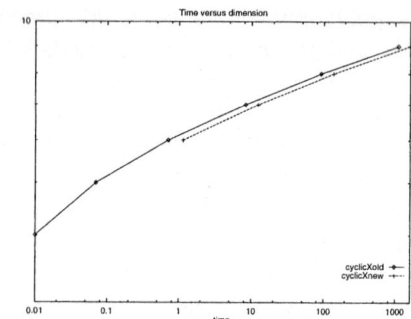

Fig. 1. Time versus number of integral points in a logarithmic scale, for both cyclic data sets combined

Fig. 2. Time versus input dimension in a logarithmic scale, for both cyclic data sets

solving the LPs: We may infer that our algorithmic improvements in applying the simplex method and its dual repeatedly have decreased the dependence upon d.

5 Experimental Comparisons

In order to demonstrate the generality of our methods and the fact that they can be easily applied within the framework of any general purpose LP library, we re-implemented our code using GLPK [13], a general-purpose LP library. Experiments with GLPK provided results similar to those of our implementation. Detailed data times are presented in [9]. We also performed experiments with the SoPlex library [16] but due to license constraints we do not present them.

For measuring the improvement due to exploiting successive LPs, we compared our program with the commercial version of ILOG PLANNER 3.3 [19] (available at the University of Athens). Detailed data appear in [9]. We observed that although PLANNER is much faster than our simple LP solver, our program is faster eventually by a factor of 3 to 6 on cyclic inputs (comparable to the savings over the Simple approach). This factor naturally decreases as the input size grows, since the LP sizes grow and PLANNER handles them faster. For small inputs, PLANNER is slower than our Simple approach due to its initialization overhead. Another point of interest is that memory consumption in PLANNER exceeded 350 MB on the `cyclic9new` problem, even if there is no storage of the output points. Experiments on `cyclic9old` and `cyclic10new` were not possible due to excessive memory consumption.

The integral points can be computed using an existing software like `porta`, if the Minkowski sum is explicitly calculated [2]. The time needed for this process is not reported. `porta` is slower on the cyclic inputs; the comparison is unclear on the multi-homogeneous inputs, since we have ignored the time to generate the description of the Minkowski sum. Another library for handling polyhedra is polylib [20]. We performed experiments using it on a 1.4 GHz 4-processor Athlon with 768 MB memory. Detailed data in [9] show similar results.

Multivariate polynomial multiplication is related to integral point computation in a Minkowski sum, although the number of terms in the polynomial product can differ significantly from the number of integral points, as shown in table 1. In order to juxtapose our algorithm to polynomial multiplication, we used the generic computer algebra packages Magma 2.8 [6], Maple 6, MuPad 2.0.0, Fermat [17] as well as the C++ library SYNAPS (version of 2004) developed by B. Mourrain at INRIA Sophia-Antipolis [18]. Due to licensing and availability restrictions, experiments were conducted on a 400 MHz SUN Ultra-SPARC with 128 MB of RAM for Maple and SYNAPS, a 700 MHz Linux i686 with 128 MB of RAM for Magma and a 533 MHz G4 Macintosh for Fermat. An important difference with our code and `porta` is that these packages do store their output.

Concerning Maple and MuPad, memory consumption is a severe drawback. Timings are faster than our code on the smaller instances of the cyclic families but become longer at `cylic9new` for both. Maple V was unable to handle `cyclic8new` because of space complexity, but is faster on the smaller instances; e.g. on `cyclic7new` it runs in 0.38 sec.

Table 2. Time and space use for Fermat

System	(secs)	(MB)
cyclic10old	80.7	860
cyclic8new	0.52	7.5
cyclic9new	5.28	60
cyclic10new	46.4	470
(1,1,1,1;3,3,3,1)	0.95	0.66

Table 3. Time and space use for Magma

System	(secs)	(MB)
cyclic8old	3.21	22
cyclic9old	23.36	171
cyclic9new	9.77	93
cyclic10new	—	—
(1,1,1,1;3,3,2,1)	2.29	17
(1,1,1,1;3,3,3,1)	2.30	21

Table 4. Time and space use for SYNAPS

System	(secs)	(MB)
cyclic9old	31.00	86
cyclic10old	—	—
cyclic8new	1.45	5.1
cyclic9new	14.82	44
cyclic10new	160.20	313
(1,1,1,1;3,3,2,1)	5.76	2.7
(1,1,1,1;3,3,3,1)	11.20	3.4

Execution timings are between 2 and 15 times faster on Magma and SYNAPS and between 26 and 29 times faster on Fermat than our software on the cyclic families, if we account for the difference of hardware (roughly approximated by the ratio of clock frequencies) and the number of output points. On the other hand, these programs are not faster (in fact, Magma and SYNAPS are slower) on multi-homogeneous systems, but we have ignored the fact that they also have to compute the product's coefficients. Memory consumption by far exceeds that of our approach and the space required to store the output.

Acknowledgements. We acknowledge partial financial support by Pythagoras project 70/3/7392 under the EPEAEK fund of the Greek Ministry of Educational Affairs and EU, and by Kapodistrias project 70/4/6452 of the Research Council of University of Athens.

References

1. S.P. Amarasinghe. *Parallelizing Compiler Techniques Based on Linear Inequalities.* Ph.D. thesis, Computer Systems Lab., Stanford University. 1997.
2. T. Christof, A. Loebel and M. Stoer. PORTA 1.3.2. Univ. of Heidelberg and ZIB Berlin, 1999. http://www.iwr.uni-heidelberg.de/groups/comopt/software/PORTA.
3. T. Christof and G. Reinelt. Combinatorial Optimization and Small Polytopes. *Top (Spanish Statistical and Operations Research Society)*, 4:1-64, 1996.
4. V. Chvátal. *Linear Programming.* W.H. Freeman & Co., New York, 1983.
5. P. Clauss. Counting Solutions to Linear and Nonlinear Constraints Through Ehrart Polynomials: Applications to Analyze and Transform Scientific Programs. In *Intern. Conf. Supercomp.*, 278-285, 1996.
6. The Computational Algebra Group. Magma 2.8. University of Sydney, Australia. http://magma.maths.usyd.edu.au/magma/.
7. D. Cox, J. Little, and D. O'Shea. *Using Algebraic Geometry.* Number 185 in Graduate Texts in Mathematics. Springer-Verlag, New York, 1998.
8. A. Dickenstein and I.Z. Emiris. Multihomogeneous Resultant Formulae by Means of Complexes. *J. Symb. Computation*, 36(3-4):317–342, 2003.
9. I.Z. Emiris and K. Zervoudakis. Successive Linear Programs for Computing all Integral Points in a Minkowski Sum. http://www.di.uoa.gr/~quasi/EmiZer.pdf
10. I.Z. Emiris. Enumerating a subset of the integer points inside a Minkowski sum. *Comp. Geom.: Theory & Appl., Spec. Issue*, 22(1–3):143–166, 2002.
11. I.Z. Emiris and J.F. Canny. Efficient incremental algorithms for the sparse resultant and the mixed volume. *J. Symbolic Computation*, 20(2):117-149, 1995.
12. I.M. Gelfand, M.M. Kapranov and A.V. Zelevinsky. *Discriminants, Resultants and Multidimensional Determinants*, Birkhäuser, Boston, 1994.
13. GNU Project, SciFace Software GmbH. GLPK 3.2.3, GNU LInear Programming Kit. http://www.gnu.org/software/glpk.
14. P. Gritzmann and V. Klee. Computational convexity. In J.E. Goodman and J. O'Rourke, eds, *The Handbook of Discrete and Computational Geometry*, pages 491-516. CRC Press, Boca Raton, Fl., 1997.
15. P. Gritzmann and B. Sturmfels. Minkowski addition of polytopes: Computational complexity and applications to Groebner bases. *SIAM J. Disc. Math.*, 6(2):246-269, 1993.
16. Konrad-Zuse-Zentrum für Informationstechnik, Berlin. SoPlex 1.2.1, Sequential Object-oriented simPLEX class library. http://www.zib.de/Optimization/Software/Soplex.
17. Fermat: A Computer Algebra System for Polynomial and Matrix Computation. R. Lewis, Fordham University, New York. http://www.bway.net/~lewis.
18. B. Mourrain. SYmbolic Numeric APlicationS, INRIA Sophia-Antipolis, 2002. http://www-sop.inria.fr/galaad/synaps/.
19. ILOG S.A. *Planner 3.3, Reference Manual.* 2001.
20. PolyLib, A library of polyhedral functions. http://icps.u-strasbg.fr/polylib, 2002.
21. A. Schrijver. *Theory of Linear and Integer Programming.* J. Wiley & Sons, Chichester, 1982.
22. B. Sturmfels and A. Zelevinsky. Multigraded Resultants of Sylvester Type. *J. of Algebra*, 163(1):115-127, 1994.
23. R.C. Whaley, A. Patitet and J.J. Dongarra. Automated empirical optimization of software and the ATLAS project. http://netlib.uow.edu.au/atlas/.

The Contribution of Game Theory to Complex Systems[*]

Spyros Kontogiannis[1,2] and Paul Spirakis[2]

[1] Department of Computer Science, University of Ioannina,
45110 Ioannina, Greece
kontog@cs.uoi.gr
[2] Research & Academic Computer Technology Institute,
N. Kazantzakis Str., Univ. Campus, 26500 Rio-Patra, Greece
{kontog, spirakis}@cti.gr

Abstract. We address several recent developments in non-cooperative as well as evolutionary game theory, that give a new viewpoint to Complex Systems understanding. In particular, we discuss notions like the anarchy cost, equilibria formation, social costs and evolutionary stability. We indicate how such notions help in understanding Complex Systems behaviour when the system includes selfish, antagonistic entities of varying degrees of rationality. Our main motivation is the Internet, perhaps the most complex artifact to date, as well as large-scale systems such as the high-level P2P systems, where where the interaction is among humans, programmes and machines and centralized approaches cannot apply.

1 Introduction

Consider a scenario where there is a number of individuals exchanging goods in a large-scale system (ie, stocks in an electronic market, music files in a p2p network, etc). Each individual wants to acquire a resource in order to get some gain from it. For example, stock buyers obtain shares at a price in order to resell them later in (hopefully) higher prices; network users buy music files for their own pleasure, or possibly resell them afterwards for their own profit. Assume the existence of a (private) utility function per individual, encoding the degree of their satisfaction. It is expected that each individual attempts to maximize his/her own degree of satisfaction, and does not care about other measures of the system, such as cumulative satisfaction of the individuals participating in this market (usually called the **system-optimum** objective), or fairness among the individuals' satisfaction degrees. The individuals participating in an exchange of goods, have to decide which goods to offer and at which price. Then they can choose whether or not to buy some of these goods offered by their opponent.

Two quite interesting approaches for studying such systems are the following: Either we study a dynamical system in which we consider an infinite chain of random clashes of pairs of individuals (each describes an exchange of goods) and check whether this system (given the *adaptation rule* of the individuals' policies) will converge to a stable state, or we consider a snapshot of the whole system and then consider that all the

---

[*] This work was partially supported by the EU within the 6th Framework Programme under contract 001907 (DELIS).

individuals will have unlimited computational power and try to do their best in a *simultaneous* action of claiming and selling arbitrary numbers of shared goods from each other. The former approach is well described by an evolutionary game: individuals keep buying goods for which they believe their prices to be low, and keep raising prices of goods that they own, and which (they believe that) they can still resell at a higher price. The latter approach is a typical instance of a congestion game: The more a good (seen as a resource) is claimed by individuals, the higher its price will be set (this is usually called the *congestion effect*). Individuals may claim service by a subset of resources from a collection of subsets of resources that would be satisfactory for them. The goal is for each individual to get a satisfactory subset of resources at the lowest possible cost.

This report aims to shed some light to the usefulness of a relatively new but vastly growing front of research in computer science that strongly intersects with (both non-cooperateive and evolutionary) game theory, to the study of mainly algorithmic questions concerning (dynamically changing) large-scale systems of interacting entities that demonstrate some kind of selfish behaviour. Our case study in this work is a large-scale system where entities of possibly conflicting interests interact for the exploitation of shared resources (seen as common goods). Paradigms of this kind are the Internet itself, high-level P2P systems where humans, programmes and machines have to interact, or electronic markets where the users themselves exchange goods.

Game theory provides us with concepts describing the stable states to which the players may end up (the Nash equilibria), or the performance degradation of the system due to lack of coordination among the individuals (quantified by the price of anarchy). Moreover, the notions of game design principles (eg, taxation) assure that players will eventually end up in equilibria that are also "socially acceptable". Evolutionary game theory studies the persistence of stable states to (temporal) irrational behaviour of a small portion of the players, ie, the invasion of erratic strategies to a stable state, and the êventual elimination of such strategies and return to the previous stable state.

Non-Cooperative vs Evolutionary Game Theory. Non-cooperative game theory is the study of *interactive* decision making, ie, those involved in the decisions are affected not only by their own choices but also by the decisions of others. This study is guided by two principles: (1) the choices of players are affected by well-defined (and not changing) *preferences* over outcomes of decisions, and (2) the layers act *strategically*, ie, they take into account the interaction between their choices and the ways other players act.

The dogma of non-cooperative game theory is the belief that players are considered to be *rational* and this rationality is *common knowledge* to all the players. This common knowledge of rationality gives hope to some equilibrium play: Players use their equilibrium strategies because of what would happen if they had not. The point of departure for evolutionary game theory is the view that the players are not always rational, due to either limited computational capabilities, or limited knowledge of other players' nature (eg, due to privacy constraints). In evolutionary games, "good" strategies *emerge* from a trial-and-error learning process, in which players discover that some strategies perform better than others. The players may do very little reasoning during this process. Instead, they simply take actions by rules of thumb, social norms, analogies for similar situations, or by other (possibly more complex) *methods* for converting stimuli into actions. Thus, in evolutionary games we may say that the players are "programmed" to adopt some strategies. Typically, the evolution process deals with a huge population of players. As time proceeds, many small games are played (eg, among pairs of players that "happen" to meet). One then expects that strategies with high payoffs will spread within the population (by learning, copying successful strategies, or even by infection).

Indeed, evolutionary games in large populations create a *dynamic process*, where the frequencies of the strategies played (by population members) *change in time* because of the learning or selection forces guiding the individuals' strategic choices. The rate of changes depends on the current strategy mix in the population. Such dynamics can be described by stochastic or deterministic models. The subject of evolutionary game theory is *exactly* the study of these dynamics. A nice presentation of evolutionary game dynamics is [10]. For a more thorough study the reader is referred to [3]. Numerous paradigms for modeling individual choice in a large population have been proposed in the literature. For example, if each individual chooses its own strategy so as to optimize its own payoff ("one against all others" scenario) given the current population state (ie, other individuals' strategies), then the aggregate behaviour is described by the **best-response dynamics** [14]. If each time an arbitrary individual changes its strategy for any other strategy of a strictly better (but not necessarily the best) payoff, then the aggregate behaviour is described by the **better-response dynamics** or **Nash dynamics** [18]. In case that pairs of individuals are chosen at random (repeatedly) and then they engage in a bimatrix game ("one against one" scenario) whose payoff matrix determines the gains of the strategies adopted by them, then we refer to **imitation dynamics**, the most popular version of which is the **replicator dynamics**[20].

If we allow sufficient time to pass, then the global "state" of the whole population will respond to the forces of selection/learning by either *self-organizing* and approaching a seemingly stationary state, or by leading to complicated behaviour, such as chaos. In fact, chaos is a very realistic possibility, appearing even in seemingly very simple systems. One of the goals of evolutionary game theory is to *characterize* those cases where such chaotic behaviour does not occur. In the "fortunate" cases where the behaviour of the system is self-organizing and approaches some stationary configuration, we start to wonder how does this configuration "looks like". One major question here is whether the stationary configuration is "structurally stable". One can easily understand non-stable stationary states by checking whether an (sufficiently small) perturbation in the specification of the system can completely alter the properties of the stationary state.

Not surprisingly, evolutionary game processes that converge to stable states have the property that those states are also self-confirming equilibria (eg, Nash equilibria). This is one of the most robust results in evolutionary game theory, the "folk theorem" that stability implies Nash equilibrium. In fact, one of the key concepts in the study of evolutionary games is that of the **Evolutionary Stable Strategies** (ESS), which are nothing more than Nash Equilibria together with an additional stability property, interpreted as follows: If an ESS is established and if a (small) proportion of the population suddenly adopts some *mutant* behaviour, then the process of selection/learning will eliminate the mutant behaviour, ie it will be able to withstand the pressures of mutation and selection.

It should be obvious by the above discussion that evolutionary game theory is a very suitable framework for the study of self-organization. The framework draws on the rich tradition of game theory. It is mathematically precise and rigorous; it is general enough to be applied in many example areas such as biology and species evolution, infection and spread of viruses in living populations or in the Internet, self-stabilization codes in distributed computing, etc. We would like to especially stress the suitability of such a theory for the study of self-stabilizing distributed protocols (eg, Dijkstra). However, evolutionary game theory will become much more useful if we can *efficiently handle* its mathematical models. For example, suppose that we adopt a dynamic model for the strategic evolution of a population. How efficiently (if ever) can we answer the model's long-run behaviour? Can we predict that an evolutionary game process will stabilize, say, to an ESS? Even more, given the simple games that the population members play (ie, their payoffs) and given the description of the adaptation and learning forces, can we claim that such an evolutionary game process will indeed have any ESS? Can we compute how this ESS will look like, in the case of an affirmative answer?

Till now, the prime concern of evolutionary game mathematicians has been to understand the dynamics of evolutionary games (usually via tools of the rich field of nonlinear differential equations). We propose here a complementary concern: namely, the precise characterization of the *computational complexity* of the question of convergence in such games. This concern is tightly coupled with the quest for *efficient* techniques by which one can predict the long-term behaviour of evolutionary systems, or compute the precise structure and properties of the equilibria involved. Such an *algorithmic* examination may in addition allow for the understanding of how the *environment* of the population (its graph of allowable motions of players, its constraints on how players meet, etc) affects the evolution. It may also allow for *efficient comparison* of the the evolution trajectories of two phenomenally different evolving populations.

The proposed blend of the algorithmic thought with evolutionary game theory, in fact, intends even to highlight *design rules* for self-organizing systems and to complement the older experimental, simulations-based approach, with efficient computational ways that calculate the impact of such design rules. A good example here is the rigorous computation of the *speed of convergence* for such self-organizing evolutionary systems. For such a problem, several paradigms of the algorithmic thought may become handy. Such a paradigm is that of the *rapid mixing* of discrete stochastic combinatorial processes and its implications on the efficient approximate enumeration of the cardinality of the stationary state space. The purpose of this paper is exactly to propose this algorithmic view of evolutionary game theory; we do so, by discussing some concrete open problems and areas of research.

2 Some Key Notions of Non-cooperative Games

Non-cooperative Games and Equilibria. We restrict our view to the class of *finite games in strategic form*. More precisely, let $I = \{1, 2, \ldots n\}$ be a set of **players**, where n is a positive integer. For each player $i \in I$, let S_i be her (finite) set of allowable actions, called the **action set**. The deterministic choice of an action $s_i \in S_i$ by player $i \in I$, is called a **pure strategy** for i. A vector $\mathbf{s} = (s_1, \ldots, s_n) \in \times_{i \in I} S_i$, where $s_i \in S_i$ is the pure strategy adopted by player $i \in I$, is called a **pure strategies profile** or a **configuration** of the players. The space of all the pure strategies profiles in the game is thus the cartesian product $S = \times_{i \in I} S_i$ of the players' action sets (usually called the **configuration space**). For any configuration $\mathbf{s} \in S$ and any player $i \in I$, let $\pi_i(\mathbf{s})$ be a real number indicating the payoff to player i upon the adoption of this configuration by all the players of the game. In economics, the payoffs are, eg, firms' profits, while in biology they may represent *individual fitness*. In computer networks, where the players are users (eg, exchanging files), the payoff may be the opposite of a user's delay, when her data travel from a source to a destination in the network.

The finite collection of the real numbers $\{\pi_i(\mathbf{s}) : \mathbf{s} \in S\}$ defines player i's payoff function. Let $\pi(\mathbf{s}) = (\pi_i(\mathbf{s}))_{i \in I}$ be the vector function of all the players' payoffs. Thus, a strategic game is described by a triplet $\Gamma = (I, S, \pi)$ where I is the set of players, S is their configuration space and π is the vector function of all the players' payoffs.

A **mixed strategy** for player $i \in I$ is a *probability distribution* (as opposed to a deterministic choice that is indicated by a pure strategy) over her action set S_i. We may represent any mixed strategy as a vector $\mathbf{x_i} = (x_i(s_{i,1}), x_i(s_{i,2}), \ldots, x_i(s_{i,m_i}))$, where $m_i = |S_i|$, $\forall j \in [m_i]^1$, $s_{i,j} \in S_i$ is the jth allowable action for player i, and $x_i(s_{i,j})$ is the probability that action $s_{i,j}$ is adopted by player i. In order to simplify notation, we shall represent this vector as $\mathbf{x_i} = (x_{i,1}, x_{i,2}, \ldots, x_{i,m_i})$. Of course, $\forall i \in I$, $\sum_{j \in [m_i]} x_{i,j} = 1$ and $\forall j \in [m_i]$, $x_{i,j} \in [0,1]$. Since for each player i all probabilities are nonnegative and sum up to one, the **mixed strategies set** of player i is the set $\Delta_i \equiv \left\{ \mathbf{x_i} \in \mathbb{R}_{\geq 0}^{m_i} : \sum_{j \in [m_i]} = 1 \right\}$. Pure strategies are then just special, "extreme" mixed strategies in which the probability of a specific action is equal to one and all other probabilities equal zero. A **mixed strategies profile** is a vector $\mathbf{x} = (\mathbf{x_1}, \ldots, \mathbf{x_n})$ whose components are themselves mixed strategies of the players, ie, $\forall i \in I$, $\mathbf{x_i} \in \Delta_i$. We denote by $\Delta = \times_{i \in I} \Delta_i \subset \mathbb{R}^m$ the cartesian product of mixed strategies sets of all the players, which is called the **mixed strategies space** of the game ($m = m_1 + \cdots + m_n$).

When the players adopt a mixed strategies profile $\mathbf{x} \in \Delta$, we can compute what is the *average* payoff, u_i, that player i gets (for $\mathbf{x}$) in the usual way: $u_i(\mathbf{x}) \equiv \sum_{\mathbf{s} \in S} P(\mathbf{x}, \mathbf{s}) \cdot \pi_i(\mathbf{s})$ where, $P(\mathbf{x}, \mathbf{s}) \equiv \prod_{i \in I} x_i(s_i)$ is the occurrence probability of configuration $\mathbf{s} \in S$ wrt the mixed profile $\mathbf{x} \in \Delta$. This (extended) function $u_i : \Delta \mapsto \mathbb{R}$ is called the **(mixed) payoff function** for player i.

Let us indicate by $(\mathbf{x_i}, \mathbf{y_{-i}})$ a mixed profile where player i adopts the mixed strategy $\mathbf{x_i} \in \Delta_i$ and all other players adopt the mixed strategies that are determined by the mixed strategies profile $\mathbf{y} \in \Delta$. This notation is particularly convenient when a single player i considers a unilateral "deviation" $\mathbf{x_i} \in \Delta_i$ from a given profile $\mathbf{y} \in \Delta$. One of the cornerstones of game theory is the notion of Nash Equilibrium (NE in short) [17]:

Definition 1. *A **best response** of player i to a mixed strategies profile $\mathbf{y} \in \Delta$ is any element of the set $B_i(\mathbf{y}) \equiv \arg\max_{\mathbf{x_i} \in \Delta_i} \{u_i(\mathbf{x_i}, \mathbf{y_{-i}})\}$ (usually called the **best response correspondence** of player i to the profile $\mathbf{y}$). A **Nash Equilibrium** (NE) is any mixed strategies profile $\mathbf{y} \in \Delta$ having the property that, $\forall i \in I$, $\mathbf{y_i}$ is a best response of player i to $\mathbf{y}$. That is, $\forall i \in I$, $\mathbf{y_i} \in B_i(\mathbf{y})$.*

The nice thing about NE is that they always exist in finite strategic games:

Theorem 1 ([17]). *Every finite strategic game $\Gamma = (I, S, \pi)$ has at least one NE.*

---
[1] For any integer $k \in \mathbb{N}$, $[k] \equiv \{1, 2, \ldots, k\}$.

Symmetric 2-Player Games. The subclass of symmetric 2-player games provides the basic setting for much of the evolutionary game theory. Indeed, many of the important insights can be gained already in this (special) case.

Definition 2. *A finite strategic game* $\Gamma = (I, S, \pi)$ *is a* **2-player game** *when* $I = \{1, 2\}$. *It is called a* **symmetric** *2-player game if in addition,* $S_1 = S_2$ *and* $\forall (s_1, s_2) \in S, \pi_1(s_1, s_2) = \pi_2(s_2, s_1)$.

Note that in the case of a 2-player strategic game, the payoff functions of Γ can be represented by two $|S_1| \times |S_2|$ real matrices Π_1, Π_2^T such that $\Pi_1[i, j] = \pi_1(s_i, s_j)$ and $\Pi_2[j, i] = \pi_2(s_j, s_i), \forall (s_i, s_j) \in S$. For any mixed profile $\mathbf{x} = (\mathbf{x_1}, \mathbf{x_2}) \in \Delta$, the expected payoff of player 1 for this profile is $u_1(\mathbf{x}) = \mathbf{x_1}^T \Pi_1 \mathbf{x_2}$, while that of player 2 is $u_2(\mathbf{x}) = \mathbf{x_2}^T \Pi_2 \mathbf{x_1}$. In a symmetric 2-player game $\Pi = \Pi_1 = \Pi_2^T$ and thus we can fully describe the game by common action set S and the payoff matrix Π of the row player. Two useful notions of 2-player games are the support and the extended support:

Definition 3. *In a 2-player strategic game* $\Gamma = (\{1, 2\}, S, \pi)$, *the* **support** *of a mixed strategy* $\mathbf{x_1} \in \Delta_1$ ($\mathbf{x_2} \in \Delta_2$) *is the set of allowable actions of player 1 (player 2) that have* non-zero *probability in* $\mathbf{x_1}$ ($\mathbf{x_2}$). *More formally,* $\forall i \in \{1, 2\}, supp(\mathbf{x_i}) \equiv \{j \in S_i : x_i(j) > 0\}$. *The* **extended support** *of a mixed strategy* $\mathbf{x_2} \in \Delta_2$ *of player 2 is the set of* pure best responses *of player 1 to* $\mathbf{x_2}$. *That is,* $extsupp(\mathbf{x_2}) \equiv \{j \in S_1 : u_1(j, \mathbf{x_2}) \in \max_{\mathbf{x_1} \in \Delta_1} \{u_1(\mathbf{x_1}, \mathbf{x_2})\}\}$. *Similarly, the* **extended support** *of a mixed strategy* $\mathbf{x_1} \in \Delta_1$ *of player 1, is the set of* pure best responses *of player 2 to* $\mathbf{x_1}$. *That is,* $extsupp(\mathbf{x_1}) \equiv \{j \in S_2 : u_2(\mathbf{x_1}, j) \in \max_{\mathbf{x_2} \in \Delta_2} \{u_2(\mathbf{x_1}, \mathbf{x_2})\}\}$.

The following lemma is a direct consequence of the definition of a Nash Equilibrium:

Lemma 1. *If* $(\mathbf{x_1}, \mathbf{x_2}) \in \Delta$ *is a NE of a 2-player strategic game, then* $supp(\mathbf{x_1}) \subseteq extsupp(\mathbf{x_2})$ *and* $supp(\mathbf{x_2}) \subseteq extsupp(\mathbf{x_1})$.

Proof. The support of a strategy that is adopted by a player is the set of actions which she adopts with positive probability. At a NE $(\mathbf{x_1}, \mathbf{x_2}) \in \Delta$, each player assigns positive probability only to (not necessarily all the) actions which are pure best responses to the other player's strategy. On the other hand, the extended support of, say, $\mathbf{x_2}$ is exactly the set of all the actions (ie, pure strategies) of player 1 that are best responses to $\mathbf{x_2}$, and vice versa. That is, $supp(\mathbf{x_1}) \subseteq extsupp(\mathbf{x_2})$ and $supp(\mathbf{x_2}) \subseteq extsupp(\mathbf{x_1})$.

When we wish to argue about the vast majority of symmetric 2-player games, one way is to assume that the real numbers in the set $\{\Pi[i, j] : (i, j) \in S\}$ are independently drawn from a probability distribution F. For example, F can be the uniform distribution in an interval $[a, b] \in \mathbb{R}$. A typical symmetric 2-player game Γ is then just an instance of the implied random experiment, described in the following definition.

Definition 4. *A symmetric 2-player game* $\Gamma = (S, \Pi)$ *is an instance of a (symmetric 2-player) random game wrt the probability distribution* F, *if and only if for all* $(s_i, s_j) \in S$, $\Pi[i, j]$ *is an iid random variable drawn from* F.

Definition 5. *A strategy pair* $(\mathbf{x_1}, \mathbf{x_2}) \in \Delta^2$ *for a symmetric 2-player game* $\Gamma = (S, \Pi)$ *is a symmetric Nash Equilibrium, if and only if (1)* $(\mathbf{x_1}, \mathbf{x_2})$ *is a NE for* Γ, *and (2)* $\mathbf{x_1} = \mathbf{x_2}$.

Not all NE of a symmetric 2-player game need be symmetric. However it is known that there is at least one such equilibrium:

Theorem 2 ([17]). *Every symmetric 2-player game has at least one symmetric Nash Equilibrium.*

3 Evolutionary Games and Stable Strategies

We will now restrict our attention to symmetric 2-player strategic games. So, fix a symmetric 2-player strategic game $\Gamma = (S, \Pi)$, for which the mixed strategies space is Δ^2. Suppose that all the individuals of a large population are programmed to play the same (either pure or mixed) *incumbent* strategy $\mathbf{x} \in \Delta$, whenever they are involved in the game Γ. Suppose also that a small group of *invaders* appears in the population. Let $\varepsilon \in (0, 1)$ be the share of invaders in the postentry population. Assume that all the invaders are programmed to play the (pure or mixed) strategy $\mathbf{y} \in \Delta$ whenever they are involved in Γ.

Pairs of individuals in this *dimorphic* postentry population are now repeatedly drawn at random to play always the same symmetric 2-player game Γ. If an individual plays, the probability that her opponent will play strategy $\mathbf{x}$ is $1 - \varepsilon$ and that of playing strategy $\mathbf{y}$ is ε. This is equivalent with a match with an individual who plays the *mixed* strategy $\mathbf{z} = (1 - \varepsilon)\mathbf{x} + \varepsilon\mathbf{y}$. The postentry payoff to the incumbent strategy $\mathbf{x}$ is then $u(\mathbf{x}, \mathbf{z})$ and that of the invaders' is just $u(\mathbf{y}, \mathbf{z})$ ($u = u_1 = u_2$). Intuitively, evolutionary forces will select *against* the invader if $u(\mathbf{x}, \mathbf{z}) > u(\mathbf{y}, \mathbf{z})$.

Definition 6. *A strategy $\mathbf{x}$ is **evolutionary stable** (ESS in short) if for any strategy $\mathbf{y} \neq \mathbf{x}$ there exists a barrier $\bar{\varepsilon} = \bar{\varepsilon}(\mathbf{y}) \in (0, 1)$ such that $\forall 0 < \varepsilon \leq \bar{\varepsilon}$, $u(\mathbf{x}, \mathbf{z}) > u(\mathbf{y}, \mathbf{z})$ where $\mathbf{z} = (1 - \varepsilon)\mathbf{x} + \varepsilon\mathbf{y}$.*

One can easily prove the following characterization of ESS, which sometimes appears as an alternative definition:

Proposition 1. *Let $\mathbf{x} \in \Delta$ be a (mixed in general) strategy profile that is adopted by the whole population. Then, $\mathbf{x}$ is an evolutionary stable strategy, if and only if $\mathbf{x}$ satisfies the following properties, $\forall \mathbf{y} \in \Delta \setminus \{\mathbf{x}\}$:*

[P1] $u(\mathbf{y}, \mathbf{x}) \leq u(\mathbf{x}, \mathbf{x})$ **[P2]** *If $u(\mathbf{y}, \mathbf{x}) = u(\mathbf{x}, \mathbf{x})$ then $u(\mathbf{y}, \mathbf{y}) < u(\mathbf{x}, \mathbf{y})$.*

Observe that the last proposition implies that an ESS $\mathbf{x} \in \Delta$ implies a symmetric Nash Equilibrium $(\mathbf{x}, \mathbf{x}) \in \Delta^2$ of the underlying symmetric 2-player strategic game Γ (due to **[P1]**), and has to be strictly better than any invading strategy $\mathbf{y} \in \Delta \setminus \{\mathbf{x}\}$, against $\mathbf{y}$ itself, in case that $\mathbf{y}$ is a best-response strategy against $\mathbf{x}$ in Γ (due to **[P2]**).

Definition 7. *A mixed strategy $\mathbf{x} \in \Delta$ is **completely mixed** iff and only if $supp(\mathbf{x}) = S$ (that is, it assigns to all the allowable actions non-zero probability).*

It is not hard to prove the following lemma:

Lemma 2 (Haigh 1975, [9]). *If a completely mixed strategy $\mathbf{x} \in \Delta$ is an ESS, then it is the unique ESS of the evolutionary game.*

Let $\mathcal{P}_k \equiv \{(v_1,\ldots,v_k) \in \mathbb{R}_{\geq 0}^k : \sum_{i\in[k]} v_i = 1\}$ be the k-dimensional simplex. Fix an evolutionary game with an action set $S = [n]$ for the players, and a payoff matrix U. For any non-negative vector $\mathbf{x} \in \mathcal{P}_k$ for some $k \in \mathbb{N}$, let $Y_\mathbf{x} \equiv \mathcal{P}_k \setminus \{\mathbf{x}\}$. The following statement, proved by Haigh, is a necessary and sufficient condition of a mixed strategy $\mathbf{s} \in \mathcal{P}_n$ being an ESS, given that $(\mathbf{s},\mathbf{s})$ is a symmetric NE of the symmetric game $\Gamma = (S, U)$.

Lemma 3 (Haigh 1975, [9]). *Let $(\mathbf{s},\mathbf{s}) \in \mathcal{P}_n \times \mathcal{P}_n$ be a symmetric NE for the symmetric game $\Gamma = (S,U)$ and let $M = extsupp(\mathbf{s})$. Let also $\mathbf{x}$ be the projection of $\mathbf{s}$ on M, and C the submatrix of U consisting of the rows and columns indicated by M. Then $\mathbf{s}$ is an ESS if and only if $\forall \mathbf{y} \in Y_\mathbf{x}$, $(\mathbf{y}-\mathbf{x})^T C(\mathbf{y}-\mathbf{x}) < 0$.*

Population Dynamics. A simple way to think about the evolution of a population whose members play a 2-player game whenever they meet, is to consider the "state" of the population at time t to be a vector $\mathbf{x}(t) = (\mathbf{x_1}(t), \mathbf{x_2}(t), \ldots, \mathbf{x_m}(t))$, where $S = \{1, 2, \ldots, m\}$ is a set of allowable actions, individuals are only allowed to adopt *pure strategies* in S, and $\mathbf{x_i}(t)$ is the population share playing strategy $i \in S$ at time (ie, round) t.

Let's assume that when two individuals meet, they play the symmetric 2-player game $\Gamma = (S, \Pi)$, where $\Pi = \Pi_1 = \Pi_2^T$. We can interpret for example the payoff value $\Pi_1[i,j]$ as the number of offsprings of the individual that played strategy i, against an individual who played strategy j. (Similarly, $\Pi_2[i,j] = \Pi[j,i]$ is the number of offsprings of the individual playing strategy j, against an individual playing strategy i). How are the generated offsprings programmed? There are various ways to define this. For example, they may play the *same strategy as their parents*. Then, we have a particular kind of dynamics (usually called the **replicator dynamics**). Of course, for the model to be complete, one has to say how often they are selected from the population.

In general, such a way of thought usually results in defining $\mathbf{x}(t)$ via either a *stochastic* process, or via a system of differential equations describing its rate of change (that is, $\dot{\mathbf{x}}(t) = f(\mathbf{x}(t), t)$, where f is usually a non-linear deterministic function). Then the model becomes a sample of a vast variety of dynamical system models and one can study its evolution by finding how $\mathbf{x}(t)$ changes in time. It is not hard to modify these models in order to capture effects like noise, random choice of the strategy $\mathbf{y}$ to play, or some particular rule of "learning" which are the good strategies, based on the payoffs that the individuals get (and perhaps, some desirable payoff values that act as thresholds for changes in strategy). For more details, we recommend that the interested readers have a look at [10,21].

4 Congestion Games

In this section our aim is to present recent developments in a broad class of non-cooperative games, which is of great interest: the **congestion games**. As already mentioned in the introduction, such games can describe very well snapshots of our dynamical (large-scale) system of selfish entities and resources.

A congestion game Γ can be described by a tuple $\langle N, E, (w_i)_{i \in N}, (S_i)_{i \in N}, (d_e)_{e \in E} \rangle$ where N is the set of (non-cooperative) selfish players, E is the set of shared resources, $\forall i \in N$, w_i is player i's **demand for service** (ie, how many stock shares would be required, how long is the music file requested from the p2p system, etc), $\forall i \in N$, $S_i \subseteq 2^E$ is the collection of all possible subsets of resources that satisfy player i (called its **action set**), and $\forall e \in E$, $c_e : \times_{i \in N} S_i \mapsto \mathbb{R}$ is the **charging function** (per player that wants to use it) of resource e, which is non-decreasing on the cumulative congestion caused to it by the players.

Existence and Construction of Nash Equilibria. There are possibly many questions that might be of interest in congestion games. We already know since the early 1950s that every finite strategic game has at least one NE. But what if in our system there is no interest by the players for mixed strategies? For example, an individual in a market will eventually have to decide whether to buy a share or not, rather than decide which (bunches of) shares to request according to some probability distribution on his/her action set. In such situations it is of great interest to be able to decide whether there is a NE in pure strategies (PNE in short), ie, a pure strategies profile that is a NE.

This has been answered for unweighted congestion games (ie, all players' demands for service are identical), no matter what kind of charging functions are adopted by the resources [18]:

Theorem 3. *Any unweighted congestion game has at least one Pure Nash Equilibrium.*

The main argument for this is the essential equivalence of the unweighted congestion games with a very important class of strategic games (which always possess at least one PNE): the (exact) potential games (see [16]).

On the other hand, [7,13] have proved that there are very simple instances of weighted congestion games with linear and $2-$wise linear[2] charging functions of the resources, that possess no PNE. For the case of congestion games on networks of resources with linear delay functions it has been proved [7,8]) that there is at least one PNE, which can be constructed in pseudo–polynomial time.

If we are interested for the construction of an arbitrary NE, it is still not known whether there is a polynomial–time for constructing such an equilibrium, even for the simplest case of a finite strategic game with 2 players. Indeed, this (the construction of an arbitrary NE in a finite strategic game) is considered to be, together with factoring, one of the most important problems at the boundary of **P** and **NP**.

Measuring the Performance of a Game. Beyond the study on the construction of NE profiles in a strategic game, another very important aspect, especially for the designer of the game, has to do with the quality of the game. Indeed, there is usually a measure of the whole system's performance for each profile chosen by the players. We consider that this measure of system performance is depicted by a function $SC : \times_{i \in N} S_i \mapsto \mathbb{R}$ when considering pure strategies profiles, that we call the **social cost** function. For the case of mixed strategies profiles (where the players adopt probability distributions according to which they choose their action *independently* of other players' choices), the system's measure is given by the expected value of the social cost function. For simplicity we denote this by $SC(\mathbf{p})$ where $\mathbf{p}$ is the mixed strategies profile adopted by the players.

---

[2] By this term we mean the maximum or the minimum of two linear functions.

The **social optimum** of the game is the minimum (over all possible configurations of the players) social cost: $OPT(\Gamma) = \min_{\varpi \in \times_{i \in N} S_i} \{SC(\varpi)\}$. The quality of the game Γ is then measured by the **price of anarchy** (PoA in short) [12]: $PoA(\Gamma) = \max_{\mathbf{p} \in NE(\Gamma)} \left\{ \frac{SC(\mathbf{p})}{OPT(\Gamma)} \right\}$. There are various measures of performance in a congestible system of resources. For example, we might be interested in optimizing the *average satisfaction* of the players participating in the game. This is achieved by the utilitarian measure of performance, ie, by setting as social cost (to be minimized) the sum of the players' costs. A thorough study has been conducted for this measure of performance, especially in the case of an infinite number of players with negligible service demands. For more details the reader is referred to [19] and the references therein.

On the other hand, if we are interested in studying the *fairness* of the produced solution, then we would like to optimize the maximum-to-minimum satisfaction of the players. This is achieved by setting as a social cost the expected value maximum cost paid among the players, which should be as small as possible. This model has been studied mainly for the case of players with non-negligible, unsplittable service demands, ie, each player has to eventually be served by a unique action from its set of allowable actions. Especially in the case of congestion games on parallel links with linear resource delays, the price of anarchy is known to be $\Theta\left(\frac{\log m}{\log \log m}\right)$ for identical players ([12,15] or $\Theta\left(\frac{\log m}{\log \log \log m}\right)$ for players with varying demands [4] (m is the number of resources). For congestion games whose resources comprise an arbitrary network, it has been shown that the price of anarchy can be unbounded for very simple networks ([19,7]). For congestion games among players of identical demands on networks of linear delays, as well as among players of varying demands but on a special class of (single–commodity) networks, it has been shown [7,8] that the PoA is again $\Theta\left(\frac{\log m}{\log \log m}\right)$.

Constructing Good Games. A very interesting and quite challenging aspect is how to set the rules of a game in such a way that the measure of its performance, ie, the price of anarchy is as small as possible. There have been several proposals to this direction in the literature. One of the more challenging ideas is for the system designer to change the charging functions of the resources so as to induce socially optimal profiles as the only Nash Equilibrium for the players. In particular, we would be interested to set an additive **toll** $\tau_e \in \mathbb{R}_{\geq 0}$ per resource in a congestion game so that, if the players consider as charging function of each resource e the function $d_e(\varpi) + t_e$ then the worst possible social cost (measured according to the original game) of a NE in the new game would be strictly less than that of the original game, and ideally equal to the social optimum of the original game. It is well known that for the case of identical players with splittable (and negligible) service demands, the **marginal cost tax** $\tau_e^* = \theta_e(\varpi) \cdot d_e(\varpi)$ induces the social optimum (wrt the utilitarian social cost) as the only NE of the game [1] ($\theta_e(\varpi)$ is the cumulative congestion on resource e according to the configuration ϖ of the players). On the other hand, recent development shows that we can compute (via linear programming) the right tolls for inducing the socially optimum profile as the unique NE even when the players value resource charging and taxes differently in polynomial time [2,5,6,11].

References

1. Beckmann M., McGuire C.B., Winsten C.B. *Studies in the Economics of Transportation.* Yale University Press, 1956.
2. Cole R., Dodis Y., Roughgarden T. Pricing network edges for heterogeneous selfish users. In *Proc. of the 35th ACM Symp. on Theory of Computing (STOC '03)*, pages 521–530. Association of Computing Machinery (ACM), 2003.
3. Cressman R. *Evolutionary dynamics and extensive form games.* MIT Press, 2003.
4. Czumaj A., Voecking B. Tight bounds for worst-case equilibria. In *Proc. of the 13th ACM-SIAM Symposium on Discrete Algorithms (SODA '02)*, pages 413–420, 2002.
5. Fleischer L. Linear tolls suffice: New bounds and algorithms for tolls in single source networks. In *Proc. of the 31st International Colloquium on Automata, Languages and Programming (ICALP '04)*, pages 544–554. Springer-Verlag, 2004.
6. Fleischer L., Jain K., Mahdian M. Tolls for heterogeneous selfish users in multicommodity networks and generalized congestion games. In *Proc. of the 45th IEEE Symp. on Foundations of Computer Science (FOCS '04)*, pages 277–285. IEEE Comput. Soc. Press, 2004.
7. Fotakis D., Kontogiannis S., Spirakis P. Selfish unsplittable flows. In *Proc. of the 31st International Colloquium on Automata, Languages and Programming (ICALP '04)*, pages 593–605. Springer-Verlag, 2004.
8. Fotakis D., Kontogiannis S., Spirakis P. Symmetry in network congestion games: Pure equilibria and anarchy cost. In *progress (submitted for publication)*, 2005.
9. Haigh J. Game theory and evolution. *Advances in Applied Probability*, 7:8–11, 1975.
10. Hofbauer J., Sigmund K. Evolutionary game dynamics. *Bulletin of the American Mathematical Society*, 40(4):479–519, 2003.
11. Karakostas G., Kolliopoulos S. Edge pricing of multicommodity networks for heterogeneous selfish users. In *Proc. of the 45th IEEE Symp. on Foundations of Computer Science (FOCS '04)*, pages 268–276. IEEE Comput. Soc. Press, 2004.
12. Koutsoupias E., Papadimitriou C. Worst-case equilibria. In *Proc. of the 16thAnnual Symposium on Theoretical Aspects of Computer Science (STACS '99)*, pages 404–413. Springer-Verlag, 1999.
13. Libman L., Orda A. Atomic resource sharing in noncooperative networks. *Telecommunication Systems*, 17(4):385–409, 2001.
14. Matsui A., Gilboa I. Social stability and equilibrium. *Econometrica*, 59:859–867, 1991.
15. Mavronicolas M., Spirakis P. The price of selfish routing. In *Proc. of the 33rd ACM Symp. on Theory of Computing (STOC '01)*, pages 510–519, 2001.
16. Monderer D., Shapley L. Potential games. *Games and Economic Behavior*, 14:124–143, 1996.
17. Nash J. F. Noncooperative games. *Annals of Mathematics*, 54:289–295, 1951.
18. Rosenthal R.W. A class of games possessing pure-strategy nash equilibria. *International Journal of Game Theory*, 2:65–67, 1973.
19. Roughdarden T., Tardos E. How bad is selfish routing? *J. Assoc. Comput. Mach.*, 49(2):236–259, 2002.
20. Taylor P. D., Jonker L. Evolutionary stable strategies and game dynamics. *Mathematical Biosciences*, 40:145–156, 1978.
21. Weibull, Jörgen W. *Evolutionary Game Theory.* The MIT Press, 1995.

Estimated Path Selection for the Delay Constrained Least Cost Path[*]

Moonseong Kim[1], Young-Cheol Bang[2], and Hyunseung Choo[1]

[1] School of Information and Communication Engineering,
Sungkyunkwan University,
440-746, Suwon, Korea +82-31-290-7145
{moonseong, choo}@ece.skku.ac.kr
[2] Department of Computer Engineering,
Korea Polytechnic University,
429-793, Gyeonggi-Do, Korea +82-31-496-8292
ybang@kpu.ac.kr

Abstract. The development of efficient Quality of Service (QoS) routing algorithms in high speed networks is very difficult since divergent services require various quality conditions. If the QoS parameter we concern is to measure the delay on that link, then the routing algorithm obtains the Least Delay (LD) path. Meanwhile, if the parameter is to measure of the link cost, then it calculates the Least Cost (LC) path. The Delay Constrained Least Cost (DCLC) path problem of the mixed issues on LD and LC has been shown to be NP-hard. The path cost of LD path is relatively more expensive than that of LC path, and the path delay of LC path is relatively higher than that of LD path in DCLC problem. In this paper, we propose Estimated Path Selection (EPS) algorithm for the DCLC problem and investigate its performance. It employs a new parameter which is probabilistic combination of cost and delay. We have performed empirical evaluation that compares our proposed EPS with the DCUR in various network situations. It significantly affects the performance that the normalized surcharge is improved up to about 105%. The time complexity is $O(l + n \log n)$ which is comparable to well-known previous works.

1 Introduction

The advanced multimedia technology in company with high speed networks generates a bunch of real-time applications. The significance of real-time transmission has grown rapidly, since high end services such as video conferencing, demand based services (Video, Music, and News on Demand), Internet broadcasting, etc. are popularized. This end-to-end characteristic is an important factor for Quality of Service (QoS) support. Since network users and their required

---

[*] This work was supported in parts by Brain Korea 21 and the Ministry of Information and Communication in Republic of Korea. Dr. Choo is the corresponding author and Dr. Bang is the co-corresponding author.

bandwidths for applications increase, the efficient usage of networks has been intensively investigated for the better utilization of network resources.

Unicast routing protocols can be classified into two general types; distance vector such as routing information protocol (RIP) [7] and link state such as open shortest path first (OSPF) [13]. The distance vector and the link state routing protocols are based on Bellman-Ford algorithm and Dijkstra's shortest path algorithm [2], respectively. If the parameter we concern is to measure the delay on that link, then the routing algorithm obtains the Least Delay (LD) path. Meanwhile, if the parameter is a measure of the link cost, then it calculates the Least Cost (LC) path. But the path cost of LD path is relatively more expensive than that of LC path, and the path delay of LC path is relatively higher than that of LD path. Therefore, it is necessary to negotiate between the cost and the delay.

For real-time applications, a path delay should be acceptable and also its cost should be as low as possible. We call it as the Delay Constrained Least Cost (DCLC) path problem. It has been shown to be NP-hard [6]. Widyono proposed an optimal centralized delay constrained algorithm, called the Constrained Bellman-Ford (CBF) algorithm [19], to solve it. But the CBF is not practical for large networks due to its exponential running time in worst case. Salama *et al.* proposed a polynomial time algorithm called Delay Constrained Unicast Routing (DCUR) [14].

The path cost which is computed by DCUR is always within 10% from the optimal CBF [14]. At the current node, the DCUR chooses the LD path when the LC path is rejected to prevent the possibility of constructing paths that violate the delay bound. This procedure is simple but if the DCUR frequently takes the next node by the LD path, then the total cost becomes high. As you see, the DCLC is desirable to find a path that considers the lower cost and the acceptable delay together. Even though there is a loss for the cost, two parameters should be carefully negotiated to reduce the delay. This is because the adjustment between the cost and the delay for the balance is important. Hence, we propose Estimated Path Selection (EPS) algorithm for the DCLC problem and investigate its performance. It employs a new parameter [10] which is probabilistic combination of cost and delay.

The rest of paper is organized as follows. In Section 2, we state the network model, the previous algorithms, and the weighted factor algorithm [10]. Section 3 presents details of the proposed algorithm. Then, in Section 4, we analyze and evaluate the proposed algorithm's performance based on simulations. We finally conclude this paper in Section 5.

2 Preliminaries

2.1 Network Model

We consider that a computer network is represented by a directed graph $G = (V, E)$ with n nodes and l links or arcs, where V is a set of nodes and E is a set of links, respectively. Each link $e = (i,j) \in E$ is associated with two parameters, namely link cost $c(e) > 0$ and link delay $d(e) > 0$. The delay of a link, $d(e)$, is the sum of the perceived queueing delay, transmission delay, and propagation delay. We define a path as sequence of links such that $(u,i), (i,j), \ldots, (k,v)$, belongs to E. Let $P(u,v) = \{(u,i), (i,j), \ldots, (k,v)\}$ denote the path from node u to node v. If all nodes $u, i, j, \ldots, k, v$ are distinct, then we say that it is a simple directed path. For a given source node $s \in V$ and a destination node $d \in V$, $(2^{s \to d}, \infty)$ is the set of all possible paths from s to d. We define the length of the path $P(u,v)$, denoted by $n(P(u,v))$, as a number of links in $P(u,v)$. The path cost of P is given by $\phi_C(P) = \sum_{e \in P} c(e)$ and the path delay of P is given by $\phi_D(P) = \sum_{e \in P} d(e)$. $(2^{s \to d}, \Delta)$ is the set of paths from s to d for which the end-to-end delay is bounded by Δ. Therefore $(2^{s \to d}, \Delta) \subseteq (2^{s \to d}, \infty)$. The DCLC problem is to find the path that satisfies $min\{ \phi_C(P_k) \mid P_k \in (2^{s \to d}, \Delta), \forall k \in \Lambda \}$ where Λ is an index set.

2.2 Previous Algorithms

Fig. 1 shows an example of the paths obtained by different routing algorithms to connect source node v_0 to destination node v_4, with a delay constraint of 29. Fig. 1(d) shows the path DCUR constructs [14]. DCUR proceeds as follows. The

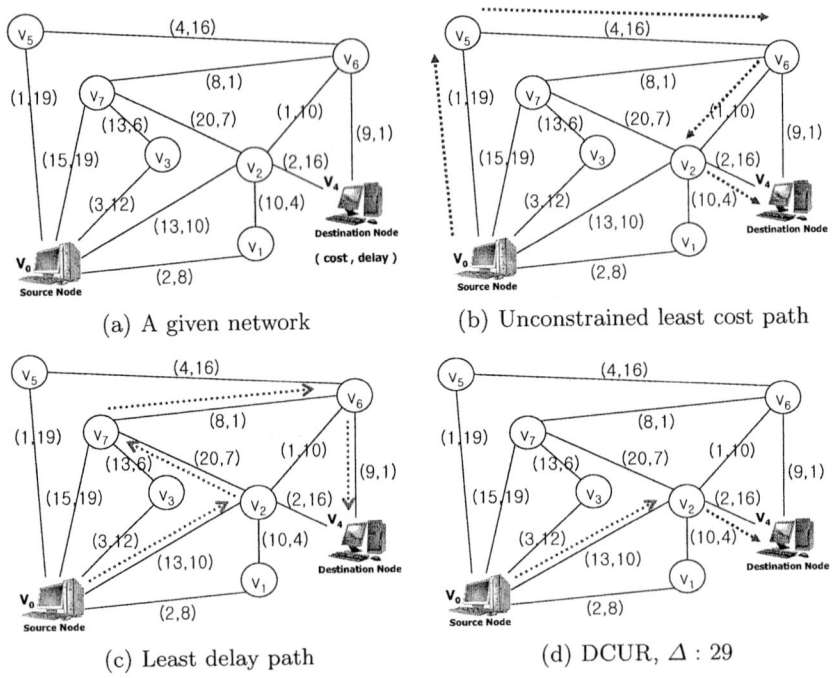

Fig. 1. Paths are constructed by different algorithms from source v_0 to destination v_4

source v_0 adds the first link on the LC path toward v_4, link (v_0, v_5), after checking that there exist delay-constrained paths from v_0 to v_4, that utilize (v_0, v_5). The source v_0 determines that the first link on its LC path toward v_4, link (v_0, v_5), cannot be used. This is because the subpath $\{(v_0, v_5)\}$ is not part of any delay-constrained path from v_0 to v_4. Thus v_0 decides to continue via the LD path direction. It adds the first link in that direction, link (v_0, v_2). Then node v_2 adds the first link on its LC path toward v_4, link (v_2, v_4), after checking that there exist delay-constrained paths from v_0 to v_4 that utilize (v_0, v_2) and (v_2, v_4). This completes the path to the destination.

2.3 The Weighted Factor Algorithm

M. Kim, et al. have recently proposed a unicast routing algorithm [10] that is based on new factor [8] which is probabilistic combination of cost and delay and its time complexity is $O((l + n\log n)|\{w_\alpha\}|)$, where $\{w_\alpha\}$ is set of weights. The unicast routing algorithm is quite likely a performance of a kth shortest path algorithm which has the high time complexity. The following steps explain a process for obtaining new factor which is introduced in [10].

Steps to calculate the new factor

1. Compute two paths P_{LD} and P_{LC} for the source and a destination.
2. Compute $\bar{C} = \frac{\phi_C(P_{LD})}{n(P_{LD})}$ and $\bar{D} = \frac{\phi_D(P_{LC})}{n(P_{LC})}$
3. Compute $F^{-1}(\frac{3}{2} - \frac{\phi_C(P_{LC})}{\phi_C(P_{LD})})$ and $F^{-1}(\frac{3}{2} - \frac{\phi_D(P_{LD})}{\phi_D(P_{LC})})$
   i.e., $z^d_{\alpha/2}$ and $z^c_{\alpha/2}$. The function F is Gaussian distribution function.
4. Compute $post_{LD} = \bar{C} - z^d_{\alpha/2} \frac{S_{LD}}{\sqrt{n(P_{LD})}}$ and $post_{LC} = \bar{D} - z^c_{\alpha/2} \frac{S_{LC}}{\sqrt{n(P_{LC})}}$
   S is a standard deviation.
5. Compute $Cfct(w, e) = max\{1, 1 + (c(e) - post_{LD}) \frac{w}{0.5}\}$ and
   $Dfct(w, e) = max\{1, 1 + (d(e) - post_{LC}) \frac{1-w}{0.5}\}$
6. We obtain the new value, $Cfct(w, e) \times Dfct(w, e)$, for each link in G.

Table 1. All paths $P(v_0, v_4)$ for each w in Fig. 1 and Fig. 2

w	$P(v_0, v_4)$ for each w	ϕ_C	ϕ_D
LD	$\{(v_0, v_2), (v_2, v_7), (v_7, v_6), (v_6, v_4)\}$	50	19
0.0	$\{(v_0, v_1), (v_1, v_2), (v_2, v_7), (v_7, v_6), (v_6, v_4)\}$	49	21
0.1, 0.2, 0.3, 0.4	$\{(v_0, v_1), (v_1, v_2), (v_2, v_6), (v_6, v_4)\}$	22	23
0.5, 0.6, 0.7, 0.8	$\{(v_0, v_1), (v_1, v_2), (v_2, v_4)\}$	14	28
0.9, 1.0	$\{(v_0, v_5), (v_5, v_6), (v_6, v_2), (v_2, v_4)\}$	8	61
LC	$\{(v_0, v_5), (v_5, v_6), (v_6, v_2), (v_2, v_4)\}$	8	61

Fig. 2 are good illustrative examples of the unicast routing algorithm [10] that is based on new weighted factor. A given network topology is G in Fig. 1(a). Link costs and link delays are shown to each link as a pair $(cost, delay)$. To construct

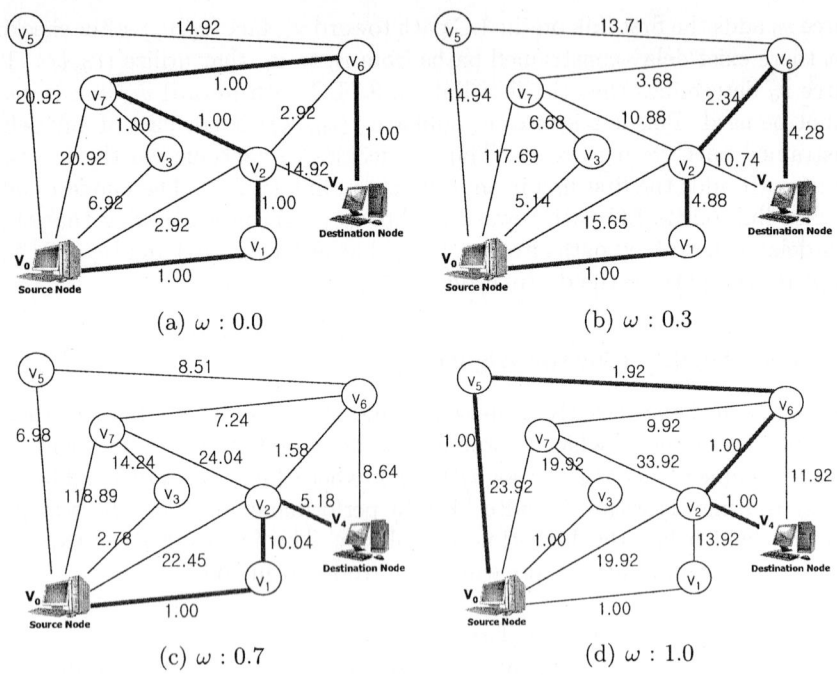

Fig. 2. The variety of paths for each ω

a path from the source node v_0 to the destination node v_4, we consider either link cost or link delay. Fig. 2 shows the paths computed by the new parameter for each weight ω. As indicated in Table 1, the path cost order is $\phi_C(P_{LC}) \leq \phi_C(P_{\omega:1.0}) \leq \phi_C(P_{\omega:0.7}) \leq \phi_C(P_{\omega:0.3}) \leq \phi_C(P_{\omega:0.0}) \leq \phi_C(P_{LD})$ and the path delay order is $\phi_D(P_{LD}) \leq \phi_D(P_{\omega:0.0}) \leq \phi_D(P_{\omega:0.3}) \leq \phi_D(P_{\omega:0.7}) \leq \phi_D(P_{\omega:1.0}) \leq \phi_D(P_{LC})$.

3 The Proposed Algorithm

M. Kim, et al. have recently proposed a unicast routing algorithm, Estimated Link Selection (ELS), for DCLC problem [9]. Basic idea of ELS is as follows. ELS computes two paths, P_{LD} and P_{LC} from source s to destination d, and calculates $\phi_D(P_{LD})$ and $\phi_D(P_{LC})$. If $\phi_D(P_{LD})$ is larger than a given bounded delay Δ, there exists no path P such that $\phi_D(P) \leq \Delta$. And it selects P_{LD} or P_{LC}. If P_{LC} is selected and $\phi_D(P_{LC}) \leq \Delta$, then no more path is considered. Otherwise, each link $(i,j) \in P$, is replaced by a minimum cost path P' connecting i and j to reduce until $\phi_D(P) \leq \Delta$. ELS significantly contributes to identify the low cost and acceptable delay unicasting path and the performance improvement is up to about 49% in terms of normalized surcharge with DCUR. The performance of ELS depends on a firstly selected path which is a LD or a LC path. However, the third path may perform better than the LC or LD path.

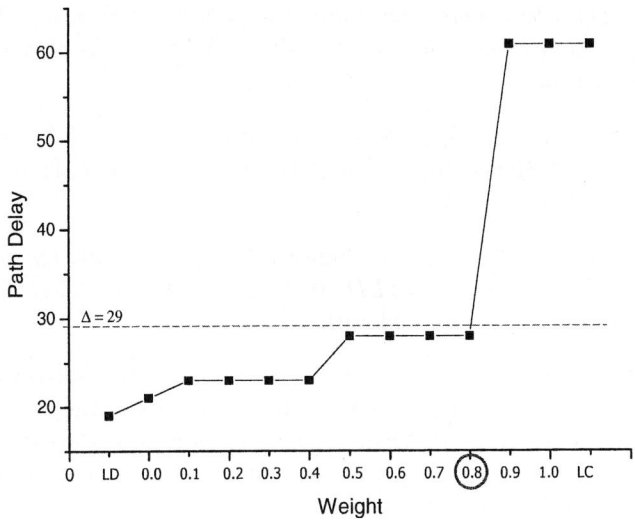

Fig. 3. The ω selection in Table 1

Our proposed algorithm, called Estimated Path Selection (EPS), considers a variety of paths that are obtained by algorithm in [10]. And EPS finds an weight ω, which can satisfy a delay constraint Δ. If we have several weights satisfied Δ, we take the largest weight. Though path delays are same or less than Δ, path costs are different. Because a path cost is decreasing as a weight is increasing [10], we choose the largest weight as ω.

A given network topology is G in Fig. 1(a). We assume the function $\psi(s, d, \omega)$ is $\phi_D(P_\omega(s,d))$. Fig. 3 shows the weight ω selection. EPS is to find ω, which can satisfy $min\{ \phi_C(P) \mid P \in (2^{v_0 \to v_4}, \Delta) \}$. EPS selects the weight 'ω: 0.8' such that $max\{0.5, 0.6, 0.7, 0.8\}$ in Fig. 3. In this way, a delay-constrained path $P_{EPS}(v_0, v_4)$ is $\{ (v_0, v_1), (v_1, v_2), (v_2, v_4) \}$. Fig. 1(d) show the path constructed by DCUR which is $\{ (v_0, v_2), (v_2, v_4) \}$. $\phi_C(P_{DCUR}) = 23$ is more expensive than $\phi_C(P_{EPS}) = 14$.

Theorem 1. *Let s be a source node and d be a destination node. Δ is a delay constraint. Assume that $\psi(s,d,\omega)$ is continuous function. If $\exists$ path P such that $\phi_D(P(s,d)) \leq \Delta$, then EPS always finds ω such that $min\{\Delta - \psi(s,d,\omega)$ and non negative$\}$.*

Proof. Let $\delta(\omega) = \Delta$ be the constant function and $\xi(\omega)$ be the continuous function $\delta(\omega) - \psi(s,d,\omega)$. If ψ is parallel line with $\delta(\omega)$, then the function ξ is constant function. So, the function ξ has a minimum. Otherwise, there always exists ω_γ such that $\xi'(\omega_\gamma - \epsilon) < 0 < \xi'(\omega_\gamma + \epsilon)$ for arbitrary positive real number ϵ. So, $\xi(\omega_\gamma)$ is locally minimum. Let ω_α be the weight such that satisfied $min\{\xi(\omega_\gamma)\}$ for every γ. Therefore $\xi(\omega_\alpha)$ is minimum for ξ. EPS takes $\omega = max\{\omega_\alpha\}$ □

Theorem 2. *Let s be a source node and d be a destination node. Δ is a delay constraint. If $\exists$ path P such that $\phi_D(P(s,d)) \leq \Delta$, then EPS always constructs a Δ-constrained path.*

Proof. By theorem 1, there exists ω such that $min\{\Delta - \psi(s,d,\omega)$ and non negative}. Hence, we find a Δ-constrained path $P_\omega(s,d)$. The path $P_\omega(s,d)$ must be $\phi_D(P_\omega) \leq \Delta$. □

Theorem 3. *Let $G(V,E)$ be a given network with $|V| = n$ and $|E| = l$. Suppose that an ordered set of weights is $\{LD, 0, 0.1, \ldots, 0.9, 1, LC\}$. The expected time complexity of EPS is $O(l + nlogn)$.*

Proof. We use the Fibonacci heaps implementation of the Dijkstra's algorithm [1]. The time complexity is $O(l + nlogn)$. The cardinality of the set of weights is 13. Because we use the above Dijkstra's algorithm for each ω, the time complexity is $O(13(l + nlogn)) = O(l + nlogn)$ for searching 13 paths. Therefore, the total time complexity is $O(l + nlogn)$. □

4 Performance Evaluation

4.1 Random Network Topology for the Simulation

Random graphs are the acknowledged model for different kinds of networks, communication networks in particular. There are many algorithms and programs, but the speed is usually the main goal, not the statistical properties. In the last decade the problem was discussed, for example, by B.M. Waxman (1993) [18], M. Doar (1993, 1996) [4,5], C.-K. Toh (1993) [17], E.W. Zegura, K.L. Calvert, and S. Bhattacharjee (1996) [20], K.L. Calvert, M. Doar, and M. Doar (1997) [3], R. Kumar, P. Raghavan, S. Rajagopalan, D. Sivakumar, A. Tomkins, and E. Upfal (2000) [12]. They have presented fast algorithms that allow generate random graph with different properties, similar to real communication networks, in particular. But none of them have discussed the stochastic properties of generated random graphs. A.S. Rodionov and H. Choo [15,16] have formulated two major demands to the generators of random graph: attainability of all graphs with required properties and the uniformity of their distribution. If the second demand is sometimes difficult to prove theoretically, it is possible to check the distribution statistically. The random graph is similar to real networks. The method uses parameters n - the number of nodes in networks, and P_e - the probability of edge existence between any node pair.

The details of the generation for random network topologies are as follows. Let us remark that if a random graph models a random network then this graph should be connected. Hence, the graph should contain at least a spanning tree. So, firstly a random spanning tree is generated. As we know, we consider cases for $n \geq 3$. A tree with 3 nodes is unique, and thus we use this as an initial tree. And we expand to a spanning tree with n nodes. After adjusting the probability P_e, we generate other non-tree edges at random for the graph based network

```
Graph Generation Algorithm
  Begin
    A_{1,2} = A_{2,1} = A_{2,3} = A_{3,2} = 1
    For i = 4 to n Do
      r = (i − 1) × random() + 1
      A_{r,i} = A_{i,r} = 1
    For i = 1 to (n − 1) Do
      For j = (i + 1) to n Do
        If P_e > random() Then A_{i,j} = A_{j,i} = 1
  End Algorithm.
```

Fig. 4. Graph Generation Algorithm

topology. Let us calculate the adjusted probability P_e^a. By $Prob\{event\}$ denote a probability of the event. Suppose e is a possible edge between a couple of nodes, then we have

$$P_e = Prob\{\,e \in \text{spanning tree}\,\} + Prob\{\,e \notin \text{spanning tree}\,\} \cdot P_e^a$$
$$P_e = \frac{n-1}{n(n-1)/2} + \left(1 - \frac{n-1}{n(n-1)/2}\right) \cdot P_e^a$$
$$\therefore P_e^a = \frac{nP_e - 2}{n - 2} \ .$$

Let us describe a pseudo code for random network topologies. Here A is an incident matrix, r is a simple variable, and $random()$ is a function producing uniformly distributed random values between 0 and 1.

4.2 Simulation Results

We now describe some numerical results with which we compare the performance for the proposed algorithm. The proposed one is implemented in C++. We randomly selected a source node and destination node. We generate 10 different networks for each size of given 25, 50, 100, and 200 nodes. The random networks used in our experiments are the probability of links (P_e) equal to 0.4 and 0.8. A source node and a destination node are picked uniformly. Moreover, we randomly choose Δ at closed interval $[\phi_D(P_{LD}), \phi_D(P_{LC})]$. We simulate 1000 times (10 different networks ×100 trials = 1000).

For the performance comparison, we implement the DCUR [14] and the ELS [9] in the same simulation environment. We employ the normalized surcharge $\bar{\delta}$, introduced in [11], of algorithm with respect to the ELS and EPS defined as follow:

$$\bar{\delta} = \frac{\phi_C(P_{DCUR}) - \phi_C(P_{new})}{\phi_C(P_{new})} \times 100 \ (\%) \ .$$

As indicated in Fig. 5, it can be easily noticed the EPS is always better than the DCUR and the ELS. And the $\bar{\delta}$ is 105% and 98% in 200-node network

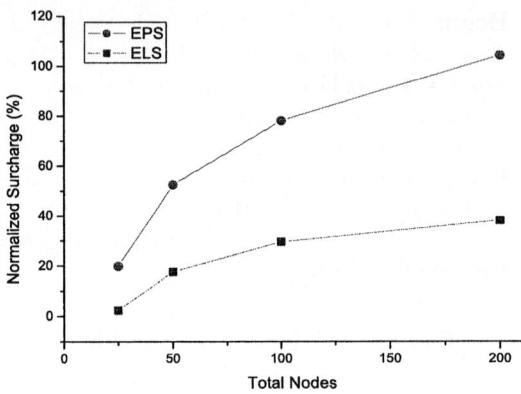

(a) Edge probability is 0.4

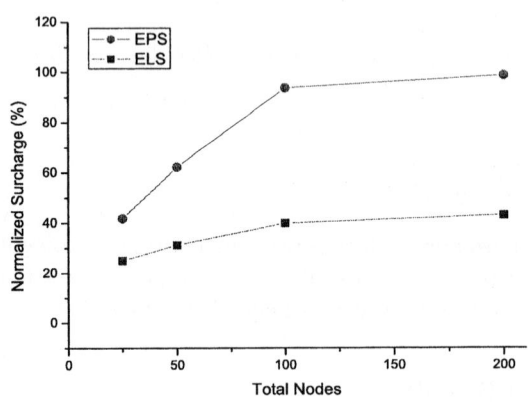

(b) Edge probability is 0.8

Fig. 5. Results with DCUR

architecture. Also, an interesting result is that the function $\bar{\delta}$ increases as the number of nodes increases.

5 Conclusion

For distributed real-time applications, the path delay should be acceptable and also its cost should be as low as possible. It is known as the DCLC path problem. In this paper, we study the DCLC problem which is NP-hard [6] and propose a heuristic algorithm, called EPS, by using a new parameter which is probabilistic combination of cost and delay. The new parameter takes in account both cost and delay at the same time. We have performed empirical evaluation that compares our proposed EPS with the DCUR in various network situations. It significantly contributes to identify the low cost and low delay unicasting path and the performance improvement is up to about 105% in terms of normalized surcharge with DCUR. In addition, we would like to extend EPS to routing of delay-constrained multicast trees.

References

1. R. K. Ajuja, T. L. Magnanti, and J. B. Orlin, *Network Flows: Theory, Algorithms and Applications*, Prentice-Hall, 1993.
2. D. Bertsekas and R. Gallager, Data Networks, 2nd ed. Englewood Cliffs, NJ: Prentice-Hall, 1992.
3. K.L. Calvert, M. Doar, and M. Doar, "Modelling Internet Topology," IEEE Communications Magazine, pp. 160-163, June 1997.
4. M. Doar, Multicast in the ATM environment. PhD thesis, Cambridge Univ., Computer Lab., September 1993.
5. M. Doar, "A Better Mode for Generating Test Networks," IEEE Proc. GLOBECOM'96, pp. 86-93, 1996.
6. M. Garey and D. Johnson, Computers and intractability: A Guide to the Theory of NP-Completeness, New York: Freeman, 1979.
7. C. Hedrick, "Routing information protocol," http://www.ietf.org/rfc/rfc1058.txt, June 1988.
8. M. Kim, Y.-C. Bang, and H. Choo, "New Parameter for Balancing Two Independent Measures in Routing Path," Springer-Verlag Lecture Notes in Computer Science, vol. 3046, pp. 56-65, May 2004.
9. M. Kim, Y.-C. Bang, and H. Choo, "Estimated Link Selection for DCLC Problem," IEEE International Conference on Communications 2004, Proc. ICC'04 vol. 4, pp. 1937-1941, June 2004.
10. M. Kim, Y.-C. Bang, and H. Choo, "On Algorithm for Efficiently Combining Two Independent Measures in Routing Paths," Springer-Verlag Lecture Notes in Computer Science, vol. 3483, pp. 989-998, May 2005.
11. V. P. Kompella, J. C. Pasquale, and G. C. Polyzos, "Multicast routing for multimedia communication," IEEE/ACM Trans. Networking, vol. 1, no. 3, pp. 286-292, June 1993.
12. R. Kumar, P. Raghavan, S. Rajagopalan, D Sivakumar, A. Tomkins, and E Upfal, "Stochastic models for the Web graph," Proc. 41st Annual Symposium on Foundations of Computer Science, pp. 57-65, 2000.
13. J. Moy, "OSPF Version 2," http://www.ietf.org/rfc/rfc1583.txt, March 1994.
14. D.S. Reeves and H.F. Salama, "A distributed algorithm for delay-constrained unicast routing," IEEE/ACM Transactions on Networking, vol. 8, pp. 239-250, April 2000.
15. A.S. Rodionov and H. Choo, "On Generating Random Network Structures: Trees," Springer-Verlag Lecture Notes in Computer Science, vol. 2658, pp. 879-887, June 2003.
16. A.S. Rodionov and H. Choo, "On Generating Random Network Structures: Connected Graphs," Springer-Verlag Lecture Notes in Computer Science, vol. 3090, pp. 483-491, August 2004.

17. C.-K. Toh, "Performance Evaluation of Crossover Switch Discovery Algorithms for Wireless ATM LANs," IEEE Proc. INFOCOM'96, pp. 1380-1387, 1993.
18. B.M. Waxman, "Routing of Multipoint Connections," IEEE JSAC, vol. 9, pp. 1617-1622, 1993.
19. R. Widyono, "The Design and Evaluation of Routing Algorithms for Real-Time Channels," International Computer Science Institute, Univ. of California at Berkeley, Tech. Rep. ICSI TR-94-024, June 1994.
20. E.W. Zegura, K.L. Calvert, and S. Bhattacharjee, "How to model an Internetwork," Proc. INFOCOM'96, pp. 594-602, 1996.

Finding Feasible Pathways in Metabolic Networks

Esa Pitkänen[1,3], Ari Rantanen[1], Juho Rousu[2], and Esko Ukkonen[1]

[1] Department of Computer Science, University of Helsinki, Finland
[2] Royal Holloway, University of London, UK
[3] Department of Computer Science,
P.O.Box 68, FIN-00014 University of Helsinki, Finland
esa.pitkanen@cs.helsinki.fi

Abstract. Recent small-world studies of the global structure of metabolic networks have been based on the shortest-path distance. In this paper, we propose new distance measures that are based on the structure of feasible metabolic pathways between metabolites. We argue that these distances capture the complexity of the underlying biochemical processes more accurately than the shortest-path distance. To test our approach in practice, we calculated our distances and shortest-path distances in two microbial organisms, *S. cerevisiae* and *E. coli*. The results show that metabolite interconversion is significantly more complex than was suggested in previous small-world studies. We also studied the effect of reaction removals (gene knock-outs) on the connectivity of the *S. cerevisiae* network and found out that the network is not particularly robust against such mutations.

1 Introduction

Information on both biochemical reactions and enzymatic function of gene products has been made available in databases such as KEGG [6] and MetaCyc [8]. This knowledge has made it possible to analyze and predict genome-scale properties of metabolism in various organisms.

Two main approaches have been proposed for global analysis of metabolism, a graph-theoretical one [5,9,1] that focuses on the topology of the metabolic network, and an approach studying the capabilities of a metabolic network in steady-state conditions using stoichiometric equations [12,11].

In the graph-theoretical approach, the focus is in identifying node ranks, path lengths and clustering properties of metabolic network. Considering metabolic networks just as graphs consisting of nodes and edges and using shortest-path length as a distance function, it was suggested that metabolic networks in general possess the *scale-free property*: metabolite rank distribution $P(k)$ follows a power-law $P(k) \approx k^{-\gamma}$, with $\gamma \approx 2.2$ for many organisms [5]. Consequently, the network contains a small number of *hub* nodes that connect otherwise distant parts of the network. Because the average path length in a scale-free network is relatively short and the network exhibits a high degree of co-clustering, such network is an example of a so-called *small world* (see, e.g., [7]). Furthermore, it was observed that random deletions of metabolites from metabolic networks have little effect on average path length between metabolites [5]. This served as a basis for claims that metabolic networks were robust against mutations.

It was quickly noticed, however, that in metabolic networks typical hub metabolites include energy and redox cofactors (e.g., ATP and NAD) that are involved with several reactions that may be otherwise non-related. Thus, the shortest paths between metabolites often were routed through these cofactors, which can be considered misleading. This observation led to studies correcting the problem via manually removing the cofactors from the analysis [9] and to the computational approach by Arita [1] that circumvented the cofactor problem by looking at atom-level behaviour of metabolic pathways; he suggested that in a valid metabolic pathway at least one (carbon) atom should be transferred from the source to the target. Analysis of these atom-level pathways in [1] yielded for *E. coli* significantly longer average path lengths than the analysis of [5] or [9]. However, both analyses consider pathways that transfer only one metabolite or atom from source to target, and disregard the other metabolites or atoms involved in the pathway.

In this paper we use stricter criteria for a valid metabolic pathway. Namely, we require that on a valid pathway all atoms of the target metabolite need to be reachable from the source. We argue that this definition is biologically more realistic than the previous definitions described above as the production of a metabolite via a pathway requires the atoms to be transferred from source to target and introduce two novel distance measures between metabolites.

We study the structural properties of two high–quality metabolic networks, the networks of *S. cerevisiae* and *E. coli*. We also compare our distance functions against the shortest-path distance function. It turns out that in these two metabolic worlds the two approaches give quite clearly differing results.

The structure of the paper is as follows. In Section 2, we formalize metabolic networks, give our distance functions and show how they relate to the shortest-path distance. In Section 3, we study the computational complexity of these distances and give algorithms for evaluating them. In Section 4, we present the results of evaluating these as well as the shortest-path distances for all metabolite pairs in metabolic networks of two microbial organisms and study the effect of reaction deletions on the distances of metabolites. Section 5 concludes the article with discussion.

2 Metabolic Networks, and-or Graphs, and Metabolic Distances

A *metabolic reaction* is a pair (I, P) where $I = (I_1, \ldots, I_m)$ are the m *input metabolites* and $P = (P_1, \ldots, P_n)$ are the n *product metabolites* of the reaction. Each member of I and P belongs to the set M of the metabolites of the metabolic system under consideration. Note that by this definition a metabolic reaction is directed and that we omit the stoichiometric coefficients which are not relevant for our current study. Bidirectional reactions are modeled by pairs of unidirectional reactions (I, P) and (P, I). Also note that when applying our theory, we want to follow how the atoms are transmitted by the reactions and will therefore omit cofactor metabolites from M, I, and P.

A *metabolic network* is given by listing the metabolic reactions that form the network. Let $R = (R_1, \ldots, R_k)$ be a set of k reactions where each $R_i = (I_i, P_i)$ for some subsets I_i and P_i of M. The corresponding *metabolic graph* which we also call a metabolic network, has nodes $M \cup R$ and arcs as follows: there is a directed arc from $M_j \in M$ to $R_i \in R$ iff $M_j \in I_i$, and a directed arc from $R_i \in R$ to $M_j \in M$ iff $M_j \in P_i$. We call the nodes of the network that are in M the *metabolite nodes* and the nodes in R the *reaction nodes*. Figure 1 gives an example graph in which the reaction nodes are shown as bullets and metabolite nodes contain abbreviated metabolite names.

A metabolic pathway in a metabolic network is a concept that is used somewhat loosely in biochemistry. It seems clear, however, that it is not sufficient to consider only simple paths in a metabolic graph. The metabolic interpretation of the network has to be taken into account: a reaction can operate only if *all* its input substrates are present in the system. Respectively, a metabolite can become present in a system only if it is produced by *at least one* reaction. We consider some (source) metabolites to be always present in a system, and denote these metabolites by A. Therefore, our metabolic network is in fact an *and-or*-graph [10] with reactions as *and*-nodes and metabolites as *or*-nodes. A similar interpretation of a metabolic network has been used in a previous study [3].

To properly take into account this interpretation, we need to define distance measures for metabolite pairs that relate to the complexity of and-or-graphs connecting the pair. Let us start with reachability from source metabolites A:

- A reaction $R_i = (I_i, P_i)$ is *reachable* from A in R, if each metabolite in I_i is reachable from A in R.
- A metabolite C is *reachable* from A in R, if $C \in A$ or some reaction $R_j = (I_j, P_j)$ such that $C \in P_j$ is reachable from A in R.

We will define metabolic pathways from A as certain minimal sets of reactions that are reachable from A and produce the target metabolite. To this end, for any $F \subseteq R$, we let $Inputs(F)$ denote the set of the input metabolites and $Products(F)$ denote the set of the output metabolites of F. Moreover, we denote by $W(A, F)$ the subset of R that is reachable from A in F. Hence $W(A, F)$ is the reactions in R that can be reached from A *without going outside F*.

A *feasible metabolism from A* is a set $F \subseteq R$ which satisfies (i) $F = W(A, F)$, that is, the entire F is reachable from A without going outside F itself. Specifically, a *feasible metabolism from A to t* is a set F for which it additionally holds that (ii) $t \in Products(F)$.

We then define that a *metabolic pathway from A to t* is any *minimal* feasible metabolism F from A to t, that is, removing any reaction from F leads to violation of requirement (i) or (ii). Thus, a metabolic pathway is a minimal subnetwork capable of performing the conversion from A to t.

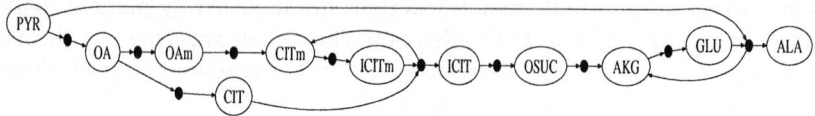

Fig. 1. A feasible metabolism (a pathway, in fact) from pyruvate (PYR) to alanine (ALA). In this network, pyruvate and glutamate (GLU) are combined to produce alanine. Here, $d_s(PYR, ALA) = 1$, $d_p(PYR, ALA) = 9$, and $d_m(PYR, ALA) = 10$.

Now, different distance measures can be defined. We define the *metabolic distance from A to t* to be the size of the smallest metabolic pathway from A to t. This distance captures the idea that the distance equals minimum number of reactions in total needed to produce t from A. The *production distance from A to t* is the smallest diameter taken over all metabolic pathways from A to t, where *diameter* of a metabolic pathway is taken as the length of the longest simple path in the pathway. Hence, production distance is the minimum number of sequential (successive) reactions needed to convert A to t. In the following we restrict ourself to a single source metabolite, that is $|A| = 1$, to be better able to compare with shortest-path analysis.

We denote by $d_p(A, t)$ the production distance and by $d_m(A, t)$ the metabolic distance from A to t. Moreover, $d_s(A, t)$ denotes the standard shortest-path distance.

It should be immediately clear that these distances satisfy:

Theorem 1. $d_s(A, t) \leq d_p(A, t) \leq d_m(A, t)$.

Figure 1 shows a feasible metabolism producing alanine from pyruvate. The reader can easily verify that this metabolism is in fact a metabolic pathway according to our technical definition: removal of any reaction would destroy the integrity of the network. Note that pyruvate is a sufficient precursor to produce all intermediates in this pathway, and no additional input substrates are needed.

Let us conclude this section by relating the metabolic distance to the shortest-path distance. The two distances can be seen as two extremes in a continuum in the following sense. We denote by S the set of auxiliary metabolites that are available as reaction substrates without explicitly producing them from A. In metabolic distance, the set S of auxiliary metabolites is empty. Therefore, all reaction substrates required for the conversion to t need to be produced from A. Let us now consider gradually extending the set of auxiliary metabolites to include all metabolite subsets of size $1, 2, 3, \ldots, |M|$. Let $S_1 \subset S_2 \subset \cdots \subset M$ be any such sequence, and denote by $d_{m,S}(A, t)$ the size of the minimum feasible metabolism from A to t with S being the set of auxiliary metabolites. It is easy to see that the distances satisfy

$$d_{m,M}(A, t) \leq \cdots \leq d_{m,S_1}(A, t) \leq d_{m,\emptyset}(A, t) = d_m(A, t),$$

as adding more and more metabolites to the set of auxiliary metabolites can only decrease the size of the required subgraph. Moreover, from some $1 \leq \ell \leq |M|$ onwards the distances equal the shortest-path distance

$$d_{m,S_\ell}(A,t) = d_{m,S_{\ell+1}}(A,t) = \cdots = d_{m,M}(A,t) = d_s(A,t)$$

as the length of shortest-path is a lower bound to the size of the feasible subgraph and the shortest-path becomes a feasible metabolism when all intermediate metabolites along the path are reachable.

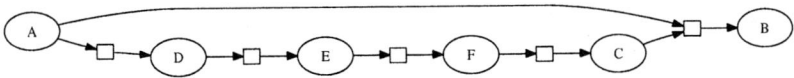

Fig. 2. In this network, metabolic distance $d_{m,S}(A,t) = 5$ when the set of auxiliary metabolites S is empty, and $d_{m,S}(A,B) = 1$ when $C \in S$

3 Algorithms and Complexity

In this section, we discuss computation of the metabolic and production distances. We then give an algorithm to quickly find a feasible, but possibly nonminimal, metabolism. Unfortunately, exact metabolic distance cannot be computed efficiently unless $P = NP$.

Definition 1. *(MINIMAL-FEASIBLE-PATHWAY). Given a set of reactions R, a set of source metabolites A, a target metabolite t and an integer k, is the metabolic distance $d_m(A,t)$ less or equal k?*

The intractability of this problem is proven via a reduction from a propositional STRIPS planning problem PLANMIN that concerns the existence of a plan from a initial state to a goal state, consisting of at most k operations [2]. We omit the proof due to the lack of space.

Theorem 2. *MINIMAL-FEASIBLE-PATHWAY is NP-complete.*

This implies that also the special case with $|A| = 1$ is NP-complete. Next, we concentrate on calculating lower and upper bounds for the metabolic distance.

Production distance $d_p(A, M_i)$ can be computed efficiently with Algorithm 1. Search starts from the source metabolites A and proceeds in breadth-first order, visiting a reaction node only after all its input metabolite nodes have been visited, and a metabolite node after any of its producing reaction nodes has been visited. The production distance to metabolite nodes is stored in table d and to reaction nodes in table w. The running time is linear in the size of the network because each metabolite node is put in the queue Q at most once.

Taking advantage of production distances, we can quickly find some feasible metabolism from A to t with Algorithm 2. The size of this metabolism gives an

Algorithm 1 Calculate production distances from A to all other metabolites

Input: A set of reactions R, a set of input metabolites A
Output: Pair (d, w), where $d[i] = d_p(A, M_i)$ and $w[i] = \max\{d_p(A, M_j) \mid M_j \in Inputs(R_i)\}$
Procedure CalculateProductionDistances(R, A):

1: **for all** $M_i \in M$ **do**
2:    **if** $M_i \in A$ **then**
3:       $d[i] \leftarrow 0$
4:    **else**
5:       $d[i] \leftarrow \infty$
6: **for all** $R_i \in R$ **do**
7:    $B[i] \leftarrow |Inputs(R_i)|$ % unsatisfied inputs
8:    $w[i] \leftarrow \infty$
9: Q : queue
10: $Q \leftarrow Q \cup A$
11: **while** $Q \neq \emptyset$ **do**
12:    $M_i \leftarrow$ remove_first(Q)
13:    **for all** $R_j \in Consumers(M_i)$ **do**
14:       $B[j] \leftarrow B[j] - 1$
15:       **if** $B[j] = 0$ **then**
16:          $w[j] \leftarrow d[i]$
17:          **for all** $M_k \in Products(R_j)$ **do**
18:             **if** $d[k] = \infty$ **then**
19:                $d[k] \leftarrow w[j] + 1$
20:                append(Q, M_k)
21: **return** (d, w)

Algorithm 2 Find a feasible metabolism from A to t

Input: A set of reactions R, a set of input metabolites A, a target metabolite t
Output: Feasible metabolism $G \subseteq R$ or **infeasible** if no feasible metabolism exists
Procedure FindFeasibleMetabolism(R, A, t):

1: $(d, w) \leftarrow$ CalculateProductionDistances(R, A)
2: **if** $d[i] = \infty$ **then**
3:    **return infeasible**
4: $V \leftarrow \{t\}$ {set of visited metabolites}
5: Q : queue {unsatisfied metabolites}
6: append(Q, t)
7: $G \leftarrow \emptyset$
8: **while** $Q \neq \emptyset$ **do**
9:    $M_i \leftarrow$ remove_first(Q)
10:    $R_j \leftarrow \mathrm{argmin}_{R_j}\{w[j] \mid M_i \in Products(R_j)\}$
11:    $G \leftarrow G \cup \{R_j\}$
12:    **for all** $M_k \in Inputs(R_j)$ **do**
13:       **if** $M_k \notin V$ **then**
14:          append(Q, M_k)
15:          $V \leftarrow V \cup \{M_k\}$
16: **return** G

upper bound $\hat{d}_m$ for the metabolic distance d_m. The algorithm maintains a list of unsatisfied metabolites. Initially the list contains only metabolite t. The idea of the algorithm is to satisfy one unsatisfied metabolite M_i in turn by adding a reaction to the network that produces M_i. If the metabolite M_i has multiple producers, a reaction with smallest production distance is chosen, breaking ties arbitrarily. The running time is again linear.

4 Experiments

To test our definition of metabolic pathway, we studied the genome-scale metabolic networks of two microbial organisms, namely *Saccharomyces cerevisiae* (yeast) [4] and *Escherichia coli* [1].

We calculated simple path lengths and production distances (Algorithm 1) in metabolic networks. In addition, we calculated a feasible metabolism for all metabolite pairs with Algorithm 2 for which such metabolism existed. While this metabolism is not necessarily minimal, the size of this metabolism gives us an upper bound for metabolic distance. To concentrate on primary metabolism and to be able to compare with previous results, we deleted 89 cofactors, such as energy and redox metabolites, from models. We also removed metabolites designated as externals and reactions either consuming or producing them.

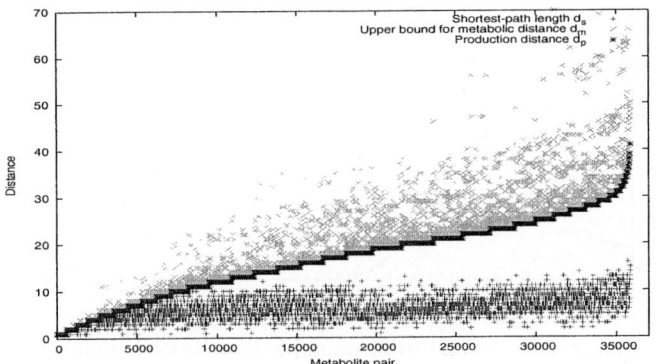

Fig. 3. Production distances, upper bounds for metabolic distance given by Algorithm 2 and shortest-path lengths in the metabolic network of *S. cerevisiae* between all metabolite pairs sorted in ascending production distance order. Only every tenth metabolite pair is included to reduce clutter.

Metabolic Distances in Two Metabolic Networks. In *S. cerevisiae*, we found that production distance was defined for 23.2% of 154803 metabolite

---

[1] Metabolic network models of *S. cerevisiae* (iFF708, 1175 reactions) and *E. coli* (iJE660a, 739 reactions) were obtained from http://systemsbiology.ucsd.edu/organisms/

pairs[2] for which there was a connecting simple path (33.6% for *E. coli*). Table 1 summarizes the results. Average production distance in both networks is significantly higher than average simple path length, implying that metabolic distance is higher as well. Results for simple paths only include paths between metabolite pairs for which a feasible metabolism exists. Figure 3 shows results for all pairs for which a metabolic pathway exists in ascending production distance order. We observe that the size of a smallest metabolic pathway is largely independent of the corresponding shortest-path length.

Table 1. Means and standard deviations (in parenthesis) of shortest-path lengths (d_s), production distances (d_p), and upper bounds for metabolic distance ($\hat{d}_m$) given by Algorithm 2 for *S. cerevisiae* and *E. coli*.

Organism	d_s	d_p	$\hat{d}_m$
E. coli	5.78	14.55	19.06 (12.5)
	(2.30)	(6.40)	
S. cerevisiae	6.11	16.72	20.34 (11.3)
	(2.40)	(7.74)	

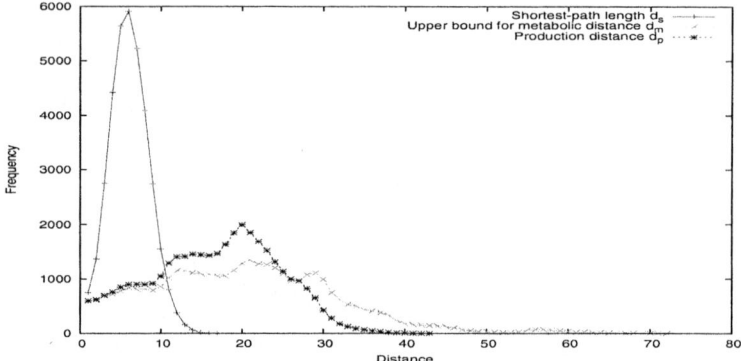

Fig. 4. Histograms of production distances, upper bounds for metabolic distance given by Algorithm 2 and shortest-path lengths for *S. cerevisiae*

This result demonstrates the shortfall of approaches using simple paths that do not transfer all atoms from source to target: not nearly all simple paths can be interpreted as biologically plausible pathways. Analysis based on simple paths does not take into account the inherent nature of metabolic networks as a system of chemical reactions. In order to proceed, all substrates of a chemical reaction must be present in the system. Therefore, since two thirds of metabolite pairs with a connecting simple path in yeast do not have a connecting metabolic

---

[2] The total of number of pairs is 352242 (cofactors excluded).

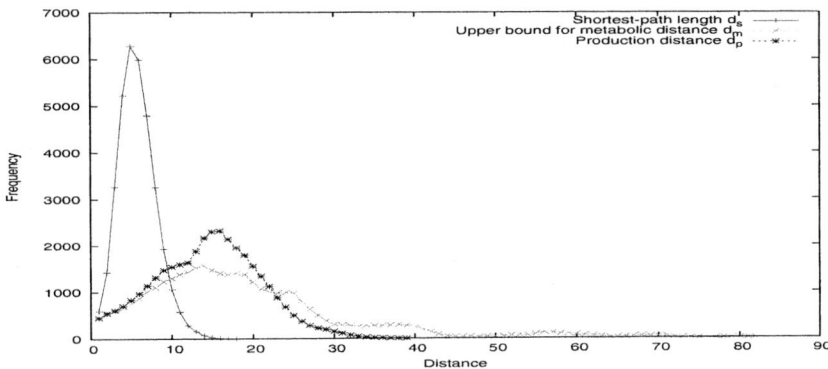

Fig. 5. Histograms of production distances, upper bounds for metabolic distance given by Algorithm 2 and shortest-path lengths for *E. coli*

pathway, we claim that previous small world analysis may produce misleading results.

Furthermore, even if two metabolites can be connected with both a simple path and a metabolic pathway, the metabolic pathway is much more complex than the simple path. This can be seen in Figures 4 and 5 which show the histograms of three distances for *S. cerevisiae* and *E. coli*, respectively. We can observe that the upper bound obtained with Algorithm 2 and production distance together give us, on the average, a good estimate of metabolic distance. The distribution of simple path lengths follows the normal distribution as expected. However, the distribution of production distances does not have similar shape, gradually increasing up to distance of 20 in *S. cerevisiae* and then descending. In *E. coli*, production distances are shorter on the average but still significantly longer than the small world hypothesis would suggest. In particular, we get the average production distance 14.6 for *E. coli* which clearly exceeds the average atom-pathway distance of 8.4 reported in a previous study [1].

Effect of Reaction Deletions to Distances. In addition to calculating pairwise distances, we observed the effect of random reaction deletions from the yeast network to our distances. Reaction deletions simulate knocking out genes with enzymatic end-products from the genome. Figure 6 shows the effect of deletions to the number of feasible metabolisms for *S. cerevisiae*. The ratio of metabolite pairs connected with a simple path in both the original network and the deletion variant decreased as the number of reaction deletions increased. However, at the same time, the ratio of connections via feasible metabolisms dropped more rapidly. This indicates that metabolic network of *S. cerevisiae* is in fact more vulnerable to gene knockouts than would be evident just by considering the simple paths.

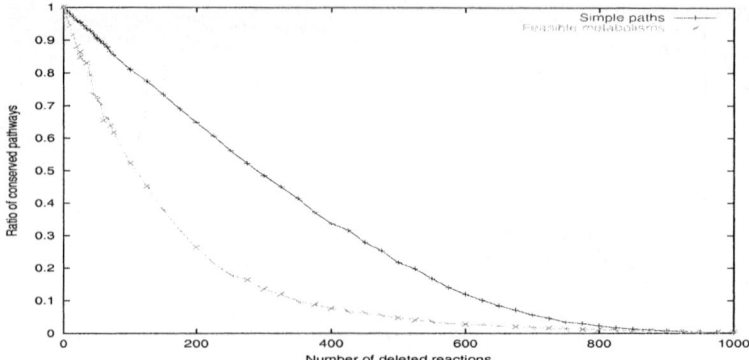

Fig. 6. Robustness of yeast against reaction deletions. The red (upper) curve gives the relative amount of connections via simple paths that are preserved after $n = 0 \ldots 1000$ deletions. The green curve gives the same quantity for connections via feasible metabolisms and indicates quite weak robustness. Averages over 100 repetitions.

5 Discussion and Conclusions

In this paper we have proposed distance measures for metabolite distances in metabolic networks. We argue that these distances have more natural biochemical interpretation than the simple shortest-path distance used in previous research. The shortest-path distance does not always have a direct correspondence to the inherent difficulty of producing a metabolite from another. The distances as we defined them take into account the fact that, in order to produce the target metabolite, all atoms of the target should be reachable from the source metabolites. Our metabolic distance, in addition, measures the genomic capacity (in terms of number of enzymes involved) that is required for the conversion.

In addition, we showed that there is a unified way to interpret the metabolic and shortest-path distances: Metabolic distance is the size of the minimal feasible metabolism from A to t when no other metabolite than A is available initially. Shortest-path distance is the size of the minimal feasible metabolism from A to t when all metabolites required by the reactions along the path are available at the outset. An interesting further research direction is to study the continuum between the two extremes by allowing some subsets of metabolites to be available besides source metabolites A, either by allowing some biologically interesting nutrients or conducting more systematic study, looking for possible phase transitions in the distances as the function of the number of allowed metabolites.

In our experiments we discovered that the average metabolic distance between pairs of metabolites in the metabolic network of *S. cerevisiae* is considerably longer than the corresponding shortest-path distance. In *E. coli* we observed the average metabolic distance to be longer than average atom-path distance reported in a previous study. This is because atom-path distance relates to transforming a single atom between metabolites, while our distance measures the complexity of total conversion. Also, the distribution of the distances takes a different shape: normal-like distribution of the shortest-path lengths is not reproduced when our more realistic measures are used.

In the second experiment, we studied the effect of random deletions of enzymes on metabolite distances. Our simulations show that the metabolic network of *S. cerevisiae* may not be as robust to mutations as stated previously.

Another future direction is to make a more comprehensive study on the effect of reaction deletions on important biological pathways, such as amino acid production and DNA synthesis. In addition we plan to apply our analysis to other organisms that have publicly available metabolic network models.

Acknowledgements. This work has been supported by the SYSBIO programme of Academy of Finland. In addition, the work by Juho Rousu has been supported by Marie Curie Individual Fellowship grant HPMF-CT-2002-02110.

References

1. M. Arita. The metabolic world of *Escherichia coli* is not small. *PNAS*, 101(6):1543–1547, 2004.
2. T. Bylander. The computational complexity of propositional STRIPS planning. *Artificial Intelligence*, 69(1-2):165–204, 1994.
3. O. Ebenhöh, T. Handorf, and R. Heinrich. Structural analysis of expanding metabolic networks. *Genome Informatics*, 15(1):35–45, 2004.
4. J. Förster, I. Famili, P. Fu, B. Palsson, and J. Nielsen. Genome-scale reconstruction of the *Saccharomyces cerevisiae* metabolic network. *Genome Research*, (13):244–253, 2003.
5. H. Jeong, B. Tombor, R. Albert, Z. N. Oltvai, and A.-L. Barabási. The large-scale organization of metabolic networks. *Nature*, (407):651–654, 2000.
6. M. Kanehisa and S. Goto. Kegg: Kyoto encyclopedia of genes and genomes. *Nucleic Acids Res.*, 28:27–30, 2000.
7. J. Kleinberg. The small-world phenomenon: An algorithmic perspective. In *Proc. 32nd ACM Symposium on Theory of Computing*, 2000.
8. C. J. Krieger, P. Zhang, L. A. Mueller, A. Wang, S. Paley, M. Arnaud, J. Pick, S. Y. Rhee, and P. D. Karp. MetaCyc: a multiorganism database of metabolic pathways and enzymes. *Nucleic Acids Research*, 32(1):D438–42, 2004.
9. H.-W. Ma and A.-P. Zeng. Reconstruction of metabolic networks from genome data and analysis of their global structure for various organisms. *Bioinformatics*, 19(2):270–277, 2003.
10. S. J. Russell and P. Norvig. *Artifical Intelligence: A Modern Approach*. Prentice Hall, 2nd edition, 2003.
11. C. H. Schilling, D. Letscher, and B. Palsson. Theory for the systemic definition of metabolic pathways and their use in interpreting metabolic function from a pathway-oriented perspective. *Journal of Theoretical Biology*, (203):228–248, 2003.
12. S. Schuster, D. A. Fell, and T. Dandekar. A general definition of metabolic pathways useful for systematic organization and analysis of complex metabolic network. *Nature Biotechnology*, 18:326–332, March 2000.

One-Dimensional Finger Searching in RAM Model Revisited

S. Sioutas, Y. Panagis, E. Theodoridis, and A. Tsakalidis

Computer Technology Institute,
N. Kazantzaki Street, University of Patras Campus,
tsak@cti.gr
Computer Engineering and Informatics Dept.,
University of Patras, Greece
{sioutas, panagis, theodori}@ceid.upatras.gr

Abstract. In the particular case we have insertions/deletions at the tail of a given set S of n one-dimensional elements, we present a simpler and more concrete algorithm than the one presented in [12] achieving the same worst-case upper bounds for finger searching queries in $\Theta(\sqrt{\log d / \log \log d})$ time. Furthermore, in the general case where we have insertions/deletions anywhere we present a new simple randomized algorithm achieving the same time bounds with high probability.

1 Introduction

By finger search we mean that we can have a "finger" pointing at a sorted key x when searching for a key y. Here a finger is just a reference returned to the user when x is inserted or searched for. The goal is to do better if the number d of sorted keys between x and y is small. Moreover, we consider finger updates, whenever for deletions one has a finger on the key to be deleted, and for insertions, one has a finger to the key after which the new key is to be inserted.

In the comparison-based model of computation Raman [2] has provided optimal bounds, supporting finger searches in $O(\log d)$ time while supporting finger updates in constant time. On the pointer machine, Brodal et al. [1] have shown how to support finger searches in $O(\log d)$ time and finger updates in constant time. Anderson and Thorup [12] presented optimal bounds on the RAM; namely $\Theta(\sqrt{\log d / \log \log d})$ for finger search with constant finger updates.

In this paper, assuming that the insert/delete operations occur at the tail of set S, we present a new algorithm based on an implicit Nested Balanced Distributed Tree (BDT), which handles finger-searching queries in optimal $\Theta(\sqrt{\log d / \log \log d})$ worst-case time in a simpler manner than that presented in [12]. Thus our method is easier to be implemented.

In the general case where we have insertions/deletions anywhere we present a new randomized algorithm based on application of oblivious on-line simple pebble games [2] upon a new 2-level hybrid data structure where the top-level structure is a Level-Linked Exponential search tree [12] and the bottom level are buckets of sub-logarithmic size. Our new randomized method results in the following complexities: $\Theta(\sqrt{\log d / \log \log d})$ w.h.p. for finger searching queries and $O(1)$ w.h.p. for updates.

In the following section we review the preliminary data structures. In section 3 we review in detail an extended outline of a new simpler than [12] method in case we have only insertions/deletions at the end. In section 4 we study the general case we have insertions/deletions anywhere constructing the randomized version of [12] achieving the same optimal time bounds with high probability. In section 5 we conclude.

2 Preliminary Data Structures

2.1 Precomputation Tables

Ajtai, Fredman and Komlos have shown in [4] that subsets of the integers $\{1,...,n\}$ of size polylogarithmic in n can be maintained in constant time so that predecessor queries (find the largest $i \in S$ such that $i \leq x$) can be performed in constant time. In fact, their result is in the cell-probe model of computation; however, on a logarithmic word size RAM their functions can be represented by tables that can be incrementally precomputed at a cost of $O(1)$ worst-case time and space per operation. The data structure occupies space that is linear in the size of the subset.

2.2 Fusion Tree

At STOC'90, Fredman and Willard [14] surpassed the comparison-based lower bounds for sorting and searching using the features in a standard imperative programming languages such as C. Their key result was an $O(\log n / \log \log n)$ time bound for deterministic searching in linear space. The time bounds for dynamic searching include both searching and updates. Since then, much effort has been spent on finding the inherent complexity of fundamental searching problems.

2.3 Amortized Exponential Search Tree

In 1996, Anderson [10] introduced *exponential search trees* as a general technique reducing the problem of searching a dynamic set in linear space to the problem of creating a search structure for a static set in polynomial time and space. The search time for the static set essentially becomes the amortized search time in the dynamic set. He got a static structure with $O(\sqrt{\log n})$ search time from Fredman and Willard [14], and thus he obtained an $O(\sqrt{\log n})$ time bound for dynamic searching in linear space. Obviously the cost for searching is worst-case while the cost for updates is amortized.

2.4 Beame-Fich (BF) Structure

In 1999 Beame and Fich [7] showed that $\Theta(\sqrt{\log n / \log \log n})$ is the exact worst-case complexity of searching a static set using polynomial space. Using the above mentioned *exponential search trees*, they obtained a fully dynamic deterministic search structure supporting search, insert, and delete in $\Theta(\sqrt{\log n / \log \log n})$ *amortized* time.

2.5 Worst – Case Exponential Search Tree

Finally, in 2000, Anderson and Thorup [12] developed a worst-case version of exponential search trees, giving an *optimal* $O(\sqrt{\log n / \log \log n})$ worst-case time bound for dynamic searching. They also extended the above result to the finger searching problem, achieving the same optimal time bound $O(\sqrt{\log d / \log \log d})$. The rebuilding operations are also very complicated and very difficult to be implemented in a standard imperative programming language such as C or C++.

2.6 BDT Structure

In a balanced distribution tree the degree of the nodes at level i is defined to be $d(i) = t(i)$, where $t(i)$ indicates the number of nodes present at level i. This is required to hold for $i \geq 1$, while $d(0) = 2$ and $t(0) = 1$. It is easy to see that we also have $t(i) = t(i-1)d(i-1)$, so putting together the various components, we can solve the recurrence and obtain for $i \geq 1$: $d(i) = 2^{2^{i-1}}, t(i) = 2^{2^{i-1}}$. One of the merits of this tree is that its height is $O(\log \log n)$, where n is the number of elements stored in it.

3 A Special Case of Finger Searching

We consider the case we have only insertions/deletions at the end of the set S, for example insert(y)/delete(y) with y >max{∀x∈ S} or y=max{∀x∈ S}, respectively. We build our structure by repeating the same kind of BDT tree-structure in each group of nodes having the same ancestor, and doing this recursively. This structure may be imposed through another set of pointers (it helps to think of these as different-color pointers). The innermost level of nesting will be characterized by having a tree-structure, in which no more than two nodes share the same direct ancestor. Figure 1 illustrates a simple example (for the sake of clarity we have omitted from the picture the links between nodes with the same ancestor).

Thus, multiple independent tree structures are imposed on the collection of nodes inserted. Each element inserted contains pointers to its representatives in each of the trees it belongs to.

We need now to determine what will be the maximum number of nesting trees that can occur for n elements. Observe that the maximum number of nodes with the same direct ancestor is $d(h-1)$. Would it be possible for a second level tree to have the same (or bigger) depth than the outermost one?

This would imply that

$$\sum_{j=0}^{h-1} t(j) < d(j) \qquad (1)$$

As otherwise we would be able to fit all the d(h-1) elements within the first h-1 levels. But we need to remember that d(i)=t(i), thus

$$d(h-1)+\sum_{j=0}^{h-1}d(j)<d(h-1) \qquad (2)$$

which would imply that the number of nodes in the first h-2 levels is negative, clearly impossible. Thus, the second level tree will have depth strictly lower than the depth of the outermost tree. As a consequence, k, which denotes the maximum number of nesting of trees that we can have, is itself O(loglogn).

At each node(leaf) of level i, say W_i, we attach a searching information array A[1..d(i)] (L[1..d(i)]), a BF(W_i) structure [7] which stores the elements of the respective array and at each leaf a number of k=O(loglogn) pointers to its respective copies at nested levels (see in Figure 1 the pointers from leaf f). Each element of S is stored at most in O(loglogn) levels, thus the space of our structure is non-linear, O(nloglogn) and the update (insertion/deletion) operation is performed in O(loglogn) worst-case time.

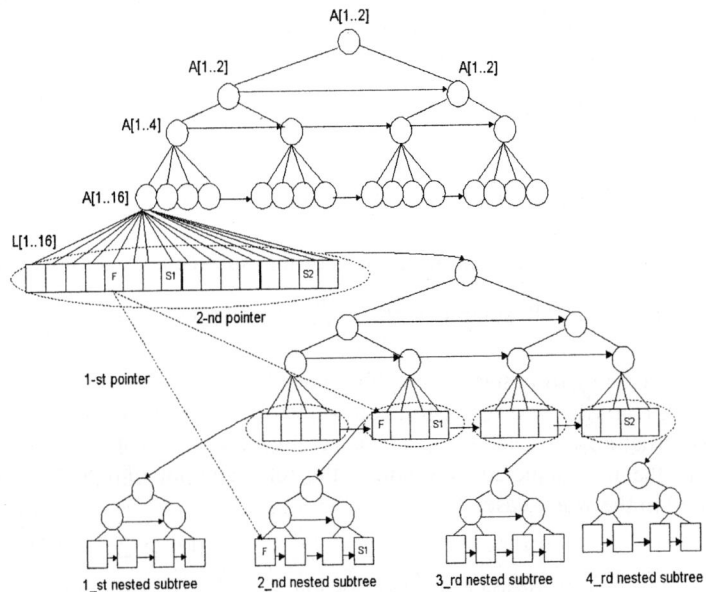

Fig. 1. Level-linked, leaf-oriented, nested BDT tree

In order to achieve linear space and O(1) worst-case update time we use the bucketing technique. The essence of the bucketing method is to get the best features of these two different structures by combining them into a two-level structure. The data to be stored is partitioned into buckets and the chosen data structure for the representation of each individual bucket is different from the representation of the top-level data structure, representing the collection of buckets (for similar applications of this data structuring paradigm see also [8], [9], [2]).

More specifically, we partition the elements of the set into contiguous buckets of size O(loglogn), with each bucket being represented by the linear list scheme and we store the first element of each bucket in the leaf-oriented nested balanced distributed tree scheme as the bucket representative. When an item is inserted it is appended to the tail of the list implementing the last incomplete bucket. If the size of this bucket becomes O(loglogn), then a new bucket is created containing only the inserted element, and we spend further O(loglogn) time, in order to insert this element into the top-level structure. We have a total of O(n/loglogn) representatives, each of which must be inserted at most in O(loglog(n/loglogn))=O(loglogn) nested levels. Furthermore, at each of these levels (leaf-levels) we must update the respective BF structures [7] in O(loglog(d(ni))) worst-case time respectively, where d(ni) the size of the respective array L, at the nith, $1 \leq ni \leq$ O(loglogn), level of nesting

More precisely the dynamic BF structure requires $O(\sqrt{\log n / \log\log n})$ amortized update time but this special semi-dynamic case of updating implies the following:

(i) If $n < 2^{(\log\log N)^2 /(\log\log\log N)}$ then the BF structure has only one part, the simple static data structure of Anderson [10]. In this case we must execute a number of **partial** rebuilding operations at the **right subtrees only** of the whole structure, ensuring always that these subtrees have size at least $\dfrac{n}{2\lceil n^{4/5}\rceil} \pm 1$ and at most $\dfrac{2n}{\lceil n^{4/5}\rceil} \pm 1$, as follows. When an update causes a right_subtree to violate this condition, we examine the sum of the sizes of that subtree and its immediate neighbor which is always a full subtree with $\dfrac{2n}{\lceil n^{4/5}\rceil} \pm 1$ elements, transferring the proper number of elements from the full neighbor node to the right-most one which we try to reconstruct. Until the next reconstruction we have all the time to spread incrementally the reconstruction cost, achieving O(1) worst-case time. Thus, for the O(loglogn) levels of the tree depicted in figure 1 the total amount of update time becomes O(loglogn) in the worst-case.

(ii) If $n \geq 2^{(\log\log N)^2 /(\log\log\log N)}$ $\Rightarrow \sqrt{\log n / \log\log n} \geq \log\log N /(\sqrt{2} \log\log\log N).$, the BF structure consists of two parts. The first part is a x-fast trie of Willard [13] with branching factor 2^k and depth u which organizes the top $1 + 2\lceil \log u \rceil$ levels for a set $s \leq n$ strings with length u, (u=2(loglogN)/(logloglogN)) $\Rightarrow \sqrt{n} \geq u^u \geq \log N.$) over the alphabet $[0, 2^k-1]$. According to [7] this reduces the predecessor and generally the dictionary problem in a set of size n from a universe of size N to the respective one in a set of size at most n from a universe of size 2^k, where $k = (\log N) / 2^{1+2\lceil \log u\rceil} \leq (\log N)/2u^2 < u^{u-2}, \lfloor 2(u-1)^2 - 1 \rfloor k < \log N \leq b$ and $b \geq \lfloor 2(u-1)^2 - 1 \rfloor k$ the number of bits we need to construct the appropriate hash functions of Lemma1 and Lemma2 of [7]. These hash functions build the second part of the whole structure that is used for each resulting subproblem. When an insertion/deletion at the end occurrs we insert/delete the appropriate hashed values in O(1) worst-case time. Hence, for the O(loglogn) levels of the tree depicted in figure 1 the total amount of update time becomes again O(loglogn) in the worst-case.

Due to the fact that $d(n_{i+1}) = \sqrt{d(n_i)}$ at level i, the total amount of update operations at the appropriate BF structures can be expressed as follows:

$$O(\log \log(d(n_1))) + O(\log \log(\sqrt{d(n_1)})) + O(\log \log(\sqrt{\sqrt{d(n_1)}})) + \cdots = O(\log \log n) \quad (3)$$

Spreading the total O(loglogn) insertion cost, over the O(loglogn) size of each bucket, we achieve an O(1) amortized insertion cost. With the same reasoning as above it is easy to prove that the total space is linear. We eliminate the amortization by spreading the time cost for the insertion of the representative over the next O(loglogn) bucket updates. Due to the fact that we have no a priori knowledge of n, we use the global rebuilding technique [3] in order to retain the buckets in within O(loglogn) size, where n the current number of elements.

The question is: does it have has any effect to the search(f,s) query the fact that the time, in which the query is done, the incremental process and consequently the insertion of the bucket's representative in all possible nested levels, has not finished yet?

In the following lemma we build the appropriate algorithm and we show that there is no possibility of such an effect.

Theorem 1. The search*(f,s) operation is correct and requires $O\left(\sqrt{\log d / \log \log d}\right)$ worst-case time

Proof: Let's give the new *search*(f,s)* algorithm.
r_f = representative of bucket in which finger f belongs to.
r_s = representative of bucket in which s belongs to.
r_n = representative of not full bucket
Search*(f,s)
1. Begin
2.   If f, s belong to same bucket (full or not) or s > r_n *then* access directly s
3.   else fsearch (r_f, r_s) /* this procedure is described next */
4. End

fsearch (f,s)
1. Begin
2.   W = Father(f)
3.   If s < A_w[right-most] then go to L_1 /* f,s have the same parent */
4.   Else Begin
5.   Repeat
6. W_1 = Father(W)
7.   If A_{w1}[right-most] < s < $A_{neighbourw1}$[right-most]
8.   /* f,s belong to neighbors nodes W_1 and neighbour_W_1 respectively */

9.   then fsearch(left_most_leaf($T_{neighbour\_w1}$), s)
10.   Until s < A_{w1}[right-most]
11.   go to L_2
12.   end
13. L_1: Begin
14.   j:= -1, f=L[i] /* Find the appropriate nested subtree such as
15.   Father(f) # Father(s) */
16.   Repeat
17.   j=j+1
18.   Until s ≤ A[⌊ i Div 2^{2^j} ⌋ 2^{2^j} + 2^{2^j}]
19.   access the (j+1)th copy of f (f_{j+1}) by Following the (j+1)th pointer from finger
20.   (leaf) f
21.   fsearch (f_{j+1}, s)
22. End
23. L_2: Begin
24.   j:=0
25.   Repeat
26.   j:=j+1
27.   search for s in BF(W_j) structure /* At each node of the W_1, W_2,.....W_k,s
            path search for s at BF(W_1),...,BF (W_k) structures respectively */
            Until s is found
28. end

(1) **Search*(f,s):** According to [4] the statement 2 requires O(1) worst-case time. In statement 3 we call the procedure fsearch(f,s) the complexity of which is analyzed as follows.

(2) **fsearch(f,s):** When f,s have the same parent (see f,s_1 in figure 1), statement 3, we must determine the appropriate nested-subtree of O(d) elements in which f,s do not belong to the same collection. So, in repeat-loop 14-16 we execute exponential steps in order to find an appropriate value j which defines the collection (of 2^{2^j} elements) in which the distance d(f,s) belongs to and consequently the appropriate (j+1)-th pointer from finger (leaf) f to its respective copy f_{j+1}. Then we call recursively the same routine (statement 18). It is obvious that the previous loop requires j=O(loglogd) steps due to the fact that the distance d between f and s is at least $d \geq 2^{2^j}$. From finger f we have a number of k = O(loglogn) pointers, so by organizing them in a structure of [4] we can access the (j+1)-th pointer in constant time. If f,s do not have the same parent we execute the repeat-loop of 5-9 statements that requires O(loglogd) steps in order to find the nearest common ancestor of f and s, W_1=nca(f,s). If f,s belong to neighbouring nodes W_1 and neighbour_W_1 respectively, (statement 7) we access the neighbour_W_1 node in O(1) time by following the neighbour pointer from W_1 to neighbour_W_1 and we call recursively the same search routine with new finger, the left-most leaf of the $T_{neighbour\_W1}$ subtree. Otherwise by executing the repeat-loop of 22-26 statements, we visit the appropriate search path W_1, W_2,..., W_r,s at each node of which we search for s at BF(W_i) structures, 1≤i≤r

and r=O(loglogd), in $O(\sqrt{\log d(w_i)/\log\log d(w_i)})$ worst-case time, where d(w_i) the degree of node w_i. This can be expressed by the following sum:

$$\sum_{i=1}^{r=O(\log\log d)} \sqrt{\frac{\log d(w_i)}{\log\log d(w_i)}} \quad (4)$$

Let L_1, L_r the levels of W_1 and W_r respectively. Thus, $d(w_1) = 2^{2^{L_l}}$ and $d(w_1) = 2^{2^{L_r}}$

However, d(w_r)=O(d), so L_r=O(loglogd). Now, the previous sum can be expressed as follows:

$$\sqrt{\frac{2^{L_1}}{L_1}} + \sqrt{\frac{2^{L_1+1}}{L_1+1}} + \ldots\ldots + \sqrt{\frac{\log d}{\log\log d}} = O\left(\sqrt{\frac{\log d}{\log\log d}}\right) \quad (5)$$

We denote that the recursive calls of statements 8, 18 are executed only once(it's obvious), consequently there is no reason to produce and solve the respective recurrence equation, hence, very simply the total time becomes $T = O(\sqrt{\log d / \log\log d})$.

4 A Randomized Algorithm with the Same Expected Time Bounds

Before we get into more detail on the data structures use, we quickly review the combinatorial pebble games [2] that lead to the development of the $O(1)$ update time data structure.

According to the definition in [2], *pebble games* are played between two players, namely player *I* (the increaser) and player *D* (the decreaser). Both players operate on an, initially empty, set of *n* piles of pebbles. The game is realized in rounds, each round consisting of a move from each player. Player I chooses a pile which he puts a pebble, while player D follows by choosing a pile from which to remove a pebble. A value M expresses the maximum value of some function on the number of pebbles at any point in the game. The objective of *I* is maximize M, whereas the objective of *D* to minimize it. Raman [2] states that typically, *I* is the environment and *D* the data structure.

A special category of pebble games is the so-called *Oblivious Pebble Games* [2]. In this type of game player *I* reveals his moves one at a time to *D*, but *D* keeps his moves secret possibly choosing randomization. In this case we are interested either in the expected value of M or the tails of M's distribution. Moreover, we typically restrict the rounds of the game, since the longer a game is played, the more likely it is that player *I* will come close to approaching his performance in the on-line version of the game (for more details you can also see [2]).

In the Oblivious On-line Discrete Zeroing Game [2] the D-strategy can lead w.h.p. to a value of M $\in$ O(cloglogn + clogc) for an integer c>1, where n denoted the number of moves. Algorithm 1 implements the D-strategy. There is a D-strategy that ensures with high probability (p> 1-n^{-a}, for any constant a > 0, for sufficiently large n) that over n moves, $M \in O(c\log\log n + c\log c)$, where c is an integer, c>1. This strategy is described from the following algorithm1:

Algorithm1: Let $c > 1$ be an integer and $\delta_1,....,\delta_n$ non-negative integers such that $\sum_{i=1}^{n}\delta_i = c$. Then player D, on his move, does the following:

1. Picks $i \in \{1,.....,n\}$ with probability δ_i / c and sets x_i to zero.
2. Picks i such that $x_i = \max_j\{x_j\}$ and that zeroes x_i.

For $c = O(\log\log n)$, $M \in O(\log^2\log n)$ with high probability. Based on D-strategy of Algorithm1 we describe our randomized algorithm2:

Algorithm2: Let n be the maximum number of keys present in the data structure at any previous time. We will show that making the buckets be of size $O(\log^2\log n)$ and using as top-level the Exponential search tree [11] with level links suffices for our purposes, yielding a simple algorithm.

We define the fullness $\Phi(b)$ of a bucket b as in [2]:

$\Phi(b) = |b| / \log^2\log n$. We will ensure that $0.5 \leq \Phi(b) \leq 2$. Also we define the criticality of a bucket b to be $\rho(b,n) = 1/\alpha \log\log n \, \max\{0, 0.7\log^2\log n - |b|, |b| - 1.8\log^2\log n\}$, for an appropriately chosen constant α. A bucket b is called critical if $\rho(b,n) > 0$. To maintain the size of the buckets, every $c = \alpha\log\log n$ updates, we do the following:

1. We check the ith bucket, $i \in \{1,.....,n/\log^2\log n\}$, with probability δ_i / c which means that we construct a randomized set of $c = O(\log\log(n/\log^2\log n)) = O(\log\log n)$ collections each of which has $O(n/\log^3\log n)$ buckets. we choose one of these collections randomly and then the bucket of the collection above where $\delta_i = \max_j\{\delta_j\}$ updates have been occurred. If this bucket has non-zero criticality apply the rebalancing transformations of step 3.
2. We check the most critical bucket and if it has non-zero criticality apply the following rebalancing transformations.
3. *Split*: if $\varphi(b) > 1.8$ split the bucket into two parts of approximately equal size.

   Transfer: If $\varphi(b) < 0.7$ and one of its adjacent buckets b' has $\Phi(b') \geq 1$ then transfer elements from b' to b.

   Fuse: If $\varphi(B) < 0.7$ and transferring is not possible, then fuse with an adjacent bucket b'.

It is clear that when a critical bucket is rebalanced, it becomes non-critical. In addition to the time required to split/fuse buckets, a bucket rebalancing step may require $O(\log\log n)$ worst-case time to insert/delete a bucket representative to/from the top-level tree. The top-level tree is the worst – case exponential search tree of Anderson and Thorup [12] that requires $O(\log\log n)$ worst - case update time as a result of an excellent combination of a variant of exponential search trees with eager partial rebuilding. Since the total work to rebalance a bucket is $O(\log\log n)$, we can perform it with $O(1)$ work per update spread over the next $\alpha\log\log n$ updates. In other words, if we can permit every bucket to be of size $\Theta(\log^2\log \hat{n})$, where $\hat{n}$ is the current number of elements, we can guarantee that between consecutive rebalancing operation at the top-level tree [7] there is no possibility for any other such operation to occur and consequently the incremental spread of work is possible. Let p be a finger. We search for a key k which is d keys away from p. If p,k belong to the same bucket of size $O(\log^2 \log n)$, we can access k directly according to [4]. Else we first check whether r_k (representative of bucket in which k belongs to) is to the left or right of r_p, (representative of bucket in which finger p belongs to) say r_k is to the right of r_p. Then we walk towards the root, say we reached node u. We check in $O(\sqrt{\log d / \log \log d})$ time according to [12] whether r_k is a descendant of u or u's right neighbor. If not, then we proceed to u's father. Otherwise, we turn around and search for k in the ordinary way.

Suppose that we turn around at node w on height h. Let v be the son of w that is on the path to the finger p. Then all descendants of v's right neighbor lie between the finger p and the key k. The subtree T_w is a Worst – case Exponential search tree for d elements with height, h=O(loglogd), so, according to [12], the time bound can be expressed as follows:

$$T(d) = O(\sqrt{\log d / \log \log d} + \sqrt{(\log d / \log \log d)^{4/5}} \qquad (6)$$
$$+ \sqrt{(\log d / \log \log d)^{16/25}} + ...) = O(\sqrt{\log d / \log \log d})$$

Thus, we have proved the following theorem:

Theorem 5: There is a randomized algorithm with O(1) update time and $O(\sqrt{\log d / \log \log d})$ for finger searching with high probability.

5 Conclusions

In this paper we presented an extended outline of a simpler than eager partial rebuilding method of finger searching for the case where we have only insertions/deletions at the end matching the worst-case upper bound $O(\sqrt{\log d / \log \log d})$ of [12]. Finally, based on Oblivious On-line Discrete Zeroing Game [2] of Raman we succeeded to limit the buckets in appropriate expected size and in combination with the worst-case Exponential search tree [12] as a top-level, we achieved $O(\sqrt{\log d / \log \log d})$ and O(1) with high probability for finger searching and update operations respectively.

References

1. Gerth Stølting Brodal, George Lagogiannis, Christos Makris, Athanasios K. Tsakalidis, Kostas Tsichlas: Optimal finger search trees in the pointer machine. JCSS. 67(2): 381-418 (2003)
2. R. Raman. Eliminating Amortization: On Data Structures with Guaranteed Response Time. PhD Thesis, University of Rochester, New York, 1992. Computer Science Dept. U. Rochester, Technical Report TR-439.

3. M. Overmars and Jan van Leeuwen, Worst case optimal insertion and deletion methods for decomposable searching problems, *Information Processing Letters*, 12:168-173, 1981.
4. M.Ajtai, M.Fredman, and J. Komlos. Hash functions for priority queues. Information and Control, 63:217-225, 1984
5. A.V.Aho, J.E.Hopcroft, and J.D.Ullman. The Design and Analysis of Computer Algorithms. Addison-Wesley, Reading, MA, 1974
6. D. Ranjan, E. Pontelli, G. Gupta and L. Longpre, The Temporal Precedence Problem, In *Algorithmica* 1999 (to appear).
7. P. Beame and F. Fich, *Optimal Bounds for the Predecessor Problem*, In Proceedings of the Thirty First Annual ACM Symposium on Theory of Computing, Atlanta, GA, May 1999.
8. M. Overmars, A O(1) average time update scheme for balanced binary search trees, *Bulletin of the EATCS*, 18:27-29, 1982.
9. A. Tsakalidis Maintaining order in a generalized linked list, *ACTA Informatica* 21 (1984)
10. A. Anderson. "Faster deterministic sorting and searching in linear space" 37th Annual IEEE Symposium on Foundations of Computer Science, 1996.
11. A. Anderson and M. Thorup. Exponential search trees for faster deterministic searching, sorting and priority queues in linear space. Manuscript.
12. A. Anderson and M. Thorup. Tight(er) Worst – Case Bounds on Dynamic Searching and Priority Queues, ACM STOC 2000.
13. D.E.Willard. Log_logarithmic worst-case range queries are possible in space $\Theta(n)$. *Information Processing Letters, 17:81-84, 1983.*
14. M.L. Fredman and D.E. Willard. Surpassing the information theoretic bound with fusion trees. Comput. Syst. Sci., 47:424-436, 1993. Announced at STOC '90.

How to Place Efficiently Guards and Paintings in an Art Gallery*

Christodoulos Fragoudakis[1], Euripides Markou[2], and Stathis Zachos[1,3]

[1] Computer Science, ECE, National Technical University of Athens
[2] Department of Informatics and Telecomunications, National University of Athens
[3] CIS Department, Brooklyn College, CUNY, USA
{cfrag, emarkou, zachos}@cs.ntua.gr

Abstract. In the art gallery problem the goal is to place guards (as few as possible) in a polygon so that a maximal area of the polygon is covered. We address here a closely related problem: how to place paintings and guards in an art gallery so that the total value of guarded paintings is a maximum. More formally, a simple polygon is given along with a set of paintings. Each painting, has a length and a value. We study how to place at the same time: i) a given number of guards on the boundary of the polygon and ii) paintings on the boundary of the polygon so that the total value of guarded paintings is maximum. We investigate this problem for a number of cases depending on: i) where the guards can be placed (vertices, edges), ii) whether the polygon has holes or not and iii) whether the goal is to oversee the placed paintings (every point of a painting is seen by at least one guard), or to watch the placed paintings (at least one point of a painting is seen by at least one guard). We prove that the problem is NP-hard in all the above cases and we present polynomial time approximation algorithms for all cases, achieving constant ratios.

1 Introduction

In the Art Gallery problem, a polygon is given and the goal is to place as few as possible guards in the polygon, so that a maximal area of the polygon is covered. This is a well known problem having the variation where a number of guards is given and the goal is to cover as many points in the polygon as possible. More variations arise when the polygon has holes and the points that must be covered lie in general on the boundary of the polygon and of its holes. On the other hand guards may be realized as vertices (vertex guards) or whole edges (edge guards) of the polygon ([2,4,5]).

We address here a closely related problem: how to place exhibits like paintings and guards in an art gallery so that the total value of guarded paintings is a maximum. More formally, a polygon is given along with a set of paintings. Each painting has a length and a value. We study how to place simultaneously a given

---

* Christodoulos Fragoudakis and Euripides Markou wish to acknowledge partial support by PYTHAGORAS, project 70/3/7392 under the EPEAEK program of the Greek Ministry of Educational and Religious Affairs.

number of guards and the paintings on the boundary of the polygon so that the total value of guarded paintings is maximum.

Some related problems that have been studied: MINIMUM VERTEX/EDGE POINT GUARD for polygons with (without) holes (known to be APX-hard and $O(\log n)$ approximable [1,6,7]), MINIMUM FIXED HEIGHT VERTEX POINT GUARD ON TERRAIN (best approximation possible $\theta(\log n)$ [6,7,8]), MAXIMUM WEIGHTED CLIQUE ON VISIBILITY GRAPH (known to be in P [11,12,13]), MINIMUM CLIQUE PARTITION ON VISIBILITY GRAPH for polygons without holes (known to be APX-hard and $O(\log n)$ approximable [6]). We prove that our problem is NP-hard and give polynomial time algorithms achieving a constant approximation ratio, based on a well known greedy algorithm which approximates the MAXIMUM COVERAGE problem ([9,10]).

The remainder of this paper is organized as follows: In section 2 we define the *Finest Visibility Segmentation (FVS)* of a polygon and settle that this construction is the finest relevant segmentation with respect to visibility: a *FVS* segment cannot be only partly visible from a vertex or an edge. In section 3 we define the MAXIMUM VALUE VERTEX GUARD WITH PAINTING PLACEMENT problem and prove that the problem is NP-hard. We present a polynomial time algorithm that achieves a constant approximation ratio and extend the result for edge guards and polygons with holes. Finally, in section 4 we present the conclusion.

2 Finest Visibility Segmentation

We start with some preliminary definitions (see figure 1). Let P be a polygon, $a, b \in P$ two points inside P and $L, M \subseteq P$ two sets of points inside P. We say that point a *sees* point b, i.e. a and b are mutually visible, if the straight line segment connecting a and b lies everywhere inside P. Notice that if point a sees point b then also point b sees point a. We say that the point set L is *visible* from the point set M or that M *oversees* L if for all points that belong to L, there exist a point that belongs to M, such that the points are mutually visible. Notice that if M oversees L, it is not necessary for L to oversee M. Finally, we say that M *watches* L if there exist a point that belongs to L and a point that belongs to M such that the points are mutually visible. Notice that if M watches L then also L watches M.

We are going to describe a method that descritizes the boundary as well as the interior of any polygon in terms of visibility. Assume any polygon P and the corresponding visibility graph $V_G(P)$: the visibility graph's vertex set is the vertex set of the polygon and two vertices share an edge in the visibility graph if and only if they are mutually visible in the polygon. By extending the edges of $V_G(P)$ inside P up to the boundary of P, see figure 2(a), we obtain a set of points *FVS* of the boundary of P, see figure 2(b), that includes of course all vertices of P. An extended edge of $V_G(P)$ generates at most two *FVS* points and there are $O(n^2)$ edges in $V_G(P)$, so there are $O(n^2)$ points in any polygon's *FVS* set. We call this construction the *Finest Visibility Segmentation* of the polygon P.

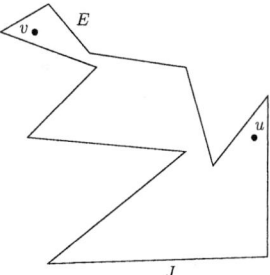

Fig. 1. Guards v and u are not mutually visible, guard v oversees edge E and guard u watches edge J

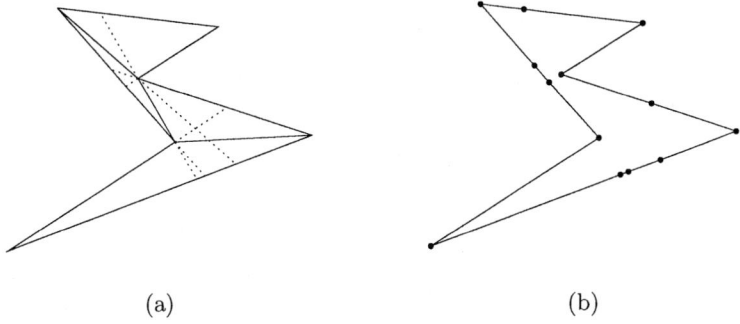

Fig. 2. Discretizing the boundary of a polygon

Any *open* segment (a,b), i.e. a and b are excluded, defined by consecutive *FVS* points, is called an *FVS* segment of P. The following two lemmas settle that a *FVS* segment cannot be **only partly** visible from a vertex or an edge.

Lemma 1. *For any vertex v of the polygon P, an* open *segment (a,b) defined by consecutive FVS points a, b, is visible by v if and only if it is watched by v.*

Proof. Of course if (a,b) is visible from v, then it is watched by v. Suppose now that (a,b) is watched by v but not overseen by v. Without loss of generality assume that v sees only (c,d) and cannot see any point between a and c, as well as, cannot see any point between d and b, see figure 3(a). So there must be an edge with endpoint vertex u that blocks v's visibility left of c and another vertex w that blocks v's visibility right of d that is $vu, vw \in V_G(P)$. The extensions of vu and vw meet the boundary at c, d respectively, hence $c, d \in FVS$. So a, b cannot be consecutive *FVS* points. □

Lemma 2. *For any edge e of the polygon P, an* open *segment (a,b) defined by consecutive FVS points a, b, is visible by e if and only if it is watched by e.*

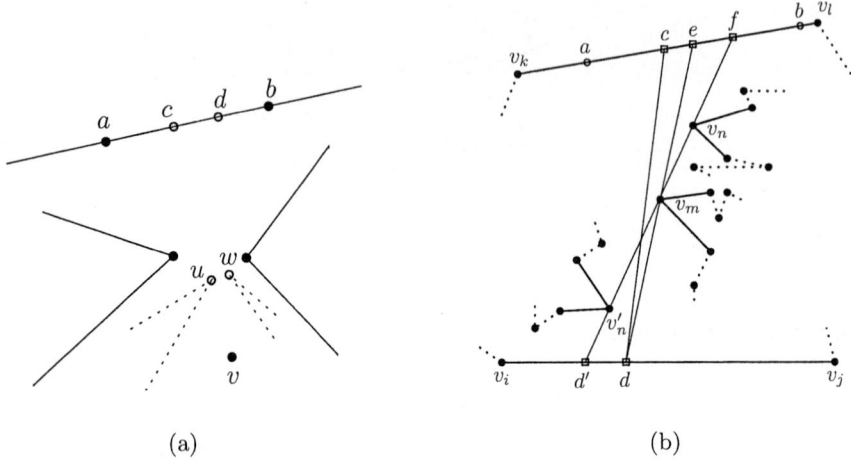

Fig. 3. Any vertex (edge) oversees a FVS segment if and only if watches the segment

Proof. Of course if (a, b) is visible from e, then it is watched by e. Suppose now that (a, b) is watched by $e = (v_i, v_j)$ but not overseen by e. The fact that e watches (a, b) implies that there exist a point $c \in (a, b)$ and a point $d \in e$ such that the line segment cd is everywhere inside the polygon, see figure 3(b). Start now an angular sweep of the line that passes through c and d, around d. If the sweep reaches b we have overseen all the cb segment, otherwise we stop at the vertex that belongs to the first edge that blocks d's visibility to (a, b) (vertex v_m in figure 3(b)). So point d oversees the ce segment and in order to see further towards b we have to consider points right of d. We start a new angular sweep of the line that passes through e and d, around v_m, that passes through different positions d' left of d. Consider the following cases:

- The sweep reaches b so we have overseen all of the cd segment.
- The sweep stops at the vertex that belongs to the first edge that blocks d''s visibility to (a, b) (vertex v_n or v'_n in figure 3(b)). This means that there is a line segment that starts from d' passes through the v_m and v_n (or v'_n) vertices and is everywhere inside P. The latter means that $v_m v_n \in V_G(P)$ and $v_m v_n$'s extension intersects P's boundary to f, hence f is a FVS point left of b, so a and b cannot be consecutive FVS points.
- The sweep reaches v_i but not b. This means that there is a line segment that starts from v_i passes through v_m, intersects (a, b) at f and is everywhere inside the polygon P. But the latter means that $v_i v_m$ is an edge of the visibility graph $V_G(P)$ and its extension intersects the boundary of P to point f, hence f is a FVS point left of b. So a and b cannot be consecutive FVS points.

Using the exact reasoning we can prove that e oversees also the ac segment. □

The above lemmas settle the following:

Theorem 1. *The boundary of any polygon P can be effectively descritized in terms of visibility to $O(n^2)$ FVS segments. Any vertex (edge) of P sees a FVS segment if and only if watches the FVS segment.*

In order to find the set of all overseen FVS segments from a polygon vertex v, namely the $FVS(v)$ set, (using lemma 1) it suffices to pick an arbitrary point p in every FVS segment. For every selection of p we have to check if vp is everywhere inside the polygon P. If this is the case, we augment the $FVS(v)$ set with the relative FVS segment. Notice that the segment inclusion in the polygon can be effectively checked in polynomial time by simple orientation tests, hence the construction of the $FVS(v)$ set costs polynomial time.

For the case of the $FVS(e)$ set, that is the set of all overseen FVS segments from a polygon edge e, (using lemma 2) it suffices to pick an arbitrary point p in every FVS segment and check if there exists a point $p' \in e$ such that pp' is everywhere inside P. This can be done by an angular sweep manner around p, stopping at the polygon vertices. If there exists a vertex v_i (possibly an endpoint of e) such that the extension of pv_i intersects e to p', we augment the $FVS(e)$ set with the relative FVS segment. Notice that again the construction of the $FVS(e)$ set costs polynomial time.

3 The MAXIMUM VALUE VERTEX GUARD WITH PAINTING PLACEMENT Problem

Given is a polygon P, a set of ordered pairs (x, y) and an integer $k > 0$. The boundary of the polygon models the walls of an art gallery while an ordered pair (x, y) represents a painting with length x and value y. The goal of the MAXIMUM VALUE VERTEX GUARD WITH PAINTING PLACEMENT problem is to place k vertex guards as well as place paintings on the boundary of P so that the total weight of the overseen paintings is maximum. Notice that in the given set of paintings $\{(x_1, y_1), \ldots, (x_i, y_i)\}$, there is an unlimited number of paintings of length x_1 and value y_1. Another restriction is that if there is an area on the boundary overseen by at least two guards, then all paintings that have their parts in this area should be overseen by the same guard. We call this problem MAXIMUM VALUE VERTEX GUARD WITH PAINTING PLACEMENT. In the following we prove that it is NP-hard to place guards on the vertices (at most k) and paintings from the given set with respect to the above restriction so that the total value of the overseen paintings is maximum.

Proposition 1. *Consider a polygon P along with a set of paintings (each painting has a length and a value assigned) and integers $k, V > 0$. It is NP-hard to decide whether we can place at most k guards on vertices of P and paintings on the walls of the gallery (boundary of P) so that the total value of overseen paintings is at least V.*

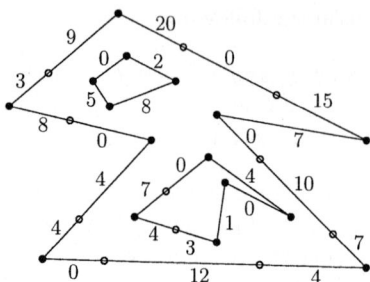

Fig. 4. A possible placement of paintings on the walls of the art gallery (zero value means that there is no painting placed)

Proof. The decision version of MINIMUM VERTEX GUARD for a polygon P reduces to the corresponding decision version of MAXIMUM VALUE VERTEX GUARD WITH PAINTING PLACEMENT. We construct an instance of the last problem as follows: We take the same polygon P. We construct the FVS, i.e. the finest line segment subdivision of the edges of P, and take a painting for each FVS segment with length the length of the segment and value also the length of the segment. Finally we take as V the total sum of values of the segments. Now the truth of the proposition is straightforward. □

Algorithm 1 is an approximation algorithm for the MAXIMUM VALUE VERTEX GUARD WITH PAINTING PLACEMENT problem. In algorithm 1 we use the MULTIPLE KNAPSACK problem. This problem is known to be NP-hard and there is a polynomial time 2-approximation algorithm for it ([3]). Actually in [14] they proved that there is a PTAS for the MULTIPLE KNAPSACK problem.

Algorithm 1 Maximum Value Vertex Guard With Painting Placement (greedy)

compute the FVS points
for all $v \in V(P)$ **do**
    compute $FVS(v)$
end for
$SOL \leftarrow \emptyset$
for $i = 1$ to k **do**
    select $v \in V$ that maximizes $W(\texttt{multknap}(FVS(v) \setminus SOL \cap FVS(v), D))$
    update SOL
end for
return $W(SOL)$

Algorithm 1 starts by calculating the FVS points and then for every $v \in V(P)$ the set $FVS(v)$. During each iteration of the algorithm, for any vertex v that hasn't been assigned a guard yet, the set $FVS(v) - SOL \cap FVS(v)$ (of the visible segments not previously overseen) is calculated. Then for every such set, the

MULTIPLE KNAPSACK problem is solved, taking as knapsacks the segments in the set (the capacity of a knapsack is the length of the corresponding segment). The solution of the MULTIPLE KNAPSACK problem results to a placement of paintings of a total maximum value in the knapsacks. The vertex that maximizes the total value of the fitted paintings is then chosen, causing an overall increase of $1 - \epsilon$ of the maximum possible increase of the solution, due to the PTAS of the MULTIPLE KNAPSACK problem. Then the algorithm updates the set SOL by adding the new FVS segments along with the fitted paintings.

In order to prove that algorithm 1 approximates MAXIMUM VALUE VERTEX GUARD WITH PAINTING PLACEMENT by a constant approximation factor, let OPT denote the collection of the set of paintings in an optimal solution and SOL denote the collection returned by the algorithm. These collections have $W(OPT)$ and $W(SOL)$ values respectively. Suppose that the algorithm places a guard at vertex v_i at iteration i, and a set of new paintings P_i. Therefore the added total value of paintings at iteration i is $W(P_i)$.

In the ordered sequence of vertices (as they have been selected by the algorithm), consider the first vertex v_l selected by the algorithm but not by the optimal solution for placing a guard. In other words, let v_l be the first vertex in the ordered sequence where there is a guard placed by the algorithm but there is no guard in the optimal solution. It holds:

$$W(P_i) = W(\cup_{m=1}^{i} P_m) - W(\cup_{m=1}^{i-1} P_m)$$

The PTAS for the MULTIPLE KNAPSACK problem implies:

$$W(P_i) \geq \alpha W(P_i'), \alpha > 0$$

where $W(P_i')$ is the new total value overseen by a guard placed on v_i in the optimal solution. We settle the following lemmas:

Lemma 3. *After l iterations of algorithm 1 the following holds:*

$$W(\cup_{i=1}^{l} P_i) - W(\cup_{i=1}^{l-1} P_i) \geq \frac{\alpha}{k}(W(OPT) - W(\cup_{i=1}^{l-1} P_i)), \quad l = 1, 2, ..., k$$

Proof. Consider vertices where guards have been placed in the optimal solution but no guard has been placed there by the algorithm. By the pigeonhole principle, there is at least one such vertex v_m so that the following holds:

$$W(P_m') \geq \frac{W(OPT) - W(\cup_{i=1}^{l-1} P_i')}{k}$$

since $W(P_i) \geq \alpha W(P_i')$, it holds:

$$W(P_m') \geq \frac{W(OPT) - W(\cup_{i=1}^{l-1} P_i)}{\alpha k}$$

Notice that

$$W(P_l) \geq W(P_m) \geq \alpha W(P_m')$$

and

$$W(\cup_{i=1}^{l} P_i) - W(\cup_{i=1}^{l-1} P_i) = W(P_l) \geq \alpha W(P_l')$$

Therefore:
$$W(\cup_{i=1}^{l} P_i) - W(\cup_{i=1}^{l-1} P_i) \geq \frac{\alpha}{k}(W(OPT) - W(\cup_{i=1}^{l-1} P_i))$$

□

Lemma 4. *After l iterations of algorithm 1 it holds:*
$$W(\cup_{i=1}^{l} P_i) \geq (1 - (1 - \frac{\alpha}{k})^l) W(OPT), \quad l = 1, ..., k$$

Proof. We are going to prove this by induction on l During the first step the algorithm chooses the set with value $W(P_1)$. It holds:
$$W(P_1) \geq \alpha W(P_1')$$

$W(P_1')$ is the biggest possible value that OPT achieves, so from the pigeonhole principle:
$$W(P_1') \geq \frac{W(OPT)}{k} \to W(P_1) \geq \frac{\alpha}{k} W(OPT)$$

Assume that the given holds for $i = l - 1$:
$$W(\cup_{i=1}^{l-1} P_i) \geq (1 - (1 - \frac{\alpha}{k})^{l-1}) W(OPT)$$

So:
$$W(\cup_{i=1}^{l} P_i) = W(\cup_{i=1}^{l-1} P_i) + (W(\cup_{i=1}^{l} P_i) - W(\cup_{i=1}^{l-1} P_i))$$

Using lemma 3:
$$W(\cup_{i=1}^{l} P_i) \geq W(\cup_{i=1}^{l-1} P_i) + \frac{\alpha}{k}(W(OPT) - W(\cup_{i=1}^{l-1} P_i)) \to$$

$$W(\cup_{i=1}^{l} P_i) \geq W(\cup_{i=1}^{l-1} P_i)(1 - \frac{\alpha}{k}) + \frac{\alpha}{k} W(OPT)$$

From the inductive hypothesis:
$$W(\cup_{i=1}^{l} P_i) \geq (1 - (1 - \frac{\alpha}{k})^{l-1}) W(OPT)(1 - \frac{\alpha}{k}) + \frac{\alpha}{k} W(OPT) \to$$

$$W(\cup_{i=1}^{l} P_i) \geq (1 - (1 - \frac{\alpha}{k})^l) W(OPT)$$

□

Theorem 2. *Algorithm 1 runs in polynomial time and achieves an approximation of $\frac{1}{1 - \frac{1}{e^\alpha}}$ with respect to the optimum of the MAXIMUM VALUE VERTEX GUARD WITH PAINTING PLACEMENT problem, where $\frac{1}{\alpha}$ is the approximation ratio of MULTIPLE KNAPSACK.*

Proof. Using lemma 4, we set $l = k$ and get:

$$W(\cup_{i=1}^{k} P_i) \geq (1 - (1 - \frac{\alpha}{k})^k)W(OPT)$$

It holds:

$$\lim_{k \to \infty} (1 - (1 - \frac{\alpha}{k})^k) = 1 - \frac{1}{e^\alpha}$$

As $(1 - (1 - \frac{\alpha}{k})^k)$ continuously gets smaller, we have:

$$1 - (1 - \frac{\alpha}{k})^k \geq 1 - \frac{1}{e^\alpha}$$

So:

$$W(SOL) > (1 - \frac{1}{e^\alpha})W(OPT)$$

That is the algorithm approximates the MAXIMUM VALUE VERTEX GUARD WITH PAINTING PLACEMENT problem with a $\frac{1}{1-\frac{1}{e^\alpha}}$ ratio. Due to the existence of the PTAS for the MULTIPLE KNAPSACK problem, $\alpha \to 1$ so $\frac{1}{1-\frac{1}{e^\alpha}} \to 1.58$. □

Similar to proposition 1, for the case of edge guards, it holds:

Proposition 2. *The* MAXIMUM VALUE EDGE GUARD WITH PAINTING PLACEMENT *problem is NP-hard.*

Algorithm 2 approximates MAXIMUM VALUE EDGE GUARD WITH PAINTING PLACEMENT. The only difference from algorithm 1 is that we need to calculate the $FVS(e)$ set using the techniques described in section 2.

Algorithm 2 Maximum Value Edge Guard With Painting Placement (greedy)

compute the FVS points
for all $e \in E(P)$ do
    compute $FVS(e)$
end for
$SOL \leftarrow \emptyset$
for $i = 1$ to k do
    select $e \in E$ that maximizes $W(\texttt{multknap}(FVS(e) \setminus SOL \cap FVS(e), D))$
    update SOL
end for
return $W(SOL)$

Similar to theorem 2 it holds:

Theorem 3. *Algorithm 2 runs in polynomial time and achieves an approximation of* 1.58 *for the* MAXIMUM VALUE EDGE GUARD WITH PAINTING PLACEMENT *problem.*

Similar results apply also for the case of polygons with holes. Algorithms 1 and 2 can be applied to polygons with holes, achieving the same approximation.

4 Conclusion

We investigated the MAXIMUM VALUE VERTEX GUARD WITH PAINTING PLACEMENT problem: we proved NP-hardness and presented a polynomial time algorithm that achieves a constant approximation ratio. The algorithm applies for a number of cases (edge guards, polygons with holes) and achieves the same approximation. While investigating the above problem we used a way to discretize the boundary of the polygon by subdividing it into $O(n^2)$ pieces of the *Finest Visibility Segmentation* which is the finest relevant segmentation with respect to visibility: a *FVS* segment cannot be only partly visible from a vertex or an edge.

References

1. Lee, D., Lin, A., Computational complexity of art gallery problems, IEEE Trans. Inform. Theory 32, 276-282, 1986.
2. O'Rourke, J., Art Gallery Theorems and Algorithms, Oxford University Press, New York, 1987.
3. Shmoys, D., Tardos, E., An approximation algorithm for the generalized assignment problem, Mathematical Programming A, 62:461-74, 1993.
4. Shermer, T., Recent results in Art Galleries, Proc. of the IEEE, 1992.
5. Urrutia, J., Art gallery and Illumination Problems, Handbook on Computational Geometry, 1998.
6. Eidenbenz, S., (In-)Approximability of Visibility Problems on Polygons and Terrains, PhD Thesis, ETH Zurich, 2000.
7. Eidenbenz, S., Inapproximability Results for Guarding Polygons without Holes, Lecture notes in Computer Science, Vol. 1533 (ISAAC'98), p. 427-436, 1998.
8. Ghosh, S., Approximation algorithms for Art Gallery Problems, Proc. of the Canadian Information Processing Society Congress, pp. 429-434, 1987.
9. Hochbaum, D., Approximation Algorithms for NP-Hard Problems, PWS Publishing Company, 1996.
10. Hochbaum, D., Approximating Covering and Packing Problems in: Approximation Algorithms for NP-Hard Problems (ed. Dorit Hochbaum), pp. 94-143, PWS Publishing Company, 1996.
11. Avis, D., Rappaport, D., Computing the largest empty convex subset of a set of points, Proc. 1st Ann. ACM Symposium Computational Geometry, pp. 161-167, 1985.
12. Dobkin, D., Edelsbrunner, H., Overmars, H., Searching for Empty Convex Polygons, Algorithmica 5, pp. 561-571, 1990.
13. Edelsbrunner, H., Guibas, L., Topologically sweeping an arrangement, J. Comput. System Sci. 38, pp. 165-194, 1989.
14. Chekuri, C., Khanna, S., A PTAS for the Multiple Knapsack problem, Proc. 11th ACM Symp on Discrete Algorithms, 213-222, 2000.

Virtual Reality Systems and Applications: The Ancient Olympic Games

A. Gaitatzes, D. Christopoulos, and G. Papaioannou

Foundation of the Hellenic World, 38 Poulopoulou St.,
11851 Athens, Greece
{gaitat, christop, gepap}@fhw.gr

Abstract. This paper presents the virtual reality systems, interaction devices and software used at the Foundation of the Hellenic World (FHW). The applications that FHW has produced, associated with the Olympic Games in ancient Greece, are then detailed. The separate virtual reality shows are presented in terms of interactivity and educational value. Technical aspects of the productions are explained, with an emphasis on surround screen projection environments. These techniques were mostly utilized in the recent production regarding the ancient Olympic Games, where much effort has been made to recreate the feeling of the games and help the user/spectator be an interacting part of the edutainment activity.

1 Introduction

The undertaking of the 28th Summer Olympiad by Athens, the capital city of Greece, has spurred an increased interest for shows and complementary edutainment contributions to the games themselves. The Foundation of the Hellenic World (FHW) has prepared a series of thematic productions related to ancient Olympia and the Olympic Games, culminating with the highly interactive and accurate representation of ancient Olympia and the pentathlon (running, long jump, javelin, discus throwing and wrestling), whose final version was released just before the beginning of the Olympic Games. The high demand for interactive and entertaining productions, apart from simple walkthrough applications, however eye-catching, has driven us to pursue an interaction model different from the classic navigator/inspector one. The virtual reality (VR) productions should be educational through creativity and active participation in events [9]. Our audience has confirmed their preference toward more "playable" environments where experimentation and first-hand experience is the most important channel leading to knowledge.

In the rest of the paper, section 2 provides the linking background and a brief insight to each one of the thematic applications, while section 3 explains the key points of the scientific and technological features related to the interactive shows and our effort to implement these in a surround screen projection environment.

2 The Productions

In 2000, as the Olympic Games were returning to their birthplace, we decided to focus the new projects on the thematic region of the Olympic History and Games for the virtual reality productions that would open in the time period before the Olympic Games in Athens. Instead of focusing on only one production, where every concept and aspect of this glorious event would be explained and presented, several productions were created, each one complementary to the previous and finally concluding in a full-scale interactive representation of ancient Olympia and its Games.

2.1 Olympic Pottery Puzzle

The study of ancient pottery has been a very important source of historical and archaeological information for understanding the life and culture in ancient Greece. Apart from the functional significance of the various types of pots, which give us clues about rituals and everyday life, the ink-paintings that cover many pot shards found at excavation sites, are priceless since they allow us to have an inside look into history. The goal of the Olympic pottery puzzle application was to educate the visitors about all this information, emphasizing on Olympic Athletic events in an entertaining and understandable way, using the constructivist's approach [13] (Fig. 1).

The user must re-assemble a number of ancient vases putting together pot shards. The users are presented with a color-coded skeleton of the vessels with the different colors showing the correct position of the pieces. They then try to select one piece at a time from a heap and place it in the correct position on the vase. When they finish the puzzle, the painting on the vase comes to life, presenting an animation of one of the ancient Olympic contests. From a technical perspective, much effort was directed towards the realistic, highly detailed representation of vases and the simulation of their material properties like specularity and glossiness, using multi-pass rendering techniques.

This VR exhibit captivates the visitors, giving them the opportunity to interact with the vases intuitively. Completing the 3D assemblage puzzle with the help of VR equipment helps them learn some important historical facts about the vases and the Olympic contests, as well as have a glimpse of the restoration procedure of earthenware. The reanimation of the depicted athletes was made in 2D (planar video over-

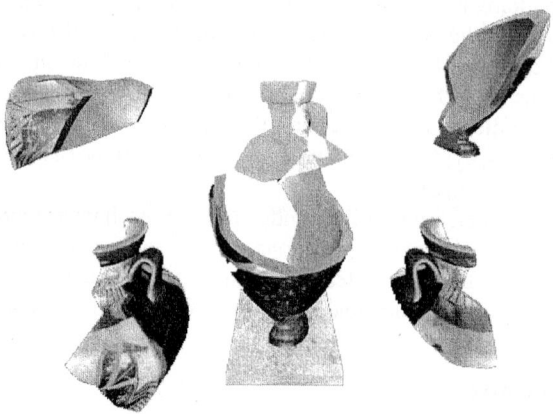

Fig. 1. The Olympic pottery puzzle

lays), preserving the colors and character of the ancient Greek ink paintings. This, in turn, helped the visitors perceive the Olympic contests and any information regarding the Olympic Games in antiquity from the perspective of an ancient Greek artist, something the public responded enthusiastically to. The "Olympic Pottery Puzzle" is suitable for presentation in both single-screen and surround screen projection systems.

2.2 Feidias' Workshop

After the successful launch of the first interactive application regarding the Olympics, it was important to build on the positive feedback and winning concepts and create an experience, which would bring the visitor one step closer to Olympia. In this VR exhibit, visitors engage themselves in another marvel of ancient Greek art, the creation of *golden ivory statues*. Golden ivory statues are regarded as the masterpieces of Greek sculpture, and were admired as such even at the time of their creation. Only statues of Gods and heroes were made using this technique.

"Feidias' Workshop" (Fig. 2) is a highly interactive virtual experience that takes place at the construction site of the 15-meter-tall golden ivory statue of Zeus. The visitors enter the two-story-high workshop and come in sight of an accurate reconstruction of an unfinished version of the famous statue of Zeus and walk among the sculptor's tools, scaffolding, benches, materials, and moulds used to construct it. The visitors take the role of the sculptor's assistants and actively help finish the creation of the huge statue, by using virtual tools to apply the necessary materials onto the statue, process the ivory and gold plates, apply them onto the wooden supporting core and add the finishing touches. Interaction is achieved using the navigation wand of the VR system [9], onto which the various virtual tools are attached. Using these tools the user helps finish the work on the statue, learning about the procedures, materials and techniques applied to the creation of these marvelous statues. The various workers and Feidias himself are displayed using *image-based rendering* techniques in the form

Fig. 2. A creative approach to interactive edutainment

of animated impostors [11]. This technique was chosen because of its low polygon count since the detail of the other models in the scene was high. In order to provide additional depth cues for the interaction and better image realism, pre-computed illumination was also applied using lightmaps.

This VR production presents an accurate reconstruction of a populated and active workshop, with interactive and educational value. The "learning by doing" concept worked well and increased the visitors' interest and active participation in the VR show. The use of the CAVE-like environment helps support the large scale and proportions of the workshop and the statue of Zeus. The positive feedback we got from the incorporation of characters, led us to the conclusion that the public was especially interested in the way of life and working habits of people in ancient Greece. The use of animated representation of characters helped the audience understand, participate and immerse themselves into the experience, giving them a reference point of interest.

2.3 A Walk-Through Ancient Olympia

In our most recent VR production "A Walk through Ancient Olympia", the user visiting the virtual historical site, learns about the ancient games themselves by interacting with athletes in the ancient game of pentathlon (Fig. 3).

We are at the end of the 2nd century BC. The day breaks and in front of us appears the majestic sanctuary of Zeus in ancient Olympia. In antiquity the Olympic Games took place here, while today it hosts the lighting of the Olympic flame. The visitors can wonder around and visit the buildings and learn their history and their function.

In addition, the public can interact virtually with 3D digital representations of Olympian athletes in the ancient pentathlon, including the 200-meter sprint, the discus throwing, the long jump, the javelin throwing and wrestling. Instead of just observing the games the visitors take part in them. They pick up the discus or the javelin and they try their abilities in throwing them towards the far end of the stadium. A role-playing model of interaction with alternating roles was tried here with pretty good success as the visitors truly immersed in the environment wish they could participate in more games.

Finally, decorated with red ribbons in his hands and legs, the glorious winner makes the tour of triumph holding a palm leaf in his hand while the spectators give him a standing ovation. The Games come to an end.

3 Production Technology

From a technical point of view, the productions of FHW are presented on two VR systems, both using projective viewing technology [8]. The larger system is a CAVE-like ReaCTor™ immersive display [5], consisting of four 3m × 3m projection screens. An 8-processor SGI® Onyx2™ drives the four projectors through four InfiniteReality2™ graphics subsystems, in active stereo. A maximum number of 10 visitors and a museum educator enter the immersive cube, all wearing stereo shutter glasses and the show is controlled by the guide via a six degrees-of-freedom tracked joystick. The museum educator also wares a hat with an attached six degrees-of-freedom sensor for the head position and orientation tracking, which affects the perspective projection on each wall.

Fig. 3. Screenshots and live capture from the production "A Walk through Ancient Olympia"

The smaller VR system consists of an ImmersaDesk™ R2 rear projection tilted screen driven in active stereo by an SGI® Octane2™. Six degrees-of-freedom head and hand tracking are provided via a head-mounted tracker and a tracked joystick. This system, having a lesser immersive effect and also a much slower computing system, is used mostly for lightweight applications. The large interactive VR shows are run in the surround-screen projection environment.

In terms of software technology, we have built our own game engine, Enhanced Visualization System (EVS) [11], [12], [8], using C++, based on OpenGL Performer™ [15] and OpenGL® for the graphics, on the CAVElib and VRPN [16] libraries for transparent access to the virtual reality hardware and stereoscopic rendering and a customary developed sound library for playing audio.

The system is divided into two major components: the scripting language, which describes the scene as a collection of nodes and their connection via events and messages and the low level core C++ classes that implement the features and interpret the scripting language commands. Thus the authors have to mostly create scene files (ascii text), where a description of the world using the scripting language is stored. The framework includes many of the features common to virtual environments and allows engineers to reuse tools and code between various applications and at the same time incorporate new features. Artists can participate more actively or even develop entire applications on their own, adjusting the final virtual environment to their needs. The framework allows for multithreaded execution, which is essential for interaction in a

Fig. 4. Character animation using bones and soft skinning

multiprocessor system such as the ones used normally in VR where each projection surface has its own Graphics/Raster engine.

For navigation and interaction a wide range of devices are supported. The VRPN [16] integration into EVS enables the usage of low-cost devices such as mice and joysticks and the usage of high-end tracker solutions such as the Intersence IS-900 using a common interface.

As natural interaction requires the presence of familiar and realistic representations not just of visual aspects of the virtual world, but also of actions and procedures, important techniques and features such as character animation and dynamics have been incorporated into the VR engine and are discussed below.

3.1 Character Animation

Real-time character animation in simulated virtual environments has progressed rapidly over the last years. This development has also been reflected by the changes of the visual style in virtual environment applications. When the experience is to be enriched with interaction in active environments where people should explore and participate in close interaction with virtual people, the use of 3D animated characters, with recognizable and natural features, gestures and fluid motion, is essential.

The animation technique, which has established itself as the defacto way in bringing articulated models to life in real-time 3D environments, is *skeletal animation* combined with *soft skinning*.

Skeletal animation uses an endoskeleton, a hierarchic structure of *joints* and *bones*, which drives a *skin*, a vertex mesh representing the outer shell of the object (Fig. 4). All the bones of the articulated object form together the skeleton. Only the skeleton is explicitly animated, which in turn implicitly animates the skin and its vertices. Using soft skinning, each vertex of the mesh can be influenced by more than one bones [18], effectively mimicking the way a bone in a real body would affect the skin of a living being. Memory usage for skeletal animation is small and requires a significantly lower amount of information to be stored when compared to other techniques. Animation data can also be generated on the fly using techniques like *inverse kinematics* [17], and applied to the model in real-time.

For our recent VR production "A Walk through Ancient Olympia" the skeletal animation technique was implemented for animating the various characters and athletes (Fig. 4). Using the *Cal3D* animation framework library [1], specialized EVS rendering and simulation nodes were created which allowed us to incorporate skeletal animations from commercial modeling and animation software into our framework. Besides the playback of animations, the ability to blend and mix multiple animations was implemented for advanced animation control, generating smooth transitions between the animations and dispensing with extra transition animation cues.

Due to the fact that models also have to interact with the environment by picking and dropping other objects, a mechanism for attachment and detachment of other scene objects on the characters was implemented.

3.2 Newtonian Dynamics

One of the challenges in the "Walk through Ancient Olympia" was to be able to actively participate in at least one of the games (Fig. 3). Considering the difficulty to move in a CAVE when surrounded by spectators, we decided to implement such interaction for the discus and javelin throwing games, which are relatively static. Both games required that the user take hold of an object and send it flying through the scene under the influence of forces in a controllable manner. The object would collide, bounce off and exchange energy with other geometry. For this purpose we used Newtonian dynamics, a well-known and extensively studied motion model for rigid bodies and their response to collisions [3], [6].

3.3 Occlusion Culling for Open Environments

As graphics cards have a limit to the fill rate and triangle count the application can pump into them, culling – or non-visible geometry elimination - is used extensively in large 3D worlds in order to minimize the geometry sent for rendering in the graphics card. In occlusion culling [2], geometry that is hidden behind objects closer to the camera point, is discarded before being subject to depth sorting algorithms. Shadow culling [10], uses predefined occlusion proxies (occluders), which consist of simplified (and usually convex) polygonal versions of actual rendered geometry, such as rectangular barriers, in order to efficiently block geometry hidden behind them. Shadow culling is best suited for our outdoor sparse environments as compared to other techniques, most of which are targeted for dense or indoor scenes.

In each frame, a semi-infinite convex frustum is created for each (convex) occluder polygon, the cap of the semi-infinite frustum being the occluder polygon itself and the sides connecting the each edge with the viewpoint (Fig. 5). The bounding boxes of the geometry to be rendered are compared for containment with these frusta. If a bounding box resides completely within all frusta, then the object it contains is hidden. This process is performed in a hierarchical manner, discarding whole sub-trees of a 3D scene graph prior to forwarding the geometry to the rendering engine. Careful construction and placement of the occluders [7], results in high hidden geometry elimination and a considerable speedup.

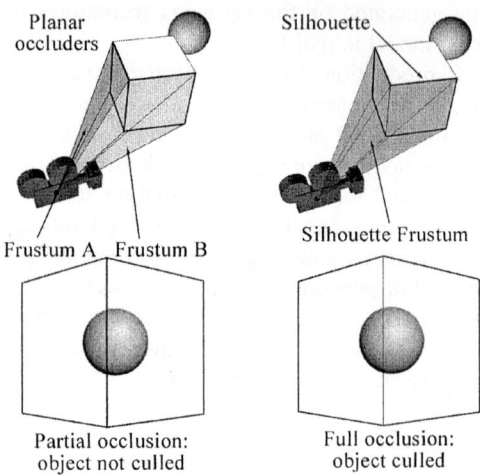

Fig. 5. Comparison between polygonal and solid occluders in shadow culling

3.3.1 Solid Occluders

In the case of outdoor scenes, like Olympia, where the static geometry is often blocky (buildings) but scattered and sparse, simple occlusion culling is not very effective due to the partial occlusion phenomenon (Fig. 5): Two or more adjoining planar occluders may partially hide a distant object but the combined occlusion area of them may hide it completely. This object cannot be eliminated if the frustum for each occluder is created separately, and the joining of frusta is an expensive operation.

To overcome this taxing limitation, we decided to use convex solid occluders [7], such as boxes and cylinders as proxies for large isolated structures (Fig. 5). A convex solid when projected on a plane is guaranteed to produce a convex polygon. The convex frustum of the projected polygon is the union of the frusta that would be generated from the individual planes of the solid occluder, thus bypassing the need to merge frusta in order to avoid partial occlusion.

For each frame, the solid occluder frustum is generated as follows. The view dependent silhouette of the solid occluder is extracted by connecting the edges belonging to adjacent polygons, which are not both visible or hidden simultaneously:

$$edge(tr_i, tr_j) \in Silhouette \Leftrightarrow$$
$$\left[\vec{N}_i \cdot (\bar{P}_{i0} - \bar{C})\right] \cdot \left[\vec{N}_j \cdot (\bar{P}_{j0} - \bar{C})\right] \leq 0 \quad (1)$$

where $\vec{N}_k$ is the normal vector of triangle tr_k, $\bar{P}_{k0}$ the triangle's first point and $\bar{C}$ the viewpoint.

The Silhouette edges do not lie on the same plane in general. Therefore, we must select a cap (near plane) for the semi-infinite frustum, based on the relative position of the viewer and the silhouette points. We chose to fix the near plane of the frustum to the furthest point of the silhouette from the viewer in order to avoid false positive culling results. This clipping plane's normal vector is the average directional vector between the viewpoint and the silhouette points $\bar{S}_i$:

$$\vec{N}_{near} = \sum_{i=0}^{K-1}(\bar{S}_i - \bar{C}) \bigg/ \left\|\sum_{i=0}^{K-1}(\bar{S}_i - \bar{C})\right\| \qquad (2)$$

3.3.2 Occluder Selection

As Hudson et al. [10] suggest, a scene may contain too many occluders for the engine to be able to test each object against each one of them. In our case, Olympia contains more than 200 occluder planes and solids. Therefore, an optimal set of occluders has to be selected for each frame at run-time in order to keep the number of "active" occluder primitives to a minimum. For this task, a "score" or optimization function f_{planar} has to be devised that takes into account the solid angle of the frustum. Hudson et al. use the area-angle approximation presented by Coorg and Teller [4]:

$$f_{planar} = \frac{-A\vec{N} \cdot \vec{V}}{\|\vec{V}\|^2} \qquad (3)$$

where A is the area of a planar occluder, $\vec{N}$ is its normal vector and $\vec{V}$ is the vector from the viewpoint to the centre of the occluder. We use the criterion in eq. (3) for planar occluders. For solid occluders we use an approximation formula that depends on the projection of the viewplane of the solid occluder's volume Vol and the squared distance of the occluder from the viewpoint:

$$f_{solid} = \frac{Vol}{\|\vec{V}\|} \cdot \|\vec{V}\|^{-2} = \frac{Vol}{\|\vec{V}\|^3} \qquad (4)$$

Keep in mind that the optimisation function for the solid occluders does not depend on angular attributes as the near plane of the constructed frustum always faces the centre of projection (eq. (2)). f_{planar} and f_{solid} are balanced and do not need further biasing to become compatible.

The effectiveness of the solid occluders becomes apparent when moving among the buildings, especially at ground level and at inspection distance (near). Planar occluders would mostly produce partial occlusion when not facing the main sides of the buildings straight on. Most of the time we view the blocky buildings from odd angles and that is where the solid occluders provide a unified contiguous frustum to take into account all sides at once.

3.4 Skylight Illumination Model

Most realistic rendering in VR has dealt with indoor scenes or has focused on objects and buildings. However, outdoor scenes differ from indoor ones in two important aspects, other than geometry: most of their illumination comes directly from the sun and sky; and the distances involved make the effects of air "aerial perspective" visible. A *Skylight Illumination Model*, once incorporated into the framework, captures and simulates the visual aspects and results of these phenomena. It changes sunlight position and colour from the pale red of dawn to the bright yellow of midday and back again. It determines the colour and brightness of the sky throughout the day and it cues us to the distance of objects by shifting their colours. All these effects vary not only based on time of day, but also depending on weather, pollution and other factors.

Traditionally, outdoor VR applications would model these phenomena using Skydomes or Skyboxes, texture-mapped with static high-resolution sky and cloud renderings. In our latest outdoor simulation of ancient Olympia, a sky simulation from sunrise to sunset and nightfall was needed. Therefore, the implementation of a Skylight model was necessary.

The analytic model of Preetham et al [14] was implemented with some modifications regarding the color conversion algorithm to produce more dramatic sunsets/sunrises and the incorporation of a nightfall simulation with rendering of stars and moon (Fig. 3).

An EVS node was created which constructs the dome geometry takes as input the sun position and weather conditions and finally, draws the dome, computing the colours for every vertex with analytic formulas. The colour and intensity of the sun is also computed and all underlying geometry is lit by its computed light attributes. Indirect skylight illumination, caused by the atmospheric scattering of light, is simulated by additional light sources placed in the perimeter of the scene. These light sources are linked to the simulation and their intensity and color is controlled to match their respective position in the skylight simulation.

The initial implementation proposed in [14] only computed values during the day. To overcome this limitation, at nightfall, the sky and sunlight colours get interpolated to a standard night bluish colour. During the night, stars and the moon are faded in, implementing a fast and easy night sky model.

All the weather parameters and the position of the sun can be animated to produce smooth animations of sunset or sunrise along with changes in weather conditions.

4 Conclusions

As the curtain of the ATHENS 2004 Olympic Games came down, the odyssey of creating this series came to an end, confirming and outlining once again the importance of combining interactivity, storyboard with culture, advanced graphics and social interest points. All these key factors lead to the success and embracement of this series of applications from the public. Encouraged from the visitor numbers (approx. 7500) during the summer of the Olympiad and their positive feedback, we feel convinced that we succeeded in the challenge of bringing Ancient Olympia to the public and comfortable in undertaking and pushing future projects into new directions.

References

1. Cal3D, Character Animation Library: http://cal3d.sourceforge.net/
2. Cohen-Or, D., Chrysanthou, Y., Silva, C., Durand, F.: A Survey of Visibility for Walkthrough Applications. IEEE TVG 9, 3 (2003), 412-431.
3. Coldet Collision Detection Library: http://photoneffect.com/coldet/

4. Coorg, S., Teller, S.: Real-time occlusion culling for models with large occluders. In Proc. ACM Symposium on Interactive 3D Graphics, 1997, 83-90.
5. Cruz-Neira, C., Sandin, D. J., DeFanti, T. A.: Surround-Screen Projection-Based Virtual Reality: The Design and Implementation of the CAVE. In Proc. ACM Computer Graphics (SIGGRAPH) 1993, 135-142
6. Eberly, D. H.: Game Physics. Morgan Kaufmann, 2004.
7. Gaitatzes, A., Christopoulos, D., Papaioannou, G.: The Ancient Olympic Games: Being Part of the Experience. In Proc. 5th International Symposium on Virtual Reality, Archaeology and Cultural Heritage (VAST) 2004.
8. Gaitatzes, A., Christopoulos, D., Roussou, M.: Reviving the Past: Cultural Heritage Meets Virtual Reality. In Proc. Virtual Reality, Archaeology and Cultural Heritage (VAST) 2001.
9. Gaitatzes, A., Christopoulos, D., Roussou, M.: Virtual Reality Interfaces for the Broad Public. In Proc. Panhellenic Conference on Human Computer Interaction (PCHCI) 2001.
10. Hudson, T., Manocha, D., Cohen, J., Liny, M., Ho, K., Zhang.: Accelerated Occlusion Culling using Shadow Frusta. In Proc. ACM 13th Annual Symposium on Computational Geometry, 1997, 1-10.
11. Papaioannou, G., Gaitatzes, A., Christopoulos, D.: Enhancing Virtual Walkthroughs of Archaeological Sites. In Proc. 4th International Symposium on Virtual Reality, Archaeology and Cultural Heritage (VAST) 2003.
12. Pape, D., Imai, T., Anstey, J., Roussou, M., DeFanti, T.: XP: An Authoring System for Immersive Art Exhibitions. In Proc. VSMM 1998, Gifu, Japan.
13. Preece, J., Rogers, Y., Sharp, H., Benyon, D., Holland, S., Carey, T.: Human - Computer Interaction. Addison - Wesley, 1994.
14. Preetham, A., Shirley, P., Smits, B. E.: A Practical Analytic Model for Daylight. In Proc. ACM SIGGRAPH 1999, 91-100.
15. Rohlf, J., Helman, J.: IRIS Performer: A High-Performance Multiprocessing Toolkit for Real-Time 3D Graphics. In Proc. ACM SIGGRAPH 1994, 381–395.
16. Taylor, R. M., Hudson, T. C., Seeger, A., Weber, H., Juliano, J., and Helser, A. T.: VRPN: A Device-Independent, Network-Transparent VR Peripheral System. In Proc. ACM Symposium on Virtual Reality Software and Technology (VRST), Banff, Alberta, Canada, November 2001.
17. Watt, A., Watt, M.: Advanced Animation and Rendering Techniques, Theory and Practice. Addison – Wesley, 1993.
18. Woodland, R.: Filling the Gaps - Advanced Animation Using Stitching and Skinning. Game Programming Gems, Ed. M. DeLoura, 2000, Charles River Media, 476-483.

Auction Scenarios of Cultural Products over the WWW

D.K. Koukopoulos

Department of Cultural Heritage Management and New Technologies,
University of Ioannina,
G. Seferi 2, 30 100 Agrinio, Greece
koukopou@ceid.upatras.gr

Abstract. Nowadays, every country faces the necessity of the demonstration of its cultural heritage over the WWW due to its increasing role in national economy through tourism. This paper studies ways of achieving this goal through electronic auctions over the WWW. More specifically, we present an electronic auction system along with several brokerage scenarios depending on different customer needs for the mediation of transactions and product searching.

Keywords: Cultural products, Electronic auctions, Brokerage scenarios.

1 Introduction

Motivation. The great value of cultural heritage is by now well recognized as it relates directly the past with important markets of current life, mainly Education, Tourism, Entertainment and Commerce. These markets are essential for any national economy. A way to enhance the benefits of the exploitation of cultural heritage is the adaptation of new technologies like WWW for the demonstration of cultural products, along with successful economic strategies like electronic commerce.

Cultural products are those that directly express attitudes, opinions, ideas, values, and artistic creativity; provide entertainment; or offer information and analysis concerning the past and present. Included in this definition are popular, mass-produced, products as well as cultural products that normally have a more limited audience, such as poetry books, antiquities, literary magazines, classical records or paintings.

WWW (World-Wide Web) is an application of a vast, rapidly growing internetwork of computers known collectively as the Internet. It is fitting for new consumers of computer communications technology to focus on the Web, for in many respects it stands alone as the Internet's commercial domain. Electronic commerce is probably the hottest Web development in the everyday life of consumers and businesses [4]. A key challenge in this scientific field is the development of novel services and their standardization. Appreciating the benefits of e-commerce has not been a straightforward issue [1] but it now seems that its momentum has been able to generate wealth (and havoc) at a significantly larger rate than traditional technologies. Still, certain types of businesses are more irresistibly drawn by the Web's promise than others. Art galleries, for instance, have been among the first segments of the business community to stake out the Web as a potentially lucrative supplemental venue for sales.

Auctions have been an important type of business to sell merchandize based upon effective pricing methods [10]. Conventionally, auctions are commonly applied to sell unique and unusual items including celebrities' personal property and art. An auction is a special type of a commercial transaction. The basic difference between an auction and a classical transaction is that in the latter the customer offers a price for a product, which is accepted or rejected or "bargained" by the seller until both agree or until the deal is broken. In an auction a product becomes an object of competition among many customers.

Participating in an auction of cultural products the gain is two-fold. The user not only tries to buy a product, but he/she is also informed about the historic background of the product. For the seller's side, which can be a memory institution (museum), auctioning can be an alternative and complementary financial source to its insufficient budgets. Also, auctioning is essential for the so called private sector of culture (galleries) which plays the role of sponsor for artists and modern art.

In this work, we consider the impact on the design of an electronic auction system of cultural products if the system have to meet different customer needs for the mediation of transactions and product searching. This work is based on a pioneering prototype [5] that has been developed in a research laboratory and that is still at the frontier of innovative concepts that seem to have created a huge marketplace of ideas, systems, services and technologies.

Network bandwidth (or the lack of it) has always been a limiting factor in the deployment of applications over the WWW. However, as the information society increasingly depends on the ability of its citizens to communicate efficiently on-line, the pace of development of products and services is not likely to settle. But then, the WWW is bound to be flooded with e-shops. Today a traditional shopper will rely on word-of-mouth, hearsay or specialized market research services to access alternative options as a consumer (or, simply, will not bother and just be loyal to a store). In a world of inexpensive bandwidth, where all shops are on-line, a shopper may much easier decide to shop around. Here, the limiting factor is time. To relieve shoppers from intensive monitoring and timely decision making, one must use software agents. A software agent is a software entity that functions continuously and autonomously in a particular environment [15]. Agents, that assume responsibilities for the users who have issued them, are slated to be the next development wave as they address exactly the above problem: act effectively with minimum supervision [19]. This work contributes to that direction.

Contribution. We use here as development platform the Voyager technology [18] which unifies distributed programming with agent technology. In this framework, we obtain the following results:

- We design an electronic auction system of cultural products. Our system implements the basic entities in an auction system (Buyers, Sellers, Auction Houses) providing a communication and interaction protocol among them. It supports a security mechanism based on user authentication in order to assure reliability. It provides a product searching mechanism that enhances the user's ability for autonomous bidding. User interface is based on the use of suitable Java applets.
- We propose novel brokerage concepts for the mediation of transactions and product searching. After specifying searching criteria, we present a number of searching strategies depending on the autonomous degree of the agents and the distributed nature of the searching algorithm.

Related Work. *Art Online.* Artists themselves have long embraced the computer as a medium of expression [14] and the Internet for creative networking [9]. Recent emphasis on technological media for digital reproduction and widespread distribution of traditional art, however, has museum and gallery administrators embrace new technology as a viable means to explore new contexts and expand their audiences. Several major museums and collections have already established Web sites dedicated to showcasing particular features and exhibits as the National Museum of Contemporary Art [13] and the Technical Museum of Thessaloniki [17]. Such institutions are virtual neighbors to private "commercial" galleries devoted to the sale of works rather than pure exhibition such as The Electronic Museum of Modern Art [8].

Online Auction Systems. There are several online auction systems which auction products including cultural ones. A widely known online auction system is eBay [7]. A lot of galleries and many auction houses like Sotheby's cooperate with eBay in order to sell their products in better prices through electronic auctioning. Especially, they take advantage of eBay's feature to conduct "live" auctions in order to combine auction house floor and online bidding maximizing consequently their profit. Yahoo [21] is a popular search engine that, also, offers auction services. A typical auction lasts several days. During this period, a bidder is informed whether some other Yahoo user has outbid him. All these auction systems require a buyer to first locate the exact product he/she is seeking and then enter a committed bidding relationship with the seller. So while the systems offers little assistance in locating a desired product, it also discourages the buyer from bidding on more than one item at a time.

Bidding Agents. The use of software agents technology in auction systems come to address the necessity for fast transactions and efficient bandwidth exploitation. Although ethical issues regarding information brokerage are not fully sorted out [11] and despite the fact that on-line transactions are not cheaper by definition [12], current research is so focused on agents and mediation systems that it is bound to produce a technological critical mass [6,16,20]. However, the design of smart bidding agents research is currently in its infancy [2,3].

Road Map. The rest of this paper is organized as follows. Section 2 presents a brief system overview. Section 3 deals with various scenarios for autonomous searching of cultural products auctions. Section 4 presents system design at the conceptual and logical level. We conclude, in Section 5, with a discussion of our results and some open problems.

2 Brief System Overview

System Architecture. The general architecture/workflow diagram for the proposed auction system is presented in Figure 1. This diagram is divided into four modules which represent the key entities of the integrated information system and, at the same time, the main research areas involved. Each module has its own technological parameters and requirement for its design and implementation.

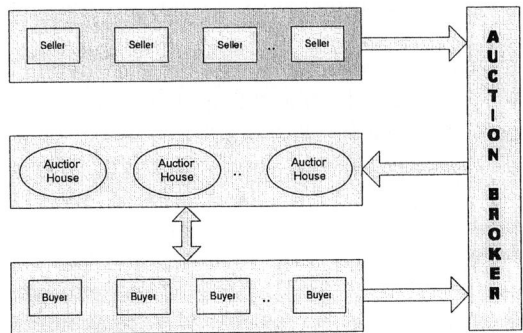

Fig. 1. System architecture

The auction system key entities are: Buyers, Sellers, Auction Houses and Auction Broker(s). A seller informs an auction house via an auction broker about products to be sold and the auction house forwards this information to a group of buyers inviting them to bid. Buyers can make bids manually or via the auction broker. Besides the implementation of auctions (mediated or not), the system affords: (i) a communication and interaction protocol between the basic system entities, (ii) a security mechanism, and (iii) a product searching feature in the Auction Broker.

Development Platform. The system was developed using Voyager technology [18]. Voyager is a dynamic object request broker that follows the object-oriented model of Java [20]. With Voyager a programmer can create remote objects (agents) easily, send them messages and move them between programs, which are located in different computers. Also, an auction house can manage system overload by transferring an auction to another computer, transparently.

Scenario of Usage. From the user point of view, an electronic auction system should support several operations, like *registration*, *product declaration*, *auction participation* and *auction observation*. These operations are implemented in our system as follows:

- A simple registration form containing only a log-in and a password field is used. Buyers and sellers are registered separately. Auction houses are accessed directly or via an auction broker.
- Registered sellers submit products for sale specifying the expected (minimum) price, a product description and an auction deadline date. Auction houses may turn down product offers.
- A buyer participates in an auction by accessing the WWW site of the auction house and being granted an authentication clearing by a login/password mechanism. Two types of bids are possible.
  - *Manual bid:* The user bids and, during the auction, he receives information about the number of users who participate in the auction and the current value of the product on sale.
  - *Autonomous bid:* In autonomous bidding, the user submits to an auction broker a product description and his authorization. Then, the auction broker takes on the responsibility to find the auction houses that auction such products and sends an agent to each of these auctions. These agents communicate with each other to achieve the best bargain.
- Any user may observe the carrying out of an auction even without registering. The marketing message will be better received when the potential user is assured of the smooth and reliable system operation. Potential sellers may also be interested in observing the carrying out of an auction.

3 Product Searching Scenarios

An important feature of our system is user ability for autonomous bidding among auctions that take place in different auction houses. For autonomous bidding, a product search algorithm runs at the auction broker and searches all the auction houses that cooperate with the broker for the desired product. The algorithm terminates successfully when a product that satisfies customer requirements is bought within the time constraints specified by the customer.

Searching Criteria. The basic criteria used to determine the purchase are: (i) the current product price, (ii) the price increment/decrement rate, and (iii) the time range of the bid (and the auction).

Search Policies. Search policies depend on two key factors: (i) the degree to which the agents are autonomous and, (ii) the degree to which the search algorithm is distributed.

Non-Risk policies. Such policies treat agents as dumb mobile objects, which have to be instructed for any bid. The auction broker sends an agent to each auction. Any information concerning the auction that reaches the agent is sent back to the broker. The broker, based on this information, decides about the best auction and it sends messages to the agents informing them about which one should make a bid. The information, which is received by an agent, is about the current product price, the number of users, and the initial price. Non-Risk policies do not allow the autonomy of agents and the broker operates as a central authority.

Risk policies. Such policies allow agents to move autonomously, running the risk of bidding for the same item at various sites simultaneously. Because the customer should not pay for more than one product, the auction broker pays the additional cost. This introduces an additional cost to the broker.

In a *Non-Risk policy*, the communication time between the broker and the agents is assumed small. But, if this time is significant, then the time the broker needs to find the best purchase and the corresponding agent to make the bid is significant. This delay introduces a problem: until the broker decides on the best purchase, the current product prices may be modified. The "waiting to bid" agent will then have received an acknowledgement that is no longer valid. If delays are substantial, agents may spend their time simply requesting permissions to bid.

On the other hand, a *Risk policy* allows agents to bid without an acknowledgement, after they have asked for one and waited some time without response. Moreover, a *Risk policy* distributes some decision workload to the agents. This may mean that agents can spot a good bargain and conclude it without having to wait for a central authorization. Obviously, such an agent does inform other agents as soon as possible, however, it can not eliminate duplicate bids (which may be both successful). The cost of duplicate bids is born by the broker, but such a broker can justifiably claim that it offers a better service to its clients; this in turn can be translated into premium subscription costs. A fitting example would be the request to obtain a good price at a last-minute ticket of a music performance. Users of such a service would probably be prepared to pay extra subscription fees, if they could count on their broker obtaining non-trivial deals for them, consistently.

Centralized policy. In such a search policy the auction broker manages the distribution of all messages between agents (Figure 2). The main disadvantage of a centralized policy is neither the heavy communication time nor the big message overhead, but the unrealistic role of the broker and the not-intuitive role of an agent. However, in special cases, a centralized policy may be acceptable (when computing power at the broker and bandwidth suffice to serve all auctions).

Distributed policy. In such a policy the role of the auction broker is limited to the creation of agents and the transmission of agents to various auctions (Figure 3).

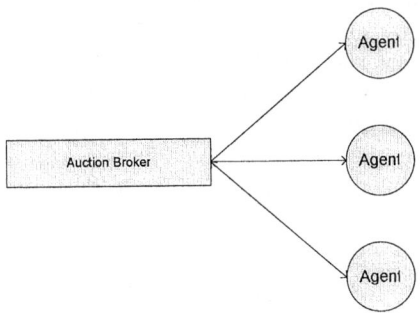

Fig. 2. Centralized policy

The auction broker creates the agents and sends one to each auction of the desired product. After that, it sends to each agent information relative to the product, which must be bought, and the addresses of the rest of the agents of the group. The agents send messages to each other about the current price of each product as well as some other information relative to the criteria, which identify the best purchase. If the purchase is completed, the winning agent informs the broker. In a distributed environment, the acknowledgement arriving at an agent about whether to bid or not has originated from another agent. It is whether the arrival of acknowledgements is essential for the bidding that differentiates the policy between *Risk* and *Non-Risk*.

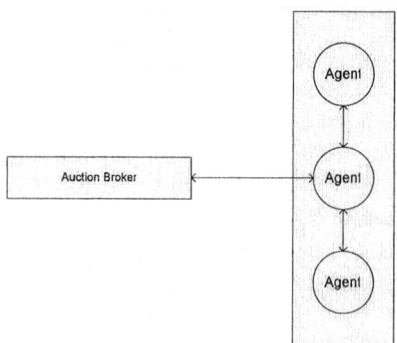

Fig. 3. Distributed policy

Additional system services. The proposed product searching scenarios hold when the world consists of any number of auction houses and the auction houses permit the cooperation with each other. In such an environment, a number of additional services are offered to users:

- A user can specify his/her requirements for a product (product description) and the auction broker takes on the responsibility to locate the appropriate auction houses. Then, agents are sent to each relative auction where they bid on behalf of the user.
- A seller can achieve less charging from an auction house for auctioning his/her product, as he/she could select among a variety of auction houses.
- Auction houses reap benefits from such a co-operation. A larger audience (of potential users) is addressed. This happens because a user of an auction house could be automatically a user of another auction house, too.
- An auction house can delegate some of its functionality to the auction broker.

4 System Design

Conceptual design. The basic objects of the system and their relations are detailed in Figure 4 in OMT notation. The system objects are: the Auction

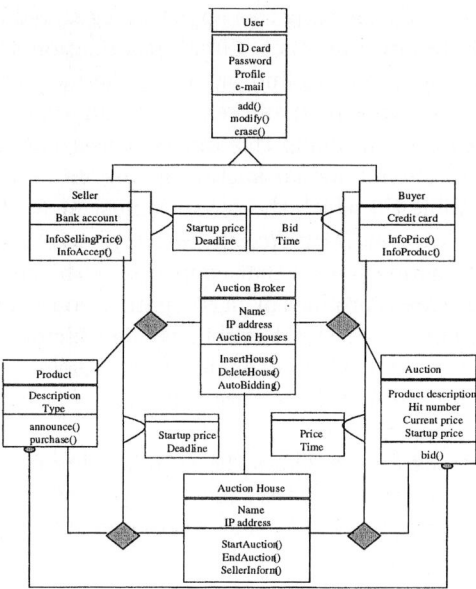

Fig. 4. Conceptual design

Broker, the Auction House, the User (Buyer or Seller), the Product and the Auction. The Auction Broker and the Auction House are the most important objects. All the other objects hook on them at some point in their lifetime. The Auction House object initializes or terminates an auction and informs a seller about the acceptance of a product. The Auction Broker object is responsible for the connection establishment with an auction house and the realization of an autonomous bidding process. The relation among the Auction House, the Seller and the Product objects describes the startup price and the deadline date till which the product must have been auctioned. The relation among the Buyer, the Auction and the Auction House objects logs the bids.

Logical Design. The implemented system uses Java applets to interact with the customers or the administrator. Applets implement all functions, including user interface ones, for the sake of fast prototyping. This has had an effect on system speed, but the proof of the concept has been established. The main applets of our system include:

- *AuctionApplet.* A user can participate in an auction, by invoking this applet. He can choose an auction, see some information relative to this auction (a description of the auctioned product) and submit a bid.
- *AutoBuyApplet.* This applet provides autonomous bidding. A user fills a form with information corresponding to the product he wants to buy and the system takes on the responsibility of searching and bidding.
- *ObserveApplet.* A user can observe an auction, by invoking this applet without having registered before.

- *TransactionApplet.* By invoking this applet, a registered user can participate in an auction or declare a product. After authorization, the user is connected to available auction houses to find out where he has been registered. Then, these auction houses are stored and sent to the auction broker for future use.
- *DeclarationApplet.* By invoking this applet a user can declare the product that he wants to submit for an auction giving its description, the desired price and a deadline till which the product must be auctioned.
- *SellerRegistrationApplet/BuyerRegistrationApplet.* These applets allow registration to the auction houses that cooperate with the auction broker. If a user wants to declare a product or participate in auctions that take place in various auction houses, he/she should firstly be registered in the corresponding auction houses as a seller or buyer giving his/her login and password. These will be checked and if they are valid, the user can declare a product or participate in an auction.
- *Administrator.* This applet allows the system administrator to operate remotely. He can manage the registry file, remove users, observe the auctioned products, the successful bidders and associated history files. He may also manipulate the status of auctions.

The implemented product search algorithm is based on a *Non-Risk Distributed policy*. The algorithm starts when the auction broker is informed by the AutoBuyApplet for a new autonomous bidding connection. Besides the product details given by the user, the AutoBuyApplet sends to the AuctionBroker the auction houses' addresses where the user has been registered. The initial actions of the AuctionBroker are described below:

1. The AuctionBroker sends a message to each auction house where the user is registered and asks for the auction schedule. Also, it informs each auction house for the product kind, so that if a new product of the same kind is declared, the auction broker is informed.
2. Each auction house sends its auction schedule to the AuctionBroker.
3. The AuctionBroker checks the auctioned products at all auctions. For each such product, it creates an agent (AgentBuyer) and sends it to the specific auction. After that, it sends to each agent the addresses of the rest of the agents.

Each agent with its arrival at the auction where it has been sent, acts as follows:

1. It informs the AuctionHouse, where it has arrived at, about its presence.
2. It is connected with its auction and notifies itself.
3. The Auction sends to the AgentBuyer information about the auctioned product and the auction itself. An agent is only interested in the current product price.
4. The agent sends to the other agents the current product price and receives the product prices of the other agents.

At this point each agent knows the current price of the other agents' target products. Consequently, all the agents know the agent with the smallest current price. This is selected as a leader to make a bid to its auction. This bid is bigger than the current product price by 5% (arbitrarily set). If the auction is finished, and the leader is the winner, it informs the other agents and the AuctionBroker that it won and it terminates its operation. Each of the other agents informs the AuctionBroker about its failure and terminates its operation. If the leader is not the winner, all the other agents attempt to elect a new leader. If the auction is not finished with the leader bid, it means that another bid has occurred. In this case, the leader is informed and sends the new price to the other agents for the election of a new leader. Each of the other agents that receives the new product price, knows that the leader election process has started. Thus, it sends the current price of its product to all the other agents including the leader. The leader election process is the same as previously with the difference that the leader initiates it.

If a new product is declared in an auction house, which belongs to the same category with the desired product, then the auction house informs the auction broker and it creates a new agent and sends it to the auction, which is created for the new product. This agent should try to get into the group of the agents that already try to buy the product for the user. For this reason, the agent sends a message to each of the group's agents. Only, the leader can answer to this message. When the leader receives this message and decides that the new agent can be a member of the group, it announces the agent to the other agents and informs the specific agent that it was accepted. If the leader decides that the agent cannot be a member of the group, it sends a message to the agent to retry. The reason an agent cannot be a member of the group of the already auctioning agents is that this particular moment may not be appropriate. This happens for example when the initial price of the new declared product is too high compared to the current price of the leader's auction.

5 Future Work

The proposed system has been developed to the level of a research prototype and it has been extensively tested in a laboratory situation, where besides a rather slow start, the registration, product declaration and bidding stages have been developed to be efficient. Among our research and development priorities are the maturing of the existent functionality and the extension of the system in order to support and other kinds of market deals beyond auctions. The full appreciation of the bandwidth limitations under real-life situations is a criterion for further system improvement. Significant progress has been achieved in this domain moving a big portion of the work load for the autonomous bidding to the auction houses from the auction broker and using client programming. It is our belief that the current system provides a suitable and indispensable infrastructure for developing solutions to electronic commerce problems of cultural products.

References

1. Y. Bakos. The Emerging Role of Electronic Marketplaces on the Internet. Communications of the ACM, Vol. 41, No. 8, August 1998, pp. 35-42.
2. R. Bapna, P. Goes and A. Gupta. Insights and Analyses of Online Auctions. Communications of the ACM, Vol 44, No. 11, November 2001, pp. 42-50.
3. R. Bapna, P. Goes and A. Gupta. Analyses and Design of Business-to-Consumer Online Auctions. Management Science, Vol. 49, No.1, January 2003, pp. 85-101.
4. M. Bichler, S. Field and H. Werthner. Introduction: Theory and Application of Electronic Market Design. Electronic Commerce Research Journal, Vol. 1, 2001, pp. 215-220.
5. C. Bouganis and D. Koukopoulos. An Electronic Auction System over the WWW. Diploma Thesis at the Dept. of Computer Engineering and Informatics, University of Patras, Greece, 1998 (in Greek).
6. D. Clark. Shopbots Become Agents for Business Change. IEEE Computer, Vol. 33, No 2, February 2000, pp. 18-21.
7. E-bay Official Web Site. http://www.ebay.com
8. The Electronic Museum of Modern Art Official Web Site. http://www.emoma.org/index.htm
9. D. Grant. Electronic news service for artists. American Artist, Vol. 57, 1993, pp. 58-60.
10. W. Hanson. Internet Marketing. South-Western College Publishing, Cincinnati, OH, 2000.
11. L. Introna, and H. Nissenbaum. Defining the Web: The Politics of Search Engines. IEEE Computer, Vol. 33, No. 1, January 2000, pp. 54-62.
12. Lee, H.G. Do Electronic Marketplaces the Price of Goods? Communications of the ACM, Vol. 41, No. 1, January 1998, pp. 73-80.
13. National Museum of Contemporary Art. http://www.emst.gr
14. A. M. Noll. The beginnings of computer art in the United States: A memoir. Leonardo, Vol. 27, No. 1, 1993, pp. 39-44
15. Y. Shoham. An overview of agent-oriented programming. In J. M. Bradshaw (Ed.) Software Agents, AAAI Press,Menlo Park, CA, 1997, pp. 271-290.
16. K. P. Sycara, M. Paolucci, J. Soudry, and N. Srinivasan. Dynamic Discovery and Coordination of Agent-Based Semantic Web Services. IEEE Internet Computing, Vol. 8, No. 3, May/June 2004, pp. 66-73.
17. Technical Museum of Thessaloniki Official Web Site. http://www.tmth.edu.gr
18. Voyager Core Technology Official Web site. http://www.recursionsw.com/voyager.htm
19. S. Wang. Analyzing Business Information Systems: An Object-Oriented Approach. CRC Press, Boca Raton, FL,1999.
20. Wong, D., Paciorek, N. and D. Moore. Java-based Mobile Agents. Communications of the ACM, Vol. 42, No. 3, March 1999, pp. 92-102.
21. Yahoo Auctions Official Web Site. http://auctions.yahoo.com

Exploring Cultural Information Interaction Design: A Case Study of a Multimedia Exhibition Based on Customizable User Interfaces

George Pehlivanides

Laboratory of Picture, Sound and Cultural Representation,
Department of Cultural Technology and Communication,
University of the Aegean, Tyrtaiou 1, 81100 Mytilini, Lesvos, Greece
g.pehlivanides@ct.aegean.gr

Abstract. The study of cultural content promotion methods, through an interdisciplinary approach, suggests new ways of information management, as well as new representation practices, which constitute the basis of new negotiation methodologies. Cultural Information Systems through a variety of possible interfaces, formed according to each given promotion strategy, suggest the study, within a broader research field, of new ways of information structure management, introducing new kinds of knowledge formation and consequently new interpretation tools of awareness. As a result of the interdisciplinary approach regarding cultural heritage management and subsequently of the possibility of parameterization regarding the forms of scientific fields and the practices of the specialities involved, a new design field is defined, the Cultural Information Interaction Design field. Under the framework of Cultural Information Interaction Design, this paper presents a case study of a multimedia exhibition implementing a method for interactive exhibit design based on Customizable User Interfaces, depended on given design problems and focused on parameterized sensorial approaches and presentation techniques. The exhibition design strategy was focused on the design of interactive exhibits with a sensorial emphasis on tangibility, proposing in that way novel forms of cultural representation practices.

1 Introduction

During their production processes, Cultural Information Systems hold, individually as well as in combination, typical features of every field involved, due to the incorporation of theoretic models and practices of various knowledge fields from a broad spectrum of sciences. This interdisciplinary aspect extends the ways of information negotiation, providing in this way, the basis of new content management and representation methodologies.

2 A Theoretic Organisation Model of the Production Processes of a Cultural Information System

In an attempt to define the knowledge fields covering the production of a Cultural Information System we could imagine a formation of levels like the one that appears in figure 1. In this schematic representation, three levels (*a,b,c*) are presented in stratified layers, which represent each category of the knowledge fields involved. In more detail, starting from below we can distinguish: **level (*a*)**, consisting of theoretic models, scientific methods and practices analysing and organising[1] cultural data, **level (*b*)**, consisting of theoretic models, scientific methods and practices structuring and applying[2] the knowledge that level (a) produced to management systems, and finally **level (*c*)**, consisting of theoretic models, scientific methods and practices expressing[3] (rendering) the subject of negotiation based on representation models.

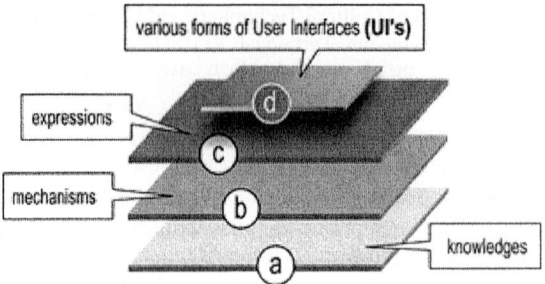

Fig. 1. Schematic representation of the knowledge fields involved, during the process of a Cultural Information System production. Starting from below, at level (*a*) specialities which analyse and organise the negotiated subject are found, at level (*b*) specialities which deal with structure and management techniques of the produced information are found, and finally, at level (*c*) specialities which render the given subject of negotiation based on representation models are found. At the top, level (*d*), consisting of the cooperative relations of the specialities, comprises all possible forms of user interfaces.

Figure 2 presents an indicative sample[4] of specialities which can cover the three above-mentioned levels (*a,b,c*), attempting to classify "in stratified layers" the various scientific fields dealing (or potentially dealing) with cultural content. Various cooperative relations can be presented in each case of group cooperation, either individually within each level (*a*), (*b*), (*c*), as for example: $(a_1 + a_2 + a_7)$ for level (*a*), $(b_1 + b_5 + b_6)$ for level (*b*), $(c_7 + c_2 + c_3)$ for level (*c*), or in stratified layers, that is, in a combinative multilevel form, as for example: $[(a) + (b)]$, $[(a) + (c)]$ or $[(a) + (b) + (c)]$,

---

[1] e.g. through museology practices.
[2] e.g. through applied informatics practices.
[3] e.g. through graphic information design practices.
[4] Representative examples of specialities dealing with issues of Cultural Heritage could be the interdisciplinary staff of institutions dealing with management, design and promotion of cultural content. For example, in Greece the specialities represented at the Department of Cultural Technology and Communication of the University of the Aegean in the year 2005 include social anthropologists, archaeologists, environmental scientists, art historians, museologists, theatrologists, filmmakers, graphic designers, 3-D graphic designers, interaction designers, programmers of multimedia applications, mechanical engineers, as well as scientists from wider knowledge fields of information technology, communication and human sciences. Source: http://www.aegean.gr/culturaltec/people_gr.htm, Date of visit: 18/11/2004.

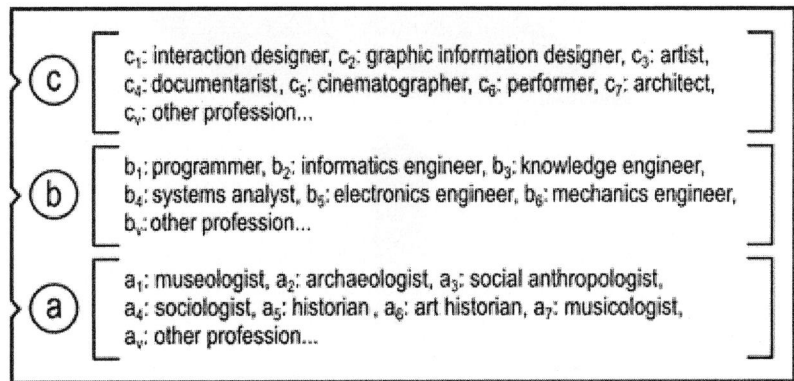

Fig. 2. Indicative sample of scientific specialities classified in groups according to the knowledge field

which, based on the previous cases, could be further analysed within each level, as for example: $[(a_6 + a_2) + (b_1 + b_2)]$, $[(a_3 + a_1) + (c_3 + c_4)]$ or $[(a_1 + a_5) + (b_1 + b_5 + b_6) + (c_1 + c_2 + c_v)]$, etc.

In an attempt of a better schematic presentation of the possible cases of cooperative relations of specialities from levels (*a*), (*b*) and (*c*), we could imagine the production process of a Cultural Information System as it is presented in figure 3. As it is shown in figure 3, a Cultural Information System can be formed either individually[5] based on each level, or in combination based on multilevel formations.

As a result of each cooperative relation, **level (*d*)** is formed on the top containing every possible form of *User Interfaces*[6] that could be shaped by the specialities from the fields involved. According to parameters, concerning the amplitude of the knowledge fields as well as the numerous specialities, every cooperative relation can provide a broad spectrum of forms of user interfaces which therefore obtain characteristic

---

[5] We could assume that a Cultural Information System could be formed even in an individual single-level basis, "borrowing" (to a certain extent) practices and theoretic models from the other levels. Although single-level data negotiation would form some kind of information systems, it is obvious that multilevel approach is more complex due to specialisation and therefore more appropriate.

[6] Although today the term *User Interface* is used for interaction environments between people and computer systems, in a broader sense, this meaning can identify "user interface" formations in every communication activity. In this regard, user interfaces are found over time and are directly related to socio-cultural criteria. As a result, in the user interfaces used every time, typical features of the implemented relative social institutions, cultural aspects and technological backgrounds are distinguished. These are parameters appeared in every formation in respect both of representation practices and interpretative approaches. So in a broader meaning of the term, *User Interface* could be defined as the negotiation boundary / reference area that functional units - systems in a mutual relation delimit among themselves. In this "communal" space, common typical characteristics are met, which contribute to the jointly adaptive approach to attributes, set of codes and interpretations.

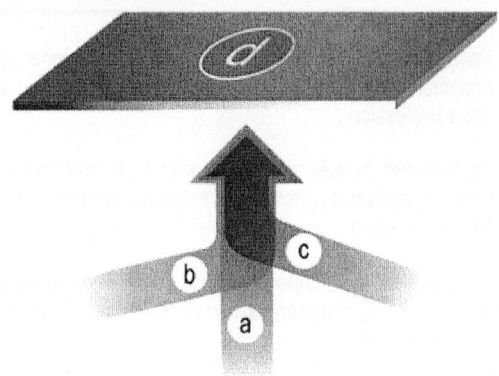

Fig. 3. Studying the production process of a Cultural Information System, cases of cooperative relations can be presented either within an individual level as for example only at level (*a*), or in a multilevel form such as in cases (*a*) + (*b*), (*a*) + (*c*), (*b*) + (*c*), (*a*) + (*b*) + (*c*). At level (*d*), according to each case, the respective user interfaces are presented (rendered).

attributes and interpretative practices that could be found in physical, virtual or combined environments.

3 Defining Cultural Information Interaction Design

In 1999, Shedroff, in his article Information Interaction Design: A Unified Field Theory of Design expressed a theory on *Information Interaction Design*, dealing with the ways of organizing and presenting data and information. According to Shedroff, Information Interaction Design is the intersection of three design fields: Information Design, Interaction Design, and Sensorial Design. Through changing design criteria, depending on the given design problem, Information Interaction Design can provide design solutions emphasizing either to Information Design practices, to Interaction Design practices or to Sensorial Design practices. Regardless of the design strategy and the selection of the main application field (depending on each case) the intersection of practices by the three above-mentioned fields, can combinatively develop content representation methods as well as content interaction modes in all communicational means, in physical or digital form or even as compound ones [1].

If we apply the above theory of Information Interaction Design in the case of cultural content negotiation, the interdisciplinary field based on which Cultural Information Systems are developed and due to its attribute of holding individual and combined typical features of each field involved, provides, according to each cooperative formation, relative representation methods, as well as interaction modes. Based on the fact that each knowledge field involved treats content according to its proper information, interaction and sensorial design practices, *Cultural Information Interaction Design*, in an interdisciplinary framework, could be defined as the interpretative tool with which each group of specialities elaborates the information to be negotiated and presents it through different forms of user interfaces.

The representation practices of a Cultural Information System - which for the purposes of this paper will be called *Cultural Representation Practices* (CUREP practices) - are established according to technical material and theoretic infrastructure, based on which these practices are designed. These infrastructures - which for the purposes of this paper will be called *Interaction Platforms* - are found in every case of design of communication practices and hold the typical features of the selected communication media and channels, regarding *both* structure techniques and presentation practices. Consequently, in each Cultural Representation Practice, the formed user interfaces hold typical characteristics of each Interaction Platform used for their presentation.

Under this prism, User Interfaces provided by different Interaction Platforms but constituting a unified Cultural Representation Practice, hold, individually and in combination, the typical features of all the selected communication media. Cultural Information Interaction Design based on theoretic approaches and practices of all the knowledge fields involved, which form each Cultural Information System, can present a broad spectrum of User Interfaces, due to the parameterizability, which would be then characterized by multiformity.

The reason of multiformity is that, depending on each cooperative relation, each user interface formed "renders" the negotiation content using the respective representation models, means of expression and interaction modes provided in each case by the knowledge fields involved. Under this interdisciplinary aspect, the major typical characteristic of Cultural Information Interaction Design is therefore parameterizability, that is, interchanging design criteria regarding the methods of representation, as well as interaction design, and the information intake process design with the use of scenarios of multimodal sensorial approaches.

Returning to the phenomenon of multiformity concerning the rendering of user interface, due to the parameterised factors in each content representation, the subjects at issue are represented in different way and medium and in different place and time. Within this framework, potential forms of user interfaces can be found in all communication media and consequently create interaction areas in physical, virtual or mixed environments, providing in that way multimodal interpretative approaches.

Combining different user interface formations by different media and environments, a unified content negotiation border is composed and formed, which for the purposes of this paper will be called *Interconnection Border*, containing all possible formations of user interfaces. The Interconnection Border, holding individually and in combination, the typical characteristics of each formed user interface, simulates at great extent, the original target idea to be negotiated. From this regard, the best application example of Cultural Information Interaction Design is found within the framework of representation practices based on contemporary Exhibition Design [2], where various representation methods are gathered together constituting a uniform cultural meta-environment.

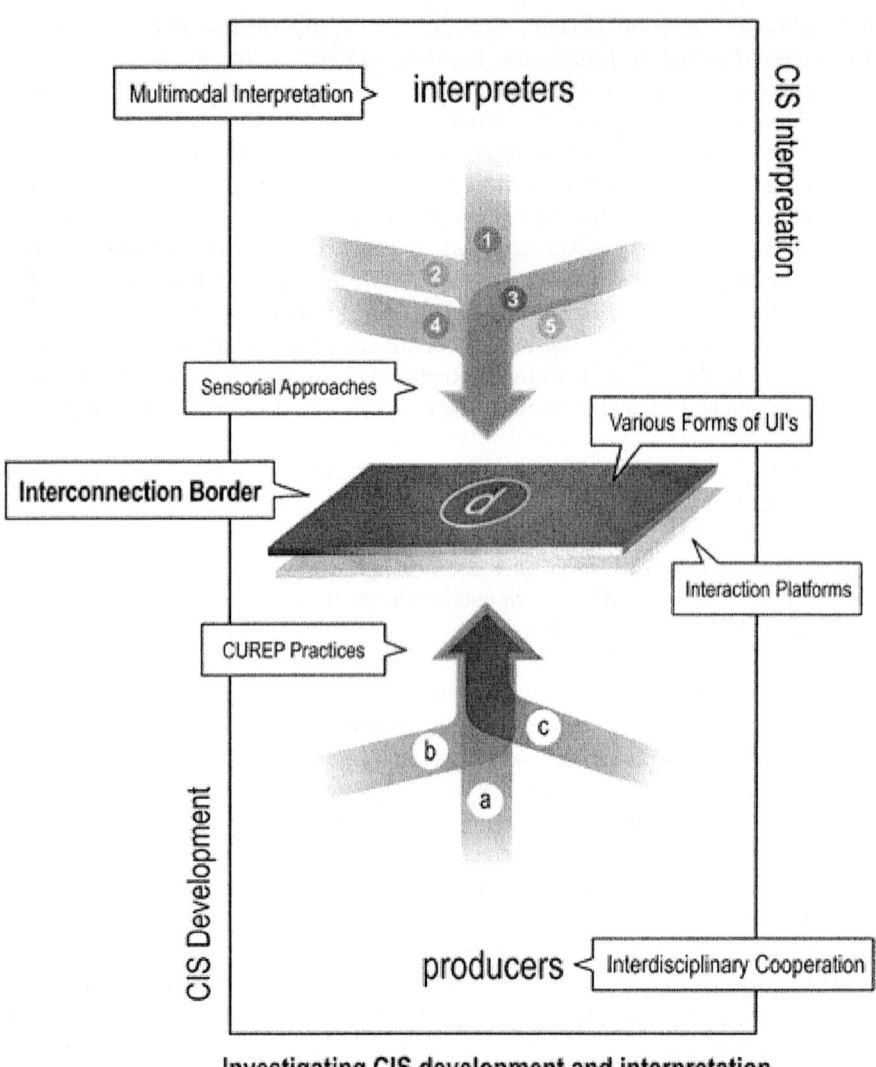

Fig. 4. Studying the production processes of Cultural Information Systems (CIS) from the producers' aspect, during each interdisciplinary cooperation of levels (*a*), (*b*) and (*c*), respective representation practices (CUREP Practices) are formed. According to each *Interaction Platform* used by each representation practice, many and different forms of user interfaces (UI's) are created. As a result, multimodal interpretation approaches are presented, from the interpreters' part, based on parameters concerning sensorial approaches, where: (1), (2), (3), (4), and (5) is vision, hearing, touch, scent and taste, respectively. The Interconnection Border created by these processes, due to its attribute to consist of a set of user interfaces of each representation practice, ideally simulates at a great extent the original target / idea.

4 Exploring Cultural Information Interaction Design: A Case Study of a Multimedia Exhibition Based on Customizable User Interfaces

An example of Cultural Information Interaction Design with representation practices based on Exhibition Design in combination with the use of *Customizable User Interfaces*[7], is the multimedia exhibition under the title: «Ermou: Symbolic, Historical, Economical and Social Centre of Mytilini»[8]. The exhibition concerned issues of the social history and material culture of Ermou Street, focusing on the following thematic fields: I) The architectural identity of Ermou street and the pertinent social web, combined with the changes in social life during the 20th century, II) The experiential experience of the inhabitants regarding economical and social life in the past, as well as in the modern reality, III) Biographical narratives of practitioners representing key points in the historical development of the local market, IV) The contemporary sound environment (soundscape) formed by everyday activities and V) A twenty-four-hour visual representation of the urban setting. For the presentation of the above-mentioned thematic fields, the design strategy of specially arranged interaction "areas" was implemented, through which the visitor could have access to different approaches of the content. In figure 5, the topographic diagram of the exhibition is presented with alphabetical definition (from A to G) of the content interaction areas. At the main exhibition area, the exhibition design strategy was focused on the design of interactive exhibits with a sensorial emphasis on tangibility [11], proposing in that

---

[7] For the purposes of this paper *Customizable User Interfaces* are defined as the forms of User Interfaces that provide physical ways of interaction with multimedia content, with the use of everyday-life objects / practices. Based on parameterization concerning sensorial approaches and presentation techniques, the forms of Customizable User Interfaces have the ability to be altered according to each given design problem / strategy. Customizable User Interfaces cover the need of producers designing the diverse representation practices of Cultural Information Systems to apply solutions according to the design problem or strategy, using various communication media and promotion tools, given the different forms of cultural content. For the interconnection of physical and virtual environments, innovative platforms, interaction design tools and relative hardware have been and constantly are elaborated suggesting alternative paths of content negotiation. Indicative examples can be found in [3, 4, 5, 6, 7, 8, 9, 10].

[8] The exhibition was presented in the city of Mytilini, Lesvos, for two years and it was the result of academic and research procedures of the department of Cultural Technology and Communication, of the University of the Aegean. The data collection and organisation, the exhibition design and the implementation of the presentation multimedia applications were effected by the students of the department of Cultural Technology and Communication, of the study division "Cultural Representation and New Technologies" during the academic years 2002-2003 and 2003-2004, in cooperation with the teaching staff, Papageorgiou Dimitris, Assistant Professor (General supervision, compilation and organisation of information material), Pehlivanides George, Adjunct Teacher (Cultural information interaction design), Boubaris Nikos, Lecturer (Soundscape supervision), Mavrofides Thomas, Adjunct Teacher (Application programming). The representation models of this cultural presentation were the result of interdisciplinary cooperation from the fields of social sciences, applied information technology and interaction design constituting in that way an interdisciplinary content negotiation framework.

way novel forms of cultural representation practices. The combination of the use of "traditional" and contemporary representation techniques created a dynamic mixed environment, providing in this way a multisensorial content negotiation possibility and consequently, multimodal interpretative approaches. The architectural arrangement of space itself where the exhibition took place, in combination with each representation model, transformed the area to a unified User Interface that contained separate interaction areas in key points. Having as main feature the multiformity concerning the content presentation, due to the use of different media and ways of presentation, each area provided a different interaction experience [12]. The interchange of content negotiation method depending on the area, created in total a unified interaction meta-environment, composed by various representation models.

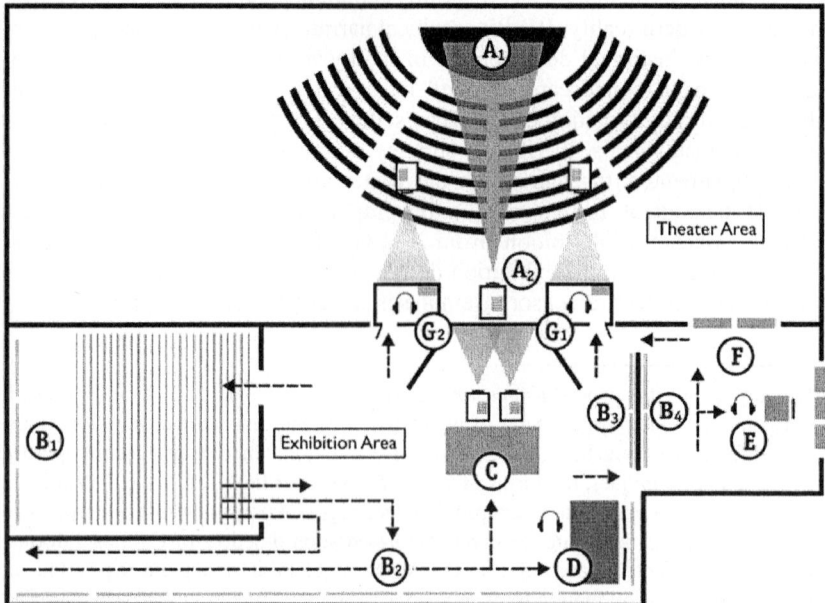

Fig. 5. Topographical diagram of the exhibition with the alphabetically defined (from **A** to **G**, starting from **A**) areas of content interaction: (A_1, A_2), Main theatre area: Introductory presentation of the subject through a series of lectures by invited lecturers and simultaneous projection of documents. Exhibition area: (B_1, B_2, B_3, B_4). Key points with information material presentation in poster form. Area (C): Interactive exhibit presenting information about the architectural identity of Ermou street, as well as the neighbouring sites. Area (D): Interactive exhibit presenting the socioeconomic framework of Ermou street through a series of inhabitants' and practitioners' narratives. Area (E): Interactive exhibit presenting biographical narratives of practitioners of Ermou street, concerning obsolete, surviving or evolving professions of today. Area (F): Information presentation in video form / Simultaneous video projection of the activities taking place in the morning (video 1) and at night (video 2) in Ermou street. Areas (G_1, G_2): Interactive exhibits presenting the soundscape of Ermou street during four time periods (morning, afternoon, evening and night).

4.1 Description of the Diverse Interaction Areas

Starting from the main theatre area (area A, consisting of key points A_1 and A_2), visitors of the exhibition, treated as audience, were originally introduced to the social economical and cultural framework of Ermou street, through a series of lectures by invited lecturers (see fig. 6.1), with simultaneous projection of documents. Proceeding to the specially arranged exhibition area, the visitors had access to historical photographic documents as well as contemporary photographic material (see fig. 6.2) in poster form (area B, consisting of key points B_1, B_2, B_3, B_4), negotiating through time issues of the architectural identity and socio-historical evolution of Ermou street. In this interaction area the large scale projected photographic material presented the negotiated issues in a predefined order. Visitors could be navigated in a natural way (by walking) to the presented information material and discuss with each other or with the representatives of the exhibition organisers issues of the presented approaches.

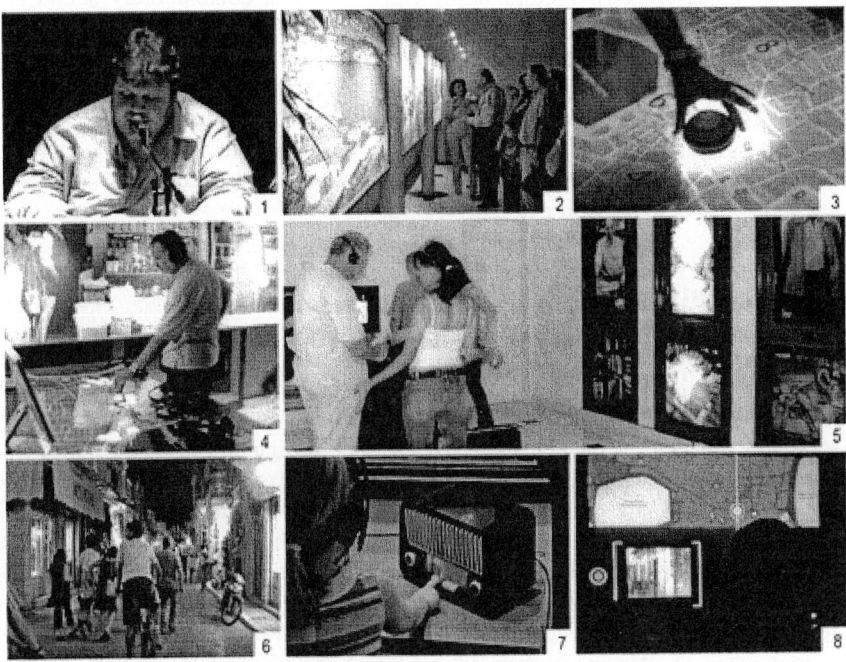

Fig. 6. Photographic material from the exhibition

In the centre of the exhibition area, the public had access to an interactive exhibit (area C), which presented information material in photograph and text form. Visitors interacted with the exhibit with the use of a specially arranged user interface, which focused on Tangible User Interface techniques [13] [14]. Visitors, placing a compass to certain points of a table map (see fig. 6.3) activated the projection of visual information (image and text) corresponding to the respective street points. In the next interactive exhibit (area D), which was also based on Tangible User Interface techniques, visitors interacted with the information material moving, like in the previous case, a symbolic object on a table map (see fig. 6.4), activating points corresponding to inhabitants' and trader's narratives about economical and social life of the past as well as of the contemporary reality. In this exhibit the relative information were conveyed at the same time in oral speech and written text. Following, visitors had access to an interactive exhibit (area E), where they could be navigated to key points of the historical evolution of Ermou street (see fig. 6.5) where three biographical narratives were presented regarding obsolete (blacksmith), surviving (tailor) or evolving today (bookseller) professions, by activating a moving cursor. The relative information was conveyed audibly (oral narrative) and visually (portrait of the practitioner in his working place and photographs of the tools and equipment of his work). In the next area (area F), visitors could watch two parallel video projections presenting Ermou street in a twenty-four-hour basis (see fig. 6.6) from selected fixed points-of-view and the activities taking place in the morning (video 1) and at night (video 2) in this street.

Finally (areas G_1, G_2), visitors were acquainted with contemporary sound environment (soundscape) of everyday activities in Ermou Street. Two identical interactive exhibits were installed in specially arranged rooms, where visitors, listened typical symbolic sounds from modern social life of Ermou street, by tuning the receiver of a radio of '50s on certain spots - "radio stations" (see fig. 6.7). In each radio tuning by the visitor, the movement of the radio "needle" was simulated by a multimedia application, which projected relative photographs of the selected street point in combination with the respective sound extracts (see fig. 6.8).

5 Conclusion

Connecting physical and virtual environments with the use of various practices and possibilities provided by digital technologies in combination with the use of everyday-life objects, the presentation of multimedia content through the common practice of keyboard - mouse - screen [15] was avoided and design strategies for mixed interactive environments were applied according to each given design problem. The reason of using a complex approach of "user interfaces" was mainly the diversity that characterises the different user profiles met in exhibition / museum [16] environments. In these environments, the context in which information is transformed to representation models usually constitutes narration and information intake methods, similar to methods used in everyday relations, in other words methods of a more experiential approach. Aiming at approaching target groups not familiar with the use of computer systems, during the stage of design, the customizability regarding the use of digital and analogue media as well as the ability of providing multimodal sensorial approaches was considered necessary. For this purpose, a methodology of user interface and interaction platform design was developed, so that the implementation of various forms of interactive applications could be easily and directly presented, as well as the ability of fast scenario interchange could be provided. For the interconnection of the interaction areas between physical and virtual environments, special encoders were used which translated in alphanumerical symbol forms, the visitors' positions and actions, activating the relative information which was stored in the computer systems. The information material was presented according to stimulus in image, text, sound, and digital video form, or it activated, in its turn, other external stimuli.

The representation techniques formed by these design criteria promoted novel ways of interaction with the content, providing ways of information access addressing to groups of the public regardless of age and knowledge background. The Cultural Information Interaction Design presented within the framework of the exhibition about Ermou Street, was a combination of practices from different design fields as well as methodologies of various specialised knowledge fields dealing with cultural content. These combinative uses suggested new ways of interpretative approaches, introducing new horizons for the promotion and presentation of Cultural Heritage.

References

1. Shedroff, N.: Information Interaction Design: A Unified Field Theory of Design, in Jacobson, R. (ed.): Information Design, MIT Press, Cambridge, Massachusetts (1999) 267-292
2. Dean, D.: Museum Exhibition: Theory and Practice, Routledge, London (1994)
3. Greenberg, S., Boyle, M.: Customizable physical interfaces for interacting with conventional applications, Proceedings of the UIST 2002, 15th Annual ACM Symposium on User Interface Software and Technology, ACM Press, Paris, France (2002) 31-40
4. Yim, J-D, Nam, T-J: Developing Tangible Interaction and Augmented Reality in Director, Conference on Human Factors in Computing Systems, CHI '04 extended abstracts on Human factors in computing systems, Vienna, Austria, ACM Press, (2004) 1541-1541
5. Borchers, J., Ballagas R.: iStuff: Searching For The Great Unified Input Theory, in UBICOMP 2002: Ubiquitous Computing, Göteborg, Sweden (2002)
6. Barragán, H.: Wiring: Prototyping Physical Interaction Design. Programming and prototyping with electronics for designers, Master Thesis, Interaction Design Institute Ivrea, Italy (2004), available at: http://people.interaction-ivrea.it/h.barragan/thesis/index.html
7. http://www.ezio.com
8. http://www.activewireinc.com
9. http://www.parallax.com
10. http://www.basicx.com
11. Milekic, S.: Towards Tangible Virtualities: Tangialities, in Bearman, D., Trant, J. (eds.): Museums and the Web 2002, Archives & Museum Informatics, Pittsburgh (2002)
12. Ciolfi, L.: Understanding Spaces as Places: Extending Interaction Design Paradigms, Cognition Technology and Work, Vol. 6, No. 1, Springer-Verlag, London (2004) 37-40
13. Ishii, H., Ullmer, B.: Tangible Bits: Towards Seamless Interfaces between People, Bits and Atoms, in Conference on Human Factors and Computing Systems, Atlanta, ACM Press, (1997) 234-241
14. Hornecker, E.: A Framework for the Design of Tangible Interaction for Collaborative Use, Proceedings of the Danish HCI Symposium, University of Aalborg, November 16, HCI Lab Technical Report no 2004/1, Copenhagen (2004) 57-61
15. Buxton, W.: Absorbing and Squeezing Out: On Sponges and Ubiquitous Computing, Proceedings of the International Broadcasting Symposium, Tokyo, (1996) 91-96
16. Mintz, A.: Interactive Multimedia: Designing for Museums, ASTC Newsletter Vol. 18, No. 6, ASTC Publications, Washington DC, (1990) 7-8

Using Personal Digital Assistants (PDAs) to Enhance the Museum Visit Experience

Katy Micha and Daphne Economou

University of the Aegean, Department of Cultural Technology and Communication,
5 Sapfous, Mytilene, Lesvos, GR – 81100,
Greece
{k.micha, d.economou}@aegean.ct.gr

Abstract. This paper addresses the design and evaluation of a Personal Digital Assistants' (PDAs) application to enhance the visit experience at the Museum/Library Stratis Eleftheriadis Teriade in Lesvos, Greece. The paper reviews the use of new technologies to enhance Museum visit experiences, and focuses on the use of PDAs for providing information and interpretation, keeping visitors interest and attention, as well as promoting various museum facilities. The paper describes the design process of the "Fables" application with the use of NaviPocket v. 2.4 by ORPHYS SYSTEMES (an authoring tool for PDA applications), includes an evaluation of the application and the authoring tool's effectiveness, and concludes with directions to further work on this area of research.

1 Introduction

There has been a considerable amount of research on the use of multimedia technologies to the museum environment to enhance the museum visit experience and provide information and interpretations for the museum collections [11], [18], [22], [15], [23]. This paper presents a study that focuses on understanding the visitors and museum requirements to develop a Personal Digital Assistants' (PDAs) application that aids the museum visit. To meet the study requirements a "real world" application is examined at the Museum/Library Stratis Eletheriadis Teriade (which will be referred to as "Teriade Museum" in this paper) in Lesvos, Greece. The museum presents a vast collection of books of special editions that have been illustrated by great painters of the 20th century.

Section 2 analyses the Museum requirements for finding ways of attracting visitors' attention, and for information provision and interpretation of collections. It reviews the ways new technologies tried to address these requirements and aid the museum visit. It also reviews the way the PDAs technology has been used to serve the museums for this reason. Section 3 presents the Teriade Museum requirements that call for the application of new technologies, which connect the exhibited collections to information (general and interpretational). Section 4 analyses design considerations related to the development of PDA applications in general and section 5 focuses specifically on issues related the development of PDA applications for museums. Section

6 presents the development process of a prototype PDA application for the Teriade Museum, which focuses on a series of illustrations by Jean de La Fontaine for the book of "Fables". Section 7 discusses the evaluation of the prototype that revealed that the use of PDA many of the visitors requirements can be served.

2 Museum Needs and New Technologies

Museums are organizations rich in content and their mission is to bring people closer to artefacts and the meanings they convey, which is manifested by the museum definition of United Kingdom Museums Association [20]. The collections of artefacts are at the core of the museums. However, the visitors must be provided with information in order to be able to assign meaning and interpretations related to the artefacts. Interpretation is the way people understand certain things [12], [13]. This is one of the roles undertaken by the museums to tell stories through their exhibitions and connect artefacts with information in order to provide meaning [3]. To do this museums tend to use mainly static ways of presenting information (like labels, photographs, catalogues etc.). However, such static ways of presenting information is not enough to fulfill their requirements. New technologies and new media should be utilized for this reason.

Multimedia and new technologies provide unique opportunities to museums as they bring new ways of communication and interpretation. Technological solutions known by now, like projection systems and info-kiosks, successfully connect artefacts to information. However, these solutions are limited to the museum physical space. Audio-guides are successful examples of connecting artefacts to information in a portable way, which is not limited by the physical environment, but to the use of audio.

PDAs technology allows the dynamic presentation of information, without being limited by, or being encroached by the aesthetics of the galleries. The introduction of handheld computers in museums for enhancing visitor experience was inspired by Zaurus, Psion, and Newton [1], that provided the museum visitor the opportunity to access multimedia, text and audio while walking through the exhibitions. Moreover, in contrast to audio-guides, users could now follow a non linear path of exploring the information provided. The "pocket curator" in 1995, was a system that made personalised experience possible by providing interactive audio and text about biographical information and interpretive annotations for 15 works of art (Fernando Quintero). In 1997 the Smithsonian Institute launched a traveling exhibition named "America's Smithsonian," which used handheld computers iGo to lead an interactive tour, which provided information on 90 objects of the exhibition using narration, and text graphics. While in 1999 the Smithsonian Institute included the handheld computer Rocket e-Book at the "On Time" exhibition which supported hypertext files, sound, and black and white graphics. Museum futurists showed great interest in wireless networks and location aware technologies. The project Hyper Interaction with Physical Space (HIPS), sponsored by the European Commission, was one of the first projects that experimented with mobile computing and location awareness in museums [11]. Also the MIT lab is known for its interest in wearable computing through the work of Sparacino in interactive exhibit design [19]. Tate Gallery gives emphasis on museum interpretation. Tate Modern Gallery launched two pilot multimedia tours whose mission was to "to test both applications of wireless technology in the gallery, and to access a wide range of approaches to content design" [18].

Although the audience's feedback was positive towards the use of PDA's in exhibitions, the museums did not incorporate them because of practical concerns. Issues included: the fragility of the devices; the frequent need to recharge batteries; the current high cost of the devices. Cultural organizations around Greece apart from Archeoguide [21], a system based on advanced IT that provides new approaches for accessing information at cultural heritage sites, there have not been many examples of using PDAs. However, the interest for enhancing the museum experience by providing information and interpretation, as well as promoting various museum facilities with the use of handheld technologies has expanded and lately and there has been a considerable amount of research activity on this subject.

The following section states the aim of this research and focuses on the Teriade Museum to examine the possible use of PDAs to enhance museum visit experience.

3 The Museum/Library Stratis Eleftheriadis Teriade

The aim of this research is to study issues related to the design and the development of PDA applications for cultural organisations. In particular, it aims to study the real requirements for the development of museum multimedia applications for PDAs that enhance visitor's experience and provide information and interpretations about the museum collection. In order to determine the requirements for the use of PDAs to enhance the museum visit experience, it is of paramount importance to study a 'real world' situation, as only in such a situation do seemingly trivial problems arise that in reality may determine the success or failure of a system. Gunton [14], characteristically said *"if they do not like the technology they will simply not use it"* (meaning the users). The choice of a good application ensures that the end users will be motivated to use it and helps in obtaining 'real' users for evaluation. To achieve the development of a multimedia application for a PDA that aids the interpretation of the collection of "Fables" by Jean de La Fontaine, which have been illustrated by Marc Chagall and are exhibited in part of the Teriade Museum is suggested. The Fables were inspired by the tales of Greek, Hindu, Persian, Arabic and Chinese writers.

The Teriade Museum opened its door to the public in 1979 and exhibits the editorial work of Stratis Eleutheriadis Teriade, which includes copies of the "Grands Livres" and "Verve" that have been illustrated by some of the greatest artists of the 20th century like Chagall, Matisse, Picasso, Braque and others, as well as copies of medieval manuscripts. The role of the Museum is of major importance to the local community of Lesvos, as it is a focal attraction for tourists and plays an important educational role for the local schools.

The collection of Fables is of great interpretational and educational interest to Greek and European audience. The Teriade Museum pays great attention to the development of educational programs. Thus, it is believed that the development of the proposed application is an important contribution to the museum visitors and it will aid the publicity of the museum.

In its galleries Teriade Museum exhibits the only illustrations of the "Grant Livres", the "Verve" and medieval manuscripts (see Fig.1(b)). Thus, the illustrations are disconnected from the story they supplement (see Fig.1(a)), which makes it difficult for the visitor to understand their meaning and appreciate their importance. The way a collection is exhibited is a decision taken by the museum curator. One of the politics of the Teriade Museum management is to preserve the way Teriade decided to present his collection, without including interpretative information. This practically means that there are no labels, photographs, catalogues etc., but very few panels with a reference to the book a particular section of exhibited illustrations originated from and the artist who created them. Then again the Teriade Museum appreciates the visitors' requirements of being provided with more information about the collection, and connecting the illustrations to the stories, however, this should not superimpose the physical site.

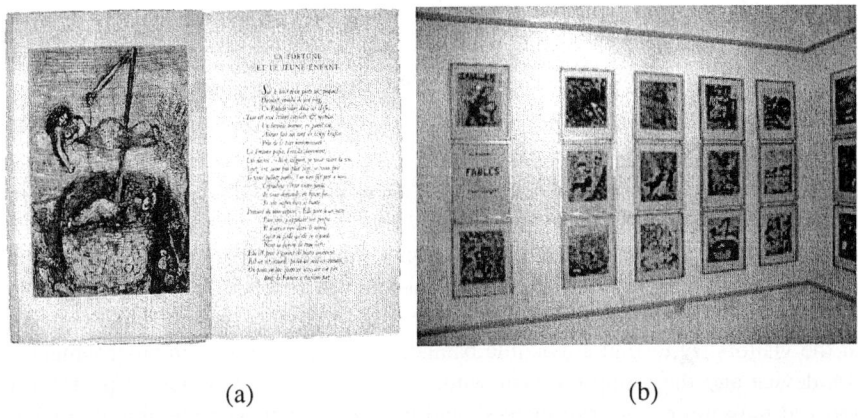

(a)   (b)

Fig. 1. (a) A snapshot of two pages of the "Fables" by Jean de La Fontaine that contains the story and the illustration by Marc Chagall. (b) One of the walls where the collection of "Fables" illustrations are exhibited at the Teriade Museum exactly the way that Teriade set it up. The stories are disconnected from their illustrations and no interpretational information about the collection is presented.

The use of PDAs technology suits adequately to the Teriade Museum requirements, as it offers a very rich way of connecting the stories to the illustrations, and providing general and interpretational information for its collections (as it incorporates visual and audio information) in an interactive, user friendly and portable way, without encroaching on the aesthetics of the gallery space.

The following sections analyse issues to be considered when developing PDA applications for museums and describes the development of the "Fables" prototype.

4 Issues Related to the Design of PDA Applications

According to Dunlop and Brewster [8] the design of successful PDA applications various factors should be considered which are mainly related to:

- the technical characteristics of the devices
- the use of the application
  These factors charge the PDA application designers with new challenges, such as:
- design for mobility
- design for a wide audience
- design for limited input/output facilities
- design for providing information based on the user location
- design for user multitasking at levels unfamiliar to most desktop users

Many times the users interact with portable appliances whilst performing many other actions (like walking etc.), therefore they cannot dedicate all their attention to the PDA monitor. Thus, the interface design should not interfere to the users' main activities [4]. To address this concern we propose the use of audio to improve usability issues. Many handheld devices use audio feedback during the typing of certain keys or in order to confirm various actions. Audio can be used to improvement the user interaction with the appliance and accordingly with the information that this contains.

5 Issues Related to the Design of PDA Applications for Museums

The design of PDA applications for museums should address the museum requirements and provide the visitors a pleasant museum experience [7]. Woodruff and his colleagues [23] studied the visitor behaviour using PDAs in museums and concluded that the visitors try to find a dynamic balance between the museum environment, the PDA device and the group the visit with. For the visitors to achieve a pleasant and improved museum experience there should be balance between the amount of information they get, the type of information made available based on various sources and the way that the information is presented. The study revealed certain issues related to the user interaction with the PDA application:

- that the visitors should be provided with visual feedback for their selection
- the information presented should be short and the system should support audio presentation of the information
- the audio information should not interfere with the interaction between visitors in the museum

In terms of the interface design, the PDA applications should pursue criteria similar to web sites development [7]. In addition, the Canadian Heritage Information Network adds some practical guidelines [5] for the graphic design of the interface:

- each screen node of the PDA application should fit the size of the PDA screen
- the navigation should be structured hierarchically

- the design of the PDA application should mach the design of the brand image of the company (museum) the application is designed for
- backtrack and easy access to the home page should be supported

The design of an aesthetically pleasing interface is important, however, the success of the system is based on accessing information in an intuitive and easy way [17].

Below the design process of the "Fables" prototype is described. User and application requirements are analysed and design solutions based on them are suggested.

6 The "Fables" Prototype

The "Fables" prototype aims to enhance the visiting experience at Teriade Museum:

- by connecting the stories to the illustrations
- by providing general and interpretative information about the Fables' illustrations that allows the visitor to understand the collection
- by helping visitors to focus their attention on specific items of the collection
- at the same time allowing the visitors to create their own personal opinion about the collection without imposing any interpretative information

In addition, the system allows the visitors to select content (text and images) that meets their personal interest and take it with them after their visit at the museum in print (a kind of a souvenir).

6.1 The Content

In order to achieve the above stated aims thorough study was required on the content to be included in the application. This was achieved by identifying the application stakeholders and their requirements. This stakeholder method of working evolved out of the Soft Systems approach [6]. The set of stakeholders consisted of the Teriade Museum curators and management, art historians who might provide various interpretations for the collection and visitors. Careful study of the above stakeholders' requirements led to the inclusion of the following content to the application:

- what are the "Fables" by Jean de La Fontaine
- what the Fables' illustrations portray, something which is not intuitive as the way the illustrations are exhibited in the museum gallery are disconnected to the text they illustrate
- why Vollard (who initially edited the Fables) chose Marc Chagall to illustrate the Fables
- what techniques Marc Chagall used to create the illustrations
- Marc Chagall's life, which helps the visitor understand the environment and the influences of the painter, also it has been stated that visitors show particular interest to finding information about people's lives [9]
- Marc Chagall as a painter
- Marc Chagall as an illustrator, which explains how Marc Chagall was involved into graphic arts

- how the Fables ended up at the Teriade Museum
- general information about the Teriade Museum
- general information about Stratis Eleutheriadis Teriade

To identify the stakeholders' needs common used techniques in requirements gathering have been used, such as interviews, focus groups and questionnaires.

Content is presented with videos made of narration and animated pictures. Text was not used as visitors cannot deal with text while moving in the gallery [22]. In addition, PDA devices are too small to provide long descriptions, therefore audio is preferred to text [18]. The videos do no exceed 1 minute duration, as long audio descriptions are tiring for the visitor [18], [23].

6.2 The Navigation System and the Prototype GUI

The user can navigate through the content by choosing the sections of their interest, or they can be automatically guided in the gallery as the system supports technology for the localisation of visitors' position in the gallery (this is based on the use of infrared technology). The user can choose to switch between manual and audio guidance at any time while using the system.

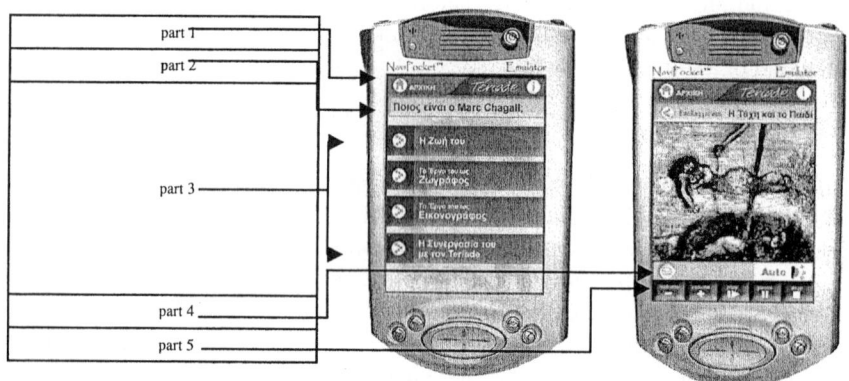

Fig. 2. The layout of the "Fables" prototype application

For the design of the application graphical user interface (GUI) and navigation system various issues of usability have been taken into consideration [16], [17]. The application interface consists of five areas as it appears in (see Fig.2):

- part 1 remains static in all pages and includes two buttons, the left one leads to the home page, and the right provides information for the Teriade Museum
- part 2 states the current section and returns to the previous page
- part 3 includes either navigation buttons that lead to the various sections and subsections of the application, or a video related to the subsections selected
- part 4 includes buttons that allow switching between auto or manual guide
- part 5 includes control buttons for the video and audio

6.3 The Prototype Implementation

One hundred illustrations of the Fables were digitised and edited for the creation of the videos. For this prototype only 5 videos have been created. For the narration a male and a female voice have been used, in order not to tire the visitor. Appropriate background sound has been incorporated to the videos.

The videos have been created with the use of Flash MX 2004 (by Macromedia) and then imported as MPEG in NaviPocket v. 2.4 by ORPHYS SYSTEMS, which was used for the implementation of the application. Navipocket, is an authoring tool which allows the creation of multimedia applications on electronic message minders of PDA type. Navipocket is a software unit intended for all the portable systems supporting an embarked OS (Version 1 functions under Microsoft Windows EC 2.xx and PocketPC). The product is a complete set of an "Editor", a "Simulator" and a "Run-time". Envisaged for a use in situation, the software privileges the speed of execution, the economy of the resources, and the facility of use without stylus.

7 The Prototype Evaluation Process and Results

The scope of the evaluation is to assess the application effectiveness, in terms of achieving its initial goal and meeting the user and application requirements, and also to assess Navipocket as an authoring tool.

For the evaluation 30 University students were used. The students went through the gallery without the use of the PDA application first and then they were interviewed to access their understanding of the collection. Then the users went through the gallery with the use of the PDA application, and they were allocated with a list of tasks (e.g. to find information about Marc Chagall – why he was involved into graphic arts, to find more about the Teriade Museum etc.) in order to be encouraged to explore the application to extract information. During their visit they were observed by the researchers, in order to identify problems with the use of the application and help them in case assistance was required. At the end of their visit the users discussed their experience with the researchers. The duration of a whole session was approximately 45 minutes. The following section states the evaluation outcome.

7.1 The Application Effectiveness

One of the main objectives of the application was to connect the illustrations to the stories they portrayed. When the users visited the gallery without using the PDA application, they did not realise which story each illustration portrayed, although they knew some of them very well (as they are very popular, for example Aesop's fables). In addition, most of the users did not know much about Marc Chagall, but they would like to get more information about him and his work. When they were asked what they thought that the illustrations portrayed, they were incapable of providing an adequate answer. This changed when the users went through the gallery with the use of the PDA application. The evaluation showed that the use of video, narration and music provides a very pleasant way for the visitor to get information. The users spent time trying to complete the tasks they have been allocated and they were able to answer most of the questions they were asked. The use of the PDA helped focussing the visitors' attention to particular areas of the gallery and the amount of time they spent at the gallery was prolonged. In the after session discussion the visitors stated that the use of the application helped them understand the meaning of the gallery and they expressed great enthusiasm using the application.

7.2 The System Usability

The scope of this part of the evaluation was to assess the effectiveness of the system in terms of usability (if they could easily find the information they required). To achieve this, the users where allocated a particular task (e.g. to locate the illustration of a particular story, to find the title of the story of a particular illustration, to find why Vollard choose Marc Chagall to illustrate the Fables, to find what technique Marc Chagall used to create the illustrations, to find particular information about the Teriade Museum). The aim was to encourage the users to navigate through various levels of the application and identify particular problems with the GUI. This is a typical method used for requirements gathering and/or for system evaluation.

The evaluation revealed that the use of the application was easy and all the users that took part in the study agreed that they were able to find the information required quickly (all the users accomplished the task that they have been allocated to find information about Chagall and how he got involved into graphic arts). The problems that have been identified were trivial and related to the wording of some titles and the icon for finding information for the Teriade Museum, which were easily updated. One of the most serious problems was the allocation of a particular illustration in the gallery. Sixty percent of the participants managed to allocate the illustration they were looking for on the wall, 20% found it after lots of difficulties and 20% did not find it at all. This task was much easier when the auto guidance was used. The users also stated some issues related to the video controls, like being able to rewind the videos forwards and backwards, to have random access of the video and provide information related to the duration of each video.

8 Conclusions

The paper presented a study for the design and the development of PDA applications to create an enhanced museum experience by providing information and interpretations about the museum collection. To address the research requirements the Teriade Museum was used as a case study. The research focused on developing a prototype application that provides interpretative information about the illustrations of the "Fables" by Jean de La Fontaine exhibited in part of a gallery of the Teriade Museum. For the development of the application a stakeholders requirements gathering approach was followed, which identified the content to be included and the way the information should be presented. The prototype evaluation revealed various issues regarding information comprehension, interpretation and usability and showed that in general the use of PDA can improve the museum experience and serve the user requirements effectively and efficiently.

Future work should focus on issues related to interpretation and the way visitors interact with museum collections with the scope to extract more information about the use of PDAs technology to better serve museum and visitors' requirements. This type of research would be particularly interesting for Greek heritage, where there is a plethora of small museums with extremely valuable collections, very often being neglected by the visitors due to ignorance or lack of information. Technological solutions like the one presented in this paper could reveal the Greek cultural heritage treasures and attract new groups of visitors.

References

1. Amirian, S.: Hand-held Mobile Computing in Museums (2001), last visited in 30/11/2004: http://www.cimi.org/whitesite/AmirianBJM.htm.
2. Archeoguide: Project Description, last visited in 19/5/2004: http://archeoguide.intranet.gr/
3. Bounia, A.: Multimedia as Interpretative Tools in the Greek Museums: General Rules and Questions. In Dascalopoulou, S. et. al (eds.): Conference Proceedings of the First International Conference of Museuology: Museum, Communication and New Technologies (2002) 17- 26.
4. Brewster, S.: Overcoming the lack of screen space on mobile computers. Personal and Ubiquitous Computing, Vol. 6 (3) (2002) 188 -205.
5. Canadian Heritage Information Network (CHIN): Tip sheets, personal digital assistants (pda), pda aesthetics and interface design, Creating and Managing Digital Content (2004), last visited in 30/11/2004: http://www.chin.gc.ca/English/Digital_Content/index.html
6. Checkland, P. & Scholes, J.: Soft Systems Methodology in Action. Chichester-NY: John Wiley & Sons. (1990)
7. Ciavarella, C. & Paterno, F.:Design criteria for location-aware, indoor, PDA applications. In Luca Chittaro (ed.): Conference Proceedings of Human-Computer Interaction with Mobile Devices and Services, 5th International Symposium Mobile HCI 2003 (2003) 131-144
8. Dunlop, M. & Brewster, S.: The challenge of mobile devices for human computer interaction. Personal and Ubiquitous Computing, Vol. 6 (4) (2002) 235 - 236
9. Economou, M.: The evaluation of museum multimedia applications: Lessons from research. Journal of Museum Management & Curatorship, Vol. 17 (2) (1998) 173-187
10. Economou, M.: New technologies in museums. Museology, International Scientific Electronic Journal, 1 (2004), last visited in 15/05/2004: http://www.aegean.gr/culturaltec/museology/papers/EconomouMaria.pdf
11. Evans, J. & Sterry, P.: Portable computers & interactive media: A new paradigm for interpreting museum collections. In D. Bearman & J. Trant (eds.): Cultural Heritage Informatics 1999: Selected papers from ICHIM 99, Kluwer Academic Publishers (1999) 93-101
12. Falk, J. & Dierking, L.: The Museum Experience. Washington, DC: Whalesback Books (1992)
13. Falk, J. & Dierking, L.: Learning from Museums: Visitor Experiences and the Making of Meaning. Walnut Creek, CA: Altamira Press (2000)
14. Gunton, T. (ed.): Information systems practice: the complete guide, Manchester: NCC Blackwell, ISBN: 1855541718 (1993)

15. Lehn, D., & Heath, C.: Displacing the object: Mobile technologies and interpretive resources. In Conference Proceedings ICHIM 03, Archives and Museum Informatics (2003)
16. Norman, D.: The Design of Everyday Things, New York: Basic Books (1998)
17. Preece, J., Rogers, Y. & Sharp, H.: Interaction design: Beyond human – computer interaction, Danvers, MA: Wiley (2002)
18. Proctor, N. & Tellis, C.: The state of the art in museum handhelds in 2003. In D. Bearman & J. Trant, (eds.): Museums and the Web 2003: Selected Papers from an International Conference. Archives & Museum Informatics (2003), last visited in 19/4/2004: www.archimuse.com/mw2003/papers/ proctor/proctor.html2003
19. Sparacino, F., Larson, K., MacNeil, R., Davenport, A.: Technologies and methods for interactive exhibit design: from wireless object & body tracking to wearable computers. In D. Bearman & J. Trant, (eds.): Cultural Heritage Informatics 1999 (1999) 147-154
20. The Museums Association (United Kingdom) definition 2002, available from World Wide Web: Defining Museums and Galleries (2002), last visited in 09/06/2005: http://www.city.ac.uk/ictop/mus-def.html
21. Vlahakis V., Ioannidis N., Karigiannis J.:ARCHEOGUIDE: Challenges and Solutions of a Personalised Augmented Reality Guide for Archaeological sites. Computer Graphics in Art, History and Archaeology, Special Issue of the IEEE Computer Graphics and Applications Magazine (2002) 52-60
22. Wilson, G.: Multimedia Tour Programme at Tate Modern. In D. Bearman & J. Trant (eds.): Museums and the Web 2004, (Arlington, Virginia / Washington DC, 31.3.2004-3.4.2004), Archives & Museum Informatics, (2004), last visited in 30/11/2004: http://www.archimuse.com/mw2004/papers/wilson/wilson.html
23. Woodruff, A., Aoki, P.M., Hurst, A. & Szymanski., M.H.: Electronic guidebooks and visitor attention. In 6th International Cultural Heritage Informatics Meeting Proceedings (2001) 437-454, last visited in 28/7/2004:
http://www2.parc.com/csl/members/woodruff/publications/2001-Woodruff-ICHIM2001-VisitorAttention.pdf

Trial Evaluation of Wireless Info-communication and Indoor Location-Based Services in Exhibition Shows

Adamantia G. Pateli, George M. Giaglis, and Diomidis D. Spinellis

Athens University of Economics and Business,
47A Evelpidon & 33 Leukados Street, 11362, Athens, Greece
{pateli, giaglis, dds}@aueb.gr

Abstract. Exhibition shows are essentially information exchange hubs. Their success relies on the quantity and quality of interaction of the involved parties: exhibitors, visitors, and organizers. The introduction of advanced wireless applications in the exhibition industry is a major opportunity for improving interaction and communications, thus leveraging the value proposition of exhibition services. This paper discusses the development and commercial trial of a Wireless Exhibition Guide that employs mobile terminals, wireless networks, and indoor location positioning technologies integrated through a set of software components, to introduce sophisticated information, communication, and navigation services for exhibition environments. Results indicate acceptance of the Wireless Exhibition Guide amongst the stakeholders of the exhibition industry, organizers, exhibitors, and visitors alike, and provide guidance towards the future of portable personalized location-sensitive information systems in information-rich environments, such as museums, conference centers, and art shows.

1 Introduction

Despite the emergence of various electronic business communication and promotion methods over the past years, exhibition fairs continue to rank as the most dynamic and effective sales and marketing tools in existence [1]. In the context of the modern economy, fairs continue to bring together market participants providing a unique opportunity for personal contact and information exchange. Moreover, fairs and exhibitions are "shop windows" offering insights into the latest industrial products and services to business and individual visitors.

As exhibition organizers compete to generate value for their shows, their attention and promotional activities have been concentrating more and more on visitors rather than on exhibitors [2]. Visitor satisfaction has become of strategic importance and has led trade fair organizers into pursuing a new strategy described by the term 'visitor orientation'. Towards implementing this strategic goal, one of the things exhibitors bear in mind, while designing and setting up their show, is the need to accomplish the 'extended-stay visit' [3]. Exhibitors are naturally interested in making visitors stay at their corporate booths as long as possible. To this end, traffic flow engineering is typically employed. Self-guided tours based on various technological means (ranging from CD-ROMs to portable computing devices) are used to direct visitors at a desired pace throughout the show. In addition, firms try to notify visitors about presentations taking place at different times of the day, so as to extend their stay in the exhibition place. At the same time, exhibitors must provide something to be remembered; this trend is referred to as 'experiential exhibiting' [4]. Technology can assist in making a sophisticated and impressive presentation of the exhibition products' unique selling points.

2 The Wireless Exhibition Guide

Drawing on the experience of previous research and commercial efforts on providing wireless services in exhibition [5, 6], museum [7] and conference settings [8], and having identified a set of technological solutions allowing for efficient peer-to-peer wireless communication and positioning of increased accuracy, a European-wide development and research team, with the participation of a number of ICT providers (Intracom Hellenic Telecommunications and Electronics Industry S, L.M. Ericsson A/S, Elisa Communications Corporation, Pouliadis Associates Corporation, Space Systems Finland Ltd.), research institutes (Research Center of Athens University of Economics and Business, Helsinki University of Technology) and exhibition venue owners (The Finnish Fair Corporation, ROTA Ltd.), initiated a research project, partially funded by the European Commission, to design and develop a Wireless Exhibition Guide (WEG). The WEG aimed to exploit the technological opportunities arising from evolution in the areas of wireless networks and indoor positioning technologies [9] to provide value-added services supporting the professionals and customers in the exhibition industry in a context-aware manner [10].

The following sections discuss in brief several aspects of the Wireless Exhibition Guide development, such as the technology applied (sub-systems and infrastructure), a usage scenario indicative of the services provided for the three stakeholders of the exhibition sector (exhibition organizers, exhibitors, and visitors), and the results from the system's testing and user evaluation in a real exhibition event.

2.1 A WEG Use Scenario

The scenario involves Philip, a visitor in the "Mobile Expo" organized by Finnish Fair Corporation (FFC) in Finland, who uses a set of value-added services provided by the WEG application.

Philip enters the exhibition center and passes through the reception. The registration staff of FFC asks for his invitation and the visitor informs them about his online pre-registration. The secretariat asks the visitor if he wishes to use the WEG. After getting all the required information, Philip agrees to download the WEG software to his device under the guidance of the FFC technical staff. While he is about to enter the exhibition hall, he meets a colleague, Charles, who is about to register onsite. Philip, who is a leader and moderator of a group comprising of the company's employees, is inviting Charles to become member of the group. After that, Charles gets his device as well, and they go on their different ways. Before splitting, they both ask to view on their devices a personalized and location-aware navigation plan.

Since Philip wishes to locate specific products, he uses his device to locate stands with the specific products on the map. After locating those stands on the navigation plan, he takes the routing advice of his device to get there. As he approaches the stand of interest, he receives alerts for offerings based on his profile as well as targeted promotional spots of certain exhibits from the exhibitors. While wandering through the stands, Philip gets recommendations for specific events as well as common announcements (e.g. the exhibition is about to close). He is visiting 3 or 4 other stands that are in his list, and he follows the exact same procedure with the previous ones.

After being in the exhibition for 3 hours, Philip decides to take a break for a snack or coffee so he moves towards the closest restaurant or rest area by using his navigation plan and routing advice on his device. On his way to the restaurant, he decides to meet with Charles, so he uses the system to track him since they both belong to the same user group. When he manages to position Charles, he sends a real-time message asking him to meet in five minutes in the restaurant area. Before sitting in the restaurant, they connect to the nearest kiosk to get information on their visit trail and movements up to this moment. Before leaving the exhibition center, Philip asks to get information on nearby means of transportation.

While being at home or in the office, Philip gets connected to the Internet, gets access to the WEG software, and downloads the material that he requested through bookmarks, as well as additional promotion material sent either by organizers or exhibitors. Furthermore, replying to the organizers' request, he uses the system to send feedback by giving his response to an online questionnaire.

2.2 The Technology Solution

The Wireless Exhibition Guide technology solution is implemented through a set of software and hardware components. The way in which these are integrated is more thoroughly discussed in prior research works [10, 11]. This section briefly discusses the WEG technology solution in terms of system architecture (*Fig. 1*).

The core component of the Wireless Exhibition Guide system is the **application server**, which is responsible for handling user requests and realizing the relevant application logic (e.g. navigation assistance, personalized recommendations, "bookmarking" capability, business cards exchange, monitoring of mobile terminal locations, content management). The application server receives user requests via either the Internet or the wireless network installations of the exhibition center. Two **wireless networking technologies** (802.11b WLAN and Bluetooth) are employed and tested to provide wireless access to visitors, exhibitors, and exhibitor organizers within the exhibition boundaries.

The delivery of location-based services and information (i.e. targeted messages [12], bookmarking, virtual trail) is enabled via **two indoor positioning technologies**; WLAN-based Positioning System and Indoor GPS System. WLAN-based Positioning is based on the WLAN infrastructure, which is also used for transferring data to and from the users. Indoor GPS constitutes a rather innovative positioning solution developed by Space Systems Finland Ltd. The indoor GPS system includes: a) a number of ground transmitters, pseudolites (pseudo-satellites) that emulate the signal of GPS satellites and replace GPS in the exhibition environment, b) a set of reference receivers that are used for signal integrity provision and synchronization of the pseudolites signals, and c) the Master Control Station (MCS) running the control software for providing monitoring, configuration, and control of the whole system.

The **wireless devices** that enable access to the application server and delivery of the WEG navigation, communication and information services include Personal Digital Assistants (PDAs) and laptops. Visitors use PDAs to make bookmark requests, receive exhibition content, and routing information. During the trial operation of the system, a specific PDA (iPAQ 3870) was selected to test visitors' services. Nevertheless, other models of PDA devices can as well be used provided that they are WLAN-enabled and have a free PCMCIA socket for a GPS receiver. Visitors can also use laptops for preparing their visit before the exhibition and review their visit after it. Exhibitors and exhibition organizers can use wireless connected laptops to receive statistics, get real-time notifications, and submit exhibition content.

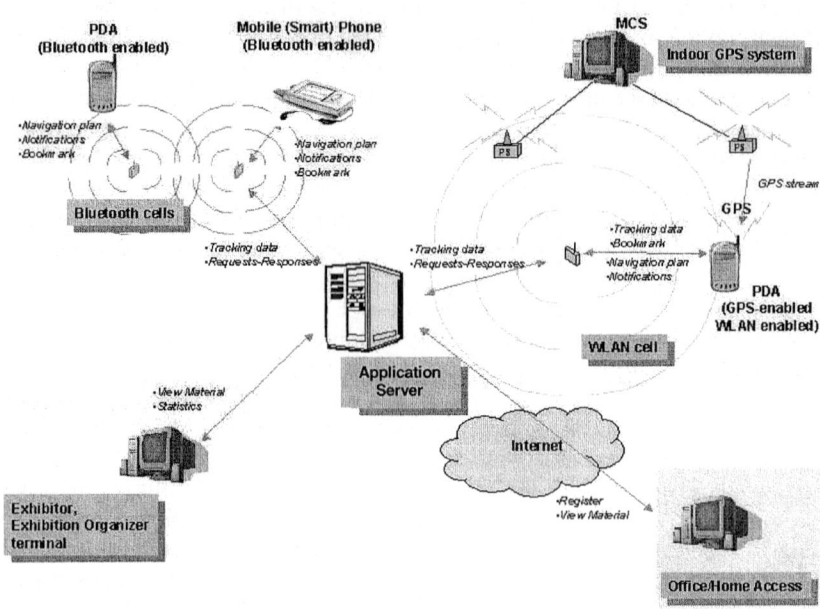

Fig. 1. Technical Architecture of the Wireless Exhibition Guide

3 Trial Design

The trial operation of the WEG prototype took place in the FFC Exhibition Center, Helsinki, Finland on 18–19 March 2004 during the ViiniExpo (The Wine Exhibition). The trial consisted of two stages. Stage I included testing of the primary technologies applied first in isolation and then in integration, while Stage II concerned the evaluation of the system's services from the end-user perspective. The whole paper is primarily focused on Stage II (user evaluation), the methodology employed and results. Regarding Stage I, due to space restrictions, we considered it important to include information on only the positioning accuracy achieved by the two principal wireless technologies (WLAN-based and Indoor GPS).

3.1 End-User Evaluation Methodology

The principal objectives set for the evaluation of the WEG included:
a) Collecting data on users' attitude towards the future use of the system,
b) Assessing overall experience and satisfaction with the WEG services.

A total of 17 persons were involved in the evaluation process of the WEG prototype: 12 visitors, 3 exhibitors, and 2 organizers. They were all interviewed and then given an evaluation form to fill in.

The trial, which lasted two days, gave emphasis on visitors' experience of the system with the use of PDAs. In addition, the trial focused on testing the delivery of position services, which had been considered as the most important feature of the Wireless Exhibition Guide during the user requirements phase. *Table 1* indicates which validation methods applied in each user group.

Table 1. Evaluation Methods applied per test-group

Evaluation Methods / Test Group	Visitors	Exhibitors	Organizers
– Test Tasks	X	X	
– Interview	X	X	X
– Observation	X		
– Evaluation Form	X	X	X
– Demonstration			X

In practice, visitors performed a set of test tasks, while being under observation. The evaluation expert went through all tests with users playing the role of moderator. Visitors were asked to perform 8 tasks in total. They were also asked to think aloud while interacting with the system. When all test tasks were completed, the moderator asked visitors some general questions and then left them some free time to fill in an evaluation form. Exhibitors performed about 10 test tasks in total. Before any task, they were shortly introduced to the WEG system from the visitor's side in order to be able to imagine how their customers interact with the system. Also exhibitors were told to think aloud and fill in an evaluation form being tailored to their interaction with the system. For organizers, there were no test tasks available. Instead, the whole functionality of the WEG system was demonstrated to them, so that they evaluate it from the viewpoint of the candidate buyer of the software. In practice, organizers were asked to evaluate the system from all the three user groups' side.

3.2 Evaluation Tool

Following, we present the main sections, which correspond to the primary evaluation criteria, of the delivered evaluation forms.

- **User Interface & Performance.** Users are asked whether the User Interface (fonts, color, position, menus, forms) is aesthetically pleasant and exciting, as well as whether the systems is easy to learn, is easy to operate and has satisfactory performance speed.
- **Value of Services.** For each essential and innovative service, its perceived value is measured. The formal definition of usefulness is "the degree to which a person believes that using a particular system would enhance his or her job performance" [13]. In the exhibition context, the system should enhance the visiting and communication experience of visitors, the communication and promotion performance of exhibitors and the management and monitoring ability of organizers in a manner complementary to curren practices.
- **General Attitude Towards the System.** Issues like trust and willingness to use are faced in this part. Users are asked to declare their willingness to use the system in the future. However, the Perceived Ease of Use and Perceived Usefulness are considered by the TAM construct as the key factors influencing the users' behavioral intention and actual use of the system [14]. Users are also asked to state their intention to pay for getting the systems' services as well as the price level they can afford for getting the system's services.
- **Overall mobile experience and satisfaction from the system.** Questions in this part examine the overall experience from using mobile devices and mobile technologies along with the overall satisfaction of using a new system to support visiting experience [15]. Users are asked to compare their experience to the one gained during exhibition visits in the "traditional" way.

4 Trial Results and Business Implications

Due to the restricted size of the test sample, the data collected from the three user groups via observation, interview and evaluation forms could not be analyzed with quantitative statistical methods. Instead, qualitative methods are employed to stress the main strengths and weaknesses of the system, as they were verbally expressed but also coded in the delivered questionnaires.

4.1 End-User Evaluation Results

Test users who played the role of visitors were very keen about the features of the WEG. Some of them rated the system very high, despite the usability problems and the relative instability of the system during the trial. Others were not so happy with their visiting experience. This was naturally reflected in their comments (interviews and forms) and can be explained by their high expectations from the system. Conversely, for those whose expectations were not so high, technical problems that were presented were not insurmountable. Regarding the positioning services that were provided, these were seen as key drivers for the use of the software. In addition to positioning features, communication features were also found interesting and useful. Especially the message service was considered to be an advantageous feature. However, users were not happy with the way in which these services were delivered, since communication features suffered from usability problems. Some key statements/ suggestions of visitors are presented in *Table 2*.

Table 2. Visitors' Suggestions for Improvement

❏ *"The real added value concretizes in bigger exhibitions (CEBIT, COMDEX, etc.)"*
❏ *"There should also be some features that show users' location and their direction when they move"*
❏ *"If users can choose the most interesting stands before, those stands should be seen in different color on map when entering to exhibition hall"*
❏ *"As, in the next two or three years, almost everyone will have a smart phone (or a similar mobile device), it would be useful to be able to use the Wireless Exhibition Guide through smart phones as well".*

Visitors were keen to use position based services in future, and they were also "happy to see the glimpse of WLAN in action" for the very first time. The positive attitude towards the system can be analyzed in the user needs context as they were set at the first place. In the case of visitors, it can be said that apart from some existing needs raised from the exhibition visiting experience, there were also needs which emerged only during the WEG use experience. General requirements like to know where you are, to locate companies and stands as easily as possible and to share your experiences with others can be considered "universal needs". The WEG satisfied this kind of needs in a satisfactory level, and this is why the majority of visitors involved to test appreciated these features. On the contrary, needs like "to avoid the information overload" and "to get just the information user wants at particular time/place" were clearly born by the usage of the WEG system. Namely, the system's ability to offer limited or regulated information based on user's location to avoid unnecessary actions (like scrolling long lists of exhibitors), were features which visitors found surprisingly useful. This is the result of the technology's ability to create new needs, not just satisfy the existing ones.

Test users in the role of exhibitors were first introduced to the features visitors used through a PDA. After this short demonstration, exhibitors were asked to conduct ten test tasks designed only for them. The expectations of exhibitors were quite neutral. Maybe this was one reason why they were considerably happy with the elements of the WEG. They identified a number of very useful and value-added tools provided by the system. Their specific comments are quoted in *Table 3*.

Overall, exhibitors were also quite satisfied with the elements and features of the WEG. In more specific terms, the ability to use tools for analyzing and reporting visitors was found as a new useful and quite valuable service. The identified usability shortcomings somehow affected the overall experience, but still exhibitors saw the whole service as a good tool that could generate added value in their exhibition experience.

There were two exhibition industry organizations involved in the trial, Finnexpo and ROTA. Representatives of those companies were first shown the visitor's part of

Table 3. Exhibitors' Suggestions for Improvement

> - *The Analyzing and Reporting Tool was found "Useful tool to know what kind of individuals or groups of individuals have been visiting the exhibition or stands" and "Very valuable tool for after-sales service".*
> - *The Virtual Business Cards facility was considered a value-added service because "It can consist of more important information of a company and its products than traditional business cards or brochures".*
> - *The Communication tool was characterized as "a very handy tool for sending messages to certain individuals characterized by some attributes vital to exhibitor's own interests".*

the system (with PDA in the exhibition hall). After this short demonstration, they were asked to use the system via PC at the same place where exhibitors did their tasks (the office set-up). Some of the WEG services, such as the online exhibitor catalogue and the pre-registration facility, were already offered by the exhibition organizers though one or more web-based information systems. However, the very added value of the WEG was the fact that organizers did not have just one system in use that would incorporate all valuable features. Thus, the system could even, in principle, somehow replace or supplement their current business practices and systems. This was the main reason why organizers also liked the WEG. But at the same time, they were skeptical about the ability of the system to integrate with their legacy systems. Despite this skepticism, several very useful and precious features were found. Especially tools for creating and viewing questionnaires, as well as extracting statistical reports, were seen very handy in order to replace their existing practice of getting feedback from visitors. However, *"if the system could generate real-time information, such as how many visitors are on-line at a particular time, which stands are the most popular ones, then it would offer even more positive feedback to organizers"*.

Organizers were the most significant test group. Their high requirements and expectations from the use of the WEG system were due to having already part of the WEG services in place through their legacy systems. However, organizers lacked an integrated system with all essential features incorporated. This was considered as the core value that the WEG system generated for exhibition organizers. Moreover, navigation and positioning services were also seen as critical source of value, since the organizers do not currently offer such services in their exhibition events.

4.2 Positioning Accuracy

The achieved positioning accuracy of the visitors is described as a part of the evaluation results, since it affects the user experience significantly and is referred frequently in the evaluation results by the test users. There were two separate positioning subsystems in operation, but it was transparent to the main server which (either one or both) of them was in use at a time.

4.2.1 iGPS Positioning Subsystem

The pseudolite system trials were conducted in a different hall of the Finnish Fair Expo Center. Although the actual usability tests were conducted in Hall 4, where the actual Wine exhibition was taking place, the pseudolite tests were performed in another exhibition hall (Hall 2) (*Fig. 2*). This was due to the lack of small and unnoticeable end-user receivers that could be used in a transparent way in the exhibition place.

The test results showed that the pseudolite system is capable of providing very good positioning accuracies in an indoor environment. In the beginning of the project, it was estimated that an accuracy of 1 meter would serve the needs of an exhibition application. During the tests, we showed that sub-meter, and even sub-decimetre, accuracies can be acquired using the pseudolites. Specifically, the achieved positioning DRMS (distance root mean square) for 2-dimensional positioning (x, y) was 0.06m and 0.24m for 3-dimensional positioning (x, y, z). Although the current system is not feasible for real exhibitions due to the inconvenient size of the end-user receiver, discussions with receiver manufacturers revealed that small and efficient receivers should be available by early 2005.

Fig. 2. The pseudolite antenna attached to the ceiling of the Exhibition Hall 2

4.2.2 Wireless LAN Positioning Subsystem

The wireless LAN access network covered the whole FFC Exhibition Centre, and thus the WLAN positioning system was available in both halls, the mock-up site in Hall 2 as well as the actual exhibition site in Hall 4. The positioning system only needed the installation of the positioning client software at the client device side. Due to this practical reason, the user tests of the final trial evaluation were performed only by using the WLAN positioning system and standard Compaq iPAQ's with WLAN accessibility in Exhibition Hall 4.

The achieved accuracy in the un-optimized network of the FFC Exhibition hall (*Fig. 3*) was fair: 4.2 meters in average. This was achieved with just a basic WLAN access network, consisting of only 2 access points per hall and without any optimization to the access point settings. The average accuracy is fairly good, but occasional errors of more than 10 meters appeared every now and then.

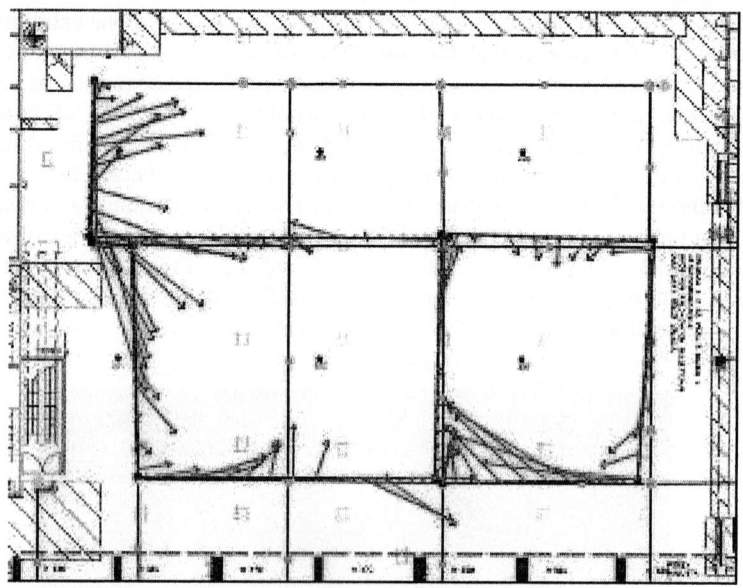

Fig. 3. Test User Walking Paths - Normal WLAN with high transmit power and low number of access points (FFC Exhibition Center)

5 Conclusions and Further Research

The evaluation trials have indicated that the WEG has achieved a high degree of overall acceptance. Despite some minor technical problems, mainly regarding the stability of the system in the case of multiple PDA users interacting with it in parallel sessions, all user groups were satisfied with the overall experience of having a personal exhibition guide, which provided them with navigation services and location-based information. User feedback has been recorded in detail in order to feed future re-design and re-development efforts on the WEG technology and service solution.

One of the primary innovative features of the WEG is the use of an indoor GPS system able to locate users with a quite great accuracy, compared to the positioning abilities of WLANs. The described indoor GPS solution has been implemented with the integration of a rather large module into the PDA device. Adding the GPS module has rendered the PDA device unacceptably large and has also significantly decreased its battery life. Future versions of the WEG should handle this problem by using either chipless GPS technology, which several device manufacturers are currently investigating, or a single chip that will handle all GPS functions [16]. Both GPS technology solutions will greatly contribute to minimizing both the power assumption and the size of the device to be used for accessing the WEG services.

Towards the purpose of convergence of voice and data services, the implementation of the same technology solution based on interconnection of wireless and mobile networks is proposed. The challenge concerns the provision of roaming services from mobile to wireless network and vice versa. To cover future inter-network roaming for users of wireless location-based services, an integrated location management architecture, much like the one proposed by Varshney [17], should be developed. Such architecture supports location tracking in other wireless networks (WLANs, PANs) as well as in cellular networks (GSM, GPRS) and satellites. The proposed solution would allow the WEG users to access multiple networks while being in the exhibition show, thus increasing the value of the WEG solution.

The current analysis of WEG business solution has triggered interest in analyzing the successful conditions, under which commercialization of WEG could be achieved. Based on alternative patterns of alliance formation, with the purpose of the WEG commercialization, among actors of the mobile and exhibition industry, a wide range of alternative business models can be identified and designed [18]. In practice, we expect that more than one business model for the exploitation of the WEG can apply given differences in the organizational and market conditions. We contend that the final selection/decision on the business model to be applied in a given situation will be based on a number of factors regarding both the internal and external environment of the candidate service providers, such as size, competitive position and corporate strategy (internal factors), but also competition degree, technology uncertainty, and market maturity (external factors).

References

1. UFI - The Global Association of the Exhibition Industry: Trade Fairs: A Powerful Marketing Tool (2004) [available online from: http://www.ufinet.org/, last accessed on: 9th August 2004].
2. Munuera, J., Ruiz, S.: Trade Fairs as Services: A Look at Visitors Objectives in Spain. Journal of Business Research 44 (1999) 17-24.
3. Spaeth F.: The Extended-stay Exhibit. EXHIBITOR Magazine, November (2001) [available online from: http://www.exhibitornet.com/exhibitormagazine /article.asp?ID=66, last accessed on: 24th April 2002].
4. Konopacki A.: New Trends In Exhibiting. Research Report (2002) [available online from: http://www.tradeshowresearch.com /pubs3/ntie.html, last accessed on 9th August 2004].
5. Bieber, G., Giersich, M.: Personal mobile navigation systems - design considerations and experiences. Computers and Graphics 25 (2001) 563-570.
6. Kraemer, R.: Bluetooth Based Wireless Internet Applications for Indoor Hot Spots: Experience of a Successful Experiment During CeBIT 2001. In: Proceedings of the 26th Annual IEEE Conference on Local Computer Networks, November 14 - 16, Tampa - USA (2001)
7. Bianchi, A., Zancanaro, M.: Tracking users' movements in an artistic physical space. In: Proceedings of the I3 Second Annual Conference, October 20-22, Siena- Italy (1999)
8. Cox, D., Kindratenko, V., Pointer, D.: IntelliBadge™. In: Proceedings of the 1st International Workshop on Ubiquitous Systems for Supporting Social Interaction and Face-to-Face Communication in Public Spaces, 5th Annual Conference on Ubiquitous Computing - UbiComp 2003, October 12-14, Seattle – WA (2003) 41-47

9. Giaglis, G.M., Pateli, A., Fouskas, K., Kourouthanassis, P., Tsamakos, A.: On the Potential Use of Mobile Positioning Technologies in Indoor Environments. In: Loebbecke, C., Wigard, R.T., Gricar, J., Pucihar, A., Lenart, G. (eds.): Fifteenth Bled Electronic Commerce Conference - e-Reality: Constructing the eEconomy, June 17-19, Bled - Slovenia, Vol. 1. (2002) 413-429
10. Mathes I., Pateli A., Tsamakos, A., Spinellis, D.: Context aware services in an Exhibition Environment- the mEXPRESS approach. In: Stanford-Smith, B. et al. (eds.): Challenges and Achievements in E-business and E-work: Proceedings of the E-business and E-work Conference, October 16-18, Prague, The Czech Republic (2002) 685-692
11. Pateli, A., Spinellis, D., Giaglis, G.: Wireless Info-Communication and Navigation Services in Exhibition Shows. In: Horwitch, M. (eds.): PROCEEDINGS – The Third International Conference on M-Business – m>Business 2004, Uncovering the Next Waves – Major Opportunities and the Essential Lessons, July 12–13, New York - USA. (2004)
12. Tsilira, A., Pateli, A., Athanasiadis, E., Spinellis, D.: Targeted Messages in Indoor Mobile Environment: A Software-Oriented Approach. In: Proceedings of the IASTED International Conference on SOFTWARE ENGINEERING ~SE~ 2004, February 17-19, Innsbruck, Austria (CD- ROM Proceedings) (2004)
13. Davis, F.: Perceived Usefulness, Perceived Ease of Use, and User Acceptance of Information Technology. MIS Quarterly (1989) 319-340
14. Lee, W., Kim, T., Chung, J.: User Acceptance of the Mobile Internet. In: Proceedings of the First International Conference on Mobile Business, July 8-9, Athens - Greece (2002)
15. Mills, J.E., Morrison, A. M.: Measuring Customer Satisfaction with Online Travel. In: Proceedings of ENTER 2003 Conference, January 29–31, Helsinki - Finland (2003)
16. Kumar, S., Stokeland, J.: Evolution of GPS technology and its subsequent use in commercial markets. International Journal of Mobile Communications 1 (2003) 180-193
17. Varshney, U.: Location management for wireless networks: issues and directions. International Journal of Mobile Communications 1 (2003) 91-118
18. Maitland, C. F., Van de Kar, E. A. M, De Montalvo, U. W.: Network Formation for Provision of Mobile Information and Entertainment Services. In: Proceedings of the 16th Bled Electronic Commerce Conference - eTrasformation, June 9-11, Bled - Slovenia (CD-ROM – Proceedings) (2003)

Epidemic Collaborative Geocast for Reliable Segmented File Sharing in Mobile Peer-to-Peer Devices

Constandinos X. Mavromoustakis and Helen D. Karatza

Department of Informatics,
Aristotle University of Thessaloniki,
54124 Thessaloniki, Greece
{cmavrom, karatza}@csd.auth.gr

Abstract. The dual problem of searching resources in the network and that of disseminating with reliability resources selectively in an infrastructureless wireless network is yet unexplored. This paper proposes an approach based on the advantages of epidemic selective dissemination through mobile Infostations. The proposed scheme combines the strengths of both proactive multicast group establishment (flexible Geocasting) and hybrid Infostation concept and attempts to fill the gap between mobility and reliable file sharing for mobile peer to peer users. This method faces the flooding problem and enables end to end reliability by forwarding requested packets to epidemically 'selected' mobile users in the network. Examination through simulation is performed for the response and reliability offered by epidemic collaborative Geocast method showing a significant robustness in reliable file sharing among mobile peers.

1 Introduction

While MP2P objects[1] sharing is user driven as happens to the internet, a crucial issue is which dissemination strategy will be used. MANets due to the frequent and unexpected changes in topology and short lived devices characteristics are not robust to host with reliability resource/file sharing among mobile peers. Thus by applying epidemiological models to information diffusion allows the evaluation of such strategies depending on the MANET characteristics, e.g. the node density. In order to choose appropriate strategies at run time, the model should be easily evaluated. Reliability in highly changing topology networks is a major issue since their moving characteristics trade off the end user's QoS. Thus optimally designed systems have to offer end user reliability and integrity by enabling reliable sharing of information.

Unlike cellular systems where users enjoy a constant connectivity, MP2P systems are "short-lived". Connections between peers on the network are prone to failures. MP2P devices have many negative characteristics like short connections times, unpredictable disconnections (range and battery failure), small network formation factor, and file's unavailability. In this paper a reliable file sharing scheme for MP2P devices is proposed taking the advantages of epidemic file dissemination through mobile users

---

[1] The term "objects" refer to a general term pointing to files or memory addresses(file references, memory references).

and mobile Infostations [1, 9, 10]. Through geographical landscapes where Infostations are set and initialized, the modified epidemic protocol creates a replicated object in order to enable MP2P reliable file sharing. This scheme proved its scalability in node's density since it does not require the knowledge of network at any single host. Additionally it does not require spatial distributions to efficiently spread information while enables reliability in supported mobility.

The organization of the paper is as follows: Section 2 discusses the related work that has been done for MP2P reliable information sharing, featuring out the basic principles and the conducted solutions by different schemes. Section 3 then introduces the proposed reliable file sharing scheme for MP2P users, followed by section 4 which provides the evaluation and simulation results of the proposed scheme in contrast to the Geocast characteristics and reliability factors for file sharing in MP2P environment. Finally, Section 5 concludes with a summary of our contribution and further research.

2 Related Work

MP2P environment represent a new class of computing with large numbers of resource-constrained computing nodes, cooperating on a single or group of applications. MP2P devices must often operate for extended periods of time unattended, where evolving analysis and environments can change application requirements, creating the need to alter the network's behavior. Totally different from the traditional method of programming a node over a dedicated link, the embedded nature of these systems requires a mechanism to propagate new code over the network.

In general, the information sharing process should require a minimal amount of time. This not only reduces any service interruptions to a deployed application, but is also reduces information sharing reliability. Recent researches in reliable information sharing require dense networks in order to bind network partitioning. However, in dense networks, the contention and collisions caused by the random interactions of neighboring nodes harms the performance since file sharing techniques rely on overhearing. In turn overhearing drives the network to generate a huge overhead in order to "hear" the peers. This issue can be disastrous for sensitive information since capacity limitations can take place in each node due to overhearing, and information will be lost[2].

For data dissemination in wireless networks, naive retransmission of broadcasts can lead to the broadcast storm problem [2], where redundancy, contention, and collisions impair performance and reliability. The authors in [2] discuss the need to have a controlled retransmission scheme and propose several schemes, such as probabilistic and location based methods. The experiments were conducted by Ganesan et al. In [3] authors identify several interesting effects at the link-layer, notably the highly irregular packet reception contours, the likeliness of asymmetric links, and the complex propagation dynamics of simple protocols. In [4] an epidemic algorithm is proposed based on strictly local interactions for managing replicated databases in a robust way for unpredictable communication failures. The epidemic property is important since

---

[2] The same time security issues arise.

MP2P devices experience high loss rates due to their unpredictable movements, their asymmetric connectivity, and to node failures in the "repopulation" process [5]. When a mobile node makes an explicit request for a resource, the whole network is flooded with a query, like mobile ad-hoc route discovery algorithms [6]. In [7] data replication schemes are proposed for ad hoc networks which are based on the improvement of data accessibility. However, this approach may not be valid when the link failure probability is taken into consideration. Another drawback is that it only considers the accessibility, without considering the query delay. Significant improvements of the basic flooding approaches using advertisements and geographic information have also been recently studied [8]. This work proposes a reliable autonomous file sharing scheme with use of the new concept of mobile Infostations where is a variant of fixed Infostation proposed in [1, 11, 13]. In this work the file sharing mechanism is essentially stateless, where neither routing information is required nor global information like knowledge of the destination nodes is required. The basic advantage, while enabling high reliability and ensuring that file sharing will complete successfully, is that this scheme does not flood the whole network. By adopting the idea of geographical landscapes where initialized Infostations are set in, the modified epidemic protocol creates a replicated object to mobile Infostations in order to enable P2P reliable file sharing in an "any cast" form.

3 Epidemic Collaborative Replication for Maintaining File Sharing Reliability in Mobile Peer-to-Peer Devices

This section describes the reliable autonomous file sharing scheme with use of the mobile Infostations, which bounds the dissemination of requested files in geographical landscapes in an epidemic way.

3.1 Cooperative Mobile Infostations in Organized Landscapes

Recently, new ideas are emerging contrasting the concept of "run anywhere, anytime" pervasive systems, such as Infostations and ad hoc networks. Such systems are based on the waterfilling concept, where the transmission occurs only when source and destination are close together to ensure reliability. Results obtained for these issues [1, 9, 11] have provided good estimates that permit such systems to become the basis for low cost, wireless data transmission.

The idea of MANETs is also contrasting the ubiquitous coverage paradigm of the cellular systems. But taking into account that the capacity of MANETs is constrained by the mutual interference of concurrent transmissions between nodes, security and reliability issues arise on a mobility based scenario. Some research results presented in [10], introduce mobility into a fixed network model, which show that the average throughput per source-destination pair can be kept constant even if the number of nodes per unit area increases. This improvement is obtained through the exploitation of the time-variation of the user's channel due to mobility. The new concept in [10] is to split the packets of each source node to as many nodes as possible. Therefore, strategies of this type incur additional delay, because packets have to be buffered until

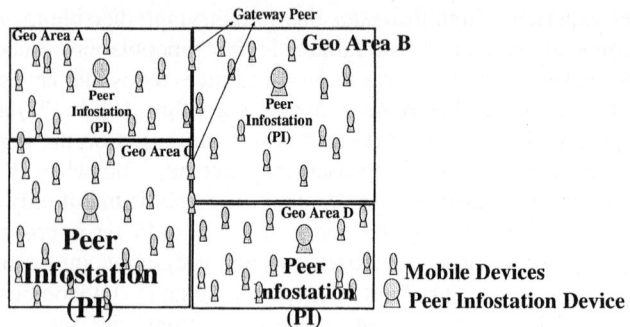

Fig. 1. Geographical landscape with the hybrid Infostation model

the channel becomes sufficiently strong for transmission(s). Taking into account all the above reasons, this paper adopts the idea of Infostation into geographical landscapes. Figure 1 shows the basic Infostation model applied in a geographical landscape.

Infostations consist of high bit rate connectivity which can be seen as independent access ports to the Internet, or (clustered) organized into groups having a common server (Cluster Infostation Controller-CIC). Different locations and characteristics of user mobility patterns for different scenarios are depicted in [11, 12]. In such scenarios[3] the controllers are connected to the internet through a backbone network. Combining the pure Infostation system with a mobility based framework we introduce the Hybrid Mobile Infostation System (HyMIS) where the primary Infostation is not static (PI) but can move with lower velocity[4] than other selected Infostations. Secondary mobile Infostations could move across an area forming a cluster with other peers and exchanging information with PI of each landscape. PI is selected only if it is set in the centre of the landscape/geographic area. A mobile user becomes a PI if is centrally located in each landscape. Additionally PI covers only a specified circle of radius R.

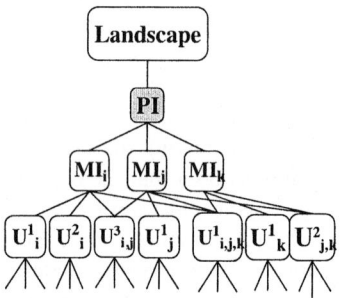

Fig. 2. The hybrid peer-to-peer Infostation based architecture (HyMIS)

---

[3] The drive through, the walk-through, and sit-through scenario(stationary users).
[4] That might be research criterion for selecting a device to be PI.

The R radius coefficient depends (as in all mobile hosts) to signal power. HyMIS architecture resolves the disadvantages of the pure MP2P architecture in terms of inefficient routing, network partitioning and lack of security.

This hybrid Infostation system adopts the basic concept of pure Infostation system in terms of capacity node but without flooding the network with unnecessary flow of information. This capacity node plays a role of control storage node [13]. On the contrary to [13] this work proposes a hybrid peer-to-peer architecture shown figure 2. PI is selected[5] and located in the center of every landscape covering a certain predetermined area. A mobile peer is chosen to be PI only if it has high residual energy and capacity and moves with low velocity (or stall). This means that for a certain time distance T (until it remains as the PI of the landscape) will be near or located at the centre of the landscape6. Additionally Mobile Infostations (MIs) are set dynamically, based essentially on the residual spare capacity as is explained in the following section. These MIs are users that are in the landscape creating a tree of MIs users and PI users. This principle is shown in figure 2. As depicted in figure 2, $U^1_{i,j,k}$ is downloading simultaneously from MI_i, MI_j, MI_k or vice versa. The coexistence of PIs (that do not change landscape every while) and MIs, simultaneously recovers from the split of the peer-to-peer network, and improves the network topology connectivity. In order to improve the inefficiency of the pure peer-to-peer flooding tactic an epidemic object replication scheme is chosen for reliable file sharing. This scheme is described in the following section.

3.2 Epidemic Object Replication Scheme for Reliable File Sharing

Distributing information within networks can be very complicated particularly if hosts do not have wider knowledge of the properties of the network. As a result many problems occur when it is highly important that a certain information or group of information (file(s)) have to reach one particular host or all hosts within the entire network. Epidemic algorithms follow a nature paradigm by applying simple rules to efficiently spread information by just having a local view of the environment. According to this fact, epidemic algorithms are easy to implement and guarantee message propagation in heterogeneous environments.

To achieve reliability in MP2P environments a dynamic gossiping scheme must be used. Secure file sharing can be determined by relying on epidemic algorithms, a breed of distributed algorithms that find inspiration in the theory of epidemics. Epidemic (or gossip) algorithms constitute a scalable, lightweight, and robust way of reliably disseminating information to a recipient or group of recipients, by providing guarantees in probabilistic terms. Based on certain characteristics, epidemic algorithms are amenable to the highly dynamic scenarios. In this work a promiscuous caching is used which means that data can be cached "anywhere, anytime". However this enables trade offs in consistency for availability which is faced with cooperative MI used in landscapes described earlier.

---

[5] Selection is based on the low velocity criterion and trajectory of each device.
[6] We assume that each node is informed about reaching each Lanscape's centre and also if is candidate to become a PI.

In a MP2P system each user might desire to share or download a file or files with other users (peers). Many conditions must be satisfied for reliable communication between mobile peers. On one hand users due to their mobility might draw away from the user (peer) that a file sharing communication takes place. On the other hand a sudden network partitioning or network split could occur because of network's dynamic topology which is continuously changing. Thus a proactive dissemination scheme must be determined in order to prevent the cutoff in file sharing communication. This work assumes an isolated system comprising of a fixed number of mobile nodes confined in a predefined geographic region. These nodes are mobile, and communicate with each other in a wireless (radio) ad-hoc manner. As studied in [8, 10, 12] there is a trade off between reliable coverage and data rate. The limited connectivity coverage that MP2P systems offer, results in significant delay in downloading a message or file (group of packets). In the proposed scenario each node carries some unique data items. During the period for which the system is studied, no new node is inserted in the network.

Each mobile host m_k has a predetermined capacity M. At any time in the network each m_k has a state. There are three states that m_k can be characterized: the susceptible state $S(t)$ represents the number of hosts in the system which are "susceptible," infected state $I(t)$ represents the number of "infected" hosts, and $R(t)$ represents the "recovered" hosts. A host is in susceptible state $S(t)$ if the device does not share any information with any other host. In turn A host is in infected state $I(t)$ if a file(s) share occurs. Finally a host is in "recovered" state $R(t)$ if any shared file(s) are no longer pending. A Markov chain model of an infectious disease with susceptible, infected, and recovered states is used shown in figure 3. Markov chain model was chosen to evaluate this extra storage requirement, for modeling of infectious diseases to determine the file sharing termination criteria.

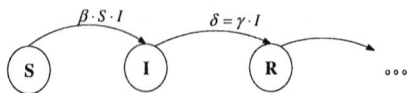

Fig. 3. Markov chain model of an infectious disease with susceptible, infected, and recovered states

The modelling of diseases in fixed networks have been studied in the past [14], and this model is used in a similar manner in this scenario. Adopting the framework from an infectious disease model [15], a host is set as "infected" if a file sharing (or a group of data packets) are pending. Suppose there are k hosts in the system, then a host is sharing a resource with $\beta(k-1)$ other hosts per unit time. $S(k-1)$ do not have yet the disease. Therefore, the transition rate from state S to state I becomes

$$Filesharin \ g = (nu\_\inf ected) \cdot (dld\_Rate) \cdot (nu\_NOT\_share) \quad (1.1)$$

$$Filesharin \ g = I[\beta(k-1)] \cdot \left[\frac{S}{k-1}\right] \quad (1.2)$$

where β is the contact rate for k hosts.

Then the downloaded (no longer pending) rate is:

$$\delta = \gamma \cdot I \tag{2}$$

where γ is the download rate and I is the number of infected devices.

The $\beta \cdot S \cdot I$ is called π coefficient which indicates the enforcement degree of the diffusion process. π has the dimension of $\left[\frac{1}{Time}\right]$. Previous examinations of the behaviour of small scale systems [15] showed that relatively small populations could be faced wit a stochastic model. Thus taking into account that π depends on the number of $S(t)$ and $I(t)$ and the probability of transmitting the information, we can derive $S(t)$ as follows:

$$\frac{dS}{dt} = -\beta \cdot S \cdot I = -\pi \tag{3.1}$$

$$\frac{dI}{dt} = \beta \cdot S \cdot I = \beta(N-I) \cdot I = \beta NI - \beta I^2$$

By solving the first order differential equation the outcome is:

$$I(t) = \frac{N}{1 + e^{-\beta \cdot N \cdot t}(N-1)} \tag{3.2}$$

According to the definition of spreading ratio equation (3.2) becomes:

$$I'(t) = \frac{I(t)}{N} = \frac{N}{N \cdot (1 + e^{-\beta \cdot N \cdot t}(N-1))} \tag{3.3}$$

$$I'(t) = \frac{1}{1 + e^{-\beta \cdot N \cdot t}(N-1)}$$

Equation 3.3 is referred as the cumulative distribution function.

An issue is when the locations will be updated. This issue can be measured as follows:

$$L(t) = L(t-1) + S_t \cdot \vec{d} \tag{4}$$

Where $L(t)$ is the new location $L(t-1)$ the previous location at step time $(t-1)$, S_t is the speed of each device and $\vec{d}$ is the directed unit vector [13]. Additionally the distance from a node to the closest PI can be measured as [(Node's position - center of PI's communication area) - (radius of area)].

Two different user-based cases exist where the communication might be disturbed: (i) when source user's communication fails and (ii) user's destination communication fails. In case (i) the source users might move to a point that no communication coverage exists and as a result connection failure will occur and the prospective resource for download will be lost.

Taking cases (i) and (ii) as a paradigm this paper proposes a solution in order to enable reliability in resource sharing between mobile peers. Considering a file[7] download from a node A to a node B it is helpful to evaluate both cases. In (i) the

---

[7] Stream(s) of packets.

user's device (mobile node) chooses in epidemic form (infection) which of user's device neighbouring nodes, will be MI. This classification is based on candidate's node residual energy, capacity and signal transmission power [19]. PI only communicates with MI and not with pure users. Node "A" then copies packets to the chosen "infected" MI for time t. MI in turn copies these packets to PI of the landscape to which is the only user which communicates directly. This file lies in PI buffer for time t and then is deleted. This mechanism occurs recursively for the forthcoming chosen MIs, in the case where MI's communication fails. Finally when downloading is completed, file is being removed from PI and "infected" MI even if time t has not yet ended. Additionally every infected node then recovers.

In case (ii) where the destination node "B" is to be moved influencing the communication between A and B, a similar mechanism is activated in the following way: if the signal transmission power is reduced which means communication between A-B is prone to failure(s), "B" sends messages to "A's" neighbours to search for MIs in an epidemic way-as explained earlier. In turn MIs copy packets to PI of the landscape and then PI to MI-cluster controllers to which an examination takes place to examine whether destination node "B" changed landscape. If "B" changed landscape then MI-cluster controllers copy file packets to PI of the nearby landscape otherwise the epidemic algorithm of case (i) takes place.

The above method spreads data load evenly in an epidemic way. Assuming that the mobility of hosts is a hybridized version of city walk and random walk [16] the epidemic selective method is applied only when any file transfer is disturbed. Each host chooses an anchor randomly as its next target destination, and moves toward the anchor at a variable speed parameterized by average speed. Epidemic packet diffusion enables reliability as shown in the results in the following section.

4 Simulation Experiments and Discussion

To demonstrate the methodology discussed in this paper, we performed exhaustive discrete time simulations of the proposed scenario under several different conditions. We assume a system consisting of several mobile nodes, e.g., mobile users equipped with notebooks or PDAs and wireless network interfaces. All mobile nodes collaborate via a shared application that uses a distributed lookup service. Radio coverage is small compared to the area covered by all nodes, so that most nodes cannot contact each other directly. Additionally, we assume IEEE 802.11x as the underlying radio technology. However, it is necessary to point out that communication and epidemic-like dissemination could be employed on any radio technology that enables broadcast transmissions inside a node's radio coverage.

4.1 Simulation and Performance Evaluation of the Proposed Scenario

To emulate the scenario described earlier, the need of a possible realistic environment must be achieved. In this section, we present some experimental and simulation results for performance evaluation and reliability in resource sharing offered by our scheme.

Two sets of experiments were performed. One set deals with the epidemic selective caching concept and the grade of contribution in enabling reliability in file sharing, and the second deals with the performance of epidemic Geocast under significant traffic, network partition limitations and the latency issues that arise.

An issue that has to be taken into account is whether the cached information destined for a proper node could be stored in a node with higher residual energy. As shown in simulation process if nodes with higher level of residual energy are chosen in the path then the network partitioning probability is further reduced [19]. For this reason cached information size and file size are chosen randomly in our scenario and files are searched for, upon queries on a recursive basis.

In simulation was used a two-dimensional network, 4 landscapes each one consisting of 25 nodes with each link (frequency channel) having max speed reaching 2Mb per sec. The propagation path loss is the two-ray model without fading. The network traffic is modeled by generating constant bit rate (CBR) flows. Each source node transmits one 512-bytes (~4Kbits-light traffic) packet. Packets generated at every time step by following Pareto distribution as depicted in [17, 18], destined for a random destination uniformly selected.

Additionally we have modeled in each node an agent which evaluates the information destined for a proper destination. In this way we have at any time measures of the information destined for each node (for a given time interval) by any node. In real time networks this agent could be client-based. Network structure has been implemented as a [N-1] row, [N-1] column for each node being a possible destination as developed in [19].

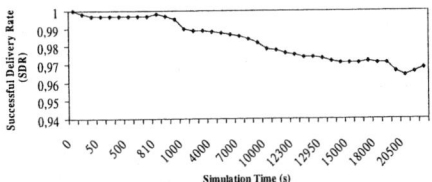

Fig. 5. The ratio of successful packet delivery

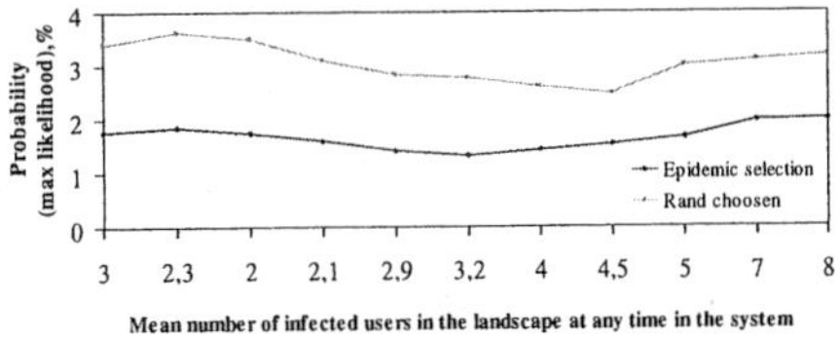

Fig. 6. Mean number of infected users in the landscape (MIs)

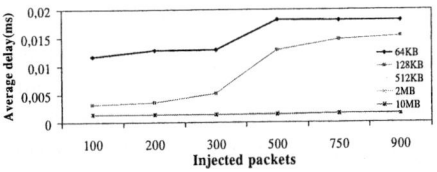
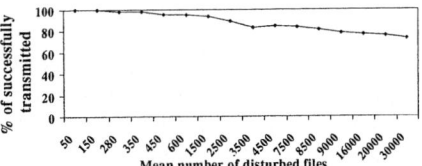

Fig. 7. Average packet delay versus the number of injected packets in the network

Fig. 8. Mean number of disturbed files with the number of successfully transmitted using epidemic selective caching

Figure 5 shows the successful packet delivery ratio. It is clearly shown that throughout simulation time the SDR drops slightly using the epidemic selection. After consecutive simulations the extracted values did not dropped below 96.5% for successful delivery of packet. Of course under self similar traffic (web traffic [18]) it is obvious that a trade off of 2,5% is expected for SDR. Future research will examine such scenario.

Figure 6 illustrates the mean number of infected users, infected by epidemic algorithm used and by randomly chosen selection, in the landscape. As seen the mean number of infected users for which epidemic algorithm is used is significantly small compared with the number of randomly chosen. This proves the robust characteristics in node selection for packet's caching in order to enable reliability.

In figure 7 the average packet delay with the number of injected packets in the network is illustrated. As the number of packets increases the average packet delay increases slightly. After consecutive simulations for this metric it has been shown that when the number of injected packets reaches 550-600, the average packet delay increases dramatically for 64KB and 128MB capacities in each peer. This occurs due to capacity limitation that binds each node. As shown for different capacity limitations the average delay remain almost the same for 128KB, 512KB, 2 MB and 10 MB.

Figure 8 shows the percentage of successfully transmitted packets using epidemic selective caching versus the mean number of disturbed files. It is remarkable to point out that for large number of file distributions the percentage of successfully transmitted packets using epidemic selective caching does not drops below 76.8%. This means that for large distributions in any landscape the packets can be successfully transmitted in high percentage compared with other schemes [1, 5, 11].

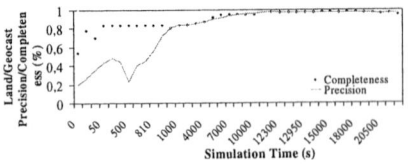
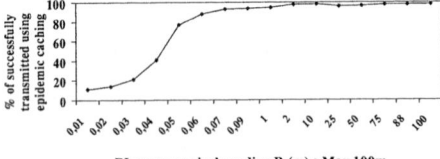

Fig. 9. Land/Geocast response during simulation

Fig. 10. PI coverage of circle with radius R (in meters) and max coverage radius of 100m, vs the number of successfully transmitted using epidemic placement

One difficult part is to ensure persistence of the data file within the geographic region after reaching the region, since the carrier nodes are free to move in and out of the region. On the other hand, as a best effort solution to the problem, the data file migrates from the current host that is moving away from the target zone to new nodes which move towards the target zone. The geographically constrained broadcast could be the paradigm for extracting useful information about the response of the algorithm in such areas. Figure 9 shows the response of epidemic file sharing in a single landscape. Precision is determined by the percentage of the reached mobile nodes that are actually interested for a certain file. Thus precision is essentially the reverse of the degree of spam caused, due to the dissemination mechanism. Precision drops if nodes are moving to another landscape for which the epidemic reliability mechanism takes place as explained earlier. However, since the nodes are assumed to be continuously moving it is difficult to achieve completeness because the membership of the target population itself keeps varying over time.

Figure 10 presents the PI's coverage with radius R and maximum coverage radius of 100m, versus the number of successfully transmitted packets using epidemic placement. After consecutive simulation runs the reliability is shown to colligate with the increase in radius. Network structure has been implemented as in [19], and in such scenario, as figure 11 depicts the highest number of successfully transmitted using epidemic placement is accomplished at radius of >1m.

5 Conclusions and Further Research

In this paper a reliable file sharing scheme for MP2P devices is presented merging the advantages of epidemic file dissemination through mobile users and mobile Infostations. The proposed recursive epidemic placement scheme creates a replicated object in order to enable P2P reliable file sharing proving its scalability in nodes' density since it does not require spatial distributions to efficiently spread information while enables reliability in supported mobility.

Next steps in our research are focused in MP2P network's connection with internet via modified Infostations. Hybrid wireless networks (Ad-hoc, MP2P-WLANs) are also in our research ongoing progress work. The main focus is on for web information retrieval by mobile users intending to access the web.

References

[1] D. J. Goodman, J. Borras, N.B. Mandayam, and R.D. Yates, "INFOSTATIONS: A New System for Data and Messaging Services," Proceedings of IEEE VTC '97 2 (1997) pp.969-973.
[2] S.-Y. Ni, Y.-C. Tseng, Y.-S. Chen, and J.-P. Sheu, "The broadcast storm problem in a mobile ad hoc network". In Proceedings of the Fifth Annual ACM/IEEE International Conference on Mobile Computing and Networking, pages 151-162. ACM Press, 1999.
[3] D. Ganesan, B. Krishnamachari, A. Woo, D. Culler, D. Estrin, and S. Wicker, "Complex behavior at scale: An experimental study of low-power wireless sensor networks". Technical Report UCLA/CSD-TR 02-0013, UCLA, 2002.
[4] A. Demers, D. Greene, C. Hauser, W. Irish, and J. Larson, "Epidemic algorithms for replicated database maintenance". In Proceedings of the Sixth Annual ACM Symposium on Principles of Distributed Computing, pages 1-12. ACM Press, 1987.
[5] J. Kulik, W. R. Heinzelman, and H. Balakrishnan, "Negotiation-based protocols for disseminating information in wireless sensor networks". Wireless Networks, 8(2-3):169-185, 2002.
[6] X. Hong, K. Xu, and M. Gerla, "Scalable routing protocols for mobile ad hoc networks". IEEE Network Magazine, 16(4):11 –21, Jul-Aug 2002.
[7] T. Hara, "Effective Replica Allocation in Ad Hoc Networks for Improving Data Accessibility," Proceedings of the IEEE INFOCOM 2001 Conference, pp. 1568-1576, 2001.

[8] J. Tchakarov and N. Vaidya, "Efficient content location in wireless ad hoc networks". IEEE International Conference on Mobile Data Management (MDM), 2004.
[9] C. D. Gavrilovich, G. Ware, L. Freindenrich, "Broadband Communication of the Higways of Tomorrow", IEEE Communications Magazine, April 2001.
[10] M. Grossglauser and D. Tse, "Mobility Increases the Capacity of Ad Hoc Wireless Networks", Proceedings of IEEE Infocom 2001, pp 312-319.
[11] A. Iacono and C. Rose, "Infostations: New Perspectives on Wireless Data Networks," WINLAB technical document, Rutgers University, 2000.
[12] O. Dousse, P. Thiran, and M. Hasler, "Connectivity in adhoc and hybrid networks," Proceedings of IEEE Infocom 2002, New York, 2002.
[13] T. Small and Z.J. Haas, "The Shared Wireless Infostation Model - A New Ad Hoc Networking Paradigm (or Where there is a Whale, there is a Way)".Proceedings of the ACM MobiHoc 2003 conference, Annapolis, Maryland, 2003, pp 233-244.
[14] M. E. J. Newman, "The Movements of North Pacific Blue Whales During the Feeding Season off Southern California and their Southern Fall Migration" Santa Fe Institute 01-12-073.
[15] F. Brauer and C. Ch´avez, "Mathematical Models in Population Biology and Epidemiology" Springer-Verlag New York, Inc., 2001.
[16] T. Camp, J. Boleng, and V. Davies, "A survey of mobility models for ad hoc network research". Wireless Communications & Mobile Computing (WCMC): Special issue on Mobile Ad Hoc Networking: Research, Trends and Applications, 2(5):483–502, 2002.
[17] K. Park, G. Kim, and M. Crovella, "On the relationship between file sizes, transport protocols and self-similar network traffic". Proceedings of ICNP 1996,pp 171-179.
[18] P. Ulanovs, E. Petersons. "Modeling methods of self-similar traffic for network performance evaluation", Scientific Proceedings of RTU. Series 7. Telecommunications and Electronics, 2002.
[19] C. Mavromoustakis, H. Karatza, "Handling Delay Sensitive Contents using Adaptive Traffic-based Control Method for Minimizing Energy Consumption in Wireless Devices". To appear in the Proceedings of 38th Annual Simulation Symposium (ANSS), IEEE Computer Society Press, SCS, Hilton Mission Valley Hotel, San Diego, CA, April 2-8, 2005.

Investigating Factors Influencing the Response Time in ASP.NET Web Applications

Ágnes Bogárdi-Mészöly[1], Zoltán Szitás[2], Tihamér Levendovszky[1], and Hassan Charaf[1]

[1] Budapest University of Technology and Economics,
Department of Automation and Applied Informatics,
Goldmann György tér 3., Budapest, Hungary, H-1111
agi@aut.bme.hu, tihamer@aut.bme.hu, hassan@aut.bme.hu
http://www.aut.bme.hu/
[2] Budapest University of Technology and Economics,
Department of Electronics Technology,
Goldmann György tér 3., Budapest, Hungary, H-1111
szitas@ett.bme.hu
http://www.ett.bme.hu/

Abstract. Distributed systems and network applications play an important role in computer science nowadays. The most common consideration is performance, because these systems have to provide cost-effective and high availability services in the long term, thus they have to be scaled to meet the expected load. The performance of a web application is affected by several factors. The goal of our work is to analyze how some of them affect the response time. The paper presents the result of performance measurements of an ASP.NET web application. We measured the average response time of a test web application while changing the parameters of the application server. The results are analyzed using statistical methods: (i) independence tests to investigate which factors influence principally the performance, (ii) in addition certain plots and hypothesis tests to determine the distribution of the response time.

1 Introduction

Software developers faced a new challenge in the middle of the past decade, as the World Wide Web became more and more popular. New, easy-to-use and user friendly network applications had to be developed to fulfill the diversified needs of the enormous and growing user community. On the other hand, the web and its services became an important sector in business world as well, because of the large number of potential customers.

Static contents, based on simple HTML pages were not sufficient any more. New frameworks and programming environments were released to aid the development of complex web applications and to support building services offering dynamic content. These new languages, programming models and techniques are in widespread use nowadays, thus developing such applications is not the only issue anymore: operating, maintenance and performance questions became of key importance. One of the most important factors is performance, because network systems have to face a large number of users, but they have to provide high availability services with low response times, in a cost-effective way. Thus performance measurements, bottleneck analysis, scalable design etc. are key concepts in the field of networking.

One of the most prominent technologies of distributed systems and network applications today is Microsoft .NET [1]. Our primary goal was to investigate factors influencing the response time, because it is the only performance metric to which the users are directly exposed. We tested a portal with concurrent user sessions, focusing on the effect of different thread pool attributes on performance. The measurement results are analyzed using statistical methods.

2 Backgrounds and Measurement Process

We have implemented a test web application, which is a real-world ASP.NET web site [2]. We have slightly modified it to suit the needs of the measurement process. The application server and the database server run on the same PC. A test environment was designed to use the most up-to-date hardware and to modify the database accesses. The effect of database was minimized to avoid the database to be the bottleneck of the system. Thus we were able to measure the performance of the web application only. This can be achieved if the threads are sent to sleep instead of some accesses to the database.

The web server is Internet Information Services (IIS) 6.0 [3] with ASP.NET 1.1 runtime environment [4], one of the most frequent technologies among commercial platforms. The database management system is SQL Server 2000 with Service Pack 3. The server runs on a 2.8 GHz Intel Pentium 4 processor with Hyper-Threading technology enabled. It has 1 GB of system memory; the operating system is Windows Server 2003.

The emulation of the browsing clients and the measuring of the response time is performed by Application Center Test (ACT), a load generator running on another PC on a Windows XP Professional computer with Service Pack 2 installed. It runs on a 3 GHz Intel Pentium 4 processor with Hyper-Threading technology enabled, and it also has 1 GB system memory. The connection among the computers is provided by a 100 Mb/s network.

ACT [5] is a well usable stress testing tool included in Visual Studio .NET Enterprise and Architect Editions. The test script can be recorded or manually created. Each test run takes 5 minutes and 1 minute warm-up time for the load to reach a steady-state. At the same time 50 simultaneous browser connections (virtual users) send a list of HTTP requests to the web server concurrently. In the user scenario sleep times are included to simulate the realistic usage of the application.

During the measurements the CPU utilization and available memory are monitored with the help of the integrated counters. As a best practice the CPU utilization should be limited to an average of 75 percent for each processor, because high CPU utilization can lead to high context switching rate which causes undesirable overhead. During our measurement process the average CPU utilization was 75.84 % and the average available memory was 498.31 MB on the server.

An application server has several settings which can affect the performance [6]. As one can see in Fig. 1, the request of the client goes through several subsystems before it is served. During our measurements the maximum and minimum numbers of certain threads in the thread pool are changed (Fig. 2).

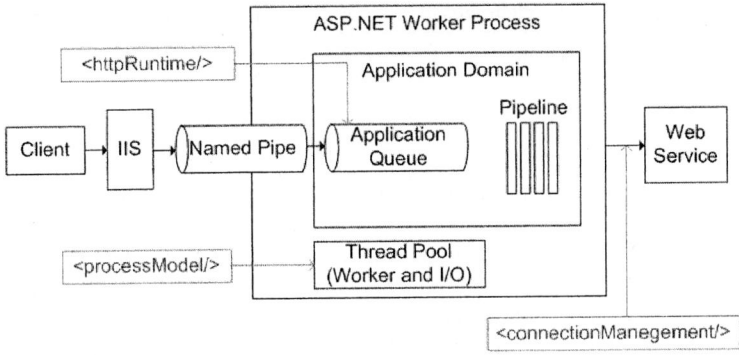

Fig. 1. Architecture of ASP.NET and its relationships to the investigated configuration elements located in the machine.config file

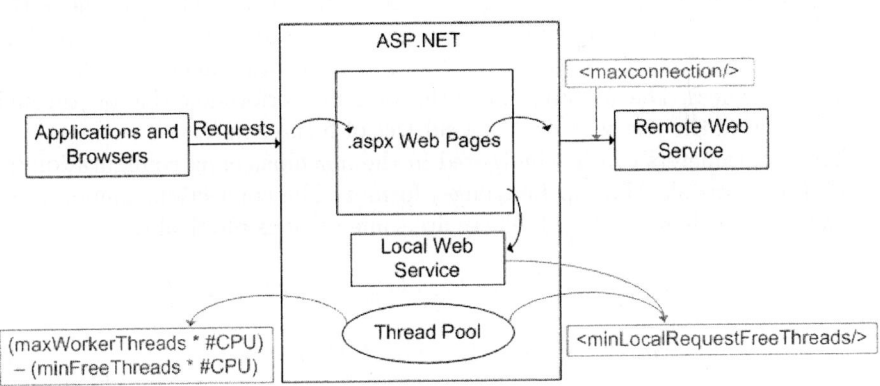

Fig. 2. Thread pool configuration options for ASP.NET

Table 1 summarizes the investigated parameters and their default and recommended values.

The *maxWorkerThreads* attribute means the maximum number of worker threads, the *maxIOThreads* parameter is the maximum number of I/O threads

Table 1. Default and recommended values for the investigated parameters. The first two are automatically multiplied by the number of available CPUs, the latter ones have to multiplied manually.

Name of parameter	Default value	Recommended value
$maxWorkerThreads$	20	100
$maxIOThreads$	20	100
$minFreeThreads$	8	88 * #CPU
$minLocalRequestFreeThreads$	4	76 * #CPU
$maxconnection$	2	12 * #CPU

in the .NET thread pool (automatically multiplied by the number of available CPUs).

The $minFreeThreads$ attribute limits the number of concurrent requests because all incoming requests will be queued if the number of available threads in the thread pool falls below the value for this setting. The $minLocalRequestFreeThreads$ parameter is similar to $minFreeThreads$, but it is related to requests from localhost (for example a local web service call). These two attributes can be used to prevent deadlocks by ensuring that a thread is available to handle callbacks from pending asynchronous requests.

The $maxconnection$ attribute defines the maximum number of the outgoing HTTP connections that can be initiated from the ASP.NET as a client (for example to a remote web service). The $maxconnection$ parameter is constant during our measurements because the test web application does not call any remote web services. The investigation of this possible performance factor (through modification of the test web site) is a subject of future work.

These parameters can be configured in the machine.config configuration file in XML (eXtensible Markup Language) format. The connections among these parameters are shown in Fig. 3. There are some obvious physical restrictions:

$$minLocalRequestFreeThreads \leq minFreeThreads, \quad (1)$$

$$minFreeThreads < maxIOThreads, \quad (2)$$

$$minFreeThreads < maxWorkerThreads. \quad (3)$$

According to the connections and limitations the settings of our measurements are demonstrated in more detail in Table 2. Hyper-Threading technology is enabled on the processor of the server. Thus it seems to have two processors, although physically there is only one processor. Therefore the recommended values which are automatically multiplied by the number of processors are divided by two.

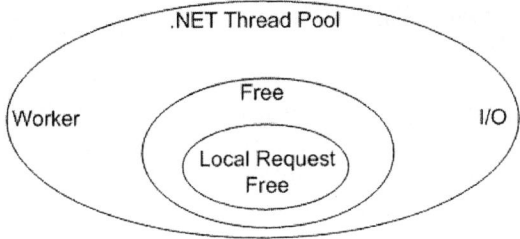

Fig. 3. Partitioning the threads in the .NET Thread Pool in accordance with the reviewed attributes

Table 2. One line means one set of measurements. In each set, one of the parameters is changed in the noted interval, the others are held on a default (d) or recommended (r) value.

$maxWorkerThreads$	$maxIOThreads$	$minFreeThreads$	$minLocalRequestFreeThreads$
5-104	20 (d)	8 (d)	4 (d)
20 (d)	5-104	8 (d)	4 (d)
50 (r)	50 (r)	4-92	4 (d)
50 (r)	50 (r)	88 (r)	2-88

3 Contributions

Thereinafter the results of measurement process are analyzed using statistical methods [7], [8], [9], [10] with the help of MATLAB [11], and optimums are calculated for the given application and environment. Our MATLAB scripts can be downloaded from [12].

3.1 Searching Factors Influencing the Performance

First of all chi square test of independence must be carried out to investigate whether each input and output is independent (whereas in case of other inputs the default or recommended values are kept).

The inputs (individual values) are classified into categories according to the increasing order with the same number of values. Since the output is a continuous distribution, it is discretized. Practically intervals of equal lengths and intervals with integer endpoints are used. The length of intervals is enlarged, until each observed (joint) frequency has been different from null. In addition the length of intervals is increased further, we would like to see as many values as possible being more than 5-6, according to the recommendations.

The null hypothesis (H_0) is: There is no relationship between each input and output (variables are independent). Alternate hypothesis (H_1) is: There is a relationship between them (variables are dependent).

The observed and expected frequencies are shown in Table 3. The first row in each cell is the observed frequency (O), the second row in each cell is the expected frequency under the assumption (E), where

$$E = \frac{k_{i.} * k_{.j}}{N} \ . \tag{4}$$

The chi square statistic is

$$\chi^2 = \sum \frac{(O-E)^2}{E} \ . \tag{5}$$

Table 3. Contingency table in case the input is *maxWorkerThreads*

		Response time				
		170-179	179-188	188-197	197-206	$\sum (k_{i.})$
maxWorkerThreads	5-24	1 / 2.6	9 / 6.8	9 / 7.8	1 / 2.8	20
	25-44	8 / 2.6	7 / 6.8	4 / 7.8	1 / 2.8	20
	45-64	2 / 2.6	9 / 6.8	8 / 7.8	1 / 2.8	20
	65-84	1 / 2.6	4 / 6.8	12 / 7.8	3 / 2.8	20
	85-104	1 / 2.6	5 / 6.8	6 / 7.8	8 / 2.8	20
	$\sum (k_{.j})$	13	34	39	14	100 (N)

The detailed results are depicted in Table 4. In case of the *maxWorkerThreads* parameter the null hypothesis is rejected at every acceptable level of significance, because the chi square statistic is larger than the critical values belonged to each acceptable level of significance. In case of the *minLocalRequestFreeThreads* the null hypothesis is rejected at 0.01 level of significance. This means that in 1 % or 1/100 cases we will reject the null hypothesis when in fact it is true. In case of *maxIOThreads* and *minFreeThreads* the null hypothesis is rejected at 0.05 level of significance. In other words, in 5 % or 1/20 cases we will reject the null

Table 4. The detailed results of the executed chi square statistics

Input	Number of intervals	Chi square statistic	Degrees of freedom	Alpha	Critical value	H_0
Worker	4	35.2273	12	0.0005	34.8213	False
I/O	4	22.9695	12	0.05	21.0261	False
				0.025	23.3367	True
Free	4	17.9158	9	0.05	16.919	False
				0.025	19.0228	True
Local Free	4	22.7033	9	0.01	21.666	False
				0.005	23.5894	True

hypothesis when it should be accepted. Therefore, these can be enough evidence to reject the H_0 hypothesis in case of every parameter.

To summarize, four influencing parameters of the performance are found, which is proven by a statistical method, namely, the chi square test of independence.

Remark 1. In IIS 5.0 [13] ASP.NET makes use of the I/O threads first, and then it jumps over to the working threads and starts to use the working threads. In IIS 6.0 worker threads have taken the role of I/O threads, and I/O threads are only related to I/O calls. Thus the response time depends on the number of I/O threads 'less' than worker threads.

3.2 Determining Optimums for a Given Application and Environment

The sizes of the thread pool are dependent upon the application and the environment, thus for determining the optimal thread pool sizes of a given application the measurements have to be performed in the real environment. The application was measured on up-to-date hardware as a test environment. On similar grade of hardware expectedly similar results are yielded. In other words, only a method is provided, but with general scope, whereas the actual measures are environment-dependent.

The best response times are summarized in Table 5. As it can be seen from the table, when the settings cause the best response times, the number of worker threads is the principally influencing factor (mostly different from the default value). The best response time is observed when the number of worker threads is set to the recommended value approximately, and other parameters are set to the default values.

Table 5. Measurement settings of the best response times

	I/O	Worker	Free	Local Free	Response time (ms)	CPU utilization (%)	Available memory (MB)
1.	20	55	8	4	170.09	74.47	512.79
2.	20	23	8	4	171.16	73.96	506.07
3.	20	84	8	4	171.5	76.47	544.28
4.	50	50	88	48	171.54	72.04	477.7
5.	50	50	21	4	171.8	74.97	460.76
6.	20	26	8	4	171.82	74.94	518.24
7.	50	50	39	4	172.05	72.45	524.45
8.	50	50	88	68	172.19	74.03	495.62
9.	50	50	88	76	173.46	80.37	517.8
10.	50	50	10	4	174.14	71.82	517.21

3.3 Determining the Distribution of the Response Time

Then we would like to have determined the (multivariate) distribution of the response time, but for multivariate normality test wide-spread, well-tried methods have not been formulated yet. Only univariate normality can be tested (when other inputs are held on the default or recommended value).

The simplest way of the determination is to plot a histogram of the observed response times (Fig. 4). But there is a key problem with histograms: depending upon the used bin size it is possible to draw very different conclusions.

A better technique is to plot the observed quantiles versus the theoretical quantiles in a quantile-quantile plot. The applied theoretical distribution is normal distribution according to the conjecture from histograms. If the distribution of observed response times is normal, the plot is close to linear. The result plot can be seen in Fig. 4. Based on the data, the response times do appear to be normally distributed.

The test of normality can be executed graphically using the normal probability plot. If the data samples are taken from a normal distribution, the plot will appear linear (other probability density functions will introduce curvature in the plot). The normal probability plot of the response times is shown in Fig. 4. The data follows a straight line but departs from it at ends. This means that the data has longer tails than the normal distribution.

The test of normality can be performed numerically with the help of certain hypothesis tests. The Bera-Jarque test statistic is based on estimates of the sample skewness and kurtosis. The test evaluates the hypothesis whether the response time is normal with unspecified mean and variance, against the alternative that response time is not normally distributed. The detailed results are represented in Table 6.

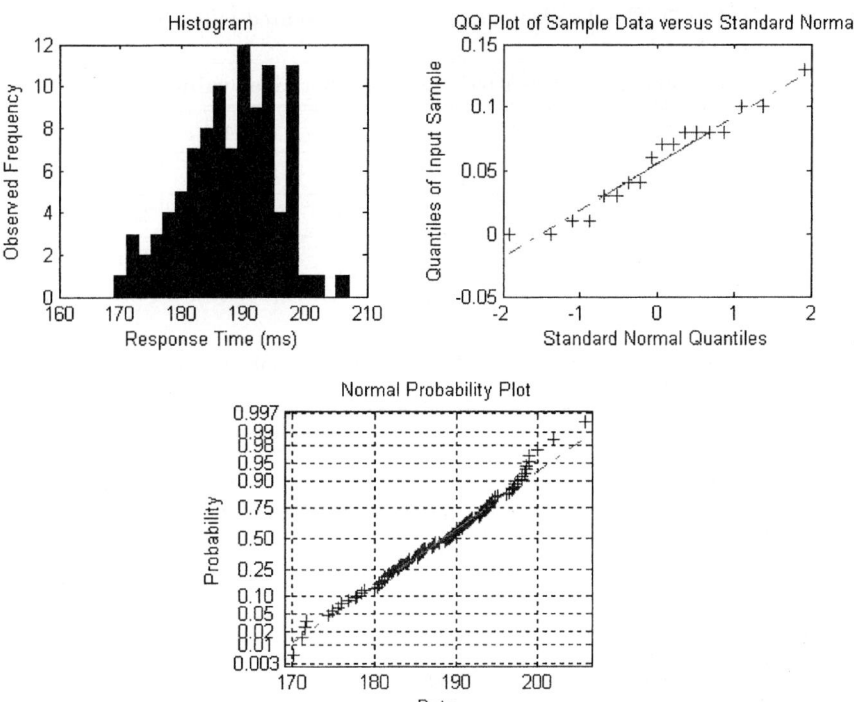

Fig. 4. Histogram (uses 20 bins), quantile-quantile plot and normal probability plot in case the input is *maxWorkerThreads*

Table 6. The detailed results of the performed Bera-Jarque tests

Parameter	Test statistic	Alphas	Critical value	H_0
Worker	1.0069	0.1	4.6052	True
I/O	1.4451	0.1	4.6052	True
Free	7.1708	0.025	7.3778	True
		0.05	5.9915	False
Local Free	1.4786	0.1	4.6052	True

In most cases the null hypothesis is true at every acceptable level of significance (in case of *minFreeThreads* the null hypothesis is rejected only at 0.01 level of significance). This would mean that the response time has a normal distribution. But this test is an asymptotic test, thus care should be taken with small sample sizes.

The hypothesises of the Lilliefors test are the same. The test compares the empirical cumulative distribution function of the response time ($S(x)$) to a nor-

Table 7. The detailed outcomes of the executed Lilliefors tests

Parameter	Test statistic	Alphas	Critical value	H_0
Worker	0.143	0.1	0.184	True
I/O	0.1507	0.1	0.201	True
Free	0.1554	0.1	0.184	True
Local Free	0.1644	0.1	0.184	True

Table 8. The maximum likelihood estimation of the parameters

	Mean	Variance	
	$\hat{\mu} = \frac{1}{n}\sum X_i$ (sample mean)	$\frac{1}{n}\sum(X_i - \hat{\mu})^2$ (sample variance)	$\frac{1}{n-1}\sum(X_i - \hat{\mu})^2$ (bias-corrected sample variance)
Worker	0.0561	0.0014	0.0014
I/O	0.0667	0.0014	0.0016
Free	0.0556	0.0017	0.0018
Local Free	0.0556	0.0011	0.0012

mal cumulative distribution function having the same mean and variance as response time (CDF). The test statistic is

$$T = \max |S(x) - CDF| \quad . \tag{6}$$

The detailed outcomes are described in Table 7. The null hypothesis is true at every acceptable level of significance. This test is not asymptotic, thus the response time is unambiguously normal in case of all four parameters.

3.4 Determining the Parameters of the Distribution

Finally, the parameters of normal response time were determined by maximum likelihood estimation with successive approximation (Table 8). The estimates are strongly consistent since the strong law of large numbers. The sample mean is unbiased estimation, but the sample variance is only asymptotically unbiased, thus it have to be corrected.

4 Conclusion and Future Work

The results of the independence tests have proven that the *maxWorkerThreads*, *maxIOThreads*, *minFreeThreads*, *minLocalRequestFreeThreads* parameters have a considerable effect on the performance, in other words they are performance factors. Based on these measurements we have determined the optimal settings for the given application and environment.

The investigation of the interaction among the parameters is the subject of future work. Its method is similar to the executed two-dimensional test, but handling the multidimensional contingency table is a little bit more complex and more measurements are required.

We have determined (in absence of multivariate normality test) the univariate distribution of the response time. The normality has been intuitively founded by graphically methods, and has been proven with hypothesis tests. The normality of the response time facilitates to construct models later on. We evaluated the parameters of the distribution by maximum likelihood estimation with successive approximation. Stemming from the property of the maximum likelihood estimation method, after the correction the calculated estimates are unbiased and strongly consistent.

References

1. Microsoft .NET Homepage - http://www.microsoft.com/net/
2. Microsoft Educational Portal (Hungary) - http://www.msportal.hu/
3. Internet Information Services 6.0 - http://www.microsoft.com/WindowsServer2003/iis/dfault.mspx
4. ASP.NET Homepage - http://asp.net/
5. Performance Testing Microsoft .NET Web Applications. Microsoft Press (2003)
6. Improving .NET Application Performance and Scalability (Patterns & Practices). Microsoft Corporation (2004)
7. Brase, C. H., Brase, C. P.: Understandable Statistics. D. C. Heath and Company (1987)
8. Bevezetés a matematikai statisztikába. Kossuth Egyetemi Kiadó (2003)
9. Móry, F. T., Székely, J. G.: Többváltozós statisztikai analízis. Műszaki Könyvkiadó (1986)
10. Jain, R.: The Art of Computer Systems Performance Analysis. John Wiley and Sons (1991)
11. MATLAB - http://www.mathworks.com/products/matlab/
12. Our MATLAB scripts can be downloaded from - http://avalon.aut.bme.hu/~agi/research/
13. Support WebCast: Microsoft ASP.NET Threading - http://support.microsoft.com/default.aspx?scid=kb;en-us;820913&Product=asp

Storing and Locating Mutable Data in Structured Peer-to-Peer Overlay Networks

Antony Chazapis and Nectarios Koziris

National Technical University of Athens,
School of Electrical and Computer Engineering,
Computing Systems Laboratory,
{chazapis, nkoziris}@cslab.ece.ntua.gr

Abstract. Structured peer-to-peer overlay networks or Distributed Hash Tables (DHTs) are distributed systems optimized for storage and retrieval of read-only data. In this paper we elaborate on a method that allows them to manage mutable data. We argue that by altering the retrieval algorithm of DHTs, we can enable them to cope with data updates, without sacrificing their fundamental properties of scalability and fault-tolerance. We describe in detail and analyze an implementation of a Kademlia network capable of handling mutable data. Nevertheless, the corresponding protocol additions can easily be applied to any DHT design. Experimental results show that although the process of managing and propagating data updates throughout the network adds up to the total cost of the lookup operation, the extra network utilization can be exploited in favor of overlay resilience to random node joins and failures.

1 Introduction

Structured peer-to-peer overlay networks represent a large class of distributed systems that focus on providing scalable and fault-tolerant key-value pair storage in a continuously changing pool of unreliable and unrelated networked computers. These systems, which are most commonly referred to as Distributed Hash Tables (DHTs), store read-only copies of key-value pairs at various nodes of the network in a way that enables them to implement an optimized "lookup" function: Given a specific key, they will return the corresponding value in a very small number of steps - usually proportional to the logarithm of the number of total participants in the network.

In fact, all DHTs use a common methodology to solve the problem of distributing the network workload and data to participating nodes: Assuming a large virtual identifier space of a predefined structure, both nodes and data are given unique IDs that correspond to specific locations within. The algorithm producing the IDs must guarantee that nodes and data will be uniformly distributed in the identifier space. Then, each node takes on the responsibility of storing values and managing lookup queries that refer to data with IDs "close" to its own. The notion of closeness depends on the details of each specific DHT implementation, as does the arrangement of the identifier space. For example,

Kademlia [1] uses an XOR metric to measure distances between the leaves of a binary tree, while Chord [2] places all IDs around a clockwise circle. A brief description of the structures and algorithms used by various structured peer-to-peer systems is provided by Balakrishnan et. al [3].

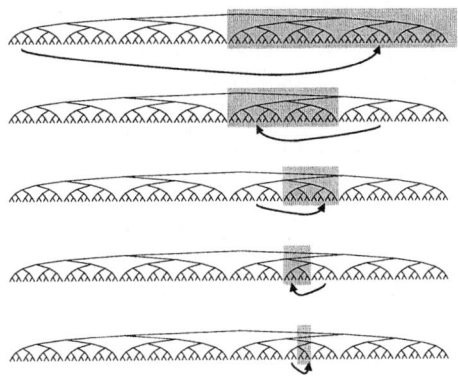

Fig. 1. Looking up a key in a Kademlia overlay

DHTs were designed from ground up to be read-only distributed key-value list storage systems. Nevertheless, in this paper we explore an algorithm based on versioning that enables the use of Kademlia as a mutable data storage and retrieval facility. In the following section we analyze the changes made to the Kademlia protocol and discuss on the differences between our system and analogous designs that have been proposed by the research community. Experimental results from an early implementation suggest that our protocol additions enable data to be inherently changed in the DHT with very few implications on the performance and scalability properties of the overlay. Before concluding, we present thoughts on applications and future extensions of our design.

2 Design

A solution to the problem of storing mutable data in a DHT is presented by the designers of Ivy [4]. Ivy is a distributed file system, that uses the read-only key-value pair storage infrastructure of the peer-to-peer network to create an archive of linked change records. Each value contains actual data, in the form of changes done to the file system, and the identifier of the next read-only tuple in the linked list (previous set of changes). By knowing the key of the latest list item put in the network, an external system can walk the list (called "log") from the most recent to the oldest change. An analogous design is followed by OceanStore [5], which implements a file management layer on top of an underlying Tapestry [6] network. In such systems, there may be a need to go through hundreds of key-value lookups in the DHT in order to find the latest aggregate value, which would incur an intolerable cost in terms of network messages. Even more, log records never get deleted as they are needed for recovery in case of network failures and there is no straight-forward way to identify which key-value pairs are no longer needed in the list. Using the model of Ivy or Oceanstore, one can store mutable data in a DHT, assuming there is another distributed system coordinating the updates of the latest keys inserted in the peer-to-peer overlay.

In the contrary, we would like to enable inherent mutable data storage at the level of each individual key-value pair stored in the system. Related work in the field has investigated the applicability of distributed mutual exclusion protocols [7] in DHTs. In order to update a key-value pair, a node must acquire the permission to do so, by requesting the lock from all servers holding replicated instances of the tuple. If the majority replies, the lock is granted and the new value can be propagated to the corresponding servers. Nevertheless, distributed mutex algorithms in general, require that there is a well defined algorithm for identifying which nodes hold replicated values. In DHTs, key-value pairs are replicated to nodes that are close to the ID of the key and cached around the network. It is extremely difficult to trace which nodes hold a particular tuple and provide guarantees that lock violations and deadlocks will not occur in an environment of continuously changing node behavior (which may in turn alter the placement of replicated data tuples). Moreover, if such an algorithm existed, there would be an easy way to compromise the peer-to-peer network's security properties [8].

Instead, we propose a method of handling mutable data in DHTs with a relaxed consistency between replicated instances of key-value pairs. Our design leaves the DHTs *store* operation unchanged, but alters the way the system handles *lookups*. Updates are routed to the overlay by storing the new value to the closest nodes of the tuple. The algorithm uses a version identifier along every data item and tries to "inform" at least the nodes returned by subsequent lookup operations of the change. In DHT semantics, a participating node receiving a *store* command for a key-value pair already present at its local repository, should check if the version of the given data item suggests a new, updated value or not. Latest versions of key-value tuples should always replace local pairs with the same ID. By utilizing versions, values can eventually be updated (or even deleted) without the need to employ new control commands at the peer level.

Nevertheless, the closest nodes to a key-value pair may change over time in an unpredictable manner. The storage procedure by itself does not guarantee that the whole network will be aware of the value change. As we have updated the replicas stored at the nodes returned by the corresponding *lookup* procedure, there is a very high probability that upon subsequent queries for the same key, at least one of the updated peers will be contacted. Thus, data changes can be propagated to nodes when key-value pairs are looked up. This requires that the algorithm for locating data items will not stop when the first value is returned, but will continue until all available versions of the pair are present at the initiator. The querying node will then decide which version to keep and send corresponding *store* messages back to the peers that seem to hold previous or invalid values.

2.1 Implementation

With the above design in mind, we have tweaked the Kademlia protocol to support mutable data storage. While these changes could have been applied to any DHT (like Chord or others), we picked Kademlia as it has a simpler routing table structure and uses a consistent algorithm throughout the lookup procedure. Kademlia nodes also support issuing multiple concurrent requests in each query step (up to α), which reduces the total time needed for queries to complete and helps in identifying and bypassing faulty peers that could stall the process. Also κ, a system-wide parameter, specifies the number of replicas maintained for each data item and controls the size of routing tables.

According to the Kademlia protocol, three RPCs take place in any data storage or retrieval operation: FIND_NODE, FIND_VALUE and STORE. To store a key-value pair, a node will first need to find the closest nodes to the key. Starting with a list of closest nodes from its own routing table, it will send parallel asynchronous FIND_NODE commands to the top α nodes of the list. Nodes receiving a FIND_NODE RPC should reply with a list of at most κ closest peers to the given ID. The requesting node will collect the results, merge them in the list, sort by distance from the key, and repeat the process of querying other nodes in the list, until all κ closest nodes have replied. Actually, the initiator does not wait for all α concurrent requests to complete before continuing. A new command can be generated every time one of the α inflight RPCs returns new closest nodes candidates. When the list is finalized, the key-value pair is sent for replication to the corresponding peers via STORE RPCs. Kademlia instructs that all key-value pairs are republished in this way every hour, and expire in 24 hours from their initial publication.

To retrieve a value from the system, a node will initiate a similar query loop, using FIND_VALUE RPCs instead of FIND_NODEs. FIND_VALUE requests return either a value from the remote node's local repository, or - if no such value is present - a list of at most κ nodes close to the key. In the later case, this information helps the querying node dig deeper into the network, progressing closer towards a node responsible for storing the value at the next step. The procedure stops immediately when a value is returned, or when the κ closest peers have replied and no value is found. On a successful hit, the querying node will also cache the data item to the closest peer in the lookup list that did not return the value, with a STORE RPC. Moreover, whenever a node receives a command from another network participant, it will check its local key-value pairs and propagate to the remote peer the ones that are closer to its ID. This guarantees that values are replicated to all of their closest nodes and helps peers receive their corresponding data items when they join the network.

Our modified lookup algorithm works similar to the FIND_NODE loop, originally used for storing values in the network. We first find all closest nodes to the requested key-value pair, through FIND_NODE RPCs, and then send them FIND_VALUE messages. The querying node will check all values returned, find the most recent (all key-value pairs have associated timestamp metadata) and notify the nodes having stale copies of the change. Of course, if a peer replies to the

FIND_VALUE RPC with a list of nodes it is marked as not up to date. When the top κ nodes have returned a result (either a value or a list of nodes), we send the appropriate STORE RPCs. Nodes receiving a STORE command should replace their local copy of the key-value pair with its updated version. Storing a new key in the system is done exactly in the same way, with the only difference that the latest version of the data item is provided by the user, so there is no need to send FIND_VALUE RPCs to the closest nodes of a key (version checking is done by the remote peers). Moreover, deleting a value equals to updating it to zero length. Deleted data will eventually be removed from the system when it expires.

2.2 Discussion

In the original Kademlia protocol, a *lookup* operation will normally require at most log(N) hops through a network of N peers. The process of searching for the key's closest nodes is complementary to the quest for its value. If an "early" FIND_VALUE RPC returns a result, there is no need to continue with the indirect FIND_NODE loop. On the other hand, the changes we propose merge the *lookup* and *store* operations into a common two-step procedure: Find the closest nodes of the given key and propagate the updated value. Cached items are ignored and lookups will continue until finding all nodes responsible for the storage of the requested data item. The disadvantage here is that it is always necessary to follow at least log(N) hops through the overlay to discover an identifier's closest peers.

Thus, getting data is not faster - it costs exactly the same as when storing it. There certainly can not be a way to support such a major change in the peer-to-peer system without paying some cost, either in terms of bytes exchanged or in terms of increased latency required for a result (two benchmarking metrics proposed as a common denominator in evaluating peer-to-peer systems [9]). Nevertheless, the penalty in messages needed by our system to to support mutable data does not come without a gain: In every such operation the latest version of a key-value pair will actually be republished on the network. There is no longer a need to explicitly redistribute data items every hour. Values are automatically republished on every usage, but also explicitly reseeded to the network when an hour passes since they were last part of a *store* or *lookup* operation. Also, by using more messages for retrieving data items, routing tables are updated more frequently and the network becomes even more resilient to failures.

We believe that the changes we propose for Kademlia can easily be adopted by other DHTs as well. There is a small number of changes required and most (if not all of them) should happen in the storage and retrieval functions of the protocol. There was no need to change the way Kademlia handles the node join procedure or routing table refreshes. Of course, every structured peer-to-peer overlay willing to use mutable data should find a new way to correlate keys and values for data items. Most networks up to date use a simple approach where keys are generated from the SHA1 hash of their value. With SHA1 hashes, if the value is to change, so will the key. Keys in networks supporting the *update* command should have a deterministic meaning of their own - much like the one filenames have for file systems - and not be dependent of their corresponding values. Also, there is still a requirement that key-value pairs expire 24 hours after their last modification timestamp. Among other advantages refreshing provides, it is the only way of completely clearing up the ID space of deleted values.

3 Evaluation

In order to study the behavior of the proposed system, we implemented the full Kademlia protocol plus our additions in a very lightweight C program. In the core of the implementation lies a custom, asynchronous message handler that forwards incoming UDP packets to a state machine, while outgoing messages are sent directly to the network. Except from the connectionless stream socket, used for communicating with other peers, the message handler also manages local TCP connections that are used by client programs. The program runs as a standard UNIX-like daemon. Client applications willing to retrieve data from the network or store key-value pairs in the overlay, first connect to the daemon through a TCP socket and then issue the appropriate *get* or *set* operations. All items are stored in the local file system and the total requirements on memory and processing capacity are minimal.

For our tests we used a cluster of eight SMP nodes, each running multiple peer instances. Another application would generate insert, update and select commands and propagate them to nodes in the peer-to-peer network.

3.1 Performance in a Static Network

To get some insight on the scalability properties of the underlying DHT, we first measured the mean time needed for the system to complete each type of operation for different amounts of key-value pairs and DHT peers. Kademlia's parameters were set to $\alpha=3$ and $\kappa=4$, as the network size was limited to a few hundred nodes.

Figures 2(a), 2(b) and 2(c) show that the prototype needs less than 2 milliseconds to complete a select operation and an average of 2.5 milliseconds to complete an insert operation in a network of 512 nodes with up to 8K key-value pairs stored in the system. The overall system seems to remain scalable, although there is an evident problem with disk latency if a specific node stores more than 8K key-value pairs as individual files in the file system. This is the reason behind the performance degradation of the four node scenario as the amount of mappings increases. As κ has been set to 4, all data items are present at all 4 nodes. When the network has 8K key-value pairs, each node has a copy of all 8K mappings. In future versions of the implementation, we intend on evaluating embedded, lightweight database engines like SQLite for the local storage requirements of each node.

Nevertheless, systems larger than 4 nodes behave very well, since the mean time to complete queries does not experience large deviations as the number data items doubles in size. Also, the graphs representing inserts and updates are almost identical. The reason is that both operations are handled in the same

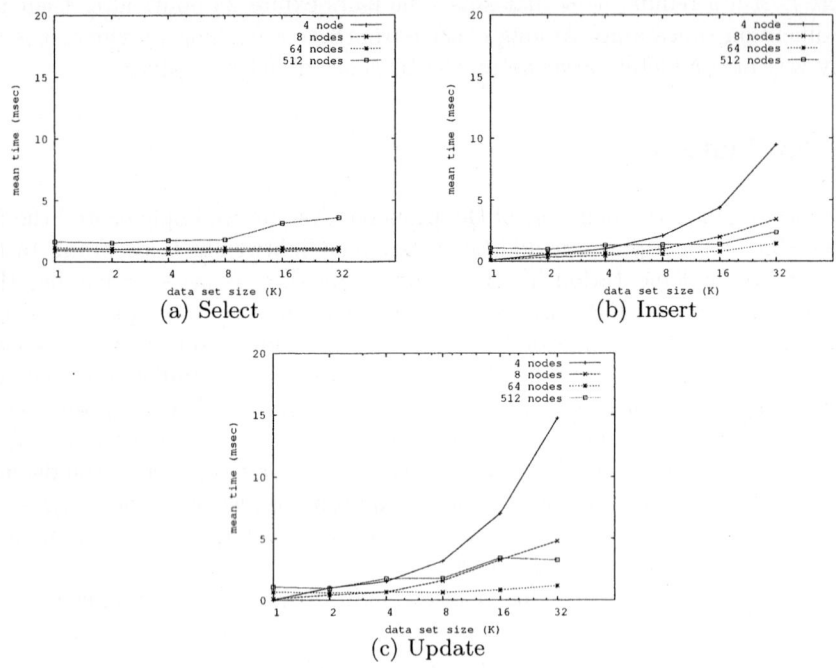

Fig. 2. Mean time to complete operations in a static network

way by the protocol. The only functional difference is that inserts are done in an empty overlay, while updates are done after the inserts, so the version checking code has data to evaluate.

3.2 Performance in a Dynamic Network

Our second goal was to measure the performance of the overlay under high levels of churn (random participant joins and failures), even in a scaled-down scenario. Using the implementation prototype, we constructed a network of 256 peers, storing a total of 2048 key-value pairs, for each of the following experiments. Node and data identifiers were 32 bits long and Kademlia's concurrency and replication parameters were set to $\alpha=3$ and $\kappa=4$ respectively. A small value of κ assures that whatever the distribution of node identifiers, routing tables will always hold a subset of the total population of nodes. Also it guarantees that values will not be over-replicated in this relatively small network.

Each experiment involved node arrivals and departures, as long as item lookups and updates, during a one hour timeframe. Corresponding *startup*, *shutdown*, *get* and *set* commands were generated randomly according to a Poisson distribution, and then issued in parallel to the nodes. We started by setting the item update and lookup rates to 1024 $\frac{operations}{hour}$, while doubling the node arrival

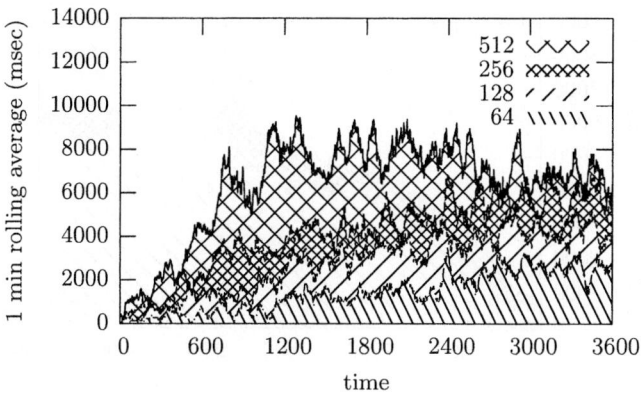

Fig. 3. Time to complete queries while increasing node arrival and departure rates

and departure rates. Initially 64 new nodes were generated per hour and 64 $\frac{nodes}{hour}$ failed. The arrival and departure rates were kept equal so that the network would neither grow nor shrink. Figure 3 shows the average query completion time during a one minute rolling timeframe for four different node join and fail rates. In the simulation environment there is practically no communication latency between peers. Nevertheless, timeouts were set to 4 seconds.

Handling Timeouts. As expected, increasing the number of node failures, caused the total time needed for the completion of each query to scale up. High levels of churn, result in stale routing table entries, so nodes send messages to nonexistent peers and are forced to wait for timeouts before they can continue. Kademlia nodes try to circumvent stale peers in *get* operations, as they take α parallel paths to reach the key in question. It is most likely that at least one of these paths will reach a cached pair, while other paths may be blocked, waiting for replies to timeout. Our protocol additions require that caching is disabled, especially for networks where key-value pairs are frequently updated.

Instead, we try to lower query completion times by making nodes dynamically adapt their query paths as other peers reply. In the first phase of the *get* operation, where FIND_NODE requests are issued, nodes are instructed to constantly wait for a maximum of α peers to reply from the closest κ. If a reply changes the κ closest node candidates, the requesting node may in turn send more than one commands, thus having more than α requests inflight, in contrast to α in total as proposed by Kademlia. This optimization yields slightly better results in total query completion times, in expense to a small increase in the number of messages. Figure 4 shows a comparison of the two algorithms in a network handling 256 node arrivals and departures per hour.

Handling Lookup Failures. High levels of churn also lead to increasing lookup failures. Experiment results shown in Table 1 suggest that as the rate of node arrivals and departures doubles, the lookup failure rate grows almost exponen-

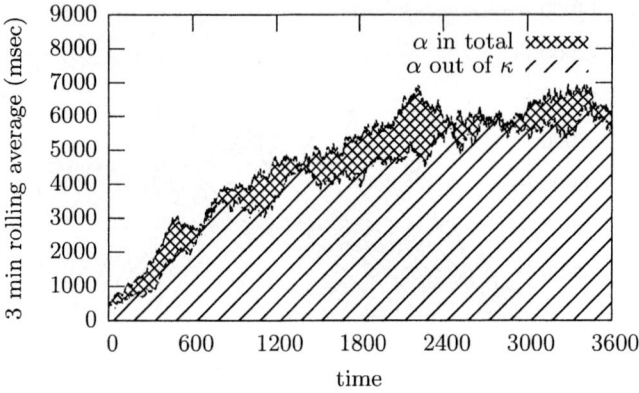

Fig. 4. Dynamically adapting α to changes in the lookup list

tially. In order to prove that the extra messaging cost by our protocol additions can be exploited in favor of overall network fault-tolerance, we reran the worst case scenario (512 node joins and 512 node failures per hour) several times, while doubling the lookup rate from 1024 up to 16384 $\frac{operations}{hour}$. It is evident from the results presented in Table 2, that even in a network with very unreliable peers, a high lookup rate can cause the corresponding failure rate to drop to values less than 1%. This owes to the fact that lookup operations are responsible for propagating key-value pairs to a continuously changing set of closest nodes, while helping peers find and remove stale entries from their routing tables.

Table 1. Increasing node node arrival and departure rates

$\frac{nodes}{hour}$	64	128	256	512
Failures	0	2	32	154
Rate	0.00%	0.19%	3.12%	15.03%

The initial high failure rate is also dependent on the way Kademlia manages routing tables. When a node learns of a new peer, it may send corresponding values for storage, but it is not necessary that it will update its routing table. For small values of κ and networks of this size, routing tables may already be full of other active nodes. As a result, lookups may fail to find the new closest peers to a key. A dominant percentage of lookup failures in our experiments were caused by nodes not being able to identify the latest closest peers of a value. Also, Kademlia's routing tables are designed to favor nodes that stay longer in the network, but the random departure scheme currently used by our simulation environment does not exploit this feature.

Table 2. Increasing the lookup rate

$\frac{operations}{hour}$	1024	2048	4096	8192	16384
Failures	162	106	172	126	84
	131	91	137	80	58
	163	63	145	116	106
	143	61	130	120	87
Rate	15.82%	5.17%	4.19%	1.53%	0.51%
	12.79%	4.44%	3.34%	0.97%	0.35%
	15.91%	3.07%	3.54%	1.41%	0.64%
	13.96%	2.97%	3.17%	1.46%	0.53%

4 Future Work

A DHT capable of handling mutable data can provide the basis of large-scale distributed mass storage and retrieval systems. Key-value pairs can either hold data or pointers to data. For example, peer-to-peer file sharing systems over mutable DHTs can follow a layered approach, deploying a distributed transfer protocol (like the one used by BitTorrent [10]) over an overlay storing a list of pointers to servers holding the actual files. BitTorrent requires that a centralized server (called "tracker") for each file is responsible for holding the list of peers that have started or completed downloading it. This list can be stored as a value in our peer-to-peer system. Dynamic changes in the list may produce inconsistencies, but the upper layer protocol will automatically bypass faulty entries - what really matters is that the list should contain at least one pointer to a valid server holding the file. Other similar applications could as well benefit from this approach. For example, the Grid Replica Location Service, manages a distributed catalog of filename to replica location mappings [11] without imposing any consistency requirements on the update mechanism of the catalog. The Replica Location Service may return a collection of replica locations to applications containing a number of false positive entries. The only requirement is that at least one entry should be correct. We plan on making our implementation work as a core component in this class of programs.

5 Conclusion

A thorough transformation of the default DHT *lookup* operation, has allowed us to implement and evaluate a structured peer-to-peer overlay network capable of handling mutable data. The new lookup procedure is coupled with a simple version management algorithm that handles the reseeding of the latest data updates to the network. Experimental results on a Kademlia-based implementation, support the effectiveness of the protocol changes and additions required, even in networks with a very high rate of changes in node membership status. Moreover, the cost of administering data updates is kept to a minimum, while allowing the overlay network to maintain its inherent characteristics and advantages. Scalability is preserved, as the propagation of data updates happens in a decentralized fashion and the extra messages needed for the maintaining data changes are used by peers to refresh their routing tables and preserve the system's overall tolerance to failures. We believe that a DHT allowing data updates, could be employed by many current and future large-scale distributed applications.

References

1. Maymounkov, P., Mazières, D.: Kademlia: A peer-to-peer information system based on the xor metric. In: Proceedings of the 1st International Workshop on Peer-to-Peer Systems (IPTPS'02), Cambridge, MA (2002)
2. Stoica, I., Morris, R., Karger, D., Kaashoek, M.F., Balakrishnan, H.: Chord: A scalable peer-to-peer lookup service for internet applications. In: Proceedings of the 2001 Conference on Applications, Technologies, Architectures, and Protocols for Computer Communications, ACM Press (2001) 149–160
3. Balakrishnan, H., Kaashoek, M.F., Karger, D., Morris, R., Stoica, I.: Looking up data in p2p systems. Communications of the ACM **46** (2003) 43–48
4. Muthitacharoen, A., Morris, R., Gil, T.M., Chen, B.: Ivy: A read/write peer-to-peer file system. In: Proceedings of the 5th Symposium on Operating Systems Design and Implementation, Boston, MA (2002)
5. Kubiatowicz, J., Bindel, D., Chen, Y., Eaton, P., Geels, D., Gummadi, R., Rhea, S., Weatherspoon, H., Weimer, W., Wells, C., Zhao, B.: Oceanstore: An architecture for global-scale persistent storage. In: Proceedings of ACM ASPLOS, ACM (2000)
6. Zhao, B.Y., Huang, L., Stribling, J., Rhea, S.C., Joseph, A.D., Kubiatowicz, J.D.: Tapestry: A resilient global-scale overlay for service deployment. IEEE Journal on Selected Areas in Communications **22** (2004) 41–53
7. Lin, S.D., Lian, Q., Cheng, M., Zhang, Z.: A practical distributed mutual exclusion protocol in dynamic peer-to-peer systems. In: Proceedings of the 3rd International Workshop on Peer-to-Peer Systems (IPTPS'04), San Diego, CA (2004)
8. Hazel, S., Wiley, B.: Achord: A variant of the chord lookup service for use in censorship resistant peer-to-peer publishing systems. In: Proceedings of the 1st International Workshop on Peer-to-Peer Systems (IPTPS'02), Cambridge, MA (2002)
9. Li, J., Stribling, J., Gil, T.M., Morris, R., Kaashoek, M.F.: Comparing the performance of distributed hash tables under churn. In: Proceedings of the 3rd International Workshop on Peer-to-Peer Systems (IPTPS'04), San Diego, CA (2004)
10. Cohen, B.: Incentives build robustness in bittorrent. (Available online: http://bittorrent.com/)
11. Chervenak, A., Deelman, E., Foster, I., Guy, L., Hoschek, W., Iamnitchi, A., Kesselman, C., Kunszt, P., Ripeanu, M., Schwartzkopf, B., Stockinger, H., Stockinger, K., Tierney, B.: Giggle: a framework for constructing scalable replica location services. In: Proceedings of the 2002 ACM/IEEE conference on Supercomputing, IEEE Computer Society Press (2002) 1–17

Performance Analysis of Overheads for Matrix - Vector Multiplication in Cluster Environment

Panagiotis D. Michailidis, Vasilis Stefanidis, and Konstantinos G. Margaritis

Parallel and Distributed Processing Laboratory,
Department of Applied Informatics, University of Macedonia,
156 Egnatia str., P.O. Box 1591, 54006 Thessaloniki, Greece
{panosm,bstefan,kmarg}@uom.gr
http://macedonia.uom.gr/~{panosm,bstefan,kmarg}

Abstract. This paper presents the basic parallel implementation and a variation for matrix - vector multiplication. We evaluated and compared the performance of the two implementations on a cluster of workstations using Message Passing Interface (MPI) library. The experimental results demonstrate that the basic implementation achieves lower performance than the other variation. Further, we analyzed the several classes of overheads contribute to lowered performance of the basic implementation. These analyses have identified cost of reading of data from disk and communication cost as the primary factors affecting performance of the basic parallel matrix - vector implementation. Finally, we present a performance model for estimating the performance of two proposed matrix - vector implementations on a cluster of heterogeneous workstations.

1 Introduction

The matrix - vector multiplication is one of the most fundamental and important problems in science and engineering. Versions for serial computers have long been based on optimized primitives embodied in the kernels of standard software packages, such as LINPACK [4]. A stable and fairly uniform set of appropriate kernels well suited to most serial machines makes these implementations hard to beat. This is not yet the case for parallel computers, where the set of primitives can so readily change from one machine to another, but the block algorithms of LAPACK [1] and ScaLAPACK [3] are one step in this direction.

Some studies of distributed matrix - vector multiplication have been made on parallel machines or homogeneous networks of workstations or PCs [5,7,15]. Recently, several parallel matrix - vector or matrix multiplication algorithms have been proposed and implemented on cluster of heterogeneous workstations [2,12,8,6]. They use different distribution schemes for several parallel matrix multiplication algorithms on heterogeneous clusters. Further, we have been proposed four variations for matrix - vector multiplication on a cluster of heterogeneous workstations [13]. These variations are based on row block decomposition scheme using dynamic master - worker paradigm. Furthermore, we have been proposed a performance prediction model of four parallel implementations in paper [13].

In this paper, we propose the basic implementation for matrix - vector multiplication and a variation on a cluster of workstations. These parallel implementations are based on block checkerboard decomposition using dynamic master - worker programming model. Further, these implementations were executed using the Message Passing Interface (MPI) [9,11] library on a cluster of heterogeneous workstations. Moreover, we analyze the overheads for the performance degradation of basic parallel implementation on a cluster of workstations. Finally, we are developing a simple heterogeneous performance model for two implementations that is general enough to cover performance evaluation of both homogeneous and heterogeneous computations in a dedicated cluster of workstations.

The rest of this paper is organized as follows: Section 2 briefly presents heterogeneous computing model and the metrics. Section 3 presents a performance analysis for estimating the performance of the basic parallel implementation and the variation for matrix - vector multiplication on a cluster of workstations. Section 4 discusses the experimental and theoretical results of parallel implementations. Finally, Section 5 contains our conclusions.

2 Heterogeneous Computing Model

A heterogeneous network (HN) can be abstracted as a connected graph HN(M,C), where

- M=$\{M_1, M_2,...,M_p\}$ is set of heterogeneous workstations (p is the number of workstations). The computation capacity of each workstation is determined by the power of its CPU, I/O and memory access speed.
- C is standard interconnection network for workstations, such as Fast Ethernet or an ATM network, where the communication links between any pair of the workstations have the same bandwidth.

Based on the above definition, if a cluster consists of a set of identical workstations, the cluster is homogeneous.

2.1 Metrics

Metrics help to compare and characterize parallel computer systems. Metrics cited in this section are defined and published in previous paper [14]. They can be roughly divided into characterization metrics and performance metrics.

2.2 Characterization Metrics

To compute the power weight among workstations an intuitive metric is defined as follows:

$$W_i(A) = \frac{min_{j=1}^{p}\{T(A, M_j)\}}{T(A, M_i)} \quad (1)$$

where A is an application and T(A,M_i) is the execution time for computing A on workstation M_i. Formula 1 indicates that the power weight of a workstation refers to its computing speed relative to the fastest workstation in the network. The value of the power weight is less than or equal to 1. However, if the cluster of workstations is homogeneous then the values of the power weights are equal to 1.

To calculate the execution time of a computational segment, the speed, denoted by S_f of the fastest workstation executing basic operations of an application is measured by the following equation:

$$S_f = \frac{\Theta(c)}{t_c} \qquad (2)$$

where c is a computational segment, $\Theta(c)$ is a complexity function which gives the number of basic operations in a computational segment and t_c is the execution time of c on the fastest workstation in the network.

Using the speed of the fastest workstation, S_f, we can calculate the speeds of the other workstations in the system, denoted by S_i ($i = 1, ..., p$), using the computing power weight as follows:

$$S_i = S_f * W_i, i = 1, ..., p, \text{ and } i \neq f \qquad (3)$$

where W_i is the computing power weight of M_i. So, by equation 3, the execution time of a segment c across the heterogeneous network HN, denoted by T_{cpu}(c,HN), can be represented as

$$T_{cpu}(c, HN) = \frac{\Theta(c)}{\sum_{i=1}^{p} S_i} \qquad (4)$$

where $\sum_{i=1}^{p} S_i$ is the computational capacity used which is obtained by summing the individual speeds of the workstations. Here, T_{cpu} is considered the required CPU time for the segment. Furthermore, substituting $S_i = 1$ in above equation for dedicated cluster of homogeneous workstations, the execution time of a segment c returns to the conventional form:

$$T_{cpu}(c, HN) = \frac{\Theta(c)}{p} \qquad (5)$$

2.3 Performance Metrics

Speedup is used to quantify the performance gain from a parallel computation of an application A over its computation on a single machine on a heterogeneous network system. The speedup of a heterogeneous computation is given by:

$$SP(A) = \frac{min_{j=1}^{p}\{T(A, M_j)\}}{T(A, HN)} \qquad (6)$$

where T(A,HN) is the total parallel execution time for application A on HN, and T(A,M_j) is the execution time for A on workstation M_j, j=1,...,p.

Efficiency or utilization is a measure of the time percentage for which a machine is usefully employed in parallel computing. Therefore, the utilization of parallel computing of application A on a dedicated heterogeneous network is defined as follows:

$$E = \frac{SP(A)}{\sum_{j=1}^{p} W_j} \quad (7)$$

The previous formula indicates that if the speedup is larger than $\sum_{j=1}^{p} W_j$, the system computing power, the computation presents a superlinear speedup in a dedicated heterogeneous network. Further, substituting $W_j = 1$ in above equation for dedicated cluster of homogeneous workstations, the utilization returns to the traditional form:

$$E = \frac{SP(A)}{p} \quad (8)$$

3 Performance Analysis of the Matrix-Vector Implementations

In this section, we describe basic parallel matrix - vector multiplication implementation. First of all, we consider the matrix - vector multiplication $y = Ax$ where A is an $n \times n$ matrix and x and y are vectors of size n. The number of workstations in the cluster is denoted by p and we assume that p is power of 2.

3.1 Basic Parallel Implementation

For the analysis, we assume that the entire matrix A stored in the local disk of the master workstation. The basic idea of this implementation is as follows: The master workstation partitions the vector x into blocks of size b elements and each block is broadcasted to all workers. Further, master partitions the matrix A into blocks of size $b \times b$ and each block is distributed to a worker. Thus, blocks of the matrix A are distributed in a cyclic fashion along vertically. Each worker must receive (horizontally) a row of $\frac{n}{b}$ blocks of matrix A so that each worker to compute the block of size b rows of the resulting vector y. Finally, each worker sends back a block of size b rows of the vector y. We must note that this implementation there is not overlapping between communication and computation phases. The execution time of this parallel implementation that is called MV1, can be broken up into six terms:

- T_a: It is the total I/O time to read the entire matrix A and the vector x from the local disk of the master workstation. The size of the matrix is n^2 elements and the size of the vector is n elements. Therefore, the master reads $(n^2 + n) * sizeof(int)$ bytes totally. Then, the time T_a is given by:

$$T_a = \frac{(n^2 + n) * sizeof(int)}{(S_{I/O})_{master}} \quad (9)$$

where $(S_{I/O})_{master}$ is the I/O capacity of the master workstation.

- T_b: It includes the startup time for partitioning of the matrix A and vector x into blocks. The time T_b is given by:

$$T_b = \frac{(n^2 + n) * sizeof(int)}{(S_{part})_{master}} \qquad (10)$$

where $(S_{part})_{master}$ is the partition capacity of the master workstation.

- T_c: It includes the communication time for broadcasting the blocks of the vector x to all workers involved in processing of the matrix vector multiplication. The number of blocks that allocated to all workers is $\frac{n}{b}$ and the size of each block is $b * sizeof(int)$ bytes. Therefore, the master will broadcast $n * sizeof(int)$ bytes totally. Then, the time T_c is given by:

$$T_c = \frac{n * sizeof(int)}{S_{comm}} \qquad (11)$$

where S_{comm} is the communication speed.

- T_d: It is the total communication time to send all blocks of the matrix A to workers. The number of blocks that allocated to workers is $(\frac{n}{b})^2$ and the size of each block is $b^2 * sizeof(int)$ bytes. So, the master sends $n^2 * sizeof(int)$ bytes totally. Then, the time T_d is given by:

$$T_d = \frac{n^2 * sizeof(int)}{S_{comm}} \qquad (12)$$

where S_{comm} is the communication speed.

- T_e: It is the average computation time across the cluster. Each worker performs a matrix vector multiplication between the block of vector and the block of matrix with size $b^2 * sizeof(int)$ bytes. Further, the cluster will perform $(\frac{n}{b})^2$ matrix - vector multiplications totally. Then, the time T_e is given by:

$$T_e = \frac{n^2 * sizeof(int)}{\sum_{j=1}^{p}(S_{comp})_j} \qquad (13)$$

where $\sum_{j=1}^{p}(S_{comp})_j$ is the computation capacity of the cluster (homogeneous or heterogeneous) when p workstations are used.

- T_f: It includes the communication time to receive p results from all workers. Each worker sends back a block of vector y of size $b * sizeof(int)$ bytes. Therefore, the time T_f is given by:

$$T_f = p * \frac{b * sizeof(int)}{S_{comm}} \qquad (14)$$

where S_{comm} is the communication speed.

Finally, the total execution time of the above parallel implementation, T_p, using p workstations, is given by:

$$T_p = T_a + T_b + T_c + T_d + T_e + T_f \qquad (15)$$

3.2 Variation of the Basic Implementation

For the analysis, we assume that the entire matrix A stored in the local disk of the master workstation. The basic idea of this implementation is similar to the above implementation. However, we assume that the blocks of the matrix and the vector are stored in the local memory of worker workstations instead of allocation of the blocks to workers. The execution time of this parallel implementation that is called MV2, can be broken up into four terms:

- T_a: It is the total I/O time to read the entire matrix and the vector from the local disk of the master workstation. The amount of this time is similar to the T_a of the previous parallel implementation.
- T_b: It includes the startup time for partitioning of the vector and matrix into blocks. The amount of this time is similar to the T_b of the previous parallel implementation.
- T_e: It includes the average computation time across the cluster. The amount of this time is similar to the T_e of the above implementation.
- T_f: It includes the communication time to receive results from all workers. The amount of this time is similar to the T_f of the above implementation.

Finally, the total execution time of the above parallel implementation, T_p, using p workstations, is given by:

$$T_p = T_a + T_b + T_e + T_f \tag{16}$$

4 Experimental and Theoretical Results

In this section, we discuss the experimental and theoretical results of two parallel algorithms. These algorithms are implemented on a cluster of heterogeneous workstations using the MPI library [9,11].

4.1 Experimental Results

The target platform for our experimental study is a cluster of heterogeneous workstations connected with 100 Mb/s Fast Ethernet network. More specifically, the cluster consists of 25 Pentium II 266 MHz with 64 MB RAM and 7 Pentium 166 MHz with 32 MB RAM. The middleware of the cluster is ROCKS of NPACI [10] with RedHat 7.1. The MPI implementation used on the network is MPICH version 1.2. During all experiments, the cluster was dedicated. Finally, to get reliable performance results 5 - 10 executions occurred for each experiment and the reported values are the average ones.

Figures 1 and 2 present for some values n, b and p the speedup curves for the MV1 and MV2 implementations, respectively.

As can be seen from Figures that as the number of workstations increases, the speedups of the MV1 and MV2 implementations appear to deviate from the ideal ones. From the experimental results we observe that the speedup curves improve

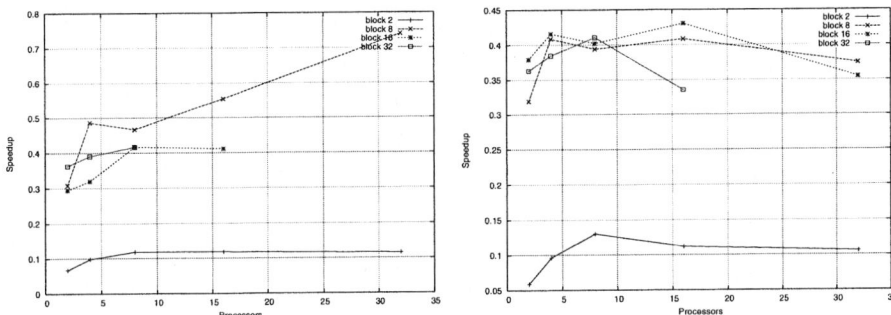

Fig. 1. The experimental speedup as a function of the number of workstations for the MV1 implementation for matrix size of 256 (left) and for matrix size of 4096 (right)

as the block size is increased. It is easy to notice that the increase in efficiency will become saturated when the number of workstations involved reaches some point. From the graph of Figure 1 for matrix size of 4096, we can observe that this saturation point seems to depend on the block size. For block size of 2, the graph of the speedup seem to flattened when the number of workstations reaches 10. For block size of 8, 16 and 32, the speedup begins to fall when the number of workstations reaches 7-10. This saturation point is due to communication and other steps which are not involved in the serial matrix - vector multiplication. Therefore, we conclude that the block size is an important parameter which can affect the overall performance. More specifically, this parameter is directly related to the I/O and communication factors. So, the low communication and I/O cost is obtained for large values of block size. However, from the graph of Figure 2 for matrix size of 4096 there is worst performance for very large values of block size because produce a poorly balanced load.

Another parameter which can affect the performance of two implementations is the matrix size. From Figures, we can see that the speedup curves of two implementations increase slightly as the matrix size is increased. Finally, we observe from the experimental results that the MV1 parallel implementation occur low speedups whereas the MV2 implementation improves the speedup results of the MV1 implementation slightly.

In order to better understand the reasons for the performance degradation of the MV1 implementation, a more detailed analysis the percentage of time for each phase of implementation was performed. The results are shown in Figure 3. It is interesting to note in this Figure that the high communication cost between master and workers is the primary factor affecting performance of the basic implementation and it achieves nearly 56,84%. In this communication cost is dominated by the communication time T_f rather than the time T_d. Another reason for the performance degradation is due to the high cost of reading of data from the local disk of the master workstation for small values of block size. We must note that the percentage of time for the phases T_a and T_b are decreased as the block size is increased. This occurs because when the matrix is read and

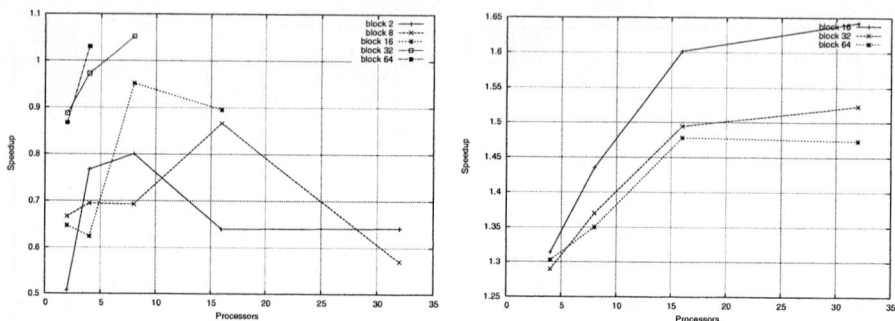

Fig. 2. The experimental speedup as a function of the number of workstations for the MV2 implementation for matrix size of 256 (left) and for matrix size of 4096 (right)

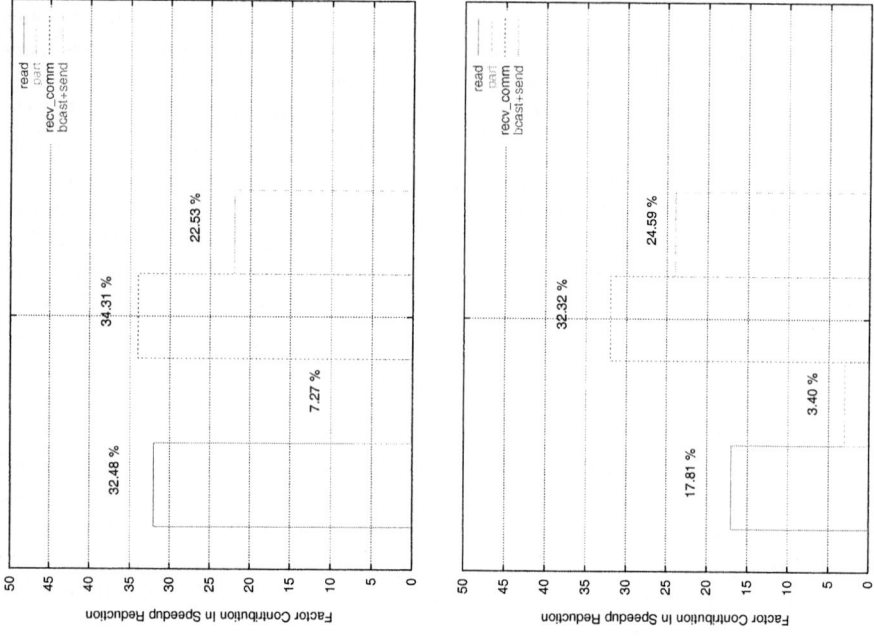

Fig. 3. Contribution factors of the MV1 implementation for matrix size of 256 with block size of 2 using 2 workstations (left) and for matrix size of 4096 with block size of 8 using 4 workstations (right)

partition in chunks of large size improves the locality. Finally, we observe that the total volume of communication (i.e. $T_d + T_f$) is constant as the matrix size and number of workstations are increased.

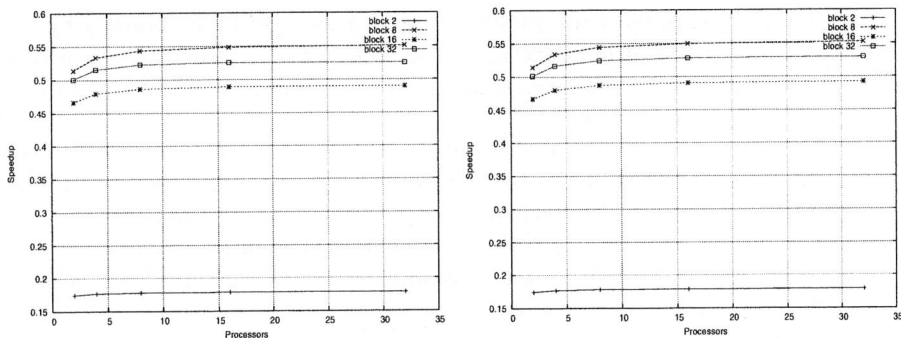

Fig. 4. The theoretical speedup as a function of the number of workstations for the MV1 implementation for matrix size of 256 (left) and for matrix size of 512 (right)

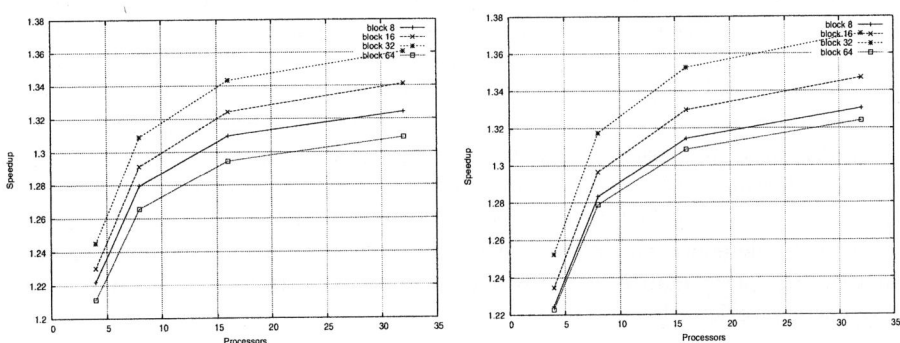

Fig. 5. The theoretical speedup as a function of the number of workstations for the MV2 implementation for matrix size of 256 (left) and for matrix size of 4096 (right)

4.2 Theoretical Results

In this subsection, we validate our proposed performance model presented in the previous section with results obtained by experiments. The performance estimated results for two implementations were obtained by the equations 15 and 16. In order to get these estimated results, we must to determine the values of the speeds $S_{I/O}$, S_{comp}, S_{part} and S_{comm} of the fastest workstation. The average speeds $S_{I/O}$, S_{comp} and S_{part} of the fastest workstation for all block sizes (b =2, 8, 16 and 32), executing the matrix - vector multiplication are critical parameters for predicting the CPU demand times of computational segments on other workstations. The speeds were measured for different matrix sizes and averaged by formula 2 as follows, $S_{I/O}$ = 4758500 ints/sec, S_{comp} = 5510072 ints/sec and S_{part} = 190040 ints/sec for five implementations. Finally, the communication speed was measured for different matrix sizes and block sizes as follows, S_{comm} = 41214492 ints/sec.

Figure 4 presents for some values n, b and p the speedups obtained by the equation 15 for the MV1 implementation on a cluster of heterogeneous workstations. Similarly, Figure 5 demonstrates the speedups obtained by the equation 16 for the MV2 implementation.

We can see that the estimated results for two implementations confirm well the computational behaviour of the experimental results. The slight difference between the two is due to the fact that our performance model did not take into account all factors affecting the performance of implementations such as network protocol characteristics and communication load. These effects will be captured in our future work in this direction.

5 Conclusions

The basic parallel matrix - vector multiplication implementation and a variation are presented and implemented on a cluster platform. These implementations are based on block checkerboard decomposition scheme and the cluster platform considered in this paper employ a master-worker model. Further, we presented the experimental results of the proposed implementations in the form of performance graphs. We observed from the results that there is the performance degradation of the basic implementation. Moreover, from the experimental analysis we identified the communication cost and the cost of reading of data from disk as the primary factors affecting performance of the basic parallel matrix - vector implementation. Finally, we have introduced a performance model to analyze the performance of the proposed implementations on a cluster of heterogeneous workstations.

References

1. Anderson, E., Bai, Z., Bischof, C., Demmel, J., Dongarra, J., Du Croz, J., Greenbaum, A., Hammarling, S., McKenney, A., Ostrouchov, S., Sorensen, D.: LAPACK Users' Guide. SIAM, Philadelphia (1992)
2. Beaumont, O., Boudet, V., Rastello, F., Robert, Y.: Matrix multiplication on heterogeneous platforms: IEEE Transactions on Parallel and Distributed Systems **12**(2001) 10 1033–1051
3. Choi, J., Dongarra, J., Pozo, R., Walker, D.W.: ScaLAPACK: A scalable linear algebra library for distributed memory concurrent computers. In: Proc. Fourth Symposium on the Frontiers of Massively Parallel Computation, McLean, Virginia, (1992) 120–127
4. Dongarra, J., Moler, C.B., Bunch, J.R., Stewart, G.W.: LINPACK User's Guide. SIAM, Philadelphia (1979)
5. Fox, G., Johnson, M., Lyzenga, G., Otto, S., Salmon, J., Walker, D.: Solving problems on concurrent processors. Vol. I, Prentice-Hall, Englewood Cliffs, NJ, (1988)
6. Kalinov, A.: Scalability analysis of matrix-matrix multiplication on heterogeneous clusters. In: Proc. ISPDC 2004-HeteroPar 04, IEEE Computer Society (2004)
7. Kumar, V., Gramma, A., Gupta, A., Karypis, G.: Introduction to Parallel Computing. The Benjamin/Cummings, Publishing Company (1994)

8. Ohtaki, Y., Takahashi, D., Boku, T., Sato, M.: Parallel implementation of Srassen's matrix multiplication algorithm for heterogeneous clusters. In: Proc. 18th International Parallel and Distributed Processing Symposium (IPDPS 2004), IEEE Computer Society, CD-ROM (2004)
9. Pacheco, P.: Parallel Programming with MPI. San Francisco, CA, Morgan Kaufmann (1997)
10. Papadopoulos, P.M., Katz, M.J., Bruno, G.: NPACI Rocks: Tools and Techniques for Easily Deploying Manageable Linux Clusters, San Diego Supercomputer Center, University of California San Siego (2001)
11. Snir, M., Otto, S., Huss-Lederman, S., Walker, D.W., Dongarra, J.: MPI: The Complete Reference, The MIT Press, Cambridge, Massachusetts (1996)
12. Tinetti, F., Quijano, A., Giusti, A.D., Luque, E.: Heterogeneous networks of workstations and the parallel matrix multiplication. In: Proc. 8th European PVM/MPI Users' Group Meeting, (2001) 296–303
13. Typou, T., Stefanidis, V., Michailidis, P., Margaritis, K.: Matrix Vector multiplication on a cluster of workstations. In: Proc. First International Conference From Scientific Computing to Computational Engineering, Athens, Greece (2004)
14. Yan, Y., Zhang, X., Song, Y.: An effective and practical performance prediction model for parallel computing on non-dedicated heterogeneous NOW. Journal of Parallel and Distributed Computing **38** (1996) 63–80
15. Wilkinson, B., Allen, M.: Parallel Programming: Techniques and Applications using Networking Workstations, 2nd edition (2005)

Middleware for Building Ubiquitous Computing Applications Using Distributed Objects

Nicolas Drosos, Eleni Christopoulou, and Achilles Kameas

Research Academic Computer Technology Institute, Research Unit 3, Design of Ambient, Intelligent Systems Group, N. Kazantzaki str., Rio Campus, Patras, Greece
{ndrossos, hristope, kameas}@cti.gr

Abstract. Ubiquitous systems are characterized by multi-fold complexity, stemming mainly from the vast number of possible interactions between many heterogeneous objects and services. Devices ranging from simple everyday objects populated with sensing, actuating and communication capabilities to complex computer systems, mobile or not, are treated as reusable "components" of a dynamically changing physical/digital environment. As even an individual object with limited functionality, may present advanced behavior when grouped with others, our aim is to look at how collections of such distributed objects can collaborate and provide functionality that exceeds the sum of their parts. This paper presents GAS-OS, a middleware that supports building, configuring and reconfiguring ubiquitous computing applications using distributed objects.

1 Introduction

The vision of Ambient Intelligence (AmI) implies a seamless environment of computing, advanced networking technology and specific interfaces [5]. In one of its possible implementations, technology becomes embedded in everyday objects such as furniture, clothes, vehicles, roads and smart materials, and people are provided with the tools and the processes that are necessary in order to achieve relaxing interactions with this environment. The AmI environment can be considered to host several Ubiquitous Computing (UbiComp) applications, which make use of the infrastructure provided by the environment and the services provided by the AmI objects therein. The target of this paper is to present the GAS-OS, a middleware that we developed and supports the composition of UbiComp applications from AmI objects. GAS-OS runs on every AmI object and collectively serves as a distributed component framework. Moreover, it provides developers of UbiComp applications with a uniform programming model that hides the heterogeneity of the underlying networks, hardware, operating systems and programming languages.

The structure of the paper is as follows. Section 2 outlines the design challenges of UbiComp applications and the requirements for a middleware that supports such applications. Section 3 describes the architecture of the GAS-OS, followed by a real life application example in section 4. Section 5 presents related approaches and section 6 lessons learned from this work. Finally we conclude in section 7.

2 Design Goals

The design goals of a middleware that supports the composition of UbiComp applications are tightly interrelated to the challenges arising from the deployment of such applications and also emerge from the requirements of generic middleware systems.

According to the AmI vision people will build "ecologies" (UbiComp applications) by configuring and using AmI objects; everyday objects augmented with Information and Communication Technology (ICT) components. AmI artefacts can be seen as distributed objects since data, behavior and services encapsulated must be accessed remotely and transparently to the overall application. An important aspect though is that these augmented objects still maintain their primary role and *autonomous* nature. Furthermore, in order to *compose* UbiComp applications using artefacts, they must provide the means to be easily used as building blocks of large and complex systems.

In addition, because of the *heterogeneity* of these objects, a key challenge that arises is the feasibility of *semantic interoperability* among them. As AmI artefacts are resource constraint devices, grouping them together could emerge more advanced behaviors. Thus their *composeability* is a challenge that can give rise to new collective functionalities. As artefacts in UbiComp applications may offer various services, the challenge of a semantic representation of services and a *semantic service discovery* mechanism is evident. UbiComp applications also need to be *adaptive* to changes, *robust* and *fault-tolerant* as they are usually created in an ad-hoc manner, and AmI objects are liable to failures. They must also be *context-aware* to understand the environment and adapt their behavior to different situations. *Scalability* is also very important since UbiComp applications are usually composed by a large number of objects.

Considering the users' perspective, a key challenge is the *ease of use, development and deployment*. The combination of objects needs to be based on a user-oriented and user-friendly model. This implies that objects' capabilities must be "advertised" to users through a comprehensible "vocabulary".

Considering the system's perspective, the heterogeneity of artefacts implies middleware systems on top of which applications can function transparently based on the infrastructure. To preserve the autonomy of artefacts and to cater for the dynamic nature of such applications ad-hoc networking has to be supported. The underlying physical networks used are heterogeneous ranging from infrared communication over radio links to wired connections. Since every node serves both as client and server (devices provide/ request services), the required communication can be seen as *p2p*.

Due to the dynamicity of UbiComp applications and the mobility of artefacts, the middleware has to consider services and capabilities of changing availability. Even a service that is both functional and reachable can become unavailable (volatility problem). Furthermore, as any object can become an artefact, regardless of its physical (e.g. power) or computational properties (e.g. memory), the core functionality should be small enough to be executed on resource constrained devices, but *extensible* to use the capabilities of more powerful devices as well. Therefore, we should not pose severe restrictions, like the assumption of a specific platform (*platform independence*). Various manufacturers should be able to implement their consumer solutions on a variety of platforms, not predefined in advance. At the same time, the middleware has to cope with the unavoidable heterogeneity in service definition and deployment.

Since UbiComp applications can be synthesized by end-users, the middleware has to support a user-oriented *conceptual model*. Additionally interacting with the system has to be done in *real time* since services must be available to users at each particular moment. Finally, middleware systems aiming at a broad range of applications, should remain *open*, capable of collaborating with established technological solutions and standards for communication, interoperability etc.

3 Designing the Middleware to Support UbiComp Applications

Before we describe the architecture and implementation of *GAS-OS*, the proposed middleware for building UbiComp applications, we first want to motivate our design rationale with respect to the challenges and requirements stated above.

GAS-OS implements the concepts encapsulated in GAS [6], a generic architectural style, which can be used to describe everyday environments populated with computational objects. The key idea behind GAS-OS is the uniform abstraction of AmI object services and capabilities via the *plug/synapse* high-level programming model that abstracts the underlying data communications and access components of each part of a distributed system. The basic idea is that users connect at a logical level a service or content provider and a client, and thus compose applications in an ad-hoc, dynamic way. Simply by creating associations between distributed objects, people cause the emergence of new applications, which can enhance activities of work, re-creation or self-expression, rendering their involvement in a natural and abstract way. Furthermore the plug/synapse model serves as a common interfacing mechanism among AmI objects providing the means to create large scale systems based on simple building blocks. Plugs are software classes that make visible the object's properties, capabilities and services to people and to other objects, while synapses are associations between two compatible plugs, which make use of value mappings and are implemented using a message-oriented set of protocols.

Typical middleware platforms address the problem of communication using the Remote Procedure Call (RPC) model. This is not applicable in our case, because each object is autonomous, having no dependencies from fixed centralized nodes. Inspired by Message-Oriented Middleware (MOM) design a fundamental characteristic of GAS-OS is to enable non-blocking message passing. Messaging and queuing allow nodes to communicate across a network without being linked by a private, dedicated, and logical connection. Every node communicates by putting messages on queues and by taking messages from queues. To cope with the requirement to adapt to a broad range of devices even the more resource constraint ones, ideas from micro-kernel design were taken under consideration, where only minimal functionality is located in the kernel, while extra services can be added as plug-ins.

Furthermore, we decided to adopt Java using a JVM layer to assume the responsibility of decoupling GAS-OS from typical local operations like memory management, communication, etc, also providing the requested platform independence. The JVM layer allows the deployment on a wide range of devices from mobile phones and PDAs to specialized Java processors. The proliferation of Java-enabled end-systems makes Java a suitable underlying layer providing a uniform abstraction for the middleware masking the heterogeneity of the underlying AmI objects, networks etc.

Using p2p communication also provides the requested support for dynamic applications over ad-hoc networks. A p2p communication module inside GAS-OS translates the high-level requests/replies into messages and by using low-level p2p networking protocols dispatches them to the corresponding remote service or device capability.

In order to support the definition and realization of collective functionality as well as to ensure the interoperability among the objects, all AmI objects should use a commonly understood language and vocabulary of services and capabilities, in order to mask heterogeneity in context understanding and real-world models. This is tackled by using the GAS Ontology [2] that describes the semantics of the basic terms of our model for UbiComp applications and their interrelations. The term "service" is a fundamental one in this ontology, which contains a service classification, since the AmI objects offer various services and the demand for a semantic service discovery mechanism is evident. Due to facts that artefacts acquire different knowledge and may have limited capabilities, we decided to divide the GAS Ontology into two layers: the GAS Core Ontology (GAS-CO) that represents the necessary common language and the GAS Higher Ontology (GAS-HO) that describes an artefact's acquired knowledge.

3.1 GAS-OS Architecture

The outline of the GAS-OS architecture is shown in Fig.1. Synapses are established at the application layer of the GAS-OS architecture (Fig. 1) using APIs and protocols provided by GAS-OS kernel. The GAS-OS kernel implements the plug/synapse model manifesting the services and capabilities of AmI objects through plugs, while providing the mechanisms (API and protocols) to perform synapses with other AmI objects via the application layer. Synapses can be considered as virtual communication channels that feed the lower communication levels with high-level data. Interfacing with networking mechanisms (transport layer) is done via the Java platform. Data are transmitted through the physical layer to the other end of the synapse where the reverse transformation process is followed. Data departing from a plug are the result of internal processing of an AmI object usually involving sensor data. Data arriving to plugs are usually translated to AmI object behavior (e.g. activate a specific actuator in order to achieve a goal). Using ontologies and the ontology manager plug-in (presented in section 3.2), this translation is done based on the commonly accepted terms of GAS, as encoded in GAS-CO. The resource manager plug-in on the other hand keeps track of available local resources and arbitrates among conflicting requests for those resources. Resources include OS-level resources (memory, CPU, power, etc) as well as high-level resources (sound, light, etc). Through the well-defined interfaces of the plug-in manager, other plug-ins (e.g. security), not currently supported, can be attached to the GAS-OS architecture.

The GAS-OS kernel is the minimum set of modules and functionalities every distributed object must have in order to participate in ubiquitous applications. The GAS-OS Kernel encompasses a Communication Module, a Process Manager, a State Variable Manager, and a Memory Manager as shown in Fig. 1.

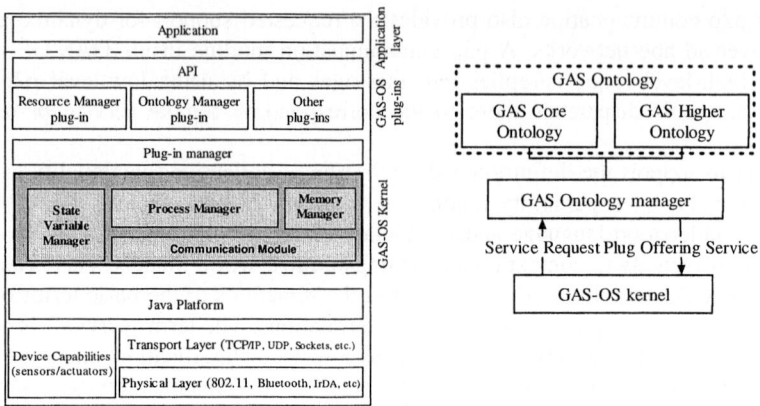

Fig. 1. Left: GAS-OS layered architecture diagram. Right: The GAS Ontology manager

The Communication Module is responsible for communication between GAS-OS nodes. P2P communication is implemented adopting the basic principles and definitions of the JXTA project. Peers, pipes and endpoints are combined into a layered architecture that provides different levels of abstraction throughout the communication process. Peers implement protocols for resource and service discovery, advertisement, routing as well as the queuing mechanisms to support asynchronous message exchange. In order to avoid large messages and as a consequence traffic congestion in the network, XML-based messages are used to wrap the information required for each protocol. Pipes correspond to the session and presentation layers of the ISO-OSI reference model, implementing protocols for connection establishment between two peers, supporting multicast communication for service and resource discovery, while at the same time guaranteeing for reliable delivery of messages. In cases where reliable network protocols are used in the transport layer (e.g. TCP/IP), pipes are reduced to acknowledging for application-level resource availability. Endpoints are associated to specific network resources (e.g. a TCP port). According to the transport layer chosen we can have many different endpoints (e.g. IP-based, Bluetooth, IrDA, etc.), which can also serve as a bridge for different networks. Finally, in order to discover and use services and resources beyond the reachability of wireless protocols (e.g. RF), we have adopted the Zone Routing (ZRP) hybrid routing protocol.

The Process Manager is the coordinator module of GAS-OS. Its most important tasks are to manage the processing policies of GAS-OS, to accept and serve various tasks set by the other modules of the kernel and to implement the Plug/Synapse model. Plugs wrap the information required to describe a service. If the ontology manager plug-in is used a higher-level / contextual description of the service may also be available. Synapses are software entities attached to plugs, wrapping the required information for the remote plug; also having properties that define the interaction patterns (e.g. interaction rules). The process manager implements the protocols required supporting creating, destroying and altering synapses and as a consequence configuring and reconfiguring a UbiComp application consisted of several AmI objects.

The State Variable Manager is a repository of the object's capabilities (e.g. sensors/actuators) inside GAS-OS reflecting at each moment the state of the hardware. An event-based mechanism is used to facilitate communication between the state variable manager and the process manager in order to set up a real time reactive system.

Finally, the Memory Manager enhances the memory management performed by the JVM towards the specific needs of GAS-OS by queuing tasks and messages, buffering sensor and actuator data, storing the state of the AmI object and caching information of other AmI objects to improve communication performance.

3.2 GAS Ontology Manager

The GAS Ontology Manager is the module that manages the GAS Ontology stored at each artefact and implements the interaction of an artefact with its stored ontology. Furthermore, it is responsible to provide to the other modules of GAS-OS any knowledge needed from the ontology. The right part of Fig. 1 demonstrates the interaction among the ontology manager and the GAS-OS kernel. An important feature of the ontology manager is that it adds a level of abstraction between GAS-OS and the GAS ontology, meaning that only the ontology manager can understand and manipulate the ontology; the GAS-OS can simply query this module for information stored into the ontology without having any knowledge about the ontology language or its structure.

Since GAS-CO must be common for all artefacts and cannot be changed during the use of UbiComp applications, this module provides only methods for acquisition of knowledge, such as the definitions of basic concepts and the service classification. Likewise it can only query the GAS-HO-static of an artefact. On the other hand, as it is responsible for keeping up to date an artefact's GAS-HO-volatile, it can both read and write it. As the GAS-HO contains only instances of the concepts defined in the GAS-CO, the basic methods of the ontology manager relevant to the GAS-HO can query for an instance and add new ones based on the concepts defined in the GAS-CO. Thus an important feature of the GAS Ontology manager is that it enforces the integrity of the instances stored in the GAS-HO with respect to the concepts described in GAS-CO.

The interoperability among AmI objects is initially established using the objects' GAS-HO; if their differences lead to infeasible interoperability, each local GAS Ontology manager is responsible for the interpretation of different GAS-HOs based on the common GAS-CO. Thus the semantic interoperability among AmI objects is greatly improved. The GAS Ontology manager also enables knowledge exchange among AmI objects by sending parts of an object's GAS-HO to another object.

One of the ontology's goals is to describe the services that artefacts provide so that to support a service discovery mechanism. Thus the ontology manager provides methods that query the ontology for the services that an artefact offers as well as for artefacts that provide specific services. The GAS-OS get from the ontology manager the necessary knowledge stored in an AmI object's ontology relevant to its services, in order to implement a service discovery mechanism. Finally the GAS Ontology manager using this mechanism and the service classification can identify

AmI objects that offer similar semantically services and propose objects that can replace damaged ones. So it supports the deployment of adaptive and fault-tolerant UbiComp applications.

4 Building a Real Life Home Application

This section demonstrates the development of a real life application starting from a high level description of the target scenario to its implementation based on the services offered by the GAS-OS middleware.

Let's take a look at the life of Patricia, a 27-year old woman, who lives in a small apartment near the city centre and studies Spanish literature. A few days ago she heard about these new AmI objects and decided to give herself a very unusual present: a few furniture pieces and other devices that would turn her apartment into a smart one! On the next day, she was waiting for the delivery of an eDesk (sensing light intensity, temperature, weight on it, proximity of a chair), an eChair (could tell whether someone was sitting on it), a couple of eLamps (could be remotely turned on and off), and some eBook tags (could be attached to a book, telling whether it is open or closed and determine the amount of light that falls on it). Pat had asked the store employee to pre-configure some of the artifacts, so that she could create a smart studying corner in her living room. Her idea was simple: when she sat on the chair and she would draw it near the desk and then open a book on it, then the study lamp would be switched on automatically. If she would close the book or stand up, then the light would go off.

The behavior requested by Pat requires the combined operation of the following set of AmI objects using their plugs: eDesk (Reading, Proximity), eChair (Occupancy), eLamp (Light_Switch) and eBook (Open/Close). Then a set of synapses has to be formed, for example, associating the Occupancy plug of the eChair and the Open/Close plug of the eBook to the Proximity plug of the eDesk, the Reading plug of the eDesk to the Light_Switch plug of the e-Lamp, etc.

The capability of making synapses is a service offered by GAS-OS and is implemented in simple steps as described below. Consider the synapsing process among the Reading plug of the eDesk and the Light_Switch plug of the eLamp.

Initially, the eDesk sends a *Synapse Request* message to the eLamp containing information about the eDesk and its Reading plug as well as the id of the Light_Switch plug. Then the eLamp activates the *Synapse Response* process by first checking the plug compatibility of the Reading and Light_Switch plugs, to confirm that they are not both service providers only (output plugs) or both service receptors only (input plugs). If the compatibility test is passed, an instance of the Reading plug is created in the eLamp (as a local reference) and a positive response is sent back to the eDesk. The instance of the Reading plug is notified for changes by its remote counterpart plug and this interaction serves as an intermediary communication channel. In case of a negative plug compatibility test, a negative response message is sent to the eDesk. Upon a positive response, the eDesk also creates an instance of the Light_Switch plug, and the connection is established (Fig. 2-left). After connection's establishment, the two plugs are able of exchanging data, using the *Synapse Activation* mechanism.

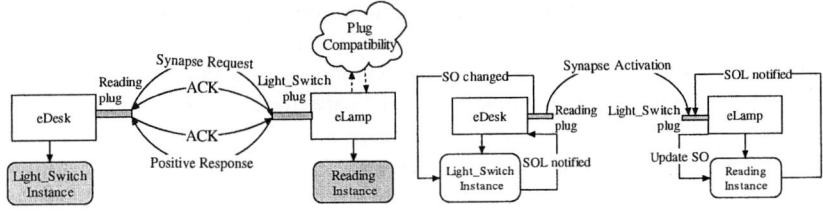

Fig. 2. Synapsing process between Reading and Light_Switch plugs

Output plugs (Reading) use shared objects (SO) to encapsulate the plug data to send, while input plugs (Light_Switch) use event-based mechanisms, called shared object listeners (SOL), to become aware of incoming plug data. When the value of the shared object of the Reading plug changes the instance of the Light_Switch plug in the eDesk is notified and a synapse activation message is sent to the eLamp. The eLamp receives the message and changes the shared object of its Reading plug instance. This, in turn, notifies the target Light_Switch plug, which reacts as specified (Fig. 2-right). Finally, if one of the two connected plugs breaks the synapse, a *Synapse Disconnection* message is sent to the remote plug in order to also terminate the other end of the synapse.

But how are the above messages actually exchanged between AmI objects? In the example, both the eDesk and the eLamp own a communication module with an IP-based (dynamically determined) Endpoint. Plug/Synapse interactions (e.g. synapse establishment) are translated to XML messages by the communication module and delivered to the remote peer at the specified IP address (Fig. 3).

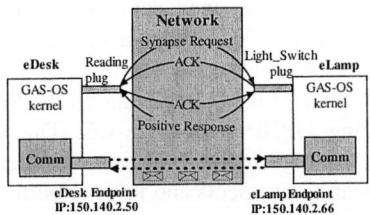

Fig. 3. From Plug/Synapse interactions to p2p communication

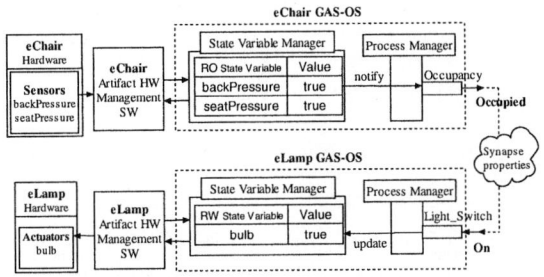

Fig. 4. Communication with hardware

Having described the ways interaction among objects is implemented using GAS-OS, what is missing to close the loop is interaction with the end-users of the UbiComp application. This interaction is done via the sensors and actuators each artefact has, but the way the sensing and actuating data are manipulated by each object is also facilitated by GAS-OS and specifically through its State Variable Manager. In Fig. 4, the eChair has two pressures sensors (back, seat) to sense that someone is sitting on it, and the eLamp has one bulb actuator, both reflected inside GAS-OS as state variables in the SVM. Through communication with the eChair hardware management software the eChair's SVM retrieves all the sensor information of the eChair and registers itself as a listener for changes of the environment. It also communicates with the Process Manager to promote the eChair-eLamp communication as it feeds the Weight plug with new data coming from the hardware that results in the Weight-Light synapse. The reverse process is followed on the other end of the synapse. The matching of the "Occupied" / "Not Occupied" values of the Occupancy plug with the "On" / "Off" states of the Light_Switch plug, is done by configuring the properties of the synapse. So by mapping the "Occupied" state of the eChair to the "On" state of the eLamp and the "Not_occupied" to "Off" we have the following (desired) behavior: "sitting on the chair switches the lamp on while leaving the chair switches the lamp off".

5 System Evaluation

The primary goal for GAS-OS was to serve as a proof of concept that users could be enabled to configure UbiComp applications by using everyday objects as components. Following we discuss if GAS-OS meets the demands of UbiComp applications.

GAS-OS proved capable of running on different devices, satisfying our requirement for supporting resource constrained devices. Devices were developed ranging from handheld computers running Win CE and Java PE, to COTS java-based boards like the EJC [10]. GAS-OS was also tested on devices using Microsoft UPNP protocol to communicate with their hardware, running on the SNAP embedded J2ME controller [12], by interfacing UPNP with GAS-OS. The overall integration process proved easy enough, providing strong indications concerning the independence of GAS-OS from communication protocols and its interfacing ability with standards.

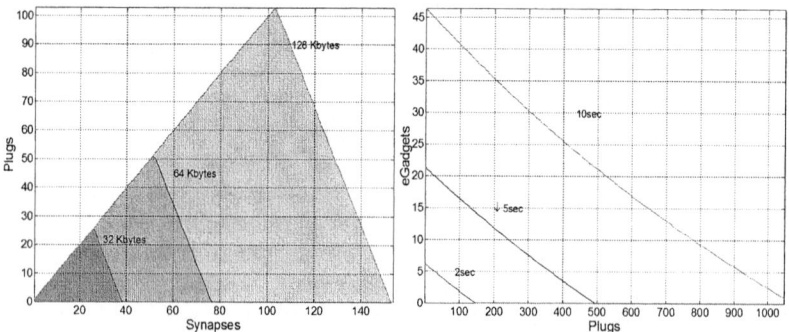

Fig. 5. L.: Max synapses when constraining memory vs # plugs that can participate. R.: # objects that can be discovered in a certain period of time vs # of plugs.

Measuring the process of discovering artefacts provided feedback on the efficiency of GAS-OS to discover a certain number of objects within a time frame and consequently an estimation of how long will the user have to wait in order to discover his ubiquitous environment. (Fig.5-right) shows the number of objects that can be discovered in successive time intervals, versus the number of plugs. To reach maximum performance overhead, we have to get to a large number of plugs per object.

As plugs and synapses are the main factors that increase memory requirements during the execution of an application, we studied the relation between the number of plugs and synapses that participate for constraint amounts of memory. Maximum memory allocation is achieved when each plug participates in only one synapse (Fig.5-left). The more plugs participating in a synapse, the more the allocated memory until we reach the memory constraint. From this point and on more synapses can only be achieved if distributed to fewer plugs.

Using code instrumentation, we measured the average synapsing and communication time in an application where 5 objects are inter-connected with 6 synapses. After creating the 1st synapse only a few milliseconds are required to create the rest, while the average time of approximately 1 sec for all 6 synapses is acceptable. For communication among 2 objects having a synapse, the average time is only a few milliseconds, which is acceptable for real time applications. These measurements include the overhead of the 802.11b protocol, while messages exchanged vary from a few bytes to 1 KB. What is important though is that after synapses' establishment communication between objects is fast, satisfying our requirement for real time response.

The use of ontologies in order to deal with heterogeneity in service definition improved interoperability of objects. Specifically the service discovery mechanism enabled the identification of semantically similar services and GAS-OS, exploiting this, could replace a failed or moved AmI object with a similar one in satisfactory time.

Finally, GAS-OS, the end-user programming tools (GAS Editor) that use it and the applications built with it, were evaluated in user and expert trials [7]. During the development and deployment of UbiComp applications from both novice and experienced users, we got fairly encouraging results regarding usability, as using GAS Editor it was proven easy to create, configure and reconfigure UbiComp applications.

6 Related Work

Several research efforts are attempting to design ubiquitous computing architectures. In "Smart-Its" [4] the aim is to develop small devices, which, when attached to objects, enable their association based on the concept of "context proximity". The collective functionality of such system is composed of the computational abilities of the Smart-Its, without taking into account the "nature" of the participating objects. A more generic approach is the one of "Oxygen" [11], which enables human-centered computing by providing special computational devices, handheld devices, dynamic networks, etc. The "Accord" [9] focuses on developing a Tangible Toolbox (based on the idea of tangible puzzle) that enables people to easily embed functionality into existing artefacts around home and permit artefacts to be integrated with each other.

The GAIA system [8] provides an infrastructure to spontaneously connect devices offering or using registered services. GAIA-OS requires a specific system software infrastructure using CORBA objects, while mobile devices cannot operate autonomously without this infrastructure. In GAIA is used an ontology server that maintains various ontologies, addressing issues like service discovery and context-awareness; a fairly different approach from ours. The BASE [1] is a component-oriented microkernel based middleware, which, although provides support for heterogeneity and a uniform abstraction of services, the application programming interface requires specific programming capabilities by users. Finally TinyOS [3] is an event driven operating system designed to provide support for deeply embedded systems, which requires concurrency intensive operations while constrained by minimal hardware resources.

7 Conclusions

In this paper we presented GAS-OS, a middleware for building UbiComp applications from individual artifacts using the plug/synapse abstraction layer. GAS-OS, being a component framework, determines the component interfaces and the rules governing their composition, and provides a clear separation between computational and compositional aspects of such applications, leaving the latter to ordinary people, while the former can be undertaken by designers or engineers. End-users only have to compose their applications as instances of the system. As a component-based application can be reconfigured to meet new requirements at a low cost, composition achieves adaptability and evolution. The possibility to reuse objects for purposes not accounted for during the design opens roads for emergent uses of artefacts that result from actual use.

References

1. Becker C. et al., "BASE - A Micro-broker-based Middleware For Pervasive Computing", in Proceedings of the 1st IEEE International Conference on Pervasive Computing and Com-munication (PerCom03), Fort Worth, USA, 2003.
2. Christopoulou E., Kameas A., "GAS Ontology: an ontology for collaboration among ubiquitous computing devices", International Journal of Human – Computer Studies, Vol. 62, issue 5, Protégé: Community is Everything (2005), pp 664-685, Elsevier Ltd.
3. Hill J. et al., "System architecture directions for networked sensors", In Architectural Support for Programming Languages and Operating Systems. (2000) 93-104
4. Holmquist L.E. et al., "Smart-Its Friends: A Technique for Users to Easily Establish Connections between Smart Artifacts", in Proc. of UbiComp 2001, Atlanta, USA, Sept. 2001.
5. IST Advisory Group, "Scenarios for Ambient Intelligence in 2010-full", February 2001.
6. Kameas A. et al., "An Architecture that Treats Everyday Objects as Communicating Tangible Components", in Proc. of the 1st IEEE PerCom, Fort Worth, USA, 2003.
7. Markopoulos P., Mavrommati I., Kameas A., "End-User Configuration of Ambient Intelligence Environments: Feasibility from a User Perspective", In the proc. of the 2nd European Symposium on Ambient Intelligence, LNCS 3295, pp. 243-254, November 2004.
8. Román M., Campbell R.H., "GAIA: Enabling Active Spaces", Proceedings of the 9th ACM SIGOPS European Workshop, pp. 229-234, Kolding, Denmark, September 2000
9. Accord project website: http://www.sics.se/accord/home.html
10. EJC website: http://www.embedded-web.com/
11. Oxygen project website: http://oxygen.lcs.mit.edu/
12. Simple Network Application Platform (SNAP) website: http://snap.imsys.se/

A Suffix Tree Based Prediction Scheme for Pervasive Computing Environments

Dimitrios Katsaros[1] and Yannis Manolopoulos[2]

[1] Department of Informatics, Aristotle University, Thessaloniki, 54124, Hellas
dimitris@skyblue.csd.auth.gr
http://skyblue.csd.auth.gr/~dimitris/

[2] Department of Informatics, Aristotle University, Thessaloniki, 54124, Hellas
manolopo@skyblue.csd.auth.gr
http://skyblue.csd.auth.gr/~manolopo/yannis.html

Abstract. Discrete sequence modeling and prediction is a fundamental goal and a challenge for location-aware computing. Mobile client's data request forecasting and location tracking in wireless cellular networks are characteristic application areas of sequence prediction in pervasive computing, where learning of sequential data could boost the underlying network's performance. Approaches inspired from information theory comprise ideal solutions to the above problems, because several overheads in the mobile computing paradigm can be attributed to the randomness or uncertainty in a mobile client's movement or data access. This article presents a new information-theoretic technique for discrete sequence prediction. It surveys the state-of-the-art solutions and provides a qualitative description of their strengths and weaknesses. Based on this analysis it proposes a new method, for which the preliminary experimental results exhibit its efficiency and robustness.

1 Introduction

The new class of computing, termed *location-aware computing*, which emerged due to the evolution of location sensing, wireless networking, and mobile computing presents unique challenges and requires high performance solutions to overcome the limitations of current wireless networks stemming from the scarcity of wireless resources. A location-aware computing system must be cognizant of its user's state, and must modify its behavior according to this information. A user's state usually consists of its physical location and information needs. If a human were given such context, s/he would make decisions in a proactive fashion, anticipating mobile client's user needs. In making these proactive decisions, the system must be able, among other things, to deduce future data requests and also to record and predict the positions of roaming clients.

The issues of data request prediction and location tracking/prediction, although diverse in nature, are simply different facets of the same coin; they can both be described in terms of a *discrete sequence prediction* problem formulation. From a qualitative point of view, this problem can be described as follows: *given a history of events, forecast the next one to come*.

Drastic solutions to the aforementioned problems have direct impact on the underlying wireless network performance. Accurate data request prediction results in effective data prefetching [18], which, combined with a caching mechanism [13], can reduce user-perceived latencies as well as server and network loads. Also, effective solutions to the mobility tracking problem can reduce the update and paging costs, freeing the network from excessive signaling traffic [4].

1.1 Motivation and Paper Contributions

The problem of discrete sequence prediction has received a lot of attention in various fields of computer science; prediction techniques have been developed in the context of Web/database prefetching [5,7,9,15,19], computational biology [1,3], mobile location tracking [4,8,17,21], machine learning [16,20]. All these techniques are related to some *lossless compression scheme*, due to the classical result about the duality between the lossless compression and the prediction of discrete sequences [11]. These algorithms can be classified in four families: a) the $\mathcal{LZ}78$ family (acronym for Lempel-Ziv-78) comprised by the works [4,7,8,15,17,21], b) the $\mathcal{PPM}$ family (Prediction by Partial Match) comprised by the works [5,7,9,19], c) the $\mathcal{PST}$ family (acronym for Probabilistic Suffix Tree) comprised by the works [1,3,16,20], and d) the $\mathcal{CTW}$ family (acronym for Context Tree Weighting) comprised by the works [24,23,22].

Each of these works has been developed in the context of a specific application field (computational biology, Web, etc) and reflects the characteristic of this field. The pervasive computing environment requires for the prediction method to posses some very specific features. The prediction method

- should be online and need not rely on time-consuming preprocessing of the available historical data in order to build a prediction model,
- should present low storage overhead,
- refrain from using administratively tunable or statistically estimated (from historical data) parameters, because they are not reliable and/or they are frequently changing.

The aforementioned prediction models do not posses all the above characteristics, as it will become evident from the discussion on the relevant research work (see Section 2). Table 1 summarizes the weaknesses of the relevant models with respect to the requirements described earlier.

Therefore our motivation stems from seeking for an online, self-tuning and with low storage requirements prediction model. Evidently, such a model should be supported by an appropriate data structure.

The present paper's purpose is to introduce the ideas of a novel prediction scheme and not to perform an exhaustive performance evaluation. In this context, it makes the following contributions. Firstly, it presents a classification of the state-of-the-art prediction methods into families and gives a qualitative comparison of their characteristics. It describes a new method for discrete sequence prediction, which meets the requirements set by the pervasive computing

Table 1. A qualitative comparison of discrete sequence prediction models

Prediction		Overheads		
Family	Model	Training	Parameterization	Storage
$\mathcal{L}Z78$	[7]	on-line	moderate	moderate
	[4]	on-line	moderate	moderate
	[21]	on-line	moderate	moderate
$\mathcal{P}PM$	[5]	off-line	heavy	large
	[7]	on-line	moderate	large
	[9]	off-line	heavy	large
	[19]	off-line	moderate	large
$\mathcal{P}ST$	[1]	off-line	heavy	low
	[3]	off-line	heavy	low
	[16]	off-line	heavy	low
	[20]	off-line	heavy	low
$\mathcal{C}TW$	[24,23]	on-line	moderate	large
	[22]	on-line	moderate	large

environement. This method is based on the ideas described in [10]. Finally, it presents a preliminary performance evaluation of the proposed method to prove its effectiveness and robustness without delving into an exhaustive comparison with all the competing techniques.

2 Relevant Work on Discrete Sequence Prediction

All the predictors, we present in the sequel, are based on the assumption that the next event to come depends on a number of previous (seen in the past) events. The "size" of the past (i.e., number of preceding events) defines the "order" of the context or the *order of the predictor*. Ideally, we would like to have predictors that do not impose any constraint on the order, but such a constraint helps the current predictors to reduce the storage requirements of the underlying data structure, which supports their operation. Suppose that the following sequence has been seen $abcdefgabcdklmabcdexabcd$; we will show the prediction models constructed by each predictor.

2.1 The $\mathcal{P}PM$ Predictor

The most famous predictor is based on the $\mathcal{P}PM$ compression algorithm [6]. The algorithm requires an upper bound on the number of consecutive events it will model. Suppose that this bound is 3, then the maximum context that $\mathcal{P}PM$ can model consists of 3 events/symbols. The predictor is supported by a *trie* and its content is illustrated in Figure 1 for our sample sequence. The trie is constructed by sliding (symbol by symbol) a window of size equal to the maximum context upon the sequence, and recording the substring inside this window in the trie.

Apparently, the need of a predetermined maximum context size is a drawback and if the sequence of events contains dependencies of larger size, then they cannot be modeled. The numbers beside each symbol record its frequency of occurrence with respect to its context. Apart from this basic $\mathcal{PPM}$ scheme several variants of it have appeared in the literature. The work in [9] presented some *selective* $\mathcal{PPM}$ models that prune some states of the predictor in case they do not appear very frequently. Similar in spirit is the work of [5]. For instance, a *frequency-pruned* $\mathcal{PPM}$ model [9] with frequency threshold equal to $\frac{1}{10}$ is illustrated in Figure 2.

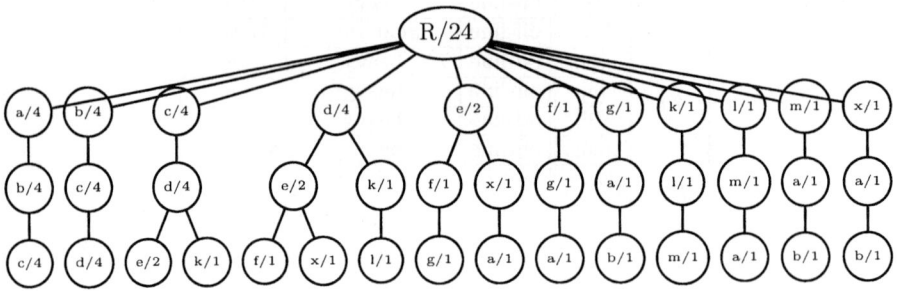

Fig. 1. The $\mathcal{PPM}$ predictor for the sequence $abcdefgabcdklmabcdexabcd$

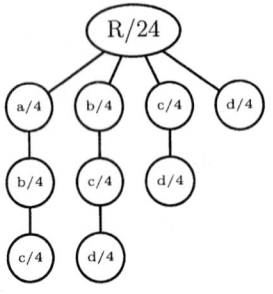

Fig. 2. The frequency-pruned $\mathcal{PPM}$ predictor with frequency threshold equal to $\frac{1}{10}$ for the sequence $abcdefgabcdklmabcdexabcd$

2.2 The $\mathcal{LZ}78$ Predictor

Another popular predictor is the $\mathcal{LZ}78$ predictor [7], which parses the input sequence into distinct substrings, such that, for all substrings, the prefix of each substring (i.e., all characters but the last one) is equal to some substring already encounter and stored into the *trie* that supports the $\mathcal{LZ}78$ predictor. Therefore the sample sequence will be parsed into the following substrings: $a, b, c, d, e, f, g, ab, cd, k, l, m, abc, de, x, abcd$. The contents of the corresponding trie are illustrated in Figure 3.

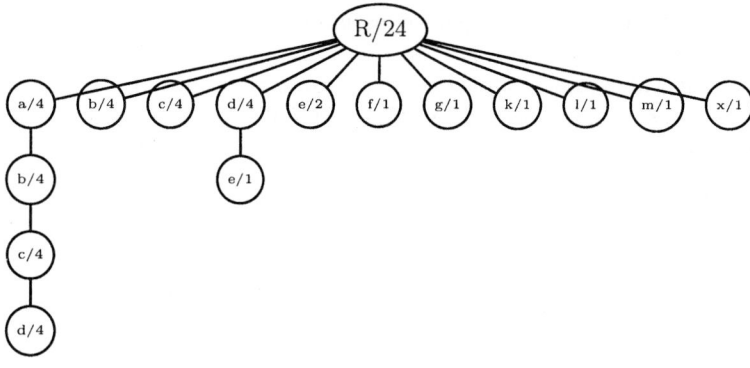

Fig. 3. The $\mathcal{LZ}78$ predictor for the sequence $abcdefgabcdklmabcdexabcd$

The drawback of this predictor is that the "decorrelation" process it uses constructs patterns only if it see them at least twice. For instance, only after seeing three times the ab pattern it is able to predict that with high probability it will be followed by a c character. This has a direct impact on the confidence it pays to some patterns. For instance, the confidence of the pattern de is only $\frac{1}{4}$, instead of the value of $\frac{2}{4}$ assigned by $\mathcal{PPM}$. Although, for very large training sequences this problem will not affect the prediction quality significantly, for short training sequences the $\mathcal{LZ}78$ will yield sparse and noisy statistics [2]. Compared with the original $\mathcal{PPM}$ predictor, the branches of the $\mathcal{LZ}78$ predictor are not of the same length, which in general is a desirable characteristic of the predictor, and also it does not use any predetermined parameters for the maximum length of the context it models.

An enhancement to the original $\mathcal{LZ}78$ method is proposed in [4,8,21], where the trie is augmented with *every prefix of every suffix* of a newly recorded pattern, but this enhancement is still not enough to compensate for the drawbacks mentioned above.

2.3 The $\mathcal{PST}$ Predictor

The $\mathcal{PST}$ predictor is very similar to $\mathcal{PPM}$ but it attempts to construct the best possible prediction model given a specific maximum context length. For this purpose it maintain in total five user defined parameters (including the context length), whose tuning is quite difficult and application-specific. Specifically, it maintains a) the threshold P_{min}, which defines the minimum occurence probability of a subsequence in order to be included into the $\mathcal{PST}$ tree, i.e., no symbol occurring with probability less than P_{min} can be encoded into the $\mathcal{PST}$, b) r, which is a simple measure of the difference between the prediction of the candidate (to be included into the $\mathcal{PST}$ tree) and its direct father node, c) γ_{min} the smoothing factor, d) a, a parameter that together with the smooting probability defines the significance threshold for a conditional appearance of a symbol.

The $\mathcal{PST}$ for our sample sequence, assuming that the maximum represented sequence length is $L = 3$, $P_{min} = \frac{1}{12}$, $r = 1$, $\gamma_{min} = 0.0001$, $a = 0$, is shown in Figure 4. This value for the threshold P_{min} means that only substrings consisting of symbols appearing at least twice in the original sequence will be encoded into the $\mathcal{PST}$ tree. Note that we do not draw the probability vector corresponding to each node.

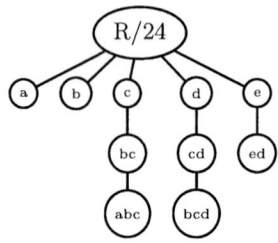

Fig. 4. The $\mathcal{PST}$ predictor for the sequence $abcdefgabcdklmabcdexabcd$

It should be noted that $\mathcal{PST}$ differ from the classical suffix tree [12], which contains all the suffixes of a given string. The two data structures have the following relation: the skeleton (nodes, edges and labels) of a $\mathcal{PST}$ for a given input string is simply a subtree of the suffix tree associated with the *reverse* of that string.

2.4 The $\mathcal{CTW}$ Predictor

This prediction technique was initially introduced for binary alphabets [24,23] and thus is not very popular in the applications's domain. Some efforts to extend it for multi-symbol alphabets [22] suffer from exponentially-growing computational cost and, in addition (as reported in chap. 4 of [22]), they perform poorly. Thus, we do not examine it further here.

3 The $\mathcal{STP}$ Prediction Method

Before proceeding to describe the proposed prediction algorithm, we provide a formal definition of the discrete sequence prediction problem.

Definition 1 (Discrete Sequence Prediction problem). *Let us assume that a sequence $s_1^n = s_1, s_2, \ldots, s_n$ of events is given. Each symbol of s_1^n belongs to a finite alphabet. Given this sequence, the goal is to predict the next event to come, i.e., the $\hat{s}_{n+1}$.*

The algorithm works as follows: a) It finds the largest suffix of s_1^n, call it ss_i^n, whose copy appears somewhere inside s_1^n. Then, it takes a suffix of ss_i^n (the length of this suffix is a parameter of the algorithm) and locates its appearances inside s_1^n. The symbols that appear after the appearances of it are the candidate predictions of the algorithm. The final outcome of the prediction algorithms is the symbol which appears most times. In pseudocode language, this is expressed as follows:

Table 2. The STP algorithm

Algorithm STP
// Current sequence is $s_1^n = s_1, s_2, \ldots, s_n$.
// Predict the symbol after s_n.
begin
STEP 1.
    Find the *largest* suffix of s_1^n, whose copy appears somewhere inside s_1^n.
        Let this suffix be named ss_1^l. Its length is l and starts at
        the position i in s_1^n, i.e.,
$$ss_1^l = (s_{n-l+1}, s_{n-l+2}, \ldots, s_n) = (s_{n-i-l+1}, s_{n-i-l+2}, \ldots, s_{n-i}).$$
STEP 2.
    Take a suffix of ss_1^l of length k with $k = \lceil \alpha * l \rceil$, where α is a parameter.
        Let this suffix be named sss_1^k, where $sss_1^k = (s_{n-k+1}, s_{n-k+2}, \ldots, s_n)$.
    Suppose that ss_1^l appears m times inside s_1^n.
    Each such occurence defines a *marker* and the m positions after
        each market are called *marked positions*.
STEP 3.
    The predicted symbol is the symbol that appears
        the most times in the marked positions.
        (In case of ties, the prediction consists of multiple symbols.)
end

To explain how STP algorithm works, we present a simple example in the sequel.

Example 1. Suppose that the sequence of symbols seen so far is the following: $s_1^{24} = abcdefgabcdklmabcdexabcd$. The largest suffix of s_1^{24} which appears somewhere in s_1^{24} is the $ss_1^4 = abcd$. Let $\alpha = 0.5$. Then $sss_1 2 = cd$. The appearances of cd inside s_1^{24} are located at the positions $3, 10, 17, 23$. Therefore, the marked positions are the $5, 12, 19, 25$. Obviously the last one is not null, since it "contains" the symbol we want to predict. In the general case, all marked positions will contain some valid symbol. Thus, the sequence of candidate predicted symbols is e, k, e. Since the symbol that appears most of the times in this sequence is the e, the output of the STP algorithm, i.e., the predicted symbol at this stage, is e.

Theorem 1. *The PST algorithm is generalization of both PPM and $LZ78$ with respect to the patterns it can discover.*

Proof. For a proof see [14].

Implementation Details. The implementation of the algorithm requires an appropriate data structure to support its basic operations, which are the following:

a) determination of the maximal suffix (at step 1) and, b) substring matching (at steps 1 and 2). These two operations can be "optimally" supported by a *suffix tree* [12]. The suffix tree of a string $x_1, x_2, \ldots, x_n$ is a trie built from all suffixes of $x_1, x_2, \ldots, x_n\$$, where *mathdollar* is a special symbol not belonging to the alphabet. External nodes of a suffix tree contain information about the suffix positions in the original string and the substring itself that leads to that node (or a pair of indexes to the original string, in order to keep the storage requirement linear in the string length). It is a well known result that the suffix tree can be built in linear (optimal) time (in the string length), and can support substring finding in this string also in linear (optimal) time (in the length of the substring). Therefore, the substring searching operation of our algorithm can be optimally be implemented. As for the maximal suffix determination operation, if we keep pointers to those external nodes that contain suffixes ending with the \$ symbol (since on of them will be the longest suffix we are looking for), then we can very efficiently support this operation, as well.

From the above discussion, we conclude the following: a) the $\mathcal{STP}$ algorithm is online; it needs no training or preprocessing of the historical data, b) the storage overhead of the algorithm is low, since it is implemented upon the suffix tree and finally, c) it has only one tunable parameter, α, which fine-tunes the algorithm's accuracy. Therefore, it meets all the requirements we set in Subsection 1.1 for the features of a good predictor for pervasive environments.

4 Performance Evaluation of $\mathcal{STP}$

We conducted some preliminary performance evaluation tests in order to examine the prediction capabilities of the $\mathcal{STP}$ method. At this stage we are not interested in its comparison with other competing algorithms. We simply aimed at examining its prediction accuracy and the impact of the α parameter on its performance. We are currently implementing all the competing approaches to perform an exhaustive comparison. At this paragraph we will present only one experiment with real data as proof of concept of the algorithm and its ability to carry out prediction.

We examined the prediction performance of the algorithm using a real web server trace, namely the *ClarkNet*, available from the site http://ita.ee.lbl.gov/html/traces.html. We used both weeks of requests and we cleansed the log (e.g., by removing CGI scripts, staled requests, etc). The user session time was set to 6 hours. As performance measures we used the prediction *precision* and *overhead*, which are defined as follows:

Definition 2. *The ratio of symbols returned by the predictor that indeed match with the next event/symbol in the sequence, divided by the total number of symbols return by the predictor defines the prediction* **precision**.

Definition 3. *The total number of symbols return by the predictor divided by the total number of events/symbols of the sequence defines the prediction* **overhead**.

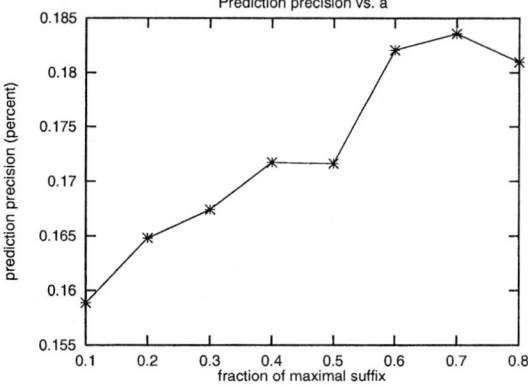

Fig. 5. Performance of the STP method. Prediction precision.

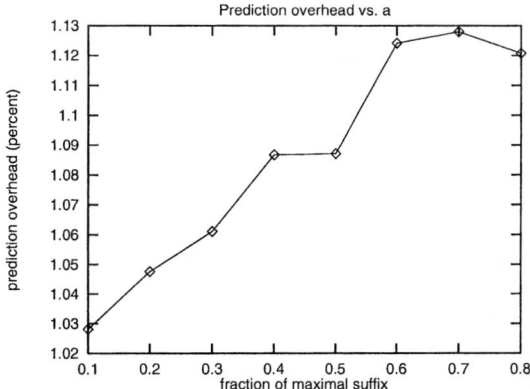

Fig. 6. Performance of the STP method. Prediction overhead.

The results are illustrated in Figures 5 and 6. Apparently, larger values for α increase the precision of the algorithm, since the predictor makes use of longer, and thus of more selective, context.

5 Future Work

This paper presents only the basic idea of the STP algorithm. Currently, we elaborate on it by developing some truncated versions of it, in order to reduce its size and to exploit any changing patterns in the client's behavior. For instance, by expelling some suffixes (e.g., the longer ones) from the suffix tree we can take advantage of a user whose data interests or habits (trajectories) evolve over time. Additionally, we are implementing all the state-of-the-art prediction algorithms in order to perform an exhaustive performance comparison to draw important conclusions under what cases each algorithm performs the best and also to verify in practice the validity of Theorem 1.

6 Concluding Remarks

Discrete sequence prediction is an effective means to reduce access latencies and location uncertainty in wireless networking applications. Due to the unique features of the corresponding mobile applications, the employed prediction scheme should be online, lightweight and accurate; though the existing prediction schemes do not satisfy all these requirements. To address all of them, we presented a new prediction scheme, named STP. This new scheme is based on the suffix tree data structure, which guarantees low storage overhead, fast and online construction. We showed the viability of the method through some preliminary experimental results.

References

1. A. Apostolico and G. Bejerano. Optimal amnesic probabilistic automata or how to learn and classify proteins in linear time and space. *Journal of Computational Biology*, 7(3–4):381–393, 2000.
2. R. Begleiter, R. El-Yaniv, and G. Yona. On prediction using variable order Markov models. *Journal of Artificial Intelligence Research*, 22:385–421, 2004.
3. G. Bejerano and G. Yona. Variations on probabilistic suffix trees: Statistical modeling and prediction of protein families. *Bioinformatics*, 17(1):23–43, 2001.
4. A. Bhattacharya and S. K. Das. LeZi-Update: An information-theoretic framework for personal mobility tracking in PCS networks. *ACM/Kluwer Wireless Networks*, 8(2–3):121–135, 2002.
5. X. Chen and X. Zhang. A popularity-based prediction model for Web prefetching. *IEEE Computer*, 36(3):63–70, 2003.
6. J. G. Cleary and I. H. Witten. Data compression using adaptive coding and partial string matching. *IEEE Transactions on Communications*, 32(4):396–402, 1984.
7. K. M. Curewitz, P. Krishnan, and J. S. Vitter. Practical prefetching via data compression. In *Proceedings of the ACM International Conference on Data Management (SIGMOD)*, pages 257–266, 1993.
8. S. K. Das, A. Cook, D. J. Bhattacharya, Heierman E. O., and T.-Y. Lin. The role of prediction algorithms in the MavHome smart home architecture. *IEEE Wireless Communications*, 9(6):77–84, 2002.
9. M. Deshpande and G. Karypis. Selective Markov models for predicting Web page accesses. *ACM Transactions on Internet Technology*, 4(2):163–184, 2004.
10. A. Ehrenfeucht and J. Mycielski. A pseudorandom sequence – How random is it? *American Mathematical Monthly*, 99(4):373–375, 1992.
11. M. Feder and N. Merhav. Relations between entropy and error probability. *IEEE Transactions on Information Theory*, 40(1):259–266, 1994.
12. D. Gusfield. *Algorithms on Strings, Trees, and Sequences: Computer science and computational biology*. Cambridge University Press, 1997.
13. D. Katsaros and Y. Manolopoulos. Web caching in broadcast mobile wireless environments. *IEEE Internet Computing*, 8(3):37–45, 2004.

14. D. Katsaros and Y. Manolopoulos. Prediction in wireless networks by variable length Markov chains. Manuscript in preparation, 2005.
15. P. Krishnan and J. S. Vitter. Optimal prediction for prefetching in the worst case. *SIAM Journal on Computing*, 27(6):1617–1636, 1998.
16. C. Largeron-Leténo. Prediction suffix trees for supervised classification of sequences. *Pattern Recognition Letters*, 24(16):3153–3164, 2003.
17. A. Misra, A. Roy, and S. K. Das. An information-theoretic framework for optimal location tracking in multi-system 4G wireless networks. In *Proceedings of the IEEE International Conference on Computer Communications (INFOCOM)*, volume 1, pages 286–297, 2004.
18. A. Nanopoulos, D. Katsaros, and Y. Manolopoulos. A data mining algorithm for generalized Web prefetching. *IEEE Transactions on Knowledge and Data Engineering*, 15(5):1155–1169, 2003.
19. J. Pitkow and Pirolli P. Mining longest repeating subsequences to predict World Wide Web surfing. In *Proceedings of the USENIX Symposium on Internet Technologies and Systems (USITS)*, pages 139–150, 1999.
20. D. Ron, Y. Singer, and N. Tishby. The power of amnesia: Learning probabilistic automata with variable memory length. *Machine Learning*, 25(2–3):117–149, 1996.
21. A. Roy, S. K. Das, and A. Misra. Exploiting information theory for adaptive mobility and resource management in future wireless cellular networks. *IEEE Wireless Communications*, 11(4):59–65, 2004.
22. P. Volf. *Weighting techniques in data compression: Theory and algorithms*. PhD thesis, Technische Universiteit Eindhoven, 2002.
23. F. J. Willems. The context-tree weighting method: Extensions. *IEEE Transactions on Information Theory*, 44(2):792–798, 1998.
24. F. J. Willems, Y. M. Shtarkov, and T. J. Tjalkens. The context-tree weighting method: Basic properties. *IEEE Transactions on Information Theory*, 41(3):653–664, 1995.

Factors That Influence the Effectiveness of Mobile Advertising: The Case of SMS

Dimitris Drossos and George M. Giaglis

Department of Management Science and Technology,
Athens University of Economics and Business,
Evelpidon 47A & Lefkados 33, Athens, GR-11362, Greece
{drosos, giagls}@aueb.gr

Abstract. Mobile advertising takes the case of one-to-one marketing one step further, since it allows companies to send personalized offers regardless of time and space boundaries. By employing all the characteristics of one-to-one marketing and augmenting them with features such as location awareness, ubiquitous customer reach, direct response and time independence, mobile advertising is emerging as a promising advertising channel. However, little is known regarding the factors that may influence the effectiveness of a mobile advertising campaign. In this paper we attempt to identify such factors in the field of SMS advertising through an empirical survey of advertisers. Factor analysis is employed for model generation and the outcome provides four main categories that may impact the effectiveness of the SMS advertising communication: campaign strategy, targeting, creative development, and source.

Keywords: Mobile applications, SMS advertising, factor analysis.

1 Introduction

Technological advancements enhance brands' capabilities to communicate and understand customer wants. Interactivity has allowed the increase of the company's knowledge, not only regarding customer data, such as demographics, but also dynamic information, such as purchasing and consumption patterns. In one-to-one marketing, companies identify potential customers, differentiate and customize their offerings according to each customer's preferences, needs, and wants. Simply stated, companies segment the market to the size of one.

Mobile advertising takes the case of one-to-one marketing one step further. Through the mobile channel companies can make on the fly personalized offers independent of time and space boundaries. By employing all the characteristics of one-to-one marketing and augmenting them with features such as location awareness, ubiquitous customer reach, direct response and time independence, mobile advertising could benefit the advertiser as well as the customer through offerings that better relate to customer-specific criteria and the time and place where the advertisement is delivered.

According to the *Interactive Mobile Advertising Platform* [1] mobile advertising is defined as "the business of encouraging people to buy products and services using the wireless channel as medium to deliver the advertisement message". Advertising has changed radically over the years due to the introduction of new techniques and technologies [2]. To this end, advertising researchers are in a perennial effort to examine factors of successful advertising campaigns through the bundle of advertising media [3, 4, 5-6]. In this study we attempt to conceptualize factors that influence the effects of a mobile messaging advertising campaign, referring especially to push advertising via Short Messaging Service (SMS). Factors have been hypothesized through literature review and were then evaluated by advertising experts through an empirical survey that took place in October 2004. In the next section, factors from traditional and contemporary channels are discussed and adjusted to the principles of mobile advertising. Following, an exploratory factor analysis provides a classification model of the corresponding factors before concluding by illustrating how further research can be employed to empirically validate the theoretical propositions put forward in this paper.

2 Factors That Influence SMS Advertising Effectiveness

In traditional marketing settings, the role of advertising and its mechanisms have been studied extensively. The history of TV, radio, and print advertising is long enough for advertisers to be familiar with the technicalities of these media and have an intuitive perception of what correlates are needed to implement a successful advertising campaign. Specific attributes of source, message, channel, and audience characteristics have been recorded and evaluated in several studies, a review of which can be traced in *Percy* [7]. Such variables and outcomes from several researches for mobile advertising have been the subject of our literature review and are integrated in this study.

Numerous factors may play a critical role as determinants of the effectiveness of an advertising campaign. The advertising procedure involves, essentially, four core segments: the brand's overall marketing strategy, the advertisement itself, the medium through which the stimuli are delivered, and the prospect (i.e. prospective customer) who receives the communication message [8]. A plethora of variables from these segments may impact the effectiveness of mobile communication to varying degrees. Characteristics of the source (for example, the advertiser's reputation), the advertiser-agency relationship, message formulation, channel and audience characteristics, all have power over the strength of communication effectiveness [3, 5, 9]. Although there is near-consensus for a few basic factors, for example the impact of the advertisement's size and colour on readership [10], there is generally no conformity on an overall set of factors that define advertising effectiveness.

As SMS advertising is just another form of communication, like TV advertising or radio advertising, it could be implicitly acknowledged that characteristics of the source, advertiser-agency relationship, message formulation, channel, audience characteristics and the like, all have power over the strength of communication effectiveness, as in the case of traditional or Internet advertising [4, 5, 11-12]. Giving rise to this implicit inheritance, several studies in the field of mobile and wireless advertising have recorded a comprehensive list of such factors. In the following table a list of such factors is depicted.

3 Empirical Results

Of the factors documented in the previous section, only a small proportion has been subjected to empirical testing (see for example, [6]). To address the current gap in validated knowledge regarding the effectiveness of mobile messaging advertising, we have conducted exploratory research to delve into the perceptions of advertising experts on SMS advertising. Two semi-structured interviews were carried out with the marketing executives of two established mobile marketing companies in Greece. The interviews were recorded and were followed by content analysis of the transcriptions.

This process yielded variables that, according to the interviewees, can affect the effectiveness of a mobile messaging advertising campaign. These variables were then cross-examined against the literature review findings (Table 1) to provide input for the development of a structured questionnaire, which was used in a subsequent survey

Table 1. Hypothesized factors of SMS advertising effectiveness

Representative Studies	Indicative Factors
[13]	Social norms, User motives, Mode, Advertisement (Ad) delivery time, Place of Ad delivery, Personal characteristics
[14]	Ad delivery time, Place of Ad delivery, Retail pricing, Ad relevance
[15]	Ad delivery time, Place of Ad delivery, Personal characteristics, Context disturbance/acceptance, Ad content, Brand commitment, Product category, Relevance
[16]	Ad delivery time, Place of Ad delivery, Product category, Message source, Fee
[17]	Ad delivery time, Place of Ad delivery, Brand commitment, Product category, Relevance
[18]	Ad delivery time, Place of Ad delivery, Ad content, Relevance, Mobile network technology, Personalization, Regulation, Incentive, Devices' technical characteristics, Campaign management, Carrier cooperation, Call to action
[19]	Ad delivery time, Place of Ad delivery, Customization
[20]	Context, Targeting, Consumer response, Opt-out
[21]	Ad delivery time, Product category
[22]	Ad delivery time, Place of Ad delivery, Personal characteristics, Managerial time
[23]	Place of Ad delivery, User profiling, Device profile, Advertiser profiling
[24]	Place of Ad delivery, Personal characteristics, Relevance, Permission Marketing, Targeting, Purchasing habits
[25]	Place of Ad delivery, Personal characteristics, Personalization
[26]	User profiling, Place of Ad delivery
[27]	Ad content, Message format, Product category, Incentive, Clutter, Consumer response, Message frequency, Message structure
[28]	Opt-in, Sales Message Control, Incentive, Customization
[29]	Creativity, Market interpretation, Relevance, Opt-in, Campaign management
[6]	Source, Irritation, Ad content

asking experts to rate (on a seven-point Likert scale) the significance of each recorded variable on the effectiveness of an SMS campaign.

Judgement snowball sampling [30] was employed as the survey's sampling method, since it is a sampling technique appropriate for special populations. We identified advertising experts through an industry group of 190 members specializing in electronic advertising (Internet and mobile alike). These individuals served as informants to identify others with the desired characteristics for our study. A total of 113 responses were collected, out of which 90 met the criteria for exploratory factor analysis.

Using Principal Components and the Varimax method, a group of four factors were obtained with KMO=0,753 indicating the appropriateness of the sample. The corresponding variables and the grouping factors are depicted in the following table.

Table 2. Factor analysis results

Factors / Variables	Campaign Strategy	Targeting	Creative Development	Source
Product Superiority	,766			
Message Persuasion	,697			
Incentive (i.e. coupon)	,663			
Message Appeal	,615			
Message Creativity	,588			
Adequate market research resources	,574			
Continuous Feedback from consumers responses	,562			
Message's Strategy (quiz, polls etc.)	,500			
Agency's knowledge of customers' wants		,715		
Place of Ad delivery		,709		
Time of Ad delivery		,689		
Agency's knowledge of customers' previous purchases		,523		
Message Language			,754	
Message Length			,655	
SMS responses' costs			,653	
Message Frequency			,519	
Depiction of source's brand name before opening the SMS				,804
Depiction of source's brand name into the SMS				,768
Source's reputation				,535
Ad clutter				,527
KMO (,753) Total Variance Explained (54%)				

The basic motivation of conducting exploratory factor analysis was to reveal the respondents' perspective for the issue in question. Thus, advertising experts see mobile advertising as a four-stage process. First, they need to decide on the campaign's strategy: they think about the advertised product in comparison to other products and decide on how to develop a communication message that reflects the product's superiority and the campaign's objectives. Given that mobile advertising is a form of permission based marketing, a determinant for the success of the campaign is adequate market research resources. As consumers gain more control of the flow of information, the advertiser must anticipate the information the consumer needs and deliver a consistent message for an identified consumer. Moreover, it is crucial to select an appropriate type of campaign (for example, one-off push vs. continued dialogs) and design appropriate service modules ("text-to-wins", polls, alerts, quizzes, coupons, loyalty point systems, and so on). Secondly, advertisers examine the features of their opt-in database so as to effectively target consumers. The growth of interactive advertising highlights the role of the consumer in the determining the effects of advertising, making traditional assumptions about how advertising works challengeable. In view of the fact that the mobile phone has the higher level of uniqueness, owners have the phone on them most of their waking hours [22], and it is the only device from which agencies can retrieve the consumers' location, targeting capabilities could augment mobile advertising in the centre of one-to-one marketing. Thirdly, respondents evaluate the dynamics of different message formats and structures. SMS has a significant social and cultural impact: new language forms have emerged, especially when teenagers are communicating with each other. When addressing young people, messages should be entertaining and show familiarity with the abbreviations typical of SMS messaging. Finally, the advertised brand is a decisive variable for the effectiveness of the campaign, since a well known brand will probably initiate more responses and overcome possible competitive SMS messages.

4 Future Research Steps

We have developed a model identifying the factors influencing the effectiveness of a mobile messaging advertising campaign. We have found four main factors (Campaign Strategy, Source, Targeting, and Creative Development), each consisting of a number of constituent variables that collectively provide a holistic view of the determinants of successful mobile messaging push advertising. Our contribution lies in the development of an empirically validated model, which is clearly lacking in the majority of existing propositions regarding the potential and critical success factors of mobile advertising.

The validity and generalizability of our results are of course limited by a number of factors. We have chosen to base our study on the views of industry experts (i.e. advertisers). Although this seems like a logical step, given the relative inexperience of the user population with mobile messaging advertising, our findings would benefit by cross-examination with mobile messaging advertisement recipients. Such research could be based on an explanatory (confirmatory) survey that is based on the model proposed in this paper or, especially in the case of inexperienced users, on focus groups and/or field experiments.

The sampling method followed in this paper may be another potential limiting factor. The representativeness of the sample is difficult to ascertain because the data collection instrument was web-based and some respondents were identified through a judgement snowball technique. While expertise with advertising was ensured through the respondent's company profile and occupation, self-selection bias problems may have found their way into the sample. However, the sample size (N=90) is large enough to alleviate most of these concerns.

However, the results of this exploratory research are far from being conclusive. Further research is required to complement our findings and associate the impact of each factor identified with overall mobile advertising effectiveness. Such evaluation can be conducted through a variety of methods, which can be classified into two major research streams: the laboratory experiment and the field study approach.

Since mobile advertising depends heavily on situational factors, the laboratory approach, despite being able to validly assess causality through the proper control of external factors, seems inappropriate for studying the collective impact of SMS advertising factors in the context of their real-life environmental influences. Conversely, in the field study approach researchers use field data as inputs to models that conclude to one dependent (outcome) measure. Although multicollinearity and reverse causality decrease internal validity, field studies can record the value of each relationship, evaluate the robustness of the aforementioned advertising model and predict the value of the effectiveness variable in real life settings.

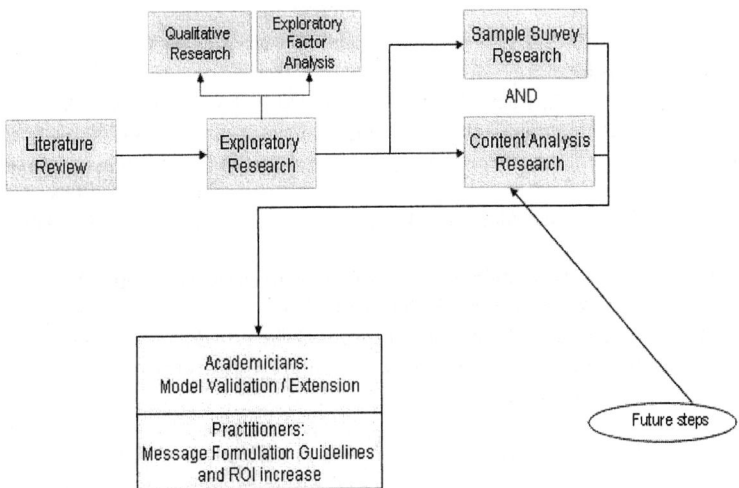

Fig. 1. Proposed research strategy

Thus, a sample survey can be initially used to identify which are the clusters of consumers that are more positively positioned towards SMS advertisements and develop a corresponding portrayal of users for more effective targeting. To shed light into which message elements elicit higher response rates, an applicable field study technique could be content analysis. Content analysis may be defined as the systematic, objective, quantitative analysis of message [10]. Content analysis is based on classifying mainly text in specific variables. An SMS Coding Book, with form and content variables, could be developed so as to record the list of variables to be researched and provide a consistent framework for conducting the research. Inter-coder classification will permit a quantitative assessment of achieved reliability (inter-judgement reliability is usually represented by Cohen's Kappa static formulae). Moreover, these message characteristics, like the number of words and size of the ad copy, could be correlated with one outcome measure, the actual customers' SMS replies to SMS advertisements. Through regression analysis, a correlation between the outcome measure and the factors will be built up resulting to statistical significant factors that impact the customers' psychological set and prompt them to respond.

References

1. IMAP: Global System Framework – Business Model, Research Report. http://www.imapproject.org/imapproject/downloadroot/public1/D2.1.b%206%2002%2003.pdf (2003)
2. Richards, J., Curran, C.: Oracles on "advertising": Searching for a definition. Journal of Advertising. 31 (2002) 63-77
3. Chittenden, L., Ruth, R.: An evaluation of e-mail marketing and factors affecting response. Journal of Targeting, Measurement & Analysis for Marketing. 11 (2003) 203-17
4. Petty, R. E., Cacioppo, J. T., Schumann, D.: Central and Peripheral Routes to Advertising Effectiveness: The Moderating Role of Involvement. Journal of Consumer Research. 10 (1983) 135-46
5. Stewart, D. W., Koslow, S.: Executional Factors and Advertising Effectiveness: A Replication. Journal of Advertising. 18 (1989) 21-32
6. Tsang, M. M., Ho, S.-C., Liang, T.-P.: Consumer Attitudes Toward Mobile Advertising: An Empirical Study. International Journal of Electronic Commerce. 8 (2004) 65-78
7. Percy, L.: A Review of the Effect of Specific Advertising Elements upon Overall Communication Response. Current Issues & Research in Advertising. 6 (1983) 77-118
8. Assael, H.: Consumer Behavior and Marketing Action. 2nd edn. Kent Publishing Company (1984)
9. Baltas, G.: Determinants of internet advertising effectiveness: an empirical study. International Journal of Market Research. 45 (2003) 505-513
10. Naccarato, J. L., Neuendorf, K. A.: Content Analysis as a Predictive Methodology: Recall, Readership, and Evaluations of Business-to-Business Print Advertising. Journal of Advertising Research. 38 (1998) 19-33
11. De Pelsmacker, P., Van den Bergh, J.: Advertising Content and Irritation: A Study of 226 TV Commercials. Journal of International Consumer Marketing. 10 (1998) 5-27
12. Moore, D. J., Harris, W. D.: Affect intensity and the consumer's attitude toward high impact emotional advertising appeals. Journal of Advertising. 25 (1996) 37-50
13. Barnes, S. J.: Wireless digital advertising: nature and implications. International Journal of Advertising. 21 (2002) 399--420
14. Balasubramanian, S., Peterson, R. A., Jarvenpaa, S. L.: Exploring the Implications of M-Commerce for Markets and Marketing. Journal of the Academy of Marketing Science. 30 (2002) 348-361
15. Heinonen, K., Strandvik, T.: Consumer Responsiveness to Mobile Marketing. http://web.hhs.se/cic/roundtable2003/papers/D22Heinonen_Strandvik.pdf (2003)

16. Yuan, S.-T., Tsao, Y. W.: A recommendation mechanism for contextualized mobile advertising. Expert Systems with Applications. 24 (2003) 399-414
17. Kannan, P.K., Chang, A., Whinston, A.: Wireless Commerce: Marketing Issues and Possibilities. Proceedings of the 34th Hawaii International Conference on System Sciences, Hawaii (2001)
18. Leppäniemi, M., Karjaluoto, H., Salo, J..: The success factors of mobile advertising value chain. EBusiness Review. IV (2004) 93-97
19. Advani, R., Choudhury, K.: Making the Most of B2C Wireless. Business Strategy Review. 12 (2001) 39-49
20. Ranganathan, A. Campbell, R.: Advertising in a Pervasive Computing Environment. Proceedings of the 2'nd ACM International Workshop on Mobile Commerce, Atlanta, Georgia, September 28 (2002)
21. Barwise, P.: TV, PC, or Mobile? Future Media for Consumer e-Commerce. Business Strategy Review. 12 (2001) 35-42
22. Watson, R. T., Pitt, L. F., Berthon, P., Zinkhan, G. M.: U-Commerce: Expanding the Universe of Marketing. Journal of the Academy of Marketing Science. 30 (2002) 333-47
23. Hristova, N., O'Hare, G.: Ad-me: Wireless Advertising Adapted to the User Location, Device and Emotions. Proceedings of the 37th Hawaii International Conference on System Sciences, January, Hawaii (2004)
24. Varshney, Upkar and Ron Vetter (2001), "A Framework for the Emerging Mobile Commerce Applications," Proceedings of the 34th Hawaii International Conference on System Sciences, IEEE Computer Society Press, Los Alamitos, CA
25. Kaasinen, E.: User needs for location-aware mobile services. Personal and Ubiquitous Computing. 7 (2003) 70-79
26. Aalto, L., Göthlin, N., Korhonen, J., Ojala, T.: Bluetooth and WAP push based location-aware mobile advertising system. Proceedings of the 2nd international conference on Mobile systems, applications, and services, Boston, MA, USA, June 6-9, (2004)
27. Barwise, P., Strong, C.: Permission-Based Mobile Advertising. Journal of Interactive Marketing. 16 (2002) 14-24
28. HPI Research on behalf of Nokia: New Nokia research shows consumers ready for m-marketing via mobile handsets. http://www.pressi.com/fi/julkaisu/42994.html (2002)
29. Kavassalis, P., Spyropoulou, N., Drossos, D., Mitrokostas, E., Gikas, G., Hatzistamatiou, A.: Mobile Permission Marketing: Framing the Market Inquiry. International Journal of Electronic Commerce. 8 (2003) 55-79
30. Churchill, G., Iacobucci, D.: Marketing Research: Methodological Foundations. 8th edn. USA, South Western (2002)

An Improved HCI Method and Information Input Device Using Gloves for Wearable Computers

Jeong-Hoon Shin and Kwang-Seok Hong

School of Information and Communication Engineering, Sungkyunkwan University,
Suwon, Kyungki-do, 440-746 Korea
only4you@chol.com, kshong@skku.ac.kr
http://only4you.mchol.com, http://hci.skku.ac.kr

Abstract. Input to small device is become an increasingly crucial factor in development for the ever-more powerful wearable computers. In this paper, we propose glove-based human-computer interaction method and information input device for wearable computers. We suggest an easy and effective alphanumeric input algorithm using gloves and conduct efficiency test. The key factor for the proposed algorithm and device is the use of unique operator-to-key mapping method, key-to-symbol mapping method. The strong points of the proposed algorithm and device is using simple and easy algorithm. As a result, users can easily learn how to use. We list and discuss traditional algorithm and method using a glove, then describe an improved newly proposed algorithm using gloves. We conducted efficiency test with 20 subjects and compared the results with 12 similar systems. We set 11 key factors as performance evaluation parameters, and then compared performance of each system using these 11 key factors.

1 Introduction

In this paper, a new gloves-based text input device and improved algorithm are introduced to provide HCI method for a wearable computer. Wearable computers are the next generation of portable machine. Worn by people, they provide constant access to various computing and communication resources. Wearable computers are generally composed of small sized PC, display mounted on head, wireless communication hardware and input device. Thus, input to small sized devices is becoming an increasingly crucial factor in development for the ever-more powerful embedded market [1].

The purpose of this paper is to introduce the HCI method for the wearable computers using gloves and an improved algorithm, and assess its performance. Because of its device independent characteristic, proposed device could be applied to all kinds of electronic applications. It could be applied to all kinds of wearable computers as well as desktop computers.

Our paper is organized as follows. In section 2, several devices for the wearable computers using gloves are introduced. In section 3, we suggest a novel HCI method and its improved algorithm for wearable computer. In section 4 we analyze proposed device and method using 11 key factors of the HCI devices. And conclusions are given in section 5.

2 Traditional Glove Based HCI Method and Device

The following subsections explain the main characteristics of traditional glove based alphanumeric input devices. In these sections, we shortly describe the features of each method, and compare between methods.

2.1 Chording Gloves

The chording glove is a chord keyboard where the buttons have been mounted directly on the fingers themselves. The 31 character limit of a chord keyboard is surpassed by using three sticky shifts, mounted on the side of the index finger, in order to be pressed by the thumb. Function keys are provided to enable quick use of rarely used utilities. The Chording Glove employs pressure sensors for each finger of the right hand in a glove to implement chording input device. There is one key for each finger. Multiple keys are pressed simultaneously in various combinations to enter characters. A chord can be made by pressing the fingers against any surface. Almost all possible finger combinations are mapped to symbols, making it potentially hard to type them. Additional buttons, located along the index finger, are used to produce more than the 2^5 distinct characters [2].

Fig 1 shows the chords for the letter Y, M and U using Chording Glove.

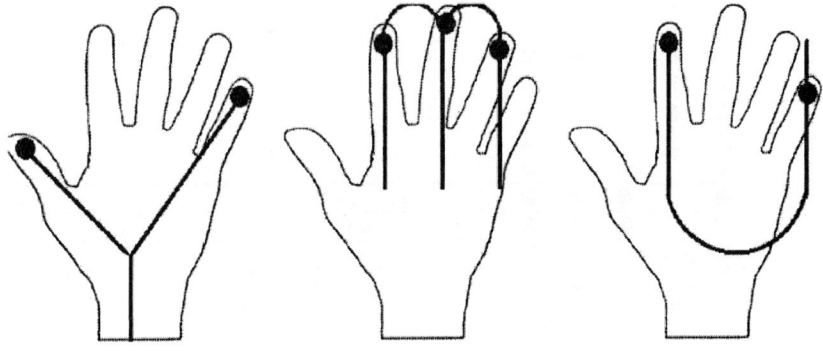

Fig. 1. Chords for the letters Y, M and U using Chording Glove

Table 1 shows the key map of the Chording Glove for the English language. As shown in Table 1, a weak point of this method is difficult to use. It needs more than 80 minutes to learn the entire chord set. After 11 hours of training, word input speed reached approximately 18 words per minute (wpm) whereas the character error rate amounted to 17%.

Table 1. Key map of the Chording Glove for the English Language

Chord					Shifts			
Thumb	Index	Middle	Ring	Little	Default	Caps	Num	Caps+Num
●	●	○	○	○	a	A	5	&
●	●	○	●	○	b	B		*
●	●	●	●	○	c	C	0	%
●	○	●	●	○	d	D	/	\
○	○	○	●	○	e	E	3	!
●	○	○	●	●	f	F	Tab	
○	○	●	●	○	g	G	)	>
○	○	●	○	○	h	H	2	@
○	○	○	○	●	i	I	4	?
●	●	●	○	●	j	J		
○	●	●	●	●	k	K	^	^
○	●	●	●	●	l	L	=	<
○	●	●	●	○	m	M	-	_
○	●	●	○	○	n	N	(	"
●	○	○	●	○	o	O	7	|
○	●	○	●	○	p	P	+	#
○	●	●	○	●	q	Q	?	
●	●	●	○	○	r	R	9	'
●	○	●	○	○	s	S	6	$
○	●	○	○	○	t	T	1	'
○	●	○	○	●	u	U	[	{
○	●	○	●	●	v	V	Escape	
●	●	○	○	●	w	W	]	}
●	●	○	●	●	x	X	*	
●	○	○	○	●	y	Y	8	~
●	○	●	○	●	z	Z		
●	○	●	●	●	, (comma)		;	
○	○	●	●	●	. (period)		:	
●	○	○	○	○	Space			
○	○	○	●	●	Back Space			
●	●	●	●	●	Return			

2.2 Finger-Joint Gesture Wearable Keypad

The Finger-Joint Gesture Wearable Keypad suggests viewing the phalanges of the fingers (besides the thumb) of one hand as the keys on phone keypad. Fig 2 shows the Finger-Joint Gesture (FJG) Keypad glove and Fig 3 shows the keypad and the various function keys on mobile phone [3].

By holding the inside of the hand in front of you, and bending the fingers toward you and aligning the fingertips of the four fingers, a 4X3 matrix is similar in shape to the traditional telephone keypad. And FJG keypad employs the same layout as that encountered on any traditional mobile telephone. Nothing else has to be learned. The FJG concept is a generic way of combining the 12 keys of the keypad with 4+1 different functions. It can be used in a variety of different interfaces.

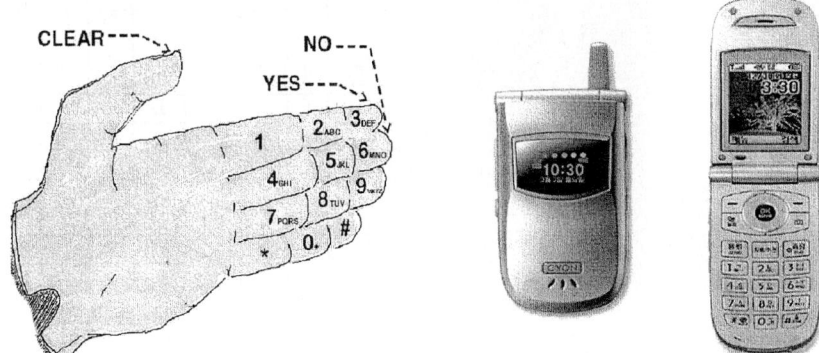

Fig. 2. The Finger-Joint Gesture (FJG) Keypad Glove

Fig. 3. The keypad and the various function keys on mobile phone

A weak point of this method is the limited number of alphabets can be aligned on the phalanges. To overcome this weak point, if the multiple numbers of alphabets are mapped on the same phalanges (one-to-many characters mapping) in the same mode (EX: ABC, DEF...), the user has to use multiple successive keystrokes on the same phalanx of the fingers. As shown in Fig 2, if you want to generate the alphabet L, then you have to depress the medial phalanx of the middle finger three times consecutively using the thumb.

2.3 Thumbcode

"Thumbcode" method defines the touch of the thumb onto the fingers' phalanges of the same hand as key strokes. Character is signed or thumbed by pressing the tip of the thumb against one of the phalanges. This defines the twelve thumb states of Thumbcode. In combination with the twelve thumb states this gives a total of 96 basic Thumbcode. Fig 4 shows external appearance of the Thumbcode and Fig 5 shows the Thumbcode assignments. Each of the eight 3X4 arrays in Fig 5 should be visualized as being superimposed on the fingers of the right hand. In Fig 5, the 4 vertical bars mean 4 fingers of right-hand. Narrow space means that the adjacent fingers are closed. And regular space means that the adjacent fingers are opened. The four fingers can touch each other in eight different ways, each basically representing a mode, or modifier key that affects the mapping for the thumb touch [4].

A weak point of this method also can be described as complexity of combining fingers. User has to combine their fingers to generate Thumbcode in complex ways. As a result of this complexity, this method also needs training time to use fluently.

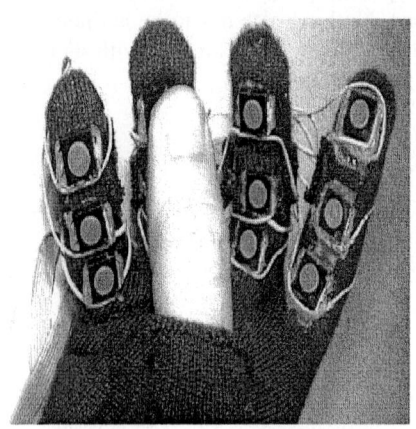

Open ‖‖			
1	t	e	a
2	s	i	n
3	4	5	6
Pair ‖‖			
7	o	h	←
8	d	r	␣
9	0	.	=
Trio ‖‖			
b	c	f	g
j	k	l	m
[	]	;	'
Closed ‖‖			
p	q	u	v
w	x	y	z
,	.	/	\

Shift Open ‖‖			
!	T	E	A
@	S	I	N
#	$	%	~
Shift Pair ‖‖			
&	O	H	
*	D	R	←
(	)	-	+
Shift Trio ‖‖			
B	C	F	G
J	K	L	M
{	}	:	"
Shift Closed ‖‖			
P	Q	U	V
W	X	Y	Z
<	>	?	|

Fig. 4. External appearance of Thumbcode

Fig. 5. Thumbcode assignments view of right-hand palm

3 An Improved HCI Method and Device

Key-to-symbol mapping methods can be divided into two classes. Exactly one key to one symbol (character) mapping (1 degree of freedom, DOF) method and one-to-many characters mapping (1.5 degree of freedom, DOF) method are typical key-to-symbol mapping methods.

In a one-to-many characters mapping method, user has to use multiple successive keystrokes to produce some character. In this paper, we propose an improved one-to-many characters mapping method.

We can produce any character using a keystroke. If the user wants to produce a character "C" in a traditional one-to-many characters mapping method, the user has to

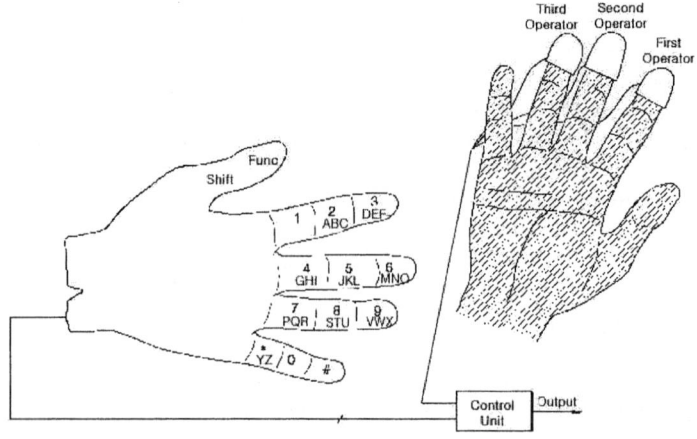

Fig. 6. Key-to-Symbol mapping and the operators

use multiple successive keystrokes on the medial phalanx of the index finger. But, in the proposed method, the user can produce a character "C" using a keystroke on the medial phalanx of the index finger with a specific operator (third operator).

First of all, we could decide the number of discrete operators and the layout of the key-to-symbol mapping according to the use of applications. In the proposed text input device, maximum number of the symbols can be mapped on a key depends on the number of using operators (the maximum number of used operators not exceeds 5). If we use 3 operators, we can map 3 characters on a key. Thus, the maximum number of characters can be mapped on the phalanges of the 4 fingers is 36. We can produce 36 different characters using a keystroke with a specific operator. This process could be finished using the control unit in Fig 6.

If the user depresses the tip phalanx of the middle finger with a first operator, then the character "M" will be produced. And, if the user depresses the tip phalanx of the middle finger with a second operator, then the character "N" will be produced. And, if the user depress the tip phalanx of the middle finger, then character "O" will be produced, and so on. Key-to-symbol mapping method is very easy and simple. Thus, nothing else has to be learned.

4 Efficiency Test and Results

To verify its efficiency, the proposed glove based text input device was built and assessed. The experiment that we conducted was designed to evaluate the input speed

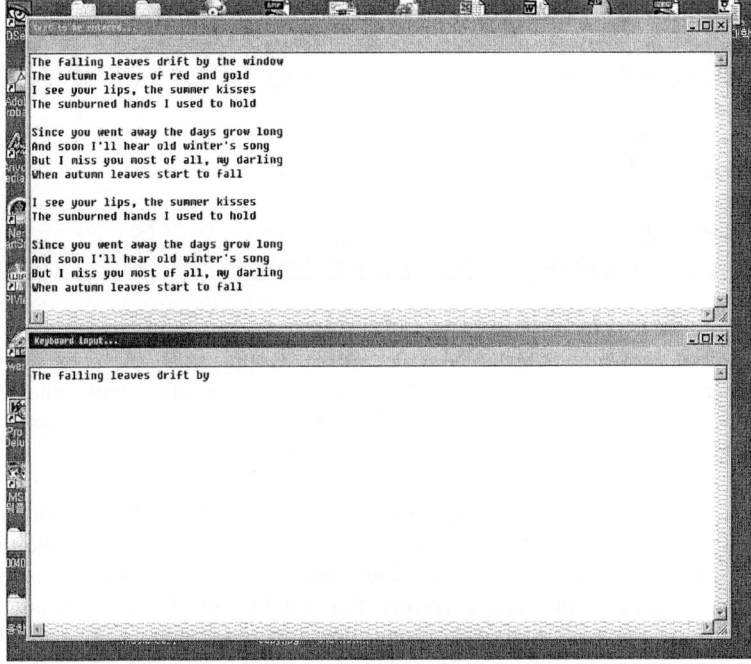

Fig. 7. Sample text for used testing and keyboard input display

and error rate of the proposed device. 20 subjects were selected from among the respondents to advertisements placed around the university campus. There were 12 males and 8 females, and all were right handed and aged between 24 and 32 years. The subjects are seated on the chair during the session. The initial session consisted of a tutorial which lasted less than a minute, and whose purpose was to teach the subjects the key-map and how to operate the device. Once this session was completed, a sample text was provided to the subjects. Fig 7 shows provided sample text.

Table 2. Efficiency test for of HCI methods using 11 key factors

Method or device		Number of discrete keys	Number of discrete operators	Key-to-symbol mapping DOF	operator-key-mapping potentially n-n	Operator-key switch time	Familiarity	Temporal significance for key press	Estimated bandwidth interval in cpm	Invisibility (+: high, o: medium)	Visual incarnation of keyboard
Visual Panel	d	52+	1	1	1-n	Medium	Medium	3s	20	o	fixed
Finger-Joint Gesture	m	12	1	1.5	1-n	High	Medium	0	100	+	no
Thumbcode	d/m	12/96	1+4	1.5	1-n	High	Low	0	70	+	no
Chording Glove	d/m	5	5	1.5	1-1	Medium	Low	0	80	o	no
FingeRing	d/m	5	5	1.5	1-1	120ms	Low	120ms	120	+	no
Touchpad	d	52	10	1	n-n	Low	High	0	250	o	fixed possible
TouchStream	d	52	10	1	1-1	Low	High	0	250	o	yes
VType	d/m	10	10	1.5	1-1	Low	Medium	0	100	o	with HMD
VKey	d	52+	10	1	1-n*	Low	High	0	250	o	yes
VKB Projection	d	52+	10	1	1-n*	Low	High	0	250	o	yes
Scurry	d	52	10	1	1-n*	Low	High	0	250	o	no
Senseboard	d	52+	10	1	1-n*	Low	High	0	250	+	no
Proposed device	d/m	52+(600)	5	1.5	1-n	High	Very High	0	·	+	no

The complete text to be entered by the subject appeared in the top window of the computer display, while their keyboard input was displayed in the bottom window. We compared the proposed device and its method of utilization with other devices which use other methods, from several points of view, namely the input speed, error rate and the time required to learn the entire key-map.

After 1 hour of training, the average input speed for the proposed device was 27.4 words per minute. For comparison, the input speed on a QWERTY keyboard for a previously untrained user after 12 hours of training is 20 words per minute [5], and the input speed for a previously untrained user using a glove after an 80 minutes tutorial is 16.8 words per minute [2]. Therefore, this result means that the proposed device offers a fast and convenient method of inputting text. The error rate was calculated as the ratio of input errors to the total number of characters and was found to be 7.8% after training. Compared with the error rate on a QWERTY keyboard (12.7%) and the traditional method of using a glove (17.4%), the proposed method constitutes an accurate text input method [2 and 6]. Furthermore, the number of keystrokes and the time required to enter the complete sample text were the same as those obtained using a QWERTY keyboard, and were much less than the corresponding values in the case of a traditional glove.

To verify the performance for user interface, we examined each of the methods and devices for a number of characteristics which we consider relevant to a user interface. Table 2 shows results of the efficiency test with proposed HCI method and device. We compared our newly suggested simple HCI method and device with other devices and methods for wearable computers. As shown in Table 2, the suggested method and device are superior to others in a large part.

The definitions of the taxonomy used in table 2 are as follows [7].

Method or device: This factor distinguishes between mere suggestions of character-producing methods without implementations and actual operating devices.

Number of discrete keys: This factor means that how many keys does the method and/or device have? This is important if other or expanded alphabets like Chinese are to accommodated.

Number of discrete operators: This factor means that are all ten fingers used to operate the keys of the proposed keyboard or is it only the index finger, thumb etc. that can press a key?

Key-to-symbol mapping DOF: This factor means that does each key correspond to exactly one symbol/character (1 degree of freedom, DOF), or is it a one-to-many characters mapping (1.5 DOF, see section 4.2), disambiguated by either temporal methods (multiple successive keystrokes), by statistical prediction or by chording methods (multiple keys pressed simultaneously produce one character).

Operator-to-key mapping: A one-to one mapping means there are as many keys as operators, and each operator works with the one key only. A one-to-many mapping is exemplified by how most people touch-type on a keyboard: One finger is responsible for a set of keys, and the key set for a finger does not intersect with any other finger's set, i.e. one key is always pressed by the same finger. Finally, a many-to-many mapping allows any operator to press any key.

Operator-key switch time: This factor is related to the number of discrete operators that can be employed with the proposed keyboards, but it is an independent quantity. It gives an idea about the human factors aspect of the time between pressing two different keys.

Familiarity: This factor is related to the appearance of the key mappings. Does the proposed keyboards have an entirely new method to input text, does it have a remote relation to conventional keyboards (same layout but does not support all its affordances), or is it very much in the style of a physical keyboard? This will have a big impact on how easily users can transition to this kind of virtual keyboard, and in our opinion also on the broad acceptance of the keyboards.

Temporal significance interval for key press: For the device to register a key press, how long does the key have to be pressed? On a physical keyboard, a key does not have to be depressed for a noticeable amount of time, but this might be different for virtual keyboards. Obviously, this has an immediate impact on the potential typing speed with the proposed keyboards.

Estimated bandwidth: This can of course be only a rough guideline to how many characters a human will likely be able to input per time when using this kind of device or method.

Invisibility: This factor defines that how apparent is the device and its use to other people? Can the proposed keyboard be used in "stealth" mode, without disturbing others or even without being noticed?

Visual incarnation of a keyboard: This factor defines that whether the proposed keyboard can display its key mappings using several mechanism available or not? Visualization of the "keys" is an important consideration for novice users.

After finishing the efficiency test in standstill state, we also conducted efficiency test in mobile condition. Fig 8 shows the configuration of conducted experiments in mobile condition.

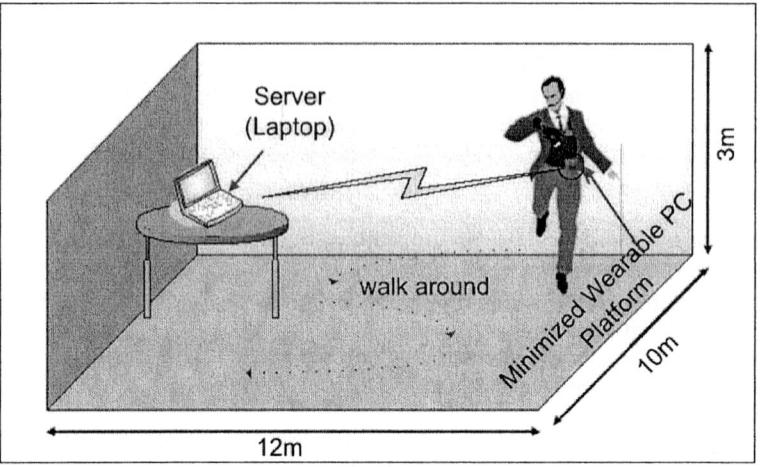

Fig. 8. Configuration of conducted experiments in mobile condition

Performance under the mobile condition is very important to the HCI method for the wearable computers. For this reason, we conducted the performance evaluation in mobile condition. The subjects wearing proposed HCI device walk around laptop computer. The provided texts are inputted under the mobile condition.

But, in this case, performance of the proposed device falls severely. To achieve usable and useful results using the proposed device as a HCI method, further work and improvements are needed.

5 Conclusions

Nowadays, many systems adapt multi-modal human computer interfaces. The reason for using multi-modal HCI system is to create a more natural experience for the user by allowing him/her to use other methods of communication than just speech or just mouse, and aid the computer in understanding what the user wants by providing multiple modality streams that can disambiguate each other.

In this paper, we proposed an improved HCI method using gloves. Although there are several benefits of using one-handed text input devices, but there are clear-cut lines of input speed and error rate. To overstep these limits, we proposed the method and the device using two hands. The proposed method and experiment gave us possibility of using gloves as a text input device. For the purpose of achieving popular use of the glove as a text input device, more convenient and swift method should be proposed.

References

1. Markus Eisenhauer, Britta Hoffman, Doro Kretschmer.: "State of the Art Human-Computer Interaction", Giga Mobile project D2.7.1, September 2002
2. Robert Rosenberg and Mel Slater. : "The Chording Glove: A Glove-Based Text Input Device" IEEE Transactions on systems, Man, And Cybernetics-Part C: Applications and reviews, May 1999
3. Goldstein, M. and Chincholle, D.: "Finger-Joint Gesture Wearable Keypad" in Second Workshop on Human Computer Interaction with Mobile Devices, 1999
4. Pratt, V. R.: "Thumbcode: A Device-Independent Digital Sign Language." http://boole.stanford.edu/thumbcode, July 1998
5. J. Noyes,: "The QWERTY keyboard: A review," Int. J. Man-Mach Studies, vol. 18, no. 3, pp. 265-281, 1983
6. K. M. Potosnak,: "Keys and keyboards," Handbook of Human-Computer Interaction, Ed. New York: Elsevier, 1988
7. Mathias Kolsch and Matthew Turk. : "Keyboards without keyboards: A survey of virtual keyboards" http://ilab.cs.ucsb.edu/projects/mathias/KolschKeyboards.pdf

Efficient Parameterization of 3D Point-Sets Using Recursive Dynamic Base Surfaces

Philip Azariadis[1,2] and Nickolas Sapidis[1]

[1] Department of Product & Systems Design Engineering, University of the Aegean,
Ermoupolis, Syros, 84100 Greece
{azar, sapidis}@aegean.gr
http://www.syros.aegean.gr

[2] ELKEDE – Technology & Design Centre SA, Research & Development Department

Abstract. Modelling a three-dimensional (3D) point cloud with smooth mathematical surfaces or high-quality triangle meshes is an essential component of many applications in Computer Graphics, Visualization and Computer-Aided Design/Engineering. A vital prerequisite for that is the construction of a *parameterization* for a given 3D point-set; this problem is the focus of the present paper. The proposed method employs ideas and tools from "point-based geometric modelling" in order to construct a set of continuous surfaces locally-fitted to a point set. Then parameterization is achieved by orthogonally projecting the point set onto these surfaces.

1 Introduction

A large variety of standard applications in Computer Graphics (CG), Visualization and Computer-Aided Design and Engineering rely on processing three-dimensional (3D) point-clouds for modelling free-form objects. Furthermore, many researchers and commercial systems are currently proposing new geometric-models based solely on *points*. A vital prerequisite for all these methods and techniques is availability of an adequate parameterization of the given point-set. Indeed, high-quality meshing, texture mapping and morphing algorithms, as well as object creation/manipulation methods rely almost exclusively on good parameterizations of the sampled geometry. Given a cloud of unorganised points $\mathbf{C} = \{ \mathbf{p}_\mu = (x_\mu, y_\mu, z_\mu) | \mu = 0, \ldots, N-1 \}$ this paper addresses the problem of assigning adequate parameter values $(u_\mu, v_\mu) \in [0,1] \times [0,1] \subset \Re^2$, $\mu = 0, \ldots, N-1$ that best represent the points' position within the rectangular domain in the plane.

Significant research has been devoted to the aforementioned parameterization problem employing an underlying 3D triangulation. Generally, through iterative steps a topologically identical two-dimensional (2D) triangulation is obtained, which defines the parameter values of the vertices in the domain plane. These methods differ from each other in how the transformation is performed from 3D to 2D. Indicative examples include Harmonic parameterizations [7], Floater's barycentric mappings [8] and the Most Isometric Parameterization [11].

Other approaches incorporate different (and usually non-linear) energy functions to minimize the metric distortion during the flattening process of the 3D mesh [3, 5, 15, 17, 18]. Several of these techniques provide "minimal distortion" solutions to the general texture mapping problem and, therefore, are tailored to that CG application [6, 14, 21]. However, all the aforementioned methods assume that the points are either structured in some kind of mesh and they seem to be slow if the number of data points is large. They are also limited if there are concave parts and hole loops within the point-cloud.

Ma and Kruth [16] use interactively defined section curves together with four boundary curves to obtain a *base surface*, which roughly approximates the shape of the point-cloud. Parameter values are then computed by projecting data points onto the base surface. A generalization of the method presented in [8] is proposed by Floater and Reimers [9] for parameterizing unorganized points by solving a global linear system. Hoppe at al. [10] introduce a method for producing "simplicial" surfaces approximating an unorganized set of points which is derived with an homogeneous sampling ratio. Pottman et al. [19] propose a scheme where a so called "active" curve or surface approximates a model shape through an iterative procedure where the quasi-Newton optimization procedure is employed to minimize, in each iteration, a quadratic objective function.

When the object surface is closed, i.e., it is represented by a 3D mesh without boundaries, "spherical mapping or embedding" is usually employed for the parameterization purposes. Several methods for direct parameterization on the sphere have been developed, i.e., [1, 13, 20, 22].

The parameterization method proposed in this paper is able to process arbitrary point-clouds or subparts of them, which are "enclosed" within a given set of boundary curves that resemble the topology of disk. The proposed method doesn't make any strict assumptions regarding the sampling density of the point-cloud nor demands the cloud points to be structured in a 3D mesh.

2 The "Dynamic Base Surface" Parametrization-Methodology

Dynamic Base Surfaces (DBS) are developed in [2] in order to solve the parameterization problem for unstructured clouds of points. The resulting parameterization is then utilised in [2] for high-accuracy surface fitting. According to the original DBS methodology (see also Fig.2(a)) an initial DBS is constructed interpolating a given closed boundary topologically equivalent to a rectangle with a bi-cubic Coons surface. A grid of points is derived along the two parametric directions of the DBS and then it is projected onto the cloud surface by minimizing a set of distance metrics. The projection direction of each grid point is set equal to the corresponding DBS normal direction. The resulting projected grid is relaxed, by resampling the corresponding parametric curves, producing a final grid of almost equally spaced points along its two parametric directions. Then, a new DBS is fitted to the relaxed projected-grid. The overall evolution procedure is repeated by calculating more parametric curves onto the new DBS, and, thus, increasing the grid size, until the termination criterion is satisfied. Finally, the required parameterization is achieved by orthogonally projecting the point-cloud onto the resulted DBS.

The preliminary DBS method algorithm in [2] fits a single spline-surface to the point-cloud. This algorithm is not efficient since it cannot guarantee an acceptable surface fit along the entire point-cloud, which is confirmed by our systematic numerical tests.

3 Projection of a Grid of Points onto a Point Cloud

As indicated in Section 2 (see also Fig. 2), an important component (subproblem) of the DBS parameterization-methodology is the projection of a point grid onto the given point cloud. Here, an efficient new "grid-onto-cloud" projection method is developed that enhances significantly the original DBS methodology.

3.1 The Directed Projection Problem

A vital component of "grid projection" is "directed projection of a point onto a cloud" reviewed here: Let $\mathbf{p} = (x, y, z)$ be an arbitrary 3D point, with $\mathbf{n} = (n_x, n_y, n_z)$ an associated projection vector. The pair $\mathbf{p}, \mathbf{n}$ is denoted by $\hat{\mathbf{p}} = \langle \mathbf{p}, \mathbf{n} \rangle$. Then, the *directed projection* $\mathbf{p}^*$ of $\hat{\mathbf{p}}$ onto the point-cloud $\mathbf{C}$ is defined as follows: each $\mathbf{p}_\mu \in \mathbf{C}$ is associated to a positive weight a_μ; these are defined below. Then, $\mathbf{p}^*$ is the solution of the problem (see extensive analysis in [2] & [4]):

$$\text{Find } \mathbf{p}^* \text{ minimizing } E(\mathbf{p}^*) = \sum_{\mu=0}^{N-1} a_\mu \left\| \mathbf{p}^* - \mathbf{p}_\mu \right\|^2 \tag{1}$$

We describe $\mathbf{p}^* = (x^*, y^*, z^*)$ as

$$\mathbf{p}^* = \mathbf{p}^*(t) = \mathbf{p} + t\mathbf{n}, \ t \in \Re. \tag{2}$$

Then, the solution of problem (1) corresponds to [4]

$$t = \frac{\lambda - \mathbf{p} \cdot \mathbf{n}}{\|\mathbf{n}\|^2}, \text{ where } \lambda = \frac{c_1 n_x + c_2 n_y + c_3 n_z}{c_0}, \ c_0 = \sum_{\mu=0}^{N-1} a_\mu, \ c_1 = \sum_{\mu=0}^{N-1} a_\mu x_\mu,$$

$$c_2 = \sum_{\mu=0}^{N-1} a_\mu y_\mu, \ c_3 = \sum_{\mu=0}^{N-1} a_\mu z_\mu \tag{3}$$

The works [2] and [4] have established that appropriate values for the weights $\{a_\mu\}$ are given by[1]:

$$a_\mu = \frac{1}{1 + \|\mathbf{p}_\mu - \mathbf{p}\|^2 \|(\mathbf{p}_\mu - \mathbf{p}) \times \mathbf{n}\|^2}, \ a_\mu \in [0,1] \tag{4}$$

---

[1] The Euclidean norm of a vector $\mathbf{v}$ is denoted by $\|\mathbf{v}\|$.

3.2 Grid Definition and Projection

Given a parametric surface $\mathbf{S} = \mathbf{S}(u,v)$, $u,v \in [0,1]$, and the point cloud $\mathbf{C}$:

(3.2.a) A set of points is selected along the two parametric directions of $\mathbf{S}$, which constitutes the so called *grid of points* denoted by $\mathbf{p}_{i,j} = \mathbf{S}(u_i, v_j)$, $i = 0,\ldots,m-1$, $j = 0,\ldots,n-1$. Each grid point is coupled with a projection direction, which is the actual surface normal direction at the given point. Thus, the grid $\mathbf{p}_{i,j}$ is associated to a *grid of normal vectors* $\mathbf{n}_{i,j}$, where $\mathbf{n}_{i,j} = \dfrac{\mathbf{S}_u(u_i,v_j) \times \mathbf{S}_v(u_i,v_j)}{\|\mathbf{S}_u(u_i,v_j) \times \mathbf{S}_v(u_i,v_j)\|}$.

(3.2.b) Every grid point is projected onto the point cloud along the associated direction. This projection is performed "row-" or "column-" wise, i.e., an entire row (resp. column) of grid points is simultaneously projected onto the point-cloud. Under this way one is able to control the smoothness of a projected *grid section* (i.e., a grid row or column) by minimizing its chord length.

The grid-projection procedure terminates when all grid sections are projected onto the point cloud.

3.3 An Algorithm for Smooth Grid-Projection

A new method for projecting the grid of points $\mathbf{p}_{i,j}$ along the associated direction vectors $\mathbf{n}_{i,j}$ onto the point cloud is proposed in this section. With respect to the previous approach, the proposed method projects the grid onto the point cloud section-by-section. In fact, in order to simplify the notation a set of row or column grid points paired with their corresponding direction vectors is considered here, i.e., $\hat{\mathbf{p}}_{i,j0} = \langle \mathbf{p}_{i,j0}, \mathbf{n}_{i,j0} \rangle$, $i = 0,\ldots,m-1$, $0 \le j0 < n$, which is regarded as a *polygonal curve*. The basic steps of the new projection algorithm are outlined in the following:

(3.3.a) A discretization of the polygonal curve $\hat{\mathbf{p}}_{i,j0}$ is performed deriving a set $\hat{p} = \{\hat{\mathbf{p}}_k = \langle \mathbf{p}_k, \mathbf{n}_k \rangle \mid k = 0,\ldots,K-1\}$ of K distinct *nodes* $\mathbf{p}_k$. This discretization constitutes a relatively dense sampling of the initial polygonal curve $\mathbf{p}_{i,j0}$.

(3.3.b) The node-set $\hat{p}$ is projected onto the point cloud by minimizing an energy function (see details below) which is a convex combination of a distance metric, a first- and a second-order smoothing functional. During the projection process the first and last nodes, $\hat{\mathbf{p}}_0$ and $\hat{\mathbf{p}}_{K-1}$, are fixed, since they lie onto the point cloud.

(3.3.c) The projected node-set (which is also considered as a polygonal curve lying onto the point cloud) is sampled deriving m new grid points $\mathbf{p}^*_{i,j0}$ on the point cloud.

The smooth projection of $\hat{p}$ onto $\mathbf{C}$ is a polygonal curve $q^* = \{\mathbf{p}^*_k\}$ which minimizes the energy function:

$$E = (1-\gamma)D + \gamma(L+C), \quad \gamma \in [0,1] \tag{5}$$

The distance between the polygonal curve and the point cloud is expressed through

$$D = \sum_{k=1}^{K-1} E(\mathbf{p}_k^*) \qquad (6)$$

While the length of the projected polygonal curve is measured through

$$L = \sum_{k=0}^{K-2} \|\mathbf{p}_k^* - \mathbf{p}_{k+1}^*\|^2 \qquad (7)$$

and the functional

$$C = \sum_{k=0}^{K-3} \|\mathbf{p}_k^* - 2\mathbf{p}_{k+1}^* + \mathbf{p}_{k+2}^*\|^2 \qquad (8)$$

resembles the second-order derivative of the polygonal curve q^*. The weight factor γ is used to fine tune the projection process. E.g., one would like to increase γ in point clouds with high-curvature regions and vice versa.

Each $\mathbf{p}_k^*$ is defined by $\mathbf{p}_k^* = \mathbf{p}_k + t_k \mathbf{n}_k$ (compare with (2)), thus, the whole polygonal curve q^* is defined by the vector $\mathbf{t} = (t_k)$ ($k = 1, \ldots, K-2$) (we set $t_0 = t_{K-1} = 0$ since the first and last nodes are fixed). Equation (5) is quadratic with respect to functionals (6), (7) and (8), and, thus, its minimization is achieved by solving a system of linear equations.

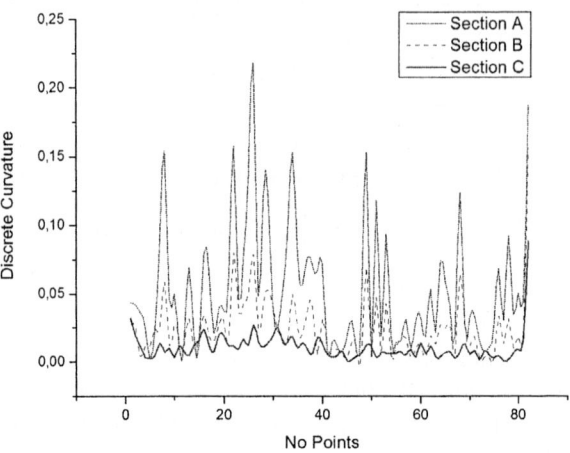

Fig. 1. The discrete-curvature plots of a grid section computed with three different approaches

Systematic numerical tests establish that the above projection method gives very satisfactory results: e.g., in Fig.1, discrete-curvature plots are presented for a gridsection projected with three different methods. "Section A" shows the discrete curvature of the resulted polygonal curve projected with $\gamma = 0$. "Section B" is the result of the straightforward method of Section 3.2, with $\gamma = 0.5$. Finally, "Section C" is the result of the new method after incorporating the new smoothing functional (Eq.(8)) with $\gamma = 0.5$. Clearly, the new method results in a projected grid-section with a much smoother discrete-curvature.

4 Recursive DBS and Point-Cloud Subdivision

A complete DBS algorithm is proposed in this section which remedies the major disadvantage of the preliminary DBS algorithm in [2]: inability to closely approximate all parts of the given cloud. The proposed remedy is based on a "divide and conquer" strategy: when an excessive approximation error is identified, the current "surface-modelling problem" is subdivided into four such problems, which are treated independently.

Figure 2(b) outlines the new DBS algorithm: Let DBS-A and **C** be the DBS and the corresponding point cloud, respectively, at the point (2) of the algorithm in Fig. 2(a). First, an accuracy criterion is applied: each point in **C** is projected onto DBS-A, so that the orthogonal distance of the point to DBS-A is calculated. If the average distance for all points in **C** is smaller than a predefined tolerance, then the algorithm terminates. Otherwise, the algorithm examines the current grid size (which depicts the number of grid rows and columns). If this is still smaller than the maximum grid size, the algorithm continues with a new iteration by increasing the grid size. In the opposite case, both the current DBS and the point cloud are subdivided in four parts as described below and the same algorithm is invoked with each one of the new parts.

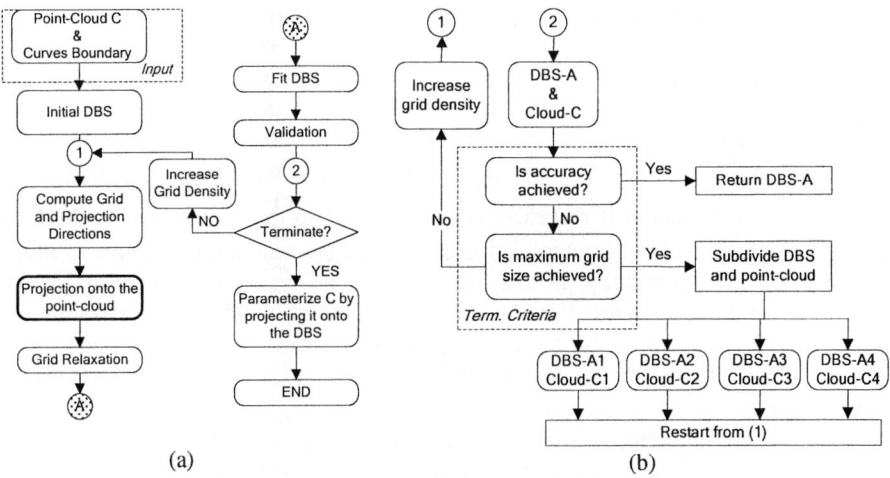

Fig. 2. (a) The basic flow chart of the preliminary DBS method. (b) The new DBS algorithm

4.1 DBS Subdivision

When subdivision is required, the given DBS-A (which is not approximating the current point cloud accurately enough) is replaced by four new surfaces DBS-A_i

($i = 1,\ldots 4$) defined as follows: the two parametric curves corresponding to $u = 0.5$ and $v = 0.5$ of DBS-A are calculated and projected onto the cloud using the grid-section projection method described in Section 3.3. These projections and the boundaries of DBS-A produce four four-sided closed boundaries. Using the existing DBS-A and the new boundaries, four grids are constructed which are used to define the four new surfaces DBS- $\mathbf{A}_i$, $i = 1,\ldots 4$.

4.2 Point-Cloud Subdivision

In order to replace the current cloud-approximation problem by an equivalent set of four approximation-problems, the present point cloud must be partitioned into four subclouds. For this purpose, the following procedure is employed to identify the subcloud $\mathbf{C}_i$ corresponding to the DBS- $\mathbf{A}_i$:

(4.2.a) For each point in the current cloud **C**: Project it orthogonally onto DBS- $\mathbf{A}_i$. The outcome is: *(4.2.a.1)* a point within the boundaries of DBS- $\mathbf{A}_i$, or *(4.2.a.2)* a point outside the boundaries of DBS- $\mathbf{A}_i$, or *(4.2.a.3)* no point at all.

(4.2.b) For each cloud point in **C** corresponding to cases (4.2.a.2) or (4.2.a.3): a new projection point is calculated by projecting the cloud point onto the nearest DBS boundary.

(4.2.c) For each cloud point in **C**, measure its distance to its projection onto DBS- $\mathbf{A}_i$. All cloud points with a distance *sufficiently small* (we use the heuristic limit-value = "25% of the diagonal dimension of the bounding box of DBS- $\mathbf{A}_i$") are included in the subcloud $\mathbf{C}_i$.

4.3 Quadtree Structure

By dividing the initial DBS-A and replacing it by four smaller parts DBS- $\mathbf{A}_i$ ($i = 1,\ldots 4$) one actually defines a parent/child relation between DBS-A and DBS- $\mathbf{A}_i$ ($i = 1,\ldots 4$). This relation is recorded and maintained so that conclusion of the DBS algorithm is followed by: (a) application of appropriate seaming operations to incorporate geometric continuity in the common boundaries, (b) appropriate point-parameterization techniques. For the purposes of point-cloud parameterization we force the DBS patches to share the same boundary curves which correspond to the two parametric curves $u = 0.5$ and $v = 0.5$ of the parent DBS-A (thick curves shown in Fig.3(a)).

The criteria to determine whether to stop or continue with the DBS subdivisions are as follows: (a) If accuracy criterion is satisfied then STOP, (b) If quadtree depth is maximum then STOP, (c) If grid size is maximum SUBDIVIDE. The accuracy criterion determines the current approximation error. In the present method we also check the quadtree depth and we force the algorithm to terminate when this depth becomes quite large.

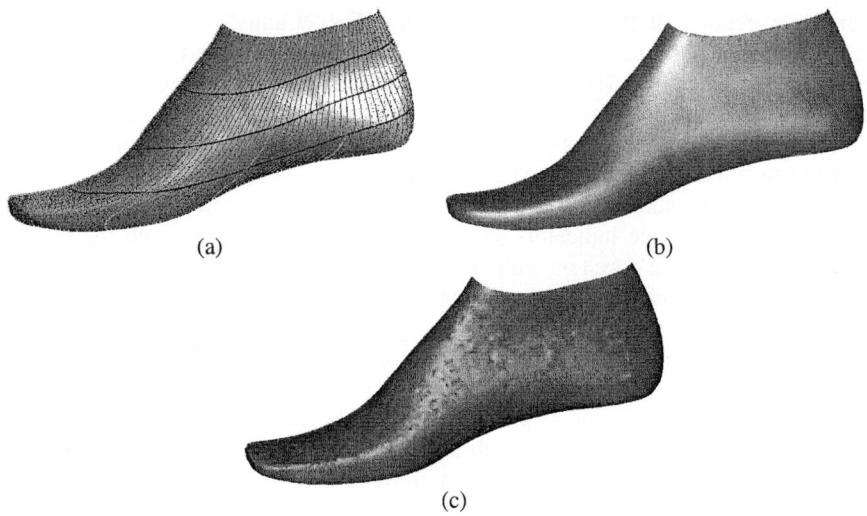

Fig. 3. (a) A point cloud of a shoe last and the corresponding DBS. The result of triangulating the point cloud using: (b) the DBS parameterization, (c) a commercial RE software.

5 Applications and Discussion

The effectiveness of the proposed DBS parameterization-algorithm is demonstrated through the reconstruction of several parts of point clouds using a well known 2D Delaunay triangulation library [12]. The first example concerns the global parameterization of a point cloud derived through a touch-based probe digitizer for the needs of shoe manufacturing. Figure 3(a) shows the result of applying the proposed DBS method to that cloud. Three levels of subdivision sufficed to approximate faithfully the given geometry (mean error < 0.1 mm). The inner thick polygonal curves correspond to the boundaries of the local DBSes, while thinner curves depict the corresponding grids of points. The given point cloud is triangulated using the present DBS parameterization resulting to the C^0-continuous surface shown in Fig.3(b); this triangulation is accurate and smooth. Figure 3(c) demonstrates the result of triangulating the same point cloud using a state-of-the-art Reverse Engineering software. Clearly this commercial software has produced a much inferior triangulation since it is sensitive to noise; a very common side-effect of acquisition techniques based on mechanical probes.

Figure 4 depicts another example of a complicated point cloud parameterized through DBS. The resulting triangulation, shown in Fig.4(b), reproduces accurately most of the geometric details in the given data.

Local parameterization is required when only a part of a point cloud needs to be parameterized. Such situations occur when one wishes to apply different texture to different surface parts, or when certain point-cloud parts should be treated separately from the others (ie., shoe or apparel industry), or when the original point cloud is too complicated in order to be parameterized globally. Three local parameterization examples are presented in Figs. 5(a)-(c). All examples illustrate the final DBS derived after the execution of the proposed algorithm. The "Bunny" point-cloud has been locally parameterized using four levels of DBS subdivisions and with a maximum grid size equal to 10x10. The "Horse" point-cloud required three levels of subdivision of the DBS in order to approximate the local geometry with a mean error less that 0.1 mm. While the "Human" point-cloud required also three levels of DBS subdivision in order to achieve a fit accuracy less than 0.1 mm.

Table 1 lists the parameters affecting every presented example along with the corresponding performance indicators showing the achieved accuracy and the required computational time for a system with an 1.5 GHz Pentium 4, with 512 MB of memory and an OpenGL enabled video adapter with 64 MB of dedicated memory. The most time-sensitive parameter is the maximum allowed depth-value of the quadtree structure, as it is clearly shown in the "Bunny" example.

All examples demonstrate: (a) The capacity of the proposed method to approximate point clouds of complex shape in various application areas, (b) the high quality of the derived parameterizations which is verified either from the resulted triangulations and/or the high fit accuracy. The derived DBSes are sets of smooth surfaces stitched together with C^0 continuity. For the purposes of point-cloud parameterization such a level of continuity is acceptable, as it is shown in the presented examples.

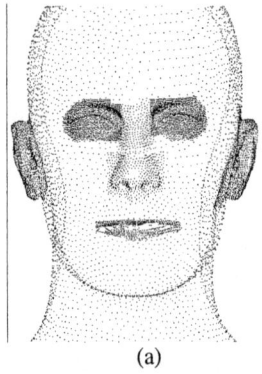
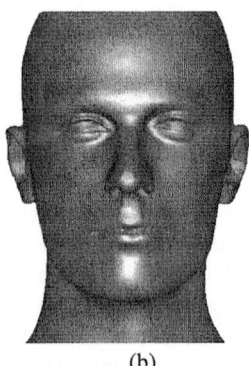

(a)   (b)

Fig. 4. (a) The point cloud of a human face. (b) The result of triangulating the "face" point-cloud using the DBS parameterization.

6 Conclusions

This paper introduced a new method for performing global and/or local parameterization of a 3D point-cloud, a problem well known in the fields of Computer Graphics, Visualization, Computational Geometry, CAD/CAM and CAE. The new approach employs ideas and tools from the new and emerging modelling framework known as "point-based modelling". The proposed DBS method succeeds to parameterize (locally and/or globally) a large variety of point clouds given an initial closed boundary topologically equivalent to disk.

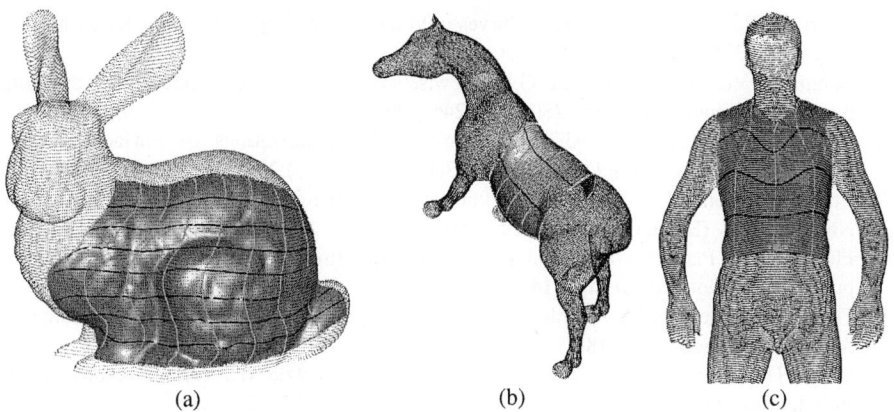

Fig. 5. Example of a local parameterization of the (a) "bunny" point-cloud and (b) "horse" point-cloud, (c) "human" point-cloud

Table 1. Summarizing the results discussed in Section 5

Surface	Bounding box (mm) dx-dy-dz	Cloud size	Max grid size	Max Depth	Mean error (mm)	Time (sec)
Shoe last	246x38x101	6K	14x14	3	0.1	24.10
Face	174x183x241	10K	14x14	3	0.1	26.23
Bunny	300x285x233	30K	10x10	4	0.1	117.19
Horse	135x300x250	49K	12x12	3	0.1	31.83
Human	300x50x117	124K	12x12	3	0.1	47.58

Acknowledgements

This work was supported by the Ministry of Development of Greece through the Research Project "E-MERIT: An Integrated E-Collaborative Environment for Product & Process Modeling Using 3D Models and Avatars". The human body data-set of Fig.5(c) was offered by Athens Technology Centre SA and originated in the European Anthropometric Database (Pilot Sizing Survey data / E-Tailor project, IST-1999-10549, funded by the European Commission). This data set was scanned at the Hohenstein Institute with a Human Solutions Vitus-Smart Scanner.

References

1. Alexa, M., Merging polyhedral shapes with scattered features, The Visual Computer, **16**, 26–37, 2000.
2. Azariadis P., Parameterization of clouds of unorganized points using dynamic base surfaces, CAD, **36**(7):607-623, 2004.
3. Azariadis P., Aspragathos N., On using planar developments to perform texture mapping on arbitrarily curved surfaces, Computers & Graphics, **24**(4):539-554, 2000.

4. Azariadis P., Sapidis N., Drawing Curves onto a Cloud of Points for Point-Based Modelling, CAD, **37**(1):109-122, 2005.
5. Bennis C., Vezien J.-M., Iglesias G., Piecewise surface flattening for non-distorted texture mapping, Computer Graphics, **25**(4):237-246, 1991.
6. Desbrun M., Meyer M., Alliez P., Intrinsic Parameterizations of Surface Meshes, EUROGRAPHICS'02 (G. Drettakis & H. Seidel eds.), **21**(3):209-218, 2002.
7. Eck, M., Hadenfeld, J., Local energy fairing of B-spline curves, in Farin, G., Hagen, H., Noltemeier, H. (Eds.), Computing, **10**, 1995.
8. Floater, M.S., Parametrization and smooth approximation of surface triangulations, Computer-Aided Geometric Design, **14**(3);231–250, 1997.
9. Floater M.S., Reiners M., Meshless parameterization and surface reconstruction, Computer Aided Geometric Design, **18**(2):77-92, 2001.
10. Hoppe H., DeRose T., DuChamp T., McDonald J., Stuetzle W., Surface reconstruction from unorganized points, Computer Graphics, **26**(2):71–78, 1992.
11. Hormann, K., Greiner, G.. MIPS: An efficient global parameterization method, in Laurent, P.-J., Sablonnière, P., Schumaker, L.L. (Eds.), Curve and Surface Design, Vanderbilt University Press, Nashville, 153–162, 2000.
12. Jonathan S., Triangle: A Two-Dimensional Quality Mesh Generator and Delaunay Triangulator, http://www-2.cs.cmu.edu/afs/cs/project/quake/public/www/triangle.html
13. Kobbelt, L.P., Vorsatz, J., Labisk, U., Seidel, H.-P., A shrink-wrapping approach to remeshing polygonal surfaces, Computer Graphics Forum, **18**(3):119-130, 1999.
14. Lévy, B., Patitjean S., Ray N., Maillot J., Least Squares Conformal Maps for Automatic Texture Atlas Generation, ACM SIGGRAPH'02, 362–371, 2002.
15. Lee A., Sweldens W., Scroder P., Cowsar L., Dobkin D., MAPS: Multiresolution Adaptive Parameterization of Surfaces, Proc. SIGGRAPH' 98, 95-104, 1998.
16. Ma W., Kruth P., Parameterization of randomly measured points for least squares fitting of B-spline curves and surfaces, Computer-Aided Design, **27**(9):663–675, 1995.
17. Ma S.D., Lin. H., Optimal texture mapping, Proc. EUROGRAPHICS' 88, 421-428, 1988.
18. Maillot, J., Yahia, H., Verroust A., Interactive texture mapping, Proc. SIGGRAPH' 93, 27–34, 1993.
19. Pottmann H., Leopoldseder S., Hofer M., Approximation with active B-spline curves and surfaces, Proc. Pacific Graphics' 02, IEEE Computer Society, 8-25, 2002.
20. Sheffer A., Gotsman C., Dyn N., Robust Spherical Parameterization of Triangular Meshes, Computing, **72**, 185–193, 2004.
21. Sander P., Gortler S., Snyder J., Hoppe H., Texture Mapping Progressive Meshes, In Computer Graphics, Proc. SIGGRAPH'01, 409-416, 2001.
22. Shapiro, A., Tal, A., Polygon realization for shape transformation, The Visual Computer, **14**, 429–444, 1998.

Interactive Dynamics for Large Virtual Reality Applications

Georgios Papaioannou

Foundation of the Hellenic World, Virtual Reality Department,
38 Poulopoulou St., 11851, Athens, Greece
gepap@fhw.gr
http://www.di.uoa.gr/~georgep

Abstract. Recent commercial virtual reality shows have become very demanding in terms of interactive credibility and visual realism. In an effort to push further the immersive quality and the sense of 'being there' in the most recent VR production of the Foundation of the Hellenic World "A Walk through Ancient Olympia", the user, apart from virtually visiting the historical site, becomes an interacting part of the edutainment activity. Described in this paper is a new script-controlled generic dynamics system devised for heavy interactive VR applications and used in the above commercial production, which utilises the notion of force-fields and also simulates aerodynamic effects in a real-time, computationally efficient manner. The impact of the interactive dynamics system on the usability and virtual presence is also discussed, in the context of a fully immersive stereoscopic surround-screen virtual reality environment and a role-playing interactive show.

Keywords: virtual reality, visualisation, game engines, real-time simulation.

1 Introduction

Virtual reality is in essence the art of illusion of simulating a fake environment where the spectator is immersed and detached from reality as effectively as possible, no matter the technical means to achieve this. Two important factors that set virtual reality apart from other content presentation methods is the ability to perceive the computer-generated environment as being part of it and not as a remote spectator and its free-style interactive quality. To this end, real-time stereoscopic visualisation of life-size proportions, smartly selected sound effects and sometimes, mechanical feedback project a convincing illusion to the spectator of the virtual reality show.

The interaction mechanism is a more delicate issue, partly because a virtual set offers far more possibilities for experimentation, exploration and manipulation of three-dimensional objects than a simple computer game and partly due to the role of interactivity as a distraction from visual imperfections, owing to display hardware incapacity or real-time software limitations. It is true that hardware technology in spatial tracking, haptics, displays and graphics processing reaches new levels of perfection and speed every day, but at the same time, the demands of the spectators are increasing with equal or more rapid rates. Even nice computer graphics and stunning effects can loose their glitter once the user becomes accustomed to the virtual environment, so the virtual show has to be expertly directed to add more and more interactive elements as the story evolves. The reader should keep in mind that virtual reality graphics are much more simplistic in appearance than the photorealistic, pre-rendered visuals often encountered in movie or IMAX theatres. An immersive VR application has the processing cost of a conventional 3D shoot-em-up real-time game with large polygonal environments, multiplied by the number of displays involved in a multi-screen virtual environment, and all that doubled for stereoscopic vision. Therefore, interaction in a virtual reality system needs to be strengthened in every possible way to focus the interest of the user on what can be performed and experienced and not on what can be purely visibly perceived.

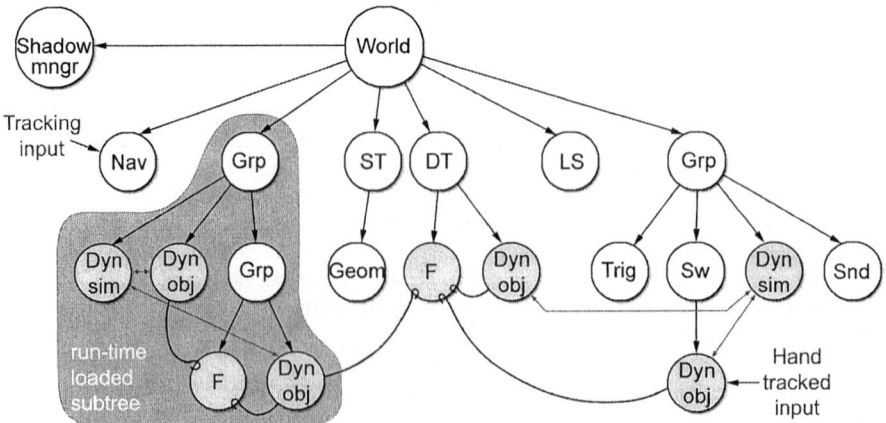

Dyn sim: Dynamic simulation, *Dyn obj*: Dynamics object, *Grp*: Group, *ST*: Static transformation, *DT*: Dynamic transformation *F*: Forcefield, *LS*: Lightsource, *Trig*: Trigger, *Sw*: Switch, *Snd*: Sound, *Nav*: Navigator, *Geom*: Geometric Node (e.g. mesh, skeletal animation, particle system etc)

Fig. 1. A typical scene-graph utilising dynamic simulation nodes in the EVS virtual reality engine. Dynamic objects are hooked on force fields and declared to local dynamic simulation nodes. Dynamic objects are controlled by the simulation nodes and the picking operations of the user simultaneously.

A typical virtual world is structured as a tree (scene-graph), with the root being a group node representing the world coordinate system along with the complete representation of geometry, effects and interaction mechanisms. This group, as every other intermediate tree level, is further analysed in geometry, transformation, trigger or event processing node. A large VR scene-graph may contain many thousands of nodes, each one performing its simulation and visualisation cycle at each frame displayed and communicating with other nodes via direct calls or a delayed message passing paradigm (Fig. 1).

In this paper, an approximate rigid-body physical simulation system is presented, which is not very demanding in terms of computational cost, although it takes into account effects such as aerodynamic behaviour of moving objects. This dynamics system is targeted for heavy, distributed three-dimensional environments, such as the one constructed for the "Walk through Ancient Olympia" virtual reality show of the Foundation of the Hellenic World [4]. The contribution of this work is in the fast approximation of aerodynamic behaviour and the scripted event-based architecture of the physics engine.

The article is structured as follows: Section 2 gives an insight on the role and common computational models of physical simulation for moving objects and explains the notion of force-fields. Section 3 discusses the integration of a dynamics system in the script-based, event-driven virtual reality engine of the Foundation of the Hellenic World (FHW) - EVS (Enhanced Visualisation System) [4], [8], the interaction mechanism and the implications of multiprocessor or cluster platforms in the process. Finally, section 4 presents the case study of the "Walk through Ancient Olympia" commercial production in the context of platform implementation, production constraints and quality of immersive experience.

2 Physical Simulation

In game engines, a number of visual effects and simulation reactions such as explosions or vehicle steering response, as well as interactive actions like picking, throwing, or smashing props depends on an iterative computational approximation of the equation of motion for unconstrained or constrained objects. Objects would collide, drag, bounce off and exchange energy with other geometry. Even deformable or articluated objects are modelled as networks of interlocked rigid bodies, softly (spring systems) or hardly (hinges and ball-point joints) constrained. Part of the process is the determination of the contact points between the moving geometry at each frame (collision detection) and the collision response as a reaction of the closed system (force generation and linear and rotation momentum modification) [3], [5]. Most physics engines (like Havoc^{TM}) rely on the Newtonian and Lagrangian models and respective motion equations. Newtonian dynamics are more suitable for the calculation of unconstrained motion of bodies, whereas the Lagrangian dynamics cover the constrained motion more effectively. The interested reader may refer to the excellent textbook by Eberly on rigid body kinematics and physical simulation for game engines [3], as further elaboration on the essentials of physical simulation are beyond the scope of this paper.

For the purposes of our virtual reality engine, we have opted not to rely on one of the commercially available physics engines for various reasons. First, a full-featured physics engine consumes a good part of the processor time for the motion estimation. Processor time in virtual reality system is a much more limited resource than in a conventional game engine due to the higher and constant refresh rate of the stereoscopic display system and the need to sort, cull and render the geometry on multiple video outputs simultaneously. Second, the virtual reality thematic shows the engine is intended for, require the fast simulation of aerodynamic control of motion (both linear and rotational) under the non-negligible presence of air resistance, a feature, which is uncommon in most implemented engines as a generic procedure.

2.1 Newtonian Dynamics

The physics subsystem implemented in the EVS virtual reality engine uses dynamics based on Newton's second law for unconstrained motion, an extensively studied motion model for rigid bodies and their response to collisions [4]. In brief, for a given time step dt, this model calculates the new position and rotation offsets of a rigid body based on the summation of the forces applied to its centre of mass and the position of the centre of mass in relation to the contact points – if any - of the object and the environment:

$$m \frac{d\vec{v}(t)}{dt} = \vec{F}_{tot}(t), \quad \frac{d\vec{x}}{dt} = \vec{v}, \quad \frac{d\mathbf{R}(t)}{dt} = \mathbf{Skew}\left(\vec{w}(t)\right)\mathbf{R}(t) \ . \tag{1}$$

In the above equation, m is the mass of the moving object, $\vec{v}$ its linear velocity and $\vec{w}$ is its angular velocity. The mass of a triangulated mesh is calculated indirectly from the mesh volume integral [7]. The skew matrix has the property $\mathbf{Skew}(\vec{a}) \cdot \vec{b} = \vec{a} \times \vec{b}$ and is defined as:

$$\mathbf{Skew}(\vec{a}) = \begin{bmatrix} 0 & -a_z & z_y \\ a_z & 0 & -a_x \\ -a_y & a_x & 0 \end{bmatrix} . \tag{2}$$

The linear offset $d\vec{x}$ and the differential rotation matrix $d\mathbf{R}$ are the unknowns obtained at each frame by solving equation (1) by integrating the velocity over the time lapsed from the previous frame and by estimating the sum of forces $\vec{F}_{tot}$ at the centre of mass and the angular velocity from the total torque applied to the object. In terms of three-dimensional transformations expressed as homogeneous matrices, a moving object V under the influence of a number of forces, which is initially located at a point $\vec{p}$ in space, is transformed at each frame as:

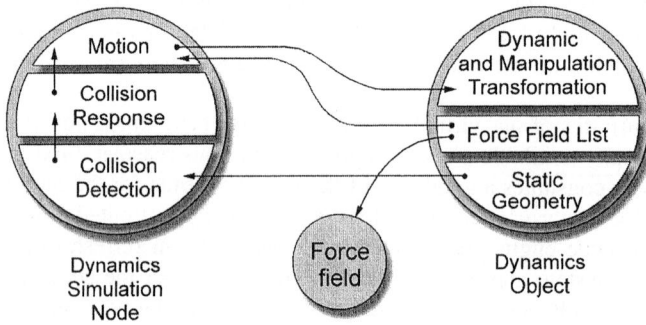

Fig. 2. Internal structure of the dynamics simulation and dynamics-enabled object scene-graph nodes and data flow between them

$$V(t+dt) = \mathbf{M}_{dyn}(t+dt) \cdot V = \mathbf{T}_{(\vec{x}+\vec{p}+d\vec{x})} \cdot d\mathbf{R} \cdot \mathbf{R} \cdot \mathbf{T}_{(-\vec{p})} \cdot V \ . \tag{3}$$

The concatenated matrix in Eq. 3 can be very easily updated because the rotational and the translational parts are well separated as sub-matrices of **M**. A dynamics-enabled three-dimensional object is represented in the scene-graph as a fixed geometrical mesh under a geometric transformation group which implements **M**(*t+dt*) (Fig. 2).

The above formation does not handle the effect of drift, both in the linear component and rotational one, due to the resistance of air or other medium. The linear velocity can be simply dampened by a factor. The air resistance has a more complex effect on the rotation of an object, which is discussed in section 2.3.

2.2 Force Fields

In order for forces to be compatible with the scene-graph representation of the virtual world, in EVS they have been designed as ordinary leaf nodes of the scene hierarchy. This means that forces can be activated or deactivated, receive and post events, get scaled, rotated and moved like geometrical entities (Fig. 1). This last property is very useful when one needs to intuitively move a force in the virtual space or have a force field attached to an object (e.g. spherical force fields for collision avoidance). As will be discussed in the case study, a transformable force field representing a linear force has been used in conjunction with a linear gravitational field in order to define the movement of a projectile held by a moving hand (6-degrees-of-freedom tracked input device).

The activation time of the force field defines the desired momentum and therefore the speed of the object. This way, throwing a projectile or pushing a box, becomes much more interactively involving than simply applying an impulse force for a predetermined time and allows for control of the dynamic response via the hand-help VR controller (analog joypad).

2.3 Aerodynamics

The rotational part of the aerodynamic correction slowly biases the object's rotational matrix so that its primary axis becomes aligned with the current velocity vector at each point of the trajectory. This approximate solution is based on the observation that for flat or elongated objects of nearly homogeneous material, their aerodynamic shape is associated with their principal axes. Objects moving through resistive media

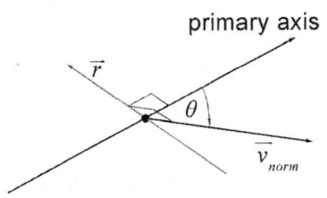

Fig. 3. Computation of the corrective rotation matrix based on the deviation θ of the primary geometry (mesh) axis from the velocity vector $\vec{v}$

tend to minimise the area exposed to the current. In order to reduce this resistive flow, the primary axis of the object, which corresponds to the wider scattering of mass over the solid shape, needs to be aligned with the flow.

In more detail, at initialisation time, the principal axes of an object are extracted from a random sampling of the object's surface vertices and they correspond to the eigenvectors of the covariance matrix of the sample set (second order central moments) [6]. The largest (primary) axis is the eigenvector that corresponds to the largest eigenvalue (Fig. 3). At each frame, the differential rotation matrix of Eq. 3 is post-multiplied by the correction matrix $\mathbf{R}_{Bias}$ before being applied to the geometry. $\mathbf{R}_{Bias}$ is derived as follows:

$$\mathbf{R}_{Bias}(t) = \mathbf{R}_{\theta,\vec{r}}(t), \ \theta = bias \cdot \frac{\pi}{2} \|\vec{a}_1 \times \vec{v}_{norm}\|$$

$$\vec{r} = \begin{cases} \vec{a}_1 \times \vec{v}_{norm} / \|\vec{a}_1 \times \vec{v}_{norm}\|, & \theta \neq 0 \\ (1,0,0), & \theta = 0 \end{cases} \quad (4)$$

where *bias* is the amount of aerodynamic influence, $\vec{r}$ is the axis of rotation, $\vec{a}_1$ is the transformed primary axis and $\vec{v}_{norm}$ is the normalised velocity direction at time *t*.

When objects travel a long way airborne, the above adjustment helps rectify the orientation of a lightweight object relative to its trajectory.

3 Virtual Reality Engine Design

The object-oriented design of the EVS virtual reality engine is based on the concept of the scene-graph and it utilises both a message-passing mechanism and direct control to communicate behaviours among the nodes and alter the state of the engine. From triggered events to static geometry and animations, all activity is handled via messages that are received and dispatched from identically structured and interfaced nodes, each one of course performing a different task (Fig. 4). Control of the engine is not centralised, but instead dispersed among the nodes. This is a very convenient

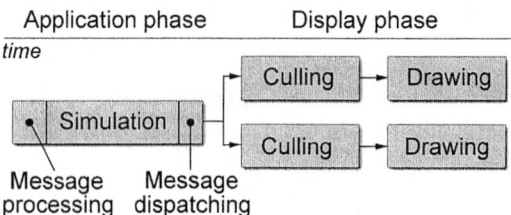

Fig. 4. Processor time distribution for each node on single display, stereoscopic system. This segmentation reflects the separation of the entire application into overlapping Application, Culling and Drawing processes. For a multi-view system, the Culling and Drawing processes are multiplied by the number of displays.

design decision in terms of engine operation because it disassociates the simulation and visualisation processes and allows the engine to run on various platform configurations, from a sequential, single-processor environment, to shared-memory or distributed platforms and clusters with replicated scene-graphs. In the later case, message communication between cluster nodes can be very limited due to the deterministic nature of the simulation and the need to pass only tracking and time-signature data to the various autonomous nodes.

The frame-cycle of a node typically consists of two phases, the application and the display phase (Fig. 4). The application phase is further broken down to a message processing stage, a pure simulation and data modification stage and a period for dispatching outbound notifications. Some nodes, like the dynamic simulation and the collision detection, which are time-critical processes, can directly affect the data of other nodes by calling their methods without passing messages, which may have a delayed effect (a few ms).

In the case of the interactive dynamics nodes, sharing the burden among the nodes has the welcome effect of easily splitting the dynamics into smaller, independent dynamics clusters of interacting objects as separate nodes. This does not only make the computations and object reference faster, but it also allows for the dynamic loading and unloading of whole sub-trees of the scene-graph, without disturbing the individual dynamic simulations. At world design time, it is inherently easier to isolate the interactive dynamics of a particular scene of the show and group it with the corresponding geometrical and action information, in a separate scene file, which can be loaded on the fly and executed upon an event-driven request.

The interactive dynamics subsystem is organised as a number of active, dynamic simulation nodes and a number of passive, dynamics objects (Fig. 1). A dynamics object consists internally of a transformation controlled by the dynamics simulation, a transformation directly associated with the input device when the object is grabbed and the geometry of the object itself. Each dynamics object maintains a list of force fields that it is currently attached to (Fig. 2). Hooking and unhooking a dynamics object from a forcefield is performed via appropriate messages.

A dynamics simulation node keeps track of a number of dynamics object assigned by the scene description script to it. At each frame, it calculates the next position and orientation of the listed objects according to Eq. 3 and the force fields that the objects are hooked on and performs collision detection. If a collision is encountered between two objects, a collision event is generated and the trajectory collision response is calculated.

In terms of software design, the dynamics simulation node is subclassed from a collision detection node, augmented by motion estimation and collision response features. Collision detection is based on the ColDet library [1], which uses object-aligned bounding box hierarchies for accelerated performance. The initial implementation has been extended to perform an iterative time step subdivision scheme with backtracking to accurately pinpoint a contact point.

Here is included a script example according to the syntax of EVS world description language, which demonstrates the use of the dynamics system, the node structure and the notification-based mechanism:

```
#EVS scene file description for kicking a ball. "Up" vector is +Z axis
#An invisible leg controlled by the user (presumably the user's leg),
#kicks a ball, which is sent bouncing across a field.

# Gravitational force, always enabled:
forcelinear( name="gravity", direction = "0, 0, -1", initstate=on)

# Kick force, initially disabled and attached to a dummy object
# that represents our leg. Node names are resolved after script parsing,
# so declaration order is not critical.

forcelinear( name="kick", direction = "0, 5, 0", initstate=off,
             duration = 0.5, #maximum force application time
             attach = "dummy_leg"
           )
# The invisible kicking foot, controlled by a tracker
object( name="dummy_leg", file=crude_foot.obj, draw=false )

# Trigger at zero point and radius 100 to give control of leg to tracker
usertrigger( sphere = "0, 0, 0, 100",
             eventmessage="enter, dummy_leg, attach all"
           )

# The ball to kick. This is the only dynamics controllable object in this
# simulation. The other objects are static and contribute only to
# collision detection. Although the object is already hooked to gravity,
# it does not move because of initial balance and friction.
dynobject( name="ball", file=football.3ds, position = "10, 0, 0",
           density = 0.5, friction = 0.3,
           hook="kick", hook="gravity"
         )

object( name="playfield", file=plane.3ds )

# The dynamic simulation node. It can take non-dynamic objects
# as participating nodes as well, but cannot animate them
dynamics( name="sim_kick",
          collider="dummy_leg", collider="playfield",
          collidee="ball",
          eventmessage="onimpact, kick, enable", #apply external force
          eventmessage="onrelease, ball, unhook kick"
        )
```

4 Implementation and Case Study

The dynamics simulation system of EVS was designed with surround-screen projective viewing environments in mind. This is the reason why special care has been taken to conform the simulation and dynamic object node operation to the pipelined processing stages of a multi-display computing system. As mentioned above, a distinctive difference in the underlying software architecture between the EVS dynamics and the widely used physics engines is its decentralised nature and the local control of simulation nodes, enabling an easy break-up of scene-graph hierarchies to smaller meaningful declarations.

Not surprisingly, the interactive dynamics system described is mostly used in the CAVE-like ReaCTor™ immersive environment of FHW. A CAVE [2] is an immersive stereoscopic display configuration, consisting of up to 6 projection walls that form a cube and completely surround the user. In the four-wall FHW CAVE, a maximum number of 10 visitors and a museum educator enter the immersive cube, all wearing stereo shutter glasses and the show is controlled by the guide via a 6-degrees-of-freedom tracked joystick (wand). The museum educator also wares a hat with an attached 6DOF sensor for the head position and orientation tracking.

In the most recent VR production of FHW for the CAVE system, "A Walk through Ancient Olympia", the user, apart from visiting the historical site, learns about the ancient games themselves by interacting with athletes in the ancient game of pentathlon, which then included a 200-meter sprint, discus and javelin throwing, long jump, wrestling. One of the challenges was to be able to actively participate in at least one of the games. Considering the difficulty to move in a CAVE when surrounded by spectators, the logical decision was to implement such interaction for the discus and javelin throwing games, which are relatively static. Both games required that the user take hold of an object and send it flying through the scene, along the stadium, under the influence of forces in a controllable manner. The object would collide, bounce off and exchange energy with other geometry. Figure 5 shows the interactive javelin and discus throw games of the production, where the dynamics system was first introduced.

The novel VR experience offered by the introduction of a completely physically interactive and controllable part in the show has been more than welcome by the visitors. Group after group of people of various ages that enter the CAVE since August 2004, when this thematic show was launched, get excited about the interaction. Being able to actually handle and manoeuvre the life-sized projectiles and challenge the pre-animated 3D characters in the games of discus and javelin throwing, has a great impact on the immersive quality of the show. Of course, people ask when will they be able to interact with the wrestler one on one or run a race. Based on this practical experiment and the impressions the museum educators get from the visitors, a role-playing model of interaction with alternating roles seems a definitely engrossing perspective in VR productions to come.

Fig. 5. Application of the interactive dynamics in the discus and javelin throwing games of the ancient pentathlon, a part of FHW VR experience "A Walk through Ancient Olympia"

Acknowlegement. The author would like to acknowledge the other EVS virtual reality engine development team members, Sakis Gaitatzes and Dimitrios Christopoulos, as well as the Foundation of the Hellenic World for supporting our creative work.

References

1. ColDet Collision Detection Library: http://photoneffect.com/coldet/
2. Cruz-Neira, C., Sandin, D. J., DeFanti, T. A.: Surround-Screen Projection-Based Virtual Reality: The Design and Implementation of the CAVE. Proc. ACM Computer Graphics (SIGGRAPH '93) (1993), 135-142
3. Eberly, D. H.: Game Physics. Morgan Kaufmann, 2004
4. Gaitatzes, A., Christopoulos, D., Papaioannou, G.: The Ancient Olympic Games: Being Part of the Experience. Proc. Eurographics 5th International Symposium on Virtual Reality, Archaeology and Intelligent Cultural Heritage (VAST 2004), 19-28
5. Hecker, C.: Physics – Part3, Collision Response. Game Developer Magazine, March 1997, 11 - 18
6. Lo, C. H., Don, H. S.: 3-D Moment Forms: Their Construction and Application to Object Identification and Positioning. IEEE Transactions on Pattern Analysis and Machine Intelligence, 11 (1989), 1053-1064
7. Mirtich, B.: Fast and Accurate Computation of Polyhedral Mass Properties. ACM Journal of Graphics Tools (1997)
8. Papaioannou G., Gaitatzes A., Christopoulos D.: Enhancing Virtual Walkthroughs of Archaeological Sites. Proc. 4th International Symposium on Virtual Reality, Archaeology and Cultural Heritage (VAST 2003), 193-201

A Pictorial Human Computer Interaction to Query Geographical Data

Fernando Ferri[1], Patrizia Grifoni[1], and Maurizio Rafanelli[2]

[1] IRPPS-CNR, via Nizza 128, 00198 Roma, Italy
{fernando.ferri, patrizia.grifoni}@irpps.cnr.it
[2] IASI-CNR, viale Manzoni 30, 00185 Roma, Italy
rafanelli@iasi.cnr.it

Abstract. This paper proposes an extension of the Pictorial Geographical Query Language GeoPQL, that allows the user to express queries pictorially. Topological and metrics operators are already presented in a previous work. This extension refers to queries in which the user uses concepts that the system implicitly interprets and transforms. In particular, the paper adds the oriented polyline to the classic three objects (point, polyline, and polygon) and defines a set of cardinal and positional operators. In order to maintain non-ambiguity in the query's visual representation, GeoPQL uses three different working spaces, the first for topological and metrics operators, the second for cardinal operators, and the third for positional operators.

1 Introduction

Geographical databases received considerable attention during the past few years due to the emergence of novel applications. Part of research focused on human computer interaction problem and, then, on visual query representation for geographical data. In a previous paper [1] the authors proposed a *pictorial* query language (GeoPQL) for geographical data. The *symbolic graphical objects* (SGOs) which form its alphabet are the classic point, polyline and polygon. The motivations of this work refer to the extension of GeoPQL by the introduction of oriented polylines, with the consequent proposal of operators regarding the relationships between two SGOs from the cardinal and the positional point of view. Three different environments (topological, cardinal, and positional) were defined in the enlarged GeoPQL. This extension allows to express queries by drawing geometric SGOs, using three different work spaces corresponding to the above mentioned environments. In particular, the paper proposes and discusses four cardinal operators, their combinations, their specializations, as well as eight positional operators.

2 Related Works

In order to satisfy the need of a friendly human-computer interaction, a new class of query languages was proposed, called visual query languages (VQLs). These VQLs are often based on the extensive use of iconic and/or graphical mechanisms [2], [3].

They are devoted to the extraction of information from databases [4]. VQLs often use icons or drawings to formulate queries, specially in GIS area. They offer an intuitive and incremental view of spatial queries, but often have a little expressive power, fairly ineffective query execution and, may offer different interpretations of the same query. Ambiguity is one of the main problems in using VQLs [1]. For example, consider the following query: "Find all the regions which are *north of* a river and *overlap* a forest". In it the user is not interested in the relationship between the river and the forest. The absence, in the user mental model, of explicit relationships between them should have, instead, produce the phrase "irrespective of the topological relationship between the river and forest" to complete the query. Only some of the proposed VQLs consider cardinal and positional operators. One of these is SVIQUEL [5], a VQL that considers 45 different types of primitives capable of representing both cardinal and topological relationships between two SGOs of type "polygon". However SVIQUEL avoids multiple interpretations by limiting the number of objects involved (to just two) and providing a tool with a low expressive power for specifying the relative spatial positions. Other VQLs enlarge the user's possibilities both by allowing more complex queries to be formulated and by giving a free interaction modality. Different important proposals [6], [7], [8], [9] use an approach based on blackboard metaphor, but also in them a query may have multiple interpretations. Formal approaches to cardinal directions can roughly be classified into two groups depending whether the spatial location of the located object is characterized by a point or a polygon. In [10] the author distinguishes cone-based and projection-based approaches to represent possible locations of a located object. In [9] the author uses the projection-based approach, partitioning space into nine regions (or zones) for an areal object (the eight cardinal zones plus the central, neutral zone). The cardinal direction from an object to a target direction is described by recording the partitions into which at least some parts of the target object fall. In this paper we consider a similar approach, based on four cardinal zones (North, South, East, and West) and subdivide the minumum bounding box in four parts by two diagonals.

3 The Cardinal Operators

In this section, for sake of brevity, we will formally define only the operator *G-North_of* and the relative specializations (*G-Partially_North_of* and *G-Weekly_North_of*) because the definition of the other operators (G-East_of, G-West_of and G-South_of and their specializations) is similar. Their composition (*G-North_East_of, G-North_West_of*, etc.) is obtained by the AND of couples of operators. In addition for all definitions herein, we will refer to two generic SGOs ψ_i, ψ_j, and to p and q as generic points respectively of ψ_i and ψ_j. Before defining the above mentioned operators, we define the concepts of *Bottom-point, Top-point, Left-point* and *Right-point* of the *minimum bounding box* of an SGO (polygon or polyline). A generic point p of an SGO ψ_i is the **Bottom-point** of this SGO (called it p_b) if its y-coordinate $p_{b,y}$ is less than or equal to the y-coordinate p'_y of all the other points $p' \in \psi_i$. Can be defined, in a similar way, the *Top-point, Left-point* and *Right-point* of an SGO. The **minimum bounding box** of an SGO ψ_i is the rectangle whose sides pass respectively for its *Bottom-point, Top-point, Left-point* and *Right-point*, and are parallel to the Cardinal axes. The *minimum bounding box*, also called *neutral zone*, is subdivided in other four sub-zones (triangles) by its diagonals.

The *Top-triangle* T_t of the minimum bounding box of ψ_i is the triangle having all its points North_of both diagonals. Analogously, can be defined in a similar way *Bottom-triangle, Left-triangle* and *Right-triangle* of an SGO. In Fig. 1(a) the North and South areas, and in Fig. 1(b) the West and East areas, are shown.

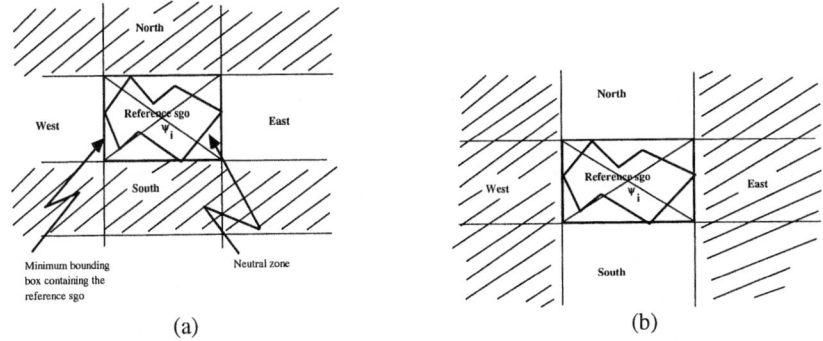

Fig. 1. North, South, West and East areas respect to the minimum bounding box

Definition: Let $\psi_i, \psi_j \in A$ be two *sgo* of any type. The **G-North_of** (N) an SGO ψ_i from the reference SGO ψ_j produces the A element $\psi_h = \psi_i$, where all points of ψ^o_i are in the north area of Top-point_of ψ_j. ❑

Analogously, all the other cardinal operators (*G-West_of (Wst), G-East_of (Est), G-South_of (Sth)*) can be defined.

Definition: Let $\psi_i, \psi_j \in A$ be two SGOs of any type. The **G-Partially_North_of** (pN) an SGO ψ_i from the reference SGO ψ_j produces the A element $\psi_h = \psi_i$, where, it exists at least a point of ψ^o_i which is G-North_of Top-point of ψ_j and it exists at least a point of ψ^o_i which is G-South_of Top-point of ψ_j. ❑

In Fig. 2(a) an example of SGO ψ_i G-North_of the reference SGO ψ_j is shown and in Fig. 2(b) examples of SGO ψ_i G-partially_North_of the reference SGO ψ_j is shown. When an SGO is totally within the minimum bounding box of the reference SGO, the cardinal relations are defined "G-Weekly_Card_of", where with *Card* we intend whatever cardinal point.

Definition: Let $\psi_i, \psi_j \in A$ be two SGOs of any type. The **G-Weakly_North_of** (wN) an SGO ψ_i from the reference SGO ψ_j produces the A element $\psi_h = \psi_i$, where it exists at least a point of ψ^o_i (internal point of ψ_i) which is internal to the Top-triangle of the minimum bounding box of ψ_j. ❑

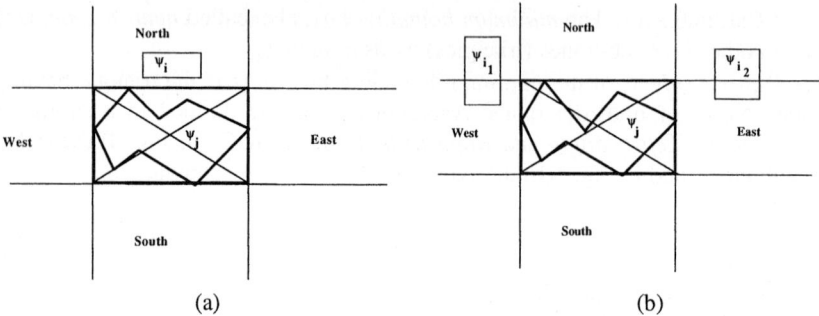

Fig. 2. Example of G-North_of and G-partially_North_of

In Fig. 3(a) an example of SGO ψ_i G-Weekly_North_of ψ_j is shown. In Fig. 3(b) an example of SGO ψ_{il} which is (G-partially_North_of $\wedge$ G-Weakly_North _of) ψ_j is shown.

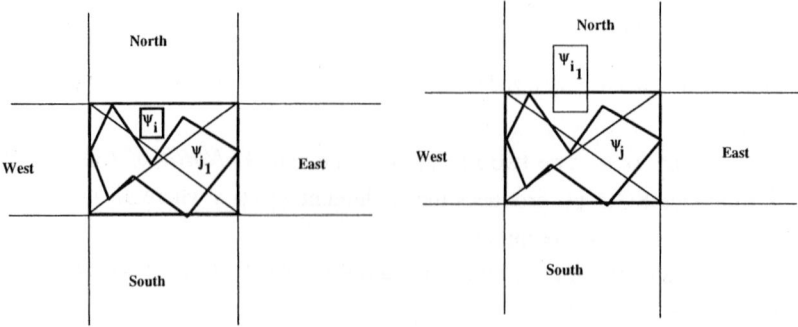

Fig. 3. Example of G- Weakly_North_of and G-partially_North_of $\wedge$ G-Weakly_North _of

3.1 Case of the Meta-operator ANY

Suppose that the query is "Find all the SGOs which are in the "North area" respect to the reference SGO ψ_t, that is, all the SGOs which are (G-North_of OR G-North-West_of OR G-North-East_of) ψ_t (Fig. 4(a)). In order to avoid to draw a molteplicity of SGOs, we inserted, similarly to the topological environment, the meta-operator ANY.

Applying this operator between the target SGO and the reference SGO (Fig. 4(b)), the system interprets this drawing as the entire drawing of Fig. 4(a).

Definition: Let $\{\psi_i\}_n$, $\psi_j \in A$ be a set of *sgo* of any type, where $\{\psi_i\}_n$ represents all the possible ways to draw sgo within the North area. The ***G-Any_Card_of*** *(AnyC)* an sgo ψ_i from the reference sgo ψ_j produces the A element $\psi_h = \psi_t$, where *Card* characterizes any cardinal position (North, South, West, East) and its specialization, and C sintetizes the generic cardinal position (and its specialization).

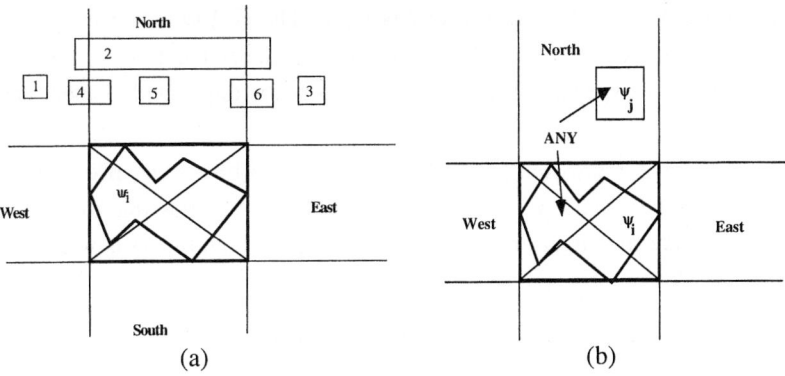

Fig. 4. Example of G- Any_North_of

We can compute the exact number of ANY relations, given n sgo represented in the pictorial query and k (always equal to 2) elements (sgo) involved in each relation. This number m is given by the following formla: $m = [\,N\,!\,/\,(k\,!\,(\,n-k\,)\,!\,)\,] - h$ (where h is the number of relations wished and expressed by the user drawing, enclosed Alias). In the case of Fig. 5(a) we have: n = 5, h = 4 (three DSJ and one Alias), k = 2, so that we have: $m = [\,5\,!\,/\,(2\,!\,(\,5-2\,)\,!\,] - 4 = [\,120\,/\,2 \times 6\,] - 4 = 10 - 4 = 6$.

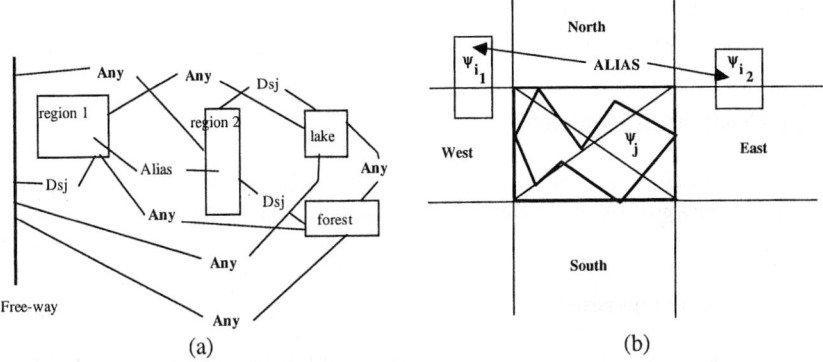

Fig. 5. Example of computation of ANY operators in a query (a) and an example of the ALIAS operator

3.2 Case of the G-ALIAS Operator

Consider the following query: "Find all the SGOs which are (G-Partially-North_of AND G-West_of the reference sgo ψ_j) OR (G-Partially-North_of AND G-East_of the reference sgo ψ_j) (Fig. 2(b)). In this case, similarly to the topological environment, it is necessary to use the G-ALIAS operator which is able to duplicate an sgo in order to can realize an expression with the OR operator (Fig. 5(b)).

Definition: Let $\psi_{i1} \in A$ be an *sgo* of any type. The *G-Alias (Als)* ψ_{i2} of an sgo ψ_{i1} produces the duplication of the element ψ_{i1} that is, the element $\psi_{i2} \in A$, whose cardinal position, or its specialization, is different from the duplicated element and is that drawn by the user. ❑

The SQL-Like expression [1], in the case of Fig. 5(b), is: (ψ_{i1} pN ψ_j AND ψ_{i1} W ψ_j) OR (ψ_{i2} pN ψ_j AND ψ_{i2} E ψ_j). In this way it will be possible to obtain the OR operation, where the target of the query is common to both the parts which are in OR between them.

3.3 Case of SGOs with Overlapping Between Them

In this section we examine the case of SGOs which are in overlapping with the reference SGO.

First case: an SGO is *completely inside the reference SGO* (for example, sgo 1 of Fig. 6(a)). In this case the query language produces the following Sql-Like expression (said ψ_i the sgo 1 and ψ_j the sgo of reference): (ψ_i INC ψ_j) ∧ (ψ_i wN ψ_j).

Second case: an SGO is overlapped with the reference SGO, but *completely inside its minimum bounding box* (the SGO 2 of Fig. 6(a)). Then, the Sql-Like expression is: (ψ_i OVL ψ_j) ∧ (ψ_i wN ψ_j).

Third case: an SGO is overlapped to the reference SGO and *Partially-North_of* its minimum bounding box (the SGO 3 of Fig. 6(a)). Then, the Sql-Like expression produced is: (ψ_i OVL ψ_j) ∧ (ψ_i pN ψ_j).

4 The Positional Operators

The proposed positional operators are: *G-Inside* (Ins), *G-Partially_Inside* (pIn), *G-Left* (Lft), *G-Right_of* (Rgt), *G-Before* (Bfr), *G-After* (Aft), *G-Nearest* (Nrt), and *G-Farthest* (Frt).

4.1 The G-Inside Operator

The *G-Inside* operator represents the particular relationship between two SGOs (disjoint or in touch), where one SGO is enclosed in the "concavity" of another one. Before defining this operator, we have to introduce the concept of *concavity*. In [11] the authors considered geometric inside and topologic inside relationships. In this paper, we only consider the later one, because we believe the topologic inside refers to a specific case of inclusion relationship, where an object is enclosed in the hole of another object.

Definition: Let $p_1, \ldots, p_n$ be a polyline (with $n \geq 3$). Let p_x, p_y and p_z three any consecutive points of the polyline. For any p_x, p_y and p_z they do not lie on the same straight line. If n = 3, then <$p_1\ p_2\ p_3$> is said a *concavity*. If n > 3, let p_i and p_j be two non-consecutive points of this polyline and let $p_i\ p_j$ be the segment which joins the two points p_i and p_j, then <$p_i\ p_k\ p_j$> (with i < k < j) is a *concavity* (in the following denoted by C < p_i p_k p_j >) if no cross exists between the segment <p_i p_j> and any other segment which is part of the polyline (Fig. 6(b)). ❏

The polygon α, defined by the C concavity, and the polyline <p_i, p_j>, is called *area of the concavity*.

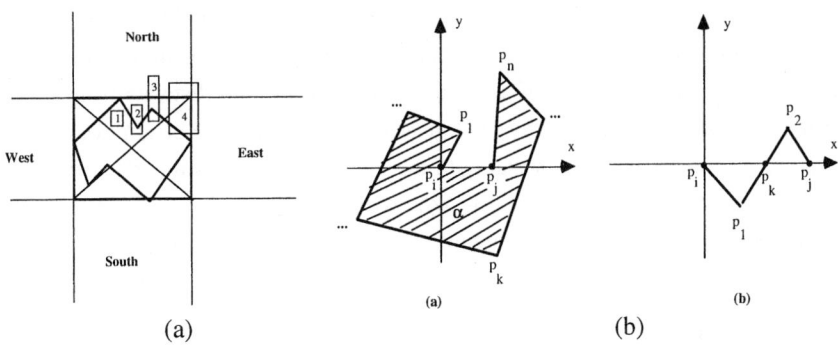

Fig. 6. Example of SGOs partially overlapped (a) and an example of concavity

Definition: Let ψ_j be an sgo of the alphabet A. Let C < p_i, p_k, p_j > = ψ_i be a concavity in the vertex set {p_1, p_k, p_n }, with 1 ≤ i < k < j ≤ n. An sgo ψ_j is *G-Inside* C < p_i, p_k, p_j > = ψ_i (and denoted by ψ_j Ins C = ψ_i), if ψ_j is completely enclosed in the polygon delimited by C < p_i, p_k, p_j > and the line joining p_j to p_i (Fig. 7(a)). ❏

Definition: Let ψ_i be an sgo of the alphabet A . Let C < p_i, p_k, p_j > = ψ_j be a concavity in the set verticies {p_1, p_k, p_n }, with 1 ≤ I < k < j ≤ n. An sgo ψ_i is *G-Partially_Inside* C < p_i, p_k, p_j > (and denoted by ψ_i pIn C) if it exists a set of points {p_{ih}} enclosed in the polygon delimited by C < p_i, p_k, p_j > and the line joining p_i to p_j, and it exists a set of points {p_{ik}} not enclosed in the polygon delimited by C < p_i, p_k, p_j > and the line joining p_i to p_j (Fig. 7(b)). ❏

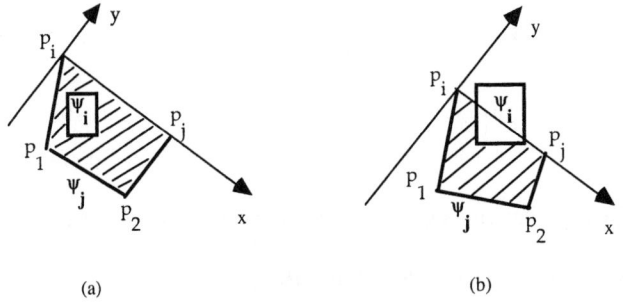

Fig. 7. Example of G-Inside (a) and an example of G-Partially_Inside

4.2 The G-Left and G-Right Operators

For the *G-Left* and *G-Right* operators the reference SGO is always an *oriented polyline*. The definition of these operators are based on the identification of the polyline segment (reference SGO) which has the the minimum distance from the other symbolic SGOs. The orientation of this segment defines the side to which the considered object belongs.

Definition: Let ψ_i be an oriented polyline (the reference SGO), and let ψ_j be any other SGO of the alphabet A. Let p_i be the point of ψ_i, which has the minimum distance from ψ_j and let p_j be the point of ψ_j which has the minimum distance from ψ_i. The SGO ψ_j is ***G-Right*** ψ_i (denoted by ψ_j Rgt ψ_i), if, translating the origin of the Y-axis onto the mentioned point p_i such that both the Y-axis, and ψ_i assume the same orientation, the x-coordinate of the point $p_j \in \psi_j$ is positive (Fig. 8(a)). ❑

Analogous definition (with the obvious changing) can be given for the *G-Left* (Lft) operator.

4.3 The G-Before and G-After Operators

Concerning *G-Before* and *G-After* operators, we only consider the case of two points which are onto an *oriented* polyline.

Definition: Let ψ_i and ψ_j be two points of the alphabet A. Let $\psi_k \in A$ be an oriented polyline onto which both ψ_i and ψ_j are located. The sgo ψ_j is ***G-Before*** the sgo ψ_i (denoted by ψ_j Bfr ψ_i) if ψ_j is enclosed in the semi-oriented polyline defined by the two points <origin of $\psi_k - \psi_i$> (Fig. 8(b)). ❑

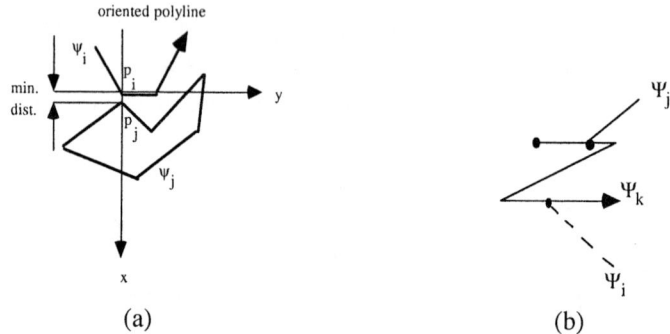

Fig. 8. Example of G-Right (a) and an example of G-Before

With the obvious changings we can define the other operator *After*.

4.4 The G-Nearest and G-Farthest Operators

The *G-Nearest* and *G-Farthest* operators are specializations of the G-Distance operator [1]. In the case of G-Nearest operator, we have to measure the distance between the reference SGO and all the other SGOs which are involved in the query, and to select the SGO which has the *Min-G -Distance* from the reference SGO. A similar reasoning is made for the G-Farthest operator, where we have to select the SGO which has the *Max-G-Distance* from the reference SGO.

Definition: Let ψ_i, $\{\psi_h\}$ (with $1 \le h \le n$) be SGOs of the alphabet A. A sgo $\psi_j \in \{\psi_h\}$ is *G-Nearest* to the reference SGO ψ_i (and we write ψ_j Nrs ψ_i) if the Min-G-Distance between ψ_i and ψ_j is the minimum value among all the Min-G-Distances between ψ_i and all the objects of $\{\psi_h\}$. ❑

Analogously we can define the operator Farthest.

5 Some Pictorial Query Example

In this section we give some examples of pictorial queries. The main characteristic of this VQL is that the user has not to know the formal syntax of the language: he has only to draw points, polylines and polygons on the screen, to assign to each of them a semantic meaning, to select his target and to click on the button called *execution*.

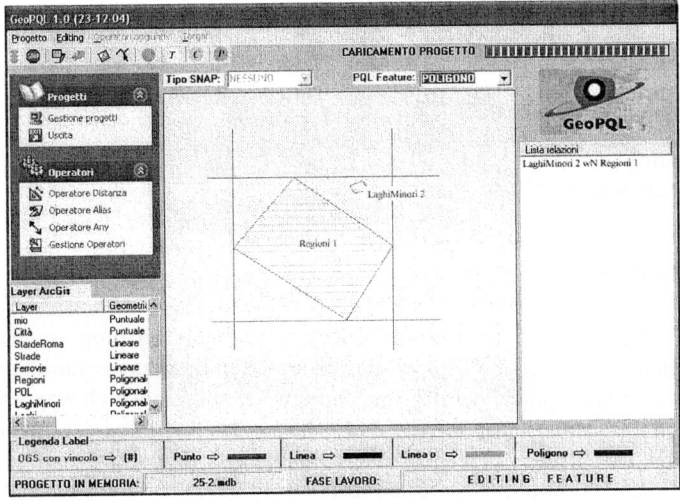

Fig. 9. The query of the example 1

Example 1. Suppose to have the following "mental model" of a query: "Find all the *Lakes* whose points are North of a given *region*, which has its top point North of all the points of the lake". The user will draw the drawing shown in Fig. 9. Translating this query in the internal language SQL-Like [1] of the system, we will find written in the relative window the following expression: "Lake *wN* region".

This representation (as those ones of the following examples) can be drawn (and seen) only if we select the suitable (cardinal) environment (characterized by the light blue color) clicking on the button C at the top of the screen.

Example 2. In this last example we suppose to have the following "mental model" of a query: "Find all the rivers which are left of a given city". The user will draw the drawing shown in Fig. 10.

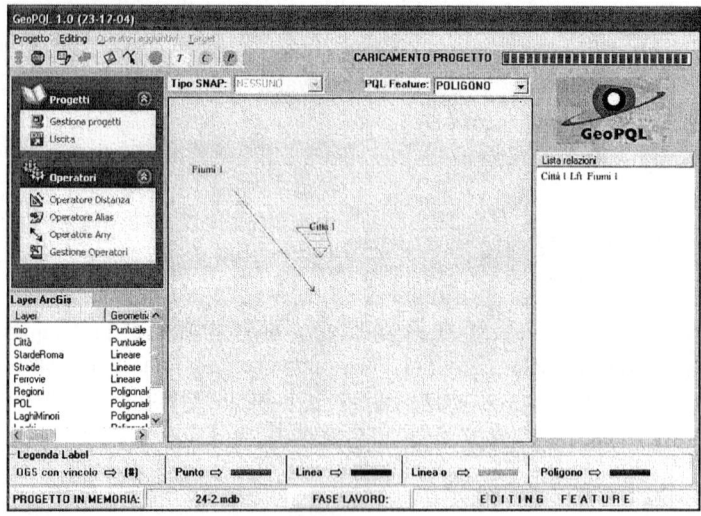

Fig. 10. The query of the example 2

Translating this query in the internal language SQL-Like of the system we will find written in the relative window the following expression: "City Lft River".

6 Conclusions

The cardinal and positional operators discussed in this paper propose an enlargement and a refinement of other set of operators proposed in literature regarding visual query languages for geographical data. In this paper we explain in which way such operators are used, in a transparet way, by the user. The system interprets the drawing made by the user and transforms it in a set of internal language (SQL-Like) instructions, whose form is <SGO_1 operator SGO_2>. The form of the clauses is always the same: SELECT target FROM database WHERE topological/cardinal/positional relations WITH constraints over the attributes of the SGO. To implement this version of GeoPQL has been necessary to enlarge the set of possible SGOs with the oriented polyline, to introduce the cardinal axes, and to create three different working spaces, each for every environment (topological, cardinal, positional).

Also this version is a stand alone extension for the suite of ESRI ArcGis 9.x tools. The system has been implemented in accordance with the ESRI standard, from which it inherits the format of the data and many functionalities, and using the same technology used by the ESRI developers (ArcObjects). In this system all the base functions which exist in ArcView® are present, as well as other functions, developed *ad hoc*, as a very power geoprocessing (which extends the already exinting one in

ArcView®), or an internal SQL-Like language which formally describes the pictorial query drawn by the user.

References

1. F.Ferri, M.Rafanelli. Resolution of ambiguities in query interpretation for geographical pictorial query languages. In Journal of Computing and Information Technologies – CIT Vol. 12, N. 2, pp.119-126, 2004
2. E.Clementini, P.Di Felice. Spatial Operators, in ACM SIGMOD Record, Vol. 29, N. 3, Sept. 2000, pp. 31-38, 2000.
3. L. Forlizzi, B. Kuijpers, E. Nardelli. Region-based query languages for spatial databases in the topological data model. SSTD 2003, LNCS n. 2750, Springer-Verlag Publ., pp. 344-371, 2003
4. T.Catarci, M.F.Costabile, S.Levialdi, C.Batini. Visual query sistems for databases: a survey. Journal of Visual Languages and Computing, Vol. 8, pp.. 215-260, 1997.
5. S. Kaushik, E.A. Rundensteiner. "SVIQUEL: A Spatial Visual Query and Exploration Language" 9th Intern. Conf. on Database and Expert Systems Applications - DEXA'98, LNCS N. 1460, pp. 290-299, 1998.
6. M. A. Aufaure-Portier, C. Bonhomme. A High Level Visual Language for Spatial Data Management. in Visual Information and Information Systems - Third Intern. Confer. Visual '99, Amsterdam, The Netherlands, June 1999, Lecture Notes in Computer Science, N.1614, Springer-Verlag, pp. 325-332, 1999.
7. Y. C. Lee, F. L. Chin. An Iconic Query Language for Topological Relationship in GIS. IJGIS 9(1): 25-46, 1995.
8. M. Mainguenaud, CIGALES: A Visual Query Language for Geographical Information System: The User Interface, International Journal of Visual Languages and Computing, Academic Press, 5, 113-126, 1994.
9. M. J. Egenhofer. Query processing in Spatial-Query-by-Sketch. International Journal of Visual Languages and Computing, Vol. 8, N. 4, pp. 403-424, 1997.
10. A.U. Frank. Qualitative spatial reasoning: Cardinal Directions as an example. International Journal of GIS, Vol. 10, N. 3, pp. 269-290, 1996
11. Z. Cui, A.G. Cohn, D.A. Randell. Qualitative and Topological Relationships in Spatial Databases. Third International Symposium on Advances in Spatial Databases, SSD'93, Singapore, June 1993, LNCS, N. 692, Springer-Verlag, pp. 296-315, 1993.

Bagging Model Trees for Classification Problems

S.B. Kotsiantis[1], G.E. Tsekouras [2], and P.E. Pintelas[1]

[1] Educational Software Development Laboratory,
Department of Mathematics, University of Patras, Greece
{sotos, pintelas}@math.upatras.gr
[2] Department of Cultural Technology and Communication,
University of the Aegean, Mytilene, Greece
gtsek@ct.aegean.gr

Abstract. Structurally, a model tree is a regression method that takes the form of a decision tree with linear regression functions instead of terminal class values at its leaves. In this study, model trees are coupled with bagging for solving classification problems. In order to apply this regression technique to classification problems, we consider the conditional class probability function and seek a model-tree approximation to it. During classification, the class whose model tree generates the greatest approximated probability value is chosen as the predicted class. We performed a comparison with other well known ensembles of decision trees, on standard benchmark datasets and the performance of the proposed technique was greater in most cases.

1 Introduction

The purpose of ensemble learning is to build a learning model which integrates a number of base learning models, so that the model gives better generalization performance on application to a particular data-set than any of the individual base models [5]. Ensemble generation can be characterized as being homogeneous if each base learning model uses the same learning algorithm or heterogeneous if the base models can be built from a range of learning algorithms.

A model tree is a regression method that takes the form of a decision tree with linear regression functions instead of terminal class values at its leaves [11]. During the construction of the model tree there are three main problems to be solved: Choosing the best partition of a region of the feature space, determining the leaves of the tree and choosing a model for each leaf.

In this study, model trees are coupled with bagging for solving classification problems. In order to apply the continuous-prediction technique of model trees to discrete classification problems, we consider the conditional class probability function and seek a model-tree approximation to it. During classification, the class whose model tree generates the greatest approximated probability value is chosen as the predicted class. We performed a comparison with other well known ensembles of decision trees, on standard UCI benchmark datasets and the performance of the proposed method was greater in most cases.

Current ensemble approaches of decision trees are described in section 2. In Section 3 we describe the proposed method and investigate its advantages and limitations.

In Section 4, we evaluate the proposed method on several UCI datasets by comparing it with bagging, boosting and other ensembles of decision trees. Finally, section 5 concludes the paper and suggests further directions in current research.

2 Ensembles of Classifiers

Empirical studies showed that ensembles are often much more accurate than the individual base learner that make them up [5], and recently different theoretical explanations have been proposed to justify the effectiveness of some commonly used ensemble methods [8].

Combining models is not a really new concept for the statistical pattern recognition, machine learning, or engineering communities, though in recent years there has been an explosion of research exploring creative new ways to combine models. Currently, there are two main approaches to model combination. The first is to create a set of learned models by applying an algorithm repeatedly to different training sample data; the second applies various learning algorithms to the same sample data. The predictions of the models are then combined according to a voting scheme. In this work we propose a combining method that uses one learning algorithm for building an ensemble of classifiers. For this reason this section presents the most well-known methods that generate sets of base learners using one base learning algorithm.

Probably the most well-known sampling approach is that exemplified by bagging [3]. Given a training set, bagging generates multiple bootstrapped training sets and calls the base model learning algorithm with each of them to yield a set of base models. Given a training set of size t, bootstrapping generates a new training set by repeatedly (t times) selecting one of the t examples at random, where all of them have equal probability of being selected. Some training examples may not be selected at all and others may be selected multiple times. A bagged ensemble classifies a new example by having each of its base models classify the example and returning the class that receives the maximum number of votes. The hope is that the base models generated from the different bootstrapped training sets disagree often enough that the ensemble performs better than the base models.

Breiman [3] made the important observation that instability (responsiveness to changes in the training data) is a prerequisite for bagging to be effective. A committee of classifiers that all agree in all circumstances will give identical performance to any of its members in isolation.

If there is too little data, the gains achieved via a bagged ensemble cannot compensate for the decrease in accuracy of individual models, each of which now sees an even smaller training set. On the other end, if the data set is extremely large and computation time is not an issue, even a single flexible classifier can be quite adequate.

Another method that uses different subsets of training data with a single learning method is the boosting approach [7]. It assigns weights to the training instances, and these weight values are changed depending upon how well the associated training instance is learned by the classifier; the weights for misclassified instances are increased. Thus, re-sampling occurs based on how well the training samples are classified by the previous model. Since the training set for one model depends on the previous model, boosting requires sequential runs and thus is not readily adapted to a parallel environment. After several cycles, the prediction is performed by taking a weighted vote of the predictions of each classifier, with the weights being proportional to each classifier's accuracy on its training set.

AdaBoost is a practical version of the boosting approach [7]. There are two ways that Adaboost can use these weights to construct a new training set to give to the base learning algorithm. In boosting by sampling, examples are drawn with replacement with probability proportional to their weights. The second method, boosting by weighting, can be used with base learning algorithms that can accept a weighted training set directly. With such algorithms, the entire training set (with associated weights) is given to the base-learning algorithm.

Melville and Mooney [12] present a new meta-learner (DECORATE, Diverse Ensemble Creation by Oppositional Re-labeling of Artificial Training Examples) that uses an existing "strong" learner (one that provides high accuracy on the training data) to build a diverse committee. This is accomplished by adding different randomly constructed examples to the training set when building new committee members. These artificially constructed examples are given category labels that disagree with the current decision of the committee, thereby directly increasing diversity when a new classifier is trained on the augmented data and added to the committee.

Random Forests [4] grows many classification trees. Each tree gives a classification (vote). The forest chooses the class having the most votes (over all the trees in the forest). Each tree is grown as follows:

- If the number of cases in the training set is N, sample N cases at random - but with replacement, from the original data. This sample will be the training set for growing the tree.
- If there are M input variables, a number m<<M is specified such that at each node, m variables are selected at random out of the M and the best split on these m is used to split the node. The value of m is held constant during the forest growing.
- Each tree is grown to the largest extent possible. There is no pruning.

3 Proposed Algorithm

Model trees are binary decision trees with linear regression functions at the leaf nodes: thus they can represent any piecewise linear approximation to an unknown function [17]. A model tree is generated in two stages. The first builds an ordinary decision tree, using as splitting criterion the maximization of the intra-subset variation of the target value. The second prunes this tree back by replacing subtrees with linear regression functions wherever this seems appropriate.

The construction and use of model trees is clearly described in [16] account of the M5 scheme. An implementation called M5' is described in [17] along with further implementation details. The learning procedure of M5' model tree algorithm effectively divides the instance space into regions using a decision tree, and strives to minimize the expected mean squared error between the model tree's output and the target values. The training instances that lie in a particular region can be viewed as samples from an underlying probability distribution that assigns class values. It is standard procedure in statistics to estimate a probability distribution by minimizing the mean square error of samples taken from it.

After the tree has been grown, a linear multiple regression model is built for every inner node, using the data associated with that node and all the features that participate in tests in the subtree rooted at that node. Then the linear regression models are simplified by dropping features if this results in a lower expected error on future data (more specifically, if the decrease in the number of parameters outweighs the increase in the observed training error). After this has been done, every subtree is considered for pruning. Pruning occurs if the estimated error for the linear model at the root of a subtree is smaller or equal to the expected error for the subtree. After pruning has terminated, M5' applies a 'smoothing' process that combines the model at a leaf with the models on the path to the root to form the final model that is placed at the leaf.

We use M5' for classification problems thus we convert the class nominal attribute with n attribute values into n − 1 binary attributes, and it generates one model tree for each class. During classification, the class whose model tree generates the greatest approximated probability value is chosen as the predicted class. Finally, the algorithm is briefly described in Fig. 1.

MODEL GENERATION
Let n be the number of instances in the training data.
For each of t iterations:
- Sample n instances with replacement from training data.
- Converts the class attribute with m attribute values into m − 1 binary attributes
- Built M5' for each m − 1 problems
- Store the resulting models.

CLASSIFICATION
For each of the t iterations:
- The class that has the greatest approximated probability value from the m − 1 models is chosen as the predicted class for this iteration

Return class that has been predicted most often from the t iterations.

Fig. 1. The proposed ensemble

A number of recent studies have shown that the decomposition of a classifier's error into bias and variance terms can provide considerable insight into the prediction performance of the classifier. Bias measures the contribution to error of the central tendency of the classifier when trained on different data. Variance is a measure of the contribution to error of deviations from the central tendency. Bias and variance are evaluated with respect to a distribution of training sets, such as a distribution containing all possible training sets of a specified size for a specified domain. Generally, bagging does tend to decrease variance without unduly affecting bias [1], [15]. M5' is not a stable algorithm and for this reason it can be effectively combined with bagging.

It must be also mentioned that the proposed ensemble can be easily parallelized. The computations required to obtain the classifiers in each bootstrap sample are independent of each other. Therefore we can assign tasks to each processor in a balanced manner. This parallel execution of the presented ensemble can achieve linear speedup.

4 Experiments Results

For the comparisons of our study, we used 26 well-known datasets mainly from many domains from the UCI repository [2]. These data sets were hand selected so as to come from real-world problems and to vary in characteristics. Thus, we have used data sets from the domains of: pattern recognition (iris), image recognition (sonar), medical diagnosis (breast-cancer, breast-w, colic, diabetes, heart-c, heart-h, heart-statlog, hepatitis, lymphotherapy, primary-tumor) commodity trading (credit-a, credit-g), computer games (kr-vs-kp, monk1, monk2, monk3), various control applications (balance) and prediction of student performance (student) [9]. Table 1 is a brief description of these data sets presenting the number of output classes, the type of the features and the number of examples.

In order to calculate the classifiers accuracy for our experiments, the whole training set was divided into ten mutually exclusive and equal-sized subsets and for each subset the model was trained on the union of all of the other subsets. Then, cross validation was run 10 times for each algorithm and the average value of the 10-cross validations was calculated. It must be mentioned that we used the free available source code for most of the algorithms by [18] for our experiments.

In Table 2, we represent as "v" that the specific algorithm performed statistically better than the proposed ensemble according to t-test with $p<0.05$. Throughout, we speak of two results for a dataset as being "significant different" if the difference is statistical significant at the 5% level according to the corrected resampled t-test [13], with each pair of data points consisting of the estimates obtained in one of the 100 folds for the two learning methods being compared. On the other hand, "*" indicates that proposed ensemble performed statistically better than the specific algorithm according to t-test with $p<0.05$. In all the other cases, there is no significant statistical difference between the results (Draws). In the last row of the table one can also see the aggregated results in the form (α/b/c). In this notation "α" means that the proposed ensemble is significantly less accurate than the compared algorithm in α out of 26 datasets, "c" means that the proposed algorithm is significantly more accurate than the compared algorithm in c out of 26 datasets, while in the remaining cases (b), there is no significant statistical difference.

It has been observed that for both bagging and AdaBoost, an increase in committee size (sub-classifiers) usually leads to a decrease in prediction error, but the relative impact of each successive addition to a committee is ever diminishing. Most of the effect of each technique is obtained by the first few committee members [1], [3], [7]. Quinlan (1996) used only 10 replicates, while Bauer & Kohavi [1] used 25 replicates, Breiman [3] used 50 and Freund and Schapire [7] used 100. For both Bagging and Boosting, much of the reduction in error appears to have occurred after ten to fifteen classifiers. But Adaboost continues to measurably improve their test set error until around 25 classifiers for decision trees [14]. The decision on limiting the number of sub-classifiers is important for practical applications. To be competitive, it is important that the algorithms run in reasonable time.

Table 1. Datasets

Datasets	Instances	Categ. features	Numer. features	Classes
Balance	625	0	4	3
breast-cancer	286	9	0	2
breast-w	699	0	9	2
Colic	368	15	7	2
Credit-a	690	9	6	2
credit-g	1000	13	7	2
Diabetes	768	0	8	2
glass	214	0	9	6
haberman	306	0	3	2
heart-c	303	7	6	5
heart-h	294	7	6	5
heart-statlog	270	0	13	2
hepatitis	155	13	6	2
iris	150	0	4	3
kr-vs-kp	3196	35	0	2
labor	57	8	8	2
lymphotherapy	148	15	3	4
monk1	124	6	0	2
monk2	169	6	0	2
monk3	122	6	0	2
primary-tumor	339	17	0	21
sonar	208	0	60	2
soybean	683	35	0	19
student	344	11	0	2
vote	435	16	0	2
wine	178	0	13	3

In the first experiment, we compare the presented ensemble with bagging, boosting and Decorate ensembles of the most well known decision tree learner - C4.5 (using 10 sub-classifiers) as well as with Random Forest ensemble using 10 random trees [4], too. We also compare the presented ensemble with simple M5' algorithm in order to show the contribution of bagging in the performance improvement. In the last raw of the Table 2 one can see the concentrated results.

The presented ensemble is significantly more accurate than both Bagging C4.5 and simple M5' algorithm in 3 out of the 26 data sets, while it has not significantly higher error rates in any data set. The presented ensemble is significantly more accurate than boosting C4.5 in 4 out of the 26 data sets whilst it has significantly higher error rates in one data set. Furthermore, the proposed ensemble has significantly lower error rates in 2 out of the 26 data sets than Decorate C4.5, whereas it is not significantly less accurate in any data set. What is more, Random Forest is significantly more accurate than the proposed ensembles in none out of the 26 data sets whilst it has significantly higher error rates in 3 data sets.

Table 2. Comparing the proposed ensemble with other well known ensembles using 10 sub-classifiers

Datasets	Bagging M5'	Bagging C4.5	Adaboost C4.5	Decorate C4.5	Random Forest	M5'
balance-scale	90.14	82.04 *	78.35 *	80.99 *	80.20 *	87.76*
breast-cancer	70.57	72.71	66.75	71.54	69.50	70.40
breast-w	96.24	96.07	96.08	96.44	95.78	95.85
colic	84.80	85.34	81.63	84.44	84.78	83.23
credit-a	86.41	85.71	84.01	85.49	85.07	85.39
credit-g	76.36	73.91 *	70.91 *	73.01 *	73.65	74.99
diabetes	76.85	75.64	71.81 *	75.35	74.44	76.56
glass	73.31	73.50	75.15	71.94	76.11	71.30
haberman	73.62	72.78	71.12	73.92	67.55 *	72.90
heart-c	82.25	78.88	78.76	78.85	80.31	82.14
heart-h	81.23	79.93	78.68	79.03	79.94	82.44
heart-statlog	82.26	80.59	78.59	80.30	80.56	82.15
hepatitis	83.36	80.73	82.38	82.57	83.06	82.38
iris	94.93	94.67	94.33	94.80	94.20	94.93
kr-vs-kp	99.34	99.42	99.59	99.21	98.90	99.21
labor	90.13	82.60*	87.17	91.10	86.90	85.13*
lymp/rapy	80.84	77.25	80.87	78.75	80.60	80.35
monk1	85.40	82.10	94.10 v	88.22	84.19	87.80
monk2	58.87	59.80	60.82	58.09	56.03	57.46
Monk3	93.37	92.38	90.01	88.60	92.71	93.29
primary-tumor	47.91	43.90	41.65 *	44.64	42.19 *	45.26
sonar	81.02	78.51	79.22	80.76	80.97	78.37*
soybean	93.38	92.78	92.83	93.78	91.86	92.90
students	81.48	79.07	77.21	79.73	78.18	80.92
vote	95.97	96.27	95.51	95.40	95.98	95.61
wine	97.35	95.16	96.45	96.90	97.13	97.19
W/D/L		0/23/3	1/21/4	0/24/2	0/23/3	0/23/3
Average accuracy	82.98	81.22	80.92	81.69	81.18	82.15

To sum up, the performance of the presented ensemble is more accurate than the other well-known ensembles that use the well known decision tree algorithm - C4.5 - using 10 sub-classifiers. The proposed ensemble can achieve a reduction in error rate about 8% compared to the other ensemble models.

Table 3. Comparing the proposed ensemble with other well known ensembles using 25 sub-classifiers

Datasets	Bagging M5'	Bagging C4.5	Adaboost C4.5	Decorate C4.5	Random Forest	M5'
balance-scale	90.38	81.99 *	76.91 *	81.48 *	80.30 *	87.76*
breast-cancer	71.16	72.64	66.57	70.58	70.18	70.40
breast-w	96.28	96.12	96.53	96.51	96.31	95.85
colic	84.75	85.29	81.76	84.90	85.21	83.23
credit-a	86.39	85.99	85.70	85.88	85.49	85.39
credit-g	76.57	74.29 *	72.85 *	73.49 *	74.50	74.99
diabetes	76.96	76.38	72.78 *	75.34	75.21	76.56
glass	73.63	74.64	77.25	73.18	78.44 v	71.30
haberman	73.49	72.62	71.12	73.12	66.88 *	72.90
heart-c	82.42	79.47	79.57	79.02	81.23	82.14
heart-h	81.44	80.11	78.18	79.64	80.22	82.44
heart-statlog	82.67	81.19	80.19	80.78	81.37	82.15
hepatitis	83.48	81.50	82.87	82.57	84.15	82.38
iris	94.80	94.67	94.40	95.07	94.40	94.93
kr-vs-kp	99.35	99.43	99.62	99.25	99.18	99.21
labor	90.47	84.20*	89.10	93.30	86.50	85.13*
lymp/rapy	81.12	78.75	83.09	79.02	83.48	80.35
monk1	85.73	82.99	96.54 v	89.62	87.22	87.80
monk2	60.25	60.33	61.86	58.03	55.10	57.46
Monk3	93.45	92.13	90.35	90.98	92.95	93.29
primary-tumor	48.32	45.16	41.65 *	44.99	43.18 *	45.26
sonar	81.27	79.78	82.88	83.15	83.29	78.37*
soybean	93.59	93.15	93.21	93.91	92.71	92.90
students	81.31	79.61	76.84 *	80.35	79.41	80.92
vote	96.02	96.50	95.28	95.51	96.28	95.61
wine	97.24	95.34	96.73	97.57	97.57	97.19
W/D/L		0/23/3	1/20/5	0/24/2	1/22/3	0/23/3
Average accuracy	*83.17*	*81.70*	*81.69*	*82.20*	*81.95*	*82.15*

In the second experiment, we compare the presented ensemble with same ensembles using 25 sub-classifiers at this time: bagging, boosting, DECORATE C4.5, as well as Random Forest ensemble using 25 random trees and simple M5' algorithm, too. In the last raw of the Table 3 one can see the concentrated results.

The presented ensemble is significantly more accurate than both Bagging C4.5 and simple M5' algorithm in 3 out of the 26 data sets, while it has not significantly higher error rates in any data set. The presented ensemble is significantly more accurate than boosting C4.5 in 5 out of the 26 data sets whilst it has significantly higher error rates in one data set. Furthermore, the proposed ensemble has significantly lower error rates in 2 out of the 26 data sets than Decorate C4.5, whereas it is not significantly less accurate in any data set. What is more, Random Forest is significantly more accurate than the proposed ensembles in 1 out of the 26 data sets whilst it has significantly higher error rates in 3 data sets.

To sum up, the performance of the presented ensemble is more accurate than the other well-known ensembles that use the C4.5 algorithm using 25 sub-classifiers. The proposed ensemble can achieve a reduction in error rate about 7% compared to the other ensemble models.

Finally, it must be mentioned that for the proposed ensemble, much of the reduction in error appears to have occurred after ten sub-classifiers. It seems that the proposed method continues to measurably improve test set error until around 25 sub-classifiers. Nevertheless, the decision on limiting the number of sub-classifiers is important for practical applications. To be competitive, our decision is to use 10 sub-classifiers.

5 Conclusion

This work has shown that when classification problems are transformed into problems of function approximation in a standard way, they can be successfully solved by constructing model trees to produce an approximation to the conditional class probability function of each individual class.

Bagging model trees outperform state-of-the-art decision tree ensembles on problems with numeric and binary attributes, and, more often than not, on problems with multi-valued nominal attributes too.

In a future work, we will combine model trees with a boosting process for solving classification problems. We will also examine the efficiency of bagging with logistic model trees [10] that use logistic regression at the leaves of the model trees, instead of linear regression.

References

1. Bauer, E. & Kohavi, R.: An empirical comparison of voting classification algorithms: Bagging, boosting, and variants. Machine Learning, Vol. 36, (1999) 105–139.
2. Blake, C. & Merz, C.: UCI Repository of machine learning databases. Irvine, CA: University of California, Department of Information and Computer Science. [http://www.ics.uci.edu/~mlearn/MLRepository.html] (1998)
3. Breiman, L.: Bagging Predictors. Machine Learning, 24 (1996) 123-140.
4. Breiman, L.: "Random Forests". Machine Learning 45 (2001) 5-32.
5. Dietterich, T.: Ensemble Methods in Machine Learning, In Proc. 1st International Workshop on Multiple Classifer Systems, LNCS, Vol 1857, (2000) 1-10, Springer-Verlag.

6. Frank, E., Wang, Y., Inglis, S., Holmes, G., Witten, I.: Using Model Trees for Classification, Machine Learning, 32, (1998) 63–76.
7. Freund Y. and Schapire, R. E.: Experiments with a New Boosting Algorithm, in proceedings of ICML'96, pp. 148-156.
8. Kleinberg, E.M.: A Mathematically Rigorous Foundation for Supervised Learning. In J. Kittler and F. Roli, editors, Multiple Classifier Systems. First International Workshop, MCS 2000, Cagliari, Italy, volume 1857 of Lecture Notes in Computer Science, (2000) 67–76. Springer-Verlag.
9. Kotsiantis, S., Pierrakeas, C., Pintelas, P.: Predicting Students' Performance in Distance Learning Using Machine Learning Techniques, Applied Artificial Intelligence (AAI), Volume 18, (2004) 411 – 426.
10. Landwehr, N., Hall, M., Frank, E.: Logistic Model Trees, Lecture Notes in Computer Science, Volume 2837, Jan 2003, Pages 241 – 252.
11. Malerba, D., Esposito, F., Ceci, M., Appice, A.: Top-Down Induction of Model Trees with Regression and Splitting Nodes. IEEE Trans. Pattern Anal. Mach. Intell. 26(5): 612-625 2004.
12. Melville P. and Mooney R.: Constructing Diverse Classifier Ensembles using Artificial Training Examples, in proceedings of IJCAI-2003, pp.505-510, Acapulco, Mexico, August 2003.
13. Nadeau, C., Bengio, Y.: Inference for the Generalization Error. Machine Learning, 52 (2003) 239-281.
14. Opitz D. & Maclin R.: Popular Ensemble Methods: An Empirical Study, Artificial Intelligence Research, Vol. 11, (1999) 169-198.
15. Quinlan, J. R.: Bagging, boosting, and C4.5. In Proceedings of the Thirteenth National Conference on Artificial Intelligence (1996) 725–730. AAAI/MIT Press.
16. Quinlan, J. R.: Learning with continuous classes, Proc. of Australian Joint Conf. on AI, (1992) 343-348, World Scientific, Singapore
17. Wang, Y. & Witten, I. H.: Induction of model trees for predicting continuous classes, In Proc. of the Poster Papers of the European Conference on ML, Prague (1997) 128–137. Prague: University of Economics, Faculty of Informatics and Statistics.
18. Witten, I., Frank, E.: Data Mining: Practical Machine Learning Tools and Techniques with Java Implementations. Morgan Kaufmann, San Mateo, CA, (2000).

On the Utility of Incremental Feature Selection for the Classification of Textual Data Streams

Ioannis Katakis, Grigorios Tsoumakas, and Ioannis Vlahavas

Department of Informatics,
Aristotle University of Thessaloniki,
54124 Thessaloniki, Greece
{katak,greg,vlahavas}@csd.auth.gr

Abstract. In this paper we argue that incrementally updating the features that a text classification algorithm considers is very important for real-world textual data streams, because in most applications the distribution of data and the description of the classification concept changes over time. We propose the coupling of an incremental feature ranking method and an incremental learning algorithm that can consider different subsets of the feature vector during prediction (what we call a feature based classifier), in order to deal with the above problem. Experimental results with a longitudinal database of real spam and legitimate emails shows that our approach can adapt to the changing nature of streaming data and works much better than classical incremental learning algorithms.

1 Introduction

The World Wide Web is a dynamic environment that offers many sources of continuous textual data, such as web pages, news-feeds, e-mails, chat rooms, discussion forums, usenet groups, instant messages and blogs. There are many interesting applications involving classification of such textual data streams. The most prevalent one is spam filtering [1]. Other applications include filtering of pornographic web pages for safer child surfing [2,3] and delivering personalized news feeds [4]. Another recent application involves the filtering of *web spam* [5], a name for web pages whose sole purpose is to mislead search engines into including an irrelevant commercial web site in the results of a query.

The dynamic nature of the above data streams requires continuous or at least periodic updates of the current knowledge in order to ensure that it always includes the information content of the latest batch of data. This is important in domains where the concept of each class and/or the data distribution changes over time. For example in spam filtering, parts of the spam concept change over time as different unsolicited commercials come into vogue [6]. Similarly, in a personalized news feeder, the interests of a user are changing over time. This phenomenon is also known as *concept drift* [7].

It is obvious that computationally efficient mining of data streams requires incremental algorithms that can update the current knowledge without reprocessing past data, that are either unavailable or too costly to be retrieved. The huge amount of data that is constantly arriving from a stream, does not allow to permanently store all data, rather a small part of it (the latest batch) or a summary of all the data that have been seen.

Textual data streams are also high-dimensional. Documents are usually represented as a bag-of-words and the feature vector for a collection of documents in a typical application comprises several thousands of words. However, not all features are necessary. Therefore, feature selection must be performed in order to reduce the dimensionality of the problem and allow learning algorithms to obtain higher quality of knowledge with less computational cost. For this reason, a lot of studies on feature selection methods for text classification have been performed in the past [8,9].

However, to the best of our knowledge, no work exists on the issue of incrementally/periodically updating the features that a text classification algorithm considers. We argue that this is very important for real-world textual data streams, because the predictive power of features changes over time: words that in the past have been important, become redundant with the passing of time and new high-predictive words arise that were not considered before.

In order to deal with this issue, this paper proposes an approach for classification of textual data streams that is incremental both with respect of the examples that arrive and with respect to the subset of features that it considers over time. To the best of our knowledge, such an approach has not been considered before, not only for textual data, but also for any other type of high-dimensional data.

Our approach requires two components: a) an incremental feature ranking method, and b) an incremental learning algorithm that can consider a subset of the features during prediction. To verify the utility of incremental feature selection, we experimentally evaluate our approach on a chronologically ordered version of a spam and legitimate email collection. The results showed that incremental feature selection offers higher accuracy compared to classical incremental learning.

The rest of this paper is organized as follows: Section 2, presents background knowledge on text classification. In Section 3, we describe the proposed approach. In Section 4 we give details about the experimental setup, including the preprocessing of the data set and the specific algorithms that were used. In Section 5 we present and discuss the results and finally in Section 6 we conclude and propose some future work on this topic.

2 Automated Text Classification

Automated text classification has gained scientific interest in the last 20 years. Applications like document organization [10], text filtering [11] and author identification [12] are some representative examples of the research outcome in the field of text classification. The impressive growth of the world wide web in the last decade resulted in many new interesting applications like web page classification [13], e-mail organization [14] and spam filtering [1] and raised new research issues [15].

An informal definition of text classification would be "the categorization of previously unseen documents into predefined classes". In author identification for example, the classes are the authors. In document organization, the classes are a number of predefined topics and in spam identification there are only two classes: a mail can be spam or legitimate. This is a binary classification problem or else a text filtering problem.

The first problem we come across in any text learning task is that the data cannot be immediately processed by a classifier. We have to first follow a procedure to convert our text to a format that is acceptable by learning algorithms. The most common approach is the vector space model, where every text document is represented as a vector of feature weights $\vec{d_j} = <w_{1j},\ldots,w_{|V|j}>$, where V is the set of words that occur at least once in a document and consists our problem's vocabulary. This is the so-called bag-of-words approach. Another option is to use phrases as features, although research has shown that this approach does not improve effectiveness [16]. The weight for each word of the vector is either tf-idf [17] (the term frequency in the collection of documents divided by the frequency in the current document), or more commonly a binary value denoting the existence or absence of the word in the document.

For text classification and especially for spam filtering applications, a widely used classifier, mainly for its simplicity and flexibility is the Naive Bayes Classifier [18] which showed decent performance in the identification of junk e-mails [1].

Feature selection has been studied extensively in the context of text classification [8,9]. The reason is that text data are usually high-dimensional and feature selection is essential for a) reducing the computational complexity of machine learning algorithms, and b) improving the accuracy of classification.

Feature selection methods fall broadly into two categories: a) the filter approach, and b) the wrapper approach. In the wrapper approach feedback from the use of the learning algorithm with the selected features is used to evaluate these features. When the best set is found the algorithm is called to make new classifications based on this set of features only. On the other hand, the filter approach is totally independent of the classifier. Another useful categorization of feature selection methods is based on whether they evaluate individual features, or subsets of features.

Wrappers are usually more computationally intensive than filters due to extensive use of the learning algorithm. Methods that evaluate subsets of features are also more computationally intensive due to the larger number of evaluations that they have to consider. For this reason in text classification tasks, where the dimensionality of the data is typically very large, filters that evaluate features are usually considered. Features are ranked based on the result of the evaluation and the top N features are selected for further classification use.

3 Our Approach

Our approach uses two components in conjunction: a) an incremental feature ranking method, and b) an incremental learning algorithm that can consider a subset of the features during prediction.

In Section 2 we noted that feature selection methods that are commonly used for text classification are filters that evaluate the predictive power of all features and select the N best. Such methods evaluate each word based on cumulative statistics concerning the number of times that it appears in each different class of documents. This renders such methods inherently incremental: When a new labelled document arrives, the statistics are updated and the evaluation can be immediately calculated without the need of re-processing past data. These methods can also handle new words by including them in the vocabulary and initializing their statistics. Therefore the first component of our approach can be instantiated using a variety of such methods, including *information gain*, the χ^2 statistic and *mutual information* [8,9].

The incremental re-evaluation and addition of words will inevitably result into certain words being promoted to/demoted from the top N words. This raises a problem that requires the second component of the proposed approach: a learning algorithm that is able to classify a new instance taking into account different features over time. This problem has not been considered before to the best of our knowledge. We call learning algorithms that can deal with it *feature based*, because learning is based on the new subset of features, in the same way that in *instance based* algorithms, learning is based on the new instance.

Two inherently feature based algorithms are *Naive Bayes* (NB) and *k Nearest Neighbors* (kNN). In both of these algorithms each feature makes an independent contribution towards the prediction of a class. Therefore, these algorithms can be easily expanded in order to instantiate the second component of our approach. Specifically, when these algorithms are used for the classification of a new instance, they should also be provided with an additional parameter denoting the subset of the selected features. NB will only consider the calculated probabilities of this subset, while kNN will measure the distance of the new instance with the stored examples based only on this subset.

It is worth noticing that the proposed approach could work without an initial training set. This is useful in personalized web-content (e-mail, news, etc.) filtering applications that we want to work based solely on our perception of the target class. However, very often an initial collection of labelled documents is available. Figure 1 presents algorithm INITIALTRAINING for the initial training of our approach, based on such a collection of **Documents** that belong to one of several **Classes**.

The first step is to build the **Vocabulary** of distinct words that appear in all documents of the collection using the BUILDVOCABULARY function. We also initialize **WordStats**, which is a construct that will hold the number of appearances of each **Word** in the **Vocabulary** for each different class of documents, for the purpose of feature ranking. Next, for each **Document** in the collection of training **Documents** we update the **WordStats**. Based on the calculated statistics, we sub-

```
input  : Documents, Classes
output: Classifier, Vocabulary, WordStats, FeatureList
begin
    Vocabulary ← BUILDVOCABULARY(Documents)
    foreach Word ∈ Vocabulary do
        foreach Class ∈ Classes do
            WordStats [Word][1][Class] ← 0
            WordStats [Word][0][Class] ← 0
    foreach <Document, DocClass> ∈ Documents do
        foreach Word ∈ Vocabulary do
            if Word ∈ Document then
                | WordStats [Word][1][DocClass] ← WordStats [Word][1][DocClass] + 1
            else
                | WordStats [Word][0][DocClass] ← WordStats [Word][0][DocClass] + 1
    FeatureList ← ∅
    foreach Word ∈ Vocabulary do
        Evaluation ← EVALUATEFEATURE(Word, WordStats)
        INSERTSORT(<Word, Evaluation>, FeatureList)
    Classifier ← BUILDCLASSIFIER(Documents, Vocabulary)
end
```

Fig. 1. Algorithm INITIALTRAINING

sequently evaluate each Word in the Vocabulary using the metric of preference and insert the Word and its Evaluation in the list FeatureList, which is sorted according to the evaluation metric. Finally we train a feature based classifier using all Documents and the complete Vocabulary. Note that the training of the Naive Bayes classifier does not demand any other statistics than those already collected in WordStats.

Figure 2 presents algorithm UPDATE for the incremental update of our approach. When a new Document arrives as an example of a DocumentClass, the first thing to happen is to check if it contains any new words. If a new Word is present then it is added to the vocabulary (ADDWORD) and the WordStats of this Word are initialized to zero. Then for each Word in the Vocabulary we update the counts based on the new document, re-calculate the evaluation metric and sort the list according to the new evaluations, as before. Finally, the classifier must also be vertically updated based on the new example and also take into account any new words. Note that for the Naive Bayes classifier updating the WordStats is enough for this purpose.

Finally, when a new unlabelled Document arrives for classification, the feature based classifier of our approach considers just the top NumToSelect ranked words from the sorted FeatureList. This process is performed by algorithm CLASSIFYDOCUMENT shown in Figure 3.

```
input  : Document, DocClass, Classes, Vocabulary
output : Classifier, Vocabulary, WordStats, FeatureList
begin
    foreach Word ∈ Document do
        if Word ∉ Vocabulary then
            ADDWORD(Word, Vocabulary)
            foreach Class ∈ Classes do
                WordStats [Word][1][Class] ← 0
                WordStats [Word][0][Class] ← 0

    foreach Word ∈ Vocabulary do
        if Word ∈ Document then
            WordStats [Word][1][DocClass] ← WordStats [Word][1][DocClass] + 1
        else
            WordStats [Word][0][DocClass] ← WordStats [Word][0][DocClass] + 1
    FeatureList ← ∅
    foreach Word ∈ Vocabulary do
        Evaluation ← EVALUATEFEATURE(Word, WordStats)
        INSERTSORT(<Word, Evaluation>, FeatureList)
    Classifier ← UPDATECLASSIFIER(Document, DocClass)
end
```

Fig. 2. Algorithm UPDATE

```
input  : Classifier, Document, FeatureList, NumToSelect
output : Class
begin
    FeatureSubset ← SELECTFEATURES(NumToSelect, FeatureList)
    Class ← USECLASSIFIER(Classifier, Document, FeatureSubset)
end
```

Fig. 3. Algorithm CLASSIFYDOCUMENT

4 Experimental Setup

In this section we present the data set, feature selection method and learning algorithm that were used in the experiments.

4.1 Data Set

In order to evaluate the utility of the proposed approach for classification of textual data streams, it is important to use real-world data. For the domain of spam filtering this means that we need real-world spam and legitimate emails chronologically ordered according to their date and time of arrival. In this way we can approximate the time-evolving nature of this problem and consequently we can evaluate properly the different approaches.

There are various collections of spam messages available on the Web, including the repository of SpamArchive[1], the public corpus of the SpamAssasin project[2] and the Ling-Spam corpus[3]. Our choice was the public corpus of SpamAssassin for two main reasons: a) Every mail of the collection is available with the headers, so we are able to extract the exact date and time that the mail was sent or received, and b) It contains both spam and ham messages with a decent spam ratio (about 20 percent).

The Spam Assassin collection comes in four parts (folders): spam, spam2, ham, and easy ham which is a collection of more easily recognized legitimate messages. In order to convert this collection into a longitudinal data set we extracted the date and time that the mail was sent. Then we converted the time into GMT time. Date was also changed where needed. We stamped each mail with its date and time by renaming it in the format yyyy_MM_dd_hh_mm_ss (yyyy: year, MM: month, dd:day, hh: hours, mm: minutes, ss: seconds). If a mail was more than once in the corpus (sometimes a user may get the same mail more than once) we kept all copies. All attachments were removed. The boolean bag-of-words approach was used for representing the mails.

4.2 Feature Selection Method and Learning Algorithm

The feature ranking method that we selected for the experiments is the χ^2 statistic, for its simplicity and effectiveness [8]. As we mentioned in the precious section, there are many other similarly simple metrics that could be used for instantiating our framework [8,9]. Here, we are not focusing on the effectiveness of different feature selection methods, rather on whether the proposed incremental feature selection approach is useful in textual data stream classification.

The algorithm that we selected is Naive Bayes. The k-NN algorithm is inefficient for data-streams, because it needs to store all data. Naive Bayes on the other hand store only the necessary statistics, and is therefore our choice for incremental learning from textual data streams.

The Naive Bayes (NB) classifier is a simplistic but practical Bayesian learning algorithm that performs extremely well in many text classification tasks. The decision of the algorithm is determined by the following equation:

$$c_{NB} = argmax P(c_j) \prod P(w_i|c_j) \qquad (1)$$

Where c_j is the $i-th$ class of our classification problem. In our case, we have only two classes. A mail can belong to class c_L (legitimate mail) or c_S (spam mail). w_i is the $i-th$ word of a vocabulary built from our corpus by collecting

---

[1] http://www.spamarchive.org
[2] http://spamassassin.apache.org/
[3] http://www.iit.demokritos.gr/skel/i-config/downloads/

all distinct words. $P(c_j)$ expresses the probability a random document to belong in the $j-th$ class. It can be approximated from the training set by dividing the number of documents of class j with the total number of training documents available.

$$P(c_j) = \frac{|docs_j|}{|Examples|} \qquad (2)$$

The $P(w_i|c_j)$ probability represents the possibility the word w_i to be present in a document of class c_j. Hence, it expresses how possible it is for our unlabelled document to belong in class c_j if it contains the word w_j. This possibility can be typically approximated by:

$$P(w_i|c_j) = \frac{NumberOfTimesWordw_iOccursinallc_jDocuments}{TotalNumberofc_jdocuments} \qquad (3)$$

The simplicity of the NB classifier is obvious from all the above equations. To classify a new document we only need to have the knowledge of the above probabilities. We have expanded the Naive Bayes implementation of the Weka library of machine learning algorithms [19] in order to be able to perform classification using a subset of all features that were used for training.

The χ^2 statistic of a word w and a class c can be calculated by the following equation.

$$\chi^2(w,c) = \frac{N \times (AD - CB)^2}{(A+C) \times (B+D) \times (A+B) \times (C+D)} \qquad (4)$$

where A is the number of times w and c co-occur, B is the number of times w occurs without c, C is the number of times c occurs without w, D is the number of times neither c nor w occur, and N is the total number of documents.

We have also expanded the implementation of the χ^2 feature ranking method of Weka [19] in order to perform incremental updates.

5 Results and Discussion

In the experiments, we compare the predictive performance of our approach (NB3) with a classical incremental Naive Bayes classifier (NB2) and a non-incremental Naive Bayes classifier (NB1). NB1 is only trained once on a percentage of the data, and uses the features that are selected based on this initial training set. NB2 also uses a static feature space, but apart from the initial training, each time a new document arrives, it updates the probabilities for each feature. Our approach (NB3) also updates the probabilities not only for the selected features but for *all* of the features and in addition it recalculates the χ^2 rank of these features based on the updated probabilities. It therefore uses a dynamic feature space, that may change over time. In addition our approach can utilize new features that appear in new documents.

We varied the percentage of documents that were used for initial training from 0.1 to 0.5 with a step of 0.1. Using a 0.1 percentage of initial training data allows us to study the behavior of the filter for a longer time (0.9 of the whole longitudinal data set), while an initial training of 0.5 simulates a short period of online filtering. The number of features to select was set to 250 and 500.

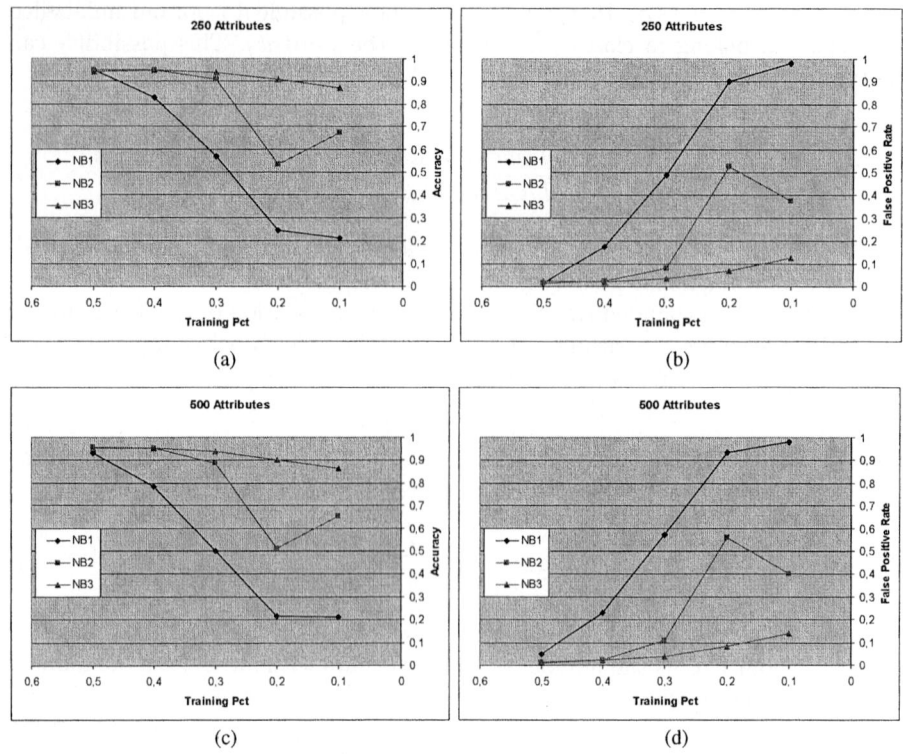

Fig. 4. (a) accuracy and (b) false positive rate when we select the top 250 features and (c) accuracy and (d) false positive rate when we select the top 500 features

Figure 4 shows (a) the accuracy and (b) the false positive rate when we select the top 250 features and (c) the accuracy and (d) the false positive rate when we select the top 500 features. We first notice that the behavior of the three approaches follows the same pattern independent of the number of features used.

The non-incremental Naive Bayes classifier (NB1) performs very badly when run for a long time (0.1 to 0.4) and approximates the other two incremental classifiers when half of the total data that it subsequently classifies are used for training. This is something expected as incremental learning is important for updating the current model with the latest data.

The incremental Naive Bayes classifier (NB2) also has problems when run for a long time (0.1 to 0.3) and approximates NB3 when 0.4 or more of the total data is used for its training. This actually shows that vertically incremental learning alone cannot catch up with the changing nature of real-world data streams.

The feature based incremental Naive Bayes classifier together with the incremental χ^2 feature ranking method (NB3) shows much better behavior than the other two classifiers even when little data is used for initial training (i.e. even when run for a long time). This verifies our initial argument that incremental feature selection is very important for classification of textual data streams.

6 Conclusions and Future Work

This paper argued that incremental feature selection is very important for the classification of textual data streams due to the changes in data distribution and class concept that occur over time. We presented an approach that combines an incremental feature selection methods with what we called a feature based learning algorithm in order to deal with the above problem. The experimental results show that the proposed approach offers better predictive accuracy compared to classical incremental learning, and are encouraging for further work.

In the future we intend to experiment with maintaining statistics for a fixed number of features over time instead of the whole vocabulary. This would increase the efficiency of the proposed approach, due to the reduced storage and processing requirements. We would like to see whether this would also increase the effectiveness of the proposed approach in dealing with fast changing data/concepts, as it focuses more aggressively on the latest data.

References

1. Sahami, M., Dumais, S., Heckerman, D., Horvitz, E.: A bayesian approach to filtering junk E-mail. In: Learning for Text Categorization: Papers from the 1998 Workshop, Madison, Wisconsin, AAAI Technical Report WS-98-05 (1998)
2. Chandrinos, K.V., Androutsopoulos, I., Paliouras, G., Spyropoulos, C.D.: Automatic web rating: Filtering obscene content on the web. In Borbinha, J.L., Baker, T., eds.: Proceedings of ECDL00, 4th European Conference on Research and Advanced Technology for Digital Libraries, Lisbon, Portugal, Springer Verlag (2000) 403–406
3. Lee, P.Y., Hui, S.C., Fong, A.C.M.: Neural networks for web content filtering. IEEE Intelligent Systems **17** (2002) 48–57
4. Lang, K.: Newsweeder: Learning to filter netnews. In: Proceedings of the 12th International Conference on Machine Learning, Tahoe City, California (1995) 331–339
5. Fetterly, D., Manasse, M., Najork, M.: Spam, damn spam, and statistics: using statistical analysis to locate spam web pages. In: WebDB '04: Proceedings of the 7th International Workshop on the Web and Databases, New York, NY, USA, ACM Press (2004) 1–6
6. Fawcett, T.: "in vivo" spam filtering: A challenge problem for data mining. KDD Explorations **5** (2003)

7. Widmer, G., Kubat, M.: Learning in the presence of concept drift and hidden contexts. Machine Learning **23** (1996) 69–101
8. Yang, Y., Pedersen, J.O.: A comparative study on feature selection in text categorization. In Fisher, D.H., ed.: Proceedings of ICML-97, 14th International Conference on Machine Learning, Nashville, US, Morgan Kaufmann Publishers, San Francisco, US (1997) 412–420
9. Forman, G.: An extensive empirical study of feature selection metrics for text classification. J. Mach. Learn. Res. **3** (2003) 1289–1305
10. Larkey, L.S.: A patent search and classification system. In Fox, E.A., Rowe, N., eds.: Proceedings of DL-99, 4th ACM Conference on Digital Libraries, Berkeley, US, ACM Press, New York, US (1999) 179–187
11. Schapire, R.E., Singer, Y., Singhal, A.: Boosting and Rocchio applied to text filtering. In Croft, W.B., Moffat, A., van Rijsbergen, C.J., Wilkinson, R., Zobel, J., eds.: Proceedings of SIGIR-98, 21st ACM International Conference on Research and Development in Information Retrieval, Melbourne, AU, ACM Press, New York, US (1998) 215–223
12. Fung, G.: The disputed federalist papers: Svm feature selection via concave minimization. In: TAPIA '03: Proceedings of the 2003 conference on Diversity in computing, New York, NY, USA, ACM Press (2003) 42–46
13. Peng, X., Choi, B.: Automatic web page classification in a dynamic and hierarchical way. In: IEEE International Conference on Data Mining. (2002) 386–393
14. Clark, J., Koprinska, I., Poon, J.: A neural network based approach to automated e-mail classification. In: IEEE/WIC International Conference on Web Intelligence (WI'03). (2003) 702–705
15. Sebastiani, F.: Machine learning in automated text categorization. ACM Computing Surveys **34** (2002) 1–47
16. Lewis, D.D.: An evaluation of phrasal and clustered representations on a text categorization task. In: SIGIR '92: Proceedings of the 15th annual international ACM SIGIR conference on Research and development in information retrieval, New York, NY, USA, ACM Press (1992) 37–50
17. Salton, G., Buckley, C.: Term-weighting approaches in automatic text retrieval. Inf. Process. Manage. **24** (1988) 513–523
18. John, G.H., Langley, P.: Estimating continuous distributions in Bayesian classifiers. In: Proceedings of the 11th Conference on Uncertainty in Artificial Intelligence, Morgan Kaufmann (1995) 338–345
19. Witten, I., Frank, E.: Data Mining: Practical machine learning tools with Java implementations. Morgan Kaufmann (1999)

Gossip-Based Greedy Gaussian Mixture Learning

Nikos Vlassis[1], Yiannis Sfakianakis[1], and Wojtek Kowalczyk[2]

[1] Informatics Institute, University of Amsterdam,
Kruislaan 403, 1098 SJ Amsterdam, The Netherlands
{vlassis,jsfakian}@science.uva.nl
[2] Department of Computer Science, Vrije Universiteit Amsterdam,
De Boelelaan 1081a, 1081 HV Amsterdam, The Netherlands
wojtek@cs.vu.nl

Abstract. It has been recently demonstrated that the classical EM algorithm for learning Gaussian mixture models can be successfully implemented in a decentralized manner by resorting to gossip-based randomized distributed protocols. In this paper we describe a gossip-based implementation of an alternative algorithm for learning Gaussian mixtures in which components are added to the mixture one after another. Our new Greedy Gossip-based Gaussian mixture learning algorithm uses gossip-based parallel search, starting from multiple initial guesses, for finding good components to add to the mixture in each component allocation step. It can be executed on massive networks of small computing devices, converging to a solution exponentially faster than its centralized version, while reaching the same quality of generated models.

Keywords: Data mining, Algorithms and Complexity, Computer and Sensor Networks, Information Retrieval.

1 Introduction

Gaussian mixture models constitute a rich family of probability distributions, with many applications in statistics, pattern recognition, machine learning, and data mining [1]. Such models postulate that the observed data are generated by a two-level process that first samples components, and then draws data from the corresponding Gaussian distributions. Gaussian mixture models have been used, e.g., for clustering large datasets [2], for dimension reduction [3], and for classification [4].

Learning the parameters of a Gaussian mixture from a given dataset is often carried out by maximum likelihood and the EM algorithm [5]. The EM algorithm is an iterative optimization technique that starts with an initial estimate of the mixture parameters, and in each step produces a new parameter estimate that increases the likelihood function. However, EM is a local optimization algorithm and therefore is likely to get trapped in a local maximum of the likelihood function. Several initialization methods have been proposed for tackling this problem [6].

A way to resolve the sensitivity of EM to initialization and to improve its convergence performance is to use a greedy learning approach [7,8,9]. In the greedy approach, components are added to the mixture one after the other until a desired number of components. The main idea is to replace the original k-component mixture problem by a sequence of 2-component mixture problems that are easier to solve. As it was shown in [8,9], the greedy approach can produce much better results than the standard EM algorithm (with random restarts) with little extra overhead. A similar approach has been proposed in [10] in which components of the mixture are split and merge in order to avoid local maxima of EM.

Recently, a decentralized implementation of the EM algorithm for Gaussian mixture learning, called Newscast EM, was proposed for data that are distributed over a the nodes of a network [11]. This method relies on a gossip-based randomized protocol that implements the M-step of the EM algorithm in a parallel-distributed fashion: each node starts with a local estimate of the mixture parameters, and then pairs of nodes repeatedly exchange their parameter estimates and combine them by weighted averaging. In such a gossip-based M-step, nodes learn the correct estimates exponentially fast, in a number of cycles that is logarithmic in the network size.

In this paper we show how similar gossip-based protocols can be used for the greedy learning of Gaussian mixture models. In particular, we derive a gossip-based distributed implementation of the greedy learning algorithm of [9]. The derived algorithm essentially resolves the sensitivity to initialization of the algorithm of [11]. Preliminary results indicate that the proposed algorithm can achieve comparable results to its centralized counterpart, but much faster.

2 Gaussian Mixtures and the EM Algorithm

For random vector $x \in \mathrm{I\!R}^d$, a k-component Gaussian mixture model is given by the convex combination

$$p(x) = \sum_{s=1}^{k} \pi_s p(x|s) \qquad (1)$$

of k Gaussian densities

$$p(x|s) = \frac{(2\pi)^{-d/2}}{|C_s|^{1/2}} \exp\left[-\frac{1}{2}(x-m_s)^\top C_s^{-1}(x-m_s)\right], \qquad (2)$$

parameterized by their means m_s and covariance matrices C_s, while the mixing weights π_s satisfy $\sum_s \pi_s = 1$, and define a 'prior' distribution over the components. For a given dataset $\{x_1, \ldots, x_n\}$ of independent and identically distributed samples from $p(x)$, the learning problem is to estimate the parameter vector $\theta = \{\pi_s, m_s, C_s\}_{s=1}^k$ of the k components that maximizes the log-likelihood function (assuming that the latter is bounded from above)

$$\mathcal{L} = \sum_{i=1}^{n} \log p(x_i) = \sum_{i=1}^{n} \log \sum_{s=1}^{k} \pi_s p(x_i|s). \qquad (3)$$

Maximization of the data log-likelihood $\mathcal{L}$ can be carried out by the EM algorithm, which is an iterative optimization algorithm that maximizes in each step a lower bound of $\mathcal{L}$ [5,12]. This bound $\mathcal{F}$ is a function of the current mixture parameters θ and a set of n 'responsibility' distributions $q_i(s)$, one for each point x_i. This lower bound, analogous to the variational free energy in statistical physics, equals

$$\mathcal{F} = \sum_{i=1}^{n} \sum_{s=1}^{k} q_i(s) \big[\log \pi_s + \log p(x_i|s) - \log q_i(s) \big]. \tag{4}$$

The standard EM algorithm starts with an initial estimate of the parameter vector θ (e.g., random or computed by a clustering method like k-means), and then it alternates between two steps. In the E-step, the energy $\mathcal{F}$ is maximized over the responsibilities q_i giving $q_i(s) = p(s|x_i)$, i.e., the Bayes posteriors given the parameters found in the previous step. In the M-step, the energy $\mathcal{F}$ is maximized over the parameters θ keeping the $q_i(s)$ fixed, giving the following equations:

$$\pi_s = \frac{1}{n} \sum_{i=1}^{n} q_i(s), \tag{5}$$

$$m_s = \frac{1}{n\pi_s} \sum_{i=1}^{n} q_i(s) x_i, \tag{6}$$

$$C_s = \frac{1}{n\pi_s} \sum_{i=1}^{n} q_i(s) x_i x_i^\top - m_s m_s^\top. \tag{7}$$

The E- and M-steps are repeated until $\mathcal{L}$ does not improve significantly between two consecutive iterations.

3 Greedy Gaussian Mixture Learning

One the limitations of the standard EM algorithm is that it is very sensitive to the initialization of the parameter vector θ. For various initialization choices EM can easily get trapped in local maxima of the log-likelihood function. An alternative approach which avoids the initialization of θ is to start with a single-component mixture (which is trivial to find) and then keep on adding components to the mixture one after the other [7,8,9]. In particular, each $(k+1)$-component mixture $p_{k+1}(x)$ is recursively defined as the convex combination of a k-component mixture $p_k(x)$ and a new component $f(x; \theta_{k+1})$, i.e.,

$$p_{k+1}(x) = (1 - a_{k+1}) p_k(x) + a_{k+1} f(x; \theta_{k+1}), \tag{8}$$

with mixing weight $a_{k+1} \in (0, 1)$. Assuming that $p_k(x)$ has already been learned, learning the parameters θ_{k+1} of the new component and the mixing weight a_{k+1} can be done by maximizing the log-likelihood of $p_{k+1}(x)$

$$\mathcal{L}_{k+1} = \sum_{i=1}^{n} \log[(1 - a_{k+1}) p_k(x_i) + a_{k+1} f(x_i; \theta_{k+1})] \tag{9}$$

with $p_k(x)$ kept fixed. As shown in [7], if optimal parameters $[a^*_{k+1}, \theta^*_{k+1}] = \arg\max_{[a_{k+1}, \theta_{k+1}]} \mathcal{L}_{k+1}$ are computed for every k, then the 'greedy' k-component mixture $p_k(x) = (1 - a^*_k)p_{k-1}(x) + a^*_k f(x; \theta^*_k)$, can be almost as good as the maximum likelihood mixture $p^*(x)$ in the following sense:

$$\sum_{i=1}^{n} \log p_k(x_i) \geq \sum_{i=1}^{n} \log p^*(x_i) - \frac{c}{k}, \qquad (10)$$

where k is the number of components of $p_k(x)$, and c is a constant independent of k.

Although the theoretical results of [7] justify the greedy approach for mixture learning, in practice it is difficult to compute the optimal parameters $[a^*_{k+1}, \theta^*_{k+1}]$ that maximize $\mathcal{L}_{k+1}$ in each component allocation step. Since $\mathcal{L}_{k+1}$ cannot be analytically maximized, an option is to perform a global search over the space of $[a_{k+1}, \theta_{k+1}]$ starting from some initial (random) estimates. This is the approach taken in [9]: a number of candidate components are generated from each one of the k components of $p_k(x)$ by randomization, and then a 'partial' EM algorithm is executed that searches locally for a vector $[\tilde{a}_{k+1}, \tilde{\theta}_{k+1}]$ with high $\mathcal{L}_{k+1}$, and which hopefully is not too far from $[a^*_{k+1}, \theta^*_{k+1}]$. In particular, assuming a fixed k-component mixture $p_k(x)$, component allocation is done as follows:

1. Data are first assigned to their 'nearest' component according to posterior probability. That is, each point x_i is assigned to component $\arg\max_s p(s|x_i)$.
2. For each component s, let A_s be the set of points assigned to component s. Repeat until m candidates (e.g., $m = 10$) are created from s:
   (a) Select two points x_s, x'_s uniformly at random from A_s.
   (b) Cluster all A_s points in two subsets, according to their nearest Euclidean distance from x_s and x'_s.
   (c) Create a candidate component f_s from each subset, having $\theta_{k+1} = [m_{k+1}, C_{k+1}]$ the mean and the covariance of the points in the subset.
   (d) Set $a_{k+1} = 0.5$ and update $[a_{k+1}, \theta_{k+1}]$ with partial EM steps, as explained below.
3. Among all mk updated parameter vectors, select the vector $[\tilde{a}_{k+1}, \tilde{\theta}_{k+1}]$ with the highest $\mathcal{L}_{k+1}$.

In the 2d step above, the parameters $[a_{k+1}, \theta_{k+1}]$ are updated by an EM algorithm that optimizes a lower bound of $\mathcal{L}_{k+1}$. The idea is to treat $p_{k+1}(x)$ as a two-component mixture, composed of the new component $f(x; \theta_{k+1})$ and the fixed mixture $p_k(x)$, and lower bound $\mathcal{L}_{k+1}$ by setting to zero the responsibility $q_i(f_s)$ of candidate components f_s for points not in A_s. This has the effect that the partial EM steps can be carried out fast, with total cost $O(mn)$. Maximizing this bound over the responsibilities $q_i(f_s)$ gives

$$q_i(f_s) = \frac{a_{k+1} f(x_i; \theta_{k+1})}{(1 - a_{k+1}) p_k(x_i) + a_{k+1} f(x_i; \theta_{k+1})}, \qquad (11)$$

which is the Bayes posterior for the two-component mixture $p_{k+1}(x)$. Similarly, maximizing the bound over the parameters a_{k+1} and $\theta_{k+1} = [m_{k+1}, C_{k+1}]$ gives:

$$a_{k+1} = \frac{1}{n} \sum_{i \in A_s} q_i(f_s), \tag{12}$$

$$m_{k+1} = \frac{1}{na_{k+1}} \sum_{i \in A_s} q_i(f_s) x_i, \tag{13}$$

$$C_{k+1} = \frac{1}{na_{k+1}} \sum_{i \in A_s} q_i(f_s) x_i x_i^\top - m_{k+1} m_{k+1}^\top. \tag{14}$$

When the best vector $[\tilde{a}_{k+1}, \tilde{\theta}_{k+1}]$ has been found in step 3 above, the new $(k+1)$-component mixture is formed as

$$p_{k+1}(x) = (1 - \tilde{a}_{k+1}) p_k(x) + \tilde{a}_{k+1} f(x; \tilde{\theta}_{k+1}), \tag{15}$$

and is subsequently updated with standard EM (all its $k+1$ components are updated). Upon convergence of EM, a new component is added to the mixture, and so on until some criterion on the number of components is satisfied, e.g., one based on MDL [7]. The above greedy algorithm is experimentally shown to outperform the standard EM with random restarts [9].

4 Gossip-Based Gaussian Mixture Learning

A recent development in Gaussian mixture modeling is the use of gossip-based protocols for distributed learning [13,14,11,15]. Such protocols apply in the case where the data x_i are not centrally available but are distributed over the nodes of a network. The main idea is to decompose the M-step of the EM algorithm into a number of cycles: each node maintains a local estimate of the model parameters, and in every cycle it contacts some other node at random, and the two nodes update their model estimates by weighted averaging. As shown in [11], under such a protocol the local estimates of the individual nodes converge exponentially fast to the correct solution in each M-step of the algorithm. In some applications the gossip approach may be more advantageous then other distributed implementations of EM that resort on global broadcasting [16] or routing trees [17].

The above distributed EM implementation relies on a gossip-based protocol that computes the average μ of a set of numbers $v_1, \ldots, v_n$ that are stored in the nodes of a network (one value per node). Each node i initially sets $\mu_i = v_i$ as its local estimate of μ, and then it runs the following protocol for a number of cycles:

1. Contact a node j that is chosen uniformly at random from $1, \ldots, n$.
2. Nodes i and j update their estimates by $\mu_i' = \mu_j' = (\mu_i + \mu_j)/2$.

It turns out that under this protocol each node learns the correct average very fast, in a number of cycles that is logarithmic in the sample size:

Theorem 1 (Kowalczyk and Vlassis, 2005). *With probability at least $1-\delta$, after $\lceil 0.581(\log n + 2\log\sigma + 2\log\frac{1}{\varepsilon} + \log\frac{1}{\delta})\rceil$ cycles holds $\max_i |\mu_i - \mu| \leq \varepsilon$, for any $\varepsilon > 0$ and data variance σ^2.*

Using this gossip-based protocol, a distributed implementation of the standard EM algorithm is possible by noting that the M-step (5)–(7) involves the computation of a number of averages. The idea is that each node i maintains a local estimate $\theta_i = \{\pi_{is}, m_{is}, \tilde{C}_{is}\}$ of the parameters of the mixture, where $C_{is} = \tilde{C}_{is} - m_{is}m_{is}^\top$, and the following protocol is executed identically and in parallel for each node i:

1. **Initialization.** Set $q_i(s)$ to some random number in $(0,1)$ and then normalize all $q_i(s)$ to sum to 1 over all s.
2. **M-step.** Initialize i's local estimates for each component s by $\pi_{is} = q_i(s)$, $m_{is} = x_i$, $\tilde{C}_{is} = x_i x_i^\top$. Then, for a fixed number of cycles, contact node j and update both i and j local estimates for each component s by:

$$\pi'_{is} = \pi'_{js} = \frac{\pi_{is} + \pi_{js}}{2}, \tag{16}$$

$$m'_{is} = m'_{js} = \frac{\pi_{is} m_{is} + \pi_{js} m_{js}}{\pi_{is} + \pi_{js}}, \tag{17}$$

$$\tilde{C}'_{is} = \tilde{C}'_{js} = \frac{\pi_{is}\tilde{C}_{is} + \pi_{js}\tilde{C}_{js}}{\pi_{is} + \pi_{js}}. \tag{18}$$

3. **E-step.** Compute $q_i(s) = p(s|x_i)$ for each s, using the M-step estimates π_{is}, m_{is}, and $C_{is} = \tilde{C}_{is} - m_{is}m_{is}^\top$.
4. **Loop.** Go to 2, unless a stopping criterion is satisfied.

As reported in [11], the above gossip-based learning algorithm produces results that are essentially identical to those obtained by the standard EM algorithm, but much faster. Resorting to Theorem 1, one can see that each node can implement the M-step in $O(\log n)$ time, whereas if the data were to be transferred to and processed by a central server, the runtime would have been $O(n)$. The communication complexity of each gossip M-step (total number of messages sent over the network) is $O(n\log n)$ since each node contacts $O(\log n)$ other nodes (one per gossip cycle).

5 Gossip-Based Greedy Gaussian Mixture Learning

A disadvantage of the gossip-based EM algorithm above is that the initialization (step 1) is random. In this section we derive a gossip-based greedy Gaussian mixture learning algorithm in which components are added sequentially to the mixture. This requires implementing a (randomized) function that computes candidate components to add to a mixture. We first note that if this function depends only on the parameters of the mixture, and since each node at the end of each M-step has converged to the same mixture parameters, then clearly each node can compute the same set of candidate components by using the same random number generator and same seed. On the other hand, if this function depends also on the data as in [8,9], then it can also be implemented by gossip-based protocols as we show below. The resulting algorithm will alternate between full mixture updating using the gossip-based EM algorithm described in the previous section, and component allocation using the gossip-based approach described next.

We show here how each one of the component allocation steps 1–3 of Section 3 can be implemented in a gossip-based manner. We assume that a k-component mixture has already been learned by the gossip-based EM algorithm above, and therefore all nodes know the same set of parameters π_s, m_s, and C_s, for $s = 1, \ldots, k$, that fully characterize $p_k(x)$. Hence each node i can evaluate for instance $p_k(x_i)$ directly, but not $p_k(x_j)$ for $j \neq i$.

1. First all data points should be partitioned to sets A_s according to their 'nearest' component in terms of posterior. For each node i we can directly evaluate $\arg\max_s p(s|x_i)$, so each i knows in which set A_s it belongs, but it does not know the assignment of a node $j \neq i$.
2. Each node $i \in A_s$ creates a local cache which initially contains only i, and which eventually will contain all nodes $j \in A_s$ (a subnetwork). To achieve this, each node i contacts random nodes from $1, \ldots, n$ until it finds a node $j \in A_s$ (note that node j knows whether it is in A_s). The probability of locating such a node j within ρ steps by sampling uniformly at random from all n nodes is approximately $1 - (1 - \pi_s)^\rho$, from which we can bound the number of steps needed so that all nodes know with high probability at least one more node in their partition sets. When all nodes have two entries in their local caches, each node i runs a protocol in which it repeatedly (for a fixed number of steps) contacts a node j uniformly at random from i's local cache and merges j's local cache with its cache. The result is a local cache for each node $i \in A_s$ that contains (almost) all nodes $j \in A_s$.
    (a) After a subnetwork has been formed for every component s, and each node $i \in A_s$ knows almost all other nodes $j \in A_s$, selecting two random points x_s, x'_s from A_s corresponds to selecting two random nodes from each subnetwork. For this, each node $i \in A_s$ chooses two random numbers in $(0, 1)$, and it repeatedly runs the following protocol (the number of steps can be easily bounded):
    – Select a node j from i's cache.
    – Both nodes i and j compute and maintain the max and the min of their numbers, together with the corresponding maximizing/minimizing x-points (which are also propagated by the same protocol).
    At the end of this protocol (which has super-exponential convergence), all nodes in A_s know the (same) two points $x_s \in A_s$ and $x'_s \in A_s$.
    (b) Each node $i \in A_s$ computes its Euclidean distance to both x_s and x'_s, so it knows in which corresponding subset it belongs, and it sets a bit $b_i \in \{0, 1\}$ accordingly.

(c) A candidate vector $[a_f, \theta_f]$, with $\theta_f = [m_f, C_f]$, is implicitly created by setting $q_i(f) = b_i$ (or $q_i(f) = \bar{b}_i$ for the other subset), for each node i in the initialization of the partial EM (see next step).

(d) Compute a good $[a_f, \theta_f]$ with gossip-based partial EM steps. Each node i maintains a local estimate $[a_{if}, \theta_{if}]$ of $[a_f, \theta_f]$ and executes the following protocol:

  i. **Initialization.** Set $q_i(f) = b_i$.

  ii. **M-step.** Initialize i's local estimates by $a_{if} = q_i(f)$, $m_{if} = x_i$, $\tilde{C}_{if} = x_i x_i^\mathsf{T}$. Then, for a fixed number of cycles, contact node j from i's cache, and update both i and j local estimates by:

$$a'_{if} = a'_{jf} = \frac{a_{if} + a_{jf}}{2}, \tag{19}$$

$$m'_{if} = m'_{jf} = \frac{a_{if} m_{if} + a_{jf} m_{jf}}{a_{if} + a_{jf}}, \tag{20}$$

$$\tilde{C}'_{if} = \tilde{C}'_{jf} = \frac{a_{if} \tilde{C}_{if} + a_{jf} \tilde{C}_{jf}}{a_{if} + a_{jf}}. \tag{21}$$

  iii. **E-step.** Using the M-step estimates a_{if}, m_{if}, and $C_{if} = \tilde{C}_{if} - m_{if} m_{if}^\mathsf{T}$, compute the posterior

$$q_i(s) = \frac{a_{if} f(x_i; \theta_{if})}{(1 - a_{if}) p_k(x_i) + a_{if} f(x_i; \theta_{if})}. \tag{22}$$

  Note that node i can compute the quantity $p_k(x_i)$, as we explained above.

  iv. **Loop.** Go to step ii, unless a stopping criterion is satisfied.

3. Note that, contrary to the centralized greedy algorithm of Section 3, here all mk candidate components can be updated in parallel. That is, steps (a)–(d) above can be replicated m times using the same gossip-based protocols. After steps 1 and 2 above, each node $i \in A_s$ knows all m candidate candidates that have been generated and EM-updated from points in A_s. The remaining task is to have all nodes agree which candidate to add to $p_k(x)$. Evaluating $\mathcal{L}_{k+1}$ from (9) for all of them would be expensive, as it would require that all nodes exchange all mk candidates. For practical purposes, one can consider an approximation of $\mathcal{L}_{k+1} = \sum_{i=1}^n \log[(1 - a_f) p_k(x_i) + a_f f(x_i; \theta_f)]$ in which the contribution of a new component f_s to $\mathcal{L}_{k+1}$ is zero for data points outside A_s. This gives:

$$\tilde{\mathcal{L}}_{k+1} = \sum_{i \in A_s} \log[(1 - a_f) p_k(x_i) + a_f f(x_i; \theta_f)]$$

$$+ \sum_{i \notin A_s} \log[(1 - a_f) p_k(x_i)]$$

$$= \mathcal{L}_k + n \log(1 - a_f) + \sum_{i \in A_s} \log\left(\frac{a_f f(x_i; \theta_f)}{(1 - a_f) p_k(x_i)} + 1\right). \tag{23}$$

Note that the term $\mathcal{L}_k$ is independent of $[a_f, \theta_f]$, while the third term is a sum that involves only points from each local subset A_s. Hence the latter can be efficiently computed with the gossip-based averaging protocol of Section 4 where each node i contacts only nodes j from its local cache. The quantity $\tilde{\mathcal{L}}_{k+1}$ is evaluated by each node $i \in A_s$ for all m candidates f_s, and the best candidate is kept. Then all nodes run the max-propagation protocol of step 2(a) above, in order to compute the component with the highest $\tilde{\mathcal{L}}_{k+1}$ among all mk components. Note that the complexity of the above operations is $O(\log n)$ as implied by Theorem 1, as compared to the $O(n)$ complexity of the centralized greedy EM of Section 3.

6 Results

In Fig. 1(left) we demonstrate the performance of the gossip-based averaging protocol as described in [11], for typical averaging tasks involving zero-mean unit-variance data. We plot the variance reduction rate (mean and one standard deviation for 50 runs) as a function of the number of cycles, for $n = 10^5$.

We also ran a preliminary set of experiments comparing the performance of the proposed greedy gossip-based mixture learning algorithm with the algorithm of [9]. We used synthetic datasets consisting of 10^4 points drawn from Gaussian mixtures in which we varied the number of components (5, 10), the dimensionality (1, 2, 5), and the degree of separation c of the components (from 1 to 8; separation c means that for each i and j holds $||m_i - m_j|| \geq c\sqrt{\max\{\text{trace}(C_i), \text{trace}(C_j)\}}$ [18]). The results are summarized in Table 1 where we see that the two methods are virtually identical in terms of log-likelihood of a test set. The gossip-based algorithm however is much faster than the centralized one, as we explained above. A typical run for a mixture of 6 components in shown in Fig. 1(right).

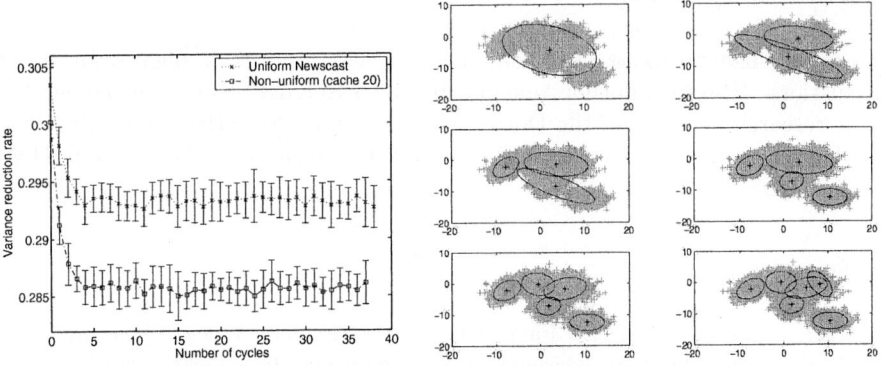

Fig. 1. (Left) Variance reduction rate of gossip-based averaging for $n = 10^5$ data. (Right) A typical run of the proposed greedy gossip-based algorithm for a 6-component mixture with 10^4 points.

Table 1. Proposed algorithm vs. centralized greedy mixture learning, for various mixture configurations

Components	Dimension	Separation	Proposed algorithm	Greedy EM
5	1	3	-3.3280	-3.3280
5	1	8	-3.4294	-3.4294
10	1	3	-3.9905	-3.9905
10	1	8	-3.9374	-3.9374
5	2	1	-5.0590	-5.0494
5	2	4	-5.3331	-5.3322
10	2	1	-5.7179	-5.7132
10	2	4	-5.8104	-5.8080
5	5	1	-10.1581	-10.1367
5	5	4	-10.4246	-10.3940
10	5	1	-10.8107	-10.7939
10	5	4	-11.2110	-11.1913

7 Conclusions

We proposed a decentralized implementation of greedy Gaussian mixture learning using gossip-based protocols. The proposed algorithm applies in cases where a (large) set of data are distributed over the nodes of a network, and where point-to-point communication between two nodes is available. Compared to the gossip-based EM algorithm of [11], the current algorithm does not require (random) initialization of the mixture, but it grows the mixture sequentially by adding components one after the other. Compared to the algorithm of [9] the algorithm is exponentially faster for data that are already distributed over a network, without compromising solution quality.

Acknowledgments

We would like to thank A. Likas, J.J. Verbeek, and S. Voulgaris for useful discussions. The first author is supported by PROGRESS, the embedded systems research program of the Dutch organization for Scientific Research NWO, the Dutch Ministry of Economic Affairs and the Technology Foundation STW, project AES 5414.

References

1. McLachlan, G.J., Peel, D.: Finite Mixture Models. John Wiley & Sons (2000)
2. Moore, A.W.: Very fast EM-based mixture model clustering using multiresolution kd-trees. In: Advances in Neural Information Processing Systems 11, The MIT Press (1999)
3. Tipping, M.E., Bishop, C.M.: Mixtures of probabilistic principal component analysers. Neural Computation **11**(2) (1999) 443–482

4. Titsias, M., Likas, A.: Shared kernel models for class conditional density estimation. IEEE Trans. Neural Networks **12**(5) (2001) 987–997
5. Dempster, A.P., Laird, N.M., Rubin, D.B.: Maximum likelihood from incomplete data via the EM algorithm. J. Roy. Statist. Soc. B **39** (1977) 1–38
6. Meila, M., Heckerman, D.: An experimental comparison of several clustering and initialization methods. In: Proc. 14th Ann. Conf. on Uncertainty in Artificial Intelligence, San Francisco, CA (1998) 386–395
7. Li, J.Q., Barron, A.R.: Mixture density estimation. In: Advances in Neural Information Processing Systems 12, The MIT Press (2000)
8. Vlassis, N., Likas, A.: A greedy EM algorithm for Gaussian mixture learning. Neural Processing Letters **15**(1) (2002) 77–87
9. Verbeek, J.J., Vlassis, N., Kröse, B.: Efficient greedy learning of Gaussian mixture models. Neural Computation **15**(2) (2003) 469–485
10. Ueda, N., Nakano, R., Ghahramani, Z., Hinton, G.E.: SMEM algorithm for mixture models. Neural Computation **12** (2000) 2109–2128
11. Kowalczyk, W., Vlassis, N.: Newscast EM. In Saul, L.K., Weiss, Y., Bottou, L., eds.: Advances in Neural Information Processing Systems 17. MIT Press, Cambridge, MA (2005)
12. Neal, R.M., Hinton, G.E.: A view of the EM algorithm that justifies incremental, sparse, and other variants. In Jordan, M.I., ed.: Learning in graphical models. Kluwer Academic Publishers (1998) 355–368
13. Karp, R., Schindelhauer, C., Shenker, S., Vöcking, B.: Randomized rumour spreading. In: Proc. 41th IEEE Symp. on Foundations of Computer Science, Redondo Beach, CA (2000)
14. Kempe, D., Dobra, A., Gehrke, J.: Gossip-based computation of aggregate information. In: Proc. 44th IEEE Symp. on Foundations of Computer Science, Cambridge, MA (2003)
15. Boyd, S., Ghosh, A., Prabhakar, B., Shah, D.: Gossip algorithms: Design, analysis and applications. In: Proc. IEEE Infocom, Miami, FL (2005)
16. Forman, G., Zhang, B.: Distributed data clustering can be efficient and exact. ACM SIGKDD Explorations **2**(2) (2000) 34–38
17. Nowak, R.D.: Distributed EM algorithms for density estimation and clustering in sensor networks. IEEE Trans. on Signal Processing **51**(8) (2003) 2245–2253
18. Dasgupta, S.: Learning mixtures of Gaussians. In: Proc. IEEE Symp. on Foundations of Computer Science, New York (1999)

A Knowledge Management Architecture for 3D Shapes and Applications

Marios Pitikakis[1,2], Catherine Houstis[1,2], George Vasilakis[1,2], and Manolis Vavalis[2]

[1] University of Thessaly, Department of Computer and Communications Engineering,
37 Glavani Str, 38221 Volos, Greece
[2] Center for Resaerch and Technology Hellas, Informatics and Telematics Institute,
1st Km Thermi-Panorama Road, 57001 Thermi-Thessaloniki, Greece
{pitikak, houstis, vasilak, mav}@iti.gr

Abstract. In this paper, we present a knowledge-based approach to 3D shape management and service composition, exploiting and extending Web Services and Semantic Web technologies. Semantic Web technology fosters semantic interoperability, while Web Services technology is utilized to construct loosely coupled components, which, combined with workflow technology enrich the processing capabilities needed for e-Science and e-Engineering. We propose an open system architecture for the formalization, processing and sharing of shape knowledge in order to efficiently support key activities: from shape creation, retrieval, post-processing and composition, to the categorization and transparent invocation of algorithms, to the automated construction and execution of complex process flows, to capturing metadata for accurate searching of shape and algorithmic resources. Two representative scenarios have been chosen, 3D shape geometry processing and 3D product development, which will demonstrate the potential of the platform in terms of establishing novel, knowledge-based and semantically enriched solutions dealing with the automation of the knowledge lifecycle.

1 Introduction

Knowledge Management (KM) has been instrumental in shifting the focus of attention to the subtle nature and value of knowledge in collaborative business and working environments. The importance of Web Services has been recognized and widely accepted by industry and academic research. The Web is now evolving into a distributed device of computation from a collection of information and computational resources. Furthermore, the need for composing existing Web Services into more complex services is also increasing. The next generation of the Web promises to deliver semantically enriched Web Services by annotating them with large amounts of semantic metadata *glue,* so that they can be utilized by software entities like application agents or other services with minimal or no human intervention at all.

Current Web Service technologies do not deal with the definition of the meaning of services, since they provide only syntactic-level descriptions of their functionalities, making it difficult for requesters and providers to interpret or represent non-trivial statements such as the meaning of inputs and outputs or applicable constraints. In many cases, Web services offer little more than a formally defined invocation interface, with some human oriented metadata that describes what the service does, and which organization developed it.

Several initiatives are taking place in industry and academia (e.g. SWWS [1], WSMF [2], WSMX [3], [4], the Integrated Project DIP [5] and SWSI [6]), which are investigating solutions for the main issues regarding the infrastructure for Semantic Web Services. Although there are various Semantic Web Services technologies proposed, no widely accepted service representation and deployment standard exists. Furthermore, these approaches are mainly business-oriented, focusing on a set of e-commerce requirements for Web Services including trust and security.

Some choreography and orchestration languages have been proposed to workflow and service composition requirements, such as WSFL [7], XLANG [8] and BPEL4WS [9], which are currently being evaluated by various industry standardization bodies. However, such initiatives generally focus on representing service compositions where the flow of the process and the bindings between the services are known a priori. The lack of machine readable semantics necessitates human intervention for automated service discovery and composition within open systems and pre-defined service sequencing and binding is not sufficient, thus obstructing their usage in complex scientific computing contexts.

Applications dealing with shapes and shape processing workflows usually involve very complicated steps, ranging from time consuming numerical computations to the gathering of the necessary resources and/or acquiring the knowledge to perform a specific step. Resources, either shape models or tools, may also come from different organizations and most probably with minimal documentation or described with different terminology. There is a number of issues that, if properly addressed, could significantly optimize such applications: (a) to have an up-to-date overview of the already existing resources, i.e. what has already been done in terms of models, tools, benchmarks, process knowledge, previous product development phases, etc.; (b) to be able to access and share in a simple way the available resources without the need of re-implementing code; (c) to be able to provide task oriented interfaces to users (defining tasks to be performed instead of traditional querying for information) through reasoning on process knowledge; (d) to be able to annotate the available resources and to transfer all or a relevant subset of information throughout the process and the various models it incorporates.

The industry and academic worlds have both proposed solutions that progress along different dimensions regarding Semantic Web Services. Academic research has been mostly concerned with expressiveness of service descriptions, while industry has focused on modularization of service layers, mostly for usability in the short term [10]

Our work intends to merge both streams of progress – expressiveness of service descriptions and modularization of service layers –, with the goal of fostering the next generation of semantically-enabled systems and services. Our aim is to define a methodology for capturing invaluable expert knowledge, implicitly contained in scientific processes, that is mostly undocumented, and therefore hard to be reused or automated. e-Science activities involve constructing complex processing chains to realize series of computations by sharing and reusing distributed and geographically dispersed resources. Similarly, e-Engineering requires the (semi-) automatic construction of processing pipelines to generate the different product model representations that in turn are used to implement downstream digital mock-ups. In the service oriented computing paradigm, this involves discovering relevant, compatible and available services and composing them into workflows.

In this paper, a knowledge-based approach to service composition and management is proposed, based on the combination of Web Services and Semantic Web technologies for constructing semantically enriched, coarse-grained components that can be integrated to form an e-Science and e-Engineering environment for collaborating services. This will provide the unifying infrastructure that is necessary for building, through workflows, more complex, yet more flexible, services, that are self describing, and can be used in diverse, potentially heterogeneous, application environments.

The rest of the paper is structured as follows. In section 2 we start by giving an overview of our approach and a proposed system architecture. In section 3 and 4 we describe key aspects of the envisioned platform. Finally, in section 5 we present two representative scenarios and in section 6 we conclude by discussing the potential impact to the industry and research sectors.

2 Semantically Enriched Web Services

Current Web Service technologies provide a set of "industry-standards" (e.g. UDDI [11], WSDL [12] and SOAP [13]). None of these standards deals with the definition of the meaning of services, since they provide only syntactic-level descriptions of their functionalities (no formal definition of what the syntactic definitions might mean), making it difficult for requesters and providers to interpret or represent non-trivial statements such as the meaning of inputs and outputs or applicable constraints. This limitation may be relaxed by providing a rich set of semantic annotations that augment the service description. In many cases, Web Services offer little more than a formally defined invocation interface, with some human oriented metadata that describe what the service does, and which organization developed it. Furthermore, these protocols do not address the need to coordinate the sequencing and execution of services as part of some larger information processing tasks.

We envisage to provide Web Services which support the user-centered processes of navigation, browsing and searching for shape processing resources. Our goal is to support e-Engineering and e-Science applications focused on the knowledge lifecycle of shapes, such as distributed scientific simulations, geometrical processing etc. The key features of the system are (a) formalization of domain knowledge through ontologies, starting from the basic building blocks (tools, applications, data sets), that will allow a shared understanding of the domain and will make explicit descriptions of generic functionalities; (b) grouping of basic functional elements in order to implement application-specific functionality, which is addressed by the development of workflow management mechanisms; (c) incorporation of semantics into service descriptions and on-the-fly service composition through the use of loosely coupled, reusable software components; (d) knowledge discovery tools to help users assemble relevant knowledge for effective decision-making and semantically enriched utility services, to improve their capability to perceive and utilize system knowledge. Also,

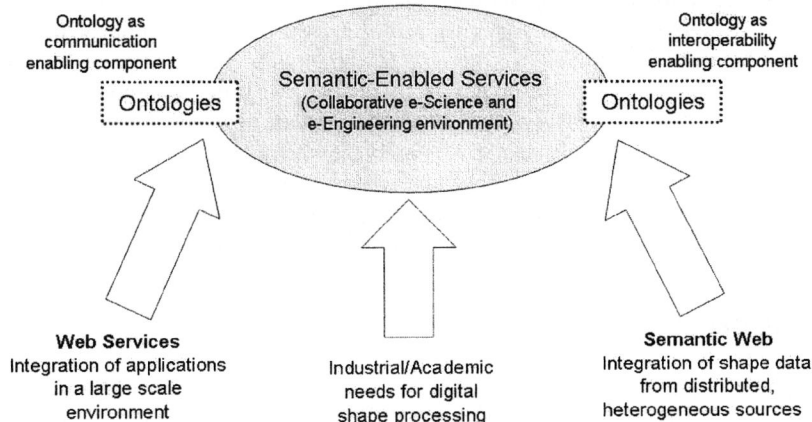

Fig. 1. Semantically enriched Web Services as a collaborative e-Science and e-Engineering environment

create new tools to help the users discover and assemble services into processes for easier and better quality of workflow executions given the increasing number and complexity of Web Services; (e) definition of Semantic Web Services through a higher-level service ontology.

The knowledge management platform will constitute a common semantic-based information avenue where industry and academia meet to address their shape processing needs. The knowledge-based approach that we propose makes extensive use of domain knowledge and combines Web Services and Semantic Web technologies (see Fig. 1).

Furthermore, it addresses two types of integration: vertical and horizontal integration. Vertical integration refers to the specification of the dynamic process of bringing together a set of functional elements, at runtime, in order to implement application-specific functionality. The aim is to provide a well-known functionality as a turn-key solution, thus, focusing on tuning the various parts of the system in order to fulfill the needs of the application in the best possible way.

On the other hand, horizontal integration is about classifying the passive functionality at a semantic level, at design-time, which could be useful for implementing a wide range of applications and/or intermediate system elements. In our case, the focus is on packaging this functionality in components that are well-documented and also easily accessible to third parties that may be interested in them.

The vast majority of shape related applications or processes to date are largely vertically integrated, and without any documentation about their "internal" structure. However, there is little or no horizontal integration. Most applications are built in a custom way, using specially built data processing and information integration elements, some times even special sensor and computational infrastructure. What is probably worse, custom stand-alone development is perpetuated since little or no effort goes into making the individual functional components universally accessible and reusable.

Admittedly, horizontal integration is a hard problem. It requires considerable experience to single out what is generally useful from a large collection of functional elements that may be available (or possible to implement). The context of design and engineering adds even more complexity to this category of integration because it faces the difficulties related to shape processing as well as processing the semantics attached to them. Having said that, this is no reason not to target better solutions, and aggressively focusing on the specific stages of the product development process is a first step to address this very high complexity. We believe that investing effort in achieving horizontal integration will yield substantial benefits.

3 Proposed Architectural Design

Our approach will be based on the semantic service descriptions, i.e. the conceptual links between services and their properties. For example, in the domain of Geometry Processing of 3D shapes, there are many different methods/algorithms and implementations, each of which is tailored to a specific type of problem. In such an algorithm, even a single method could have different configurations of control parameters that may produce very different results. In the area of design and engineering, geometry processing of 3D shapes is combined with complementary semantics attached to them (material, technological data, boundary conditions etc), which further increase the diversity of methods/algorithms and implementations used. Knowledge about the most appropriate method to choose in a particular situation as well as the best possible configuration parameters is an important feature that constitutes expert-knowledge and a vital ingredient of problem-solving success. Any system concerned with the appropriate selection of these methods, therefore, requires access to a detailed representation of the knowledge contingencies relating to problem characteristics with the appropriate selection and configuration of available methods.

Our knowledge-based system for service composition will have the advantage of providing specific advice at multiple levels of granularity during the service composition process. At the highest level, the system can help determine what kind of service is required that includes problem-solving goals and procedural knowledge. Once all the services that can fulfill the required function are discovered, the system can recommend an appropriate service, taking into account both problem characteristics and performance considerations. More specialized, in-depth advice can also be given, for example, on how to initialize and configure the control parameters of a service. Such knowledge is usually only available from experienced users or domain experts.

The notion of a workflow, defined as a partially ordered sequence of tasks or activities, will be used to describe the computational aspect of shape processing scenarios. Taking into account current workflow technology, a framework for the execution of workflows within Semantic Web Services will be implemented. It will be comprised of a description language for the specification of the services, a mechanism to publish and discover the services, and a Web Service container to handle the execution of services and the interaction with the web server. The description language will be an extension to OWL-S [14], while the discovery and publication mechanism will utilize the ontology structure.

Intuitive user interfaces will be built for transparently accessing the information in the system and efficiently managing the available tools and services. They will form the top access layer of the system, providing a way to interact with the multi-faceted ontology structures and the associated metadata, amplifying the user's perspective in the search for appropriate information, the refinement of search criteria, the composition of services and service workflows, etc.

Our objective is to build an open system architecture for formalizing, processing and sharing knowledge about digital shapes and applications, supporting the conceptual search and retrieval of shape content, as well as the definition and execution of Semantic Web Services for 3D shape processing. The backbone of the platform is formed by the knowledge management system and the computational system. A possible architecture is shown in Fig. 2.

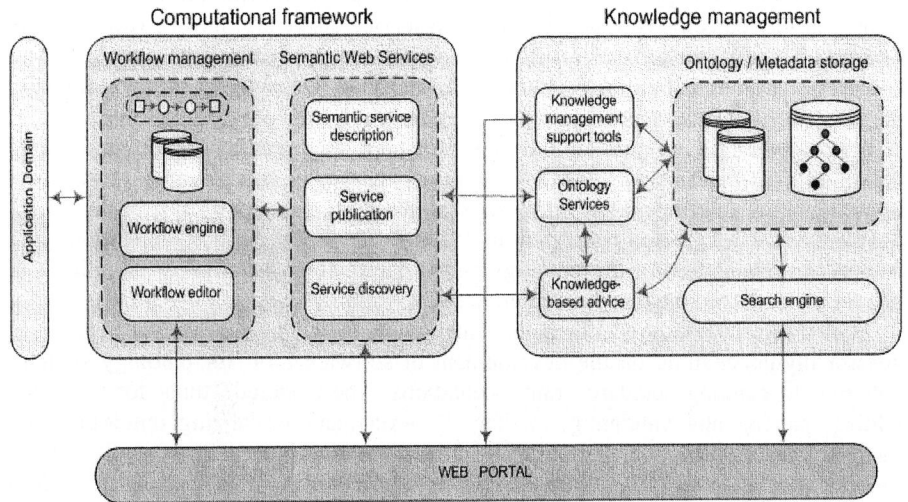

Fig. 2. Overview of the proposed architecture

4 Knowledge Management

Ontologies will be used as a vehicle for representing knowledge and augmenting the various stages of shape processing scenarios with semantics, thus, facilitating knowledge sharing and re-use. This will enable semantic searching for shape resources, as well as providing semantic interoperability between different shape programs and tools. Capturing the concepts involved in shape processing and formally representing them with ontologies will also allow for a coarse-grained specification of the components and/or steps involved, thus making the infrastructure more manageable and more flexible.

The OWL-S language, which has enough expressive power and is well established in the research community, will be used for the description of Semantic Web Services. OWL-S provides an upper ontology for describing not only the input and output but also the properties and capabilities of Web Services. The main contribution of the OWL-S is its service ontology, which builds on the Semantic Web stack of standards.

A service ontology will be designed that will utilize lower level knowledge captured in the application ontologies, and provide a higher level ontology and metadata framework for the composition of Semantic Web Services. The engineering of the service ontology will follow a combination of the OntoKnowledge [11] and OntoClean [12] methodologies, and will form a semantic layer on top of the application layers defined in the scenarios. The OntoClean methodology is one of the most advanced methodologies in creating foundational and higher-level ontologies while OntoKnowledge is probably the most established general methodology for building ontologies. This will help in making the service ontology a reusable, fairly discipline-independent resource.

The service ontology will constitute the core semantic information that will be exploited in service composition and automated service discovery. Its size will therefore be kept relatively small in order to be as manageable and flexible as possible.

Part of ontology evolution is ontology maintenance. When the size of the ontology is increasing, the task of storing, maintaining and re-organizing it to secure successful re-use is challenging. While an ontology evolves it will need restructuring, aligning and other maintenance tasks. Furthermore, the instances of an evolved ontology must be reorganized and transferred into a valid structure. For this purpose a change management methodology and corresponding administrative tools will be defined in order to prevent invalidation of the ontology and to facilitate an automated migration and adaptation of respective metadata reference descriptions.

Tools for efficient knowledge management will also be developed. Our efforts will specifically concentrate on the development of software tools for ontology support, adhering to existing standards implementations. These include tools for: creating, editing, parsing and validating, loading, browsing and visualizing ontologies and metadata descriptions. Furthermore, a unified web interface to these tools will be provided, in order to, along with the knowledge discovery mechanisms, provide a single point of access to ontology management operations.

5 e-Engineering and e-Science Scenarios

For demonstrating the potential of the proposed approach, two specific application domains will be used that involve complex flows of operations. The implementation of these e-Engineering and e-Science workflows will show how existing code can be easily re-used (syntactic interoperability) and shared (semantic interoperability).

5.1 e-Engineering Scenarios

When computer support systems started being used for the different stages of the digital shape life cycle, the standardization focused on specific steps and not on the entire process of computer assisted solutions. The result was an information flow with much need for domain expert intervention. Like in other major industries, aeronautic products development are supported by numerical tools like Digital Mock-Ups

(DMUs) based on Computer Aided Design (CAD) models, physical simulation models (such as Finite Element models) and Virtual Reality (VR) applications, for the construction, capitalization, simulation, evaluation and visualization of alternative design proposals.

A typical design process is marked by several milestones separating the principal stages of the process. Each stage corresponds to a particular type of DMU, adapted to the information available at that stage of the process. In this context, during all the design steps (from specification steps to usage steps) geometric models are considered a priori to be "sharable" objects, and geometric model processing is defined as a "shared" requirement among all the users of geometric models. In fact, various applications (assembly simulation, physical simulation etc) are committed in processes where geometrical data are required as a part of a "geometrical reference model" (which is often the most detailed CAD model existing at the current step of the project) and the shape of a component often needs to be modified through tedious geometric operations, to fit the requirements of the corresponding application.

Each user involved in the design process has experience in the tools and processes to access, use and modify the shape of a component. These processes are not shared at all, or not shared enough, to create a real integration of shape models as specific views of the product.

A better understanding of these needs and a formalization of knowledge, semantic information, tools and processes corresponds to a step forward for subsequent industrial applications. The open system architecture envisaged will formalize, process and share knowledge related to shape models, and is well suited to answer the difficulties and end-user needs.

5.2 e-Science Scenarios

In the last few years, digital shape research relies on huge software packages, each of them developed by research teams over time periods greater than ten years. Therefore it becomes crucially important to share a formal conceptualization of the domain and, on the practical side, to allow the sharing of software packages and the reuse of the huge amount of work it represents. The main building blocks of knowledge in this domain are tools (i.e., pieces of code), applications (e.g., sets of functionalities managed through a graphic user interface) and data sets (i.e., digital shape models). Further elaboration on these basic elements leads to workflows, benchmarking and statistics of use.

However, the scientific community of actors (i.e. researchers, teachers, students etc) does not share the geographic location of the laboratories, the specific expertise, the algorithmic tools to solve similar problems or, when they share the algorithms, they frequently use different implementations. Moreover they are not used to work together (i.e. use the same programs or models) on a regular basis and the terminology they rely on is sometimes not precisely defined and agreed upon.

The first scenario concerns geometry processing and has to do with the implementation of workflows for benchmarking algorithms, which is a typical and important activity involved in the development of any new tool. For example, in a shape-retrieval application context, benchmarking algorithms means to execute the algorithms on different datasets of shape models, in order to highlight advantages and drawbacks of the approach. For obtaining reasonable results, data sets should contain a high number of models, sometimes several thousands. The process is therefore very long and collecting all the results takes a lot of time. The results of the experiments are usually represented as distance matrices or precision-recall diagrams, which need specific tools for their visualization. The interpretation of the experiments is left to the readers and there is no automatic way to document the benchmark suite with shape-specific data (e.g., the presence of form features and how they influence the results) or with algorithm-specific data (e.g., the setting of some parameters). The aim of this scenario is to develop a scientific tool, able to keep track of the experiments results, to visualize them and to share the results.

The second scenario that will be addressed concerns shape matching, which is currently a very active research field. Assessing the similarity among shapes is a highly complex task, which requires knowledge about the context, the types of shapes, their representation and their semantics. Different methods can be used, either based on point-wise measures, or based on structural similarities, or based on functional requirements of the shapes. The choice of one method over another depends on the application context of the similarity results, and the workflow will guide the user through the different choices according to the requirements and knowledge available.

6 Conclusion and Impact to Industry and Research

There is a great challenge in tackling knowledge related to 3D content and associated processing workflows. Information encoded in media representing shapes (e.g., images, videos or 3D models) is implicit, based on data formats that have no relation with data interpretation and offer no grasp to their direct access and easy understanding. In contrast, through semantics, this information can be captured and be made explicit and closer to natural language. It can then be used as a key to access the underlying knowledge.

While there has been quite an effort in the recent past on handling and extracting semantics out of images or videos, only initial steps on taking forward the processing of fully-3D digital content have been made. Product design is the best example of an application domain which requires different representation for shapes at the different stages of the design pipeline.

Academic research in geometry processing is being gradually slowed down by the need to master or integrate many different theoretical and technological aspects. Geometry processing relies on huge software packages, each of them developed by research teams over time periods greater than ten years. It is of paramount importance to enable the sharing and the combination of these software packages and the reuse of the huge amount of work they embody.

Similarly, the product development process involves several steps from the design office, where the shape of components and subsystems are defined, to the so-called downstream engineering stages where these shapes need to suit the requirements of analysis models for design review, simulation of product behavior, ergonomics assessment, marketing presentations etc. This leads to the concept of downstream digital mock-ups requiring the (semi-) automatic construction of workflows to generate them for the previously listed stages of the product development process.

Current approaches in design and engineering are based either on human assessment, which is slow, expensive and does not ensure completeness, or on cheap semi-automatic methods with limited precision and characteristic misinterpretations.

The necessity for human intervention results in poor communication of expert knowledge, traditionally being passed on from domain expert to domain expert, and forfeits the potential for sharing and re-use of this knowledge in a much more efficient way. The problem stems from the fact that currently expert knowledge is implicit, existing only inside the domain experts' minds; and far worse, it is typically lost once they leave the workplace. Until today, most of the *semantic* information needed for such intervention has not been formally described and captured; it simply constitutes knowledge of the domain experts.

Capturing and formally representing expert knowledge will make it machine accessible and processable resulting in automating the process and improving efficiency and manageability. It will also make possible the automation of consistency checking resulting in more reliable software. Furthermore, it will allow for more cost-effective solutions for complex design and engineering processes, thus, achieving higher levels of productivity.

The proposed platform addresses these issues by dealing with expert knowledge and tools in the product development process, using Semantic Web Services to represent the different stages. These services can in turn be chained to form corresponding workflows. Creating a platform that integrates, combines, adapts, and enhances existing tools with semantic information to assist in efficient discovery and interoperability.

The architecture presented in this paper offers the potential to move beyond current approaches, applying Knowledge Management best practices into the knowledge lifecycle of digital shapes and coupling them with other major IT advances.The leveraging, integration and application of Knowledge Management technologies on a large scale is a critical missing factor in Product Design and Engineering and offers a new cost-effective paradigm.

Acknowledgements

The authors would like to thank the AIM@SHAPE Network of Excellence Consortium and especially CNR-IMATI, Fraunhofer-IGD, SINTEF and INPG for their valuable contributions. Also, the authors would like to thank EADS Corporate Research Center France.

References

1. Bussler, C., Fensel, D., Maedche, A.: A conceptual architecture for semantic web enabled web services, ACM SIGMOD Record, v.31 n.4 (2002)
2. Fensel, D., Bussler, C.: The Web Service Modeling Framework WSMF, Electronic Commerce: Research and Applications, 1 (2002) 113-137
3. Moran, M., Mocan, A.: WSMX - An Architecture for Semantic Web Service Discovery, Mediation and Invocation. Proceedings of the 3rd International Semantic Web Conference (ISWC2004), Hiroshima, Japan (2004)

4. Moran, M., Zaremba, M., Mocan, A., Bussler, C.: Using WSMX to bind Requester & Provider at Runtime when Executing Semantic Web Services. Proceedings of the 1st WSMO Implementation Workshop, Frankfurt, Germany (2004)
5. DIP (Data, Information and Process Integration with Semantic Web Services), http://dip.semanticweb.org
6. SWSI (Semantic Web Services Initiative), http://www.swsi.org
7. WSFL 1.0, http://www-3.ibm.com/software/solutions/webservices/pdf/WSFL.pdf
8. XLANG, http://www.gotdotnet.com/team/xml_wsspecs/xlang-c/default.htm
9. Curbera, F., Goland, Y., Klein, J., Leymann, F., Roller, D., Thatte, S. and Weerawarana, S.: Business Process Execution Language for Web Services, Version 1.0. http://www-106.ibm.com/developerworks/webservices/ library/ws-bpel/
10. Sollazzo, T., Handschuh, S., Staab, S., Frank, M.: Semantic Web Service Architecture - Evolving Web Service Standards toward the Semantic Web. Proceedings of the 15th Interntional FLAIRS Conference. Pensacola, Florida, May 16-18. AAAI Press (2002)
11. UDDI. The UDDI technical white paper. 2000. http://www.uddi.org/
12. Chinnici, R., Gudgin, M., Moreau, J. and Weerawarana, S.: Web Services Description Language (WSDL) 1.2, W3C Working Draft. http://www.w3.org/TR/wsdl12/ (2002)
13. SOAP 1.2 Working draft, http://www.w3c.org/TR/2001/WD-soap12-part0-20011217/
14. OWL-S Coalition: OWL-S 1.0 Release. http://www.daml.org/services/owl-s/1.0/ (2003)
15. OntoKnowledge, http://www.ontoknowledge.org/
16. Guarino, N., Welty, C.: Evaluating ontological decisions with OntoClean. Communications of the ACM, v.45 n.2. (2002)

Using Fuzzy Cognitive Maps as a Decision Support System for Political Decisions: The Case of Turkey's Integration into the European Union

Athanasios K. Tsadiras[1] and Ilias Kouskouvelis[2]

[1]Department of Informatics,
Technological Educational Institute of Thessaloniki,
P.O.BOX 14561, 54101 Thessaloniki, Greece
tsadiras@it.teithe.gr
[2] Department of International & European, Economic & Political Studies,
University of Macedonia,
Egnatias 156, P.O.Box 1591Thessaloniki 54006, Greece
iliaskou@uom.gr

Abstract. In this paper we use Fuzzy Cognitive Maps (FCMs), a well-established Artificial Intelligence technique that incorporates ideas from Artificial Neural Networks and Fuzzy Logic, to create a dynamic model of Turkey's course towards its integration into the European Union, after the decision of December 18, 2004, according to which in October 3, 2005, Turkey will start negotiating its access to the European Union. FCMs create models as collections of concepts and the various causal relations that exist between these concepts. The decision capabilities of the FCM structure are examined and presented using a model developed based on the beliefs of a domain expert in the political situation in Turkey & European Union. The model is examined both statically using graph theory techniques and dynamically through simulations. Scenarios are introduced and predictions are made by viewing dynamically the consequences of the corresponding actions.

1 Introduction to Fuzzy Cognitive Maps

Decision Support Systems are defined as "interactive computer-based systems, which help decision makers utilize data and models to solve unstructured problems" [1]. Unstructured problems are defined as "fuzzy, complex problems for which there are no cut-and-dried solutions" [2]. In International Relations theory, negotiations and crisis management [3] are consider unstructured or semistructured areas where Decision Support Systems can assist by providing new potentials to the decision making process.

Cognitive Map (CM) models were introduced by Axelrod in the late 1970s and were widely used for Political Analysis and Decision Making in International Relations [4]. The structural and decision potentials of such models were studied and the explanation and prediction capabilities were identified [4], [5]. The introduction of Fuzzy Logic gave new representing capabilities to CMs and led to the development of Fuzzy Cognitive Maps (FCM) by Kosko in the late 1980s [6], [7].

FCMs models are created as collections of concepts and the various causal relationships that exist between these concepts. The concepts are represented by nodes and the causal relationships by directed arcs between the nodes. Each arc is accompanied by a weight that defines the degree of the causal relation between the two nodes. The sign of the weight determines the positive or negative causal relation between the two concepts-nodes.

Certainty Neuron Fuzzy Cognitive Maps (CNFCMs) were introduced in 1997 [8], giving additional fuzzification to the FCM structure. CNFCMs allow the activation of each concept's activation to be a number from the whole interval [-1,1] (or, as in our case, in the interval [0,1]) allowing the representation of both the sign of the activation and its degree, while on the contrary, FCM allows each concept to have a binary value (-1 or 1), representing a negative or a positive activation and not the degree of the activation. Furthermore in CNFCM, the aggregation of the influences that each concept receives from other concepts is handled by function f_M () that was used in MYCIN Expert System [9], [10] for certainty factors' handling. The dynamical behavior and the characteristics of this function are studied in [11]. The artificial neurons that use this function as their threshold function are defined as Certainty Neurons [12].

2 Development of FCM Model for the Case of Turkey's Integration into European Union

The reliability of an FCM model depends on whether its construction method follows rules that ensure its reliability. Since the model is created by the personal opinions and points of view of the expert(s) on the specific topic, the reliability of the model is heavily depended on the level of expertise of the domain expert(s). There are two main methods for the construction of FCMs :
a) The Documentary Coding method [13], which involves the systematic encoding of documents that present the assertions of a specific person for the specific topic.
b) The Questionnaire method [14], [15], which involves interviews and filling in of questionnaires by domain experts.

In our case we used the second method, discussing, interviewing, analysing and also supplying with questionnaires a domain expert. The domain expert (a faculty member of the Department of International & European, Economic & Political Studies of the University of Macedonia) provided the international context, the actors and factors, the possible alternative scenarios, as well as the analysis of the findings.

2.1 The Case of Turkey's Integration into the European Union: Important Actors/Concepts

After the European Union's European Council at Helsinki, the speed of Turkey's course towards its integration into the Union has been increased. This course led to the decision of December 18, 2004, according to which in October 3, 2005, Turkey will start negotiating its access to the EU. This was not an easy decision to make and, yet, it is just the beginning of another road for Turkey and definitely not the end, as provided by the decision itself. The decision was not easy to make given the large variety of the EU's member states interests, the opposition by large parts of their public opinion, the moderate progress of Turkey in fulfilling the EU's enlargement criteria and the consistent support of Turkey from the United States government. And the decision to start negotiations is not the end, because the final integration of Turkey depends on a large variety of factors and actors.

Through extensive interviews with the domain expert, the actors involved and considered important for the case, were identified as the following: The United States of America, The European Union, Greece, Cyprus, The European Union public opinion, The Turkish Government, The Turkish Armed Forces, The Turkish public opinion.

It is a common place that the European future of Turkey depends not only on the willingness or the wishes of the various actors, but to a great extent from the fulfillment of the EU criteria. Fulfilling the criteria will be translated, perceived and advertised as a positive course for all those who more or less sincerely support Turkey's European drive; the opposite will happen for those opposing Turkey's entry into the Union. As indicators of a Turkish successful drive, the domain expert suggested five areas: Economy, Human Rights, The Turkish Armed Forces, The Greek – Turkish Relations, The Cyprus invasion problem.

According the above, the list of the concepts that were identified as playing important role in our case and should appear in the FCM model, are the following:

Concept 1. USA Position	Concept 10. Improvement of Human Rights in Turkey
Concept 2. European Union Position	
Concept 3. Greek Position	Concept 11. Improvement of the Democratic Role of Turkish Army
Concept 4. Cypriot Position	
Concept 5. European Public Opinion	
Concept 6. Turkish Government Position	Concept 12. Improvement to Greek - Turkish Relations
Concept 7. Turkish Army Position	
Concept 8. Turkish Public Opinion	Concept 13. Improvement to Cypriot - Turkish Relations
Concept 9. Improvement of Turkish Economy	

2.2 Identification of Causal Relations Between Actors/Concepts

A number of questionnaires were presented to the domain expert, in order to define the causal relationships that exist between the identified concepts of the case. Moreover, in these relationships, the degree to which a concept influences each other concept was extracted. The format of the questionnaire is given in figure 1. The expert had to fill in with + or – whether he believed that there is a positive or negative causal relationship between the concepts. The degree of these causal relationships was captured by allowing the expert to fill in the sign in one of the fields "Very Big",

What is influence of the USA position on this case, will influence and to what degree to the following	Very Big	Big	Moderate	Small	Very Small	No
The European Union Position						
European Public Opinion Position						
Turkish Army Position						
......						

Numerical weights	1	0.9	0.8	0.7	0.6	0.5	0.4	0.3	0.2	0.1	0

Fig. 1. Part of questionnaire concerning the case of Turkey's Integration into European Union

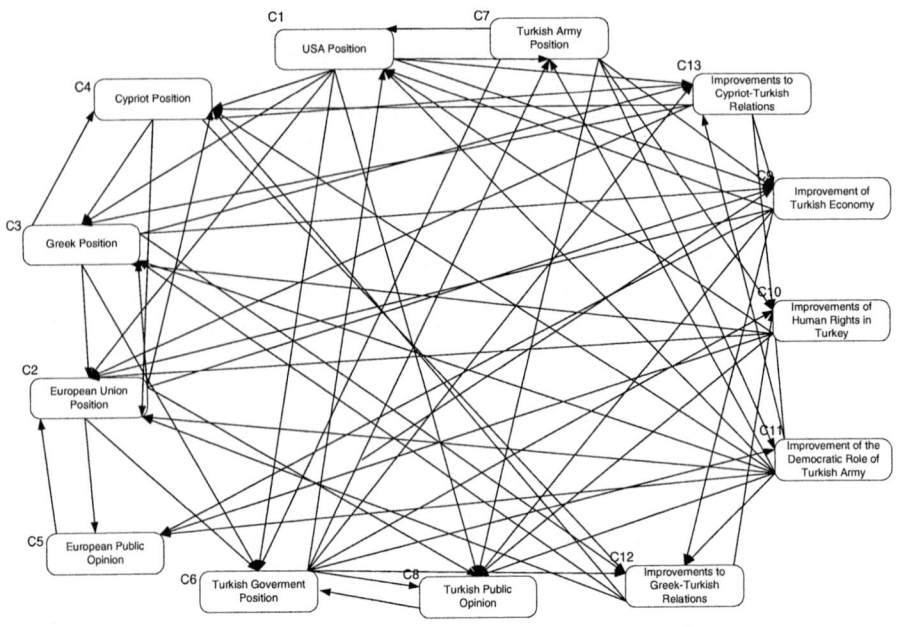

Fig. 2. FCM model for the case of Turkey's Integration into European Union

"Big", "Moderate", "Small", "Very Small". These linguistic values could be transformed into numerical weights by assigning weights from the interval [0,1] according to the way that is shown in figure 1. To justify his opinion, additional questionnaires were presented to the expert.

After studying the questionnaires and taking the weights identified by expert, the model presented in figure 2 was developed. In figure 2, only the signs of the arcs-causal relationships are shown. The weights of the arcs are given in Appendix A.

3 Static Analysis

The static analysis of the model is based on studying the characteristics of the weighted directed graph that represent the model, using graph theory techniques. The first way to examine statically the model's graph is by calculating its density [5]. The density d is defined as

$$d = \frac{m}{n(n-1)}$$

where m is the number of arcs in the model and n is the number of concepts of the model. Product $n(n-1)$ is equal to the maximum number of arcs that a graph of n nodes can have. Density gives an indication of the complexity of the model. High density indicates increased complexity in the model and respectively to the problem that the model represents. Typical values of density are in the interval [0.05, 0.3]. The density of the graph in figure 2 is 69/(13x12) = 0.44 which is extremely high, and gives an indication of the great complexity of the problem that it represents.

Graph Theory provides also the notion of node's importance [4] that assists the static analysis of FCM models. Node's importance (or cognitive/conceptual centrality as it is called by others [16], [17]) gives an indication of the importance that the node/concept have for the model, by measuring the degree to which the node is central to the graph. The importance of a node i is evaluated as

$$imp(i) = in(i) + out(i)$$

where in(i) is the number of incoming arcs of node i and out(i) is the number of outcoming arcs of node i. According to this definition, the importance of the nodes of the FCM model for "Turkey's Integration into European Union" is given in Table 1.

Table 1. Importance of nodes

	C1	C2	C3	C4	C5	C6	C7	C8	C9	C10	C11	C12	C13
In	8	6	6	4	1	8	6	1	4	5	10	4	6
Out	5	9	7	6	4	5	3	7	6	5	2	5	5
Imp	13	15	13	10	5	13	9	8	10	10	12	9	11

It is found that the most central/important concepts were C2: "European Union Position", C1: "USA Position", C6: "Turkish Government Position" and C3: "Greek Position".

4 Dynamical Behavior of CNFCM Model

The model of the case of "Turkey's Integration into European Union" was simulated using the CNFCM technique that was mentioned in section 1. Various scenarios can be imposed, after inserting to the CNFCM simulation program we developed, the 13 concepts of the model and the causal relationships that exist among these concepts. The "what-if" scenarios that were tested were chosen in order to show the decision making capabilities of the method presented to the paper. The scenarios are shown in Table 2.

Table 2. "What –if" Scenarios

Scenario	Description
#1	All concepts are free to interact. Activation of C1: "USA Position" is initialized to +0.7 and C6: "Turkish Government Position" is initialized to +0.9
#2	All concepts are free to interact. Activation of C1: "USA Position" is initialized to -0.5 and C6: "Turkish Government Position" is initialized to -0.5 (moderate negative)
#3	Activation of C1: "USA Position" is set & kept to -0.4. All other concepts are free to interact.
#4	Activation of C1: "USA Position" is set & kept to -0.7. All other concepts are free to interact.
#5	Activation of C3: "Greek Position" is set & kept to -0.8. All other concepts are free to interact.

4.1 Scenarios with All Concepts to Be Free to Interact

In the first two scenarios (#1 & #2), all 13 concepts of the model are free to interact. In scenario #1, the initial activations of the 13 concepts are those imposed by the domain expert, representing the activations of the current state of our case. The activation of C1: "USA Position" is initialized to +0.7 and C6: "Turkish Government Position" is initialized to +0.9, representing the strong willingness of USA & Turkish Government in the course of Turkey's Integration into European Union. The system is set free to evolve dynamically. The dynamical behavior of the model is shown in figure 3 where we can see that reaches equilibrium at a fixed point.

The equilibrium point is interpreted in the following way: The strong willingness of the Turkish Government and the USA towards Turkey's Integration into European Union, influences a lot all other concepts of the system, leading gradually to high

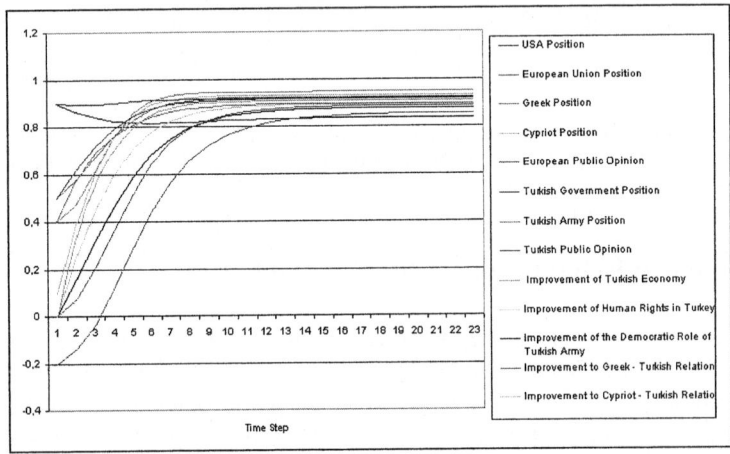

Fig. 3. Simulation of CNFCM Model of "the case of Turkey's Integration into European Union". Transition phase to equilibrium for scenario #1.

positive activation of all concepts, meaning that the road of Turkey's Integration into European Union is open, according the current political state.

Applying other scenarios to the system, with the activation of either of C1: "USA Position" or C6: "Turkish Government Position" to be initialized to a positive value and the other to a negative value, show similar dynamical behaviour (equilibrium to high positive values for the concepts). This means that even if one of these concepts ("USA Position" or "Turkish Government Position") changed to a negative position towards the Turkey's integration into European Union, the other is strong enough, together with the other concepts of the model, to lead the first one from a negative position to a positive position towards Turkey's integration into European Union and so finally Turkey's integration will be successful.

In scenario #2, both concepts "Turkish Government Position" and "USA Position" are initialized to a moderate negative value (-0.5 and -0.5). This means that they both do not believe in Turkey's Integration into European Union. The dynamical behavior of the model for this scenario is shown in figure 4 where we can see that reaches equilibrium at a high negative fixed point position.

This equilibrium point is interpreted in the following way: The negative position of the Turkish government and the USA towards Turkey's integration into the European Union, influences crucially all other concepts of the system, leading gradually to high negative activation of all concepts. The position of all factors becomes negative. It can be concluded that in this case, Turkey did not manage to integrate into the EU.

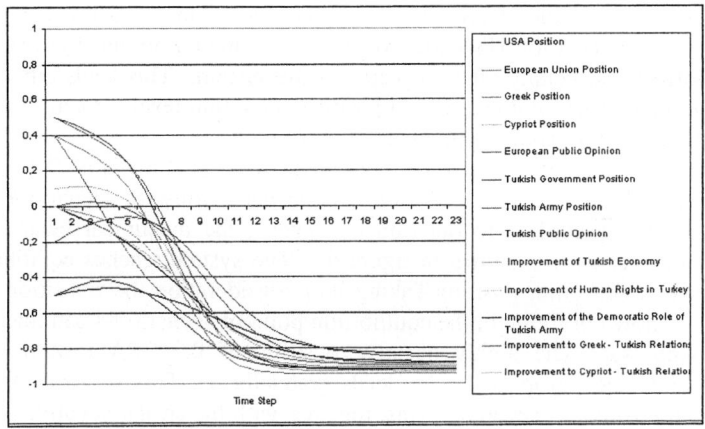

Fig. 4. Simulation of CNFCM Model of "the case of Turkey's integration into European Union". Transition phase to equilibrium for scenario #2.

4.2 Scenarios with Selected Concepts to Be Set Steady to a Level

In the following two scenarios, concept "USA position" will be set steady to a level and will not change even if affected by other concepts (this is the case where USA government is strongly determined to follow its own position and not be influenced

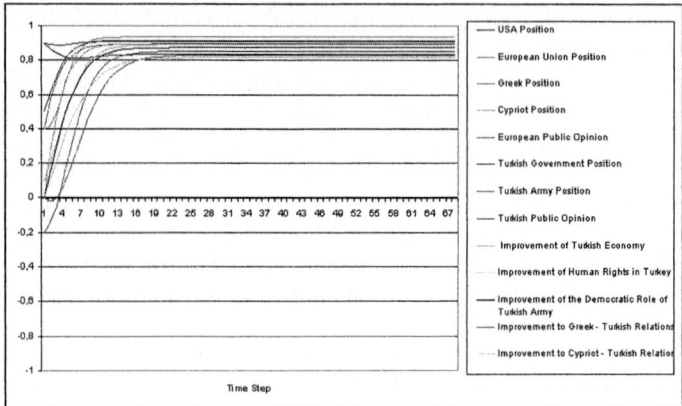

Fig. 5. Simulation of CNFCM Model of "the case of Turkey's Integration into European Union". Transition phase to equilibrium for scenario #3 (USA Position" is set to -0.4).

by other factors). In scenario #3 the USA position is moderate negative (-0.4). The initial activations of other concepts are those of scenario #1 (current political position according to our domain expert). The dynamical behavior of the model for this scenario is shown in figure 5 where we can see that reaches equilibrium at a high positive fixed point position.

The equilibrium point of scenario #3 is interpreted in the following way: The moderate negative position USA towards Turkey's integration into European Union, does not influence crucially other concepts of the system. This leads other concepts to carry on their transition towards to a positive activation level. It can be concluded that in this case Turkey manage to integrate into Europe.

In scenario #4, the USA position is highly negative (-0.7, towards -0.4 of scenario #3). Having the initial activations of other concepts as those of scenario #1 (current political position according to our domain expert), the dynamical behavior of the model for this scenario is shown in figure 6. The system reaches equilibrium at a high negative fixed point position. Taking into consideration the transition phase of this case, as shown in figure 6, the equilibrium point of scenario #4 can interpreted in the following way: The highly negative position of the USA towards Turkey's integration into the European Union, leads gradually the Turkish Army Position to change from positive to negative. This, together with the strong negative position of the USA, leads also to the change a) first of the position of Turkish Government, and then b) of the position of Turkish Public Opinion (both from positive to negative). After these, all concepts move towards high negative positions. It can be concluded that in this scenario Turkey does not manage to integrate into the European Union (even if its initial will is to integrate into European Union).

In the final scenario, concept "Greek Position" will be set steady to a level and will not change even if affected by other concepts (this is the case where the Greek Government is strongly determined to follow its own position no matter the influences of other factors). So, in scenario #5 the Greek Government is strongly

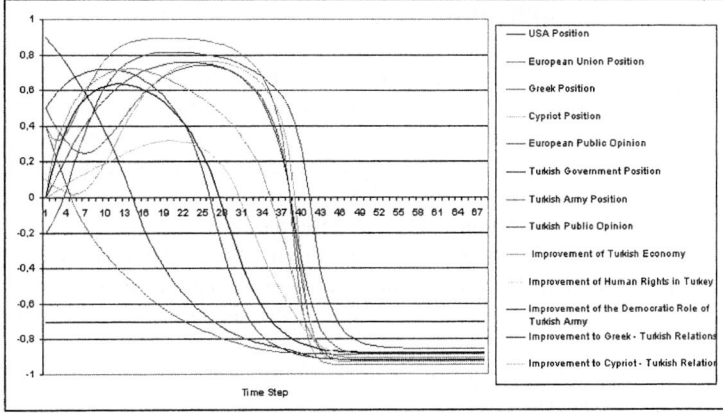

Fig. 6. Simulation of CNFCM Model of "the case of Turkey's integration into the European Union". Transition phase to equilibrium for scenario #4 ("USA Position" is set to -0.7).

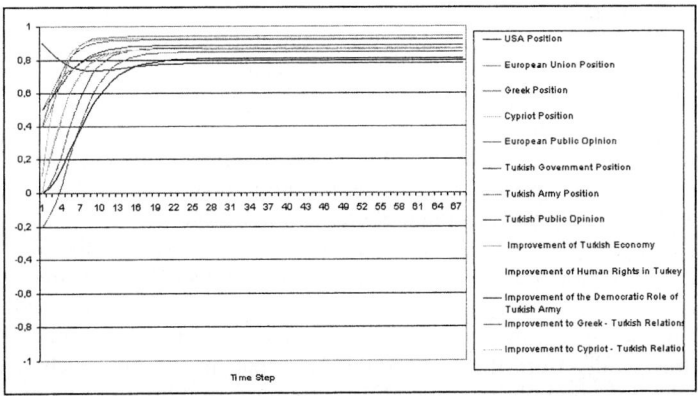

Fig. 7. Simulation of CNFCM Model of "the case of Turkey's Integration into European Union". Transition phase to equilibrium for scenario #5 ("Greek Government Position" is set to -0.8).

negative towards Turkey's integration into European Union (its activation set to -0.8), without exercising its veto power. The initial activations of other concepts are those of scenario #1 (current political position according to our domain expert). The dynamical behavior of the model for this scenario is shown in figure 7. It can be seen that system reaches equilibrium at a high positive fixed point position.

Equilibrium point of scenario #5 can be interpreted in the following way: The initial positive position of the other concepts of the model, leads the system to a positive fixed point, even with Greek Government to have an opposite opinion. It can be concluded that Turkey manages to integrate into Europe, even with Greek Government to have a steady opposite position.

5 Summary – Conclusions

Using the FCM method, a model was created for the case of Turkey's integration into European Union, based on the opinion of a domain expert. The model was first examined statically. The density of model's graph was calculated and found extremely high, indicating the complexity of the case. The conceptual centralities of the concepts that exist in the model were also calculated and the most central, and consequently the most important concepts of the model were found.

The model was then simulated in a computer and it was predicted that
a) According to the current political state and if this situation is maintained (rebus sic standibus), Turkey can successfully move towards its integration into European Union.
b) An occasional/initial change of position of the Turkish government (towards a negative position) can lead to the failure of the Turkey's integration into the European Union, only if this is accompanied by a corresponding negative position of the USA on the matter.
c) A determined moderate negative position of USA on Turkey's integration into European Union cannot stop Turkey's successful move towards its integration into European Union.
d) On the contrary, a determined highly negative position of the USA on Turkey's integration into the European Union can stop Turkey's successful move towards its integration into the Union.
e) A determined highly negative position of Greece on Turkey's integration into European Union (without the exercise of the veto power and not accompanied with changes of other actors towards a negative position) cannot stop Turkey's successful move towards its integration into the Union.

Through the above static and dynamic studies of the FCM model, the CNFCM system was identified as an important and useful Decision Support System, since it is capable to provide support to decision makers, by making predictions on various scenarios that are imposed to the model that CNFCM creates. Conclusions on these scenarios are not drawn only from the final equilibrium that the system reaches, but also by studying the transition phase of the FCM system to equilibrium. The decision maker can test his decisions, by applying them to the CNFCM system and see the consequences to the other concepts of the model.

References

[1] G. M. Gorry and M. S. S. Morton, "A Framework for Management Information Systems", *Sloan Management Review*, 1971.
[2] Turban and J. E. Aronson, *Decision Support Systems and Intelligent Systems* (5th edition): Prentice Hall, 1998.
[3] I. Kouskouvelis, *Decision Making, Crisis, Negotiation* (in Greek): Papazisis, 1997.
[4] R. Axelrod, *Structure of Decision. The Cognitive Maps of Political Elites*. Princeton, New Jersey: Princeton University Press, 1976.
[5] J.A. Hart, "Cognitive Maps of Three Latin American Policy Makers," *World Politics*, vol. 30, pp. 115-140, 1977.
[6] B. Kosko, "Fuzzy Cognitive Maps," *International Journal of Man-Machine Studies*, vol. 24, pp. 65-75, 1986.

[7] B. Kosko, *Fuzzy Thinking. The New Science of Fuzzy Logic*. London: Harper Collins, 1994.
[8] A. K. Tsadiras and K. G. Margaritis, "Cognitive Mapping and the Certainty Neuron Fuzzy Cognitive Maps," *Information Sciences*, vol. 101, pp. 109-130, 1997.
[9] E. H. Shortliffe, *Computer-based Medical Consultations: MYCIN*. Elsevier, 1976.
[10] B. G. Buchanan and E. H. Shortliffe, *Rule-Based Expert Systems. The MYCIN Experiments of the Stanford Heuristic Programming Project*. Reading, MA: Addison-Wesley, 1984.
[11] A. K. Tsadiras and K. G. Margaritis, "The MYCIN Certainty Factor Handling Function as Uninorm Operator and its Use as Threshold Function in Artificial Neurons," *Fussy Set and Systems*, vol. 93, pp. 263-274, 1998.
[12] A. K. Tsadiras and K. G. Margaritis, "Using Certainty Neurons in Fuzzy Cognitive Maps," *Neural Network World*, vol. 6, pp. 719-728, 1996.
[13] M. T. Wrightson, "The Documentary Coding Method," in *Structure of Decision. The Cognitive Maps of Political Elites*, R. Axelrod, Ed. Princeton, New Jersey: Princeton University Press, 1976, pp. 291-332.
[14] F. R. Roberts, "Strategy for The Energy Crisis: The Case of Commuter Transportation Policy," in *Structure of Decision. The Cognitive Maps of Political Elites*, R. Axelrod, Ed. Princeton, New Jersey: Princeton University Press, 1976, pp. 142-179.
[15] F. S. Roberts, "Weighted Digraph Models for the Assessment of Energy Use and Air Pollution in Transportation Systems," *Environment and Planning*, vol. 7, pp. 703-724, 1975.
[16] K. Nakamura, S. Iwai, and T. Sawaragi, "Decision Support Using Causation Knowledge Base," *IEEE Transactions on Systems, Man, and Cybernetics*, vol. 12, pp. 765-777, 1982.
[17] J. D. Ford and W. H. Hegarty, "Decision Makers' Beliefs about the Causes and Effects of Structure: An Exploratory Study," *Academy of Management Journal*, vol. 27, pp. 271-291, 1984.

Appendix A – Weights of Causal Relationships between Concepts

Concepts / Weights	C1	C2	C3	C4	C5	C6	C7	C8	C9	C10	C11	C12	C13
C1: USA Position	0	0	0	0	0	0,2	0,2	0	0,1	0,2	0,1	0	0
C2: European Union Position	0,4	0	0,2	0,3	0,3	0	0	0	0,4	0,5	0,4	0,1	0,2
C3: Greek Position	0,5	0,2	0	0,3	0	0	0	0	0	0,1	0,2	0,2	0,4
C4: Cypriot Position	0,6	0,4	0,4	0	0	0	0	0	0	0	0,2	0,1	0,4
C5: European Public Opinion	0	0,4	0	0	0	0	0	0	0,1	0,2	0,2	0	0
C6: Turkish Government Position	0,7	0,3	0,1	0	0	0	0,5	0,2	0	0	0	0	0
C7: Turkish Army Position	0,8	0	0	0	0	0,2	0	0	0	0	0,4	0	0
C8: Turkish Public Opinion	0,2	0,2	0	0	0	0,4	0,4	0	0,1	0,2	0,2	0	0
C9: Improvement of Turkish Economy	0,2	0,5	0,1	0	0	0,5	0,1	0	0	0	0	0	0,1
C10: Improvement of Human Rights in Turkey	0	0	0	0	0	0,4	0,2	0	0	0	0,2	0,1	0,2
C11: Improvement of the Democratic Role of Turkish Army	0	0	0	0	0	0,1	0,3	0	0	0	0	0	0
C12: Improvement to Greek - Turkish Relations	0	0	0,2	0,1	0	0,1	0	0	0	0	0,3	0	0,5
C13: Improvement to Cypriot - Turkish Relations	0,4	0	0,3	0,1	0	0,2	0	0	0	0	0,3	0	0

Developing a Robust Part-of-Speech Tagger for Biomedical Text

Yoshimasa Tsuruoka[1,2], Yuka Tateishi[1,2], Jin-Dong Kim[1,2], Tomoko Ohta[1,2], John McNaught[3,5], Sophia Ananiadou[4,5], and Jun'ichi Tsujii[2,3]

[1] CREST, JST (Japan Science and Technology Agency),
Honcho 4-1-8, Kawaguchi-shi, Saitama 332-0012, Japan
{tsuruoka, yucca, jdkim, okap}@is.s.u-tokyo.ac.jp
[2] University of Tokyo,
7-3-1 Hongo, Bunkyo-ku, Tokyo 113-0033, Japan
tsujii@is.s.u-tokyo.ac.jp
[3] School of Informatics, University of Manchester,
P.O.Box 88, Sackville St, Manchester M60 1QD, UK
[4] School of Computing, Science and Engineering, Salford University,
Salford, Greater Manchester M5 4WT, UK
S.Ananiadou@salford.ac.uk
[5] The National Centre for Text Mining,
P.O.Box 88, Sackville St, Manchester M60 1QD, UK

Abstract. This paper presents a part-of-speech tagger which is specifically tuned for biomedical text. We have built the tagger with maximum entropy modeling and a state-of-the-art tagging algorithm. The tagger was trained on a corpus containing newspaper articles and biomedical documents so that it would work well on various types of biomedical text. Experimental results on the Wall Street Journal corpus, the GENIA corpus, and the PennBioIE corpus revealed that adding training data from a different domain does not hurt the performance of a tagger, and our tagger exhibits very good precision (97% to 98%) on all these corpora. We also evaluated the robustness of the tagger using recent MEDLINE articles.

1 Introduction

Since a huge amount of biomedical knowledge is described in the literature, automatic information extraction from biomedical documents is increasingly important for many researchers in this domain.

For extracting information from text, many natural language processing (NLP) techniques can be employed. For example, a simple approach to extracting information about protein-protein interactions would involve scanning the text for particular verbs and neighboring noun phrases by applying some linguistic patterns on words and their part-of-speech (POS) tags. A more sophisticated way would be to use parsers to deeply analyze the syntactic and semantic relations among the entities in the sentences.

In order to carry out noise-free information extraction, the very basic step in natural language processing of POS tagging must be performed with high precision. The precision of POS tagging not only directly affects the performance of pattern-based approaches but also influences the accuracy of parsing which in general uses the POS tags on the words as part of the input [1,2].

For documents like newspaper articles, there are a number of publicly available NLP tools including POS taggers, chunkers (shallow parsers), and syntactic parsers. However, the problem for researchers working on biomedical information extraction is that such tools do not necessarily work well on biomedical documents because the characteristics of biomedical text are considerably different from those of newspaper articles, which are often used as the training data for NLP tools [3,4] . Table 1 lists some examples of tagging errors made by the TnT tagger [5], a popular HMM-based POS tagger, which is trained on the Wall Street Journal corpus, when it is applied to biomedical text.

Recently, two large biomedical corpora that are annotated with POS tags have become publicly available: the GENIA corpus [6] and the PennBioIE corpus [3]. In building these corpora, the developers used a POS tagger to reduce manual annotation effort and reported that they could achieve better performance than with a standard tagger by using an already annotated portion of their corpus for training the tagger. Their observation clearly suggests that we might be able to build a good POS tagger for biomedical documents if we use their corpora as the training data.

However, since each corpus consists of text extracted from a particular domain (e.g. transcription factors for the GENIA corpus) and does not cover the entire characteristics of biomedical text, there are still remaining issues to be addressed: (1) Which corpus should we use for training? (2) Should we use a single corpus or combine two corpora? (3) Does the combination of corpora from different domains have a bad effect on trained tagger performance? if so, how much?

The purpose of this paper is to clarify these issues and develop a reliable POS tagger that can be used as a fundamental tool for biomedical text mining. In this paper we evaluate the performance of a part-of-speech tagger by using different combinations of corpora as the training data, and show how the domain of the training corpus affects the tagging performance. We also investigate the robustness of the trained taggers using recent MEDLINE articles.

2 POS Tagging Algorithm

As our POS tagging algorithm, we adopt a method based on a Cyclic Dependency Network proposed by Toutanova et al. [8], which is currently one of the best algorithms for English POS tagging. Unlike the popular Maximum Entropy Markov Modeling (MEMM) approach, this method can incorporate features about the tags on both sides of the classification target. Toutanova et al. achieved an accuracy of 97.24% on sections 22-24 in the Wall Street Journal corpus, using sections 0-18 for training. On the same sets for training and testing, Gimenez

Table 1. Examples of tagging errors made by an HMM-based tagger trained on the Wall Street Journal corpus. The tagset includes NN (Noun, singular or mass), JJ (Adjective), VBP (Verb, non-3rd ps. sing. present), VBG (Verb, gerund/present participle), JJR (Adjective, comparative), RBR (Adverb, comaparative), IN (Preposition/subordinating conjunction), and FW (Foreign word). For the complete information about the tagset, see [7].

Tagging Errors	Correct Tagging
... and membrane potential after mitogen binding. CC NN NN IN NN JJ	binding NN
... two factors, which bind to the same kappa B enhancers ... CD NNS WDT **NN** TO DT JJ NN NN NNS	bind VBP
... by analysing the Ag amino acid sequence. IN VBG DT **VBG** JJ NN NN	Ag NN
... to contain more T-cell determinants than ... TO VB **RBR** **JJ** NNS IN	more T-cell JJR NN
Stimulation of interferon beta gene transcription in vitro by NN IN JJ JJ NN NN **IN NN** IN	in vitro FW FW

and Marquez [9] achieved an accuracy of 97.05% with support vector machines and Collins [10] achieved an accuracy of 97.11% with a discriminative HMM model.

2.1 POS Tagging with a Cyclic Dependency Network

We briefly describe the POS tagging algorithm based on a cyclic dependency network. For further details of the algorithm, see [8].

Given a sentence $\{w_1...w_n\}$, the task of POS tagging is to find the tag sequence that maximizes the following score:

$$score = \prod_{i=1}^{n} p(t_i|t_{i-2}t_{i-1}t_{i+1}t_{i+2}w_1...w_n) \qquad (1)$$

where t_i is the POS tag of the ith position. The best tag sequence can be computed in polynomial time by dynamic programming.

A probabilistic classifier is employed for estimating the local probabilities $p(t_i|t_{i-2}t_{i-1}t_{i+1}t_{i+2}w_1...w_n)$, which give the probability distribution for the tags on each token.

The advantage of this modeling over the standard left-to-right decomposition is that we can incorporate the information about the tags on both sides of t_i, i.e. $(t_{i-2}t_{i-1})$ and $(t_{i+1}t_{i+2})$ in performing local classification.

2.2 Local Probabilistic Classifier

We use maximum entropy modeling with inequality constraints [11] as the local probabilistic classifier. This modeling has a comparable generalization capacity

Table 2. Feature templates used in POS tagging experiments. Tags are parts-of-speech.

Current word	w_i	& t_i
Previous word	w_{i-1}	& t_i
Next word	w_{i+1}	& t_i
Bigram features	w_{i-1}, w_i	& t_i
	w_i, w_{i+1}	& t_i
Previous tag	t_{i-1}	& t_i
Tag two back	t_{i-2}	& t_i
Next tag	t_{i+1}	& t_i
Tag two ahead	t_{i+2}	& t_i
Tag Bigrams	t_{i-2}, t_{i-1}	& t_i
	t_{i-1}, t_{i+1}	& t_i
	t_{i+1}, t_{i+2}	& t_i
Tag Trigrams	$t_{i-2}, t_{i-1}, t_{i+1}$	& t_i
	$t_{i-1}, t_{i+1}, t_{i+2}$	& t_i
Tag 4-grams	$t_{i-2}, t_{i-1}, t_{i+1}, t_{i+2}$	& t_i
Tag/Word combination	t_{i-1}, w_i	& t_i
	t_{i+1}, w_i	& t_i
	t_{i-1}, t_{i+1}, w_i	& t_i
Prefix features	prefixes of w_i (up to length 10)	& t_i
Suffix features	suffixes of w_i (up to length 10)	& t_i
Lexical features	whether w_i has a hyphen	& t_i
	whether w_i has a number	& t_i
	whether w_i has a capital letter	& t_i
	whether w_i is all capital	& t_i

to that of Gaussian priors [12], which is a popular method for regularization in maximum entropy modeling. The advantage of this modeling is that most of the parameters become zero after training, resulting in a compact set of parameters. This advantage is especially useful in developing practical NLP tools because compact models require less computational cost and memory at run-time. This modeling has one meta-parameter called *width factor* for regularization. We tuned this parameter using the development data and set it to be 1.0.

For the features used in local classification, we adopted the feature set provided by [8] except for complex features like crude company name detection features because they are too specific to newspaper articles. Table 2 lists the feature templates used in our experiments.

2.3 Pruning

One problem of the tagging algorithm based on a cyclic dependency network is the computational cost for decoding (finding the best tag sequence) because the search space is very large.

To reduce the search space of Viterbi decoding in POS tagging, Ratnaparkhi [13] proposed to use a *Tag Dictionary* by which we consider only the tag-word pairs that appear in the training sentences as the candidate tags. However, in our preliminary experiments, the use of a tag dictionary limits precision because the training set does not cover all the tag-word pairs which appear in unseen data. We thus take a different approach to reducing the computational cost for decoding.

We first generate the candidate tags on each word using the zero-th order probability $p(t_i|w_1...w_n)$ given by the local classifier trained without the information about the adjacent tags. If the probability of a candidate is lower than one hundredth of that of the tag with the highest probability, the candidate is not considered in the decoding. This pruning method gave considerable speed-up with little loss of tagging accuracy.

3 Experiments on Annotated Corpora

The first set of experiments was carried out on the three corpora that are annotated with POS tags.

3.1 Corpora

We used the following three corpora for training and testing.

- Wall Street Journal (WSJ) corpus
  The corpus is included in the Penn Treebank [7] and consists of 1 million words of 1989 Wall Street Journal material. Each word is annotated with part-of-speech tags. We split the corpus into the training and the test set, following a standard splitting criterion provided in [8]: Sections 0-18 for training, 19-21 for development, and 22-24 for testing. The development set was used for feature selection and parameter tuning.
- GENIA corpus (version 3.02) [6]
  The corpus consists of 2,000 MEDLINE abstracts that have the three MeSH keywords, "Human", "Blood", and "Transcription Factors". We constructed the training set using 90% of the corpus and the test set using the rest.
- PennBioIE corpus (Release 0.9) [3]
  The corpus contains the MEDLINE abstracts in two domains of biomedical knowledge: (1) inhibition of the cytochrome P450 family of enzymes (1100 texts) (2) molecular genetics of cancer (1157 texts). We constructed the training data by merging the first 90% of the text from each domain. The rest was used as the test data.

The statistics are shown in Table 3. Training sets and test sets are mutually exclusive: no sentences in the training sets were included in the test sets.

3.2 POS Tagging Performance

We evaluated the performance of POS tagging with the following seven different combinations of the corpora as the training data.

Table 3. Statistics of the corpora used in the experiments

	# tokens	# sentences
WSJ for training	912,344	38,219
GENIA for training	450,492	18,508
PennBioIE for training	641,838	29,422
WSJ for testing	129,654	5,462
GENIA for testing	50,562	2,036
PennBioIE for testing	70,713	3,270

Table 4. POS tagging accuracy on the test sets

	WSJ	GENIA	PennBioIE
WSJ	97.05	85.19	86.14
GENIA	78.57	98.49	86.59
PennBioIE	85.45	93.20	97.74
WSJ + GENIA	96.96	98.32	91.98
WSJ + PennBioIE	96.94	93.34	97.75
GENIA + PennBioIE	85.60	98.35	97.63
WSJ + GENIA + PennBioIE	96.89	98.20	97.68

- WSJ
- GENIA
- PennBioIE
- WSJ + GENIA
- WSJ + PennBioIE
- GENIA + PennBioIE
- WSJ + GENIA + PennBioIE

Table 4 shows the accuracies on the test sets. The tagger trained on the WSJ corpus achieved an accuracy of 97.05% on the test set of the WSJ corpus. Since this test set is the same as that used in [8], the accuracies are directly comparable. Our accuracy is slightly lower than their accuracy (97.24%). This might look strange because our tagger employs the same tagging algorithm. The suspected reason is that they used features which are specifically tuned to the WSJ corpus such as company-name detection features. We did not use such features because our target is biomedical text. The feature set we used in this paper is almost identical to those in [10], and our tagger gives comparable performance to that achieved by Perceptron (97.11%) [10] and SVMs (97.05%) [9].

The tagger trained on the GENIA corpus achieved an accuracy of 98.49% on the test set of the GENIA corpus, which is slightly better than the above-mentioned performance on the WSJ corpus. This suggests that the texts in the GENIA corpus are less diverse than the WSJ corpus.

An interesting observation is that the performance on the PennBioIE corpus was improved from 86.59% to 91.98% by adding the WSJ corpus on top of the

Table 5. POS tagging accuracy on the test sets (without the distinction between proper nouns and nouns)

	WSJ	GENIA	PennBioIE
WSJ	97.20	91.55	90.51
GENIA	85.27	98.55	92.21
PennBioIE	87.35	93.44	97.92
WSJ + GENIA	97.20	98.54	93.60
WSJ + PennBioIE	97.21	94.03	97.97
GENIA + PennBioIE	88.34	98.41	97.84
WSJ + GENIA + PennBioIE	97.20	98.35	97.87

GENIA corpus. This indicates that even the text from a considerably different domain could contribute to the improvement of the tagger.

The most important observation in Table 4 is that the taggers trained on multiple corpora give good performance on all the test sets corresponding to the training corpora. In other words, adding text from a different domain did not deteriorate the precision of the tagger, which clearly indicates the robustness of our tagger.

In analyzing the tagging results, we found that the evaluation scheme was too strict. As pointed out in [4], the distinction between proper nouns and (normal) nouns is often ambiguous in the biomedical domain. The majority of the errors were caused by failure to make this distinction correctly, and the precisions shown in Table 4 are thus correspondingly depressed.

Since this distinction is often unnecessary from the natural language processing point of view, we also calculated the precisions achieved by ignoring the distinction between nouns and proper nouns. The results are shown in Table 5. The tagger trained on the WSJ corpus achieved accuracies of about 90% on the GENIA corpus and the PennBioIE corpus, which are considerably better than those given by the strict evaluation scheme.

The key observation revealed in Table 4 becomes much clearer: no loss of accuracy on the WSJ corpus was observed by adding the GENIA corpus and the PennBioIE corpus to the WSJ corpus.

4 Experiments on Recent MEDLINE Articles

In the previous section we evaluated the performance of our tagger on existing annotated corpora, and the tagger trained on the combination of all the three corpora exhibited very good performance. This suggests that the tagger is robust and would work well on other types of biomedical documents. Nevertheless, we cannot rule out the possibility of over-fitting: The tagger might have shown good performance on the text in the particular domain from which the training data was constructed. To fully evaluate the robustness of the tagger, we need to use totally unseen text for the taggers.

Table 6. Relative performance on recent MEDLINE articles

	NAR	NMED	JCI	Total (Accuracy)
WSJ	43	19	35	97 (26.6%)
GENIA	121	74	132	327 (89.8%)
PennBioIE	124	65	118	307 (84.3%)
WSJ + GENIA	106	73	129	308 (84.6%)
WSJ + PennBioIE	127	69	117	313 (86.0%)
GENIA + PennBioIE	123	75	134	332 (91.2%)
WSJ + GENIA + PennBioIE	128	72	131	331 (90.9%)

Table 7. Relative performance on recent MEDLINE articles (without the distinction between proper nouns and nouns)

	NAR	NMED	JCI	Total (Accuracy)
WSJ	109	47	102	258 (70.9%)
GENIA	121	74	132	327 (89.8%)
PennBioIE	129	65	122	316 (86.8%)
WSJ + GENIA	125	74	135	334 (91.8%)
WSJ + PennBioIE	133	71	133	337 (92.6%)
GENIA + PennBioIE	128	75	135	338 (92.9%)
WSJ + GENIA + PennBioIE	133	74	139	346 (95.1%)

In order to investigate the robustness of the tagger, we collected several recent abstracts of papers in three popular biomedical journals: Nucleic Acid Research (NAR), Nature Medicine (NMED), and Journal of Clinical Investigation (JCI). We randomly chose three abstracts from the latest issue of each journal, which are all published later than March 2005. The total number of tokens was 1,835.

Because the purpose is to evaluate the relative performance of the taggers, we focused only on the tokens where the taggers showed discrepancies. Of all the 1,835 tokens in the text, 330 tokens are tagged differently. We manually annotated the tokens with correct POS tags and evaluated the accuracies of the taggers.

The results are shown in Table 6 and 7. The tables show the numbers of correct tags given by individual taggers. Again, the tagger trained on the combined corpus performed best, which confirms the robustness of the tagger.

4.1 Error Analysis

Our experimental results revealed that the tagger trained on texts from all three corpora gives the best performance. We investigated what types of errors are still remaining.

Some are errors that could be corrected with parsing. For example, in the sentence

"These amplicons consist of a long inverted repeat with telomeric repeats at *both* ends and contain either the two different targeting cassettes used to inactivate JBP1 , or one cassette and one JBP1 gene ."

where *both* is incorrectly recognized as part of a *both – and* construction and labeled *CC*, the word can be assigned a proper POS if the coordination is correctly analyzed and 'ends' and 'contain' cannot be coordinated.

In the sentences

"Both RNase E and RNase III *control* the stability of sodB mRNA upon translational inhibition by the small regulatory RNA RyhB ."

and

"Using neutralizing antibodies and lactadherin-deficient animals , we show that lactadherin interacts with alphavbeta3 and alphavbeta5 integrins and *alters* both VEGF-dependent Akt phosphorylation and neovascularization .",

where *control* and *alters* are wrongly tagged as nouns, parsing will predict that they should be verbs (*VBN* and *VBZ* respectively) because a sentence needs a main verb.

There was one error, the correction of which would need deeper analysis. In the sentence

"In the absence of VEGF , lactadherin administration induced alphavbeta3- and alphavbeta5-dependent Akt phosphorylation in endothelial cells in vitro and strongly *improved* postischemic neovascularization in vivo ."

even syntactic parsing cannot determine whether *improved* is a past form or past participle of a verb. Sentences like this one suggest that it may be dangerous to assign a single POS to a word before deeper syntactic and semantic analysis. Our future work should encompass allowing the tagger to output multiple candidate tags for each word and investigating the cost in parsing that would stem from this ambiguity.

The remaining errors have more lexical nature involving words that have several possible POSs but one is preferred over the others in the context of biomedical research abstracts. For example, in

"Each long repeat within the linear amplicons corresponds to sequences covering the JBP1 locus , starting at the telomeres upstream of JBP1 and ending in a approximately 220 bp sequence repeated in an inverted (palindromic) orientation *downstream* of the JBP1 locus .",

the word 'downstream' is incorrectly labeled as a noun (*NN*), but in biomedical literature the word is more frequently used as adjective and that is true with this sentence. The error is expected to be eliminated if we can add more annotated biomedical texts to the training data. A similar result can be expected for the word 'set' (past participle incorrectly labeled as *NN*) in

"In experiments with Leishmania tarentolae *set* up to disrupt the gene encoding the J-binding protein 1 (JBP1) , a protein binding to the unusual base beta-D-glucosyl-hydroxymethyluracil (J) of Leishmania , we obtained JBP1 mutants containing linear DNA elements (amplicons) of approximately 100 kb ."

and 'bleeding' (a nominal modifier incorrectly labeled as a verb taking object) in

"In vivo , these inhibitors eliminate occlusive thrombus formation but do not prolong *bleeding* time .".

In the sentence

"Mutations in these genes may increase smooth swimming of the bacteria, potentially allowing *more* effective interactions with and invasion of host cells to occur ."

the word 'more' would be correctly labeled as an adverb *RBR* if it is known that a word 'more' is rarely used as 'greater in number' in academic texts. In

"These amplicons consist of a *long* inverted repeat with telomeric repeats at both ends and contain either the two different targeting cassettes used to inactivate JBP1 , or one cassette and one JBP1 gene .",

the word 'long' would be assigned the correct POS (adjective) if the word 'inverted' is not usually modified by an adverb 'long' (meaning 'for a long time').

5 Conclusion

This paper presented a part-of-speech tagger which is specifically suitable for processing biomedical text.

We have built the tagger based on a cyclic dependency network with maximum entropy modeling with inequality constraints, and evaluated the tagger on three corpora: the WSJ corpus, the GENIA corpus and the PennBioIE corpus.

Experimental results revealed that adding training data from a different domain does not hurt the performance of our POS taggers, and the tagger trained on the combined set of all three corpora offers very good performance (97% to 98% precision). We confirmed the robustness of the tagger by testing it further on several recent MEDLINE abstracts.

Acknowledgments

The UK National Centre for Text Mining is funded by the Joint Information Systems Committee, the Biotechnology and Biological Sciences Research Council, and the Engineering and Physical Sciences Research Council.

References

1. Kudo, T., Matsumoto, Y.: Chunking with support vector machines. In: Proceedings of NAACL 2001. (2001) 192–199
2. Bikel, D.M.: Intricacies of collins' parsing model. Computational Linguistics **30** (2004) 479–511
3. Kulick, S., Bies, A., Libeman, M., Mandel, M., McDonald, R., Palmer, M., Schein, A., Ungar, L.: Integrated annotation for biomedical information extraction. In: Proceedings of HLT/NAACL-2004. (2004)
4. Tateisi, Y., Tsujii, J.: Part-of-speech annotation of biology research abstracts. In: Proceedings of 4th International Conference on Language Resource and Evaluation (LREC2004). (2004) 1267–1270
5. Brants, T.: TnT – a statistical part-of-speech tagger. In: Proceedings of the 6th Applied NLP Conference (ANLP). (2000)
6. Ohta, T., Tateisi, Y., Kim, J.D., Tsujii, J.: Genia corpus: an annotated research abstract corpus in molecular biology domain. In: Proceedings of the Human Language Technology Conference (HLT 2002). (2002)
7. Marcus, M.P., Santorini, B., Marcinkiewicz, M.A.: Building a large annotated corpus of english: The penn treebank. Computational Linguistics **19** (1994) 313–330
8. Toutanova, K., Klein, D., Manning, C., Singer, Y.: Feature-rich part-of-speech tagging with a cyclic dependency network. In: Proceedings of HLT-NAACL 2003. (2003) 252–259
9. Gimenez, J., Marquez, L.: Fast and accurate part-of-speech tagging: The SVM approach revisited. In: Proceedings of RANLP 2003. (2003) 158–165
10. Collins, M.: Discriminative training methods for hidden markov models: Theory and experiments with perceptron algorithms. In: Proceedings of EMNLP 2002. (2002) 1–8
11. Kazama, J., Tsujii, J.: Evaluation and extension of maximum entropy models with inequality constraints. In: Proceedings of EMNLP 2003. (2003)
12. Chen, S.F., Rosenfeld, R.: A gaussian prior for smoothing maximum entropy models. Technical Report CMUCS -99-108, Carnegie Mellon University (1999)
13. Ratnaparkhi, A.: A maximum entropy model for part-of-speech tagging. In: Proceedings of EMNLP 1997. (1997)

Weaving Aspect-Oriented Constraints into Metamodel-Based Model Transformation Steps

László Lengyel, Tihamér Levendovszky, and Hassan Charaf

Budapest University of Technology and Economics,
Goldmann György tér 3., 1111 Budapest, Hungary
{lengyel, tihamer, hassan}@aut.bme.hu

Abstract. Graph rewriting is a widely used approach to model transformation. In general, graph rewriting rules parse graphs only by topological concerns, but they are not sophisticated enough to match a graph with a node which has a special property. In case of diagrammatic languages, such as the Unified Modeling Language (UML), the exclusive topological parsing is found to be not enough. To define the transformation steps in a more refined way additional constraints must be specified, which ensures the correctness of the attributes among others. Dealing with OCL constraints provides a solution for the unsolved issues. Often, the same constraint is repetitiously applied in many different places in a transformation. It would be beneficial to describe a common constraint in a modular manner, and to designate the places where it is to be applied. This paper presents the problem of the crosscutting constraints in graph transformation steps, provides an aspect-oriented solution for it, and introduces the weaving algorithms used to propagate aspect-oriented constraints to graph transformation steps.

Keywords: Metamodel-Based Graph Transformation Steps, Aspect-Oriented Constraints, Crosscutting Constraints, Weaving AO Constraints, OCL, VMTS.

1 Introduction

OMG's Model Driven Architecture [1] offers a standardized framework to separate the essential, platform independent information from the platform dependent constructs and assumptions. A complete MDA application consists of a definitive platform-independent model (PIM), and one or more platform-specific models (PSM) and complete implementations, one on each platform that the application developer decides to support. The platform independent artifacts are mainly UML and other software models containing enough specification to automatically generate the platform-dependent artifacts by so-called model compilers. Hence software model transformation provides a basis for model compilers which plays central role in the MDA architecture.

The increasing demand for visual languages (VL) in software engineering (Unified Modeling Language, UML; Domain Specific Languages, DSLs) requires more sophisticated parsing mechanisms of the diagrammatic languages. Although these VLs can often be modeled with labeled, directed graphs, the complex attribute dependencies peculiar to the individual software engineering models cannot be treated with this general model. Consequently, often it is not enough to parse graphs based on the topological information only, we want to restrict the desired match by other properties, e.g. we want to match a node with a special *integer* type property which value is between 4 and 12. Previous work [2] has shown that the rules can be made more relevant to software engineering models if the metamodel-based specification of the transformations allows assigning OCL [3] constraints to the individual transformation steps. The OCL constraints enlisted in the transformation steps affect the matched instances of the rewriting rules.

Often, the same constraint is repetitiously applied in many different places in a transformation. Aspect-Oriented Software Development (AOSD) [4] is a new technology that has introduced the separation of concerns (SoC) in software development. The methods of AOSD facilitate the modularization of crosscutting concerns within a system. Aspects may appear in any stage of the software development lifecycle (e.g. requirements, specification, design, implementation, etc.). Crosscutting concerns can range from high-level notions of security to low-level notions like caching and from functional requirements such as business rules to non-functional requirements like transactions. AOSD has started at the programming level of the software development life-cycle, and over the last decade several aspect-oriented programming languages have been introduced (e.g. AspectJ [5]). Aspect-oriented programming eliminates the crosscutting concerns in the programming language level, but the aspect-oriented techniques must be applicable on a higher abstraction level as well to solve this issue. The modularization of crosscutting concerns is also useful in model transformation. It would be beneficial to describe a common constraint in a modular manner, and mark the places where it is to be applied.

The paper discusses the problem of the crosscutting constraints in graph transformation steps, introduces the concept of the aspect-oriented constraints, provides an aspect-oriented solution for crosscutting constraints, and presents the weaving algorithms used to propagate aspect-oriented constraints to graph transformation steps.

2 Backgrounds and Related Work

Graph rewriting [6] is a powerful tool for graph transformation with a strong mathematical background. The atoms of graph transformation are rewriting rules, each rewriting rule consists of a left hand side graph (LHS) and right hand side graph (RHS). Applying a graph rewriting rule means finding an isomorphic occurrence (match) of the LHS in the graph the rule being applied to (host graph), and replacing this subgraph with RHS. Replacing means removing elements that are in the LHS but not in the RHS, and gluing elements that are in the RHS but not in the LHS.

Models can be considered special graphs; simply contain nodes and edges between them. This mathematical background makes possible to treat models as labeled graphs and to apply graph transformation algorithms to models using graph rewriting [2] [7]. Previous work [2] has introduced an approach, where LHS and RHS of the rules are built from metamodel elements. It means that an instantiation of LHS must be found in the host graph instead of the isomorphic subgraph of the LHS. Hence the LHS and RHS graphs are the metamodels of the graphs which we search and replace in the host graph.

The Object Constraint Language (OCL) [3] is a formal language for analysis and design of software systems. It is a subset of the UML standard [8] that allows software developers to write constraints and queries over object models. A constraint is a restriction on one or more values of an object-oriented model or system: a precondition (postcondition) to an operation is a restriction that must be true at the moment that the operation is going to be executed (the operation has just ended its execution).

Aspect-oriented programming (AOP) [9] is based on the idea that computer systems are better programmed by separately specifying the various concerns of a system and some description of their relationships, and then relying on mechanisms in the underlying AOP environment to weave or compose them together into a coherent program.

In [10] an aspect oriented approach is introduced for software model containing constraints where the dominant decomposition is based upon the functional hierarchy of a physical system. This approach provides a separate module for specifying constraints and their propagation. To provide the weaver with the necessary information to perform the propagation, a new type of aspect is used: the strategy aspect. Strategy aspect provides a hook that the weaver may call in order to process the node specific constraint propagations.

The Visual Modeling and Transformation System (VMTS) [2] [11] is an implemented n-layer multipurpose modeling and metamodel-based transformation system. Using this environment, it is easy to edit metamodels, design models according to their metamodels, transform models using graph rewriting [2] [12], and facilitates to check constraints specified in the metamodel during the metamodel instantiation, and the rewriting rule constraints during the graph transformation process. The results discussed in this paper have been validated in VMTS as a proof-of concept implementation.

3 Contributions

A *precondition* (*postcondition*) assigned to a rewriting rule is a *boolean* expression that must be true at the moment when the rewriting rule is fired (after the completion of a rewriting rule). If a *precondition* of a rewriting rule is not true then the rewriting rule fails without being fired. If a *postcondition* of a rewriting rule is not true after the execution of the rewriting rule then the rewriting rule fails. A direct corollary of this is that an OCL expression in LHS is a precondition to the rewriting rule, and an OCL expression in RHS is a postcondition to the rewriting rule. A rewriting rule can be fired if and only if all conditions enlisted in LHS are true. Also, if a rewriting rule finished successfully then all conditions enlisted in RHS must be true. The nodes contained by the LHS and RHS graphs of the rewriting rules in our approach are called *Pattern Rule Nodes (PRN)*.

3.1 Crosscutting Constraints

Transformation consists of several steps, many times not only a transformation rule but a whole transformation is required to validate, preserve or guarantee a certain property. To meet this expectation all the transformation steps have to be taken into consideration. If one defines a constraint for more transformation steps or for a whole transformation, then the same constraint appears numerous times in the transformation.

E.g. we have a transformation which modifies the properties of *Company* type objects and we would like the transformation to validate that the number of employees of a *Company* is always between 50 and 300 (*50 ≤ Company.NumbeOfEmployees ≤ 300*). It is certain that the transformation preserves this property if the constraint is defined for all PRN whose type is *Company*. It means that the constraint can appear in every transformation step several times, and therefore the constraint crosscuts the whole transformation, its modification and deletion is not consistent, because such an operation has to be performed on all occurrences of the constraint. Besides this it is often difficult to reason the effects of a complex constraint when it is spread out among the numerous PRNs in rewriting rules [14]. Fig. 1 introduces a metamodel and a transformation with 2 graph transformation steps. *const_NumOfEmployees* constraint appears at several places in this transformation.

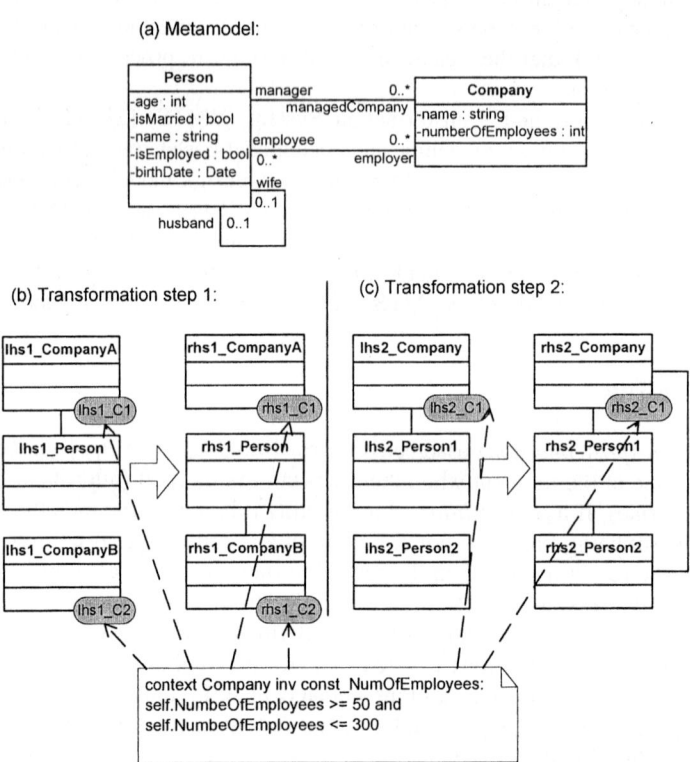

Fig. 1. (a) Metamodel, (b-c) A transformation with replicated structure, built from metamodel types

3.2 Weaving OCL Constraints to Transformations (Global Constraint Weaver)

A disadvantage of our earlier metamodel-based graph transformation approach [15] can be seen in many tangling constraints throughout of our rewriting rules. We need a mechanism to separate this concern. Having separated the constraints from the PRNs, we need a weaver method which facilitates the propagation (linking) of constraints to PRNs. The propagation of OCL constraints in VMTS is solved with the Global Constraint Weaver (GCW) algorithm. The GCW algorithm is passed a transformation with optional number of transformation steps and a constraint list and it links the constraints to the PRNs contained by the transformation steps.

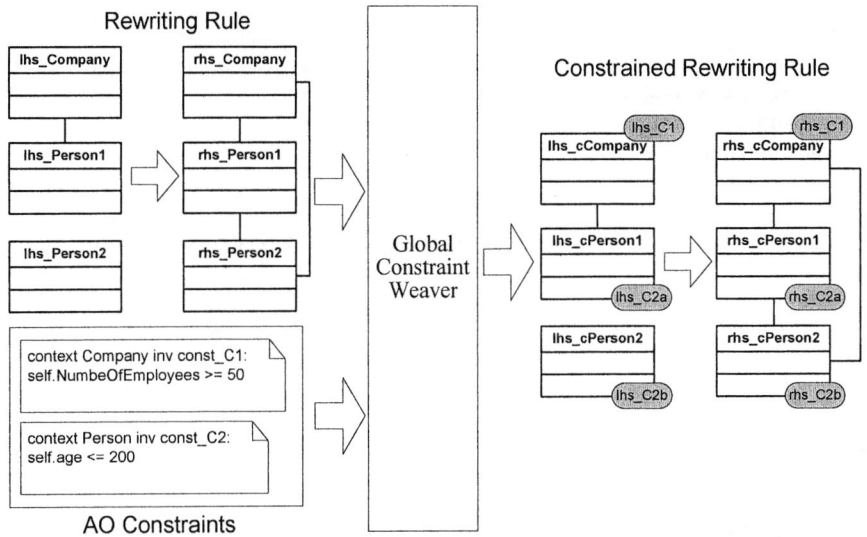

Fig. 2. The inputs and the output of the Global Constraint Weaver

This method means that our new approach manages constraints using AO techniques [16]: constraints are specified and stored independently of any graph rewriting rule or PRN and are linked to the PRNs by the GCW. Fig. 2 introduces the weaving process.

The output of the weaver is not stored as a new rewriting rule; the result is handled as a linking between the constraints and a transformation rule. This linking is the so-called *Weaving Configuration*.

The Global Constraint Weaver algorithm has three main steps. (i) It selects the PRNs from the transformation steps with corresponding type to the context information of the constraint. (ii) If the constraint contains navigation steps then the algorithm checks the topology of the rewriting rule for each formerly obtained PRN whether it satisfies the pattern required by the constraint The pattern of the rewriting rule is suitable for a constraint if starting from the PRN one can walk through the paths described by the navigation paths contained by the constraint. In other words the pattern of the rewriting rule contains nodes with appropriate type and relation between them which facilitates to walk trough the navigation paths of the constraint. (iii) In the third step, examining the transformation steps, the algorithm decides if it is necessary to assign the constraint to each transformation step, or it is sufficient to assign only to the first one as a precondition and to the last step as a postcondition. If an intermediate state modifies one of the properties contained by the constraint, the algorithm assigns the constraint to this intermediate state to prevent that a violated condition not being revealed until the end of the transformation. The pseudo code of the Global Constraint Weaver algorithm is as follows.

GLOBALCONSTRAINTWEAVING(Constraint[] *Cs*, Transformation *T*)
1 **foreach** Constraint *C* in *Cs*
2   **foreach** Transformation Step *S* in *T*
3   *nodesWithProperMetaType* = METATYPEBASEDSEARCHING(*ContextInfo* of *C*, *S*)
4   *nodesToCheck* = CHECKTOPOLOGY (*nodesWithProperMetaType*, *S*, *C*)
5   **if** (ISREQUIREDTOWEAVE(*C*, *nodesToCheck*, out *nodesToWeave*, true)) **then**
6   WEAVECONSTRAINT(*C*, *nodesToWeave*)
7   **endif**
8   **end foreach**
9 **end foreach**

3.3 Weaving Constraint Aspects to Transformations (Constraint Aspect Weaver)

This section introduces the concept of the constraint aspect and the algorithms we used to create constraint aspect from OCL constraint and to propagate constraint aspect to transformation steps. Before we introduce the algorithms for the unified treatment we give our definitions (Fig. 3).

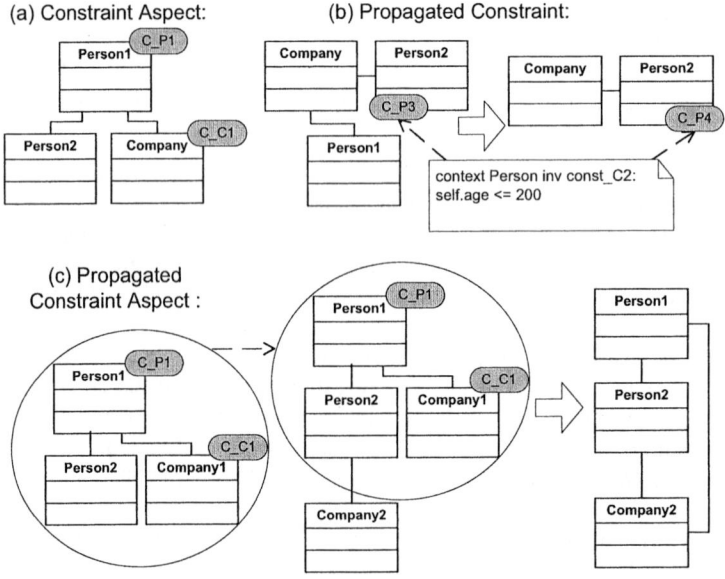

Fig. 3. (a) Constraint Aspect, (b) Propagated Constraint, (c) Propagated Constraint Aspect

Definition 1 (Constraint Aspect):
A *Constraint Aspect* is a pattern built from metamodel elements which contains at least one OCL constraint. A *Constraint Aspect* contains not only textual conditions

described by the OCL constraints but topology conditions as well. The topology and type conditions are checked at propagation time, while the OCL constraints are validated during the transformation.

Definition 2 (Propagated Constraint, Propagated Constraint Aspect):
A *Propagated Constraint* (*Propagated Constraint Aspect*) is an OCL constraint (Constraint Aspect) linked to a rewriting rule, and forms a Weaving Configuration, which contains the OCL constraint (Constraint Aspect) and the rewriting rule.

Definition 3 (Canonical Constraint Form and Pure Canonical Constraint Form):
The *Canonical Constraint Form* (*Pure Canonical Constraint Form*) of a Constraint Aspect is the form which contains the fewest possible navigation steps (does not contain navigation steps).

A constraint aspect is visually more expressive than an OCL constraint, therefore better suits into the visual transformation system as the OCL constraint.

Evaluating a constraint which contains navigations requires more computational complexity than a constraint without any navigation steps. To resolve the problem of the navigation steps we can create constraint aspect from an OCL constraint and normalize the constraint aspect to get the Canonical Constraint Form. A Normalized Constraint Aspect incorporates the constraints on their adequate places, therefore it includes the fewest possible navigation steps.

Fig. 4 introduces the creation process of the constraint aspects from an OCL constraint, and the normalization of the created Constraint Aspect. The lines with numbers from 1 to 4 show the steps of the constraint aspect creation: (i) the algorithm identifies the context type (*Person1*), (ii) and the referred types by the association ends (*managedCompany – Company, wife – Person*), based on this information it builds the pattern, and finally (iii) the algorithm assigns the OCL constraint to the root PRN of the created Constraint Aspect. In Fig. 4b the dashed lines denote that the constraint *C_P1* contains path expressions. Finally, the lines 5 and 6 show the constraint decomposition and replacement.

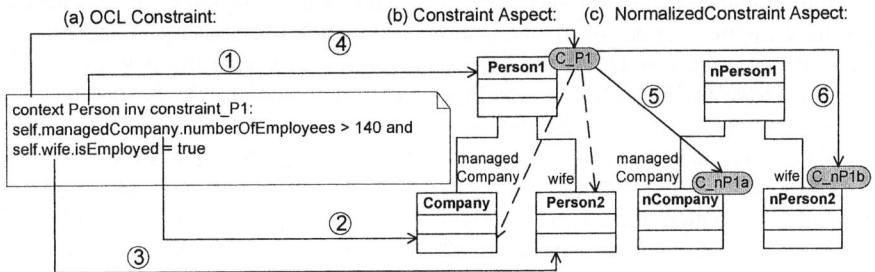

Fig. 4. (a) OCL Constraint, (b) Generated Constraint Aspect, (c) Normalized Constraint Aspect – Canonical Constraint Form

The constraint evaluation during the transformation process consists of two parts. (i) The selection of the object and its properties we need to check against the constraint and (ii) the execution of the validation method. The eliminated navigation steps accelerate the first part of the constraint evaluation.

The pseudo code of the NORMALIZECONSTRAINT algorithm, which generates the (Pure) Canonical Form of the constraint aspect is as follows.

```
NORMALIZECONSTRAINT (ConstraintAspect CA)
1  foreach PropagatedConstraint C in CA which contains navigation
2    if (C.DestinationNodes.Count == 1) then
3      RELOCATE C to DestinationNode of the C
4    else
5      minNumberOfSteps = CALCULATENAVIGATIONSTEPS(DestinationNodes of the C, CurrentNode of the C)
6      optimalNode = CurrentNode of the C
7      foreach Pattern Rule Node PRN in PatternRuleNodes of the CA
8        numberOfSteps = CALCULATENAVIGATIONSTEPS(DestinationNodes of the C, PRN)
9        if (numberOfSteps < minNumberOfSteps) then
10         minNumberOfSteps = numberOfSteps
11         optimalNode = PRN
12       endif
13     end foreach
14     if (optimalNode != CurrentNode of the C) then
15       UPDATENAVIGATIONPATS of the C
16       RELOCATE C to optimalNode
17     endif
18   endif
19 end foreach
```

The NORMALIZECONSTRAINT algorithm processes the OCL constraints propagated to the constraint aspect one by one. The main *foreach* loop examines the navigation paths of the actual constraint: if all the paths have the same destination node then the algorithm removes the navigations from the constraint and relocates it to the destination node. Otherwise the constraint has more than one navigation path and the destination nodes of the paths are different. In this case the algorithm calculates the number of all navigation steps for each PRN contained by the constraint aspect. This calculation sums the number of the navigation steps which is necessary in aggregate to reach all destination nodes of the original constraint (C) from the new place. The algorithm stores the best node (*optimalNode*) and finally updates the navigation paths and relocates the constraint to the optional node.

VMTS facilitates to create constraint aspect from an OCL constraint with CREATECONSTRAINTASPECT algorithm or to specify a pattern and the constraints assigned to the pattern directly as a constraint aspect. In both cases after the constraint aspect creation we can use the NORMALIZECONSTRAINT algorithm to get the canonical form of the constraint aspect.

The pseudo code of the algorithm (CONSTRAINTASPECTWEAVING) which weaves Constraint Aspects to transformation steps is as follows.

```
CONSTRAINTASPECTWEAVING(ConstraintAspect[] CAs, Transformation T)
1  foreach ConstraintAspect CA in CAs
2    foreach Transformation Step S in T
3      matches = METATYPEBASEDMATCHING(pattern of the CA, S)
```

```
4    foreach Constraint C in CA
5       nodesToCheck = GETNODESBYTYPE(ContextType of C, matches)
6       if (ISREQUIREDTOWEAVE(C, nodesToCheck, out nodesToWeave)) then
7          WEAVECONSTRAINTASPECT(CA, nodesToWeave)
8          break
9       endif
10   end foreach
11   end foreach
12 end foreach
```

In general it is more efficient to work with constraint aspects than OCL constraints, because during the propagation of the constraint aspects we can use the metatype-based searching for pattern matching to reduce the possible places of the constraint assignment, and we have to run the ISREQUIREDTOWEAVE algorithm on the selected places only to decide based on the constraints if it is necessary to assign the constraint aspect. Contrary to it, in the case of simple OCL constraints the GCW algorithm has to use the CHECKTOPOLOGY method to find the topologically appropriate places in the transformation steps.

Proposition. The normalized constraint aspect CA' is created from the OCL constraint C with the CREATECONSTRAINTASPECT and NORMALIZECONSTRAINT algorithms. T_1 and T_2 are two identical transformations (which contain optional number of transformation steps). C is propagated to the T_1 using Global Constraint Weaver algorithm and CA' is propagated to the T_2 using Constraint Aspect Weaver algorithm. Then transformations T_1 and T_2 produce the same result models step by step.

Proof: We assume that one has two identical host graphs (H_1 and H_2) and applies T_1 to H_1 and T_2 to H_2. After each transformation step one compares the result of the actual transformation steps and in step n^{th} steps T_{1n} and T_{2n} produce different results - one of them is successful but the other fails because of a constraint failure.

(a) The inputs of the GCW algorithm (GLOBALCONSTRAINTWEAVING) are OCL constraint(s) and a transformation (let it be constraint C and transformation T_1). The GCW checks all the possible places of the passed rewriting rules ($T_{11}...T_{1n}$) where the constraint can be assigned; the algorithm selects the PRNs with the type that corresponds to the context information of the constraint C (line 3), in those places it checks if the topology of the actual transformation step satisfies the pattern required by the navigation paths of the constraint C (line 4). For the topologically selected PRNs the algorithm checks if their step requires the constraint C to be propagated to it. It decides whether it is the first or the last step in the transformation or whether it can modify the property contained by the constraint C (ISREQUIREDTOWEAVE method). Finally the GCW algorithm propagates the constraint C to the required places (line 6).

(b) The inputs of the ACW algorithm are constraint aspect(s) and a transformation (let it be the constraint aspect CA and the transformation T_2). The CAW algorithm checks the transformation steps one by one. In each step it searches for matches by the pattern of CA (line 3) and for each constraint ($CA\_C_1...CA\_C_n$) contained by CA the algorithm selects the PRNs from the matches with the type which corresponds to the context information of the actual constraint (lines 4-5). Similarly to the GCW algorithm CAW also uses the ISREQUIREDTOWEAVE method to decide if a transformation step requires *CA* to be propagated to the actual PRN (line 6). If at least one of the constraints ($CA\_C_1...CA\_C_n$) contained by *CA* requires to be propagated, the whole constraint aspect is linked (lines 7-8).

The difference between the GCW and CAW algorithms is that the GCW checks the pattern of the transformation step according to the text of the OCL constraint, while the CAW utilizes that the constraint aspect includes the pattern in its topology. Since the two approaches differ in their data representation only, the algorithm cannot give different results. That contradicts the initial assumption.

The aspect-oriented constraint management does not reject the classical constraint assignment; it extends the possibilities of constraint handling in metamodel-based model transformation frameworks.

4 Conclusions

The extension of the algebraic graph rewriting with OCL constraints makes transformations sophisticated enough to parse diagrammatic graphs with optional conditions.

We have found that the source of our rewriting problems is often related to a lack of support for modularizing constraints. As we have adopted an aspect-oriented approach to our metamodel-based transformation process, it is illustrated that the maintainability and understandability of our transformation steps and constraints has been enhanced.

In this work (i) the relation between the pre- and postconditions and OCL constraints assigned to the rewriting rules was presented, (ii) the problem of the crosscutting constraints contained by the graph transformation steps was discussed and (iii) a summary of the aspect-oriented solution with propagation algorithms was provided.

References

1. MDA Guide Version 1.0.1, OMG, doc. number: omg/2003-06-01, 12th June 2003 www.omg.org/docs/omg/03-06-01.pdf
2. Levendovszky T, Lengyel L, Mezei G, Charaf H, A Systematic Approach to Metamodeling Environments and Model Transformation Systems in VMTS, ENTCS, International Workshop on Graph-Based Tools (GraBaTs) Rome, 2004
3. Object Constraint Language Specification (OCL), www.omg.org
4. AOSD Homepage. http://www.aosd.net/
5. The AspectJ Programming Guide, http://www.aspectj.org
6. Rozenberg (ed.), Handbook on Graph Grammars and Computing by Graph Transformation: Foundations, Vol.1 World Scientific, Singapore, 1997
7. Levendovszky T, Lengyel L, Charaf H, Implementing a Metamodel-Based Model Transformation System, Buletinul Stiintific al Universitatii "Politehnica" din Timisoara, ROMANIA Seria AUTOMATICA si CALCULATOARE PERIODICA POLITECHNICA, Transactions on AUTOMATIC CONTROL and COMPUTER SCIENCE Vol.49 (63), 2004, ISSN 1224-600X
8. UML 2.0 Specifications, http://www.omg.org/uml/

9. Tzilla Elrad, Robert E. Filman, and Ataf Bader, Aspect-oriented Programing, CACM Volume 44, Issue 10, October 2001
10. Jeff Gray, Ted Bapty, Sandeep Neema, Aspectifying Constraints in Model-Integrated Computing, OOPSLA Workshop on Advanced Separation of Concerns in Object-Oriented Systems, Minneapolis, MN, October 2000
11. The VMTS Homepage. http://avalon.aut.bme.hu/~tihamer/research/vmts/
12. Levendovszky T, Lengyel L, Charaf H, Software Composition with a Multipurpose Modeling and Model Transformation Framework, IASTED 2004, Innsbruck, pp.590-594
13. PROGRES system can be downloaded from http://www-i3.informatik.rwth-aachen.de/research/projects/progres/main.html
14. Lengyel L, Levendovszky T, Charaf H, Managing Crosscutting Constraints in Metamodel-Based Model Transformation Frameworks, International Carpathian Control Conference, ICCC'2005, Volume II, Miskolc-Lillafüred, Hungary, May 24-27, 2005, pp. 41-46
15. Lengyel L, Levendovszky T, Kozma P, Charaf H, Compiling and validating OCL constraints in metamodeling environments and visual model compilers, IASTED on SE, February 15-17, 2005, Innsbruck, Austria, pp. 48-54
16. Lengyel L, Levendovszky T, Charaf H, Weaving Crosscutting Constraints in Metamodel-Based Transformation Rules, 8th International Conference on Information Systems Implementation and Modeling, ISIM '05, April 19-20, 2005, Czech Republic, pp. 119-126
17. Levendovszky T, Charaf H, Pattern Matching in Metamodel-Based Model Transformation Systems, submitted to Periodica Polytechnica Electrical Engineering, ISSN 0324-6000

A Graphical Rule Authoring Tool for Defeasible Reasoning in the Semantic Web

Nick Bassiliades[1], Efstratios Kontopoulos[1], Grigoris Antoniou[2], and Ioannis Vlahavas[1]

[1] Department of Informatics, Aristotle University of Thessaloniki,
GR-54124 Thessaloniki, Greece
{nbassili, skontopo, vlahavas}@csd.auth.gr
[2] Institute of Computer Science, FO.R.T.H.,
P.O. Box 1385, GR-71110, Heraklion, Greece
antoniou@ics.forth.gr

Abstract. Defeasible reasoning is a rule-based approach for efficient reasoning with incomplete and inconsistent information. Such reasoning is useful for many applications in the Semantic Web, such as policies and business rules, agent brokering and negotiation, ontology and knowledge merging, etc. However, the syntax of defeasible logic may appear too complex for many users. In this paper we present a graphical authoring tool for defeasible logic rules that acts as a shell for the DR-DEVICE defeasible reasoning system over RDF metadata. The tool helps users to develop a rule base using the OO-RuleML syntax of DR-DEVICE rules, by constraining the allowed vocabulary through analysis of the input RDF namespaces, so that the user does not have to type-in class and property names. Rule visualization follows the tree model of RuleML. The DR-DEVICE reasoning system is implemented on top of the CLIPS production rule system and builds upon an earlier deductive rule system over RDF metadata that also supports derived attribute and aggregate attribute rules.

1 Introduction

The development of the Semantic Web [8] proceeds in layers, each layer being on top of other layers. At present, the highest layer that has reached sufficient maturity is the ontology layer, with OWL [11], a description logic based language, being the standard. The next step in the development of the Semantic Web will be the logic and proof layers and rule systems appear to lie in the mainstream of such activities. Rule systems can play a twofold role in the Semantic Web initiative: (a) they can serve as extensions of, or alternatives to, description logic based ontology languages; and (b) they can be used to develop declarative systems on top of (using) ontologies.

Defeasible reasoning is a simple rule-based approach to reasoning with incomplete and inconsistent information. It can represent facts, rules, and priorities among rules. This reasoning family comprises defeasible logics ([3]) and Courteous Logic Programs [14]. The main advantage of this approach is the combination of two desirable features: a) enhanced representational capabilities, allowing one to reason with incomplete and contradictory information, coupled with b) low computational complexity compared to mainstream nonmonotonic reasoning.

Defeasible logic can easily express conflicts among rules. Such conflicts arise, among others, from rules with exceptions, which are a natural representation for policies and business rules [2]. And priority information is often implicitly or explicitly available to resolve conflicts among rules. Potential applications include security policies ([5], [16]), business rules [1], personalization, brokering [4], bargaining, and automated agent negotiations ([13], [19]).

However, defeasible logic is certainly not an end-user language but rather a developer's one, because its syntax may appear too complex. In this paper, we present a graphical rule authoring tool for defeasible logic that acts as a shell for the DR-DEVICE [6] defeasible reasoning system for the Semantic Web. This rule authoring tool is built in Java and helps users to develop a rule base using the OO-RuleML [9] syntax of DR-DEVICE rules. Among others, the tool constrains the allowed vocabulary, by analyzing the input RDF namespaces; therefore, it removes from the user the burden of typing-in class and property names and prevents potential semantical and syntactical errors. The visualization of rules follows the tree model of RuleML.

DR-DEVICE supports multiple rule types of defeasible logic, as well as priorities among rules. Furthermore, it supports two types of negation (strong, negation-as-failure) and conflicting (mutually exclusive) literals. DR-DEVICE has a RuleML-compatible [9] syntax, which is the main standardization effort for rules on the Semantic Web. Input and output of data and conclusions is performed through processing of RDF data and RDF Schema ontologies. The system is built on-top of a CLIPS-based [10] implementation of deductive rules, namely the R-DEVICE system [7]. The core of the system consists of a translation of defeasible knowledge into a set of deductive rules, including derived and aggregate attributes.

The paper is organized as follows. Section 2 briefly introduces the syntax and semantics of defeasible logics. Section 3 presents the architecture of the DR-DEVICE reasoning system. Section 4 describes the RuleML syntax of defeasible logic rules in DR-DEVICE. Section 5 presents the graphical rule authoring tool. Finally, section 6 discusses related work, and section 7 concludes the paper with a summary and description of current and future work.

2 An Introduction to Defeasible Logics

A *defeasible theory D* is a couple $(R,>)$ where R a finite set of rules and $>$ a superiority relation on R. Each rule has a unique rule label. There are three kinds of rules: strict rules, defeasible rules, and defeaters.

Strict rules are denoted by $A \rightarrow p$ and are interpreted in the classical sense: whenever the premises are indisputable, then so is the conclusion. An example of a strict rule is *"Penguins are birds"*. Written formally: r_1: penguin(X) $\rightarrow$ bird(X). Inference from strict rules only is called *definite inference*. Strict rules are intended to define relationships that are definitional in nature and such an example is ontological knowledge.

Defeasible rules are denoted by $A \Rightarrow p$, and can be defeated by contrary evidence. An example of such a rule is r_2: bird(X) $\Rightarrow$ flies(X), which reads as: *"Birds typically fly"*.

Defeaters are denoted as $A \leadsto p$ and are not used to actively support conclusions, but only to prevent some of them. An example of such a defeater is: r_4: `heavy(X) ~> ¬flies(X)`, which reads as: *"Heavy birds may not fly"*.

A *superiority relation* on R is an acyclic relation > on R (that is, the transitive closure of > is irreflexive). When $r_1 > r_2$, then r_1 is called *superior* to r_2, and r_2 *inferior* to r_1. This expresses that r_1 may override r_2. For example, given the defeasible rules r_2 and r_3: `penguin(X) => ¬flies(X)`, no conclusive decision can be made about whether a penguin flies, because rules r_2 and r_3 contradict each other. But if we introduce a superiority relation > with $r_3 > r_2$, then we can indeed conclude that a penguin does not fly.

3 The DR-DEVICE System Architecture and Functionality

The DR-DEVICE reasoning system consists of two major components (Fig. 1): the RDF loader/translator and the rule loader/translator. The user submits to the rule loader a rule program (a URL or a local file name) that contains a) one or more rules in RuleML-like syntax [9], b) the URL(s) of the RDF input document(s), which is forwarded to the RDF loader, c) the names of the derived classes to be exported as results, and d) the name of the RDF output document.

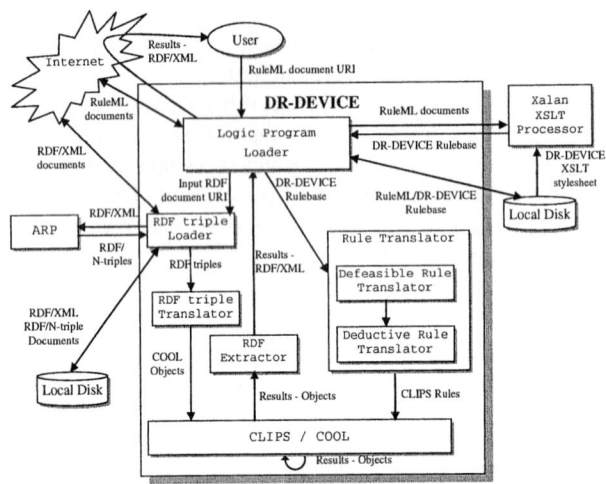

Fig. 1. Architecture of the DR-DEVICE reasoning system

The RuleML file is transformed into the native CLIPS-like syntax through an XSLT stylesheet. The DR-DEVICE rule program is then forwarded to the rule translator. The *RDF loader* downloads the input RDF documents, including their schemas, and translates RDF descriptions into CLIPS objects, according to the RDF-to-object translation scheme of R-DEVICE [7].

The *rule translator* compiles the defeasible logic rules into a set of CLIPS production rules in two steps: First, the defeasible logic rules are translated into sets of deductive, derived attribute and aggregate attribute rules of the basic R-DEVICE rule language, using the translation scheme described in [6]. Then, all these R-DEVICE rules are translated into CLIPS production rules [10], according to the R-DEVICE rule translation scheme [7]. All compiled rule formats are kept in local files, so that the next time they are needed they can be directly loaded, improving speed.

The inference engine of CLIPS performs the reasoning by running the production rules and generates the objects that constitute the result of the initial rule program or query. The compilation phase guarantees correctness of the reasoning process according to the operational semantics of defeasible logic.

Finally, the result-objects are exported to the user as an RDF/XML document through the RDF extractor. The RDF document includes the RDF Schema definitions for the exported derived classes and the instances of the exported derived classes, which have been proven (positively or negatively, defeasibly or definitely).

4 The Defeasible Logic Language of DR-DEVICE

DR-DEVICE has both a native CLIPS-like syntax ([6]) and a RuleML-compatible syntax [9]. Rules are encoded in an imp element and they have a label (_rlab element), which also includes the rule's unique ID (ruleID attribute) and the type of the rule (ruletype attribute). The names (rel elements) of the operator (_opr) elements of atoms are class names, since atoms actually represent CLIPS objects. Atoms have named arguments, called slots, which correspond to object properties. In DR-DEVICE, RDF resources are represented as CLIPS objects; therefore, atoms correspond to queries over RDF resources of a certain class with certain property values. For example, the following fragment represents the defeasible rule r_2 of section 2:

```
<imp><_rlab ruleID="r2" ruletype="defeasiblerule"><ind>r2</ind></_rlab>
    <_head>   <atom>  <_opr><rel>flies</rel></_opr>
                      <_slot name="name"><var>X</var></_slot>   </atom>
    </_head>
    <_body>   <atom>  <_opr><rel>bird</rel></_opr>
                      <_slot name="name"><var>X</var></_slot>   </atom>
    </_body>
</imp>
```

Superiority relations are represented as attributes of the superior rule. For example, rule r_3 (of section 2) is superior to rule r_2. In RuleML, this is represented via a superiority attribute in the rule label of rule r_3. Negation is represented via a neg element that encloses an atom element.

```
<imp>   <_rlab ruleID="r3" ruletype="defeasiblerule" superior="r2">
            <ind>r3</ind> </_rlab>
    <_head><neg>   <atom>  <_opr><rel>flies</rel></_opr>
                           <_slot name="name"><var>X</var></_slot>   </atom>
        </neg>
    </_head>
    <_body><atom>  <_opr><rel>penguin</rel></_opr>
                   <_slot name="name"><var>X</var></_slot>      </atom>
    </_body>
</imp>
```

Apart from rule declarations, there are `comp_rules` elements that declare groups of competing rules which derive competing positive conclusions, also known as *conflicting literals*.

```
<comp_rules c_rules="r10 r11 r12">
   <_crlab> <ind>cr1</ind> </_crlab>
</comp_rules>
```

Further extensions to the RuleML syntax, include function calls that are used either as constraints in the rule body or as new value calculators at the rule head. Additionally, multiple constraints in the rule body can be expressed through the logical operators: `_not, _and, _or`.

Finally, in the header of the rulebase several important parameters are declared; the input RDF file(s) are declared in the `rdf_import` attribute of the `rulebase` (root) element of the RuleML document. There exist two more attributes in the `rulebase` element: the `rdf_export` attribute, which is the RDF file with the exported results, and the `rdf_export_classes` attribute, which are the derived classes, whose instances will be exported in RDF/XML format. An example is shown below:

```
<rulebase rdf_import="http://lpis.csd.auth.gr/.../carlo.rdf#"
          rdf_export_classes="acceptable rent"
          rdf_export="http://lpis.csd.auth.gr/.../export-carlo.rdf">
```

5 The Graphical Rule Authoring Tool

As the previous section shows, expressing or even viewing rules in RuleML syntax can often be highly cumbersome. In order to enhance user-friendliness and efficiency, DR-DEVICE is supported by a Java-built graphical authoring tool, which also acts as a graphical shell for the DR-DEVICE core reasoning system.

The graphical shell facilitates the development and invocation of rulebases, by calling the external applications that constitute the DR-DEVICE system. Users can evoke local or remote RuleML rulebases by starting new projects. The rulebase is then displayed in the left frame in XML-tree format, also offering the user the capability of navigating through the entire tree (Fig. 2). When the rule base is compiled and run, the DR-DEVICE core system, described in section 3, is evoked. The execution trace is watched via a DOS Window which can be later re-examined using the 'Run Trace' window (Fig. 3). Users can set the level of detail during the trace, using the Parameters menu. The exported results of the inference process can be examined via an Internet Explorer window (Fig. 3). Finally, users can also re-run already compiled projects considerably (10-times) faster.

The graphical authoring tool facilitates rulebase developers via constrained yet flexible deployment of pre-defined rule templates, according to both the RuleML-compatible syntax and the RDF-oriented semantics.

While traversing the XML tree, the user can add or remove elements, according to the DTD limitations. In general, the rule editor allows only a limited number of operations performed on each element, according to the element's meaning within the rule tree. The main principle of tree expansion is the following: when a new element is added, then all the mandatory sub-elements are also added. When there are multiple alternative sub-elements, none is added, but the user can select one of them to add by right-clicking on the parent element. Furthermore, the user can alter the textual content (PCDATA) of the tree leafs. The `atom` element has a special treatment because it can be either negated or not. To facilitate this, the wrapping/unwrapping of an `atom` element within a `neg` element is performed via a toggle button.

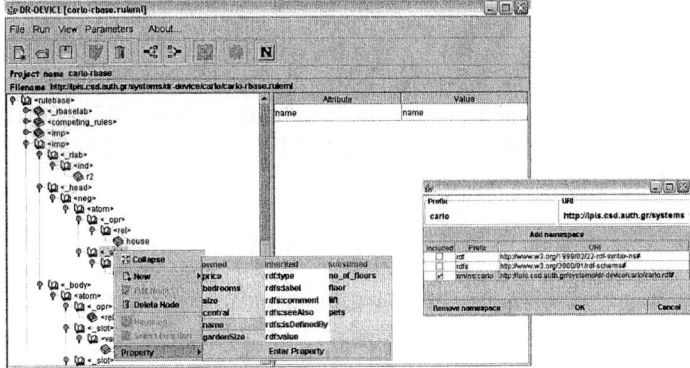

Fig. 2. The graphical rule authoring tool of DR-DEVICE and the namespace dialog window

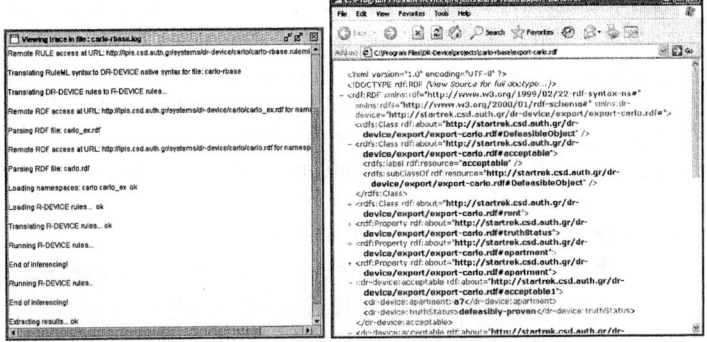

Fig. 3. The Run Trace and Results windows of the graphical DR-DEVICE shell

The attribute editing area (in the right-hand frame) shows the XML attributes, corresponding to the selected tree node in the XML navigation-editing area. All the attributes (both mandatory and optional) are shown in this area, but the final XML document will contain only the non null ones. Rule IDs are treated specially, since they uniquely represent rules within the rulebase. Some IDREF attributes, such as the `superior` attribute of the `_rlab` element, use the list of rule IDs to constrain the list of possible values. Names of functions appearing in an `fcall` element are constrained to be among the system-defined CLIPS functions.

One of the important aspects of the rule editor is the namespace dialog window (Fig. 2), where the user can declare all the XML namespaces that will be used throughout the rulebase. Actually, namespace declarations are addresses of RDF

Schema documents that contain the vocabulary for the input RDF documents over which the rules of the rulebase will be run. Namespaces are analyzed by the authoring tool in order to discover the allowed class and property names for the rulebase being edited. These names are used in pull-down menus and name lists throughout the authoring of the RuleML rulebase, in order to constrain the allowed names that can be used, to facilitate rule authoring and, consequently, reduce the possible semantical (and syntactical) errors of the rule developer.

More specifically, RDF Schema documents are parsed, using the ARP parser of Jena [18], a flexible Java API for processing RDF documents, and the names of the classes found are collected in the *base class vector* (CV_b), which already contains rdfs:Resource, the superclass of all RDF user classes. Therefore, the vector is constructed as follows:

rdfs:Resource $\in CV_b$
$\forall C$ (C rdf:type rdfs:Class) $\rightarrow C \in CV_b$

where ($X\ Y\ Z$) represents an RDF triple found in the RDF Schema documents.

. Except from the base class vector, there also exists the *derived class vector* (CV_d), which contains the names of the derived classes, i.e. the classes which lie at rule heads (conclusions). This vector is initially empty and is dynamically extended every time a new class name appears inside the rel element of the atom in a rule head.

The vector CV_d is used for loosely suggesting possible values for rel elements of the atom in a rule head, but not constraining them, because rule heads can either introduce new derived classes or refer to already existing ones.

The *full class vector* (CV_f), which is a union of the above two vectors $(CV_f = CV_b \cup CV_d)$, is used for constraining the allowed class names, when editing the contents of the rel element inside atom elements of the rule body.

Furthermore, the RDF Schema documents are also parsed for property names and their domains. The properties are placed in a *base property vector* PV_b, which already contains some built-in RDF properties (*BIP*) whose domain is rdfs:Resource:

BIP = {rdf:type, rdfs:label, rdfs:comment, rdfs:seeAlso,
  rdfs:isDefinedBy, rdf:value} $\subseteq PV_b$
$\forall P$, (P rdf:type rdf:Property) $\rightarrow P \in PV_b$

Except from the base property vector, there also exists the *derived property vector* (PV_d), which contains the names of the properties of the derived classes, i.e. the properties of classes which lie at rule heads (conclusions). This vector is initially empty and is dynamically extended every time a new property name appears inside the _slot element of the atom in a rule head. Therefore, the *full property vector* (PV_f) is a union of the above two vectors: $PV_f = PV_b \cup PV_d$.

For each property P in the PV_f vector an object is created that maintains all the RDF Schema information needed. More specifically, each P object maintains two sets: *superproperty set SUPP(P)* and *domain set DOM(P)*.

The $SUPP(P)$ set initially contains all the direct superproperties of P. The rest of the properties (including the derived class properties) have an empty $SUPP(P)$:

$\forall P \in PV_b\ \forall SP \in PV_b$, ($P$ rdfs:subPropertyOf SP) $\rightarrow SP \in SUPP(P)$

The $SUPP(P)$ set is then further populated with the indirect superproperties of each property, by recursively traversing upwards the property hierarchy. Existing duplicates due to multiple inheritance are subsequently merged, since $SUPP(P)$ is a set:

$\forall P \in PV_b, \forall SP \in SUPP(P) \; \forall SP' \in SUPP(SP) \rightarrow SP' \in SUPP(P)$

The $DOM(P)$ set of domains is initially constructed, by examining the domain of each property declared in the RDF Schema documents. The domain of each derived class property is the corresponding derived class:

$\forall P \in PV_b, \forall C, (P \; \texttt{rdfs:domain} \; C) \rightarrow C \in DOM(P)$

The domain of the RDF built-in properties BIP is `rdfs:Resource`:

$\forall P \in BIP, \texttt{rdfs:Resource} \in DOM(P)$

If a property does not have a domain, then `rdfs:Resource` is assumed:

$\forall \; P \in (PV_b\text{-}BIP), (\neg\exists C \; P \; \texttt{rdfs:domain} \; C) \rightarrow \texttt{rdfs:Resource} \in DOM(P)$

The $DOM(P)$ set is then further populated, by inheriting the domains of all the superproperties (both direct and indirect):

$\forall P \in PV_b, \forall SP \in SUPP(P) \; \forall C \in DOM(SP), C \in DOM(P)$

This follows from the RDFS semantics, which dictate that the domains (and ranges) of the superproperties are inherited by the subproperties conjunctively.

The domains of the properties are needed, in order to constrain the possible values that the slot names can take, when editing the RuleML tree. More specifically, for each atom element appearing inside the rule body, when the class name C is selected, the names of the properties that can appear inside the _slot subelements are constrained only to those that have C as their domain, either directly or inherited. Furthermore, subsumed properties are also allowed, as it is explained below.

In order to link each class with the allowed properties, for each class C in the CV_f vector an object is created that maintains all the RDF Schema information needed. More specifically, each C object maintains five sets: *superclass set $SUPC(C)$, subclass set $SUBC(C)$, owned property set $OWNP(C)$, inherited property set $INHP(C)$,* and *subsumed property set $SUBP(C)$*.

The $SUPC(C)$ set initially contains all the direct superclasses of C:

$\forall C \in CV_b, \forall SC \in CV_b, (C \; \texttt{rdfs:subClassOf} \; SC) \rightarrow SC \in SUPC(C)$

If a class does not have a superclass, then it is considered to be a subclass of `rdfs:Resource`:

$\forall C \in CV_b, C \neq \texttt{rdfs:Resource} \land (\neg\exists SC \; SC \in CV_b \rightarrow (C \; \texttt{rdfs:subClassOf} \; SC))$
$\rightarrow \texttt{rdfs:Resource} \in SUPC(C)$

Derived classes are considered to be subclasses of `rdfs:Resource`:

$\forall C \in CV_d, \texttt{rdfs:Resource} \in SUPC(C)$

The $SUPC(C)$ set is then further populated with the indirect superclasses of each class, by recursively traversing upwards the class hierarchy. Potential duplicates due to multiple inheritance are again subsequently merged, since $SUPC(C)$ is a set:

$\forall C \in CV_b \ \forall SC \in SUPC(C) \ \forall SC' \in SUPC(SC) \rightarrow SC' \in SUPC(C)$

The $SUBC(C)$ set is constructed, by inversing all the subclass relationships (both direct and indirect):

$\forall C \in CV_b \ \forall SC \in SUPC(C) \rightarrow C \in SUBC(SC)$

The $OWNP(C)$ set of owned properties is constructed, by examining the domain set of each property object in the full property vector:

$\forall P \in PV_f \ \forall C \in DOM(P) \rightarrow P \in OWNP(C)$

The inherited property set $INHP(C)$ is constructed, by inheriting the owned properties from all the superclasses (both direct and indirect):

$\forall C \in CV_b \ \forall SC \in SUPC(C) \ \forall P \in OWNP(SC) \rightarrow P \in INHP(C)$

This follows from the RDFS semantics, which dictate that the instances of a subclass are also instances of its superclass; therefore, properties which have the superclass as domain can also have any of its subclasses as domain.

Finally, the subsumed property set $SUBP(C)$ is constructed, by copying the owned properties from all the subclasses (both direct and indirect):

$\forall C \in CV_b \ \forall SC \in SUBC(C) \ \forall P \in OWNP(SC) \rightarrow P \in SUBP(C)$

Although the domain of a subsumed property of a class C is not compatible with class C, it can still be used in the rule condition for querying objects of class C, implying that the matched objects will belong to some subclass C' of class C, which is compatible with the domain of the subsumed property. For example, consider two classes A and B, the latter being a subclass of the former, and a property P, whose domain is B. It is allowed to query class A, demanding that property P satisfies a certain condition; however, only objects of class B can possibly satisfy the condition, since direct instances of class A do not even have property P.

The above three property sets comprise the *full property set FPS(C)*:

$FPS(C) = OWNP(C) \cup INHP(C) \cup SUBP(C)$

which is used to restrict the names of properties that can appear inside a _slot element (see Fig. 2), when the class of the atom element is C.

6 Related Work

There exist several previous implementations of defeasible logics. *Deimos* [17] is a flexible, query processing system based on Haskell. It implements several variants, but not conflicting literals nor negation as failure in the object language. Also, it does not integrate with Semantic Web (for example, there is no way to treat RDF data and RDFS/OWL ontologies; nor does it use an XML-based or RDF-based syntax for syntactic interoperability). Therefore, it is only an isolated solution. Finally, it is propositional and does not support variables.

Delores [17] is another implementation, which computes all conclusions from a defeasible theory. It is very efficient, exhibiting linear computational complexity. Delores only supports ambiguity blocking propositional defeasible logic; so, it does not support ambiguity propagation, nor conflicting literals, variables and negation as failure in the object language. Also, it does not integrate with other Semantic Web languages and systems, and is thus an isolated solution.

SweetJess [15] is another implementation of a defeasible reasoning system (situated courteous logic programs) based on Jess. It integrates well with RuleML. However, SweetJess rules can only express reasoning over ontologies expressed in DAMLRuleML (a DAML-OIL like syntax of RuleML) and not on arbitrary RDF data, like DR-DEVICE. Furthermore, SweetJess is restricted to simple terms (variables and atoms). This applies to DR-DEVICE to a large extent. However, the basic R-DEVICE language [7] can support a limited form of functions in the following sense: (a) path expressions are allowed in the rule condition, which can be seen as complex functions, where allowed function names are object referencing slots; (b) aggregate and sorting functions are allowed in the conclusion of aggregate rules. Finally, DR-DEVICE can also support conclusions in non-stratified rule programs due to the presence of truth-maintenance rules [6].

Mandarax [12] is a Java rule platform, which provides a rule mark-up language (compatible with RuleML) for expressing rules and facts that may refer to Java objects. It is based on derivation rules with negation-as-failure, top-down rule evaluation, and generating answers by logical term unification. RDF documents can be loaded into Mandarax as triplets. Furthermore, Mandarax is supported by the Oryx graphical rule management tool. Oryx includes a repository for managing the vocabulary, a formal-natural-language-based rule editor and a graphical user interface library. Contrasted, the rule authoring tool of DR-DEVICE lies closer to the XML nature of its rule syntax and follows a more traditional object-oriented view of the RDF data model [7]. Furthermore, DR-DEVICE supports both negation-as-failure and strong negation, and supports both deductive and defeasible logic rules.

7 Conclusions and Future Work

In this paper we argued that defeasible reasoning is useful for many applications in the Semantic Web, such as modeling policies and business rules, agent brokering and negotiation, ontology and knowledge merging, etc., mainly due to conflicting rules and rule priorities. However, the syntax of defeasible logic may appear too complex for many users; therefore, we have developed a graphical authoring tool to facilitate users in developing a rulebase using a RuleML-compatible defeasible logic rule language. DR-DEVICE is a defeasible reasoning system over RDF metadata, which is implemented on top of the CLIPS production rule system. The rule authoring tool constrains the allowed vocabulary by analyzing the input RDF namespaces, so that the user does not have to type-in class and property names, preventing potential syntactical and semantical errors. Rule visualization follows the tree model of RuleML.

In the future, we plan to delve into the proof layer of the Semantic Web architecture by developing further the graphical environment into a full visual IDE that includes rule execution tracing, explanation, proof exchange in an XML or RDF format, proof visualization and validation, etc. These facilities would be useful for increasing the trust of users for the Semantic Web agents and for automating proof exchange and trust among agents in the Semantic Web.

Acknowledgments

This work is partially funded by the Greek Ministry of Education (EPEAEK) and the European Union under the Pythagoras II programme.

References

[1] Antoniou G. and Arief M., "Executable Declarative Business rules and their use in Electronic Commerce", *Proc. ACM Symposium on Applied Computing*, 2002.
[2] Antoniou G., Billington D. and Maher M.J., "On the analysis of regulations using defeasible rules", *Proc. 32nd Hawaii International Conference on Systems Science*, 1999.
[3] Antoniou G., Billington D., Governatori G. and Maher M.J., "Representation results for defeasible logic", *ACM Trans. on Computational Logic*, 2(2), 2001, pp. 255-287.
[4] Antoniou G., Skylogiannis T., Bikakis A., Bassiliades N., "DR-BROKERING – A Defeasible Logic-Based System for Semantic Brokering", *IEEE Int. Conf. on E-Technology, E-Commerce and E-Service*, pp. 414-417, Hong Kong, 2005.
[5] Ashri R., Payne T., Marvin D., Surridge M. and Taylor S., "Towards a Semantic Web Security Infrastructure", *Proc. of Semantic Web Services*, 2004 Spring Symposium Series, Stanford University, California, 2004.
[6] Bassiliades N., Antoniou, G., Vlahavas I., "A Defeasible Logic Reasoner for the Semantic Web", 3rd Int. Workshop on Rules and Rule Markup Languages for the Semantic Web (RuleML 2004), Springer-Verlag, LNCS 3323, pp. 49-64, Hiroshima, Japan, 2004.
[7] Bassiliades N., Vlahavas I., "R-DEVICE: A Deductive RDF Rule Language", 3rd Int. Workshop on Rules and Rule Markup Languages for the Semantic Web (RuleML 2004), Springer-Verlag, LNCS 3323, pp. 65-80, Hiroshima, Japan, 2004.
[8] Berners-Lee T., Hendler J., and Lassila O., "The Semantic Web", *Scientific American*, 284(5), 2001, pp. 34-43.
[9] Boley H., Tabet S., *The Rule Markup Initiative*, www.ruleml.org/
[10] *CLIPS Basic Programming Guide* (v. 6.21), www.ghg.net/clips/CLIPS.html
[11] Dean M. and Schreiber G., (Eds.), OWL Web Ontology Language Reference, 2004, www.w3.org/TR/2004/REC-owl-ref-20040210/
[12] Dietrich J., Kozlenkov A., Schroeder M., Wagner G., "Rule-based agents for the semantic web", Electronic Commerce Research and Applications, 2(4), pp. 323–338, 2003.
[13] Governatori G., Dumas M., Hofstede A. ter and Oaks P., "A formal approach to legal negotiation", *Proc. ICAIL 2001*, pp. 168-177, 2001.
[14] Grosof B. N., "Prioritized conflict handing for logic programs", *Proc. of the 1997 Int. Symposium on Logic Programming*, pp. 197-211, 1997.
[15] Grosof B.N., Gandhe M.D., Finin T.W., "SweetJess: Translating DAMLRuleML to JESS", *Proc. Int. Workshop on Rule Markup Languages for Business Rules on the Semantic Web (RuleML 2002)*.
[16] Li N., Grosof B. N. and Feigenbaum J., "Delegation Logic: A Logic-based Approach to Distributed Authorization", *ACM Trans. on Information Systems Security*, 6(1), 2003.
[17] Maher M.J., Rock A., Antoniou G., Billington D., Miller T., "Efficient Defeasible Reasoning Systems", *Int. Journal of Tools with Artificial Intelligence*, 10(4), 2001, pp. 483-501.
[18] McBride B., "Jena: Implementing the RDF Model and Syntax Specification", *Proc. 2nd Int. Workshop on the Semantic Web*, 2001.
[19] Skylogiannis T., Antoniou G., Bassiliades N., Governatori G., "DR-NEGOTIATE – A System for Automated Agent Negotiation with Defeasible Logic-Based Strategies", *IEEE Int. Conf. on E-Technology, E-Commerce and E-Service*, pp. 44-49, Hong Kong, 2005.

Initial Experiences Porting a Bioinformatics Application to a Graphics Processor

Maria Charalambous[1], Pedro Trancoso[1], and Alexandros Stamatakis[2]

[1]Department of Computer Science, University of Cyprus,
75 Kallipoleos Ave., P.O.Box 20537, 1678 Nicosia, Cyprus
{cs00cm, pedro}@ucy.ac.cy
http://www.cs.ucy.ac.cy/~pedro
[2]Institute of Computer Science, Foundation for Research and Technology-Hellas,
P.O. Box 1385, Heraklion, Crete, GR-771 10 Greece
stamatak@ics.forth.gr
http://www.ics.forth.gr/~stamatak

Abstract. Bioinformatics applications are one of the most relevant and compute-demanding applications today. While normally these applications are executed on clusters or dedicated parallel systems, in this work we explore the use of an alternative architecture. We focus on exploiting the compute-intensive characteristics offered by the graphics processors (GPU) in order to accelerate a bioinformatics application. The GPU is a good match for these applications as it is an inexpensive, high-performance SIMD architecture.

In our initial experiments we evaluate the use of a regular graphics card to improve the performance of RAxML, a bioinformatics program for phylogenetic tree inference. In this paper we focus on porting to the GPU the most time-consuming loop, which accounts for nearly 50% of the total execution time. The preliminary results show that the loop code achieves a speedup of 3x while the whole application with a single loop optimization, achieves a speedup of 1.2x.

1 Introduction

The demands from the game application market have been driving the development of better and faster architectures. One such example is the development of the Graphics Cards and more specifically the Graphics Processing Units (GPU). The GPUs are the responsible entities for drawing the fast moving images that we observe on the computer screens. To achieve those real-time realistic animations, the GPUs must perform many floating-point operations per second. As such, and given that the work performed by the GPUs is dedicated to these applications, the GPUs are forced to offer many more computational resources than the general purpose processors (CPU). Given the characteristics of these applications, performance can easily be improved from the use of vector units, *i.e.* using the SIMD programming model. In some way these GPUs have similar characteristics with the classical supercomputers (*e.g.* Cray supercomputers).

While the first GPU models were only capable of handling graphics operations, as they were hardwired, the latest models offer the capability of executing user code. This was originally done for users, and game writers in particular, to be able to write their own graphics operations. Nevertheless, the programmability has opened the power of the GPU for other non-graphics applications. This has lead to the rising interest in a new research field known as General Purpose Computation on Graphics Processing Units or GPGPU [1].

Although different manufacturers offer different models of GPUs, the interface exported for their programming is standard and supported by the graphics card drivers. Currently the two major standards for the GPU interface are OpenGL [2] and DirectX [3]. Because these interfaces were written for programming graphics operations, they are not trivial to be used by general-purpose applications. Consequently, there are some efforts into making environments and tools that make the GPU programming easier for general-purpose applications. One such environment is BrookGPU [4]. Brook makes some extensions to ANSI C in order to support the execution of general-purpose applications on the GPU, making it relatively easy to port an application.

Several general-purpose applications have been mapped to the GPU: dense matrix multiply [5], linear algebra operations [6], sparse matrix solvers for conjugate gradient and multigrid [7], and database operations [8] among others.

In this paper we present our initial experiments in porting a bioinformatics application, RAxML, to execute on the GPU. RAxML is a program for inference of evolutionary trees based on the Maximum Likelihood method. After profiling RAxML's execution we focused on the porting to the BrookGPU environment of a single loop which accounts for nearly 50% of the original execution time. With this program we study the applicability of BrookGPU to real-world applications as RAxML has approximately 10000 lines of source code. In our experiments we compared the execution on a mid-class GPU (NVIDIA FX 5700LE) with a high-end CPU (Pentium 4 3.2GHz). The results show that the loop code may be accelerated by a factor of 3 when executing on the particular GPU. Given that we only optimized a single loop and also that we did not make a considerable effort yet into eliminating all the overheads, the overall improvement observed for the complete application is of 20%. These results are very encouraging and show that the GPU is a cost-effective solution for this application.

This paper is organized as follows: Section 2 presents the GPU architecture, its characteristics and limitations, along with its programming environment. Section 3 describes the bioinformatics application and its porting to the GPU. Section 4 shows the experimental setup and Section 5 discusses the experiments and results obtained. Finally the conclusions are presented in Section 6.

2 Graphics Processing Unit

2.1 Architecture

The GPU is an interesting architecture as it offers a large degree of parallelism at a relatively low cost. Its operations are similar to the well known *vector processing model*. This model is also known from Flynn's taxonomy [9] as *Single Instruction, Multiple Data* or *SIMD*. As such, it is natural that the GPU will be able to perform well on many of the applications that in the past were executed on vector supercomputers.

Another characteristic of the simple parallel architecture of the GPU is that it allows for its performance to grow at a rate faster than the well known Moore's law. In fact the GPU has been increasing at a rate of 2.5 to 3.0x a year as opposed to 1.4x for the CPU.

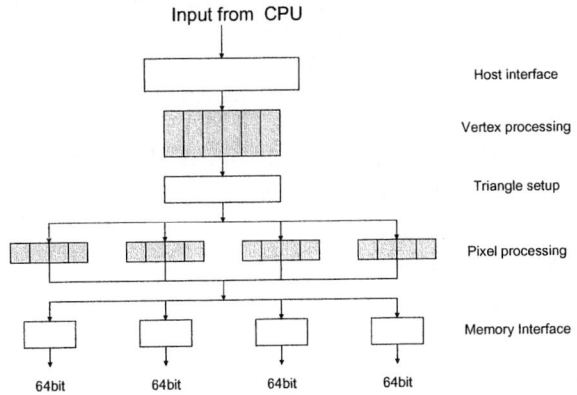

Fig. 1. GPU architecture

The general architecture of the GPU is depicted in Figure 1. Notice that the GPU includes two different types of processing units: vertex processors and pixel (or fragment) processors. This terminology comes from the graphics operations that each one is responsible for. For example, the vertex processor performs mathematical operations that transform a vertex into a screen position. This result is then pipelined to the pixel or fragment processor, which performs the texturing operations.

2.2 Programming Environment

As mentioned before, programming the GPU in an high-level language is a recent development. The first high-level language programming environments were developed for graphics applications in mind. Such examples are Cg from NVIDIA [10] and OpenGL Shading Language [11]. Although helpful, they make the job of mapping a general purpose application a considerable task. Therefore, some research teams are working on developing high-level language programming environments for general purpose programming. One such environment is BrookGPU [4] from Stanford University.

Brook is an extension to the standard ANSI C and is designed in order to facilitate the porting of general purpose applications to the GPU. The main differences from the standard C language are the introduction of the concept of *stream* variables, and *kernel* and *reduction* functions. The programming model offered by BrookGPU for the functions to be executed on the GPU is a *streaming* model. In this model a function processes streams, *i.e.* sequences of data, but operates on a single element at a time.

Using Brook, a function that is executed on the GPU, can be of two types: *kernel* and *reduction*. The former is a general function that accepts multiple input and output parameters which may be of type stream or not. The latter is a function that takes only one stream parameter and returns a single stream output or scalar value. This is used to execute the known reduction operations such as a sum of all the values in a stream.

Finally, BrookGPU has the advantage that it is necessary to write the code once and its runtime will take care of selecting the correct implementation. For example, the same code can execute either on the CPU, or the GPU, using the OpenGL or the DirectX interface. In addition, it also provides an indirection layer such that the user does not need to be aware if the card has a NVIDIA or an ATI chip, for example.

3 GPU-RAxML

3.1 RAxML

RAxML (Randomized Axelerated Maximum Likelihood) [12,13] is a program for inference of evolutionary (phylogenetic) trees from DNA sequence data based on the Maximum Likelihood (ML) Method [14].

Phylogenetic trees are used to represent the evolutionary history of a set of n organisms. An alignment with the DNA or protein sequences of those n organisms can be used as input for the computation of phylogenetic trees. In a phylogeny the organisms of the input data set are located at the tips (leaves) of the tree whereas the inner nodes represent extinct common ancestors. The branches of the tree represent the time which was required for the mutation of one species into another new one.

The inference of phylogenies with computational methods has many important applications in medical and biological research, such as e.g. drug discovery and conservation biology [15]. Due to the rapid growth of sequence data over the last years it has become feasible to compute large trees which comprise more than 1.000 organisms. The computation of the tree-of-life containing representatives of all living beings on earth is considered to be one of the *grand challenges* in Bioinformatics.

The fundamental algorithmic problem computational phylogeny faces is the immense amount of alternative tree topologies which grows exponentially with the number of organisms n, e.g. for $n = 50$ organisms there exist $2.84 * 10^{76}$ alternative trees (number of atoms in the universe $\approx 10^{80}$). Thus, for most biologically meaningful optimality criteria the problem is NP-hard. Moreover, there is a speed/quality *trade-off* among the various evolutionary models which have been devised for tree reconstruction. This means that a phylogenetic analysis with an elaborate model such as ML requires significantly more time but yields trees with superior accuracy than Neighbor Joining [16] or Maximum Parsimony [17,18]. However, due to the higher accuracy it is desirable to infer complex large trees with ML.

The current version of RAxML incorporates novel fast hill climbing and simulated annealing heuristics and is, to the best of our knowledge, the currently fastest and at the same time most accurate program for phylogenetic inference with ML on real world sequence data. Moreover, it has significantly lower memory requirements than comparable implementations [19]. Finally, like every ML-based program, RAxML exhibits a source of fine-grained loop-level parallelism in the likelihood functions which consume over 90% of the overall computation time (see Section 3.2).

3.2 RAxML Profiling

Before porting the application to BrookGPU we profiled its execution time in order to identify the most time-consuming portions of the code. We concentrated our analysis on the loops that had been parallelized for the OpenMP version of RAxML [20]. For each loop we added instructions to measure the time consumed by the corresponding loop execution and also to measure its frequency. The execution time was measured with accuracy using the processor's hardware performance counters [21]. The results obtained for the *test150* input data set (see Section 4) are presented in Figure 2.

These results show that the most time-consuming piece of code is *loop2*, which is visited 4489449 times and accounts for 47% of the total execution time. Equally important is the fact that the five loops that were identified in the profiling phase account altogether for 90% of the total execution time. Also, an analysis of the code shows that the code of the loops is vectorizable without

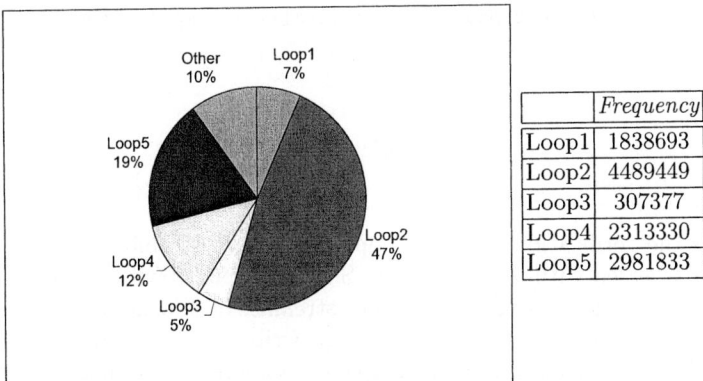

Fig. 2. Execution time and loop frequency profile of RAxML for test150

major changes. Consequently, the profiling results indicate that this application has a good potential for speedup when ported to the GPU.

3.3 Porting RAxML to the GPU

Based on the results presented in the last Section, in our initial experiments we focus on porting *loop2* to execute on the GPU. To achieve this goal we use the BrookGPU system as presented in Section 2.2. This porting is a good case-study for studying the applicability of BrookGPU as a platform for real-world applications as RAxML is composed of approximately 10000 lines of source code.

In BrookGPU there are two types of source files: regular C++ (or C) source files (*.c* files) and Brook source files (*.br* files). The latter are the ones containing the code that is to be executed on the GPU. The code to execute on the GPU has to be included in special functions named *kernel*. These *kernel* function perform the same set of operations on different data elements belonging to the same *stream* of data.

The first step in porting the application is to identify the code to execute on the card. To be effective this has to be a loop in the original source code. Once this loop is identified, a pre-condition for it to be ported to the GPU is that there are no dependencies in the data accesses in the loop's operations across different iterations. This means that the data accesses in a certain iteration are different from the ones in any other iteration, therefore independent, and consequently iterations may safely be executed in parallel, without resulting in any conflicts. In practice this is the definition of a loop being vectorizable. For our example an excerpt of the code is presented in Figure 3.

```
...
for (i = 0; i < tr->cdta->endsite; i++) {
    fxqr = tr->rdta->freqa * lqa[i] + tr->rdta->freqg * lqg[i];
    fxqy = tr->rdta->freqc * lqc[i] + tr->rdta->freqt * lqt[i];
    fxqn = fxqr + fxqy;
    ...
    lpa[i] = sumaq * (zzr * (lra[i] - tempi) + tempj);
    ...
}
...
```

Fig. 3. Original loop2 code

After the verification that the loop code is vectorizable, we need to identify the data accessed within an iteration. Simple variables will not be changed but arrays will have to be transformed into streams. In addition, we need to determine if the data is accessed in a read-only, write-only, or read-write fashion.

The next step is to extract the loop code and create a kernel function with it. The function parameters are the variables as identified in the previous step. In addition, the keyword *out* needs to be used for all returning parameters. Notice that this function, as it contains the code to be executed on the GPU, needs to be placed in a separate file, a *Brook* file (*.br*), in order for the corresponding code to be correctly generated by the system. For our example mentioned above, the Brook kernel function is the one presented in Figure 4.

```
kernel void
second_loop(float4 lq<>, out float lp_x<>, ...
            float i_freqa, float i_freqg, float i_freqc, float i_freqt,...)
{
    float fxqr, fxqy, fxqn;
    ...
    fxqr = i_freqa * lq.x + i_freqg * lq.y;
    fxqy = i_freqc * lq.z + i_freqt * lq.w;
    fxqn = fxqr + fxqy;
    ...
    lp_x = sumaq * (zzr * (lr.x - tempi) + tempj);
    ...
}
```

Fig. 4. Brook kernel function for loop2 code.

In the original code, the loop code is replaced with a function call to the new kernel function. In addition, it is necessary to pack the arrays into streams before the kernel call and unpack the output streams into regular arrays after the kernel call. The packing function is called *streamRead* and the unpacking one *streamWrite*. For our example the code looks like the one presented in Figure 5.

```
    ...
    streamRead(lq, lq_array);
    second_loop(lq,lp_x,...,i_freqa,i_freqg,i_freqc,i_freqt,...);
    streamWrite(lp_x, lpa);
    ...
```

Fig. 5. Application with call to kernel function

It is necessary to note that this procedure may not be straightforward in all cases as the use of the graphics card imposes some limitations. Examples of such limitations are the size of the stream used, the type and number of parameters that may be passed to the kernel function, and the operations performed within the kernel function. A detailed analysis of some of these limitations and proposed solutions is presented in [22].

4 Experimental Setup

For the experiments presented in this paper we used one graphics card and one computer setup. The graphics card used was a NVIDIA GeForce FX 5700

LE [23]. This card has a NV36 graphics processor clocked at 250MHz, 128MB DDR video memory clocked at 200MHz and the data transfers with the PC are done through the AGP interface. The NV36 processor includes 3 vertex and 4 pixel pipelines [24].

As for the computer system we used a *high-end* Intel Pentium 4 3.2GHz based system with 1GB RAM.

The application used is RAxML as described in Section 3.1. The input data set used in these experiments is composed of an alignment of 150 sequences or organisms where each organism is represented by a DNA sequence of a length of 1269 nucleotides. This input set is named *test150*.

The environment used was BrookGPU version 0.3 [4] as described in Section 2.2. For the experiments, Brook was compiled using the Intel C++ compiler with the release compile flag, *i.e.* with full code optimizations.

For the experiments we compare the execution time of running the code on the regular CPU of the system and on the GPU of the graphics card. We measure these two situations using the same code as the BrookGPU runtime allows the user to decide where the code should be executed depending on the value of an environment variable (*BRT_RUNTIME*). If we set the variable *BRT_RUNTIME* to *cpu* the code will execute on the system's CPU while if we set the variable to *nv30gl* it will execute on the card's GPU.

5 Experimental Results

As previously described, in this preliminary study we focused on porting one loop, *loop2*, from the original code to execute on the GPU. The speedup obtained from executing the modified application on the GPU comparing to the execution on the CPU is shown in Figure 6.

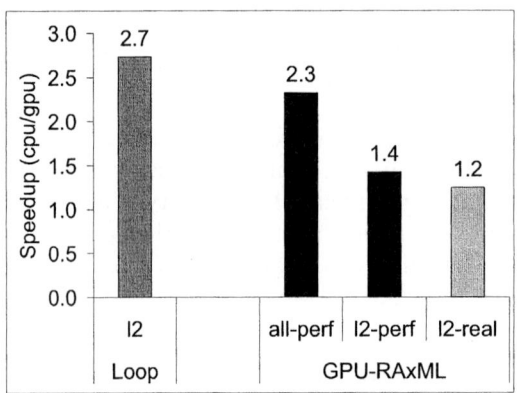

Fig. 6. Speedup of GPU-RAxML when executing on GPU compared to CPU

In this Figure we present four bars separated into two groups: *Loop* on the left, which represents the results for the speedup of the *loop2* loop code; and *GPU-RAxML* on the right, which represents the results for the speedup of the complete RAxML application compared to the execution on the CPU. In the latter group we have three bars: two dark ones representing predicted speedup and a lighter one representing measured speedup. From left to right, the first bar, *all-perf*, represents the predicted speedup for the complete application, assuming that all loops have been ported to the GPU and that each loop achieves the same speedup as the one observed for *loop2*. The second bar, *loop2-perf*, represents the predicted speedup for the complete application, assuming that only *loop2* has been ported to the GPU. Both predicted values have been determined using Amdahl's law, the profiling information, as well as the speedup measured for *loop2*. Finally, the third bar, *loop2-real*, represents the speedup measured for the whole application in the situation where only *loop2* has been ported to the GPU. Notice that both the *loop2* and predicted speedup values do not take into account any extra overheads of sending and receiving data to and from the GPU, hence the suffix *perf* for perfect speedup, while the *loop2-real* includes all overheads.

From the results in the Figure 6 it is possible to observe that the use of the GPU is very effective. For the code of the loop we optimize, the GPU achieves a speedup of nearly 3x. It is important to notice that the GPU used is not a high-end model while the CPU used is a high-end model. As a consequence, this is not a very fair comparison for the GPU. A more realistic setup would have either a high-end GPU or a lower-end CPU. This would result in a much larger advantage for the GPU.

Regarding the overall application speedup, notice that the observed real speedup is only 1.2, *i.e.* the GPU performs only 20% better than the CPU. Nevertheless, this is 86% of the perfect speedup of 1.4. The 14% of the "lost" speedup is due to data transfer and other overheads related to the preparation of the data to be sent and received from the GPU. At this point we did not concentrate in eliminating these overheads as we are still studying the potential for the use of the GPU for this application. In the near future we will study some changes to the original program in order to reduce these overheads and bring the *real* speedup closer to the *pref* one. In addition, we are currently porting the rest of the loops to the GPU and therefore we expect an increase in the observed speedup that could reach the predicted value of 2.3 shown in the *all-perf* bar.

Notice that the speedup observed is even more impressive when we consider the cost and power consumption of the processors used. If we consider the price information in PriceWatch [25], the NVIDIA 5700LE card costs approximately US$75 while the Pentium 4 US$200, *i.e.* 2.7 times more expensive. Furthermore, while the NVIDIA chip consumes approximately 24W [26], the Pentium 4 3.2GHz consumes approximately 5.5x more power, as it consumes more than 130W. This leads to the conclusion that the use of the GPU is a very cost- and power-effective solution for this type of application.

6 Conclusions

In this paper we presented our initial experiments in evaluating the potential of porting a bioinformatics application to execute on the Graphics Processor Unit. For the preliminary results presented in this paper we focused on porting to the BrookGPU environment a single loop from the RAxML application, which typically accounts for nearly 50% of the original execution time.

In our experiments, we compared the execution on a mid-class GPU (NVIDIA FX 5700LE) with a high-end CPU (Pentium 4 3.2GHz). In the experiments performed, the loop code achieved a speedup of 3x when executing on the GPU compared to the high-end CPU. Although this has resulted in only an improvement of 20% in the overall application, this value will increase as we port the rest of the loops to the GPU and perform some code modifications to reduce certain overheads.

Overall, the loop speedup results are very encouraging and lead us to conclude that the GPU is a solution that is able to achieve high-speedup with lower cost and less power consumption compared to high-end systems.

Acknowledgments

We would like to thank Michael Ott from Technical University of Munich for his help with the RAxML code and the anonymous reviewers for their valuable comments. Finally, we thank the German Academic Exchange Service (DAAD) for funding the postdoctoral research of A. Stamatakis.

References

1. GPGPU: General-Purpose Computation Using Graphics Hardware. http://www.gpgpu.org/ (2005)
2. Segal, M., Akeley, K.: The OpenGL Graphics System: A Specification (Version 2.0) (2004)
3. Peeper, C.: DirectX High Level Shading Language. Microsoft Meltdown UK Presentation, Microsoft Corporation (2002)
4. Buck, I., Foley, T., Horn, D., Sugerman, J., Fatahalian, K., Houston, M., Hanrahan, P.: Brook for GPUs: Stream Computing on Graphics Hardware. ACM Transactions on Graphics **23** (2004) 777–786
5. Larsen, E., McAllister, D.: Fast matrix multiplies using graphics hardware. In: Supercomputing '01: Proceedings of the 2001 ACM/IEEE conference on Supercomputing (CDROM), ACM Press (2001) 55–55
6. Kruger, J., Westermann, R.: Linear algebra operators for GPU implementation of numerical algorithms. ACM Transactions on Graphics **22** (2003) 908–916
7. Bolz, J., Farmer, I., Grinspun, E., Schrooder, P.: Sparse matrix solvers on the GPU: conjugate gradients and multigrid. ACM Transactions on Graphics **22** (2003) 917–924
8. Govindaraju, N., Lloyd, B., Wang, W., Lin, M., Manocha, D.: Fast Computation of Database Operations using Graphics Processors. In: SIGMOD '04: Proceedings of the 2004 ACM SIGMOD international conference on Management of data, ACM Press (2004) 215–226

9. Flynn, M.: Very high-speed computing systems. Proceedings of the IEEE **54** (1966) 1901–1909
10. Mark, W., Glanville, R., Akeley, K., Kilgard, M.: Cg: a system for programming graphics hardware in a C-like language. ACM Transactions on Graphics **22** (2003) 896–907
11. Kessenich, J., Baldwin, D., Rost, R.: The OpenGL Shading Language (2004)
12. Stamatakis, A., Ludwig, T., Meier, H.: RAxML-III: A Fast Program for Maximum Likelihood-based Inference of Large Phylogenetic Trees. Bioinformatics **21** (2005) 456–463
13. Stamatakis, A.: An Efficient Program for phylogenetic Inference Using Simulated Annealing. In: Proceedings of IPDPS2005, Denver, Colorado, USA (2005)
14. Felsenstein, J.: Evolutionary trees from DNA sequences: A maximum likelihood approach. Journal of Molecular Evolution **17** (1981) 368–376
15. Bader, D., Moret, B.M., Vawter, L.: Industrial Applications of High-Performance Computing for Phylogeny Reconstruction. In: Proceedings of SPIE ITCom: Commercial Applications for High-Performance Computing, Denver, Colorado, USA (2001) 159–168
16. Gascuel, O.: BIONJ: An improved version of the NJ algorithm based on a simple model of sequence data. Molecular Biology and Evolution **14** (1997) 685–695
17. Guindon, S., Gascuel, O.: A Simple, Fast, and Accurate Algorithm to Estimate Large Phylogenies by Maximum Likelihood. Systematic Biology **52** (2003) 696–704
18. Williams, T., Moret, B.M.: An Investigation of Phylogenetic Likelihood Methods. In: Proceedings of 3rd IEEE Symposium on Bioinformatics and Bioengineering (BIBE'03), Bethesda, Maryland, USA (2003)
19. Stamatakis, A., Ludwig, T., Meier, H.: New Fast and Accurate Heuristics for Inference of Large Phylogenetic Trees. In: Proceedings of IPDPS2004, Santa Fe, New Mexico, USA (2004)
20. Stamatakis, A., Ott, M., Ludwig, T.: RAxML-OMP: An Efficient Program for Phylogenetic Inference on SMPs. In: Proceedings of 8th International Conference on Parallel Computing Technologies (PaCT2005), Krasnojarsk, Russia (2005) Preprint available on-line at www.ics.forth.gr/~stamatak.
21. Intel: IA-32 Intel Architecture: Software Developers Manual. Volume 3 of System Programming Guide. Intel (2003)
22. Trancoso, P., Charalambous, M.: Exploring Graphics Processor Performance for General Purpose Applications. In: Proceedings of the Euromicro Symposium on Digital System Design, Architectures, Methods and Tools (DSD 2005). (2005)
23. NVIDIA: NVIDIA GeForce FX: Performance. http://www.nvidia.com/page/fx_5700.html (2005)
24. TechPowerUp: GPU Database. http://www.techpowerup.com/gpudb/ (2005)
25. PriceWatch: Price Comparison Search Engine. http://www.pricewatch.com (2005)
26. Tscheblockov, T.: Power Consumption of Contemporary Graphics Accelerators. http://www.xbitlabs.com/articles/video/display/ati-vs-nv-power.html (2004)

Improving the Accuracy of Classifiers for the Prediction of Translation Initiation Sites in Genomic Sequences

George Tzanis, Christos Berberidis, Anastasia Alexandridou, and Ioannis Vlahavas

Department of Informatics, Aristotle University of Thessaloniki,
Thessaloniki 54124, Greece
{gtzanis, berber, aalexan, vlahavas}@csd.auth.gr
http://mlkd.csd.auth.gr

Abstract. The prediction of the Translation Initiation Site (TIS) in a genomic sequence is an important issue in biological research. Although several methods have been proposed to deal with this problem, there is a great potential for the improvement of the accuracy of these methods. Due to various reasons, including noise in the data as well as biological reasons, TIS prediction is still an open problem and definitely not a trivial task. In this paper we follow a three-step approach in order to increase TIS prediction accuracy. In the first step, we use a feature generation algorithm we developed. In the second step, all the candidate features, including some new ones generated by our algorithm, are ranked according to their impact to the accuracy of the prediction. Finally, in the third step, a classification model is built using a number of the top ranked features. We experiment with various feature sets, feature selection methods and classification algorithms, compare with alternative methods, draw important conclusions and propose improved models with respect to prediction accuracy.

1 Introduction

The rapid progress of computer science in the last decades has been closely followed by a similar progress in molecular biology. Undoubtedly, the use of computational tools has given a boost in the collection and analysis of biological data, creating one of the hottest areas of research, namely bioinformatics. Molecular biology deals with the study of the structure and function of biological macromolecules. During the last decade, the field of data mining and knowledge discovery provided the biologists with a new set of tools for high performance processing of large volumes of data. As a multidisciplinary field, data mining uses techniques from various other areas, such as artificial intelligence, machine learning, statistics, database technology, etc.

Genomic sequences represent a large portion of the biological data that require the use of computational tools in order to be analyzed. Despite the rapid developments of the ongoing research in this field, there is still limited knowledge about the role that each part of these molecules plays and how this relates to other parts. The large size of the sequences and the numerous possible features are the main reasons behind the urgent need for representation, algorithmic and mathematical methods that allow for the efficient analysis of such data and the delivery of accurate and reliable knowledge to the domain expert. Depending on the problem tackled, pattern discovery and classification are two of the most common tasks usually performed on these symbolic sequences, that consist of an alphabet of nucleotides or amino acids.

Translation, along with transcription and replication, are the major operations that relate to biological sequences. The recognition of Translation Initiation Sites (TISs) is essential for genome annotation and for better understanding of the process of translation. It has been recognized as one of the most critical problems in molecular biology that requires the generation of classification models, in order to accurately and reliably distinguish the valid TISs from a set of false ones. However, the traditional machine learning methods are not directly applicable to these data.

The necessity to adapt these methods to this kind of problems has been the motivation behind our research. Although many approaches have been proposed to deal with this problem, there is a great potential for the improvement of their accuracy. In this paper we apply data mining to tackle the problem of the prediction of TISs in DNA sequences. We use a large number of features and different classifiers in order to build more accurate models. Some of the features are directly extracted from the raw sequences, concerning the nucleotides present at each position of the sequence, but most of them are generated. Along with the features already discussed in other papers, we generate and propose the use of some new ones. We show that a combination of these features improves the accuracy of the prediction models. In order to select the best features, various ranking algorithms are utilized to evaluate the contribution of each feature to the accuracy of prediction. After a number of the best features is selected, we use various algorithms to build classification models. We present the results of our experiments, we compare them with other methods and finally, we draw interesting conclusions. For our experiments we used a real world dataset that contains processed DNA sequences collected from vertebrate organisms.

This paper is outlined as follows: In the next section we briefly present the relative work in the area of TIS prediction. In section three we describe the problem and provide the background knowledge. In section four we present the dataset and the approach selected. Section five contains the results of our experiments and finally, in section six we present our conclusions as well as some directions for future research.

2 Related Work

Since 1982 the prediction of TISs has been extensively studied using biological approaches, data mining techniques and statistical models. Stormo et al. [17] used the perceptron algorithm to distinguish the TISs. Meanwhile, in 1978 Kozak and Shatkin [9] had proposed the ribosome scanning model, which was later updated by Kozak [7]. According to this model, translation initiates at the first start codon that has an appropriate context. Later, in 1987 Kozak developed the first weight matrix for the identification of TISs in cDNA sequences [6]. The following consensus pattern was derived from this matrix: GCC[**AG**]CCatg**G**. The bold residues are the highly conserved positions.

Pedersen and Nielsen [13] made use of artificial neural networks (ANNs) to predict which AUG codons are TISs achieving an overall accuracy of 88% in Arabidopsis thaliana dataset and 85% in vertebrate dataset. Zien et al. [20] studied the same vertebrate dataset, but instead of ANNs employed support vector machines using various kernel functions. Hatzigeorgiou [3] proposed an ANN system named "DIANA-TIS" consisting of two modules: the consensus ANN, sensitive to the conserved motif and the coding ANN, sensitive to the coding or non-coding context around the initiation codon. The method was applied in human cDNA data and 94% of the TISs were correctly predicted. Salamov et al. [16] developed the program ATGpr, using a linear discriminant approach for the recognition of TISs by estimating the probability of each ATG codon being the TIS. Nishikawa et al. [12] presented an improved program, ATGpr_sim, which employs a new prediction algorithm based on both statistical and similarity information. This new algorithm exploits the similarity to known protein sequences achieving better performance in terms of sensitivity and specificity.

Zeng et al. [19] used feature generation and correlation based feature selection along with machine learning algorithms. In their study, used a large number of k-gram nucleotide patterns. Using a ribosome scanning model and the selected features they achieved an overall accuracy of 94% on the vertebrate dataset of Pedersen and Nielsen. In [11] the three-step approach followed in [19] (feature selection, feature generation and feature integration) is also presented. They discuss various methods for feature selection and describe the use of different classification algorithms. Later, in [10] the same three-step method was used, but k-gram amino acid patterns were generated, instead of k-gram nucleotide patterns. A number of the top ranked features were selected by an entropy based algorithm and a classification model was built for recognition of TISs applying support vector machines or ensembles of decision trees.

3 Background Knowledge and Problem Description

The main structural and functional molecules of an organism's cell are proteins. Another important family of molecules are nucleic acids. The most common nucleic acids are deoxyribonucleic acid (DNA) and ribonucleic acid (RNA). DNA is the genetic material of almost every living organism. RNA has many functions inside a cell and plays an important role in protein synthesis. Both proteins and nucleic acids are linear polymers of smaller molecules (monomers). The term sequence is used to refer to the order of monomers that compose the polymer. A sequence can be represented as a string of different symbols, one for each monomer. There are twenty protein monomers called amino acids and five nucleic acid monomers called nucleotides. Every nucleotide is characterized by the nitrogenous base it contains: adenine (A), cytosine (C), guanine (G), thymine (T), or uracil (U). DNA may contain a combination of A, C, G, and T. In RNA U appears instead of T. A sequence of nucleotides has two ends called the $5'$ and the $3'$ end. Moreover, it is directed from the $5'$ to the $3'$ end ($5' \rightarrow 3'$). Proteins and nucleic acids are called macromolecules, due to their length.

Proteins are synthesized by the following process. DNA is transcribed into a messenger RNA (mRNA) molecule (transcription). Then mRNA is used as template for the synthesis of a protein molecule (translation). In our setup, we focus on the process of translation, which is further explained below.

An organelle called ribosome is the "factory" where translation takes place. The mRNA sequence is scanned by the ribosome, which reads triplets of nucleotides named codons. Thus, a protein of n amino acids is coded by a sequence of $3n$ nucleotides. Some amino acids are coded by more than one codon. There are three different ways to read a given sequence in a given direction. Each of these ways of reading is referred to as reading frame. The first reading frame starts at position 1, the second at position 2 and the third at position 3 of the sequence. The reading frame that is translated into a protein is named Open Reading Frame (ORF).

Translation, usually, initiates at the AUG codon nearest to the 5' end of the mRNA sequence. However, there are some escape mechanisms that allow the initiation of translation at following, but still near the 5' end AUG codons. These mechanisms of translation initiation make more difficult the recognition of the TIS on a given genomic sequence. Also, GUG and UUG sometimes are used as start codons, but this rarely happens in eukaryotes [8]. Moreover, there are three stop codons encoding the termination of translation (UAG, UAA and UGA). After the initiation of translation, the ribosome "reads" the mRNA codon by codon. For each codon "read" a transfer RNA (tRNA) molecule brings the proper amino acid. The amino acid is added to the protein chain, which, by this way, is elongated until a stop codon is reached.

A codon that is contained in the same reading frame with respect to another codon is referred to as "in-frame codon". The coding region of an ORF is bounded by the initiation codon and the first in-frame stop codon. The direction of translation is $5' \rightarrow 3'$. We name upstream the region of a nucleotide sequence from a reference point towards the 5' end. Respectively, the region of a nucleotide sequence from a reference point towards the 3' end is referred to as downstream. In TIS prediction problems the reference point is an AUG codon. The above are illustrated in Fig. 1.

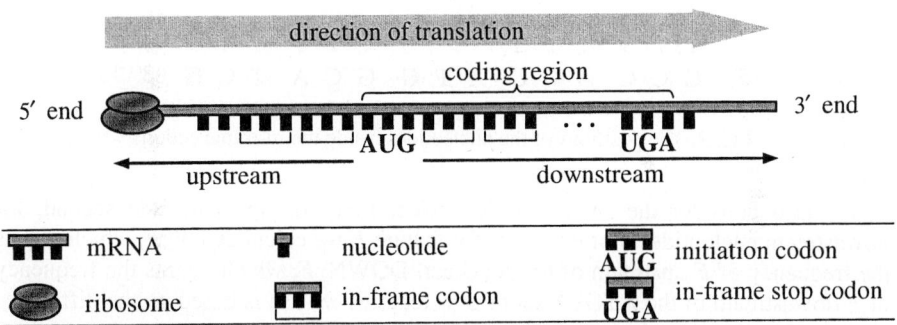

Fig. 1. Translation initiation - The ribosome scans the mRNA until it reads an AUG codon. If the AUG codon has appropriate context, then probably the translation initiates at that site.

4 Materials and Methods

In this section we describe the dataset and the three step approach we followed in order to improve the classification accuracy.

4.1 Dataset

The original dataset we use consists of 3312 genomic sequences collected from various vertebrate organisms. These sequences were extracted from GenBank, the US

NIH genetic sequence database [2] and only those sequences with an annotated TIS are included. The dataset is publicly available in [5]. The DNA sequences have been processed in order to remove the interlacing non-coding regions (introns) and their alphabet consists of the letters A, C, G and T. Thus, a candidate initiation codon is referred to as ATG codon instead of AUG codon. These sequences contain 13503 ATG codons in total, whereof 3312 of them are TISs.

4.2 Feature Generation

In order to build the classification models, we generate a large number of frequency counting features. Among them is a set of k-gram nucleotide patterns, i.e. nucleotide sequences of length k. For example, A, C, G and T are the four 1-grams for a DNA sequence. AA, AC, AG, AT are four of the sixteen possible 2-grams. Each k-gram nucleotide pattern is an individual feature. Also, the in-frame $3n$-grams are generated (n is a positive integer). For instance, the feature IN_GCC counts the in-frame GCC codons.

Apart from k-grams, we also generate a new set of features of the form IN_POS_k_X, where $1 \leq k \leq 3$ and X is any nucleotide. By POS_k we mean the position k at an in-frame codon. For example, in the sequence of Fig. 2 the value of IN_POS_2_C is 4. Moreover, we generate a number of new features to count the differences of the frequencies between the nucleotides. For example, we consider the feature A/G-T/C_DIF, which counts the difference of thymines and cytosines from the adenines and guanines (A + G – T – C).

Fig. 2. The positions of the nucleotides inside the in-frame codons

We also consider the same features twice; first, for upstream and second, for downstream nucleotides. For example, for feature F we calculate UP_F, which counts the frequency of F upstream of the ATG and DOWN_F, which counts the frequency of F downstream of the ATG. A set of new features we use is based on the difference between upstream and downstream occurrences. These features are denoted as UP_DOWN_F_DIF. For example, UP_DOWN_A/G_DIF counts the difference between upstream and downstream frequencies of adenines and guanines.

The following binary features are also included: DOWN_IN_STOP and A/G_POS_-3. The former indicates the existence of a downstream stop codon (TAA, TAG or TGA) inside the same reading frame of the ATG. The latter indicates the presence of an adenine or a guanine at position –3, according to Kozak's consensus pattern. The position of the A of the ATG codon is considered to be the position +1 and the numbering increases for the next nucleotides. The nucleotide preceding the A of the ATG codon is at position –1, and the numbering decreases for upstream nucleotides (Fig. 3). Finally, each position of the window is also considered as an individual feature (i.e. POS_+3).

```
-6 -5 -4 -3 -2 -1 +1 +2 +3 +4 +5 +6 +7 +8 +9
5'  G  C  C  A  C  C  A  T  G  G  C  A  T  C  G  3'
```

Fig. 3. The positions of the nucleotides relative to an ATG codon

We have developed an iterative algorithm to generate all the above described features. At each iteration a sequence is read from the given dataset. Then, the sequence is scanned and when an ATG codon is found, a window centered at this codon is created. The window covers N nucleotides upstream and N nucleotides downstream of the ATG. N is given by the user. After the window is created, it is scanned once for each feature in order to calculate its value. The calculated value for a certain feature may be a frequency count, a binary value or a nominal value for the features concerning the nucleotide presence at each position of the window. The positions that do not correspond to any nucleotide, because the segment of the sequence is shorter than the end of the window, are denoted as unknown by the symbol "?". When the values of all the features have been calculated, they are stored in an output file as a new record. This file is the input for the feature selection algorithms.

4.3 Feature Selection

Zeng et al. in [19] used k-gram nucleotide patterns for $1 \leq k \leq 5$. Their study illustrated that the use of 4-grams or 5-grams does not improve the classification accuracy. We used k-grams for $1 \leq k \leq 6$ (also in-frame 3-grams and 6-grams were used) and observed that k-grams for $k > 3$ could not improve the classification accuracy. Therefore, we focused on the k-gram nucleotide patterns for $k \leq 3$. We experimented with various

Table 1. The basic features considered in our study

Features in [19]	New Features	Best Features
POS_-3	DOWN_IN_POS_2_T	POS_-3
UP_IN_ATG	DOWN_IN_POS_3_C	UP_ATG
DOWN_IN_CTG	DOWN_IN_POS_1_G	UP_IN_ATG
DOWN_IN_TAA	UP_DOWN_A/G_DIF	DOWN_IN_STOP
DOWN_IN_TAG	UP_DOWN_C/T_DIF	DOWN_IN_POS_2_T
DOWN_IN_TGA		DOWN_IN_POS_3_C
DOWN_IN_GAC		DOWN_IN_POS_1_G
DOWN_IN_GAG		UP_DOWN_A/G_DIF
DOWN_IN_GCC		UP_DOWN_C/T_DIF

window lengths and we present detailed results for a window of 189 nucleotides. We used three evaluation measures, information gain measure, gain ratio measure and chi-squared statistic in order to rank the candidate features. A number of features exposing a good ranking in all tests were selected. Table 1 shows the feature set proposed in [19], the new features we propose and the best ones finally selected.

4.4 Classification

We use three different classification algorithms to test the improvement in accuracy achieved by the use of the new features. The first is C4.5 [15], a decision tree construction algorithm. The second is a propositional rule learner, called Repeated Incremental Pruning to Produce Error Reduction or RIPPER in short [1]. The last algorithm is a Naïve Bayes classifier [4]. We run each algorithm applying 10-fold cross validation, which is generally considered to be one of the most reliable accuracy estimation methods. Moreover, each experiment is repeated ten times and the average results are used for the comparisons.

The results of cross validation are evaluated according to some standard performance measures (Table 2). *Sensitivity* or *TP Rate* measures the proportion of the correctly classified TISs over the total number of TISs. *Specificity* or *TN Rate* measures the proportion of the correctly classified non-TISs over the total number of non-TISs. *Precision* measures the proportion of the correctly classified TISs over the total number of the instances classified as TISs. Finally, *accuracy* measures the proportion of the correctly classified instances over the total number of instances. Zeng et al. [19] use another performance measure, named *adjusted accuracy*. This measure is useful when the dataset is skewed, namely when one class has significantly more instances than the other. This is also the case with our dataset, since the number of non-TISs is significantly larger than the number of TISs and so we included it in our experiments.

Table 2. Measures of cross validation performance (TP: True Positives, TN: True Negatives, FP: False Positives, FN: False Negatives)

Sensitivity (TP Rate)	$\dfrac{TP}{TP + FN}$	Accuracy	$\dfrac{TP + TN}{TP + FP + TN + FN}$
Specificity (TN Rate)	$\dfrac{TN}{TN + FP}$		
Precision	$\dfrac{TP}{TP + FP}$	Adjusted Accuracy	$\dfrac{Sensitivity + Specificity}{2}$

5 Experiments and Discussion

For the conduction of our experiments we used the Weka library of machine learning algorithms [18]. In order to compare our new features with the features proposed in the work of Zeng et al. [19] we have built classifiers using C4.5, RIPPER, and Naïve Bayes and three feature sets. The first feature set (denoted as [19]) contains the nine features proposed in [19]. The second (denoted as [19] + New) contains the features proposed in [19] along with the new features we propose and the third (denoted as Best) contains the best features selected, namely a combination of the features contained in the second feature set with some already studied features (see Table 1). We discovered that the new features improve the classification accuracy of the three classifiers. When the second of the aforementioned feature sets is used with the C4.5

classifier the accuracy increases from 88.63% to 91.44% (3.17% improvement). With the RIPPER classifier the accuracy increases from 88.31% to 92.11% (4.30% improvement) and finally with the Naïve Bayes classifier the accuracy increases from 85.21% to 87.08% (2.19% improvement). Better results are reported when the third feature set is used, where the improvement in accuracy ranges from 6.23% to 6.70%. The results of our experiments are listed in Table 3, while the graphs in Fig. 4 display the accuracy and the adjusted accuracy achieved by each of the three classifiers.

Table 3. Classification performance of the three classifiers using 10-fold cross validation for the features presented in Table 1

Features	Algorithm	Sensitivity	Specificity	Precision	Adjusted Accuracy	Accuracy
[19]	C4.5	93.78 %	72.79 %	91.38 %	83.29 %	88.63 %
	RIPPER	92.52 %	75.36 %	92.03 %	83.94 %	88.31 %
	Naïve Bayes	85.77 %	83.49 %	94.11 %	84.63 %	85.21 %
[19] + New	C4.5	94.95 %	80.64 %	93.78 %	87.80 %	91.44 %
	RIPPER	94.83 %	83.74 %	94.72 %	89.29 %	92.11 %
	Naïve Bayes	85.75 %	91.17 %	96.76 %	88.46 %	87.08 %
Best	C4.5	97.09 %	85.65 %	95.42 %	91.37 %	94.28 %
	RIPPER	96.66 %	86.77 %	95.74 %	91.71 %	94.23 %
	Naïve Bayes	90.58 %	90.32 %	96.64 %	90.45 %	90.52 %
[19] + DIST	C4.5	96.33 %	88.48 %	96.26 %	92.40 %	94.40 %
	RIPPER	95.83 %	88.95 %	96.39 %	92.39 %	94.14 %
	Naïve Bayes	87.49 %	87.52 %	95.57 %	87.50 %	87.50 %
[19] + New + DIST	C4.5	96.73 %	89.11 %	96.47 %	92.92 %	94.86 %
	RIPPER	96.15 %	90.23 %	96.80 %	93.19 %	94.70 %
	Naïve Bayes	85.73 %	91.54 %	96.89 %	88.63 %	87.15 %
Best + DIST	C4.5	98.07 %	93.07 %	97.75 %	95.57 %	96.84 %
	RIPPER	97.62 %	93.08 %	97.75 %	95.35 %	96.51 %
	Naïve Bayes	89.41 %	90.65 %	96.71 %	90.03 %	89.72 %
[19] + ORDER	C4.5	95.08 %	76.29 %	92.50 %	85.69 %	90.47 %
	RIPPER	94.89 %	76.56 %	92.57 %	85.72 %	90.39 %
	Naïve Bayes	85.40 %	87.77 %	95.55 %	86.59 %	85.98 %
[19] + New + ORDER	C4.5	95.71 %	81.12 %	93.98 %	88.42 %	92.14 %
	RIPPER	95.34 %	83.55 %	94.69 %	89.44 %	92.45 %
	Naïve Bayes	85.56 %	91.20 %	96.76 %	88.38 %	86.94 %
Best + ORDER	C4.5	97.04 %	85.63 %	95.41 %	91.34 %	94.24 %
	RIPPER	96.56 %	86.89 %	95.77 %	91.72 %	94.19 %
	Naïve Bayes	87.59 %	90.23 %	96.50 %	88.91 %	88.24 %

In order to further improve the accuracy of classifiers we include the distance feature (DIST) used in [19], which counts the distance of the current ATG codon from the beginning of the sequence. This feature improves sensibly the accuracy in all cases. However, in many occasions the sequence length is not precisely known. It is possible for a sequence to lack some nucleotides from its start. Generally, the error-free sequences are rare. Thus, the use of feature DIST is not appropriate for every dataset. Aiming to treat this problem we use a new feature that counts the order of the ATG codon inside the sequence (ORDER). Although this feature is also affected by the aforementioned problem, it is less sensitive in such situations. For instance, if a part from the 5′ end of a sequence that does not contain any ATGs is missing, then the feature DIST will not measure the actual distance of an ATG from the beginning of the sequence. On the other hand, the feature ORDER will refer to the actual order. Under these conditions, the scientist who wishes to deal with TIS classification should focus more on the features related to the context of the ATG codon than the use of distance or order features.

As shown in the graphs of Fig. 4, the feature DIST improves sensibly the prediction accuracy. The feature ORDER also improves the prediction accuracy, but less notably. However, this is not the case when the Naïve Bayes classifier is used. In this

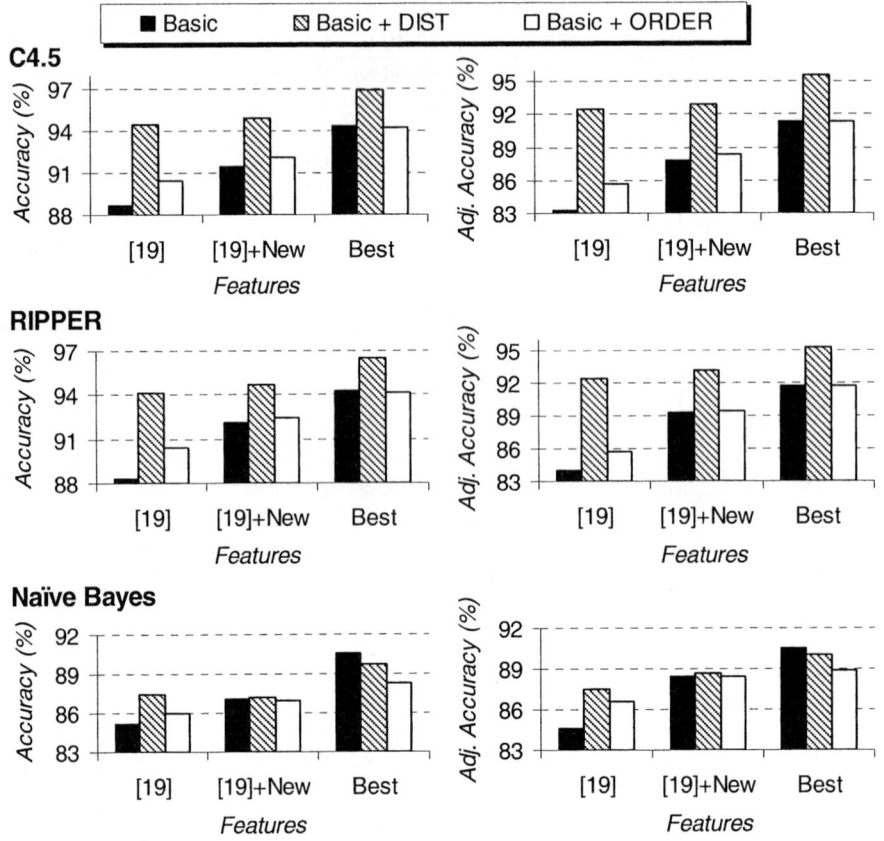

Fig. 4. Comparison of the accuracy and adjusted accuracy achieved by the three classifiers using 10-fold cross validation for the features presented in Table 1. The experiments were repeated, once including the feature DIST (*Basic + DIST*), once including the feature ORDER (*Basic + ORDER*) and once including none of the above two features (*Basic*).

case the use of the DIST or ORDER feature decreases the classification accuracy, when the best features are used. Moreover, all the metrics indicate an improvement in performance. In particular, the increase in sensitivity and specificity together denotes that both TISs and non-TISs are classified more accurately. However, some exceptions are observed. For example, sensitivity decreases when using the second feature set ([19] + New) along with Naïve Bayes classifier. Also, in the same case specificity increases more than sensitivity is reduced. Since our dataset is skewed, as already discussed, the accuracy of prediction decreases as opposed to the adjusted accuracy that increases. More detailed results of our experiments can be found in the following URL: http://mlkd.csd.auth.gr/TIS/index.html.

6 Conclusions and Future Work

The prediction of a TIS in a genomic sequence is very interesting topic in molecular biology. It is not a trivial task and the reasons for this are manifold. First of all, the knowledge about the process of translation is limited. It is known that in more than 90% of the mRNA of eukaryotic organisms the translation initiates at the first AUG codon. However, there are some mechanisms that prevent the initiation of translation at the first AUG codon. Moreover, the available sequences are not always complete and contain errors. For example, due to errors in the dataset used in our study more than 40% of the sequences contain an ATG codon downstream of the true TIS. The same observation was made by Peri and Pandey [14]. They also noticed that most initiation codons contain three or more mismatches from Kozak's consensus pattern. Finally, the translation is affected not only by the primary structure of mRNA (the order of nucleotides in the sequence), but by the secondary structure as well (the structure that forms mRNA after folding). This is a point to wonder if any significant improvement in accuracy of classifiers can be achieved by just considering the primary structure of the genomic sequences.

In this paper, we considered the utilization of a set of new features in order to achieve better accuracy for the prediction of Translation Initiation Sites in genomic sequences. For this purpose we developed a feature generation algorithm, which uses a window of variable length in order to calculate the values of each feature. We applied our algorithm on a real-world dataset that contains processed DNA sequences from vertebrates. We used various algorithms for the evaluation and selection of the features. After extensive experimentation we discovered that the use of these features improves the accuracy of a number of different classifiers. In some cases the accuracy reaches 97%, which, under the issues discussed is considered more than satisfactory.

We conclude by providing some directions for future work. There is a great variety of features that can be generated and describe a genomic sequence. Only a portion of them has been so far studied. Our future plans involve the experimentation with novel features, especially those that indicate periodic occurrences of nucleotides. The study of features that incorporate information about the secondary structure of mRNA is also another concern. Additionally, we aim to use more datasets in order to verify the results and study the impact of the features we proposed in other kind of organisms. Finally, experiments with a larger range of window sizes are also under consideration.

References

1. Cohen, W.: Fast Effective Rule Induction. In Proceedings of the 12th International Conference on Machine Learning. Morgan Kaufmann, Lake Tahoe, California, USA (1995) 80-89
2. GenBank Overview. http://www.ncbi.nlm.nih.gov/Genbank/index.html
3. Hatzigeorgiou, A.: Translation Initiation Start Prediction in Human cDNAs with High Accuracy. Bioinformatics (2002) 18(2) 343-350
4. John, G.H., Langley, P.: Estimating Continuous Distributions in Bayesian Classifiers. In Proceedings of the 11th Conference on Uncertainty in Artificial Intelligence. Morgan Kaufmann, San Mateo, California, USA (1995) 338-345
5. Kent Ridge Bio-medical Data Set Repository. http://sdmc.i2r.a-star.edu.sg/rp/
6. Kozak, M.: An Analysis of 5'-Noncoding Sequences from 699 Vertebrate Messenger RNAs. Nucleic Acids Research (1987) 15(20) 8125-8148
7. Kozak, M.: The Scanning Model for Translation: An Update. The Journal of Cell Biology (1989) 108(2) 229-241
8. Kozak, M: Initiation of Translation in Prokaryotes and Eukaryotes. Gene (1999) 234(2) 187-208
9. Kozak, M., Shatkin. A.J.: Migration of 40 S Ribosomal Subunits on Messenger RNA in the Presence of Edeine. Journal of Biological Chemistry (1978) 253(18) 6568-6577
10. Liu, H., Han, H., Li, J., Wong, L.: Using Amino Acid Patterns to Accurately Predict Translation Initiation Sites. In Silico Biology (2004) 4(3) 255-269
11. Liu, H., Wong, L.: Data Mining Tools for Biological Sequences. Journal of Bioinformatics and Computational Biology, (2003) 1(1) 139-168
12. Nishikawa, T., Ota, T., Isogai, T.: Prediction whether a Human cDNA Sequence Contains Initiation Codon by Combining Statistical Information and Similarity with Protein Sequences. Bioinformatics (2000) 16(11) 960-967
13. Pedersen, A.G., Nielsen, H.: Neural Network Prediction of Translation Initiation Sites in Eukaryotes: Perspectives for EST and Genome analysis. In Proceedings of the 5th International Conference on Intelligent Systems for Molecular Biology, AAAI Press, Menlo Park, California, USA (1997) 226-233
14. Peri, S., Pandey, A.: A Reassessment of the Translation Initiation Codon in Vertebrates. Trends in Genetics (2001) 17(12) 685-687
15. Quinlan, J.R.: C4.5: Programs for Machine Learning, Morgan Kaufmann, San Mateo, California, USA (1993).
16. Salamov, A.A., Nishikawa, T., Swindells, M.B.: Assessing Protein Coding Region Integrity in cDNA Sequencing Projects. Bioinformatics (1998) 14(5) 384-390
17. Stormo, G.D., Schneider, T.D., Gold, L., Ehrenfeucht, A.: Use of the 'Perceptron' Algorithm to Distinguish Translational Initiation Sites in E. coli. Nucleic Acids Research (1982) 10 (9) 2997-3011
18. Witten, I.H., Frank, E.: Data Mining: Practical Machine Learning Tools with Java Implementations. Morgan Kaufmann, San Francisco (2000)
19. Zeng F., Yap H., Wong, L.: Using Feature Generation and Feature Selection for Accurate Prediction of Translation Initiation Sites. In Proceedings of the 13th International Conference on Genome Informatics, Tokyo, Japan (2002) 192-200
20. Zien, A., Rätsch, G., Mika, S., Schölkopf, B., Lengauer, T., Müller, K.R.: Engineering Support Vector Machine Kernels that Recognize Translation Initiation Sites. Bioinformatics (2000) 16(9) 799-807

A New Test System for Stability Measurement of Marker Gene Selection in DNA Microarray Data Analysis

Fei Xiong[1], Heng Huang[1], James Ford[1],
Fillia S. Makedon[1], and Justin D. Pearlman[2]

[1] Department of Computer Science, Dartmouth College,
Hanover, NH 03755, USA
[2] Advanced Imaging Center, Dartmouth-Hitchcock Medical Center,
Lebanon, NH 03766, USA

Abstract. Microarray gene expression data contains informative features that reflect the critical processes controlling prominent biological functions. Feature selection algorithms have been used in previous biomedical research to find the "marker" genes whose expression value change corresponds to the most eminent difference between specimen classes. One problem encountered in such analysis is the imbalance between very large numbers of genes versus relatively fewer specimen samples. A common concern, therefore, is "overfitting" the data and deriving a set of marker genes with low stability over the entire set of possible specimens. To address this problem, we propose a new test environment in which synthetic data is perturbed to simulate possible variations in gene expression values. The goal is for the generated data to have appropriate properties that match natural data, and that are appropriate for use in testing the sensitivity of feature selection algorithms and validating the robustness of selected marker genes. In this paper, we evaluate a statistically-based resampling approach and a Principal Components Analysis (PCA)-based linear noise distribution approach. Our results show that both methods generate reasonable synthetic data and that the signal/noise rate (with variation weights at 5%, 10%, 20% and 30%) measurably impacts the classification accuracy and the marker genes selected. Based on these results, we identify the most appropriate marker gene selection and classification techniques for each type and level of noise we modeled.

Keywords: Gene Selection, Stability Measurement, Sample Classification, Microarray Data

1 Introduction

DNA microarray technology has already become a significant method to support decision making in biological and biomedical research. It provides a comprehensive picture of gene expression levels in biological samples in which thousands of genes can be studied simultaneously for their behaviors under different conditions. Many applications have been developed with this technology, supplying the scientific community with more powerful recognition tools to detect undefined patterns or clusters. The significance of gene expression analysis has also been demonstrated in numerous clinical cases by its prominent ability to facilitate the process of diagnosis, prognosis and therapy.

A key step in gene-based feature selection and sample classification is the preparation of microarray data. It is generally not easy to get enough samples for a specific DNA microarray study, either because of missing data due to an impure experimental environment, the rareness of a specimen type, or noise that obscures the real patterns. As discussed in [1], the accuracy of microarray data analysis is highly dependent on the quality of data being used. Many analytical techniques have been developed, such as the replicated measurements used in [1,2,3], the resampling methods used in [4,5,6], and the missing value estimation used in [7,8,9]. Nevertheless, these works only focused on ways to assess the repeatability of clustering patterns observed in the microarray data. Few of them clearly addressed the problem of how to measure the accuracy and stability of gene selection results with similar approaches.

Feature selection was introduced as an efficient method to choose a subset of attributes from the original data while still keeping the most distinguishing characteristics of that data. It conducts dimensionality reduction and enhances data mining results by eliminating irrelevant or noisy features. In DNA microarray data analysis, we treat genes as features and each gene is assigned a score indicating its power to discriminate the sample classes according to certain ranking criteria. Genes with top ranks will be selected as marker genes and then used to conduct statistical or computational study in a new subspace with reduced dimensionality.

The smaller "candidate" gene set derived from gene selection approaches offers new opportunities for biologists to find the most "promising" genes possibly included in a crucial biological pathway. However, the gene selection problem is complicated by the fact that the number of genes typically far exceeds the number of samples ("the curse of dimensionality"). Here uncertainty arises from both the interaction of marker genes with each other and the sensitivity of feature selection algorithms to the noise in data. The reliability of gene selection results is the major concern of biologists. There is an immediate need for an effective validation system to evaluate different gene selection algorithms under different training conditions and ensure the quality and stability of marker gene selection results. Previous work to assess the reproducibility/reliability of gene selection results can be found in [1,10,11].

In this paper, we will focus on the assessment of robustness and stability of marker gene selection results. Gene Selection is different from gene clustering because 1) genes are selected by a rank of their distinctness across different sample classes 2) we want as few genes as possible in the result list while still keeping a very high classification accuracy on test samples. The purpose of our study is to build an efficient test system for biologists to use to generate synthetic DNA microarray data and verify their analysis methods for quality assurance. In this paper, We use resampling techniques and PCA-based linear noise distribution to generate some reasonable synthetic data sets. We then tested for the effects of pertubations by applying three popular feature selection algorithms, Relief-F, Information Gain, and the χ^2-statistic, on the synthetic data. A classifier was then built with k-Nearest Neighbor (K-NN), Support Vector Machines (SVMs) or Decision Tree (C4.5). The results with each type and level of noise and each feature selection algorithm were then calculated and compared.

2 Methods

2.1 Marker Gene Selection

A set of DNA microarray data can be representd as a $m \times n$ matrix where m is the number of genes and n is the number of samples. This is usually an "unbalanced" matrix since a typical microarray experiment measures thousands of genes using only tens or hundreds of specimen samples. Assume that each sample is labeled by a tag c_i, where $i = 1 \cdots k$ is one of the k classes in the data. The goal of feature selection is to find the minimum subset of m in which the n samples still can be classified properly by referring to the expression values of the reduced feature set. Feature selection methods fall broadly into two categories, namely the wrapper model and the filter model [12]. The wrapper model exploits a predetermined mining algorithm to build a classifier and thoroughly examine all possible subsets in the original feature space. In contrast, a filter model doesn't use a classifier but instead chooses an optimal subset based on the intrinsic characteristics of the training data. In practice, the filter model is generally preferable because of its computational efficiency.

One of the most important problems in feature selection is to find an appropriate ranking algorithm to identify which features are better than others in distinguishing different sample classes. Usually they are based on statistical computation on the features to evaluate the amount of information they provide for sample classification. Another problem with feature selection in microarray data analysis is that selected genes are often highly correlated. This is partially because those genes may have similar biological functions or might have been enrolled in the same biological pathway. If one gene is selected, another highly correlated gene is also likely to be selected. This will not only incur redundancy in the marker gene selection result but will also increase the misclassification rate. Wang et al. [16] applied clustering algorithm on the gene selection problem to obtain a succinct marker gene set with less redundancy and still competitive classification accuracy.

Some popular feature selection methods have been applied to search for marker genes, including Relief-F [13], Information Gain [14], and χ^2-statistics [15]. Selection methods are either based on statistical computation or information theory. Features are ranked based on computed values of their contributions to sample class discrimination. For a detailed introduction to each algorithm, please refer to Wang et al. [16].

2.2 Sample Classification

Classification algorithms have been used to identify the distinctness between different specimen sample types in microarray data analysis. The underlying problem is to partition the sample set into statistically or biologically meaningful classes according to the gene expression values. K-nearest neighbors (KNN [17]) is a nonparametric classification algorithm where each sample is represented by a vector of m gene expression values and then classified according to the class membership of its k nearest neighbors in the m-dimensional vector space. The similarity between two sample vectors is usually measured by either Euclidean distance or a Pearson correlation coefficient. If the majority of the k nearest neighbors of a sample were in class C_i, the sample will then be classified as in class C_i. Otherwise, that sample will be treated as unclassified.

Support vector machines (SVMs [18]) and other kernel-based supervised learning algorithms elegantly solve the classification problem by mapping the data into a higher-dimensional feature space and defining a hyerplane to separate them. As a simplified version, the linear SVMs seek a thresholding plane $\alpha \cdot d + b$ where α maximizes the distance of any training point from the linear hyperplane. The class label of a sample is either $+1$ or -1 depending on to which side of the hyperplane the corresponding data point is mapped. Given a margin, defined as the sum of distances from the separating hyperplane to the closest positive or negative training samples, linear SVMs search for a tradeoff between maximizing the margin and minimizing classification errors.

Decision tree is a tree whose internal nodes are tests on one or more features and whose leaf nodes are categories that reflect classification outcomes. An instance is classified by starting from the root node, testing the attributes specified by that node, and then moving down the decision tree branches according to the attribute values. The outcomes from each test would be exclusive and exhaustive. This process will repeat until it finally reaches the leaf nodes where a unique classification result is given with some conditional probability. In machine learning society, the most popular implementation of decision tree algorithm is C4.5 [19]. We will use it to evaluate our gene selection results together with the other two algorithms for a comparison.

2.3 Stability Measurement

Cross Validation. Cross validation [20] is usually used to test the generalization of a statistical classifier to recognize previously unknown data. The original data set is divided into k disjoint subsets, and a new model is trained on each group of $k-1$ subsets. The remaining subset is used as test data. Cross validation makes good use of the current data set by treating each portion in it as both the training and the test data. Therefore it is especially useful when the amount of available data is insufficient to be split as a training and a test partition, where each should adequately represent the intrinsic patterns belonging to each class. For mathematical simplicity, an extreme form of cross validation is to let k equal to the size of original data set, resulting in the Leave One Out Cross Validation (LOOCV).

Principal Components Analysis. Principal components analysis (PCA) [21] is a very popular dimensionality reduction technique that is widely used in the analysis of high-dimensional microarray data. Given n observations on p variables, PCA seeks to reduce the dimensionality of the data matrix by finding k new principal components (PCs), where k is less than p. Each principal component is a linear combination of the original variables, and they are mutually uncorrelated and orthogonal. PCA defines a projection of the original space that captures the maximum variance present in the initial data set by minimizing the error between the original data set and the reduced dimensional data set.

PCA analysis of high-dimensional microarray data can consider either genes or samples as variables. For gene-based analysis, gene components are created to indicate the features of genes that best explain the sample responses they generate. For sample-based analysis, sample components are created to indicate the features of samples that best explain the gene behaviors they correlate to.

3 Experimental Design

3.1 Overview

In this paper, we are interested in the problem that whether the fluctuation of gene expression values in the sample set can significantly affect marker gene selection results. An overview of the marker gene selection and result stability measurement system we employ is given in Figure 1. For different test purposes, we generate the new training data set by using resampling methods like cross validation, and linear transformation methods like principal components analysis. Each original data set was preprocessed by removing rows and columns containing missing data and applying a logarithm transformation. We use 10-fold cross validation for each data set. Principal components analysis is applied to every sample class, and to preserve data precision, all principal components are returned to construct the lower dimensional feature space. Sample data are then mapped to the new space by a linear transformation. To obtain data perturbations, our method is to add noise to the weights of sample vectors on each principal component dimension. Here noise was randomly generated on a designated scale to simulate natural phenomenon. Finally, different feature selection algorithms are compared to measure their sensitivities regarding to the variation of gene expression values.

3.2 Data Sets

- *Smoking-induced Changes in Airway Transcriptome:* This data set was published by Spira et al. [23] in 2004. It uses gene expression profiling to describe how cigarette smoking affects normally expressed genes in human airway epithelial cells and defines the reversible and irreversible genetic effects thereafter. Seventy five patient samples are divided into 3 types: "current smoker", "never smoked" and "former smoker". The number of samples is 34, 23, and 18, respectively. Each sample contains 22215 probe sets.

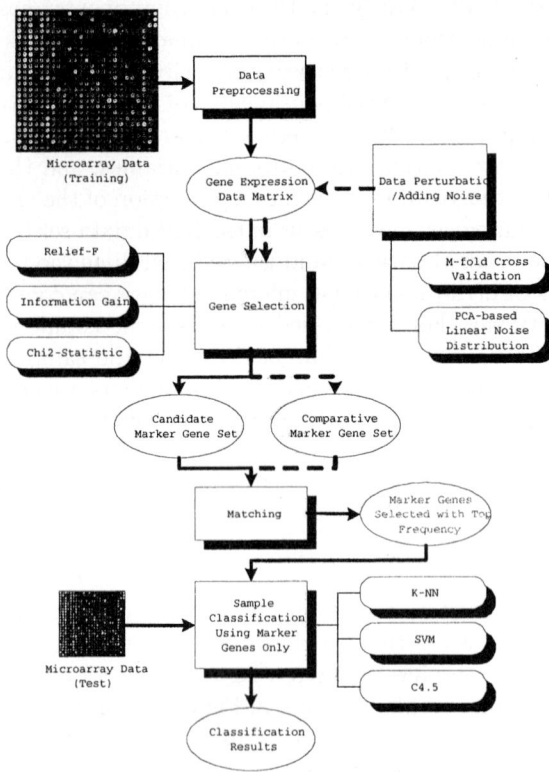

Fig. 1. Overview of the Marker Gene Selection and Result Stability Measurement System

- *Lung Cancer:* This data set was published by Gordon et al. [22] in 2002. It focuses on the pathological distinction between malignant pleural mesothelioma (MPM) and adenocarcinoma (ADCA) of the lung. There are 181 tissue samples, including 31 MPM and 150 ADCA. Thirty two samples (16 MPM and 16 ADCA) are used for training and the remaining 149 samples are used for testing. Each sample contains the expression values of 12533 genes.

3.3 Implementation

We used MATLAB 7 to write programs for generating new samples of the microarray data by resampling and through PCA-based linear noise distribution. A Java based data mining toolkit (Weka 3.4.4 [24]) was employed to implement the feature selection algorithms and sample classification algorithms. All the experiments were conducted on a dual Pentium 4 XEON 2.8GHz processor system with 1G memory and the RedHat Linux 9 operating system.

4 Results

4.1 Smoking-Induced Changes in Airway Transcriptome

We first applied 10-fold cross validation (CV) on the smoking-related microarray data as described previously. Samples were randomly divided into ten partitions. We employed each of the three feature selection algorithms (Relief-F, Information Gain, χ^2-statistic) for gene ranking and then chose the top 100 genes as a candidate marker gene set. There is an obvious change in the marker gene set selected by each CV round compared with the default 100 genes selected by using all samples (Table 1).

Table 1. Ten-fold cross validation for marker gene selection (RF=Relief-F, IG=Information Gain, $\chi^2=\chi^2$-statistic)

	Common	CV1	CV2	CV3	CV4	CV5	CV6	CV7	CV8	CV9	CV10
RF	39	81	83	69	80	80	77	78	77	79	83
IG	54	84	80	84	84	77	77	75	79	84	85
χ^2	49	81	75	80	80	78	79	77	81	80	81

In the table above, the number in each CV column represents how many genes selected by the corresponding algorithm could be found in the default 100 top ranked genes. The second column "Common" indicates how many genes have been selected by all the ten CV rounds and also appear in the default 100 top ranked genes. Using only those "common" genes as features, the classification accuracy for the total 75 samples based on LOOCV is given in Table 2. The best classification result was obtained by using Relief-F to derive the common marker gene set with an SVM classifier.

Table 2. Sample classification results based on different gene selection results

	K-NN	SVMs	C4.5
Relief-F	73.3333%	78.6667%	68%
Information Gain	72%	77.3333%	74.6667%
χ^2-statistic	74.6667%	73.3333%	72%

The cross validation method doesn't introduce any new data into the original sample set; However, researchers are also interested to see the stability of gene selection results given the existence of extra noise. Therefore, we need an appropriate simulation system to examine different algorithms under this case. As introduced before, we apply a PCA-based noise distribution model. For each PC dimension, noise is randomly added at a threshold of 5%, 10%, 20% and 30%. Here we assume that adding noise to each sample won't change its class membership (otherwise the generated synthetic data may estray far away from the ground truth). The experimental results regarding to three feature selection algorithms are given in Table 3. The number under each noise level represents that how many genes in the top 100 genes ranked by each algorithm would still be selected after the noise induction.

Table 3. Gene selection results after PCA-based linear noise distribution (Smoking)

	5%	10%	20%	30%
Relief-F	94	89	84	76
Information Gain	88	84	81	76
χ^2-statistic	88	82	75	69

4.2 Lung Cancer

To further investigate the stability of gene selection results in relation to data perturbation and extra noise, we repeated the experiments above in the lung cancer data [22]. The ten-fold cross validation result is compatible with the one discussed in 4.1, and the size of overlapped marker genes is 52, 45, and 47 for RF, IG and the χ^2-statistic respectively. Sample classification results are quite good as near to 100% in all the cases. When we applied the PCA-based linear noise distribution on the sample data, the gene selection results are like below (Table 4).

Table 4. Gene selection results after PCA-based linear noise distribution (Lung Cancer)

	5%	10%	20%	30%
Relief-F	97	91	91	89
Information Gain	88	81	79	66
χ^2-statistic	88	81	80	68

5 Discussion and Conclusion

From the results shown in each case study, we find that the m-fold cross validation turned to be a reasonable method to test the stability of gene selection results. We chose the most commonly accepted genes from each CV round, and constructed a new marker gene set. The sample classification accuracies by using the derived marker genes as features are relatively good compared with using all the 100 top ranked genes. Here the cross validation steps ensure the reproducibility of marker genes in case of data perturbation. For comparison, we also tested the bootstrapping method as mentioned in [4] but the marker gene selection results turned to be very "bumpy" and quite a few genes are consistently preserved from round to round (results not included in this paper). A similar problem was also reported by Fu and Youn [11]; thus we decided to only use cross validation for assessment of error and stability. Meanwhile, another interesting question is how robustly the gene selection approach performs when extra noise is added to the samples. We implemented a test bed to generate synthetic microarray data by applying the PCA-based linear noise distribution to the original data set. Our experimental results indicate that the three gene selection algorithms all have rather good tolerance to noise until its percentage is considerably high (e.g. $\geq 30\%$). The number of overlapped marker genes between the "noise" data set and the default data set is significantly large as well.

Our empirical stability measurement seems to support the Relief-F algorithm. Compared with the other two gene selection algorithms, Relief-F has the best performance in either the sample classification accuracy or the number of marker genes preserved after noise is included (for both the smoking-related data and the lung cancer data). This could be partially because that Relief-F has the ability to cope with features that are highly interdependent while the other two algorithms are merely good at detecting irrelevant features. Nevertheless, this observation still needs to be verified by experiments on more test data sets.

The marker gene selection results from our case studies also hold very suggestive biological meanings. Some of the "common" marker genes selected from our experiment on the smoking-related data set have matched the results in [23]. For instance, TU3A and CX3CL1, which are both claimed as potential tumor suppressor genes, were found in the 39 marker genes obtained from 10-fold cross validation on Relief-F. In addition, an antioxidant gene GPX2 has been identified as a marker gene because of its distinct increase in gene expression in current smokers. As from the discussion in [23], those abnormal expression levels might be permanent and that might explain the persistent risk for former smokers to have lung cancer even long time after they discontinued smoking. We expect our work could supply biologists a comparative method to measure the stability of gene selection and provide useful information in the problem domain, such as clinical disease sample classification and biological pathway determination.

Acknowledgements

The work in this paper was supported by a grant from the Flight Attendant Medical Research Institute (FAMRI).

References

1. Medvedovic, M., Yeung, K. and Bumgarner, R. E.: Bayesian mixture model based clustering of replicated microarray data. Bioinformatics **20(8)** (2004) 1222-1232.
2. Dougherty, E. R., Barrera, J., Brun, M., Kim, S., Cesar, R. M., Chen, Y., Bittner, M. and Trent, J. M.: Inference from clustering with application to gene-expression microarrays. J. Comput. Biol. **9** (2002) 105-126.
3. Yeung, K. Y., Fraley, C., Murua, A., Raftery, A. E. and Ruzzo, W. L.: Model-based clustering and data transformations for gene expression data. Bioinformatics **17** (2001) 977-987.

4. Kerr, M. k. and Churchill, G. A.: Bootstrapping cluster analysis: assessing the reliability of conclusions from microarray experiments. Proc. Natl. Acad. Sci. USA **98** (2001) 8961-8965.
5. Pollard, K. S. and Van der Laan, M. J.: Multiple testing for gene expression data: an investigation of null distributions with consequences for the permutation test. Proceedings of the 2003 International MultiConference in Computer Science and Engineering, **METMBS'03** Conference, (2003) 3-9.
6. Ge, Y., Dudoit, S. and Speed, T. P.: Resampling-based multiple testing for microarray data analysis. Technical Report **633**, Department of Statistics, UC Berkeley, (2003).
7. Troyanskaya, O., Cantor, M., Sherlock, G., Brown, P., Hastie, T., Tibshirani, R., Botstein, D. and Altman, R. B.: Missing value estimation methods for DNA microarrays. Bioinformatics **17** (2001) 520-525.
8. Zhou, X., Wang, X. and Dougherty, E. R.: Missing-value estimation using linear and non-linear regression with Bayesian gene selection. Bioinformatics **19(17)** (2003) 2302-2307.
9. Kim, H., Golub, G. and Park, H.: Missing value estimation for DNA microarray gene expression data: local least squares imputation. Bioinformatics **21(2)** (2005) 187-198.
10. McShane, L., Radmacher, M., Freidlin, B., Yu, R., Li, M. and Simon, R.: Methods for assessing reproducibility of clustering patterns observerd in analyses of microarray data. Bioinformatics **18(11)** (2002) 1462-1469
11. Fu, L. and Youn E.: Improving Reliability of Gene Selection From Microarray Functional Genomics Data. IEEE Transactions on Information Technology in Biomedicine **7(3)** (2003) 191-196
12. Kohavi, R. and John, G.: Wrapper for feature subset selection. Artifical Intelligence **97(1-2)** (1997) 273-324
13. Kononenko, I.: Estimating attributes: analysis and extensions of relief. In Proceedings of the European conference on machine learning on Machine Learning. Springer-Verlag, New York, Inc. (1994) 171-182
14. Mitchell, T.: Machine Learning. McGraw-Hill, New York. (1997)
15. Liu, H. and Setiono, R.: Chi2: feature selection and discretization of numeric attributes. In Proceedings of the Seventh International Conference on Tools with Artifical Intelligence. (1995) 388-391
16. Wang, Y., Makedon, F., Ford, J. and Pearlman, J.: HykGene: a hybrid approach for selecting marker genes for phenotype classification using microarray gene expression data. Bioinformatics **21(8)** (2004) 1530-1537
17. Massart, D., Vandeginste, B., Deming, S., Michotte, Y. and Kaufman, L.: The k-nearest neighbor method. In Chemometrics: A Textbook (Data Handling in Science and Technology, *vol. 2*. Elsevier Science, New York. (1988) 395-397
18. Vapnik, V.: Statistical Learning Theory. Wiley-Interscience, New York. (1998)
19. Quinlan, J. R.: C4.5: Programs for Machine Learning. Morgan Kauffman, San Francisco, USA. (1993)
20. Stone, M.: Cross-Validatory choice and assessment of statistical predictions. J. R. Stat. Soc. **B 36(1)** (1974) 111-147
21. Jolliffe, I.: Principal Component Analysis (Second Edition): Springer-Verlag, New York. (2002)
22. Gordon, G., Jensen, R., Hsiao, L., Gullans, S., Blumenstock, J., Ramaswamy, S., Richards, W., Sugarbaker, D., and Bueno, R.: Translation of Microarray Data into Clinically Relevant Cancer Diagnostic Tests Using Gege Expression Ratios in Lung Cancer And Mesothelioma. Cancer Research **62** (2002) 4963-4967

23. Spira, A., Beane, J., Shah, V., Liu, G., Schembri, F., Yang, X., Palma, J., and Brody, J.: Effects of cigarette smoke on the human airway epithelial cell transcriptome. Proc. Natl. Acad. Sci. USA **101(27)** (2004) 10143-10148
24. Witten, I. and Frank, E.: Data Mining: Practical Machine Learning Tools and Techniques with Java Implementations. Morgan Kaufmann, San Francisco, Calif. (1999)

Protein Classification with Multiple Algorithms

Sotiris Diplaris[1], Grigorios Tsoumakas[2], Pericles A. Mitkas[1], and Ioannis Vlahavas[2]

[1] Dept. of Electrical and Computer Engineering, Aristotle University of Thessaloniki,
54126, Thessaloniki, Greece
{diplaris, mitkas}@danae.ee.auth.gr
[2] Dept. of Informatics, Aristotle University of Thessaloniki,
54126, Thessaloniki, Greece
{greg, vlahavas}@csd.auth.gr

Abstract. Nowadays, the number of protein sequences being stored in central protein databases from labs all over the world is constantly increasing. From these proteins only a fraction has been experimentally analyzed in order to detect their structure and hence their function in the corresponding organism. The reason is that experimental determination of structure is labor-intensive and quite time-consuming. Therefore there is the need for automated tools that can classify new proteins to structural families. This paper presents a comparative evaluation of several algorithms that learn such classification models from data concerning patterns of proteins with known structure. In addition, several approaches that combine multiple learning algorithms to increase the accuracy of predictions are evaluated. The results of the experiments provide insights that can help biologists and computer scientists design high-performance protein classification systems of high quality.

1 Introduction

A crucial issue in bioinformatics is structural biology, i.e. the representation of the structure of several biological macromolecules. The knowledge of the 3D structure of proteins is a strong weapon in combating many diseases, since most of them are caused by malfunctions of the proteins involved in several functions of the human cells. Until now the biological effect of proteins could be identified only by expensive in vitro experiments. In the recent years, though, large databases were created for the recording and exploitation of biological data, due to the human DNA and protein decoding. With the contribution of modern data analysis techniques, such as machine learning and knowledge discovery, the issue has been approached computationally, thus providing fast and more flexible solutions.

The function of a protein is directly related to its structure. Proteins are grouped into several families according to the functions they perform. All proteins contained in a family feature a certain structural relation, thus having similar properties. Patterns are short amino acid chains that have a specific order, while profiles are computational representations of multiple sequence alignments using hidden Markov models. We will refer to both profiles and patterns as motifs. Motifs have been widely used for the prediction of a protein's properties, since the latter are mainly defined by their motifs. Prosite [1], Pfam [2] and Prints [3] are the most common databases where motifs are being recorded.

Machine learning (ML) algorithms [4] can offer the most cost effective approach to automated discovery of a priori unknown predictive relationships from large data sets in computational biology [5]. A plethora of algorithms to address this problem have been proposed, by both the artificial intelligence and the pattern recognition communities. Some of the algorithms create decision trees [6,7], others exploit artificial neural networks [8] or statistical models [9].

An important issue however that remains is which from the multitude of machine learning algorithms to use for training a classifier in order to achieve the best results. The plot thickens if we also consider the recent advances in ensemble methods that combine several different classification algorithms for increasing the accuracy. This creates a problem to the ML expert who wants to provide the biologist with a good model for protein classification.

In this paper we perform an empirical comparison of the performance of several different classification algorithms for the problem of motif-based protein classification. Moreover, we exploit the combination of different classification algorithms in order to achieve accuracy improvement. Two main paradigms in combining different classification algorithms are used: classifier selection and classifier fusion. The first one selects a single algorithm for classifying a new instance, while the latter combines the decisions of all algorithms.

The rest of this paper is organized as follows. Section 2 presents the biological problem of motif-based protein classification, as well as methods for combining multiple classification algorithms in order to optimize the predictive performance. Section 3 describes the details of the performed classification experiments for the comparison of several different classification algorithms. In Section 4 the results are presented and discussed, and finally, Section 5 concludes this work and points at the future outlooks.

2 Problem Description

2.1 The Motif-Based Protein Classification Problem

The basic problem we are trying to solve can be stated as follows: "Given a set of proteins with known properties (that have been experimentally specified), we aim to induce classifiers that associate motifs to protein families, referred to as protein classes." In Fig.1 this approach is designated.

Any protein chain can be mapped into a representation based on attributes. Such a representation supports the efficient function of data-driven algorithms, which represent instances as classified part of a fixed set of attributes. A very important issue in the data mining process is the efficient choice of attributes. In our case, protein chains are represented using a proper motif sequence vocabulary [10].

Suppose the vocabulary contains N motifs. Any given protein sequence typically contains a few of these motifs. We encode each sequence as an N-bit binary pattern where the ith bit is 1 if the corresponding motif is present in the sequence; otherwise the corresponding bit is 0. Each N-bit sequence is associated with a label that identifies the functional family of the sequence (if known). A training set is simply a collection of N-bit binary patterns each of which has associated with it, a label that identifies the function of the corresponding protein. This training set can be used to train a

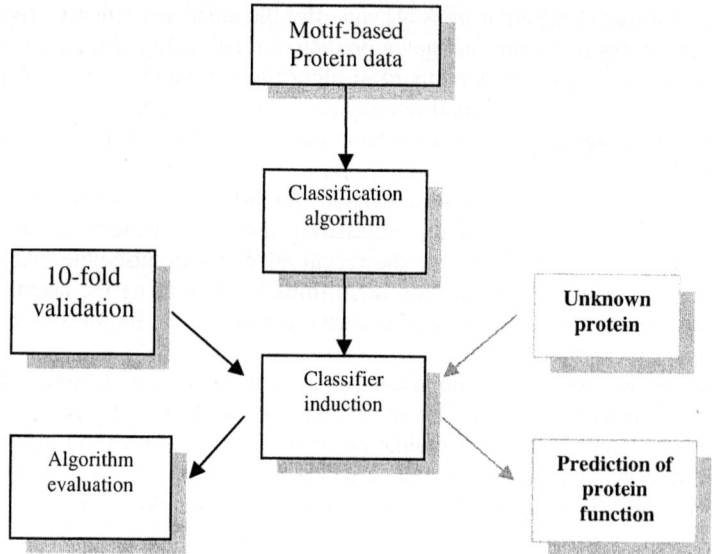

Fig.1. The protein classification problem

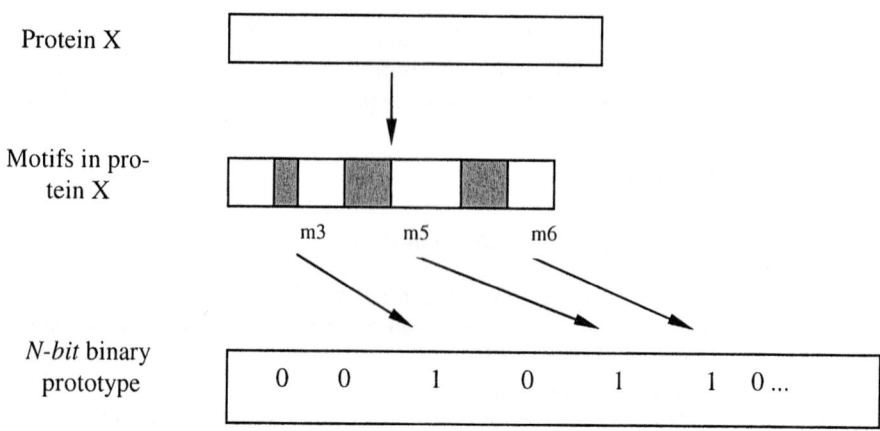

Fig. 2. Data representation

classifier which can then be used to assign novel sequences to one of the several functional protein families represented in the training set. The data representation procedure is depicted in Figure 2.

2.2 Combining Multiple Classification Algorithms

The main motivation for combining different classification algorithms is accuracy improvement. Different algorithms use different biases for generalizing from examples and different representations of the knowledge. Therefore, they tend to err on different parts of the instance space. The combined use of different algorithms could lead to the correction of the individual uncorrelated errors. There are two main paradigms for handling an ensemble of different classification algorithms: *Classifier Selection* and *Classifier Fusion*. The first one selects a *single* algorithm for classifying a new instance, while the latter fuses the decisions of *all* algorithms. This section presents the most important methods from both categories.

Classifier Selection
A very simple method of this category is found in the literature as Evaluation and Selection or SelectBest. This method evaluates each of the classification algorithms (typically using 10-fold cross-validation) on the training set and selects the best one for application on the test set. Although this method is simple, it has been found to be highly effective and comparable to other more complex state-of-the-art methods [11].

Another line of research proposes the selection of a learning algorithm based on its performance on similar learning domains. Several approaches have been proposed for the characterization of learning domain, including general, statistical and information-theoretic measures [12], landmarking [13], histograms [14] and model-based data characterizations [15]. Apart from the characterization of each domain, the performance of each learning algorithm on that domain is recorded. When a new domain arrives, the performance of the algorithms in the k-nearest neighbors of that domain is retrieved and the algorithms are ranked according to their average performance. In [12], algorithms are ranked based on a measure called Adjusted Ratio of Ratios (ARR), that combines accuracy and learning time of algorithm, while in [16], algorithms are ranked based on Data Envelopment Analysis, a multicriteria evaluation technique that can combine various performance metrics, like accuracy, storage space, and learning time.

In [17,18] the accuracy of the algorithms is estimated locally on a number of examples that surround each test example. Such approaches belong to the family of Dynamic Classifier Selection [19] and use a different algorithm in different parts of the instance space.

Two similar, but more complicated approaches that were developed by Merz[20] are Dynamic Selection and Dynamic Weighting. The selection of algorithms is based on their local performance, but not around the test instance itself, rather around the meta-instance comprising the predictions of the classification models on the test instance. Training meta-instances are produced by recording the predictions of each algorithm, using the full training data both for training and for testing. Performance data are produced by running m k-fold cross-validations, and averaging the m evaluations for each training instance.

Classifier Fusion
Unweighted and Weighted Voting are two of the simplest methods for combining not only Heterogeneous but also Homogeneous models. In Voting, each model outputs a class value (or ranking, or probability distribution) and the class with the most votes (or the highest average ranking, or average probability) is the one proposed by the ensemble. Note that this type of Voting is in fact called Plurality Voting, in contrast to the frequently used term Majority Voting, as the latter implies that at least 50% (the majority) of the votes should belong to the winning class. In Weighted Voting, the

classification models are not treated equally. Each model is associated with a coefficient (weight), usually proportional to its classification accuracy.

Stacked Generalization [21], also known as Stacking, is a method that combines multiple classifiers by learning a meta-level (or level-1) model that predicts the correct class based on the decisions of the base-level (or level-0) classifiers. This model is induced on a set of meta-level training data that are typically produced by applying a procedure similar to k-fold cross-validation on the training data:

Let D be the level-0 training data set. D is randomly split into k disjoint parts $D_1 \ldots D_k$ of equal size. For each fold $i=1..i$ of the process, the base-level classifiers are trained on the set $D \setminus D_i$ and then applied to the test set D_i. The output of the classifiers for a test instance along with the true class of that instance form a meta-instance.

A meta-classifier is then trained on the meta-instances and the base-level classifiers are trained on all training data D. When a new instance appears for classification, the output of all base-level classifiers is first calculated and then propagated to the meta-level classifier, which outputs the final result.

Ting and Witten [22] have shown that Stacking works well when meta-instances are formed by probability distributions for each class instead of just a class label. A recent study [11] has shown that Stacking with Multi-Response Model Trees as the meta-level learning algorithm and probability distributions, is the most accurate heterogeneous classifier combination method of the Stacking family.

Selective Fusion [23,24] is a recent method for combining different classification algorithms that exhibits low computational complexity and high accuracy. It uses statistical procedures for the selection of the best subgroup among different classification algorithms and subsequently fuses the decision of the models in this subgroup with (Weighted) Voting.

3 Experimental Setup

This section provides information on the dataset, participating algorithms and combination methods that were used for the experiments.

3.1 Dataset

The protein classes considered in are the 10 most important protein families: PDOC00064 (a class of oxydoreductases), PDOC00154 (a class of isomerases), PDOC00224 (a class of cytokines and growth factors), PDOC00343 (a class of structural proteins), PDOC00561 (a class of receptors), PDOC00662 (a class of DNA or RNA associated proteins), PDOC00670 (a class of transferases), PDOC00791 (a class of protein secretion and chaperones), and PDOC50007 (a class of hydrolases). For clarity of presentation, the Prosite documentation ID, i.e. the PDOCxxxxx number was used to represent that class. Similarly, the Prosite access number i.e. the PSxxxxx was used to represent that motif pattern or profile. During the preprocessing, a training set was exported, consisting of 662 proteins that belong in barely 10 classes. Some proteins belonged in more than one class, thus the problem could be defined as a multi-label classification problem. The approach taken was to create separate classes in order to represent the classification of each multi-labeled protein. Thus, for a protein that belonged in two or more classes, a new class was created that was named after both the protein classes in which the protein belonged. This resulted to a total of 32 different classes. GenMiner [25] was used for the preparation of data.

3.2 Learning Algorithms and Combination Methods

We used 9 different learning algorithms at the base-level. These are general-purpose machine learning algorithms spanning several different learning paradigms (instance-based, rules, trees, statistical). They were obtained from the WEKA machine learning library [26], and used with default parameter settings unless otherwise stated:

- *DT*, the decision table algorithm of Kohavi [27].
- *JRip*, the RIPPER rule learning algorithm [28].
- *PART*, the PART rule learning algorithm [29].
- *J48*, the decision tree learning algorithm C4.5 [7], using Laplace smoothing for predicted probabilities.
- *IBk*, the *k* nearest neighbor algorithm [30].
- *K**, an instance-based learning algorithm with entropic distance measure [31].
- *NB*, the Naive Bayes algorithm [32] using the kernel density estimator rather than assume normal distributions for numeric attributes.
- *SMO*, the sequential minimal optimization algorithm for training a support vector classifier using polynomial kernels [33].
- *RBF*, WEKA implementation of an algorithm for training a radial basis function network [34].

The above algorithms were used alone and in conjunction with the following five different classifier combination methods: Stacking with Multi-Response Model Trees (SMT), Voting (V), Weighted Voting (WV), Evaluation and Selection (ES) and Selective Fusion (SF).

4 Results and Discussion

For the evaluation of the algorithms and combination methods, we used 10-fold stratified cross-validation. The original data set was split in 10 disjoint parts of approximately equal size and approximately equal class distribution. Each of these parts was sequentially used for testing and the union of the rest for training.

Table 1 presents the results concerning the mean error for each of the algorithms. We notice that the lowest error is exhibited by SMO followed closely by IBk, DT, J48, K* and PART. JRip is a bit worse, while NB and RBF exhibit quite low performance. The results verify the reputation of Support Vector Machines as a state-of-the-art classification method. Decision Trees (J48) and Instance-Based Learning methods (IBk, K*) also perform well, while Rule Based methods (JRip, PART) follow in performance.

After this evaluation the biologist might choose to use SMO for modeling the protein classification algorithm. However, the rest of the well-performing algorithms could also be used and might generalize better than SMO. In addition the combination of all these algorithms, or perhaps a subset of them could give better results. To investigate this issue we experimented with the combination methods that were mentioned in the precious section.

Table 1. Mean error rate of the learning algorithms

	DT	JRip	PART	J48	IBk	K*	NB	SMO	RBF
Er.	0.024	0.035	0.026	0.024	0.023	0.024	0.610	0.021	0.739

Table 2 presents the results concerning the mean error for each of the combination methods. ES simulates the process followed by someone that would like to use just the single best algorithm. 10-fold cross-validation is applied on the training set and the result of the evaluation guides the selection of the algorithm in the test set. This result, although good, it is worse than combining all the algorithms with Weighted Voting. This shows that the correction of uncorrelated errors through the voting process has helped in reducing the error rate. Simple Voting on the other hand did not perform well, due to the existence of bad performing models, such as NB and RBF. The state-of-the-art method of SMT performed very badly. The reason is that the large number of classes (32) leads to a very high dimensionality for the meta-level data set, which does not allow a good model to be induced. The best overall method is SF, which combines the best subset of the models that is selected using statistical tests. This result indicates that selection of the proper models and their combination can lead to very good results. It is worth noticing that SF selects and combines 6.3 models on average on the 10 folds. This result reinforces the previous conclusion that the combination of multiple algorithms results in error reduction, especially when coupled with a method for selecting the appropriate models.

Table 2. Mean error rate of the combination methods

	SB	V	VW	SF	SMT
Er.	0.024	0.195	0.021	0.019	0.558

5 Conclusions and Future Work

We have presented a comparative study of different classification algorithms and algorithm combination methods for the problem of motif-based protein classification. The results show that for a successful practical application of machine learning algorithms in such a real-world problem, one requires: a) a number of different classification algorithms, and b) a proper combination method that can automatically discard low performing models and combine the best models.

One of the issues that need to be investigated in the future is the approach taken for dealing with the multiple classes that each protein belongs to. This problem is common in biological domains and has not been considered extensively by the machine learning community. In the sequel of this work we intend to explore the effectiveness of alternative representations of the learning problem for the domain of protein classification.

References

1. Falquet, L., Pagni, M., Bucher, P., Hulo, N., Sigrist, C.J., Hofmann, K., Bairoch, A.: The PROSITE database, its status in 2002. Nucleic Acids Res. **30** (2002) 235–238
2. Bateman, A., Birney, E., Durbin, R., Eddy, S.R., Howem, K.L., Sonnhammer, E.L.L.: The Pfam protein families database. Nucleic Acids Res. **28** (2000) 263–266
3. Attwood, T.K., Croning, M.D.R., Flower, D.R., Lewis, A.P., Mabey, J.E., Scordis, P., Selley, J., Wright, W.: PRINT-S: the database formerly known as PRINTS. Nucleic Acids Res. **28** (2000) 225–227
4. Mitchell, T.: Machine Learning. McGraw Hill, New York (1997)
5. Baldi, P.F., Brunak, S.: Bioinformatics: The Machine Learning Approach. The MIT Press, Cambridge, MA (2001)
6. Wang, D., Wang, X., Honavar, V., Dobbs, D.: Data-driven generation of decision trees for motif-based assignment of protein sequences to functional families. In: Proceedings of the Atlantic Symposium on Computational Biology, Genome Information Systems & Technology (2001)
7. Quinlan, R.: C4.5: Programs for Machine Learning. Morgan Kaufman, San Mateo (1993)
8. Bishop, C.: Neural Networks for Pattern Recognition. Oxford University Press, New York (1995)
9. Duad, R., Hart, P.: Pattern Classification and Scene Analysis. Wiley, New York (1973)
10. Bairoch, A.: Prosite,: A dictionary of protein sites and patterns – User Manual. Swiss Institute of Bioinformatics, Geneva (1999)
11. Dzeroski, S., Zenko, B.: Is Combining Classifiers with Stacking Better than Selecting the Best One?. Machine Learning **54** (2004) 255–273
12. Brazdil, P.B., Soares, C., Da Costa, J.P.: Ranking Learning Algorithms: Using IBL and Meta-Learning on Accuracy and Time Results. Machine Learning **50** (2003) 251-277
13. Pfahringer, B., Bensusan, H., Giraud-Carrier, C.: Meta-learning by landmarking various learning algorithms. In: International Conference on Machine Learning, (2000)
14. Kalousis, A., Theoharis, T.: Noemon: Design, implementation and performance results of an intelligent assistant for classifier selection. In: Intelligent Data Analysis, (1999)
15. Bensusan, H., Giraud-Carrier, C., Kennedy, C.: A higher-order approach to meta-learning. In: ECML'2000 workshop on Meta-Learning: Building Automatic Advice Strategies for Model Selection and Method Combination, (2000)
16. Keller, J., Paterson I., Berrer, H.: An integrated concept for multi-criteria ranking of data mining algorithms. In: ECML-00 Workshop on Meta-Learning: Building Automatic Advice Strategies for Model Selection and Method Combination, (2000)
17. Giacinto, G., Roli, F.: Adaptive selection of image classifiers. In: Proceedings of the 9th International Conference on Image Analysis and Processing, (1997) 38-45
18. Woods, K., Kegelmeyer, W. P., Bowyer, K.: Combination of multiple classifiers using local accuracy estimates. IEEE Transactions on Pattern Analysis and Machine Intelligence **19** (1997) 405–410
19. Ho, T.K., Hull, J.J., Srihari, S.N.: Decision combination in multiple classifier systems. IEEE Transactions on Pattern Analysis and Machine Intelligence **16** (1994) 66–75

20. Merz, C.J.: Dynamical selection of learning algorithms. In: Fisher, D., Lenz, H. J., eds: Learning from Data: Artificial Intelligence and Statistics, Springer-Verlag, (1995)
21. Wolpert, D.: Stacked generalization. Neural Networks **5** (1992) 241–259
22. Ting, K.M., Witten, I.H.: Issues in stacked generalization. Journal of Artificial Intelligence Research **10** (1999) 271–289
23. Tsoumakas, G., Katakis, I., Vlahavas, I.: Effective Voting of Heterogeneous Classifiers. In: Proceedings of the 15th European Conference on Machine Learning, Pisa, Italy (2004) 465–476
24. Tsoumakas, G., Angelis, L., Vlahavas, I.: Selective Fusion of Heterogeneous Classifiers. Intelligent Data Analysis **9** (2005) to appear.
25. Hatzidamianos, G., Diplaris, S., Athanasiadis, I., Mitkas, P.A.: GenMiner: A Data Mining Tool for Protein Analysis. In: Proceedings of the 9th Panhellenic Conference on Informatics, Thessaloniki, Greece (2003)
26. Witten, I., Frank, E.: Data Mining: Practical machine learning tools with Java implementations. Morgan Kaufmann (1999)
27. Kohavi, R.: The power of decision tables. In: Proceedings of the 12th European Conference on Machine Learning (1995) 174–189
28. Cohen, W.: Fast effective rule induction. In: Proceedings of the 12th International Conference on Machine Learning (1995) 115–123
29. Witten, I., Frank, E.: Generating accurate rule sets without global optimization. In: Proceedings of the 15th International Conference on Machine Learning (1998) 144–151
30. Aha, D., Kibler, D., & Albert, M. Instance-based learning algorithms. Machine Learning **6** (1991) 37–66
31. Cleary, J., Trigg, L.: K*: An instance-based learner using an entropic distance measure. In: Proceedings of the 12th International Conference on Machine Learning (1995) 108–114
32. John, G., Langley, P.: Estimating continuous distributions in bayesian classifiers. In: Proceedings of the 11th Conference on Uncertainty in Artificial Intelligence (1995) 338–345
33. Platt, J.: Fast training of support vector machines using sequential minimal optimization. In: Scholkopf, B., Burges, C., Smola, A, eds: Advances in Kernel Methods - Support Vector Learning, MIT Press (1998)
34. Bishop, C: Neural Networks for Pattern Recognition. Oxford University Press (1995)

Computational Identification of Regulatory Factors Involved in MicroRNA Transcription[†]

Praveen Sethupathy[1,2,5,*], Molly Megraw[1,2,5,*], M. Inmaculada Barrasa[4], and Artemis G. Hatzigeorgiou[1,2,3]

[1] Center for Bioinformatics, University of Pennsylvania, Philadelphia PA 19104, USA
agh@pcbi.upenn.edu
[2] Department of Genetics, School of Medicine, University of Pennsylvania, Philadelphia, PA 19104, USA
[3] Department of Computer and Information Science, School of Engineering, University of Pennsylvania, Philadelphia, PA 19104, USA
[4] Department of Cancer Biology, Abramson Family Cancer Research Institute, School of Medicine, University of Pennsylvania, Philadelphia, PA 19104, USA
ibarrasa@mail.med.upenn.edu
[5] Genomics and Computational Biology Graduate Group, School of Medicine, University of Pennsylvania, Philadelphia, PA 19104, USA
{praveens, megraw}@mail.med.upenn.edu

Abstract. MicroRNAs (miRNAs) are non-coding RNA molecules that bind to and translationally repress mRNA transcripts. Currently ~1345 miRNAs have been identified in at least twelve species through experimental and computational approaches. Here, we report on a field not yet thoroughly investigated: the transcriptional regulation of miRNAs. Adequately locating miRNA promoter regions will provide a reasonable search space for computational and experimental studies to determine regulatory factors that drive miRNA transcription. Insight in to the factors that control miRNA transcription may provide clues regarding more complicated mechanisms of miRNA expression control in a developing organism. We use a novel Expressed Sequence Tag (EST) based approach to approximate promoter regions for intergenic miRNAs in order to detect specific and over-represented regulatory elements. We find that miRNA promoter regions may be enriched for binding sites that recruit transcription factors (TFs) involved in development, including several homeobox TFs such as HOXA3 and Ncx. Additionally, we use clustering techniques to cluster miRNAs according to tissue specificity to find tissue-specific regulatory elements. We find a few over-represented binding sites in brain-specific miRNA promoter regions, some of which recruit TFs involved specifically with the development of the nervous system. Based on the results we suggest an interesting mechanism for in vivo miRNA expression control. The EST-based pri-miRNA assembly program will be made available at the website of the DIANA-group by the time of publication (http://diana.pcbi.upenn.edu).

[†] A.G.H, M.M., and P.S. are supported in part by an NSF Career Award Grant (DBI-0238295).
[*] These authors contributed equally to this work.

1 Introduction

MiRNAs are ~22 nt non-protein-coding RNA molecules that have been identified in at least twelve species. MiRNAs are derived from precursor sequences, often termed hairpins due to their secondary structure. These hairpin structures are derived from a primary transcript, termed pri-miRNA, which is the original unprocessed transcript of the miRNA gene. These tiny RNAs are known to be involved in important roles in cellular development and differentiation in several species ([1], [4], [19]). They function by binding to portions of particular mRNA transcripts and either cleaving them or repressing their translation without cleavage. This binding is generally done with perfect complementarity in plants, and often imperfect complementarity in other species ([4]).

Some miRNAs can be difficult to clone since it is possible for their expression to be restricted to a particular cell type or to a particular environmental condition ([4]). Therefore, within the last three years, significant efforts have been made to predict miRNA genes via computational methods ([9], [15], [17]). To understand the specific functions of these miRNAs, recent work also attempts to predict the target genes whose expression profiles are regulated by each miRNA ([8], [12], [14], [16], [20], [24]).

The transcriptional regulation of miRNAs themselves has not yet been thoroughly examined. Although there is evidence that miRNAs can be transcribed by both pol-II and pol-III ([6], [27]), the locations of the miRNA promoters, the identity of the polymerases involved, and the identity of the transcription factors involved are all largely unknown. A few studies of putative cis-elements driving miRNA transcription have emerged ([13], [25]), but there are still many open questions and substantial work to be done. For example, adequately locating miRNA promoter regions will be an important step toward a more coherent understanding of miRNA transcription, and this will allow increased flexibility for medical scientists to research methods of miRNA control for the purpose of positively altering gene expression levels in diseased states.

MiRNAs, just as protein coding genes, can be characterized as either intergenic or intragenic. It is reasonable to assume that the transcription of an intergenic miRNA is activated by promoter elements upstream of the primary-miRNA transcript from which the miRNA is derived. This assumption is not necessarily appropriate for intragenic miRNAs. Some intragenic miRNAs could be transcribed via the promoter elements of the host gene ([21]), and others via promoter elements within the intron of the host gene and upstream of the miRNA. Given these differences, it is appropriate to consider intergenic and intragenic miRNAs separately when studying their transcriptional processes. The purpose of this study is to identify regulatory motifs and putative transcription factor binding sites for intergenic miRNAs.

The goals of this study are to: (A) locate the likely promoter regions for each miRNA considered, (B) find motifs and transcription factor binding sites (TFBSs) enriched in these putative promoter regions, and (C) use recently available miRNA expression information to search for binding sites enriched in tissue-specific miRNA promoters.

In this paper, we present a novel method for approximating the promoter regions. We use these approximations to find regulatory regions that may play a role in intergenic miRNA transcription. Results of this work suggests that miRNA promoter regions may be enriched for binding sites of transcription factors known to be involved in development. Additionally, we have found that half of the development related transcription factors with binding sites in the promoters of brain-specific miRNAs have detailed involvement in the development of the nervous system.

2 Materials and Methods

2.1 Data Sets

2.1.1 MiRNAs and ESTs

We downloaded from the Rfam miRNA registry all known human and mouse miRNAs. We also downloaded the genomic locations of the precursors for these miRNAs from the UCSC Genome Browser (http://genome.ucsc.edu) miRNA track, using the most current genome builds for human and mouse (hg17 and mm5 respectively). We then determined which of the miRNAs were most likely to be intergenic by the following procedure: We downloaded the Known Genes and Genscan Genes lists provided by UCSC (using the hg17 and mm5 builds) and wrote a script to identify all miRNAs in human and mouse which do not overlap known or Genscan predicted genes. There are 39 such miRNAs in human and 26 in mouse. We then further eliminated a few miRNAs in both species which were observed to overlap with a gene from the Ensemble set or other predicted gene sets having strong UCSC-mapped EST support for the gene.

2.1.2 Promoters and Transcription Factors

Human promoter sequences were downloaded from the Eukaryotic Promoter Database (EPD). EPD provides the experimentally verified transcription start sites (TSSs) for ~1,800 human genes. We chose ~100 unrelated human genes and downloaded 4kb upstream of their TSSs to search for ubiquitous motifs and transcription factor binding sites.

2.1.3 MiRNA Expression Data

Dataset #1
Type of data: Northern blot ([23]); *Scale:* 0-28; *Mouse tissues:* brain, liver, heart, muscle, lung, kidney and spleen; *Human tissues:* brain, liver, heart and muscle;
Source: Table with northern quantifications, no further processing; *Numbers of miRNAs assayed for expression:* 112 (includes mouse and human miRNAs), 86 and 70 in common with Dataset #2 and #3, respectively.

Dataset #2
Type of data: Microarray ([26]); *Scale:* -4 to 4; *Mouse Tissues:* ES cells, six stages of embryo development, and seven adult tissues (liver, kidney, lung, ovary, heart, brain and thymus); *Source:* The data was downloaded from GEO-NCBI (accession number GSE1635), the downloaded file contained the normalized log of ratios (R/G) of each of the arrays or hybridizations performed, the normalization used by the authors was a global median centering normalization; *Numbers of miRNAs assayed for expression:* 124 (includes mouse and human miRNAs), 70 in common with Dataset #3.

Dataset #3
Type of data: Microarray ([2]); *Scale*: 0-8; *Mouse Tissues:* ES cells and 38 tissues, for the clustering we have used ES cells and the following 12 tissues- brain, femur, heart, intestine, liver, lung, mammary gland, muscle, spleen, stomach, testis; *Source:* The data was downloaded from the GEO-NCBI (accession numbers: GSM30346, GSM30347, GSM30350, GSM30351, GSM30352); *Numbers of miRNAs assayed for expression:* 141 (includes mouse and human miRNAs).

2.2 Find Regulatory Elements in MiRNA Promoter Regions

2.2.1 Approximation of the Promoter Region for Each MiRNA

We created a program which assembles ESTs into putative primary transcripts for intergenic miRNAs. Essentially, we built the probable transcribed region around a miRNA precursor by piecing together a series of adjacent or overlapping ESTs on the same strand as the precursor. However, it was necessary to keep in mind that working with ESTs can be an error-prone process and we wished to avoid piecing together ESTs which have the "pitfall properties" described next.

It was not desirable to consider ESTs which are too long (much longer than the longest expected primary transcript, we cut off at 10kb) as they may be chimeric, ESTs which map to multiple locations on the genome since they cannot be reliably placed in any single location, or ESTs which overlap a neighboring gene since it is not reasonable to expect that primary miRNA transcripts overlap the exonic region of a gene. Therefore, using ESTs from dbEST that have been mapped onto the most recent genome builds for human and mouse by UCSC, we performed a putative pri-miRNA assembly process by finding ESTs not having any of these "pitfall properties" which overlap an intergenic miRNA precursor, and then sequentially extending the EST assembly in both directions with adjacent or overlapping ESTs until no ESTs free of the "pitfall properties" can be added.

Because we are aware that the strand annotation of ESTs can be unreliable, we also performed the assembly process without the restriction that ESTs added to the assembly be on the same annotated strand as the relevant miRNA precursor. We then compared the two results and were comforted to find that generally the length and location of the resulting putative primary transcript was not greatly changed by including oppositely annotated ESTs in the assembly. One reason for this is that there were often many fewer candidate ESTs on the oppositely annotated strand than on the like-annotated strand, providing additional support for the idea that ESTs free of the "pitfall properties" in the precursor region were transcribed as portions of the primary transcript and for whatever reason exited the nucleus (or represent EST "contaminants" from nuclear material).

The putative primary transcripts are used conservatively in subsequent steps of this study as guides to a minimum length for each primary transcript, as opposed to an absolute representation of the pri-miRNAs. Thirteen of the human miRNAs and ten of the mouse miRNAs in the intergenic subset we studied had precursor coverage by these assembled "EST Blocks".

2.2.2 Search for Motifs and TFBSs

We considered the 5' upstream regions of the set of putative primary transcripts deduced from *2.2.1* as the search space for conventional motif finding algorithms. We used two motif finding algorithms, MEME ([3]) and AlignACE ([10]). MEME (Multiple Em for Motif Elicitation) is a probabilistic local alignment tool useful for conserved motif discovery. We used MEME with the following options: Background- Single-nucleotide frequencies; Motif length- 6 - 25 bases; Motif mode- "Any number of motif repititions"; E-val cutoff- 1.

MEME E-values refer to the expected number of motifs of the same width with equal or higher likelihood in the same number of random sequences with the same nucleotide composition as the considered set of sequences. AlignACE is a Gibbs-sampling based probabilistic approach for motif discovery. We used AlignACE with the default options. AlignACE reports each putative motif with a MAP (Maximum A Priori Log Likelihood) score, a score which measures the motif's degree of over-representation. Because motif searching algorithms are heuristic, attention must be given to the false positive rate. We placed more confidence in those motifs which were reported as significant by both programs. The significant motifs reported by these programs were further considered as the search space for an in-house transcription factor binding site (TFBS) scanning program. The scanning was accomplished via a script that performs the following steps:

1. Convert reported motifs in to probability matrices (motif matrices). A probability matrix indicates the probability of each of the four nucleotides occurring in each of the motif's nucleotide positions
2. Convert all TRANSFAC vertebrate transcription factor frequency matrices to probability matrices (TF matrices)
3. Since the reported motifs are generally longer than transcription factor binding sites, perform a local matrix alignment between each motif matrix and each TF matrix and record the score of each alignment ("similarity score")
4. Generate 100 random probability matrices and perform local alignments between all pairs and record the score of each alignment ("random score")
5. Set one standard deviation from the mean of the random scores as the cutoff for "similarity" between any two matrices being aligned (and set two standard deviations from the mean as the cutoff for "strong similarity")
6. Filter the set of similarity scores from step 3 to those that satisfy the cutoff requirements
7. Report this final set of similarity scores as indicators of the presence of putative TFBSs

Strong hits found by this program were recorded as putative TFBSs. For example, suppose the mean of the random scores is 1.15 and the standard deviation is 0.25. We consider any similarity score under 0.90 (1.15 – 0.25) as a putative TFBS, and any similarity score under 0.65 (0.90 – 0.25) as indicative of a strong candidate TFBS.

2.3 Find Regulatory Elements Specific for Certain Tissues

In addition to the possibility that there are motifs and TFBSs common to most or all of the intergenic miRNAs, it is also possible that several motifs and TFBSs are found only in miRNAs with a certain tissue-specificity. Therefore, we clustered the miRNAs according to tissue-specificity and searched for motifs within the promoters of each cluster.

2.3.1 Cluster MiRNAs According to Expression

Several recent studies have published data on miRNA expression profiles based on northern blots and microarrays ([2], [23], [26]). These studies included different sets of miRNAs, different sets of tissues, reported expression values in different scales, and used slightly different in-house technologies to measure expression. For these reasons, merging the data from the three studies was a task harboring many complications. Therefore, we considered each dataset separately. We used Hierarchical and K-means clustering to cluster the miRNAs from each dataset according to their expression profiles. We then searched for clusters within a dataset which indicated tissue-specificity, and corroborated this finding across the other datasets. These clusters were recorded as tissue-specific clusters for further analysis.

2.3.2 Search for Motifs and TFBSs Within Each Cluster

Within each tissue-specific cluster, we searched the promoters of the miRNAs for over-represented motifs, again using MEME and AlignACE. We further scanned these motifs for the presence of putative transcription factor binding sites and recorded the strong hits as described previously.

2.4 Computational Validation of TFBS Predictions

Not every TFBS in the set of predicted miRNA promoter TFBSs is likely to be functional. Many TFs have binding sites that are non-specific, ubiquitous, and frequently occurring across the genome. We used motif searching and TFBS scanning programs on 91 unrelated human promoters and labeled the resulting frequently occurring TFBS predictions as "non-specific". Any TFBS from the set of predicted miRNA promoter TFBSs that does not match any TFBS in the "non-specific" list is considered as potentially "specific".

3 Results

3.1 Find regulatory Elements in MiRNA Promoter Regions

3.1.1 Approximation of the Promoter Region for Each miRNA

Table 1 displays the EST blocks identified by the EST assembly program described in *2.2.1* of the Materials and Methods section. Thirteen miRNAs were found to have EST blocks. Each EST block is a contiguous assembly of acceptable ESTs (those not having any of the "pitfall properties"). Figure 1 provides a visual example of a same-strand EST block. The miRNA in consideration is hsa-mir-122a. ESTs shown in red are the members of the block, identified by the program as not having any of the "pitfall properties".

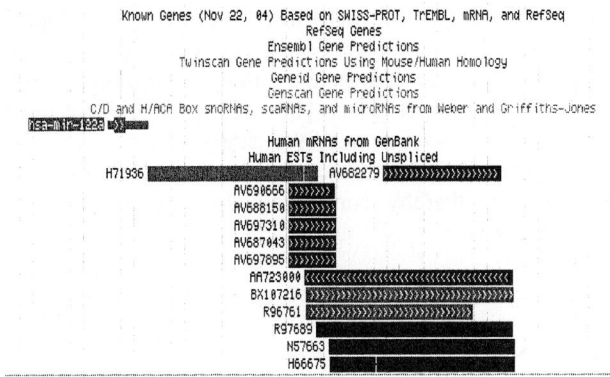

Fig. 1. ESTs shown in red are members of hsa-mir-122a's EST block

3.1.2 Search for Motifs and TFBSs

Motif searching algorithms can generally be grouped into two categories: enumerative, such as the ST algorithm, and alignment-based. The alignment-based approach can itself be grouped in to two categories: Expectation Maximization, such as MEME, and Gibbs-sampling, such as AlignACE.

Using MEME ([3]), we searched in the first 4kb upstream of all the 5' EST block ends deduced from 2.2.1 for sequence motifs which might be involved in miRNA transcription. MEME reported eight significant motifs, each ~20-25 nts long. We repeated this search using AlignACE ([10]) and found that this algorithm reported seven out of the eight of these motifs as highly significant and frequently occurring. Details of the options used with MEME and AlignACE are provided in the Materials and Methods section.

The seven significant motifs were scanned for putative vertebrate transcription factor binding sites. Details of the scanning procedure are provided in the Materials and Methods section. Twenty-nine unique putative transcription factor binding sites (TFBSs) were found within the motifs. We surmised that many of the 29 TFBSs recruit TFs that are non-specific in their binding and highly common in promoters of Pol II transcribed genes. To test this, we repeated the above motif searching and TFBS scanning procedure on a set of 91 unique and unrelated Eukaryotic Promoter Database (EPD) promoters from human genes of human promoters. At least 11 of the 29 predicted TFBSs are present in high frequency across this set. The remaining 18 TFBSs are further considered as those sites that are more likely to recruit TFs which are more specific in binding and function. Of these 18, 7 are especially noteworthy (Table 2). Two of the 7 are sites that recruit the proteins C/EBP and CREB, both of which are already predicted as transcriptional activators of miRNAs in previous studies ([11], [25]). Interestingly, the remaining five are homeo-box and forkhead-box transcription factors – proteins well known for their involvement in development.

We repeated the motif searching and TFBS scanning procedures in the regions 4kb to 8kb upstream of the 5' EST block ends deduced from 2.2.1. Again, we find several strong transcription factor binding sites that are known to recruit transcription factors involved in development (Table 3).

MiRNAs are known to play a vital role in the proper development of C.elegans ([22]), D.melanogaster ([1]) and plants ([19]). For example, lin-4 and let-7 are two C.elegans miRNAs known to control the timing of postembryonic events via the translational repression of target genes ([1]). It is probable that miRNAs also play a critical role in human development. We suggest that it is very likely for the aforelisted TFs to be transcriptional activators (such as HOXA7) and repressors (such as Msx1) of miRNAs, thereby controlling the precise timing and duration of expression of target genes.

3.2 Find Regulatory Elements Specific for Certain Tissues

3.2.1 Cluster MiRNAs According to Expression

Details of the clustering techniques and miRNA expression datasets are provided in the Materials and Methods section. Section 2.1.3 conveys the relationship between the datasets considered in this study. The clustering procedures revealed three notable clusters (Table 4).

3.2.2 Search for Motifs and TFBSs Within Each Cluster

Among the clusters identified, we chose the brain cluster for further analysis. Genes expressed in the brain are often restricted to specific compartments (substantia nigra, cerebellum, etc), perhaps implying the presence of compartment specific silencers and enhancers in the promoter regions of these genes. So, by considering all brain-expressed miRNAs in one cluster, we may lose information about compartment specific cis-elements. However, compartment specific expression data for miRNAs are not currently available. Therefore, it is reasonable to consider the brain as a whole entity and search for a higher order group of cis-elements – tissue(brain)-specific cis-elements.

None of the miRNAs in the brain cluster had EST block support. Therefore, we approximated the promoter region for each of these miRNAs by considering both 1.5kb and 4kb upstream of the 5' end of the precursor. We used MEME and AlignACE to search for motifs in these regions and used the in-house TFBS scanning procedure to search for putative transcription factor binding sites in exactly the same manner as previously described. Of the 20 predicted TFs, nine can be considered in the promiscuous/highly common category. Of the remaining 11 TFs, four are known to play key roles in development: En-1, MZF1, HOXA3, and Ncx.. Also, it is confirmatory that all four have moderate to high levels of expression in the brain (http://expression.gnf.org). It is unlikely for MZF1, HOXA3, and Ncx to be brain-specific transcription factors because their binding sites are also found in the putative promoter regions of a set of miRNAs with heterogeneous expression profiles (Table 2, 3). We believe that more likely brain-specific miRNA transcription factors can be identified if more ESTs are published in dbEST such that our EST-based pri-miRNA assembly program can build EST blocks and provide more accurate promoter regions for motif and TFBS search.

We believe that more likely brain-specific miRNA transcription factors can be identified if more ESTs are published in dbEST such that our EST-based pri-miRNA assembly program can build EST blocks and provide more accurate promoter regions for motif and TFBS search.

Table 1. The results of the EST-based pri-miRNA assembly program. The * indicates that the EST Block was determined by using ESTs on both strands. The # indicates that the EST Block was determined by using ESTs on the miRNA strand only.

miRNA Name	Chr	Str	Precursor Left	Precursor Right	EST Block Left*	EST Block Right*	EST Block Length*	EST Block Left#	EST Block Right#	EST Block Length#
hsa-mir-197	1	+	109853556	109853631	109853556	109853877	321	109853556	109853877	321
hsa-mir-196b	7	-	26982338	26982422	26981757	26982560	803	26981757	26982560	803
hsa-let-7a-1	9	+	94017793	94017873	94017084	94017873	789	94017084	94017873	789
hsa-let-7d	9	+	94020670	94020757	94019622	94021501	1879	94020440	94021501	1061
hsa-mir-223	X	+	65021732	65021842	65018323	65022692	4369	65018323	65022692	4369
hsa-mir-34c	11	+	110889373	110889450	110889114	110889823	709			
hsa-mir-135a-2	12	+	96460057	96460157	96459502	96461548	2046	96459502	96461281	1779
hsa-mir-22	17	-	1563946	1564031	1561550	1566304	4754	1561650	1566304	4654
hsa-mir-142	17	-	53763591	53763678	53763243	53764036	793	53763243	53763702	459
hsa-mir-122a	18	+	54269285	54269370	54269285	54270130	845	54269285	54270127	842
hsa-mir-27a	19	-	13808253	13808331	13808239	13808331	92			
hsa-let-7a-3	22	+	44829147	44829221	44829147	44830190	1043	44829147	44829941	794
hsa-let-7b	22	+	44830084	44830167	44829592	44830190	598			

Table 2. The TFs predicted to be enriched in the first 4kb upstream of miRNA transcription start sites. The * indicates a homeo-box or forkhead-box transcription factor.

TF ID	Gene Ontology (GO) Function
Ncx*	T-cell leukemia homeobox 2; development
HOXA7*	Homeobox A7; development
HOXA3*	Homeobox A3; development
Msx1*	Muscle-Seg. Homeobox 1; development
FOXD3*	Forkhead Box D3; development
CREB	Transcription; signal transduction
C/EBP	Transcription; CCAAT enhancer binding

Table 3. The development related TFs predicted to be enriched in the 4kb to 8kb upstream region of miRNA transcription start sites

TF ID	Gene Ontology (GO) Function
Ncx	T-cell leukemia homeobox 2; development
FAC1	Fetal Alzheimer's Clone 1; development
FOXD3	Forkhead Box D3; development
Msx1	Muscle-Segment Homeobox 1; development
HOXA3	Homeobox A3; development
MZF1	Myeloid Zinc Finger 1, differentiation
SRY	Sex Determining Region Y; differentiation

Table 4. The results of expression-based clustering of miRNAs

Brain	Low in ES cells	Ubiquitous
hsa-mir-10b	mmu-mir-139	hsa-let-7b
hsa-mir-125a	mmu-mir-22	hsa-mir-223
mmu-mir-222	hsa-mir-22	hsa-mir-27a
mmu-mir-154	hsa-mir-30a	hsa-mir-23a
--	hsa-mir-24-2	--

3.3 Computational Validation of TFBS Predictions

Complete validation of the TFBS predictions can be accomplished via chromatin immunoprecipitation (ChIP) assays. However, further credence can be given to the TFBSs via simple computational methods. We have shown that at least nine putative TFBSs are not as frequently found in other appropriate background promoter sets, thereby concluding that they are generally more specific and apparently enriched in promoters of miRNAs.

Bona fide transcription factors will have binding sites preferentially located proximal to the transcription start site (TSS), rather than distal to the TSS. In other words, although it is certainly possible to have enhancers and other cis-elements significantly upstream of the TSS, most effective TFBSs are found clustered within the first 8kb upstream of the TSS. Only roughly half of the ten predicted TFs have binding sites as far as 8kb-12kb upstream of the putative TSS. Furthermore, even some of the sites that are found 8kb-12kb upstream are less convincing as bona fide cis-elements because their similarity scores based on the TFBS scanning procedures are very low.

4 Discussion

In this study we report on a novel algorithm which utilizes EST information to approximate a primary-miRNA transcript from a miRNA precursor for the purpose of making a reasonable assumption about the promoter location. We also searched these promoter regions for novel motifs and TFBSs regulating miRNA transcription. We have predicted at least ten TFs that may be important in the transcriptional regulation of human miRNAs. Many of these are TFs that have previously been found to have a role in development. We predict miRNA promoter regions to be enriched for TFBSs that recruit TFs known to be involved in development.

Several of the predicted TFs are homeobox proteins. These proteins are known to be likely targets of miRNAs ([18]). Taken together, these two observations suggest the possibility of a negative feed-back loop whereby miRNAs may control their own expression (Figure 2).

We have also used recently available miRNA expression data to cluster miRNA genes according to tissue-specificity. This enabled us to search for tissue-specific motifs and TFBSs. We predict four development related TFs that may be important in the transcriptional regulation of the brain-specific miRNAs. Two of these four TFs have specific roles in either neurogenesis or general CNS development.

MiRNAs are known to play vital roles in many biological functions, including developmental timing, differentiation, apoptosis, fat metabolism, and growth control ([12]). Additionally, miRNAs have specific and varied expression patterns across developmental stages, tissues, and cell types ([12]). We believe that gaining insight in to the transcriptional regulation of miRNAs will help to understand the range of miRNA expression regulation and to more coherently describe the functional importance of miRNAs. We present here a novel approach to locate miRNA promoter regions and search for cis-elements that may partially control miRNA expression patterns.

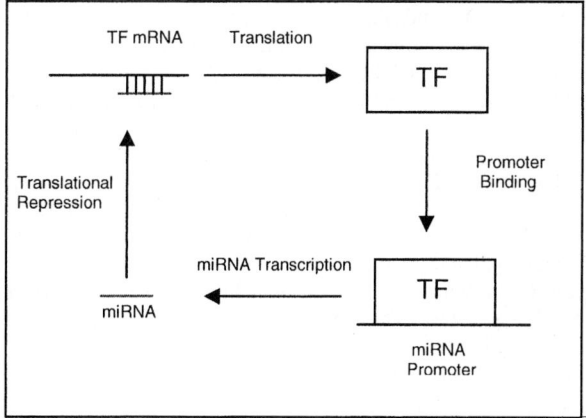

Fig. 2. Simplified version of a hypothetical negative feed-back loop to control miRNA expression

References

1. Ambros, V. (2003) MicroRNA pathways in flies and worms: growth, death, fat, stress, and timing. *Cell*, 113, 673-676.
2. Babak, T., Zhang, W., Morris, Q., Blencowe, B.J., Hughes, T.R. (2004) Probing microRNAs with microarrays: Tissue specificity and functional inference. *RNA*, 10, 1813-1819.
3. Bailey, T.L., Elkan, C. (1995) Unsupervised Learning of Multiple Motifs in Biopolymers Using Expectation Maximization. *Machine Learning Journal*, 21, 51-83.
4. Bartel, D.P. (2004) MicroRNAs: genomics, biogenesis, mechanism, and function. *Cell*, 116, 281-297.
5. Berger, E.M., and Ambros, V. (2003) Temporal regulation of microRNA expression in *Drosophila melanogaster* mediated by hormonal signals and broad-Complex gene activity. *Developmental Biology*, 259, 9-18.
6. Chen, C.Z., Li, L., Lodish, H.F., and Bartel, D.P. (2004) MicroRNAs modulate hematopoietic lineage differentiation. *Science*, 303, 83-86.
7. Church, G.M., Ruvkun, G., Kim, J. (2003) Computational and Experimental Identification of *C.elegans* microRNAs. *Molecular Cell*, 11, 1253-1263.
8. Enright, A.J., B. Jino, U. Gaul, T. Tuschl, C. Sander, and D.S. Marks. (2003). MicroRNA Targets in *Drosophila*. *Genome Biology*, 5.
9. Grad, Y., Aach, J., Hayes, G.D., Reinhart, B.J., Ohler, U., Yekta, S., Lim, L.P., Bartel, D.P., Burge, C.B. (2004) Patterns of flanking sequence conservation and a characteristic upstream motif for microRNA gene identification. *RNA*, 10, 1309-1322.
10. Hughes, J.D., Estep, P.W., Tavazoie, S., Church, G.M. (2000) Computational Identification of *Cis*-regulatory Elements Associated with Groups of Functionally Related Genes in *Saccharomyces cerevisiae*. *J. Mol. Bio*, 296, 1205-1214.
11. Impey, S., McCorkle, S.R., Cha-Molstad, H., Dwyer, J.M., Yochum, G.S., Boss, J.M., McWeeney, S., Dunn, J.J., Mandel, G., and Goodman, R.H. (2004) Defining the CREB regulon: a genome-wide analysis of transcription factor regulatory regions. *Cell*, 119(7):1041-1054.
12. John, B. Enright, A.J., A. Aravin, T. Tuschl, C. Sander, and D.S. Marks. (2004) Human MicroRNA targets. *PLoS Biology*, 5:2(11).

13. Johnson, S.M., Lin, S.Y., and Slack, F.J. (2003) The time of appearance of the *C.elegans let-7* microRNA is transcriptionally controlled utilizing a temporal regulatory element in its promoter. *Developmental Biology*, 259, 364-379.
14. Kiriakidou, M., Nelson, P.T., Kouranov, A., Fitziev, P., Bouyioukos, C., Mourelatos, Z., and Hatzigeorgiou, A. (2004) A combined computational-experimental approach predicts human microRNA targets. *Genes & Development*, 18, 1165-1178.
15. Lai, E.C., Tomancak, P., Williams, R.W., Rubin, G.M. (2003) Computational identification of *Drosophila* microRNA genes. *Genome Biology*, 4, R42.
16. Lewis, B.P., I.H. Shih, M.W. Jones-Rhoades, D.P. Bartel, and C.B. Burge. (2003) Prediction of mammalian microRNA targets. *Cell*, 115, 787-98.
17. Lim, L.P., Lau, N.C., Weinstein, E.G., Abdelhakim, A., Yekta, S., Rhoades, M.W., Burge, C.B., Bartel, D.P. (2003) The microRNAs of *Caenorhabditis elegans*. *Genes & Development*, 17, 991-1008.
18. Mansfied, J.H., Harfe, B.D., Nissen, R., Obenauer, J., Srineel, J., Chaudhuri, A., Farzan-Kashani, R., Zuker, M., Pasquinelli, A.E., Ruvkun, G., Sharp, P.A., Tabin, C.J., McManus, M.T. (2004) MicroRNA-responsive 'sensor' transgenes uncover Hox-like and other developmentally regulated patterns of vertebrate microRNA expression. *Nat. Genetics*, Vol 36, No. 10.
19. Palatnik, J.F., Allen, E., Wu, X., Schommer, C., Shwab, R., Carrington, J.C., and Weigel, D. (2003) Control of leaf morphogenesis by microRNAs. *Nature*, 425, 257-263.
20. Rajewsky, N. and Socci, N. D. (2004) Computational identification of microRNA targets. *Developmental Biology*, 267, 529-535.
21. Rodriguez, A., Griffiths-Jones, S., Ashurst, J.L., and Bradley, A. (2004) Identification of Mammalian microRNA Host Genes and Transcription Units. *Genome Research*, 14.
22. Sempere, L.F., Sokol, N.S., Dubrovsky, E.B., Lin, S.Y., Johnson, S.M., Abraham, M., Vella, M.C., Pasquinelli, A., Gamberi, C., Gottlieb, E., and Slack, F.J. (2003) The *C.elegans* hunchback, hb-1, controls temporal patterning and is a probable microRNA target. *Dev Cell*, 4(5), 639-650.
23. Sempere, L.F., Freemantle, S., Pitha-Rowe, I., Moss, E., Dmitrovsky, E., Ambros, V. (2004) Expression profiling of mammalian microRNAs uncovers a subset of brain-expressed microRNAs with possible roles in murine and human neuronal differentiation. *Genome Biology*, 5:R13.
24. Stark, A., J. Brennecke, R.B. Russell, and S.M. Cohen. (2003) Identification of *Drosophila* MicroRNA Targets. *Plos Biology*, 1, 1-13.
25. Sun, Y., Koo, S., White, N., Peralta, E., Esau, C., Dean, N.M., and Perera, R.J. (2004) Development of a micro-array to detect human and mouse microRNAs and characterization of expression in human organs. *Nucleic Acids Research*, 32, No.22.
26. Thomson, J.M., Parker, J., Perou, C.M., and Hammond, S.M. (2004) A custom microarray platform for analysis of microRNA gene expression. *Nature Methods*, 1, 47-53.
27. Zeng, Y. and Cullen, B.R. (2003) Sequence requirements for microRNA processing and function in human cells. *RNA* 9, 112-123.

Web Service-Enabled Grid-Based Platform for Drug Resistance Management

P. Gouvas[1,*], G. Magiorkinis[2,*], A. Bouras[1], D. Paraskevis[2], D. Alexandrou[1], A. Hatzakis[2], and G. Mentzas[1]

[1] National Technical University of Athens, School of Electrical and Computer Engineering,
Information Management Unit, 9 Iroon Polutexneiou Str. Zografou Campus,
15780 Zografou, Athens, Greece
{pgouv, bouras, dalex, gmentzas}@mail.ntua.gr
http://imu.iccs.ntua.gr

[2] University of Athens, Medical School, Department of Hygiene and Epidemiology,
75 Mikras Asias Str., 11527 Athens, Greece
{gmagi, dparask, ahatzak}@med.uoa.gr

Abstract. HIV Drug Resistance testing has been established as a routine test in several cases. Estimation of genotypic resistance is a laborious task consisting of experimental procedure and complicated algorithmic interpretation of mutational pattern (sequence data). Since the sequencing procedure is not error free, it is often necessary to proceed into quality checking and manual editing of the raw data (chromatograms). This paper presents the design and development of a grid-based platform that assists the storage and analysis of HIV nucleotide sequences both for clinical practice and research purposes. Modular software components were implemented for sequence uploading, quality verification, mutation identification, genotypic resistance interpretation, phylogenetic analysis, multiple-sequence alignment and sophisticated mutation querying. Moreover these services have been exported as web services in order to provide a high layer of abstraction and enhanced collaboration among researchers. The platform has been validated and tested with more than 500 HIV sequences.

1 Introduction

Nowadays, virologists and related researchers have high expectations towards bioinformatics software applications and applications integration. They intend to access, process and analyze the genomic resources they need, while these resources must be accurate and free of redundancy due to the significance and complication of the expected results. In order research institutes and laboratories to meet all needs that derive from both users and research, they increasingly demand strictly integration and interoperability between bioinformatics applications and genomic resources, improving the communication and cooperation with academic and research partners.

On the other hand, genome sequence management and especially drug resistance estimation uses computer science and information technology extensively across its

---
[*] These authors have equally contributed to the study.

area. The increased reliance on technology in this field has motivated the creation of bioinformatics, which concerns the development of new tools for the analysis of genomic and molecular biological data, including sequence analysis, phylogenetic inference, genome database organization and mining, biologically inspired computational models, genetic algorithms, neural networks, machine learning and artificial life.

Medical Research Institutes (MRIs) undertake the task to estimate the levels of the viral resistance developed in patients after treatment failure and, subsequently, by this way, to assist physicians to choose the most potent (active) future therapy. The results of the MRIs are known as Genotypic Resistance Reports and in most of the cases are based on Genotypic Resistance Algorithms (GRAs).

These algorithms (which in most cases are rule based) estimate the potential effectiveness of a drug according to a set of viral mutations associated with resistance to different drugs. In other words, resistance algorithms interpret the genotypic score (resistance mutations) to different levels of resistance for each drug, which is directly associated with the possibility for a patient to respond to treatment with a drug. More specifically, a virus can be characterized as fully, intermediately resistant or sensitive to a particular drug and, then treatment prescription should be chosen according to the estimated resistance pattern.

Although the clinical utility of resistance testing has been shown by several prospective and retrospective studies there are still some cavities concerning the dynamic medical treatment derived mainly from a) the high complexity of resistance due to high number of drugs and different drug combinations and b) the Genotypic Resistance Algorithms are continuously updated.

The continuous update of the GRAs is due to the upcoming findings of new associations between resistance mutations and response to treatment (based on heuristic/statistical and AI based methods as a result of clinical research). Therefore, the update of GRA is essential given the new rules for estimating resistance to different drugs. We should note that there is considerable diversity of GRA (rules) among different Medical Research Institutes.

In this paper, the vision of the integration of research effort in the areas of bioinformatics, and in HIV drug resistance in particular, will be examined. A complete genome organization and mining platform which emphasizes in HIV drug resistance and enables the research integration will be described.

2 Integration Challenge

In biology research, the experimental, complicated estimation of HIV genotypic drug resistance is critically dependent to wide genome-based data analysis that requires interoperability among multiple databases and analytic tools. Although, a large number of genome sequence databases and bioinformatics applications are available through the web, the crucial advantage of automatic integration of such resources is not yet a reality. The main obstacles identified [1] include: 1) heterogeneous genomic resources, 2) incompatible bioinformatics applications running environments, 3) the application web interface, user-friendly though, is neither machine-friendly nor machine-comprehensive, 4) the use of a non-standard format for data input and output, 5) lack of standardization in defining application interface and message exchange, and

6) existing protocols for remote messaging are often not firewall-friendly. To overcome these interoperability and standardization issues, web services have emerged as a standard XML-based model for message exchange between heterogeneous applications integrating resources, data, and processes.

2.1 Web Services in Bioinformatics

A Web Service is a software system designed to support interoperable machine-to-machine interaction over a network [2]. It has an interface described in a machine-processable format (specifically WSDL). Other systems interact with the Web Service in a manner prescribed by its description using SOAP-messages, typically conveyed using HTTP with an XML serialization in conjunction with other Web-related standards. Web Services architecture [3] and model [4] comprise three emerging key technologies: WSDL, SOAP and UDDI.

A typical web service process includes a service provider (e.g. a research institute) that deploys web services representing its available services, applications and system features and publishes them in a UDDI registry, and a service requester that searches the registry, which offers categorization and discovery services, trying to find the composed service required and uses it binding with the service provider.

As web services provide a common reference base for deploying, representing and formatting both input and output data of already existing bioinformatics applications and processes, there is no need for researchers to customize and modify the pre-developed applications and pre-defined genomic resources and database schemas in order to fit with a unifying bioinformatics application and resources model. As a result, the web services technology converts, in a way, the system-based architecture of current bioinformatics applications, serving specific needs in specific laboratories or research centers, to a holistic component-based architecture. The deployed web services implementing specific, single system features are considered as "closed" components with specific, machine-processable and interpretable input and output data structure, while the potential services requester, apart from the web services profiles, is not aware of the functional and technical specifications of the components s/he uses and the service provider can change the inter-component structure without altering the overall functionality of the component – web service.

2.2 The Drug Resistance Scenario

More specific, in our drug resistance case, the adaptation of the web services technology in bioinformatics and drug resistance (Figure 1) will lead to the creation and administration of web services realizing pre-selected and pre-existing features of various bioinformatics platforms. Additionally, the creation of descriptions for the deployed web services will be completed (profiling), while the web services' profiles will be registered in the corresponded web repository publishing, thus, the deployed web service on the UDDI registry.

In particular, for each bioinformatics platform, specific features are chosen, among the existing set of the platform functional applications (i.e. sequence upload, quality verification, mutation identification, phylogenetic analysis, genotypic resistance interpretation and sophisticated mutation query). The service provider (i.e. research laboratory) deploys several web services that implement these pre-selected features. The provider will now create the web service profile describing in a standard XML-based format technical information, syntactical description, and content and context information about the specific web service. Special effort is given to the XML-based description of the data structures referring to the input and output of the feature.

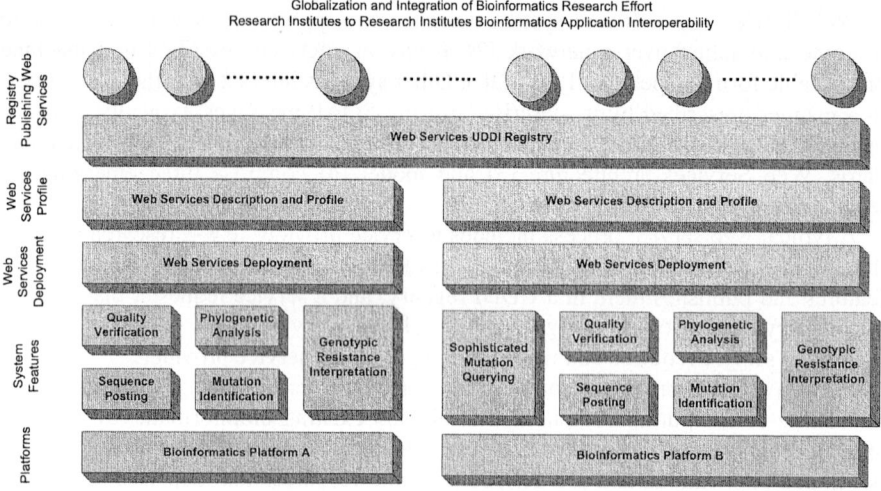

Fig. 1. Web services in drug resistance

The service provider publishes the deployed web services to the common UDDI bioinformatics registry that serves as "yellow pages" for bioinformatics applications enabling the globalization of bioinformatics systems features and distributed research efforts, and strengthening and realizing an upper-level integration of heterogeneous genomic resources, the interoperability of drug resistance platforms and the composition of bioinformatics research at global scale.

2.3 Realizing the Challenge

In the following sections, the design and implementation lifecycle of a grid-based platform that assists the storage and analysis of HIV nucleotide sequences both for clinical practice and research purposes will be thoroughly discussed. Given the above, modular software components have been implemented for several tasks regarding HIV drug resistance management. Moreover these services have been exported as web services in order to provide a high layer of abstraction and enhanced collaboration among researchers.

3 Architecture

Expertise consultation from virologists (i.e. Department of Hygiene and Epidemiology, Medical School-University of Athens) was firstly taken into account so as a concrete architecture to be formulated. Furthermore all algorithms that were routine procedures which were accomplished manually up to now have been interpreted to automatic procedures and integrated to the final architecture.

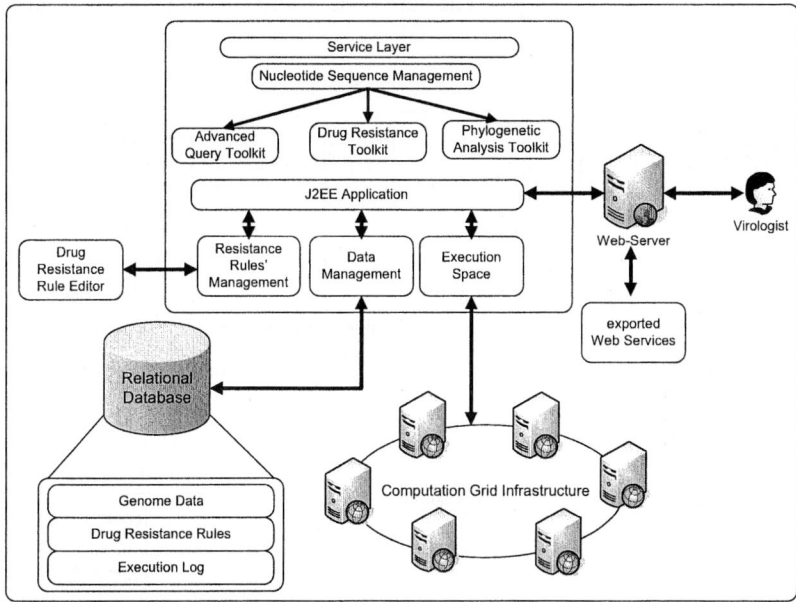

Fig. 2. Platform Architecture

The final platform architecture is presented in Figure 2. More specific, the proposed architecture constitutes the composition of various discrete components, which are presented below in detail, regarding a) the data layer, b) the application layer, c) the computational grid infrastructure and d) finally a high level integration mechanism using the web services technology.

3.1 Data Layer

At first a relational schema of the database was designed and implemented. The database has been designed in order to undertake the storage of a) Genome Data b) Execution Log Metadata and finally c) Drug Resistance Rules. The Genome Data consists of the DNA sequences along with some crucial metadata such as sequence name, virus extraction date, virus Genome Region, validation procedure, starting point-ending point, and amino-acid sequence. All these characteristics are vital for research purposes and forthcoming sequence analysis. The execution log metadata are related to statistical variables such as amount of analyzed sequences, cluster utilization report info, etc.

As far as drug resistance rules are concerned several Medical Research Institutes (MRIs) are responsible for publishing Genotypic Resistance Algorithms (GRAs). These rule based algorithms are firstly interpreted in standardized XML format and after stored in the database. As mentioned above the continuous update of the GRAs is due to the upcoming findings of new associations between resistance mutations and response to treatment. So, it is of major importance the continuous update of GRAs.

In our platform the Relational Database is based on MySQL 5.0 DBMS running on Linux (Fedora Core 3 distribution). The core SQL schema of the platform is presented below:

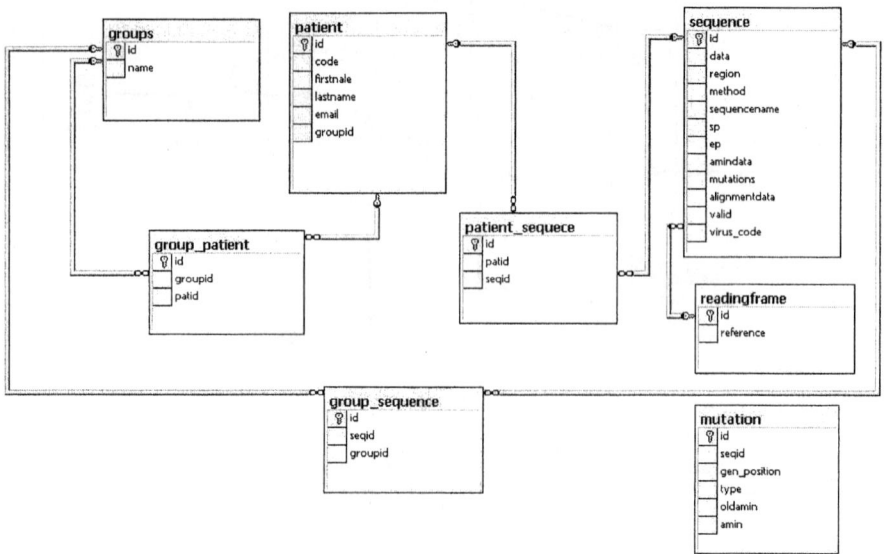

Fig. 3. Database Core Schema

3.2 The Necessity for Grid Infrastructure

The endmost goal of the platform is the facilitation of virus sequence analysis and especially drug resistance estimation and reporting. However, it is a fact that most of the algorithms that relate to virus analysis which will be discussed later on this paper are computational-intensive. In order to meet these requirements and tackle the barrier of computational intensiveness[5] a computational grid infrastructure has been utilized.

A computational grid is a hardware and software infrastructure that provides dependable, consistent, pervasive, and inexpensive access to high-end computational capabilities. In the last five years, toolkits and software environments for implementing Grid applications have become available. These include Legion (http://legion.virginia.edu), Condor (http://www.cs.wisc.edu/condor), Unicore (http://www.unicore.org), Globus (http://www.globus.org/toolkit) etc. These toolkits coordinate resources that are not subject to centralized control, use standard open, general-purpose protocols and interfaces and deliver nontrivial qualities of service.

In our platform the computational grid infrastructure consists of a six-processor Linux cluster (3GHz CPU-1GB RAM) running Fedora Core 3, equipped with Giga-Ethernet Interfaces and interconnected with one Giga-Ethernet switch. All software components used or implemented utilize the MPICH API (version 1.2.7) in order to take advantage of the computational grid infrastructure. In the next section a thorough description of the platform applications will be analyzed.

3.3 Application Layer

Modular software components were implemented from scratch and several of-the-self components were integrated throughout a single point of use for the following tasks: a) sequence uploading, b) quality verification, c) mutation identification, d) genotypic resistance interpretation, e) phylogenetic analysis, f) multiple sequence alignment and g) sophisticated mutation querying. These services have also been exported as web services as described in the previous section.

As far as DNA sequence uploading is concerned a web based sequence uploading tool has been implemented allowing both the upload of one sequence at a time and the automatic upload of many sequences (batch mode). For the latter mode a formalization of multiple FASTA format was considered to automatically update the patient and sample identification codes.

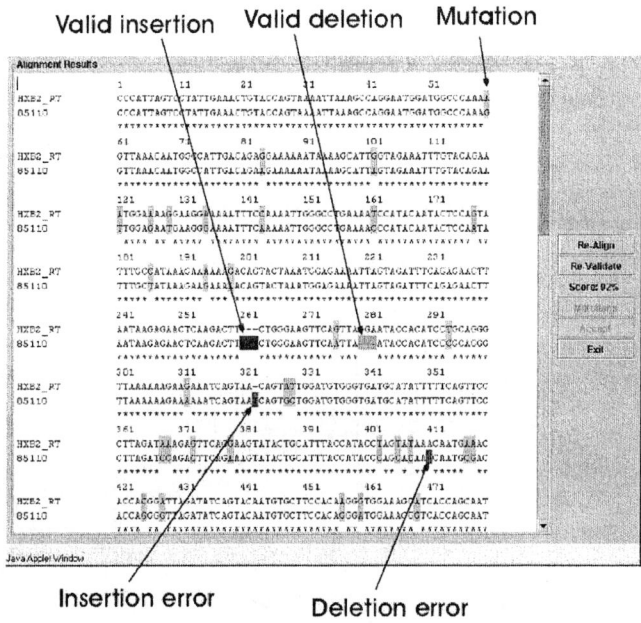

Fig. 4. Implemented Alignment Editor

Concerning quality verification, in order to facilitate the interactive error checking of the sequence data, a sophisticated Java based Alignment Editor has been implemented. The quality validation algorithm that this utility relies on is based on three crucial criteria such as a) the percentage of sequence similarity to the gene's reference sequence, b) the maintenance of the reading frame and c) the identification of potential premature 'stop codons'. This utility is accompanied by a user friendly environment that pinpoints DNA insertion/deletion/mutation errors and 'stop codons'. Beyond the visualisation functionalities of the utility this component is responsible for updating the database with the validated sequence, post the alignment file and enrich the database with the mutation information which is essential for drug estimation. The Graphical User Interface of this utility is presented in Figure 4.

Regarding identification of mutations, reference sequences of the HXB2 isolate (HIV) were obtained in order to be used as norms for the mutations' identification. Mutation interpretation algorithm was developed taking also into account the IUPAC nucleotide ambiguity codes so as to achieve tolerance to sequencing impuissance and quasi-species' diversity. Mutations' identification can be only performed for the qualified data that have passed quality verification control.

Furthermore, Genotypic Resistance interpretation of the unknown sequence is carried out using the Rega Genotypic Resistance Algorithm [6], while the program can only perform this task (resistance interpretation) only for sequences passed the quality control step. In case of multiple amino acids at resistance sites (due to minor populations), resistance interpretation is carried out for all possible amino acids and, finally, the "worst case scenario" in terms of resistance interpretation is reported.

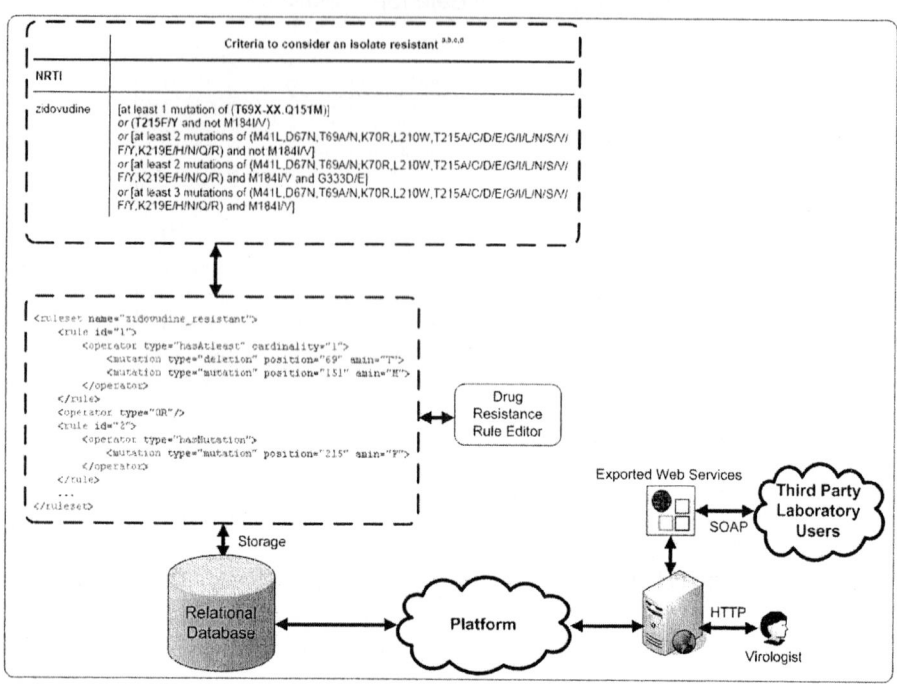

Fig. 5. Web based query interface

The next component that has been integrated to the platform is related to Phylogenetic analysis. Phylogenetic analysis is used for the inference of the evolutionary relationships between different nucleotide or amino acid sequences sampled from a single or different organisms or species. Although sufficient software exists [7] for all kinds of phylogenetic analyses, analysis of big datasets (like those existing for viral sequences: > 950 full-length and 122,000 partially available sequences) cannot be efficiently performed in a reasonable time, using non-parallel environment. Although there were several initiatives in the past to perform large scale evolutionary analyses of HIV-1, computation time provided always as a barrier for performing such a kind of studies.

Subtype reference sequences were obtained from the Los Alamos sequence database (http://hiv-web.lanl.gov) and source code was modified from the linux version of the PHYLIP program for automated phylogenetic analysis workflow. The final output includes a neighbour joining tree and a bootstrap analysis consensus tree.

Finally the platform has been enriched with a query interface supporting both statistical and research purposes. The query interface was developed to facilitate two goals a) BLAST similarity search on existing sequences and b) the discovery of sequences that meet a certain genotypic resistance rule-set. The first goal has been achieved by the integration of BLAST source code in order to perform fast similarity searches among big datasets.

The second goal is achieved throughout the standardized procedure described in Figure 5.

At first an XML representation of the Genotypic Resistance Rules mentioned above are interpreted in XML-based rules and stored in the local Database. This interpretation is accomplished by the use of the drug resistance rule editor which is a web based component developed using Java Server Pages (JSP) Framework. These rules stored in the database consist of the core component of the inference subsystem. The inference sub-system undertakes the task of combining the mutation information derived from all sequences existing in the data base with the drug resistance rules existing in the database. For every single existing Drug a predefined rule-set exists in the database and is used for drug resistance check. However, the end user-researcher may query the database which a custom rule. Hence, a web based component for creating formatted rules have been developed (Figure 6).

Finally, all services developed in the scope of our platform have been exported to web services making use of Apache AXIS framework.

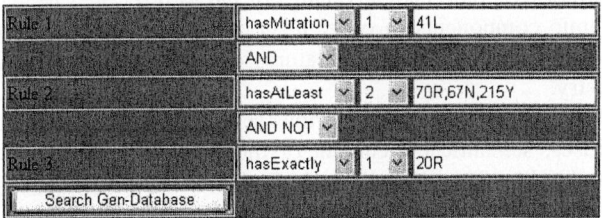

Fig. 6. Web based query interface

4 Results

A flexible and modular system concerning the adjustment of genes and resistance algorithm's updating was implemented. The various software components implemented/integrated cover a range of research and clinical demands. The alpha-testing was based on more than 500 PR/RT sequences with previous manual interpretation of resistance and HIV-1 subtype and confirmed that the use of this platform accelerates the process of genotypic interpretation and secures the quality, storage and analysis of massive sequence data. The mutations' query component provides an excellent way to perform mutational pattern analysis.

Furthermore, the lack of an interoperability infrastructure can be easily, effectively compensated by a top level XML-based structure ensuring both the interoperability of bioinformatics applications and the integration of heterogeneous genomic resources. Additional benefits arising from the use of web services are listed below:

- XML-based data and services model serving as a common base and format in the deployment and publishing of heterogeneous distributed bioinformatics applications;
- Service-oriented, component-based architecture;
- Provision of environment- and programming language- independent bioinformatics services;
- Provision of a centralized UDDI registry publishing, categorizing and discovery of web services implementing applications and features of bioinformatics systems;
- Integration and interoperability among heterogeneous bioinformatics systems and applications providing access to multiple bioinformatics web-deployed services, aggregating and processing genomic data from multiple sources; and
- Direct, widespread and no-barriers access to drug resistance and bioinformatics applications, and reuse of distributed genomic resources.

5 Conclusions and Future Work

Although, a lot of work has already been done towards the endmost goal that is an integrated, global bioinformatics platform serving HIV drug resistance management, a lot of steps have to be implemented in the direction of the research community awareness to the adoption of widely accepted platforms. The various research institutes and laboratories should take advantage of the web services technology and grid-based algorithmic components in order to develop high level drug resistance management systems and export specific features of these systems to a common bioinformatics registry.

As the UDDI registries may store various services relative to drug resistance for a variety of viruses, semantic enrichment of the web services is necessary to allow researchers easily, directly and intelligently find and take advantage of the appropriate bioinformatics resources and applications.

In this paper a web service-enabled Grid-based platform dedicated for drug resistance management has been designed and implemented. Our vision is to enhance the architecture by creating a semantically-enabled Problem Solving Environment in the virology domain. Such environment pre-requires a a software repository with grid-enabled and semantically-enhanced virology software applications including applications for the phylogenetic analysis of virus isolates and for the support of gene sequence processing. Additionally a reliable inference engine that will use stored Genotypic Resistance Algorithms (GRAs) should be developed. Among researchers using drug resistance rule-sets in various bioinformatics applications a strong necessity of standardised logic-based representation exists to provide large scale interpretability and processability.

References

1. Remko de Knikker, Y. Guo1, J. Li1, A. Kwan, K. Yip, D. Cheung and K. Cheung, "A web services choreography scenario for interoperating bioinformatics applications", 10 March 2004, BMC Bioinformatics 2004, 5:25
2. W3C, "Web Services Glossary", 11 February 2004, W3C Working Group Note, [http://www.w3.org/TR/ws-gloss/]
3. W3C, Web Services Architecture, 11 February 2004, W3C Working Group Note, [http://www.w3.org/TR/ws-arch/]
4. Basic Profile of the Web Services Interoperability model, [http://www.wsi.org/Profiles/Basic/2003-05/BasicProfile-1.0-WGAD.htm]
5. Biogrid Project [http://biogrid.icm.edu.pl]
6. Leuven Genotypic Resistance Algorithm [www.kuleuven.be/rega/cev/ pdf/ResistanceAlgorithm6_22.pdf]
7. Phylip program suite[http://evolution.genetics.washington.edu/phylip.html]

The Enhancement of Class Model Development Using Business Rules[*]

Tomas Skersys[1] and Saulius Gudas[1,2]

[1] Kaunas University of Technology, Studentu 50-309, LT-51368 Kaunas, Lithuania
skertoma@pit.ktu.lt, gudas@soften.ktu.lt
[2] Kaunas Faculty of Humanities of Vilnius University, Muitines 8,
LT-3000 Kaunas, Lithuania
gudas@vukhf.lt

Abstract. Paper deals with the principles of model-driven UML Class model enhancement using business rules (BR) as a source of domain knowledge. Business rules are stored in BR repository which is defined by the business rules meta-model. Templates for business rules formalization are presented. Co-relations between BR meta-model and extended UML Class meta-model are also presented and discussed in this paper. Basic steps of the algorithm for the extended UML Class model enhancement are presented and illustrated with example.

1 Introduction

Modern tools for computer-aided system engineering (CASE) influence and improve the content of information systems (IS) development life cycle (ISDLC). However, IS development projects still suffer from the poor quality of models used in system analysis and design stages. At some degree, quality of models that are developed by CASE tools can be assured using various automated model comparison, syntax checking procedures. It is also reasonable to check these models against the business domain knowledge, but the domain knowledge stored in the repository of CASE tool is insufficient [1], [2]. Involvement of business domain experts into these processes is complicated because non-IT people often find it difficult to understand models that were developed by IT professionals using some specific modeling language (e.g. UML, DFD, etc.).

Building the Class model (CM) for a problem domain is among the main objectives of the OO software development. Nevertheless, there is still no clear, well-developed process proposed to help the software engineers solve this problem successfully [3], [4]. It is a common practice when system designer develops models of the system by analyzing earlier created models and relying on his own experience and knowledge about the problem domain. In other words, transition from stage to stage in the ISDLC is done empirically. In such situation model verification and approval by business domain experts becomes a very important activity. Yet there is no CASE tool or method that could propose a sufficient technique of UML CM (or other IS design model) verification against the business domain knowledge approved by business expert.

---

[*] The work is supported by Lithuanian State Science and Studies Foundation according to Eureka programme project "IT-Europe" (Reg. No 3473).

From our point of view one of the most promising techniques to verify Class model (CM) against the business domain knowledge is the business rules (BR) approach [5], [6], [7]. Business rules are among the core elements of structured business domain knowledge; moreover, BR can be understood and therefore verified by business domain experts. However, clearly expressed, formalized BR are still not commonly used in novel CASE systems. These systems are usually limited to the use of constraints that describe and specify data structures and are expressed as an integrated part of the graphical notation of the models. The usage of other types of BR is limited to the description fields of model elements, where BR can be written as plain text.

As far as BR are not realized as a separate component of the CASE system repository, there is no possibility to uniquely identify and use them in other phases of the ISDLC. Another reason is that most of the CASE tools are mainly based on the modeling languages that are not well suited for BR modeling. UML is the most widely used object-oriented modeling language and it also lacks support for business rules modeling [8]. Nevertheless, it should be pointed out that the OMG group has already begun an initiative to find ways of BR integration with the OMG standards (UML and MDA in particular) [9], [10].

The approach for BR integration in the IS development process was already proposed in [11]. This paper is focused on the principles of BR-based UML Class model verification. The Business rules meta-model, extended UML Class meta-model are presented, and formalized steps are developed to verify an extended UML Class model.

2 Business Rules Repository Model

According to the BR approach, business rules should be represented and managed as a separate and at the same time tightly integrated component of IS. For that reason it is essential to store BR in a separate business rules repository (BRR) [12], [13], [14]. None of the analyzed repository models provide a mechanism for structuring BR, as there are no constructs for the decomposition of BR to its atomic elements defined in those repositories. Moreover, for the purposes of IS development the BR repository must be integrated with other business objects via constructs of the Enterprise model [1], [2], [11]. Structure of BR repository is defined by the business rules meta-model (Fig. 1).

Constructs of the Business rules repository model are as follows:

- *BRInformal*, *BRStructured* represent BRs written in natural language and structured (formalized) forms respectively. Informal BRs (*BRInformal*) are gathered from the sources (*Actor*) within the organization. A structured BR (*BRStructured*) is extracted from the informal rule (informal BR may be transformed into one or more structured BR). Structured BR may have events (*Event*) that initiate this rule, and preconditions (*Condition*) that must hold true in order to process the rule. A rule is a part of an information activity (*InfActivity*) that is also the element of the Enterprise model (EM elements are darkened in Fig. 1) [1], [2].
- BR is a composition of certain elements (*BRElement*). Elements may be:
  - Business rule itself (*BRStructured*);
  - Term (*BRTerm*) – a word or phrase that is relevant to business;

- Fact (*BRFact*) – a statement that asserts a relationship between two (or more) terms;
- Reserved word (*BRResWord*) – a reserved symbol, word or phrase that has particular, well-defined meaning in a business rule;
- Value (*BRValue*) – a particular symbolic or numerical value in a business rule;
- Action (*BRAction*) – an action that can be performed with business object.

In the context of this paper two features of *BRResWord* will be used: *Meaning* and *Type*. Values assigned to *Meaning* can be *Relationship* or *Feature*; values of *Type* can be *Association, Aggregation, Composition* or *Generalization*.

• We propose to structure BR using a predefined system of templates (Sec. 3). Therefore, BRR model contains elements aimed to implement this feature: Template (*Template*), Template element (*TempElement*). Template includes elements of the following types: Value (*Value*), Reserved word (*ResWord*), Action (*Action*), Fact (*Fact*), Term (*Term*), Business rule (*BR*).

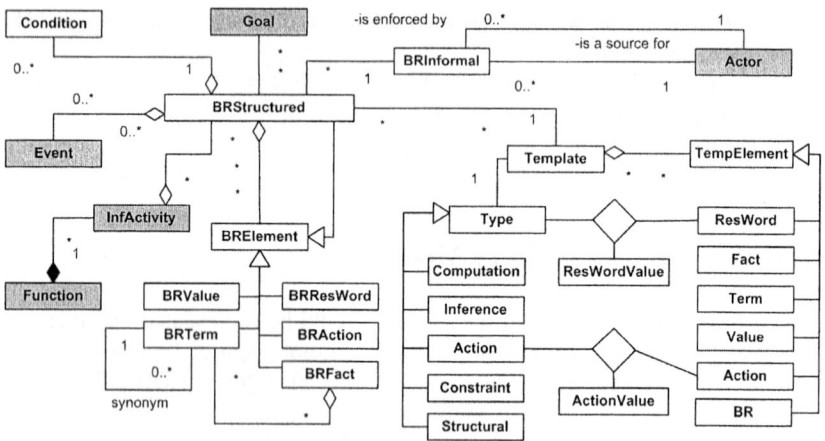

Fig. 1. Business rules repository model (UML notation)

Table 1. The classification of business rules

Type	Definition
Term	A word or phrase that is relevant to the business.
Fact (Structural)	A statement that asserts a relationship between two (or more) terms.
Constraint	A statement that specifies a mandatory feature of the business entity.
Inference	A statement where logic operations are used to derive a new fact.
Action assertion	A statement that defines conditions for the initiation of a certain business action.
Computation	A statement that derives a value of the fact by using a certain algorithm.

Business rules templates have to be classified in order to define their structure. This classification is close to the ones presented in [15], [16]. Type of the template itself is defined by the *Type*: Computation (*Computation*), Inference (*Inference*), Action (*Action*), Constraint (*Constraint*), Structural (*Structural*). The classification of templates coincides with the classification of business rules (Table 1).

The BR repository presented in Fig. 1 plays a major role in Class model verification and augmentation process using business rules.

3 Templates for Business Rules Formalization

One of the major problems in the area of IS engineering today is the communication gap between the business people and systems developers [17]. Communicating requirements through the formalized business rules narrows this gap.

Business rules structuring using templates is an acceptable way of BR formalization [11]. National (i.e., Lithuanian) language-based templates were developed with respect to the basic recommendations on BR templates construction [18], [19] – this is important in order to reach maximum compatibility with the English-based template analogues. Consequently, this will let to minimize efforts of mapping structured BR to other formalized forms and reach the implementation level of the rules. Business rules templates were developed on the basis of elements that define the structure of the Template (*Template*) in the BR repository model (Fig. 1). Basic structures of the classified BR templates (EBNF notation) are as follows:

- <Template_Fact>::= <Term> <ResWord> <Term> – template for a Fact;
- <Template_Constraint>::= (<Fact> | <Term>) <ResWord> {[<ResWord>] | [<ResWord> <Value>]} [(<Fact> | <Term> | <Value>)] – the template for a Constraint;
- <Template_Inference>::= <ResWord> <Fact> <ResWord> (<Fact>|<Value>) [{<ResWord> <Fact> <ResWord> (<Fact>|<Value>)}] <ResWord><Fact> <ResWord>(<Fact> | <Value>) – the template for an Inference BR.
- <Template_Action>::= <ResWord> <Fact> <ResWord> (<Fact> | <Value>) [{<ResWord> <Fact> <ResWord> (<Fact> | <Value>)}] <ResWord> <Action> (<Term> | <Fact> |
) – the template for an Action BR.
- <Template_Computation>::= <Fact> <ResWord> (<Fact> | <Value>) {[<ResWord> (<Fact> | <Value>)]} – the template for a Computation BR.

4 Extended UML Class Meta-model

In object-oriented (OO) methods class models are typically used: as domain models to explore domain concepts; as conceptual/analysis models to analyze requirements; as system design models to depict detailed design of OO software [20]. Class model is also a part of OMG standard, namely Unified Modeling Language (UML). Class model in UML-based CASE systems serves as a main source of knowledge for the development of information system prototype: database specification, graphical user interface (GUI), application code.

However, from our point of view it is important to note that UML meta-model does not have sufficient set of constructs for business modeling [1], [2], [21]. The construct of business rules is also omitted UML meta-model even though BR is recognized as one of the main aspects of business modeling. We have proposed extended UML Class meta-model (Fig. 2) that is based on the core of the UML meta-model, but also incorporates constructs from the Enterprise meta-model [1], [2] and BR meta-model (see Sec. 2 and [11] for more details on BR meta-model).

Constructs of the extended UML Class meta-model are as follows:

- Class model (*ClassModel*) is composed of the model elements (*ModelElement*). Class model elements can be either classes (*Class*) or relationships (*Connector*) that relate these classes to each other. Each relationship has at least two connection ends (*ConnectionEnd*) and also may have some constraints or structural rules (*Rule*) that specify that relationship.
- Traditionally, classes have attributes and operations. We enriched construct *Class* with certain subtypes: *Process, Flow, Actor* and *Function*. Such modification is based on the specification of the Enterprise model introduced in [1], [2]. The classification of classes is not a new idea – P. Coad's UML modeling in color [22], Robustness diagrams are just a few examples. Techniques that classify classes pursue certain practical goals. In our case this classification is made in order to make a close link between the business environment (Enterprise model) and the IS design models (in this case, extended UML Class model).
- Classes of type *Flow* may have states (*FlowState*).

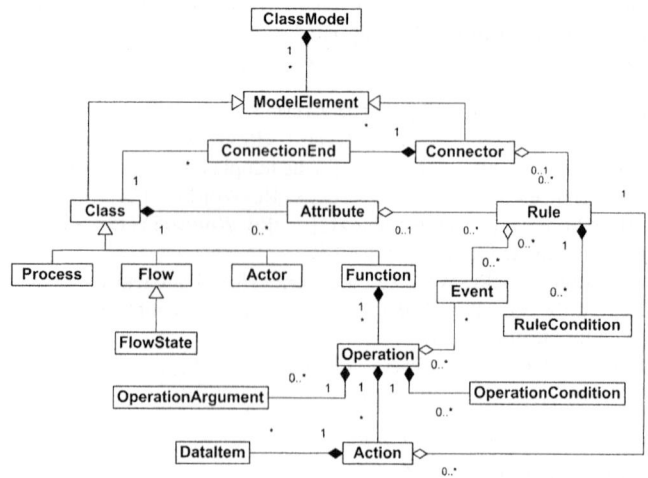

Fig. 2. Extended UML Class meta-model (UML notation)

- In the extended UML Class meta-model each class may have attributes (*Attribute*), but the operation level (*Operation*) is specific only to the *Function* type classes. Construct *Operation* represents algorithmically-complex operations [23], and algorithmically-simple operations (such as Create, Connect, Access, Release) are not modeled in order to reduce the complexity of the class models. Classes of type *Function* are at some degree similar to the controller type classes in Robustness diagrams. Class' attribute (*Attribute*) may have number of constraining rules (*Rule*).
- Class operation (*Opperation*) is composed of actions (*Action*) and may have arguments (*OperationArgument*) and conditions (*OperationCondition*) that must be true in order to fire the operation.
- Structure of the action may contain certain data items (*DataItem*) from the Data base (BD) of the system. Action represents single business rule (*Rule*) of type *Computation, Action assertion* or *Inference* (Table 1). These rules may have certain condi-

tions (*RuleCondition*) that need to be true for the business rule to fire out. Rules may be triggered by the events (*Event*).

5 UML Class Model Development Using Business Rules

5.1 Algorithm of Class Model Enhancement

The algorithm of business rules-based enhancement of CM represents the activities of model verification against the knowledge of business domain and model augmentation. Knowledge of business domain is expressed in a form of structured business rules. Making reference to the OMG's Model Driven Architecture (MDA) [24], verification of the Domain model (in our case represented as a Class model) must be done on the platform-independent level, and this is the level where business rules naturally reside.

Table 2. BRMM to CMM mappings (BRMM → CMM)

BR meta-model element	Mapping	Extended UML Class meta-model element
<BRMM.BRStructured>	φ1	<CMM.Rule>
<BRMM.Condition>	φ2	<CMM.RuleCondition>
<BRMM.Event>	φ3	<CMM.Event>

Table 2 presents relationships between the Business rules meta-model (BRMM, Fig. 1) and extended UML Class meta-model (CMM, Fig. 2). This is done by showing how elements of the BRMM map to the elements of the CMM (φ: <BRMM> → <CMM>). Formalized business rule (*CMM.Rule* in Table 2) can be applied either to specify (or constrain) attribute of the class or relationship between two specific classes, or to specify the action (in platform independent manner) that is a composing part of the operation of the class. In the Class meta-model (Fig. 2) construct *Rule* is related with the *Attribute, Relationship* and *Action* via the aggregation relationship.

The algorithm of UML Class model enhancement using business rules is composed of three steps:

- **Step 1.** Verification and specification of *relationships* among the classes of the CM (Fig. 3). Missing relationships are identified and inserted into the model during the interactive communication with model developer. Additionally, the model is augmented with the *roles* that classes play communicating with each other; *types* and *cardinalities* of these relationships are also specified. Business rules of types *Constraint* and *Structural (Fact)* are used in the first step of the algorithm.
- **Step 2.** Verification and specification of classes' *attributes* (Fig. 4). Attributes are verified against the BR of types *Constraint* and *Structural (Fact)*. Missing attributes are also identified and assigned to the classes of CM.
- **Step 3.** The *composition of classes' operations* (methods) is defined in the third step. In traditional and object-oriented IS development methods business logic is usually buried within lines of application code – this causes a lot of problems in rapidly

changing business environments [Skersys and Gudas 2004]. In business rules-extended IS development process every line of code that expresses business logic can be identified and tracked. This can be achieved because these lines of procedural code are the implementation of particular business rules that are stored and managed separately from the application code itself. Computation, inference and action assertion business rules compose the core of application. On the platform independent CM development stage we suggest to fill the content of the class' operation with structured rules represented in platform independent manner. Such specification can be elaborated and transformed into procedural code in later stages of ISDLC.

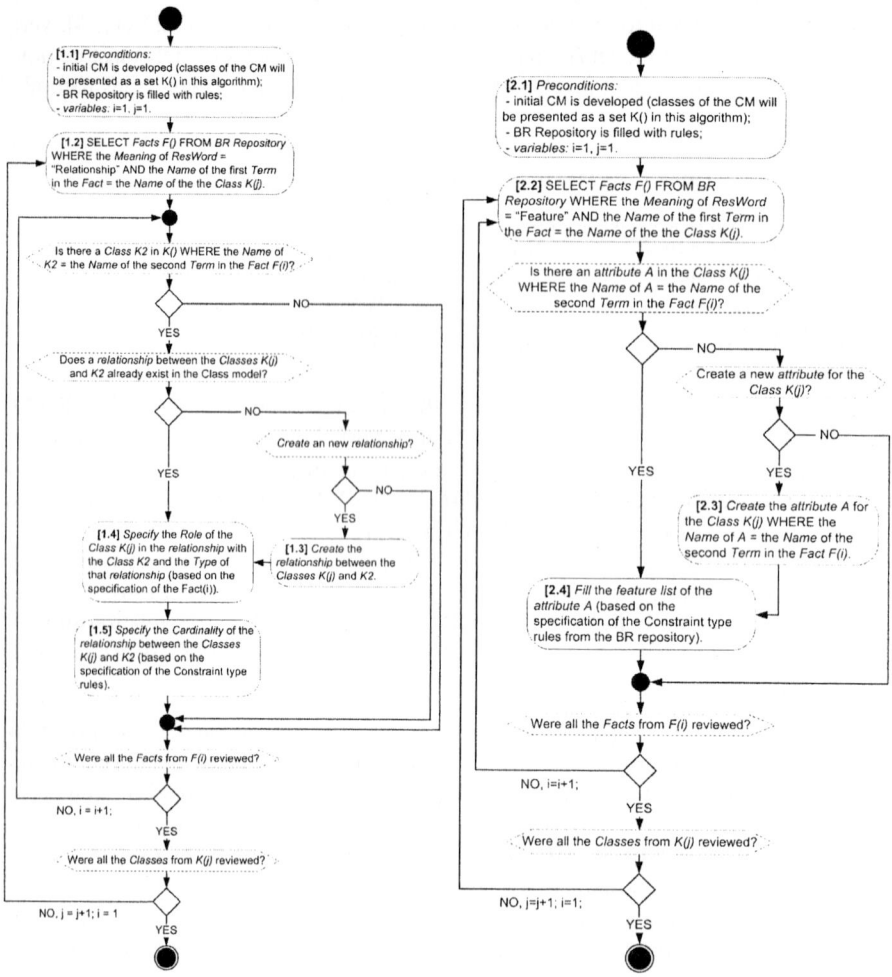

Fig. 3. Business rules-based specification of relationships among classes of the Class model

Fig. 4. Business rules-based specification of attributes of classes of the Class model

The first two steps are presented in Sec. 5.2; the first step is also illustrated with example in Sec 5.3. The example is written in English in this paper. However, in real situation problem domain should be specified and modeled using national language, in order to reach the best understanding among business experts and system development team (Sec. 3). In general, the proposed BR repository allows the construction of BR in any language.

5.2 Description of the Algorithm

Let's consider BR repository filled with business rules (Table 3) and the initially developed Class model which we want to enhance (Fig. 5) using domain knowledge stored in BR repository. The presented set of rules is just enough to illustrate the main principles of the algorithm. The enhanced Class model is depicted in Fig. 6.

Table 3. List of business rules stored in BR repository

No.	Business rule	Comments
1.1	Shipping department performs Product shipment.	List of Facts describing relationships and roles among business objects. Formal structure of the Fact is presented in Sec. 3.
1.2	Shipping department reports to Head office.	
1.3	Product shipment is performed by Shipping department.	
2.1	Workload schedule is composed of exactly three Scenarios.	List of Constraints describing cardinalities of relationships among business objects. Formal structure of the Constraint is presented in Sec. 3.
2.2	Scenario belongs to exactly one Workload schedule.	
3.1	Scenario has a feature Scenario ID.	This is a list of Facts describing features (attributes) of business objects in the business domain.
3.2	Scenario has a feature Scenario instructions.	
3.3	Scenario has a feature Estimated duration.	
4.1	Scenario Scenario ID is unique.	This is a list of Constraints describing constraints on business objects' attributes.
4.2	Scenario Estimated duration must be greater than zero.	

Let us briefly go through the first part of the algorithm (Fig. 3):

- *Step 1.1.* Preconditions are declared.
- *Step 1.2*: *The selection of Facts F() from BRR*. A set of Facts $F()$ is selected from the BR repository. Selected Facts are related with a certain class $K(j)$ from the Class model through the Fact's first Term *Name*; second condition is that the *Meaning* of the reserved word *ResWord* of these Facts is *"Relationship"*.

In our case let us assume that $K(1) = $ "Shipping department". Then F(1)= "Shipping department performs Product shipment." and F(2) = "Shipping department reports to Head office.".

- If there is a class $K2$ in the Class model where the *Name* of $K2$ equals to the Fact's $F(i)$ second Term *Name* of the Fact $F(i)$, one proceeds to the next step. If there is no such $K2$ then the Fact $F(i)$ is skipped and the next Fact from the set $F()$ is selected ($F(i+1)$) and the step is repeated.

In our case only the Fact $F(1)$ satisfies the condition. $F(2)$ is skipped because second Term *Name* of the $F(2)$ is *"Head office"* and there is no such class *"Head office"* in the Class model *"Schedule processing"*.

- If there is a class *K2*, the algorithm checks if there is a relationship between the classes *K(j)* and *K2* already exist in the Class model. If so, one proceeds to the step 1.4, otherwise, step 1.3 is the next one.

In our case there is a relationship between the classes *"Shipping department"* and *"Product shipment"* therefore one proceeds to the step 1.4.

- **Step 1.3:** *The creation of the relationship between the classes K(j) and K2 of CM.* One proceeds to the step 1.3 when there is no relationship between the classes *K(j)* and *K2* in the Class model detected and the suggestion to create this relationship on the basis of the Fact *F(i)* is accepted by the system analyst. One proceeds to the step 1.4 after the relationship between the classes *K(j)* and *K2* is created.
- **Step 1.4:** *The specification of the Role that K(j) plays in the relationship with K2 and the Type of that relationship.* The *Role* of the class *K(j)* in the relationship with the class *K2* and the *Type* of that relationship is characterized by a *Reserved word* (*ResWord*) in *F(i)*. The results of this step are marked with tag 1 in Fig. 6.

In our example *ResWord Name* of *F(1)* is equal to *"performs"* – this is the *Role* that the class *"Shipping department"* plays in the relationship with the class *"Product shipment"*. *Type* of the *ResWord* was *"Association"*.

- **Step 1.5:** *The specification of the Cardinality of the relationship.* Cardinality of the relationship is specified on the basis of Constraint type business rules stored in BR repository. Constraints are selected using a simple condition – a rule must implement some constraint between two business objects that are represented as classes in the Class model.

In our case Constraints 2.1 and 2.2 (Table 4) are selected because they implement constraints on the cardinality of the relationship between the existing classes of the Class model (see tag 2 in Fig. 6).

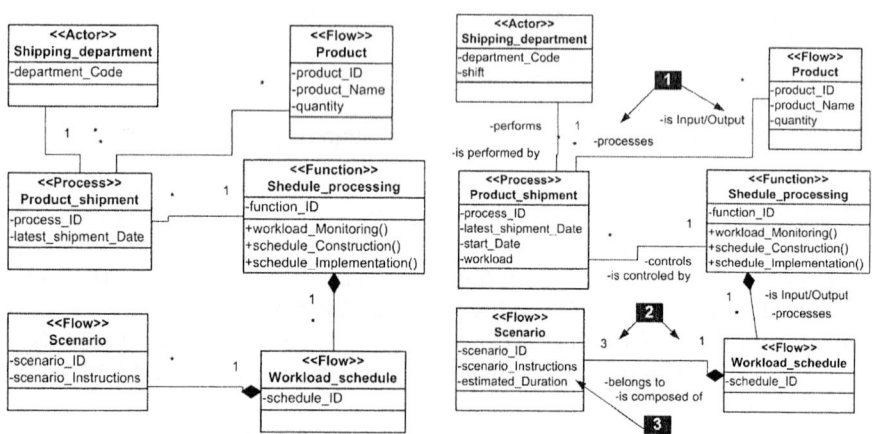

Fig. 5. The initial UML Class model "Schedule processing"

Fig. 6. The final UML Class model "Schedule processing"

- The inner cycle of the algorithm depicted in Fig. 3 closes with the conditional check if all the Facts from the set *F()* are reviewed. Otherwise, one begins a new cycle with the new Fact *F(i+1)*.

- The outer cycle closes with the conditional check if all the Classes from the Class model are reviewed. If not, one begins a new cycle with the Class $K(j+1)$. Otherwise, the first part of the algorithm is finished.

The second part of the Class model enhancement algorithm is depicted in Fig. 4. Rules that are used in this part are also presented in Table 3 (rules 3.1-4.2). Results received after the execution of this part are marked with the tag 3 in Fig. 6.

6 Conclusions

Paper deals with the principles of extended UML Class model (CM) verification and augmentation using business rules. Business rules (BR) are among the main elements composing the core of structured business domain knowledge. The UML meta-model, however, does not distinguish business rules as a separate construct. This makes it problematic to use UML as a modeling language in the projects of agile IS development for ever-changing business environment.

In order to implement such business rules-based approach the structure of business rules repository is formally defined as a meta-model. Major constructs of the Business rules repository model are defined. A predefined set of BR templates is developed and described in EBNF notation. Templates are used to structure business rules and to minimize efforts of mapping structured BR to other formalized forms (or to the implementation level of the business rules).

UML meta-model construct *Class* is concerned as a set of subtypes: *Process, Flow, Actor* and *Function*. This modification is based on the specification of the Enterprise model introduced in [1], [2]. The co-relation of domain model (Enterprise model), business rules and IS design models is a mandatory precondition for the verification of these models against domain knowledge.

The major steps of model-driven UML Class model enhancement using domain knowledge include verification and specification of relationships among the classes of CM, verification and specification of classes' attributes, the specification of composition of classes' operations (methods).

References

1. Gudas, S., Lopata, A., Skersys, T.: Approach to Enterprise Modelling for Information Systems Engineering. INFORMATICA, Vol. 16, No. 2. Institute of Mathematics and Informatics, Vilnius (2005) 175-192
2. Gudas, S., Skersys, T., Lopata, A.: Framework for Knowledge-based IS Engineering. In: Advances in Information Systems ADVIS'2004. LNCS Vol. 3261. Springer-Verlag, Berlin , (2004) 512-522
3. Dong, L., Subramaniam, K., Eberlein, A., Far, B.H.: Automating Transition from Use-Cases to Class Model. In: IEEE Canadian Conference on Electrical and Computer Engineering CCECE'03 (2003)
4. Wahono, R.S., Far, B.H.: A framework of object identification and refinement process in object-oriented analysis and design. In: Cognitive Informatics ICCI'02 (2002)
5. Ross, R.G.: Principles of the Business Rule Approach. Addison-Wesley (2003)

6. Dorsey, P.: The business rules approach to systems development. BRIM® Information Documents. www.dulcian.com (2002)
7. Hay, D., Healy, K.A.: Defining business rules – what are they really? Final Report - revision 1.3. The Business Rules Group (2000)
8. Haggerty, N.: Modeling business rules using the UML and CASE. In: Business Rules Forum'2000. www.brcommunity.com (2000)
9. Business Rules in Models RFI. OMG Document: br/2002-09-13. Object Management Group (2002)
10. Business Semantics of Business Rules RFP. OMG Document: br/2003-06-03. Object Management Group (2003)
11. Skersys, T., Gudas, S.: Business rules integration in information systems engineering. In: Information Systems Development ISD'2004. Technika, Vilnius (2004) 253-263
12. Herbst, H., Myrach, T.: A repository system for business rules. Database Application Semantics, London, (1997) 119-138
13. Kapocius, K., Butleris, R.: The business rules repository for information systems design. In: Research Communications of 6th East European Conference ADBIS'02. Bratislava (2002) 64-77
14. Plotkin, D.: Business rules everywhere. Intelligent Enterprise, Vol. 2, No. 4 (1999) 37-44
15. von Halle, B.: Building a business rules system. DM Review Magazine. www.dmreview.com (2001)
16. Kadir, M.,N., Loucopoulos, P.: Relating evolving business rules to software design. In: Software Engineering Research and Practice'03 (2003) 129-134
17. Ross, R.G., Lam, G.S.W.: The do's and don'ts of expressing business rules. The BRS RuleSpeak™ Practitioner Kit. www.brsolutions.com (2001)
18. Ross R.G., Lam, G.S.W.: RuleSpeak Sentence Templates. The BRS RuleSpeak™ Practitioner Kit. www.brsolutions.com (2001)
19. Reeder, J.: Templates for capturing business rules. www.brcommunity.com (2002)
20. Ambler, S.W.: The Elements of UML Style. Cambridge University Press (2003)
21. Vernadat, F.: UEML: Towards a Unified Enterprise modelling language. In: MOSIM'01. Troyes, France (2001) 178–186
22. Coad, P., Lefebvre E., de Luca J.: Java Modeling in Color with UML: Enterprise Components and process. Yourdon Press, Prentice Hall (1999)
23. Coad, P., Yourdon, E.: Object-oriented analysis. 2nd edn. Yourdon Press (1991)
24. Mellor, S.J., Kendall, S., Uhl, A., Weise, D.: MDA Distilled: Principles of Model-driven Architecture. Addison-Wesley (2004)

Scenario Networks: Specifying User Interfaces with Extended Use Cases

Demosthenes Akoumianakis and Ioannis Pachoulakis

Department of Applied Informatics and Multimedia,
Technological Educational Institution of Crete,
P.O. Box 1939 Heraklion, Crete, Greece, GR 71500
{da, ip}@epp.teicrete.gr

Abstract. In this paper, we present the rationale and the baseline of a notation which can be used on its own or as an extension to standard UML to facilitate specification of an interactive system's global execution context (GEC). The GEC graph is a visual construction consisting of (a) nodes, which represent interaction scenarios, and (b) directed links, which represent scenario relationships designating alternate execution, concurrency, ordering, and set-oriented relationships between two scenario nodes. The technique is particularly useful for specifying adaptable and adaptive behaviours across interaction platforms, contexts of use and target user communities. In the paper, we demonstrate the application of the technique using a file-exchange application which runs on a portable device such as a PDA and implements a lightweight ftp process to connect to a server wirelessly and offer standard ftp functionality (get/put/delete).

1 Introduction

Modelling user interfaces is a complex engineering task and a popular research topic. In the past three decades it has been studied from a variety of perspectives (i.e. psychological, sociological, knowledge engineering) by Human Computer Interaction (HCI) researchers, yielding substantial results and a broad collection of methods for describing interaction tasks, object classes, lower-level dialogs, as well as mental activities of users interacting with application software. In the majority of these efforts the distinct assumption has been the loose separation of the user interface modelling activity from the software engineering tasks typically involved in addressing functional requirements of interactive software systems. As a result, user interface modelling methods and tools do not couple easily with application modelling and vice versa. This status quo brings about several drawbacks for the software design community, as frequently the integration effort required to bridge across the user interface and software engineering tasks is far from trivial. Recent attempts towards establishing effective methods for closing the gap between the two engineering communities [see 17-20] have explored concepts such as scenarios [21], use cases [1,2], dedicated dialogue description techniques such as event modelling and more recently the UML - Unified Modelling Language [3]. UML departs from the commitment of model-based user interface development tools which focus on domain modelling to describe the data over which the interface acts, to provide a more encompassing frame of reference for modelling the functionality of the application for which the interface is being constructed. This, however, is widely acknowledged as insufficient support for user interface modelling [4-7]. As a result, extending UML to establish additional expressive power for user interface modelling is an active track of on going research activities.

In this paper, we investigate current work in this area and describe the rationale and baseline of a notation, which can be used on its own or as an extension to UML, to facilitate specification of an interactive system's global execution context (GEC). The extended facilities can be used to compile a task's GEC graph as a visual construct, which consists of (a) nodes, representing interaction scenarios, and (b) directed links representing scenario relationships such as alternate execution, concurrency, ordering, and set-oriented relationships between two scenario nodes.

2 Related Work

At present, no current research effort is known of, which seeks to extend a particular user interface modelling technique to facilitate application modelling. All activities in this area aim to advance (some of) the following targets: use specific UML notations to model user interfaces; extend UML so as to facilitate user interface modelling; couple UML components with user interface modelling techniques. A representative effort in the direction of using specific UML notations to model user interfaces is presented in [22]. The authors suggest an approach for requirement engineering, linking scenarios with user interface prototypes. Scenarios are acquired in the form of UML collaboration diagrams and are enriched with user interface information. These diagrams are automatically transformed into UML Statechart specifications of all objects involved. These specifications are, in turn, used to generate a UI prototype, which is embedded in a UI builder environment for further refinement. The approach has been demonstrated to work for relatively simple user interfaces (such as those used in ATMs) using conventional user interface objects. As a result, it deals only with interactions at the lexical level. Syntactic and/or semantic interaction levels are ignored and no account of HCI knowledge is exploited. These shortcomings have motivated research proposals for either explicit coupling between UML and user interface modelling notations, or UML extensions.

Several researchers have investigated integrating interface modelling techniques with UML. The rationale for such coupling is derived on the one hand from the insufficiency of UML to model user interface aspects and on the other from the maturity of some well-established user interface modelling notations. For example, one approach assesses UML models for use in interface modelling, comparing them with a collection of specialist interface modelling notations [4]. Another approach suggests how one can use several UML models — particularly class diagrams and use case diagrams — along with task models for user interface modelling [5]. The latter work proposes coupling the ConcurTaskTrees notation to available UML diagramming techniques, while creating semantic mappings of the ConcurTaskTrees concepts into UML meta-model [6].UML extension mechanisms could then be used to support smooth coupling. The primary benefit resulting from coupling UML to existing user interface modelling techniques is that each component remains atomic in the sense that no extension is required to accommodate new expressive or representational power. Hence, since the coupling is typically undertaken by semantic mappings across the notations, this needs to be done only once. In this manner, application and user interface designers continue to work on their own perspectives using their own tools, while relying on these mappings to undertake the required integration.

A different line of research includes efforts which seek to extend UML to support user interface modelling, without reference to a particular user interface technique or task model. These efforts typically add notations to the already rich set of UML diagrams. A representative of this category is UMLi [7], which attempts to use the UML extensibility mechanisms to support user interface modelling. An alternative research track concentrates on building UML profiles for specific tasks of user interface design such as GUI (layout). A representative effort is reported in [8], where the author describes a profile intended to provide an easily comprehensible abstract representation of an actual screen based on designers' sketches. A GUI Layout Diagram is proposed, consisting of a Screen, which contains multiple ScreenAreas, each of which may be decorated with one or more Stereotypes, representing performed functionalities like text, image or link. By nesting and arranging properly stereotyped ScreenAreas within each other, the developer is able to create an abstract version of a user interface. The Navigational Diagram provides UML-based support for common design artefacts like storyboards and sitemaps. The diagrams created can be linked to Use Case modelling using existing UML to specify requirements and context of a particular screen.

One issue of significance to the present work is the sufficiency of the proposals described above and other similar efforts reported in the literature to cope with the emerging requirements for nomadic applications and ubiquitous access. Specifically, our concern relates to the suitability of existing notations to facilitate the novel requirements prevailing in nomadic and ubiquitous applications - such as scalability, object mobility / migration, security, platform independence, location awareness, personalization / individualization - commonly referred to as non-functional requirements (NFRs) or quality attributes [9].

To this end, the established UML notations offer no obvious mechanism to allow designers to model explicitly and address such software quality attributes in the course of analysis and design. The work described in [22] is a partial on-going effort towards such an end, which deals only with class diagrams. This realization has been the driving concern in recent efforts aiming to extend UML so as to facilitate support for modelling global applications [10] and their respective properties and quality attributes (e.g., mobility, performance, object migration, security). On the other hand, the model-based user interface development paradigm seems to address some of these concerns partially and in an ad hoc manner. In particular, model-based development has indeed delivered a number of possible solutions to generating user interfaces for multiple platforms (for instance [11]) but these do not result from an explicit account of designated NFRs. In fact, model-based development practitioners need not be aware of such constructs as NFRs. Instead, in the majority of cases, platform-aware user interfaces are generated by manipulating, automatically or semi-automatically, an abstract task model that is incrementally transformed to a concrete instance.

It should be noted that our premise is not that model-based development cannot cope with such challenges. On the contrary, we strongly believe that it is perhaps the only engineering paradigm that can be refined to cope with the emerging requirements. However, this would require a substantial shift from task-level to goal-oriented and activity modelling and linking with recent advances in goal-oriented requirements engineering and requirements-driven system development such as the Tropos project [12]. To this end, it is claimed that in modern applications, the designer is increasingly required to be able to articulate the GEC of the systems tasks, rather than being solely concerned with the development of an abstract task model from which incrementally, either through mappings or transformations, a platform-aware user interface is generated. The remainder of this paper develops a proposal for a specifications-based technique to facilitate an insight to the GEC of a system's tasks.

3 Specifying the Global Execution Context of Tasks

The premise of the present work is that HCI design lacks a coherent and detailed macro-level method (in the sense defined in [13]), for including change management in the user interface development process. In other words, although there is a plethora of micro-level techniques useful to study change in the context of HCI, there is no integrated frame of reference for identifying and propagating change across stages in the course of the design and development processes. It is also argued that formalizing change management in relation to designated NFRs, which are explicitly accounted in the context of human-centred development, can provide a useful frame of reference.

3.1 Definition of Terms

Change in interactive software is inherently linked with the context in which a task is executed. Typical context parameters include the target user, the platform providing the computational host for the task or the physical or social context in which the task is executed. Traditionally, interactive software was designed to cope with minimal and isolated changes, related primarily to the user, since no other part of the system's execution context (i.e. platform or context of use) was viable to change. As more and more software and information systems adopt Internet technologies and protocols for greater openness and interoperability, the changes that can take place are far more complex and demanding, as the closed computing environment is replaced by the open, dynamic and almost unbounded nature of the Internet. In the new distributed and networked information-processing paradigm, change management entails a thorough understanding of the GEC of tasks.

In our previous work [14] we presented a methodology and a suite of tools for designing user interfaces as a composition of task contexts. A task context was defined as an interactive manifestation (or a style) of an abstract task (i.e. a task comprising abstract interaction object classes). For example, a selection is an abstract task, which can be interactively manifested either as an explicit choice from a list box, or choice from a check box or selection from a panel of options. Each alternative was designated as a distinct task context with explicit rationale and interaction style, describing conditions for style activation/deactivation, object classes, attributes of object classes, preference and indifference expressions, default conditions, etc.

Building on this early conception of a task context, we define the GEC of an abstract task T as a five tuple relation $<T, g, S, f, C>$ where g is the task's goal to be achieved by alternative scenarios $s_i \in S$, and a function $f(s_i)$ which defines the maximally preferred option of S, given a designated set of constraints C. Such a definition, allows us to model change in interactive software in terms of certain conditions or constraints which propagate alternative interactive behaviours to achieve task-oriented goals. Each constraint in C is a predicate of type *c(type, parameter, value)*. Three types of constraints are relevant, namely user constraints, platform constraints and context constraints. In light of the above, it is now argued that change δ in the execution context of a software system occurs if and only if there exists at least one constraint in C whose parameter value has been modified. The result of recognizing δ and putting it into effect causes the deactivation of an $s_i \in S$, which was the status prior to recognizing δ, and the activation of a new $s_j \in S$, which becomes the new status. In the context of user interface design, it is therefore of paramount importance to identify the changes which may reasonably take place in a system's execution context, model them in terms of constraints relevant to user interface, and detail the interactive scenarios through which the user interface can cope with the designated changes. To this effect, the study of NFRs early in the design process can help populate and structure the required design space.

3.2 Goal Modelling of Designated NFRs

In the context of detailed user interface modelling work, two aspects of NFRs become prominent. The first is explicitly modelling designated NFRs, while the second amounts to modelling how the NFRs intertwine. One possible approach is to use the concepts and notation of the NFR Framework [15] to develop the softgoal interdependency graph for adaptability by identifying and decomposing NFR in conceptual models. Figure 1 presents the hierarchical decomposition for the NFR of adaptability, summarizing how it may be related to other NFRs such as scalability, individualization and platform independence. Softgoals are represented as clouds and can be decomposed to other softgoals either through AND- or OR-decompositions, represented by single and double arcs respectively. An AND-decomposition refines an overall goal into a set of subgoals, which should all be achieved. OR-decompositions refine a softgoal into an alternative set of refinements; one suffices to satisfy the softgoal. The softgoal hierarchy of Figure 1 is typically read from the top. Thus, adaptability requires that a system is capable of detecting the need for change, deciding what change is needed and putting the required change into effect. Deciding on changes needed is considered to be an internal system function, responsible for implementing context-sensitive processing and thus, it does not usually have an interactive manifestation. Consequently, it suffices to explicitly mention it, but no further decomposition is attempted. Detecting the need for change, as pointed out in the previous section entails detecting changes of scale, changes in interaction platform or changes in users and context of use or any combination of them. In all cases detection can be automatic or manual. Figure 1 depicts that change of interaction platform and changes in users and contexts of use constitute AND-decompositions of the ubiquity softgoal, thus linking explicitly ubiquity and adaptability. On the other hand, putting a change into effect entails an OR-decomposition denoting that changes may be propagated either on the user interface or on the content to be presented or on both. User interface change is OR-decomposed to physical changes (i.e., lexical aspects of interaction), syntactic changes (i.e. modifications in the dialogue such as confirmation box, alternate feedback, etc) and semantic changes (i.e. alternative overall interactive embodiment such as symbolic versus pictographic presentation of interaction objects, for example [16]). In all cases, the system can effect the changes either automatically or manually (see following section).

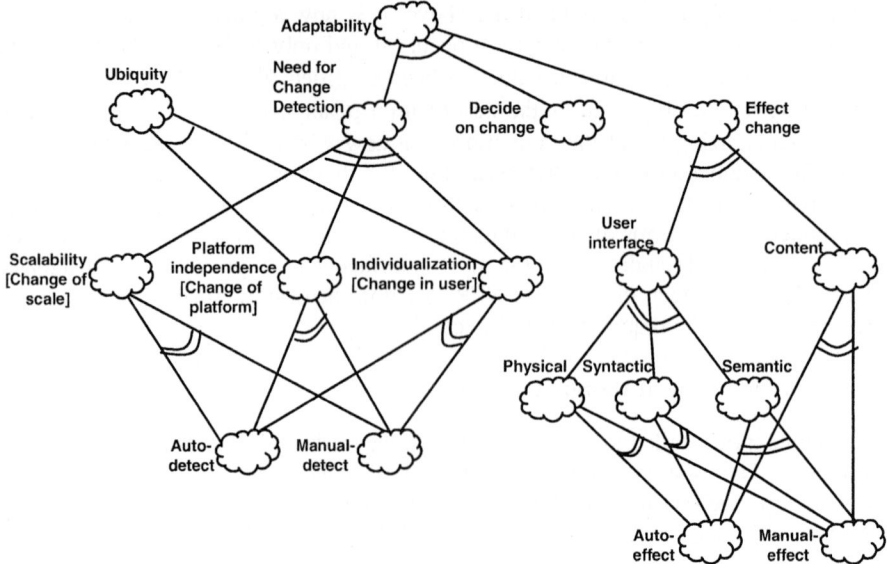

Fig. 1. Softgoal hierarchy for adaptability

3.3 Scenario Crafting

A first step in translating a softgoal hierarchy into concrete user interface requirements is to capture softgoals in terms of a small set of reference scenarios to provide a concrete resource for reflection and/or envisioning. Typically, the mapping of goals to scenarios follows the structure of the softgoal hierarchy and thus it is common to start with a top-level scenario describing an abstract task to be achieved and progressively refine the scenario as surrogate goals are considered. It is worth pointing out that at this stage of the analysis, it is really indifferent whether a system already exists or is to be designed. Instead, the only concern of the analyst is to compile narrative descriptions of desirable interactions. This is illustrated by means of an example in Figure 2, which depicts at the top an abstract scenario that is incrementally articulated (i.e. made concrete) through navigating the hierarchy. The dashed lines indicate a link between a goal node in the hierarchy and the corresponding draft scenario. The example is motivated by a file exchange application where a user is required to carry out standard ftp functionality. This is a simple application, which allows authorised users to connect to a server and subsequently manipulate files (i.e. transfer, delete, view).

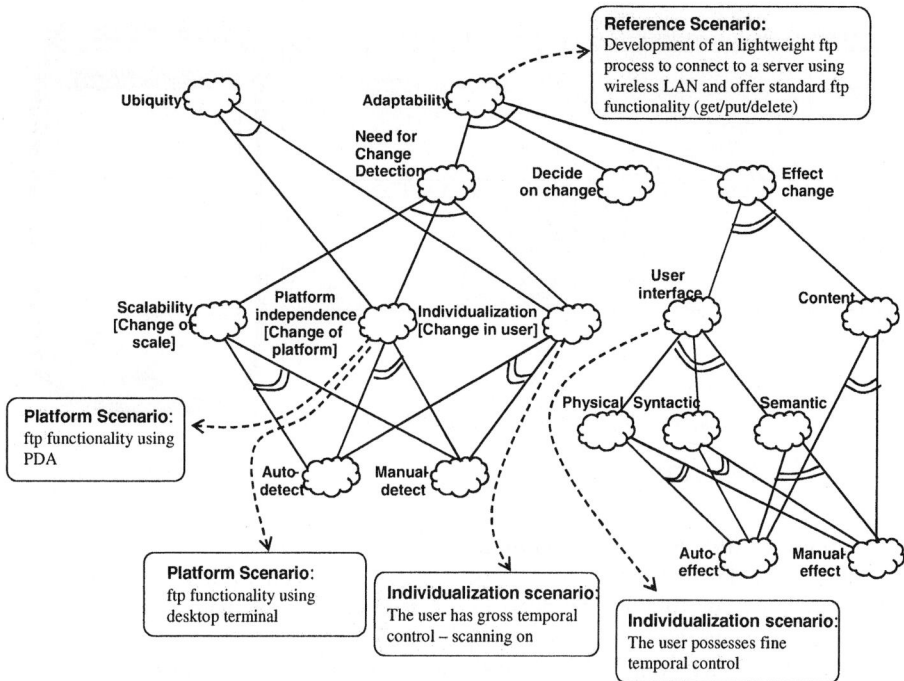

Fig. 2. Exemplar scenarios

In subsequent sections of this paper, we will assume a tentative prototype, such as that depicted in Figure 3, and we will be concerned with populating the GEC of the respective tasks taking into account representative adaptability scenarios as described in Figure 2.

3.4 Scenario Relationships

Scenario relationships are the primary mechanism for specifying the GEC of a reference scenario. To demonstrate their scope, we will assume a base (or reference) scenario, which executes the tasks of our example case study on a desktop through a style S_B (see Fig. 3). There may be several styles serving the same goal through different interaction elements, resulting in different interaction scenarios. Moreover, any two styles may be aggregated to an abstract style, while an abstract style can be segregated to one or more concrete styles. Style aggregation and segregation form two semantic relationships, which are further elaborated through a set of operators, with the most important briefly described below in the context of our reference case study.

Alternative_to: Two styles are related with the alternative_to relationship when each serves exactly the same goals and one and only one can be active at any time. For instance, Figures 3 and 4 describe two alternative styles for carrying out the same tasks (on a desktop and PDA respectively). This is typically expressed as follows $\forall$ g $\in$ Goal, $g(S_i)$ alternative_to $g(S_j)$. Alternative_to is the main operator for specifying

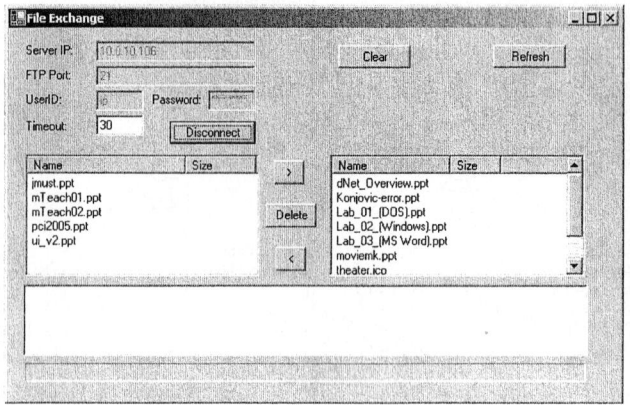 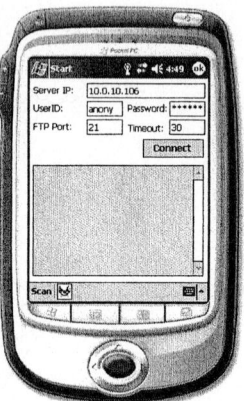

Fig. 3. FTP on the desktop   Fig. 4. FTP on a PDA

adaptability of a system with regards to designated quality attribute (e.g., platform independence). Two alternative scenarios are considered as indifferent with regards to all other quality attributes except the ones designated in the alternative_to declaration. This leads to the preference operator described below.

Preference: This relationship extends the alternative_to relationship for cases where, given a goal g and $g(S_i)$ alternative_to $g(S_j)$ where i # j and i, j > 1. In such cases, there should be a preference order for S_i and S_j specified by a preference condition or rule. When executed, the preference condition should place candidate scenarios in a preference ranking (indifference classes), while the most preferred scenario (first indifference class) is the one to be activated. Typically, the range of scenarios in a preference class may be used to augment one another under certain conditions.

Augmentation: Augmentation captures the situation where one scenario in an indifference class is used to support or facilitate the mostly preferred (active) scenario within the same indifference class. In general, two scenarios related with an augments relationship serve precisely the same goal through different interaction means. An example illustrating the relevance of the augments to relationship is depicted in Fig. 5. In the example, the scanner is explicitly activated upon button press. There are cases, however, which are better served by an implicit activation of the scanning function (i.e., case of a user with gross temporal control).

Parallelism: Parallelism in the execution of interaction scenarios (or concurrent activation) is a common feature in a variety of interactive applications and one which, when properly supported, can serve a number of desirable features such as adaptivity, multimodality and increased usability. For the purpose of the present work, two scenarios are related with a parallel_to relationship when they serve the same goal and are active concurrently.

Figure 6 shows an example of parallel scenarios for selecting multiple files to download, where selection from the taskbar by file type (e.g., .ppt) results in automatic checking of all files (in the current selection list) with the appropriate extension. In general, such a feature, which is provided in parallel with selecting through browsing the list and manually checking options, is useful to easily select files in a category.

Specifically, it avoids: (a) scrolling the list up/down to view the file extension of each file separately, and (b) having to increase the width of the "Name" column by hand for long filenames, which is awkward on a PDA.

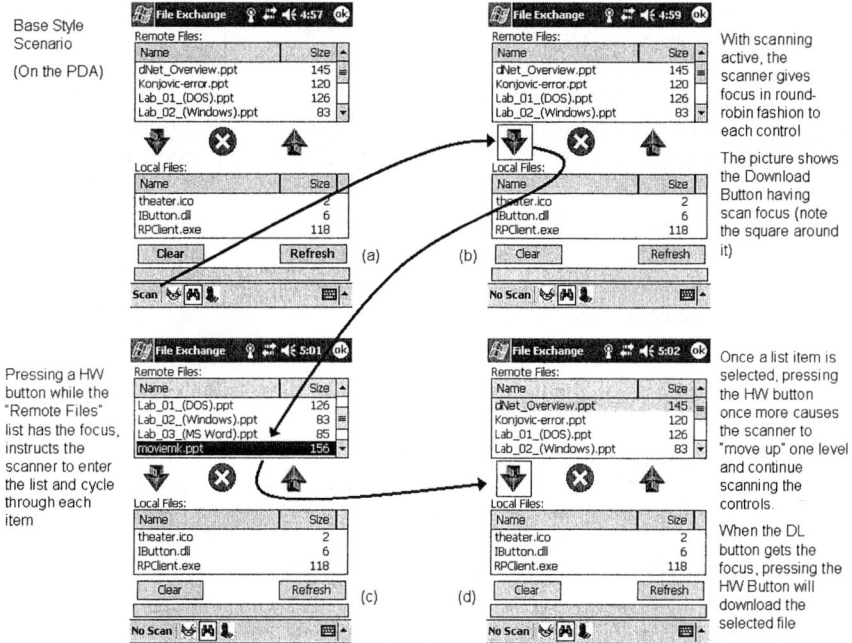

Fig. 5. Example of augmentation

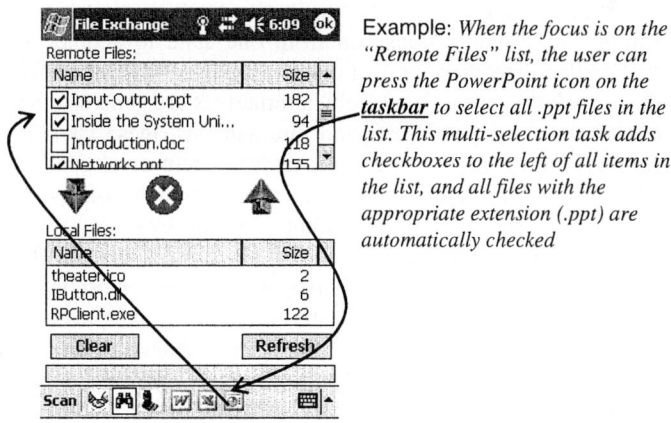

Example: When the focus is on the "Remote Files" list, the user can press the PowerPoint icon on the taskbar to select all .ppt files in the list. This multi-selection task adds checkboxes to the left of all items in the list, and all files with the appropriate extension (.ppt) are automatically checked

Fig. 6. Parallel scenarios for selection

3.5 Building the Global Execution Context Graph

Having presented the basic scenario relationships, we can now illustrate the GEC graph of our reference example as an extended use case model (see Figure 7). The diagram elaborates a base scenario "Select file with desktop style", characterizing file selection as a polymorphic task accomplished in parallel through two concurrent scenarios namely selection-by-type and selection-by-checking. The base scenario has two alternatives representing respectively PDA- and HTML-like styles. All alternatives can be augmented by scanning, which is specialized into two alternatives versions, namely one button auto scanning and two button auto scanning, with the former being the preferred option.

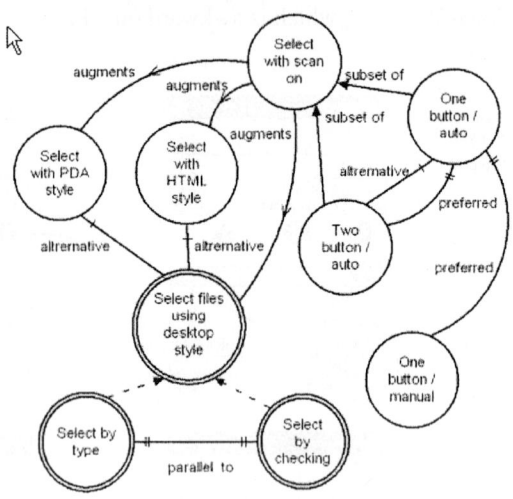

Fig. 7. The global execution context graph

4 Discussion and Concluding Remarks

From the discussion, so far, two main conclusions can be drawn. Firstly, an analysis of the GEC of a system's tasks entails an account of all relevant NFRs in terms of the task T these relate to, the goal g served, the scenarios S which can facilitate them, the function f defining the system's transition from one state to another and the constraints C which rationalize these transitions. Secondly, NFR-based user interface design requires an analytic approach whereby alternatives are generated and evaluated in terms of suitability, design trade-offs and rationale. All these alternatives should aim to capture plausible interaction scenarios under different softgoal regimes. It is worth noting that this is considered to be a distinct contribution of the present work, as existing proposals for design rationale capture and retrieval are seldom related to NFRs in the course of user interface design. Thirdly, the designated NFRs raise explicit demands upon the outcomes of HCI design and the corresponding artefacts, such as the user interface software architecture, the interaction styles devised to capture alternatives and the way in which they are to be managed in the course of user interface development. For instance, requiring that a quality goal is to realize the auto-detect and auto-effect softgoals for all superior softgoals of the hierarchy in Figure 1 implies a single implementation capable of managing a broad range of interaction styles. This however entails novel user interface engineering practices and tools, which at present are not widely available.

References

1. Carroll, J. M., Mack, R., Robertson, S., Rosson, M. B.: Binding objects to scenarios of use, International Journal of Human Computer Studies, 21, 1994, 243-276.
2. Jacobson, I.,: Object-oriented Software Engineering – A use case driven approach, Reading, MA: Addison Wesley, 1992.
3. OMG, Unified Modelling Language 1.3, Object Management Group, 1999.
4. Markopoulos, P., Marijnissen, P.: UML as a Representation for Interaction Designs, Proc. Australian Conf. Computer-Human Interaction, CHISIG, 2000, pp. 240–249.
5. Paternò, F.: Towards a UML for Interactive Systems, *Proc. 8th IFIP Working Conf. Eng. for Human-ComputerInteraction* (EHC 01), Springer-Verlag, 2001, pp. 7–18.
6. Mori, G., Paternò, F., Santoro: CTTE: Support for Developing and Analyzing Task models for interactive system design. IEEE Trans. on Software Engineering, 28(9), 2002, 1-17.
7. Pinheiro da Silva, P., Paton, W.N.: User interface modelling in UMLi, IEEE Software, 2003 (July/August), 62-69.
8. Blankenhorn, K.: A UML Profile for GUI Layout, Master's Thesis, University of Applied Sciences Furtwangen, Department of Digital Media, 2004.
9. Mylopoulos, J., Chung, L., Nixon, B. : Representing and using NFRs: a process-oriented approach, IEEE Trans. Software Engineering 18 (6), 1992, pp. 483-497.
10. Hubert Baumeister, Nora Koch, Piotr Kosiuczenko, Perdita Stevens, and Martin Wirsing. UML for global computing. In Corrado Priami, editor, *Global Computing. Programming Environments, Languages, Security, and Analysis of Systems. LNCS* 2874, November 2003.
11. Mori, G., Paternò, F., Santoro: Design and Development of Multidevice user interfaces through multiple logical descriptions. IEEE Trans. on Soft. Engineering, 30(8), 2004, 1-14.
12. Castro, J., Kolp, M., Mylopoulos, J.: Towards requirements-driven information systems engineering: the Tropos project. Information Systems 27 (2002) 365–389.
13. Olson, J. S., Moran, T. P., 1996, Mapping the method muddle: Guidance in using methods for user interface design. In HCI design: Success stories, emerging methods, and real-world context, edited by Rudisill, M., Lewis, C., Polson, P. B., & McKay, T. D., (San Francisco, CA: Morgan Kaufmann Publishers), pp. 101-121.
14. Akoumianakis, D., Savidis, A., & Stephanidis, C., 2000, Encapsulating intelligent interaction behaviour in unified user interface artefacts, Interacting with Computers, 12, 383-408.
15. Chung, L., Nixon, B., Yu, E. and Mylopoulos,J. "Non-Functional Requirements in Software Engineering" Kluwer Academic Publishers 2000.
16. Miller, L. A. and Stanney: The effect of pictogram-based design on human - computer performance, International Journal of Human - Computer Interaction, 9, 1997, 119-132.
17. Nunes, N.J., et al., Interactive System Design with Object Models, in Reader, A. Moreira, S. Demeyer (eds.), ECOOP'99 Workshop, Springer-Verlag, 1999.
18. Constantine, L.L. and L.A.D. Lockwood, Software for use : a practical guide to the models and methods of usage-centered design, Reading, Mass.: Addison Wesley, 1999.
19. Mark van Harmelen, et al., Object Models in UI Design. SIGCHI Bulletin, 29(4), 1998.
20. Artim, J., et al., Incorporating work, process and task analysis into industrial object-oriented systems development. SIGCHI Bulletin, 30(4), 1998.
21. Elkoutbi, M., Khriss, I., Keller, R.: Generating User Interface Prototypes from Scenarios. In 4th IEEE Int. Symposium on Requirements Engineering, Limerick, Ireland, June 1999.
22. Cysneiros, L-M., Leite, JCSP.: Using UML to reflect non-functional requirements. Proceedings of CASCON 2001, IBM Press, Toronto, 2001, pp: 202-216.

Teaching Programming with Robots: A Case Study on Greek Secondary Education

Maya Sartatzemi[1], Vassilios Dagdilelis[2], and Katerina Kagani

[1] Department of Applied Informatics, University of Macedonia, 156 Egnatia str.,
P.O.Box 1591, Thessaloniki, Greece
maya@uom.gr

[2] Department of Educational and Social Policy, University of Macedonia, 156 Egnatia str.,
P.O.Box 1591, Thessaloniki, Greece
dagdil@uom.gr

Abstract. The teaching of programming in the Greek education system begins at the secondary level. The aims of the programming syllabus include the attainment of knowledge and skills, which are related to problem solving and the design of algorithms. In order to acquire the students knowledge and skills, the usual approach that is followed is: the use of a programming language of general aim (Pascal, Basic, etc), the use of a professional environment for this programming language, the development of programs that solve problems which treat numbers and symbols. According to researches that have been realized, this approach of teaching programming to beginners constitutes important factor that complicates its learning. In this work we propose a framework of teaching the programming fundamentals to beginners that is based on using LEGO Mindstorms technology. This paper analyzes the results from a pilot research that was carried out on Greek secondary school students.

1 Introduction

The teaching of programming in the Greek education system begins at the secondary level (junior high school [three years] and senior high school – Lyceum [three years]). The aims of the programming syllabus include the attainment of knowledge and skills, which are related to problem solving and the design of algorithms. Within this framework, various programming types, techniques, environments are used and data structures, algorithmic structures as well as other topics related to the development of programs are taught. In order for the students to acquire this knowledge and these skills, a general language is usually used (such as Pascal, Basic, C etc), as well as a professional programming environment for each respective language. Within this context, problems are solved, which as a rule, concern the processing of numbers and symbols.

Nevertheless, according to a great deal of research with similar results, the programming principles of the teaching approach described above are not always functional and can create problems of understanding in novice programmers. The most important problems that novices come up against are due to the fact that [3, 9]:

The *professional programming languages* offer a large range of statements, which as a consequence are complex. Therefore, in teaching the process of solving a problem, the students tend to focus their attention on the use of the language rather than the actual solution to the problem. Correspondingly, the expression of an algorithm into a programming language requires a high mental effort.

Professional programming environments do not in fact meet the needs of novice programmers in as much as they offer functions which are extraneous to the novices and which do not provide any support at the beginner level; they do not get support in identifying syntactical errors, neither from the error messages nor from the use of the debugging tool, which usually requires a specific set up, understood only by professional programmers.

In order to *solve interesting problems*, students must learn a wide range of statements of the language as well as develop large programs, which is unfeasible, since teaching time is limited.

Besides the problems inherent in the teaching approach to programming, the students also encounter other difficulties related to the basic structures; the syntax of the programming language; the properties of the "machine" which the student controls; as well as the ability to determine, the development, the control and the debugging of a program with the available tools.

Many researchers propose a variety of approaches in order to confront the problems and difficulties of programming. These approaches entail either different programming paradigms (procedural versus object oriented) or educational programming languages with respective programming environments [2].

In this paper, we present a way in which a relatively new technology, Lego Mindstorms, can be used in secondary education for the teaching of programming, allowing students to explore ideas, which are prescribed in the school curriculum in novel ways. It has to be noted that the aim of this pilot study was to conclude whether we can make use of new teaching approaches of programming so that we can cure problems without changing the curriculum, which we are obliged to follow while teaching in a class. This research is being funded by the Greek Ministry of Education and the European Union as part of the project "Pythagoras II- Funding of research groups in University of Macedonia".

2 Description of Mindstorms and ROBOLAB Environment

The LEGO company in 1998 introduced a robotic construction kit, based on related research conducted by Seymour Papert at MIT Media Lab. This kit, known as LEGO® Mindstorms™ [4, 5], is an excellent tool for the learning of Engineering, Robotics and Computer Programming, for students at all three levels of education.

There are many schools and universities which did not hesitate to integrate Lego Mindstorms into their course work, either as a basic subject or as a tool for other subjects [1, 6, 7]. Students have used the robotic kit to build a large range of constructions with specific behaviours, such as a robot, a machine, which moves in reaction to the movements of a person or of another machine. By attaching sensors to the LEGO's electronic bricks, students can transform a simple door into a door that "talks" and "welcomes" whoever goes through it, or a door that counts how many people go through it each day [8].

The kit includes a) the RCX brick, a programmed LEGO brick, which includes a micro-processor (tiny computer), case for batteries, a monitor, and a circuit which moves motors and connects sensors, b) motors and various sensors such as touch, light, temperature, rotation, c) a large range of the classic LEGO bricks as well as wheels and other mechanical parts.

With the relevant programming of RCX one can create a wide range of autonomous robots made out of LEGO bricks. The creation and management of an autonomous robot is recommended in four steps:

1. Constructing a robot in accordance with the designs included in the kit or using their own imagination.
2. Developing a program using the visual programming environment accompanying the kit or another programming language.
3. Loading of the program on the robot, using the infra-red transmitter.
4. Program execution.

In order for the robot to demonstrate specific behaviour, steps 2 to 4 are usually repeated several times.

The LEGO company makes their product available with a choice of two types of programming environments, a basic one, known as *RSX Code*, and a more complex one, which requires a higher degree of knowledge in programming, known as *Robolab*.

The features of *Robolab* are presented in two modules, in order to be able to meet the needs of students at various levels. In both modules, icons are used for the representation of commands and structures. The first and more basic module, the Pilot, has limitations concerning the number and the sequence of icons that a student can use, in order to accomplish their attempt successfully. The second and more advanced module, the Inventor, was created in order to satisfy the needs of users in higher grades who had more programming abilities. The environment in this module is likewise graphical, however, it offers more user flexibility. Here there are four (4) levels of increasing complexity. In the Inventor, the commands which modulate a program are chosen from a pallet of functions offering a higher level of programming structures, such as loops, variables, choice structures and the ability to create subroutines. Programmers can in this way take advantage of all the RCX features.

As far as the transition from the Pilot to the Inventor is concerned, this presupposes that the user understands the logic behind the choice of the command-icons and is able to connect them to each other in order to develop a program. An important advantage of Robolab is that it uses a learning model where most of the commands available are dependent on the level that the user has actually reached [7].

3 Description of the Lessons and Data Analysis

In accordance with the syllabus for programming for the 3rd grade of junior high school and the 1st grade of senior high school respectively, ten (10) hours in the school year of teaching time only are available. Therefore, taking into account this limitation, we propose five two-hour lessons as an introductory course for these classes in high school. In the first part of each lesson, the teacher presents on an overhead projector the new programming structures in connection with the possibilities of the programming environment Robolab. In each lesson, after the presentation of the new concepts, the students study ready programs and modify their parameters. By studying these ready programs, students are given the opportunity to pinpoint important aspects; to become acquainted with particular syntactical features; and to clarify points which are difficult to understand. In addition, before the students proceed to developing their own programs, they are called on to study ready programs and give written descriptions on the results of the program of the robot's behaviour.

In the second part of each lesson, exercises are performed – programs for the control of the robot's behaviour. The construction of the robot is done in the very first lesson and is used in all the following lessons.

For each lesson the following are given out: two information sheets, two icon cards, a lesson plan, the lesson presentation on an overhead projector (use of software presentation), a question-check sheet and a worksheet.

On completion of the teacher's presentation and the examples, a question-check sheet is handed out to the students which they answer individually enabling the teacher to monitor the knowledge they have acquired. In the second part of each lesson, a worksheet is handed out containing exercises on the programming of the robot's behaviour. In this section, the students are organized into pairs and attempt to solve the given problems. In the framework of this activity, students have the opportunity to take initiative in the design, the construction and the improvement of the autonomous robot's behaviour. The teacher observes the students' work, intervenes when considered necessary, offers assistance and guidance in their endeavour.

The exercises on the worksheets relate to the development of programs which control the movements of a vehicle. More specifically, they presuppose a LEGO vehicle, which has a motor (in port A), a lamp (in port C), two touch sensors (in ports 1 and 2) and a light sensor (in port 3). These exercises with appropriate modification can control the behaviour of other constructions which have the same sensors and the same output devices in the corresponding ports.

During the school year 2004-2005 three (3) out of the five programmed lessons were conducted. This happened for reasons not related to teaching as such, but rather due to external factors such as pressure of the school curriculum and the like. The lessons were repeated with two different classes of fourteen (14) students each. In this pilot application, only one LEGO robot was installed in a PC. Whatsoever, the programming environment Robolab had been installed in all PCs in the computer laboratory. Each group of students had been planning the solution of the exercise on its PC and when it was syntactically correct, students were able to transfer it onto the PC with the robot and apply it, processing possible errors and omitted details. If the program has syntactic errors or omissions Robolab does not allow the loading of the program in RCX processor. In case the program is syntactically articulate but contains logical mistakes, the teacher helps students towards the right solution, making the necessary observations. At the end of each exercise, the right solution is presented and a brief mentioning of evident errors is made.

During these lessons, data was collected from two sources: the question-check sheet which consisted of questions on the knowledge students had acquired; and the worksheets with the programs that students had developed in order to solve the proposed problems. This comprised the main body of data analysed. To this must be added a series of informal data, acquired directly through classroom experience.

Below we present a summary of the findings of each lesson; an overall analysis of the findings, in allotted categories.

In the first lesson no worksheet was given, only a question-check sheet.

Table 1. 1st question-check sheet and the students' responses. After the percentages for each situation, some characteristic responses are given.

Questions	Correct responses	Wrong or incomplete responses %	Did not respond %
What is RCX?	60	32(*)	8
What is an InfraRed tower?	48	47	4
What does "loading" a program mean?	40	37(**)	24
In which way is a program executed?	32	28	40

(*) the processor of a vehicle
(**)
- the vehicle will start moving
- it gives a command for the robot to start
- I transmit the program and I give a command to RCX to start the program

Table 2. 1st question-check sheet (continue). The students were called on to report the RCX buttons and to describe their functions.

Button	Responses %	Correct responses %
On/Off	80	71
View	49	59
Prgm	69	72
Run	35	0
none	12	4

In the third question they are given a figure which depicts the RCX processor and a motor connected to an input port. They are then asked to ascertain why the motor is not moving. 31% of the students responded correctly, 48% gave wrong or incomplete responses, whereas 20% did not respond. Some characteristic student expressions are given below:

- because it is not connected to the robot and it cannot give movement to the robot
- it does not work because the RCX processor and the transmitter have no communication

- because the transmitter is not positioned in the right place to enable the motor to work

In the last test we asked students to correspond the icon buttons of RCX with the actions which each symbolizes, and in this test the responses of the students were 100% correct.

In the second lesson, there was a worksheet and a question-check sheet.

Table 3. 2nd question-check sheet and the students' response

Questions	Correct responses %	Wrong or incomplete responses %	Did not respond %
Explain the difference between the input and output commands	15	54	31
State the categories of sensors	15	54	31

Table 4. 2nd question-check sheet (continue) and the students' responses. After the percentages for each situation, some characteristic responses are given.

Question	Icon	Correct responses %	Wrong or incomplete responses %	Did not respond %
Fig. 1. Describe in one sentence what each of the icons mean	1	29	64(*)	7
	2	57	29	14
	3	36	43	21
	4	7	71	21
Fig. 2. What is the role of the Wait For command? Explain the forms which we meet in Robolab. (Use the icons).	1	0	79	21
	2	0	79(**)	21
	3	0	71	29
	4	0	57(***)	43
	5	21	29	50

(*)
- to start the motor which is in position 2 backwards
- the motor will go backwards at speed 2
- the motor goes backwards and then stops. Then it has sound and moves for 10' until the sound is heard for 4'

(**)
- to move until it finds darkness.
- to move until it finds a place which is brighter/has more light.
- wait until you meet darkness.
- wait until you meet light.

(***)
- wait until the motor is compressed
- wait until the motor is freed

Table 5. 2nd question-check sheet (continue) and the students' responses

Problem: Where is the mistake/error?	Correct responses %	Wrong or incomplete responses %	Did not respond %
Fig. 3. The program must activate the motor which is found in port A at level 1.	43	43	14
Fig. 4. The program must activate motor A for 4 seconds and then to stop it.	57	21	21

Table 6. 2nd worksheet and the students' responses. After the percentages for each situation, some characteristic responses are given.

Proposed problem	Correct responses %	Wrong or incomplete responses %	Did not respond %
Program the vehicle, which you constructed to move forward for 6 seconds and then stop.	83	0	17
Program your vehicle to move forward for 4 seconds, to stop for 2 seconds and then to move in the opposite direction for 4 seconds.	71	4	25

Program the vehicle which you constructed to produce a sound, then to move forward for 6 seconds, to stop and produce a different sound (use a modifier to choose the sound which is made each time).	50	33(*)	17
Create a program which will light the lamp of the vehicle until it runs into some object or a wall.	4	79(**)	17
Program the vehicle which you constructed to move forward until the light sensor detects an increase in the level of light by 5.	0	79(***)	21

(*)
- 6 programs without sound.
- 1 program without stop.
- 1 program with the use of an incorrect symbol for the representation constant.

(**)
- 6 programs without a stop motor
- 10 programs without a stop lamp
- 14 programs without an input Modifier
- 13 programs used the motor icon in the opposite direction

(***)
- 17 programs without constant, which determines the level of light
- 1 program without a stop motor
- 2 programs without an input modifier

In the third lesson, whose main aim was repetition structures, the students were likewise given a Worksheet and a question-check sheet.

Table 7. 3rd question-check sheet and the students' responses

Questions	Correct responses %	Wrong or incomplete responses %	Did not respond %
What is the difference between Loop and the Jump/Land pair?	88	12	0
What do we gain by using Loops?	56	12	32
Correspond the icons with the phrases (Sound production, modifier which regulates the level of the power of the motor to 1, Red jump, End Loop, Start Loop, Red land) which best describe them	100	0	0

Table 8. 3rd question-check sheet (continue) and the students' responses

Problem type: identify the errors	Correct responses %	Wrong or incomplete responses %	Did not respond %
Fig. 5. The program must produce a sound 3 times.	52	29	19
Fig. 6. The program must produce an audio signal continually.	85	11	4
Fig. 7. This program must produce an audio signal continually.	89	8	3

Table 9. 3rd worksheet and the students' responses. After the percentages for each situation, some characteristic responses are given.

Proposed problem	Correct responses %	Wrong or incomplete responses %	Did not respond %
Program the vehicle which you constructed to produce an audio signal and then to wait for 1 second. This procedure will be repeated continually.	83	0	17
Program the vehicle you constructed to produce an audio signal many times (for a random number of repetitions).	83	0	17
Program the vehicle you constructed to produce the audio signal beepbeep 10 times.	42	42(*)	16
Create a program which will turn on the lamp of the vehicle at a random level. This will be repeated 10 times and at each repetition the lamp will light up at a different level.	0	67(**)	33

(*)
- 5 programs did not have constant sound

(**)
- *10 programs did not have the time for the lamp to stay on*
- *1 program did not have a stop lamp.*

4 Results and Conclusions

The environment of the robots Mindstorms presents itself as a most interesting solution, to an alternative, more effective teaching introduction to programming for secondary education students. The above data, enabled us to reach the following conclusions:

The students have a general functional perception of the way in which the subsystem of the robotic mechanism is interconnected, since they did not have any great difficulty in constructing a functioning robot. Nevertheless, Table 1 shows that the students do not fully understand these interconnections, nor the way in which the information circulates. In each situation, the phrases they use indicate an inadequate perception at this level. The data in Table 2, as well as the first questions in Table 4 reinforce this hypothesis. Analogous (but not exactly the same) is the confirmation that often students have difficulty in memorizing the exact function which each icon symbolizes. This is perhaps an indication of the relative complexity which icons present, especially the fact of there being a large number of them. There were certain icons, such as those with modifiers and with the random number generator, which proved to be observably difficult for students. Naturally, it must be noted that both of these symbolized functions unusual and non-existent outside the programming environments of their previous experience. Although students recognize the function of these when they come across them in a ready program, they have difficulty in using them in the creation of programs. An important problem, which we had not foreseen (which turned out to be serious, since in one way or another it was ascertained in other lessons) arose in relation to distinguishing between the input and output ports. The vast majority of students (as is shown in Table 3) failed to define their role exactly. This may be attributed to the fact that the use of ports with a specific character is rather unusual in daily life.

The language used in order to program the robot turned out to be easy to understand, which of course, is quite different to the fact that the students had difficulty in memorizing the commands. In fact, the responses in the third lesson, both in the question-check sheet, and the worksheet, definitely show that students have understood certain basic functions of the repetition structures. Of course, certain lexical constructions, such as the Wait for type of commands, are a major source of difficulty. In our opinion, we believe that this happens because of the fact that the repetitive structure, is indirect, it cannot be expressed nor explicitly formulated and the logical condition also remains indirect. Furthermore, loops that are executed for a specific number of times seem to be easier to use than those of the type while-do or repeat-until. Of course, the proposed problems explicitly specify the need for repetition and thus indirectly indicate the use of the repetition structures. It is worth noting that the difficulties ascertained in the use of these repetition structures is in complete accordance with the findings of research which has been conducted for over twenty years now. They do not merely confirm them but reinforce the more general hypothesis that the difficulty of these structures is almost independent of the programming environment and the programming language being used.

The fact that the students had to solve problems associated with the function of real systems comprised, in principle, a positive condition, from a teaching perspective. In systems such as Lego Robots, the validity of each solution is made apparent through the execution of the corresponding program. The system will either have the anticipated behaviour or not and in each situation it is obvious which of the two has occurred. Nevertheless, the functioning of a real system in daily life cannot be described by a formal system and leaves room for innuendoes. In this way, the responses in Table 5 and in the tables with the proposed problems (Table 6 & Table 9) show that the students attach a wider meaning to the commands than the actual one. For example, the students regard that the presence of a clock means that the system (robot) returns to its prior situation after the time that is written on the clock passes and often they omit the time. In addition, very frequently, as their responses show, students omit the commands which signal the end of an action (stop).

Summarizing, the lessons showed the following:

Students acquire procedural knowledge relatively quickly and can control the robots relatively easily. However, in many situations, this knowledge is lacking and inaccurate. The use of a real system for the formulation and solution of a problem is positive since it allows the familiarization, up to a point, with the advanced technology of robots. In addition, it allows the control of the results of a program's execution in an obvious way. However, it appears that it is difficult to connect the existence of a real system with the typical behaviour of a robotic system and this, perhaps comprises an unforeseen source of difficulties.

The students appear to easily understand the programming concepts of the environment Mindstorms. Nevertheless, it was observed that the difficulties novice programmers encounter in other environments, which are connected to the intrinsic difficulty of certain programming structures, also exist in the environment Mindstorms.

References

1. Barnes J. David, Teaching Introductory Java through LEGO Mindstorms Models, Proceedings of the 33rd SIGCSE Technical Symposium on Computer Science Education, (2002)
2. Brusilovsky, P., Calabrese, E., Hvorecky, J., Kouchnirenko, A., Miller, P., Mini-languages: a way to learn programming principles, Journal of Education and Information Technologies, 2, (1997), 65-83
3. Kagani K., Programming with Robots, Master Thesis, University of Macedonia, (2003)
4. LEGO Homepage, http://www.lego.com/eng/
5. Martha N. Kyr, ROBOLAB Getting Started, Teacher's Guide for ROBOLAB Software, The LEGO Group, Tufts University, National Instruments Corporation, (1998)
6. Patterson-McNeill Holy, Binkerd Carol, Resources for Using LEGO® MINDSTORMS™, Proceedings of the Seventh Annual Consortium for Computing in Small Colleges Central Plains Conference on The Journal of Computing in Small Colleges, (2001), 147-151.
7. Programming and Alternative Learning Group, http://www.umcs.maine.edu/~pbrick/.
8. Resnick Mitchel, Behavior Construction Kits, Communications of the ACM, Vol. 36, Issue 7, (1993), 64-71
9. Xinogalos Stelios, Satratzemi Maya and Dagdilelis Vassilios, An introduction to object-oriented programming with a didactic microworld: objectKarel, Computers & Education, Elsevier, In Press (Available online 8 December 2004)

ASPIS: An Automated Information System for Certification and Analysis of Examination Process[*]

Georgios Katsikis[1], Naoum Mengoudis[2], Alexandros Nanopoulos[1],
Ioannis Samoladas[1], and Ioannis Stamelos[1]

[1] Department of Informatics, Aristotle University of Thessaloniki,
541 24, Thessaloniki, Greece
katsikis@gmail.com, alex@delab.csd.auth.gr
{ioansam, stamelos}@csd.auth.gr
[2] Aristotle Certification Training and Assessment,
26is Octovriou No. 10, 546 27, Thessaloniki, Greece
mengoudis@acta.edu.gr

Abstract. One of the innovations that the usage of Internet has introduced is distance learning. Along with distance learning came the requirement for distance certification. While there are organizations that support the certification process, the provided support in Greece is relatively limited inflexible. In this paper we describe the first to our best knowledge, system that automates the certification process. The proposed system takes into account various learning parameters and makes use of the feedback of the process, along with the help of the data mining on the certification results. In this paper, we describe processes necessary for distance certification, the system itself and we present some results of the data mining we applied on the systems preliminary data.

1 Introduction

During the past years, the wide usage of Internet has introduced the notion of distance learning. A number of organizations are, now, offering courses that are conducted over the web and a large number of people are enrolled in them. Additionally, big multinational companies use the Internet to keep their employees up-to-date with their job area, offering to them life long education. These courses cover a wide range of subjects, but the majority of them involve information technology areas.

All these organizations that provide distance learning courses need a mechanism to support this life-long learning process in order to track the performance of their students, a mechanism that provides distance certification. While there are a number of companies in other countries that offer a distance certification application and procedure, this is not the case in Greece. Furthermore, the support for the certification process is limited and there are certain problems with the inflexible process. The

---

[*] This work has been funded by the Greek General Secretariat for Research and Technology under the 3rd European Union's Community Support Framework, Operational Program "Information Society", Measure 3.3, Action 3.3.1, Project: "Electronic Learning".

certification process does not take account of the learning process (teaching methods, training centers, educational staff, etc.) and there is not a formal process to accredit learning providers (or learning centers) and examination centers. Additionally, the results of the certification process are not used as a feedback in order to evaluate and make the process better.

In order to address the problems mentioned, we propose the ASPIS (the name ASPIS is the Greek acronym for "Automated Certification System") system. To our best knowledge, this is the first system in Greece that offers an online automation of both the certification process and the accreditation process for learning centers and the examination centers. The system keeps track of the whole learning and examination process.

The ASPIS system provides data (e.g., about examinees, education centers, tests, etc) that can be exploited in order to find useful information, which can be used to assess the whole educational process and carefully monitor specific parts of it. For this purpose, we describe the use of the analysis module that is included in ASPIS, which performs data mining on the data collected by the system. Up to the authors knowledge, relatively little interest has been given during the past years in applying data mining for educational-related purposes. We detail the data-mining methodology that is used and illustrate some sample results.

Next, we are going to present the processes for the certification and the accreditation. Furtherance, we describe the ASPIS system in detail, followed by initial results obtained from the implementation of the system so far. In the last section we present the the data mining results of the ASPIS database, followed by our conclusion.

2 Certification - Accreditation Processes

Before implementing the ASPIS system it was necessary to define a certification process both for the examination process and the accreditation process of the examination centers and learning providers by a central authority (in our case the Aristotle University of Thessaloniki). These processes were used in order to specify the system's requirements [5]. To take an idea of such process we have conducted interviews with the industrial partners of the ASPIS project, from those interviews we have modeled a general framework that can be easily applied and altered in order to capture a specific process of a learning organization.

Organizations wishing to offer courses leading to certificates have to be accredited by the central authority mentioned above, according to already established standards [4], [7]. Likewise, organizations wishing to implement the process of examinations and offer it to candidates have to be accredited. Once accredited, learning centers (learning providers) and examination centers are monitored in a variety of ways to ensure that standards are fulfilled.

The general process for certifying the candidate is shown in Figure 1. The candidate is registered in the examination center by bringing complete probative elements of his identity. He acquires a unique username and password to log into the examination system and take exams in the required module(s) (e.g. word processing, spreadsheets). The examinations can be written offline or online (in our case, the

ASPIS system accommodates only online examinations). Examination results are published shortly after.(e.g. either online or with regular post) and candidates have the right to appeal to any step of the process.

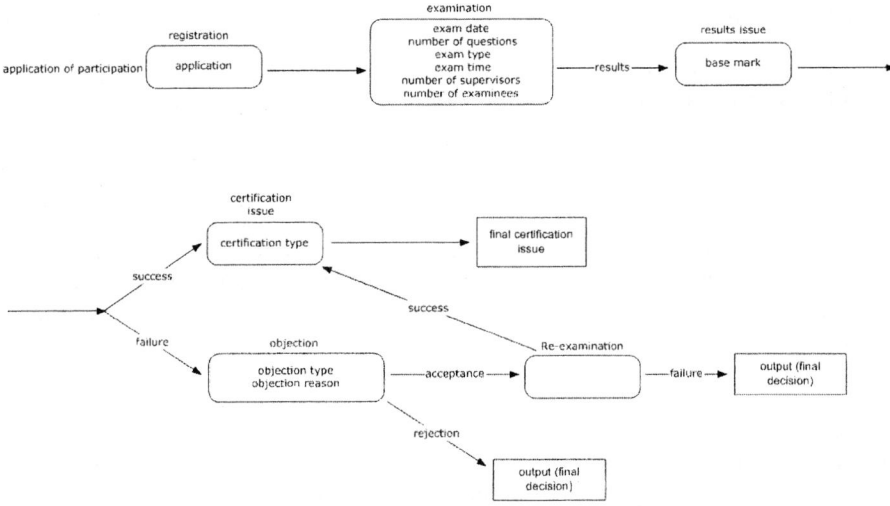

Fig. 1. Process diagram for the exam

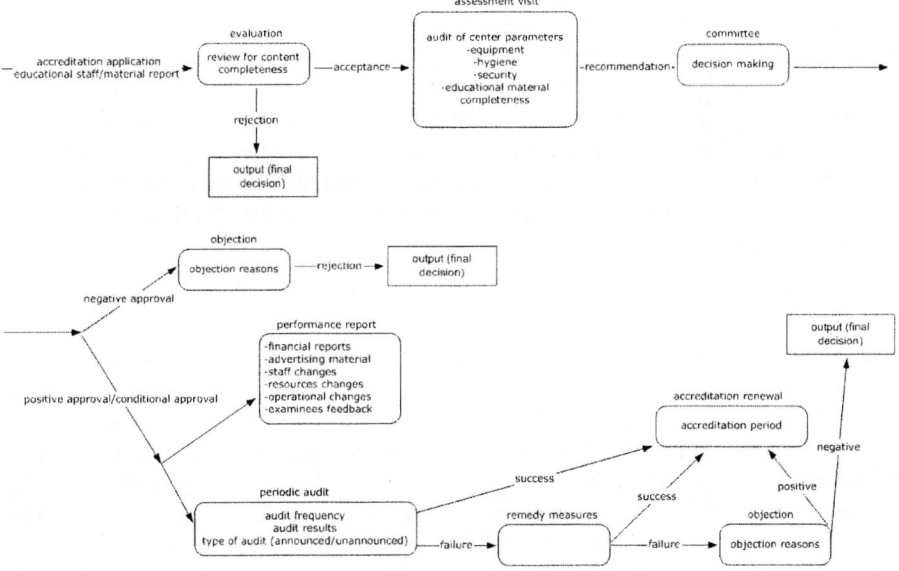

Fig. 2. Process diagram for center accreditation

The general process for accrediting the organizations wishing to act either as learning providers or examination centers is shown in Figure 2. The interested organization submits an application to the central authority. After a visit of evaluation, the authority decides whether to grant the accreditation. If the accreditation is not granted, the rejected organization has the right to appeal. If the accreditation is granted, the organization that was accredited must comply with the accreditation rules.

3 The ASPIS System

3.1 Overview

The ASPIS system is a modern web based system, i.e. a web based database application. The system supports two functions, accreditation and examination. For the first, it offers automation regarding the tracking of the process for the accreditation and the maintenance of the existing accredited centers (e.g. reminders for the periodic audit). It does not support cases and processes that include strong human interference, for example decision making regarding the grant of the accreditation.

For the second function the system support almost full automation of the certification process (the automation is not supported when the examination process demands a written exam, which is not the usual case for such system). There are three kinds of users in the system: the students who give tests and take exams, the educator who specify tests, and the administrators who perform tasks such as adding new students to the system. Some other system details are:

- Each student belongs to one or more classes. The same is true for the educator.
- A question belongs to a specific chapter. A chapter belongs to a study area.
- There are three types of questions: multiple choice, fill in the blanks and match the phrases. A question may additionally include static images such as diagrams.
- An educator enters the specifications of a test (e.g. number, type and difficulty level of questions) not the questions included in that test. When a student takes the test, the latter is created on the fly randomly according the specifications that the educator entered.

3.2 Architecture

The ASPIS system is a three-tier application, like most of the recent web based systems. The base of the system is the relational database management system (RDBMS) or the database tier, which is the MySQL database management system [reference]. Above that tier there is the application logic or the middle tier, which performs most of the systems functions and it is also responsible for the communication between the upper tier of the system and the database tier. The language we used to write this tier was PHP, a server side scripting language suitable for building web based applications. This tier also includes the web server that stands above the PHP engine. On the top there is the client tier which is the web browser that interacts with the user. All these three tiers are cooperating in order to carry out the functions that the ASPIS system performs. The general architecture is shown in Figure 3.

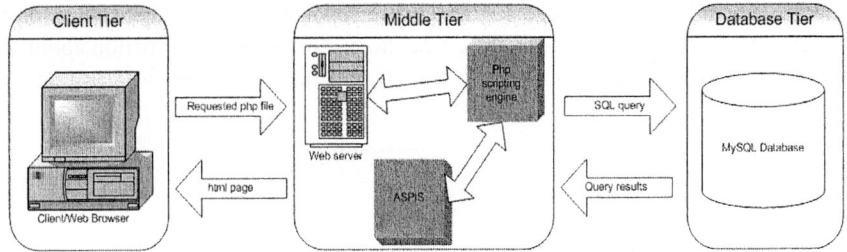

Fig. 3. The 3-tier architecture

Particularly, when a client or more precisely a web browser makes a request to the web server (middle tier) for a specific page, five steps occur:

1. The web server passes the request to the PHP engine's web server interface.
2. The web server interface calls the PHP engine and passes the parameters to the engine.
3. The appropriate PHP script from the ASPIS system is retrieved from the disk by the engine.
4. The script is executed by the engine and the output is returned to the web server interface.
5. The web server interface returns output to the web server which in turn returns the output as an http (common html file) response to the client's web browser.

Although PHP can be easily embedded in html web pages, for the ASPIS system this was not the case. Instead, PHP was used to build the web pages from scratch without using existing html code. These pages are built according to specific parameters as an input to PHP and the user's rights. This means, for example, that there are no separate pages for the main page of the student or the administrator, but a single script builds the page according to the role of the user logged into the system. This feature gives an advantage to the whole system in terms of maintainability. New features can be easily implemented by adding new function to the module that builds the pages instead of adding new raw script files to the application.

The ASPIS system consists of two main modules and one auxiliary module. The main modules are the *Pagebuilder module* and the *Database module*. The architectural view is shown in Figure 4. The auxiliary or Data Mining module is separate from the other two (not shown here). This module is not written in PHP and it directly interacts with the database, bypassing the PHP engine that the rest of the system uses. The functionality contained in the first two modules is further divided into other scripts or modules:

- There are three important scripts in ASPIS that contain information for the two main modules. The first script is access.php, which is responsible for user authentication and passes the appropriate role parameters to the Pagebuilder module. The second important script, metadata.php, contains all of the system's information - the database schema and all the information that the second script wants in order to build pages, e.g. information about forms. Additionally, it implements all the validation functionality, e.g. whether the user has entered an incorrect email address. The globals.php script is in fact the configuration file for the application and the database connections, containing information about how to log into the database and other system and database specific constants and parameters.

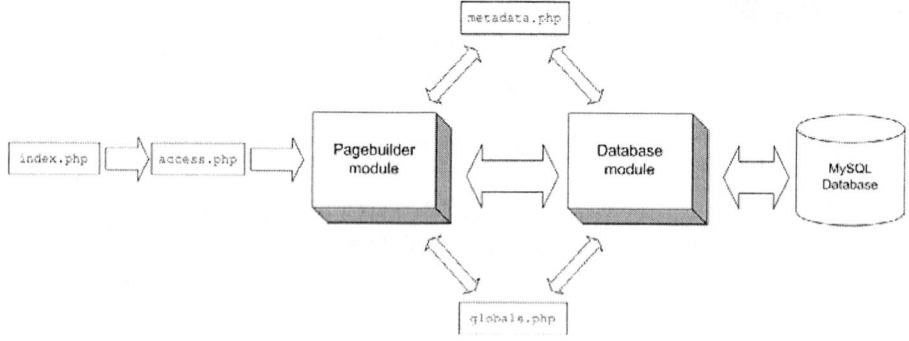

Fig. 4. ASPIS architecture

- The Pagebuilder module, as its name implies, is responsible for the construction of the majority of the web pages that the ASPIS consists of. It constructs the pages that data is entered or displayed in, i.e. the whole application. For each of one displayed item, it uses a separate function; we could say that it is the API for these functions. For example, the function buildMenu constructs the menu of the main page of the user according to his rights (for example, the student has a menu in order to take a test and the administrator has options like adding a new user to the system). It also adds the appropriate html tags, cascading style sheets and javascript code to the page constructed and uses the scripts mentioned in the first bullet.
- The Database module contains all the appropriate functions that the system uses in order to communicate with the MySQL database management system and either inserts new data or processes old ones. This module uses the information from the metadata.php and the globals.php mentioned before. This module has all the functions that interact with the database in the lower level through the PHP engine, i.e. the sql queries. Whenever access to the database is needed, this script is used through the function it provides. If a new query has to be inserted to the system, here is where we implement it. This allows, apart from the modularity of the system, future migration to another database system.

Of course there are web pages that do not belong to the above, like the login page, which passes parameters to the Pagebuilder module.

It worths mentioning that the whole application is written according to the most up-to-date web standards as these are specified by the World Wide Web Consortium

(W3C). This means that the content is separate from the presentation. The content is coded in pure xhtml (a reformulation of html as an xml application) and the presentation or the style is applied by various CSS (Cascading Style Sheets) without affecting the content. This means, first that by applying different style sheets the user interface can be replaced easily, leaving content untouched, and second that having the content free from the way it is presented, it can be easily displayed in other media than the computer screen, i.e. handheld devices e.t.c.

4 Case Study – IL

In order to evaluate the ASPIS system, we first implemented a prototype and performed a pilot operational use in a real educational environment. The system was installed by a large Greek educational organization (and an industrial partner of the ASPIS project) that offers computer training in a number of cities across Greece. During that period a lot of data was collected and users provided a lot of feedback about the system itself. This feedback helped in improving the system, especially its user interface which changed, without altering its core design and functionality. The final system is also online and used by the same educational organization mentioned before. Some numbers that indicate the massive usage of the system until March 2005 are shown in Table 1. The size of the database has reached 291.4 megabytes.

Table 1. Usage statistics of the ASPIS system

Total number of accounts	2403
Total number of students	2309
Total number of educators	77
Total number of administrators	17
Total number of classes	448
Total number of study areas	16
Total number of chapters (of study areas)	80
Total number of questions	1329
Total number of test specifications submitted	27077
Total number of tests submitted	81561

5 Data Mining

5.1 Objectives of Applying Data Mining in ASPIS

During its operation, the ASPIS system produces a relatively large volume of data. This includes data about examinees (personal data like address, education center); data about education centers (name, address); data about the tests, i.e., the contents of the database of questions asked to and answers provided by the examinees during their tests; etc. Evidently, such data can be transformed to valuable information, which can be used to (i) improve the ability to assess the whole process and (ii) to monitor specific parts of it in order to adjust accordingly.

As it has been recognized during the previous years, the technology to attain objectives analogous to the aforementioned ones is data mining. Data mining is the extraction of interesting (non-trivial, implicit, previously unknown and potentially useful) information or patterns from data in large databases [2]. Data mining has been primarily used in financial/marketing applications like target marketing, determination of customer purchasing patterns, and cross-market analysis. Other application areas include telecommunications, insurance, astronomy, etc. However, relatively little interest has been given during the past years in applying data mining for education-related purposes.

Given the two (i and ii) objectives described previously, we consider the following data mining tasks:

1. Mine relationships between data about the examinees (e.g., region of lodging, level of class, etc), data about the examination centers (their names), and data about their examination results (total score). The discovered relationships of this kind will allow for better assessment of the educational process (objective i), since it is helpful to understand how the aforesaid factors interrelate and which of them affect the success or failure of examinees.
2. Mine relationships and investigate patterns between the answers of the participants. The discovered relationships allow for better monitoring of the educational part of the system, that is, the questions used in the tests and, accordingly, their educational value. If, for example, one can find questions, or categories of questions, that tend to be answered in the same way (i.e., correctly or incorrectly), then one may have a better understanding on how the taught subjects interrelate and obtain a picture of the educational model the particular student develops through the interaction with the system. So, one could adjust the initial educational approach in order to meet students' expectations and developed cognitive models on the particular domain.

The data mining method that we used to examine the previous issues is association-rules mining, which is detailed in the following.

5.2 Mining Association Rules in ASPIS

Association-rules mining concerns the finding of frequent patterns called associations (other names: correlations, causal structures) among sets of items or objects in transaction databases, relational databases, and other information repositories. An almost legendary example of a discovered association rule is:

- buys(x, "diapers") → buys(x, "beers") [0.5%, 60%]
- which states that if one purchases diapers, then he is also likely to purchase beer. As shown, an association rule is characterized by two measures:
- The support s% (in previous example: 0.5%), which reflects the statistical significance of the rule, that is, how many transactions include the items of the rule.

- The confidence c% (in previous example: 60%), which reflects the assurance of the rule, that is, how sure we are that the items in the head and the body of the rule really relate.

The problem of association-rules mining is, therefore, to find all rules with support higher than a given threshold s% and a confidence higher than a given threshold c%. This problem has attracted a lot of interest and many algorithms have been developed [1]. We focus on the family of algorithms that are based on *pattern-growth* and more particularly on *FP-growth* [3], since they have been reported to have very good properties.

In ASPIS, we created a separate module in the architecture, which is responsible for probing the database of questions and answers, and for finding association rules of type 1 and 2, that have been described previously. In particular, the analyst can query the database and formulate a view containing information about the total scores (case 1) or the correctly/incorrectly answered questions per examinee (case 2). The selection can be further focused by including the time period of interest. Each record in the aforementioned views corresponds to transactions, and we use the FP-growth algorithm to mine associations. Examples of discovered patterns, which indicate the usefulness of this module, are given in the following.

5.3 Examples of Mined Results

By using a sample of the tests' database, consisting of 81561 tests, we mined association rules for cases 1 and 2 that were described previously.

For the former case (1), we have discretized the ratings of examinees (originally in 0-100 scale) in 8 levels: A, B, ... G, by equi-partitioning the original scale. We focused on relationships between the city of residence of examinees and their rating. The rules we detected (support threshold 1%, confidence threshold 55%) were the following:

- Residence(x, "Kozani") → Rating(x, "G") [2%, 67%]
- Residence(x, "Thessaloniki") → Rating(x, "A") [6%, 66%]
- Residence(x, "Florina") → Rating(x, "A") [1%, 58%]

The utility of this kind of rules is evident, because they are significant (the original sample was large) and one can detect clear relationships. Thus, such rules can help in monitoring the educational process, since regions that tend to have low ratings can be looked more carefully to examine the reasons. Moreover, it is also useful to know the regions where the education process has good results.

For the case 2, we have mined association rules between the correctly and incorrectly answers by each examinee. A sample of the detected rules for the former case is the following:

- "What appears after then end of booting?", "Give a way to terminate a program that got stuck" → "Which icon do we use to undelete a file?" [76%]
- "What appears after then end of booting?", "Give a way to terminate a program that got stuck" → "Which of the listed actions cannot be performed with the mouse?" [76%]

A sample of detected rule for the latter case is the following:

- "Is it possible to minimize a dialog box?", "In which way can we minimize all opened windows?" → "From the listed items, which is not a component of MS Windows?" [73%]

From such rules one can see topics that tend to be understood (correctly answered) or not understood (incorrectly answered), for instance the minimization procedure, and react accordingly by emphasizing such topics (and their relation) during classes.

6 Conclusions

In this paper we have presented a case study of a distance certification system. The system automates a large portion of the processes that a certification authority wants, namely the examination process itself and the accreditation process of the organizations wishing to offer both courses and exams for the specific certification. In order to build that system we modeled both of the mentioned processes, examination and accreditation, in order to better understand the requirements of our system. The latter is a web based system with three tier architecture; increased modularity in order to address future extensions, an interface build in accordance with the latest web standards and it also includes data mining functionality. Last, we presented some preliminary results on the data produced during the pilot period of the system operation.

Although the majority of the functionality of the system is already done, there are things to be done. Our primary next goal is to automate more parts for the examination and the accreditation processes and connect the system with other systems that are out of the processes (e.g. a learning management system). Additionally there is ongoing effort to enhance the data mining facility and integrate it into the core of the ASPIS system.

References

1. Agrawal, R., Imielinski, T., Swami, A. N. Mining Association Rules between Sets of Items in Large Databases. ACM SIGMOD Conference (1993) 207-216
2. Fayyad, U. M., Piatetsky-Shapiro, G., Smyth, P., Uthurusamy, R. Advances in Knowledge Discovery and Data Mining. AAAI/MIT Press (1996)
3. Han, J., Pei, J., Yin, Y. Mining Frequent Patterns without Candidate Generation. ACM SIGMOD Conference (2000) 1-12
4. Kirkpatrick, D. Evaluating training programs: The four Levels, San Francisco, CA:Berrett-Koehler (1996)
5. Mooij, T., & Smeets, E. Modeling and supporting ICT implementation in secondary schools. Computers & Education, 36 (2001), 265-281
6. MySQL AB. http://www.mysql.com
7. Wisher, R. A., & Champagne, M. V. Distance learning and training: An evaluation perspective. In J. D. Fletcher and S. Tobias (Eds.), Training and Retraining: A Handbook for Business, Industry, Government and the Military. MacMillan Reference USA (2000)

Bridging the Contextual Distance: The e-CASE Learning Environment for Supporting Students' Context Awareness

Stavros N. Demetriadis, Pantelis M. Papadopoulos, and Ioannis A. Tsoukalas

Informatics Department, PO BOX 888, Aristotle University of Thessaloniki,
54124 Thessaloniki, Greece
{sdemetri, pmpapad, tsoukala}@csd.auth.gr

Abstract. Supporting students' awareness of the complex way that contextual issues affect knowledge application in authentic situations is a critical instructional mission and can lead to improved problem solving in the workplace. In this work we present the design of e-CASE (Context Awareness Supporting Environment), which is a case based learning environment for supporting instruction in the domain of software development. In designing e-CASE we employ a model for context which further guides the use of script and narrative control techniques as external representations for enhancing students' context awareness. Our system applies an appropriate metadata scheme for connecting various pieces of information and creating crossing paths for the learner, in the web of authentic application cases. It also provides functionality for updating and extending its content allowing people from the workplace to become content providers. Thus, we argue, e-CASE can help bridging the contextual distance, supporting the development of an extended learning community by establishing flexible and instructionally efficient links between the traditional educational settings and the workplace.

1 Introduction

The instructional effort to encode knowledge at a higher level of abstraction and present it outside of any specific application context, underestimates the role of context in learning and results in limited knowledge transfer to real world problems solving and inflexible forms of learning [1]. To efficiently deal with these problems instructional designers have strongly focused on anchoring learning in the context of real world situations. Context sensitive instructional designs such as case and problem based learning ([2], [3]) offer to students a more authentic learning experience by engaging them in the processing of contextually rich material. In these approaches one major challenge for instructors is how to support students in developing adequate domain content understanding and metacognitive information processing, skills. Moreover, learning in context brings out the necessity for a more effective connection between traditional learning settings and the workplace, which is usually the source of authentic learning experiences concerning knowledge application.

In relation to the above deliberations we argue that in designing technology enhanced environments for contextualized learning, one can offer better learning conditions when addressing the following issues:

- (a) How to design and instructionally integrate in the environment appropriate external representations to support students' processing of the contextually rich material and understanding of the role that context plays in real world situations.
- (b) How to design the environment in such way that it promotes the participation of broader social groups in the learning process, providing services for the update and extension of the learning material.

In this work we present the design of e-CASE (Context Awareness Supporting Environment), which is a case based learning environment for supporting instruction in the domain of software development. In designing e-CASE we employ a model for context which further guides the use of script and narrative techniques as external representations for enhancing students' context awareness. Our system applies an appropriate metadata scheme for connecting various pieces of information and creating crossing paths for the learner, in the web of authentic application cases. It also provides functionality for updating and extending its content encouraging people from the workplace to become content providers. In the following we present:

- (a) The basic theoretical issues in our approach, namely a model for context and the use of scripts and narrative for supporting students' context awareness.
- (b) The design of e-CASE as a case based learning environment for supporting instruction in the domain of software development and also as an "extended community" supporting environment, enabling the update of its content in the form of learning experiences from the workplace.

2 Theoretical Considerations

2.1 Context and Context Awareness

Researchers generally do not agree on a universally accepted definition of context and on the way that it affects the processes of problem-solving and learning. Kokinov [4] describes context as "the set of all entities that influence human cognitive behavior on a particular occasion" and emphasizes that context should be considered as a "state of mind", thus focusing strongly on the reasoner's internal cognitive processes. Other researchers, however, conceptualize context as emerging both from the mind and the "situation". Ozturk and Aamodt [5] talk about the "situational context" which comprises all contextual elements that exist in a situation independent of the observer; these elements exist in the environment before and after the observer notices them.

Although it is not our purpose to offer a conclusive definition of context, we would like to introduce a working definition of the term in order to render it operational for the purposes of our work. We maintain, therefore, that the concept of context presents two important aspects:

- *Availability*: Contextual information is collateral information available to the reasoner, not directly emerging from the focus of her activity.

- *Relevance*: There is a varied degree of relevance between contextual information and the focus of reasoner's activity.

Based on the above we describe context as "the set of all elements of collateral information, which enable people to reason meaningfully in relation to the purpose of their activity". According to Kokinov [6], the elements that compose the context of a situation can be made available (are induced) from at least three mental processes: perception, reasoning and memory.

- *Perception induced context*: Contextual elements may be available through perception (observation) of the environment. This information may also activate older representations from the memory.
- *Memory induced context*: Elements which are recalled from memory and older representations which are reactivated.
- *Reasoning induced context*: Representations that are derived from the reasoning process (i.e. setting goals, defining strategy, etc.).

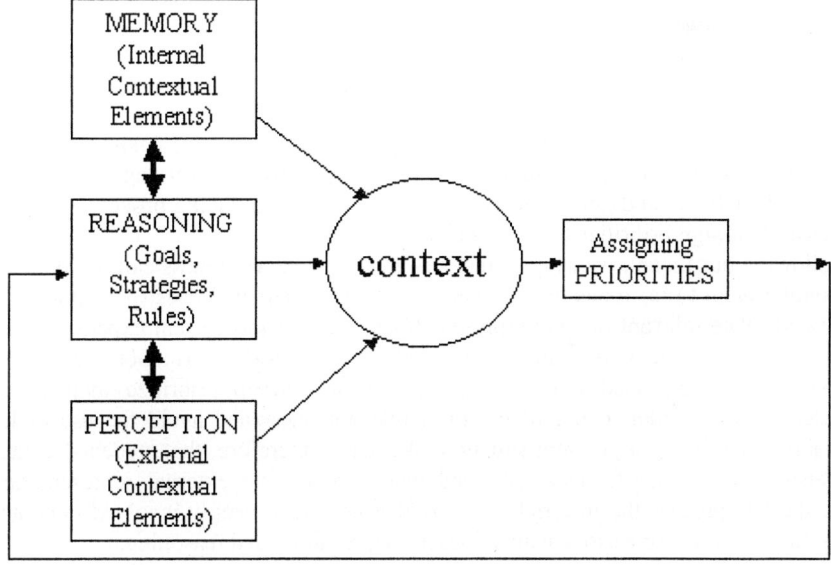

Fig. 1. A model for context, highlighting the context inducing processes (perception, memory recall, reasoning), the priorities assigning process and the feedback loop

Relevance is another important issue of context. It refers to the degree of affinity between contextual elements and the focus of the activity. Relevance can be considered as a measure of the priorities assigned to all mental representations and operations in a given moment (which constitutes the essence of context) [4]. Relevance is, therefore, directly related to the quality of the solution produced for a problem" [5]. By successfully assigning priorities to the problem solving operations, the reasoner builds an effective course of action to accomplish the goal.

Fig. 1 graphically depicts the above ideas. In this model the two-way arrows between reasoning, memory and perception emphasize that these three processes interact with each other (for example, a learner may have initially chosen a strategy for problem solving which affects the kind of representations that she recalls from memory and the specific external information that attract her attendance). The induced contextual information affects the assignment of priorities to the problem solving actions (a "relevance" defining process). These priorities in turn affect the reasoning process and the interacting memory recall and perception process (feedback loop), thus leading to a contextually adapted behavior of the reasoner.

"Contextual distance" results from the differences in the context of two comparable situations. A typical example is the difference in context between the educational setting where learning takes place and the real world situation where knowledge is applied. During the learning process student's problem solving actions and, therefore, knowledge encoding are affected by the priorities assigned due to the specific contextual elements. The difference in context between the learning situation and the application situation can result to poor students' performance either because of their inability to efficiently recall and use relevant knowledge (lack of appropriate memory trails) or even because of lack of any knowledge at all which could be of use in the different application context

2.2 Context Awareness

We describe a learner's "context awareness" as her ability to (a) acknowledge and understand the role of contextual elements in her problem solving activity, (b) consciously activate and get seriously involved in context inducing processes, and (c) successfully assign priorities to problem solving actions.

Following our model, we suggest that students' context awareness can be supported by guiding them to (a) focus on externally perceived contextual cues (perception), (b) recall and relate relevant internal representations (memory) to current experiences and external cues, and (c) make inferences based on contextual information (reasoning). Eventually it is expected that students should be able to prioritize their mental representations in order to use of the most relevant ones (and avoid the use of less relevant) when facing a problem situation. We argue, therefore, that students' context awareness can be significantly enhanced when appropriate external representations guide them to process the material in a way that gets them deeply involved in context generating cognitive processes, namely observing, recalling and reasoning.

One may ask whether supporting students' context awareness is really necessary or students become automatically context aware when working in a specific context. According to Bargh [7] the awareness of the role of the external contextual elements is a cognitive process that can be executed simultaneously in different layers and as a result these elements are not fully utilized. For example, the learner may not perceive an external element of the context but be influenced by it subconsciously. Moreover, the learner may perceive an external element but not the way that this element is interpreted. Finally, the learner may understand the way that an external element is interpreted but may not understand the way that this element affects her decisions and behavior. In these cases supporting context awareness would mean to have the student consciously observe the external elements, focus on their interpretation and reflect on the way that these elements affect (or should affect) the decision taking process.

2.3 Representations for Supporting Context Awareness

We argue that scripts and narrative are two types of external representations which can significantly enhance students' learning and consequently (when this is the focus of study) their context awareness.

Scripts. Scripts are prescriptions which guide in a structured way students' task related interactions and processing of the material. Epistemic scripts as external representations have been used extensively in collaborative learning environments to support learners in argumentative knowledge construction ([8], [9]). We suggest that scripts can also be used in individual instruction to support students' context awareness. To achieve this, designers should embed appropriate scripts, based on models for context, and help learners focus on contextual elements, improving their awareness of the effect that these elements may have on real world situations.

Narrative. Narrative refers to the use of external representations which present a meaningful plot (not necessarily in textual form) as a means for learning and instruction. The use of narrative seems to have an influence on many high-level cognitive abilities and hence be important for instruction. For instance, Luckin et al. [10] point out that narrative is a process involving both recognizing and giving structured meanings which can be shared and articulated. In the following we are going to describe how we have embedded scripts and narrative in the design of e-CASE. The instructional efficiency of these representations is one major research objective of our project.

3 Designing e-CASE

3.1 Learning in Context: Case Based Learning

In designing e-CASE (Context Awareness Supporting Environment) we have selected to implement case based instruction as an appropriate method for learning in authentic context. A case is essentially "a story with a point, a written narrative of a real-world event, situation, or experience that connects particular situations, faced by a single individual or many, to more general principals, theories, methods, or standards" [11]. Case based method of instruction employs real of fictional incidences, events or situations to present real world problems along with their surrounding context. By doing so, it establishes a link between the learning environment and the practice field. Perhaps the most convincing argument in favor of case based learning (CBL) is its potential to bridge the gap and forge connections between theory and professional practice [12]. CBL provides realistic and complex issues in a safe context for students to explore alternatives and judge their consequences [13]. Case-based learning can support a range of different epistemologies although the most powerful implementations seem to be based on constructivist theories, which propose the use of diverse and complex case-based material in order for the learner to criss-cross the domain landscape through common themes and multiple perspectives. In this way it is expected that the method facilitates flexible schema assembly, the gradual acquisition of deeper, more abstract domain understanding, and successful transfer to new situations ([1], [11], [13], [14]). Finally, case-based learning appears to foster communities of learning and to develop collaborative skills needed for professional practice. Students typically come to value open discussion and develop mutual respect as they develop their ability to articulate and defend their positions ([15]).

3.2 Learning from Software Development Failures

e-CASE supports instruction in the domain of software development. More specifically it presents to students cases dealing with software development failures. According to Ewusi-Mensah [16], the study of software development failures offers a picture of the plurality and diversity of factors involved in software development, outside of the technical "prescriptive and deterministic" view of software development typically covered in the software engineering and computer science curriculums. This will hopefully provide students with a broader perspective and appreciation of the complexity of the cofactors that are the real bane of software development projects.

Software Development Failures. A software project can be threatened by failure in two stages. The first stage is the development process and as a failure in this phase can be characterized the inability of the project team to produce a working system, meaning that the problems occurred during the project development dictated the total, substantial or partial abandonment of the project. The second stage where the failure occurs is when a project is completed and delivered to the users, but it cannot perform the functions expected, meaning that the project does not meet its requirements. In e-CASE we focus mainly on the first stage and especially on the factors that lead the project team to a failure.

Table 1. A summary of software project abandonment factors groupings into the three categories

Abandonment factor category	Dominant factors
Socio-organizational	Unrealistic project goals and objectives
	Changing requirements
	Lack of executive support and commitment
	Insufficient user commitment and involvement
Socio-technical	Unrealistic project goals and objectives
	Inappropriate project-team composition
	Project management and control problems
	Inadequate technical know-how
	Problematic technology base/infrastructure
	Changing requirements
Economic	Cost overruns and schedule delays
	Unrealistic project goals and objectives
	Changing requirements

Abandonment Factors. The abandonment of software development projects is caused in most cases by a multiplicity of cofactors. Ewusi-Mensah [16] suggests nine abandonment factors as the most important (Table 1). These factors can be grouped in three overlapping categories: the socio-organizational, the socio-technical and the economic.

3.3 e-CASE Design Features

The nine factors and three categories, mentioned in Table 1, constitute the basis for a metadata scheme that we implemented in e-CASE. In order to further clarify the role of factors we will analyze the three main entities in the e-CASE: the case, the scenario and the path.

The Case. A case is a multiple media based presentation of a software development project that for some reason(s) failed. Every case has a unique title, a subtitle, an abstract and media files (text, images and video). The case presentation is organized in "frames". Each of these frames analyzes one of the nine abandonment factors and there is a value (impact factor) assigned to it, denoting the relative importance of the factor in the project failure. The impact factor is a metadata value that allows the system to suggest connections and similarities between cases.

Although structuring the case into frames according to the factors is mandatory, the existence of all the nine frames is not. This means that it is possible to have a case with data about only some of the nine factors. On the other hand, the environment is flexible enough to accept new factors and categories. The idea behind this is that in time the nine abandonment factors might not be sufficient to describe all the possible aspects of a case.

The Scenario. A scenario is the main study unit in e-CASE (fig. 2). Each scenario is a text based narrative (with links to media files) presenting a plausible software development case but with no factor based structure. The scenario presents some background history of the case until a certain point is reached, where open-ended questions are posed to students about the continuation of the described project. The objective is to actively engage students in decision making process in order to deal with the problematic situation depicted in the scenario. Every scenario has a number of paths which suggest the relative frames that the students should study before attempting to answer the questions that the scenario poses to them.

The Path. A path has a title, a subtitle, an introduction and content comprising several case frames. The path content is essentially a collection of case frames. There are two main types of paths: the "horizontal" and the "vertical" path. A vertical path has as content the case abstract and some of the frames belonging to this specific case. Usually, a vertical path contains frames that analyze factors of the same category. A horizontal path respectively contains frames that analyze the same factor (or group of factors) and belong to different cases. The objective of using paths is to provide multiple criss-crossings through the domain field in order to support deeper understanding of the complexity and the diversity of abandonment factors.

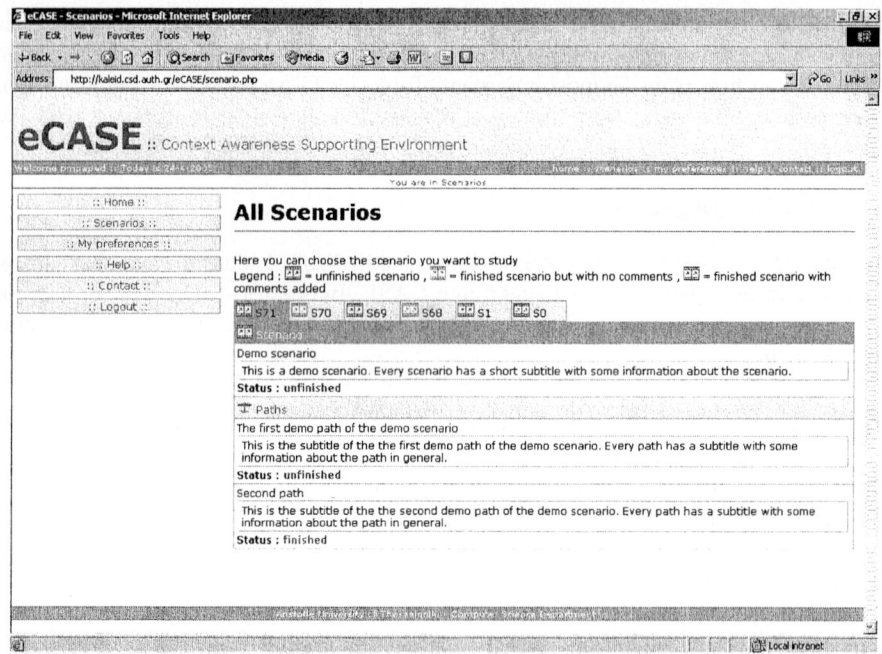

Fig. 2. Demo screen dump from e-CASE presenting all available scenarios to students

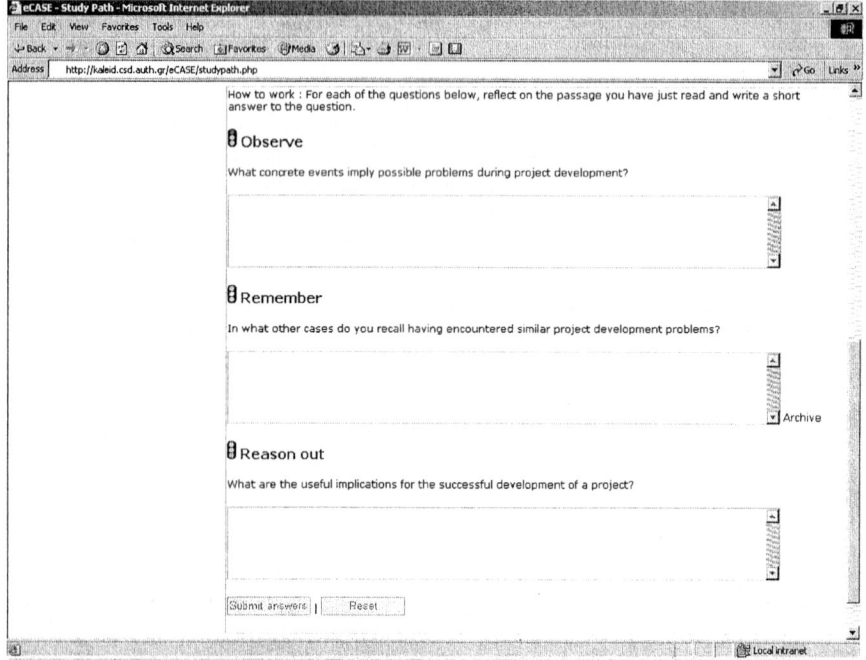

Fig. 3. An example of script for supporting students' context awareness

Every frame inside a path is accompanied by a script representation that supports students focusing on contextual information. One possible design of such a script is presented in fig. 3. The three questions of the script guide the learners to sequentially focus on the "perception", "memory", and "reasoning" dimensions of the context model by asking them to (a) identify concrete events which imply possible problems during the problem solving process, (b) recall other instances where similar development problems were encountered, and (c) reason out some useful implications for the successful problem solving process (i.e. the software development process). Hence, students inside the e-CASE have to first answer the questions in the scripts before going on answering the open-ended questions of the scenario they study. The script engages them in a cognitive task which activates context generating processes, by guiding them to focus on elements which can be (a) perceived, (b) recalled from memory, and (c) produced by reasoning and contribute to the context of the situation.

3.4 "Extended" Learning Communities

In order to enhance the quality of learning in authentic contexts, instructional material should present in the best possible way the conditions in real world application cases. However, the conditions of such socio-technical environments may change, subject to the evolutionary changes affecting all related factors. How is it possible to integrate in the learning environment new significant learning experiences emerging in the context of knowledge application?

Towards this objective, we believe that it is important to foster the development of "extended" learning communities, that is, networked communities which allow the participation of other social groups in the educational process, apart from the traditional instructors and students groups.

The meaning and importance of a learning community is highlighted by the conceptual framework known as "activity theory". Activity theory [17] provides the theoretical background for understanding the way that human relations interweave to synthesize what theorists call an "activity system". In the activity system of a learning organization instructors and students are the "subjects" that are getting involved in the instructional activity. The "object" is the intended result of their activity, which is effective learning and instruction respectively. The "tools" (which may be traditional - blackboards, textbooks, etc. - or technology enhanced) are mediating subjects' activity towards the successful production of the object. The activity of the subjects takes place in a social framework (within a community) that includes people and organizations (i.e. peer learners, co-instructors, administration, institutional partners) which affect the relation between subjects and object, either by setting "rules" in their interaction (defining what is and what is not acceptable for their actions in the activity system), or by setting the way that the workload is distributed among the partners. Any specific activity system is a complex social network with its own context, emerging from the relations between all engaged participants.

Instruction takes place traditionally in different activity system than the workplace where real world experiences take place. We argue that technology can support the development of a transformed socio-cognitive activity system which facilitates the communication and collaboration between traditional institutionalized activity systems and external activity systems which apply knowledge (the workplace). The main idea in such an effort is that the context of knowledge application systems should be transferred in the form of instructional material within the traditional learning setting. Towards this end, we have integrated in e-CASE design the opportunity for users (characterized as "content providers") to contribute raw instructional material (their learning experiences). Instructors later may review the raw material, transform it into the established instructional form (case-frame format), define appropriate metadata, scripts and paths and approve it for further distribution to learners.

4 Conclusions

In this paper we presented our initial design of the e-CASE learning environment highlighting its theoretical underpinnings and major design considerations. We maintain that supporting students' context awareness is an important instructional objective and it can improve problem solving in real world knowledge application situations. We further argue that e-CASE can help bridging the contextual distance in the domain of software development, (a) by integrating appropriate external representations for supporting students' efficient processing of the contextualized material, and (b) by supporting the development of an extended learning community offering flexible and instructionally efficient connection between the traditional educational setting and the workplace.

Acknowledgements

This research is partly funded by the European "Kaleidoscope Network of Excellence" project (contract number 507838).

References

1. Spiro, R.J., Jehng, J.: Cognitive flexibility and hypertext: Theory and technology for the non-linear and multidimensional traversal of complex subject matter. In: Nix, D., Spiro, R. (eds.): Cognition, Education, and Multimedia. Ehrlbaum, Hillsdale NJ (1990)
2. Morrison, T.: Action Learning: A Handbook for Capacity Building Through Case-Based Learning. (2001). Retrieved December 11, 2001 in .pdf format from the Asian Development Bank Institute's Web site at http://www.adbi.org.
3. Duch, B.J., Groh, S.E., Allen, D.E.: Why Problem-Based Learning? A Case study of institutional change in undergraduate education. In: Duch, B.J., Groh, S.E., Allen, D.E. (eds.): The Power of Problem-Based Learning. Stylus, Sterling Virginia (2001) 3-11
4. Kokinov, B.: A Dynamic Approach to Context Modeling. In: Brezillon, P., Abu-Hakima S. (eds.): Proceedings of the IJCAI-95 Workshop on Modeling Context in Knowledge Representation and Reasoning. LAFORIA 95/11 (1995)
5. Ozturk, P., Aamodt, A.: A context model for knowledge-intensive case-based reasoning, Int. J. Human–Computer Studies 48 (1998) 331–355
6. Kokinov, B.: Dynamics and Automaticity of Context: A Cognitive Modeling Approach. In: Bouquet, P., Serafini, L., Brezillon, P., Benerecetti, M., Castellani, F. (eds.) : Modeling and Using Context. Lecture Notes in Artificial Intelligence, Vol. 1688. Springer, Berlin (1999)

7. Bargh, J.: The Four Horsemen of Automaticity: Awareness, Intention, Efficiency and Control in Social Cognition. In: Wyer, R. & Srull, Th. (eds.): Handbook of Social Cognition, Vol. 1. Basic Processes. 2nd Edition. Erlbaum, Hillsdale NJ (1994)
8. Kollar, I., Fischer, F.: Internal and external scripts in web-based collaborative inquiry learning. In: Gerjets, P., Kirschner, P. A., Elen, J., Joiner, R. (eds.): Instructional design for effective and enjoyable computer-supported learning. Proceedings of the first joint meeting of the EARLI SIGs "Instructional Design" and "Learning and Instruction with Computers". Knowledge Media Research Center Tübingen (2004) 37-47
9. Mäkitalo, K., Weinberger, A., Häkkinen, P., Järvelä, S., Fischer, F.: Epistemic cooperation scripts in online learning environments: Fostering learning by reducing uncertainty in discourse? Computers in Human Behavior 21 (2005) 603-622
10. Luckin R., Plowman L., Laurillard D., Stratford M., Taylor J., Corben S.: Narrative evolution: learning from students' talk about species variation, International Journal of Artificial Intelligence in Education 12 (2001) 100-123
11. Hachen, D.: Sociology cases database project. (1996). Retrieved January 16, 2001, from University of Notre Dame Web site at http://www.nd.edu/~dhachen/cases/
12. Kinzie, M.B., Hrabe, M.E., Larsen, V.A.: Exploring professional practice through an instructional design team case competition. Educational Technology Research & Development 46(1) (1998) 53-71
13. Jonassen, D.H.: Scaffolding diagnostic reasoning in case based learning environments. Journal of Computing in Higher Education. 8(1) (1996) 48-68
14. Demetriadis, S., Pombortsis, A.: Novice Student Learning in Case Based hypermedia Environment: A Quantitative Study. Journal of Educational Multimedia and Hypermedia 8(1) (1999) 241-269
15. Benham, M.K.P.: The practitioner-scholars' view of school change: A case-based approach to teaching and learning. Teaching and Teacher Education 12(2) (1996) 119-135
16. Ewusi-Mensah, K.: Software Development Failures. The MIT Press, Cambridge MA (2003)
17. Kaptelinin, V.: Computer-Mediated Activity: Functional Organs in Social and Developmental Contexts. In: Nardi B.A. (ed.): Context and Consciousness, Activity Theory and Human-Computer Interaction. The MIT Press, Massachusetts (1996)

Designing Mobile Learning Experiences

Giasemi Vavoula[1] and Charalampos Karagiannidis[2]

[1] Institute of Educational Technology, The Open University, UK
g.vavoula@open.ac.uk
[2] University of the Aegean, Department of Cultural Technology and Communication,
Mytilini, Lesvos Island, Greece
karagian@acm.org

Abstract. This paper reviews existing applications of mobile learning, and discusses some design issues for the development of mobile learning experiences.

1 Introduction

The emergence of the knowledge society poses new requirements for education and training: the knowledge-based economy requires a flexible, very well-trained workforce; and the citizens of the information society need to be continuously (re)trained in order to remain competitive within this workforce and to fully exploit the learning opportunities offered by the knowledge society for their personal development, fulfillment and enjoyment.

The rapid evolution of learning technologies – exploiting the respective developments in information and communication technologies (ICT) – create numerous new opportunities for meeting these requirements: web-based learning environments (learning management systems, learning content management systems, etc) deliver life-long education and training applications and services to *anyone, anytime, anyplace*. However, most of these applications realize a learning model that is rather "traditional" in nature: it is based on the notion of one (or more) tutors, who help learners acquire a specific body of knowledge (through learning material, learning activities, etc), which can be measured through specific assessment methods. Such a model does not fit instances of learning that occur in the process of specific problem solving in the course of everyday life: "When the person's central concern is a task or decision, he will not be very interested in learning a complete body of subject matter. Instead, he will want just the knowledge and skill that will be useful to him in dealing with the particular responsibility of the moment" ([1], pp. 51).

Recent developments in ICT, and especially in mobile and wireless technologies, facilitate the departure from traditional learning models, since learning can be easily "carried", and even embedded, into our everyday environment. The exploitation of this potential brings about a new era for learning: just-in-time, just-enough, on-demand personalized learning experiences, seamlessly integrated within our everyday activities.

This is the context where the paradigm of mobile learning is emerging. In the following section we present an overview of the current state-of-the-art in learning technologies and identify the gap that the emerging paradigm of mobile learning aims to fill in. We then introduce mobile learning and present a brief overview of the area in section 3. In section 4 we analyze the dimensions of, and discuss some design issues for mobile learning systems.

2 The Present: State-of-the-Art in Learning Technologies

Learning technologies[1] are attracting increasing interest worldwide, since they can meet the requirements of the knowledge society and knowledge-based economy for high-quality life-long learning. Over the past decades, a number of applications and services have been made available out of these efforts, reflecting, or even driving a paradigm shift in technology-enhanced learning: from computer-assisted learning, to web-based learning, to mobile learning.

Over the last decade, a major transformation has taken place due to the wide adoption of the internet. The main drivers for this transformation can be summarized as follows:[2]

- *demand*: rapid obsolescence of knowledge and training; need for just-in-time training delivery; search for cost-effective ways to meet learning needs of a globally distributed workforce; skills gap and demographic changes which drive the need for new learning models; demand for flexible access to lifelong learning; etc;
- *supply*: internet access is becoming standard at work and at home; advances in digital technologies enable the creation of interactive, media-rich content; increasing bandwidth and better delivery platforms make e-learning more attractive; a growing selection of high-quality e-learning products and services are made available; emerging technology standards facilitate compatibility and reusability of e-learning products; etc.

As a result, the interest in learning technologies in the past few years has turned mainly into:

- the *development* of learning *material*, *activities* and *software*, which is of high-quality, exploiting multimedia, interactive, immersive and mobile technologies and
- the *delivery* and *management* of such material, activities and software.

Figure 1 depicts the idea of learning content management systems (LCMSs), as they reflect the development, management and use stages of the learning technology development cycle. Re-usable learning objects ("any digital resource that can be reused to support learning"), learning activities, software, etc, are created by instructional designers, subject experts, or even learners and are published within a common repository, together with their description (which is based on a common format, e.g. through learning technologies specifications and standards, or following the specific conventions of a learning community). Learners and teachers can search this repository to retrieve, access and share learning objects according to their profile

---

[1] We use this term to refer to applications of ICT for learning.
[2] Source: SRI Consulting and WR Hambrecht + Co.

and learning objectives (which can also be described through a common format) and annotate and augment them with personal notes, ideas and interpretations and share them back with other learners and the community.

LCMSs offer a number of advantages, including: re-usability of learning material (facilitating the development of economies of scale), personalized access to learning material, just-in-time, on-demand and just-enough learning.

These developments facilitate the departure from a number of constraints, relating to time and place, as the learning resources become available at all times, outside classrooms or libraries. However, the current state-of-the-art still realizes a learning model which is rather "traditional" in nature: learners access a common repository to acquire a body of knowledge, which can be assessed against specific measures. This misses out the conversational and situational nature of learning and knowledge.

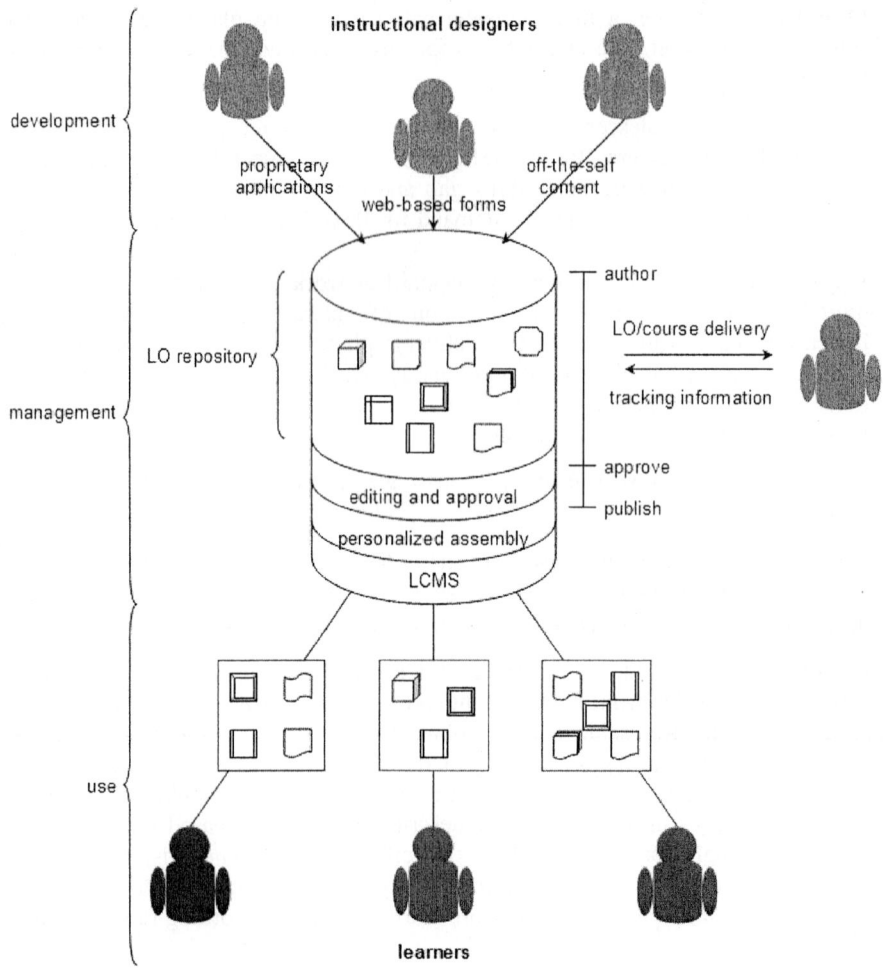

Fig. 1. Learning Content Management Systems (adopted from [2])

Moreover, a number of constraints are not yet overcome: learners need to be in specific places where they have internet access through a desktop or laptop machine.

The next section describes mobile learning, as the emerging paradigm that bares the potential to overcome some of these constraints: learners can learn anytime, anywhere, accessing location and context-specific learning resources as the need arises, in continuous contact and collaboration with fellow learners and tutors.

3 The Emerging Paradigm: Mobile Learning

Mobile learning is usually defined as learning that takes place via wireless devices, such as mobile phones, personal digital assistants, tablet computers, etc. That is, in most definitions encountered in the literature, it is only the employment of specific types of technology that seems to differentiate mobile learning from other forms of learning. However, when considering mobility from the learner's point of view, it can be argued that mobile learning can take place everywhere: pupils can revise for exams on the bus to school, doctors can update their medical knowledge while on hospital rounds, language students can improve their language skills while traveling abroad. In this context, a definition of mobile learning should therefore be widened to include any sort of learning that happens when the learner is not at a fixed, predetermined location, or learning that happens when the learner takes advantage of the learning opportunities offered by mobile technologies [3].

There are a number of reasons which make mobile technologies and devices attractive for learning, including: palmtops are relatively inexpensive, compared with full-sized desktop or laptop computers; they offer the possibility of ubiquitous computing; they facilitate access to information and promote the development of information literacy; they offer the possibility of collaborative learning and independent learning [3].

During the past few years, mobile devices and technologies have become mainstream and, as a result, a number of prototype learning applications have been deployed and tested in different contexts (extensive reviews are included in [3], [4], [5], [6]). Table 1 presents a categorization of such applications according to their underlying learning model, based on [5].

The above description demonstrates that learning and teaching with mobile technologies is beginning to make a breakthrough from small-scale pilots to institution-wide implementations. A number of key issues need to be taken into account in the development of these implementations, which can be summarized as follows:

- *context*: gathering and utilizing contextual information may clash with the learner's wish for anonymity and privacy;
- *mobility*: the ability to link to activities in the outside world also provides students with the capability to "escape" the classroom and engage in activities that do not correspond with either the teacher's agenda or the curriculum;
- *learning over time*: effective tools are needed for the recording, organization and retrieval of (mobile) learning experiences;

Table 1. Review of Mobile Technologies for Learning (adopted from [5])

Theme	Key Theorists	Activities	Example Systems
Behaviorist learning	Skinner, Pavlov	– drill and feedback – classroom response systems	– Skills Arena: a mathematics video game where drills in addition and subtraction are presented as a game with advanced scoring and recordkeeping, character creation and variable difficulty level – BBC Bitesize: provides revision materials via mobile phones; it has been running since 2003 and has proved to be very popular (over 650,000 GCSE students, as well as a number of curious adult learners) – m-phones for language learning: SMS is used as part of an English language course, where students receive frequent vocabulary messages (which also act as reminders to revise) – classroom response systems: e.g. Classtalk which engages students in communication with the classroom, for articulating and presenting their ideas
Constructivist learning	Piaget, Bruner, Papert	– participatory simulations	– the virus game: each student wears a badge-tag which shows whether they are "infected"; students can watch the "spread of the disease", through their communication – savannah: students play the role of lions roaming in the wild in an area 100m x 50m; each student carries a PDA that gives them a "window" into the gameworld, displaying content and actions that were appropriate to their current location and what was going on in the rest of the game – environmental detectives: a scenario was built around a spill of a toxin; students develop a suitable remediation plan, assisted by their PDAs which allow them virtual activities based on their virtual location
Situated learning	Lave, Brown	– problem and case-based learning – context awareness	– ambient wood: integrates physical and digital interaction; digital information is coupled with novel arrangements of electronically-embedded physical objects; a series of activities are designed around the topic of habitats, focusing on the plants and animals in the different habitats of woodland and the relationships between them – natural science learning: a butterfly-watching system; a database of different butterfly species is used with a content-based image retrieval system; students visit a butterfly farm, take photographs of the butterflies and query the database for possible matches

Table 1. Review of Mobile Technologies for Learning (adopted from [5]) continued

Theme	Key Theorists	Activities	Example Systems
Situated learning (continued)	Lave, Brown	– problem and case-based learning – context awareness	– Tate modern: allows visitors to view video and still images, listen to expert commentary and reflect on their experience by answering questions or mixing a collection of sound clips to create their own soundtrack for an artwork; the wireless network is location-sensitive, which means that users do not have to search out the information – MOBIlearn: context-awareness is being explored, not just as a way to deliver appropriate content, but to enable appropriate actions and activities, including interactions with other learners in the same or similar contexts
Collaborative learning	Vygotsky	– mobile computer-supported collaborative learning (MCSCL)	– MCSCL: activities are distributed through the teacher's hand-held device; the teacher downloads the activity from the project website and then transmits the activity to the students; the students are automatically assigned to collaborative groups; upon completion of the activity, the teacher's Pocket PC collects the students work, which can then be downloaded to the school's PC for analysis
Informal and lifelong learning	Eraut	– supporting intentional and accidental learning episodes	– m-learn: mobile technology to teach basic literacy and numeracy skills; custom content was created, for example an urban soap opera about two characters moving into a flat for the first time to help with language and provide advice about how to set up a home – breast cancer care: delivers personalized education of breast cancer patients; the users can query specific subject knowledge bases through a content specialist, to gain the information they need
Learning and teaching support	n/a	– personal organization – support for administrative duties (e.g. attendance)	– student learning organizer: an integrated suite of software tools enabling students to create, delete and view timetable events and deadlines, as well as download course material packages – support for teachers and administrators: managing teachers' workloads and supporting teaching and learning – SMS supports computing students at risk: develops, delivers and evaluates blending learning opportunities that exploit SMS, WAP and VLE technologies; students use SMS text messaging, receive noticeboard information such as room changes, appointments, feedback and exam tips via SMS

- *informality*: students may abandon their use of certain technologies if they perceive their social networks to be under attack; and
- *ownership*: students want to own and control their personal technology, but this presents a challenge when they bring it in to the classroom [5].

The following section scrutinizes the process of designing mobile learning applications and lists related, more specific, design issues that need to be addressed.

4 Mobile Learning Design Issues

A number of issues need to be taken into account when designing mobile learning applications. For example, the rapid advancements in mobile technology, the general incompatibility between devices, operating systems and applications, and the limited resources in relation to desktop technologies, make the choice of mobile technologies and infrastructures a very important decision.

In the following we examine the main dimensions of mobile learning systems in relation to (currently available) technologies, and suggest corresponding checklists to inform and evaluate design choices.

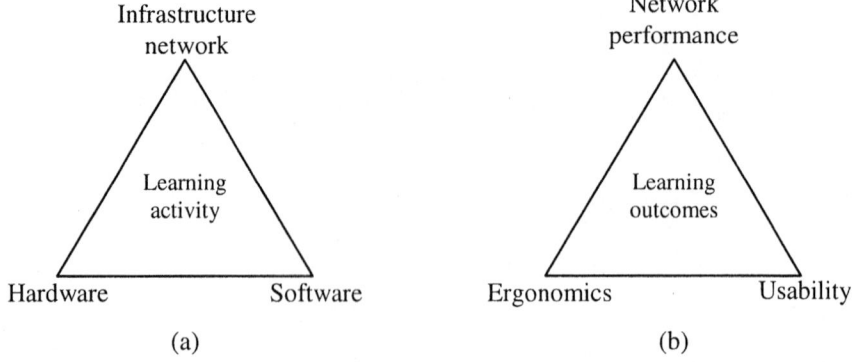

Fig. 2. Dimensions for the (a) design and (b) evaluation of mobile learning systems

As Figure 2 depicts, the choices of infrastructure networks, hardware and software are interdependent and intertwined with the design of the learning activities.

The design of the learning activities for mobile learning is governed by the same principles as the design of any other technology based learning activities, and the choice of the type of activity to implement has to be guided by the learning objectives. What the designer needs to bear in mind is that they design for the learning, not for the technology. The use of (mobile) technology is not the objective; rather, it is a means to enable activities that were otherwise not possible, or to increase the benefits for the learner(s). It is possible that the use of mobile technologies is suitable for only a part of the learning activity, whereas other parts are better supported by other technologies – or even by no technology at all.

The infrastructure network component includes decisions about the selection of communication networks and, in the case of location-aware applications, the selection of positioning systems. The available communication networks include satellites, mobile telephony, wireless local networks, personal ad-hoc networks, etc. The selection of an infrastructure network is informed by the number of users, the need for range, connectivity and data access, the time and place of use, possible interference with other devices, security requirements, the costs to the provider and/or the user and the network configuration.

The available positioning technologies include infrared, Bluetooth, WiFi and Ultra Wide Band, radio frequency systems such as GPS and RFID and hybrid radio frequency systems that make use of ultrasound (for a concise review see [7]). The selection of a positioning technology is informed by the requirements for precision (for example, the requirements are looser for outdoors than indoors applications), the need for real-time positioning, and whether the location tracking is automatic (e.g. the user is continuously tracked) or user-initiated (e.g. the user deliberately declares their position using, for example, RFID tags/readers).

With regard to the hardware, there is a wide range of mobile devices to choose from including laptops/notebooks, tablet computers, personal digital assistants (PDAs) and smart phones. The selection of a device depends on the requirements for processing power, battery life, robustness and ergonomics factors (for example, whether the user has only one or both hands available, if they are moving or standing still, the weight they can bear, environmental factors such as temperature and noise, etc.). Another issue that needs to be taken into account is the management of the hardware, especially in the case where it is provided by an educational institution as part of a course: are the devices for individual or for group use? Can the learners take the devices home? Who is responsible for damage? Etc.

Related to hardware are also the sensors and probes often used in context-aware mobile learning applications [8]. Context-awareness in mobile learning enables the delivery of context-specific content, options and services [9]. Available context attribute sensors include environmental sensors for measuring, for example, light, sound, atmospheric elements, pressure, humidity, precipitation and air temperature; activity sensors for recognizing, for example, body and eye movement, touch and limb orientation; and body sensors for measuring, for example, heart rate, blood pressure and brain activity (ECG). The type of sensors to use depends on the context attributes that are judged relevant to the learning experience.

With regard to the software a great challenge lies in the design of the user interface, the help system and the interaction. The typically small screen size and limited processing power limit designer choices and resources. Example interfaces are map-, menu-, voice-, text-based – and many more. Nielsen's usability heuristics [10] offer a good summary of the desired attributes of user interfaces.

The help system is there to provide easy recovery from errors and faults, to assist in the performance of all functions (trivial or not), to adapt to the user and their actions. Possible components to incorporate in a help system include tutorials, FAQ lists, troubleshooting guides, hypertext documentation, etc. Issues to consider are the accuracy and completeness of the content, the appropriateness of the structure, the appearance, and the extent to which the help system adapts to the user.

To design the interactions, we need to study the users, their activities and their environment in relation to the learning activity. For example, the use 'on the go'

Table 2. Designer checklists for components of mobile learning systems

	Component	Example choices	Checklist	Technical Evaluation
Activity	Learning activity	Drill-and-practice, problem-based learning, classroom response, etc	Learning objectives	Relative learner performance
Infrastructure	Communications Network	Satellites, mobile telephony, WLAN, personal ad-hoc, etc	Number of users, Range coverage, Connectivity and data access, Time and place of use, Interference, Security, Costs, Configuration, Management	Reliability, Security, Quality of service, Seamlessness
	Positioning System	Infrared, Bluetooth, WiFi, Ultra Wide Band, RF (GPS, RFID), Hybrid RF, etc	Precision, Real-time, Automatic vs. user-initiated	
Hardware	Devices	Laptops/notebooks, tablets, PDAs, smart phones, etc	Processing power, Battery life, Robustness, Ergonomics	Ergonomics, Robustness, Performance, Accuracy, Reliability, Unobtrusiveness
	Sensors and probes	Environmental sensors (sensors for light, wind, CO, Radon, sound, pressure, humidity, precipitation, air temperature, smoke), Activity sensors (movement, touch, accelerometers, eye-trackers, skin conductance, limb orientation), Body sensors (heart rate, blood pressure, blood composition, exhaled air composition, ECG, EEG), etc	Required context attributes	Ergonomics, Robustness, Performance, Accuracy, Reliability, Unobtrusiveness
Software	Interface	Map-based, menus, voice, textual, etc	System status visibility, match with real world, user control, consistency and standards, error prevention, recognition, flexibility, aesthetics	Usability: learnability, performance, effectiveness, error tolerance and recovery, user satisfaction
	Help system	Tutorials, FAQs, troubleshooting, hypertext-based documentation, etc	Content, Structure, Appearance, Dynamics and adaptivity	
	Interaction	Speech interface, handwriting, etc	User needs, Privacy, Ownership, Context of use (environment and activity)	

means limited ability for scrolling, possible use with only one hand available, possible need for use in 'silent' mode and possible need for synchronization. Especially when the mobile application is for young children, the designer needs to remember their limited skills in hand-eye coordination and in the manipulation of small objects. Example interaction techniques make use of speech, handwriting, haptics, etc.

An important step in the design of mobile learning applications, as in any other type of application, is the continuous evaluation and re-design. Figure 2 illustrates the dimensions towards which mobile learning systems need to be evaluated, in correspondence to the design dimensions. The outcomes of the learning activity need to be evaluated against preset educational objectives, using appropriate evaluation instruments (questionnaires, quiz, drill-and-practice, etc.). The evaluation needs to compare the performance of the learner(s) before and after the mobile learning activity; and also the performance of the learner(s) who used the mobile learning application against other learner(s) who did not use it. The infrastructure network needs to be evaluated for its reliability, security, quality of service and seamlessness. The hardware needs to be evaluated with regard to ergonomics issues, including comfortable use (appropriate form, size, etc.) during the supported activities in the specified context of use, and also with regard to robustness, performance, reliability, unobtrusiveness and, in the case of sensors and probes, accuracy. The software needs to be evaluated with regard to its usability and more specifically its learnability, performance, effectiveness, error tolerance and recovery, and user satisfaction.

Table 2 summarizes the above design issues for mobile learning.

5 Conclusions

Mobile learning is an important area for research and development, as it offers new forms of communication, collaboration and learning that were not possible a few years ago. Mobile technologies have become widely available and affordable only in the recent years, therefore few commercial educational applications are currently available. We can expect rapid developments in mobile learning as the technology offers greater range at lower prices.

This paper discusses some issues that designers of mobile learning experiences need to take into account when making design choices - most of them being rather technological. However, apart from the technological issues, the full exploitation of mobile technologies, especially from a pedagogical point of view, requires a sound theoretical basis which is rather not available today: as Falk and Dierking argue, "most of what is known about learning is based on studies from either classrooms or psychology laboratories, and so may be inappropriate as a basis for considering learning outside of these settings" [11]. This is clearly not in line with the new opportunities offered by mobile technologies, therefore new learning theories and instructional models may need to be developed, which can form the educational and social basis for the delivery of effective mobile learning experiences.

References

1. Tough, A.: The Adult's Learning Projects: a Fresh Approach to Theory and Practice in Adult Learning. Toronto: Ontario Institute for Studies in Education (1971).
2. Nichani, M.: LCMS = LMS + CMS [RLOs]. elearningpost (2001) Electronically available at http://www.elearningpost.com/features/archives/001022.asp.
3. O'Malley, C., Vavoula, G., Glew, J., Taylor, J., Sharples, M., Lefrere, P.: Guidelines for Learning, Teaching and Tutoring in a Mobile Environment. MOBIlearn Project Deliverable D4.1 (2003).
4. Gay, G., Rieger, R., Bennington, T.: Using Mobile Computing to Enhance Field Study: In Proceedings International Conference on Computer-Supported Collaborative Learning, Boulder, CO, USA (2002).
5. Naismith, L., Lonsdale, P., Vavoula, G., Sharples, M.: Literature Review in Mobile Technologies and Learning, NESTA FutureLab Report (2005).
6. Savill-Smith, C., Kent, P.: The Use of Palmtop Computers for Learning: A Review of the Literature. Learning and Skills Development Agency Research Report (2003).
7. Dempsey, M.: Indoor Positioning Systems in Healthcare: a basic overview of technologies. Radianse Inc White Paper (2003).
8. Rudman, P. Sensing the world – what's 'sensable'. Electronically available at http://www.dcs.gla.ac.uk/~rudmanp/Documents/Sensable.pdf
9. Lonsdale, P., Baber, C., Sharples, M., Byrne, W., Arvanitis, T., Brundell, P., and Beale, H. Context awareness for MOBIlearn: creating an engaging learning experience in an art museum. In Proceedings of MLEARN 2004, Bracciano, Rome, LSDA (2004).
10. Neislen, J.: Usability Heuristic Evaluation. In Nielsen, J., Mack, R.L. (Eds.). Usability Inspection Methods. John Wiley & Sons, New York, NY (1994).
11. Falk, J., Dierking L.: Lessons Without Limit: How Free-Choice Learning is Transforming Education. AltaMira Press (2002).

From e-Business to Business Transformation[*]
(Extended Abstract)

Christos Nikolaou[1,2], Jakka Sairamesh[2], and Markus Stolze[2]

[1] Department of Computer Science, University of Crete, Greece
nikolau@csd.uoc.gr
[2] IBM T.J. Watson Research Center, Hawthorne, NY 10532, US
jramsh@us.ibm.com, mrs@zurich.ibm.com

Now that the first wave of excitement on e-commerce has subsided, and after the sobering experience of the dot-com bubble burst, there is a growing understanding that e-commerce is not about a different way of doing commerce, and e-business is not about a different way of doing business. E-Business is about doing business – in a better, more competitive and productive way. To improve business, one has to transform business and the processes that it uses.

Globalization of the world economy has led to an increased ability of companies to spread the planning, design, manufacturing and distribution functions of their products and services around the globe. Rapid technological advances and the complexity of the design and manufacturing of products in a wide range of industries (electronics, car manufacturing, aerospace, retail, etc.) have pushed to the modularization of corporate functions, see [1]. Modularization has led to increased autonomy of the modules-functions even within the same multinational corporation. Moreover, as competition intensifies and becomes global, corporations are protecting what they consider as their core competencies. These competencies are also called in the literature the strategic differentiators of a company. In addition, they are willing to shed modules that are not differentiating them and are not competitive enough, and ally themselves with best-of-breed companies that can supply the functionality of these modules in an optimal or near-optimal fashion. For example, when Mercedes-Benz planned their new sport-utility vehicle assembly plant in Alabama, they structured the whole supply system into modules, and they assigned the entire driver's cockpit as a module to a nearby plant owned by Delphi Automotive Systems, a spin-off of the General Motors Corporation (see [1]). Corporations are also willing to "mutate" their strategic differentiators to serve "nearby" markets, thereby taking advantage of innovation in their field and emerging new niche markets. The disaggregation of until now vertically organized companies and industries has led to the emergence of value nets and of business ecosystems.

Emerging technologies such as RFID for all kinds of sensing and tracking, web service composition and workflows, business process modeling, supply chain optimization techniques, data mining technologies to detect emerging new patterns, etc. have increasingly penetrated all parts of a value network lifecycle. However, despite the significant progress made in the use of technology for transforming or creating value nets, critical questions remain open:

---

[*] Invited paper.

- How do value net companies sense and quickly react to challenges from innovators in the markets the net serves, how is the value net transformed, including its own products and services, and how can it monitor and evaluate the performance of these strategic changes?
- Innovation not only creates new markets, it may also radically transform the way a business process is executed. How can a company or a value net detect this on time, and quickly transform its business processes so as to stay competitive?
- Is it possible to move from KPIs and future market indicators to business strategy, then to business processes and finally to their implementation through human and software agents and then back again to monitor and evaluate process performance against the KPIs, in an automatic or even semi-automatic way? Notice that this should be done not for a single company but for a group of companies belonging to a value net, with possibly conflicting KPIs.
- How does one devise strategies for companies to follow, which will allow them to decide which value net(s) to join? How do companies in a value net decide whether or not to accept a newcomer? Notice that IT (strategic) outsourcing and Business Process Transformation Services (BPTS), see [2], are special cases of these more general questions.
- Strategic vs. "Grounded" Innovation: most of the discussion about "On Demand Business" and "Business Process Management" is strongly influenced by the assumption that the direction and impulse for innovation comes top down. Management changes the business strategy to respond to new market situations or analysis of the CBM of the organization. The question then is how to communicate and implement the new strategy given the corporate culture, organization and IT landscape. Another (maybe less fundamental but equally important) direction of innovation is bottom up. The help desk people hear from unhappy customers, people in the production observe ineffective processes, efficiency and quality of some processes have high (unexplained) variance. This is the area of quality management, lean sigma, etc. Here the basic question is how to enable employees to see the business impact of their actions and how to empower them to collaborate to continuously improve their performance. We call this the "grounded" approach to innovation as suggestions for change will be grounded in the experience and observations of the employees and the ideas for improvements will equally be grounded in what they know. The challenge here is more to provide employees with visibility of their impact, with sensible benchmarks and with knowledge of best practices and possible improvements.
- Trust management and security policy issues: the extra value created for value nets both for the value net partners themselves and for their customers is the tight linkage of the partners achieved within the value net. This presupposes a high level of trust between the partners, which has to be built-up as the value net evolves, and could be easily destroyed if one of the partners behaves unreliably, or even maliciously. Therefore, trust building and relationship monitoring is an important operational issue of every value net.

We are proposing a theoretical framework for estimating the value of a value net. Through this framework, we are also proposing a methodology for addressing the issues listed above and for guiding the transformation of the value net and of its business processes, all with the general objective of achieving a higher overall value for the value net.

References

1. Carliss Y., Clark Kim B., "Managing in an Age of Modularity", *in* Harvard Business Review on Managing the Value Chain, Harvard Business School Press, 2000.
2. Torto Stephanie, M., Danilenko Anna, "IBM's Next Big Bet: Business Performance Transformation Services", December 2004, IDC #32666, Volume: 1, Tab: Vendors.

Trust, Privacy and Security in E-Business: Requirements and Solutions

Sokratis K. Katsikas[1], Javier Lopez[2], and Günther Pernul[3,*]

[1] Dept. of Information & Communication Systems Engineering,
University of the Aegean, Greece
ska@aegean.gr
[2] Dept. of Languages and Computation Sciences, University of Malaga, Spain
jlm@lcc.uma.es
[3] Dept. of Management Information Systems, University of Regensburg, Germany
guenther.pernul@wiwi.uni-regensburg.de

Abstract. An important aspect of e-business is the area of e-commerce. One of the most severe restraining factors for the proliferation of e-commerce, is the lack of trust between customers and sellers, consumer privacy concerns and the lack of security measures required to assure both businesses and customers that their business relationship and transactions will be carried out in privacy, correctly, and timely. This paper considers trust privacy and security issues in e-commerce applications and discusses methods and technologies that can be used to fulfil the pertinent requirements.

1 Introduction

Diffusion, general availability, and the benefits of information and communication technologies are rapidly changing our society, economy, and the way we do business. Digital business is much more than just buying and selling over the Net: digital business means doing business electronically, both within enterprises and externally, using computer networks or telecommunications. As such it includes any transaction completed over a computer-mediated network that transfers or supports the transfer of "value" for goods and services sold including property rights, like ownership of, or rights to make use of the goods or services.

An important aspect of digital business is the area of electronic commerce. The current state of e-commerce is a good example that the supporting technology has not yet reached its full potential. During the late 90's there were a lot of predictions about how e-commerce would develop in the near future. For example, in 1999 Forrester Research predicted a volume of US$ 184 billion of US online retail sales in 2004 [1] whereas the actual value is only approximately US$ 69 billion [2], representing a big gap of almost 167 %. One of the major reasons for the gap between predicted value and actual development that has been suggested by the research community and backed by many studies is simply the lack of *trust, privacy and security in digital business*.

---
* Authors' names in alphabetical order.

In order for digital business to reach its full potential the obvious conclusion is that either companies involved need to increase the level of confidence and trust provided by them to their customers or technologies need to be created having strong built-in features to protect the individuals' privacy and the security of the digital business transaction.

Because these areas transcend any single function or discipline within digital business, it is necessary to develop a global view. In this paper we are discussing the major issues involved. We will start with a general discussion on trust issues, followed by a discussion on the general meaning of privacy and privacy enforcing technologies and will conclude with the current major fields related to providing the security of the underlying technical infrastructures for digital business. Of importance are also complex psychological and social aspects how people react towards risks but due to lack of space they had to be omitted from our discussion.

2 Trust

Trust is a core issue in every business transaction. When considering an Internet-based scenario, this issue becomes extremely essential and, as we will see later, its definition is not trivial. Moreover, in order for Internet-based digital business to achieve similar levels of acceptance as traditional commerce, trust needs to become a built-in part of electronic transactions.

This is not easy because customers tend to perceive the Internet as a more or less anarchic environment that not only can provide good business liaisons but also multiple potential threats. It seems that it does not matter that the number of transactions where dishonest behaviour is detected is negligible in comparison with the number of transactions where the behaviour of participant is totally honest. Consumers and merchants are still worried about the threats, and their lack of trust has a negative influence on the wide deployment of the technology.

The problem becomes bigger if we consider the problem of the everyday more distributed nature of Internet commerce applications, where trust relationships of a specific user with other entities, companies, organizations, etc. differ depending on many different parameters. Moreover, recent pervasive aspects of the network itself provide new considerations to bear in mind [3].

2.1 Meaning of Trust

Different definitions of trust have been proposed in the literature during the last years. Some authors have tried to define the concept of trust in a global or general way, while others have defined it attending to the relation with specific types of applications.

One of the first attempts to define the concept of trust in e-commerce can be found in [4], where trust in a system is defined as "a belief that is influenced by the individual's opinion about certain critical system features". As pointed out in [5], that definition "concentrated on human trust in electronic commerce, but did not address trust between the entities involved in an e-commerce transaction".

In fact, Grandison and Sloman in [5] argue that the lack of consensus with regards to trust led them to use the terms trust, authorization, and authentication interchangeably. Further, they define trust as "the firm belief in the competence of an entity to act dependably, securely, and reliably within a specified context (assuming dependability covers reliability and timeliness)". Similarly, they define distrust as "the lack of firm belief in the competence of an entity to act dependably, securely, and reliably within a specified context."

2.2 Relation with Authentication and Authorization

Trust, authorization and authentication can not be used interchangeably because authorization and authentication have to be considered as basic security services of applications, while trust can not be considered as a basic security service but as an outcome resulting as a combination of the appropriate use of basic services.

Additionally, we also agree on the importance given to authentication and authorization, as both services are essential to get trust from consumers and merchants. In this sense, the concept of digital certificate has risen as a technical solution that greatly contributes to increase trust on the e-commerce security technology in general, and on authentication and authorization services in particular.

Identity certificates (or *public-key certificates*) provide the best solution to integrate the authentication service into most applications developed for the Internet that make use of digital signatures [6]. However, new applications, particularly in the area of digital business, need an authorization service to describe what a user is allowed to do. In this case privileges to perform tasks should be considered. *Attribute certificates* provide an appropriate solution, as these data objects have been designed for use in conjunction with identity certificates [7].

It is widely known that the use of a wide-ranging authentication service based on identity certificates is not practical unless it is complemented by an efficient and trustworthy means to manage and distribute all certificates in the system. This is provided by a *Public-Key Infrastructure* (PKI), which at the same time supports encryption, integrity and non-repudiation services. Without its use, it is impractical and unrealistic to expect that large scale digital signature applications can become a reality.

Similarly, the attribute certificates framework provides a foundation upon which a *Privilege Management Infrastructure* (PMI) can be built. PKI and PMI infrastructures are linked by information contained in the identity and attribute certificates of every user. The link is justified by the fact that authorization relies on authentication to prove who you are, but it is also justified by the fact that the combined use of both types of certificates contribute to increase users' trust. Although linked, both infrastructures can be autonomous, and managed independently. Creation and maintenance of identities can be separated from PMI, as authorities that issue certificates in each of both infrastructures are not necessarily the same ones. In fact, the entire PKI may be existing and operational prior to the establishment of the PMI.

2.3 Trust Management

When dealing with trust issues in e-commerce, its management is probably the most difficult problem to face. Blaze et al. introduced [8] the notion of trust management.

In that original work they proposed the PolicyMaker scheme as a solution for trust management purposes. KeyNote was proposed [9] to improve two main aspects of PolicyMaker: to achieve standardization and to facilitate its integration into applications.

Afterwards, other similar systems have been proposed for trust management purposes. As argued in [5], a common problem is that those solutions are used to identify a static form of trust (usually at the discretion of the application coder). However, trust can change with time, and that is the reason why it is generally considered that digital certificates (identity and attribute) can be also considered for trust management purposes. More precisely, the infrastructures used to manage those certificates, PKIs and PMIs, provide procedures and functions that can be seen as an advanced method to manage trust. These are better solutions than the ones mentioned in the previous paragraph in the sense that are less static, but they are too biased towards authentication and authorization services.

In fact, trust management is tremendously dynamic, especially in digital business scenarios. Dillon et al [10] have elaborated on this issue. In their work, they argue that trust of one entity in another changes with a number of factors. Additionally, they define the dynamic nature of trust as "the change in the trustworthiness value of an entity, assigned to it by a given trusting entity with the passage of time in different time slots".

3 Privacy

In the digital business arena privacy is usually related to the use of customer information. Transacting typically makes the exchange of large amounts of personal data necessary. This may either be necessary for the e-business transaction itself (for example: credit card information, banking account details, delivery details) or desired by the e-business partner: collecting customer data that later may be analyzed, shared with other businesses or even be sold. Altogether, privacy in our context may be defined as the individual right of humans to determine, when, how, and to what extent information is collected about them during the course of the digital business transaction; the right to be aware and to control the beginning of any interaction or data gathering process; and the right to choose when, how, and to what extent their personal information is made available to others.

At a first glance the two viewpoints, the first one supporting a corporate view and favouring the business interests and thereby strengthening the global economy, and the second one supporting the individuals view seem to be mutually exclusive. In practice, however, we face the need to reach a compromise and to arrive at a solution that is mutually beneficial to all. In the literature such a compromise is called *consumer-centric privacy*: for the individual this means to gain the maximum amount of privacy and for the e-businesses through the maximisation of privacy for their customers to gain substantial economic benefit. The economic benefit may be resulting from direct effects, like the improvement of the public image of the vendors (resulting in additional customers and in long lasting trust relationships) or from side effects, like improved brand recognition or more generally, a reduced trust barrier (as discussed in the introduction), leading to an increased e-commerce level and making many more individuals comfortable participating in digital business.

3.1 Methods to Preserve Privacy

These methods can generally be placed in three categories: privacy through legislation, privacy through organizational means, and privacy through technology. Combining solutions from the different fields may also be applicable.

Privacy Through Legislation

Governments in many countries have established legislation in order to protect consumers. Moreover, international guidelines, treaties, convention and regulation are also in place.

In the age of digital business, technology has advanced so far and so fast that the approach of protecting privacy through legal regulations is no longer as effective as it was in the past. Legislators are often far behind the new developments and the legal systems are not fast enough to properly react. Additionally, laws are generally country- specific. This means that a customer from a country that protects his privacy does purchase in a web store in a country without similar regulations does only have little or does not have any protection at all.

Privacy Through Organizational Means

Both the shop owners as well as the users have simple organizational means that considerably help in protecting the privacy of individuals during digital business. For example, consumer data can be physically separated into personally identifiable and non-identifiable information. Of course, it should not be possible to combine the separated data buckets.

Another organizational means is to involve into the business transaction a third party transaction service. Such a service would act as a trusted intermediary that guarantees the outcome of the transaction. Other organizational means to increase trust and privacy are delivering some sort of belief to the consumer that a merchant complies with a certain privacy policy. This may be achieved by privacy seals issued by a trusted authority (for example TRUSTe, the "online privacy seal") or through technologies such as the Platform for Privacy Preferences (P3P), that allow customers to evaluate whether the published privacy policy of the business satisfies their own preferences. However, both approaches do mainly show the awareness of a business of their customers' privacy concerns; they cannot guarantee that the business actually will behave as expected.

Privacy Through Technology

Privacy Enhancing Technologies (PET) attempt to achieve anonymity by providing unlinkability between an individual and any of their personal data. Several levels of anonymity have been defined in the literature, ranging from full anonymity (no one can find out who you really are) to pseudo-anonymity (the identity is generally not known but may be disclosed if necessary) to pseudonymity (several virtual identities can be created and used under different situations). Anonymity can be achieved by either anonymising the transport medium, or by allowing anonymous access, or by using statistical databases.

Technologies for anonymising the transport medium aim at hiding the original identity of the consumer in a way that his identity cannot be revealed. One of the simplest possible ways to achieve this for a user is to simply set up an account with a free email service provider the user trusts that they will not log communication details. Another possibility is to use an anonymising server. When an individual is using such a service, all communications are routed through the anonymising server, thus the recipient has no way to determine the IP address or the identity of the user.

A further step in technical complexity is a setting without a trusted third-party. Crowds [15] groups users into large groups (crowds) and instead of directly connecting requests to a web site, the system passes it to the crowd. There the request passes a randomized number of crowd members and finally is submitted to the recipient who is not able to identify who in the crowd is the originator of the request. Another well-known and prominent technology is Chaum Mixes [16], whereby messages of equal size are cryptographically changed and finally delivered to the recipients in different order. Chaum Mixes have been extended by onion routing protocols, which use a network of dynamically changing mixes and the user submits a request in form of a data structure reminding on the layers of an onion.

In systems allowing anonymous access to a service, users are known only by a pseudonym (credential) to the organization they are doing business with. A single user can use different pseudonyms which cannot be linked to each other.

Related to anonymous access is the use of an authentication and authorisation infrastructure (AAI). Such infrastructures arose from the fact that it is not always necessary to exactly know who a user is but sufficient to know that the user is authorized to perform a certain action. Often this is outsourced to another organization, which is responsible for registering users, user authentication and equipping users with proper credentials. This of course implies that the AAI is trusted to the organization relying on such services. Different types of AAIs and their use are surveyed in [17].

A statistical database is a data collection, for example all customers and their items bought but not revealing information that uniquely identifies the individuals. The value of such databases is the statistical information, not the data itself. Therefore, techniques are essential that can keep the statistics of the data set valid but keep the individuals data itself private. All these techniques have the disadvantage that they make the data less useful. Additionally, it has been shown that by repeating slightly changing queries database trackers revealing individuals' privacy may be constructed. Statistical databases have their potential in CRM (customer relationship management) and general data mining.

4 Security

Recognising the fact that, in any given e-commerce scenario, there are five interconnected and interacting components (people, software, hardware, procedures and data), one comes to the conclusion that e-commerce systems are (and should be looked upon as) information systems, comprising a technological infrastructure and an organisational framework, rather than pure technological infrastructure. Therefore, addressing the problem of security in e-commerce must be done in an information system setting.

In such a setting, security can be defined as an organised framework consisting of concepts, beliefs, principles, policies, procedures, techniques, and measures that are required in order to protect the individual system assets as well as the system as a whole against any deliberate or accidental threat [18]. Operationally, in order to compile such a framework, the pertinent requirements must be identified first.

4.1 The Security Requirements

E-commerce applications may seem quite dissimilar, at a first glance. However, closer inspection reveals that there exist distinct phases in all of them, a fact that allows a generic model to be built, which can describe all of them. Such a model has been proposed in [19] for business transactions and has been shown [20] to be good for describing commercial transactions as well. In an exchange transaction, two parties, A and B, agree to and fulfill mutual conditions of satisfaction. The first party, A, is usually called the *customer* or *buyer*; the second, B, is usually called the *performer* or *seller*. B accepts A's request to provide something for A, in exchange for which A will provide a payment to B. The transaction can be visualized as a cycle of four phases:

- *Request:* A makes a request of B to provide the service. (Often this amounts to taking B up on an offer B has made).
- *Negotiation:* A and B come to an agreement on exactly what will be provided (A's condition of satisfaction) and what payment will be made (B's condition of satisfaction).
- *Performance:* B carries out the actions needed to fulfill his part of the bargain and notifies A when done.
- *Settlement:* A accepts B's work, declares it satisfactory, and pays.

The last two phases can be combined into one composite phase, called the *Execution* phase [21]. The model is good for any kind of transaction, not only electronic transactions.

During the Request phase, the buyer needs to be sure that an offer s/he is considering is valid, i.e. s/he has to be sure that the integrity of the information that is presented to her/him has not been compromised. On the other hand, the seller must be sure that the offer s/he makes is available to the buyer. If the transaction is not a retail one, the seller may want her/his offers to remain confidential to the buyer, lest any competitor interferes with the transaction. The need for confidentiality is also apparent, for both parties, in the Negotiation phase, in particular when this pertains to contract negotiations. Important in this phase is also the inability of either party to repudiate their offers. But non-repudiation is even more important in the last, the Execution, phase. In this phase, secure payment must also be ensured, as well as secure delivery of goods. Finally, observe that what is fundamentally different between e-commerce and traditional commerce is the absence of human face-to-face communication. Machines have no way of knowing who is *really* on the other end of the line once presented with pre-agreed information that convinces them of her/his identity.

Therefore, e-commerce security requirements revolve around the need to preserve the *confidentiality*, the *integrity* and the *availability* of information and systems, the *authenticity* of the communicating parties and the *non-repudiation* of transactions.

4.2 Addressing the Requirements

From a structural point of view, an efficient framework for preserving security in information systems comprises actions that are categorised as legal, technical, organisational and social. Legal actions consist of adopting suitable legislation; these should be and have been undertaken by governments at an international, national, and even local level. Technical and organisational actions need to be undertaken by individual organisations (or by bodies representing organisations of a similar nature and purpose). Last, but by no means least, social actions consist of enhancing the awareness of the public on the need for security and on their rights and obligations stemming from this need.

Even though there are numerous legal issues associated with e-commerce [22-23], the major ones are:

- The protection of privacy, an issue that has already been discussed previously.
- The protection of intellectual property rights. This entails the protection of copyrights for literary, musical, dramatic, and artistic works, as well as of sound recordings, films, broadcasts, and cable programs. It also entails the protection of trademarks, as domain names may be seen as a variation of such. Related to this is the problem of cybersquatting, i.e. the practice of registering domain names in order to sell them later at a higher price. Finally, protecting patents in e-commerce settings is also an issue. National legislation for the protection of intellectual property rights exists mostly everywhere [24]. At an international level, most prominent role is played by the World Intellectual Property Organization – WIPO, who is also administering a total of 23 relevant international treaties [25]. Similar is the situation with the protection of trademarks and patents.
- The protection of the right to free speech against the need to control offensive, illegal and potentially dangerous information. This includes the issue of controlling spam.
- The protection of both consumers and merchants against fraud. This entails the protection of all parties signing electronic contracts, protection against identity fraud, protection against computer crime, regulation of taxation, protection against money laundering etc.

Legislation exists for most of the above issues in a traditional commerce setting. However, it is not always straightforward to apply laws and regulations developed for such a setting in an e-commerce environment. Therefore, legal action in the direction of ensuring the applicability of existing and/or for developing new pertinent legislation is required.

From a conceptual point of view, the task of technically securing an information system can be broken down into securing its application and communication components. Applications are secured through the combined use of technologies including those for identification and authentication, identity management, access control and authorization, trusted operating systems, secure database systems, malware detection, data integrity preservation, intrusion detection and prevention, audit, and applied cryptology. On the other hand, communications are secured through the combined use of technologies including those for applied cryptology, firewalls, secure transactions, secure messaging, secure executable content, secure network management, network oriented intrusion detection and prevention, web access control, digital rights protection.

It can be seen, therefore, that all of the security requirements of e-commerce that we have identified can be addressed by a variety of technical measures, of differing strength and efficiency. Different measures can be and are used for different aspects of these requirements. However, the only measure that can adequately address all but one (the availability) of these requirements is encryption. This is why it deserves particular discussion in the current context.

The numbers of entities involved in e-commerce applications prohibits the use of symmetric encryption. Therefore, a more automated and consolidated approach is required, based on a Public Key Infrastructure (PKI) [26].

User requirements from a PKI have been recorded in several applications, and are, understandably, quite dissimilar. However, a common ground can be and has been found [27]. A comprehensive list of services that satisfy the above requirements can be found in [28]. The functions required to perform each of these services can subsequently be defined [28].

It appears, then, that we do know the way and we do have the technologies to solve most of the technical problems associated with securing e-commerce. If this was indeed the case, then all the real security breeches that we encounter everyday in e-commerce should not have been happening. What is, then, the problem?

The most usual problem is that, while everyone recognizes the need for securing e-commerce, what they do not know is that security is more than erecting physical and electronic barriers. The strongest encryption and most robust firewall are practically worthless without a set of organizational security measures, built around a security policy that articulates how these tools are to be used, managed and maintained. Such a policy concerns risks. It is high-level and technology neutral. Its purpose is to set directions and procedures, and to define penalties and countermeasures for non-compliance [29].

5 Conclusion

Even though there are useful laws focusing on several aspects of e-commerce trust, privacy and security, common agreements between the different countries are still missing. For the seller and the consumer engaged in digital business it should not make any difference, from a legal point of view, where the user, the e-business and any intermediary service is geographically located. Such an effort must start with a common agreement and understanding leading to an all-encompassing legal and moral protection of consumers' rights. In the past, legislators had to fight against specific violations as they appeared, resulting in a patchwork of various legal protections that only help to guard against isolated aspects of trust, privacy and security in digital business.

E-businesses should better support for third-party transaction services, trust infrastructure, privacy platforms and security solutions. Consumers should more carefully choose the services and products based on statements related to privacy and security and on the existence of certified characteristics, such as privacy or site authentication seals. This would increase acceptance of the seals and put some additional pressure on e-businesses to have their conformance with their published statements certified. However, privacy through organizational means does not actually enforce individual privacy. All approaches are only a help to guide decision-making about whom to trust. This is only a first step; technologies are needed that also attempt to enforce the preservation of privacy.

Current technologies make a significant achievement to preserving the trust, privacy and security in digital business. However, more research is needed to perform this automatically (without user involvement) and with less involvement of trusted third parties. Finally there is a need to develop technologies that better fit the general security requirements. In today's world strong anonymity is sometimes regarded as a potential risk to the security of the society or a country. Additional research is needed in order to understand how the two sets of conflicting requirements can be balanced and met under a single umbrella.

Overall, the issues of trust, privacy and security seem to be attractive to the research community at large, as demonstrated by the large number of contributions presenting recent developments in a number of specialized conferences (e.g. [30]-[31]).

References

1. Forrester Research. Post-web retail. Sept. 1999. http://forrester.com/.
2. US Census Bureau – http://www.census.gov/estats
3. B. Bhargava, L. Lilien, M. Winslett. Pervasive Trust. IEEE Intelligent Systems, pp. 74-77, September 2004.
4. Anil Kini, Joobin Choobineh: Trust in Electronic Commerce: Definition and Theoretical Considerations. HICSS (4) 1998: 51-61.
5. T. Grandison, M. Sloman. A Survey of Trust in Internet Applications. IEEE Communications Surveys & Tutorials, 2000.
6. ITU-T Recommendation X.509, "Information Technology - Open systems interconnection - The Directory: Authentication Framework", June 1997.
7. ITU-T Recommendation X.509, "Information Technology - Open systems interconnection - The Directory: Public-key and attribute certificate frameworks", March 2000.
8. M. Blaze, J. Feigenbaum, J. Lacy. Decentralized Trust Management. IEEE Symposium on Security and Privacy, pp.164-173, 1996.
9. M. Blaze, J. Feigenbaum, J. Ioannidis, A. Keromytis. The KeyNote Trust-Management System Version 2. RFC 2704, 1999.
10. 10.T. Dillon, E. Chang, F. Khadeer. Managing the Dynamic Nature of Trust. IEEE Intelligent Systems, pp. 79-82, September 2004.
11. R. Clarke. Internet Privacy Concerns Confirm the Case for Intervention. Comm. of the ACM. Vol. 42, No. 2, 1999.
12. W. Chung, J. Paynter. Privacy Issues on the Internet. Proc of the 35th Hawaii Int. Conf. on System Sciences. Jan. 2002.

13. M. Brown, R. Muchira. Investigating the relationship between Internet Privacy Concerns and Online Purchasing Behaviour. Journal of Electronic Commerce Research. Vol. 5, No. 1, 2004.
14. I. Araujo. Privacy Mechanisms supporting the building of trust in e-commerce. Proc. IEEE International Workshop on Privacy Data Management, Tokyo, Japan, April 2005.
15. M. K. Reiter, A. D. Rubin. Anonymous web transaction with Crowds. Comm. of the ACM. Vol. 42, No. 2, 1999.
16. 16.D. L. Chaum. Untraceable electronic mail, return address, and digital pseudonyms. Comm. of the ACM. Vol. 24, No. 2, 1981.
17. 17.J. Lopez, R. Oppliger, G. Pernul. Authentication and Authorization Infrastructures (AAIs): A Comparative Survey. Computers & Security Journal. Elsevier (North Holand), Vol. 23, 2004.
18. 18.E. Kiountouzis: Approaches to the security of information systems. In S. Katsikas, D. Gritzalis and S. Gritzalis (Eds.): Information Systems Security, New Technologies Publications, Athens, Greece, 2004 (In Greek).
19. 19.T. Winograd and F. Flores, *Understanding Computers and Cognition*, Addison-Wesley, 1997.
20. 20. P. J. Denning, "Electronic Commerce", in D. E. Denning & P. J. Denning (Eds), *Internet Besieged*, Addison-Wesley & ACM Press, 1998.
21. 21.G. Pernul, A. Rohm and G. Herrmann, "Trust for Electronic Commerce Transactions", in *Proceedings, ADBIS '99*, Springer-Verlag, 1999.
22. R. Burnett. Legal aspects of e-commerce. Computing & Control Engineering Journal, 2001.
23. E. Turban. Electronic Commerce A Managerial Perspective. Prentice Hall. 2004.
24. http://www.wipo.int/clea/en/index.jsp
25. http://www.wipo.int/treaties/en
26. A. Arsenault and S. Turner, IETF PKIX WG, Internet draft, Internet X.509 Public Key Infrastructure PKIX Roadmap, March 10, 2000.
27. D. Lekkas, S.K. Katsikas, D.D. Spinellis, P. Gladychev and A. Patel, "User Requirements of Trusted Third Parties in Europe", in Proceedings, User identification and Privacy Protection Joint IFIP WG 8.5 and WG 9.6 Working Conference, pp. 229-242, 1999.
28. S. Gritzalis, S.K.Katsikas, D. Lekkas, K. Moulinos, E. Polydorou, "Securing the electronic market: The KEYSTONE Public Key Infrastructure Architecture", Computers and Security, Vol. 19, no. 8, pp. 731-746, 2000.
29. S.K. Katsikas and S.A. Gritzalis. A Best Practice Guide for Secure Electronic Commerce. Upgrade, Vol. III, no.6, December 2002. http://www.upgrade-cepis.org. Also in Novatica Journal of the Associacion de Tecnicos de Informatica, http://www.ati.es/novatica. Also in Tecnoteca Online of ALSI, http://www.tecnoteca.it.
30. Sokratis K. Katsikas, Javier Lopez, Günther Pernul (Eds.): Trust and Privacy in Digital Business, First International Conference, TrustBus 2004, Zaragoza, Spain, August 30 - September 1, 2004, Proceedings. Lecture Notes in Computer Science 3184 Springer 2004
31. Sokratis K. Katsikas, Javier Lopez, Günther Pernul (Eds.): Trust, Privacy and Security in Digital Business, Second International Conference, TrustBus 2005, Copenhagen, Denmark, August 2005, Proceedings. Lecture Notes in Computer Science 3592, Springer 2005

Adoption of Enterprise Resource Planning Systems in Greece

Angeliki K. Poulymenakou and Spiros A. Borotis

Athens University of Economics and Business,
Department of Management Science and Technology,
ELTRUN – The eBusiness Center,
Organization Information Systems Group,
76 Patission Str., 10434, Athens, Greece
{akp, borotis}@aueb.gr

Abstract. Enterprise Resource Planning Systems (ERP) comprises the dominant business information systems currently implemented in the global market. In this survey, the authors explore the adoption of these systems in enterprises that operate in the Greek market. The scope of the adoption is focused on the level of business processes, in terms of the incentives and the real benefits, that ERP applications offer to enterprises. The survey indicated significant results in the areas of the transformation of incentives for adoption to actual benefits, and on the significance of business process reengineering before the implementation of the systems. Other interesting results are focused on the business use of those systems, the future enhancements, and their contribution in solving the issue of fragmentation of information in disparate legacy applications.

1 Introduction

Enterprise Resource Planning Systems (ERP) are commercial software packages that enable the integration of transactions-oriented data and business processes throughout an organization (and perhaps eventually throughout the entire interorganisational supply chain) [18]. This objective is primarily served through the extensive use of computer networks, database management systems, and information-related transaction processing subsystems. Moreover, ERP systems offer ready-to-use business scenarios, which facilitate the planning and management of business information. Subsequently, it is recognized that those systems model current working activities of every organization that adopts them. ERP applications contribute to the integration of information – solving the problem of "islands of automation" [1] – offer best practice solutions through predefined scenarios [25], and act also as tools for business management and planning. Moreover, they support the concept of horizontal organization structure, achieving the optimization of information flow, the automation of processes, and the improvement of monitoring. The standardization arising is codified in the term "business scenario".

Organizations nowadays, strive for flexibility and adaptability to changing market demands, in order to cope with the challenges that appear in the competitive business environment. In order to be successful in this effort, organizations must integrate business functions into a single system by efficiently utilizing information technology, and by sharing data with third-party vendors and customers [17]. Major organization functions integrated through ERP applications include sales, distribution, financial management, manufacturing, and human resources [2].

Reviewing the literature, the authors identified some academic and professional studies that try to scrutinize the business use of those applications [8, 11, 16], but also revealed a lack of studies concerning the characteristics of ERP adoption in particular national socio-economic contexts, like the Greek one. The main objective of this research is to investigate the incentives of adopting ERP applications in the Greek market, the realization of the corresponding benefits, and the business use of such systems. Moreover, two other critical issues arising in practice, i.e. the management of change and the future enhancement with new functionalities, will also be investigated in depth. The outcomes of this study will facilitate organizations to avoid obstacles that may lead them to failures, an issue that has appeared prominently in the extant literature [7, 18].

2 Enterprise Resource Planning Systems

The problem of fragmentation of enterprise information was prevalent in the beginning of the '90s, and was emanating from the loose linkage between legacy applications which were used to support different – or even the same – business activities. Deficiencies and multiple entries of unconsolidated data hindered daily operations and created insuperable obstacles in smoothing organization operations. Wasteful utilization of resources to maintain the current operations led organizations to explore in depth the adoption and use of a new type of information systems, namely enterprise resource planning systems. These applications promise extensive and seamless integration of all information systems between inter- and intra-organization functions, thus dealing substantially the issue of fragmentation of information in disparate islands of automation [1, 7]. Moreover, organizations adopt ERP applications for several other reasons [7, 8, 16, 23], which focus on the various levels of organization, i.e. operational, managerial, or strategic [26].

Designing the ERP application is a complicated and critical project. This effort includes not only the parameterization of the application, but also the pre-design of business processes that will be embedded in the operation of the new system. In order to achieve this, three approaches are used in practice. The first one necessitates the reengineering of business processes, and then, the implementation of the new business model through the use of the new ERP application [7, 11]. Business Process Reengineering (BPR) is described by its supporters as a means of facilitating significant, even fundamental, change in the way an organization operates [5, 6, 13, 19]. In the second approach, the organization first selects the ERP software, and tries to take full advantage of its capabilities, in order to enhance business performance, and improve the way work is done [15, 25]. In this way, the organization is "fastened" on the new system. In the third approach, an effort takes place that aims at bridging the gap between the current business processes and the predefined business scenarios of the ERP application. This work is usually achieved through additional code development in the predefined scenarios, in order to "fasten" them with the current business activities [7]. This approach usually endangers the realization of the motivations to adopt and the success of the system, and impedes organizations from taking advantage of future releases of the system, which are delivered by the manufacturers on a frequent basis.

3 Methodology

This study comprises a quantitative survey which aims at scrutinizing the adoption of ERP applications from companies operating in the Greek market environment. The study design involves quantitative data collection and analysis methods. The literature was reviewed extensively, and a questionnaire tool was constructed to facilitate the procedure. The questionnaire was based extensively on the one used by Deloitte [8].

Sample data was collected in the end of 2001 through a questionnaire delivered to organizations using or currently implementing an enterprise system, and were filled in by the owner of the ERP project. The sample was based on customer lists furnished by the most ERP providers operating in the Greek market. Following data cleaning, 229 questionnaires were derived usable for analysis, and in terms of the customer lists, they comprise the 30 – 40% of the organizations using or implementing an ERP application that time. 44 of them were in the phase of implementation, and 185 of them were using the ERP system in daily operations. The data was codified and analyzed with the use of SPSS 10.0. Due to the nature of the questionnaire, the statistical techniques used include description statistics – and especially frequencies – cross-tabulation, and correlation analysis [12].

4 Findings and Discussion

4.1 Organizations' Profile

The organizations that participated in the survey belonged to all industrial sectors, composing a mosaic that corresponds roughly to the Greek market proportions (Table 4, Appendix). More than half of them occupied 51 – 500 employees, an indicator suggesting the popularity of ERP applications in SMEs. Moreover, almost 20% of respondents were Large Organizations, i.e. occupied more than 500 employees. As far as their annual turnover is concerned, almost the 60% of them surpass the limit of 15m Euros. Moreover, the 64.5% of the organizations invest on ICT – on average – more than 2% of their turnover. Based on the European Information Technology Observatory [10], the average company in Greece invests about 1% of annual budget on ICT, an issue indicating that ERP adopters invest much more financial resources on ICTs as compared to industry average. Moreover, the aforementioned corollaries confirm the conclusion that, the majority of large organizations have already adopted ERP applications, and now is the time for SMEs [11]. This is also confirmed nowadays by the efforts of ERP providers to produce and deliver to the market products oriented in the needs of SMEs. Moreover, on 80% of those organizations, more than 40% of employees used a PC for their work, a number near the average use identified for white-collar workers in Europe [10].

Last but not least, the organizations were asked to denote whether they belong to a multinational group. The 69% of them were national companies or belonged to a national group, an indicator that shows the trend of such organizations to adopt those modern information systems.

4.2 Adoption and Implementation of the ERP Project

In this section, major issues concerning the phases of planning and implementation of the ERP applications are examined. Specifically, we review in depth the issue of fragmentation of information, the motivations for adopting the ERP application and the corresponding realization of perceived benefits. Finally, issues of implementing the system and management of change will facilitate the reader to synthesize a rich picture of the ERP adoption context.

4.2.1 Motivations for Adoption and Realization of Perceived Benefits

The primary objective when adopting an enterprise application is to harmonize the technological imperatives with business priorities. Integration of stand-alone applications, automation of transactions, reengineering of processes, acquisition and retention of competitive advantage consist the primary components of the transformation of information management in organizations.

The aforementioned issues analyzed further, and the corresponding motivations and their transformation to real benefits were defined and delivered to the sample, in order to identify which of those were the most critical. Moreover, the authors constructed a new metric, the "realization of perceived benefit", which is the percentage of real benefits in terms of the pre-selected motivations. The results (Table 5) are based on the answers of organizations that have adopted the ERP applications and were using it in practice. Some of them did not declare perceived benefits, possibly because it was too early for them, so the sample is constituted by 168 organizations.

First of all, organizations adopt ERP applications in order to support their daily operations in the operational level. Results indicated that the vast majority of them strive for automating their procedures and for integrating their applications (85.1%), achieve flexibility and completeness of information infrastructure (76.8%), improvements in access, use, consolidation (72%), standardization, and homogenization of information systems and infrastructures (61.3%). Obviously, these issues reveal deficiencies in the bottom line of the business pyramid, and necessitate immediate actions to be undertaken to solve the problem.

Organizations also aspire to boost the middle level of the management hierarchy. In order to do that, they need the "right information in the right place", i.e. consolidated reporting. Reduction of time required to produce financial close cycle reporting was rated with 61.3% (in contrast to 10% appeared in [8]), supporting the aforementioned statement. Moreover, they need to survive and succeed in the arising competitive environment, an issue that calls for improvements in business image (58.3%), and reducing several costs (personnel, inventory, procurement, etc.). Those corollaries mobilize the need for reengineering of processes (53%), which direct the investigation to more strategic objectives.

Strategic motivations contribute to the implementation of corporate strategy and business objectives. Improving relations with customers and suppliers, and adopting a new business model customized to contemporary needs were rated as significant from the studied organizations, but not as much as expected. Improvements in customer responsiveness was rated with 39.9%, in supply chain performance with 32.1% and adoption of new business model with only 28.6%. Those outcomes sensitized the researchers on the manner of use of the ERP applications. Although many IT managers view them as "strategic computing platforms" [24], Greek organizations tended to adopt them for tactical uses.

In order to explore the aforementioned conjunction, the authors estimated the average percentage degree of benefit realization for each motivation category (Table 1). Results indicated that strategic motivations were not very "popular". Ratings are somewhat better in the case of managerial motivations. But, operational motivations are by far the most frequent realized after the adoption of the system (almost 75%). Moreover, the first five popular motivations are operational, whereas the first strategic one, was in the tenth place (Table 5).

Table 1. Motivation categories and realization of each (n = 168)

Motivation Category	Average Percentage	Average Realization
Strategic	22.5 %	57.5 %
Managerial	38.5 %	58.5 %
Operational	54.6 %	74.7 %

So, organizations operating in the Greek market, do not primarily adopt the ERP applications for strategic or managerial reasons, but in order to cover their operational needs. As data indicated, enterprise applications achieved this target. The paradox here is that, although ERP systems are sold as strategic systems, in Greek market they are used to cover operational needs, an issue that necessitates further investigation on local ERP practice.

4.2.2 Fragmentation of Information Before the ERP

Information infrastructure of Greek organizations was significantly fragmented as, the ERP applications replaced 1 – 5 legacy applications (72.4%) fully or partially isolated in the 71.1% of the sample (Table 6). The severity of the problem was also indicated by particular motivations for adoption, like the automation of procedures, integration of applications, and flexibility of information infrastructure, which were rated extremely high in the survey (Table 5). Those results were taken from organizations having already adopted and were using in practice an ERP application. The data demonstrated the existence of the problem, in a percentage between 32.1% - 85.1% (average: 61.2%).

Those organizations were also asked to declare whether the problem was solved with the adoption of the ERP application. The corresponding realization for perceived benefits (for the aforementioned motivations) was fluctuating (for the aforementioned motivations) between 61.1% - 78.3% (average: 70.7%).

Therefore, arguably, the problem of fragmentation of information existed in a significant degree, and that it was solved – in a significant degree – with the adoption of enterprise resource planning applications.

4.2.3 Implementing the System: Process Engineering and Reengineering

Survey results indicated that the 20.5% of respondents made first a BPR project and then implemented the system. This result can be partially justified by the complication, extensive effort and risks of those projects [6, 13, 21]. The 60.3% of the studied organizations first selected the ERP software and then tried to take full advantage of its capabilities, in order to enhance business performance, and improve the way work is done. This approach is quite common as organizations acquire the system not only due to the offered functionalities of the systems, but also for the best practices they include. Finally, the 16.6% of them tried to bridge the current organization practices with the offered business scenarios. Although literature indicates the significance of process reengineering before ERP implementation, the practice points at taking full advantage of the capabilities offered by the ERP applications.

A critical question arises here is, "which is the best of the three aforementioned approaches for ERP implementation"? The best way to answer it is to combine those three approaches with the success of the system, i.e. the realization of perceived benefits. Using correlation analysis, we found that business process reengineering contributed positively to the realization of *reducing personnel costs, cash management, automation of procedures and integration of applications, process reengineering, flexibility and completeness of information infrastructure, and improvement in access, use, and consolidation of information, adoption of new business model, and improve of business image*. On the other hand, bridging the gap through additional code development, contributed negatively to the feasibility of automation of procedures and integration of applications, process reengineering, improvement in access, use, and consolidation of information, improve customer responsiveness and supply chain performance. The analysis indicated for the organizations that first selected the ERP software and then tried to take full advantage of its capabilities that, it could operate negatively only in the implementation of a new business model.

Furthermore, the authors estimated the average realization of perceived benefits for each of the approaches. In cases were a BPR had been led up the implementation process, the average realization metric reached the 82.3%. The corresponding percentage for the second approach was 66.9%, and for the third was 42.7%. Those results suggest first the need for business process reengineering before the adoption of an ERP application, and second, the significance of BPR for the success of the system.

4.2.4 Change Management and ERP Adoption

A common issue arising in the agenda of information systems adoption concerns the management of change, an issue belonging to the wider agenda of organizational change [4, 22]. Since ERP philosophy is process-based rather than function-based, its adoption is likely to bring disruptive organizational changes [14]. Introducing a new information system can be also considered as a "tool" to operationalize the prescribed change [3]. Issues like resistance to change also occur in those circumstances for several reasons and many organizations try to implement their enterprise system as quickly as possible and with minimal organizational change [20]. The aforementioned issues necessitate the existence of a change management plan, which will facilitate the procedure of adoption and mitigate the impediments.

Survey results indicated that only 18.3% of organizations considered change management as a criterion for selecting the consultants to implement the system, and only 18.8% used a change management plan to facilitate the adoption. Probably, the reason is allocated in the procedure of implementation as, in the 76.9% of organizations did not follow a business process reengineering route, which suggests an implementation route focusing on minimal disruption of the business status quo. Resistance to change was reported only by the 14.8% of the organizations.

4.3 The Business Use of the ERP

ERP systems are used to automate the information flow and to support the operation of business processes. Regardless of the managerial structure of an organization, the primary functions that the aforementioned systems are called to automate and integrate include management of financials, production, quality, sales and distribution, inventory, human resources, projects, services, cost accounting and auditing.

Several organizations were viewing the adoption of the enterprise application as an ongoing process and, were operating in a complicated way (Table 2). Many of them had removed all previous systems and adopted fully the ERP (60%). Others, were using the ERP for some business functions, or both ERP and some previous applications for some other (21.1%). Some other were using the ERP for some functions and legacy applications for some other (13.5%). A small sample of them was also operating with a mix of the aforementioned infrastructures (4.9%). Finally, some of them denoted that they intended to enhance new functionalities to their ERP application soon.

Table 2. Business Process Support (n = 185)

Business Function	Only ERP	ERP and Legacy	Only Legacy	Forecasted Increase
Financial Management	89.2 %	9.7 %	0.5 %	1.6 %
Production Management	30.3 %	2.7 %	1.1 %	5.9 %
Quality Management	8.6 %	2.2 %	2.2 %	5.4 %
Sales & Distribution	71.4 %	9.2 %	2.2 %	3.2 %
Inventory Management	67.0 %	3.8 %	1.6 %	7.0 %
Human Resources Management	25.4 %	6.5 %	13.5 %	13.5 %
Project Management	11.4 %	1.6 %	4.3 %	6.5 %
Services Management	9.7 %	1.1 %	1.6 %	4.3 %
Cost Accounting & Auditing	70.8 %	8.1 %	0.5 %	4.9 %

Financial management seems to be the first and most popular business function automated through an ERP system. Possibly this result can be attributed to the volume of financial data accrued and have to be manipulated by every organization. Secondly, sales, distribution, cost accounting and auditing appealed significantly for ERP support for organizations, as they focus on the satisfaction of customers and the creation of consolidated models and reports. The simultaneous use of ERP and legacy applications was under 10% for all functions, and can be interpreted as the linkage of ERPs with particular applications supporting very special needs of the respondents. Moreover, management of services and quality revealed to be the most unpopular functions automated both by an ERP or some legacy application, suggesting the immaturity of such practices in Greek organizations.

Data analysis revealed also that automation of human resource management was the most non-integrated function in the organizations of the sample, indicating the need for reconsidering it the modern knowledge society [9], where people comprise a strategic resource. On the positive side, the market seems to realize the significance of this function which was voted as the first candidate for enhancement (13.5%) in the immediate future.

Finally, 111 (almost 60%) organizations were using only the ERP to support their business functions, abolishing all legacy applications. Obviously, these organizations had understood the meaning of integration of information, and tried to take full advantage of the capabilities of ERP applications.

4.4 The Second Wave

Literature indicates that "going live is not the end of the journey" for ERP adoption [8]. Organizations obtain real benefits only after the implementation of the system, as time is needed for them to appear and be conceived by the users and the upper management, return-on-investment metrics have to be applied, and the new business model has to be operationalized efficiently and effectively. Following that, organizations usually enhance the system with more functionalities, reaching the phase of *Onward and Upward* [18].

The second wave (or onward and upward) phase has three stages [8]. In the *stabilization* phase, the organization tries to gain efficiencies from smooth-running ERP-enabled processes. In the second stage, i.e. *synthesize*, the organization tries to realize additional effectiveness from the better decision-making capabilities offered by the ERP. In the last stage of *synergizing*, the organization aims at acquiring new competencies, redefining business processes, and generally, achieving new, sweeping changes that primarily benefit it.

Reviewing the results, it is more than obvious that organizations were undertaking actions concerning primary the first stage, and specifically improvement of processes and auditing, changes in information technology operations, and new functionalities. Estimating the average of each category, we discover that the average rating of actions undertaken in the stabilization phase is 53.5%, in the *synthesizing* phase is 18.4%, and in the phase of *synergize*, the percentage reaches 19.3%. The result extracted is that, more than half of the organizations that had adopted by that time an ERP application, were trying to stabilize it and take the first advantages of it.

The second wave could be facilitated if organizations were talking actions towards this objective. These actions are presented under the phases of *synthesize* and *synergize*, and should be taken under consideration for the corporate strategic information planning.

Table 3. Actions Undertaken by the Organizations after the ERP Implementation (n = 185)

Stage	Action	Percentage
Stabilize	Process Improvement	83.2 %
	Improve Auditing	55.7 %
	Changes in IT Operations	51.9 %
	Performance Measurement	23.2 %
Synthesize	New ERP Functionalities	38.9 %
	Data Warehouses	33 %
	Knowledge Management	16.2 %
	Electronic Data Interchange (EDI)	14.6 %
	Supply Chain Management (SCM)	11.9 %
	Electronic Commerce	11.8 %
	Customer Relationship Management (CRM)	11.4 %
	Electronic Procurement	9.2 %
Synergize	Changes in Strategy concerning Products and Services	20.5 %
	Changes in Strategy concerning Suppliers and Distribution	19.5 %
	Changes in Strategy concerning Customers	17.8 %

5 Conclusions

The survey above comprises the first comprehensive attempt to scrutinize the adoption of ERP applications in the Greek market. Although a comparison with international studies on the aforementioned issues would be interesting, its presentation is beyond the scope of this paper. Organizations intending to adopt such a system will also find helpful the presented results, in order to conceive the real benefits that can be obtained with an ERP application, and avoid mistakes that can endanger the success of the effort. The first finding indicates that ERP systems dominate in the information infrastructure of large organizations. The SMEs' market currently seems to be the most appealing and growing "arena" for ERP providers. Possibly, the solution of ASP provision could facilitate their penetration to SMEs.

In this study we found that the reengineering of business processes before the adoption of the ERP system contributes positively to desirable outcomes for organizations. Although this effort is quite difficult, assuming and requires a comprehensive and systematic planning, it becomes imperative for organizations in order to improve their internal operations and become competitive and innovative with their customers and suppliers. Organizations that try to bridge the gap between current business processes and predefined ERP business scenarios with additional code development, endanger the realization of the motivations to adopt, and the success of the system. Moreover, they become unable to take advantage of future releases of the system, which are delivered from the manufacturers of the systems in a frequent basis.

Furthermore, the ERP applications appeared to solve the problem of information fragmentation, which was experienced by many Greek organizations. To a great extent, they were successful in this objective, operating either only with the ERP or "in a mix". Moreover, those organizations primarily use their newly acquired ERP applications for supporting their operational needs, a fact consistent with a "first wave" of ERP adoption. Malfunctions in the bottom line are obvious and raise immediate actions, which ERPs are called to support. Although ERP systems are sold as strategic systems by their providers, Greek organizations use them in a limited manner, loosing the opportunity to take advantage of their strategic capabilities.

However, the aforementioned systems offered a lot to the organizations that adopted them. Multiple information systems loosely interfaced and containing the same data elements were eliminated to a great extent. Data in different systems often inconsistent was replaced with consolidated information kept in unique databases. ERPs used in practice now, cover all the major functions of Greek enterprises, while dominant use is in the areas of data processing concerning the internal financial operation, the management of the relation with customers and suppliers, and business planning.

References

1. Applegate, L.M., McFarlan, F.W., McKenney, J.L.: Corporate Information Systems Management. Text and Cases. 5th edn. Irwin McGraw-Hill (1999).
2. Arinze, B., Anandarajan, M.: A framework for using OO mapping methods to rapidly configure ERP systems. Communications of the ACM 46 (2003) 61-65.
3. Bjorn-Andersen, N.,Turner, J.A.: Creating the 21st century organization: the metamorphosis of Oticon. In Baskerville, R., Smithson, S., Ngwenyama, O., DeGross, J.I. (eds.): Transforming Organizations with Information Technology. Amsterdam North-Holland (1994).
4. Boudreau, M.-C., Robey, D.: Organizational Transition to Enterprise Resource Planning Systems: Theoretical Choices for Process Research. In Proceedings of the 1999 International Conference on Information Systems, Charlotte, NC (1999) 291-299.
5. Champy, J.: Re-engineering Management. Harper Collins New York (1999).
6. Currie, W.L., Willcocks, L.: The New Branch Columbus project at Royal Bank of Scotland: the implementation of large-scale business process re-engineering. Journal of Strategic Information Systems, 5 (1996) 213-236.
7. Davenport, T.H.: Putting the Enterprise into the Enterprise System. Harvard Business Review, (July – August 1998) 121 – 131.
8. Deloitte Consulting: ERP's Second Wave (1998).
9. Drucker, P.F.: The age of social transformation. Atlantic Monthly 274 (1995) 53-80.
10. EITO: European Information Technology Observatory (2001).
11. Everdingen, Y.V., Hillegersberg, J.V., Waarts, E.: ERP adoption by European midsize companies. Communications of the ACM 43 (April 2000) 27-31.
12. Hair, J.F., Anderson, R.E., Tatham, R.L., Black, W.C.: Multivariate data analysis. 5th edn. Prentice-Hall (1998).
13. Hammer, M., Champy, J.: Re-engineering the Corporation: a manifesto for business revolution. Nicholas Brearley Publishing London (1993).
14. Hong, K.K., Kim, Y.G.: The critical success factors for ERP implementation: an organizational fit perspective. Information & Management, 40 (2002) 25-40.

15. Kremers, M., Dissel, H.V.: ERP Systems migrations – A provider's versus a customer's perspective. Communications of the ACM 43 (April 2000) 53-56.
16. Kumar, V., Maheshwari, B., Kumar, U.: Enterprise resource planning systems adoption process: a survey of Canadian organizations. International Journal of Production Research 40 (2002) 509-523.
17. Lee, J., Siau, K., Hong, S.: Enterprise integration with ERP and EAI. Communications of the ACM 46 (2003) 54-60.
18. Markus, M.L., Tanis, C.: The Enterprise System Experience – From Adoption to Success, In: Zmud, R.W., Price, M.F. (eds.): Framing the Domains of IT Management. Pinnaflex Educational Resources Inc (2000) 173 – 207.
19. Morris, D., Brandon, J.: Re-engineering Your Business. McGraw-Hill London (1993).
20. Nah, F., Zuckweller, K., Lau, J.: ES implementation: CIOs' perceptions of critical success factors. International Journal of Human-Computer Interactions 16 (2003) 5-22.
21. Newell, S., Cooprider, J.G., David, G., Edelman, L.F., Logan, T.A.: Analyzing different strategies to enterprise system adoption: reengineering-led vs. quick-development. International Journal of Enterprise Information Systems, 1 (2005) 1-16.
22. Orlikowski, W.J.: Improvising Organizational Transformation Over Time: A Situated Change Perspective. Information Systems Research. 7 (1996) 63-90.
23. Ross, J.W., Vitale, M.R.: The ERP Revolution: Surviving vs. Thriving. Information Systems Frontiers. 2 (2000) 233-241.
24. Sweat, J.: ERP: enterprise application suits are becoming a focal point of business and technology planning Information Week (1998) 42-52.
25. Sprott, D.: Componentizing the enterprise application packages. Communications of the ACM 43 (April 2000) 63-69.
26. Turban, E., McLean, E., Wetherbe, J.: Information technology for management: transforming business in the digital economy. 3rd edn. John Wiley & Sons, Inc (2001).

Appendix

Table 4. Responded Profile by Industry Sector (n = 229)

Industrial Sector	Percentage	Industrial Sector	Percentage
Manufacturing	37.5 %	Banking and Financial	5.7 %
Trade	34.1 %	Construction	3.5 %
Services	16.6 %	Other	8.3 %
ICT	6.6 %		

Table 5. Motivations for ERP Adoption, Perceived Benefits, and Degree of Realization of Benefits (n = 168)

	Motivations for Adoption	Perceived as Motivation	Perceived as Real Benefit	Degree of Benefit Realization
Strategic	Improve customer responsiveness	39.9 %	25 %	62.7 %
	Improve supply chain performance	32.1 %	19.6 %	61.1 %
	Adoption of new business model	28.6 %	18.5 %	64.6 %
	Adoption from partners	6.5 %	3.6 %	54.5 %
	Adoption from competitors	5.4 %	2.4 %	44.4 %

	Motivations for Adoption (c'td)	**Perceived as Motivation**	**Perceived as Real Benefit**	**Degree of Benefit Realization**
Managerial	Reduction of time to produce financial close cycle report	61.3 %	41.7 %	68 %
	Improve business image	58.3 %	41.1 %	70.4 %
	Process reengineering	53 %	38.7 %	73 %
	Reduce personnel costs	43.5 %	23.2 %	53.4 %
	Improve cash management	36.9 %	22 %	59.7 %
	Reduce inventory costs	33.3 %	17.9 %	53.6 %
	Organization / products / services / processes expansion	33.9 %	19.6 %	57.9 %
	Reduce procurement costs	27.4 %	13.1 %	47.8 %
	Reduce data costs	23.2 %	11.9 %	51.3 %
	New cooperation / takeover / merging support	14.3 %	7.1 %	50 %
Operational	Automation of procedures, integration of application	85.1 %	66.7 %	78.3 %
	Flexibility and completeness of information infrastructure	76.8 %	56 %	72.9 %
	Improvement in access, use and consolidation of information	72 %	53.6 %	74.4 %
	Standardization and homogenization of information systems and infrastructures	61.3 %	47.6 %	77.7 %
	Prospective integration to stock market	18.5 %	10.7 %	58.1 %
	Loosing support from previous software provider	13.7 %	11.9 %	87 %
	Other	4.2 %	2.4 %	57.1 %

Table 6. Number and Type of Legacy Applications Replaced by the ERP (n = 185)

Number	Percentage	Type	Percentage
none	4.9 %	Legacy applications partially integrated	40.0 %
1 – 5	72.4 %		
5 – 10	10.8 %	Legacy applications fully integrated	34.6 %
10 – 15	4.9 %	Legacy stand-alone applications	33.0 %
15 – 20	1.1 %	Other	3.2 %
> 20	4.3 %		

Supply Chains of the Future and Emerging Consumer-Based Electronic Services

Georgios Doukidis and Katerina Pramatari

Athens University of Economics & Business,
Department of Management Science and Technology,
76 Patision Str., 104 34 Athens, Greece
{gjd, k.pramatari}@aueb.gr
http://www.eltrun.gr

Abstract. This paper focuses on the supply-chain opportunities provided by emerging wireless and mobile commerce technologies coupled with automatic product identification technologies (RFID) as well as collaborative environments for sharing information. Speed and visibility have become supply chain imperatives and it is foreseen that the above technologies will transform the supply chain, delivering multiple benefits, such as improved on-self availability and customer service, reduced losses and theft, improved inventory, traceability, warehouse/ back-room, and shelf management. The paper identifies the four major supply chain transformations: sharing information to collaborate, automatic identification of individual items (RFID), product and consumer safety with traceability, and consumer value management (CVM). On these four aspects of S.C. transformations it identifies emerging electronic services with examples from the consumer goods industry.

1 Introduction

The advent of e-business has created several challenges and opportunities in the supply chain environment. The Internet has made it easier to share information among supply chain partners and the current trend is to try to leverage the benefits obtained through information sharing across the supply chain to improve operational performance, customer service, and solution development [1]. Depicting this trend on a continuum, we see companies moving from information sharing and coordination to knowledge sharing and advanced collaboration practices.

Furthermore, the emergence of new technologies, such as automatic product identification (RFID), is expected to revolutionize many of the supply chain operations, affecting both intra- and inter-company processes. This technology represents a great opportunity for cost-reduction and improved service levels, while the expected benefits are to grow substantially if its scope of implementation is extended from internal warehouse and distribution processes to supply-chain processes involving collaborating partners.

At the same time there is a clear turn and focus on the customer, on increasing consumer value and ultimately on building consumer enthusiasm. This turn has been expressed through various strategies and activities, such as the increasing concern for food and consumer safety, the development of advanced shopping environments capitalizing on new technological capabilities and pervasive computing, and the proliferation of several electronic service offerings through such disperse environments as the Web, the mobile, and digital interactive television.

The above trends represent major forces that are expected to revolutionize the supply chains of the future. In this paper we analyze each of these trends, summarizing the current developments in each area and potential benefits but also the open issues and risks associated with their deployment.

In section two of the paper we discuss supply chain collaboration practices and underlying technologies. In section three we summarize the characteristics of RFID technology, its impact on retail and supply chain management as well as its potential to enhance collaboration. In section four we refer to the concept of traceability, which imposes the consumer safety imperative on supply chain operations, and comment on how the technology of RFID can support its efficient implementation. In section five we introduce the term consumer value management (CVM) and refer to some cases of electronic services delivered through various electronic media that enhance the consumer shopping experience with the ultimate objective to build consumer enthusiasm.

2 Sharing Information to Collaborate

Since the early 1990s, there has been a growing understanding that supply chain management should be built around the integration of trading partners. Bowersox et al. [2] state that firms collaborate in the sense of "leveraging benefits to achieve common goals". Anthony [3] suggests that supply chain collaboration occurs when "two or more companies share the responsibility of exchanging common planning, management, execution, and performance measurement information". He goes further suggesting that "collaborative relationships transform how information is shared between companies and drive change to the underlying business processes". Research carried out by Andersen Consulting, Stanford University, Northwestern University, and INSEAD, as reported in Anderson and Lee [4], recommends that industry participants "collaborate on planning and execution" of supply chain strategy to achieve a "synchronized supply chain".

Some scholars suggest using the term demand chain management (DCM) instead of supply-chain management (SCM). This puts emphasis on the needs of the market and designing the chain to satisfy these needs, instead of starting with the supplier/manufacturer and working forward. The main stimulus behind this has been the shift in power away from the supplier towards the customer [5].

In retailing, supply-chain collaboration has taken the form of practices such as Continuous Replenishment Program (CRP), Vendor Managed Inventory (VMI) and Collaborative Planning, Forecasting and Replenishment (CPFR). VMI is a technique developed in the mid 1980s, whereby the manufacturer (supplier) has the sole responsibility for managing the customer's inventory policy, including the replenishment process, based on the variation of stock level in the customer's main warehouse or distribution centre [6]. VMI is probably the first trust-based business link between suppliers and customers. CRP moves one step ahead of VMI and reveals demand from the retailers' stores. The inventory policy is then based on the sales forecast, built from historical demand data and no longer purely based on the variations of inventory levels at the customers' main stock-holding facility.

Collaborative Planning, Forecasting and Replenishment (CPFR) can be seen as an evolution from VMI and CRP, addressing not only replenishment but also joint demand forecasting and promotions planning, focusing on promotions and special-line items. CPFR is based on extended information sharing between retailer and supplier, including point-of-sales (POS) data, forecasts and promotion plans.

Pramatari et al. [7] provide a framework for classifying the various CPFR initiatives undertaken to date, by examining the implementation scope of CPFR across the axes of place, product, time and extent of information sharing. This classification shows that the focus of the various CPFR projects reported is around the replenishment of the retailer's distribution centre. These projects deal with promotion items and new introductions, rather than regular line products, while the information shared is POS data (mainly electronically) and promotion plans. They also refer mainly to mid/long-term replenishment planning and not to the day-to-day replenishment in the store. However, Holmström et al. [8] suggest that collaborative planning will only be successful if it involves very little extra work for the retailers. Collaborative planning cannot just be a solution between close partners. The goal must be solutions that enable mass collaboration in order to obtain economies of scale.

Pramatari et al. [7] further suggest a new form of CPFR, which they name Process of Collaborative Store Ordering (PCSO), addressing the daily store replenishment process. This process is supported by special Internet-based IT infrastructure (collaborative platform) allowing the daily online sharing of store-level information (e.g. POS sales data, store assortments, stock-level in the store, promotion activities, out-of-shelf alerts, etc), the sales forecasting and order generation, the online collaboration of the trading partners, and finally the order exchange and order status tracking.

Based on these short descriptions, VMI and CRP address more the supply-chain collaboration, whereas CPFR puts more emphasis on the demand side. What makes the distinction in the evolution path followed by these collaboration practices is the amount of information exchanged between the trading partners and the process(es) enabled by this information sharing. In the traditional ordering process, retailers provided manufacturers with only data on quantities of goods required once a week (through ordering). VMI/CRP and CPFR dramatically increase the total volume of information transmitted between retailers and suppliers. Pramatari et al. [9] summarize the evolution in information exchange from pure ordering to CPFR and the underlying technology supporting the exchange of information and collaboration between the trading partners.

3 Automatic Identification of Individual Items (RFID)

Radio-Frequency Identification Technology (RFID) falls under the umbrella of Automatic Identification (Auto-ID) technologies along with technologies such as magnetic stripe, smart cards, voice data entry, touch memory and so on [10]. RFID technology has been extensively used for a diversity of applications ranging from access control systems to airport baggage handling, livestock management systems, automated toll collection systems, theft-prevention systems, electronic payment systems, and automated production systems. Nevertheless, recent advances have made possible the identification of consumer products using RFID.

Traditionally, the retail sector uses barcodes as the main identifier for cases, pallets and products. Today, over 5 billion products are scanned everyday in 141 countries. Whilst it is clear to retailers and manufacturers that the barcode's relevance and importance to the industry will remain for years ahead, many in the industry are now looking to the business case of RFID as the "next generation of barcode".

The identification is done by storing a serial number, and perhaps other information, on a microchip that is attached to an antenna. This bundle is called an RFID tag. The antenna enables the chip to transmit the identification information to a reader. The reader converts the radio waves reflected back from the RFID tag into digital information that can be passed on to an enterprise information system. RFID technology has two main advantages. Firstly, it does not require line-of-sight for a tag to be read, contrast to barcode. Secondly, a tag may carry much more information than a barcode, thus enabling the identification of each individual product instance rather than product type.

EPCglobal, which replaced Auto-ID Centre in 2003, sets the standards for implementing RFID technology in the supply chain. These include frequency transmission, software compatibility, data communication and system integration. Moreover, recent EAN-UCC standardization developments in the field of RFID have set specific standard in the format of EPC [11]. EPC (Electronic Product Code) is a globally unique serial number that uniquely identifies each product and may include other numbers that support information regarding the producer, supplier and the type of product. EPCglobal suggests an architecture in which unique product code observation data are available globally through a distributed information service structure. Thus, every company can ask information about a specific product code from the appropriate company that holds this information.

The prospects of RFID have attracted the attention of large retailers and suppliers. Over the past few years, we have witnessed several initiatives in the retail sector that have tried to field-test RFID in different application areas; Metro has launched the 'store-of-the-future' initiative in Rheinberg, Germany, a converted traditional supermarket that uses RFID technology as a means to enhance the shoppers' experience during their visit to the retail outlet [12]. As another example, Gillette investigated the potential of RFID in store management focusing on the elimination of out-of-shelf conditions [13]. The increased interest of the retail sector in the RFID technology can also be depicted from Wal-Mart's decision to have its top 100 suppliers to begin shipping tagged pallets and cases by January 2006 [14].

RFID can thus enhance core supply and demand chain management operations, ranging from the upstream to the downstream side. Figure 1 illustrates the different classes of RFID-enhanced applications [9].

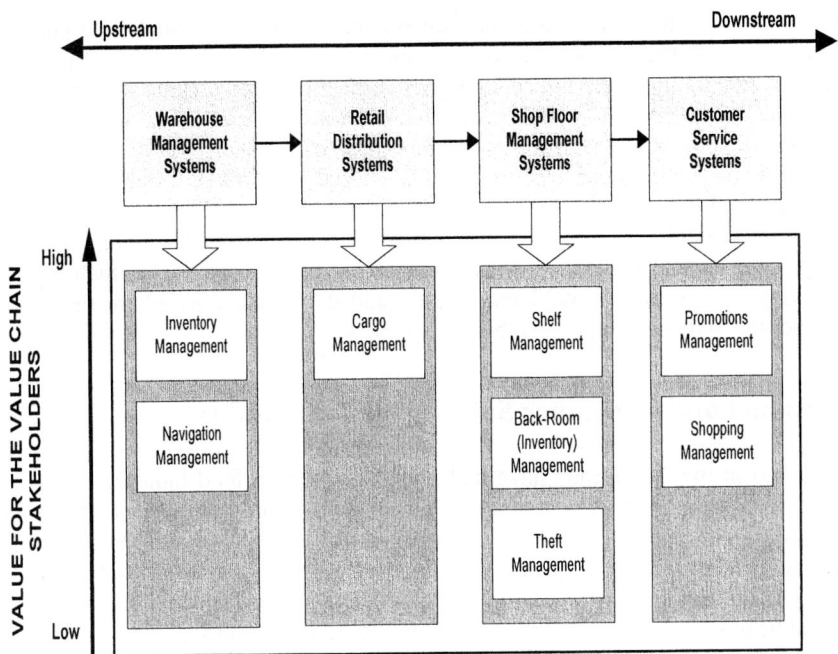

Fig. 1. A taxonomy of different classes of RFID-enhanced applications

The prospective RFID-enhanced applications are classified across two axes: The first axis spans across the value chain, from the upstream side (referring to applications targeted to the supplier and intermediate distribution centers), down to the retail outlet, and finally, the end consumer. The second axis refers to the perceived value of the individual application for the interested stakeholder. This value derives from the nature of the application and its perceived benefits; high value applications introduce totally new means to operate a particular process resulting, in most cases, to increased business effectiveness; low value applications simply automate or provide an alternative means to conduct a particular operation.

Agarwal [10] gives a good insight in the potential benefits that rise with RFID use, including stock reduction, reduced labor costs and mass customization. However, the full benefits of RFID will be achieved only when all firms within a supply chain implement the technology.

Moreover, RFID solutions need be integrated with the existing back-end infrastructures of retailers and suppliers and this requires significant overhead, especially if we take into account that such infrastructures have been developed incrementally over a rather long period of time and thus their current architectures have been evolved rather than designed. Still, this integration represents the initial phase for the retail sector in order to benefit from the rich information provided by RFID. In this phase, companies investing in RFID systems will reap the expected benefits by creating proprietary systems owned and controlled solely by them.

The second phase will require the creation of the necessary infrastructures that support information sharing and collaboration among the retail value chain. While the

Internet has provided new means for retailers and suppliers to collaborate and share information using dedicated platforms, we argue that RFID will significantly enhance the depth and quality of the information exchanged over such collaborative platforms, leading to smarter forms of collaboration [9]. Indeed, the capability to know on a real-time basis the current stock level at the warehouse or the shelf will lead to gradually eliminating out-of-stock and out-of-shelf situations. Similarly, tracking a product along the supply chain on a real-time basis, even within the retail outlet, will enable suppliers to effectively manage replenishment and product recalls, have better forecasting accuracy and provide more tailor-made promotional plans. Ultimately, RFID technology can generate 'intelligent' supply and demand chains where the product instead of the end user triggers the business process.

4 Product and Consumer Safety with Traceability

Food crises in the last decade have had a great impact on food industry. Food deficiencies have led not only to contamination but also in some cases even to death. BSE crisis and dioxin crisis in the 1990s are the most striking examples of the above. As a consequence, food sales drop dramatically; pointing out the vulnerability of food industry upon food quality and how poor quality may affect not only the consumer's physical health, but the business's commercial health as well [15].

A survey (October 2000) by the UK Food Standard Agency showed that 75% of consumers are concerned about food safety. The restoration of consumer confidence is a major challenge for food industry [16]. Moreover, retailers have invested heavily in the establishment of quality departments and demand from their suppliers to do the same. On top of these, the EU has edited a series of directives and regulations (most recent 2001/95/EC & 178/2002) regarding food quality assurance and traceability issues. All these indicate that there is an imperative need for food quality across the supply chain, which partly relies on physical traceability throughout the chain.

A generic definition for traceability is given by ISO [17]: Traceability is the ability to trace the history, application or location of an entity, by means of recorded identifications. Van Dorp [18] provides an extended list of definitions on traceability, pointing out that the differences between them derive from the different type of activities that are included and the organizational context in which they are performed.

Product traceability can be distinguished in two types, according to the direction in which information is recalled in the chain. Backward traceability [15], or tracing, is the ability, at every point of the supply chain, to find origin and characteristics of a product from one or several given criteria. Forward traceability, or tracking, is the ability, at every point of the supply chain, to find the localization of products from one or several given criteria. It is important for an information system to support both the above types of traceability, as the effectiveness for one type does not necessarily imply the effectiveness for the other.

The business scope at which tracking and tracing take place can further distinguish traceability in external or supply chain traceability and internal. Indeed, as Moe [19] remarks, traceability is the ability to track a product batch and its history through the whole, or part, of a production chain from harvest through transport, storage, processing, distribution and sales or internally in one of the steps in the chain. The former refers to chain traceability while the latter refers to internal traceability.

The emerging technology of RFID raises great potentials for effective and efficient traceability system design. Wireless data acquisition can lead to high quality location information, which can be utilized for traceability purposes using the appropriate information infrastructure. This information can be obtained at significantly reduced labor costs and with small changes in the enterprise's business processes [20].

Table 2. RFID potential in meeting traceability requirements

Traceability Requirement	RFID Potential
Item Identification	Effective unique identification of traceable units. Potentially provision of extra information about the product.
Bill of Lots Recording	Automatic detection and identification of lots used in a specific batch production, using wireless identification
Operation Recording	Automatic detection and identification of batches that are subject to specific operations and hosted in specific capacity units
Item Observation/ Data capture	Effective and efficient item observation with reduced labor costs
Traceability data communication	Efficient data capture and information sharing with minor investment through the EPC infrastructure

Existing traceability systems implement identification in batch/lot level. The identification is done using either barcode EAN-UCC 128 or more informal non-standardized numbering. Traceability based on lot numbering creates a serious problem: each partner in the chain must synchronize his data to comply with the identification applied by the lot producer. Only if all partners in the chain synchronize their data is traceability feasible. Applying RFID tags on the packages (either cases or pallets) of each lot can solve this problem. All chain partners can use the EPC for identification with no fear for data inconsistency. Thus, no data synchronization is required.

With respect to the means of identification, the use of barcode requires significant labor costs, as each item should be scanned in a line-of-sight range. The costs depend on the level of the identification that the barcode is applied, i.e. identification at case level includes more costs than that at pallet level. RFID technology provides an efficient way for identification. Several hundred RFID tags can be read in a second with no need for line-of-sight, using radio waves. As a consequence, items can be easily identified with no special requirements in business processes (product counting, scanning etc.).

Moreover, by establishing an RFID-reader and simple EPC information system at every node in a supply network, unique product identification and location information can be efficiently communicated among supply chain partners with no need for integration with internal information systems. This fact significantly reduces the cost and risk associated with system integration and data synchronization, making RFID the best candidate for implementing traceability across a complex supply network with various partners involved [20].

Table 2 summarizes the potential of RFID technology in meeting traceability requirements.

5 Consumer Value Management

Value traditionally refers to a preferential judgment like an interactive, relativistic preference experience, whereas values refer to the criteria by which such preferential judgments are made [21]. Values, in this way, become deeply held and enduring beliefs, while value results as a trade-off of, for example, benefits and sacrifices associated with a particular good or service [21].

In Roland Berger [22], Consumer Value is defined as 'providing functional and emotional benefits tailored to the individual needs of consumers that continuously enhance overall experience of life'. In the same report, co-innovation and co-revolution are discussed as strategic levers towards delivering increased consumer value. Co-innovation implies cooperation of several partners with the joint objective of bringing about substantial growth to a market by collaborating across the innovation process. Co-revolution implies the involvement of internal and external partners in the management of relevant parts of the value chain in order to achieve broader growth opportunities at reduced costs for all partners. Furthermore, the report suggests three areas in which excellence in implementation has to be secured: employee enthusiasm, business transformation and in-store implementation.

In the marketing literature we find consumer value management as the strategy to guide consumers to the ultimate level of consumer commitment: from consumer *satisfaction*, where the company understands and satisfies the most important consumer expectations, to consumer *loyalty*, where consumers trust the company's offers and a continuous relationship between the consumer and the company's offer is established, and ultimately to consumer *enthusiasm*, the state where the company surprises the consumers by anticipating or creating new – also unarticulated – needs and desires. In this latter case, consumers have a strong emotional link with the company's offer, which becomes part of their lives.

On the other hand, there is a growing discussion on the increased complexity of the shopping environment and that understanding people's complicated lives is a critical business issue [23]. According to Wilmott [23], retailers need to actually deliver in terms of a shopping experience that is both easy, helpful and an enjoyable experience, whereas Scandroglio [24] stresses simplicity as a new consumer need.

Thus, user-friendly technologies helping consumers overcome frustrations, offering an experience (rather than shopping) trip and provide personalized services at store and home become critical. Services designed to enhance the physical product offer are becoming a key, differentiating factor with huge growth potential as retailers seek to create solution-driven concepts.

MyGROCER, a European project in which Procter & Gamble and the Greek supermarket retail chain ATLANTIC participated, investigated the potential of RFID to the downstream environment and in particular its effect on the traditional shopping experience [25]. This was supported through an intelligent shopping cart equipped with a display device and an RFID sensor capable of scanning the contents of the cart. Shoppers could use their loyalty card to log in the system and receive the following facilitating services [25]:

- continuous monitoring of the products that are currently in their shopping cart along with their cumulative value;
- a reminding list of products they wish to purchase during their shopping visit;
- a list of all available promotions;
- fully personalized based on their shopping behavior and past consumption patterns;
- display of valuable information for each product (such as nutritional value, recipes and so on) complementing or even extending the information available on the product packaging;
- and advanced navigation capabilities.

The same project included a home replenishment scenario based on RFID technology and an on-the-move shopping scenario based on mobile technology. Roussos et al. [26] describe the above consumer shopping experience using the term "retailtainment experience". Such a system transforms grocery shopping into a retailing entertainment. Hence, the design of systems and supporting appliances alike, should be approached from the point of view of entertainment service provision [26].

Apart from in-store shopping, consumer value management has to deal with an increasing number of channel alternatives. These channels are not limited to off-line catalogues or web-based electronic stores but include mobile and digital interactive television environments as well. In this context retailers and suppliers need to understand the specific relationship between the utilitarian values consumers derive from each channel in order to define and synchronize multiple, complementary channel strategies. These channels change both the consumer experience but also the supply chain relationships and structures. Furthermore, these channels represent opportunities for new revenue streams and emerging business models [27].

6 Conclusions

In this paper we have highlighted what we characterize as the four major supply chain transformations currently: sharing information to collaborate, automatic identification of individual items (RFID), product and consumer safety with traceability, and consumer value management (CVM). These transformations represent the emerging trends, challenges and opportunities in the retail industry, under the perspective of the changing consumer and business behavioral patterns, the reconfiguration of intra and inter-organizational relationships and the evolving technological capabilities [28].

Our objective has not been to give a thorough analysis of the research and development in each of these areas but, on the contrary, to give an overall view and attract academic and business interest on the emerging techniques and technologies for supply chain management and collaboration, as well as on the emerging relationships and the electronic transformations governing multi-channel retailing. Each of these transformations represents a vast area of research that should be approached from various academic perspectives and disciplines.

The application of the latest technological inventions to enthuse consumers through accurate targeting along with the identification of the potential of the new technologies, processes and strategies for transforming the supply chain are expected to be a major stream of research and business development in the years to come [28]. We hope that the work presented in this paper has provided some basic insight towards this direction.

References

1. Swaminathan, J.M., Tayur, S.R.: Models for Supply Chains in E-Business. Management Science, 49 (2003) 1387-1406.
2. Bowersox, D.J., Closs, D.J., Stank, T.P.: Ten mega-trends that will revolutionize supply chain logistics. Journal of Business Logistics, 21 (2000) 1-16.
3. Anthony, T.: Supply chain collaboration: success in the new Internet economy, Achieving Supply Chain Excellence Through Technology, Montgomery Research Inc (2000) 241-44.
4. Anderson, D.L., Lee, H. (1999) Synchronised supply chains: the new frontier, 112-21, Achieving Supply Chain Excellence Through Technology, Montgomery Research Inc.,
5. Soliman, F., Youssef, M. (2001). The impact of some recent developments in e-business on the management of next generation manufacturing. International Journal of Operations and Production Management, Vol. 21, pp. 538-564.
6. Cooke, J.A. (1998). VMI: very mixed impact?. Logistics Management Distribution Report, Vol. 37, No. 12, pp. 51.
7. Pramatari, K., Papakiriakopoulos, D., Poulymenakou, A., Doukidis, G.I. (2002) New forms of CPFR. The ECR Journal-International Commerce Review, Vol. 2, No. 2, pp. 38-43.
8. Holmstrom, J. Framling, K. Kaipia, R. and Saranen, J (2002) "Collaborative planning forecasting and replenishment: new solutions needed for mass collaboration", Supply Chain Management: An International Journal Vol 7. No 3. pp. 136-145
9. Pramatari, K.C., Doukidis, G.I., Kourouthanassis, P. (2005). Towards 'smarter' supply and demand-chain collaboration practices enabled by RFID technology. In Vervest P., Van Heck E., Preiss K. and Pau L.F, (Eds.), Smart Business Networks, Springer Verlag (ISBN: 3-540-22840-3).
10. Agarwal, V. (2001). Assessing the benefits of Auto-ID Technology in the Consumer Goods Industry, Auto-ID Centre. Available online at: www.epcglobalinc.org
11. ECR. (2004). ECR - Using Traceability in the Supply Chain to meet Consumer Safety Expectations: ECR Europe.
12. Wolfram, G., Scharr, U., and Kammerer, K. (2004). RFID: Can we realise its full potential?. The ECR Journal, Vol. 3, No. 2, pp. 17-29.
13. Cantwell, D. (2003). RFID Real World Applications: The case of Gillette. GCI Intelligent Tagging Working Group, Berlin 2003.
14. Roberti, M. (2004). Wal-Mart Begins RFID Rollout. RFID Journal.
15. Jansen-Vullers, M. H., van Dorp, C. A., & Beulens, A. J. M. (2003). Managing traceability information in manufacture. International Journal of Information Management, 23, 395-413.
16. Viaene, J., & Verbeke, W. (1998). Traceability as a key instrument towards supply chain and quality management in the Belgian poultry meat chain. Supply Chain Management, 3(3), 139-141.

17. ISO, E. S. (1995). EN ISO 8492.1995. European Committee for Standardization, Point 3.16.
18. van Dorp, K. J. (2002). Tracking and Tracing: a structure for development and contemporary practices. Logistics Information Management, 15(1), 24-33.
19. Moe, T. (1998). Perspectives on traceability in food manufacture. Trends in Food Science and Technology, 9, 211-214.
20. Kelepouris, T., Pramatari, K. (2005) An information infrastructure for rfid-enabled traceability. WP 2005-003, Eltrun Working Paper Series, 2005. Available online at: www.eltrun.gr.
21. Holbrook, M. B. (1994). The nature of customer value. In R. T. Rust, & R. L. Oliver (Eds.), Service quality: New directions in theory and practice (pp. 21–71). Thousand Oaks, CA7 Sage Publications.
22. Roland Berger (1999) How to implement Consumer Enthusiasm Strategic Consumer Value Management, ECR Europe Publications, www.ecrnet.org
23. Willmott, M. (2004) Too much of a good thing? The ECR Journal – International Commerce Review, Vol. 4, No. 1, pp. 19-25
24. Scandroglio, G. (2004) Do we really need 10 varieties of salt? The ECR Journal – International Commerce Review, Vol. 4, No. 1, pp. 19-25
25. Kourouthanassis, P., and Roussos, G. (2002). Developing Consumer-Friendly Pervasive Retail Systems. IEEE Pervasive Computing, Vol. 2, No. 2, pp. 32-39.
26. Roussos, G., Kourouthanassis, P., and Moussouri, T. (2003). Appliance Design for Mobile Commerce and Retailtainment. Personal and Ubiquitous Computing, Vol. 7, No. 3-4, pp. 203-209.
27. Pramatari, K.C., Mylonopoulos, N., Papakiriakopoulos, D, Lekakos, G. (2000) Personalised Interactive TV Advertising: The iMEDIA Business Model. Electronic Markets Journal, Vol. 11, No. 1, pp. 17-25.
28. Doukidis, G. and Vrechopoulos, A.P. (2005) (Eds.), Consumer Driven Electronic Transformation, Springer Verlag (ISBN: 3-540-22611-7).

A Quantum Computer Architecture Based on Semiconductor Recombination Statistics

D. Ntalaperas[1,2], K. Theodoropoulos[1], A.Tsakalidis[1,2], and N.Konofaos[1]

[1] Computer Engineering and Informatics Dept., University of Patras, Patras, Greece
[2] Research Academic Computer Technology Institute, Riga Feraiou 61, Patras, Greece
nkonofao@ceid.upatras.gr

Abstract. A new architecture for the practical implementation of a quantum computer is presented in this paper. The architecture makes use of the recombination statistics that govern semiconductor devices and I particular quantum phenomena occurring inside the forbidden gap of a semiconductor filled with a controlled amount of impurities. The occupation of a single trap by an electron is used for the representation of the qubit, whereas illuminating techniques are used for the controlled transition of the electrons between gap levels. The way these transitions correspond to the logical equivalent of quantum gates is being demonstrated by the implementation of the quantum Controlled-NOT (CNOT) gate. Measuring techniques of the final computational outcome based on macroscopic properties of a semiconductor are discussed.

The above techniques are then combined for the design of a quantum circuit, which implements the Shor's factoring algorithm. The physical model for the interconnection of quantum gates scaled to a full quantum computer is given along with the design of the algorithm. Finally, some error estimations are given together with some proposed mechanisms to reduce this error to acceptable levels using known quantum error correction techniques.

Keywords: Quantum computer, qubit, CNOT gate, semiconductor traps, Shor's algorithm.

1 Introduction

Quantum Computers are known for their capability to solve specific computational tasks faster than their computational counterparts. The physical development of a quantum computer still remains an open challenge despite many efforts up to date [1]. Quantum computers are also seem to be a necessity, if the Moore 's Law is still to be valid. Various implementation models for a Quantum Computer have been proposed [1]. Most of them take the representation of the quantum bit (or qubit) to be a two level quantum observable of some system, such as the spin of an electron or that of an atom nuclei. In most of them, there is a one-to-one correspondence between the quantum system and the qubit, i.e. each two level physical system corresponds to a single qubit. Recentluy, new techniques have been proposed, such as Nuclear Magnetic Resonance (NMR) in which the single qubit is represented by an averaging process over a collection of two level systems [1] but also quantum systems based on well known phenomena appearing at semiconductor devices have also been considered [2 and references therein].

In this paper a new mechanism for the development of a quantum computer is being proposed. This mechanism is based on the physical properties of semiconductors, and in particular on the phenomena governing the energy gap of a semiconductor filled with impurities [3]. This work follows the results of previous efforts on the use of the properties of the energy levels existing within the semiconductors forbidden energy gap which are called traps [4,5].

In order to present a full picture of the proposed quantum computer architecture, five consecutive steps are followed and they include: a) The representation of the quantum bit in terms of traps being occupied by electrons, b) a description on the way the response of the states to external signals is equivalent to a quantum computational gate (notably to the physical mechanism for implementing the Controlled–Not gate, c) the formation of a quantum circuit through the interconnection of single quantum gates, d) a demonstration on how such techniques can be combined in order to perform a known quantum algorithm and finally, e) the development of the initialization and measuring mechanisms for the model.

2 The Qubit Representation

The quantum bit (or qubit) representation in this model is derived from the different trap levels existing within the semiconductor forbidden gap. It results from Pauli's Exclusion Principle, that predicts that each trap can be occupied by at most one electron. This fact is being exploited so that an unambiguous qubit representation can be defined. In particular, two adjacent traps are being used, thus the computational base is a four state base, instead of a two state one [5]. This can be demonstrated by considering the four possible states, regarding the occupation by electrons and it is depicted in figure 1 where two adjacent traps appear and their state of occupation reflects the four state basis.

These four states are mutually exclusive, therefore they can be used as the eigenstates of the observable Q, defined as the observable corresponding to the outcome of the measurement corresponding to the occupation of two adjacent traps. The set of the four states also forms a complete set, since they constitute the only possible outcomes. Therefore, a correspondence between the physical states and the quantum computational basis can be made.

Having four possible quantum states the computational set consists of the elements $\{|00>, |01>, |10>, |11>\}$. The correspondence between physical and computational states is then defined to be:

State 1 → $|00>$
State 2 → $|10>$
State 3 → $|11>$
State 4 → $|01>$

The computational bases which have one (1) as their first element correspond to physical states which have exactly one trap occupied by an electron. This result is used for the implementation of quantum gates as shown in the next paragraph.

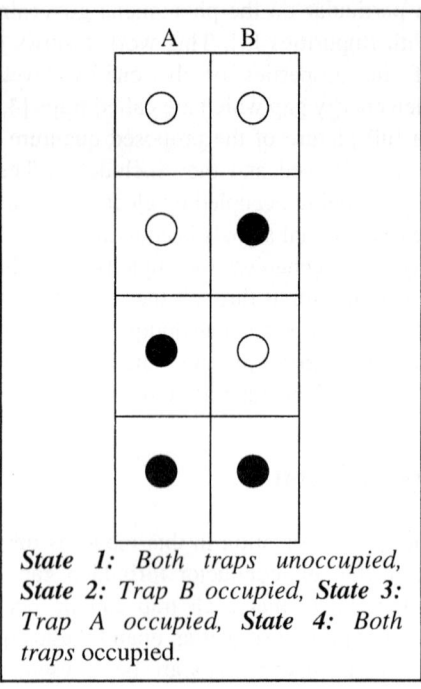

State 1: Both traps unoccupied, **State 2:** Trap B occupied, **State 3:** Trap A occupied, **State 4:** Both traps occupied.

Fig. 1. The four possible states two adjacent traps can be in. Here, $E_A < E_B$, where E_A, E_B are the energy levels of traps A and B respectively.

3 Quantum Computation – The CNOT Gate

If a physical system is to be capable to perform quantum computation, then there must be a way that the system resembles to a logical equivalent of a quantum logic gate. It has been showed, that for a quantum computer to be able to perform universal computation, there are exactly three gates that need to be implemented. These are the Controlled-Not (CNOT), the Phase and the Hadamard gates.

The way in which the CNOT gate can be implemented in the physical system described in the previous section, will be presented in the following paragraphs. It is well known that the truth table for the CNOT gate is [1]:

$$|00\rangle \rightarrow |00\rangle$$
$$|01\rangle \rightarrow |01\rangle$$
$$|10\rangle \rightarrow |11\rangle$$
$$|11\rangle \rightarrow |10\rangle$$

The above table means that the CNOT gate flips the second (target) qubit if the first (control) qubit is equal to one, otherwise the target qubit remains unaffected. The way that the CNOT gate is implemented in our quantum computer system, is by the operation knowing as "electron swap". This operation can be achieved by the use of an external signal in the form of a laser pulse having the appropriate frequency and its physical effect is that the position of two electrons of adjacent traps is flipped [6].

Referring to Figure 1, the effect of the "electron swap" can be described as:

$$State\ 1 \rightarrow State\ 1$$
$$State\ 2 \rightarrow State\ 3$$
$$State\ 3 \rightarrow State\ 2$$
$$State\ 4 \rightarrow State\ 4$$

Substitution of the physical states by their corresponding computational ones, will result to the truth table of the CNOT operation being obtained:

$$|00\rangle \rightarrow |00\rangle$$
$$|10\rangle \rightarrow |11\rangle$$
$$|11\rangle \rightarrow |10\rangle$$
$$|11\rangle \rightarrow |11\rangle$$

Therefore, the operation of the "electron swap", in computational terms is equivalent to the CNOT gate.

4 Circuit Interconnection

The next step is the construction of the quantum circuit, since for a quantum computation to take place, the different quantum gates must be connected and form such a quantum circuit. Therefore, for the model to be complete, there must be a physical way, allowing for the output of a quantum gate to be given as an input to a next level gate level.

In semiconductors this can be achieved by using appropriate electrical signals. These signals have the effect of moving electrons of a trap of given energy level, to a next trap of higher energy level. This is demonstrated in figure 2.

Thus, the two step complete mechanism of the quantum gate is:

a) First a laser pulse performs the logical operation of the CNOT gate.
b) Then, an electrical signal shifts the output to the next level and the process is repeated.

The frequency of the laser pulse for step (a) depends on the energy level of the traps being involved. Thus, the frequency of each one of the quantum circuit levels is distinct and well defined, therefore a frequency "overlap" can never occur.

The circuit can be scaled up by increasing the number of the traps in the gap. This can be achieved by introducing extra impurities, so that the scale of the quantum circuit can be controlled with accuracy.

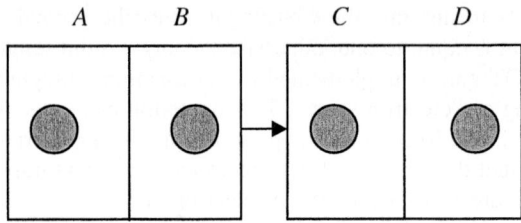

Fig. 2. The circuit interconnection. Here $E_A < E_B < E_C < E_D$. Gray color indicates that whether the traps are occupied or not is irrelevant.

5 Implementation of the Algorithms and Measurement

A demonstration on the way the above techniques can be combined in order to develop the different gates that and the circuit construction is presented in the following paragraphs. The demonstration examines the implementation of the well known quantum algorithm known as the Shor's factorization algorithm [1,7].

First, the system is prepared in a known and predefined quantum state. This state is chosen to be equal to |000....>, that is the state where all qubits are equal to one. This can be achieved by illumination techniques so that the vast majority of the traps of the starting energy level are unoccupied at the start of the experiment. It must be noticed that the starting energy level must be chosen to be fairly far from the valence band, so that decoherence effects between the valence band electrons and trap level electrons can be avoided.

Having prepared the system, the next step is to perform the application of the series of signals described on the above sections. Then, the algorithm under test is implemented via a measurement technique determining the outcome as a result of the applied signal on the initial system condition.

As an example, the logical circuit for the Quantum Fourier Transformation, which is the quantum routine used in Shor's Algorithm and given schematically in Figure 3, can be implemented as described in [5]. The corresponding operations are then defined as:

The Hadamard operation, denoted as H, is well defined as:

$$|0\rangle \rightarrow 1/\sqrt{2}\ (|0\rangle + |1\rangle)$$
$$|1\rangle \rightarrow 1/\sqrt{2}\ (|0\rangle - |1\rangle)$$

and R_n is the Phase Operation:

$$a|0\rangle + b|1\rangle \rightarrow a|0\rangle + exp(2\pi j/2^n)\ |1\rangle$$

Provided that these two gates are implemented, $O(n^2)$ steps are required to transform a given matrix of length n. After the computation is completed, a measuring process should then be performed for the outcome to be obtained.

Since measuring a single trap is in practice very difficult if not impossible, a sampling technique is used and the outcome is then determined by majority voting. This can be achieved by measuring a macroscopic property of the semiconductor, such as the conductance. The measured electrical property will provide information regarding the status of the traps at the energy level corresponding to the final output gates of the circuit. The final outcome is then determined by comparing the electrical property to a predefined threshold; if the property value exceeds the threshold value, then the outcome is to be taken as one (1), otherwise as zero (0).

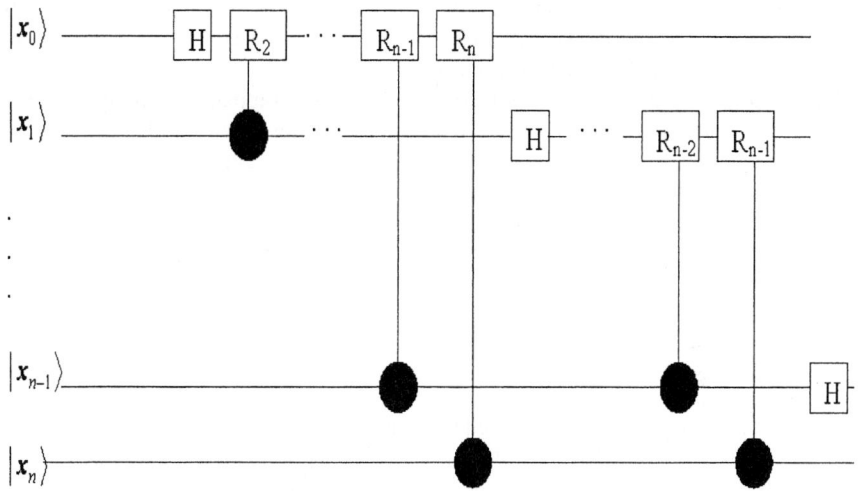

Fig. 3. The Quantum Fourier Transform

6 Error Correction

Errors can be introduced in the course of a quantum computation resulting in loss of information or computational faults. Two major error factors are considered [1,7,8].

First, electrons between adjacent traps can partly occupy different traps than those they ought to (overlapping). This introduces interference between different level gates and causes computational errors. One way to remove this error is by means of enlarging the energy separation between adjacent traps. This can be done in the same manner as with scaling up, by controlling the doping impurities inside the semiconductor.

Second, loss of information can occur due to decoherence effects present in all quantum systems. In this system, decoherence can occur because of the coupling between the semiconductor electrons and the external signaling (pulses). This coupling factor is small, since theoretically laser pulses and electrons react in a coherent way [6]. Nevertheless, this error could be added up in the course of a computation, so that the total error increases linearly on the length of the circuit. That means that the total error factor can take a maximum value of ne, where e is the order of the initial error and n the length of the circuit. This factor can be evaluated within reasonable approximation and then is subtracted from the final outcome.

7 Conclusions

The mechanism involving the implementation of a quantum computer architecture using existing semiconductor properties has been presented. The mechanism is based on a four state computational basis using well known properties of semiconductor traps. As semiconductors have already been thoroughly studied and used for years, this mechanism has the advantage that the transition from classical to quantum computing can be made on existing platforms, an idea that recently has come upon the attention of scientists [1,2 and references therein].

The proposed architecture is compatible to already established techniques and can be applied to solve well known quantum algorithms using a standard CNOT gate.

Further work includes the development of the other two universal quantum gates as well as further models on the semiconductors being used currently by computer industry. This procedure, together with suitable simulation is currently on.

References

1. Nielsen M A, Chuang I L , *Quantum Computation and Quantum Information*, Cambridge University Press, 2000.
2. Hollenberg L C L, Dzurak A.S, Wellard C., Hamilton A.R., Reilly D J, Millburn G J, Clark, R G, 2004 *Physical Review B* 69 113301
3. Grove A S, *Physics and Technology of Semiconductor Devices*, New York, John Wiley & Sons, 1967 pp. 126-140.
4. K.Theodoropoulos, D.Ntalaperas, I.Petras, A.Tsakalidis, N.Konofaos, Proceedings (in press by Springer-Verlag) of ICPS2004, 27th Int. Conference on the Physics of Semiconductors, July 26-30, 2004, Flagstaff, Arizona, USA.
5. K.Theodoropoulos, D.Ntalaperas, I.Petras, N.Konofaos, 2nd International Conference on Microelectronics Microsystems and Nanotechnology, Athens, Greece 14-17 November 2004.
6. R.Bube, *"Photoelectronic Properties of Solids"*, John Wiley and Sons, New York, 1997.
7. Barenco C H, Bennett R, Cleve D P, diVincenzo N,. Margolus N, Shor P W, Sleator T, Smolin J, Weinfurter H, 1995 *Phys. Review A* **52** 3457
8. Takarabe K, Landsberg PT, Liakos JK, 1997 *Semicond. Sci. Techn.* 12 687

TSIC: Thermal Scheduling Simulator for Chip Multiprocessors

Kyriakos Stavrou and Pedro Trancoso

Department of Computer Science, University of Cyprus,
75 Kallipoleos Ave., P.O.Box 20537, 1678 Nicosia, Cyprus
{tsik, pedro}@cs.ucy.ac.cy

Abstract. Increased power density, hot-spots, and temperature gradients are severe limiting factors for today's state-of-the-art microprocessors. However, the flexibility offered by the multiple cores in future Chip Multiprocessors (CMPs) results in a great opportunity for controlling the chip thermal characteristics. When a process is to be assigned to a core, a thermal-aware scheduling policy may be invoked to determine which core is the most appropriate.

In this paper we present TSIC, Thermal SImulator for CMPs, which is a fully parameterizable, user-friendly tool that allows us to easily test different CMP configurations, application characteristics, and scheduling policies. We also present a case study where the use of TSIC together with simple thermal-aware scheduling policies allows us to conclude that there is potential for improving the thermal behavior of a CMP by implementing new process scheduling policies.

1 Introduction

Technology scaling, together with frequency and complexity increase, result in a rise of the power density, which is becoming a key limiting factor to the performance of current state-of-the-art microprocessors [1,2,3,4]. In addition, power dissipation is not uniformly distributed in modern microprocessors leading to localized hot-spots [2,5] whereas application's behavior varies during their execution leading to significant temporal temperature gradients [6]. For example, Skadron et al. [7] observed a gradient of 40 ^oC for the gzip benchmark. Nevertheless, peaks in the temperature are not the only power-related problem observed in microprocessors. Skadron et al. [3] report the negative effect of temporal and spatial temperature gradients on the lifetime of microprocessors inferring that "a constant temperature T will always yield a longer expected lifetime than a time-varying temperature with an average of T". The need of mechanisms that will limit both the temporal and spatial divergence of chip's temperature is therefore highlighted.

There are several techniques that target the temperature problem. Dynamic Thermal Management (DTM) techniques [2,8,9] try to guarantee that the operation temperature of a microprocessor will never exceed a given threshold.

Dynamic Voltage Scaling (DVS) [10] reduces the frequency and voltage of microprocessors at run time to decrease power consumption during periods of moderate computation needs or of dangerous temperature levels. Activity Migration [5] proposes spreading the heat by migrating computation to different locations on the die. Cluster-Hopping [11] proposes execution using a variable subset of the available clusters to decrease both the spatial temperature divergence over the chip and the temperature peaks.

One approach to avoid several of the problems previously mentioned and still increase the performance of a processor is to shift to Chip Multiprocessors (CMP) architecture. Nevertheless, CMPs also suffer from high temperatures, spatial and temporal diversities [4,5]. These parallel execution engines are likely to execute workloads of significantly different temperature profiles leading to large spatial and temporal thermal diversities over the chip. In addition, when CMPs are used in multiprocessing environments, there will be periods during which some cores will be idle while others will be executing high demanding applications, further increasing the problem. Finally, as the number of cores on the chip increases, these diversities are expected to worsen.

However, an increase in the number of cores available on the chip will result in new opportunities for thermal management. In particular, we believe that in future CMPs, it will be possible to improve the thermal efficiency of the chip by applying *thermal-aware process scheduling*, through mapping the processes to the most appropriate cores.

The main contribution of this work is the design and implementation of TSIC, a fully parameterizable graphical **T**hermal **SI**mulator for **C**MPs. TSIC uses information for the position of each core and the thermal stress caused by the process running on it to determine it's temperature dynamically taking into account the ambient and the inter-core heat transfer rate. The simulator models context switches due to I/O operations, page faults or quantum exhaustion to provide more realistic results.

As a case study, several scheduling policies have been implemented to examine the impact of the scheduling algorithm on the temperature behavior of the chip. Our results show that simple heuristics can improve both the fraction of time during which the temperature of the cores is above a critical threshold and the temperature diversities over the chip.

The rest of the paper is organized as follows. Section 2 discuses the general thermal model, Section 3 the core scheduling whereas Section 4 presents TSIC. Our case study is presented in Section 5 and Section 6 shows the conclusions to this work.

2 Thermal Model

The main factors affecting the temperature of a core are: inter-core heat exchange, heat abduction from the ambient and the power consumption of the core itself. Equation 1 describes core's temperature as a function of the factors mentioned above [2,6,7].

$$\Delta T_i = \left[\sum_{m=1, m\neq i}^{n} f_c(T_i - T_m)\right] - \left[f_a(T_i - T_{ambient})\right] + \left[f_p(Process_i, T_i)\right] \quad (1)$$

What follows is a brief analysis of the previous equation.

Inter-Core Heat Exchange: There is heat exchange between each pair of cores in the chip, that obeys both the principle of superposition and reciprocity. Superposition, which is modeled by the summation in equation 1, means that the total effect of inter-cores heat exchange is the sum of the effect of heat exchange between each pair of cores. Reciprocity, which defines that if core A is cooler than core B the temperature of A due to heat exchange with B will increase by the same "amount" that the temperature of B will decrease, is modeled by $f_c(x) = -f_c(-x)$ in equation 1.

Heat Abduction from the Ambient: Heat transfer to the ambient, which is the only way of cooling the chip, is a function of the difference between core's and ambient's temperature. The larger the difference the larger the heat abduction rate [2,12,13].

Local Power Consumption: The local power consumption of the core is the last, but probably the most important, factor in the heat equation. As mentioned earlier, applications have significant differences in their thermal behavior. TSIC takes this diversity into account by modeling applications of five different thermal types ranging from applications with minimal impact on temperature to "thermal viruses" (section 4.1).

The first term of equation 1, models the inter-core heat exchange, implying that such an exchange exists among *any* pair of cores in the chip. Skadron *et al.* [2] found that modeling only the heat exchange between adjacent cores (cores having a common edge) has minimal effect on accuracy and provides significant improvement on computational efficiency of the algorithm. Thermal transfer between non adjacent cores still exists but now is implicit. For example, in Figure 1 the temperature of core 1 is modeled to be explicitly affected only by the cores 1-L, 1-R, 1-U and 1-D and not by the diagonally adjacent cores (1-LU,1-LD, 1-RU and 1-RD). However core 1-LU, for example, still affects the temperature of core 1, but implicitly, through affecting the temperature of cores 1-L and 1-U (this applies in the same way to the rest of the diagonally adjacent cores).

Cores neighboring with the edge of the chip, have the ability to dissipate more heat to the ambient than the other cores, due to the increased "free" cross-sectional area. TSIC takes this into account by modeling increased heat abduction rate for these cores.

3 Core Scheduling

Whenever a process is scheduled for execution, *Process Scheduling Policies* are used to determine the core on which it will run. In TSIC, the user is able to

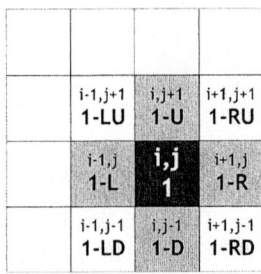

Fig. 1. A chip multiprocessor with 16 cores

choose one out of the several available policies. The modularity of TSIC allows new policies to be implemented with just few lines of code. The scheduling policies available in TSIC are briefly described below.

Random: The new process is assigned to a randomly selected *idle* core. It is guaranteed that an idle core exists as the simulator never generates more processes than the number of idle cores.

Random is the simplest policy among those available in TSIC but the less efficient. However, as explained in the results section, when the utilization of the chip is high, little potential for optimizations exists without process migration. Consequently, in such a scenario, the *Random* policy could be applicable.

Always Coolest: The new process is assigned to the coolest *idle* core. This is the simplest heuristic used to optimize thermal behavior and the easiest to implement as it requires no state. What is needed is just one temperature sensor for each core. This however will not be a problem taking into account that currently Power5 [14] embeds 24 such sensors.

Our results show that even this simple heuristic can be beneficial revealing the potential offered by scheduling policies.

Neighborhood Aware: This policy benefits cores adjacent to the edge of the chip and cores that reside in "cooler" neighborhoods. The rationale behind this heuristic is that the lower the temperature of the core's neighborhood is, the easier it will be to keep its temperature at low levels due to the inter-core heat exchange. Cores neighboring with the edge of the chip are beneficial due to the increased heat abduction rate from the ambient.

Neighborhood aware is found to perform the best among the other two policies and can be implemented with negligible cost.

Figure 2 depicts an example of operation of the available policies, assuming that all cores are idle. *Random* policy can select any core of the chip. *Always Coolest* policy will select the core noted with **C** whereas *Neighborhood Aware* policy will select the core noted with **N**. If the new process is mapped to core **C** it is likely that its temperature will significantly increase due to both the process just assigned to it and due to the heat exchange with the *hotter* neighboring

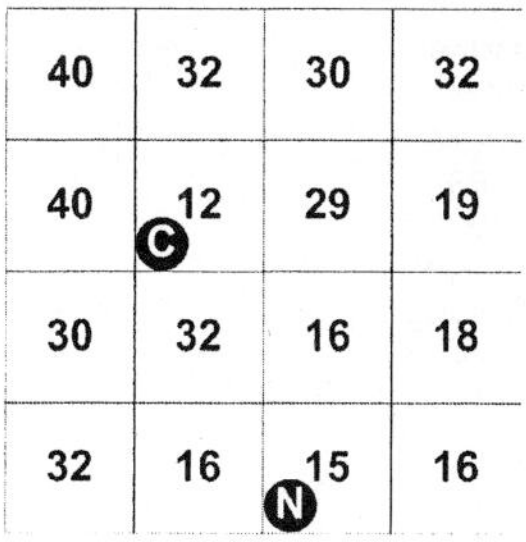

40	32	30	32
40	12 ⓒ	29	19
30	32	16	18
32	16	15 ⓝ	16

Fig. 2. An example of operation of scheduling policies

cores. Assigning the new process to core **N** will lead to better thermal behavior due to the low temperature of the neighborhood.

None of these two locations is however guaranteed to be optimal as the execution time and thermal type (section 4.1) of *future* processes is not known. Implementing such an *Oracle Scheduling Algorithm* is what our future work will focus on, as it will allow us to more accurately evaluate the efficiency of the available scheduling algorithms and guide the implementation of new, more efficient ones.

4 TSIC: Thermal SImulator for CMPs

4.1 Application Processes

To better understand the operation of TSIC, this section presents the way processes are handled by the simulator.

Real workloads consist of applications of varying demands, varying execution time and varying temperature profiles [6,7]. The *Thermal Type* of an application represents the thermal stress it causes to the processor on which it is running, in terms of power consumption and heat dissipation. To better represent real workloads, TSIC models applications of five different thermal types, ranging from applications with minimal impact on temperature (Thermal Type 1) to "thermal viruses" (Thermal Type 3).

Additionally, TSIC allows defining the average execution time of processes between context switches (*process lifetime*). An important advantage of TSIC is that it models *independent* context switches among the cores of the chip. This models real systems better as, when a process has a page fault on one processor, the operating system would likely switch to another process immediately in order to avoid the performance penalty.

On each *"Process Cycle"* the simulator generates a number of new processes and removes those that either completed their execution or suffered a context switch. Although the number of processes generated on each cycle is random, the average utilization of the chip is controlled by a parameter in TSIC, set by the user. If for example, in a CMP of 64 cores, the average utilization was defined to

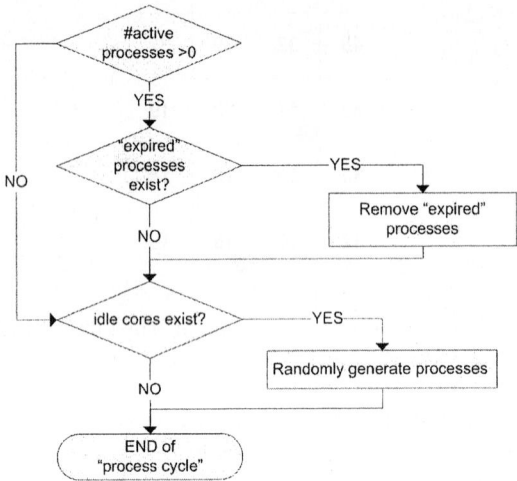

Fig. 3. The process manipulation algorithm - the "Process Model"

be 75%, it is guaranteed that *on average*, at a certain point in time, 48 cores will be active, whereas periods of less and more utilization will exist. This is another advantage of TSIC as it models what would occur in a real system.

The thermal type of the processes being generated is randomly defined and guaranteed to meet the average defined by the user. The same stands for the time that a process will run on a core before an I/O or a quantum triggered context switch event occurs.

Figure 3 depicts the algorithm executed by the simulator for process manipulation (the *"Process Model"*). If *expired processes* exist, *i.e.* processes that their execution is interrupted due to I/O or quantum triggered context switch, the simulator removes these processes and classifies the cores on which those processes were running as *Idle Cores*. A random event, that is repeated as many times as the number of currently idle cores, determines if a new process will be generated. If this is the case, the lifetime and the thermal type of the process are randomly defined.

4.2 Operation of the Simulator

In order to estimate the temperature of each core, a predefined number of *"Thermal Cycles"* are interleaved between successive *"Process Cycles"*, allowing the *Thermal Model* to spread the temperature differences over the chip (Figure 4).

4.3 Temperature Metrics

Several metrics have been proposed [2,3,4,10,12] to quantify the temperature distribution over the chip. The most obvious metric is the average temperature of each core. Although the temporal average provides an indication for the core's

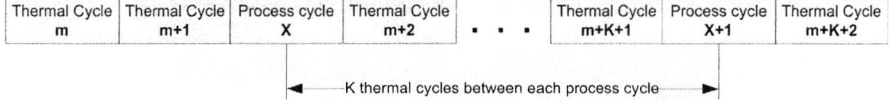

Fig. 4. The simulator combines both the thermal and the process model

thermal stress, it hides information about periods during which its temperature was above a critical threshold (periods in thermal violation). Therefore other metrics, such as percentage of cycles in thermal violation and the temporal and spatial divergence of temperature should also be considered.

The metrics previously mentioned are only a subset of those reportable by TSIC which are listed below. We are however, trying to identify whether these metrics provide a complete picture of the thermal history of the chip.

- Chip-wide average temporal temperature
- Per core average temporal temperature
- Per core temporal temperature distribution
- Chip-wide temporal temperature distribution
- Chip-wide spatial temperature divergence
- Chip-wide temporal temperature divergence

Quantifying the benefits of improving the thermal characteristics of the chip, is another aspect related to the temperature metrics and an important part of our future work.

4.4 TSIC Interface

TSIC is a powerful, fully parameterizable thermal simulator for CMPs with a Graphical User Interface. It embeds a thermal and a process model, and offers three different process scheduling policies.

The main window of TSIC is presented in Figure 5. TSIC allows simulation of only the *Thermal Model*, only the *Process Model* or of the *Combined Model*. All parameters (the number of cores, the average usage, the average thermal behavior of the workload, the average execution time of each process, all parameters of the thermal model and the scheduling algorithm) can be configured through the *Settings Menu* that is presented in Figure 6-a.

Another advantage of TSIC is the functionality it provides for defining the initial temperatures of the cores. This is done through the menu presented in Figure 6-b.

5 Case Study: Evaluation of Scheduling Algorithms

As a case study, we analyze the effect of different process scheduling policies on the thermal behavior of the chip, for four different cases, two different chip sizes

596   K. Stavrou and P. Trancoso

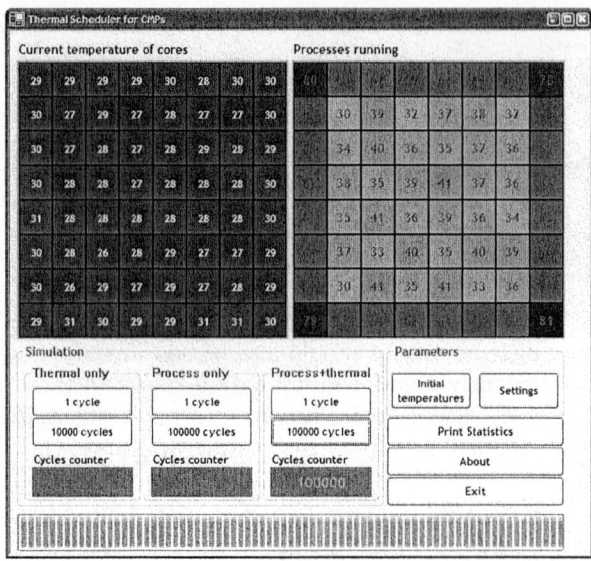

Fig. 5. TSIC: Temperature SImulator for CMPs

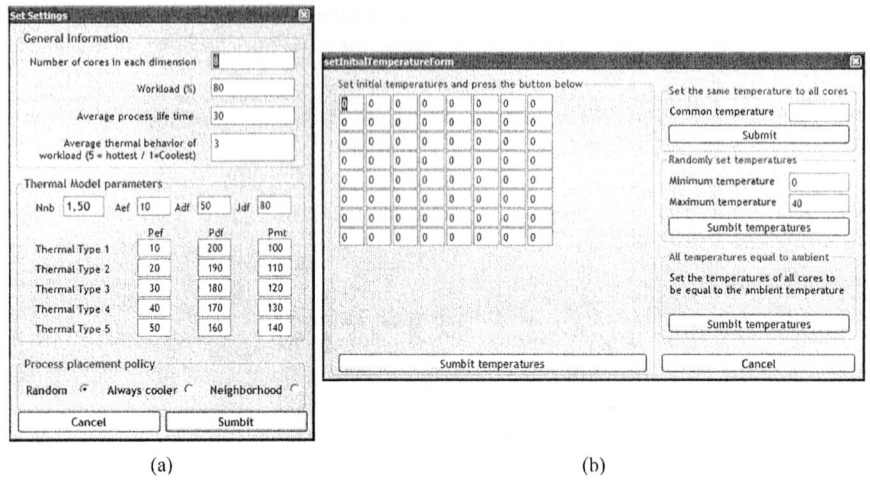

Fig. 6. (a)Settings menu, (b)TSIC allows setting the initial temperatures of cores

(36 and 64 cores) and two different chip utilizations (load of 50% and 80%). For all cases we simulated 10^6 cycles with a Thermal Type 3 workload (section 4.1), that is a workload of *medium* thermal stress.

Figure 7 (a) depicts the average temporal temperature of the whole chip, *i.e.* the average temperature of the chip during the simulation period. It must be

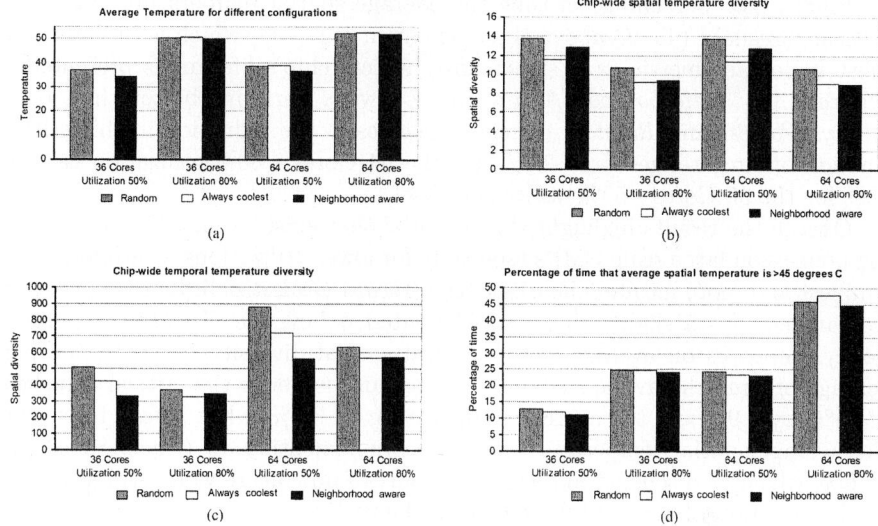

Fig. 7. Experimental results

noted here that the average temperature of the *chip* at a certain point in time is the average temperature of *all cores* at that specific point in time. *Neighborhood Aware* policy decreases the average temperature for the 50% utilization case but offers smaller benefit for the higher utilization case. This is due to the larger cooling ability the chip has when more cores are idle. Specifically, for the 36 Cores - 50% utilization case, a maximum reduction of 2.8 °C was observed between the *Always Coolest* and the *Neighborhood Aware* policy. It is worth mentioning that *Always Coolest* policy is always slightly worse than *Random* policy which implies that *local* temperature optimizations do not necessarily have a *global* effect.

Chip-Wide temporal temperature diversity, which is depicted in Figure 7 (b), is an indication of the uniformity of the average *temporal* temperature of the chip over the time. The smaller its value the more uniform the average chip temperature is. As explained in section 4.3 large temporal diversities are likely to reduce the reliability and lifetime of the chip. Both *Always Coolest* and *Neighborhood Aware* heuristics decrease the Chip-Wide temporal temperature diversity compared to the *Random* policy, especially for the 50% utilization case. As mentioned earlier, this is due to the increased number of idle cores on the chip during its operation. For the case of 36 Cores - 50% utilization this reduction reaches 43%.

Respectively to Chip-Wide *temporal* temperature diversity, Chip-Wide *spatial* temperature diversity, is an indication of the uniformity of the temperature among the cores of the chip. The results shown in Figure 7 (c), indicate that *Always Coolest* policy performs better than *Neighborhood Aware* policy, due to *Always Coolest* policy targeting local and not a chip-wide temperature reduction. This also explains why *Neighborhood Aware* performs better on average than *Always Coolest* for Chip-Wide *temporal* temperature diversity.

Finally, the percentage of time the average spatial temperature is above a critical threshold (45 °C above the ambient in our case) which is probably the most important metric as it significantly affects chip's lifetime is presented in Figure 7 (d). *Neighborhood Aware* policy always performs better than both, *Always Coolest* and *Random* policies. Specifically the reduction in this critical fraction of time ranges from 2.5%, for the 64 Cores - 80% utilization case, to 15% for the 36 Cores - 50% utilization case.

Overall the results highlight the potential that exists from different scheduling policies on large scale CMPs especially for lower utilizations. Considering the simplest and more intuitive heuristic, the *Always Coolest* policy, as the baseline, we can see that a slightly more sophisticated policy, the *Neighborhood Aware* policy, improves on average, the temporal spatial diversity by 9.5%, the percentage of time the average spatial temperature is above the critical threshold of 45°C by 3.9% and the average temperature by 3.7%, while it fails improving the average spatial temperature diversity. Implementing an *Oracle Scheduling Policy*, which as discussed in section 3 is part of our future work, will guide the implementation of new and more efficient heuristics.

Finally, we believe that if the scheduling policy can also force process migration, the potential will significantly increase providing benefits even for large utilizations. We are currently studying several alternatives.

6 Conclusions

In this paper we have presented TSIC (**T**hermal **SI**mulator for **C**MPs), a fully parameterizable, user-friendly tool that allows us to easily test different CMP configurations, application characteristics, and scheduling policies.

We have also presented a case study where the use of TSIC together with simple thermal-aware scheduling policies allowed us to conclude that there is potential for improving the thermal behavior of a CMP through using efficient process scheduling policies.

Even simple heuristics, such as the *Always Coolest* policy can achieve notable improvements on the thermal behavior of the chip especially for low workloads. Considering the simplest and more intuitive heuristic, the *Always Coolest* policy, as the baseline, we can see that a slightly more sophisticated policy, the *Neighborhood Aware* policy, improves on average, the temporal spatial diversity by 9.5%, the percentage of time the average spatial temperature is above the critical threshold of 45°C by 3.9% and the average temperature by 3.7%, while it fails improving the average spatial temperature diversity motivating us for further research.

References

1. Mudge, T.: Power: A First Class Architectural Design Constraint. IEEE Computer **34** (2001) 52–57
2. Skadron, K., Stan, M.R., Huang, W., Velusamy, S., Sankaranarayanan, K., Tarjan, D.: Temperature-Aware Microarchitecture: Extended Discussion and Results. Technical Report TR-CS-2003-08, University of Virginia (2003)

3. Huangy, W., Luy, Z., Ghoshy, S., Lachy, J., Stany, M., Skadron, K.: The Importance of Temporal and Spatial Temperature Gradients in IC Reliability Analysis. Technical Report TR-CS2004-07, University of Virginia (2004)
4. Li, Y., Brooks, D., Hu, Z., Skadron, K.: Performance, Energy, and Thermal Considerations for SMT and CMP Architectures. In: Proc. of the 11th IEEE International Symposium on High Performance Computer Architecture (HPCA). (2005) 71–82
5. Heo, S., Barr, K., Asanovic, K.: Reducing Power Density through Activity Migration. In: Proc. of the 2003 International Symposium on Low Power Electronics and Design,. (2003) 217–222
6. ElEssawy, W., Albonesi, D.H.: A Microarchitectural Level Step Power Analysis Tool. In: Proc. of the 2002 international symposium on Low power electronics and design. (2002) 263–266
7. Lee, K.J., Skadron, K.: Using Performance Counters for Runtime Temperature Sensing in High-Performance Processors. In: Proc. of the Workshop on High-Performance, Power-Aware Computing (HP-PAC). (2005) 232–239
8. Brooks, D., Martonosi, M.: Dynamic Thermal Management for High-Performance Micro-processors. In: Proc. of the 7th IEEE International Symposium on High Performance Computer Architecture (HPCA). (2001) 171–182
9. Srinivasan, J., Adve, S.V.: Predictive Dynamic Thermal Management for Multimedia Applications. In: Proc. 17th International Conference Supercomputing. (2003) 109–120
10. Magklis, G., Scott, M.L., Semeraro, G., Albonesi, D.H., Dropsho, S.: Profile-based Dynamic Voltage and Frequency Scaling for a Multiple Clock Domain Microprocessor. In: Proc. of the 30th annual International Symposium on Computer Architecture. (2003) 14–27
11. Chaparro, P., Gonzalez, J., Gonzalez, A.: Thermal-Aware Clustered Microarchitectures. In: Proc. of the 2004 IEEE International Conference on Computer Design,. (2004) 48–53
12. Deeney, J.: Thermal modeling and measurement of large high power silicon devices with asymmetric power distribution. In: Proc. of the 2002 Symposium on Microelectronics. (2002)
13. Lall, B.S., Guenin, B.M., Molnar, R.J.: Methodology for Thermal Evaluation of Multichip Modules. IEEE Transactions on Components, Packaging and Manufacturing Technology **18** (1995) 72–79
14. Kalla, R., Sinharoy, B., Tendler, J.M.: IBM Power5 Chip: A Dual-Core Multithreaded Processor. IEEE Computer **24** (2004) 40–47

Tuning Blocked Array Layouts to Exploit Memory Hierarchy in SMT Architectures

Evangelia Athanasaki, Kornilios Kourtis, Nikos Anastopoulos,
and Nectarios Koziris

National Technical University of Athens,
School of Electrical and Computer Engineering,
Computing Systems Laboratory,
{valia, kkourt, anastop, nkoziris}@cslab.ece.ntua.gr

Abstract. Cache misses form a major bottleneck for memory-intensive applications, due to the significant latency of main memory accesses. Loop tiling, in conjunction with other program transformations, have been shown to be an effective approach to improving locality and cache exploitation, especially for dense matrix scientific computations. Beyond loop nest optimizations, data transformation techniques, and in particular blocked data layouts, have been used to boost the cache performance. The stability of performance improvements achieved are heavily dependent on the appropriate selection of tile sizes.

In this paper, we investigate the memory performance of blocked data layouts, and provide a theoretical analysis for the multiple levels of memory hierarchy, when they are organized in a set associative fashion. According to this analysis, the optimal tile size that maximizes L1 cache utilization, should completely fit in the L1 cache, even for loop bodies that access more than just one array. Increased self- or/and cross-interference misses can be tolerated through prefetching. Such larger tiles also reduce mispredicted branches and, as a result, the lost CPU cycles that arise. Results are validated through actual benchmarks on an SMT platform.

1 Introduction

The ever increasing gap between processor and memory speed, necessitates the efficient use of memory hierarchy to improve performance on modern microprocessors [15]. Compiler optimizations can efficiently keep reused data in memory hierarchy levels close to processors. Loop tiling is one of the well-known control transformation techniques, which, in combination with loop permutation, loop reversal and loop skewing attempt to modify the data access order to improve data locality. Combined loop and data transformations were proposed to avoid any negative effect to the number of cache hits for some referenced arrays, while increasing the locality of references for a group of arrays.

The automatic application of nonlinear layouts in real compilers is a really time consuming task. It does not suffice to identify the optimal layout either blocked or canonical one for each specific array. For blocked layouts, we also need an automatic and quick way to generate the mapping from the multidimensional iteration indices to the correct location of the respective data element in the linear memory. Any method of fast indexing for non-linear layouts will allow compilers to introduce such layouts along with row or column-wise ones, therefore further reducing memory misses. In [1], in order to facilitate the automatic generation of tiled code that accesses blocked array layouts, we proposed a very quick and simple address calculation method of the array indices. Our method has proved to be very effective at reducing cache misses.

In this paper, we further extend our previous work by providing a tile selection formula that applies to blocked array layouts. All related work selects tiles smaller than half of the cache capacity (they usually refer to L1 cache or cache and TLB concurrently). However, blocked array layouts almost eliminate self-interference misses, while cross-interference can be easily obviated. Therefore, other factors, before negligible, now dominate cache and TLB behaviour, that is, code complexity, number of mispredicted branches and cache utilization. We have managed to reduce code complexity of accesses on data stored in a blocked-wise manner by the use of efficient indexing, described in detail in [1]. Experimentation has proved that maximum performance is achieved when L1 cache is fully utilized. At this point, tile sizes fill the whole L1 cache. Proper array alignment obviates cross-conflict misses, while the whole cache is exploited, as all cache lines contain useful data. Such large tiles reduce the number of mispredicted branches, as well. Experimental results were conducted using the Matrix Multiplication.

The remainder of the paper is organized as follows: Section 2 briefly reviews the related work. Section 3 presents a theoretical analysis of cache performance and demonstrates the need of optimizing L1 cache behaviour, as it is the dominant factor on performance. A tight lower bound for cache and TLB misses is calculated, which meets the access pattern of the Matrix Multiplication kernel. Section 4 illustrates execution results of optimized numerical codes, giving heuristics of tile size selection. Finally, concluding remarks are presented in Section 5.

2 Related Work

Loop tiling is a control transformation technique that partitions the iteration space of a loop nest into blocks in order to reduce the number of intervening iterations and thus data fetched between data reuses. This allows reused data to still be in the cache or register file, and hence reduces memory accesses. Without tiling, contention over the memory bus will limit performance. Conflict misses [20] may occur when too many data items map to the same set of cache locations, causing cache lines to be flushed from cache before they may be used, despite sufficient capacity in the overall cache. As a result, in addition to eliminating capacity misses [11], [23] and maximizing cache utilization, the tile should be selected in such a way that there are no (or few) self conflict misses, while cross conflict misses are minimized [3], [4], [5], [10], [17].

To model self conflict misses due to low associativity cache, [24] and [12] use the effective cache size $q \times C$ ($q < 1$), instead of the actual cache size C, while [3], [4], [10] and [19] explicitly find the non-conflicting tile sizes. Taking into account cache line size as well, column dimensions (without loss of generality, assume a column major data array layout) should be a multiple of the cache line size [4]. If fixed blocks are chosen, Lam et al. in [10] have found that the best square tile is not larger than $\sqrt{\frac{aC}{a+1}}$, where a = associativity. In practice, the optimal choice may occupy only a small fraction of the cache, typically less than 10%. What's more, the fraction of the cache used for optimal block size decreases as the cache size increases. The desired tile shape has been explicitly specified in algorithms such as [5], [3], [4], [23], [24], [10]. Both [23] and [10] search for square tiles. In contrast, [3], [4] and [24] find rectangular tiles or [5] even extremely tall tiles (the maximum number of complete columns that fit in the cache). However, extremely wide tiles may introduce TLB thrashing. On the other hand, extremely tall or square tiles may have low cache utilization.

Unfortunately, the performance of a tiled program resulting from existing tiling heuristics does not have robust performance [13], [17]. Instability comes from the so-called pathological array sizes, when array dimensions are near powers of two, since cache interference is a particular risk at that point. Array padding [8], [13], [16] is a compiler optimization that increases the array sizes and changes initial locations to avoid pathological cases. It introduces space overhead but effectively stabilizes program performance. Cache utilization for padded benchmark codes is much higher overall, since padding is used to avoid small tiles [17]. As a result, more recent research efforts have investigated the combination of both loop tiling and array padding in the hope that both magnitude and stability of performance improvements of tiled programs can be achieved at the same time. An alternative method for avoiding conflict misses is to copy tiles to a buffer and modify code to use data directly from the buffer [5], [10], [21]. Copying in [10] can take full advantage of the cache as it enables to use tiles of size $\sqrt{C} \times \sqrt{C}$ in each blocked loop nest. However performance overhead due to runtime copying is low if tiles only need to be copied once.

Cache behaviour is extremely difficult to analyze, reflecting its unstable nature, in which small modifications can lead to disproportionate changes in cache miss ration [20]. Traditionally, cache performance evaluation has mostly used simulation. Although the results are accurate, the time needed to obtain them is typically many times greater than the total execution time of the program being simulated. To try to overcome such problems, analytical models of cache behaviour combined with heuristics have also been developed, to guide optimizing compilers [6], [16] and [23], or study the cache performance of particular types of algorithm, especially blocked ones [3], [7], [10], and [22]. Code optimizations, such as tile size selection, selected with the help of predicted miss ratios require a really accurate assessment of program's code behaviour. For this reason, a combination of cache miss analysis, simulation and experimentation is the best solution for optimal selection of critical transformations.

The previous approaches assumed linear array layouts. However, as aforementioned studies have shown, such linear array memory layouts produce unfavorable memory access patterns, that cause interference misses and increase memory system overhead. In order to quantify the benefits of adopting nonlinear layouts to reduce cache misses, there exist several different approaches. In [18], Rivera et al. considers all levels of memory hierarchy to reduce L2 cache misses as well, rather than reducing only L1 ones. He presents even fewer overall misses, however performance improvements are rarely significant. Park et al. in [14] analyze the TLB and cache performance for standard matrix access patterns, when tiling is used together with block data layouts. Such layouts with block size equal to the page size, seem to minimize the number of TLB misses.

3 Theoretical Analysis

In this section we study the cache and TLB behaviour, while executing the matrix multiplication benchmark, which is the building block of many scientific applications. The analysis is devoted to set associative caches. Arrays are considered to be stored in memory according to the proposed blocked layouts, that is, elements accessed in consecutive iterations are found in nearby memory locations. Blocked layouts eliminate all self-conflict misses. We examine only square tiles. Such tile shapes are required for symmetry reasons, to enable the simplification of the benchmark code. As a result, while optimizing nested loop codes and selecting tile sizes, we should focus on dimishing the remaining factors that affect performance. The following analysis is an effort to identify such factors.

3.1 Machine and Benchmark Specifications

The optimized ([9], [16], [1]) matrix multiplication code has the following form:

```
for (ii=0; ii < N; ii+=T)
   for (jj=0; jj < N; jj+=T)
      for (kk=0; kk < N; kk+=T)
         for (i = ii; (i < ii+T && i < N); i++)
            for (j = jj; (j < jj+T && j < N); j++)
               for (k = kk; (k < kk+T && k < N); k++)
                  C[i,k]+=A[i,j]*B[j,k];
```

Table 1 contains the symbols used in this section to represent the machine characteristics.

3.2 Data L1 Misses

In case of set associative caches, apart from capacity misses, neither self- nor cross-interference misses arise. Even 2-way set associativity is enough for kernel codes such as matrix multiplication, where data elements from three different arrays are retrieved. Array alignment should be carefully chosen, so that no more

Table 1. Table of hardware specifications and respective symbols used in this section

	Xeon DP	symbol
CPU freq. :	2,8GHz	
L1 cache :	16KB 8-way set asssoc.	C_{L1}
L1 line :	64B	L_1
L1 miss penalty:	4 clock cycles	c_{L1}
total L1 misses :		M_1
L2 cache :	1MB 8-way set asssoc.	C_{L2}
L2 line :	64B	L_2
L2 miss penalty:	18 clock cycles	c_{L3}
total L1 misses :		M_2
TLB entries (L1):	64 addresses	E (# entries)
page size :	4KB	P
TLB miss penalty:	30 clock cycles	c_{TLB}
total L1 misses :		M_{TLB}
mispred. branch penalty:	20 clock cycles	c_{br}

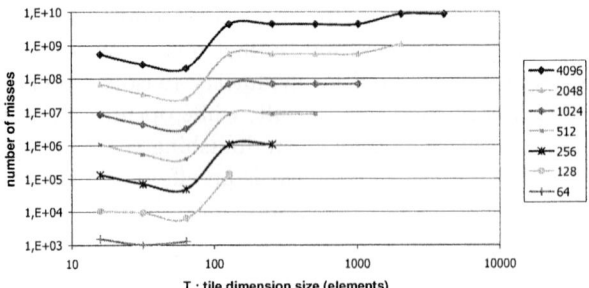

Fig. 1. Number of L1 cache misses on the Xeon DP architecture

than two arrays are mapped in the same cache location, concurrently. For this purpose, the starting mapping distances of arrays (that is, elements $A[0]$, $B[0]$, $C[0]$), should be chosen to be from L_1 to T^2 elements. Further analysis is beyond the scope of this paper.

$N^2 < C_{L1}$: In this case, all three arrays can exploit reuse, both in-tile and intra-tile. For example, array C reuses one tile row along loop j (in-tile reuse) and a whole row of tile along loop jj (intra-tile reuse). In both cases, the working set fit in L1 cache. As a relult, for array C:
$M_C = x^2 \cdot \frac{T^2}{L_1} = \left(\frac{N}{T}\right)^2 \frac{T^2}{L_1} = \frac{N^2}{L_1}$
Similarly, $M_A = M_B = \frac{N^2}{L_1}$

$N^2 \geq C_{L1}, T \cdot N < C_{L1}$: As in the previous case: $M_A = M_C = \frac{N^2}{L_1}$

On the other hand, for array B only in-tile reuse can be exploited, as loop ii reuses N^2 elements, and the cache capacity is not adequate to hold them. As a result, each ii iteration will have to reload the whole array in the cache:

$$M_B = x^3 \cdot \frac{T^2}{L_1} = \left(\frac{N}{T}\right)^3 \frac{T^2}{L_1} = \frac{N^3}{TL_1}$$

In case that $N^2 = C_{L1}, T = N$, there is in fact no tiling, so reuse takes place in loops k and j for arrays A and C, containing just 1 element and one row of the array (N elements) respectively. As a result, reuse is exploited as above. However, the reference to array B reuses N^2 elements (the whole array) along loop i. In each iteration of i, two rows of B elements ($2N$ elements) have been discarded from the cache, due to references to arrays A and C. That is:

$$M_B = \frac{N^2}{L_1} + (N-1) \cdot \frac{2N}{L_1}$$

$N^2 > C_{L1}, 3T^2 < C_{L1} \leq T \cdot N$: Three whole tiles fit in the cache, one for each of the three arrays. For arrays B, C reuse along loops ii and jj respectively can not be exploited, as there is not enough L1 cache capacity to hold N^2 and $T \cdot N$ elements respectively. The number of misses are:

$$M_B = M_C = \frac{N^3}{TL_1}$$

On the other hand, reuse along loop kk for array A can be exploited (only T^2 elements are included):

$$M_A = \frac{N^2}{L_1}$$

$N^2 > C_{L1}, T^2 \leq C_{L1} < 3T^2$: There is enough space for at most two whole tiles. Only in-tile reuse can be exploited in the arrays along the three inner loops. Thus:

$$M_A = M_B = M_C = \frac{N^3}{TL_1}$$

$N^2 > C_{L1}, T^2 > C_{L1} > T$: As in the previous case, no whole-tile reuse can be exploited. Additionally, in array B, in-tile reuse (along loop i) can not be exploited, either. Therefore, the total number of misses for each array is:

$$M_A = M_C = \frac{N^3}{TL_1}$$
$$M_B = \frac{N^3}{L_1}$$

Summary of the Data L1 Misses: Figure 1 illustrates the graphic representation of the total number of Data L1 cache misses ($M_1 = M_A + M_B + M_C$) for different problem sizes. The cache capacity and organization have the characteristics of the Xeon DP architecture (table 1).

L1 cache misses increase sharply when the working set, reused along the three innermost loops, overwhelms the L1 cache. That is, the tile size overexceeds the L1 cache capacity (C_{L1}), and no reuse can be exploited for at least one array.

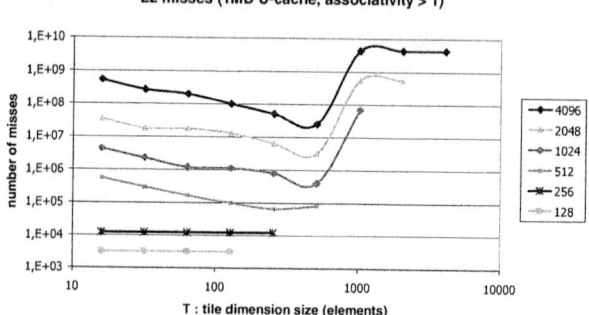

Fig. 2. Number of L2 cache misses on the Xeon DP architecture

3.3 L2 Misses

This cache level has similar behaviour as the L1 cache. As a result, we skip the detailed analysis and provide only with the corresponding graphs. Figure 2 presents the number of L2 cache misses in case of a set associative cache, with size equal the L2 cache of the Intel Xeon platform (table 1).

We note that L2 cache is unified (for data and instructions). However, the number of misses hardly increases (less than 1%) compared to an equal-sized data cache, when caches are large, like the one of the Xeon platform.

The number of L2 misses, for all array sizes, are minimized for $T^2 = C_{L2}$, when the whole cache is been used and a whole tile fits in the cache so that tile-level reuse can be exploited. However, L1 misses are 1 order of magnitude more than L2 misses. As a result, the L1 misses dominate the total memory behaviour, as illustrated in figure 4.

3.4 Data TLB Misses

This cache level is usually fully associative. So, there is no need to take care of array alignment. The TLB miss analysis is similar to the L1 cache analysis. Due to space limitations, we provide only with the corresponding table. Table 2 summarizes the total number of Data TLB misses M_{TLB} for all problem sizes. According to this table, the number of Data TLB misses has the form of figure 3.

The number of TLB misses for all array sizes, for an example of 64 entries (as the TLB size of Xeon is), are minimized when $T = 256$. At this point, the pages addresses of a whole tile fit in the TLB entries, so that tile-level reuse can be exploited.

3.5 Total Miss Cost

Taking into account the miss penalty of each memory level, as well as the penalty of mispredicted branches (as presented in [2]), we derive the total miss cost of

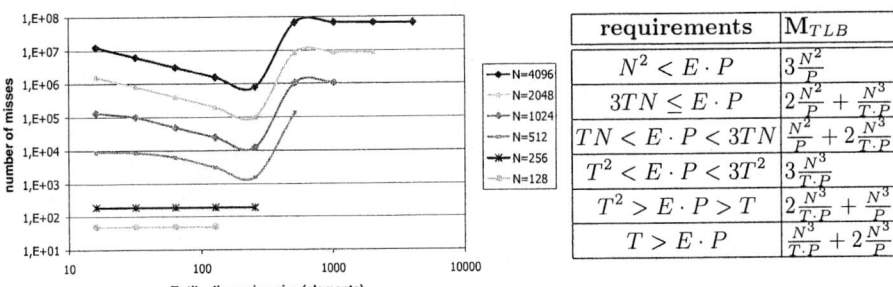

Fig. 3. Number of TLB misses for various array and tile sizes

Table 2. D-TLB misses

requirements	M_{TLB}
$N^2 < E \cdot P$	$3\frac{N^2}{P}$
$3TN \leq E \cdot P$	$2\frac{N^2}{P} + \frac{N^3}{T \cdot P}$
$TN < E \cdot P < 3TN$	$\frac{N^2}{P} + 2\frac{N^3}{T \cdot P}$
$T^2 < E \cdot P < 3T^2$	$3\frac{N^3}{T \cdot P}$
$T^2 > E \cdot P > T$	$2\frac{N^3}{T \cdot P} + \frac{N^3}{P}$
$T > E \cdot P$	$\frac{N^3}{T \cdot P} + 2\frac{N^3}{P}$

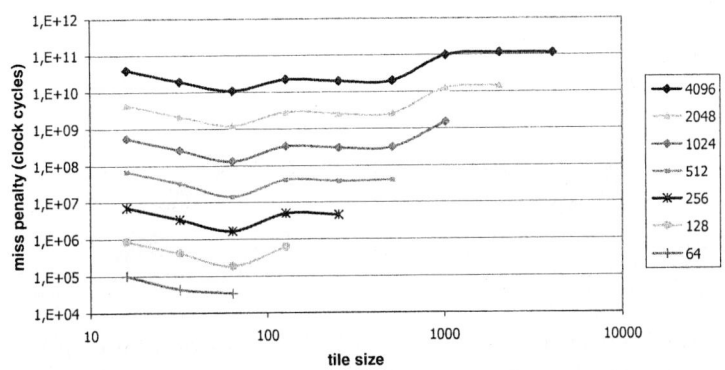

Fig. 4. Number of L2 cache misses on the Xeon DP architecture

figure 4. Figure 4 makes clear that L1 misses dominate cache and, as a result, total performance in the Xeon DP architecture. Maximum performance is achieved when $T = 64$, which is the optimal tile size for L1 cache (the maximum tile that fits in L1 cache). L1 cache misses are more than one order of magnitude more than L2 misses and three orders of magnitude more than TLB misses. Notice that the Xeon DP architecture bears quite a large L2 cache (1Mbytes), which reduces the number of L2 misses significantly, and leaves L1 cache to dominate total performance. Thus, even though L1 misses cost fewer clock cycles, they are still the most weighty factor.

4 Experimental Results

In this section we present experimental results using the Matrix Multiplication benchmarks. The experiments were performed on a Dual SMT Xeon (Simulta-

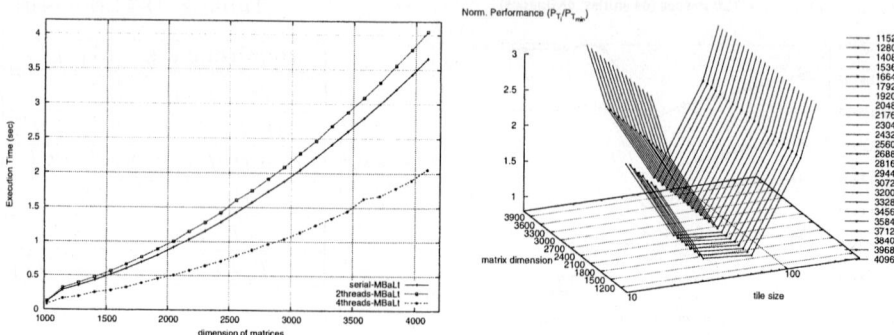

Fig. 5. Xeon - The relative performance of the three different versions

Fig. 6. Xeon - Normalized performance of the matrix multiplication benchmark for various array and tile sizes (serial MBaLt)

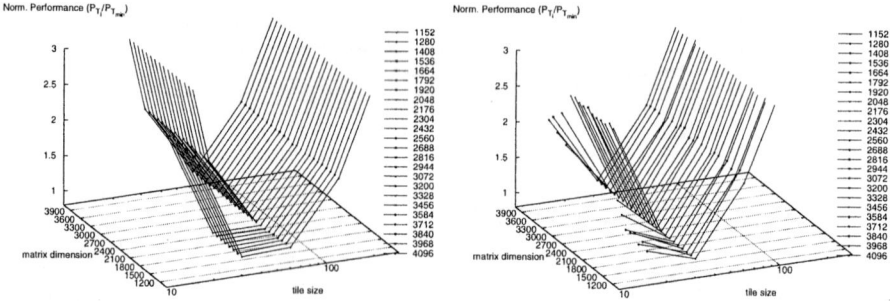

Fig. 7. Xeon - Normalized performance of the matrix multiplication benchmark for various array and tile sizes (2 threads - MBaLt)

Fig. 8. Xeon - Normalized performance of the matrix multiplication benchmark for various array and tile sizes (4 threads - MBaLt)

neous Multi-Threading supported). The hardware characteristics were described in table 1.

The dual Xeon platform needed special attention, in order to efficiently exploit the hyperthreading technology. We conducted three different experiments. Firstly, the serial blocked algorithm of Matrix Multiplication (MBaLt code - with use of fast indexing) was executed. Secondly, we enabled hyperthreading running 2 threads in the same physical cpu. For large tile sizes, execution times obtained with the 2threads-MBaLt version are quite larger than those of the serial version. Smaller tile sizes lead to more mispredicted branches and loop boundary calculations, thus increasing the overhead of tiling implementation. In the case of 2threads-MBaLt, this tiling overhead gets almost doubled, since the two threads are executing the same code in an interleaved fashion. In other words, the total overhead introduced overlaps the extra benefits we have with the simultaneous execution capabilities of the hyperthreaded processor. This is not the case for larger tile sizes, where the tiling overhead is not large enough to overlap the advantages of extra parallelism. Figure 5 illustrates only best performance measurements for each different array dimension (tile sizes are equal to the one minimize execution time). The serial-MaLt version seems to have better performance compared to the 2threads-MBaLt version, as execution time is minimized for small tile sizes. Finally, we executed a parallel version of matrix multiplication MBaLt code (4threads-MBaLt), where 2 threads run on each of the 2 physical cpus, that belong to the same SMP. Execution time is reduced, and performance speed up reaches 44% compared to the serial-MBaLt version.

As far as the optimal tile size is concerned, serial MBaLt obey to the general rule, this is $T_{optimal} = \sqrt{C_{L1}} = 64$. However, when hyperthreading had been enabled, $T_{optimal}$ seams to be shifted to the just smaller size, in order to make room in the L1 cache for the increased number of concurrently used array elements. This behaviour is observed, both when two threads run on the same physical cpu (2threads-MBaLt), as well as in the parallel version (4threads-MBaLt) where $T_{optimal} = 32$ (figures 6, 7 and 8). Note that for the 2threads-MBaLt version $T_{optimal} = 32$ when $N < 2048$. For larger arrays, the 2threads-MBaLt version behaves similarly to the serial one, filling the whole L1 cache with useful array elements.

5 Conclusion

A large amount of related work has been devoted to the selection of optimal tile sizes and shapes, for numerical nested loop codes where tiling has been applied. In this paper, we have examined blocked array layouts with an addressing scheme that uses simple binary masks. We have found theoretically and verified through experiments and simulations that, when such layouts are used, in direct mapped caches, with a large L2 cache, L1 cache misses dominate overall performance. Prefetching in combination with other code optimization techniques, set optimal tiling to be $T_1 = \sqrt{C_{L1}}$. On the other hand, when L2 cache has a moderate capacity, L2 misses weight overall performance to larger tile sizes and determine the optimal tile size to be $T \leq \sqrt{C_{L2}}$.

References

1. E. Athanasaki and N. Koziris. Fast Indexing for Blocked Array Layouts to Improve Multi-Level Cache Locality. In *8-th Work. on Interaction between Compilers and Computer Architectures*, Madrid, Spain, Feb 2004. In conjuction with HPCA-10.
2. E. Athanasaki and N. Koziris. A Tile Size Selection Analysis for Blocked Array Layouts. In *9-th Work. on Interaction between Compilers and Computer Architectures*, San Francisco, CA, Feb 2005. In conjuction with HPCA-11.
3. J. Chame and S. Moon. A Tile Selection Algorithm for Data Locality and Cache Interference. In *Int. Conf. on Supercomputing*, Rhodes, Greece, June 1999.
4. S. Coleman and K. S. McKinley. Tile Size Selection Using Cache Organization and Data Layout. In *Conf. on Programming Language Design and Implementation*, La Jolla, CA, June 1995.

5. K. Esseghir. Improving Data Locality for Caches. Master's thesis, Department of Computer Science, Rice University, Houston, TX, Sept 1993.
6. S. Ghosh, M. Martonosi, and S. Malik. Cache Miss Equations: A Compiler Framework for Analyzing and Tuning Memory Behavior. *ACM Trans. on Programming Languages and Systems*, 21(4), July 1999.
7. J. S. Harper, D. J. Kerbyson, and G. R. Nudd. Analytical Modeling of Set-Associative Cache Behavior. *IEEE Trans. Computers*, 48(10), Oct 1999.
8. C.-H. Hsu and U. Kremer. A Quantitative Analysis of Tile Size Selection Algprithms. *The J. of Supercomputing*, 27(3), Mar 2004.
9. M. Kandemir, J. Ramanujam, and A. Choudhary. Improving Cache Locality by a Combinaion of Loop and Data Transformations. *IEEE Trans. on Computers*, 48(2), Feb 1999.
10. M. S. Lam, E. E. Rothberg, and M. E. Wolf. The Cache Performance and Optimizations of Blocked Algorithms. In *Int. Conf. on Architectural Support for Programming Languages and Operating Systems*, Santa Clara, CA, April 1991.
11. K. S. McKinley, S. Carr, and C.-W. Tseng. Improving Data Locality with Loop Transformations. *ACM Trans. on Programming Languages and Systems*, 18(04), July 1996.
12. N. Mitchell, K. Högstedt, L. Carter, and J. Ferrante. Quantifying the Multi-Level Nature of Tiling Interactions. *Int. J. of Parallel Programming*, 26(6), Dec 1998.
13. P. R. Panda, H. Nakamura, N. D. Dutt, and A. Nicolau. Augmenting Loop Tiling with Data Alignment for Improved Cache Performance. *IEEE Trans. on Computers*, 48(2), Feb 1999.
14. N. Park, B. Hong, and V. Prasanna. Analysis of Memory Hierarchy Performance of Block Data Layout. In *Int. Conf. on Parallel Processing*, Vancouver, Canada, Aug 2002.
15. D. Patterson and J.Hennessy. *Computer Architecture. A Quantitative Approach.* San Francisco, CA, 3rd edition, 2002.
16. G. Rivera and C.-W. Tseng. Eliminating Conflict Misses for High Performance Architectures. In *Int. Conf. on Supercomputing*, Melbourne, Australia, July 1998.
17. G. Rivera and C.-W. Tseng. A Comparison of Compiler Tiling Algorithms. In *Int. Conf. on Compiler Construction*, Amsterdam, The Netherlands, March 1999.
18. G. Rivera and C.-W. Tseng. Locality Optimizations for Multi-Level Caches. In *Int. Conf. on Supercomputing*, Portland, OR, Nov 1999.
19. Y. Song and Z. Li. Impact of Tile-Size Selection for Skewed Tiling. In *5-th Work. on Interaction between Compilers and Architectures*, Monterrey, Mexico, Jan 2001.
20. O. Temam, C. Fricker, and W. Jalby. Cache Interference Phenomena. In *Conf. on Measurement and Modeling of Computer Systems*, Nashville, TN, May 1994.
21. O. Temam, E. D. Granston, and W. Jalby. To Copy or Not to Copy: A Compile-Time Technique for Assessing When Data Copying Should be Used to Eliminate Cache Conflicts. In *Conf. on Supercomputing*, Portland, OR, Nov 1993.
22. X. Vera. *Cache and Compiler Interaction (how to analyze, optimize and time cache behaviour)*. PhD thesis, Malardalen University, Jan 2003.
23. M. E. Wolf and M. S. Lam. A Data Locality Optimizing Algorithm. In *Conf. on Programming Language Design and Implementation*, Toronto, Canada, June 1991.
24. M. E. Wolf, D. E. Maydan, and D.-K. Chen. Combining Loop Transformations Considering Caches and Scheduling. In *Int. Symposium on Microarchitecture*, Paris, France, Dec 1996.

A Tool for Calculating Energy Consumption in Wireless Sensor Networks

G. Dimitriou[1], P.K. Kikiras[2], G.I. Stamoulis[1], and I.N. Avaritsiotis[2]

[1] Dept. of Computer and Communications Engineering,
University of Thessaly, Volos, Greece
{dimitriu, georges}@inf.uth.gr
[2] Dept. of Electrical & Computer Engineering,
National Technical University of Athens, Athens, Greece
kikirasp@mail.ntua.gr, abari@cs.ntua.gr

Abstract. Energy and total useful lifetime are primary design concerns of fundamental importance, in a variety of real life applications, where the deployment of a Wireless Sensor Network is desired. In this paper the authors introduce AVAKIS, a tool for calculating the energy consumption of the various components of a sensor node. The proposed tool is an architectural level simulator, in which the system building blocks are described by a high level behavioral model. The methodology used in order to estimate power consumption is based on both the characteristics of the components, and on a number of user-defined initialization parameters.

1 Introduction

One of the main concerns and constraints when designing a wireless sensor network (WSN) is energy consumption. In most of the real life application scenarios, where WSNs are deployed, energy is a limited and valuable resource. In order to overcome energy shortage, the sensor node, the processing algorithms and the communication - routing protocols must be energy aware.

In the study of WSNs, three key disciplines are converging: digital circuitry and sensors, wireless communications, and signal processing software and algorithms. Furthermore, the energy efficient implementation of a wireless network requires cross-layer optimizations, starting from the physical up to the application level. Having in mind the characteristics and limitations of WSNs, we have been motivated to develop a tool that addresses the problem of estimating the energy consumption of the node during its operation.

The rest of this paper is organized as follows. Section 2 presents the methods and tools that are used in this work. In section 3 a case study of a WSN for perimeter protection is presented, and the analytical capabilities of the tool and its findings are commented on. Finally, in section 4, concluding remarks and an outline of future work are discussed.

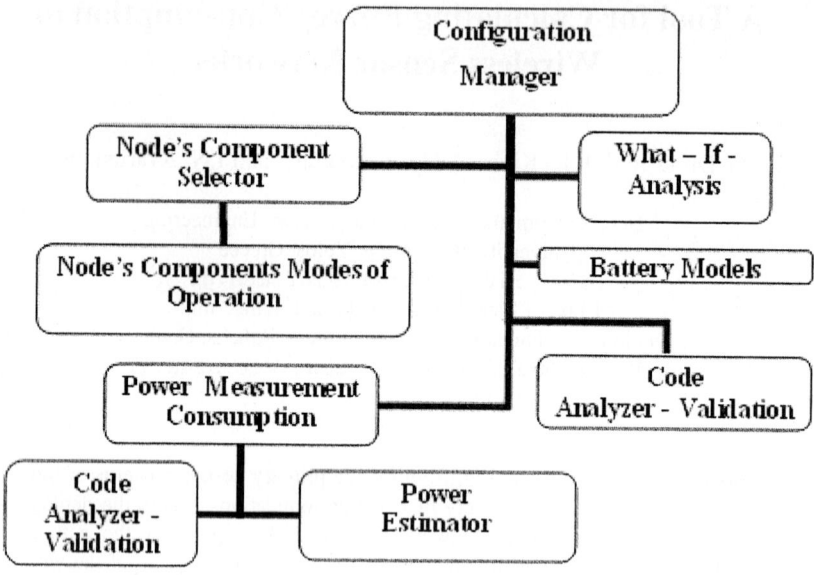

Fig. 1. Configuration Manager Components

2 Tool Architectural and Functional Overview

2.1 Architectural Overview

The proposed tool, AVAKIS, is an architectural level simulator in which the system building blocks are described by a high-level behavioral model:

Configuration Manager: This is the main component of the tool. The configuration manager is responsible for conducting any needed calculation for the estimation of power consumption at the components of a selected node. It provides appropriate modules for configuring any aspect of the wireless node, as shown in Figure 1.

Protocol interface: This protocol interface provides appropriate tools for the definition of the network protocol that it is going to be implemented by the configuration manager. Additionally, this component can act as a hook to other simulators that work on the upper layers.

Component Expansion Interface: This module provides the user with advanced customization features for adding supplementary components, whenever the main node's generic components are not suitable for a specific implementation.

Reporting Mechanism: This mechanism provides a number of reports and graphs presenting the power consumption of the node in any given simulation. More on this mechanism will be discussed in Section 3.

2.2 Functional Overview

The estimation of the sensor node energy consumption is a multi-parameter problem, depending on the hardware characteristics and the protocol decisions throughout the OSI layer range.

The main energy consumers in the node are the microprocessor, the sensing device and the RF link. The power consumed by the microprocessor is related to the frequency of its clock, to the voltage supply, to the time that is needed to perform a given task, which in turn is related to the code that is executed, and to the power saving features that are implemented. On the other hand, the energy consumption of the RF link is comprised of the energy required transmitting a bit over a given distance and of the energy required for the operation of the RF circuitry. Similarly, the energy consumption of the sensor device is divided into the energy required by its electronic circuitry and the energy required sensing a bit of information. The former is related to the power supply voltage and the latter is highly correlated with the sampling frequency. Thus, we have modeled a "threshold" operational status, where, even though the sensor is active, it has a much lower power supply voltage than in its usual operation, which means that the sensor at this state performs sampling in less frequent time intervals and at lower sensitivity. For the rest of the components of the node, such as the DSP, the GPS, and the memory, the energy consumption model is derived from the characteristics provided by their manufacturers.

The selection of the components was based on their power consumption profiles. Especially for the DSP, a number of different profiles have been modeled, due to the fact that, while it is in its active state (FFT, Compress, Encrypt, and Decrypt), each of the above operations present different needs of energy consumption.

In order to maximize the operational lifetime of the node, the components of the node that operate in full operational mode must be constrained to those explicitly needed to perform the required task at any given time. Thus, different operational states, for all the energy consuming components of the node, have been modeled, in an attempt to maximize the accuracy of the energy consumption estimate.

At this point it must be stressed, that the state in which the node will operate in, depends on the operational needs and planning, the application goals defined prior to deployment, and on the expected activity at the deployment area.

Radio and Battery Models

Radio Model. The radio model used is based on the models of [1,2], which are extended, by taking in account the power consumption required for the transceiver to shift between different operational states and by considering the probability of retransmissions due to errors or collisions. In general, each node of the network can communicate with any other neighboring node in its effective transmission range, and with the base station in three different ways: direct, multihop and clustering. For each of these communication methods, we have modeled situations such as overhearing and relaying of transmissions for linear or non-linear distribution of network nodes.

1. *Direct.* Each node communicates directly with the base station without any collaboration of any other node. Under this scheme, communication can occur either with overhearing (with or without relays) or without overhearing of neighboring nodes. In this case, the energy needed to transmit a packet of size K bits between two nodes A and B in distance d equals to:

a) *Without overhearing:*

$$E_{AB} = E_{transmit} * K * d^a. \quad (1)$$

b) *With overhearing:*
   (i) *Without relays.* In order to transmit a packet from a node to the base station with overhearing from other N nodes which are on listen mode:

   $$E_{AB} = E_{transmit} * K * d^a + N * E_{receive} * K. \quad (2)$$

   (ii) *With relays.* Likewise:

   $$E_{AB} = E_{transmit} * K * d^a + N * E_{receive} * K + \sum_{1}^{N-1} E_{D(i)B}, \quad (3)$$

   where $D(i)$ represents each node's distance from node B.

2. *Multihop.* The nodes are communicating with base station by using other nodes of the network as relaying points.
   a) *Linear model:* Let us assume a network with n nodes and distance between nodes equal to r. If we consider the energy expended in transmitting a single K-bit message from a node located at distance nr from the base station using a routing protocol, each node sends a message to the closest node on the way to the base station. Thus the node located at distance $(n-1)r$ from the base station would require n transmits at distance r and $n-1$ receives, plus *one* transmit for distance d. The energy needed to transmit a K-bit packet from a node to the base station would then equal to:

   $$E_{AB} = (n-1)(E_{transmit} * K * r^a + E_{receive} * K) + E_{transmit} * K * d^a. \quad (4)$$

   b) *Non-linear model:* The solution to this problem is highly correlated with the transmission routing protocol. We can assume that in a dense non-linear network topology, although it is possible that L nodes will be overhearing the transmissions, they would be prevented from relaying the transmission by the routing protocol and only a subset of them (let it be n) will relay the transmission. Therefore, we can assume that the energy required to transmit a K-bit packet from A to B is as follows (provided that all nodes are transmitting in their effective range d):

   $$E_{AB} = E_{transmit} * K * n * d^a + E_{receive} * K * L. \quad (5)$$

3. *Clustering.* This type of communication scheme requires the presence of a node, which will serve as a cluster head. This node is responsible for the collection and fusion of the selected data from its area and for the implementation of communication and security tasks between the nodes of its cluster area and the base station. In that case the energy needed to transmit a K-bit packet from node A to cluster head B (let their distance be d) equals to:

$$E_{AB} = E_{transmit} * K * d^a + E_{receive} * K * N + E_{ReceiveClusterHead} * K. \quad (6)$$

In all the above cases, $E_{transmit}$ is the energy expenditure in the node's transmitter electronics, N is the number of the nodes that overhear, $E_{receive}$ is the energy cost spent at the overhearing nodes while receiving the K-bit packet, $E_{ReceiveClusterHead}$ is the energy expenditure in the cluster's transmitter electronics needed to receive K bits of data and α is the path loss exponent, with value between two and five and which expresses the RF propagation path loss suffered over the wireless channel at distance d.

Battery Model. The available energy and consequently the overall lifecycle of a node is depending on the capacity of its battery. A battery's capacity is measured in milli-ampere-hours (mAh). In theory that means that a 100 mAh battery could support a node consuming 10 mA for 10 hours. But this is not the case in a real world scenario. The available energy is a function of the battery's technology and discharge profile (which both are heavily depending on the chemistry of the battery), and from the way the energy is extracted from the battery. In the literature, a number of battery models have been proposed, but in this work the linear battery model introduced in [3] has been adopted, which treats the battery as a linear current storage.

Power Estimation Procedure Overview. In the following paragraphs, the power consumption estimation methodology with the help of the proposed tool will be presented. First, the user selects the components of the node and their specific characteristics (e.g microcontroller frequency, RF required start-up time, operational state, etc.). Subsequently, the user selects the operational requirements of the node such as sampling rate, instructions executed per clock, and compression ratio.

The user then enters the code that will be executed by the processing elements of the node. In order to estimate the microprocessor power component, a plug-in has been developed, which calculates power, by measuring the number of machine instructions that the code is expected to execute. The power consumption plug-in (further PCPI) is essentially an interpreter, which produces an intermediate representation for a C input program and simulates its execution through a traversal of that representation. The overall power consumption can be estimated by summing up the expected power consumption of individual machine instructions.

PCPI tool. The first part of PCPI is the front end of a C compiler/interpreter that we built from scratch, which analyzes a C program and produces a corresponding intermediate representation. An intermediate representation based on the abstract syntax tree (AST) has been chosen, which allows an easy interpretation through a tree traversal. Most features of the C programming language are supported, except for preprocessor directives, which must be translated into C code, before the application of PCPI. Full type checking has been incorporated into PCPI, although not required for the purpose of this project, minimizing interpretation errors that would later appear due to incorrect source code.

The second part of PCPI is a simulator that interprets a program given in the form of an AST-based intermediate representation. The execution environment is created, and the AST is traversed in the order dictated by the program execution. For each node visited, all necessary actions are taken to update the data space, and to estimate the power consumed by that node.

For the purpose of power estimation, a load-store architecture model is assumed, so that all data items are loaded from memory before, and stored back to memory after any operation on them. Nonetheless, operations within the same C expression communicate data through registers, i.e. with no memory access, unless there is a side effect that forces a memory update, or a function call that forces register spilling of values that must stay alive through the call.

Individual machine instructions are divided into 12 types, depending on the operation they perform and the data type – integral or floating point – they involve. A user-defined table provides estimated power consumption for all different types of machine instructions, in a way that allows power consumption estimation for different processor architectures. The power consumption of each memory and each branch operation includes an average expected cost for cache misses and branch mispredictions. The PCPI simulator emulates calls to all basic C library functions, in order to support I/O, string and heap operations. Power consumption is not modeled for those functions, though.

An example run of PCPI on a C program, possible core of a cryptography application, is shown in Figure 2. The source code is given in Figure 2a, whereas the PCPI output is given in Figure 2b. Power measurement is given in some abstract power units that show the relative consumption with a base unit corresponding to the power consumed by a single unconditional jump instruction.

```
unsigned char a[10000],c[10000];
unsigned long long k[9];
main(){
   unsigned long long *aull, *cull;
   int i=0,j;
   while (i<10000) {
      aull = (unsigned long long*) &a[i];
      cull = (unsigned long long*) &c[i];
      for (j=0;j<9;j++) cull[j] = aull[j] ^ k[j];
      cull[9] = aull[9] ^ cull[8] ^ cull[0];
      i+=80;
   }
}
```

(a)

Simulation Statistics

8126 Integer ALU instructions; power = 24378
1250 Unconditional jump instructions; power = 1250
1376 Conditional jump instructions; power = 11008
11626 Memory load instructions; power = 104634
2877 Memory store instructions; power = 20139
3625 Integer multiply instructions; power = 25375
Total: 28880 instructions; 186784 power units

(b)

Fig. 2. Example run of PCPI

Consequently, the number of instructions to be executed along with the calculated energy consumption and the initialization parameters defined by the user are forwarded to the power estimator. In this stage the power consumption at the components defined by the user is computed and the results of the calculations are presented to the user in tabular and graphical form. At this point, the user can perform what-if analysis by modifying any user defined parameters prior to execution of the estimator, and visualize the new results in either graphical or tabular form.

3 Case Study: A WSN for Perimeter Protection

3.1 System Description and Architecture

A surveillance network [4] is assumed, composed of three areas of interest, with a number of nodes deployed in each area.

The node is equipped with a low power GPS (Global Positioning System) receiver, which is used at the early stages of deployment for the exact geolocation discovery of the node. Furthermore, the node has an A/D converter attached to the microcontroller unit, in order to convert analog sensed signals to digital, for further processing. For performing communication tasks, the nodes are equipped with an RF radio. Finally, the node has a microcontroller unit (MCU), a low-power storage unit and a power module (two rechargeable Lithium batteries). The footstep detection algorithm used, is based on [5] and was designed to require minimum computations and memory resources; therefore, in order to complete its detection task, it requires only 840 instructions to be executed by the MCU, including the control instructions required by the protocol.

3.2 Analysis of Energy Consumption

In the following paragraphs the analysis capabilities of the proposed tool for a node as the one mentioned previously are exhibited.

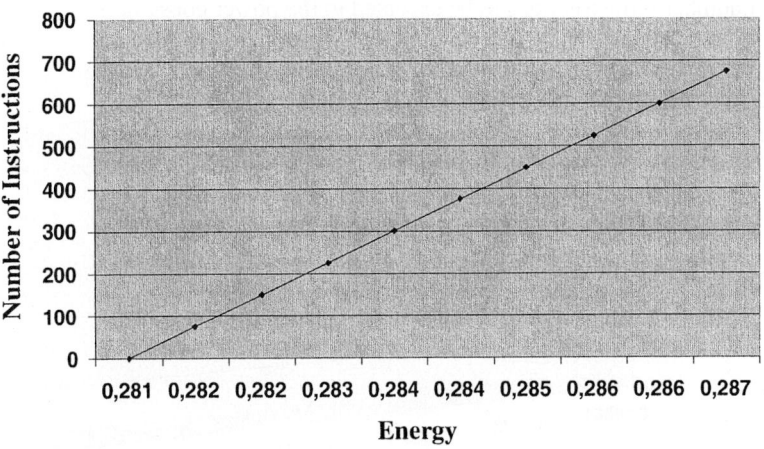

Fig. 3. Node's total energy consumption per instruction executed at the MCU

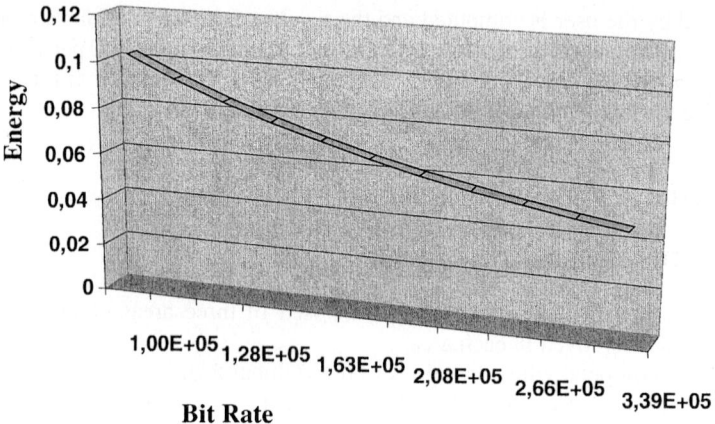

Fig. 4. Energy consumed at the node vs. number of bits to transmit

Power Consumption per Instructions to be Executed. The number of the instructions that the MCU is going to execute is proportional to the energy that the MCU is going to consume. As we can see in Figure 3, the power of the MCU increases linearly with the number of instructions executed. Thus, the importance of the development of power aware algorithms and protocols is obvious, because an increase of 10% in the number of instructions to be executed leads to an increase of 2% of the energy consumed at the node.

Power Consumption per bit. The number of bits that a node must send in order to fulfill its task is highly affecting its power consumption, and as seen in Figure 4, the higher the number of bits to transmit, the more energy the node consumes. This fact correlated with the results of the analysis performed earlier, considering the impact of the total number of instructions to be executed to the power consumption of the MCU.

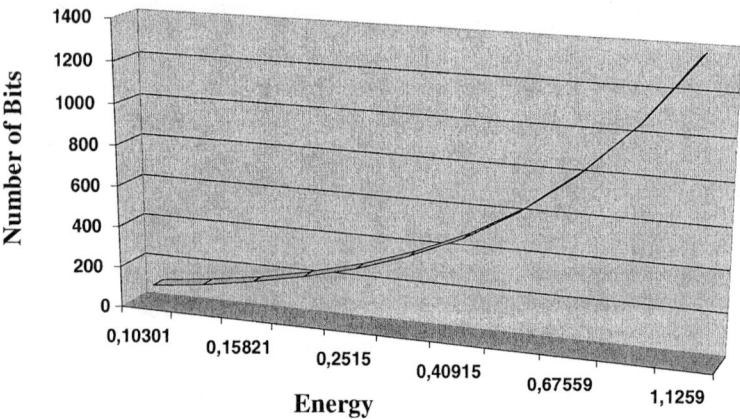

Fig. 5. Energy consumed at the node vs. transmission bit rate

This can lead us to the conclusion that it is less energy consuming to process locally the sensed data and then to transmit the results of the processing, than to transmit raw or semi-processed data to other parts of the network. However, this is mitigated by the distance the signal needs to be transmitted

Power Consumption vs. Bit Rate. As we can see from Figure 5, as the bit rate increases, the energy consumed by the node decreases. That is explained, if we consider that the bit rate affects the time that the RF works at its active state, which is the state of operation that the power consumption of the RF peaks.

Power Consumption per Compression Ratio and Sampling Rate. As we can see from Figure 6a, as the compression ratio increases, the total amount of energy

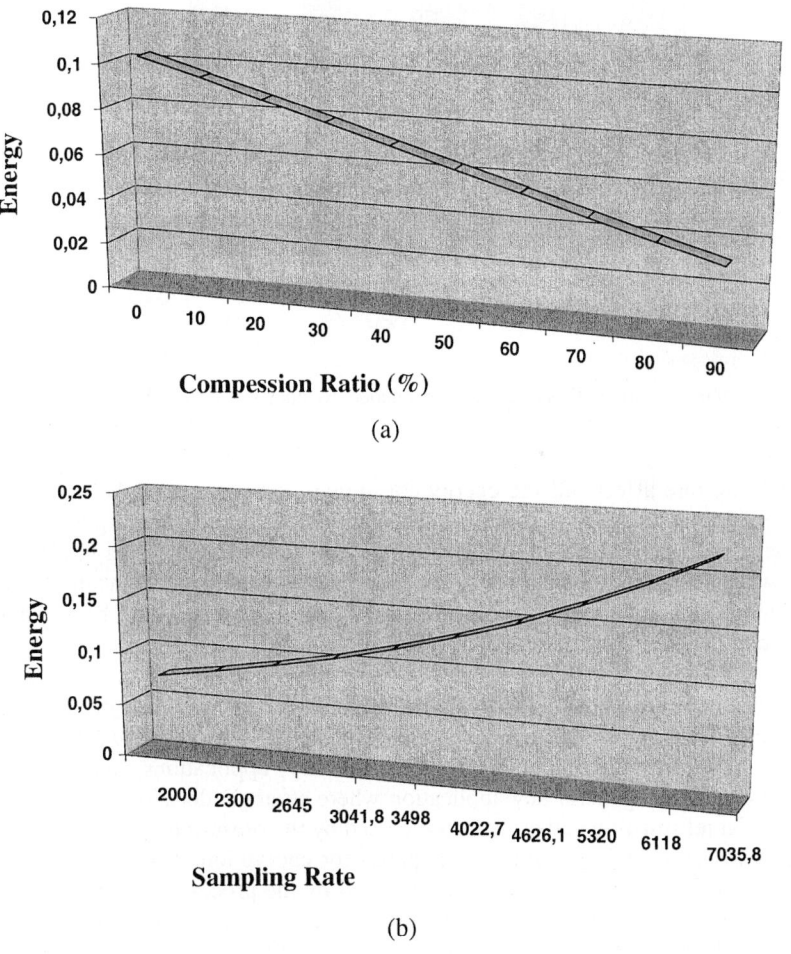

Fig. 6. Energy consumed at the node vs. (a) compression ratio and (b) sampling rate

consumed at the node decreases. This happens, because the compression ratio affects the number of total bits that the node is going to transmit, and thus, as presented earlier, the more bits the node transmits, the more energy it consumes.

We have chosen to evaluate symmetric algorithms and hash functions due to their energy efficiency, especially when compared with the energy required to implement a public key security mechanism [6].

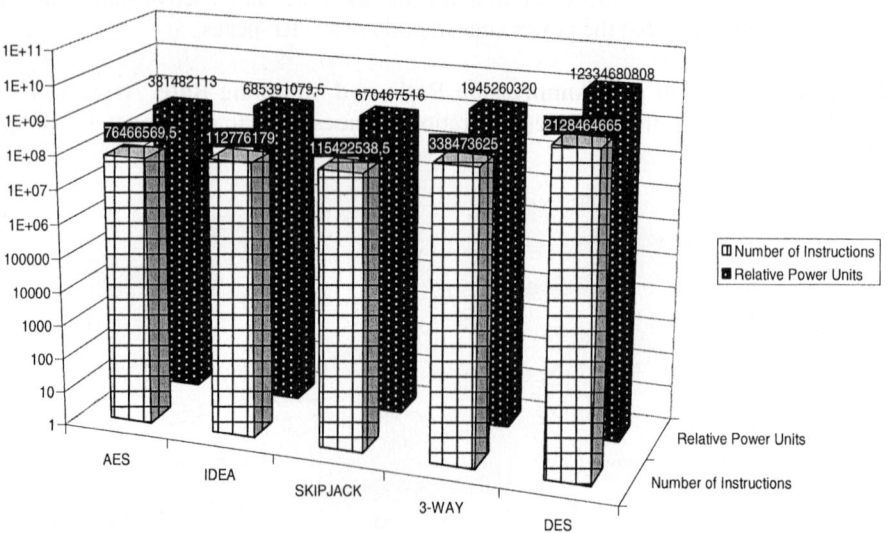

Fig. 7. Number of instructions and power needed to encrypt a 512KB file per encryption algorithm

Sampling rate affects all the energy consuming components of the node, by prolonging the time that the MCU, the sensor, and the RF circuitry are required to stay in their active operation state, in which they consume the maximum energy (Figure 6b). Thus, when designing sensing algorithms, special provision must be taken to ensure a) sample at a slow rate until a predefined threshold is exceeded, and b) to sample at such a rate that satisfies the network sensing requirements.

Power Consumption vs. Encryption Algorithm. Security is of fundamental importance for a variety of applications for which WSNs are deployed. For example, biomedical applications, security (including military) applications, industrial control applications and in general any application where strategic decisions are expected to be based on information gathered and processed by the sensor nodes.

Our tool can calculate the energy required for encryption. The amount of energy consumed by a security algorithm is determined by the processor or DSP power consumption on active state, on MCU frequency, and on the number of clock cycles needed by the processor to compute the security function. Figure 7 shows the number of instructions and the power consumption required encrypting a 512KB file.

4 Conclusions

A novel tool for estimating the energy consumption of a sensor node along with its breakdown at the component level has been presented. The analysis is based on both the characteristics of the components, and on a number of user defined initialization parameters.

The contribution of this work is that the main network operations and all node functions are linked to the physical layer and the actual implementation of the sensor node, providing accurate and reliable estimates, along with a new perspective on node design practices. The clear tradeoffs between local processing, raw data transmission, and communication range, as well as the relationships between all aspects of sensor network design and the total energy consumed are accounted for in AVAKIS.

This enables designers to easily incorporate and validate energy saving features, specific to the application their sensor network will be used for, allowing reliable cross-layer optimizations.

References

1. Prithwish Basu, Jason Redi, "Effect of Overhearing Transmissions on Energy Efficiency in Dense Sensor Networks," IPSN'04, April 26–27, 2004, Berkeley, California, USA.
2. Wendi Heinzelman, Anantha Chandrakasan, and Hari Balakrishnan, "Energy-Efficient Communication Protocol for Wireless Microsensor Networks," Proceedings of the 33rd Hawaii International Conference on System Sciences - 2000.
2. Sung Park, Andreas Savvides and Mani. B. Srivastava, "Simulating Networks of Wireless Sensors," Proceedings of the 2001 Winter Simulation Conference.
3. P.K. Kikiras, J.N Avaritsiotis, "Unattended Ground Sensor Network for Force Protection," Journal of Battlefield Technology Vol 7, No 3, November 2004.
4. G.P. Mazarakis, J.N Avaritsiotis, "A Prototype Sensor Node for Footstep Detection", Proceedings of EWSN'05 January 31 – February 2, 2005, Istanbul, Turkey.
5. D.W. Carman, P.S. Kruss, and B.J. Matt. Constraints and Approaches for Distributed Sensor Network Security. In NAI Labs Technical Report 00-010, September 2000.

Hardware Support for Multithreaded Execution of Loops with Limited Parallelism[†]

Georgios Dimitriou[1] and Constantine Polychronopoulos[2]

[1] Dept. of Computer & Communications Engineering,
University of Thessaly, Volos 38221, Greece
`dimitriu@uth.gr`
[2] Dept. of Electrical & Computer Engineering,
University of Illinois at Urbana-Champaign, Urbana, Illinois 61801, USA
`cdp@csrd.uiuc.edu`

Abstract. Loop scheduling has significant differences in multithreaded from other parallel processors. The sharing of hardware resources imposes new scheduling limitations, but it also allows a faster communication across threads. We present a multithreaded processor model, Coral 2000, with hardware extensions that support Macro Software Pipelining, a loop scheduling technique for multithreaded processors. We tested and evaluated Coral 2000 on a cycle-level simulator, using synthetic and integer SPEC benchmarks. We obtained speed-ups of up to 30% with respect to highly optimized superblock-based schedules on loops that exhibit limited parallelism.

1 Introduction

For more than thirty years the appearance of novel processor architectures has signaled the introduction of new loop-scheduling techniques, at both the iteration and the instruction level, that attempt to exploit the respective hardware capabilities. The development of multiprocessors, for instance, led to the design of iteration-level loop scheduling techniques in the 1970s. Likewise, the development of multiple-issue processors led to the design of instruction-level loop scheduling techniques in the 1980s.

Multithreaded processors support multiple hardware threads that share their resources. Loop scheduling is significantly affected by multithreading at all code granularity levels, from the coarse-grained iteration level, to the fine-grained instruction level. For instance, at the iteration level, loop scheduling through partitioning of the loop iteration space hurts data cache locality, since cache is shared among threads. At the instruction level on the other hand, a function call can be included in a software-pipelined schedule and executed through a context switch to another thread, since the context switch will preserve the instruction schedule and the private register contents of the first thread.

[†] This work was supported in part by the National Science Foundation, the Office of Naval Research, by a research grant from the National Security Agency and a research donation from Intel Corp. Most development and testing were done on the computers of the National Center for Supercomputing Applications at the University of Illinois.

In this paper we present our multithreaded processor model, *Coral 2000*, with architectural support for *Macro Software Pipelining* (MSWP) [1], a multithreaded-processor loop-scheduling technique that we have developed in an attempt to address the aforementioned issues. MSWP pipelines a loop at the task level, using the loop distribution transformation [2], and can be applied on loops with abundant, as well as with limited parallelism. Coral 2000 architectural support for MSWP includes:

- A zero-cycle thread context-switch mechanism, based on the α-*Coral* concept at the University of Illinois [3], that allows threads to be frequently switched.
- An inter-thread communication means, which enables threads to execute asynchronously, when they are working on a common loop.
- The ability to recognize branches at the fetch stage of the processor front end and to rapidly switch threads involved in branches.
- Thread-level speculation that handles loop-carried dependencies and control flow abnormalities, like early loop exits and multithreaded recursion.
- A thread scheduler with priorities, to boost non-speculative threads and minimize misspeculation overhead, and with a buffering mechanism that allows the front end to mix instructions from more than one thread within the same stage.

We tested and evaluated the architectural features of Coral 2000 on a cycle-level simulator that implements all the above multithreading support, using several synthetic benchmarks, as well as an integer SPEC benchmark.

This paper is organized as follows. Section 2 discusses multithreaded processor architecture and loop scheduling at both the iteration and the instruction level. MSWP is briefly presented in Section 3. The following section presents Coral 2000, with all hardware support for multithreading. Section 5 discusses simulation results for a number of benchmarks. The last section summarizes our conclusions.

2 Multithreaded Processor Architecture and Loop Scheduling

2.1 Multithreaded Processor Architecture

Multithreaded processors support multiple active threads in hardware, switching context among them to exploit parallelism and utilize hardware resources. The *interleaved* multithreaded architectures switch context at each cycle, whereas the *blocked* multithreaded architectures switch context on demand.

Two early multithreaded processors were the *Heterogeneous Element Processor* (HEP) [4] and the *Sparcle* processor [5]. The HEP was interleaving threads at each cycle, in order to hide memory access latency. In the Sparcle, each thread was continuously fetching instructions until a miss on a remote memory access, or until a synchronization failure, in which case context was switched to another thread.

In the last decade, interleaved multithreaded processors have been enhanced with superscalar capabilities [6]. The *Simultaneous MultiThreading* (SMT) processor has further extended interleaved multithreading to allow multiple threads to be fetching instructions at the same time, in an attempt to fill the unused slots in the processor pipeline [7]. Recent work on SMT includes extensions for multiple-path branch-level speculation [8] and single-chip clustered SMT processors [9].

Another approach to multithreading, closer to on-chip multiprocessors than to multithreaded processors though, has been the *Multiscalar* processor [10], which additionally supports *thread-level speculation* [11,12]. A combination of the SMT and the Multiscalar processor has also been considered [13].

2.2 Loop Scheduling and Parallelism Exploitation

Program parallelism is mostly exploited within loops, either at coarse granularity level through loop parallelization, or at fine granularity level through code compaction.

Traditional loop scheduling in parallel machines schedules different loop iterations on separate processors. In the absence of loop-carried dependencies [14], a loop is transformed to a completely parallel or *doall* loop. Otherwise, synchronization operations are inserted in the loop body, resulting in a partially parallel or *doacross* loop. Alternatively, the loop can be partitioned across tasks of the loop body, resulting in the *dopipe* loop. Loop transformations that attempt to remove dependencies and break dependence cycles can be utilized to optimize scheduling in all the above cases [15].

At the instruction level, on the other hand, the prevailing loop scheduling technique is *Software Pipelining* (SWP) [16]. Circular instruction reordering across multiple loop iterations is performed together with code compaction, in order to exploit instruction-level parallelism (ILP). The minimum number of cycles between consecutive iteration schedules is called *Minimum Initiation Interval* (MII). A class of SWP algorithms that produce schedules with the MII is known as *modulo scheduling* [17]. Recently, *superblock scheduling* [18], based on the principles of *trace scheduling* [19], has been combined with modulo scheduling to schedule control-intensive loops [20].

Parallelism exploitation can be enhanced via speculation. Instructions can be speculatively scheduled, only with adequate hardware support to defer exceptions and state updates until speculation is committed [21]. More aggressive coarse-grained speculation at the task level requires extensive compiler and hardware support [22, 23, 24].

3 Macro Software Pipelining

Macro Software Pipelining (MSWP) is a four-step loop scheduling technique that simultaneously exploits both coarse- and fine-grained parallelism in the execution of a loop on a multithreaded processor [25].

MSWP has been based on the dopipe loop, rather than the doall or the doacross loop. By assigning different tasks of the loop body on separate threads, the loop is pipelined at the task level, and any iteration-level parallelism is exploited. Furthermore, the dissimilarity of code in the loop tasks results in a better exploitation of functional and instruction-level parallelism. Any communication across tasks forces them to operate on the same or adjacent data sets, thus better exploiting cache locality. A further exploitation of parallelism at the iteration level can be achieved through task-level speculation.

At the instruction level, ILP can be independently exploited through the application of SWP within each task. In particular, by assigning function bodies or branch targets on separate threads, we can allow operations like function calls and unpredictable branches, to be included in the schedule, and rely on the thread context-switch mechanism to preserve the schedule, as well as the register state, of the SWP thread.

3.1 The MSWP Scheduling Algorithm

The four steps of the application of MSWP are briefly described next:

Step 1. *Partition the code into threads.* Thread extraction is performed in a top-down manner, by applying loop distribution on outer loops, and moving recursively into inner loops. The selection of target loops is based on profile information. Code partitioning assumes a hierarchical representation of the input code, like the Hierarchical Task Graph (HTG) [26].

Step 2. *Apply thread-level speculation.* Each loop-carried dependence that involves multithreaded code is analyzed, to determine if a speculative calculation of the value carried is possible. In such a case, the thread at the dependence sink starts the next loop iteration speculatively, after executing the code for that calculation. Any compensation code necessary to handle misspeculation is inserted at this step.

Step 3. *Add inter-thread communication.* New code is only inserted, if existing code cannot be used to satisfy communication requirements for data and control dependencies. This step is highly dependent on the particular communication means supported by the underlying architecture.

Step 4. *Apply SWP within threads.* With step 1, we have reduced the size of the loop body in each resulting loop. If the original loop could not be pipelined at the instruction level, it is now possible that several of the new loops will.

4 Coral 2000: A Blocked Multithreaded Processor Architecture

Our processor model, *Coral 2000*, is a blocked multithreaded architecture, built on top of a superscalar out-of-order issue microprocessor. Multithreading is exported to the processor instruction set, allowing several compiler-controlled thread operations, like thread creation and termination, as well as thread speculation start, commit, wait and abort.

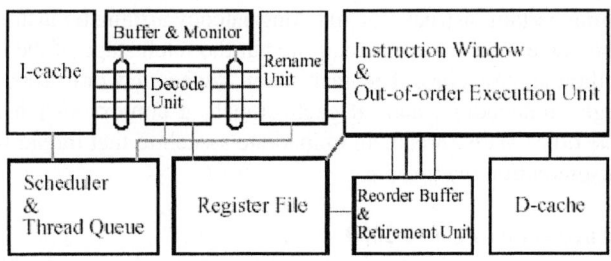

Fig. 1. Coral 2000 Architecture

The processor consists of three parts: The in-order front end includes the Fetch/Decode/Rename (FDR) pipeline, the instruction cache and the thread controller. The out-of-order part includes the window from which instructions are issued out of order, multiple integer and floating-point functional units, the memory access unit and the data cache. The in-order back end includes the reorder buffer, the register file and the instruction retirement unit. A block diagram of Coral 2000 is shown in Figure 1.

In the rest of this section, we will focus on the multithreading support of Coral 2000. Further details on Coral 2000 can be found in [25].

4.1 Threads in Coral 2000

A *hardware thread* is defined as a processor state set that corresponds to a piece of code with sequential control flow and contains state from any stage of the processor pipelines, associated with instructions from that code. Any user code may spawn up to a certain number of hardware threads.

Threads communicate with each other through registers or through memory. Some registers may be shared among threads, others are private to each thread. Speculative execution of conditional branches is supported within threads. Additionally, Coral 2000 supports speculation at the thread level.

4.2 Thread Context Switches in Coral 2000

In the blocked multithreading paradigm, threads are switched on demand, after certain hardware events. In an attempt to eliminate the thread context-switch overhead, hardware may provide support for *pending instructions*, i.e. instructions that have been suspended at a context switch and placed in an appropriate instruction queue, from where they can be later resumed [3].

In order to keep hardware cost low in Coral 2000, we provide support for pending instructions only in the FDR pipeline. This means that context switches that are triggered at that part of the processor can be serviced with zero overhead, whenever there are ready threads with pending instructions in that pipeline. Service latency for other context switches is tolerated through the out-of-order execution mechanism.

Most Coral 2000 context switches are requested at the rename stage of the FDR pipeline. Switches resulting from a rename failure suspend the corresponding thread. For example, an attempt to rename a memory load instruction with a full load buffer triggers such a switch. The rename stage may also request a context switch *after* successfully renaming certain instructions, like long-latency arithmetic instructions.

The only case context switches are requested at the fetch stage of the FDR pipeline appears at conditional branches. The instruction cache of Coral 2000 marks such branches through predecoding, and, at each branch, a context switch is requested. With at least one other ready thread, an immediate switch to that thread will eliminate any possible misprediction overhead.

4.3 Thread Scheduling in Coral 2000

All scheduling decisions in Coral 2000 are made by a centralized thread scheduler and are only applied to the FDR pipeline. A certain thread feeds each FDR pipeline stage at each cycle and is called the *primary* thread for that stage. Through the FDR support for pending instructions, up to two *secondary* threads may also supply a limited number of instructions to the FDR pipeline stages, in an attempt to fill its unused slots.

Using information collected at previous cycles, the scheduler selects ready threads to replace the primary and secondary threads, in each of the FDR pipeline stages. With thread priorities associated with speculative execution, it picks the threads with the highest priorities, or, in case of ties, the ones with the fewest unresolved conditional branches. Selections are made at each cycle, even if there is no context switch request, to provide secondary threads for instruction mixing. Nevertheless, having a candidate always available allows a thread context switch to occur instantly.

4.4 Thread Communication and the Coral 2000 Registers

In Coral 2000, thread communication is performed mainly through shared registers. Two types of shared registers are implemented for each of two different communication paradigms. Each thread is also associated with a set of private registers.

Shared Register Structures. The shared registers of the first type are called *shared register structures* (S-structures). Each S-structure is a short queue, holding a number of values that are read in the order they were written. S-structures simplify inter-thread communication, because they automatically enforce data dependencies. By holding multiple values, they also allow communicating threads within a loop body to proceed asynchronously, thus reducing thread context-switch pressure.

Accesses to S-structures are hardware controlled, so that a read will only succeed if the queue is not empty, and a write will only succeed if the queue is not full; otherwise, the failed instruction will not leave the FDR pipeline and the accessing thread will be suspended. In order to eliminate overhead of read failures, S-structures support a delayed suspension of the reading thread that allows a failed read to be renamed; the corresponding write will later forward its value to the waiting operation.

Both reads and writes change the state of an S-structure. Since any change in the processor state is only allowed at the final pipeline stage of the instruction involved, any change in the state of an S-structure before that stage must be reversible. For this reason, S-structure reads are speculative and are validated at instruction commit.

The communication mechanism of the S-structures is based on communication elements with full/empty bits that appeared in older multithreading architectures, like the HEP, the Sparcle processor and a handful of other multithreaded architectures [27, 28,29]. Similar queue structures have also been used in systolic communication [30, 31].

Global Shared Registers. The S-structures are not suitable for holding values of read-only shared variables in the execution of multithreaded code, because each value in the S-structure is valid for only one read. To remedy this, we added the second type of shared registers, the *global shared registers*, which are implemented as plain general-purpose registers without any access control, and are visible by all threads.

4.5 Thread Speculation in Coral 2000

Coral 2000 supports thread-level speculation. Thread speculative instructions are allowed to retire and store their result into the Coral 2000 registers. A special mechanism is employed in order to monitor and annul register updates in the case of misspeculation. Hardware support for effective thread speculation includes:

- Deferral of speculative exceptions.
- Consideration of thread speculation in the thread priority mechanism.
- A speculation queue associated with each thread that allows nested speculation.
- Deferral of speculative stores until the end of speculation.
- Ability to transfer control to a user-specified address at any speculation abort.

Coral 2000 does not restore register contents in thread misspeculation. The compiler must produce compensation code that reverses any register content changes performed by speculative threads. Nevertheless, there is provision for saving and restoring the content of a single private register at each speculation start and abort, as well as for resetting shared register structures at each speculation abort.

5 Experimental Results

We tested and evaluated Coral 2000 together with MSWP on a cycle-level simulator that was based on the *SuperDLX* simulator, a general-purpose simulator of a MIPS-like superscalar microprocessor [32].

We extended SuperDLX to match our model and implemented all multithreading support. Our experiments tried to cover all our work. However, since our research multiplexed loop scheduling and architecture issues, it was often hard to distinguish performance results due to scheduling, from results due to architecture.

5.1 Benchmarks

Goal of our testing was to prove that Coral 2000 and MSWP can successfully address the issues of loop scheduling on multithreaded processors. To this end, we based our experiments mostly on synthetic benchmarks. Nevertheless, we also tested MSWP on *perl*, an integer SPEC95 benchmark that exhibits limited parallelism.

All synthetic benchmarks are described through the HTGs of Figure 2. For simplicity, some nested conditional branches and loops are not shown. An outer loop is implied in all synthetic benchmarks. More specifically:

- *do*. The body of the outer loop of this program exhibits the dependencies shown in Figure 2a. Task T_2 contains long latency integer operations.
- *loop*. The body of the outer loop of this program exhibits the dependencies shown in Figure 2b.
- *func*. The body of the outer loop of this program exhibits the dependencies shown in Figure 2c. Task T_4 contains a function call, which is actually made in 50% of the loop iterations.
- *perl*. This integer SPEC95 benchmark exhibits a highly sequential behavior, due to loop-carried dependencies and abnormal control flow.

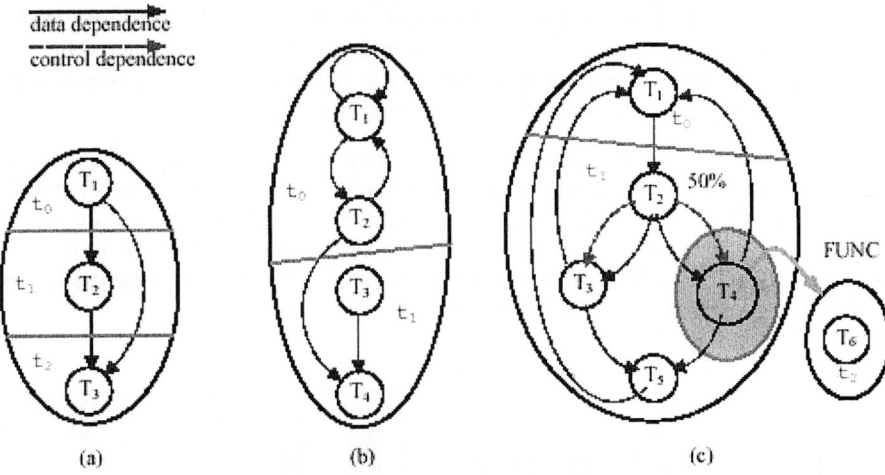

Fig. 2. HTGs of the three synthetic benchmarks

The partitioning of all synthetic benchmarks into threads is shown in Figure 2, with the shaded compound task in *func* serving as a thread interface. In particular, *perl* was partitioned into four threads.

5.2 Experiments

In order to evaluate our research, we compared execution of multithreaded to execution of single-threaded code. In each comparison, we used codes as similar as possible, with differences that resulted only from multithreading and the application of the MSWP algorithm. In order to obtain the best possible single-threaded codes, we applied superblock-based SWP on many of those codes.

The basic simulator configuration we used was that of a 3-way superscalar machine, with a reorder buffer of 40 entries and a store buffer of 36 entries. We assumed simple 32K L1 caches with one port, a hit time of 1 cycle and a miss time of 6 cycles. We ignored instruction misses, though. Finally, we used a single-level 2-bit dynamic branch prediction with a BTB of 512 entries.

For each program tested, we obtained results from four modes of simulation, depending on whether cache or dynamic branch prediction (dbp) was enabled.

Synthetic benchmarks. Figure 3a-c shows the simulation results for the three synthetic benchmarks. More specifically:

- Figure 3a depicts the execution times for *do*, using compiler-produced SWP codes, single-threaded (O3), 2-threaded with doall (2O3A), 4-threaded with doall (4O3A) and 3-treaded with MSWP dopipe (3O3P).
- Figure 3b depicts the execution times for *loop*, using superblock-based SWP codes, single-threaded without and with 2 times unrolling (O2NU and O2U2), and 2-threaded MSWP code without, with 2 and with 4 times unrolling (2O2NU, 2O2U2 and 2O2U4).

- Figure 3c depicts the execution times for *func*, using superblock-based SWP codes, single-threaded without and with 2 times unrolling (O2 and O2U2), and 3-threaded MSWP code with 5 times unrolling (3O2U5C). In the last case, t_2 is conditionally executing only those iterations that actually perform a function call.

In all the above cases we obtained speedups of up to 30% with respect to optimized single-threaded code. The unrolling factor used in each case was maximized, in order to obtain the optimal MII. Although *do* is inherently parallel and the rest are not, all three synthetic benchmarks provide a good evaluation of Coral 2000, due to their extensive use of Coral 2000 multithreading features, mainly its rapid context switches and its thread communication mechanism.

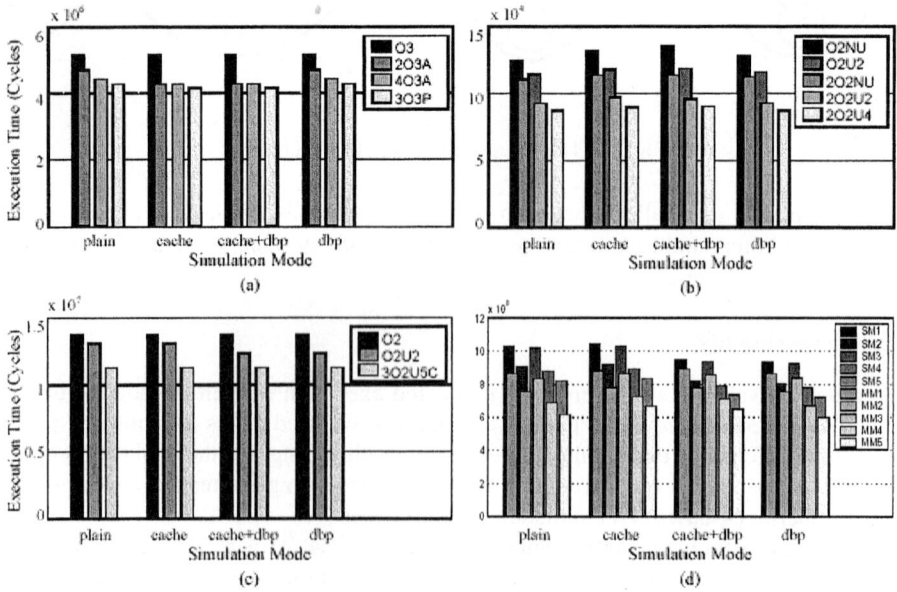

Fig. 3. Benchmark execution times

SPEC95 results. In experiments with *perl*, we varied machine configuration, from the basic (M1), to a 3-way superscalar with two (M2), a 4-way superscalar with one (M3), a 4-way superscalar with two (M4), and a 6-way superscalar with three memory ports (M5). Figure 3d shows the resulting execution times for *perl*, using a reduced *ref* input data set. We tested single-threaded (S) and 4-threaded (M) code, based on compiler-optimized code.

The speedup we obtained was up to 25%, which would not have been possible without the architectural support of Coral 2000. This is mainly due to the limited parallelism available within *perl* that cannot be exploited by multithreading without rapid context switches, fast communication means, or thread speculation. Thread speculation, in particular, was used both for loop-carried data dependencies and for abnormal control flow, along certain code paths that were selected through profiling.

6 Conclusions

In this paper we identify issues in traditional loop scheduling techniques, at both the iteration and the instruction level, that can be addressed quite successfully with multithreading. With MSWP, we provide a loop scheduling technique that is suitable for multithreaded architectures. Coral 2000 proves to enhance performance of multithreaded loop scheduling through MSWP. In particular, the hardware support we proposed has contributed to a significant speedup in the execution of loops with limited parallelism, the exploitation of which is usually outbalanced by multithreading overhead. We plan to further validate the advantages of our multithreading model through additional measurements and simulations in a hardware description language.

References

1. G. Dimitriou, C. Polychronopoulos, "Loop Scheduling for Multithreaded Processors", *IEEE Int. Conf. on Parallel Computing in Electrical Engineering*, 2004, pp. 361-366.
2. D.A. Padua, D.J. Kuck, and D.H. Lawrie, "High-speed Multiprocessors and Compilation Techniques", *IEEE Trans. on Computers*, C-29(9), 1980, pp. 763-776.
3. 3 C.D. Polychronopoulos, α-Coral: A New Multithreaded Processor Architecture, its Compiler Support, and Simulation of a multi-α-Coral Parallel System, Project Proposal, CSRD, University of Illinois at Urbana-Champaign, 1997.
4. B.J. Smith, "A Pipelined, Shared Resource MIMD Computer", *Int. Conf. on Parallel Processing*, 1978, pp. 6-8.
5. A. Agarwal, J. Kubiatowicz, D. Kranz, et al., "Sparcle: An Evolutionary Processor Design for Multiprocessors", *Int. Symp. on Microarchitecture*, 1993, pp. 48-61.
6. J.P. Laudon, Architectural and Implementation Tradeoffs for Multiple-Context Processors, PhD dissertation, Stanford University, 1994.
7. D.M. Tullsen, S.J. Eggers, and H.M. Levy, "Simultaneous Multithreading: Maximizing On-chip Parallelism", *Int. Symp. on Computer Architecture*, 1995, pp. 392-403.
8. S. Wallace, B. Calder, and D.M. Tullsen, "Threaded Multiple Path Execution", *Int. Symp. on Computer Architecture*, 1998, pp. 238-249.
9. V.S. Krishnan, and J. Torrellas, "A Clustered Approach to Multithreaded Processors", *Int. Parallel Processing Symp.*, 1998.
10. G.S. Sohi, S.E. Breach, and T.N. Vijaykumar, "Multiscalar Processors", *Int. Symp. on Computer Architecture*, 1995, pp. 414-425.
11. P. Marcuello, A. Gonzalez, and J. Tubella, "Speculative Multithreaded Processors", *Int. Conf. on Supercomputing*, 1998, pp. 77-84.
12. J. Tsai, and P. Yew, "The Superthreaded Archtecture: Thread Pipelining with Run-time Data Dependence Checking and Control Speculation", *Conf. on Parallel Architectures and Compilation Techniques*, 1996, pp. 35-46.
13. H. Akkary, and M.A. Driscoll, "A Dynamic Multithreading Processor", *Int. Symp. on Microarchitecture*, 1998, pp. 226-236.
14. U. Banerjee, *Dependence Analysis for Supercomputing*, Kluwer Academic Publishers, Boston, 1988.
15. D.A. Padua, and M.J. Wolfe, "Advanced Compiler Optimizations for Supercomputers", *Communications of the ACM*, 29(12), 1986, pp. 1184-1201.
16. B.R. Rau, and J.A. Fisher, "Instruction-level Parallel Processing: History, Overview and Perspectives", *Journal of Supercomputing*, 7(1), 1993, pp. 9-50.

17. B.R. Rau, and C.D. Glaeser, "Some Scheduling Techniques and an Easily Schedulable Horizontal Architecture for High-performance Scientific Computing", *14th Annual Microprogramming Workshop*, 1981, pp. 183-198.
18. W.W. Hwu, S.A. Mahlke, W.Y. Chen, et al., "The Superblock: An Effective Technique for VLIW and Superscalar Compilation", *Journal of Supercomputing*, 7, 1993, pp. 229-248.
19. J.A. Fisher, "Trace Scheduling: A Technique for Global Microcode Compaction", *IEEE Trans. on Computers*, C-30(7), 1981, pp. 478-490.
20. D.M. Lavery, *Modulo Scheduling for Control-intensive General-purpose Programs*, PhD dissertation, University of Illinois at Urbana-Champaign, 1997.
21. R.A. Bringmann, *Enhancing Instruction-level Parallelism through Compiler-controlled Speculation*, PhD dissertation, University of Illinois at Urbana-Champaign, 1995.
22. P.K. Dubey, K. O'Brien, K.M. O'Brien, and C. Barton, *Single-program Speculative Multithreading (SPSM) Architecture: Compiler-assisted Fine-grained Multithreading*, Res. Rep. RC 19928, IBM T. J. Watson Research Center, 1995.
23. M. Prvulovic, M.J. Garzaran, L. Rauchwerger, and J. Torrellas, "Removing Architectural Bottlenecks to the Scalability of Speculative Parallelization", *Int. Symp. on Computer Architecture*, 2001, pp.204-215.
24. A. Zhai, C.B. Colohan, J.G. Steffan, and T.C. Mowry, "Compiler Optimization of Scalar Value Communication between Speculative Threads", *Int. Conf. on Arch. Support for Programming Languages and Operating Systems*, 2002, pp.171-183.
25. G. Dimitriou, *Loop Scheduling for Multithreaded Processors*, PhD dissertation, University of Illinois at Urbana-Champaign, 2000.
26. 26 M.B. Girkar, *Functional Parallelism: Theoretical Foundations and Implementations*, PhD dissertation, University of Illinois at Urbana-Champaign, 1992.
27. Arvind, R.S. Nikhil, and K.K. Pingali, "I-structures: Data Structures for Parallel Computing", *ACM Trans. on Programming Language and Systems*, 11(4), 1989, pp. 598-632.
28. D.E. Culler, and G.M. Papadopoulos, "The Explicit Token Store", *Journal of Parallel and Distributed Computing*, 10, 1990, pp. 289-308.
29. D. Kranz, B. Lim, A. Agarwal, and D.Yeung, "Low-cost Support for Fine-grained Synchronization in Multiprocessors", in *Multithreaded Computer Architecture: A Summary of the State of the Art*, edited by R.A. Iannucci, G.R. Gao, R.H. Halstead, Jr., and B. Smith, Kluwer Academic Publishers, Boston, 1994, pp.139-166.
30. H.T. Kung, "Deadlock Avoidance for Systolic Communication", *Int. Symp. on Computer Architecture*, 1988, pp.252-260.
31. S. Borkar, R. Cohn, G. Cox, et al., "Supporting Systolic and Memory Communication in iWarp", *Int. Symp. on Computer Architecture*, 1990, pp.70-81.
32. C. Moura, SuperDLX – A Generic Superscalar Simulator, ACAPS Tech. Memo 64, School of Computer Science, McGill University, 1993.

A Low – Power VLSI Architecture for Intra Prediction in H.264

Georgios Stamoulis[1], Maria Koziri[1], Ioannis Katsavounidis[2], and Nikolaos Bellas[3]

[1] University of Thessaly, Department of Computer and Communication Engineering,
Glavani 37, 382 21 Bolos, Greece
{georges, mkoziri}@uth.gr
[2] InterVideo, Inc., 46430 Fremont Blvd., Fremont, CA 94538, USA
ioannis@intervideo.com
[3] Motorola, Inc., 1030 E. Algonquin. Rd, IL01-Annex A, Schaumburg, IL 60196, USA
bellas@labs.mot.com

Abstract. The H.264 video coding standard can achieve considerably higher coding efficiency than previous standards. The key to this high code efficiency are mainly the Intra and Inter prediction modes provided by the standard. However, the compression efficiency of the H264 standard comes at the cost of increased complexity of the encoder. Therefore it is very important to design video architectures that minimize the cost of the prediction modes in terms of area, power dissipation and design complexity. A common aspect of the Inter and Intra Prediction modes, is the Sum of Absolute Differences (SAD). In this paper we present a new algorithm that can replace the SAD in Intra Prediction, and which provides a more efficient hardware implementation.

1 Introduction

Video has always been the backbone of multimedia technology. In the last two decades, the field of video coding has been revolutionized by the advent of various standards like MPEG-1 to MPEG-4 and H.261 to H.263, each addressing different aspects of multimedia. The H.264 standard [1] pushes the envelope of video compression efficiency and provides a complete solution for a wide range of applications. The standard is being developed by the Joint Video Team(JVT) from the ISO/IEC and ITU-T. The primary goal of H.264 is to achieve higher compression while preserving video quality. The motivation of compression is to compensate for the ever present constraints of the limited channel capacity. This video coding technique follows a straight –forward "back to basics approach" providing flexibility to be used in low-delay real-time applications.

Each picture of a video, which can either be a frame or a field, is partitioned into fixed-size macroblocks that cover a rectangular picture area of 16×16 samples of the luma component and 8×8 samples of each of the two chroma components. All luma and chroma samples of a macroblock are either spatially or temporally predicted, and the resulting prediction residual is transmitted using transform coding. Therefore, each color component of the prediction residual is subdivided into blocks. The macroblocks are organized in slices, which generally represent subsets of a given picture that can be decoded independently. The H.264/AVC standard supports five different slice-coding types. The simplest one is the I slice (where "I" stands for intra). In I slices, all macroblocks are coded without referring to other pictures within the video sequence. On the other hand, prior-coded images can be used to form a prediction signal for macroblocks of the predictive-coded P and B slices (where "P" stands for predictive and "B" stands for bi-predictive). The remaining two slice types are SP (switching P) and SI (switching I), which are specified for efficient switching between bitstreams coded at various bit-rates.

The H.264 standard uses block sizes of 4x4 and 16x16 pixels to compress I-Macroblocks for intra-prediction. Intra coding refers to the case where only spatial redundancies within a video picture are exploited. The resulting frame is referred to as an I-picture. I-pictures are typically encoded by directly applying spatial transform to the different macroblocks in the frame. As a consequence, encoded I-pictures are large in size since a large amount of information is usually present in the frame, and no temporal information is used as part of the encoding process. In order to increase the efficiency of the intra coding process in H.264, spatial correlation between adjacent macroblocks in a given frame is exploited. The idea is based on the observation that adjacent macroblocks tend to have similar properties. Therefore, as a first step in the encoding process for a given macroblock, one may predict the macroblock of interest from the surrounding macroblocks, typically the ones located on top and to the left of the macroblock of interest, since those macroblocks would have already been encoded. After a prediction block P is formed based on previously encoded and reconstructed blocks, it is subtracted from the current block prior to encoding. For the luma samples, the P block is formed for each 4x4 block or for a 16x16 macroblock. There are a total of nine optional prediction modes for each 4x4 luma block, four modes for a 16x16 luma block and four modes for the chroma components. The encoder typically selects the prediction mode for each block that minimises the difference between P and the block to be encoded. The selection is done by using SAD which indicates the magnitude of the absolute error.

In the context of hardware implementation, the calculation of SAD for each block requires a significant number of additions. In an attempt to reduce encoder's complexity and power consumption, this paper introduces a new technique that replaces SAD, without having major effects in the quality of the encoded image and time required for encoding. This technique can easily be translated to a simple yet effective low power VLSI architecture for H.264 Intra Prediction. Based on the concept of comparison, the proposed architecture, instead of adding the differences between the predicted and the original pixels and then comparing the resultant sums, compares these differences. At the end of the comparisons the prediction mode with the minimum difference is selected. This new architecture results in a much more simple circuit, than that required for the complete calculation of SAD. Therefore, significantly reduction of the time required for Intra Prediction and low-power consumption will be achieved. In section 2 of the paper, we outline the H.264 intra prediction mode, and in section 3 we discuss our algorithm and explain how it reduces the computational complexity of the intra prediction mode. In section 4, we present the experimental evaluation of our algorithm, and we conclude in section 5.

2 Intra Prediction for H.264

The H.264 standard exploits the spatial correlation between adjacent macroblocks/blocks for Intra prediction. That is, the current macroblock/blocks is predicted using adjacent pixels in the upper and the left macroblocks/blocks that are decoded earlier. The H.264 standard offers a rich set of prediction patterns for Intra prediction, *i.e.* nine prediction modes for 4x4 luma blocks and four prediction modes for 16x16 luma blocks. Each mode has its own direction of prediction and the predicted samples are obtained from a weighted average of decoded values of neighbourhood macroblocks/blocks [2].

Suppose that we have a 4x4 luma block that is required to be predicted. The samples above and to the left, which are labelled A–M, have previously been encoded and reconstructed and are therefore available in the encoder and decoder to form a prediction reference. The samples a, b, c, ..., p of the prediction block P (Figure 1) are calculated based on the samples A–M as follows. Mode 2 (DC prediction) is modified depending on which samples A–M have previously been coded; each of the other modes may only be used if all of the required prediction samples are available. Note that if samples E, F, G and H have not yet been decoded, the value of sample D is copied to these positions and they are marked as 'available'.

M	A	B	C	D	E	F	G	H
I	a	b	c	d				
J	e	f	g	h				
K	i	j	k	l				
L	m	n	o	p				

Fig. 1. Labeling of prediction samples

In Figure 2 we can see a schematic representation of the nine available modes for intra prediction of a 4x4 block of luma samples. Table 1 gives us more details about how the nine modes predict the 4x4 block.

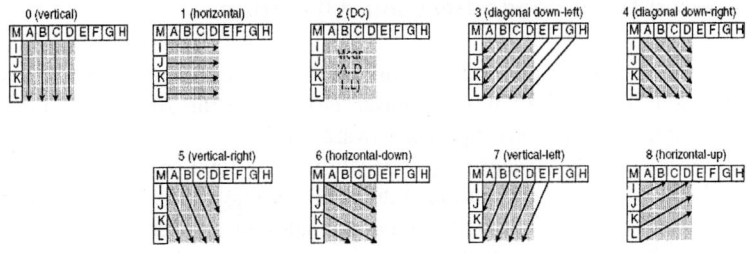

Fig. 2. 4x4 luma prediction modes

Table 1. The nine 4x4 luma block Intra prediction modes in H.264

Mode 0 (Vertical)	The upper samples A, B, C, D are extrapolated vertically.
Mode 1 (Horizontal)	The left samples I, J, K, L are extrapolated horizontally.
Mode 2 (DC)	All samples in P are predicted by the mean of samples A ... D and I ... L.
Mode 3 (Diagonal Down-Left)	The samples are interpolated at a 45· angle between lower-left
Mode 4 (Diagonal Down-Right)	The samples are extrapolated at a 45· angle down and to the right.
Mode 5 (Vertical-Right)	Extrapolation at an angle of approximately 26.6· to the left of vertical (width/height = 1/2).
Mode 6 (Horizontal-Down)	Extrapolation at an angle of approximately 26.6· below horizontal.
Mode 7 (Vertical-Left)	Extrapolation (or interpolation) at an angle of approximately 26.6· to the right of vertical.
Mode 8 (Horizontal-Up)	Interpolation at an angle of approximately 26.6· above horizontal.

To decide which mode will be selected the Sum of Absolute Differences (SAD) is calculated for each mode. Intuitively speaking, a good prediction should produce a small value of the sum of absolute differences (SAD), which can be written as

$$SAD = \sum_{i=0}^{N-1} \sum_{j=0}^{N-1} |C_{ij} - P_{ij}| \qquad (1)$$

where C and P represent the current block and its prediction, respectively[3]. According to these, the mode which has the minimum SAD is the one to be selected. The SAD computations are very expensive because they require a large number of computations for each 4x4 block. Going down to hardware level the cost for this is not negligible.

3 Proposed Intra-Mode Decision Algorithm

In this section we introduce a new technique for approaching the problem of Intra – Mode decision. The base of this technique is to avoid the stage of addition, which augments significantly the cost in the hardware level.

For a given 4x4 block, according to equation (1), a total of 16 subtractions and 15 additions is needed in order to produce the SAD for one mode. Therefore for the nine modes we conclude to 144 subtraction and 135 additions. After computing all modes, a comparison between the results will give us the decided mode. Since all that is needed in this stage of Intra Prediction is to find the prediction mode, a qualitative approach may give the same results as a quantitative one.

Based on the above observation, the proposal is, after calculating the differences among the predicted and the original pixels instead of adding them, to compare the differences for the nine available modes. The comparison will conclude to the mode with the most minimum differences. In this way, the addition stage is completely by-passed.

We first calculate the absolute difference between the corresponding pixels for each mode. This can be written as

$$M_{k_{ij}} = |C_{ij} - P_{k_{ij}}| \qquad (2)$$

where M, C, P are 4x4 arrays and k (with $0 \leq k \leq 8$) indicates the mode.

After the nine 4x4 arrays are created, a comparison among two successive arrays is done. The array with the largest number of minimum values is chosen. Lets assume that we have the following function,

$$F_k = \begin{cases} 1, M_k \leq M_{k+1} \\ 0, M_k > M_{k+1} \end{cases} \qquad (3)$$

where M_k is the array with the differences for mode k. According to equation (3) we chose M_k if $F_k < F_{k+1}$, otherwise we chose M_{k+1}.

The above algorithm may be more easily understood if presented with a code-like form.

```
for (k=0;k<NO_INTRA_PMODE;k++) {
k1=0;
            counter1=0;
            counter2=0;
            for (j=0;j<4;j++) {
              for (i=0;i<4;i++) {
                M[k][i][j] = abs(C[i][j] - P[k][i][j]);
                k1=k+1;
                M[k1][i][j] = abs(C[i][j] - P[k1][i][j]);
                if (M[k][i][j]>= M[k1][i][j])
                  Mode[next] = k;
                else
                  Mode[next] = k+1;
              }
            }
            k=k1;
            next++;
}
```

A total of 8 comparisons can produce the mode with the least number of differences from the original 9 candidates.

Therefore for the proposed algorithm we have a total of 160 comparisons instead of 135 additions and 8 comparisons which are needed with the use of SAD. Nevertheless, when thinking about a hardware implementation, these results are quite inviting, especially if one takes into account the fact that the comparison is a stage which is also met into an implementation with SAD.

4 Experimental Results

The proposed mode decision scheme has been integrated with the H.264 JM9.3 codec for the performance evaluation. It is compared with the Intra mode decision of H.264 (with SAD) in terms of the size of the file produced after the total encoding process and the average PSNR as a function of the frames encoded and as a function of the quantization parameter QP for the foreman test sequence recommended in [4]. Fig. 3 shows the % difference of the size of the files produced by the encoder for the foreman sequence of various number of frames and various QPs at coding rate 15 frames/sec. As one can notice the new algorithm only in one case causes a % increase in the file size that exceeds 5%. Fig. 4 shows the % difference of the average PSNR performance of the encoder for the foreman sequence of various number of frames various QPs at coding rate 15 frames/sec. The % difference in this case in negligible.

The above results are produced by the values presented in Tables 2 and 3. Table 2 shows the size of files (in bits) produced by the encoder for various numbers of frames and various QPs. Table 3 shows the average PSNR performance of the two

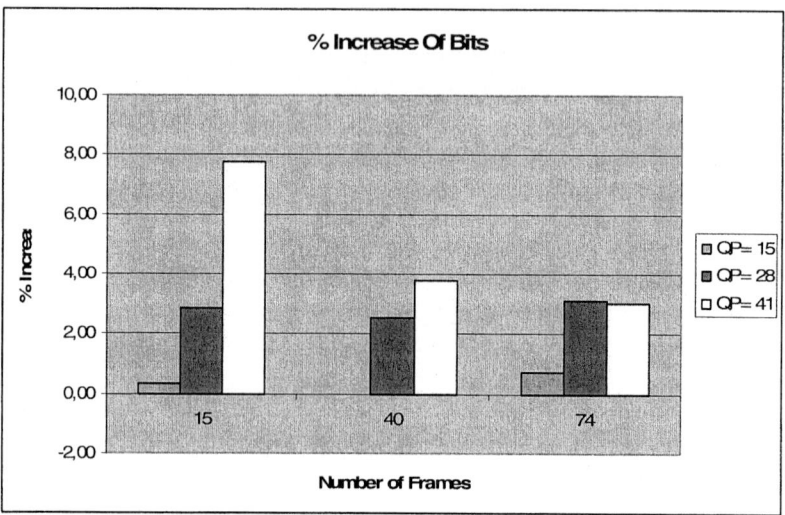

Fig. 3. Percentage of the increase in the file size produced by the encoder with the new algorithm instead of SAD

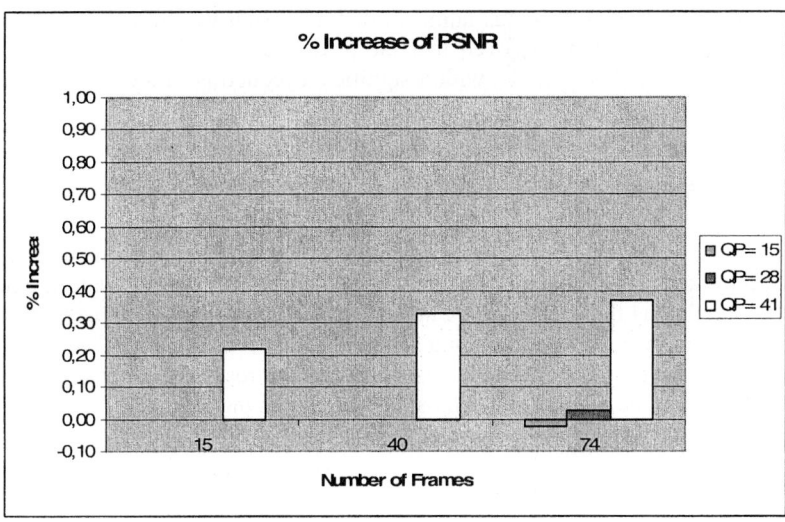

Fig. 4. Percentage of the increase in PSNR produced by the encoder with the new algorithm instead of SAD

Table 2. File size(in bits) comparison

S =SAD P= Proposed		Bits/File {Number of frames=15~74]		
		15	40	74
QP= 15	S	587160	1520848	2955568
	P	589160	1520752	2977432
QP= 28	S	127208	317464	598776
	P	130960	325816	617960
QP= 41	S	28128	69640	133328
	P	30496	72384	137472

Table 3. PSNR Comparison

S =SAD P= Proposed		PSNR (db) {Number of frames=15~74]		
		15	40	74
QP= 15	S	45.83	45.83	45.75
	P	45.83	45.83	45.74
QP= 28	S	36.12	36.10	35.65
	P	36.12	36.10	35.66
QP= 41	S	27.32	27.38	26.97
	P	27.38	27.47	27.07

compared algorithms for various numbers of frames and various QPs. From the results presented it can be approved that the proposed algorithm achieves nearly the same efficiency as that of SAD, with a significant reduction in the complexity of the encoder.

5 Conclusions

To conclude, the proposed algorithm by replacing the addition presented in the SAD algorithm with simple comparison, can be implemented in a hardware architecture which, by reducing the complexity, can achieve quite smaller time of execution and a grate reduction in power consumption. The algorithm was integrated with the H.264 JM9.3 codec for the performance evaluation, and the results show that the performance of the proposed algorithm is almost the same with that of SAD.

References

1. ITU-T Rec. H.264 / ISO/IEC 11496-10, "Advanced Video Coding", Final Committee Draft, Document **JVT-J010d1**, December 2003
2. Thomas Wiegand, Gary J. Sullivan, Gisle Bjontegaard, and Ajay Luthra, "Overview of the H.264/AVC video coding standard, " *IEEE Transactions on Circuits, System and Video Technology*, vol. 7, no. 1-19, July 2003.
3. Iain E G Richardson, "H.264 and MPEG-4 Video Compression – Video Coding for Next-generation Multimedia", John Wiley & Sons, 2003
4. JVT Test Model Ad Hoc Group, .Evaluation sheet for motion estimation,. in *ISO/IEC JTC1/SC29/WG11 and ITU-T SG16 Q.6*, Draft version 4, February 2003.

Reducing TPC-H Benchmarking Time

Pedro Trancoso[1], Christodoulos Adamou[1], and Hans Vandierendonck[2]

[1]Department of Computer Science, University of Cyprus,
75 Kallipoleos Ave., P.O.Box 20537, 1678 Nicosia, Cyprus
{pedro, cs98ca1}@cs.ucy.ac.cy
[2]Dept. of Electronics and Information Systems,
Ghent University, Sint-Pietersnieuwstraat 41, 9000 Ghent, Belgium
hvdieren@elis.UGent.be

Abstract. Benchmarking a system can be a time consuming operation. Therefore, many researchers have developed kernels and micro-benchmarks. Nevertheless, these programs are not able to capture the details of a full application. One such example are the complex database applications.

In this work we present a methodology based on a statistical method, Principal Component Analysis, in order to reduce the execution time of TPC-H, a decision support benchmark. This technique selects a subset of queries from the original set that are relevant and may be used to evaluate the systems. We use the subsets to determine the ranking of different computer systems. Our experiments show that with a small subset of 5 queries we are able to rank different systems with more than 80% accuracy in comparison with the original order and this result is achieved with as little as 20% of the original benchmark execution time.

1 Introduction

Benchmarking is a common practice for the evaluation of new computer systems. By executing certain benchmarks, the manufacturers are able to highlight the characteristics of a certain system and also to rank the system against the rest. In addition, benchmarking is widely used for computer architecture research where the programs are executed on simulated proposed architectures. As more realistic programs are used, the benchmarking process becomes more time-consuming.

Common benchmark programs are grouped into suites which represent a specific class of applications. Common examples are the SPEC [1] benchmark suite for scientific applications, EEMBC [2] benchmark suite representative of applications for embedded systems, and TPC-C [3] and TPC-H [4] representing database applications belonging to the class of online transaction and decision support system, respectively.

Reduced benchmark suites have much value when analyzing computer performance, especially in those cases where performance analysis is time-consuming, which is the case in computer architecture research. For this purpose, the Minne-SPEC reduced inputs were proposed for computer architecture research [5]. These inputs attempt to mimic the behavior of the SPEC benchmark suite while limiting instruction count. The MinneSPEC inputs were constructed manually which is time-consuming and not very accurate [6,7].

Saavedra and Smith [8] analyze Fortran programs. They measure program similarity by counting the types of operations in the programs. They interpret these counts as the coordinates of the benchmark in the program space. They apply cluster analysis techniques on these values to determine clusters of similar programs. Their method seems to be restricted to Fortran programs.

Detecting program similarity was again taken up by Eeckhout, Vandierendonck and De Bosschere [9,10]. In this work, programs are characterized at the ISA-level and lower levels by metrics such as instruction mix, branch prediction accuracies and cache miss rates. These metrics are applied to select inputs for benchmarks in order to limit simulation time without changing the characteristics of the simulated program.

The data memory behavior of the SPEC benchmarks is analyzed in [11], where it is shown that some benchmarks have characteristics that are strongly different from the majority of benchmarks. Other benchmarks have a behavior that varies strongly with small changes in the source code and/or input.

Yi and Lilja [12] present a statistically rigorous technique to determine the relative importance of processor parameters such as issue width, reorder buffer size, cache parameters, etc. The importance of these parameters varies over the benchmarks and defines a fingerprint of the benchmarks, making them useful to determine program similarity. These metrics have the benefit that they take correlations between processor parameters into account, e.g., reorder buffer size looses importance when the branch missprediction rate is high.

Vandierendonck and De Bosschere [13] have proposed a technique to compute a subset of the SPEC benchmark suite, based on published SPEC measurements for a wide range of computers. This method was further refined and analyzed in [14] and a comparison to other clustering algorithms was made. The latter paper also showed the importance of comparing the quality of a benchmark subset to randomly generated subsets, as the randomly generated subsets may already be quite good on the average.

In this paper we apply a similar technique as presented in [13] for finding representative subsets of queries from the original set of queries from the TPC-H decision support benchmark [4]. One challenge in our work is the fact that the technique used for subsetting, the Principal Component Analysis (PCA) requires more measurements than the number of programs being used for evaluation and there are only a few measurements available while the original number of queries is 22.

To test the proposed technique we use the results published in the Transaction Processing Council (TPC) [15] to rank the different computer systems. The experimental results show that a small subset of 5 queries can be used to produce a rank that is 80% accurate with a cost of only 20% of the execution time of the complete benchmark. The results also show that the method presented results in subsets that may be significantly more accurate than randomly selected sets thus guaranteeing a minimum level of accuracy on the query subsets.

This paper is organized as follows: Section 2 briefly describes the TPC-H benchmark, Section 3 presents the method used for subsetting queries, Section 4 discusses the results obtained, and in Section 5 we present the conclusions to this work.

2 TPC-H Benchmark

TPC-H is a decision support benchmark that consists of a suite of business oriented queries. Both the queries and the data that populate the database were carefully chosen in order to keep the benchmark's implementation easy but at the same time to be relevant. The benchmark is composed of 22 read-only queries and 2 update queries. These queries are performed on considerably large amounts of data, have a high degree of complexity, and were chosen to give answers to critical business questions. The queries represent the activity of a wholesale supplier that manages, sells, or distributes a product worldwide.

Both the queries and data are provided by TPC. In particular, queries are created by a program named *qgen* while data is generated by a program called *dbgen*. The data size ranges from 1GB up to 100000GB. The data is loaded and the queries are executed on a regular DBMS system.

As with other benchmarks, in the case of TPC-H, the results obtained from the execution of the benchmark on a particular computer system are published by the manufacturers of the system and found on the TPC website [15].

3 Query Subsetting

3.1 Principal Component Analysis

Principal components analysis (PCA) is a multi-variate data analysis technique that reduces the dimensionality of a data set, without removing a significant amount of information, i.e., variation between data points [16]. Hereto, it transforms the axes of the multi-dimensional space such that some axes contain most of the variation and most axes contain little variation. The axes with little variation can be removed without significantly impacting the overall variation.

Starting from the initial dimensions, PCA computes a new set of dimensions, called the principal components. The p original dimensions $X_i, i = 1, \ldots, p$ are linearly transformed into p principal components $Z_i, i = 1, \ldots, p$ with $Z_i = \sum_{j=1}^{p} a_{ij} X_j, i = 1, \ldots, p$. The principal components are constructed such that they are sorted in order of decreasing variance ($Var[Z_i] \geq Var[Z_j]$ if $i < j$) and are uncorrelated ($Cov[Z_i, Z_j] = 0$ if $i \neq j$). One typically finds that s small number of principal components has high variance, i.e., they explain a large fraction of the information in the data set, while others have almost no variance.

All points in the space described by the original dimensions X_i can be mapped in the space described by the new dimensions Z_i without loss of information. By removing the least important principal components, the dimensionality of the data set is reduced. Note that the user has control over the amount of information that is removed this way by selecting an appropriate number of principal components to retain.

3.2 Clustered PCA

One limitation with the applicability of the PCA method described in the previous Section is that in order for the algorithm to work it requires a number of samples larger than the number of dimensions. In the case of the TPC-H queries though, the total number of queries is 22 but the results reported for each different data size are always less than 22. Consequently, we propose to use PCA on clusters of queries of size n out of an original set of N queries. The algorithm works as shown in Figure 1.

```
Pick a random set of n queries from the original N
For (N-n) elements do the following:
   Run PCA on the n set
   Select the query with the lowest PCA rank and replace it
       with another one from the (N-n) set
Endfor
```

Fig. 1. Clustered PCA

Given the heuristic used for removing at each step the lowest ranked query, we are able to effectively find the n most relevant queries.

In our experiments we tested this algorithm with three different cluster sizes: 5, 10, and 15 queries.

3.3 Evaluating the Subsets

After determining the query subsets we need to evaluate and categorize them. It is relevant to notice that with this technique we use a smaller query subset to test the different systems and produce a rank that is accurate enough compared to the original rank obtained using all the queries. Therefore, we evaluate the subsets based on the similarity of the rank obtained with the subset and the original one reported on TPC's website. We call this rank quality metric the *rank accuracy*. This metric is based on the correlation metric proposed by Kendall [17] and known as Kendall's Tau. To analyze the rank we have to analyze each different pair of elements that is on the rank. For any pair (A, B) of elements in the rank, if their relative position on both the original and subset ranks is the same, *i.e.* if A is higher than B or B is higher than A in both, this pair accounts as a *Concordance*. If the case is that the relative positions do not agree on both ranks, *i.e.* A is higher than B on one rank and B is higher than A on the other rank, than the pair accounts as a *Discordance*. Considering these definitions, Kendall's Tau correlation may be defined as follows:

$$KendallTau = \frac{\sum Concordances - \sum Discordances}{\sum Pairs}$$

The *rank accuracy* as mentioned in the rest of this work is determined as the Kendall's Tau correlation, described above.

4 Results

In this Section we present the evaluation of the query subsetting technique, as described in the previous section, for a 5, 10, and 15 query cluster.

The data used for these experiments was collected from the results published on the TPC website [15]. In particular, this data corresponds to the benchmarking results for 17 computer systems tested with a standard database of 100 GByte. The data can be found in Appendix A.

In the first three charts (Figure 2) we present the results of the PCA query subsetting for the cases where the cluster of 5, 10, and 15 queries is used, respectively. In each chart we can see two lines. The top one (*AVG Accuracy*) represents the *rank accuracy* obtained using Kendall's Tau correlation. The lower line (*AVG Execution*) represents the execution time required to perform the benchmark using a reduced number of queries, normalized to the sum of the execution time for all queries. Notice that both lines represent the average of the results for five different subsets obtained by applying PCA to five distinct randomly selected initial sets. For each point of the line we represent y-bars which represent the range from the lowest to highest value of both *rank accuracy* and *execution time* for the tested subsets. On the X-axis we represent the number of queries in the subsets.

From the three charts it is possible to observe that, as expected, as we increase the number of queries in the subset, the *rank accuracy* and the *execution time* both increase. The interesting fact is that for a subset of 5 queries and clustering of 10 queries, the *rank accuracy* reaches levels higher than 80% with only 20% of the total execution time. It is also relevant to notice that comparing the clustering sizes 5, 10, and 15, the *rank accuracy* achieves higher values for the clustering of 15 queries. Also, in general, the error bars for the clustering of 15 queries are smaller. One fact to notice is that while the *rank accuracy* achieves a very high value (93%) for a set of 15 queries for the clustering of 15, the execution time cost becomes too high (69%). Therefore, such a subset is not very interesting, in terms of reduced execution time.

Overall, we believe that we can significantly reduce the benchmarking cost by using this technique as with a subset of only 5 queries it is possible to achieve a *rank accuracy* higher than 80% at an *execution time* cost of only 20% of the original one. Also, performing the PCA analysis with larger clusters seems to result in higher values for the *rank accuracy*, for the same subset size.

The chart in Figure 3 compares the results of the *rank accuracy* obtained using the PCA method for different cluster sizes and the results that could be achieved with a random selection for a subset of the same size. We represent the random subset as the area between two lines: the *worst* and *best* subset. Due to the large number of possible combinations for subsets with more than two queries, we present an approximation to the absolute worst and best results.

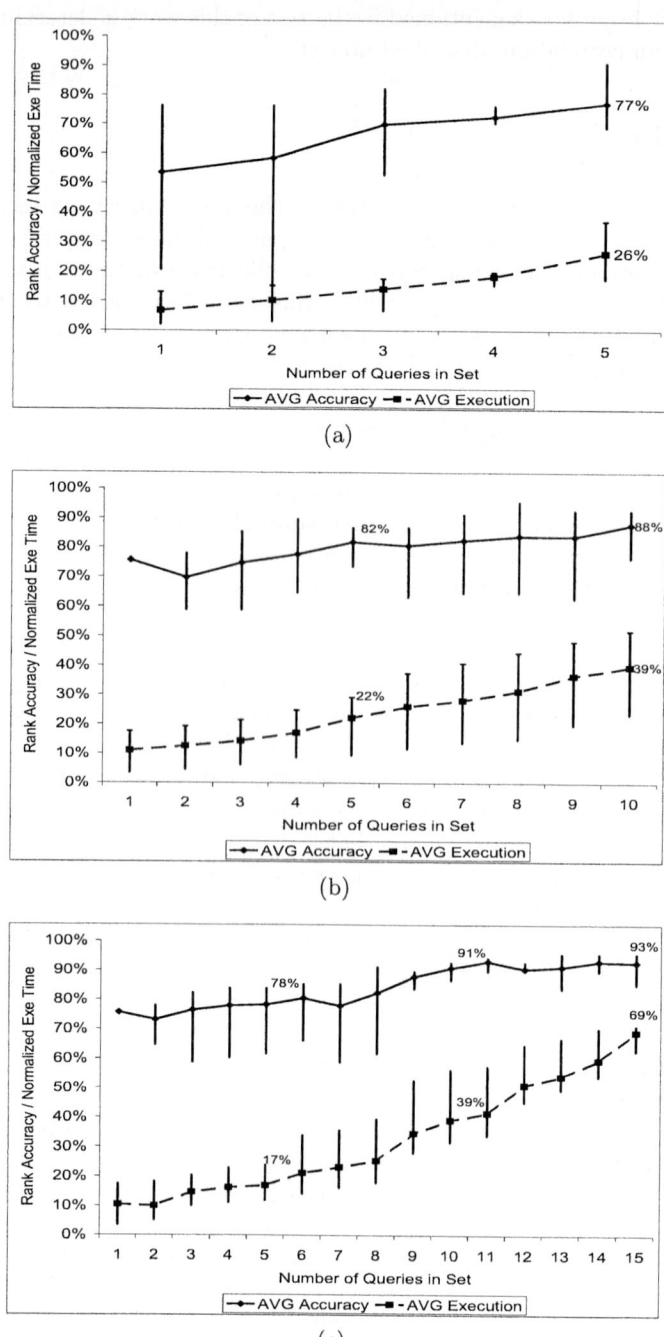

Fig. 2. Rank accuracy and execution time for PCA subsetting for: (a) 5, (b) 10, and (c) 15 query cluster

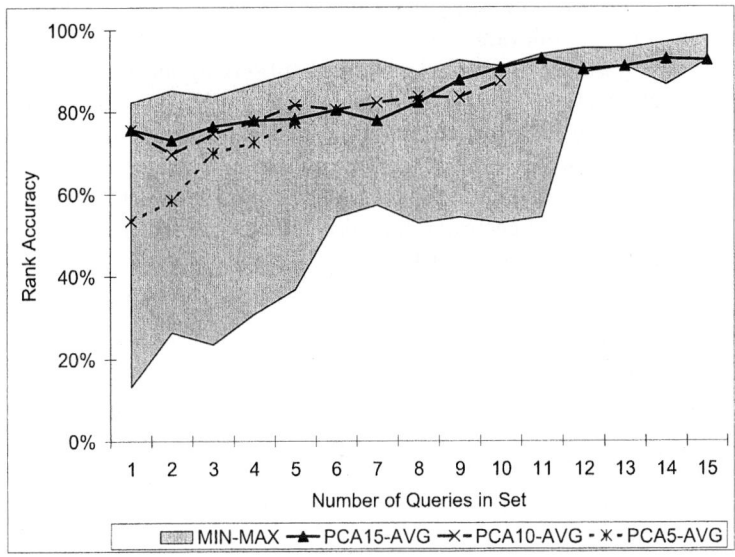

Fig. 3. PCA for 5, 10, and 15 query cluster versus random selection subset

For this approximation we used a heuristic based on the ordering of the queries obtained for a subset with a single query. Let's assume that for the subset of a single query we obtained the following results, where the first query (Q_0) is the one achieving the highest *rank accuracy* and the last one (Q_n) the lowest: Q_0, Q_1, ..., Q_{n-1}, Q_n. Consequently, we apply the simple heuristic that the subset with two queries that will achieve the best result should be the subset with the two best queries from the single subset (Q_0 and Q_1). Analogous, the subset with two queries that achieves the worst results according to the heuristic is the one composed by the two queries at the end of the list from the single query analysis (Q_{n-1} and Q_n).

It is relevant to notice that although the lower bound for the results obtained with the random subset improves significantly for subsets larger than five queries and is very close to the upper bound for subsets larger than twelve queries, the PCA results are always at a much higher value than the worst random and very close to the best random. From the same Figure it is also important to notice that the larger the cluster size used with the PCA method, the better the results obtained. The *rank accuracy* for subsets of the same size obtained with a cluster of 15 queries is most of the times higher than the one obtained with a cluster of 10 queries. This result is a consequence of the clustered PCA method used and described in Section 3.2. As on every iteration of the clustered method we select the lowest ranked query to evict from the cluster, in order to add a new query to the evaluation, the smaller the cluster, the smaller the difference between the best and worst query within the cluster. This may result to selecting wrong queries to be evicted as the selection set may be too limited. In larger clusters this problem is not as relevant.

Overall, it is possible to conclude that the subsetting methodology presented in this paper is effective, as a small subset (five queries out of 22) can achieve a high *rank accuracy* at a low execution time. In addition, results show that the PCA subset can achieve much higher *rank accuracy* than most cases of the random selection subset. The subsetting methodology presented in this paper not only results in higher accuracy but also in a guarantee that the values will be closer to the best possible subset.

5 Conclusions

Benchmarking is becoming a time-consuming operation as programs become more complex. This is a serious problem for computer architecture research as the benchmark programs are executed on a simulated architecture which usually executes orders of magnitude slower than real execution.

In this work we proposed a technique to reduce the execution of the complex TPC-H database benchmark. We do this by using a statistical method in order to reduce the number of queries to a small subset of the original ones. Our experiments showed that with the proposed technique, we were able to obtain query subsets with only 5 out of the original set of 22 queries, which may be used to rank the computer systems with an accuracy of more than 80%. It is important to notice that this was achieved with only 20% of the execution time of the complete benchmark. Also relevant is the fact that the subsets obtained with this technique are considerably better than if the subset was obtained with a random selection of queries.

References

1. Henning, J.L.: SPEC CPU2000: Measuring CPU Performance in the New Millennium. IEEE Computer **33** (2000) 28–35
2. Levy, M.: EEMBC 1.0 Scores, Part 1: Observations. Microprocessor Report (2000) 1–7
3. Transaction Processing Performance Council: TPC Benchmark^{TM} C, Standard Specification (2004)
4. Transaction Processing Performance Council: TPC Benchmark^{TM} H (Decision Support), Standard Specification (1999)
5. KleinOsowski, A.J., Lilja, D.A.: MinneSPEC: A new SPEC benchmark workload for simulation-based computer architecture research. Computer Architecture Letters (2002)
6. Eeckhout, L., Vandierendonck, H., De Bosschere, K.: Designing computer architecture research workloads. IEEE Computer **36** (2003) 65–71
7. Gòmez, I., Pinuel, L., Prieto, M., Tirado, F.: Analysis of simulation-adapted SPEC 2000 benchmarks. SIGARCH Computer Architecture News **30** (2002) 4–10
8. Saavedra, R.H., Smith, A.J.: Analysis of benchmark characteristics and benchmark performance prediction. IEEE Transactions on Computers **14** (1996) 344–384

9. Eeckhout, L., Vandierendonck, H., De Bosschere, K.: Workload design: Selecting representative program-input pairs. In: Proceedings of the 2002 International Conference on Parallel Architectures and Compilation Techniques. (2002) 83–94
10. Eeckhout, L., Vandierendonck, H., De Bosschere, K.: Quantifying the impact of input data sets on program behavior and its applications. Journal of Instruction-Level Parallelism **5** (2003) 1–33
11. Vandierendonck, H., De Bosschere, K.: Eccentric and fragile benchmarks. In: 2004 IEEE International Symposium on Performance Analysis of Systems and Software. (2004) 2–11
12. Yi, J.J., Lilja, D.J., Hawkins, D.M.: A Statistically Rigorous Approach for Improving Simulation Methodology. In: Proceedings of the Ninth International Symposium on High Performance Computer Architecture (HPCA9). (2003) 281–291
13. Vandierendonck, H., De Bosschere, K.: Many benchmarks stress the same bottlenecks. In: Workshop on Computer Architecture Evaluation Using Commercial Workloads (CAECW-7). Held in conjunction with HPCA-10. (2004) 57–64
14. Vandierendonck, H., De Bosschere, K.: Experiments with subsetting benchmark suites. In: Proceedings of the Seventh Annual IEEE International Workshop on Workload Characterization. (2004) 55–62
15. Transaction Processing Performance Council: http://www.tpc.org (2005)
16. Dunteman, G.: Principal Components Analysis. Volume 69 of Quantitative Applications in the Social Sciences. Sage Publications, Inc, Newbury Park (1989)
17. Kendall, M.: Rank and Product-Moment Correlation. Biometrika **36** (1949) 177–193

A Collected TPC-H Results for a 100 GByte Database

Table 1. Systems tested for TPC-H 100GB

System	Label
PowerEdge 6650/2.0/8GB	SysA
HP ProLiant DL580G2 4P	SysB
HP Proliant DL580 G2	SysC
HP Proliant DL760 G2 8P	SysD
HP ProLiant ML370 G3 2P	SysE
HP ProLiant DL580 G2 4P	SysF
HP ProLiant DL 760 G2 8P	SysG
IBM eServer xSeries 445 8P	SysH
IBM eServer OpenPower 720 w/DB2 UDB	SysI
IBM eServer xSeries 346	SysJ
IBM eServer 325	SysK
Langchao SP3000	SysL
MAXDATA Platinum 9000-4R	SysM
SunFire V440	SysN
SunFire V440	SysO
SunFire V250	SysP
SunFire V240 Server	SysQ

Table 2. TPC-H Results for 100GB

	Q1	Q2	Q3	Q4	Q5	Q6	Q7	Q8	Q9	Q10	Q11
SysA	1925.7	183.4	562.6	976.3	1153.5	339.4	781.7	954.6	2998.8	1027.6	151.1
SysB	1549.7	202.4	648.7	688.6	1144.8	164.8	844.6	962.1	3369.5	485.9	161.8
SysC	2620.8	291.5	1280.2	989.2	1285.1	460.8	1045.9	737.8	5192.7	1193.3	621.2
SysD	959.0	162.0	431.6	494.8	784.0	145.2	484.6	575.0	2063.2	344.3	185.0
SysE	1968.7	386.2	680.1	635.0	1326.8	82.9	999.5	4658.8	2568.6	735.9	1391.7
SysF	1174.9	291.3	503.6	664.7	937.3	110.3	673.8	737.8	2451.7	352.8	251.1
SysG	737.1	146.1	310.9	343.6	637.9	88.5	368.9	394.9	1047.5	200.0	87.9
SysH	534.3	89.8	95.8	63.1	261.6	90.2	346.7	357.2	1022	137.8	95.6
SysI	603.4	53.4	73.0	35.3	253.9	43.8	301.7	204.0	798.5	206.6	53.7
SysJ	601.8	163.6	102.2	997.0	2787.4	67.9	1214.2	3724.2	1170.3	1404	134
SysK	117.2	15.9	21	12.2	84.5	12.9	114.3	97.4	414	55.4	40.5
SysL	570.68	168.46	71.74	60.12	355.52	61.06	295.54	384.42	1077.32	188.26	85.28
SysM	1187	95.1	62.6	87.3	316	57	466.9	220.9	1076.8	305.4	156.2
SysN	3050.5	38.46	289.2	387.34	351.18	103.9	295.43	253.73	774.57	877.39	72.21
SysO	3508.4	22	307	359.5	385.3	80.1	370.1	211.5	929.8	837.6	56.1
SysP	4703.2	48.7	643	2025.9	858.2	164.7	1124.3	355	2370.5	1435.7	128
SysQ	6407.6	57.6	1123.4	2817.1	1233.4	237.7	1391.4	651.6	3414.5	1751.9	200.9

	Q12	Q13	Q14	Q15	Q16	Q17	Q18	Q19	Q20	Q21	Q22
SysA	1264.6	1456.1	669	1463.1	538.6	294.8	4424.9	211.3	1060.2	2943.3	119.2
SysB	407.9	2174.2	817.1	1598.3	483.5	339.2	5039.3	327.0	180.6	2544.9	132.6
SysC	1303.3	1629.0	690.2	1520.4	629.9	428.2	4964.4	221.3	224.7	3226.9	151.2
SysD	260.1	1039.6	745.1	1285.2	307.9	145.9	2670.0	95.2	75.3	1608.0	73.2
SysE	586.8	1382.4	118.2	1576.8	389.7	1316.9	4441.8	543.4	1453.1	2694.1	134.1
SysF	265.1	1182.7	814.8	1193.7	334.8	370.2	3857.5	327.9	180.0	2251.9	102.6
SysG	181.7	626.1	375.5	1289.8	219.7	150.2	2307.9	64.7	425.1	1191.4	44.4
SysH	123.3	567.4	35.2	83.2	137.7	613.7	934.9	698.8	206.5	2007.1	197.4
SysI	51.6	995.3	49.5	214.7	216.5	334.3	1368.5	256.0	83.3	1071.3	301.5
SysJ	1690.4	706.7	51.4	402.2	196.8	657.5	2111.3	667.6	1093.4	1879.2	192.0
SysK	24.8	218.9	16.4	62.2	73	123.6	449.8	117.9	31.2	445	56.9
SysL	160.16	471.3	50.12	82.28	372.7	516.08	1103.4	547.86	329.4	1705.18	240.04
SysM	151.7	1171	76.9	215.3	254.3	358.5	2971.5	314.2	265.5	2374.9	286.5
SysN	210.55	880.67	180.16	187.04	260.03	249.83	2178.4	393.5	326.8	1457.48	150.24
SysO	215.4	1173.9	128.1	191.5	259.6	167.6	2657.5	329	190.7	2493.2	161.6
SysP	444.3	2720.7	274.9	368.9	390.2	210.1	5816.3	641.8	354.6	5022.8	318.6
SysQ	660.3	4596.6	415.1	615.2	471.6	336.3	8711.2	971.7	611.4	6928.1	516.1

CryptoPalm: A Cryptographic Library for PalmOS

Georgios C. Alexandridis, Artemios G. Voyiatzis, and Dimitrios N. Serpanos

Department of Electrical and Computer Engineering,
University of Patras, GR-26504, Patras, Greece
GAlexandridis@myrealbox.com, {bogart, serpanos}@ee.upatras.gr

Abstract. PDAs and other handheld devices are commonly used for processing private or otherwise secret information. Their increased usage along with their networking capabilities raises security considerations for the protection of the sensitive information they contain and their communications.

We present CryptoPalm, an extensible cryptographic library for the PalmOS. The library integrates a large set of cryptographic algorithms and is compatible with the IEEE P1363 standard. Furthermore, the library offers performance comparable with that of independent, application-centric implementations of the cryptographic algorithms. CryptoPalm is beneficial for PalmOS software developers, since it provides established cryptographic algorithms as an infrastructure for meeting their applications' security requirements.

1 Introduction

The PalmOS platform is a well-known and wide-spread PDA platform. It has been used by PalmOne (formerly Palm Inc.), Sony, and Handspring for PDAs of varying capabilities. PalmOS dominated the market of PDAs, reaching a worldwide penetration of 68% by 1999. Nowadays, the PalmOS operating system is incorporated in smartphones i.e., mobile phones with PDA capabilities.

The increasing use of PDAs for processing private information and for securely accessing enterprise information drives the need for support of cryptographic operations in them. Furthermore, PDAs are complete computing systems that can interface with larger systems through communication ports like infrared ports, modems, and wireless network cards. Combined with their "personal" character, PDAs can be an attractive means for two-factor authentication methods.

Given the large installation base of PalmOS-based devices and the numerous applications, it is desirable to have a cryptographic library that incorporates most common operations, like public and secret-key algorithms and cryptographic hashing functions.

In this paper, we introduce CryptoPalm, an extensible library of cryptographic operations for the PalmOS. The library incorporates some unique characteristics. At first, it implements all the aforementioned algorithm families under a common programming interface, allowing a developer to choose the best algorithm for his needs from a set of available ones. At second, it offers compatibility with the IEEE P1363 standard for public-key cryptography, ensuring the correctness and validity of the implementation [1]. At third, it provides an extensible platform, where more algorithms can be incorporated, under the same programming interface, if needed. At fourth, it achieves comparable performance with that of independent implementations of specific algorithms. Finally, the library is compatible with all PalmOS versions, from 3.0 up to 6.0.

The paper is organized as follows. Section 2 provides a short presentation of the PalmOS platform and a review of previous attempts of cryptography implementation on the PalmOS platform. Section 3 provides an analysis of the implementation of the CryptoPalm library and the performance optimizations we incorporated, while Section 4 provides a comparison between the CryptoPalm library and independent implementations of specific algorithms. Finally, Section 5, presents the conclusions and the directions of this work.

2 Cryptography in the PalmOS

Palm PDAs are small-factor, battery-operated devices, in the size of a wallet. They offer functionalities such as calendaring, todo lists, and addressbook. The first generation of PDAs are based on the Motorola M68000 processor family, operate at 16 and later 33 MHz and have 512KB–32MB of memory. The word size is 16 bit, stored in big-endian form. They do not have a hard disk or a file system and communicate with a personal computer for data synchronization through a serial port. The second generation of Palm PDAs are based on the ARM 4T processor family, operating in much higher frequencies. The word size is now 32 bit, stored in little-endian form.

Palm PDAs run PalmOS, an operating system with a pre-emptive mutlitasking kernel. The user applications run, until PalmOS 6, as a single task and thus, no more than one user applications can run concurrently. PDAs based on the PalmOS enjoyed high market penetration. The manufacturer provides all necessary programming tools to third parties for developing new applications on top of the operating system. By the end of 2002, more than 20 million PalmOS-based devices have been sold and more than 10,000 third-party applications have been developed.

Among these applications, there have been attempts to implement various cryptographic algorithms for the PalmOS. The cryptographic algorithms are used for encrypting private information stored in the device and for supporting the SSH protocol over TCP/IP connections. The latter was based on pilotSSL, an attempt to port the SSLeay library to the PalmOS [2],[3]. Both SSLeay and pilotSSL have ceased development for quite some years now; the pilotSSL is far from a complete cryptographic library. Daswani and Boneh experimented on the capability of the Palm devices for supporting secure electronic transactions [4]. They conclude that there are some functions, like RSA key generation, that are not feasible to run on PalmOS and support the view that cryptography in such environments should be based on elliptic curve cryptography. To support this view, they provide comparisons between the pilotSSL library and a commercial SDK for elliptic curve cryptography. Lately, Copera Inc. has introduced AESLib, a high-performance implementation of the AES algorithm for the PalmOS [5].

Previous attempts to implement cryptography on the PalmOS can be characterized as application-centric. The cryptographic algorithms are built as part of larger applications and their maintainance is tight to that of the application. Furthermore, algorithms implemented in an application cannot be reused by another application. It is our view that cryptographic operations are a requirement for the majority of applications handling sensitive, private data on a PalmOS-based device and thus, they should be implemented as a library accessible from all applications. Thus, all applications can benefit from the existence of a correctly-implemented and high-performance library. PalmOS 5 headed for this option by providing a "Cryptography Provider Manager" in the operating system. However, currently it supports only two algorithms, namely RC4 for encryption and SHA-1 for hashing. In the next sections we present CryptoPalm, an attempt to provide a unified cryptographic library supporting all the popular algorithms under a common API for the PalmOS.

3 The CryptoPalm Library

The CryptoPalm is a complete cryptographic library for the PalmOS operating system. The CryptoPalm library provides implementations for the following algorithms:

- RSA public key algorithm. The implementation is compatible with the IEEE P1363 standard.
- symmetric key algorithms: DES, and two implementations of AES.
- ECC algorithms: ECDSA, compatible with the IEEE 1363 standard and supporting operations over primary and binary fields ($GF(p)$ and $GF(2^m)$).
- Hashing algorithms: SHA-1 and MD5.

The CryptoPalm cryptographic library is based on the MIRACL big number library [1]. The MIRACL library is a collection of optimized routines for handling multi-precision arithmetic, with emphasis on cryptographic operations.

The selection of the MIRACL library was driven by the fact that it offers a well-tested set of cryptographic operations and all the necessary primitives for implementing new algorithms. Furthermore, MIRACL has the following advantages for the PalmOS platform:

- There are no available general-purpose cryptographic libraries for the PalmOS. The available port of the SSLeay library to the PalmOS has ceased development for some years now and the port was made for supporting specific operations.
- MIRACL is known to be one of the top high-performance libraries for cryptographic operations [6].

---

[1] MIRACL library is available from `http://indigo.ie/~mscott/`.

- The library is developed with portability in mind, which was expected to ease the port to the PalmOS platform.
- The library supports both big and little endian architectures, which is a desirable feature, given that the Motorola M68000 processor family follows a big endian architecture.

The development of CryptoPalm library consisted of the following steps: *i.* Porting the MIRACL library to the PalmOS environment, *ii.* Implementation of public key algorithms compatible with the IEEE P1363 standard, *iii.* Integration of symmetric-key and hashing algorithms, *iv.* Implementation of algorithmic optimizations, and *v.* Development of a static and a shared library for use by other programs.

3.1 Port of the MIRACL Library to PalmOS

The MIRACL library provides the necessary support for big number arithmetic. It has been actively developed since 1988 and currently version 4.85 is available. The library is available in source code and executable forms for various processors and is free for academic and non-profit use. The library is characterized by its compactness, portability, and efficiency. Various processor families are supported and optimizations in the form of assembly code are provided for specific families.

The Motorola M68000 processor family is not currently supported, so the first step was to port the MIRACL library to this processor family. The first step of porting the library to a new environment is to correctly structure the MIRACL Definitions header file `mirdef.h`. The required changes for supporting the PalmOS environment were:

- Define a word size of 16 bits and big-endian storage.
- Disable support for optimized assembly code, since no assembly code is available for the M68000 processor.
- Disable support for standard I/O and file I/O, since the PalmOS platform neither has standardized input/output functions, e.g. ANSI C `printf()` and `scanf()`, nor a file system.

There are some points that must be taken into account when creating a library in the PalmOS environment. A first point is to decide if the library is built as a static or dynamic one. A static library introduces less overhead and the linker, if it supports it, can integrate into the application only the functions of the library that are called. This results to smaller programs. However, if the library code is updated, all programs that are linked with the previous version of the library must be upgraded too, in order to incorporate the necessary updates. Dynamic libraries can be built and installed only once in a Palm device. Programs that use the library have the extra overhead of opening the library and calling the necessary functions. The advantages of dynamic libraries are the maintainability and the fact that programs can break the 64 KB barrier (dynamic libraries can be 64 KB each).

Another point of attention is the code model, which specifies the type of jumps within the code. There are three approaches to this option: use absolute addresses for calling functions (large model), use only small addressing (small model) and use a mixed model of absolute and relative addresses (smart model). The second approach results in faster code, since it introduces minimum overhead (one jump instruction). However, code jumps must not exceed 32 KB forward or backward (as the jump instruction takes a 16 bit offset value as a parameter). Therefore, a careful link order must be defined for the use of the small model without hitting the jump limit.

The previous work allowed the creation of a static library version of CryptoPalm. The static library comes as a standalone file, `PalmMir.lib`, that contains all the necessary functionality for implementing cryptographic computations. It can be integrated with third-party code. We also developed a shared library version of CryptoPalm, in order to further assist developers of cryptographic software. Since PalmOS shared libraries must not exceed the 64 KB limit, CryptoPalm is composed of four smaller libraries; one for algebraic operations (including the P1363 RSA Implementation), one for elliptic curve operations (including the P1363 ECDSA Implementation), one containing the symmetric ciphers (DES and AES) and the hash functions (SHA-1 and MD5), and one containing Brian Gladman's AES Code. All four PRC files can be transferred to the the PDA during a HotSync operation and can be manipulated like any other Palm OS Shared library.

3.2 Public-Key Algorithms

The implementation of public key algorithms has been standardized in the IEEE P1363 standard [1]. The standard defines all the necessary steps for implementing a public-key algorithm, from the generation and validation of keys, to the encryption, decryption, signing, and signature verification functions. The MIRACL library provides "wrapper" functions for implementing only the public-key cryptography primitives.

We independently implemented a large set of IEEE P1363 functionality, supporting all cryptographic operations for both RSA (IFEP-RSA, IFDP-RSA) and Elliptic Curves (ECSP-DSA, ECVP-DSA). The implementation was validated for conformance with the standard, using the provided test vectors and checking for correct output.

3.3 Secret-Key and Hashing Algorithms

The symmetric-key algorithms implemented in the CryptoPalm library are DES and two versions of AES. The MIRACL library contains only an implementation of AES. As to support DES, we ported Eric Young's software DES implementation. This implementation is considered the fastest one in software currently freely available [6]. We also ported to the CryptoPalm library Brian Gladman's implementation, which is considered the most optimized software implementation of AES [7].

CryptoPalm provides the MD5 and SHA-1 hashing algorithms [8,9]. We ported to the PalmOS the reference implementation of MD5 provided in [8]. The SHA-1 implementation is contained in the MIRACL library.

Initial performance measurements suggested that the public-key algorithms did not achieve comparable performance with the ones provided in the literature. We further examined the implementations in order to seek for areas of improvements.

3.4 RSA Optimizations

Profiling the RSA implementation revealed that the computation of the modular exponentiation operation x^y (mod n) was the dominant one in time, accounting for over 99.5% of the time. Careful inspection of execution traces revealed four areas of algorithmic optimization [10]:

- Usage of the Chinese Remainder Theorem (CRT).
- Improving the exponentiation computation.
- Improving the modular multiplication computation.
- Improving the multiplication operation.

Usage of the CRT theoretically contributes an improvement by a factor of four. A comparison of methods for exponentiation verified that MIRACL is already using the best available method, that is of an adaptive sliding window of 5 bits. The modular multiplication method used in MIRACL, the Montgomery reduction, is almost optimal, since it is 2.5% slower than the table lookup method [10]. We opted for Montgomery reduction, since it requires less space and allows for the next optimization. The multiplication operation can be enhanced by combining the Karatsuba-Ofman multiplication method with the Montgomery reduction for the modular multiplication. The combination of the two methods offers an asymptotic improvement from $O(n^2)$ to $O(n^{1.58})$, where n is the number of binary digits of the modulo.

In summary, CryptoPalm contains an optimized RSA implementation using the Chinese Remainder Theorem, an adaptive sliding window exponentiation of 5 bits and the combination of Montgomery reduction and Karatsuba-Ofman method for the modular multiplication operation. CryptoPalm with this setup achieved an significant improvement by a factor of 5 compared to the default implementation.

3.5 Elliptic Curve Optimizations

Profiling the Elliptic Curve Cryptography implementation revealed that the computation of the scalar product of a number with a point of a curve was the most time consuming task, accounting for over 98% of the time. The scalar multiplication can be improved in four areas:

- Improving the multiplication algorithm.
- Improving the doubling and addition operation.

- Improving the modular multiplication algorithm.
- Improving the multiplication method.

The analysis of the profiling revealed that the computations could be improved by using the Brickell method [11]. This applies to both primary and binary fields. The improvement is almost halving the required time for the computation. Furthermore, for computations over prime fields, it is possible to use the combined Karatsuba-Ofman multiplication method and the Montgomery reduction method as before, along with the Brickell method. All combined, we achieved an improvement by an order of magnitude for the computations over a prime field.

4 Performance Analysis

In this section we present performance diagrams for the algorithms supported by CryptoPalm. All performance measurements were taken in the PalmOS Profiler, a special version of the PalmOS Emulator (POSE) [12]. The Profiler provides detailed timing analysis of application execution with high accuracy. For shake of comparison with other works, we provide diagrams of the performance on the Motorola Dragonball 16 MHz processor. We note that we took measurements for other processors too (Dragonball EZ 20 MHz, VZ 20 MHz, VZ 33 MHz), and on a real device (Handspring Visor Pro having a Motoral Dragonball VZ 33 MHz processor). All measurements indicate that cryptographic operations are processing-bounded (performance improves linearly with the speed of processor). Furthermore, performance on the POSE and the real device are identical, further supporting the confidence on the POSE measurements. All measurements presented are the weighted average of 100 experiments.

Table 1 provides a comparison between the CryptoPalm optimized RSA implementation and the one provided by the pilotSSLeay for encryption and decryption. The two implementations provide almost identical performance; for decryption pilotSSLeay is slighty better, for encryption CryptoPalm is slightly better. This is rather encouraging, since pilotSSLeay implements the time-critical functions in assembly code, while CryptoPalm does not.

Table 1. RSA (n=512, e=17) performance on DragonBall 16 MHz

	pilotSSLeay	CryptoPalm
Decryption	7028 ms	7343 ms
Encryption	1376 ms	1338 ms

Table 2 provides a comparison between the CryptoPalm optimized ECC implementation and the Certicom Security Builder SDK 2.1 for PalmOS, as reported in [4]. Clearly, the commercial product is achieving better performance (4–5 times faster). This is an area of improvement for the CryptoPalm library.

We should note however that the commercial product contains highly-optimized code in assembly language, while CryptoPalm is written entirely in ANSI C.

Table 2. ECC (160/163 bit) performance on DragonBall 16 MHz

	pilotSSLeay	CryptoPalm
Key generation	597 ms	3465 ms
Signature generation	776 ms	3684 ms
Signature verification	2448 ms	10084 ms

Table 3 provides a comparison between DES and AES of CryptoPalm. The AES algorithm is considered more secure than the DES algorithm; the results indicate that it is also provides higher performance, so there is no practical reason to prefer DES rather AES.

Table 3. DES and AES performance (bytes/sec)

	DES	AES 128	AES 192	AES 256
Dragonball 16 MHz	4343	7547	6501	5710
Dragonball EZ 16 MHz	4343	7547	6501	5710
Dragonball EZ 20 MHz	5305	9217	7940	6975
Dragonball VZ 33 MHz	8705	15123	13019	11429

Table 4 provides a comparison between three AES implementations: the one contained in MIRACL and ported to PalmOS, Brian Gladman's ANSI C code ported in the CryptoPalm library, and AESLib, a commercial product using also Gladman's code along with assembly language optimizations. We note that the performance for AESLib is taken by the manufacturer, so actual performance may slightly differ from the one reported. In any case, our port and AESLib offer comparable performance.

Table 4. AES 128 encryption performance on DragonBall 16 MHz (bytes/sec)

	MIRACL	Gladman	AESLib
Encryption	7733	8316	10296

Table 5 provides a comparison for various input sizes for the performance of the SHA-1 and the MD5 algorithms, as implemented in CryptoPalm. The authors are not aware of other implementations of the two algorithms for the PalmOS in order to make a comparison. From the table, it is clear that there is a logarithmic relationship between input size and time to complete a hash operation. We also note that for input sizes smaller than 256 bits the performance is the same in both cases, due to padding (the input is padded to 256 bits and then hashed). Furthermore, it is clear that MD5 is about four times faster than SHA-1.

Table 5. SHA-1 and MD5 performance (time, in milliseconds)

Input size (bits)	160	256	512	1024	2048	4096
SHA-1, DragonBall 16 MHz	9223	9210	16991	24737	40229	71212
SHA-1, DragonBall VZ 33 MHz	4605	4598	8483	12350	20085	28749
MD5, DragonBall 16 MHz	2843	2843	4722	6468	9944	16894
MD5, DragonBall VZ 33 MHz	1423	1423	2367	3233	4963	8424

5 Discussion and Future Work

We have presented CryptoPalm, a high-performance cryptographic library for the PalmOS platform. The library is compatible with the IEEE P1363 standard, a unique characteristic for the specific platform that further raises the confidence for the correctness of the implementation. The library achieves high-performance on the platform; the performance of the algorithms is comparable with other works that focus exclusively on a specific algorithm or family of them. Furthermore, CryptoPalm offers a unified API for accessing all algorithms, which is a highly desirable feature and incorporates a set of algorithms for each fundamental operation. Thus, it allows the developer to choose the algorithm that best matches his needs, without requiring to learn and install another library. CryptoPalm remains an extensible platform, where new cryptographic algorithms can be added.

There are some areas of improvement for the library that we plan to work in the future. One direction is the inclusion of more cryptographic algorithms in the library. Another direction is the further optimization of the code, by implementing computational-intensive parts in assembly language, where possible. Finally, it is desirable to further port natively the library on the PalmOS 5 and 6 platform. The library now can run as-is on these platforms through the PACE compatibility layer provided by the newer versions of the operating system. However, this layer introduces some unavoidable overhead that we would like to overcome. Newer versions of the operating system include a limited cryptographic library by incorporating licensed technology from other companies. It would be interesting to compare the performance of CryptoPalm and the licensed libraries in the new operating systems. Furthermore, newer versions of the PalmOS operating system are not supported by the emulator and the profiler, thus it is necessary to develop a new testbed environment and methodology for performance measurements on this platform.

References

1. IEEE: The IEEE P1363 Working Group. (http://grouper.ieee.org/groups/1363/. Available, April 25, 2005)
2. Goldberg, I.: pilotSSLeay-2.01. (http://www.isaac.cs.berkeley.edu/pilot/. Available, December 20, 2005)
3. Hudson, T., Young, E.: SSLeay. (http://www2.psy.uq.edu.au/~ftp/Crypto/. Available, December 20, 2005)
4. Daswani, N., Boneh, D.: Experimenting with Electronic Commerce on the PalmPilot. In: Proceedings of Financial Cryptography '99. Volume 1648 of Lecture Notes in Computer Science., Springer-Verlag (1999) 1–16
5. Copera Inc.: AESLib for Palm OS. (http://www.copera.com/AESLib/. Available, December 20, 2005)
6. Dai, W.: Speed comparison of popular crypto algorithms. (http://www.eskimo.com/~weidai/benchmarks.html. Available, December 2, 2004)
7. Gladman, B.: AES Implementation. (http://fp.gladman.plus.com/AES/. Available, April 25, 2005)
8. Rivest, R.: The MD-5 Message-Digest algorithm. (IETF RFC 1321)
9. Federal Information Processing Standards Publication 180-2: Secure Hash Standard (SHA). FIPS PUB 180-2 (2002)
10. Koc, C.: High-Speed RSA Implementation. RSA Laboratories (1994)
11. Brickell, E., Gordon, D., McCurley, K., Wilson, D.: Fast exponentiation with precomputation: Algorithms and lower bounds. In: Advances in Cryptology: Eurocrypt '92. Volume 658 of Lecture Notes in Computer Science., Springer-verlag (1992) 200–207
12. Palm Inc.: Palm OS Emulator (POSE). (http://www.palmos.com/dev/tools/emulator/. Available, December 20, 2005)

On the Importance of Header Classification in HW/SW Network Intrusion Detection Systems

Vassilis Dimopoulos[1], Giorgos Papadopoulos[1], and Dionisios Pnevmatikatos[1,2]

[1] Electronic and Computer Engineering Department,
Technical University of Crete, Chania, GR 73 100, Greece
{dimopoulos, gpap, pnevmati}@mhl.tuc.gr
[2] Institute of Computer Science (ICS), Foundation for Research and
Technology-Hellas (FORTH), Vasilika Vouton, Heraklion, GR 71110, Greece
pnevmati@ics.forth.gr

Abstract. In this paper we examine the impact of various levels of (partial) hardware acceleration levels on a software based Network Intrusion Detection System. While complete hardware solutions are possible and have been studied extensively, they are costly and may suffer from scalability and flexibility limitations. The flexibility of software is attractive to address these concerns. We show in this paper that (unexpectedly) a modest amount of hardware acceleration such as simple header classification can achieve respectable and cost-effective system throughput. We also find that further acceleration in the form of approximate filtering offers very small incremental improvement.

1 Introduction

With the proliferation of high-speed and always-on Internet connections, the demand for network security is steadily increasing. Network Intrusion Detection Systems (NIDS) such as SNORT [9] attempt to detect and prevent attacks from the network using pattern-matching rules in a way similar to anti-virus software. NIDS systems running in general purpose processors can only achieve up to a few hundred Mbps throughput [2]. Given this limitation, considerable effort has been invested in accelerating NIDS systems in hardware. Researchers have proposed complete systems [8], or have focused on the pattern matching aspect of NIDS [4,5,10]. These designs vary in cost and performance ranging from a few to more than 10Gbps throughput, usually at a considerable area cost. Complete hardware solutions must leave enough free resources to accommodate the constant additions of new rules. Furthermore, the handling of IP *fragments*, is difficult without reassembling the packet, at considerable complexity. Therefore it is desirable to have a software layer in the system to handle the difficult or exceptional cases and to perform the actual reporting or other rule matching actions.

To deal with the size limitations, hardware/FPGA-based approximate filtering has been proposed. The idea is to device a filter (for example a Bloom filter [6]) that guarantees that a negative answer is correct, but that may give "high probability" positive answers, allowing for a small fraction of *false positives*. The existence of false positives unless is extremely infrequent, requires the presence of a verification mechanism, most probably in software.

This paper addresses two concerns: First is to address criticism on earlier research (including from our own research group) that ignored the header matching portion of packet processing and concentrated on the payload string matching; we wanted to implement a full header matching sub-system and evaluate its cost and performance. Second and most important, to quantify the effects of hardware acceleration on the *system* performance. Our goal was (a) to verify several assumptions made by ourselves and other researchers in the field regarding the actual cost of header matching in hardware-based NIDS, and (b) to quantify the impact of various acceleration levels on the software and system performance. To do so, we implemented a full-fledged Snort-like intrusion detection system we call T-Gate, and we modify it to accept processed and annotated input stream from a potential hardware accelerator. We performed experiments with synthesized traffic varying the header- and payload- match probabilities to evaluate scenarios for approximate filtering, the performance of which depends on the characteristics of the input stream. We show that the most important preprocessing step is header classification, which accounts for 55% - 80% of the processing time for typical network traffic Then, if the software is instructed about the matching header group, it can perform the payload search very quickly. We also found that additional preprocessing using approximate filtering does help, but only when false positives answers are very infrequent. We implemented hardware header classification on a Xilinx FPGA for the entire SNORT rule set (2060 rules), and found that the cost is in the order of 1750 slices, or about 0.86 slices per rule. We achieved an operating frequency of 230/390 MHz (depending on the device) and a throughput of 7/12 Gbits per second, processing 4 bytes per cycle. This cost is very affordable and in a modest device leaves ample space for the ever growing rule set.

This paper is organized as follows: Sections 2 and 3 describe the functionality of Snort, and our implementation, the T-Gate. In Section 4 we evaluate T-Gate, and in Section 5 we present and evaluate the FPGA-based implementation of the header classification module. Finally in Section 6 we offer some conclusions.

2   SNORT Network Intrusion Detection

Snort [9] is one of the fastest and most effective Intrusion Detection Systems. It is an open-source, lightweight and reliable platform with constant support, and is claimed to be capable of inspecting network connections at speeds of several Gigabits per second.

Snort's operation is based on rules, which specify what is considered as suspicious network traffic. Snort inspects the header of each incoming packet in order to find an applicable set of rules. If a matching set exist, the packet body is checked (if needed) for suspicious strings. Snort rules are written using a simple language:

```
alert tcp $EXTERNAL_NET !80 -> $10.20.30.0/24 any (msg: ".", sid: .)
```

The part up to the opening parenthesis specifies the rule *header* and indicates which packets are of interest in this rule, while the part inside the parentheses specifies the rule *options*, i.e. what we are looking for inside the packet. Each rule header is formed from up to 7 specific fields, which are (From left to right): (i) *action*: what to do if this rule is verified, (ii) *protocol*, (iii-iv) *source IP and port number*, (v) *simple (->) or bidirectional (<>) rule*, and (vi-vii) *destination IP and port number*.

Rule options are written in a less strict form, using a set of keywords that specify additional packet header fields (e.g. the 'ttl' field), suspicious strings or regular expressions contained in the payload of the packet, etc. A packet matches a rule when it matched all of the rule's options.

3 The T-Gate NIDS Implementation

T-Gate is an in-house, C++ implementation of the Snort intrusion detection functionality that consists of a total of 7,600 lines of code. T-Gate operates in two phases: the *setup* and the *inspection* phase. The setup phase occurs once and creates the data structures necessary for the subsequent inspection of network traffic. Then the inspection phase begins and is repeated for every incoming packet, scanning the header and possibly the payload of incoming packets for intrusion signs. The major components of T-Gate are:

Rule classification: After reading the Snort's rule specification files we use the rule header parameters to classify each rule into a proper rule set: we use its protocol, source and destination IP addresses and the following protocol-specific fields: (i) TCP and UDP: source and destination ports, (ii) ICMP: ICMP type, and (iii) IP: transport protocol id. All rules with identical classification values are combined into a single rule set.

Rule set optimization: Many times some rule sets which are proper subsets of other sets. A trivial example of this would be rule set A: ``alert tcp $EXTERNAL_NET any -> HOME_NET any'' and rule set B: ``alert tcp any any -> any any'' ``. Rule set optimization is to avoid scanning a packet's payload more than once. This is accomplished by finding all the pairs of rule sets where one is a proper subset of the other and including the rules of the larger set into the smaller one. Thus, if the header of a packet matches rule set A we compare the payload once against the rules in set A and all supersets of A.

Rule set sorting: We assign a "generality index" to each rule set, and we sort the contents of each of the four rule set arrays (one for each protocol) in increasing order of their generality indices.

Conflict Definition. A packet header may match two different rule sets where each set is *not* a subset of the other. This is a conflict between rule sets and in this case the packet must be checked against the rules contained in both sets.

Algorithm Selection. Each rule set is paired with one of four string matching algorithms:

- Boyer-Moore-Horspool (BMH) [7]: simplification of the classic Boyer- Moore [3] algorithm. Very fast average case but useful only for a single string.
- Aho-Corasick (AC) [1]: offers guaranteed linear search cost. All strings are combined into a single finite state machine and the text is processed one character at a time.
- Wu-Manber (WM) [11]: an evolution of the BMH algorithm, capable of concurrent searching for a set of signatures. Fast on the average but only if the length of the shortest string is not very small (less than 4).
- Hybrid Aho-Corasick-Boyer-Moore: our combination of the BMH shift ability with the AC fsm. All strings are used to create a single shift table, which contains in each position the minimum value for all the strings. Much like in the BMH algorithm, we use the shift table to jump over segments of the text. Whenever the shift table gives us a value of 0, we move back m-1 characters and apply the AC fsm, where m is the length of the shortest string in the set. We keep using the fsm until it returns to its initial state, at which point we leap over m characters and start using the shift table again.

We select which algorithm for a specific rule set based on (i) the number of rules in the set which require string matching and (ii) the length of the shortest string. We found experimentally that it is best to use AC when we have a minimum length of two characters or less, BMH when the set contains only one string, ACBM when the set has less than 50 strings and WM in all other cases.

Packet Header Classification. The first level of inspection is applied to all packets. From the packet header we extract the necessary data (protocol, source and destination IP, ports, etc) and perform a sequential comparison with all the rule sets for the specific protocol. Should the packet header match a rule set, we will also have to check the payload.

Payload Scanning. After we find a matching rule set, the payload is examined for suspicious strings using the algorithm assigned to this set. The algorithm returns a list containing the id's of the strings that were located inside the payload and the positions where those strings were discovered. If no strings are found, we compare the packet's header with the entries inside the list of possible conflicts of the rule set that initially matched. If this comparison produces another set which matches the packet then the payload is scanned again.

4 T-Gate Evaluation

First we compare the speed and effectiveness of T-Gate with that of Snort. We used Snort v. 2.1.3 with all included rule files. Measurements were performed on an 1.2 GHZ Athlon processor with 256 KB cache and 256 MB RAM under very light load conditions.

for the comparison we generated a large number of traces, each containing 250,000 packets with a protocol ratio of 70% TCP and 30% UDP, and described by three variables: the mean packet size, the probability h by which a packet header will match with at least one rule set, and the probability p by which a packet matching the header of a rule set will also contain a string indicated in one of the set's rules. We ran experiments with mean packet length values: 300, 560 and 1000. Due to space limitations we show results only for average size of 300 bytes which is representative of the average internet traffic. The results for larger packet sizes offer similar comparisons and conclusions.

4.1 T-Gate Performance

T-Gate was designed as a simple NIDS and supports only one 'content:' option per rule as well as the 'nocase' option for case insensitive string matching. To perform a fair comparison we processed all the rule files used in Snort and T-Gate so that all rule options are removed except 'msg:', 'sid:', 'ip_proto:', 'itype:' and the first 'content:' and 'nocase'. Also, we disable all preprocessors of Snort as well as checksum verification. In addition, we disable event logging and alert generation in Snort since they are computationally expensive. Finally, all rules with an "any any -> any any" header were omitted since all packet headers would match the equivalent rule set (giving a probability h of 100%).

Figure 1 plots the total execution time of the two systems when processing identical traces of packets with an average size of 300 bytes. By default Snort uses the Wu-Manber string matching algorithm, but we also plot Snort using the Aho-Corasick algorithm.

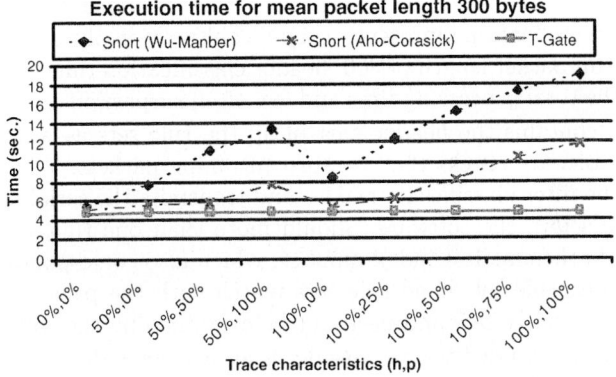

Fig. 1. Execution time for T-Gate and both cases of Snort, with a mean packet size of 300 bytes and varying trace characteristics h and p

It is interesting to observe that in several traces for Snort with AC (not shown in Figure 1) and in all traces for T-Gate, the execution time is practically stable regardless of the amount of matching headers and payload strings. This is due to the cost of reading the large traces files from the hard drive. Packet processing is done so quickly that an increase of the processing time due to the h and p parameters goes unnoticed due to the slow disk access. We modified T-Gate to measure the time spent exclusively on packet processing, we found that the packet processing time reaches at most 54% of the total execution time, supporting the hypothesis that packet processing and disk accesses are done in parallel and that disk access time dominates over that of packet processing.

The second observation is that T-Gate is significantly faster than Snort under conditions of "attack" traffic, i.e. traces with h being 100% and a large p. The execution time for Snort increases significantly under these conditions, while the execution time of T-Gate remains almost constant. We also performed experiments with additional traces with an average packet length of 560 and 1000 bytes. The resulting curves were of similar form as those of Figure 1. T-Gate is also more memory efficient, requiring about 17 MB while Snort required about 35 MB for the WM algorithm and 180 MB for the AC algorithm. The above facts suggest that T-Gate achieves comparable or better performance than Snort using less than 10% of the memory of Snort, making T-Gate a good platform to evaluate the effects of hardware acceleration.

4.2 Impact of Hardware Acceleration

We now investigate how a software IDS could benefit by the use of relatively simple hardware filters. We came up with two hardware filters that could be used to reduce both the number of packets processed by the software and the process time for each packet.

The first filter we consider is a *packet header classification* filter, since software-based header classification represents a significant portion of the total processing time: for a mean packet length of 300, header classification time represents more than 28% of the total processing time and can often surpass 50%.

This filter contains the header part of all the rule sets as well as the order in which the software checks them against incoming packets. When receiving a new packet, the filter classifies its header and transmits the serial number of the matching rule set to the software. Should more than one rule sets match, the hardware sends the smallest index number, which also corresponds to the most *specific* matching rule set. If no rule sets match with the packet's header then the packet is obviously safe and need not be examined by the software.

The second hardware filter we consider is an *approximate string match* filter. Such a filter could reduce the number of computationally expensive payload scans performed by the software. This filter is used in conjunction with the header classification filter described previously. After a packet has been classified, the packet along with the classification data arrives at the approximate string match filter. The filter then selects a specific group of strings which contains all strings of the matching rule set as well as all the strings of all possibly conflicting rule sets. The filter then performs a scan of the payload using an approximate string matching method (e.g. Bloom filter [6]) and responds either with an accurate negative answer indicating a clean packet, or a possibly incorrect positive answer, which means that most probably a string was located in the payload. If we receive a negative answer there is no need for the software to perform a payload scan, and the probability of false positives depends on the quality of the implementation.

To perform a quick exploration of the design space we developed simple theoretical models for the two filters, using the h and p probabilities, f, the probability of receiving a false positive answer, and the average processing time for header and payload processing of a packet. For The predicted execution times from the model were within 6.5% from the actual measured values.

The operation of both filters was simulated by properly preprocessing the traces we used and generating the information that the software IDS would receive if the filters were actually implemented. Figure 2 shows the impact of the two hardware accelerators on the processing time of T-Gate. From Figure 2 we can easily see that the packet header classification filter can significantly reduce processing time, and that the addition of a approximate string match filter reduces the processing time even further, but by a much smaller amount.

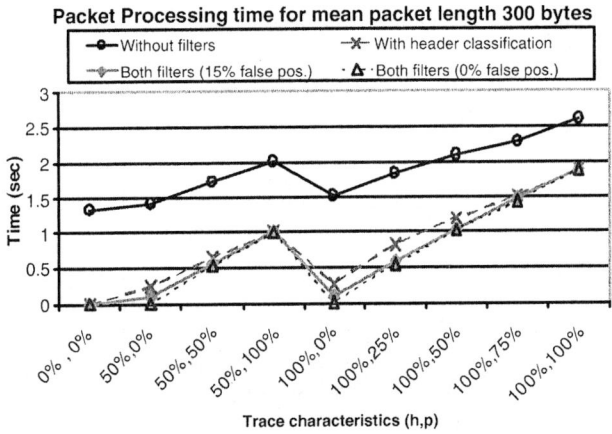

Fig. 2. Packet processing times for a mean packet length of 300 bytes and varying trace characteristics h and p

Figure 3 shows the total achieved operating bandwidth. We see that during normal operation the software-only system can achieve less that 500Mbps. Hardware acceleration helps dramatically under normal operation or light matching conditions. When the matches become very common, the involvement of the software negates any possible acceleration benefits.

5 FPGA-Based Header Matching and Classification

To establish the cost of header matching and classification for hardware/FPGA based NIDS, we implemented a full such system. The organization of the subsystem is simple and is shown in Figure 4. A single input feeds packet (header) data into the first module that performs header delineation, and field separation. For header classification, only six of all the possible header fields are necessary:

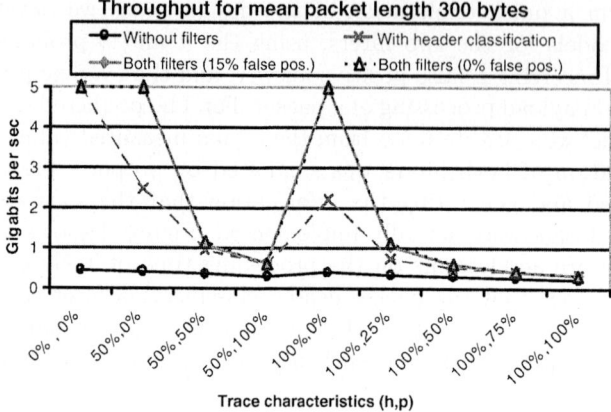

Fig. 3. Throughput in Gbps. Values over 5 Gbps were cropped in order to make the figure more readable.

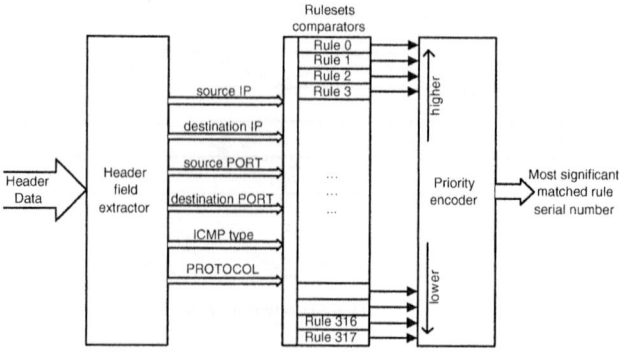

Fig. 4. Header Classification Module Organization

source and destination IP address and ports, the protocol type and the ICMP type. Here we have to make two observations: (a) these fields involve the IP header as well as the TCP/UDP headers (source and destination ports), and the ICMP header, and (b) additional header fields can be used in the Snort rules, but are *not* used for the header classification, so as to avoid excessive number of small groups.

The six header fields are registered and forwarded to the rule set comparator module. The output of this module is a bitmask indicating all possible matching rules. The matches are strictly prioritized, as mandated from the software (Snort and T-Gate). Therefore, the rule match indications are fed to a priority encoder to identify the most significant matched rule and to provide its encoding along with the packet data to the next processing level. All the modules are pipelined in fine-grain stages in order to achieve the best performance. Processing is per-

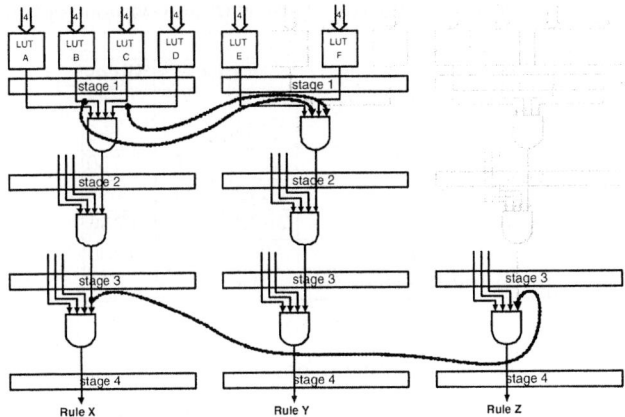

Fig. 5. Pipeline comparators with sharing. The 6 shaded FFs and the 2 shaded AND gates can be optimized away saving 8 LUTs.

formed 4 packet bytes per cycle and we use parallel comparators in order to process all the required header fields concurrently.

5.1 Pipelined Comparator Module

To achieve high operating frequency we implemented the comparator module using fine-grained pipeline, and to reduce the area cost of our implementation, we took advantage of the repeated instances of same comparators for various rules. These repetitions occur from similar rules that for example distinguish different addresses within the same domain, etc. We exploit comparator sharing at any level of the comparator tree at the minimum logic size, which is a 4-bit LUT, or even final result of the entire field value. The last case occurs when some rules have common sub-rules, for example when looking for the same destination address in a header.

Figure 5 shows both the four fine-grained pipeline stages and sketches the sharing of comparator's portions across different rules. In this diagram the light gray portions are removed and the corresponding results are obtained by shared logic cells. At the first pipeline level rule X compares against the hex value 0xABCD, rule Y compares against 0xEBFD, and rule Z compares against 0xABCD. Rule Z has more common parts with rule X not shown for space limitations. In the optimized implementation, rule Y shares two LUTs with rule X, and rule Z shares the output of stage three with rule X, with a total benefit of eight LUTs.

5.2 Performance Evaluation

For the evaluation of our design we used Xilinx Core generation tool for the multiplexer used in the encoder and the Xilinx ISE 6.2 tools for synthesis and

Table 1. Header Classification Area Cost with and without optimizations

Module	F/Fs	LUTs	Slices
Header Field Extractor	120	49	64
Comparators	1152	778	886
Priority encoder	1295	704	750
Control	112	112	56
Total Optimized	**2679**	**1643**	**1756**
No Optimizations	8904	7003	5120
Area Improvement (%)	332	426	291

Table 2. Utilization and operating frequency for three small Xilinx devices

Family	Device	Utilization (%)	Frequency (MHz)
Virtex2Pro	x2vp4	58	388
Virtex2	x2v500	57	388
Spartan3	x3s200	91	229

place and route operations. We used three devices from different FPGA families: a Virtex 2PRO x2vp4, a Virtex 2 x2v500 and a Spartan3 x3s200. The internal cell structure of these devices is similar and the results both for the area cost are practically identical. Table 1 lists the area lists the cost of our design in terms of flip-flops, LUTs and total device slices. The total cost is dominated by the Flip-Flops, and for the entire Snort rule set is 2679 FFs, that fit into 1756 slices. Table 1 also offers a break-down of this area cost per module, and as expected the majority of the FFs and logic is consumed by the field comparators and the priority encoder, i.e. the parts of our design that scale with the number of rules. In Table 1 we also show results without any LUT and FF sharing optimization: the number of FFs jumps to 8904 and the number of LUTs to 7003! This corresponds to a net increase of about 3 times in area.

Table 2 lists the area utilization and operating frequency for three devices we used in our experiments. We selected these small devices so as to keep design density in realistic levels. The operating frequencies we achieved are almost 390 MHz for the Virtex devices and about 230 MHz for the Spartan device. Since our design is capable of processing 4 packet bytes per cycle, these frequencies correspond to a processing throughput exceeding 12 and 7 Gbps respectively. It is clear that the header classification is both small and fast, and will not be a bottleneck when used in a larger design.

6 Conclusions

A complete hardware solution is by far superior in performance, and a very effective acceleration approach. However, if a software component is necessary for some reason (handling of fragments, approximate filtering, etc.), then a significant portion of the acceleration is lost, and the software becomes the bottleneck.

We discovered that in that context, a simple and small header classification is a very effective hardware acceleration technique, offering significant performance improvement with few resource demands. Using a modest personal computer together with header classification acceleration we were able to achieve (few) Gigabit software processing throughput when the system is not under attack.

To our surprise we also discovered that more sophisticated acceleration mechanisms such as approximate filtering offered limited additional performance gain because the software was the actual bottleneck.

These results offer evidence that guide us towards complete hardware/FPGA based NIDS systems, either (a) using exact matching techniques, or (b) using approximate matching techniques but accepting the fact that false positives exist and not attempting to verify whether they were actually false or not.

Header classification essentially "prunes" the search space, distinguishing between active and inactive groups of search strings. We plan to investigate ways to exploit this property and disabling a large part of the content search circuits in order to achieve hopefully significant power consumption savings.

References

1. A. Aho and M Corasick. Fast pattern matching: an aid to bibliographic search. In Commun. ACM, volume 18(6), pages 333–340, June 1975.
2. S. Antonatos, K. G. Anagnostakis, E. P. Markatos, and M. Polychronakis. Performance analysis of content matching intrusion detection systems. In Proceedings of the International Symposium on Applications and the Internet, 2004.
3. R. Boyer and J. Moore. A fast string match algorithm. In Commun. ACM, volume 20(10), pages 762–772, October 1977.
4. Young H. Cho, Shiva Navab, and William Mangione-Smith. Specialized hardware for deep network packet filtering. In Proceedings of 12th International Conference on Field Programmable Logic and Applications, 2002.
5. C. R. Clark and D. E. Schimmel. Efficient reconfigurable logic circuit for matching complex network intrusion detection patterns. In Proceedings of 13th International Conference on Field Programmable Logic and Applications, September 2003.
6. Sarang Dharmapurikar, Praven Krishnamurthy, Todd Spoull, and John Lockwood. Deep Packet Inspection using Bloom Filters. In Hot Interconnects, August 2003. Stanford, CA.
7. R. Horspool. Practical fast searching in strings. In Software - Practice & Experience, volume 10(6), pages 501–506, 1980.
8. J. W. Lockwood. An open platform for development of network processing modules in reconfigurable hardware. In IEC DesignCon '01, January 2001. Santa Clara, CA, USA.
9. M. Roesch. Snort - lightweight intrusion detection for networks. In Proceedings of LISA'99: 13th Administration Conference, November 7 -12 1999. Seattle Washington, USA.
10. I. Sourdis and D. Pnevmatikatos. Pre-decoded CAMs for efficient and high-speed nids pattern matching. In IEEE Symposium on Field-Programmable Custom Computing Machines, April 2004.
11. S. Wu and U. Mander. A fast algorithm for multi-pattern searching. In Techical Report TR-94-17, University of Arisona, 1994.

NGCE - Network Graphs for Computer Epidemiologists

Vasileios Vlachos[1], Vassiliki Vouzi[2],
Damianos Chatziantoniou[1], and Diomidis Spinellis[1]

Department of Management Science and Technology,
Athens University of Economics and Business (AUEB),
Patission 76, GR-104 34, Athens, Greece
[1] {vbill, damianos, dds}@aueb.gr
[2] vavouzi@dmst.aueb.gr

Abstract. Graphs are useful data structures capable of efficiently representing a variety of technological and social networks. They are therefore utilized in simulation-based studies of new algorithms and protocols. Inspired by the popular TGFF (Task Graphs For Free) toolkit, which creates task graphs for embedded systems, we present the NGCE, an easy to use graph generator that produces structures for the study of the propagation of viral agents in complex computer networks.

Keywords: Network graphs, Computer epidemiology, Malicious software

Designated track: Computer Security

1 Introduction

The design and evaluation of robust network protocols and algorithms is a difficult and tedious problem, mainly due to the effort and the economic cost required to deploy a prototype system in a large scale network in order to test the proposed designs. Moreover, some cases cannot conceivably be studied *in vivo*. For example, when studying malicious software or biological infectious agents, it is not possible to examine the spread of worms or viruses simply by releasing live viral code to the Internet or virulent strains to the society. The scientific community addresses these problems primarily by making extensive use of simulations.

The most accurate results come from simulations that utilize real-data topologies, but since most of the time these data are not available [1], synthetic graphs are used instead. Unfortunately the creation of artificial graphs imposes an additional effort, because they have to be built from scratch. Furthermore, as a result of the burden of constructing graph structures, researchers are forced to build only a small number of them in order to study their ideas. We believe that the existence of an easy to use graph generator will help the scientific community to evaluate the proposed algorithms under a broader scope using multiple topologies. This approach would offer the opportunity to gain insights on the weighted algorithms and to uncover their strengths and weaknesses in a much finer granularity than by using a single example or a limited number of graphs. The paper [2] showed the impact of graph generators in simulation outcomes, and [3] pointed out the correlation between the physical infrastructure and the problem under investigation during the design of graph models. Most of the recent research related to the generation of network graphs has focused on routing, resource preservation, and performance problems. On the contrary, to the best of our knowledge, little attention has been paid to the development of graph generation tools specially crafted for the study of the spread of malicious applications.

Another important issue concerns the difficulties that different research groups face in comparing their results because of the absence of a standard set of graphs or an application capable of constructing reproducible graphs. Given that it is quite difficult to generate a single set of graphs large enough to cover all needs, our goal was to introduce a tool that could regenerate graphs with predefined and repeatable properties. We focus on malcode propagation dynamics, because we believe that it represents a situation where alternative study methodologies, besides the use of simulations, are limited and not acceptable. Moreover, some studies take place during the outbreak of an epidemic, leaving insufficient time for the preparation of various graph topologies. We believe that this kind of support tool will be useful to speed up the research on the spread of viral code, especially during crisis situations. The embedded systems design community benefited a lot from the existence of tools such as the TGFF [4], which are able to generate specially crafted reproducible task-graphs for embedded systems. We hope that similar gains will also arise for the worm containment community.

Our decision was to incorporate within this application the most common topologies that have been and are still widely used to simulate the virulent activity of malware. We presume however, that this tool may also be useful for other studies related to social and technological networks as it is quite easy to add new topologies by developing appropriate plug-ins.

The rest of this paper is organized as follows. In section 2 we survey the most representative network topologies and we present their applications in a number of different circumstances. In section 3 we summarize the available graph generators. Section 4 describes the design of our tool and discusses various aspects of its implementation, while section 5 analyzes the graphs produced by our tool and comment on their characteristics. In section 6 we present possible use-case scenarios for the NGCE tool. Finally section 7 concludes this paper.

2 Network Graph Topologies

Although graphs have been widely used thoroughly to study a variety of interesting theoretical problems, only a small percentage of them are appropriate for network related problems and have been utilized in this scope. The most suitable topologies for this type of research are homogenous graphs, random graphs, random graphs with fixed connectivity, scale-free graphs and some variations of them that we will discuss below.

2.1 Homogeneous Graphs

Homogeneous or fully connected graphs were for many years the epidemiologists' preferred choice for describing the spread of infectious diseases. This topology has been recently adapted to model the growth of computer viruses and worms [5,6,7,8,9,10,11,12,13,14,15]. NGCE supports homogeneous graphs because they offer significant advantages. First, analytical mathematical models can be easily applied to them; second, they provide a good abstraction of very large networks when the majority of the susceptible hosts are accessible from an infectious agent and third, performing simulations using a homogeneous graph and comparing their outcomes with the mathematical analytical results is an excellent way to ensure that implementation details did not corrupt the simulation model. Homogeneous graphs can be built as follows.

1. Start with N vertices and no edges.
2. Connect each vertex with all the other vertices.

A homogeneous graph with N nodes will always end up with $(N^2 - N)/2$ edges.

2.2 Random Graphs

Until recently, it was believed that random graphs provide a good approximation to very large networks such us the Internet. Barabási et al [16] proved however, that the connectivity of the Internet, along with that of many other technical and social networks, obeys a power law distribution forming scale-free graphs. Prior to these findings, a large number of simulations that investigated the spread of malicious code, had been performed on random graphs [6,7,8,17,15]. Due to this fact, and, more importantly, in order to allow the comparison between older and current studies, we decided to include them in our tool. Since numerous algorithms have been proposed to construct random graphs, we selected to implement the most widely adopted one, in particular the Erdős-Rény algorithm [18] or the Gilbert algorithm according to others [19]. The algorithm works as follows.

1. Start with a graph with N nodes and no edges.
2. Connect each pair of two nodes with probability P_{er}.

This results in an Erdős-Rény graph. The shape of the connectivity distribution however is highly dependent on the value of the P_{er} probability.

2.3 Scale-Free Graphs

Scale-free structures exist in a stunning range of heterogeneous systems ranging from biological and social to purely technological [20] networks such as the World Wide Web (WWW) [21,22,23], the physical connectivity of the Internet [24,25] or the network of people connected by e-mail [26]. Studies have explored the spread of malicious code in scale-free computer networks with interesting but conflicting results [27,15,28] while [29] investigated the resilience of the Internet to random breakdowns. We assume that, in light of these recent evidences, simulation research will increasingly be based on scale-free topologies and thus we support them in the NGCE tool. Barabási and Albert demonstrated that the creation of scale-free networks should include two definitive characteristics: *Incremental growth* and *preferential connectivity*. *Incremental growth* is the process of adding new nodes to an existing graph. *Preferential connectivity* or preferential attachment describes the tendency of a newly added node to be connected with highly connected nodes. The elimination of either of these properties lead to graphs with temporal scale-free characteristics. Under certain circumstances it is possible to construct scale-free graphs without enforcing growth and preferential connectivity simultaneously. We felt that the inclusion of a flexible model that allows the experimentation with either of these modes or a combination of them would leverage the development of a larger variety of scale-free graphs.

Preferential connectivity. In order to construct a BA (Barabási and Albert) graph working with a fixed number of nodes without the incremental growth property, but with the preferential connectivity, we have to use a limited number of edges [30]. The algorithm consists of the following phases.

1. If the number of edges is less than the number of nodes, select randomly a vertex and connect it with probability

$$P(k_i) = \frac{k_i}{\sum_j k_j} \qquad (1)$$

   to the vertex i.
2. Repeat step 1.

If the number of edges is approximately equal to the number of nodes the constructed graph exhibits scale-free characteristics.

Incremental Growth. One, but not sufficient ingredient, of the scale-free networks is the incremental growth property, but without the preferential connectivity option; as new nodes are added to the graph the scale-free nature of the network diminishes. We thought that it would be best, if we enabled the construction of graphs based solely on the incremental growth for further study and experimentation. The algorithm has the following structure.

1. Create a pool K and add to it m_o initial nodes.
2. Create a pool L of all the other nodes.
3. Remove randomly a node i from the pool L and connect it to a randomly chosen node from the pool K.
4. Add node i to the pool K.
5. While the pool L is not empty, repeat step 3.

It is also possible to connect a node with $m > 1$ other nodes from pool K as long as the size of the pool K is larger than m.

Complete Model. By combining both of the incremental growth and preferential connectivity properties our system will approximate the BA model as closely as possible. The algorithm is constituted by two major parts. For the first m_o nodes:

1. Create a pool K and add to it m_o initial nodes.
2. Create a pool L of all the other nodes.
3. Remove randomly a node l from the pool L and connect it to a randomly chosen node from the pool K.
4. Add node l to the pool K.

And for the rest of the nodes, we follow closely the BA's algorithm.

1. Remove randomly a node i from the pool L.
2. Select randomly a vertex from the pool K and connect it with probability

$$P(k_i) = \frac{k_i}{\sum_j k_j} \qquad (2)$$

   to the vertex i.
3. Add i to the pool K.

The first part of the algorithm is arbitrary since Barabási and Albert, did not describe how to connect the $m_o + 1$ node.

To verify that the produced graphs obey the power law distribution necessary to characterize a graph as scale-free, we developed scripts to parse the constructed graph and extract the connectivity probabilities in a *gnuplot* format file.

2.4 Random Graphs with Fixed Connectivity

Random graphs with fixed connectivity constitute a nontrivial network topology that is often encountered in grid systems. Considering the significant importance of such systems and the fact that older studies have been based on them [6,8], we also included these structures in our NGCE tool. We implemented a custom algorithm for the creation of random graphs with fixed connectivity. In our approach, the user chooses the number of nodes and the number of edges each node should contain. Then the algorithm works as follows.

1. Create an unconnected graph with N nodes.
2. Add all nodes to a pool L.
3. Pick randomly a vertex v and a vertex u from the pool L, if the pool L has at least two elements, else exit.
4. Connect vertex v with vertex u and decrease their available connectivity by one.
5. If vertex's v or vertex's u available connectivity is 0, remove it from the pool L.
6. Repeat step 3.

2.5 Custom Graphs

Sometimes it is necessary to measure the effects of various algorithms in non-standard graphs. We therefore added an option to our system that gives the ability to an experienced user to create non-typical graphs with custom properties based either on the random graph algorithm or on the scale-free algorithm.

3 Network Graph Generators

The recent evidence from Barabási and Albert regarding the scale-free nature of the World Wide Web and the Internet [24] raised a number of issues concerning the structure of other technological networks. Several researchers proposed algorithms that provide improved models for the representation of these networks or uncover insufficiencies of the current models, such as [31,32] for the Internet or [22] for the World Wide Web. Despite these interesting advances, little effort has been put into developing tools to automate the creation of graphs in an efficient and reproducible way.

The Georgia Tech Internetwork Topology Models (GT-ITM)[33] is a widely used tool to generate random and hierarchical graphs that model the topological structure of networks. GT-ITM requires some knowledge of graph theory and is operable only via the command line. Furthermore, the types of the constructed graphs are more suitable for studying network-related problems (routing, resource reservation), rather than the spread of malicious software. Many of these concerns have been addressed by [34], which added visualization capabilities and optimized the graph creation algorithms. The GT-ITM work however is still focused on routing policies.

Inet[35] is an effective tool that aims to construct Internet topologies. While it produces sufficiently good results that approximate closely the actual Internet structure, it works only in the Autonomous Systems (AS) level leaving out finer-grain topologies, as the IP connectivity. Furthermore, Inet doesn't handle Wide Area Networks (WAN) often found in large enterprises and doesn't produce random or homogeneous graphs, which are important for the study of the spread of viral code.

Closest to our work is the BRITE [36,37] system, because of the similar architectural design with NGCE. BRITE clearly separates the Graphical User Interface from the main application and allows the development of specific plug-ins in order to have other topologies covered. Additionally, BRITE provides an analysis engine to process the constructed graphs and to extract their properties. Overall, BRITE is a very effective and mature tool that efficiently covers the majority of Internet related researches. Even so, it will need some further fine-tuning to produce some popular topologies for the study of malware epidemics.

Dreier [38] presented a user-friendly graphical graph generator which builds scale-free graphs based on the Barabási and Albert model. The main shortcoming of this tool is that is not designed to handle any other topologies.

4 Design and Implementation

NGCE tool is written in Java. It consists of 15 Java classes, with more than 5000 lines of code besides the 150 lines of scripts.

Various scripts calculate the probability distribution function $P(k)$, which gives the probability that a node has exactly k edges. After the completion of this step, $P(k)$ is automatically plotted using the gnuplot program. Every plot is displayed graphically, but is also stored in the Encapsulated PostScript (EPS) format. In addition, the title of each plot is created dynamically, in the form of an opaque Uniform Resource Identifier (URI) [39].

The title is adequate to provide all the necessary information of the plotted graph. Thus, every graph built and analyzed by NGCE can be easily reconstructed. Especially in the case of random graphs, besides the experimental data, the expected theoretical distribution function is plotted as well.

We believe that the most important instrument to analyze the output graphs is the extraction of their statistical properties via NGCE's embedded scripts. On the other hand, we are aware that a visual representation of the generated graphs would provide additional means to researchers to decide whether a graph meets their needs. In order to add this type of functionality to NGCE, we took advantage of the popular Pajek [40] tool, which is able to draw graphs in a variety of different 2 and 3-dimensional plots. To accomplish this task, we made NGCE's output graph files compatible with the Pajek tool.

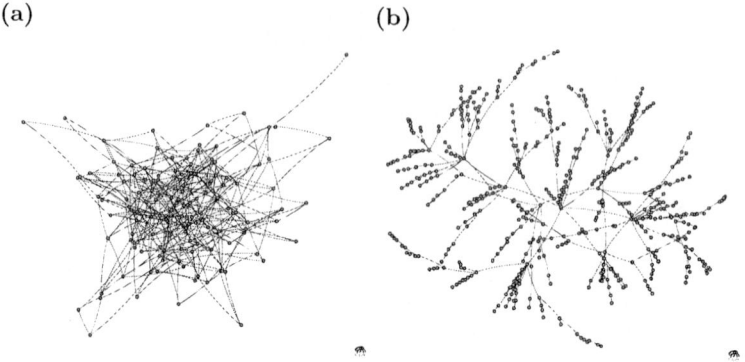

Fig. 1. Custom random and scale-free graphs visualized by the Pajek tool

NGCE's design is modular, based on a general-purpose Graph class that provides the main functionality for all the graph operations such as adding, removing and counting edges[1]. For each different graph topology a specific plug-in has been developed to implement the appropriate algorithm, making the development of new algorithms as separate plug-ins extremely easy.

---

[1] The base Graph class was based on L. Li "*Java Data Structures and Programming*" [41] book's source code used with the author's kind permission.

5 Analysis

In this section we analyze and comment on the graphs produced by the NGCE tool and evaluate them against the expected theoretical results.

1. **Random Graphs and Custom Random Graphs.** Following Barabási and Albert's reasoning [42], we expect the distribution connectivity of a random graph to fit well within a Poisson distribution. Indeed, numerous different random graph generation experiments confirmed our intuition, as can be see in Figure 2a. The degree distribution of the constructed graphs, in all cases, was close to the following Poisson distribution, which is valid for sufficiently large N.

$$P(k) = e^{-pN} \frac{(pN)^k}{k!} \qquad (3)$$

2. **Scale-Free Graphs and Custom Scale-Free Graphs.** A large number of experimental runs indicated that the graphs built with the preferential attachment and incremental growth behavior follow closely the BA model (Figure 3a). The connectivity distribution of these graphs follows a power law with an exponent approximately equal to 3, as it was predicted by Barabási and Albert. Note the capability of this algorithm to produce stationary scale-free graphs; on the other hand, the model which is solely based on the preferential attachment factor exhibits temporal scale-free behavior (Figure 2b). Finally, the observed results indicate that when only the incremental growth property is enabled (Figure 3b) the scale-free characteristics of the graph tend to be diminished as the number of nodes increases. Our results are in alignment with [42], which also used numerical simulations to conclude that this model exhibits power-law scaling in its early stages where N is close to T.

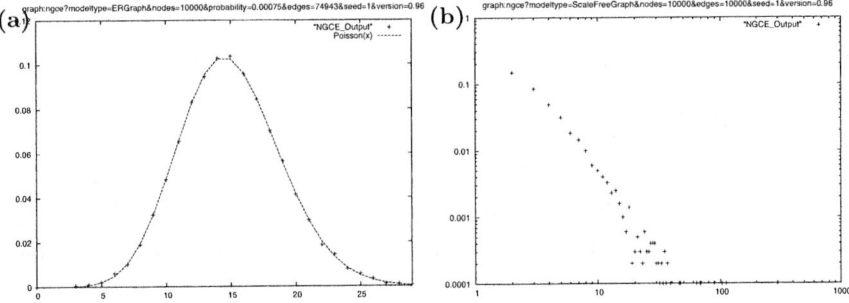

Fig. 2. Random graph based on the Erdős-Rény algorithm, 10000 nodes (left) and scale free graph with preferential connectivity only, 10000 nodes (right)

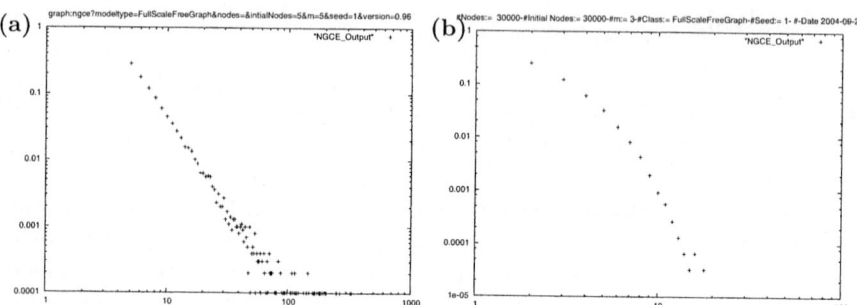

Fig. 3. Scale free graph with incremental growth and preferential attachment, 10000 nodes (left) and scale-free graph with incremental growth only, 30000 nodes (right)

6 Applications in Epidemiological Research

Our primary target for the NGCE tool was its use as a graph generator suite for research groups focused on computer epidemiology.

The comparison of the results between recent and older simulation-based studies can be a source of significant insight. The main drawback of this approach is the required effort to build identical or similar graphs in order to perform meaningful comparisons. Especially if an older study is based on different graph topologies, then the necessary additional work becomes prohibitive. As a result, very few research papers contain detailed comparisons between different algorithms on different graph topologies. NGCE's goal is to fill this gap in an efficient and effective way. We selected four of the most cited papers in the area of the computer epidemiology and reconstructed with NGCE, as close as we could, various graphs of their experiments. The outcome of this effort has been made available in the NGCE's web site for further evaluation and inspection.

We used NGCE to create most of the graph topologies which were found in Kephart's remarkable paper "How Topology Affects Population Dynamics" [8] with minimal effort. Building the homogeneous graph required only a few clicks in the NGCE's GUI or editing 3 lines in the configuration file. On the other hand, constructing Kephart's random graphs was a considerably more difficult problem, because the applied algorithm was not named or described. The author did provide, however, the statistical properties of the constructed graphs. By taking advantage of the graph analysis functions of our tool we were able to produce similar graphs. In the future, researchers can avoid such pitfalls by providing the NGCE's graph URI in their work.

Another well cited paper is "On Computer Viral Infection and the Effect of Immunization" [27] . The author describes the testbed simulation environment as a clustered topology which is typical of many transportation and energy-control networks. The above cases are among the most characteristic examples of scale-free networks, which lead us to build a scale-free graph of equal size.

Pastor-Satorras and Vespignari presented their seminal paper "Epidemic spreading in scale-free networks" [28], in which they used the Barabási-Albert algorithm to construct scale-free graphs for their experiments. We built a comparable graph using the scale-free model of our application.

Concluding this section, we note that we generated a number of graphs for own usage, as we plan to evaluate malcode containment algorithms. Specifically, we simulated the spread of a worm using the S-I [43] epidemiological model in various graphs. Where it was possible, the analytical results were evaluated against the experimental outcome of our simulator to ensure the correctness of our implementation of the algorithm and that of the underlying topology.

7 Conclusions

The source code of the NGCE tool as well as an extended version of this paper with additional results and figures are available at http://istlab.dmst.aueb.gr/~vbill/ngce/ .

The NGCE tool has been designed to allow the development of the most utilized network graph topologies in an easy and reproducible way. Our aim is to assist scientists from related fields to create and use graphs without detailed knowledge of graph theory, and give them the possibility to compare their results with previous or current studies without additional effort. We are convinced that with tools, such as the NGCE, researchers can concentrate their efforts on developing efficient algorithms and understand complex system dynamics, rather than trying to build testing infrastructure.

Acknowledgments

The work of Vasileios Vlachos is funded under the Iraklitos fellowships for research of Athens University of Economics and Business program and the European Social Fund.

References

1. Paxson, V., Floyd, S.: Why we don't know how to simulate the internet. In: Proceedings of the Winder Communication Conference. (1997)
2. Palmer, C., Steffan, J.: Generating networks topologies that obey power laws. In: Proceedings of the GLOBECOM 2003, San Francisco, USA (2000)
3. Tangmunarunkit, H., Govindan, R., Jamin, S., Shenker, S., Willinger, W.: Network topology generators: Degree-based vs. structural. In: Proceedings of ACM SIGCOMM '02, Pittsburgh, Pennsylvania, USA (2002) 147–159
4. Dick, R., Rhodes, D., Wolf, W.: Tgff: Task graphs for free. In: Proceedings of International Workshop on Hardware/Software Codesign (Codes/CACHE '97). (1998) 97–101
5. Berk, V., Bakos, G., Morris, R.: Designing a framework for active worm detection on global networks. In: Proceedings of the IEEE International Workshop on Information Assurance, Darmstad, Germany (2003)

6. Kephart, J., Chess, D., White, S.: Computers and epidemiology. IEEE Spectrum **30** (1993)
7. Kephart, J., White, S.: Measuring and modeling computer virus prevalence. In: Proceedings of the 1999 IEEE Computer Society Symposium on Research in Security and Privacy, Oakland, California (1999) 2–14
8. Kephart, J.: How topology affects population dynamics. In: Proceedings of Artificial Life 3, New Mexico,USA (1992)
9. Chen, Z., Gao, L., Kwiat, K.: Modeling the spread of active worms. In: Proceedings of the IEEE Infocom. (2003) San Francisco, USA.
10. Zou, C., Gong, W., Towsley, D.: Code red worm propagation modeling and analysis. In: Proceedings of the 9th ACM Conference on Computer and Communication Security (CCS), Washington DC, USA (2002)
11. Staniford, S., Paxson, V., Weaver, N.: How to 0wn the internet in your spare time. In: Proceedings of the 11th USENIX Security Symposium. (2002)
12. Staniford, S.: Containment of scanning worms in enterprise networks. Journal of Computer Security (2003)
13. Scandariato, R., Knight, J.: An automated defense system to counter internet worms. Submitted to SRPS 2004, 23rd Symposium on Reliable Distributed Systems (2004) Florianapolis, Brazil.
14. Zou, C., Gao, L., Gong, W., Towsley, D.: Monitoring and early warning for internet worms. In: Proceedings of the 10th ACM Conference on Computer and Communication Security, Washington DC, USA (2003)
15. Leveille, J.: Epidemic spreading in technological networks. Hpl-2002-287, School of Cognitive and Computing Sciences, University of Sussex at Brighton, Bristol (2002)
16. Barabási, A., Albert, R., Jeong, H.: Scale-free characteristics of random networks: the topology of the world-wide web. Physica A **281** (1999)
17. Zou, C., Towsley, D., Gong, W.: Email virus propagation modeling and analysis. Technical report, University of Massachusetts Amherst, ECE TR-03-CSE-04 (2003)
18. Barabási, A., Albert, R., Jeong, H.: Mean-field theory for scale-free random networks. Physica A **272** (1999) 173–187
19. Virtanen, S.: Properties of nonuniform random graph models. Research Report HUT-TCS-A77, Helsinki University of Technology, Laboratory for Theoretical Computer Science (2003)
20. Barabási, A., Bonabeau, E.: Scale-free networks. Scientific American (2003) 60–69
21. Kanovsky, I., Mazor, S.: Models of web-like graphs: Integrated approach. In: Proceedings of the 7th World Multiconference on Systematics, Cybernetics and Informatics (SCI 2003), Orlando, Florida, USA (2003) 278–283
22. Adamic, L., Huberman, B.: Power-law distribution of the world wide web. Science **287** (2000)
23. Bornholdt, S., Ebel, H.: World wide web scaling exponent from simon's 1955 model. Physical Review E **64** (2001) 0345104 (R)–1 0345104-4
24. Faloutsos, M., Faloutsos, P., Faloutsos, C.: On power-law relationships of the internet topology. In: Proceedings of ACM SIGCOMM, Cambridge, MA, USA (1999) 251–262
25. Medina, A., Matta, I., Byers, J.: On the origin of power laws in internet topologies. ACM Computer Communication Review **30** (2000) 160–163
26. Ebel, H., Mielsch, L., Bornloldt, S.: Scale-free topology of e-mail networks. Physical Review **E 66** (2002)

27. Wang, C., Knight, J., Elder, M.: On computer viral infection and the effect of immunization. In: Proceedings of the 16th Annual Computer Security Applications Conference (ACSAC),New Orleans, Louisiana, USA. (2000) 246–256
28. Pastor-Satorras, R., Vespignani, A.: Epidemic spreading in scale-free networks. Physical Review Letters **86** (2001) 3200–3203
29. Cohen, R., K.Erez, ben Avraham, D., Havlin, S.: Resilience of the internet to random breakdowns. Physical Review Letters **85** (2000) 4626
30. Barabási, A., Albert, R.: Emergence of scaling in random networks. Science **286** (1999) 509–512
31. Yook, S., Jeong, H., Barabási, A.: Modeling the internet's large scale topology. In: PNAS Proceedings of the National Academy of Science. (2002) 13382–13386
32. Zegura, E., Calvert, K., Donahoo, M.: A quantitative comparison of graph-based models for internet topology. IEEE/ACM Transactions On Networking **5** (1997) 770–783
33. Zegura, E., Calvert, K., Bhattacharjee, S.: How to model an internetwork. In: Proceedings IEEE Infocom. Volume 2., San Francisco, CA (1996) 594–602
34. Eagan, K.C.A., Merugu, S., Namjoshi, A., Stasko, J., Zegura, E.: Extending and enhancing gt-itm. In: Proceedings of the ACM SIGCOMM 2003 Workshops, Karlsruhe, Germany (2003) 23–27
35. Winick, J., Jamin, S.: Inet-3.0: Internet topology generator. Technical Report UM-CSE-TR-456-02, EECS, University of Michigan (2002)
36. Medina, A., Lakhina, A., Matta, I., Byers, J.: Brite: An approach to universal topology generation. In: Proceedings of the International Workshop on Modeling, Analysis and Simulation of Computer and Telecommunications Systems- MASCOTS '01, Cincinnati, Ohio, USA (2001)
37. Medina, A., Lakhina, A., Matta, I., Byers, J.: Brite: Universal topology generation from a user's perspective. In: Proceedings of the International Workshop on Modeling, Analysis and Simulation of Computer and Telecommunications Systems (MASCOTS '01), Cincinnati, OH (2001)
38. Dreier, D.: Manual of Operation: Barabási Graph Generator v1.0. University of California Riverside, Department of Computer Science. (2002)
39. Berners-Lee, T., Fielding, R., Irvine, U., Masinter, L.: rfc2396. Available at (October 2004): http://www.ietf.org/rfc/rfc2396.txt (1998)
40. Batagelj, V., Mrvar, A.: Program for Analysis and Visualization of Large Networks, Ljubljana, Slovenia. (2004)
41. Li, L.: Java Data Structures and Programming. Springer-Verlag, Berlin, DE (1998)
42. Albert, R., Barabási, A.: Statistical mechanics of complex networks. Reviews of Modern Physics **74** (2002) 47–97
43. Daley, D., Gani, J.: Epidemic Modelling. Cambridge University Press, Cambridge (1999)

Workflow Based Security Incident Management

Meletis A. Belsis[1], Alkis Simitsis[2], and Stefanos Gritzalis[1]

[1] University of the Aegean,
Department of Information and Communication Systems Engineering,
Samos, Greece
meletis_belsis@yahoo.com, sgritz@aegean.gr
[2] National Technical University of Athens,
Department of Electrical and Computer Engineering,
Athens, Greece
asimi@dblab.ntua.gr

Abstract. Security incident management is one of the critical areas that offers valuable information to security experts, but still lacks much development. Currently, several security incident database models have been proposed and used. The discrepancies of such databases entail that worldwide incident information is stored in different formats and places and, so, do not provide any means for Computer Security Incident Response Teams (CSIRTs) collaboration. This paper presents an architecture based on advance database techniques, able to collect incident related information from different sources. Our framework enhances the incident management process by allowing the law enforcement units to (a) collect the required evidence from incident data that are spread through a number of different incident management systems; (b) transform, clean, and homogenize them; and, finally, (c) load them to a central database management system. Such architecture can also be beneficial by minimizing the mean time between the appearance of a new incident and its publication to the worldwide community.

1 Introduction

Today's incidents sought the need for collaboration. This can be easily proven when one thinks of the number of steps, actors and internet sites that modern security incidents use. Today's hacking community posses a huge number of tools that redirect hackers' IP packets, the method is called proxying, from a number of Internet sites in order to hide, their true identity. Along with this, experience hackers usually gain unauthorized access to unprotected computer terminals (e.g. usually university terminals) and use those to forward their attacks to their final target.

One requirement regarding the usability of an incident structure is cooperation. Most of the time fighting against incidents includes the cooperation of many different Computer Security Incident Response Teams (CSIRTs) around the globe. Such cooperation enables the tracking of the path an incident followed. This assists CSIRTs in identifying the potential originating source of the attack and even helps them to prosecute the perpetrator. Providing a structure and an underline system that allows the sharing of incident information in a secure and controlled way is a vital requirement.

Unfortunately, operating such a system is not likely using today's approaches. Modern incident management systems use different approaches and mechanisms to store incident related information (i.e. databases, text files, log files). Enterprises usually deploy their own internal incident management system and most public available CSIRTs use their own models and languages to describe and store incident related data. The semantics of each database differ substantially. The discrepancies of such databases entails that worldwide incident information is stored in different formats and places and, so, does not provide any means for CSIRTs collaboration. Unfortunately, providing a common incident structure is not an easy task. Such an observation is based on the fact that CSIRTs are built for different purposes (i.e., enterprise, department, or country level) and follow different social and technical rules.

At the moment, incident data collection and exchange is usually performed in semi-automated ways; e.g., telephone, email or transport of text files. Such techniques delay the process and usually affect the integrity of the incident data. Deploying a system able to automatically gather, and correlate incident information from a number of places is vital for the security of many organizations.

In this paper, we present a novel centralized incident management system based on advance Extraction Transformation Loading (ETL) database techniques. The proposed system provides a framework for CSIRT collaboration, by shaping the *balkanized model* that current approaches use into *federated model* on which each different incident management teams may hold their own databases, but the system is able to collect and correlate information stored on them. This is performed by allowing the fully automated extraction of incident data from different CSIRTs and storing these in a central incident database. Moreover, while the incident information is stored in a common format, it is possible to further manipulate it, in order to produce full incident descriptions.

In brief, the main contributions of this paper are as follows.

- We employ advance database techniques to tackle the problem of designing a centralized incident database management system.
- We identify the main problems that are underlying the population of a central incident database.
- We propose a method based on ETL workflows for the incremental maintenance of such a centralized database.
- We present a framework for incident correlation in order to keep track of a full attack that its component incidents are stored in different databases.

Outline. Section 2 presents the state of the art concerning incident databases. In section 3, we describe a method for the collection of incidents for different databases and their propagation to a central one. Section 4 presents the technology of Extraction-Transformation-Loading workflows. In Section 5, we describe the system architecture for the incident management. Finally, in section 6, we conclude our discussion with a prospect to the future.

2 Related Work

Currently, there are a number of research efforts that propose data models able to store information related to a security incident. These efforts have been developed and used either for internal use by specific organizations or as a common centralized incident database solution. Example of the former efforts include the IBM's VULDA [1] incident database that has been developed and used exclusively by the IBM's Global Security Analysis Lab (GSAL), the IDB from the Ohio State University (OSU) [10] which stores only high level incident information that are based on the TCP/IP protocol, and the numerous databases that are developed to support the CSIRTs around the world (i.e. CERT/CC).

Along with the previous models there is a number of proposals that have been developed as worldwide centralized incident database solutions. The European project S2003 proposed a simple data model that can be used to build a library of security incidents [9]. This model can be used by European Computer Security Incident Response Teams (CSIRTs) as the means of storing data collected from security incidents.

The Incident Data Model [4] provides a centralized incident model that allows both managerial and technical incident related information to be stored while considering an incident a collection of steps.

Another paradigm of a vulnerability database is the Internet – Categorization of Attacks Toolkit (ICAT) developed by NIST [19]. The ICAT database is a Microsoft Access database that can be found on the Internet and includes a number of vulnerability descriptions.

Based on the second category the CERIAS Incident Response Database (CIRDB) [22] from Purdue University provides a database that can be either access on-line or be downloaded and installed for enterprise internal use.

One of the most interesting efforts is the Incident Object Description and Exchange Format (IODEF) [6] developed by the Incident Taxonomy and Description Working Group (TF-CSIRT) which is based on the Intrusion Detection Exchange Format Data Model (IDEFDM). The model was created to assist CSIRTs exchange incident data presented in an XML form. The work on this model has now been concluded and the results have been superseded by the FINE (Format of Incident Report Exchange) model, which is developed by the IETF INCH (Extended Incident Handling) working group [7, 5].

The Open Vulnerability and Assessment Language (OVAL) [21] provides a common ground on which vulnerability assessment tools can be developed. OVAL comprises three different XML schemas: (a) the System Characteristics Schema records the characteristics of a system; (b) the Definition Schema stores specific vulnerabilities, patches and compliance definitions; and (c) the Results Schema keeps track of the information produced by the vulnerability analysis. The OVAL community has already produced a Definition Interpreter which gathers the specific characteristics of a system and compares them against an OVAL Definition in order to produce a Result File that contains specific vulnerabilities of the aforementioned system. OVAL results are used to allow the exchange of the security related information among experts and system developers. Such a common understanding of system and vulnerability specifics enhance the sharing of security related information and accelerate the incident response process.

Unfortunately, the use of current designs, with possibly the exception of the IODEF and the OVAL, leaves little, if any opportunities for collaboration among different incident management teams. Clearly, the current luck of cooperation greatly delays the process of identifying the perpetrators that organized an attack. The existent ways of performing such collaboration is using manual procedures, which inherit many problems. These are associated with the facts that not all people are native English speaking and that humans usually use different expressions to express the same incident. The integrity of an incident record could be greatly jeopardized by the previous facts.

3 Incident Collection

Collecting incident information from different databases includes providing solutions to a number of challenges. These challenges relate with several technicalities of a database system; e.g., the type and size of database fields, as well as, with further logic on deciding the incidents that can be grouped as steps in a common incident record.

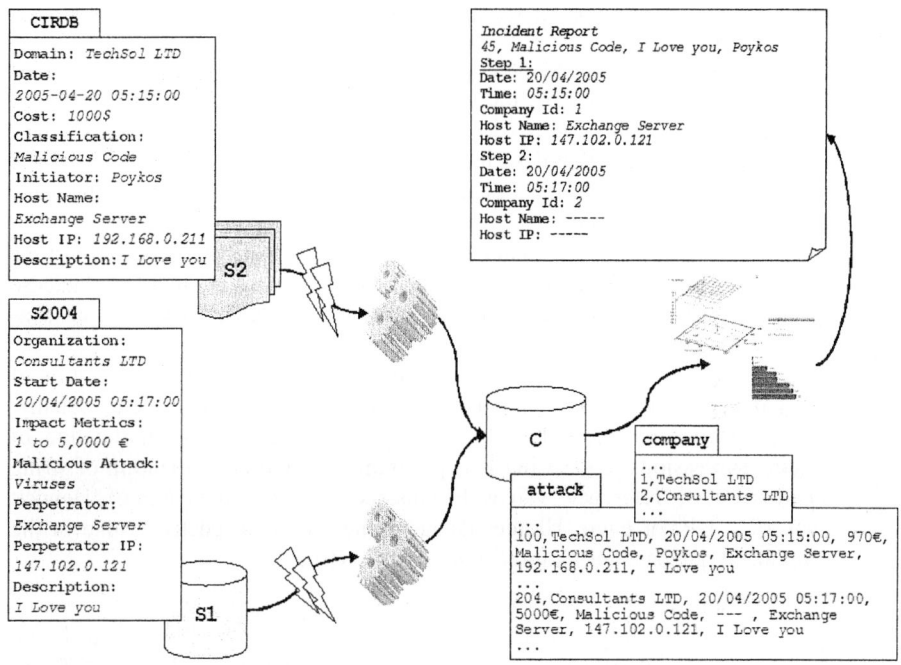

Fig. 1. Collecting and correlating incident information

To motivate our discussion consider the case depicted in Fig. 1 that involves incident records of two different incident management systems S1 and S2, and a centralized incident database C. The first record stored in an incident database S1, is presented as it is recorded in the 'European S2004 Incident Database'. The second one stored in a flat file S2, is presented as it is recorded in the 'CIRDB' database. This scenario concerns the population of C by collecting data from both S1 and S2.

The centralized database C contains homogenized incident information. Thus, it is eligible to apply further business analysis with data mining techniques in order to discover similarities and relations between the incident records.

In summary, by collecting, cleaning, transforming, and homogenizing distinct incident records from different incident sources, the system is able to identify that some of these are actually steps of the same incident. For instance, in Fig. 1 the correlation of the two source incident records results to the existence of an instance that involves a hacker nickname Poykos which emails an infected attachment with the I Love you virus to a company named TechSol LTD and more specific to the company's Exchange server with IP address 192.168.0.211. Then, this server retransmits the infected email two minutes later to a company named Consultants LTD. The overall cost of the incident is estimated up to 5970€.

A careful examination of such scenarios results in a list of problems that we have to deal with, in order to populate a centralized incident database. In terms of the transformation tasks, we can categorize the problem in two main classes of problems [17]: conflicts and problems at the schema level, and, data level transformations (i.e., at the instance level). In more detail, we have to tackle the following problems.

1. *Naming conflicts.* The same name is used for different objects (homonyms) or different names are used for the same object (synonyms). Observe in Fig. 1, that attributes Impact Metrics (S2004) and Cost (CIRDB) represent the same real world entity that describes the cost of a certain incident.
2. *Structural conflicts.* One must deal with different representations of the same object in different sources.
3. *Data formatting.* Equivalent data values are stored in different format into the incident databases. Observe in Fig. 1 the cost values: S2004 incident database stores costs as a range of values in Euro currency, while CIRDB stores costs as single values in Dollars.
4. *String Problems.* A major challenge is the cleaning and the homogenization of string data, e.g., data that stands for addresses, acronyms, names etc. Usually, the approaches for the solution of this problem include the application of regular expressions (e.g., using Perl programs) for the normalization of string data to a set of 'reference' values. For instance, consider the cases of 'Hewlett Packard', 'HP' or even 'Hioulet Pakard' where their respective value in the centralized database for all three cases can be 'HP'.

In addition, there are a lot of variations of data-level conflicts across sources: duplicated or contradicting records, different value representations, different interpretation of the values (e.g., measurement units Dollar vs. Euro), different aggregation levels (e.g., attacks per company department vs. attacks per company) or reference to different points in time (e.g. current attacks as of yesterday for source 1 vs. as of last week for source 2). The list is enriched by low-level technical problems like data type conversions, applying format masks, assigning fields to a sequence number, substituting constants, setting values to NULL or DEFAULT based on a condition, or using simple SQL operators; e.g., UPPER, TRUNC, and SUBSTR.

Moreover, a crucial issue is that the population of the centralized database should be executed in an incremental fashion. Obviously, the time window for the population of the centralized database is rather too small to repeat the same job more than once.

Thus, instead of extracting, transforming, and loading the same data, we choose to employ this procedure only on those incident records that have been changed during the last execution of the process. So, this means that we are interested only to the (a) newly inserted, (b) updated, and (c) deleted incident data.

In order to deal with such problems, we use advance database techniques. The Extraction-Transformation-Loading (ETL) workflows can be used to facilitate the population of a centralized incident database from several different incident databases. Thus, before proceeding to the presentation of system architecture that concretely deals with the aforementioned problems, we present in brief the technology of the ETL workflows.

4 Extraction – Transformation – Loading (ETL) Workflows

The integration of data from several sources to a centralized database management system is a well-studied subject in the field of databases [17]. The practice in real-world environments has shown that the integration problem is more complicated and involves complex operational processes, in order to clean, homogenize and customize the data as the management requirements demand. Recently, both researchers [11, 24, 25, 28] and practitioners [16] have started to study the problem of the collection of data from several sources (e.g., databases, flat files, web), their transformation and cleaning, and finally, their loading to a central database called *Data Warehouse* (DW) in order to facilitate business analysis in large organizations.

These operational processes normally compose a labor intensive workflow and constitute an integral part of the back-stage of data warehouse architectures, where the collection, extraction, cleaning, transformation, and transport of data takes place, in order to populate the central database. To deal with this workflow specialized tools are already available in the market, under the general title ETL tools [13, 14, 18, 20].

Extraction-Transformation-Loading (ETL) tools are pieces of software responsible for the extraction of data from several sources, their cleansing, their customization, their transformation in order to fit business needs, and finally, their loading into a central database. To give a general idea of the functionality of these tools we mention their most prominent tasks, which include: (a) the *identification* of relevant information at the source side; (b) the *extraction* of this information; (c) the *transportation* of this information to the Data Staging Area (DSA), where all the transformations take place; (d) the *transformation*, (i.e., customization and integration) of the information coming from multiple sources into a common format; (e) the *cleaning* of the resulting data set, on the basis of database and business rules; and (f) the *propagation* and *loading* of the data to the central data warehouse.

In Fig.2, we abstractly describe the general framework for ETL workflows. In the left side, we can observe the original data stores (Sources) that are involved in the overall process. Typically, data sources are relational databases and files. The data from these sources are extracted by specialized routines or tools, which provide either complete snapshots or differentials of the data sources. Then, these data are propagated to the data staging area (DSA) where they are transformed and cleaned before being loaded into the data warehouse. Intermediate results, again in the form of (mostly) files or relational tables are part of the data staging area. The central database

DW is depicted in the right part of Fig. 2 and comprises the target data stores. The loading of the central warehouse is performed from the loading activities depicted in the right side before the DW data store.

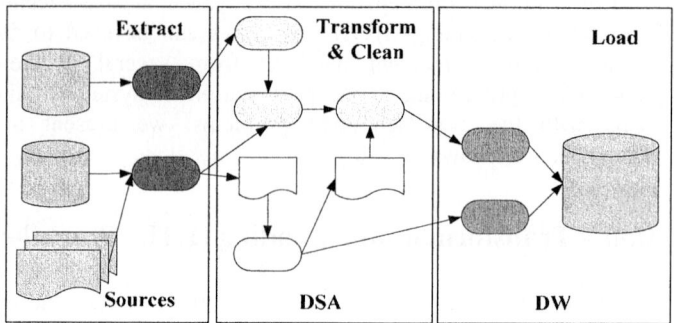

Fig. 2. The environment of Extraction-Transformation-Loading workflows

Several research efforts stress the fact that ETL workflows can be used to an area broader than just the data warehousing. Specifically, in [25, 26, 27] the authors describe ETL workflows as a generic framework, called ARKTOS II, capable to represent any process that can be modeled as an ETL workflow, through a customizable and extensible model that comprises a design tool, template transformations, a metadata repository, and an optimizer. In this work, we built upon the state of the art concerning ETL workflows. We reuse the modeling constructs of ARKTOS II upon which we subsequently proceed to build our contribution.

5 System Architecture

The management system proposed is based on the Common Object Request Broker Architecture (CORBA) architecture. Currently a number of research publications have proposed the use of CORBA to access databases [3, 2, 8]. Using CORBA the system allows for a number of client applications to access the incident database. The ability of adding new services and allow clients to dynamically discover them using the CORBA's DII is crucial.

A vital requirement for any such incident management system is security [12]. Such incident information could become a valuable tool for adversaries all over the world. For the current stage of this research, it has been agreed that only law enforcement units will be able to access the incident database. In later stages, the system will became available to the public in a way that does not sacrifice the confidentiality or the integrity of the incident data.

The system provides access control and encryption using the SSL/TLS protocol. TLS is selected because it is an already widely deployed security protocol and the computing community already has a number of implementations. The protocol in conjunction with client and server side certificates allows for strong access control, confidentiality and integrity to be applied. Along with this there are a number of the CORBA Security implementations based on the SSL/TLS protocol.

Every CSIRT wishing to participate must obtain a digital certificate. Both client and server side certificate are exchanged to force authentication and access control. The CSIRTs certificates (Fig.3) are used to ensure that data are collected only from trusted sources and thus the integrity and non repudiation properties are ensured. During the initiation of the ETL process a handshake agreement is performed. The handshake is performed using the digital certificates enabling the authentication and key exchange process work. The incident data are then encrypted/decrypted using a session key (Skey). The X.509 certificates include the access rights that the holder posses on the incident data.

Registered law enforcement organisations can contact the DBMS system to access full incident records stored in the database, by sending their digital certificates (Fig.3). This can be performed through a WEB based interface or through custom developed clients. To enable access through the WEB, law enforcement units need to download a java client from the system's WEB site. The client will then perform CORBA's structured requests to the Incident management system. The process of accessing the system is described below:

1. *Web Browser downloads HTML page.* In this case, the page includes references to embedded java applets.
2. *Web browser retrieves Java applet from HTTP server.* The Http server retrieves the applet and downloads it to the browser in the form of byte codes.
3. *Web Browser loads applet.* The applet is first run through the java run – time security engine (i.e. checks the applet for suspicious code) and then loaded into memory.
4. *Applet invokes CORBA server Objects.* The Java applet can include IDL-generated client stubs, which let it invoke objects on the ORB server. Alternatively, the applet can use the CORBA DII to generate server requests "on-the-fly". The session between the Java applet and the CORBA server objects will persist until either side decides to disconnect

The Certification Server is responsible for creating, signing and revoking the certificates. To revoke certificates the pull model is used. Each client and the server have to pull the Certification Revocation List (CRL) from the server.

We model the collection of data from a number of incident databases and their propagation to a centralized incident database as an ETL workflow.

It is possible to determine typical tasks that take place during the transformation and cleaning phase of the population of a central database. We adopt the approach of [23] and we further detail this phase in the following tasks: (a) incident data analysis; (b) definition of transformation workflow and mapping rules; (c) verification; (d) transformation; and (e) backflow of cleaned incident data.

After, collecting the incident data from the databases and store them in a common format, the system has to decide if and which of these belong to a specific incident, and which aren't. This decision is based on the fact that attacks belonging to the same incident have common fields, especially in the section of the target and source IP addresses. To facilitate this procedure, further business analysis with the application of data mining techniques can be applied.

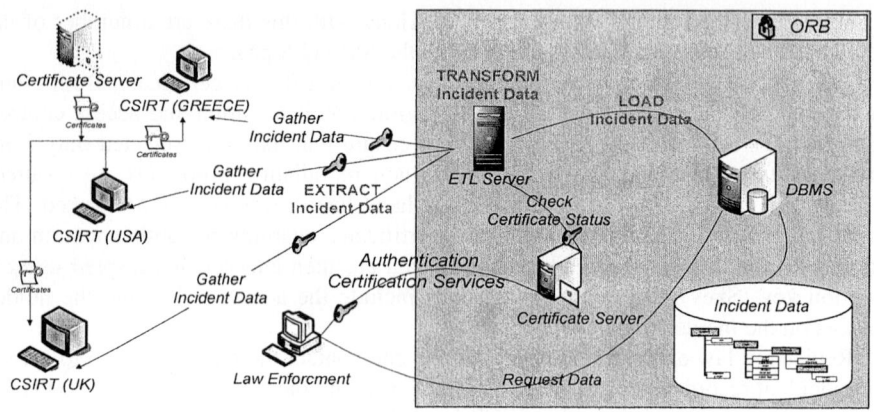

Fig. 3. System architecture for incident correlation

The system runs the ETL process on a daily bases to collect the required incident information. Usually, such procedures are executed during the night, to avoid overload the incident databases with an extra operational cost.

The structure of the centralized incident database is orthogonal to the usage of the ETL workflow. However, we propose the model described in [4] as the model of the centralized incident database due to the fact that it is developed in order to be a general incident database and thus can store a wide number of incident managerial and technical data. Along with that, this model considers an incident not as a one step process. The model is able to record all data associated with every step an incident include. Such consideration and structure will allow us to store incident records collected from different CSIRTs as steps of the same incident. For lack of space, we refer the interested user to [4] for a complete analysis of the incident model.

6 Conclusions and Future Work

In this work, we have provided a framework for automated incident management. We have presented an architecture based in advance database techniques able to collect and correlate incident related information from different sources. Our framework enhances the incident management process by allowing the law enforcement units to (a) collect the required evidence from incident data that are spread through a number of different incident management systems; (b) transform, clean, and homogenize them; and, finally, (c) load them to a central database management system. In that way, we provide a common representation of security incidents and thus, we minimize the mean time between the appearance of a new incident and its publication to the worldwide community.

As far as future work is concerned, we are currently working on the optimization of incident correlation procedure by optimizing the ETL process for the population of the centralized incident database. Also, we are interested in finding optimized methods for the correlation of incident data in the central database through the usage of data mining techniques. Finally, a challenge will be the personalized access of the central incident database, in the sense of [15], for different levels of authorization allowing not just the law enforcement units, but, also, a number of different user types to access part of the stored incident data.

Acknowledgments

This work is co-funded by the European Social Fund (75%) and National Resources (25%) - Operational Program for Educational and Vocational Training II (EPEAEK II) and particularly the Program PYTHAGORAS.

References

[1] D. Alessandri, M. Dacier. VulDa. A Vulnerability Database. In Proceedings of the 2nd Workshop on Research with Security Vulnerability Databases, 1999.
[2] B. Athman, B. Benatallah, M. Ouzzani, H. Lily. Using Java and CORBA for Implementing Internet Databases. In Proceedings of the 15th International Conference on Data Engineering (ICDE'99), pp.218-227, 1999.
[3] B. Athman, B. Benatallah, L. Hendra, J. Beard, S. Kevin, O. Mourad. World Wide Database-Integrating the Web, CORBA and Databases. In Proceedings of the ACM SIGMOD Conference (SIGMOD'99), pp. 594-596, 1999.
[4] M. Belsis, L. Smalov. Building an Enterprise IT Security Management System. In Proceedings of the 18th IFIP International Conference on Information Security, Athens, Greece, 2003.
[5] D. Corner. IDMEF-"Lingua Franca" for Security Incident Management. SANS GIAC Security Certification, V.1.4b, 2003.
[6] Y. Demechenko. Incident Object Description and Exchange Format Data Model and Extensible Markup Language (XML). Internet Draft, 2001.
[7] Y. Demchenko, H. Ohno, G. Keeni. Requirements for Format for Incident Report Exchange (FINE) (draft-ietf-inch-requirements-00.txt), 2003.
[8] K. Ebru, O. Gokhan, D. Cevdet, K. Nihan, K. Pinal, D. Asuman. Experiences in Using CORBA for a Multidatabase Implementation. In Proceedings of the 6th International Workshop on Database and Expert System Applications, London, 1995.
[9] Commission of the European Communities Security Investigations Projects. Project S2003-Incident Reporting a European Structure "Final Feasibility and Strategy Report". Report No19733, version 1.0., 1992.
[10] M. Fullmer, S. Romig. The OSU Flow-Tools Package and Cisco NetFlow Logs. In Proceedings of the 14th Systems Administration Conference, pp. 291-303, 2000.
[11] H. Galhardas, D. Florescu, D. Shasha and E. Simon. Ajax: An Extensible Data Cleaning Tool. In Proceedings of ACM SIGMOD (SIGMOD'00), pp. 590, Texas, USA, 2000.
[12] S. Gritzalis, D. Spinellis. Addressing Threats and Security Issues in World Wide Web Technology. In Proceedings of CMS '97 3rd IFIP TC6/TC11 International Joint Working Conference on Communications & Multimedia Security, IFIP, Chapman & Hall, pp.33-46, 1997.
[13] IBM. IBM Data Warehouse Manager. Available at: www-3.ibm.com/software/data/db2/datawarehouse
[14] Informatica. PowerCenter. Available at: www.informatica.com/products/data+integration/power-center/default.htm

[15] G. Koutrika, Y. Ioannidis. Personalization of Queries in Database Systems. In Proceedings of the 20th IEEE International Conference on Data Engineering (ICDE'04), pp. 597-608, Boston, USA, 2004.
[16] R. Kimball, L Reeves, M. Ross, W. Thornthwaite. The Data Warehouse Lifecycle Toolkit: Expert Methods for Designing, Developing, and Deploying Data Warehouses. John Wiley & Sons, New York, 1998.
[17] M. Lenzerini. Data Integration: A Theoretical Perspective. In Proceedings of 21st Symposium on Principles of Database Systems (PODS), pp. 233-246, Wisconsin, USA, 2002.
[18] Microsoft. Data Transformation Services. Available at www.microsoft.com
[19] NIST, New tool for identifying Vulnerabilities Up and Running. Journal on Research of the Nat. Institute of Standards and Technologies, 2001.
[20] Oracle Corp. Oracle9i™ Warehouse Builder User's Guide, Release 9.0.2, 2001. Available at: http://otn.oracle.com/products/warehouse/content.html
[21] MITRE. Oval Web Site. 2005. Available at: http://oval.mitre.org/
[22] PURDUE University. 2005. Available at: https://cirdb.cerias.purdue.edu/website/
[23] E. Rahm, H.Hai Do. Data Cleaning: Problems and Current Approaches. Bulletin of the Technical Committee on Data Engineering, 23(4), 2000.
[24] V. Raman, J. Hellerstein. Potter's Wheel: An Interactive Data Cleaning System. VLDB'01, pp. 381-390, Roma, Italy, 2001.
[25] A. Simitsis. Modeling and Optimization of Extraction-Transformation-Loading (ETL) Processes in Data Warehouse Environments. National Technical University of Athens: PhD Thesis, Athens, Greece, 2004.
[26] A. Simitsis, P. Vassiliadis, T. Sellis. Optimizing ETL Processes in Data Warehouse Environments. In Proceedings of the 21st IEEE International Conference on Data Engineering (ICDE'05), Tokyo, Japan, 2005.
[27] A. Simitsis, P. Vassiliadis, T. Sellis. State-Space Optimization of ETL Workflows. Accepted in Journal of IEEE Transactions on Knowledge and Data Engineering (TKDE).
[28] P. Vassiliadis, A. Simitsis, P. Georgantas, M. Terrovitis, S. Skiadopoulos. A Generic and Customizable Framework for the Design of ETL Scenarios. Accepted in Journal of Information Systems.

A Deterministic Approach to Balancedness and Run Quantification in Pseudorandom Pattern Generators*

Amparo Fúster-Sabater[1] and Pino Caballero-Gil[2]

[1] Instituto de Física Aplicada, C.S.I.C.,
Serrano 144, 28006 Madrid (Spain)
amparo@iec.csic.es
[2] DEIOC, University of La Laguna,
38271 La Laguna, Tenerife, Spain
pcaballe@ull.es

Abstract. An easy method of computing the number of $1's$ and $0's$ (balancedness) as well as the number of runs (run quantification) in the sequence obtained from a LFSR-based pseudorandom patter generator has been developed. The procedure is a deterministic alternative to the traditional application of statistical tests. The computation method allows one to check deviation of balancedness and run distribution goodness from standard values. As a straight consequence of the above procedure, simple rules to design pattern generators with adequate pseudorandomness properties are also derived.

Keywords: Deterministic approach, pattern generator, algorithm, cryptography.

1 Introduction

Confidentiality makes use of an encryption function currently called *cipher* that converts the *plaintext* into the *ciphertext*. Ciphers are usually divided into two large classes: stream ciphers and block-ciphers. Stream ciphers are very fast (in fact, the fastest among the encryption procedures) so they are implemented in many technological applications e.g. algorithms A5 in GSM communications [3] or the encryption system E0 used in the Bluetooth specifications [1]. Stream ciphers try to imitate the ultimate one-time pad cipher and are supposed to be good pseudorandom pattern generators capable of stretching a short secret seed (the secret key) into a long sequence of seemingly random bits. This binary sequence is then XORed with the plaintext in order to obtain the ciphertext. Most generators with application in stream ciphers are based on Linear Feedback Shift Registers (LFSRs) [4]. The pseudorandom output sequence is a periodic sequence generated as the image of a nonlinear Boolean function in the LFSR

---

* Work supported by Ministerio de Educación y Ciencia (Spain) Projects SEG2004-02418 and SEG2004-04352-C04-03.

stages. Desirable properties for such sequences can be enumerated as follows: 1) large period, 2) large linear complexity, 3) good statistical properties. There are well-known proposals ([6], [9], [11], [12]) for which conditions 1) and 2) above are perfectly satisfied. Nevertheless, how to generate sequences with good statistics is a feature that even now remains quite diffuse. Balancedness and adequate distribution of $1's$ and $0's$ in the output sequence are necessary (although not sufficient) conditions that every pseudorandom pattern generator must satisfy. Roughly speaking, a binary sequence is balanced if it has approximately the same number of $1's$ as $0's$. On the other hand, a run of $1's$ ($0's$) of length k is defined as a succession of k consecutive $1's$ ($0's$) between two $0's$ ($1's$). The runs of $1's$ are called *blocks* while the runs of $0's$ are called *gaps*. According to second postulate of Golomb [4], in a pseudorandom binary sequence of period T there are $T/2$ runs distributed as follows: half the runs have length 1, one quarter of the runs length 2, one eighth of the runs length 3, and so forth. Moreover, half the runs of any length are gaps, the other half are blocks. In brief, in a pseudorandom binary sequence the number and distribution of digits is perfectly quantified.

Due to the long period of the output sequence ($\simeq 10^{50}$), it is unfeasible to produce an entire cycle of such a sequence and then analyze the number and distribution of $1's$ and $0's$. Therefore, in practice, portions of the output sequence are chosen randomly and different statistical tests [9](monobit test, run test, poker test, serial test ...) are applied to all these subsequences. Nevertheless, passing the previous tests merely provides *probabilistic* evidence that the LFSR-based pattern generator produces a sequence with certain characteristics of pseudorandomness.

In this work, *deterministic* expressions to compute the degree of balancedness and number of runs in one period of the output sequence are proposed. If the computed values are not in the expected range, then the generator must be rejected. The procedure here presented is based on the expansion of the generating function in global *minterms*. As a straight consequence of this method, simple rules to design generators with good balancedness and run distribution are also derived. Some illustrative examples complete the work.

2 Fundamental Concepts and Basic Notation

Any L-variable Boolean function can be expressed canonically in terms of its *minterms* [5], that is the logic product of the L variables (a_1, a_2, ..., a_L) where each variable can be in its true or complementary form. Examples of minterms of L variables are:

$$a_1 a_2 ... a_L, \quad \bar{a}_1 a_2 ... \bar{a}_L, \quad \bar{a}_1 \bar{a}_2 ... \bar{a}_L$$

where the superposition of variables represents the logic product. In addition, any L-variable Boolean function can be uniquely expressed in *Algebraic Normal Form* (A.N.F.) or *Muller expansion* [10] by means of the sum exclusive-OR of logic products of different orders in the L variables. A simple example of Boolean function in A.N.F. is:

$$f(a_1, a_2, ..., a_L) = a_1 a_2 \oplus a_2 a_{L-1} \oplus a_L$$

where $\oplus$ represents the exclusive-OR logic operation.

In mathematical terms, a LFSR-based generator is a L-variable nonlinear Boolean function, $F : GF(2)^L \to GF(2)$, whose L input-variables are the stages of the LFSRs. At each clock pulse the LFSRs generate new stage contents that will be the new input-variables of F. In this way, the generator produces the successive bits of the *output sequence* or *generated sequence*. A LFSR-based pseudorandom pattern generator is nothing but a nonlinear Boolean function F given in its A.N.F. Moreover, the LFSRs involved in this kind of generator are *maximal length*-LFSRs ([4]), that is LFSRs whose characteristic polynomials are primitive. In this case, their output sequences are called *PN-sequences*.

Let A be an arbitrary *maximal length*-LFSR of length L_A and a_i ($i = 1, ..., L_A$) the binary content of the i-th LFSR stage. A minterm of L_A variables is denoted by $A_{i...j}$ whether such a minterm includes the variables $a_i ... a_j$ in their true form while the other variables are in complementary form.

Let Λ_L denote the set of L-variable Boolean functions in A.N.F. and Φ_F the *minterm function* of F. In fact, $\Phi_F : \Lambda_L \to \Lambda_L$ such that, given F, the function Φ_F substitutes every term of F by its corresponding minterm. For a nonlinear function in A.N.F., e.g. $F(a_1, a_2, a_3) = a_1 a_2 a_3 \oplus a_1 a_3 \oplus a_2 \oplus a_3$, we have:

$$\Phi_F = A_{123} \oplus A_{13} \oplus A_2 \oplus A_3.$$

On the other hand, every minterm considered as a generator applied to the L_A stages of A generates a canonical sequence [11] with an unique 1 and period $T = 2^{L_A} - 1$. Let us see for a simple example the particular form of the minterms and their corresponding canonical sequences.

Example 1: For a LFSR of $L = 3$ stages, characteristic polynomial $P(D) = D^3 + D + 1$ and initial state $(1, 1, 0)$ we have:

$$A_{123} = a_1 a_2 a_3 \longleftrightarrow \{0,0,0,0,0,0,1\}$$
$$A_{23} = \bar{a}_1 a_2 a_3 = a_1 a_2 a_3 \oplus a_2 a_3 \longleftrightarrow \{0,0,0,0,0,1,0\}$$
$$A_{13} = a_1 \bar{a}_2 a_3 = a_1 a_2 a_3 \oplus a_1 a_3 \longleftrightarrow \{0,0,0,0,1,0,0\}$$
$$A_2 = \bar{a}_1 a_2 \bar{a}_3 = a_1 a_2 a_3 \oplus a_2 a_3 \oplus a_1 a_2 \oplus a_2 \longleftrightarrow \{0,0,0,1,0,0,0\}$$
$$A_3 = \bar{a}_1 \bar{a}_2 a_3 = a_1 a_2 a_3 \oplus a_2 a_3 \oplus a_1 a_3 \oplus a_3 \longleftrightarrow \{0,0,1,0,0,0,0\}$$
$$A_1 = a_1 \bar{a}_2 \bar{a}_3 = a_1 a_2 a_3 \oplus a_1 a_2 \oplus a_1 a_3 \oplus a_1 \longleftrightarrow \{0,1,0,0,0,0,0\}$$
$$A_{12} = a_1 a_2 \bar{a}_3 = a_1 a_2 a_3 \oplus a_1 a_2 \longleftrightarrow \{1,0,0,0,0,0,0\}.$$

The left column represents the ordered succession of the corresponding minterms while the right column shows their generated sequences. The expansion of each minterm in A.N.F. is perfectly typified [7] in what form and number of terms are concerned. The cyclic succession of minterms is computed by increasing the previous minterm indexes by 1 and applying the linear recurrence relationship of the LFSR. Indeed, $a_1 a_2 a_3 \to a_2 a_3 a_4 = a_2 a_3 (a_2 \oplus a_1) = \bar{a}_1 a_2 a_3$; $\bar{a}_1 a_2 a_3 \to \bar{a}_2 a_3 a_4 = \bar{a}_2 a_3 (a_2 \oplus a_1) = a_1 \bar{a}_2 a_3 ...$ and so forth. Thus, the ordered minterm succession is:

$$A_{123}, A_{23}, A_{13}, A_2, A_3, A_1, A_{12}.$$

Once the nonlinear function F given in its A.N.F. has been converted into its minterm expansion, the basic ideas of this work can be summarized as follows:

1. The number of minterms in the representation of F equals the number of $1's$ in the output sequence as every minterm provides the generated sequence with an unique 1.
2. The contiguity of such minterms in the ordered minterm succession determines the run distribution in the output sequence.

Let us now generalize the previous statements to more than one LFSR. Let $A, B, ..., Z$ be LFSRs whose lengths are respectively $L_A, L_B, ..., L_Z$ (supposed $(L_i, L_j) = 1, i \neq j$). We denote by a_i ($i = 1, ..., L_A$), b_j ($j = 1, ..., L_B$), ..., z_k ($k = 1, ..., L_Z$) their corresponding stages. The *global minterms* associated with the generator have now $L_A + L_B + ... + L_Z$ variables and are of the form, e.g. $A_{ij} B_{pqr} ... Z_s$, that is to say the ordered product of the individual minterms of each LFSR. As before every global minterm considered as a generator applied to the stages of the LFSRs generates a sequence with an unique 1 and period $T = (2^{L_A} - 1)(2^{L_B} - 1) ... (2^{L_Z} - 1)$ [11]. In brief, every LFSR-based generator can be expressed in terms of its global minterms as well as global minterms determine balancedness and run distribution in the output sequence.

3 Conversion from A.N.F. to Global Minterm Expansion

Previously to the conversion algorithm, the following facts are introduced:

Fact 1: For every Boolean function F the following equality holds [7]

$$F = \Phi_F \circ \Phi_F \tag{1}$$

where the symbol $\circ$ denotes the composition of functions.

Fact 2: For every LFSR A, the exclusive-OR of all the minterms [8] is:

$$A_{12...L_A} \oplus A_{12...L_A-1} \oplus ... \oplus A_{2...L_A} \oplus ... \oplus A_{L_A} \oplus ... \oplus A_2 \oplus A_1 = 1. \tag{2}$$

The previous equation can be rewritten as:

$$A'_1 \oplus A_1 = 1. \tag{3}$$

On the other hand, the total number of terms in (2) is:

$$\sum_{i=1}^{L_A} \binom{L_A}{i} = 2^{L_A} - 1 \tag{4}$$

while the number of terms in $A_1 = a_1 \bar{a}_2 ... \bar{a}_{L_A}$ is [7]:

$$N_t(A_1) = 2^{L_A - 1}. \tag{5}$$

Thus, the number of terms in A'_1 will be:

$$N_t(A'_1) = 2^{L_A - 1} - 1. \tag{6}$$

Appropriate notation will be used for the rest of LFSRs.

3.1 Conversion Algorithm

Input: N_Z (number of LFSRs), $L_A, L_B, ..., L_Z$ (lengths of the LFSRs) and a nonlinear function F in A.N.F.

For instance, $N_Z = 2$, $L_A = 2$, $L_B = 3$ and $F(a_1, a_2, b_1, b_2, b_3) = a_2 b_3$.

- *Step 1:* Compute Φ_F

$$\Phi_F = A_2 B_3.$$

- *Step 2:* Substitute every minterm by its corresponding function in A.N.F. and cancel common terms

$$\Phi_F = (a_1 a_2 \oplus a_2)(b_1 b_2 b_3 \oplus b_1 b_3 \oplus b_2 b_3 \oplus b_3) =$$
$$a_1 a_2 b_1 b_2 b_3 \oplus a_1 a_2 b_1 b_3 \oplus a_1 a_2 b_2 b_3 \oplus a_1 a_2 b_3 \oplus$$
$$a_2 b_1 b_2 b_3 \oplus a_2 b_1 b_3 \oplus a_2 b_2 b_3 \oplus a_2 b_3.$$

- *Step 3:* Compute $F(a_i, b_j) = \Phi_F \circ \Phi_F$

$$F(a_i, b_j) = \Phi_F \circ \Phi_F = A_{12} B_{123} \oplus A_{12} B_{13} \oplus A_{12} B_{23} \oplus A_{12} B_3 \oplus$$
$$A_2 B_{123} \oplus A_2 B_{13} \oplus A_2 B_{23} \oplus A_2 B_3.$$

Output: F expressed in terms of its global minterms.

Once the function F has been expressed in terms of its minterms, balancedness and run distribution in the output sequence can be analyzed.

4 Balancedness in the Output Sequence

The number of 1's in the generated sequence coincides with the number of global minterms in the expression of F or, equivalently, the number of terms in Φ_F (*Step 2*). An illustrative example of application of such a procedure to a well-known generator is presented.

4.1 A Numerical Example

Let A, B, C be three LFSRs of lengths L_A, L_B, L_C respectively. The *generating function* is chosen:
$$F = a_1 b_1 \oplus a_1 c_1 \oplus b_1 c_1, \tag{7}$$
that corresponds to the Threshold's generator with three LFSRs [13]. Next, the *minterm function* Φ_F is computed:

$$\Phi_F = A_1 B_1 \oplus A_1 C_1 \oplus B_1 C_1$$
$$= A_1 B_1 (C_1' \oplus C_1) \oplus A_1 (B_1' \oplus B_1) C_1 \oplus$$
$$\oplus (A_1' \oplus A_1) B_1 C_1$$
$$= A_1 (B_1 C_1' \oplus B_1' C_1) \oplus (A_1' \oplus A_1) B_1 C_1.$$

The number of 1's in the output sequence N_1 can be directly obtained by counting the number of terms in Φ_F via the equations (5) and (6). In fact,

$$N_1 = 2^{L_A-1}(2^{L_B-1}(2^{L_C-1}-1)+(2^{L_B-1}-1)2^{L_C-1})+(2^{L_A}-1)2^{L_B-1}2^{L_C-1} \quad (8)$$

which gives us a general expression for the number of 1's in the sequence obtained from a Threshold's generator with three LFSRs. Remark that the previous expression is function exclusively of the lengths of the LFSRs. In a practical range, we say $L_i \simeq 120$, and keeping in mind that the sequence period is $T = (2^{L_A} - 1)(2^{L_B} - 1)(2^{L_C} - 1)$, the number of 1's in the output sequence is:

$$N_1 \simeq T/2.$$

Consequently, the output sequence can be considered as a balanced sequence.

5 Run Distribution in the Output Sequence

The ordered minterm succession of a *maximal length*-LFSR of length L can be treated as a PN-sequence. Indeed, if the minterms including an arbitrary index i are replaced by 1 and the minterms not including the index i are replaced by 0, then the resulting binary sequence is the reverse version of the PN-sequence generated by the LFSR. This fact is a straight application of the LFSR linear recurrence relationship given by its characteristic polynomial [11]. Now, keep in mind the following remarks:

1. The number of runs of any length of a PN-sequence is perfectly quantified.
2. Each m-gram (that is every one of the 2^m possible configurations of m bits ($m = 1, ..., L$)) in a PN-sequence will appear exactly 2^{L-m} times.
3. In the global minterm succession each m-gram of any LFSR will coincide once with each one of the m-grams of the other LFSRs.

In order to simplify the notation, Y denotes an arbitrary minterm including the index i while N denotes an arbitrary minterm not including the index i. Based on these considerations, the computation of runs in the output sequence can be carried out as it is shown in the following algorithm.

Input: A nonlinear function F in the stages of the LFSRs $A, B, ..., Z$, (A being the shortest LFSR).

Step 1: From F, compute the minterm formation rule in Y/N format.
Step 2: For $j = 1, ..., L_A - 2$:
    2.1 Determine the minterm configurations generating a *block* of length j.
    2.2 Compute the number of each one of the previous configurations.
    2.3 Repeat *(2.1)* and *(2.2)* for *gaps*.

Output: The final number of blocks and gaps of length j ($j = 1, ..., L_A - 2$) for the given generator.
    Let us see an illustrative example.

Table 1. Global minterm formation rule for F in Example 2

SecB	SecA	Output bit
Y	Y	1
N	Y	0
Y	N	0
N	N	0

Example 2: For two LFSRs, A and B, of lengths L_A and L_B respectively ($L_A < L_B$) and generating function $F = a_1 b_1$, the previous steps are:

$$\Phi_F = A_1 B_1 = (a_1 \oplus a_1 a_2 \oplus \ldots \oplus a_1 a_2 \ldots a_{L_A})(b_1 \oplus b_1 b_2 \oplus \ldots \oplus b_1 b_2 \ldots b_{L_B})$$

$$F = \Phi_F \circ \Phi_F = (A_1 \oplus A_{12} \oplus \ldots \oplus A_{12\ldots L_A})(B_1 \oplus B_{12} \oplus \ldots \oplus B_{12\ldots L_B})$$

The minterm formation rule appears in Table 1. It is clear that an 1 in the output sequence corresponds to a minterm product YY (for example, $A_1 B_{12}$) while a 0 in the output sequence corresponds to the minterm products YN, NY or NN (for example, $A_1 B_2$, $A_{23} B_{13}$ or $A_3 B_2$).

Runs of Length 1

Blocks: They are runs of the form "0 1 0". The different configurations of minterms able to generate a block of length 1 are depicted in Table 2 at columns with heading "Configurations". The columns with heading "No. of config." show the number of times that such configurations appear on their corresponding minterm sequences. The symbol $*$ denotes Y or N. The 3-gram NYN will appear 2^{L_A-3} times in $SecA$ and 2^{L_B-3} times in $SecB$, the 2-gram $NY*$ will appear 2^{L_A-2} times in $SecA$ and 2^{L_B-2} times in $SecB$, and so forth. Thus,

Table 2. Configurations of minterms producing blocks of length 1

	Configuration	No. of config.	Configuration	No. of config.
SecB	$*Y*$	2^{L_B-1}	$*YN$	2^{L_B-2}
SecA	NYN	2^{L_A-3}	NYY	2^{L_A-3}
SecB	$NY*$	2^{L_B-2}	NYN	2^{L_B-3}
SecA	YYN	2^{L_A-3}	YYY	2^{L_A-3}

the number of blocks of length 1 will be the sum of all suitable configurations multiplied by the number of times that such configurations appear

$$N_B(1) = (2^{L_B-1} + 2 \cdot 2^{L_B-2} + 2^{L_B-3}) 2^{L_A-3}. \tag{9}$$

Gaps: They are runs of the form "1 0 1". The different configurations of minterms able to generate a gap of length 1 are depicted in Table 3.

Table 3. Configurations of minterms producing gaps of length 1

	Configuration	No. of config.	Configuration	No. of config.
SecB	Y N Y	2^{L_B-3}	Y * Y	2^{L_B-2}
SecA	Y Y Y	2^{L_A-3}	Y N Y	2^{L_A-3}

Table 4. Configurations of minterms producing blocks of length n

	Configuration	No. of config.	Configuration	No. of config.
SecB	N Y ... Y N	$2^{L_B-(n+2)}$	* Y ... Y N	$2^{L_B-(n+1)}$
SecA	Y Y ... Y Y	$2^{L_A-(n+2)}$	N Y ... Y Y	$2^{L_A-(n+2)}$
SecB	N Y ... Y *	$2^{L_B-(n+1)}$	* Y ... Y *	2^{L_B-n}
SecA	Y Y ... Y N	$2^{L_A-(n+2)}$	N Y ... Y N	$2^{L_A-(n+2)}$

Thus, the number of gaps of length 1 will be the sum of all suitable configurations multiplied by the number of times that such configurations appear

$$N_G(1) = (2^{L_B-3} + 2^{L_B-2}) 2^{L_A-3} . \qquad (10)$$

Runs of Length n

The procedure can be generalized to compute the number of runs of length n ($n = 1, ..., L_A - 2$).

Blocks: They are runs of the form "0 1 ... 1 0" (with n consecutive 1's). The different configurations able to generate a block of length n and their number are depicted in Table 4.

Thus, the number of blocks of length n will be:

$$N_B(n) = (2^{L_B-(n+2)} + 2 \cdot 2^{L_B-(n+1)} + 2^{L_B-n}) 2^{L_A-(n+2)} . \qquad (11)$$

Gaps: They are runs of the form "1 0 ... 0 1" (with n consecutive 0's). Notice that in *SecA* there will be 2^n different configurations able to generate a gap of length n ranging from Y N ... N Y up to Y Y ... Y Y. Some of such configurations and their number are depicted in Table 5.

Thus, the number of gaps of length n will be:

$$N_G(n) = \left(\sum_{i=0}^{n} \binom{n}{i} 2^{L_B-(n+2-i)} \right) \cdot 2^{L_A-(n+2)}. \qquad (12)$$

Therefore, the number of runs of any length up to $L_A - 2$ can be easily computed in the proposed example. Equations (11) and (12) give us the exact number of blocks and gaps that can be found in the output sequence. Remark that N_B and N_G depend exclusively on the LFSR's lengths (L_A, L_B) and on the run length (n). There is no dependency on the characteristic polynomials. Consequently, different LFSRs of the same length will produce output sequences with the same number of blocks and gaps.

Table 5. Configurations of minterms producing gaps of length n

	Configuration	No. of config.	Configuration	No. of config.
SecB	$Y * \ldots * Y$	2^{L_B-2}	$Y N \ldots N Y$	$2^{L_B-(n+2)}$
SecA	$Y N \ldots N Y$	$2^{L_A-(n+2)}$	$Y Y \ldots Y Y$	$2^{L_A-(n+2)}$

Table 6. Numerical example

n	No. of blocks	%Deviation(blocks)	No. of gaps	%Deviation(gaps)
1	4608	13,8 %	1536	62,0 %
2	1152	43,1 %	1152	43,1 %
3	288	71,5 %	864	14,6 %
4	72	85,7 %	648	28,1 %
5	18	92,8 %	486	92,1 %

According to these expressions, it can be seen that the analyzed function F does not match the expected values. For a numerical example $L_A = 7$ and $L_B = 8$, see results in Table 6. For $n = 1$, $N_B > N_G$. For $n = 2$, equations (11) and (12) coincide. For $n \geq 3$, $N_B < N_G$. As expected, there are more gaps than blocks because the formation rule in Table 1 is not balanced.

The upper limit $L_A - 2$, L_A being the length of the shortest LFSR, follows from the fact that blocks and gaps of length n include $n+2$ bits but we can only guarantee the presence of at most L_A-grams. At any rate, the designer of binary pseudorandom pattern generators is basically interested in the runs of low length (e.g. up to length 15) while in cryptographic applications every LFSR length takes values in the range $L_i \simeq 120$.

5.1 Simple Design Rules

The nonlinear function F is a compensated function if for every minterm sequence the number of symbols Y's (N's) corresponding to bits 1 equals the number of symbols Y's (N's) corresponding to bits 0 in the output sequence. Moreover, for general balanced formation rules the more the formation rule is compensated the better the output sequence matches the standard distribution of runs. For a binary sequence generator with N LFSRs there will be 2^{2^N} possible formation rules of which $\binom{2^N}{2^{N-1}}$ will be balanced. So, simple design rules can be enumerated as follows:

1. Choose one of the balanced formation rule (as compensated as possible).
2. Determine its corresponding minterm function Φ_F.
3. Compute the generating function F by means of the composition of Φ_F.

In this way, the output sequence of the obtained LFSR-based pattern generator will exhibit the desired characteristics of pseudorandomness. At the same time and following the same procedure as before, specific expressions for the number of $1's$ and number of runs in the output sequence can be obtained.

6 Conclusions

A method of computing the number of $1's$ and $0's$ as well as the run distribution in the output sequence of LFSR-based pattern generators has been developed. The procedure allows one to reject the generators not satisfying expected values of balancedness and run distribution goodness.

The method here described has been applied exclusively to nonlinear combining functions. Nevertheless, these ideas concerning the analysis of the global minterms seem to be suitable for more general pattern generators. Consider, for instance, the *multiple-speed generators* that can be expressed in terms of a more complex generating function or the *shrinking generator* whose global minterms can be obtained by removing certain individual minterms from the selector register. In both cases, the developed method can be adapted and applied to these schemes in order to evaluate certain aspects of pseudorandomness in the generated sequences.

References

1. Bluetooth, *Specifications of the Bluetooth system*, Version 1.1, February 2001, available at http://www.bluetooth.com/
2. A. Fúster-Sabater and P. García-Mochales, On the Balancedness of nonlinear generators of binary sequences, Information Processing Letters, 85 (2003), 111-116.
3. GSM, *Global Systems for Mobile Communications*, available at http://cryptome.org/gsm-a512.htm
4. S.W. Golomb, Shift Register-Sequences, Aegean Park Press, Laguna Hill, 1982.
5. W.K. Grassman and J.P. Trembley, Logic and Discrete Mathematics, Prentice-Hall, 1996.
6. A. Klapper, Large Families of Sequences with Near Optimal Correlations and Large Linear Span, IEEE Trans. on Information Theory, 42 (1996), 1241-1248.
7. D. Mange, Analysis and Synthesis of Logic Systems, Artech House, INC., Norwood 1986.
8. W. Meier and O. Staffelbach, Nonlinearity Criteria for Cryptographic Functions, Proc. of EUROCRYPT'89, LNCS Springer-Verlag, 434 (1990), 549-563.
9. A.J. Menezes et al., Handbook of Applied Cryptography, New York:CRC Press, 1997.
10. V.P. Nelson et al., Digital Logic Circuit Analysis and Design, Prentice-Hall International 1995.
11. R.A. Rueppel, Analysis and Design of Stream Ciphers, New York:Springer-Verlag, 1986.
12. I.E. Shparlinski, On the Linear Complexity of the Power Generator, Design, Codes and Cryptography, 23 (2001), 5-10.
13. G.J. Simmons (ed.), Contemporary Cryptology: The Science of Information Integrity, New York:IEEE Press, 1991.

Protecting Intellectual Property Rights and the JPEG2000 Coding Standard

B. Vassiliadis, V. Fotopoulos, A. Ilias, and A.N. Skodras

Digital Systems & Media Computing Laboratory,
Computer Science, School of Science and Technology, Hellenic Open University,
13-15 Tsamadou st., GR-26222, Patras, Greece
{bb, vfotop1, ilias, skodras}@eap.gr

Abstract. The ever-increasing use of the Internet and file sharing applications based on Peer to Peer networks has alarmed content authors, providers and resellers of digital content. Techniques proposed for protecting digital media include watermarking, use of metadata and self-protection and self-authentication. In this paper we review the most important of these methods and analyse their potential use in Digital Rights Management systems. The main focus is on IPR management through watermarking for digital images coded with the new and a lot promising compression standard: JPEG2000.

1 Introduction

According to recent studies, the amount of information produced and digitized in the last three years is equal to that produced in all the previous years of human history. Pervasive digital media distribution through the Internet has increased the cases of digital media unauthorised use. The loss of profits for the media industry is already calculated in billions of euros [1].

Economic loss has alarmed content authors, distributors, providers and resellers alike and has created an initial movement for the development of advanced and cost-effective techniques for IPR (Intellectual Property Rights) management and protection of digital media. Although IPR protection is currently considered a strategic goal for many organisations, vendors are not willing to invest substantial resources to achieve it [2]. Following the initial enthusiasm from research and private organisations about the potentials of IPR protection and the use of advanced information systems for their management, cost effectiveness seems to be the major requirement for using them [3].

The two main strategies proposed for achieving IPR for digital media include a priori protection (copy prevention) and a posteriori protection (copy detection). Initially, IPR focused on security and encryption as a means of solving the issue of unauthorized copying. The shortcomings of CD/DVD copy prevention systems have shown that a priori protection alone is still not as effective as predicted. A posteriori protection mechanisms, such as digital watermarking, are considered as a valid solution for multimedia data in a networked environment. New trends such as self-protecting content, metadata embedding or linking in digital artifacts are proposed or used for right management purposes. New coding standards such as JPEG2000 and metadata standards such as MPEG7 have already shown significant potential in terms of flexibility, interoperability and cost-effectiveness.

IPR protection is closely linked to IPR management since digital media are produced, resold, transferred through vendor channels. The need for advanced management of digital property rights has spawned an entire race of new information systems called Digital Rights Management systems (DRM systems). These systems make use of, among other technologies, IPR protection techniques in order to efficiently and flexibly manage property rights.

In this paper we review the most important IPR protection techniques for digital images, namely watermarking and metadata with a special focus on the new JPEG2000 coding standard, and self-protecting content. We also analyse the basic characteristics of a DRM system and how the above mentioned techniques can be efficiently embedded in them.

The rest of this paper is organised as follows: section 2 introduces DRM systems and briefly discusses security policies while section 3 describes the concept of watermarking, current developments for the JPEG2000 standard and metadata enabled IPR protection methods. Section 4 briefly discusses the new proposition for self-protecting content and finally, section 5 draws the conclusions.

2 DRM Systems: An Overview of Basic Concepts and Enabling Technologies

Digital Rights Management is a set of technologies that enables the management of licenses for media artifacts throughout their lifecycle. In other words it provides a complete set of functionalities for managing IPR. The area of DRM is unique in the sense that it involves many diverse sub-areas: cryptography, legal and social aspects, signal processing, information theory, and business analysis, just to mention a few.

DRM systems rely on licenses which specify the content usage rules. Content is distributed with or without licenses but it cannot be used without them. Rules can be either attached or embedded to content, or delivered independently [4,18].

Modern DRM systems cover the full range of IPR management including the description, identification, trading, protection, monitoring and tracking of all forms of rights' usage. They are applied over both tangible and intangible assets including rights workflow and rights owner relationships [5]. The information architecture of a classic DRM system is depicted in figure 1.

The typical business model of a DRM system is presented in figure 2. The creator produces the digital content and provides the usage rules to a third party (authority) which is responsible for supervising its proper use. Distributors receive the content from the creators and distribute it through the appropriate channels (e.g. e-shops) to the end-users (buyers). In order for the buyer to use the content, the appropriate license must be obtained by the authority. This happens after the appropriate request is sent to the authority by the buyer. The transaction is concluded when the authority pays royalties to the creator.

Encryption, a key technology for any DRM system, is used to ensure that public-key certificates owned by the Buyer and the Distributor are digitally signed by the Authority. A handshake protocol makes sure that both sides have the secret keys that correspond to the public keys described in the license to use the digital media. This approach is called 'Crypto101'. Newer approaches such as broadcast encryption avoid the costly, in terms of data transmitted, two-way handshake with single way broadcast of public keys [6].

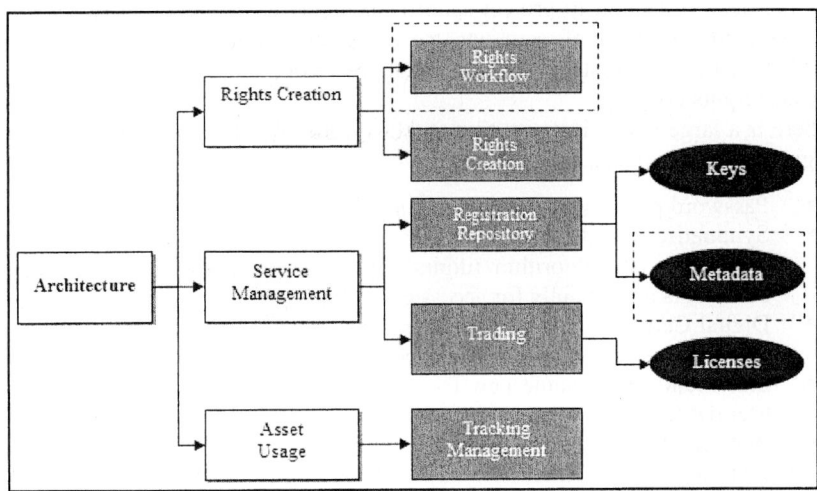

Fig. 1. The Information architecture of a classic DRM system (modified from [5])

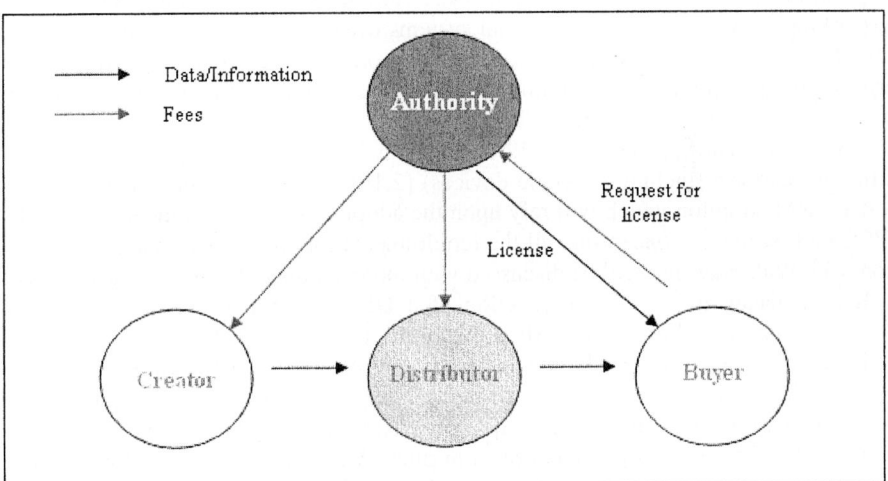

Fig. 2. The common business model of DRM systems

An interesting variation of DRM systems uses special plug-ins in order to decode digital information and communicate with the creator or the content provider. Nevertheless, this model suffers from the obvious lack of interoperability since there is no common framework for encoding the information prior to its use. This situation has led to a number of different plug-ins which are used with specific DRM systems only and thus are inflexible. Plug-ins are usually content viewers and players [7].

DRM systems provide persistent content protection meaning that they need to do more than simply manage digital licenses to authorized users. Restrictions of the content usage rights have to be maintained after the content is delivered to the end user including data protection to protect against unauthorized interception and modification, unique identification of recipients to enable access control for the digital content, and effective tamper-resistant mechanisms to process protected data and enforce content usage rights [16].

There is a large number of security methods used by DRM systems to protect IPR of digital content artifacts, among them:

- Password protection: it is used mainly for access control.
- Symmetric and Asymmetric Encryption: the content is encrypted using a symmetric key algorithm (digital signatures, one-way hash functions, or both). It is used mainly for access control and pirate prevention.
- Digital Certificates: used to authenticate or verify the identity of the parties involved in the distribution of the content
- Individualization: some new DRM systems rely on unique identification of user devices.
- Watermarking: used for binding (embedding) information to digital content, such as content owners, the buyer of the content and payment information (annotation watermarks).

Recent studies [2] have shown that, apart from standard security technologies such as password protection and encryption, most current DRM implementations use watermarking as well. Several commercial systems offer special crawling functions that scan the Internet for finding instances of the protected (watermarked) artifacts and produce usage reports. Although this method works only for on-line content, it might be successful in preventing piracy [21].

One of the major problems of DRM systems is interoperability and transfer across different platform (including mobile devices) [2,16]. This is a major requirement for wider DRM adoption which will rely upon the adoption of common media standards. JPEG2000 seems to concentrate all the requirements for still digital images (see section 3.1). Watermarking will be discussed with more details in the following sections.

Rights management, a basic function of a DRM system, is possible via RELs (Rights Expression Language). After numerous proposals, XrML was chosen for wider adoption since it was adopted as the REL for the MPEG21 standard.

There is a plethora of DRM business models: pay as you use, try first buy later, pay per view etc. Payment rules are closely connected to the way the content is supposed to be used and as such they are described in rules. A useful analysis of DRM business models, standards and core technologies can be found in [21].

3 IPR Protection and JPEG2000

Watermarking and authentication for digital images are relatively new technologies a posteriori, descendants of the last decade. The main reason for their introduction was the fact that digital images are quite easy to duplicate, forge or misuse in general.

Watermarking is mainly focused towards the protection of the images' copyright while authentication aims to the verification of the content, investigate if an image is tampered or not and if it is, to identify the locations that the alterations have occurred. For both technologies to succeed, side information needs to be embedded and/or linked with the original image file. That is obviously the reason why lossy compression schemes are often difficult to be used. Part of the watermarking or authentication information is discarded along with insignificant parts of the original image's information to achieve better compression.

Digital watermarking has been proposed as a valid solution to the problem of copyright protection for multimedia data in a networked environment [8]. The two most important characteristics a watermarking scheme should provide are imperceptibility and robustness. A digital watermark is usually a short piece of information, that is difficult to erase, intentionally or not. In principle, a digital watermark is an invisible mark inserted in digital media such as digital images, video and audio so that it can be detected at a later stage as evidence of copyright or it can generally be used against any illegal attempt to either reproduce or manipulate the media.

Watermarking has been extensively researched in the past few years as far as common image formats are concerned. By identifying the rightful creator/owner, watermarks may be used to prevent illegal use, copy or manipulation of digital content, as proof of ownership or tampering [9]. The problem that these techniques have to encounter is the robustness of the watermark against common processing tasks. Any attempt to remove the ownership information from the original image is called an attack. Some common attacks for still images include filtering, compression, histogram modification, cropping, rotation and downscaling. Image watermarking techniques can generally be divided in two main groups, depending on the processing domain of host image that the watermark is embedded in. The first one is the spatial domain group of techniques, according to which the intensity values of a selected group of pixels are modified. The other is the frequency domain group, where a group of the transform coefficients of the image are altered. Up to date, frequency domain approaches have been proved more successful for image watermarking. The transforms usually employed are the discrete versions of the Fourier, Cosine and Wavelet transform (DCT, DFT and DWT) [9,10]. In these schemes, the image is being transformed via one of the aforementioned frequency transforms and watermarking is performed by altering the resulting transform coefficients of the image. New standards such as JPEG2000 create new possibilities for the IPR protection industry and have already attracted much attention by the scientific community. In the next subsections we review the basic characteristics of the coding standard and the most important watermarking and metadata-enabled techniques proposed so far.

3.1 The JPEG2000 Image Compression Standard

Since the mid 1980s, both ITU (International Telecommunications Union) and ISO (International Organization for Standardization) have joined their efforts to establish an international Standard for compression of greyscale and colour still images. The result of this process has been called "JPEG" (Joint Photographic Experts Group) and become an International Standard in 1991. Very soon, the JPEG image format (jpg) has become the most commonly used format. However, the development of a standard is a continuous process. Thus it was reasonably expected that a new standard should appear to satisfy the increased needs and requirements of today for multimedia and Internet applications. Under these circumstances, almost a decade later, JPEG2000 emerged. The new standard provided a unified coding system for different types of still images (bilevel, gray scale, colour, multi-component) with different characteristics (natural, medical, remote sensing etc.) allowing different imaging models (client/server, real time transmission, image library archival etc.) [11]. The system performs better than older standards by achieving great compression ratios while retaining image quality at the same level. Part I of the standard (depicted in figure 3) can be used on a royalty and fee-free basis. All these lead to the conclusion that it is only a matter of time before JPEG2000 will become widely accepted.

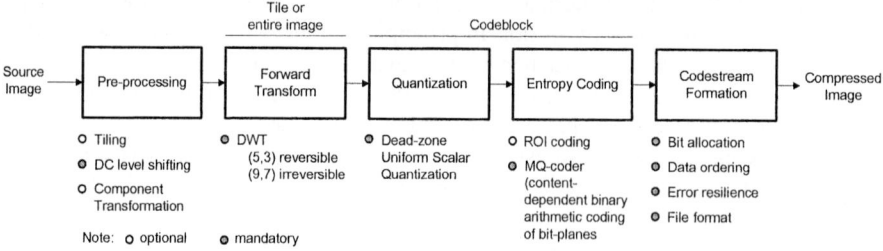

Fig. 3. JPEG2000 encoding process

The new standard has come to serve a wide variety of applications like the Internet, mobile communications, medical imagery, remote sensing, colour facsimile, printing and scanning, digital photography, e-commerce, digital libraries and many more. Each of these areas, imposes certain requirements that the new standard should fulfil in the best possible way. The implementation of JPEG2000 provides the following:

- Superior low bit-rate performance: JPEG2000 performs superior to its predecessors for very low bit-rates. Internet and mobile communications, as well as network applications greatly benefit from this feature.
- Continuous-tone and bi-level compression: Various kinds of images are supported by the new compression system. The encoding algorithm is capable of compressing images of various dynamic ranges (e.g. from 1 to 16 bpp for each colour component). This benefits a variety of applications like compound document compression, facsimile, graphics and images with binary and near to binary regions, alpha and transparency planes.
- Lossless and lossy compression: The new standard provides both kinds of compression within the same codestream. There are applications like medical imaging, digital libraries and prepress imagery, in which image information loss can not be tolerated. In these cases, the lossless part of the codestream is used while in the other cases (web browsing, network transmission over client/server applications) the lossy part can be used instead. JPEG2000 also allows progressive lossy to lossless buildup.
- Progressive transmission and decoding: It is possible to transmit images progressively and decode at the receiver with increasing pixel accuracy or spatial resolution. This a valuable feature for web browsing and digital libraries.

- Regions of Interest: In almost every image, there are regions that contain more important information content than others. In JPEG2000 one can define these regions of interest (ROI) and allocate more bits for their coding than for the rest of the image.
- Open Architecture: JPEG2000 allows optimization for different image types and applications.
- Error resilience: The new standard provides robustness to bit errors that may cause catastrophic decoding failures. This is essential, especially when images are transmitted over noisy channels (e.g. wireless networks).
- Fixed-rates, fixed-sizes, limited workspace memory: It is possible to specify the exact number of bits allocated for a group of consecutive pixels or for the whole codestream. Except for the profound advantage of this feature, it is also possible for devices of limited memory (like scanners and printers) to function with the new format.

3.2 Watermarking and JPEG2000

Watermarking against lossy compression has always been an interesting challenge. Most of the existing literature techniques are not very efficient against the JPEG standard. With the new JPEG2000 standard, superior quality for the same compression ratio can be achieved or similar quality for higher compression ratio, may be used depending on user needs. Since it is easier now to retain quality by achieving smaller file sizes, this is quite desirable. Thus compression ratios of less than 0.5bpp will become common practice. The problem is, that although these images will be visually pleasant, watermarking methods have to evolve in order to survive such high compression. Is the watermarking community ready to undertake this challenge?

Very few works directly relate watermarking with JPEG2000. In the majority of the literature, the new standard is considered as yet another attack. Others examine the effects that the various JPEG2000 coding parameters cause to the watermark's detection. There is also a third category that proposes incorporating watermarking into the JPEG2000 coding pipeline or using it as an important factor in the marking/retrieval process. These may be few but they are of great practical interest. Significant research effort has addressed watermarking in the wavelet domain. Since the heart of the new standard is the wavelet transform, these works may be seen as the pioneers of watermarking in the JPEG2000 domain. Some of these categories will be briefly discussed in this section.

The first wavelet based watermarking schemes appeared around 1995. As far as embedding is concerned, the approximation image is selected. For a 3-level wavelet decomposition, this band of coefficients is actually a miniature of the original image (dimensions are 1/8 of the originals). This way, traditional spread spectrum and spatial techniques can be easily used since these methods do not exploit the special features that the wavelet decomposition provides. Examples of these works can be found in [12-13].

Detail based methods [17] are a bit different. Coefficient distribution in the detail bands is different when compared to the approximation. There are only a few coefficients large enough to carry the watermark and a careful selection strategy is required. To define a selection threshold, the level of decomposition, orientation and subband energy can be utilized. Since the number of appropriate coefficients in each band is small, usually contribution is gathered from all the detail bands in all decomposition levels. An advantage of this practice is that if the watermark is found in one of them, there's no need to search the others, thus reducing the detection's computational cost. This characteristic makes such methods appealing for real time applications. There are also techniques that use all of the bands, approximation and details for additional robustness [18].

Usually, when watermarking methods are tested for lossy compression, the parameter involved is compression ratio. In JPEG2000, compression ratio is only one of the available options to the coder. Other equally important parameters include the filter kernels used, regions of interest, levels of decomposition, tile size and many more. Such an advanced (and consequently complex) compression algorithm, is definitely multi-parametric and it is not wise to ignore all these parameters during the testing procedure.

In a category of works, JPEG2000 is simply considered as yet another attack. No special care is taken during the algorithm's design which is simply tested against compression with various bit rates. One of the two publicly available versions of the encoder is usually used, JJ2000 or Jasper. Testing is always based on the bit rate parameter. The lowest the bit rate, the worst the detectors perform. It seems that 0.3-0.1 bpp is the range in which the watermarks start finding great difficulties to survive and under 0.1 bpp the majority of the methods easily fail (speaking of blind detection algorithms). By far, the most complete comparative study of various schemes for different bit rates can be found in Meerwald's webpage [19].

3.3 Metadata-Enabled IPR Protection and JPEG2000

JPEG2000 coding standard offers features such as Region of Interest Coding, Scalability, Error Resilience, Visual Frequency Weighting. Although all of the above mentioned features of the compression standard are very important, the application of watermarking in JPEG2000 compressed images is closely related with its IPR capabilities. These capabilities include the embedding of XML-formatted information into the image file in order to annotate/link image data with metadata. These metadata are associated with the image vendor, the image properties, the existence of IPR information in the image data etc. The new format (JP2) [11] gives the opportunity to accompany the data that correspond to the image with extra metadata but it doesn't replace the watermarking mechanisms that are used today for copyright protection and authentication, provided through watermarking process. It rather complements them.

In order to address the increasing need for security, the international community is already researching the incorporation of IPR protection characteristics within the JPEG2000 standard. This initiative will produce JPEG 2000 Secured (JPSEC) also known as Part 8 of JPEG2000 [14]. Applications addressed by JPSEC include, among others encryption, source authentication, data integrity, conditional access, ownership protection etc. It is expected that the new standard will be available by 2007.

In a different approach, metadata may be linked and not directly inserted in an image. For this purpose, a special kind of watermarking is used: annotation watermarking. Watermarks, combined with digital signature methods, may contain information about proprietary, copyright, the author, the user, the number of copies and/ or other important information. The insertion of multiple watermarks for the identification of distribution channels is also possible. It must be noted however that there is an upper limit for the number of watermarks that can be embedded in an image, before the quality of reproduction is significantly altered. In order to maintain a high Quality of Service, a consensus must be found between multiple watermarking and its perceptibility in the digital object. Multiple watermarks can be inserted at the production level, for the identification of the distribution path and/or to identify the end-user path.

4 Self Protecting Content

Self protecting content was recently suggested as a solution to the ever-increasing problem of DRM interoperability and immature economics. This type of content includes special logic which can decide by itself how it will be used by the client machine which provides only basic functionality [15]. For example, an image encoded with a self protecting standard is loaded in a palmtop. The logic is loaded into the palmtop, reads the appropriate information (ID, user acquired licenses etc.) and decides whether it will be viewed in full or reduced resolution, whether it will be copied or reproduced etc. It is obvious that apart from the logic encapsulated into the content, appropriate mechanisms need to be available to the user machine. These mechanisms should at least include a virtual machine for the code to run and a ROM for storing keys and licenses. If the end-user machine is a personal computer there is no obvious disadvantage but what happens when it is a CD-player or a home DVD device?

Although the notion of self-protecting content is extremely innovative and attractive in many aspects, several shortcomings of technological, cultural and economic nature exist: there are no standards for encoding logic into content, what happens to the size of the media artifact when code is added to it, are the manufacturers of player devices willing to add new machinery to their products, are content creators willing to pay for new content creation tools? Although the self protecting content idea has already attracted criticism, it remains to be seen if it will be adopted in the future [20].

5 Conclusions

The extensive use of digital media in networked applications increases security requirements. The protection of the IPR of digital media is increasingly considered as one of the most important areas of e-commerce. Increased concern by companies and academia has led to the development of numerous methods and techniques that manage and protect IPR. DRM is one of the most important and complete frameworks that enable end-to-end management of digital rights through the media lifecycle. Enabling technologies for DRM systems include, among other, watermarking, an information hiding technique. Watermarking can be used for embedding or connecting usage rules in/with the content itself.

New standards, such as JPEG2000 offer new possibilities for IPR protection and DRM systems that use watermarking and may lead to the development of more advanced security services. In this work we surveyed recent development in watermarking for the JPEG2000 domain which is currently a very promising research area.

JPEG2000 offers many places in its coding pipeline in which the watermarks can be embedded. There are various arguments about the place of embedding: into the transform, after it, in the quantization stage, in the coding stage. Each of these cases has specific advantages and disadvantages. Experiments justify the suspicion that the parameters used during encoding are very important for the detector's expected performance, however there are many more aspects of such a complex compression standard like JPEG2000 that still need to be investigated. In conclusion, it seems that in the next years the field of watermarking of digital images coded with the JPEG2000 standard will attract even more the interest of the research community and the upcoming format will be supported with powerful protection mechanisms.

Acknowledgements

This work was funded by the European Social Fund, Operational Programme for Educational and Vocational Training II (EPEAEK II), programme Pithagoras (contract no. 89188).

References

1. International IPR Alliance, Special 301 Recommendations, [available online http://www.iipa.com/pdf/2004SPEC301LOSS.pdf] (2004)
2. Fetscherin, M., Schmid, M.,: Comparing the usage of digital rights management systems in the music, film, and print industry. Proceedings of the 5th international conference on Electronic commerce (2003) 316–325
3. Eskicioglu, E.M.: Protecting Intellectual Property in Digital Multimedia Networks. Computer, Vol. 36 39-45 (2003)
4. Cohen, J.E.: DRM and Privacy. Communications of the ACM, Vol. 46(4) 46-49 (2003).
5. Iannella, R.:Digital Rights Management (DRM) Architectures. D-Lib Magazine, Vol.7(6) (2001)
6. Lotspiech, J., Nusser, S., Pestoni, F.:Anonymous Trust: Digital Rights Management Using Broadcast Encryption. Proc. of IEEE Vol. 92(6) 898-909 (2004)
7. Liu, Q., Safavi-Naini, R., Sheppard, N.P.: Digital Rights Management for Content Distribution. Australian Information Security Workshop (2003)
8. Voyatzis, G., Pitas I.: Image Watermarking for Copyright Protection and Authentication. In: Bovik, A. (ed.): Handbook of Image & Video Processing. Academic Press (2000)
9. Fotopoulos, V., Skodras, A.N.: Digital Image Watermarking: An Overview. EURASIP Newsletter, Vol.14 (4) (2003)
10. Fotopoulos, V., Skodras, A.N.: A Subband DCT Approach to Image Watermarking. Proc. X European Signal Processing Conference (2000)
11. Taubman, D.S., Marcellin, M.W.: JPEG2000: Image Compression Fundamentals, Standards and Practice. Kluwer Academic Publishers, (2002)
12. Liang, J., Xu, P., Tran, T.D.: A universal robust low frequency watermarking scheme. IEEE Transactions on Image Processing, (2000)
13. Perreira, S., Voloshynovskiy, S., Pun, T.: Optimized wavelet domain watermark embedding strategy using linear programming. In Szu, H.H. (ed.): SPIE AeroSence 2000: Wavelet Applications VII (2000)
14. JPEG 2000 Secured (JPSEC), [available online http://www.jpeg.org/jpeg2000/j2kpart8.html] (2000)

15. Kocher, P., Jaffe, J., Jun, B., Lawson, N.: Self protecting digital content. Cryptographic Research Inc, CRI [available online http:// www.cryptography.com/resources/ whitepapers/SelfProtectingContent.pdf] (2005)
16. Koenen, R.H., Lacy, J., Mackay, M., Mitchell, S.:The long march to interoperable digital rights management. Proc. of IEEE Vol. 92(6) (2004) 883-897
17. Kim, Y.S., Kwon, O.H., Park, R.H.: Wavelet based watermarking method for digital images using the human visual system. Electronic Letters Vol.35, (1999) 466-467
18. Davoine, F.: Comparison of two wavelet based image watermarking schemes. Proceedings of the IEEE International Conference on Image Processing (2000)
19. Meerwald, P.: Quantization Watermarking in the JPEG2000 Coding Pipeline. Communications and Multimedia Security Issues of the New Century, IFIP TC6/TC11, Fifth Joint Working Conference on Communications and Multimedia Security, CMS'01, Kluwer Academic Publishing, Darmstadt, Germany, (2001)
20. DRMWatch: Analysis of CRI's Self Protecting Digital Content. [available online http://www.drmwatch.com/special/article.php/3095031] (2005)
21. Rosenblatt, B., Trippe, B., Mooney, S.: Digital Rights Management-Business and Technology. M&T Books, (2002)
22. Hwang, S.O., Yoon, K.S., Jun, K.P., Lee, K.H.: Modeling and implementation of digital rights. Journal of Systems and Software Vol. 73(3) (2004) 533-549

Computationally Efficient Image Mosaicing Using Spanning Tree Representations

Nikos Nikolaidis and Ioannis Pitas

Artificial Intelligence and Information Analysis Laboratory,
Department of Informatics, Aristotle University of Thessaloniki,
GR-54124 Thessaloniki, Greece
{nikolaid, pitas}@zeus.csd.auth.gr
http://poseidon.csd.auth.gr

Abstract. Optimal image mosaicing has large computational complexity, that becomes prohibitive as the number of sub-images increases. Two methods are proposed, which require less computation time by performing mosaicing in pairs of two sub-images at a time, without significant reconstruction losses, as evidenced by simulation results.

1 Introduction

Very high resolution digital image acquisition is a process that stresses the limits of acquisition devices. Even high-end CCD devices can not offer the level of detail that is required in certain applications. To overcome this obstacle, digitization structures have been proposed that utilize observation of different, albeit overlapping, fields of view (sub-images), sometimes with the aid of sensor/detector arrays, and positioning mechanisms. Mosaicing is a process which is used to reconstruct or re-stitch a single, continuous image from a set of overlapping images. Several mosaicing techniques have been proposed in the literature [1,2,3,4,5]. Image mosaicing is essential for the creation of high-resolution large-scale panoramas for virtual environments. Image mosaicing is also important in other areas that include image-based rendering, creation of high resolution digital images of architectural monuments and works of art (especially of those with considerable dimensions like frescoes and large-size paintings) for archival purposes (Fig. 1) and digital painting restoration, medical imaging [1] aerial and satellite imaging etc [2]. If the field of view is split into M_1 rows of M_2 images, it should be trivial to show that an M_1M_2-fold increase in resolution may be attained, compared to sensor resolution.

The mosaicing process may be broken down into two steps. The first step involves the estimation of optimal displacement of each sub-image with respect to each neighboring one (assuming only translational camera motion and no rotation or zooming). This represents the most computationally intensive part of the entire process. In the general case of an M_1 by M_2 image mosaic, a search should be performed in a m-dimensional space, where $m = 2(2M_1M_2 - M_1 - M_2)$. The term in parenthesis represents the number of all pairs of neighboring sub-images.

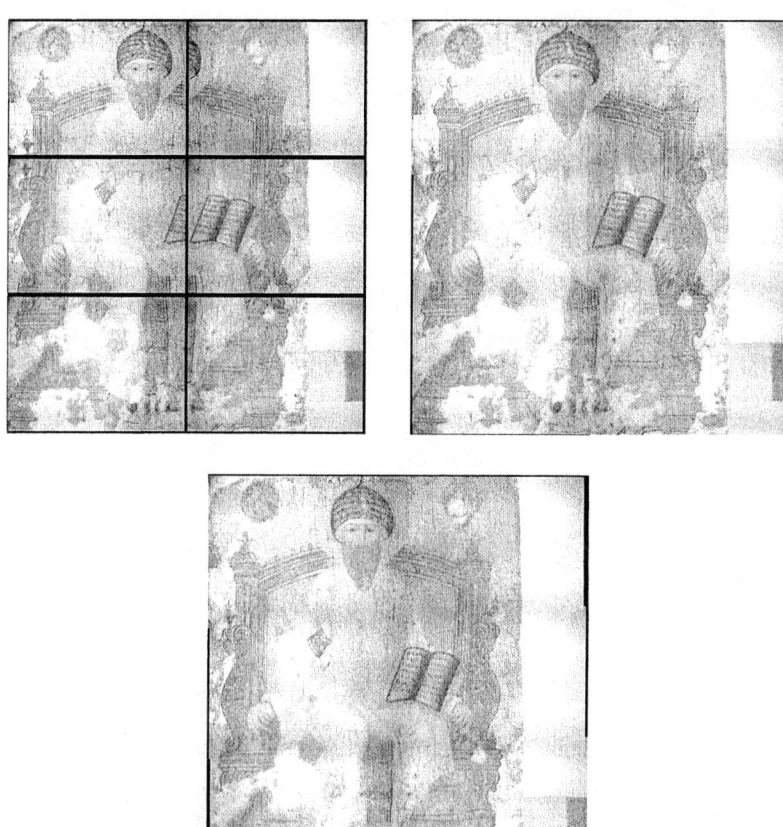

Fig. 1. (a) A $M_1 = 3$ by $M_2 = 2$ sub-image acquisition of a painting. (b) Reconstructed images after STM processing. (c) Reconstructed images after SGSTM processing.

Since these are 2-d searches, this term is multiplied by two. It is evident that computation cost becomes prohibitive, as the number of sub-images increases. Optimal displacement is researched, under the assumption that acquired images are not free of distortions [3]. The second step of the mosaicing process utilizes the previously generated displacement information in order to combine each pair of neighboring sub-images with invisible seams.

This paper shall focus on the first step. The proposed methods attempt to reduce the number of computations required to compute the sub-image displacements. Despite the fact that the methods are illustrated for the particular case where sub-images are only displaced (translated) with respect to each other, the proposed matching methodology is applicable to more complex cases, e.g. cases that involve camera rotation or zooming.

2 Mosaicing Techniques for Two Images

Before we proceed to the general case of mosaicing an arbitrary number of sub-images, the case of two images should be studied first, since it provides significant insight to the problem. In the following it is assumed that the displacement vector **d** is constrained to take values in the following set:

$$\mathbf{d} \in \{[d_1 \; d_2]^T : d_i \in \{d_{i_{min}}, \ldots, d_{i_{max}}\}, \; i = 1, 2\} \quad (1)$$

If $I_j(\mathbf{n})$, $j = 1, 2$, is the intensity of the j-th image at pixel coordinates $\mathbf{n} = [n_1 \; n_2]^T \in W(\mathbf{d})$, where $W(\mathbf{d})$ denotes the overlap area, then a quantitative expression for the matching error $E(\mathbf{d})$, which is associated with a specific displacement **d**, can be derived as follows:

$$E(\mathbf{d}) = \frac{\sum_{\mathbf{n} \in W(\mathbf{d})} |I_1(\mathbf{n}) - I_2(\mathbf{n})|^p}{||W(\mathbf{d})||} \quad (2)$$

where $||W(\mathbf{d})||$ denotes the number of pixels in the overlap area $W(\mathbf{d})$. For $p = 1, 2$ (2) expresses the Matching Mean Absolute Error E_{MMAE} and the Matching Mean Square Error E_{MMSE}, respectively. Subsequently, an optimal value $\mathbf{d}_{opt}$ for the displacement can be estimated as follows:

$$\mathbf{d}_{opt} = \arg\min_{\mathbf{d}} E(\mathbf{d}) \quad (3)$$

From (1) and (3) it should be evident that this minimization process requires a repeated evaluation of (2) over all possible values of **d**. Since matching error calculation is the most computationally intensive part of the mosaicing process, alternative forms of (3) should be researched. Block matching techniques can be employed in order to avoid the computation cost which is associated with the exhaustive minimization procedure, which is implied by (3). In this context, procedures such as the 2-d logarithmic search, the three-point search and the conjugate gradient procedure may be utilized for this purpose [6]. These procedures may provide estimates $\hat{\mathbf{d}}_{opt}$ of the optimal displacement value $\mathbf{d}_{opt}$. The 2-d logarithmic search was employed throughout our simulations.

3 Spanning Tree Mosaicing of Multiple Images

Let us suppose that $M_1 \times M_2$ sub-images should be mosaiced. In this case, a displacement matrix **D** plays a role similar to that of the displacement vector **d** of Sect. 2. The $2M_1M_2 - M_1 - M_2$ columns of **D** are 2-dimensional vectors, each one corresponding to a displacement value between two neighboring sub-images. An expression for the quality of matching, similar to the two-image case, can be derived in the multiple image case, by substituting **d** with **D** in (2) and extending the summation over all neighboring images. The optimal value $\mathbf{D}_{opt}$ of the displacement matrix can be derived from the following expression:

$$\mathbf{D}_{opt} = \arg\min_{\mathbf{D}} E(\mathbf{D}) \quad (4)$$

Unfortunately, (4) imposes prohibitive computational requirements, since the search is now performed in a much larger space. Indeed, let us suppose that for each one of the column vectors of $\mathbf{D}$, eq (1) holds. It can be shown that $\mathbf{D}$ may assume $((d_{1_{\max}} - d_{1_{\min}} + 1)(d_{2_{\max}} - d_{2_{\min}} + 1))^{2M_1 M_2 - M_1 - M_2}$ different values. Thus, computational complexity increases exponentially. Additionally, calculation of $E(\mathbf{D})$ poses other computation problems, since the overlap area W is now a multi-dimensional set.

In order to avoid this exhaustive matching process, certain constraints can be imposed on the way images are matched. Indeed, a faster method may be devised by performing simple matches only, i.e. matches between an image and one of its neighbors. The proposed method may be easily understood with the aid of a mosaicing example. In Fig. 2 (a) a mosaic of $M_1 = 2$ by $M_2 = 2$ sub-images is depicted. By associating each image with a graph node and each local matching of two sub-images with an edge, the mosaicing of the four images can be described by the graph of Fig. 2 (b). Computation of $\mathbf{D}_{opt}$ requires an exhaustive search in 8-dimensional space. To avoid this complexity, the entire mosaicing process is decomposed into simpler steps of mosaicing two images at a time. *Spanning trees* offer an elegant representation of the possible mosaicing procedures, under this constraint. Figs. 2 (c)-(f) illustrate the four spanning trees that correspond to the graph of Fig. 2 (b). For example, in the case depicted in Fig. 2 (c) three two-image matches should be performed: image A to B, A to C, and C to D, while in Figs. 2 (d)-(f) the other three possible mosaicing procedures are illustrated. The final resulting image is the one produced by the procedure which is associated with the smallest matching error. It should be obvious that this sub-optimal procedure offers a significant decrease in computational complexity. The number of trees of a graph can be calculated by the matrix-tree Theorem [7]:

Theorem 1 (Matrix-Tree Theorem). *Let G be a non-trivial graph with adjacency array $\mathbf{A}$ and degree array $\mathbf{C}$. The number of the discrete spanning trees of G is equal with each cofactor of array $\mathbf{C} - \mathbf{A}$.*

Both $\mathbf{A}$ and $\mathbf{C}$ are matrices of size $(M_1 M_2) \times (M_1 M_2)$. If node v_i is adjacent to node v_j, $\mathbf{A}(i,j) = 1$, otherwise $\mathbf{A}(i,j) = 0$. Additionally, the degree matrix is of the form:

$$\mathbf{C} = diag(d(v_1), \ldots, d(v_{M_1 M_2})) \qquad (5)$$

where $d(v_i)$ denotes the number of nodes adjacent to v_i.

The spanning tree mosaicing (STM) procedure is outlined below:

1. For each pair of neighboring images, calculate the optimal displacement and the associated matching error. Notice, that each pair of neighboring images corresponds to an edge of the graph.
2. For each spanning tree that is associated with the specific graph, calculate the corresponding matching error, by summing the local matching errors which are associated with the two-image matches depicted by the given tree.
3. Select the tree that is associated with the smallest matching error.
4. Perform mosaicing of two images at a time, following a route of the selected spanning tree.

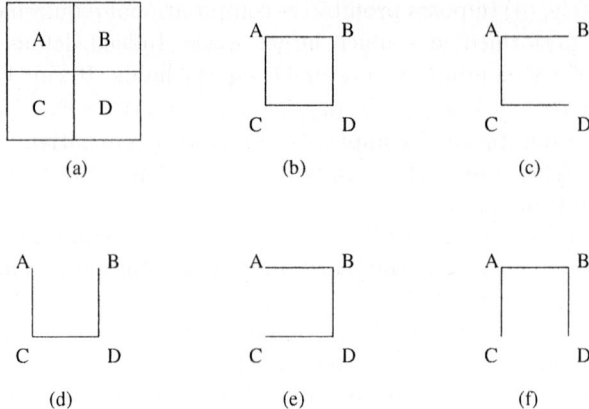

Fig. 2. (a) A labelled mosaic of $M_1 = 2$ by $M_2 = 2$ sub-images, (b) the corresponding graph, (c)-(f) the four possible spanning trees

It should be clarified that sub-optimal results are obtained when the STM approach is followed. Specifically, an approximation $\hat{\mathbf{D}}_{opt}$ of the optimal matrix is computed. However, this is contemplated by the speed gains provided by the algorithm.

As will be shown in Sect. 5, similar results are obtained by using either the MMAE or the MMSE criterion. Thus, MMAE may be preferred since it is faster to compute.

4 Sub-graph STM

The number of trees that correspond to graphs of sizes up to 5 by 5 images are tabulated in Table 1. Unfortunately, for large values of M_1 and M_2 this method can not be utilized, since the number of trees grows very fast with respect to grid size.

Sub-graph STM (SGSTM) may, partially, address this issue. In SGSTM, a graph may be partitioned into sub-graphs, by a process that splits the original

Table 1. Number of spanning trees in a graph-grid of size $M_1 \times M_2$

		1	2	M_2 3	4	5
	1	0	1	1	1	1
	2	1	4	15	56	209
M_1	3	1	15	192	2415	30305
	4	1	56	2415	100352	4140081
	5	1	209	30305	4140081	5.6×10^8

graph vertically and/or horizontally. In Fig. 3, a sample partitioning of this form is depicted. By splitting vertically first and then horizontally, four sub-graphs are created. STM can be applied separately to each one of the four sub-graphs of Fig. 3 (d). Using data of Table 1, it can be easily shown that a total of $192 + 1 + 0 + 1 = 194$ spanning trees should be examined. Since four images will be produced by the STM process (one for each sub-graph), a further STM step will be required, in order to produce the final image. Thus, 4 more trees should be added to the 194 trees examined in the previous step, to produce a total of 198 trees. In contrast, an STM of the original image set would require matching error calculations in 100352 cases.

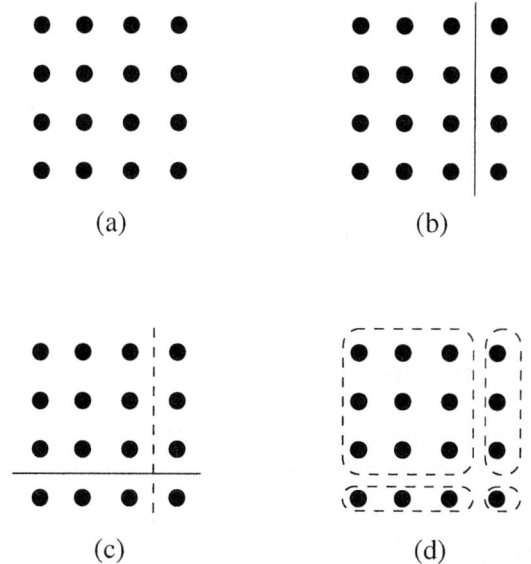

Fig. 3. (a) A graph of $M_1 = 4$ by $M_2 = 4$ image mosaic. (b) Vertical split of (a). (c) Horizontal split of (b). (d) Resulting partition of graph.

If the original graph is of size $M \times M$ ($M = 2^\nu$), the image can be gradually mosaiced by decomposing the original graph into an appropriate number of 2×2 sub-graphs, performing STM on each one, decompose once more the resulting $\frac{M}{2} \times \frac{M}{2}$ graphs and so on, until one image emerges. After mosaicing a partition's sub-graphs, new displacement matrices should be calculated that correspond to the resulting sub-images. It is obvious that the number of 2×2 graphs is equal to $\frac{M}{2}\frac{M}{2} + \frac{M}{4}\frac{M}{4} + \ldots + 1 = \frac{M^2-1}{3}$. Since four spanning trees exist for a 2×2 graph, the matching error of only $4\frac{M^2-1}{3}$ trees should be evaluated. Speedup values are depicted in Fig. 4. It is obvious that SGSTM represents a vast improvement over the STM approach, in terms of computation needs. The results of both methods on an image consisting of 6 sub-images can be seen in Fig. 1. Obviously, SGSTM

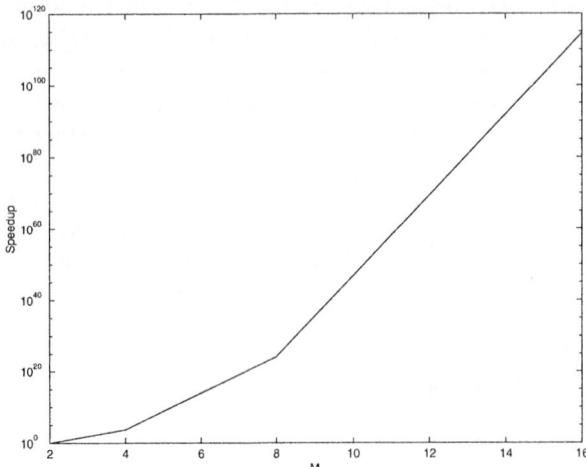

Fig. 4. Theoretical speedup of SGSTM compared to STM, for $M \times M$ ($M = 2^\nu$) graphs

mosaicing quality may be inferior to the one provided by STM, since a smaller number of possible sub-image displacements is examined.

5 Simulation Results

Simulations were carried out in order to assess the performance of the proposed methods, on several image sets. In the following, comments and results are presented for one of these sets, consisting of 12 sub-images, which were arranged in a grid of $M_1 = 4$ rows of $M_2 = 3$ sub-images each. Each sub-image had a resolution of 951×951 pixels. For this graph 2415 spanning trees exist.

For each one of the $2M_1M_2 - M_1 - M_2 = 17$ pairs of neighboring sub-images, matching errors were calculated under both the MMAE and the MMSE criteria. The 2-d logarithmic search was utilized in order to obtain the optimal displacement. Subsequently, for each one of the 2415 spanning trees, the total matching error (MMAE and MMSE) was calculated.

The total time that was required to find all spanning trees that correspond to the given graph, calculate optimal neighboring image displacements under a specific criterion, and output the overall matching error of each tree is tabulated in Table 2, in seconds. Results are included for both STM and SGSTM approaches. In the SGSTM case, the graph was decomposed into four sub-graphs: two 2×2 and two 2×1, which required the calculation of overall error for 14 trees, compared to the 2415 of STM. It is evident that SGSTM is more than an order of magnitude faster than STM. More specifically, the speedup provided by the SGSTM method over the STM method was 13.9 when the MMSE criterion was used and 11.4 for the MMAE criterion, albeit with a significant increase in the matching error. Furthermore, the use of MMAE proved to be faster than that of the MMSE. Sample minimum, maximum, mean and variance of matching error, over the entire spanning tree set for the STM approach, are recorded in Table 3.

Table 2. STM and SGSTM performance results under the MMAE and MMSE criteria

Method	MMAE		MMSE	
	Error	Time	Error	Time
STM	6.4	782.7	107	1265
SGSTM	9.7	68.9	228	91

Table 3. STM matching error statistical measures

Measure	MMAE	MMSE
Maximum	10.7	378
Minimum	6.4	107
Mean	7.9	186
Variance	0.45	1771

By studying the spanning trees that exhibited the lowest MMAE scores the following observations were made:

- MMAE optimality is closely related to MMSE optimality. Indeed, the trees that exhibited the lowest MMAE figures, exhibited also the lowest MMSE figures.
- The most characteristic feature of the trees with the lowest error figures was that optimal matching began from the center and proceeded outwards. In other words, the central nodes of the graph were connected in the best performing trees. Currently, it is assumed that matching quality of the central nodes is more crucial to the overall mosaicing quality, than matching quality of the other nodes. This issue is currently under investigation.

6 Conclusions

In this paper two novel methods that can be used for the mosaicing of large images were proposed. Spanning trees are utilized for describing the order of the mosaicing process. Since matches are performed between pairs of neighboring images, an exhaustive search for the optimal placement of sub-images with respect to each other is avoided. The SGSTM method offers significant speedup, when compared to the STM method. Despite the fact that this performance improvement comes at the cost of increased matching error, SGSTM can be utilized for fast visualization of mosaicing results (e.g. mosaic previews).

Acknowledgement

The presented work was developed within VISNET, a European Network of Excellence (http://www.visnet-noe.org), funded under the European Commission IST FP6 program.

References

1. V. Swarnakar, M. Jeong, R. Wasserman, E. Andres and D Wobschall, "Integrated distortion correction and reconstruction technique for digital mosaic mammography", in *Proc. SPIE Medical Imaging 1997: Image Display*, Vol. 3031, p. 673-681, 1997.
2. H.-Y. Shum and R. Szelisky", Construction of Panoramic Image Mosaics with Global and Local Alignment", *International Journal of Computer Vision*, vol 36, no 2, pp. 101-130, February 2000.
3. H. S. Sawhney and R. Kumar, "True multi-image alignment and its application to mosaicing and lens distortion, in *Proc. CVPR 1997*, pp. 450-456, 1997.
4. W. Puech, A. G. Bors, I. Pitas and J-M. Chassery, "Projection distortion analysis for flattened image mosaicing from straight uniform generalized cylinders", *Pattern Recognition*, vol. 34, no. 8, pp. 1657-1670, August 2001.
5. S. Peleg and J. Herman, " Panoramic Mosaics with VideoBrush", in *Proc IUW-97*, pp. 261-264, May 1997.
6. A. N. Netravali and B. G. Haskell, *Digital Pictures: Representation and Compression*, Plenum Press, 1988.
7. N. L. Biggs, E. K. Lloyd and R. J. Wilson, *Graph Theory 1736-1936*, Clarendon Press, 1986.

An MPEG-7 Based Description Scheme for Video Analysis Using Anthropocentric Video Content Descriptors

N. Vretos, V. Solachidis, and I. Pitas

Department of Informatics University of Thessaloniki, 54124, Thessaloniki, Greece
phone: +30-2310996304, fax: +30-2310996304
{vretos, vasilis, pitas}@aiia.csd.auth.gr
www.aiia.csd.auth.gr

Abstract. MPEG-7 has emerged as the standard for multimedia data content description. As it is in its early age, it tries to evolve towards a direction in which semantic content description can be implemented. In this paper we provide a number of classes to extend the MPEG-7 standard so that it can handle the video media data, in a more uniform and anthropocentric way. Many descriptors (Ds) and description schemes (DSs) already provided by the MPEG-7 standard can help to implement semantics of a media. However, by grouping together several MPEG-7 classes and adding new Ds, better results in the video production and video analysis tasks can be produced. Several classes are proposed in this context and we show that the corresponding scheme produce a new profile which is more flexible in all types of applications as they are described in [1].

1 Introduction

Digital video is the most essential media nowadays. It is used in many multimedia applications such as communication, entertainment, education etc. It is very easy to conclude that video data increase exponentially with time and researchers are focusing on finding better ways in classification and retrieval applications for video databases. The way of constructing videos has also changed in the last years. The potential of digital videos gives producers better editing tools for a film production. Several applications have been proposed that help producers in doing modern film types and manipulate all the film data faster and more accurately. For a better manipulation of all the above, MPEG-7 standardizes the set of Ds, DSs, the description definition language (DDL) and the description encoding [2]-[5]. Despite its early age, many researchers have proposed several Ds and DSs to improve MPEG-7 performance in terms of semantic content description [6], [7].

In this paper we will try to develop several Ds and DSs that will describe digital video content in a better and more sophisticate way. Our efforts originate from the idea that a video entity is a part of several objects prior to and past to the editing process. We incorporate information provided by the preproduction process improve semantic media content description. The structure of the remainder of this paper is as follows. In Section 2 we describe the Ds and DSs. Section (3), we give some examples of use of real data. Finally in Section 4, a conclusion and future work directions are described.

2   MPEG-7 Video Descriptors

In the MPEG-7 standard several descriptors are defined which enable the implementation of video content descriptions.We believe that MPEG-7 must provide mechanisms that can propagate semantic entities from the preproduction to the postproduction phase.Table 1 illustrates a summary of all the classes that we propose in order to assure this connectivity between the pre and the post production phases.

Before going any further in providing the classes' details, we explain the characterization of those classes and their relations (figure 1). Three types of classes are introduced: container, object and event classes. Container classes, as indicated by their name, contain other classes. For instance, a movie class contains scenes that in turn contain shots or takes, which in turn contain frames (optionally). This encapsulation can therefore be very informative in the relation between semantics characteristics of those classes, because parent classes can propagate semantics to child classes and vice versa. For example, a scene which is identified as a night scene, can propagate this semantic entity to its child classes (Take or Shot). This global approach of semantic entities not only facilitates the semantic extraction, but also gives a research framework in which low-level features can be statistically compared very fast in the semantic information extraction process. The object oriented interface (OOF) which is applied in this framework provides flexibility in the use and the implementation of algorithms

Table 1. Classes introduced in the new framework in order to implement semantics in multimedia support

Class Name	Characterization
Movie Class	Container Class
Version Class	Container Class
Scene Class	Container Class
Shot Class	Container Class
Take Class	Container Class
Frame Class	Object Class
Sound Class	Container Class
Actor Class	Object CLass
Object Appearance Class	Event Class
High Order Semantic Class	Container Class
Camera Class	Object CLass
Camera Use Class	Event Class
Lens Class	Object Class

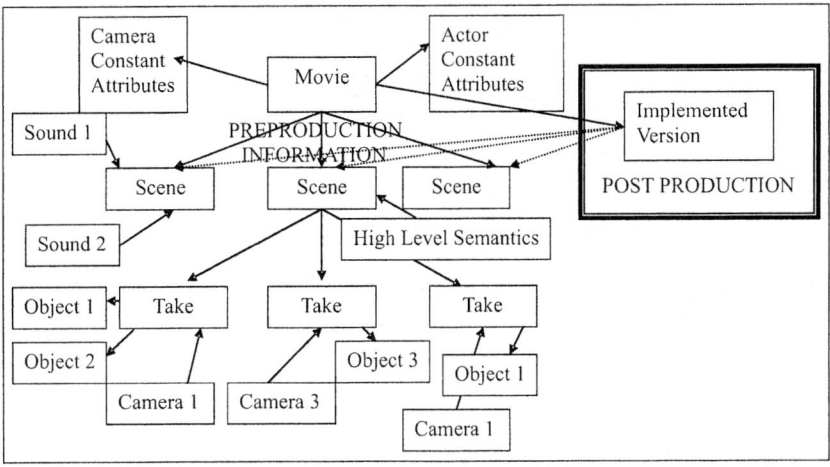

Fig. 1. The interoperability of all the classes enforce semantic entities propagation and exchange in the preproduction phase

for high semantic extraction. On the other hand, object classes are constant physical objects or abstract objects that interact with the media. Any relations of the form "this object interacts with that object" are implemented within this interface. For example a "specific actor is playing in a specific movie", or "a specific camera is used in this take", or "a specific frame is contained by this take or shot". Finally, the events classes are used to implement the interaction of the objects with the movie. An example of this is "the specific camera object is "panning" on this take". From the examples we can clearly conclude that high semantics relation can be easily implemented with the use of those classes. More specifically:

The Movie Class is the root class of the hierarchy. It contains all other classes and describes semantically all the information for a piece of multimedia content. The movie class holds what can be considered as static movie information, such as crew, actors, cameras, director, title etc. It also holds the list of the movie's static scenes where different instances of the Scene class(described later) are stored. Finally, the movie class combines different segments of the static information in order to create different movie versions, within the Version class.

The Version Class encodes (contains) the playable versions of a movie. A movie can be built using this class. It makes references to the static information of the movie in order to collect different movie parts (take fragments) and construct a shot sequence (figure 2). It can also reference a part of an already defined version's scene. For instance, a movie resume (summary) can be made out of the director's scenes.

The Scene Class contains low-level information with respect to timing, like the start and end timecode of a scene and the duration. A scene theme tag

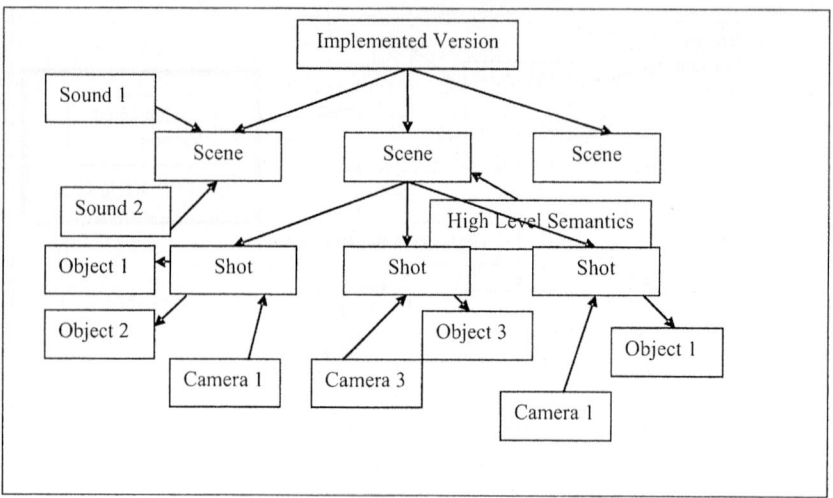

Fig. 2. Implemented versions collect static movie information in order to make a sequential playable movie. This can be achieved either with references from the static movie parts (Takes from pre production phase) or with new instantiated shot classes.

is made in order to make possible a semantic definition of each scene. The High Semantic tag is an instance of the High Order Semantic Class(described later), which gives the possibility to describe semantic actions and events by means of semantic data from the audiovisual content. It correlates higher-level information to provide a narrative description of the scene. Expert systems can be used to provide information for those tags. A sound array tag has also been introduced in a sense that sound and scene are highly correlated in a film. The sound array stores all instances of sounds that are present in a scene. The sound array, as we will see later in more detail, along with low-level information holds high level information, such as the persons that are currently talking or the song that is actually playing or the ambient sounds. Additionally the sound array also captures timecode information for every sound that is heard within the scene. Timecodes can of course overlap (for example flirting while dancing in a fine tune) and this information can be used for extraction of high level scene features. The take and shot array are restricted fields of the scene class, which means that one of them can be active for a particular instance. That class can be used for both pre and postproduction levels. The takes are used in the preproduction environment and the shots in the postproduction environment (within the Version Class).

The Shot Class holds semantic and low-level information about the shot. Two versions are proposed: one with frames and one without. In the second version, we consider the shot as the atom of the movie, which means that it is the essential element of a movie that cannot be divided any further. Several attributes of this class are common in both versions, like the serial number of the shot, the list of appearance and disappearance of an actor, the camera use, and others. The frameless version has a color information tag and a texture information tag, which give information about the color and the texture within the shot. The version with frames provides this feature within the frame class.

The Take Class implements the description of a take. Low-level and high level information is gathered within this class to provide semantic feature extraction, content description and also to facilitate the implementation of a production tool. A take is actually a continuous shot from a specific camera. In the production room the director and his/her colleagues segment takes in order to create a film version. This implementation tries to provide the users with editing ability, as well as assists the directors. For instance, if a director stores all the takes in a multimedia database and then creates an MPEG-7 file with this description scheme he/she will have the ability to easily operate on his film. The "Synchronized With" tag holds information about simultaneous takes. For example in a dialog scenario, where three takes are simultaneous, but taken from different cameras. Algorithms can be built to easily extract the simultaneous takes from a already produced film.

The Frame Class is the lowest level where feature extraction can take place. Within the frame class there are several pieces of information that we would like to store. In contrast with all other classes the frame is a purely spatial description of a video instance. No time information is stored in it. There is, of course, the absolute time of the frame and the local (in take / in shot) time of the frame but whatever information is associated with actor position, actor emotions, dominant color etc. does not have a time dimension. The non-temporality of the frame can be used for low-level feature extraction and also in a production tool for a frame-by-frame editing process (figure 3).

The Sound Class interfaces all kind of sounds that can appear in multimedia. Speech, music and noise are the basic parts of what can be heard in a movie context. This class holds also the time that a particular sound started and ended within a scene, and attributes that characterize this sound. The speech tag holds an array of speakers within the scene and also the general speech type (narration, monolog, dialog etc). The sound class provides useful information for high level feature extraction.

The Actor Class & The Object Appearance Class: The actor class implements all the information that is useful to describe an actor and also gives the possibility to seek one in a database, based on a visual description. Low-level information for the actor interactions with shots or takes is stored in the Object Appearance Class. This information include the time that the actor enters and leaves the shot. Also, if the actor re-enters the shot several times this class holds a list of time-in and time-out instances in order to handle that. A semantic list of what the actor/object is actually doing in the shot, like if he/she is running or just moving or killing someone, is stored for high-level feature extraction in the High Order Semantic Class. The Motion of the actor/object is held as low-level information. The Key Points List is used to describe any possible known Region Of Interest (ROI), like the bounding box, the convex hull, the features point etc. For instance, this implementation can

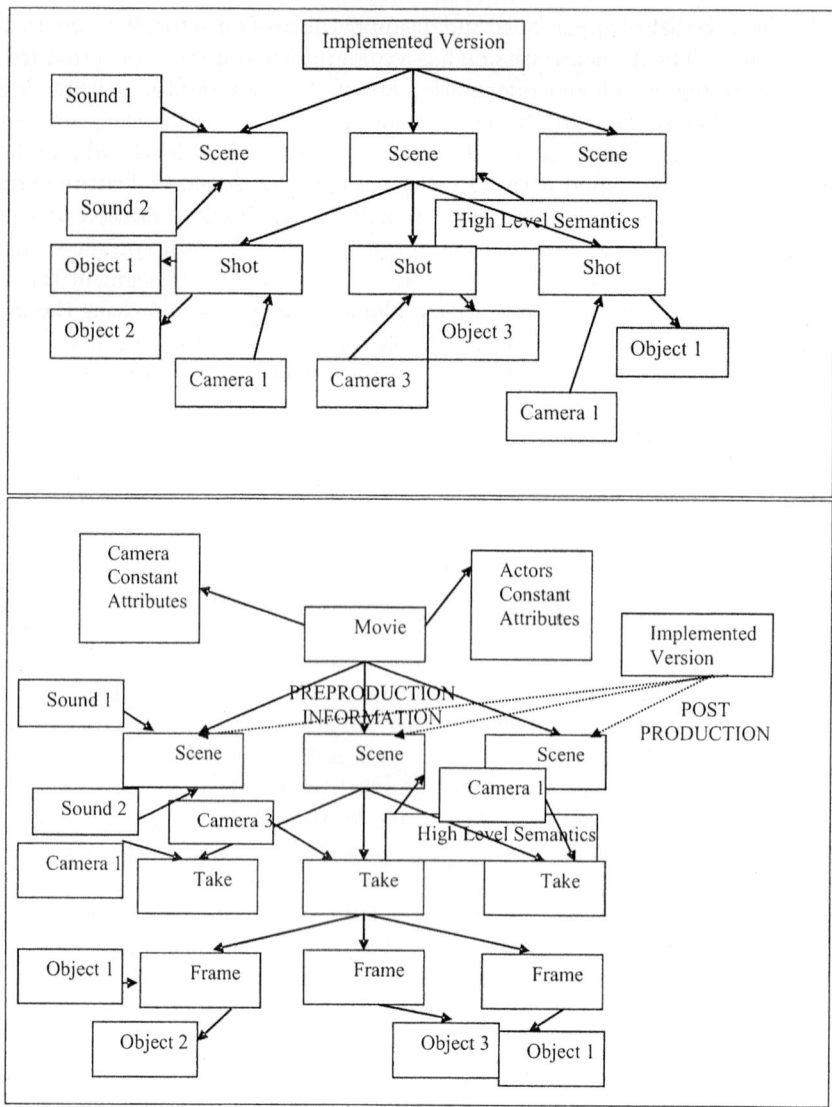

Fig. 3. Frames can be used with Take and Shot classes for a deeper analysis, giving rise to an exponential growth of the MPEG-7 file size

provide the trajectory of a specific ROI like the eye or a lip's lower edge etc. The pose estimation of the face and the emotions of the actor (with an intensity value) within the shot can also be captured. The latter three tags can be used to create high-level information automatically. The sound class also holds higher-level information for the speakers and in combining the information we can generate high-level semantics based also in the sound content of the multimedia to provide instantiations of the High Order Semantic Class.

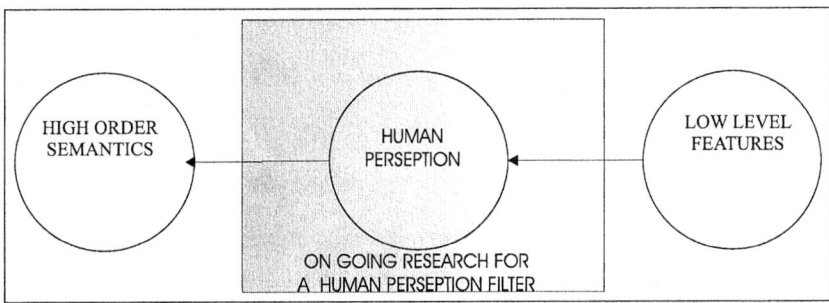

Fig. 4. Low-level features space is captured by human perception algorithms and this mechanism will produce the semantic content of the frame

The High Order Semantic Class organizes and combines the semantic features, which are derived from the audiovisual content. For example, if a sequence of actors shaking hands is followed by low volume crowd noise and positives emotions this could probably be a countries leaders handshake. The Object's Narrative Identification hosts semantics of actors and objects in a scene context, for example (Tom's Car) and not only the object identification like (Tom, Car). The Action list refers to actions performed by actors or other objects like "car crashes before a wall" or "actor is eating". The events list holds information of events that might occur in a scene like "A plane crashes". Finally, the two semantic tags, Time and Location, define semantics for narrative time (night, day, exact narrative time etc) and narrative location (indoor, outdoor, cityscape, landscape etc).

The Camera & The Camera Use Class: The camera class holds all the information of a camera, such as manufacturer, type, lenses etc. The Camera Use class, which contains the camera's interaction with the film. The latter is very useful for low-level and high-level feature extraction from the film. The camera motion tag uses a string of characters that conform to the traditional camera motion styles. New styles have no need to re-implement the class. The current zoom factor and lens is used for feature extraction as well.

The Lens Class implements the characteristics of several lenses that will be used in the production of a movie or documentary. It is useful to know and store this information in order to better extract low-level features from the movie. Also for educational reasons one can search for movies that are recorded with a particular lens.

This OOF essentially constitutes a novel approach of digital video processing. We believe that in a video retrieval application one can post queries in a form that only simple low-level features cannot answer yet. Also, video annotation, has been proven [6]to be non productive, because of the objectivity of the annotators and the time consuming annotation process. The proposed classes have the ability to standardize the annotation context and they are defined in a way that low-level features can be integrated, in order to enable an automatic extraction of those high-level features. In figure 4 one can see the relation between semantic space and technical (low-level) features space. The proposed classes are an amalgam of low-level features, like histograms, FFTs etc, and high semantic entities, like scene theme, person recognition, emotions, sounds qualification, etc. Nowadays researchers are very interested in extracting high semantic features [8],[9],[10]. Having this in mind, we believe that the proposed template can give the genre of a new digital video processing approach.

3 Examples of Use

3 types of examples, will be provide in this section . These include one for preproduction environment, one for postproduction and the combination of preproduction and postproduction.

- In preproduction environment the produced xml will have a movie class in witch takes,scenes,sound information and all the static information of the movie will be encapsulated. In Figure 5, one can visualize the encapsulation of those classes. Applications can handle the MPEG-7 file in order to produce helpful tips for the director while he/she is in the editing room or better assist him in editing with a smart agents application.

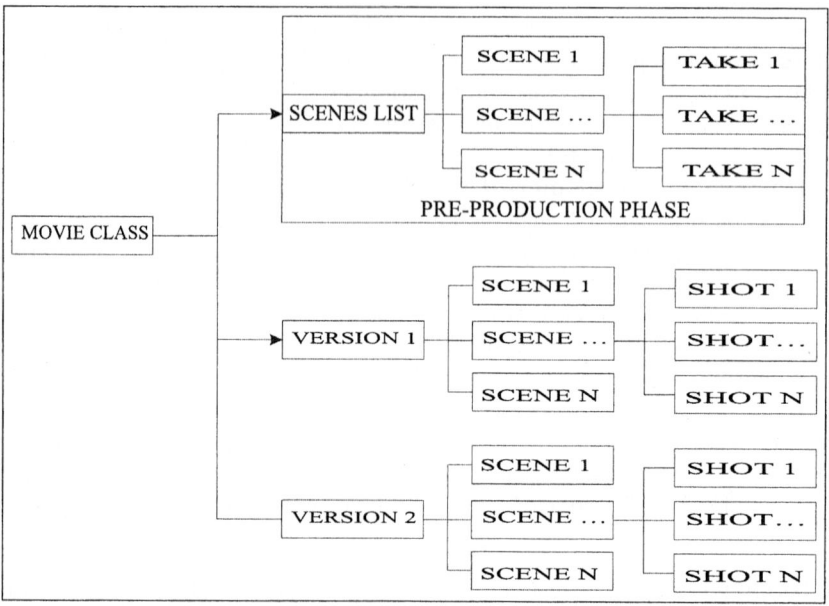

Fig. 5. Shots exist only in the post-production phase as fragments of takes from the pre-production phase, and inherit all semantic and low-level features extracted for the takes in the pre-production phase.This constitutes the semantic propagation mechanism. Several versions can be implemented without different video data files.

- In the second type of application all the types of the pull and push applications, as defined in the MPEG-7 standard[1] can be realized or improved. Retrieval application, will be able to handle in a more uniform way all kinds of request whether the latter are associated with low-level features or high semantic entities.
- Finally the 3d type of application, is the essential reason for implementing such a framework. In such an application a total interactivity with the user can be established, by providing even the ability to reediting a film and create different film version with the same amount of data. For example, by saving the takes of a film and altering the editing process, the user can reproduce the film from scratch and with no additional storage of heavy video files.Creating different permutation arrays of takes and scenes results in different versions of the same film. Nowadays media supports (DVD,VCD,etc) can hold a very large amount of data. Such an implementation can be realistic, if we consider that already produced DVDs provides users something more than just a movie e.g. (behind the scene tracks, or director's cuts, actors' interviews etc).Media Interactivity in media seems to gain a big share in the market, the proposed OOF can provide a very useful product. It is obvious that such a tool can give rise to education programs, interactive television and all the new revolutionary approaches of multimedia world.

4   Conclusion and Further Work Areas

As a conclusion we underline the fact that this framework can be very useful for the new era of image processing witch is focusing in semantic feature extraction and we believe that it can provide specific research goals. Having this in mind, in the future we will concentrate our research in filling automatically the classes' attributes. On going research has already underdevelopment tools for extraction of high semantic feature.

Acknowledgement

The work presented was developed within NM2, a European Integrated Project (http://www.ist-nm2.org), funded under the European Commission IST FP6 program.

References

[1] ISO (International Organization for Standardization): Information technology – multimedia content description interface - part 6: Reference software. ISO Standard ISO/IEC JTC1/SC29 N4163, International Organization for Standardization, Geneva, Switzerland (2001)

[2] ISO (International Organization for Standardization): Information technology – multimedia content description interface - part 1: Systems. ISO Standard ISO/IEC JTC 1/SC 29 N 4153, International Organization for Standardization, Geneva, Switzerland (2001)
[3] ISO (International Organization for Standardization): Information technology – multimedia content description interface - part 2: Description Definition Language ISO Standard ISO/IEC JTC 1/SC 29 N 4155, International Organization for Standardization, Geneva, Switzerland (2001)
[4] ISO (International Organization for Standardization): Information technology – multimedia content description interface - part 3: Visual. ISO Standard ISO/IEC JTC 1/SC 29 N 4157, International Organization for Standardization, Geneva, Switzerland (2001)
[5] ISO (International Organization for Standardization): Information technology – multimedia content description interface - part 4: Audio. ISO Standard ISO/IEC JTC 1/SC 29 N 4159, International Organization for Standardization, Geneva, Switzerland (2001)
[6] ISO (International Organization for Standardization): Information technology – multimedia content description interface - part 5: Multimedia description schemes. ISO Standard ISO/IEC JTC 1/SC 29 N 4161, International Organization for Standardization, Geneva, Switzerland (2001)
[7] Eakins, J.P.: Retrieval of still images by content. (2001) 111–138
[8] Vakali, A., Hacid, M., Elmagarmid, A.: Mpeg-7 based description schemes for multi-level video content classification. IVC **22** (2004) 367–378
[9] Krinidis, M., Stamou, G., Teutsch, H., Spors, S., Nikolaidis, N., Rabenstein, R., Pitas, I.: An audio-visual database for evaluating person tracking algorithms. In: Proc. of IEEE International Conference on Acoustics, Speech and Signal Processing, Philadelphia, USA (2005) 452–455
[10] Kyperountas, M., Cernekova, Z., Kotropoulos, C., Gavrielides, M., Pitas, I.: Scene change detection using audiovisual clues. In: Proc. of Norwegian Conference on Image Processing and Pattern Recognition (NOBIM 2004), Stavanger, Norway (2004)
[11] Sikudova, E., Gavrielides, M.A., Pitas, I.: Extracting semantic information from art images. In: Proc. of International Conference on Computer Vision and Graphics 2004 (ICCVG 2004), Warsaw, Poland (2004)

Detecting Abnormalities in Capsule Endoscopic Images by Textural Description and Neural Networks

V.S. Kodogiannis, E. Wadge, M. Boulougoura, and K. Christou

Mechatronics Group, School of Computer Science, University of Westminster,
London, HA1 3TP, UK
kodogiv@wmin.ac.uk

Abstract. In this paper, a detection system to support medical diagnosis and detection of abnormal lesions by processing endoscopic images is presented. The endoscopic images possess rich information expressed by texture. Schemes have been developed to extract texture features from the texture spectra in the chromatic and achromatic domains for a selected region of interest from each colour component histogram of images acquired by the new M2A Swallowable Capsule. The implementation of an advanced neural network scheme and the concept of fusion of multiple classifiers have been also adopted in this paper. The preliminary test results support the feasibility of the proposed method.

1 Introduction

In medical practice, endoscopic diagnosis and other minimally invasive imaging procedures, such as computed tomography, ultrasonography, con-focal microscopy, computed radiography, or magnetic resonance imaging, are now permitting visualisation of previously inaccessible regions of the body. Their objective is to increase the expert's ability in identifying malignant regions and decrease the need for intervention while maintaining the ability for accurate diagnosis. For more than 10 years, flexible video-endoscopes have a widespread use in medicine and guide a variety of diagnostic and therapeutic procedures including colonoscopy, gastroenterology and laparoscopy [1]. Conventional diagnosis of endoscopic images employs visual interpretation of an expert physician. Since the beginning of computer technology, it becomes necessary for visual systems to "understand a scene", that is making its own properties to be outstanding, by enclosing them in a general description of an analysed environment. Computer-assisted image analysis can extract the representative features of the images together with quantitative measurements and thus can ease the task of objective interpretations by a physician expert in endoscopy. Endoscopic images possess rich information, which facilitates the abnormality detection by multiple techniques. However, from the literature survey, it has been found that only a few techniques for endoscopic image analysis have been reported and they are still undergoing testing. In addition, most of the techniques were developed on the basis of features in a single domain: chromatic domain or spatial domain. Applying these techniques individually for detecting the disease patterns based on possible incomplete and partial information may lead to inaccurate diagnosis. For example, regions affected with bleeding and inflammation may have different colour and texture characteristics. Parameters in the spatial domain related with lumen can be used to suggest the cues for abnormality. For instance, small area of lumen implies the narrowing of the lumen which is often one of the symptoms for lump formation and not the presence of possible bleeding. Therefore, maximizing the use of all available image analysis techniques for diagnosing from multiple feature domains is particularly important to improve the tasks of classification of endoscopic images. Krishnan, et al.[2] have been using endoscopic images to define features of the normal and the abnormal colon. New approaches for the characterisation of colon based on a set of quantitative parameters, extracted by the fuzzy processing of colon images, have been used for assisting the colonoscopist in the assessment of the status of patients and were used as inputs to a rule-based decision strategy to find out whether the colon's lumen belongs to either an abnormal or normal category. The analysis of the extracted quantitative parameters was performed using three different neural networks selected for classification of the colon. The three networks include a two-layer perceptron trained with the delta rule, a multilayer perceptron with back-propagation (BP) learning and a self-organizing network. Endoscopic images contain rich information of texture. Therefore, the additional texture information can provide better results for the image analysis than approaches using merely intensity information. Such information has been used in CoLD (colorectal lesions detector) an innovative detection system to support colorectal cancer diagnosis and detection of pre-cancerous polyps, by processing endoscopy images or video frame sequences acquired during colonoscopy [3]. It utilised second-order statistical features that were calculated on the wavelet transformation of each image to discriminate amongst regions of normal or abnormal tissue. A neural network based on the classic BP learning algorithm performed the classification of the features. CoLD integrated the feature extraction and classification algorithms under a graphical user interface, which allowed both novice and expert users to utilise effectively all system's functions. The detection accuracy of the proposed system has been estimated to be more than 95%.

Intra-operative endoscopy, although used with great success, is more invasive and associated with a higher rate of complications. Though the gastrointestinal (GI) endoscopic procedure has been widely used, doctors must be skilful and experienced to reach deep sites such as the duodenum and small intestine. The cleaning and sterilisation of these devices is still a problem leading to the desire for disposable instruments. In GI tract, great skill and concentration are required for navigating the endoscope because of its flexible structure. Discomfort to the patient and the time required for diagnosis heavily depend on the technical skill of the physician and there is always a possibility of the tip of the endoscope injuring the walls. Standard endoscopic examinations evaluate only short segments of the proximal and distal small bowel and barium follow-through has a low sensitivity and specificity of only 10% for detecting pathologies. Hence, endoscopic examination of the entire small bowel has always been a diagnostic challenge. Limitations of the diagnostic techniques in detection of the lesions located in the small bowel are mainly due to the length of the small intestine, overlying loops and intra-peritoneal location. This caused also the desire for autonomous instruments without the bundles of optical fibres and tubes, which are more than the size of the instrument itself, the reason for the objections of the patients. The use of highly integrated microcircuit in bioelectric data acquisition systems promises new insights into the origin of a large variety of health problems by providing lightweight, low-power, low-cost medical measurement devices. At present, there is only one type of microcapsule which has been introduced recently to improve the health outcome. This first swallowable video-capsule for the gastroenterological diagnosis has been presented by Given Imaging, a company from Israel, and its schematic diagram is illustrated in Fig. 1 [4].

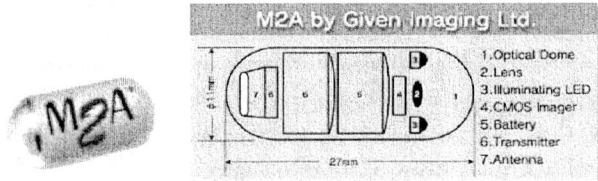

Fig. 1. Given Imaging Capsule

The system consists of a small swallowable capsule containing a battery, a camera on a chip, a light source, and a transmitter. The camera-capsule has a one centimetre section and a length of three centimetres so it can be swallowed with some effort. In 24 hours, the capsule is crossing the patient's alimentary canal. For the purpose of this research work, endoscopic images have been obtained using this innovative endoscopic device. They have spatial resolution of 171x151 pixels, a brightness resolution of 256 levels per colour plane (8bits), and consisted of three colour planes (red, green and blue) for a total of 24 bits per pixel. The proposed methodology in this paper is considered in two phases. The first implements the extraction of image features while in the second phase an advanced neural network is implemented / employed to perform the diagnostic task. Texture analysis is one of the most important features used in image processing and pattern recognition. It can give information about the arrangement and spatial properties of fundamental image elements. Many methods have been proposed to extract texture features, e.g. the co-occurrence matrix, and the texture spectrum in the achromatic component of the image. The definition and extraction of quantitative parameters from endoscopic images based on texture information in the chromatic and achromatic domain is been proposed. This information is initially represented by a set of descriptive statistical features calculated on the histogram of the original image. Additionally, in this study an alternative approach of obtaining those quantitative parameters from the texture spectra is proposed both in the chromatic and achromatic domains of the image. The definition of texture spectrum employs the determination of the texture unit (TU) and texture unit number (N_{TU}) values. Texture units characterise the local texture information for a given pixel and its neighbourhood, and the statistics of the entire texture unit over the whole image reveal the global texture aspects. For the diagnostic part, the concept of multiple-classifier scheme has been adopted, where the fusion of the individual outputs was realised using fuzzy integral. An intelligent classifier-scheme based on the methodology of Extended Normalised Radial Basis Function (ENRBF) neural networks has been implemented.

2 Image Features Extraction

A major component in analysing images involves data reduction which is accomplished by intelligently modifying the image from the lowest level of pixel data into higher level representations. Texture is broadly defined as the rate and direction of change of the chromatic properties of the image, and could be subjectively described as fine, coarse, smooth, random, rippled, and irregular, etc. For this reason, we focused our attention on nine statistical measures (standard deviation, variance, skew, kurtosis, entropy, energy, inverse difference moment, contrast, and covariance) [5]. All texture descriptors are estimated for all planes in both RGB {R (Red), G (Green), B (Blue)} and HSV {H (Hue), S (Saturation), V (Intensity)} spaces, creating a feature vector for each descriptor $D_i=(R_i,G_i,B_i,H_i,S_i,V_i)$. Thus, a total of 54 features (9 statistical measures x 6 image planes) are then estimated.

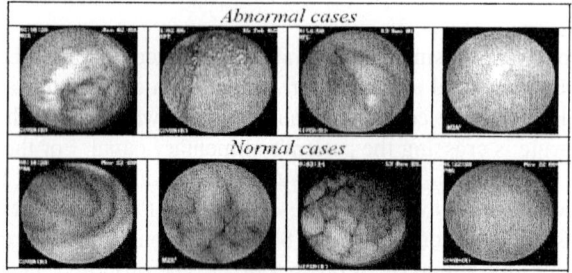

Fig. 2. Selected endoscopic images of normal and abnormal cases

For our experiments, we have used 70 endoscopic images related to abnormal cases and 70 images related to normal ones [6]. Fig. 2 shows samples of selected images acquired using the M2A capsule of normal and abnormal cases. Generally, the statistical measures are estimated on histograms of the original image (1st order statistics). However, the histogram of the original image carries no information regarding relative position of the pixels in the texture. Obviously this can fail to distinguish between textures with similar distributions of grey levels. We therefore have to implement methods which recognise characteristic relative positions of pixels of given intensity levels. An additional scheme is proposed in this study to extract texture features from texture spectra in the chromatic and achromatic domains, for a selected region of interest from each colour component histogram of the endoscopic images.

2.1 N_{TU} Transformation

The definition of texture spectrum employs the determination of the texture unit (TU) and texture unit number (N_{TU}) values. Texture units characterise the local texture information for a given pixel and its neighbourhood, and the statistics of all the texture units over the whole image reveal the global texture aspects. Given a neighbourhood of $\delta \times \delta$ pixels, which are denoted by a set containing $\delta \times \delta$ elements $P=\{P_0,P_1,....,P_{(\delta \times \delta)-1}\}$, where P_0 represents the chromatic or achromatic (i.e. intensity) value of the central pixel and $P_i\{i=1,2,...,(\delta \times \delta)-1\}$ is the chromatic or achromatic value of the neighbouring pixel i, the $TU=\{E_0,E_1,....,E_{(\delta \times \delta)-1}\}$, where $E_i\{i=1,2,...,(\delta \times \delta)-1\}$ is determined as follows:

$$E_i = \begin{cases} 0, & if \quad P_i < P_0 \\ 1, & if \quad P_i = P_0 \\ 2, & if \quad P_i > P_0 \end{cases} \quad (1)$$

The element E_i occupies the same position as the ith pixel. Each element of the TU has one of three possible values; therefore the combination of all the eight elements results in 6561 possible TU's in total. The texture unit number (N_{TU}) is the label of the texture unit and is defined using the following equation:

$$N_{TU} = \sum_{i=1}^{(\delta \times \delta)-1} E_i \times \delta^{i-1} \quad (2)$$

Where, in our case, $\delta = 3$. The texture spectrum histogram ($Hist(i)$) is obtained as the frequency distribution of all the texture units, with the abscissa showing the N_{TU} and the ordinate representing its occurrence frequency. The texture spectra of various image components {I (Intensity), R (Red), G (Green), B (Blue), H (Hue), S (Saturation)} are obtained from their texture unit numbers. The statistical features are then estimated on the histograms of the N_{TU} transformations of the chromatic and achromatic planes of the image (R,G,B,H,S,V).

3 Image Features Extraction

Recently, the concept of combining multiple classifiers has been actively exploited for developing highly reliable "diagnostic" systems [7]. One of the key issues of this approach is how to combine the results of the various systems to give the best estimate of the optimal result. A straightforward approach is to decompose the problem into manageable ones for several different sub-systems and combine them via a gating network. The presumption is that each classifier/sub-system is "an expert" in some local area of the feature space. The sub-systems are local in the sense that the weights in one "expert" are decoupled from the weights in other sub-networks. In this study, six subsystems have been developed, and each of them was associated with the six planes specified in the feature extraction process (*i.e.* R, G, B, H, S, & V). Each subsystem was modelled with an appropriate intelligent learning scheme. In our case, a neuro-fuzzy scheme has been proposed.

Such scheme provides a degree of certainty for each classification based on the statistics for each plane. The outputs of each of these networks must then be combined to produce a total output for the system as a whole as can be seen in Fig. 3. While a usual scheme chooses one best subsystem from amongst the set of candidate subsystems based on a winner-takes-all strategy, the current proposed approach runs all multiple subsystems with an appropriate collective decision strategy. The aim in this study is to incorporate information from each plane/space so that decisions are based on the whole input space. The adopted in this paper methodology was to use the fuzzy integral concept.

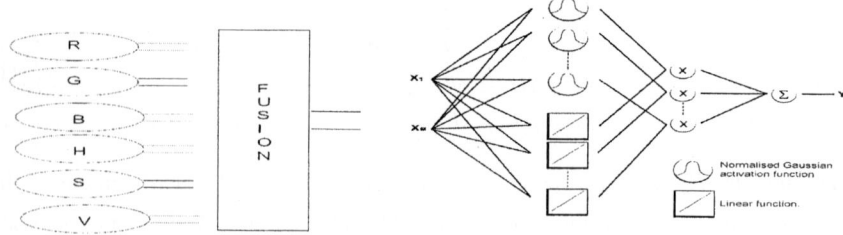

Fig. 3. Proposed fusion scheme and the neural classifier

Fuzzy integral (FI) is a promising method that incorporates information from each space/plane so that decisions are based on the whole input space in the case of multiple classifier schemes. FI combines evidence of a classification with the systems expectation of the importance of that evidence. By treating the classification results a series of disjointed subsets of the input space Sugeno defined the g_λ-fuzzy measure [8].

$$g(A \cup B) = g(A) + g(B) + \lambda g(A) g(B);$$
$$\lambda \in (-1, \infty) \qquad (3)$$

Where the λ measure can be given by solving the following non-linear equation.

$$\lambda + 1 = \prod_{i=1}^{K} (1 + \lambda g^i) \qquad \lambda > -1 \qquad (4)$$

The $g^i, i \in \{1, ..., K\}$ values are fuzzy densities relating to the reliability of each of the K feature networks and satisfy the conditions of fuzzy sets laid out by Sugeno.

3.1 Extended Normalised RBF Network

The first classification scheme utilised here is an artificial neural network known as an Extended Normalised Radial Basis Function Network (ENRBF) [9], which utilises a series of linear models instead of the linear combiner in an RBF network. Fig. 3 illustrates its structure. We propose in this paper a supervised training method for this scheme that is fully supervised and self organising in terms of structure. The method incorporates training techniques from Bayesian Ying-Yang (BYY) [10] training which treats the problem of optimisation as one of maximising the entropy between the original non-parametric data distribution based on Kernel estimates or user specified values and the parametric distributions represented by the network. This is achieved through the derivation of a series of Expectation Maximisation (EM) update equations using a series of entropy functions as the Q function or log-likelihood function. The ENRBF network can be represented by the following equations.

$$E(z \mid x, \Theta) = \frac{\sum_{j=1}^{K}\left(W_j^T x + c_j\right) p\left(x \mid j, \theta_j\right)}{\sum_{j=1}^{K} p\left(x \mid j, \theta_j\right)} \quad (5)$$

Where z is the output of the network $z \in Z$, x is an input vector $x \in X$, $\Theta = [W, c, \theta]$ are the network parameters and $\theta = [m, \Sigma]$ are the parameters of the Gaussian activation functions given by:

$$p(x \mid j, \theta_j) = \exp\left\{-\tfrac{1}{2}(x - m_j) \Sigma_j^{-1} (x - m_j)\right\} \quad (6)$$

The BYY method attempts to maximise the degree of agreement between the expected value of z from the network and the true value of z from the training data. It is guaranteed to lead to a local optimum and unlike the original EM algorithm for learning the parameters of Gaussian functions this method encourages coordination between the input and output domains. Like the EM algorithm this method is also very fast in terms of the number of iterations needed for the parameters to converge. However, as BYY is an EM based technique it is still susceptible to locally maximal values. The Split and Merge EM (SMEM) concept for Gaussian Mixture Models (GMM) proposed initially by Ueda, has been applied to the ENRBF scheme. The original SMEM algorithm is able to move neurons from over populated areas of the problem domain to underrepresented areas by merging the over populated neurons and splitting the under-populated. The use of Eigenvectors to split along the axis of maximum divergence instead of randomly as in original SMEM has been proposed recently. The SMEM algorithm suffers from the fact that before terminating all possible combinations of Split and Merge operations must be examined. Although many options can be discounted, the training time still increases exponentially with network size and again suffers from problems inherent with k-means and basic EM in that it is essentially unsupervised. In this work we incorporate the supervised nature of BYY training with improved statistical criteria for determining the neurons which poorly fit their local areas of the problem domain.

4 Results

The proposed approach was evaluated using 140 clinically obtained endoscopic M2A images. For the present analysis, two decision-classes are considered: abnormal and normal. Seventy images (35 abnormal and 35 normal) were used for the training and the remaining ones (35 abnormal and 35 normal) were used for testing. The extraction of quantitative parameters from these endoscopic images is based on texture information. Initially, this information is represented by a set of descriptive statistical features calculated on the histogram of the original image. The ENRBF scheme is incorporated into a multiple classifier scheme, where the structure of each individual (for R, G, B, H, S, & V planes) classifier is consisted of 9 input nodes (i.e. nine statistical features) and 2 output nodes. In a second stage, the nine statistical measures for each individual image component are then calculated though the related texture spectra after applying the (N_{TU}) transformation.

4.1 Performance of Histograms-Based Features

The multiple-classifier scheme using the ENRBF network has been trained on the six feature spaces. The network trained on the R feature space and it then achieved an accuracy of 94.28% on the testing data incorrectly classifying 2 of the normal images as abnormal and 2 abnormal as normal ones. The network trained on the G feature space misclassified 2 normal images as abnormal but not the same ones as the R space. The remaining 3 images were misclassified as normal ones.

Table 1. ENRBF Performance

	ENRBF Accuracy (70 testing patterns)	
Modules	*Histogram-based*	N_{TU}-*based*
R	94.28% (4 mistakes)	92.85% (5 mistakes)
G	92.85% (5 mistakes)	97.14% (2 mistakes)
B	94.28% (4 mistakes)	95.71% (3 mistakes)
H	91.43% (6 mistakes)	94.28% (4 mistakes)
S	88.57% (8 mistakes)	91.43% (6 mistakes)
V	94.28% (4 mistakes)	97.14% (2 mistakes)
Overall	**94.28% (4 mistakes)**	**95.71% (3 mistakes)**

The B feature space achieved an accuracy of 94.28% on the testing data with 4 misclassifications, i.e. 3 abnormal as normal ones and the remaining one image as abnormal ones. The network trained on the H feature space achieved 91.43% accuracy on the testing data. The network trained on the S feature space achieved an accuracy of only 88.57% on the testing data. Finally, the network for the V feature space misclassified 2 normal cases as abnormal and 2 abnormal as normal ones, giving it an accuracy of 94.28% on the testing data.

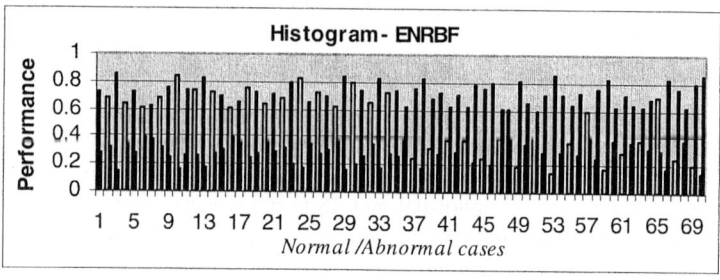

Fig. 4. Histogram-based Performance for ENRBF

The fuzzy integral (FI) concept has been used here to combine the results from each sub-network and the overall system misclassified 1 normal cases as abnormal and 3 abnormal as normal ones, giving the system an overall accuracy of 94.28%. These results are illustrated in Fig. 4, while Table 1 presents the performance of individual components. It can be shown that in general the confidence levels for each correct classification is above 0.6.

4.2 Performance of N_{TU}-Based Features

In the N_{TU}-based extraction process, the texture spectrum of the six components (R, G, B, H, S, V) have been obtained from the texture unit numbers, and the same nine statistical measures have been used in order to extract new features from each textures spectrum. In a similar way, a multi classifier consisting of ENRBF networks with 9 input nodes and 2 output nodes was trained on each of the six feature spaces. The N_{TU} transformation of the original histogram has produced a slight but unambiguous improvement in the diagnostic performance of the multi-classifier scheme. Table 1 illustrates the performances of the network in the individual components. The ENRBF network trained on the R feature space and it then achieved an accuracy of 92.85% on the testing data incorrectly classifying 3 of the normal images as abnormal and 2 abnormal as normal ones. The network trained on the G feature space misclassified 2 normal images as abnormal but not the same ones as the R space. The B feature space achieved an accuracy of 95.71% on the testing data with 3 misclassifications, i.e. 2 abnormal as normal ones and the remaining one image as abnormal one. The network trained on the H feature space achieved 94.28% accuracy on the testing data. The network trained on the S feature space achieved an accuracy of only 91.43% on the testing data. Finally, the network for the V feature space misclassified 1 normal case as abnormal and 1 abnormal as normal one, giving it an accuracy of 97.14% on the testing data.

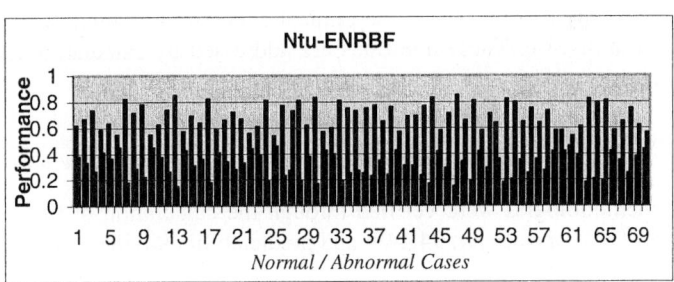

Fig. 5. N_{TU}-based Performance for ENRBF

The fuzzy integral (FI) concept has been used here to combine the results from each sub-network and the overall system provided an accuracy of 95.71%. More specifically, 1 normal case as abnormal and 2 abnormal as normal ones provide us a good indication of a "healthy" diagnostic performance. However the level of confidence in this case was slight less than the previous case (i.e. the histogram), that is 0.54 as shown in Fig. 5.

However, medical diagnostic tests are often perceived by physicians as providing absolute answers or as clarifying uncertainty to a greater degree than is warranted. When a diagnosis turns out to be at variance with the results of a diagnostic test, the clinician's assumption may be that the test was either misinterpreted or that the test is no good. Such a binary approach to the interpretation of diagnostic testing, i.e., assuming a clearly positive or negative result (like an off-on switch), is too simplistic and may be counterproductive in the workup of a patient. Instead, the results of a diagnostic test should be viewed on a continuum from negative to positive and as giving the likelihood or probability of a certain diagnosis. The performance of a neural network is usually expressed in terms of its estimation and prediction rates, that is, the number of correctly classified objects in the train and prediction sets, respectively. While these estimators may be adequate in certain instances, e.g., general classification tasks, they should not be employed when medical data is involved [11]. This is because such variables give only a measure of overall performance. In the case of human beings it is crucial to assess the capacity of a test to distinguish between people with (true positive) and without (true negative) a disease, as those individuals may or may not be subjected to further evaluations that may be stressing, costly, etc., depending upon the result of the test. In these cases, the sensitivity and the specificity are more adequate. The performance of all the classification tools evaluated in the present work was thus assessed in terms of these variables which are estimated according to [11]:

$$sensitivity = \frac{\sum true\ positive\ alarms}{\sum true\ positive\ alarms + \sum false\ negative\ alarms}$$

$$specificity = \frac{\sum true\ negative\ alarms}{\sum true\ negative\ alarms + \sum false\ positive\ alarms}$$

However, although sensitivity and specificity partially define the efficacy of a diagnostic test, they do not answer the clinical concern of whether a patient does or does not have a disease. These questions are addressed by calculating the predictive value of the test

$$predictability = \frac{\sum true\ positive\ alarms}{\sum true\ positive\ alarms + \sum false\ positive\ alarms}$$

The above methodologies were verified through the calculation of these parameters: sensitivity, 97.05%, specificity, 94.44% and predictability 94.28% for the N_{TU} case.

5 Conclusions

The major contribution of the proposed system in the process of medical diagnosis is that it can provide additional information to physicians on the characterization of the endoscopic images / tissues, by exploiting its textural characteristics, which are consequently used for the classification of the corresponding image regions as normal or abnormal. An approach on extracting texture features from endoscopic images using the M2A Given Imaging capsule has been developed. Statistical features based on texture are important features, and were able to distinguish the normal and abnormal status in the selected clinical cases. The multiple classifier approach used in this study with the inclusion of an advanced neural network algorithm provided encouraging results. Two approaches on extracting statistical features from endoscopic images using the M2A Given Imaging capsule have been developed. In addition to the histogram-based texture spectrum, an alternative approach of obtaining those quantitative parameters from the texture spectra is proposed both in the chromatic and achromatic domains of the image by calculating the texture unit numbers (N_{TU}) over the histogram spectrum. Future studies will be focused on further development of this "diagnostic" system by incorporating additional features, investigation of algorithms for reduction of input dimensionality as well as the testing of this approach to the IVP-endoscopic capsule which is under development through the "IVP- Intracorporeal Videoprobe" European research project.

References

1. Haga, Y., Esashi, M.,: Biomedical Microsystems for Minimally Invasive Diagnosis and Treatment, Proceedings of IEEE, **92** (2004) 98-114.
2. Krishnan, S., Wang, P., Kugean, C., Tjoa, M.: Classification of endoscopic images based on texture and neural network, Proc. 23rd Annual IEEE Int. Conf. in Engineering in Medicine and Biology, **4** (2001) 3691-3695.
3. Maroulis, D.E. Iakovidis, D.K., Karkanis, S., Karras, D.: CoLD: a versatile detection system for colorectal lesions endoscopy video-frames, Computer Methods and Programs in Biomedicine, **70** (2003) 151–166.
4. Idden, G., Meran, G., Glukhovsky A., Swain P.: Wireless capsule endoscopy, Nature, (2000) 405-417.
5. Haralick, R.M.: Statistical and structural approaches to texture, IEEE Proc., **67** (1979) 786- 804.
6. Boulougoura, M., Wadge, E., Kodogiannis, V., Chowdrey, H.S.: Intelligent systems for computer-assisted clinical endoscopic image analysis, 2nd IASTED Int. Conf. on Biomedical Engineering, Innsbruck, Austria, (2004) 405-408.
7. Wadge, E., Kodogiannis, V.S.,: Intelligent diagnosis of UTI in vivo using gas sensor arrays, Int. Conf. on Neural Networks and Expert Systems in Medicine and HealthCare, NNESMED 2003, (2003) 93-98.
8. Kuncheva, L.I.: Fuzzy Classifier Design, Physica-Verlag (2000).
9. E. Wadge, V. Kodogiannis, D. Tomtsis: Neuro-Fuzzy Ellipsoid Basis Function multiple classifier for diagnosis of urinary Tract Infections, Proc. ICCMSE 2003, Greece, (2003) 673-677.
10. Xu, L.: RBF Nets, Mixture Experts, and Bayesian Ying-Yang Learning, Neurocomputing, **19** (1998) 223-257.
11. Szczepaniak, P., Lisboa, P. Kacprzyk, J.: Fuzzy Systems in Medicine, Springer (2000).

Unsupervised Learning of Multiple Aspects of Moving Objects from Video

Michalis K. Titsias and Christopher K.I. Williams

School of Informatics, University of Edinburgh,
Edinburgh EH1 2QL, UK
M.Titsias@sms.ed.ac.uk, c.k.i.williams@ed.ac.uk

Abstract. A popular framework for the interpretation of image sequences is based on the layered model; see e.g. Wang and Adelson [8], Irani et al. [2]. Jojic and Frey [3] provide a generative probabilistic model framework for this task. However, this layered models do not explicitly account for variation due to changes in the pose and self occlusion. In this paper we show that if the motion of the object is large so that different aspects (or views) of the object are visible at different times in the sequence, we can learn appearance models of the different aspects using a mixture modelling approach.

1 Introduction

We are given as input a set of images containing views of multiple objects, and wish to learn appearance models of each of the objects. A popular framework for this problem is the layer-based approach which models an image as a composite of 2D layers each one modelling an object in terms of its appearance and region of support or mask, see e.g. [8] and [2].

A principled generative probabilistic framework for this task has been described in [3], where the background layer and the foreground layers are synthesized using a multiplicative or alpha matting rule which allows transparency of the objects. Learning using an exact Expectation-Maximization (EM) algorithm is intractable and the method in [3] uses a variational inference scheme considering translational motion of the objects. An alternative approach is that presented in [9] where the layers strictly combine by occlusion and learning of the objects is carried out sequentially by extracting one object at each stage.

Layered models do not explicitly represent variation in object appearance due to changes in the pose of the object and self occlusion. In this paper we describe how the generative model in [9] can be properly modified so that the pose of an object can vary significantly. We achieve this by introducing a set of mask and appearance pairs each one associated with a different viewpoint of the object. Such a model learns a set of different views (or aspects, [4]) of an object.

To learn different viewpoint object models we consider video training data and we first apply approximate tracking of the objects before knowing their full structure. This provides an estimate of the transformation of the object in each frame so that by reversing the effect of the transformation (frame stabilization) the viewpoint models for that object can be learned using a mixture modelling approach. The tracking algorithm finds first the background while moving foreground objects are tracked at later stages. For the foreground objects our tracking algorithm is based on a dynamic appearance model of the object (appearance and mask) which is updated recursively as we process the frames.

The structure of the remainder of the paper is as follows: In section 2 we describe the layered generative model which can learn a single aspect for each foreground object. In section 3 we extent this model so that to learn multiple views of the same object. In section 4 we describe an algorithm for tracking multiple objects in image sequence. In section 5 we show some results in two video sequences and we conclude with a discussion in section 6.

2 Generative Layered Model

For simplicity we will present the generative model assuming that there are two layers, i.e. a foreground object and a static background. Later in this section we will discuss the case of arbitrary number of foreground layers and a moving background.

Let **b** denote the appearance image of the background arranged as a vector. Assuming that the background is static, **b** will have the same size as the data image size (although note that for moving backgrounds, **b** will need to be larger than the image size). Each entry b_i stores the ith pixel value which can either be a grayscale intensity value or a colour value. In our implementation we allow coloured images where $\mathbf{b}_i$ is a three-dimensional vector in the RGB space. However, for notation convenience next we assume that b_i is a scalar representing a grayscale value.

In contrast to the background, the foreground object occupies some region of the image and thus to describe this layer we need both an appearance **f** and mask π. The foreground is allowed to move so there is an underlying transformation j that e.g. corresponds to translational or affine motion and a corresponding transformation matrix so that $T_j \mathbf{f}$ and $T_j \pi$ is the transformed foreground and mask, respectively. We assume that the foreground and background strictly combine by occlusion, thus a pixel in an observed image is either foreground or the background. This is expressed by a vector of binary latent variables **s**, one for each pixel drawn from the distribution [9]

$$P(\mathbf{s}|j) = \prod_{i=1}^{P}(T_j\pi)_i^{s_i}(1 - T_j\pi)_i^{1-s_i}. \tag{1}$$

Note that each variable s_i is drawn independently so that for pixel i, if $(T_j\pi)_i \simeq 0$, then the pixel will be ascribed to the background with high probability, and if $(T_j\pi)_i \simeq 1$, it will be ascribed to the foreground with high probability. Note that **s** is the binary mask of the foreground object in an example image, while π is the prior untransformed mask that captures roughly the shape of the object stored in **f**.

Selecting a transformation j using an uniform prior P_j over J possible values and a binary mask **s**, an image **x** is drawn by a Gaussian

$$p(\mathbf{x}|j,\mathbf{s}) = \prod_{i=1}^{P} N(x_i;(T_j\mathbf{f})_i,\sigma_f^2)^{s_i} N(x_i;b_i,\sigma_b^2)^{1-s_i}, \tag{2}$$

where each pixel is drawn independently from the above conditional density.

To express the likelihood of an observed image $p(\mathbf{x})$ we marginalise out the latent variables which are the transformation j and the binary mask $\mathbf{s}$. Particularly, we first sum out $\mathbf{s}$ using (1) and (2) and obtain

$$p(\mathbf{x}|j) = \prod_{i=1}^{P} (T_j\boldsymbol{\pi})_i N(x_i; (T_j\mathbf{f})_i, \sigma_f^2) + (1 - T_j\boldsymbol{\pi})_i N(x_i; b_i, \sigma_b^2). \quad (3)$$

Using now a uniform prior over the transformation P_j, the probability of an observed image $\mathbf{x}$ is $p(\mathbf{x}) = \sum_{j=1}^{J} P_j p(\mathbf{x}|j)$. Given a set of images $\{\mathbf{x}^1, \ldots, \mathbf{x}^N\}$ we can adapt the parameters $\theta = \{\mathbf{b}, \mathbf{f}, \boldsymbol{\pi}, \sigma_f^2, \sigma_b^2\}$ maximizing the log likelihood using the EM algorithm.

This model can be extended so that to have a moving background and L foreground objects. For example, for two foreground layers with parameters $(\mathbf{f}_1, \boldsymbol{\pi}_1, \sigma_1^2)$ and $(\mathbf{f}_2, \boldsymbol{\pi}_2, \sigma_2^2)$ and also a moving background the analogous of equation (3) is

$$p(\mathbf{x}|j_1, j_2, j_b) = \prod_{i=1}^{P} (T_{j_1}\boldsymbol{\pi}_1)_i N(x_i; (T_{j_1}\mathbf{f}_1)_i, \sigma_1^2) + (1 - T_{j_1}\boldsymbol{\pi}_1)_i \times$$
$$\left[(T_{j_2}\boldsymbol{\pi}_2)_i N(x_i; (T_{j_2}\mathbf{f}_2)_i, \sigma_2^2) + (1 - T_{j_2}\boldsymbol{\pi}_2)_i N(x_i; (T_b\mathbf{b})_i, \sigma_b^2) \right], \quad (4)$$

where j_1, j_2 and j_b denote the transformation of the first foreground object, the second foreground object and the background, respectively.

Applying an exact EM algorithm to learn the parameters of the above model is in general intractable. For example, for the case of L foreground objects that can be transformed in J ways, there exist J^{L+1} configurations that can generate an observed image, which grows exponentially with the number of objects. For this reason approximate algorithms should be considered, e.g. in [3] an approximate variational method has been applied.

3 Incorporating Multiple Viewpoints

In this section we generalize the layer-based model for multiple moving objects so that the viewpoint of each foreground object can arbitrarily change. Section 3.1 describes the generative layered model for changeable viewpoints and section 3.2 discusses training the model.

3.1 Multiple Viewpoints

The layered model presented in section 2 assumes that each layer can change mainly due to a 2D planar motion. However, in many video sequences this assumption will be hardly true e.g. a foreground object can undergo 3D rotation so that at different times we may see the object from different viewpoints. For example, Figure 2a shows three frames of a sequence capturing a man walking; clearly the man's pose changes substantially during time. Next we generalize the layered model so that the appearance of a foreground object can be chosen from a set of possible appearances associated with different viewpoints.

Assume again that there are two layers: one static background and one moving foreground object. We introduce a discrete latent variable v, that can obtain V possible values indexed by integers from 1 to V. For each value v we introduce a separate pair of appearance $\mathbf{f}^v$ and mask $\boldsymbol{\pi}^v$ defined as in section 2. Each pair $(\mathbf{f}^v, \boldsymbol{\pi}^v)$ models the appearance of the object under a certain viewpoint.

To generate an image $\mathbf{x}$ we first select a transformation j and a viewpoint v using uniform prior probabilities P_j and P_v respectively. Then we select a binary mask $\mathbf{s}$ from the distribution

$$P(\mathbf{s}|j,v) = \prod_{i=1}^{P}(T_j\boldsymbol{\pi}^v)_i^{s_i}(1 - T_j\boldsymbol{\pi}^v)_i^{1-s_i}, \qquad (5)$$

and draw an image $\mathbf{x}$ from the Gausssian

$$p(\mathbf{x}|j,v,\mathbf{s}) = \prod_{i=1}^{P} N(x_i; (T_j\mathbf{f}^v)_i, \sigma_f^2)^{s_i} N(x_i; b_i, \sigma_b^2)^{1-s_i}. \qquad (6)$$

Note the similarity of the above expression with equation (2). The only difference is that now the appearance $\mathbf{f}$ and mask $\boldsymbol{\pi}$ are indexed by v to reflect the fact that we have also chosen a viewpoint for the foreground object.

To express the probability distribution according to which an image is generated we sum first out the binary mask and the viewpoint variable and obtain

$$p(\mathbf{x}|j) = \sum_{v=1}^{V} P_v p(\mathbf{x}|j,v), \qquad (7)$$

where $p(\mathbf{x}|j,v)$ is given as in (3) with $\mathbf{f}$ and $\boldsymbol{\pi}$ indexed by v. Notice how the equation (7) relates to equation (3). Clearly now $p(\mathbf{x}|j)$ is a mixture model of the type of model given in (3). For example, if we choose to have a single viewpoint the latter expression reduces to the former one.

It is straightforward to extent the above model to the case of L foreground layers with varying viewpoints. In this case we need a separate viewpoint variable v_ℓ for each foreground object and a set of appearance and mask pairs: $\{\mathbf{f}_\ell^{v_\ell}, \boldsymbol{\pi}_\ell^{v_\ell}\}$, $v_\ell = 1, \ldots, V_\ell$. For example, when we have two foreground objects and a moving background the conditional $p(\mathbf{x}|j_1, j_2, j_b, v_1, v_2)$ is given exactly as in (4) by introducing suitable indexes to the foreground appearances and masks that indicate the choices made for the viewpoint variables.

3.2 Learning the Model

Training the above model using an exact EM algorithm is intractable. For L foreground objects and a moving background, each one undergoing J transformations and assuming V aspects for each foreground object, the time complexity is $O(J^{L+1}V^L)$. Approximate training methods such as the variational EM algorithm of [3] or the one-object-at-a-time method of [9] could be applied. However, it is clear that adding V views of each object will complicate the training process, and there is a danger of confusion between views of one object and different objects.

A reliable method for training the model can be based on two stage learning framework. In the first stage we compute the 2D planar transformations of a foreground object in images, while in the second stage we learn the different viewpoint models by carrying out simple clustering. Particularly, we first approximate the transformation of an object in each frame, which is simply a motion according to which this frame is matched to a reference frame. Given these transformations it is easy to reverse their effect so as to transform each image into a reference frame where the viewpoint models for that object can be learned using a mixture model. Intuitively, what is happening here is that we are transforming the video so as to stabilize a given object; this greatly facilitates the learning of the viewpoint models for that object.

Assuming a set of training images $\{\mathbf{x}^1, \ldots, \mathbf{x}^N\}$ the steps of this algorithm are the following:

1. Track first the background b in order to approximate the transformation j_b^n of each image $\mathbf{x}^n$ and then learn the background by maximizing the log likelihood

$$L_b = \sum_{n=1}^{N} \log p_b(\mathbf{x}^n | j_b^n) = \sum_{n=1}^{N} \log \prod_{i=1}^{P} p_b(x_i^n; (T_{j_b^n} \mathbf{b})_i) \tag{8}$$

and $p_b(x_i; (T_{j_b} \mathbf{b})_i)$ is given by equation (12).

2. Compute all the planar transformations $\{j_\ell^n\}$ of a foreground object ℓ using tracking (see section 4)

3. Learn the parameters of the object by maximizing the log likelihood

$$L_\ell = \sum_{n=1}^{N} \log \sum_{v_\ell=1}^{V_\ell} P_{v_\ell} p(\mathbf{x} | j_\ell^n, j_b^n, v_\ell). \tag{9}$$

In (9) the conditional density $p(\mathbf{x}|j_\ell^n, j_b^n, v_\ell)$ is given by

$$p(\mathbf{x}|j_\ell^n, j_b^n, v_\ell) = \prod_{i=1}^{P} (T_{j_\ell} \pi_\ell^{v_\ell})_i p_{f_\ell}(x_i; (T_{j_\ell} \mathbf{f}_\ell^{v_\ell})_i) + (1 - T_{j_\ell} \pi_\ell^{v_\ell})_i p_b(x_i; (T_{j_b^n} \mathbf{b})_i), \tag{10}$$

where we have replaced the Gaussian foreground and background pixel densities by the following robustified counterparts

$$p_f(x_i; f_i) = \alpha_f N(x_i; f_i, \sigma_f^2) + (1 - \alpha_f) U(x_i). \tag{11}$$

and

$$p_b(x_i; f_i) = \alpha_b N(x_i; b_i, \sigma_b^2) + (1 - \alpha_b) U(x_i). \tag{12}$$

Here $U(x_i)$ is an uniform distribution in the range of all possible pixel values and α_f and α_b express prior probabilities that a foreground (resp. background) pixel is not occluded. This robustification allow us to deal with occlusion caused by all the other foreground objects except the ℓth object. Clearly, these objects can occlude the background and sometimes also the foreground object of interest. Thus, any time a foreground or background pixel will be occluded that will be explained by the uniform component $U(x_i)$ [5,9].

It is straightforward to maximize the log likelihood in (9) using the EM algorithm to deal with the missing information concerning the viewpoint variable, the binary mask s and the indicators of the outlier process. Once models for all objects have been learned in this fashion it is possible to refine the masks and appearances by optimizing them jointly, using an analogue of equation (4).

So far we have not discussed how we learn the background and approximate the transformations of the foreground objects. We doing this based on tracking that is described in the next section.

4 Tracking the Objects

In this section we present a tracking algorithm that applies to a sequence of frames $(\mathbf{x}^1, \ldots, \mathbf{x}^N)$ and approximates the corresponding set of transformations $(j^1, \ldots, j^N)$ that describe the motion of a single object.

We wish first to track the background and ignore all the other motions related to the foreground objects. To introduce the idea of our tracking algorithm assume that we know the appearance of the background $\mathbf{b}$ as well as the transformation j_b^1 that associates $\mathbf{b}$ with the first frame. Since motion between successive frames is expected to be relatively small we can determine the transformation j_b^2 for the second frame by searching over a small discrete set of neighbouring transformations centred at j_b^1 and inferring the most probable one, i.e. the one giving the highest likelihood $p_b(\mathbf{x}^2 | j_b^2)$ (see equation (8)), assuming a uniform prior. This procedure can be applied recursively to determine the sequence of transformations in the entire video. However, the background $\mathbf{b}$ is not known in advance, but we can still apply roughly the same tracking algorithm by suitably initializing and updating the background $\mathbf{b}$ as we process the frames. This algorithm is described in detain in [7]. Once tracking of the background is completed we can learn its full structure by maximizing the log likelihood (8).

Assume now that the background has been learned. The pixels which are explained by the background in each image $\mathbf{x}^t$ are flagged by the background responsibilities $\mathbf{r}^t(j_b^t)$ computed by the equation

$$r_i(j_b) = \frac{\alpha_b N(x_i; (T_{j_b}\mathbf{b})_i, \sigma_b^2)}{\alpha_b N(x_i; (T_{j_b}\mathbf{b})_i, \sigma_b^2) + (1-\alpha_b)U(x_i)}. \quad (13)$$

Clearly the mask $\bar{\mathbf{r}}^t(j_b^t) = 1 - \mathbf{r}^t(j_b^t)$ roughly indicates all the pixels of frame $\mathbf{x}^t$ that belong to the foreground objects. By focusing only on these pixels we wish to start tracking one of the foreground objects through the entire video sequence and ignore for the moment the rest foreground objects.

Our algorithm tracks the first object by simultaneously updating its mask π_1 and appearance $\mathbf{f}_1$. The mask and the appearance are initialized so that $\pi_1 = 0.5 * \bar{\mathbf{r}}^t(j_b^t)$ and $\mathbf{f}_1 = \mathbf{x}^1$, where $\mathbf{0.5}$ denotes the vector with 0.5 values[1]. Due to this initialization

---
[1] The value of 0.5 is chosen to express our uncertainty about whether these pixels will ultimately be in the foreground mask or not.

we know that the first frame is untransformed, i.e. j_1^1 is the identity transformation. To determine the transformation of the second frame and in general the transformation j_1^{t+1}, with $t \geq 1$, of the frame $\mathbf{x}^{t+1}$ we find the most probable value of j_1^{t+1} according to the posterior

$$R(j_1^{t+1}) \propto \exp\left\{\sum_{i=1}^{P} (\mathbf{w}_1^{t+1})_i \log\left((T_{j_1^{t+1}} \pi_1^t)_i \times \right.\right.$$
$$\left.\left. p_f(x_i^{t+1}; (T_{j_1^{t+1}} \mathbf{f}_1^t)_i) + (1 - T_{j_1^{t+1}} \pi_1^t)_i U(x_i^{t+1})\right)\right\}, \quad (14)$$

where $\mathbf{w}_1^{t+1} = \bar{\mathbf{r}}^{t+1}(j_b^{t+1})$. $R(j_1^{t+1})$ measures the goodness of the match at those pixels of frame $\mathbf{x}^{t+1}$ which are not explained by the background. Note that as the objects will, in general, be of different sizes, the probability $R(j_1^{t+1})$ over the transformation variable will have greater mass on transformations relating to the largest object. Recall that $p_f(x_i^{t+1}; (T_{j_1^{t+1}} \mathbf{f}_1)_i)$ includes an outlier component so that some badly misfit pixels can be tolerated.

Once we determine j_1^{t+1} we update both the mask π_1 and appearance $\mathbf{f}_1$. The mask is updated according to

$$\pi_1^{t+1} = \pi_1^t + \beta_\pi \left(T_{j_1^{t+1}}^{-1}[\bar{\mathbf{s}}^{t+1}(j_1^{t+1})] - \pi_1^t\right), \quad (15)$$

where T^{-1} denotes the inverse transformation and β_π takes values in the range $[0, 1]$. The vector $\bar{\mathbf{s}}^{t+1}(j_1^{t+1})$ expresses the segmentation of the object in the frame $\mathbf{x}^{t+1}$ so that each $\bar{s}_i^{t+1}(j_1^{t+1})$ stores the probability

$$\bar{s}_i^{t+1}(j_1^{t+1}) = \frac{(T_{j_1^{t+1}} \pi_1^t)_i p_{f_1}(x_i^{t+1}; (T_{j_1^{t+1}} \mathbf{f}_1^t)_i)}{(T_{j_1^{t+1}} \pi_1^t)_i p_{f_1}(x_i^{t+1}; (T_{j_1^{t+1}} \mathbf{f}_1^t)_i) + (1 - T_{j_1^{t+1}} \pi_1^t)_i p_b(x_i^{t+1}; (T_{j_b^{t+1}} \mathbf{b})_i)}, \quad (16)$$

for the pixel i. The update (15) defines the new mask as a weighted average of the stabilized segmentation in the current frame (i.e. $T_{j_1^{t+1}}^{-1}[\bar{\mathbf{s}}^{t+1}(j_1^{t+1})]$) and the previous value of the mask. β_π is the weight of the stabilized segmentation in each current frame, e.g. if $\beta_\pi = 1$, then $\pi_1^{t+1} = T_{j_1^{t+1}}^{-1} \bar{\mathbf{s}}^{t+1}(j_1^{t+1})$. The update for the foreground appearance $\mathbf{f}_1$ is given by

$$\mathbf{f}_1^{t+1} = \mathbf{f}_1^t + \beta_f \left(T_{j_1^{t+1}}^{-1}[\bar{\mathbf{s}}(j_1^{t+1}) * \mathbf{r}^{t+1}(j_1^{t+1}) * \mathbf{x}^{t+1}] - \mathbf{f}_1^t\right), \quad (17)$$

where $\mathbf{y} * \mathbf{z}$ denotes the element-wise product of the vectors $\mathbf{y}$ and $\mathbf{z}$. The vector $\mathbf{r}^{t+1}(j_1^{t+1})$ is defined similarly to equation (13) and stores the probabilities that the pixels of the object in the current frame have not changed dramatically (e.g. due to occlusion). Again the above update is very intuitive. For pixels which are ascribed to the ℓth foreground (i.e. $\bar{\mathbf{s}}^{t+1}(j_1^{t+1}) * \mathbf{r}^{t+1}(j_1^{t+1}) \simeq 1$), the values in $\mathbf{x}^n$ are transformed by $T_{j_1^{t+1}}^{-1}$ into the stabilized frame which allows the foreground pixels found in the current frame to be averaged with the old value $\mathbf{f}^t$ in order to produce $\mathbf{f}^{t+1}$. Notice that $\mathbf{f}_1$

adapts slowly to large changes of the object appearance (caused e.g. by occlusion) due to the semantics of the vector $\mathbf{r}^{t+1}(j_1^{t+1})$. Note also that as the frames are processed tracking becomes more stable since π_1 approximates the mask of a single object and $\mathbf{f}_1$ will contain a sharp and clear view for only the one object being tracked while the rest of the objects will be blurred; see Figure 1b for an illustrative example.

Once the first object has been tracked we learn the different viewpoint models for that object as explained in section 3.2. When these models has been learned we can go through the images to find which pixels are explained by this object. Then we can remove these pixels from consideration by properly updating each $\mathbf{w}^t$ vector which allows tracking a different object on the next stage. Note also that the new mask π_ℓ when we track the ℓth object is initialized to $0.5 * \mathbf{w}_{\ell+1}^t$, while the appearance $\mathbf{f}_\ell$ is always initialized to the first frame $\mathbf{x}^1$.

5 Experiments

We will consider two video sequences: the Frey-Jojic (FJ) sequence available from http://www.psi.toronto.edu/layers.html (see Figure 1) and the man-walking (see Figure 2). We will also assume that the number of different aspects that we wish to learn for each foreground object is known.

The FJ sequence consists of 44 118 × 248 images (excluding the black border); it was also used in experiments shown in [3,9]. Three frames of this sequence are displayed in Figure 1a. This sequence can be well modelled by assuming a single view for each of the foreground objects, thus we set $V = 1$ for both objects. The results in Figure 1c were obtained using a 15 × 15 window of translations in units of one pixel during the tracking stage. This learning stage requires EM which converged in about 30 iterations. Figure 1b shows the evolution of the initial appearance and mask ($t = 1$) through frames 10 and 20 as we track the first object (Frey). Notice that as we process the frames the mask focuses on only one of the two objects and the appearance remains sharp only for this object. The real running time of our MATLAB implementation for processing the whole sequence was 3 minutes.

The man-walking sequence consists of 85 144 × 360 coloured images. Figure 2a displays three frames of that sequence. We assume that the number of different aspects of the foreground object that we wish to learn is five, i.e. $V = 5$. Figure 2b shows the learned appearance and mask pairs of the different viewpoint models for the foreground object. When we applied the tracking algorithm we used a window of 15 × 15 translations in units of one pixel. Notice that each different pair of mask and appearance has modelled a different pose of the man. However, some of the masks are noisy. We hope to improve on that by adding spatial continuity constraints (e.g. using a MRF for the binary variable s). Processing the whole video took about 20 mins, where the most of the time was spent in fitting the mixture model for learning the object views.

6 Discussion

Above we have extended the generative model for learning multiple moving objects so that to deal with large viewpoint variation. Particularly, we introduced multiple view-

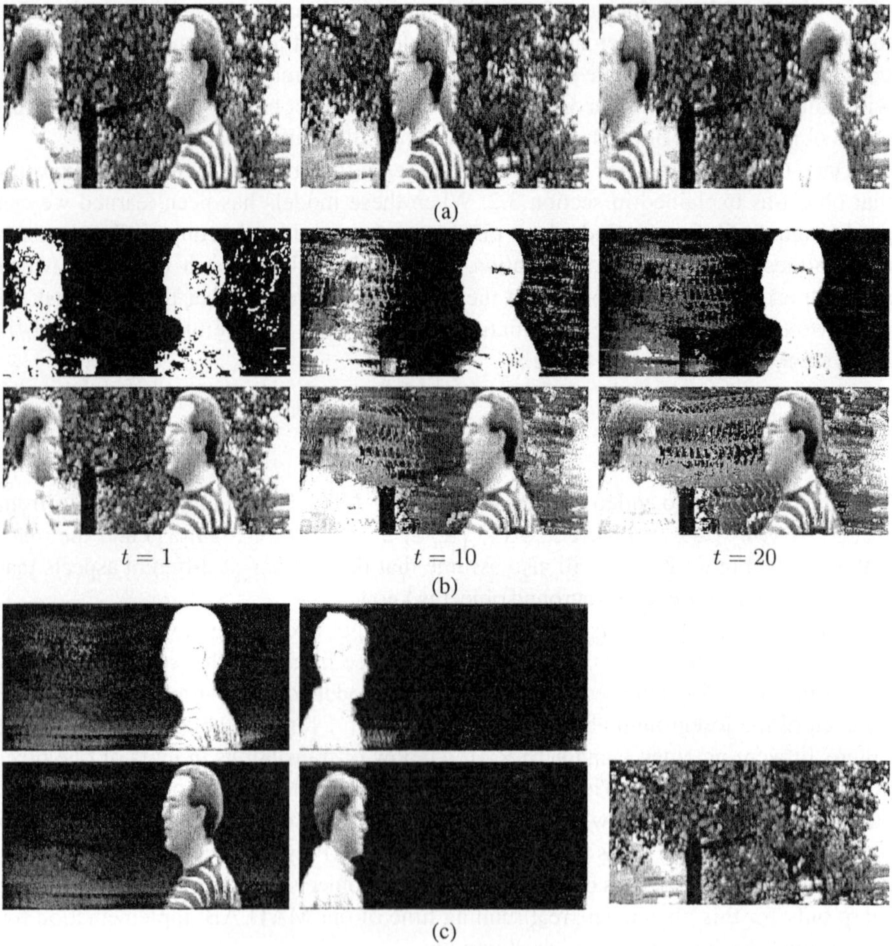

Fig. 1. Panel (a) shows three frames of the Frey-jojic sequence. Panel (b) shows the evolution of the mask π_1 (top row) and the appearance $\mathbf{f}_1$ (bottom row) at times 1, 10 and 20 as we track the first object (Frey). Notice how the mask becomes focused on one of the objects (Frey) and how the appearance remains clear and sharp only for Frey. Panel (c) shows the mask and the element-wise product of the mask and appearance model ($\pi * \mathbf{f}$) learned for Frey (first column from the left) and Jojic (second column) using the algorithm described in the text. The plot in the third column shows the learned background.

point models for each foreground object. These models are learned using a mixture modelling approach applied to the stabilized frames. To stabilize the frames we approximate the transformations of each object in the video using a tracking algorithm.

The mechanism for dealing with multiple viewpoints using mixture models has been considered before in [1]. However, in this method they consider a single object present in the images against a clutter background and only appearance images of different poses of the object are learned (not masks). In contrast, our method can be applied to

Fig. 2. Panel (a) shows three frames of the man-walking sequence. Panel (b) shows the the pairs of mask and the element-wise product of the mask and appearance model (showing against a grey background) for all different viewpoint models.

images with multiple objects and learn the background as well as the appearances and masks of the foreground objects.

Regarding tracking methods for learning moving layers, the method of [2] is much relevant to ours. They do motion estimation using optical flow by matching the current frame against an accumulative appearance image of the tracked object. Although they do not take into account issues of occlusion, so that if a tracked object becomes occluded for some frames, it may be lost. The work of [6] is also relevant in that it deals with a background model and object models defined in terms of masks and appearances. However, note that the mask is assumed to be of elliptical shape (parameterised as a Gaussian) rather than a general mask. The mask and appearance models are dynamically updated during tracking, however the initialization of each model is handled by a "separate module", and is not obtained automatically.

Some issues for further work include dealing with objects that have internal variability, and modelling non-articulated moving objects. Another issue is to automatically identify how many views are needed to efficiently model the appearance of each object and also to determine the number of objects in the images.

References

1. B. J. Frey and N. Jojic. Transformation Invariant Clustering Using the EM Algorithm. *IEEE Trans Pattern Analysis and Machine Intelligence*, 25(1):1–17, 2003.
2. M. Irani, B. Rousso, and S. Peleg. Computing Occluding and Transparent Motions. *International Journal of Computer Vision*, 12(1):5–16, 1994.
3. N. Jojic and B. J. Frey. Learning Flexible Sprites in Video Layers. In *Proceedings of the IEEE Conference on Computer Vision and Pattern Recognition 2001*. IEEE Computer Society Press, 2001. Kauai, Hawaii.
4. J. J. Koenderink and A. J. van Doorn. The internal representation of solid shape with respect to vision. *Biological Cybernetics*, 32:211–216, 1979.
5. S. Rowe and A. Blake. Statistical Background Modelling For Tracking With A Virtual Camera. In D. Pycock, editor, *Proceedings of the 6th British Machine Vision Conference*, volume volume 2, pages 423–432. BMVA Press, 1995.
6. H. Tao, H. S. Sawhney, and R. Kumar. Dynamic Layer Representation with Applications to Tracking. In *Proceedings of the IEEE Conference on Computer Vision and Pattern Recognition*, pages II:134–141, 2000.
7. M. K. Titsias and C. K. I. Williams. Fast unsupervised greedy learning of multiple objects and parts from video. In *Proc. Generative-Model Based Vision Workshop*, 2004.
8. J. Y. A. Wang and E. H. Adelson. Representing Moving Images with Layers. *IEEE Transactions on Image Processing*, 3(5):625–638, 1994.
9. C. K. I. Williams and M. K. Titsias. Greedy Learning of Multiple Objects in Images using Robust Statistics and Factorial Learning. *Neural Computation*, 16(5):1039–1062, 2004.

The Feature Vector Selection for Robust Multiple Face Detection

Seung-Ik Lee and Duk-Gyoo Kim

School of Electronic Engineering and Computer Science,
Kyungpook National University,
1370, Sankyug-Dong, Buk-Gu, Daegu, 702-701, Korea
{tonme, dgkim}@ee.knu.ac.kr

Abstract. This paper presents the robust feature vector selection for multiple frontal face detection based on the Bayesian statistical method. The feature vector for the training and classification are integrated by means, amplitude projections, and its 1D Harr wavelet of input image. And the statistical modeling is performed both for face and nonface classes. Finally, the estimated probability density functions (PDFs) are applied by the proposed Bayesian method to detect multiple frontal faces in an image. The proposed method can handle multiple faces, partially occluded faces, and slightly posed-angle faces. Especially, the proposed method is very effective for low quality face images. Experiments show that detection rate of the propose method is 98.3% with three false detections on SET3 testing data which have 227 faces in 80 images.

1 Introduction

Face detection is becoming a key task in many applications such as authentication, video surveillance, and video conferencing and so on. Also it is the first step in any automated system. For the face detection, several applications and researches have been developed in recent years and categorization of face detection methods was clearly summarized by Yang and Kriegman [1]. Among the face detection methods, the one based on learning algorithms have attracted much attention recently and have demonstrated excellent results. Scheneiderman and Kanade described a naive Bayes classifier to estimate the joint probability of local appearance and position of face patterns at multiple resolutions [2]. But one of the problems of the statistical method is the dimensionality for the learning algorithm and dimensionality reduction is usually carried out for the sake of computation efficiency and detection efficacy. Liu presented a Bayesian discriminating features method based on the learning algorithms and feature vectors were composed of the input image, its 1D Harr wavelets, and its amplitude projections [3]. And principal component analysis (PCA) was applied for the dimensionality reduction in his paper. In this paper, a new method for feature vectors of the input image is proposed for robust face detection and the dimensionality of feature vectors is reduced by proposed method while the performance of the face detection is the same or better for occluded face patterns than that of other statistical methods. For the training, 1200 frontal faces from the BioID face database and 5,000 nonface images from the natural scene images were used for nonface class modeling. First, the feature vectors are selected with input images, its vertical and horizontal amplitude projections, and its 1D Harr wavelet. Instead of using the whole amplitude projections of input image and 1D Harr wavelet, we selected the half of vertical and horizontal amplitude projection and half of 1D Harr wavelet. In the computer simulation, we found that the half part of the horizontal and vertical amplitude projections is good enough to be the important information of the face. Also only half of 1D Harr wavelet of vertical and horizontal direction is used for feature vectors. With these vectors, the feature vectors are formed to be the criterion of face and nonface class by the proposed method. After feature vectors are formed, the covariance matrixes of face and nonface class are calculated for classification. Second, the naive Bayes classifier is applied to classify the face and nonface class. And PCA method to reduce the dimensionality was used to reduce computational complexity of the covariance matrix.

2 Proposed Feature Vector Composition

The training image for face and nonface image is resolution of 16 × 16. For the face training, BioID face database was used for face training and natural images for nonface training were used shown in Fig. 1. We extracted 1,200 frontal faces from the BioID face database and 5,000 face-like images are chosen from the natural images.

The Harr wavelet is effective for human face [4] and amplitude projections of input image present the vertical and horizontal characteristics of human face [3]. In this paper, we use half parts of the Harr wavelet and amplitude projections of the input images instead of whole parts of those. Let $I(i,j)$ represent an input image with resolution 16 × 16 shown and Fig. 2 shows the block diagram of the proposed feature vector composition and training process of each class. And amplitude projections of and 1D Harr wavelet vectors of each vertical and horizontal direction are defined as follow, respectively:

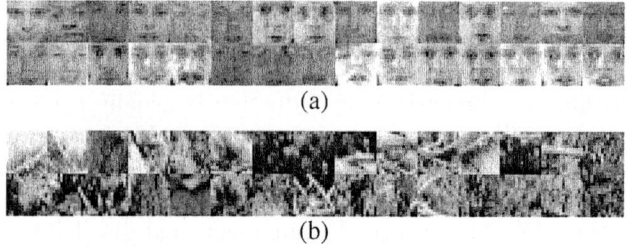

Fig. 1. Face and nonface images with resolution of 16 × 16. (a) Examples of face data from BioID face database (b) Nonface examples from natural images.

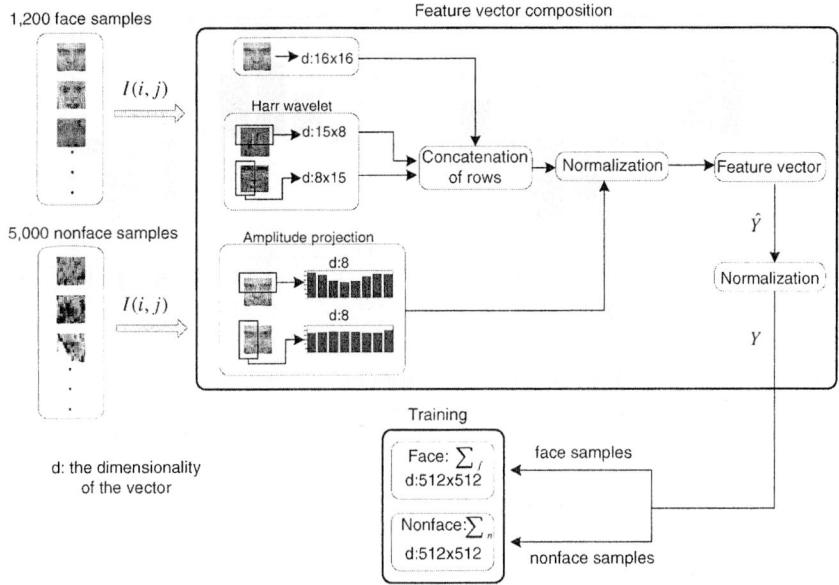

Fig. 2. The block diagram of feature vector composition and training process of each class

$$X_{ah}(i) = \sum_{i=1}^{16} I(i,j) \qquad 1 \leq i \leq 8 \qquad (1)$$

$$X_{av}(j) = \sum_{j=1}^{16} I(i,j) \qquad 1 \leq j \leq 8 \qquad (2)$$

$$X_{H\_h}(j) = I(i+1,j) - I(i,j) \qquad 1 \leq i \leq 16, 1 \leq j \leq 8 \qquad (3)$$

$$X_{H\_v}(i) = I(i,j+1) - I(i,j) \qquad 1 \leq i \leq 8, 1 \leq j \leq 16 \qquad (4)$$

After each vector is acquired, normalization by subtracting the means of their component and dividing by their standard deviation is performed before forming the feature vector Y. After that, the feature vector Y is obtained after the normalized procedure mentioned above. The feature vector $\hat{Y}$ is defined as follow:

$$\hat{Y} = (\hat{X}^t \ \hat{X}^t_{ah} \ \hat{X}^t_{av} \ \hat{X}^t_{H\_h} \ \hat{X}^t_{H\_v})^t \qquad (5)$$

where t is transpose of matrix and the dimensionality of the vector Y is 512.

In this paper, we use only half part of the amplitude projections and 1D Harr wavelet vectors and this makes dimensionality reduction of vectors. And also the detection performances of the low quality face images and the occluded faces detection are better than [3]. The amplitude characteristics of face are shown in Fig. 3 and we choose only 8 rows and 8 columns from upper and left side, respectively.

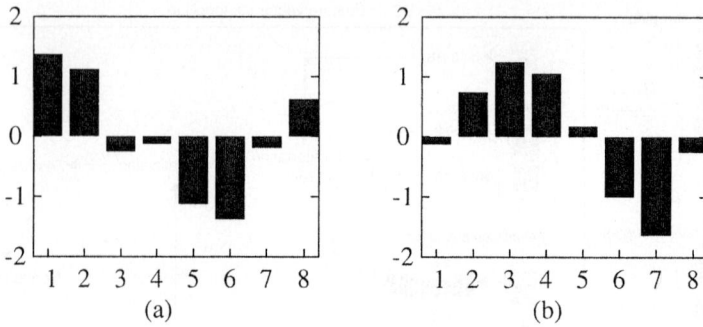

Fig. 3. An example of amplitude characteristics of face after normalization. (a) Horizontal characteristic and (b) vertical characteristic.

3 Feature Classification

The classification based on the statistical methods is to estimate the conditional PDFs and we use the Liu's method [3] in this paper for the classification. The conditional PDF of the face and nonface class is modeled as a multivariate normal distribution:

$$p(Y|W_f) = \frac{1}{(2\pi)^{N/2}|\Sigma_f|^{1/2}} exp\left(-\frac{1}{2}(Y-M_f)^t \Sigma_f^{-1}(Y-M_f)\right) \quad (6)$$

$$p(Y|W_n) = \frac{1}{(2\pi)^{N/2}|\Sigma_n|^{1/2}} exp\left(-\frac{1}{2}(Y-M_n)^t \Sigma_n^{-1}(Y-M_n)\right) \quad (7)$$

where N is dimensionality of Y. And M_f and M_n are mean vector of face and nonface, respectively. Also Σ_f and Σ_n are covariance matrix of each class.

The equation (6) and (7) can be expressed as log formations:

$$\ln[p(Y|W_f)] = -\frac{1}{2}\left((Y-M_f)^t \Sigma_f^{-1}(Y-M_f) \right.$$
$$\left. +N\ln(2\pi) + ln(|\Sigma_f|)\right) \quad (8)$$

$$\ln[p(Y|W_n)] = -\frac{1}{2}\left((Y-M_n)^t \Sigma_n^{-1}(Y-M_n) \right.$$
$$\left. +N\ln(2\pi) + ln(|\Sigma_n|)\right) \quad (9)$$

The covariance matrix can be decomposed by PCA and only small components are used to calculate the PDFs of the input images [5]:

$$\Sigma_f = \Phi_f \Lambda_f \Phi_f, \quad \Phi_f \Phi_f^t = \Phi_f^t \Phi_f = I_N \qquad (10)$$

$$\Sigma_n = \Phi_n \Lambda_n \Phi_n, \quad \Phi_n \Phi_n^t = \Phi_n^t \Phi_n = I_N \qquad (11)$$

where $\Lambda^f = diag\{\lambda_1^f, \lambda_2^f, \lambda_3^f, \ldots, \lambda_N^f\}$ and $\Lambda^n = diag\{\lambda_1^n, \lambda_2^n, \lambda_3^n, \ldots, \lambda_N^n\}$.

In equation (10) and (11), Φ is an orthogonal eigenvector matrix and Λ is a diagonal eigenvalue matrix with diagonal elements in decreasing order ($\lambda_1 \geq \lambda_2 \geq \lambda_3 \geq \ldots \geq \lambda_N$). And I_N is an identity matrix and principal components are defined as follow:

$$C_f = \Phi_f^t(Y - M_f), \quad C_n = \Phi_n^t(Y - M_n) \qquad (12)$$

From the equation (12), only first M principal components are used to estimate the conditional PDFs for each class and the remaining $N - M$ eigenvalues for C_f and C_n are estimated by [5], respectively:

$$\rho_f = \frac{1}{N-M} \sum_{k=M+1}^{N} \lambda_k^f, \quad \rho_n = \frac{1}{N-M} \sum_{k=M+1}^{N} \lambda_k^n \qquad (13)$$

where we set $M = 10$ and N is 512. Finally, from (8), (9), (10), (11), (12), and (13), the conditional PDFs for face and nonface class are obtained as follow forms for classification:

$$\ln[p(Y|W_f)] = -\frac{1}{2}\left\{\sum_{i=1}^{M} \frac{C_i^f}{\lambda_i^f} + \frac{\|Y - M_f\| - \sum_{i=1}^{M}(C_i^f)^2}{\rho_f}\right.$$
$$\left. + \ln\left(\prod_{i=1}^{M} \lambda_i^f\right) + (N-M)\ln(\rho_f) + N\ln(2\pi)\right\} \qquad (14)$$

$$\ln[p(Y|W_n)] = -\frac{1}{2}\left\{\sum_{i=1}^{M} \frac{C_i^n}{\lambda_i^n} + \frac{\|Y - M_n\| - \sum_{i=1}^{M}(C_i^n)^2}{\rho_n}\right.$$
$$\left. + \ln\left(\prod_{i=1}^{M} \lambda_i^n\right) + (N-M)\ln(\rho_n) + N\ln(2\pi)\right\} \qquad (15)$$

where C_i^f and C_i^n are the components of C_f and C_n, respectively.

And a posterior probability for each class can be obtained by the Bayes theorem:

$$P(W_f|Y) = \frac{P(W_f)p(Y|W_f)}{p(Y)}, \quad P(W_n|Y) = \frac{P(W_n)p(Y|W_n)}{p(Y)} \qquad (16)$$

From (8),(9), and (16), the decision rule is defined:

$$Y \text{ is } \begin{cases} face & if \ (\sigma_f < 500) \ and \ (\sigma_f + 50 < \sigma_n) \\ nonface & otherwise \end{cases} \qquad (17)$$

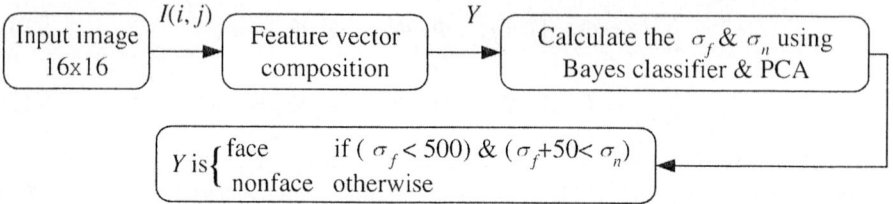

Fig. 4. The block diagram of the detection process

where σ_f and σ_n are defined as follows:

$$\sigma_f = -\frac{1}{2}\left\{\sum_{i=1}^{M}\frac{C_i^f}{\lambda_i^f} + \frac{\|Y - M_f\| - \sum_{i=1}^{M}(C_i^f)^2}{\rho_f}\right.$$
$$\left. + \ln\left(\prod_{i=1}^{M}\lambda_i^f\right) + (N-M)\ln(\rho_f)\right\} \quad (18)$$

$$\sigma_n = -\frac{1}{2}\left\{\sum_{i=1}^{M}\frac{C_i^n}{\lambda_i^n} + \frac{\|Y - M_n\| - \sum_{i=1}^{M}(C_i^n)^2}{\rho_n}\right.$$
$$\left. + \ln\left(\prod_{i=1}^{M}\lambda_i^n\right) + (N-M)\ln(\rho_n)\right\} \quad (19)$$

The block diagram of the detection process is shown in Fig. 4 and the resolution of input image is 16 × 16. And to detect the variable size of face and rotated face, the image is rescaled and rotated at the predefined angles.

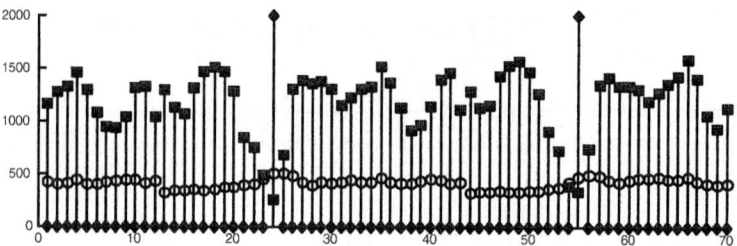

Fig. 5. An example of the value σ_f and σ_n. The box shapes represent the σ_f and circle represents the σ_n. The two lines with max vertical-value represent the location of faces in the image.

The Feature Vector Selection for Robust Multiple Face Detection   763

Fig. 6. Examples of the face detection

4 Experiments and Discussion

The training samples are 1,200 frontal faces obtained from BioID databases and 5,000 training samples generated from the natural images are used for nonface in this paper. To compare the performance, we use SET3 from the MIT-CMU test sets [6] and Fig. 4 shows the example of value σ_f and σ_n. In Fig. 5, the location of face is detected when $\sigma_f < 500$ and the condition, $\sigma_f + 50 < \sigma_n$, is chosen for better performance. The threshold 50 is chosen empirically. And also the predefined rotation degrees are chosen such as $\pm 5°$, $\pm 10°$, $\pm 15°$, and $\pm 20°$ to detect the slightly rotated faces in the input image. And the trained images of face and nonface have the standard resolution of 16×16 and each input image needs to be rescaled to detect the variable size of the faces. Fig. 6 shows the results of the face detection from the SET3 test images and the bottom-left face in Fig. 1(a) and the old man's face in Fig. 1(c) (upper-left) are detected by the propose method while those are missed in [3]. And the false detection is shown in Fig. 1(d).

The performance of face detection is compared with Liu's and experiments shows that detection rate of the propose method is 98.3% on SET3 testing data which have 227 faces in 80 images while Liu's detection rate is 97.4% on the same testing date set. And also the dimensionality of the input feature vector is 512 in the proposed method but Liu's is 768. And with this advantage, we reduce the dimensionality of the matrix by using the proposed feature selection together with PCA. But during the experiments on SET3, we have three false detections although while Liu's have one false detection. In the future research, the optimal threshold value is needed to reduce the false detection.

References

1. M.H. Yang, N. Ahuja, and D. Kreigman: Face Detection Using Mixture of Linear Subspaces. Proc. Fifth Int'l Conf. Automatic Face and Gesture Recognition (2000) 70-76
2. H.Schneiderman and T. Kanade: Probabilistic Modeling of Local Appearance and Spatial Relationships for Object Recognition. Proc. Conf. Computer vision and Pattern Recognition (1998) 45-51
3. C. Liu: A Bayesian Discrimination Features Method for Face Detection. IEEE Trans. Pattern Analysis and Machine Intelligence, vol. 25, no. 6 (2003) 725-740
4. C. Liu and H. Wechsler: Robust Coding Schemes for Indexing and Retrieval from Large Face Database. IEEE Trans. Image Processing, vol. 9, no. 1 (2000) 132-137
5. B. Moghaddam and A. Pentland: Probabilistic Visual Learning for Object Representation. IEEE Trans. Pattern Analysis and Machine Intelligence, vol. 19, no. 7 (1997) 696-710
6. H. A. Rowley, S. Baluja, and T. Kanade: Neural Network-Based Face Detection. IEEE Trans. Pattern Analysis and Machine Intelligence, vol. 20, no. 1 (1998) 23-38

A Low Complexity Turbo Equalizer

Dimitris Ampeliotis and Kostas Berberidis

Dept. of Computer Engineering and Informatics and CTI/R&D,
University of Patras, 26500, Rio-Patras, Greece
phone: + 30 2610 960425, fax: + 30 2610 991909
{ampeliot, berberid}@ceid.upatras.gr

Abstract. In this paper a new Soft Input - Soft Output (SISO) equalizer of linear complexity is developed. The algorithm can be used in the so-called Turbo Equalization scheme as a low cost solution in place of the Maximum A-Posteriori (MAP) equalization algorithm which has a prohibitive complexity for most real world applications. The proposed equalizer consists of two parts, namely, a Soft Interference Canceller (SIC) and a pre-processing part which is a new Variable-Threshold Decision Feedback Equalizer (VTDFE). The main difference in the proposed equalizer as compared to the SIC is that the input to the cancellation filter is computed not only using a-priori probabilities, but information from the received signal as well. Simulation results have shown that the proposed turbo equalizer exhibits a superior performance as compared to the turbo equalization scheme based on the conventional SIC as well as other linear complexity SISO equalizers.

1 Introduction

Turbo Equalization [1] was motivated by the breakthrough of Turbo Codes [2], and has emerged as a promising technique for drastical reduction of the intersymbol interference effects in frequency selective wireless channels. A *Turbo Equalization* procedure, in its generic form, exhibits the following two traits [3]: a) the decoder and the equalizer exchange *soft information* between each other, with this soft information being interpreted as a-priori probability information, and   b) the decoder and the equalizer exchange *extrinsic information*, that is, their output at time instant n should not directly rely on their soft input for the same time index but only on information gained by using the soft information about symbols at adjacent (past and future) time instants.

Unfortunately, the trellis-based turbo equalizer of [1] can be a heavy computational burden for wireless systems with limited processing power, especially in cases the wireless channel has long delay spread. For such reasons, a number of low complexity alternative equalization methods that can be properly incorporated in the generic Turbo Equalization scheme have been proposed, offering good complexity/performance trade-offs.

In this context, it was proposed in [4] to replace the trellis-based equalizer by an adaptive Soft Interference Canceller with linear complexity. In [5], an improved extension of the algorithm of [4] was presented. In [3] an MMSE-optimal equalizer based on linear filters was derived and it was proved that several other algorithms (such as the one in [4]) could be viewed as approximations of this one.

The SIC of [4] and its fixed (i.e. non-adaptive) version studied later in [3], turn out to be good choices for easy to medium difficulty channels at relatively high SNR. The aim in this work is mainly to improve the above fixed SIC by means of a suitable pre-processor so that it may be applicable to hostile channels with severe ISI and low SNR as well. The role of the pre-processor is to extract information from the received signal and combine this information with the a-priory probabilities coming from the decoder. The proposed pre-processor is a Variable-Threshold DFE (VTDFE) of linear complexity whose decisions' thresholds are varying by using a Bayesian classification rule that incorporates a-priory probabilities coming from the decoder. The information extracted from the received sequence via the VTDFE and the a-priori probabilities coming from the decoder, are combined by computing the conditional expectation of the transmitted symbols given the a-priory probabilities and the output of the VTDFE. This combined information is subsequently entering the SIC's cancellation filter. The overall turbo equalization scheme based on the so-called VTDFE-SIC equalizer exhibits a superior performance as compared to the turbo equalization scheme based on the conventional SIC as well as other linear complexity SISO equalizers.

The rest of this paper is organized as follows: In section 2, the communication system model is formulated. In section 3, the MMSE Soft Interference Canceller, which is a constituent part of the new scheme, is briefly reviewed. In section 4, the new VTDFE-SIC equalizer is derived concerning BPSK modulation and in section 5 we include some notes on the extension of the proposed equalizer to higher order modulations. Finally, in section 6, simulation results verifying the performance of the proposed equalizer are provided.

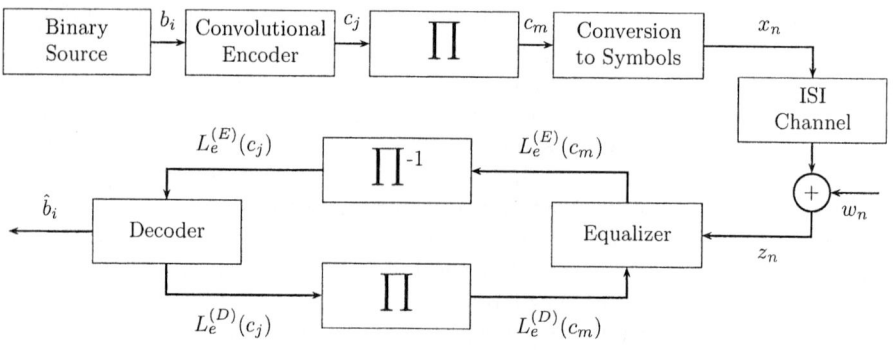

Fig. 1. The Model of Transmission

2 System Model

Let us consider the communication system depicted on Figure 1. The system transmits blocks of data, with each block containing a number of S information bits. A discrete memoryless source generates binary data $b_i, i = 1\ldots S$. These data, in blocks of length S, enter a convolutional encoder of rate R, so that new blocks of S/R bits ($c_j, j = 1\ldots S/R$) are created, where S/R is assumed integer and we do not use trellis termination. The output of the convolutional encoder is then permuted by an interleaver, denoted as Π, so as to form the block of bits $c_m, m = 1\ldots S/R$. The output of the interleaver is then grouped into groups of q bits each (with $\frac{S}{Rq}$ also assumed integer) and each group is mapped into a 2^q-ary symbol from the alphabet $A = \{\alpha_1, \alpha_2, \ldots, \alpha_{2^q}\}$. The resulting symbols $x_n, n = 1\ldots \frac{S}{Rq}$ are finally transmitted through the channel.

We assume that the communication channel is frequency selective and constant during the packet transmission, so that the output of the channel (and input to the receiver) can be modelled as

$$z_n = \sum_{i=-L_1}^{L_2} h_i x_{n-i} + w_n ,\qquad(1)$$

where L_1, $L_2 + 1$ denote the lengths of the anti-causal and causal parts, respectively, of the channel impulse response. The output of the multipath channel is corrupted by complex-valued Additive White Gaussian Noise (AWGN) w_n.

At the receiver, we employ an equalizer to compute soft estimates about the transmitted symbols. Part of the equalizer is also a scheme that transforms the soft estimates of the symbols into soft estimates of the bits that correspond to those symbols. The output of the equalizer is the log likelihood $L_e^{(E)}(c_m), m = 1\ldots S/R$, where the subscript stands for "extrinsic" and the superscript denotes that they come from the equalizer. The operator $L(\cdot)$ applied to a binary random variable y is defined as

$$L(y) = \ln\left(\frac{Pr(y=1)}{Pr(y=0)}\right).$$

In the sequel, the log likelihoods $L_e^{(E)}(c_m)$ are deinterleaved so as to give the log likelihoods $L_e^{(E)}(c_j)$ and enter a soft convolutional decoder, implemented here as a MAP decoder. We stretch the fact that the convolutional decoder operates on the code bits c_j of the code and not on the information bits b_i. The extrinsic log likelihoods $L_e^{(D)}(c_j)$ at the output of the decoder, after interleaving, enter the SISO equalizer as a-priori probabilities information and the iterative procedure is repeated until a termination criterion is satisfied. Here we choose to use a fixed number of iterations. At the last iteration, the decoder operates on the information bits b_i and delivers the hard estimates $\hat{b}_i$.

For the rest of this paper, BPSK modulation ($q = 1$) with alphabet $A = \{+1, -1\}$ and real valued white noise is mainly assumed. In section 5, the extension of the proposed algorithm to higher order constellations is briefly discussed.

3   The Fixed SIC

In this section we first briefly review the conventional Soft Interference Canceller which is a constituent part of the proposed equalizer. The SIC [4], [3] consists of two filters, the matched filter

$$\mathbf{p} = [p_{-k} \cdots p_0 \cdots p_l]^T, \quad M = k + l + 1 \qquad (2)$$

and the cancellation filter

$$\mathbf{q} = [q_{-K} \cdots q_{-1} \; 0 \; q_1 \cdots q_N]^T . \qquad (3)$$

The input to filter $\mathbf{p}$ is the sampled output of the channel at the symbol rate, whereas the input to the cancellation filter consists of past and future symbols. The output s_n of the SIC is the sum of the outputs of the two filters, i.e.,

$$s_n = \mathbf{p}^H \mathbf{z}_n + \mathbf{q}^H \mathbf{x}_n , \qquad (4)$$

where $\mathbf{z}_n = [z_{n+k} \cdots z_n \cdots z_{n-l}]^T$ and $\mathbf{x}_n$ is a vector whose entries are past and future symbol estimates. If we choose to minimize the mean square error $E[|s_n - x_n|^2]$ and assume that the cancellation filter contains correct symbols, then the involved filters are given by the equations

$$\mathbf{p} = \frac{1}{\sigma_w^2 + E_h} \mathbf{Hd} , \qquad (5)$$

and

$$\mathbf{q} = -\mathbf{H}^H \mathbf{p} + \mathbf{dd}^T \mathbf{H}^H \mathbf{p} \qquad (6)$$

where $N = l + L_2$, $K = L_1 + k$, $E_h = \mathbf{d}^T \mathbf{H}^H \mathbf{Hd}$ is the energy of the channel and $\mathbf{H}$ is the channel convolution matrix. $\mathbf{H}$ and $\mathbf{d}$ are defined as

$$\mathbf{H} = \begin{bmatrix} h_{-L_1} & \cdots & h_{L_2} & 0 & \cdots & 0 \\ 0 & \ddots & h_{L_2-1} & h_{L_2} & \cdots & 0 \\ \vdots & \ddots & \ddots & \ddots & \ddots & \vdots \\ 0 & \cdots & 0 & h_{-L_1} & \cdots & h_{L_2} \end{bmatrix}, \qquad (7)$$

$$\mathbf{d} = [\mathbf{0}_{1 \times k+L_1} \; 1 \; \mathbf{0}_{1 \times l+L_2}]^T . \qquad (8)$$

Up to this point the SIC is identical to the classical canceller. It is the incorporation of a-priori information from the decoder which mainly differentiates SIC from classical canceller. Incorporation of a-priori information is achieved if the input to the cancellation filter is not the detected symbols but the corresponding expected values of the symbols, which in turn depend on the constellation used and the a-priori probabilities coming from the channel decoder. For BPSK, it can be seen that $\bar{x}_n = \tanh(L_e^{(D)}(c_m)/2)$. For the first iteration, where no a-priori information is available, it is common to use another equalizer to initiate the iterative procedure. For example, a DFE has been used in [5].

Table 1. Summary of the SIC equalization method

Input: $\mathbf{h}, L_1, L_2, \sigma_w^2, L_e^{(D)}(c_m) = L_e^{(D)}(x_n), z_n, k, l \quad m,n = 1\ldots S/R$
Output: $L_e^{(E)}(c_m) = L_e^{(E)}(x_n) \quad m,n = 1\ldots S/R$
1. Compute $\mathbf{p}, \mathbf{q}$ from (5), (6)
2. $\bar{x}_n = \tanh(L_e^{(D)}(x_n)/2) \quad n = 1\ldots S/R$
3. $v_n = 1 - \bar{x}_n^2 \quad n = 1\ldots S/R$
4. $\mu = \frac{E_h}{\sigma_w^2 + E_h}$
5. for $n = 1\ldots S/R$
$\quad \mathbf{z}_n = [z_{n+k} \cdots z_n \cdots z_{n-l}]^T$
$\quad \bar{\mathbf{x}}_n = [\bar{x}_{n+K} \cdots \bar{x}_n \cdots \bar{x}_{n-N}]^T$
$\quad s_n = \mathbf{p}^H \mathbf{z}_n + \mathbf{q}^H \bar{\mathbf{x}}_n$
$\quad \mathbf{V}_n = diag([v_{n+K} \cdots v_n \cdots v_{n-N}])$
$\quad \sigma_n^2 = \sigma_w^2 \mathbf{p}^H \mathbf{p} + \mathbf{q}^H \mathbf{V}_n \mathbf{q}$
$\quad L_e^{(E)}(x_n) = 2\mu s_n / \sigma_n^2$

The SIC can produce soft outputs in the form of log likelihood ratios using the assumption that its output s_n is normally distributed. For BPSK, the desired mapping is

$$L_e^{(E)}(c_m) = L_e^{(E)}(x_n) = \ln\left(\frac{p(s_n|x_n = +1)}{p(s_n|x_n = -1)}\right) = \frac{2\mu s_n}{\sigma_n^2} \quad (9)$$

where $p(x|x_n = a_i)$ is the p.d.f. of the soft output of the SIC given $x_n = a_i$. The parameters μ and σ_n^2 that correspond to symbol $+1$ can be computed via the relations[1]

$$\mu = \frac{|\alpha_1| E_h}{\sigma_w^2 + E_h}, \quad \sigma_n^2 = \sigma_w^2 \mathbf{p}^H \mathbf{p} + \mathbf{q}^H \mathbf{V}_n \mathbf{q} \quad (10)$$

where $|\alpha_1|$ is the amplitude of the symbol α_1, (here set to $+1$) and $\mathbf{V}_n$ is a diagonal covariance matrix defined by:

$$\mathbf{V}_n = Cov[\mathbf{x}_n, \mathbf{x}_n^H] = diag([v_{n+K} \cdots v_n \cdots v_{n-N}])$$

where the variances v_n (for BPSK) are given by

$$v_n = E[x_n^2] - E^2[x_n] = 1 - \bar{x}_n^2 .$$

From the above formulation, it is clear that the output log likelihood ratios are extrinsic, since neither s_n nor μ and σ_n^2 depend on $L_e^{(D)}(x_n)$. The SIC equalization method as described above, is summarized in Table 1.

---

[1] To compute these statistics it is assumed that the output z_n of the channel is random and distributed as dictated by the a-priori probabilities and the p.d.f. of the noise.

4 The New SIC Technique

4.1 Enhancing the A-Priori Information

It has been proved [3] that the SIC is the MMSE optimal soft equalizer for Turbo Equalization in the case of perfect a-priori information (i.e. $|L_e^{(D)}(x_n)| \to \infty$, or equivalently, as assumed earlier, the cancellation filter is fed by correct symbols). On the other hand, in the presence of weak a-priori information (i.e. low SNR and/or initial iterations) the SIC becomes suboptimal and its performance deteriorates significantly. To alleviate this problem we seek a way to enhance the a-priori log likelihood ratios $L_e^{(D)}(x_n)$ coming from the decoder. This can be achieved by incorporating information from sequence z_n in addition to using the a-priori probabilities coming from the channel decoder. Furthermore, for the sake of computational complexity, we choose to use a linear complexity device in order to "extract" such additional information from z_n.[2] To this end, a linear complexity equalizer which processes sequence z_n and yields a soft estimate s'_n can be employed. In the sequel, s'_n is combined with a-priori probabilities so as to replace $E[x_n]$ (computed only using a-priori probabilities) by $E[x_n|s'_n]$. For BPSK, the conditional probabilities

$$Pr\{x_n = \pm 1|s'_n\} = \frac{Pr\{x_n = \pm 1\}\phi(s'_n|x_n = \pm 1)}{\phi(s'_n)}$$

correspond to the conditional (superscript "C") log likelihood ratio

$$L^{(C)}(x_n) = \ln\left(\frac{Pr\{x_n = +1\}\phi(s'_n|x_n = +1)}{Pr\{x_n = -1\}\phi(s'_n|x_n = -1)}\right) = L_e^{(D)}(x_n) + L_e^{(P)}(x_n)$$

where $\phi(x|x_n = \alpha_i)$ is the p.d.f. of the soft output of the pre-processor given $x_n = \alpha_i$, $Pr\{x_n = \alpha_i\}$ stand for the a-priori probabilities coming from the decoder and the superscript "P" denotes that the respective quantity comes from the pre-processor.

The pre-processor we propose to use here for the computation of s'_n is a Variable Threshold Decision Feedback Equalizer (VTDFE) described in the next section. The block diagram of the combined scheme, so-called VTDFE-SIC, is depicted on Figure 2.

For this modification to be valid we have to ensure that the output of the SIC remains extrinsic. Clearly, $L^{(C)}(x_{n+K}), \ldots, L^{(C)}(x_{n+1})$ and $L^{(C)}(x_{n-1}), \ldots, L^{(C)}(x_{n-N})$ should not depend on $L_e^{(D)}(x_n)$, because otherwise these LLRs, via the cancellation filter of the SIC, will contribute to $L_e'^{(E)}(x_n)$ at the output of the VTDFE-SIC scheme.

---

[2] If computational complexity is a design goal less important than performance, one can use all available information from z_n by designing an optimal estimator. This option, not studied here, currently under investigation.

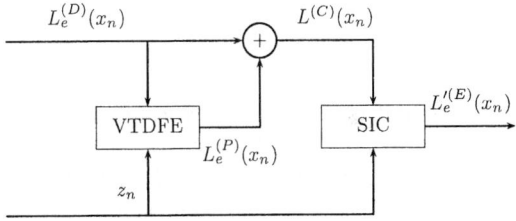

Fig. 2. The proposed VTDFE-SIC equalizer

4.2 A Variable Threshold DFE

In deriving the DFE we will use a similar notation as in the previous section. The feedforward and the feedback filters are denoted as

$$\mathbf{a} = [a_{-k'} \cdots a_0 \cdots a_{l'}]^T, \quad M' = k' + l' + 1$$

and

$$\mathbf{b} = [b_1 \cdots b_{N'}]^T$$

respectively. As in standard DFE the input to $\mathbf{a}$ is the sampled output of the channel, while the input to $\mathbf{b}$ are past detected symbols. The soft output of the DFE is

$$s'_n = \mathbf{a}^H \mathbf{z}'_n + \mathbf{b}^H \hat{\mathbf{x}}_n \ . \tag{11}$$

where $\mathbf{z}'_n = [z_{n+k'} \cdots z_n \cdots z_{n-l'}]^T$ and $\hat{\mathbf{x}}_n$ is a vector whose entries are past hard symbol estimates. Hard decisions about the transmitted symbols are taken by passing s'_n through a decision device. The optimal filter coefficients that minimize the mean square error $E[|s'_n - x_n|^2]$, given the assumption that the feedback filter contains correct symbol estimates (optimal DFE) are given by the relations [6]:

$$\mathbf{a} = \left(\mathbf{H}_1 \mathbf{H}_1^H + \sigma_w^2 \mathbf{I}\right)^{-1} \mathbf{H}_1 \mathbf{d}' \tag{12}$$

and

$$\mathbf{b} = -\mathbf{H}_2^H \mathbf{a} \tag{13}$$

with matrix $\mathbf{H}_1$ containing the first $L_1 + k' + 1$ columns and matrix $\mathbf{H}_2$ the rest $L_2 + l'$ columns of $\mathbf{H}$. We also assume $N' = L_2 + l'$. Vector $\mathbf{d}'$ is given by $\mathbf{d}' = [\mathbf{0}_{1 \times (k'+L_1)} \ 1]^T$.

In the standard DFE, hard decisions $\hat{x}_n$ are made by comparing s'_n to a threshold equal to zero and subsequently are fed back to filter $\mathbf{b}$. Such a strategy, however, would deteriorate the performance of the succeeding SIC. To alleviate this problem we suggest using time-varying thresholds for the decision device by using a Bayesian classification rule which incorporates a-priory probabilities coming from the decoder. In particular the threshold t_n used for the decision $\hat{x}_n$ is found as the solution of

$$Pr\{x_n = +1\}\phi(x|x_n = +1) = Pr\{x_n = -1\}\phi(x|x_n = -1) \tag{14}$$

which becomes

$$t_n = -\frac{\sigma'^2 L_e^{(D)}(x_n)}{2\mu'} \qquad (15)$$

if we assume that the output of the DFE is Normally distributed with variance σ'^2 and mean corresponding to symbol $+1$ equal to μ'. For higher order modulations ($q > 1$), the equalizer must be supplied with the a-priori probabilities $Pr\{x_n = \alpha_i\}, i = 1 \ldots 2^q$. Then, the decision rule consists in calculating all $Pr\{x_n = \alpha_i\}\phi(x|x_n = \alpha_i), \forall i = 1 \ldots 2^q$ given $x = s_n$, and then deciding in favor of the symbol a_j that yields the maximum value. Clearly, in the presence of perfect a-priori information the VTDFE is identical to the optimal DFE, while for weak a-priori information it combines both information from the channel and a-priori probabilities.

The soft output s'_n can be mapped to LLRs using

$$L_e^{(P)}(x_n) = \ln\left(\frac{\phi(s'_n|x_n = +1)}{\phi(s'_n|x_n = -1)}\right) = \frac{2\mu' s'_n}{\sigma'^2}. \qquad (16)$$

Concerning the parameters μ' and σ'^2 of the VTDFE output, first we assume $\mu' = \alpha_1$ (here $+1$) i.e. the VTDFE is an unbiased estimator of the unknown symbols, which is true for high SNR, while for the variance σ'^2, we have:

$$\sigma'^2 = \sigma_w^2 \mathbf{a}^H \mathbf{a} + \mathbf{b} \mathbf{C}_n \mathbf{b}^H$$

where $\mathbf{C}_n$ is the covariance matrix of the contents of the feedback filter, which is zero only when the filter contains the correct symbols. Here we choose to approximate $\mathbf{C}_n$ by:

$$\mathbf{C}_n \approx c \cdot \bar{v} \mathbf{I}$$

where $\bar{v}$ is the mean value of all v_n and c is a positive constant smaller than unity. Estimating the variance by the above relation, reveals that in the limiting case where $|L_e^{(D)}(x_n)| \to +\infty$ (and $v_n \to 0$), only the feedforward filter of the DFE inserts variance term in the output s'_n. In any other case, the variance of s'_n is greater, amounting for the fact that the feedback filter may contain erroneous symbols. The addition of the constant c, which is smaller than unity, reflects the fact that (on the average) the variance of s'_n is somewhat smaller than the variance $\bar{v}$ since we expect that the VTDFE increases the reliability of the symbol estimates. All these approximations will be verified (to some extend) by the simulation results presented in Section 6.

The pre-processing performed by the VTDFE reveals clearly that $L_e^{(P)}(x_{n+1})$, $\ldots$, $L_e^{(P)}(x_{n+N})$ depend on the decision $\hat{x}_n$ whose computation in turn depends on $L_e^{(D)}(x_n)$ (that was used to determine the threshold t_n). It can be seen, however, that this dependence is very weak, due to the use of hard decisions. Therefore, we deduce that, using the VTDFE as a preprocessing stage the output of the SIC remains extrinsic. This would not be the case if another soft equalizer were used at the pre-processing stage. Table 2 summarizes the VTDFE pre-processor.

Table 2. Summary of the VTDFE pre-processor

Input: $\mathbf{h}, L_1, L_2, \sigma_w^2, L_e^{(D)}(x_n), z_n, k', l'$ $n=1\ldots S/R$
Output: $L_e^{(P)}(x_n)$ $n=1\ldots S/R$
1. Compute $\mathbf{a}$ and $\mathbf{b}$ from (12) and (13)
2. $\mu' = \alpha_1$, $\sigma'^2 = \sigma_w^2 \mathbf{a}^H \mathbf{a} + c \cdot \bar{v} \mathbf{b}^H \mathbf{b}$

3. for $n = 1\ldots S/R$
    $\mathbf{z}'_n = [z_{n+k'},\ldots,z_{n-l'}]^T$
    $\hat{\mathbf{x}}_n = [\hat{x}_{n-1},\ldots,\hat{x}_{n-N'}]^T$
    $s'_n = \mathbf{a}^H \mathbf{z}'_n + \mathbf{b}^H \hat{\mathbf{x}}_n$
    if $(s'_n \geq t_n)$ $\hat{x}_n = +1$ else $\hat{x}_n = -1$
    $L_e^{(P)}(x_n) = 2\mu' s'_n / \sigma'^2$

5 Extension to Higher Order Modulations

In this section, we study the extension of the proposed equalizer to higher order modulations ($q > 1$) with general symbol alphabets $\mathcal{A}$. We assume that symbol x_n is given by the function:

$$x_n = \mathcal{A}(c_{(n-1)\cdot q+1}, c_{(n-1)\cdot q+2}, \ldots, c_{(n-1)\cdot q+q})$$

and that the mapping from bits to symbols is $\alpha_i = \mathcal{A}(\beta_{i,1}, \beta_{i,2}, \ldots, \beta_{i,q})$. The SISO equalizer is supplied with $L_e^{(D)}(c_m)$, $m = 1,\ldots, S/R$ and must provide soft information $L_e'^{(E)}(c_m)$.

Firstly, based on the assumption that the bits c_m are independent, we have

$$Pr\{x_n = \alpha_i\} = \prod_{j=1}^{q} Pr\{c_{(n-1)\cdot q+j} = \beta_{i,j}\}$$

where the latter probabilities come from the decoder after converting log likelihood ratios to bit probabilities. As we have already mentioned, the VTDFE has now to compute all

$$Pr\{x_n = \alpha_i | s'_n\} = \frac{Pr\{x_n = \alpha_i\}\phi(s'_n | x_n = \alpha_i)}{\phi(s'_n)}, \quad i = 1,\ldots,2^q \quad (17)$$

and make the decision $\hat{x}_n = argmax(Pr\{x_n = \alpha_i | s'_n\})$. The value of the p.d.f. $\phi(s'_n | x_n = \alpha_i)$ is equal to $\mathcal{N}(\alpha_i, \sigma_w^2 \mathbf{a}^H \mathbf{a} + c \cdot \bar{v} \mathbf{b}^H \mathbf{b})|_{s'_n}$ and

$$\phi(s'_n) = \sum_{i=1}^{2^q} Pr\{x_n = \alpha_i\}\phi(s'_n | x_n = \alpha_i)$$

The input to the cancellation filter, is simply computed as the conditional expectation, which in turn is based on the conditional probabilities of (17), i.e.:

$$E[x_n | s'_n] = \sum_{i=1}^{2^q} \alpha_i Pr\{x_n = a_i | s'_n\}$$

The soft information about bits on the output of the SIC, is computed as

$$L'^{(E)}_e(c_m) = L'^{(E)}_e(c_{(n-1)\cdot q+j}) = \ln\left(\frac{Pr\{c_{(n-1)\cdot q+j}=1|s_n\}}{Pr\{c_{(n-1)\cdot q+j}=0|s_n\}}\right)$$

$$= \ln\left(\frac{\sum_{\beta_{i,j}=1} Pr\{x_n=a_i|s_n\}}{\sum_{\beta_{i,j}=0} Pr\{x_n=a_i|s_n\}}\right)$$

$$= \ln\left(\frac{\sum_{\beta_{i,j}=1} Pr\{x_n=a_i\}p(s_n|x_n=a_i)/p(s_n)}{\sum_{\beta_{i,j}=0} Pr\{x_n=a_i\}p(s_n|x_n=a_i)/p(s_n)}\right)$$

where the term $p(s_n)$ can be eliminated from nominator and denominator. Note that when computing $Pr\{x_n=a_i\}$ in the nominator and denominator we must set the probability of bit j to unity. Also, $p(s_n|x_n=a_i) = \mathcal{N}(\mu,\sigma_n^2)|_{s_n}$, with μ and σ_n^2 given from (10).

6 Simulation Results and Conclusion

To test the performance of the proposed VTDFE-SIC technique we performed some typical experiments. Information bits were generated in bursts of $S = 2048$ bits. Then an R.S.C. code with generator matrix $G(D) = [1 \frac{1+D^2}{1+D+D^2}]$ of rate 1/2 was applied, and the resulting bits were BPSK modulated. The 4096 symbols per burst were interleaved via the use of a random interleaver and then transmitted over a channel whose impulse response was set either $h_{-1} = 0.407, h_0 = 0.815, h_1 = 0.407$ (channel B of [7]) or $h_{-2} = 0.227, h_{-1} = 0.46, h_0 = 0.688, h_1 = 0.46, h_2 = 0.227$ (channel C of [7]).

We have compared the new VTDFE-SIC with the so-called APPLE scheme [8] which has a comparable computational complexity, and the conventional SIC [3] where a linear equalizer was used for the first iteration. The performance of the VTDFE alone has been tested as well, and we have set $c = 0.7$. The performance curves depicted in Figures 3(a) and 3(b) have been taken after 5 iterations and for at least 1000 symbol error events.

As shown in Figure 3(a) the VTDFE-SIC scheme has a superior performance compared to the other linear complexity schemes approaching the performance of the AWGN channel. The SIC performance is poor for low SNRs but it achieves the AWGN bound at higher SNRs. The APPLE and the VTDFE equalizers exhibit poor performance at all SNR regions.

As we can see in Figure 3(b) the MAP equalizer performs best followed by the VTDFE-SIC scheme and the APPLE. The VTDFE scheme approaches the performance of the APPLE at high SNR, while the SIC cannot achieve good results.

Concluding, the performance of the Soft Interference Canceller has been improved by modifying its input Log-Likelihood ratio via the use of a new low-complexity DFE. The so-called VTDFE equalizer seems to be a good preprocessor for this task. The resulting overall scheme has linear complexity and

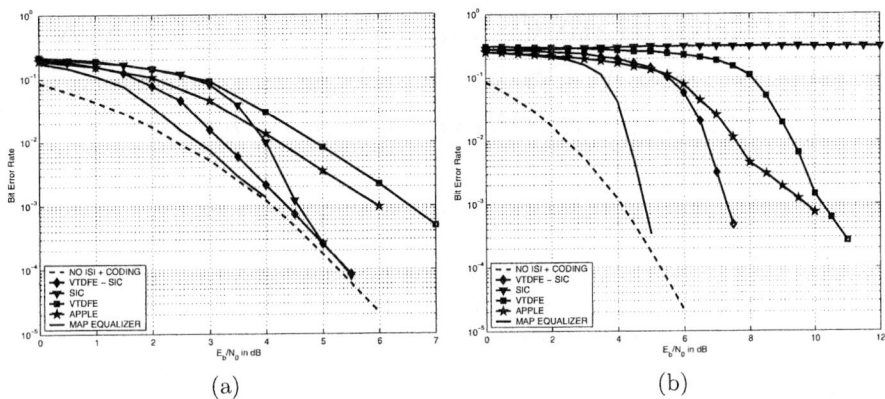

Fig. 3. (a) Performance results over the Proakis B channel. (b) Performance results over the Proakis C channel.

attains better performance than equalizers with comparable complexity. Future work will focus on unknown and time varying channels.

Acknowledgments. The authors would like to thank Prof. Jacques Palicot, Dr. Athanasios Rontogiannis and Dr. Aline Roumy for helpful discussions concerning this work.

References

1. C. Douillard, M. Jezequel, C. Berrou, A. Picard, P. Didier and A. Glavieux, "Iterative correction of intersymbol interference: Turbo Equalization," *European Transactions on Communications*, vol. 6, pp. 507-511, September/October 1995.
2. C. Berrou, A. Glavieux and P. Thitimajshima, "Near Shannon limit error-correcting coding and decoding: Turbo Codes," in *Proc. IEEE Int. Conf. on Communications*, Geneva, Switzerland, May 1993.
3. M. Tuchler, R. Koetter and A. C. Singer, "Turbo Equalization: Principles and New Results," *IEEE Trans. on Comm.*, vol. 50, no. 5, pp. 754-767, May 2002.
4. C. Laot, A. Glavieux and J. Labat, "Turbo Equalization: adaptive equalization and channel decoding jointly optimized," *IEEE Journal on Selected Areas on Communication*, vol. 19, no. 9, pp. 1744-1752, September 2001.
5. I. Fijalkow, A. Roumy, S. Ronger, D. Pirez and P. Vila "Improved Interference cancellation for Turbo-equalization," *In Proc.of ICASSP, IEEE Int. Conference on Acoustics, Speech and Signal Processing*, Turkey, June 2000.
6. K. Berberidis, A. Marava, P. Karaivazoglou and J. Palicot, "Robust and Fast Converging Decision Feedback Equalizer Based on a New Adaptive Semi-Blind Channel Estimation Algorithm," in *Proc. of the 2001 IEEE GLOBECOM*, San Antonio, USA, Nov. 2001
7. J. Proakis, *Digital Communications*, 3rd ed. New York: McGraw-Hill, 1995.
8. M. Tuchler and J. Hagenauer, "Linear time and frequency domain Turbo equalization", in *Proc. 53rd Vehicular Technology Conf.* (Spring), Rhodes, Greece, pp. 1449-1453, May 2001.

Bit Error Rate Calculation for DS-CDMA Systems with WDS in the Presence of Rayleigh Fading and Power-Control Error

Ibrahim Develi, Cebrail Ciftlikli, and Aytekin Bagis

Department of Electrical and Electronics Engineering, Erciyes University,
38039, Kayseri, Turkey
{develi, cebrailc, bagis}@erciyes.edu.tr

Abstract. This paper reports work in which modified expressions for the bit error rate (BER) calculation of DS-CDMA systems with weighted despreading sequences (WDS) in the presence of Rayleigh fading and power-control error are proposed. The focus of the modified expressions is based on a simple equality which was proposed in the open literature. The major benefit from using the proposed expressions which are obtained for both coherent and noncoherent receptions is that they require less definition about the spreading sequences for the BER calculation.

1 Introduction

Direct sequence-code division multiple access (DS-CDMA) is a promising multiplexing approach where a number of users simultaneously and asynchronously access a common channel. In DS-CDMA communications, the users are multiplexed by separate spreading sequences, rather than by orthogonal frequency bands, as in frequency-division multiple access (FDMA), or by orthogonal time slots, as in time-division multiple access (TDMA). For secure communications, DS-CDMA signals are hard to detect by unauthorized users and have good resistance against intentional jamming. Other main features of DS-CDMA are efficient spectrum utilization, narrowband interference rejection, higher voice quality in noisy environment, low transmission power and soft hand-off capacity [1]-[8].

Three major factors that limit the bit error rate (BER) performance and capacity of DS-CDMA systems are multipath fading, multiple access interference (MAI) and imperfect power control. Most performance analyses of CDMA systems in the open literature are based on the assumption that the received signals from all users are equal and constant using a perfect power control assumption [9]-[18]. In practice, an equal and constant received power level can not be achieved because of imperfect power control.

A recent paper by Huang and Ng [19] analyzes the BER performance of a DS-CDMA system with imperfect power control for both coherent and noncoherent receptions operating over a multipath Rayleigh fading channel. The receivers considered in [19] employ exponentially weighted despreading sequences (WDS) optimized for MAI rejection. The chip weighting waveforms employed are determined by only one parameter that leads to easy tuning of the waveforms in practice to achieve the best performance. It is useful to note that the derived closed-form solutions, which enable to calculate the BER in [19], require perfect definition of the spreading sequences for the signals of all active users. Also, a number of computational efforts are needed to define the parameters of each spreading sequence. Therefore, a simple expression for the BER calculation is always desirable.

In this paper, we show how the performance expressions derived in [19] can be modified to further simplify the BER calculations. An overview of the organization of this paper is as follows: In Section 2, some technical preliminaries, including the transmitter model, channel model and receiver model used in this work are described. In Section 3, the BER performance expressions derived for both coherent and noncoherent receptions in [19] are reviewed. In Section 4, the modified performance expressions for the BER calculation are developed with the help of the simple equality proposed in [20] and [21]. In Section 5, the conclusion is presented.

2 Preliminaries

2.1 Transmitter and Channel Models

In the following, transmitter and channel models for a DS-CDMA system presented in [19] are briefly reviewed. It is assumed that there are K users assigned to the phase-shift keyed DS-CDMA system and that the kth user's transmitted signal is given by

$$S_k(t) = (2P)^{1/2} G_k a_k(t) b_k(t) \cos(\omega_0 t + \theta_k) \qquad (1)$$

where the transmitted power P and the carrier frequency ω_0 are common to all users and θ_k is the phase angle introduced by the kth modulator. The parameter G_k represents the power control error for the kth user and is modeled as a random variable uniformly distributed in $[1-\varepsilon_m, 1+\varepsilon_m]$ where ε_m represents the maximum value of power control error for all users. The kth user's data signal, $b_k(t)$, is given by

$$b_k(t) = \sum_{j=-\infty}^{\infty} b_j^{(k)} P_{T_b}(t - jT_b) \qquad (2)$$

where $b_j^{(k)}$ is the data sequence of the kth user and $P_{T_b}(\cdot)$ is a unit rectangular pulse of duration T_b. The kth user's data sequence can take on values +1 or -1, with probability 1/2 each. The kth user's spreading signal, $a_k(t)$, is given by

$$a_k(t) = \sum_{j=-\infty}^{\infty} a_j^{(k)} P_{T_c}(t - jT_c) \qquad (3)$$

where $a_j^{(k)} \epsilon \{-1,+1\}$ and T_c is the chip duration. It is assumed that the spreading sequence is periodic with period $N = T_b/T_c$, that is, $a_j^{(k)} = a_{j+N}^{(k)}$.

The channel is assumed to be a frequency selective multipath channel for the uplink. The equivalent complex lowpass representation of the channel for the kth user is given by

$$h_k(t) = \sum_{l=0}^{L_p-1} \beta_{kl} \delta(t - \tau_{kl}) e^{j\eta_{kl}} \qquad (4)$$

where random variables β_{kl}, τ_{kl} and η_{kl} are the lth path gain, delay and phase, respectively, for the kth user. In this study, the following assumptions are considered as in [19]:

i) For different users and paths in each link, the random variables $\{\beta_{kl}\}$, $\{\tau_{kl}\}$ and $\{\eta_{kl}\}$ are all statistically independent,

ii) The random phases $\{\eta_{kl}\}$ are uniformly distributed over $[0, 2\pi]$ and the path delays t_{kl} are uniformly distributed over $[0, T_b]$,

iii) There are L_p paths for each user and these different paths are separated in time from each other by more than $2T_c$,

iv) For each user, the path gain β_{kl}, is a random variable with Rayleigh distribution,

v) The fading rate in the channel is slow compared to the bit rate, so that the random parameters associated with the channel do not vary significantly over two consecutive bit intervals.

The received waveform at the central station is given by $r(t) = n(t) + m(t)$, where $n(t)$ denotes additive white Gaussian noise (AWGN) with 2-sided spectral density $N_0/2$, and $m(t)$ denotes the multiple-access component of the received waveform. As a result, the received waveform $r(t)$ can be represented by

$$r(t) = (2P)^{1/2} \sum_{k=1}^{K} \sum_{l=0}^{L_p-1} G_k \beta_{kl} a_k(t - \tau_{kl}) b_k(t - \tau_{kl}) \cos(\omega_0 t + \phi_{kl}) \\ + n_c(t) \cos \omega_0 t - n_s(t) \sin \omega_0 t \qquad (5)$$

where $\phi_{kl} = \theta_k + \eta_{kl} - \omega_c \tau_{kl}$, and the terms $n_c(t)$ and $n_s(t)$ are lowpass equivalent components of the AWGN $n(t)$.

2.2 Receiver Model

For BPSK modulation, the structure of one of the paths of a RAKE receiver using coherent detection [19] is shown in Fig. 1.

In order to reject the MAI, a bank of single-path matched filters, each of which is matched to different paths, have the same impulse response matched to $2\hat{a}_k(t)\cos(\omega_0 t) P_{T_b}(t)$ where $\hat{a}_k(t)$ is the weighted despreading function with details given below. The outputs of all single-path matched filters represented by $\xi_{kl}(\kappa)$, $l \epsilon [0, L_R - 1]$ where L_R is the order of diversity, are weighted by the corresponding path gains and then summed to form a single decision variable $\xi_k(\kappa)$.

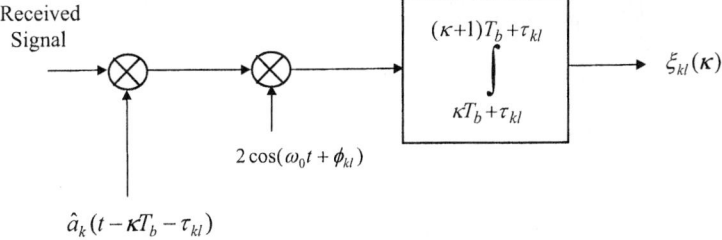

Fig. 1. Path l's matched filter structure for the kth user

The weighted despreading function of the kth user's RAKE receiver can be expressed as

$$\hat{a}_k(t) = \sum_{j=-\infty}^{\infty} a_j^{(k)} w_j^{(k)} \left(t - jT_c \middle| \left\{c_j^{(k)}, c_{j+1}^{(k)}\right\}\right) \tag{6}$$

where $c_j^{(k)} = a_{j-1}^{(k)} a_j^{(k)}$ and $w_j^{(k)}(t \backslash \{c_j^{(k)}, c_{j+1}^{(k)}\}$, for $0 \le t \le T_c$, is the jth chip weighting waveform for the kth receiver, conditioned on the status of three consecutive chips $\{c_j^{(k)}, c_{j+1}^{(k)}\} = \{a_{j-1}^{(k)} a_j^{(k)}, a_j^{(k)} a_{j+1}^{(k)}\}$. The jth conditioned chip weighting waveform for the kth user is defined as

$$w_j^{(k)}\left(t \middle| \left\{c_j^{(k)}, c_{j+1}^{(k)}\right\}\right) = \begin{cases} cw_1(t) & \text{if } c_j^{(k)} = +1 \text{ and } c_{j+1}^{(k)} = +1 \\ cw_2(t) & \text{if } c_j^{(k)} = -1 \text{ and } c_{j+1}^{(k)} = -1 \\ cw_3(t) & \text{if } c_j^{(k)} = -1 \text{ and } c_{j+1}^{(k)} = +1 \\ cw_4(t) & \text{if } c_j^{(k)} = +1 \text{ and } c_{j+1}^{(k)} = -1 \end{cases} \tag{7}$$

with the elements of the chip weighting waveform vector $\{cw_1(t), cw_2(t), cw_3(t), cw_4(t)\}$ selected as

$$\begin{aligned} cw_1(t) &= e^{-\gamma/2} P_{T_c}(t) \\ cw_2(t) &= e^{-\gamma t/T_c} P_{T_c/2}(t) + e^{-\gamma(1-t/T_c)} P_{T_c/2}(t - T_c/2) \\ cw_3(t) &= e^{-\gamma t/T_c} P_{T_c/2}(t) + e^{-\gamma/2} P_{T_c/2}(t - T_c/2) \\ cw_4(t) &= e^{-\gamma/2} P_{T_c/2}(t) + e^{-\gamma(1-t/T_c)} P_{T_c/2}(t - T_c/2 \end{aligned} \tag{8}$$

where $\gamma \in [0, \infty]$ is the parameter of the chip weighting waveforms. For DPSK modulation, the structure of path l of kth user's RAKE demodulator that employs noncoherent detection [19] is shown in Fig. 2. In this case, the outputs of all single-path receiver $\mathrm{Re}[\vartheta_{kl}(\kappa) \vartheta_{kl}^*(\kappa - 1)]$, $l = 0, 1, ..., L_R - 1$, are directly summed to form a single decision variable $\vartheta_k(\kappa)$.

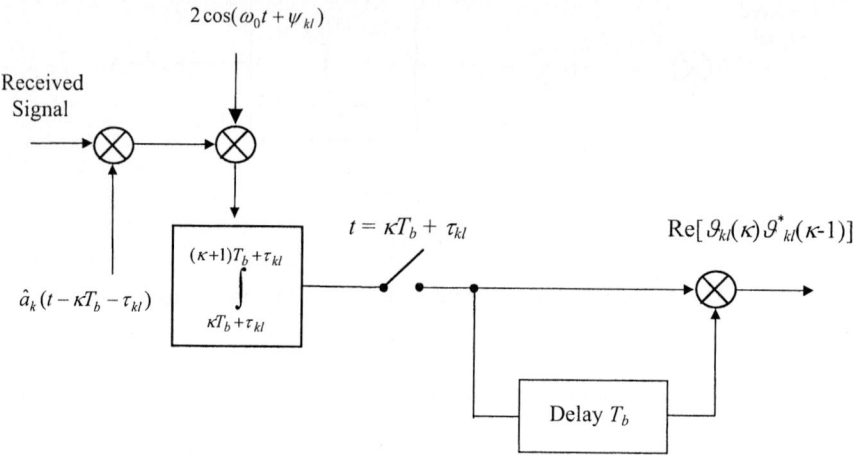

Fig. 2. Path l's noncoherent receiver structure for the kth user

3 Review of Previous Performance Expressions

According to the detailed analyses in [19], the performance expressions which enable to calculate the BER for coherent ([19], eq. (38)) and noncoherent ([19], eq. (55)) reception can be given as

$$P_e^{(k)} = \frac{1}{2} - \sum_{d=1}^{L_R} \frac{\binom{2d-2}{d-1}}{2^{2d}\varepsilon_m \bar{H}(2d-3)} \left\{ (b^2+1)^{(3-2d)/2} - (a^2+1)^{(3-2d)/2} \right\} \quad (9)$$

(for coherent reception)

$$P_e^{(k)} = \begin{cases} \left(\frac{1}{4\varepsilon_m \bar{H}}\right) \arctan\left(\frac{a-b}{1+ab}\right), & L_R = 1 \\ \left(\frac{1}{2\varepsilon_m \bar{H}}\right) \sum_{k=0}^{L_R-1} \binom{L_R-1+k}{k} \sum_{q=L_R}^{L_R+k} (-1)^{q-L_R} \left(\frac{1}{2}\right)^q \binom{k}{q-L_R} \\ \cdot \left\{ \left(\frac{1}{2^{2q-3}}\right) \binom{2q-3}{q-1} \arctan\left(\frac{a-b}{1+ab}\right) + \frac{1}{2q-1} \sum_{n=1}^{q-1} \left[\frac{q}{(q-n)2^{2n}}\right] \right. \\ \left. \cdot \binom{2q}{q} \left[\frac{a}{(a^2+1)^{q-n}} - \frac{b}{(b^2+1)^{q-n}}\right] \bigg/ \binom{2q-2n}{q-n} \right\}, & L_R \geq 2 \end{cases}$$

(10)

(for noncoherent reception)

where $a = (1+\varepsilon_m)\bar{H}$, $b = (1-\varepsilon_m)\bar{H}$, and $\bar{H}$ is the average signal to interference plus noise ratio per channel, given by ([19], eq. (36))

$$\bar{H} = \left\{ \frac{\gamma[(\hat{N}_k/N)(1-e^{-\gamma})+\gamma[1-(\hat{N}_k/N)]e^{-\gamma}]}{\bar{\gamma}_b[2(\hat{N}_k/N)(1-e^{-\gamma/2})+\gamma[1-(\hat{N}_k/N)]e^{-\gamma/2}]^2} + \frac{(KL_p-1)(1+\varepsilon_m^2/3)\Xi^{(e)}(\Gamma^{\{c_j^{(k)}\}},\gamma)}{N[2(\hat{N}_k/N)(e^{\gamma/2}-1)+\gamma[1-(\hat{N}_k/N)]]^2} \right\}^{-1/2} \quad (11)$$

where,
γ = parameter of the exponential chip weighting waveforms,
$\hat{N}_k$ = random variable which represents the number of occurrences of $c_j^{(k)} = -1$ for all $j \in [0, N-1]$,
N = processing gain,
$\bar{\gamma}_b$ = signal to noise ratio (in dB),
K = number of active users,
$\Xi^{(e)}(\Gamma^{\{c_j^{(k)}\}},\gamma)$ in (11) is defined as ([19], eq. (20))

$$\Xi^{(e)}\left(\Gamma^{\{c_j^{(k)}\}},\gamma\right) = \frac{1}{N} \left\{ \Gamma^{(k)}_{\{-1,-1,-1\}} \left[4 + \frac{12}{\gamma} - \frac{16e^{\gamma/2}}{\gamma} + \frac{4e^\gamma}{\gamma}\right] \right.$$
$$+ \left(\Gamma^{(k)}_{\{-1,-1,1\}} + \Gamma^{(k)}_{\{1,-1,-1\}}\right) \left[\frac{5}{2} - \frac{\gamma}{4} + \frac{\gamma^2}{24} + \frac{19}{2\gamma} + e^{\frac{\gamma}{2}} - \frac{12e^{\gamma/2}}{\gamma} + \frac{5e^\gamma}{2\gamma}\right]$$
$$+ \left(\Gamma^{(k)}_{\{-1,1,1\}} + \Gamma^{(k)}_{\{1,1,-1\}}\right) \left[-\frac{3}{2} - \frac{3\gamma}{4} + \frac{19\gamma^2}{24} - \frac{1}{2\gamma} + e^{\gamma/2} + \frac{e^\gamma}{2\gamma}\right] \quad (12)$$
$$+ \Gamma^{(k)}_{\{-1,1,-1\}} \left[-3 - \frac{3\gamma}{2} + \frac{7\gamma^2}{12} - \frac{1}{\gamma} + 2e^{\gamma/2} + \frac{e^\gamma}{\gamma}\right]$$
$$+ \Gamma^{(k)}_{\{1,-1,1\}} \left[1 - \frac{\gamma}{2} + \frac{\gamma^2}{12} + \frac{7}{\gamma} + 2e^{\gamma/2} - \frac{8e^{\gamma/2}}{\gamma} + \frac{e^\gamma}{\gamma}\right] + \Gamma^{(k)}_{\{1,1,1\}}[\gamma^2] \right\}$$

where $\Gamma^{(k)}_{\{v_1,v_2,v_3\}}$ is the number of occurrence of $\{c_{j-1}^{(k)}, c_j^{(k)}, c_{j+1}^{(k)}\} = \{v_1, v_2, v_3\}$ for all j in the kth user's spreading sequence and each v_n, $n \in [1, 2, 3]$, takes values +1 or -1 with equal probabilities.

For the simplicity in presentation, let

$$\Gamma_a^{(k)} = \Gamma^{(k)}_{\{-1,-1,-1\}}$$

$$\Gamma_b^{(k)} = \left(\Gamma^{(k)}_{\{-1,-1,1\}} + \Gamma^{(k)}_{\{1,-1,-1\}}\right)$$

$$\Gamma_c^{(k)} = \left(\Gamma^{(k)}_{\{-1,1,1\}} + \Gamma^{(k)}_{\{1,1,-1\}}\right) \quad (13)$$

$$\Gamma_d^{(k)} = \Gamma^{(k)}_{\{-1,1,-1\}}$$

$$\Gamma_e^{(k)} = \Gamma^{(k)}_{\{1,-1,1\}}$$

$$\Gamma_f^{(k)} = \Gamma^{(k)}_{\{1,1,1\}}$$

As can be seen from (11), the following computations are required for a random spreading sequence to calculate the BER of a DS-CDMA receiver:

$\{\Gamma_a^k, \Gamma_b^k, ..., \Gamma_f^k\}$ and $\hat{N}_k$

Based on the definitions given above, there is a need to scrutinize the entire chips of a random spreading sequence to determine both the $\Gamma_{\{v_1,v_2,v_3\}}^{(k)}$ and $\hat{N}_k$ for using in the calculation of the BER. Clearly, it is not easy to compute these occurrences in practice when the spreading codes have large length.

4 Proposal of Modified Performance Expressions

Since the $\hat{N}_k$ can be determined by summing the $\Gamma_a^{(k)}$, $\Gamma_b^{(k)}$ and $\Gamma_e^{(k)}$, there is no need for scrutinizing the chip transitions in a random spreading sequence to compute the $\hat{N}_k$.

In order to simplify the BER calculation, let us first briefly mention the following equality introduced in [20] and [21]:

$$\hat{N}_k = \Gamma_a^{(k)} + \Gamma_b^{(k)} + \Gamma_e^{(k)} \tag{14}$$

In order to summarize the validity of the equality, various spreading sequences are considered. Table 1 shows the calculated number of $\{\Gamma_a^{(k)}, \Gamma_b^{(k)}, ..., \Gamma_f^{(k)}\}$ and $(\Gamma_a^{(k)} + \Gamma_b^{(k)} + \Gamma_e^{(k)})$ belonging to spreading sequences selected [22]. The $\hat{N}_k$s which are determined by scanning each code are also included in this table. As the results indicate, for each of the sequences, $(\Gamma_a^{(k)} + \Gamma_b^{(k)} + \Gamma_e^{(k)})$ is equal to $\hat{N}_k$. As a result, the required knowledge belonging to a code for the user of interest is only the number of $\{\Gamma_a^{(k)}, \Gamma_b^{(k)}, ..., \Gamma_f^{(k)}\}$ (Table 2). Detailed information about the derivation of the equality can be found in [20] and [21]. Substitution of (14) into (11), $\bar{H}$ can now be rearranged as

$$\widehat{H} = \left\{ \frac{\gamma[\varsigma_k(1-e^{-\gamma})+\gamma(1-\varsigma_k)e^{-\gamma}]}{\bar{\gamma}_b[2\varsigma_k(1-e^{-\gamma/2})+\gamma(1-\varsigma_k)e^{-\gamma/2}]^2} + \frac{(KL_p-1)(1+\varepsilon_m^2/3)\Xi^{(e)}(\Gamma^{\{c_j^{(k)}\}},\gamma)}{N[2\varsigma_k(e^{\gamma/2}-1)+\gamma(1-\varsigma_k)]^2} \right\}^{-1/2} \tag{15}$$

where, $\varsigma_k = (\Gamma_a^{(k)}+\Gamma_b^{(k)}+\Gamma_e^{(k)})/N$. As a result, the BER performance expressions given in (9) and (10), can then be modified as follows:

$$\widehat{P}_e^{(k)} = \frac{1}{2} - \sum_{d=1}^{L_R} \frac{\binom{2d-2}{d-1}}{2^{2d}\varepsilon_m \widehat{H}(2d-3)} \left\{ \left(\widehat{b}^2+1\right)^{(3-2d)/2} - \left(\widehat{a}^2+1\right)^{(3-2d)/2} \right\} \tag{16}$$

(for coherent reception)

Table 1. Calculated number of $\{\Gamma_a^{(k)}, \Gamma_b^{(k)}, ..., \Gamma_f^{(k)}\}$, $(\Gamma_a^{(k)} + \Gamma_b^{(k)} + \Gamma_e^{(k)})$ and $\hat{N}_k$ for random spreading sequences with various code lengths

N	$\Gamma_a^{(k)}$	$\Gamma_b^{(k)}$	$\Gamma_c^{(k)}$	$\Gamma_d^{(k)}$	$\Gamma_e^{(k)}$	$\Gamma_f^{(k)}$	$\left(\Gamma_a^{(k)} + \Gamma_b^{(k)} + \Gamma_e^{(k)}\right)$	$\hat{N}_k$
16	6	4	2	1	0	2	10	10
16	0	4	6	1	2	2	6	6
16	2	4	4	2	2	1	8	8
16	4	4	4	0	0	3	8	8
16	4	6	4	1	0	0	10	10
31	1	6	14	1	5	4	12	12
31	9	10	10	1	1	0	20	20
31	5	10	6	3	1	6	16	16
31	3	6	6	7	7	2	16	16
31	2	8	8	2	2	9	12	12
63	4	8	24	4	12	11	24	24
63	18	20	12	6	2	5	40	40
63	8	16	16	8	8	7	32	32
63	2	12	12	10	10	17	24	24
63	12	24	8	12	4	3	40	40
127	28	32	32	12	12	11	72	72
127	12	24	40	12	20	19	56	56
127	22	28	36	10	14	17	64	64
127	10	28	36	14	18	21	56	56
127	14	28	36	18	22	9	64	64
511	76	136	104	76	60	59	272	272
511	64	128	128	64	64	63	256	256
511	84	136	136	52	52	51	272	272
511	52	120	136	60	68	75	240	240
511	60	104	136	60	76	75	240	240

Table 2. Comparison of the BER performance expressions

BER PerformanceExpressions	$\left\{\Gamma_a^{(k)}, \Gamma_b^{(k)}, \ldots, \Gamma_f^{(k)}\right\}$	$\hat{N}_k$
$P_e^{(k)}$ (introduced in [19] for coherent reception)	Required	Required
$\widehat{P}_e^{(k)}$ (proposed in this paper for coherent reception)	Required	Not required
$P_e^{(k)}$ (introduced in [19] for non-coherent reception)	Required	Required
$\widehat{P}_e^{(k)}$ (proposed in this paper for coherent reception)	Required	Not required

$$\widehat{P}_e^{(k)} = \begin{cases} \left(\dfrac{1}{4\varepsilon_m \widehat{H}}\right) \arctan\left(\dfrac{\widehat{a}-\widehat{b}}{1+\widehat{a}\,\widehat{b}}\right), & L_R = 1 \\[2mm] \left(\dfrac{1}{2\varepsilon_m \widehat{H}}\right) \displaystyle\sum_{k=0}^{L_R-1} \binom{L_R-1+k}{k} \sum_{q=L_R}^{L_R+k}(-1)^{q-L_R}\left(\tfrac{1}{2}\right)^q \binom{k}{q-L_R} \\[2mm] \cdot \left\{\left(\dfrac{1}{2^{2q-3}}\right)\binom{2q-3}{q-1}\arctan\left(\dfrac{\widehat{a}-\widehat{b}}{1+\widehat{a}\,\widehat{b}}\right) + \dfrac{1}{2q-1}\displaystyle\sum_{n=1}^{q-1}\left[\dfrac{q}{(q-n)2^{2n}}\right] \right. \\[2mm] \left. \cdot \binom{2q}{q}\left[\dfrac{\widehat{a}}{(\widehat{a}^2+1)^{q-n}} - \dfrac{\widehat{b}}{(\widehat{b}^2+1)^{q-n}}\right] \Big/ \binom{2q-2n}{q-n}\right\}, & L_R \geq 2 \end{cases}$$

(17)

(for noncoherent reception)

where

$$\widehat{a} = (1+\varepsilon_m)\widehat{H} \tag{18}$$

and

$$\widehat{b} = (1-\varepsilon_m)\widehat{H} \tag{19}$$

5 Conclusions

Performance analyses of CDMA systems in the open literature are mainly based on the assumption that the received signals from all users are equal and constant using a perfect power control assumption. In practice, an equal and constant received power level can not be achieved because of imperfect power control. In this paper, modified expressions for the BER calculation of DS-CDMA systems with weighted despreading sequences in the presence of Rayleigh fading and power-control error are introduced. The focus of the modified expressions is based on a simple equality which was proposed in the open literature. As a conclusion, a major benefit from using the proposed expressions is that they require less definition about the spreading sequences for the BER calculation. The method proposed in this paper move in the areas of BER calculation for DS-CDMA receivers with weighted despreading sequences one step further.

Acknowledgement

This work was supported by the Research Fund of Erciyes University with the Project number FBA-04-21.

References

[1] Peterson, R.L., Ziemer, R.E., Borth, D.E.: Introduction to Spread Spectrum Communications. Englewood Cliffs NJ, (1995) Prentice Hall.
[2] Kohno, R., Meidan, R., Milstein, L.B.: Spread spectrum access methods for wireless communications. IEEE Commun. Mag. **33** (1995) 58–67.
[3] Pickholtz, R.L., Schilling, D.L., Milstein, L.B.: Theory of spread-spectrum communications-A tutorial. IEEE Trans. Commun. **COM-30**(1982) 855–884.
[4] Gilhousen, K.S., Jacobs, I.M., Padovani, R., Viterbi, A.J., Weaver, L.A., Wheatly, C.: On the capacity of a cellular CDMA system. IEEE Trans. Veh. Technol. **40** (1991) 303–312.
[5] Jung, P., Baier, P.W., Steil, A.: Advantages of CDMA and spread spectrum techniques over FDMA and TDMA in cellular mobile radio applications. IEEE Trans. Veh. Technol. **42**(1993) 357–364.
[6] Turin, G.L.: Introduction to spread-spectrum antimultipath techniques and their application to urban digital radio. Proc. IEEE **68** (1980) 328–353.
[7] Adachi, F., Sawahashi, M., Suda, H.: Wideband DS-CDMA for next-generation mobile communications systems. IEEE Commun. Mag. **36** (1998) 56–69.
[8] Baier, A., Fiebig, U.C., Granzow, W., Koch, W., Teder, P., Thielecke, J.: Design study for a CDMA-based third generation mobile radio system. IEEE J. Select. Areas Commun. **12** (1994) 733–743.
[9] Yoon, S., Ness, Y.B.: Performance analysis of linear multiuser detectors for randomly spread CDMA using Gaussian approximation. IEEE J. Select. Areas Commun. **20** (2002) 409–418.
[10] Kim, D.K., Sung, D.K.: Capacity estimation for a multicode CDMA system with SIR-based power control. IEEE Trans. Veh. Technol. **50** (2001) 701–710.
[11] Liu, Y., Wong, T.F.: Performance analysis of an adaptive decision-feedback receiver in asynchronous CDMA systems. IEEE Wireless Communications and Networking Conference, (2002) 531-536.
[12] Veeravalli, V.V., Mantravadi, A.: The coding-spreading tradeoff in CDMA systems, IEEE J. Select. Areas Commun. **20** (2002) 396–408.
[13] Lim, H.S., Rao, M.V.C, Tan, A.E.C, Chuah, H.T.: Multiuser detection for DS-CDMA systems using evolutionary programming. IEEE Commun. Lett. **7** (2003) 101–103.
[14] Vijayan, L., Roberts, J.: BER performance of 2D-RAKE receivers in DS-CDMA over frequency-selective slow Rayleigh fading. IEEE Commun. Lett. **6** (2002) 434–436.
[15] Qinghua, S., Latva-aho, M.: Exact bit error rate calculations for synchronous MC-CDMA over a Rayleigh fading channel. IEEE Commun. Lett. **6** (2002) 276–278.
[16] Huang, Y., Ng, T.S.: A DS-CDMA system using despreading sequences weighted by adjustable chip waveforms. IEEE Trans. Commun. **47** (1999) 1884–1896.
[17] Ciftlikli, C., Develi, I.: A simple and useful approach for the determination process of the weighted despreading sequences in a DS-CDMA system. Euro. Trans. Telecomms. **14** (2003) 361–366.
[18] Develi, I.: Detection of optimal spreading codes for DS-CDMA wireless systems with despreading sequences weighted by adjustable chip waveforms. Journal of the Franklin Institute-Engineering and Applied Mathematics **342** (2005) 69–84.
[19] Huang, Y., Ng, T.S.: DS-CDMA with power control error using weighted despreading sequences over a multipath Rayleigh fading channel. IEEE Trans. Veh. Technol. **48** (1999) 1067–1079.

[20] Develi, I., Ciftlikli, C.: Computation of the tuning values of exponential chip weighting waveforms for DS-CDMA communications over AWGN channels. IEE Proc. Commun. **151** (2004) 132–136.
[21] Develi, I., Ciftlikli, C.: A simple method for calculating the SINR in DS-CDMA systems with despreading sequences weighted by stepping chip waveforms. Canadian Journal of Electrical and Computer Engineering **28** (2003) 163–167.
[22] Kärkkäinen, K.H.A., Leppänen, P.A.: The influence of initial-phases of a PN code set on the performance of an asynchronous DS/CDMA system. Wireless Personal Commun. **13** (2000) 279–293.

Multivariate AR Model Order Estimation with Unknown Process Order

Stylianos Sp. Pappas, Assimakis K. Leros, and Sokratis K. Katsikas

Dept. of Information & Communication Systems Engineering,
University of the Aegean, Karlovassi GR-83200
{spappas, aleros, ska}@aegean.gr

Abstract. A new method for simultaneous order estimation and parameter identification of a multivariate autoregressive (AR) model is described in this paper. The proposed method is based on the well known multimodel partitioning theory. Computer simulations indicate that the method is 100% successful in selecting the correct model order in very few steps. The results are compared with another two established order selection criteria the Akaike's Final Prediction Error (FPE) and Schwarz's Bayesian Criterion (BIC).

1 Introduction

In real world applications it is often assumed that a multivariate (MV) autoregressive (AR) process is used to generate a given set of time series. Based on that assumption one can model and use the data generation process, for example, for predicting future values of the considered variables. The problem of fitting a multivariate autoregressive (AR) model to a given time series is an essential one in system identification and spectral analysis. Moreover, it arises in a large variety of applications, such as multichannel data analysis, EEG and ECG analysis, geophysical data processing, clutter suppression in airborne radar signal processing, etc [1], [2].

An m-variate AR model of order θ [AR(θ) model] for a stationary time series of vectors observed at equally spaced instants n is defined as:

$$y_n = \sum_{i=1}^{\theta} A_i y_{n-i} + v_n, \quad E[v_n v_n^T] = R \tag{1}$$

where the m-dimensional vector v_n is uncorrelated random noise vector with zero mean and covariance matrix R, and $A_1,...,A_\theta$ are the m × m coefficient matrices of the AR model.

The problem can be described as follows: given a set of samples from a discrete time process {y (k), 0 ≤ k ≤ N – 1}, it is desired to obtain the set of coefficients {A_i} which yields the best linear prediction of y(N) based on all past samples:

$$\hat{y}(N/N-1) = \sum_{i=1}^{\theta} A_i \, y \, (N-i) \tag{2}$$

where (N / N – 1) denotes the predicted value of y(N) based on the measurements up to and including y(N – 1).

It is obvious that the problem is twofold. The first task is the successful determination of the predictor's order θ and the second is the computation of the predictor's matrix coefficients Ai. Determining the order of the AR process is usually the most delicate and crucial part of the problem. Over the past years substantial literature has been produced for this problem and various different criteria, such as Akaike's [3], Rissanen's [4], [5], Schwarz's [6], Wax's [7] have been proposed to implement the AR order selection process (for a survey see [8]).

The multivariate AR model order estimation problem is an extension of the scalar case. Recently, Broesrsen and Waele [9], introduced a new order selection criterion, based on the calculation of an optimal penalty factor, a "trade off" of underfit and overfit. Also Neumaier and Schneider [10] proposed a stepwise least squares algorithm for order and parameter estimation of vector AR models.

Once the model order selection task is completed, one proceeds with the identification of the prediction coefficients.

The above mentioned criteria are not optimal and is also known to suffer from deficiencies; for example, Akaike's information criterion suffers from overfit. Also their performance depends on the assumption that the data are Gaussian and upon asymptotic results. In addition to this, their applicability is justified only for large samples; furthermore, they are two pass methods, so they cannot be used in an on line or adaptive fashion.

The problem of simultaneous selection of the AR model order and of the AR parameters identification was first considered for the scalar case in [11], where a new method for scalar AR models was introduced, that overcomes these deficiencies.

In this paper, a new method for multivariate AR model order selection and parameter identification is presented, as an extension to the one proposed in [11] for scalar AR models. The method is based on the well known adaptive multimodel partitioning theory [12] – [13], it is not restricted to the Gaussian case, it is applicable to on line/adaptive operation and it is computationally efficient. Furthermore, it identifies the correct model order very fast.

This paper is organized as follows: in Section 2 the AR model order selection problem is reformulated so that it can be fitted into the state space under uncertainty estimation problem framework. In the same section the multimodel partitioning filter (MMPF) is briefly described and its application to the specific problem is discussed. In Section 3, simulation examples are presented, which demonstrate the performance of our method in comparison with previously reported ones. Finally, Section 4 summarizes the conclusions.

2 AR Model Order Selection Reformulated

If we assume that the model order fitting the data is known and is equal to θ, we can re-write equation (1) in standard state-space form as:

$$x(k+1) = x(k) \tag{3}$$

$$y(k) = h^T(k)x(k) + v(k) \tag{4}$$

where x(k) is made up of the matrices $A_1...A_\theta$, and $h^T(k)$ is the observation history of the process $\{y(k)\}$ up to the time $k - \theta$.

$$x(k) = [A_1 \mid A_2 \mid ... A_\theta]^T,$$

where the general form of the matrix A_θ is $\begin{bmatrix} a_{\theta 11} & \cdots & a_{\theta 1m} \\ \vdots & \ddots & \vdots \\ a_{\theta m1} & \cdots & a_{\theta mm} \end{bmatrix}$.

$$h^T(k) = [\, y_1(k-1) \times I \mid ... y_m(k-1) \times I \mid ... y_m(k-i) \times I\,]$$

where I is the m × m identity matrix and $i = 1, 2, ... \theta$.

In this case, where the system model and its statistics are completely known, the Kalman filter (KF), in its various forms is the optimal estimator in the minimum variance sense.

Remarks

1) Notice that $h^T(k)$ cannot be defined for $k<\theta$, unless values are assumed for $y(k)$, $k < \theta$. To enable us to define it, we assume that $y(k) = 0$ for $k < \theta$. This technique is well known as "pre – windowing."

2) In the case where the prediction coefficients are subject to random perturbations (1), (3) become respectively

$$y(k) = \sum_{i=1}^{\theta} A_i(k) y(k-i) + v(k) \tag{5}$$

$$x(k+1) = x(k) + w(k) \tag{6}$$

Now, A_i has been replaced by $A_i(k)$, to reflect the possibility that the coefficients are subject to random perturbations of the form

$$A_i(k+1) = A_i(k) + v_i \tag{7}$$

and $v(k)$, $w(k)$ are independent, zero–mean, white processes, not necessarily Gaussian.

Let us now consider the case where the system model is not completely known. The adaptive multimodel partitioning filter (MMPF) is one of the most widely used approaches for similar problems. This approach was introduced by Lainiotis in [12] - [13] and summarizes the parametric model uncertainty into an unknown, finite dimensional parameter vector whose values are assumed to lie within a known set of finite cardinality. A non - exhaustive list of the reformulation, extension and application of the MMPF approach as well as its application to a variety of problems by many authors can be found in [16] and [18] – [21]. In our problem assume that the model uncertainty is the lack of knowledge of the model order θ. Let us further assume that the model order θ lies within a known set of finite cardinality: $1 \le \theta \le M$. The MMPF operates on the following discrete model:

$$x(k+1) = F(k+1, k/\theta) x(k) + w(k) \tag{8}$$

$$z(k) = h^T(k/\theta) x(k) + v(k) \tag{9}$$

where θ is the unknown parameter, the model order in this case and F the state transition matrix. A block diagram of MMPF is presented in Fig. 1.

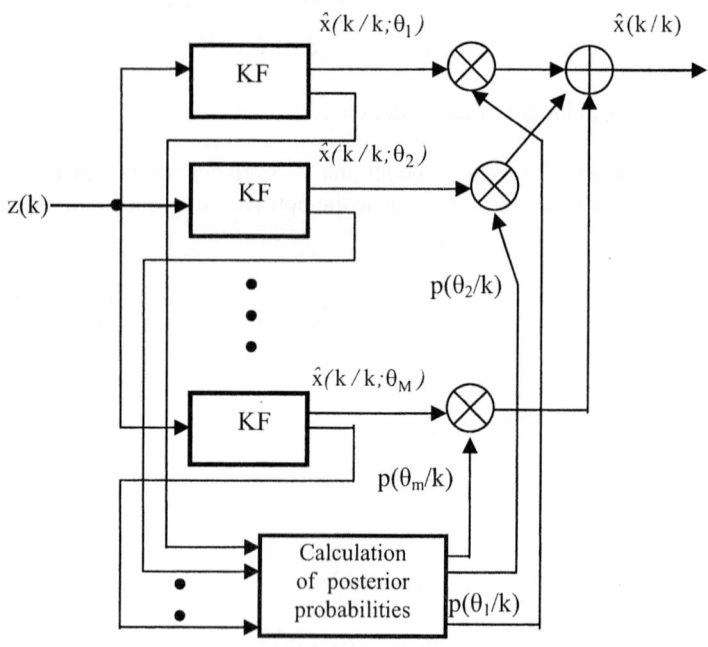

Fig. 1. MMPF Block Diagram

A finite set of models is designed, each matching one value of the parameter vector. If the prior probabilities p for each model are already known, these are assigned to each model. In the absence of any prior knowledge, these are set to 1/M where M is the cardinality of the model set.

A bank of conventional elemental filters (non adaptive, e.g Kalman) is then applied, one for each model, which can be run in parallel. At each iteration the MMPF selects the model which corresponds to the maximum posteriori probability as the correct one. This probability tends to one, while the others tend to zero. The overall optimal estimate can be taken either to be the individual estimate of the elemental filter exhibiting the highest posterior probability, called the maximum *a posteriory* (MAP) estimate, in [15], which is the case used in this paper, or the weighted average of the estimates produced by the elemental filters, as described in Eq (10). The weights are determined by the posterior probability that each model in the model set is in fact the true model.

The optimal Minimum Mean Square Error (MMSE) estimate of $x(k)$ is given by

$$\hat{x}(k/k) = \sum_{i=1}^{M} \hat{x}(k/k;\theta)\, p(\theta/k)d\theta \qquad (10)$$

The probabilities are calculated on – line in a recursive manner as follows:

$$p(\theta/k) = \frac{L(k/k;\theta)}{\sum_{i=1}^{M} L(k/k;\theta)\, p(\theta/k-1)d\theta}\, p(\theta/k-1) \qquad (11)$$

where

$$L(k/k;\theta) = \left|P_z(k/k-1;\theta)\right|^{1/2} \cdot \exp\left\{-1/2\,\|\tilde{z}(k/k-1;\theta)\| \cdot P_z^{-1}(k/k-1;\theta)\right\} \qquad (12)$$

and P_z^{-1} is given by the Kalman filter equations.

Remarks

1) An important feature of the MMPF is that all the Kalman filters needed to implement can be independently realized. This enables us to implement them in parallel, thus saving us enormous computational time [15].

2) Equations (10), (11) refer to our case where the sample space is naturally discrete. However in real world applications, θ's probability density function (pdf) is continuous in θ, and an infinite number of Kalman filters have to be applied for the exact realization of the optimal estimator. The usual approximation considered to overcome this difficulty is to somehow approximate θ's pdf by a finite sum. Many discretization strategies have been proposed at times and some of them are presented in [14], [16] and [17].

3 Examples

In order to assess the performance of our method, simulation experiments were conducted. All of these experiments were conducted 100 times (100 Monte Carlo Runs – MCRs). The models used were that of (3) and (4), with noise covariance $R = \begin{bmatrix} 0.02 & 0.35 \\ 0.35 & 7.6 \end{bmatrix}$ and cardinality M = 10.

Example 1: The data generating process is a first order MV AR (AR(1)) model of the form y(k) = A_1 y(k-1) + v(k), where $A_1 = \begin{bmatrix} -0.99101 & 8.80512*10^{-3} \\ -0.80610 & -0.77089 \end{bmatrix}$.

Table 1 summarizes our results as well as those obtained by the BIC and the FPE order selection criteria. Estimated AR parameters and the Root Mean Square Errors (RMSE) are shown in Table 2. Fig. 2 shows a data set (for 1 MCR, Sample Size 35), which includes a random noise sequence, used for the order determination and parameter estimation and also the posterior probabilities associated with each value of θ.

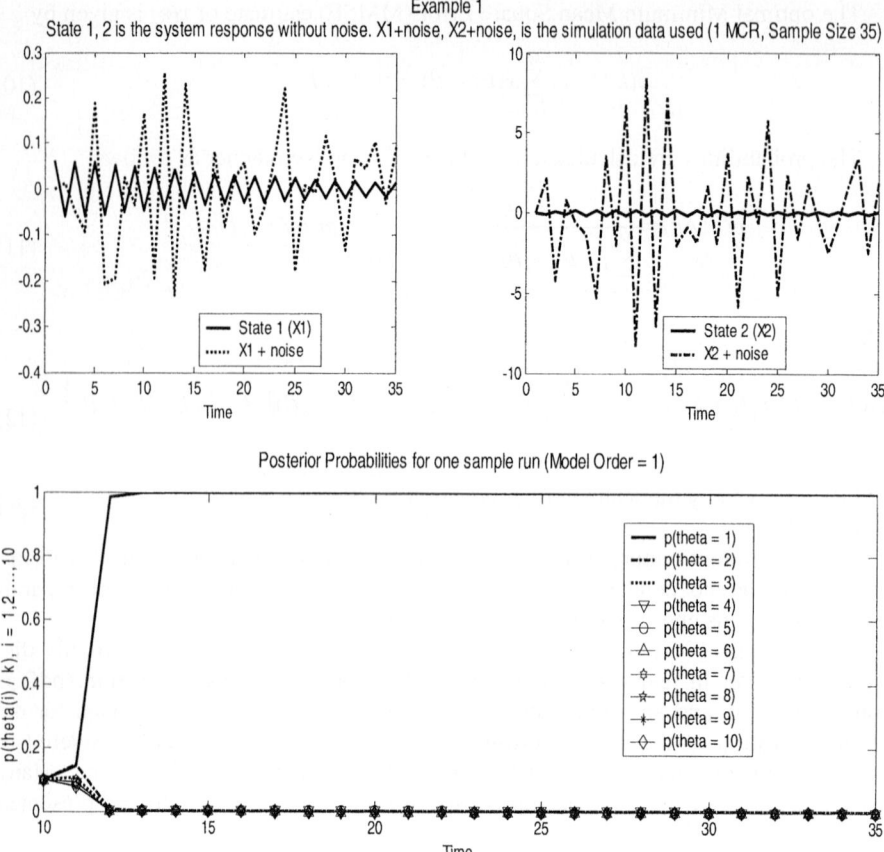

Fig. 2. Example 1, Simulation Results

From Fig 2. is obvious that the presence of the noise changes significantly the system's response. The results presented in Table 1 demonstrate that the MMPF is 100% successful in selecting the correct model order either using a small, or a larger data record set and it does so very fast; it needs only two iterations, as can be seen in Fig. 2, which depicts the posterior probabilities of all the proposed models for only one sample run. BIC is almost as efficient as MMPF for this case, there is an 8% difference for the sample size of 35. On the other hand, FPE is not able to reach the performance of the former criteria and obviously suffers from overfit.

Example 2: A second order data generating process of the form $y(k) = A_1 y(k-1) + A_2 y(k-2) + v(k)$, is used with: $A_1 = \begin{bmatrix} -0.67285 & 0.08017 \\ -4.08017 & -1.99446 \end{bmatrix}$, $A_2 = \begin{bmatrix} -0.19968 & -0.20746 \\ 3.48119 & 1.58868 \end{bmatrix}$.

Table 1. Frequencies of Estimated Order in 100 Monte Carlo Runs for AR(1), with sample sizes 35, 50 (in parenthesis) and 100 (in square brackets)

Criterion	\multicolumn{6}{c}{Estimated Order}					
	0	1	2	3	4	5-10
FPE	0	60 (84) [87]	13 (5) [7]	2 (4) [0]	3 (2) [1]	22 (5) [5]
BIC	0	92 (100) [100]	3 (0) [0]	0 (0) [0]	0 (0) [0]	5 (0) [0]
MMPF	0	100 (100) [100]	0 (0) [0]	0 (0) [0]	0 (0) [0]	0 (0) [0]

Table 2. Estimated Parameters and RMS Error for AR(1) Model, Sample size 100

AR Parameters	Estimated Parameters	RMS Error
-0.9910	-0.8458	0.1452
-0.8061	-1.4682	0.6621
0.0088	0.0022	0.0066
-0.7709	-0.7484	0.0225

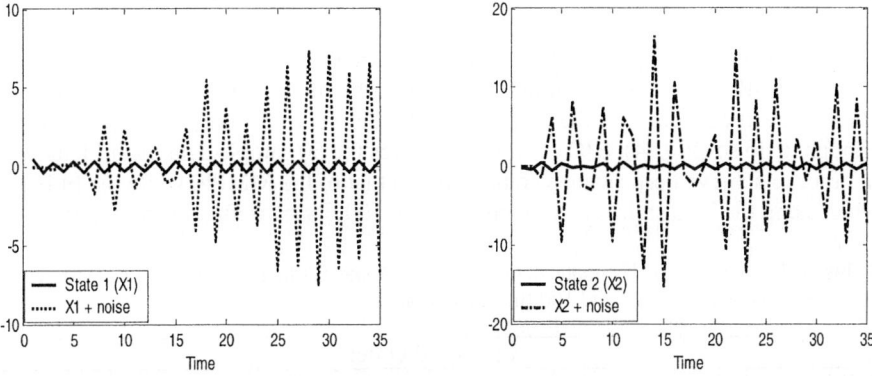

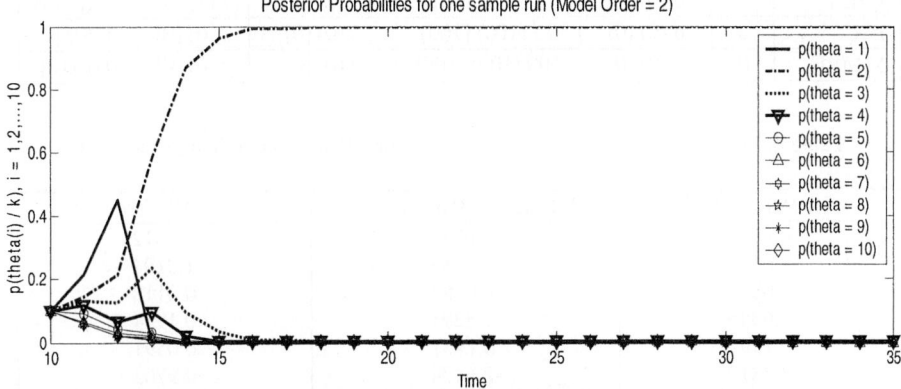

Fig. 3. Example 2, Simulation Results

Table 3 summarizes the comparison results between the three criteria. Estimated AR parameters and the Root Mean Square Errors (RMSE) are shown in Table 4.

The results presented in Table 3 demonstrate that the MMPF is like before 100% successful in selecting the correct model order (which is two in this case) either using a small, or a larger data record set and it does so very fast; it needs only four iterations, as can be seen in Fig. 3, which depicts the posterior probabilities of all the proposed models for only one sample run. BIC is also efficient, when using a sample size of 50 samples or more. Once more FPE is not able to reach the performance of the former criteria and its performance can be considered acceptable in the cases for the sample sizes of 50 and 100.

Example 3: A third order data generating process of the form $y(k) = A_1 y(k-1) + A_2 y(k-2) + A_3 y(k-3) + v(k)$, is used with: $A_1 = \begin{bmatrix} 0.0819 & 0.0615 \\ 0.0391 & 0.2874 \end{bmatrix}$, $A_2 = \begin{bmatrix} 0.1851 & 0.3291 \\ 0.0870 & 0.0498 \end{bmatrix}$, $A_3 = \begin{bmatrix} 0.3220 & 0.5795 \\ 0.0449 & 0.0471 \end{bmatrix}$.

Table 5 summarizes the comparison results of AR(3) between the three criteria. Estimated AR parameters and the Root Mean Square Errors (RMSE) are shown in Table 6. Fig. 4 shows a set of data (1 MCR, Sample Size 35) used for the simulation and also the posterior probabilities associated with each value of θ.

The MMPF was again infallible for all lengths of the data record set (Table 5). Once more, it converges to the correct model order very fast; only seven iterations are enough to do so (Fig. 4). BIC obviously requires the 50 sample data record length in in order to achieve performance comparable to that of the MMPF, while the FPE even when using the largest data record length is not 100% successful, due to overfit.

Table 3. Frequencies of Estimated Order in 100 Monte Carlo Runs for AR(2), with sample sizes 35, 50 (in parenthesis) and 100 (in square brackets)

Criterion			Estimated Order			
	0	1	2	3	4	5-10
FPE	0	0 (0) [0]	41 (79) [78]	8 (12) [15]	7 (1) [3]	44 (8) [4]
BIC	0	0 (0) [0]	75 (100) [100]	5 (0) [0]	0 (0) [0]	20 (0) [0]
MMPF	0	0 (0) [0]	100 (100) [100]	0 (0) [0]	0 (0) [0]	0 (0) [0]

Table 4. Estimated Parameters and RMS Error for AR(2) Model, Sample size 100

AR Parameters	Estimated Parameters	RMS Error
-0.6728	-0.6233	0.0612
-4.0802	-3.1855	1.0194
0.0802	0.0887	0.0118
-1.9945	-1.8291	0.1954
0.1997	0.2467	0.0591
-3.4812	-2.6474	0.9763
0.2075	0.2166	0.0127
-1.5887	-1.4149	0.2078

Table 5. Frequencies of Estimated Order in 100 Monte Carlo Runs for AR(3), with sample sizes 35, 50 (in parenthesis) and 100 (in square brackets)

Criterion	0	1	2	Estimated Order 3	4	5-10
FPE	0	0 (0) [0]	0 (0) [0]	52 (81) [84]	7 (6) [8]	49 (13) [8]
BIC	0	0 (0) [0]	0 (0) [0]	70 (100) [100]	5 (0) [0]	25 (0) [0]
MMPF	0	0 (0) [0]	0 (0) [0]	100 (100) [100]	0 (0) [0]	0 (0) [0]

Table 6. Estimated Parameters and RMS Error for AR(3) Model, Sample size 100

AR Parameters			Estimated Parameters			RMS Error		
0.0819	0.1851	0.3220	0.0781	0.1856	0.3196	0.0193	0.0198	0.0170
0.0391	0.0870	0.0449	-0.0064	0.0823	0.0091	0.2447	0.2343	0.2062
0.0615	0.3291	0.5795	0.0603	0.3261	0.5810	0.0148	0.0127	0.0145
0.2874	0.0498	0.0471	0.2422	-0.0056	0.0326	0.1291	0.1361	0.1560

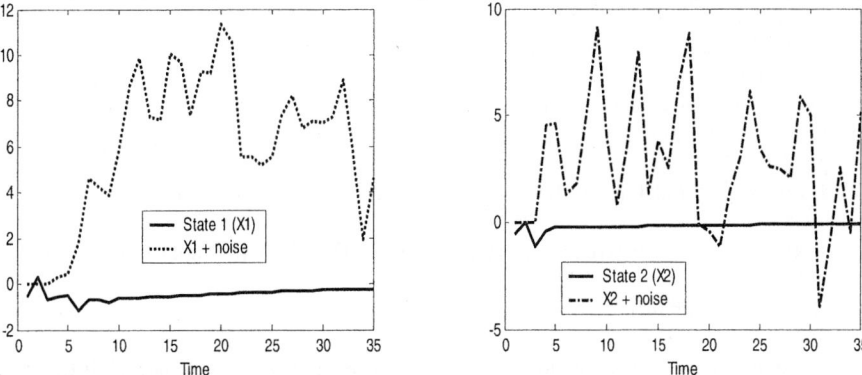

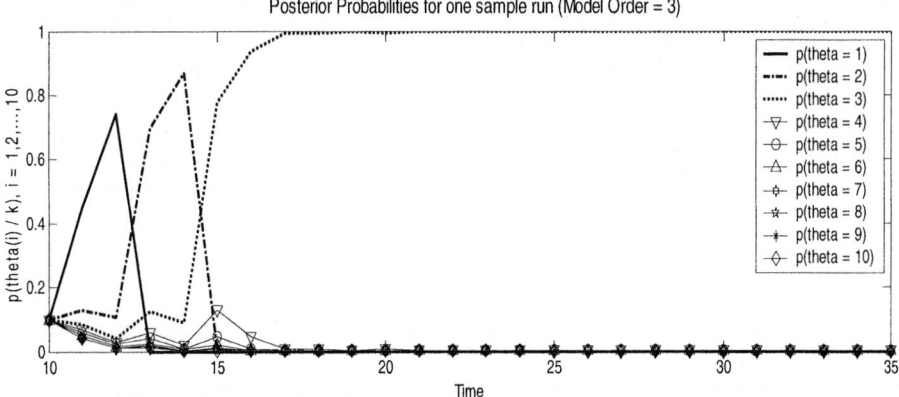

Fig. 4. Example 3, Simulation Results

4 Conclusions

A new method for simultaneously selecting the order and for estimating the parameters of a multivariate autoregressive (AR) model has been developed. The proposed method is 100% successful in selecting the correct model order in very few steps for the presented MV AR models. The results were compared to other established order selection criteria such as the Akaike's Final Prediction Error (FPE) and the Schwarz's Bayesian Criterion (BIC), in order to demonstrate the efficiency of the proposed method. As it was shown MMPF needs the smallest data set for successful order identification for all the simulated models, while the other two criteria require a larger data set as the model order increases in order to achieve a performance comparable to that of MMPF. Bearing in mind the high level of the noise used in these simulations it can be said that the RMSE of the estimated AR parameters lies in an acceptable range.

References

1. C. W. Anderson, E. A. Stolz, S. Shumsunder, "Multivariate autoregressive models for classification of spontaneous electroencephalographic signals during mental tasks ," IEEE Trans. Biomedical Eng, vol. 45, pp. 277 – 286, 1998.
2. J. Li, G. Liu, and P. Stoica, "Moving target feature extraction for airborne high-range resolution phased-array radar," IEEE Trans. Signal Processing, vol. 49, pp. 277 – 289, 2001.
3. H. Akaike, "Fitting autoregressive models for prediction," Ann. Inst. Stat. Math., vol. 21, pp. 243 – 247, 1969.
4. J. Rissanen, "Modeling by shortest data description," Automatica, vol. 14, pp. 465 – 471, 1978.
5. J. Rissanen, "A predictive least squares principle," IMA J. Math. Contr. Inform., vol. 3, pp. 211 – 222, 1986.
6. G. Schwarz, "Estimation of the dimension of the model," Ann. Statist., vol. 6, pp. 461 – 464, 1978.
7. M. Wax, "Order selection for AR models by predictive least squares," IEEE Trans. Acoust., Speech, Signal Processing, vol. 36, pp. 581 – 588, 1988.
8. H. Lutkepohl, "Comparison of criteria for estimating the order of a vector AR process," J. Time Ser. Anal. 6, pp. 35 – 52, vol. 6, 1985.
9. Stijn de Waele and Piet M. T. Broersen, "Order selection for vector autoregressive models," IEEE Trans. Sig. Proc. vol. 51, 2003.
10. A. Neumaier and T. Schneider "Estimation of parameters and eigenmodes of multivariate autoregressive models," ACM Trans. Math. Soft. vol. 27, pp. 27 – 57, 2001.
11. S. K. Katsikas, S. D. Likothanassis and D. G. Lainiotis, "AR model identification with unknown process order," IEEE Trans. Acoustics, Speech and Signal Processing, vol. 38, pp. 872 – 876, 1990.
12. D. G. Lainiotis , "Partitioning: A unifying framework for adaptive systems I: Estimation," Proc. IEEE, vol. 64, pp. 1126 – 1143, 1976.
13. ——, "Partitioning: A unifying framework for adaptive systems II: Control," Proc. IEEE, vol. 64, pp. 1182 – 1198, 1976.
14. R. L. Sengbush and D. G. Lainiotis, "Simplified parameter quantization procedure for adaptive estimation," IEEE Trans. Automat. Contr., vol AC-14, pp. 424 – 425, 1969.

15. D. G. Lainiotis, S. K. Katsikas and S. D. Likothanassis, "Adaptive deconvolution of seismic signals: Performance, computational analysis, parallelism," IEEE Trans. Acoust., Speech, Signal Processing, vol. 36, no. 11, pp. 1715 – 1734, 1988.
16. K.. Watanabe, Adaptive Estimation and Control: Partitioning Approach. Englewood Cliffs, NJ: Prentice Hall, 1992.
17. B. D. O. Anderson, T. S. Brinsmead, F. De. Bruyne, J. Hespanha, D. Liberzon, and A. S. Morse, "Multiple model adaptive control, Part 1: Finite controller coverings," Int. J. Robust Nonlinear Contr., vol 10, pp. 909 – 929, 2000.
18. 18. Katsikas, S.K.; Leros, A.K.; Lainiotis, D.G, "Passive tracking of a maneuvering target: an adaptive approach," Signal Processing, IEEE Transactions on, vol 42, Issue 7, pp. 1820 – 1825, 1994
19. Katsikas, S.K.; Likothanassis, S.D.; Beligiannis, G.N.; Berkeris, K.G.; Fotakis, D.A, "Genetically determined variable structure multiple model estimation," Signal Processing, IEEE Transactions on, vol 49, Issue 10, pp. 2253 – 2261, 2001
20. Lainiotis, D.G.; Papaparaskeva, P, "A partitioned adaptive approach to nonlinear channel equalization," Communications, IEEE Transactions on, vol 46, Issue 10, pp. 1325 – 1336, 1998
21. Moussas, V.C.; Likothanassis, S.D.; Katsikas, S.K.; Leros, A.K, "Adaptive On-Line Multiple Source Detection," Acoustics, Speech, and Signal Processing, 2005. Proceedings. (ICASSP '05). IEEE International Conference on Vol. 4, March 18-23, 2005 pp. 1029 – 1032

Cortical Lateralization Analysis by Kolmogorov Entropy of EEG

Lianyi Zhang and Chongxun Zheng

Key Laboratory of Biomedical Information Engineering of EducationMinistry Xi'an,
Jiaotong University Xi'an 710049, China
d310zlyi@sohu.com, cxzheng@mail.xjtu.edu.cn

Abstract. Based on nonlinear dynamic method, mean Kolmogorov entropy (KE) is introduced to analyze and localize the cortical lateralization. The results indicate that: 1) the lateralization determined by Kolmogorov entropy of EEG proposed in this paper is consistent with previous known studies. But this method is more sensitive to cortical lateralization. This method can identify the differences of cortical lateralization between different brain function areas. 2) The dominant hemisphere is not always the same one for some particular task. 3) The cortical lateralization may involve in several different cortical areas synchronously and for different brain areas the lateralizations of the same mental task may be not on the same side. 4) To analyze and localize cortical lateralization, mean Kolmogorov entropy based on spontaneous EEG is a good method.

1 Introduction

It is well known that certain higher cortical abilities are distributed quite unequally between the two halves of the forebrain. A number of functional cerebral asymmetries are recognized to exist in humans. Current understanding of lateralization and of how the cerebral hemispheres interact is surprisingly limited. For example, in spite of a century of experimental research, it remains unclear today which recognized underlying cortical asymmetries (regional size, connectivity, neurotransmitter levels, etc.) actually lead to cerebral specialization, whether the overall influence of one hemisphere on the other is excitatory or inhibitory, and the extent to which the intact contralateral hemisphere contributes to recovery following cortical damage [1, 2]. There are many different views on cortical lateralization. Based on early neurological observations, it has been postulated that only one hemisphere is functional during particular cognizance. Some researchers consider that both hemispheres are equipped with the same mechanisms and the hemispheres are like horses involved in a race, the faster one would win and perform the task [3]. Some propose that the dominant hemisphere is not always the same one for some particular task [4]. There is also the proposal that the hemispheres inhibit each other [5]. At present, it is not clear what physiological mechanisms are responsible for individual lateralization of functions.

The cortical lateralization can be confirmed through experiments such as injecting sodium amytal into a hemisphere (Wada test), measuring RT (Radioisotope Tracer), the split brain, hemispherectomy, and so on. Neuroimaging studies (PET, FMRI, CT, SPECT) have also help localize lateralization effects in specific cortical areas [6, 7].

The Wada test, the split brain, hemispherectomy, measuring RT (Radioisotope Tracer) and other techniques have been used in clinic for several decades and they are invasive testing. Functional magnetic resonance imaging (fMRI) measures may provide a practical and reliable substitute strategy for invasive test in recent years [6]. If the cerebral asymmetries are not obvious enough, fMRI may be not useful. In other words, fMRI may be not sensitive to some potty cerebral asymmetries. A promising, noninvasive, substitute strategy for invasive test may have been the subject of investigation for many years.

A common practice in estimating humain brain activity during performance of a mental task is to process the electroencephalogram (EEG) in order to detect signal changes that could be related to mental processes. Quantified analysis of the EEG (q-EEG) can also be used to characterize specific cortical areas that are activated under experimentally controlled conditions. Techniques that are used to investigate EEG lateralization include power analysis, coherence analysis and interelectrode correlation of activity [8]. These techniques seek out synchronicity between pairs of bilateral homologous EEG recording sites. Another EEG analysis technique proven useful to characterize EEG hemispheric specialization is the study of lateralization coefficients. This is obtained by computing the ratio of EEG power recorded in right over left homologous recording sites. Lateralization coefficients represent the capacity of EEG neural substrates to generate equipotent signals in homologous bilateral EEG recording sites. In this paper, we present a new q-EEG method, Kolmogorov entropy, to analyze and localize specific cortical lateralization areas.

Babloyantz [9] pointed out that brain activities manifested chaos. EEG signals can be considered to be chaotic. So nonlinear dynamics and deterministic chaos theory may supply effective quantitative descriptors of EEG dynamics and of underlying chaos in the brain [10]. Recently nonlinear dynamics analysis, as a powerful feature extraction method for nonlinear time series analysis, has been successfully applied to EEG data. Kolmogorov entropy (KE) is one of widely used measures of chaotic behavior and it describes the rate at which information about the state of the dynamic process is lost with time. Based on nonlinear dynamic theory, here we have introduced mean Kolmogorov entropy within one second and have used mean Kolmogorov entropy to study spontaneous EEG in order to: (1) investigate the probability of analysis and localization cortical lateralization with nonlinear dynamics methods, (2) investigate whether the dominant hemisphere is always the same one for some particular task, (3) investigate whether the dominant hemisphere only exists in one brain area.

The rest of the paper is organized as follows. Section 2 explains the methods proposed in this paper. Experiment task and data collection are described in section 3. Data analysis is in section 4. Conclusions are in section 5. Discussion is given in section 6.

2 Methods

Kolmogorov entropy (KE) describes the rate at which information about the state of the dynamic process is lost with time. The calculation of KE from a time series typically starts from reconstructing the system's trajectory in an embedding space. The EEG signals generated from brain can reflect the status of brain activity. The EEG can be represented by projections of all variables in a multi-dimensional state space. Let x_i, $i=1,\cdots,N$ be a sample series of EEG. It is a discrete time series. Then, a m-dimensional time delay vector (in an N-dimensional space) $X(n)$ can be constructed as follows:

$$X(n) = \{x(n), x(n+\tau), x(n+2\tau), \cdots, x(n+(m-1)\tau)\}. \tag{1}$$

Where τ is the time delay and m is the embedding dimension of the system. Then we can calculate the correlation sum $C_m(e)$ introduced by Grassberger and Procaccia [11]:

$$C_m(e, N_m) = \frac{2}{N_m(N_m-1)} \sum_{i=1}^{N} \sum_{j=i+1}^{N} \Theta(e - \| x_i - x_j \|). \tag{2}$$

$$N_m = N - (m-1)\tau \tag{3}$$

where Θ is the Heaviside step function, $\Theta(x) = 0$ if $x \leq 0$ and $\Theta(x) = 1$ for x>0. e is a given distance in a particular norm. If an attractor is presence in the time series, then, the values $C_m(e, N_m)$ should satisfy $C_m(e, N_m) \propto e^D$ for small e and large m and N_m, where D is the correlation dimension of the attractor and given by:

$$d_m(N_m, e) = \frac{\partial \ln C_m(e, N_m)}{\partial \ln e}. \tag{4}$$

$$D = \lim_{e \to 0} \lim_{N_m \to \infty} d_m(N_m, e). \tag{5}$$

The correlation dimension is a tool to quantify self-similarity when it is known to be present. If e is small enough and d_m does not vary with m, then Kolmogorov entropy (KE) can be calculated as follows:

$$KE = \lim_{e \to 0} \lim_{m \to \infty} \frac{1}{\tau} \ln(\frac{C_m(e)}{C_{m+1}(e)}). \tag{6}$$

Higher and finite positive KE suggests that the system would be chaos. KE=0 implies an ordered system, KE=∞ corresponds to a totally stochastic situation. The higher the KE, the more close to a stochastic the system is.

Eckmann [16] proved fundamental limitation for estimating dimensions and Lyapunov exponents in dynamical system. That is:

$$N_m \geq 10^{\frac{d_{m\max}}{2}}. \tag{7}$$

d_m could be considered unchanged if $|d_{m+1} - d_m| \leq 0.01$.

In practical applications the proper choice of the delay time t is quite important. If it is too small, then there is almost no difference between the different elements of the delay vectors, such that all points are accumulated around the bisectrix of the embedding space. If t is very large, the different coordinates may be almost uncorrelated. In this case the reconstructed attractor may become very complicated, even if the underlying 'true' attractor is simple. Actually, t can be determined by auto-covariance function $c(t)$:

$$c(t) = \frac{\frac{1}{N}\sum_{n=1}^{N-t}(x(n+t)-\bar{x})(x(n)-\bar{x})}{\frac{1}{N}\sum_{n=1}^{N}(x(n)-\bar{x})^2}. \tag{8}$$

$$\bar{x} = \frac{1}{N}\sum_{n=1}^{N}x(n). \tag{9}$$

A reasonable way is to choose $\tau = t$ when the autocorrelation function decays to 1/e [12].

Actually, EEG signal is always changing with time. So the KE of EEG is not a constant over time. To measure the unorderly degree of EEG signal, mean Kolmogorov entropy within one second is introduced:

$$\text{Mean } KE = \frac{1}{N}\sum_{n=1}^{N}KE(n) \tag{10}$$

In the following of this paper the time series indicate EEG time series and KE refers the mean KE of EEG.

3 Experiment Tasks and Data Collection

The EEG data in this paper was from Keirn and Aunon [13]. (The data is available online at http://www.cs.colostate.edu/~anderson.). In this paper we choose the EEGs of four subjects to study. All subjects are mail. Subjects 1 and 2 were employees of a university. Subject 1 was left-handed and aged 48. Subject 2 was right-handed and aged 39. Subject 3 and subject 4 were right-handed college students. Subjects were placed in a dim, sound controlled room. The electrodes were placed at O1, O2, P3, P4, C3 and C4 reference to the 10-20 system. The impedances of all electrodes were kept below 5 KΩ. Recordings were made with reference to electrically linked mastoids A1 and A2. Fig. 1 shows the placement of electrodes. The data was sampled at 250 Hz and signals were recorded for 10 s during each task, so each segment gave 2500 samples per channel. In this paper, EEG segments from four subjects performing three different mental tasks are used. The electrodes were connected through a bank of Grass 7P511 amplifiers whose bandpass analog filters were set at 0.1~100 Hz. The data were recorded using an IBM-AT controlling a Lab Master analog to digital converter with 12 bits of accuracy. The following is a description of the tasks.

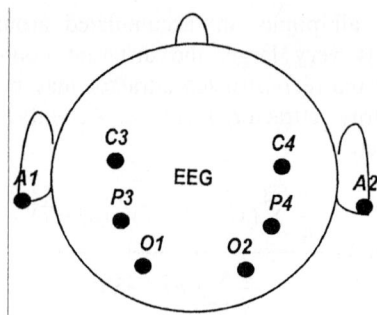

Fig. 1. Electrode placement

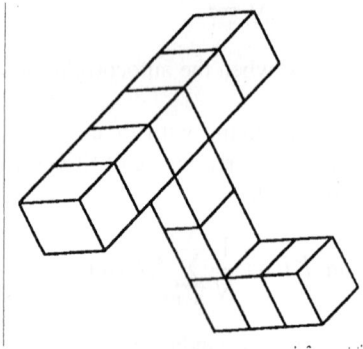

Fig. 2. Example of one of the figures used for the geometric figure rotation task

Task 1-Baseline Measurements

The subject was asked to simply relax and try to think of nothing in particular. This task was used as a control and as baseline measure of electroencephalogram.

Task 2-Complex Problem Solving

The subject was given a nontrivial multiplication problem to solve and, as in all of the tasks, was instructed not to vocalize or make over movements while solving the problem.

Task 3-Geometric Figure Rotation

The subjects was given 30 s to study a drawing of a complex three dimensional block figure after which the drawing was removed and the subject was instructed to visualize the object being rotated about an axis. An example is shown in Fig. 2. The EEG was recoded during the mental rotation period.

4 Data Analysis

In order to obtain the data of spontaneous EEG signals, a FIR with bandpass filter 0.5-30 Hz was used. At the beginning of calculation KE of four subjects' EEG signal piece by piece, first 4 seconds (1000 sample) data are chosen as basic data and step length is 25 samples (the samples within 0.1s). To compare the effects of left hemisphere and right hemisphere during different mental tasks, the mean KE of 5th, 6th, 7th, 8th, 9th, 10th second of every subject in different channel are calculated respectively. For the same time interval, the same task and the same subject, the left channel's mean KE and the right channel's mean KE of each cortical function area consist of a pair of data. So for each brain function area (Central, Parietal and Occipital) under the different mental task, every subject has 6 pair of KE data.

The properties of KE for different types of dynamics are: KE=0 implies an ordered system, KE=∞ corresponds to a totally stochastic situation. The higher the KE, the closer to a stochastic the system is. So for the bilateral of the same cortical function, the small value of KE corresponds to the dominant hemisphere.

4.1 Task 1-Baseline Measurements

For each cortical area (Central, Parietal and Occipital), four subjects have 24 pair of KE data (shown in Fig. 3). During task 1, the KEs in P3 channel (left) are obviously smaller than that in P4 channel (right). It means that all subjects presented significant left parietal lateralization for the total frequency spectrum ($\bar{d}$ =3.2722, S_d=3.0124, n=24, t=5.3215, p<0.001). From Fig. 3, it can also be found that sometime the mean KE on the left (P3) is larger than that on the right (P4). This indicates that sometime the right half may be the dominant hemisphere and sometime the dominant hemisphere may change from one hemisphere to the other for some particular task. There are no significant lateralization in the central area and occipital area.

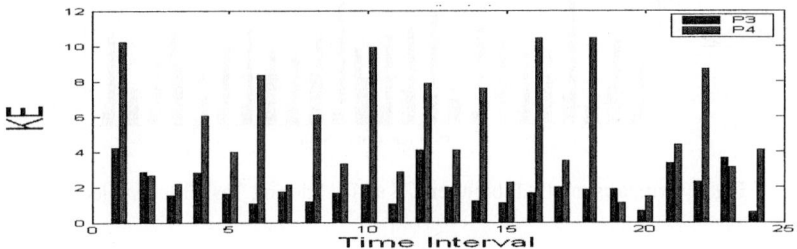

Fig. 3. Comparison of KE between P3 and P4 during Task 1 (all subjects)

4.2 Task 2-Complex Problem Solving

Fig. 4 shows the 24 pair of KE data in parietal area for all subjects during task 2. From Fig. 4, it can be seen that the KEs in P4 channel (right) are obviously greater than that in P3 channel (left). It means that all subjects presented significant left parietal lateralization for the total frequency spectrum ($\bar{d}$ =2.0714, S_d=3.352, n=24, t=3.0274,

0.01<p<0.05). It can also be found from Fig. 4 that sometime the mean KE on the left (P4) is smaller than that on the right (P4) and this indicate that sometime the right half may be the dominant hemisphere. There are no significant lateralization in the central area and occipital area, too.

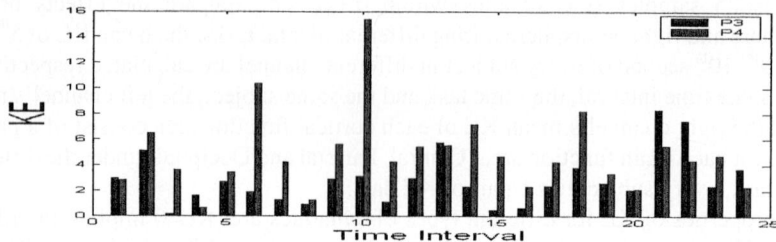

Fig. 4. Comparison of KE between P3 and P4 during Task 2 (all subjects)

4.3 Task 3-Geometric Figure Rotation

Fig. 5, Fig. 6 shows the pairs of KE data in central and occipital area during task 3 respectively. From Fig. 5 and Fig. 6 it can be seen that the KEs in left channels (C3 and O1) are obviously greater than that in right (C4 and O2) in central and occipital area. It means that all subjects presented significant right central lateralization and right occipital lateralization for the total frequency spectrum (For central area: $\overline{d}$ =5.7585, S_d=4.6901, n=24, t=6.015, p<0.001; For occipital area: $\overline{d}$ =1.8117, S_d=4.0335, n=24, t=2.2004, 0.02<p<0.05). It can also be found that right central lateralization is more obvious and significant than right occipital lateralization.

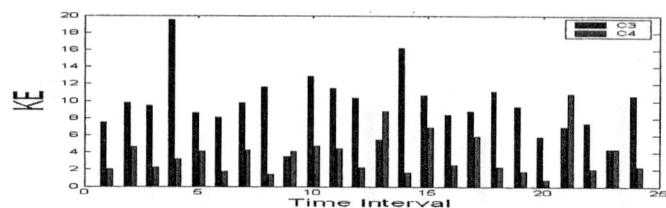

Fig.5. Comparison of KE between C3 and C4 during Task 3 (all subjects)

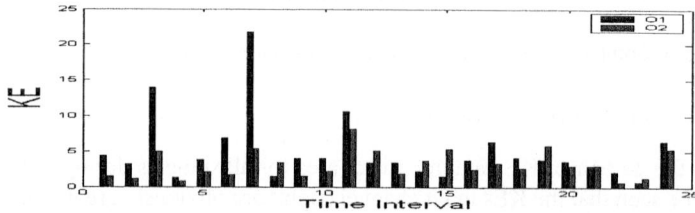

Fig. 6. Comparison of KE between O1 and O2 during Task 3 (all subjects)

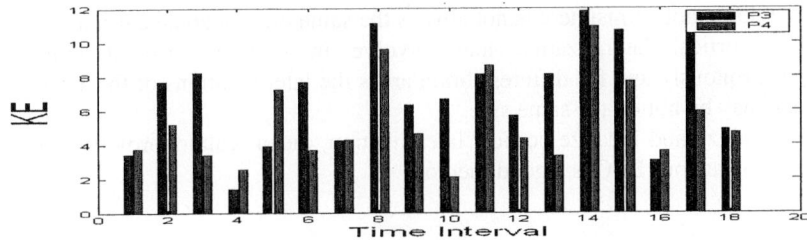

Fig. 7. Comparison of KE between P3 and P4 during Task 3 (right-handed subjects)

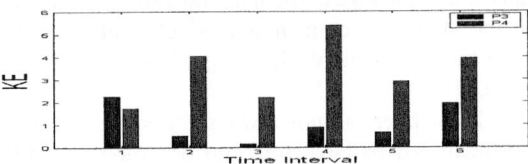

Fig. 8. Comparison of KE between P3 and P4 during Task 3 (left-handed subject)

With regard to parietal area, there is obvious difference for right-handed and left-handed. Fig. 7 shows the pairs of KE data in parietal area for all right-handed subjects. It can be seen from Fig. 7 that the KEs in left channel (P3) are obviously greater than that in right (P4) in parietal area. This means that all right-handed subjects presented significant right parietal lateralization for the total frequency spectrum ($\bar{d}$ =1.5119, S_d=2.4163, n=18, t=2.6547, 0.01<p<0.02). In parietal area, the left-handed subject is contrary to the right-handed. Fig. 8 shows the pairs of KE data of the left-handed in parietal area during task 3. It can be seen from Fig. 8 that the KEs in left channel (P3) are obviously smaller than that in right (P4) and this indicates that the left-handed presented significant left parietal lateralization for the total frequency spectrum ($\bar{d}$ =2.327, S_d=1.6969, n=6, t=3.359, 0.02<p<0.05).

During task 3, the phenomena of lateralization exist in three different brain areas synchronously. But the right central lateralization is the most obvious and significant. This can be seen from Fig. 5 to Fig. 8.

From Fig. 5 to Fig. 8, it can also be found that sometime the dominant hemisphere changes from one lateral to the contralateral.

5 Conclusions

Cortical lateralization analysis by Kolmogorov entropy of EEG is based on brain neural activity and nonlinear dynamics theory. From analysis above, the following results can be educed:

1) The lateralization determined by Kolmogorov entropy of EEG proposed in this paper is consistent with previous known studies [14,15, 8]. But this method is more sensitive to cortical lateralization. This method can identify the differences of cortical lateralization between different brain function areas.

2) The dominant hemisphere is not always the same one for some particular task
3) The cortical lateralization may involve in several different brain areas synchronously and for different brain areas the lateralizations of the same mental task may be not on the same side.
4) To analyze and localize cortical lateralization, mean Kolmogorov entropy based on spontaneous EEG is a good method.

6 Discussion

A new method to analyze and localize cortical lateralization of mental activity has been described, based on the statistical comparison of left and right mean Kolmogorov entropy of EEG. With the new method, investigations explore some interested and meaningful phenomena.

First, the dominant hemisphere is not always the same one for some particular mental task. For the mean KE pairs of bilateral homologous EEG recordings, the dominant hemisphere is not always smaller than that of the non-dominant. Sometime the mean KE of the dominant hemisphere is larger than that of the non-dominant. All subjects in this study presented this characteristic. This indicates that the dominant hemisphere is not always the one that actuall controls performance on a particular task.

Second, the lateralization for some particular mental task may involve in several brain areas synchronously. On the task of geometric figure rotation all subjects presented significant right central lateralization, right occipital lateralization and parietal lateralization synchronously. But the degree of lateralization is different. Adock J. E. had found the phenomena in patients with temporal lobe epilepsy [6]. It is possible to explore the dominant lateralization of different brain area on a particular mental task with this method proposed in present study.

Third, for different brain areas the lateralizations of the same mental task may not be on the same side. Cortical lateralization has been used in scientific reports and in daily life. Whether the cortical areas involved in a particular mental task present the same side laterlization, which has not been investigated yet. Moreover, it is not known that how many brain areas involve in a particular mental task. In present study, the left-handed subject may present right central lateralization, right occipital lateralization and left parietal lateralization synchronously on the task of geometric figure rotation. So we think that the view of 'the lateralization in some brain area' is more exact than that of 'the cortical lateralization'.

The method to analyze and localize cortical lateralization of mental activity based on Kolmogorov entropy and spontaneous EEG may provide new, promising, noninvasive test for lateralization in clinic

References

1. Davidson, R., Hugdahl, K. (Eds.), (1995). Brain asymmetry. MIT Press.
2. Hellige, J. (1993). Hemispheric asymmetry. Harvard University Press.

3. Zaidel, E., Rayman, J.: Interhemispheric control in the normal brain: evidence from redundant bilateral presentation. In: Ultima, C.; Moscovith, M., eds. Attention and performance XV: conscious and subconscious information processing. Boston: MIT Press, 1994: 477-504.
4. Hellige, J. B.: Hemispheric asymmetry: what's right and what's left. Cambridge, MA: Harvard University Press, 1993.
5. Braitenberg, V., Schuz, A.: Anatomy of the cortex. Atatistics and geometry. Berlin: Springer; 1991.
6. Adock, J. E., Wise, R. G., Oxbury, J. M., Oxbury, S. M., Matthews P. M.: Quantitative fMRI assessment of the differences in lateralization of language-related brain activation in patients with temporal lobe epilepsy. Neuroimage, Volume: 18, Issue: 2, February, 2003, pp. 423-438.
7. Brockway, P, John, P.: fMRI may replace the WADA test for language lateralization/localization. Neuroimage, Volume: 11, Issue: 5, Supplement, May, 2000, pp. S277.
8. Bolduc, C., Daoust, A.M., Limoges, E., Braun, C.M.J., Godbout, R.: Hemispheric lateralization of the EEG during wakefulness and REM sleep in young healthy adults. Brain and cognition, Volume: 53, Issue: 2, November, 2003, pp. 193-196.
9. Babloyantz, A.: Evidence of chaotic dynamics of brain activity during the sleep cycle. Phys Lett (A), 1985; 111: 152~156.
10. Sarbadhikari, S.N., Charabarty K.: Chaos in the brain: a short review alluding to epilepsy, depression, exercise and lateralization. Medical Engineering & Physics, 23 (2001), 445~455.
11. Grassberger, P., Procaccia I.: Measuring the strangeness of strange attractors. Physica 9D: 189-209, 1983.
12. Kantz, H., Schreiber, T.: Nonlinear Time Series Analysis. Cambridge University Press 1997, pp. 70-75.
13. Keirn, Z.A., Aunon, J.I.: A new mode of communication between man and his surroundings. *IEEE Trans. Biomed. Eng.*, Vol. 37, pp. 1209–1214, Dec. 1990.
14. Benson, D.F.: Aphasia and the lateralization of language. Cortex. 1986, vol. 12, pp. 71-86.
15. Liegeois, F., Connely, A., Salmond, H., Gadian, D. G., Vargha-Khadem, F., Baldeweg T.: A direct test for lateralization of language activation using fMRI: comparison with invasive assessments in children with epilepsy. NeuroImage 17, 1861-1867 (2002).
16. Eckmann, J.P., Ruelle, D.: Fundamental limitations for estimating dimensions and Lyapunov exponents in dynamical systems. Physica D, 1992, 56: 185-187.

Source-Based Minimum Cost Multicasting: Intermediate-Node Selection with Potentially Low Cost*

Gunu Jho, Moonseong Kim, and Hyunseung Choo

School of Information and Communication Engineering,
Sungkyunkwan University,
440-746, Suwon, Korea +82-31-290-7145
{jhogunu, moonseong, choo}@ece.skku.ac.kr

Abstract. In this paper, we propose a novel heuristic algorithm for constructing a minimum cost multicast tree. Our work is based on a directed asymmetric network and shows an improvement in terms of network cost for general random topologies close to real networks. It is compared to the most effective scheme proposed earlier by Takahashi and Matsuyama (TM) [18]. We have experimented comprehensive computer simulations and the performance enhancement is up to about 4.7% over TM. The time complexity of ours is $O(kn^2)$ for an n-node network with k members in the multicast group which is comparable to those of previous works [12,18].

1 Introduction

The advances in high-speed Internet technology coupled with the advent of high-speed desktop computing, data processing, and data storage technology have resulted in the rapid development of large-scale computing and communication systems to support multimedia applications. These applications usually require large bandwidth, stringent delay and delay-jitter, and multireceiver connections. And there is an urgent need to design and implement efficient routing algorithms with quality-of-service (QoS) support.

Multicasting refers to the data transmission from a node (called a source) to a group of selected nodes (called members or destinations) in communication networks. Multicast routing uses trees, called multicast routing trees, over the network topology for transmission to minimize resource usage such as cost and bandwidth by sharing links. Data generated by the source flow through the multicast tree, traversing each tree edge exactly once. As a result, multicasting is more resource-efficient and is well-suited to applications such as video distributions.

---

* This work was supported in parts by BK 21 and the Ministry of Information and Communication, Republic of Korea. Corresponding author: H. Choo

The multicast routing problem is well-studied in the area of computer networks and graph theory. Depending on the performance criterion including cost, delay, and bandwidth etc., the problem could be of varying levels of complexity [19]. The Steiner tree studied extensively earlier is very useful in representing a solutions to such problems, and deals with the cost minimization for a multicast routing tree [8,21]. It has a natural analog of the general multicast tree in computer networks [9,11,20].

The Steiner tree problem is known as NP-complete [7,8,10,21], and has a vast literature on its own [1,2,6,8,12,18,14,21]. Two most popular polynomial-time algorithms called KMB and TM are proposed in [12] and [18], respectively. Also, an interesting polynomial-time algorithm for a fixed parameter has been proposed in [14], wherein an overview of several other approximation algorithms are also provided; distributed algorithms based on Steiner heuristics are provided in [1].

In this paper, we propose a new heuristic algorithm for the Steiner tree problem. It is based on the efficient selection of intermediate nodes with potentially low cost on each phase which eventually affects overall multicast tree cost. Extensive simulations are carried out to compare the performance of our proposed algorithm with TM. The empirical evaluation has shown that the new algorithm generates more efficient multicast tree than that of TM in terms of tree cost. Also the time complexity of our algorithm is analyzed. The rest of this paper is organized as follows. In Section 2, we state the network model for the multicasting, and Section 3 presents details of the proposed algorithm. Then in Section 4, we evaluate our proposition by the simulation model. Finally, Section 5 concludes this paper.

2 Preliminaries

2.1 Network Model for Multicasting

A network is modeled as a directed asymmetric simple graph $G = (V, E)$ with a node set V and an edge set E. Each edge $(i, j) \in E$ has a link cost $c_{ij} > 0$. We shall denote a path in G by a sequence of nodes, $u_1, u_2, ..., u_p$, such that for all k, $1 \le k < p$, $(u_k, u_{k+1}) \in E$. We shall say that the path is from u_1 to u_p and its path cost is $\sum_{k=1}^{p-1} c_{u_k u_{k+1}}$. A minimum cost path from u_1 to u_p is a path from u_1 to u_p whose cost is minimal among all the possible paths from u_1 to u_p. $P(u_1, u_p)$ denotes the minimum cost path from u_1 to u_p and $C(u_1, u_p)$ denotes the path cost of $P(u_1, u_p)$. Let $P^*(W, n)$ denote a path whose cost is minimum among all minimum cost paths from each node in W to a node n where $W \subseteq V$ and $n \notin W$. Denote by $C^*(W, n)$ the path cost of $P^*(W, n)$.

A tree $T = (VT, ET)$ of G is a connected subgraph of G such that the removal of any edge in ET will make it disconnected. And the tree cost $C_T(T)$ is $\sum_{(i,j) \in ET} c_{ij}$. Given a network topology $G = (V, E)$, let $D \subset V$ be a set of destination nodes, and $s \in V \setminus D$ be the source node. The minimum cost multicast routing problem is that of finding a directed routing tree $T(VT, ET)$ which spans the source node s and destination nodes in D, satisfying the requirement to minimize $C_T(T)$.

2.2 Related Works

The Steiner tree is very effective on solving multicast routing problems. It is employed mostly when there is just one active multicast group and the minimum cost tree is wanted. Here, we discuss the most efficient heuristic for the Steiner tree problem. This is compared to our proposed algorithm in Section 4.

The TM [18] which has a resulting tree cost practically within 5% to that of the optimal one [5,14,17] is a shortest path based algorithm and is further studied and generalized in [14]. It generates a multicast tree as follows:

Step 1. Start with subgraph $T_1 = (V_1, E_1)$ consisting a single source node s, say v_1, that is, set $V_1 = \{v_1\}$ and $E_1 = \emptyset$.
Step 2. For each $i = 2, 3, ..., |D|$ do
Find a node in $D \setminus V_{i-1}$, say v_i, such that
$C^*(V_{i-1}, v_i) = min\{C^*(V_{i-1}, v_j) \mid v_j \in D \setminus V_{i-1}\}$
Construct tree $T_i = (V_i, E_i)$ by adding $P^*(V_{i-1}, v_i)$ to T_{i-1},
i.e. $V_i = V_{i-1} \cup \{nodes\ in\ P^*(V_{i-1}, v_i)\}$ and
$E_i = E_{i-1} \cup \{edges\ in\ P^*(V_{i-1}, v_i)\}$.

Since $P^*(V_{i-1}, v_i)$ can be computed in time complexity $O(|V|^2)$ by Dijkstra's algorithm [4], TM requires at most $O(|D||V|^2)$. And it is proved that the algorithm constructs a tree whose cost is within twice that of optimal one [18].

3 The Proposed Algorithm

3.1 Overview

The new proposed algorithm assumes that the source node has complete information for all network links to construct a multicast tree. This requirement can be supported by any one of many topology-broadcast algorithms, which can be based on flooding (as is the case in OSPF and IS-IS) or other techniques [3]. The proposed algorithm consists of following major steps.

Input. Network topology $G = (V, E)$, source node s, set of destination nodes D.
Output. Minimum cost multicast tree $T = (VT, ET)$ spanning s and all nodes in D.
Step 1. Find all minimum cost paths from each node in V to each node in D.
Step 2. Start from initial tree $T = (VT, ET)$, where $VT = \{s\}$ and $ET = \emptyset$.
Step 3. Find an *intermediate-node* $v \in V \setminus VT$ and if found, connect v to T through $P^*(VT, v)$.

Step 4. If $v \notin D$ or not found v at Step 3, then find $d_{min} \in D \setminus VT$, such that $C^*(VT, d_{min}) = min\{C^*(VT, d) \mid d \in D \setminus VT\}$. And connect d_{min} to T through $P^*(VT, d_{min})$.
Step 5. Repeat Steps 3 and 4 until VT contains all nodes in D.
Step 6. Prune the leaves which are not the member of D.

Since the Dijkstra's algorithm [4] can find the minimum cost paths from one node to all nodes in G at most $O(|V|^2)$ time, we can apply the algorithm to find the minimum cost paths from all nodes in V to one node in D. And we can execute Step 1 at most $O(|D||V|^2)$ time. Step 1 is for the preparation and Step 2 is for the initialization on Steps 3, 4 and 5. One of our contributions here except the performance improvement is to employ the *intermediate-node*. The *intermediate-node* is a node in $V \setminus VT$ which will be included to the current tree to have cost-effective extension to the remaining destination nodes. Before we can describe the proposed algorithm in detail, we need to define new concepts. They are used to select the *intermediate-node* at each loop where the minimum cost multicast tree spans a destination node.

Definition 1. *Potential Cost(PC)*: The potential cost of node $i \in V \setminus VT$ is the sum of costs of each minimum cost path from i to each $d \in D \setminus VT$.

$$1) \quad PC(i) = \sum_{d \in D \setminus VT} C(i, d), \text{ for each } i \in V \setminus VT$$

And the potential cost of a tree $T = (VT, ET)$ is the sum of costs of each minimum cost path from a node in VT to each $d \in D \setminus VT$.

$$2) \quad PC_T = \sum_{d \in D \setminus VT} C^*(VT, d)$$

Definition 2. *Spanning Cost(SC)*: The spanning cost of node $i \in V \setminus VT$ is the sum of cost of the minimum cost path from a node in VT to i and the potential cost of i.

$$SC(i) = C^*(VT, i) + PC(i), \text{ for each } i \in V \setminus VT$$

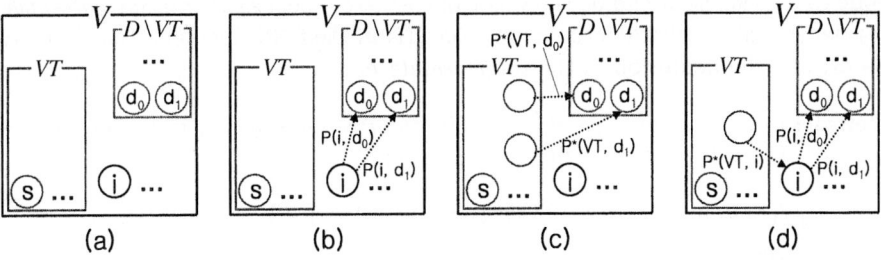

Fig. 1. Venn diagram-like representation. (a)Sets V, VT, and $D \setminus VT$ at the status on generating minimum cost multicast tree. (b)The potential cost of $i \in V \setminus VT$, $PC(i)$ is the sum of $C(i, d_0)$, $C(i, d_1)$, and so on. (c)The potential cost of $T = (VT, ET)$, PC_T is the sum of $C^*(VT, d_0)$, $C^*(VT, d_1)$, and so on. (d)The spanning cost of $i \in V \setminus VT$, $SC(i)$ is the sum of $PC(i)$ and $C^*(VT, i)$.

The potential cost of $T = (VT, ET)$, PC_T means the possible maximum cost that is needed for the current tree T to connect the remaining destination nodes through the minimum cost paths. Similarly, the potential cost of node $i \in V \setminus VT$, $PC(i)$ means the possible maximum cost that is needed for the node i to connect the remaining destination nodes through the minimum cost paths. So, the spanning cost of $i \in V \setminus VT$, $SC(i)$ means the possible maximum cost needed for the algorithm to span the remaining destination nodes in $D \setminus VT$, if the connection is via the node i. If $SC(i)$ is smaller than PC_T, we can assume that the node i may be useful to minimize the overall multicast tree cost. In addition to the spanning cost concept, we have another measure to select an *intermediate-node*.

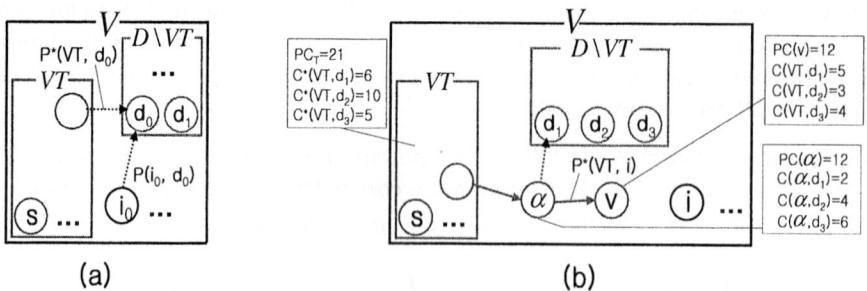

Fig. 2. Venn diagram-like representation. (a)The role of $\chi(i)$. (b)The situation after Step 3 for describing why pruning is required. Node v is the currently selected *intermediate-node* and node α is a node in $P^*(VT, v)$.

Let us suppose the condition (see Fig. 2 (a)) that $SC(i_0)$ is smaller than PC_T but $C(i_0, d_0)$ is larger than $C^*(VT, d_0)$, where $i_0 \in V \setminus VT$ and $d_0 \in D \setminus VT$. Then, i_0 is useless for now, the current spanning state which is to connect one destination node to T, because it can be the waste of cost to connect i_0 as *intermediate-node*. We denote this as characteristic function $\chi(i)$ in the following definition. Finally, we present the definition of the *intermediate-node v*.

Definition 3. *Intermediate-node v*: The *intermediate-node v* is a node in $V \setminus VT$, such that $SC(v) < PC_T$ and

$$f(v) = min\{f(i) = SC(i) \times \chi(i) \mid i \in V \setminus VT\}$$

where,

$$\chi(i) = \begin{cases} 1, & if\ C(i,d) < C^*(VT,d)\ \forall d \in D \setminus VT \\ \infty, & otherwise \end{cases}$$

If there are several is with minimum $f(i)$ value, select the one with minimum $C^*(VT, i)$.

The pruning at the last step of the proposed algorithm is needed. We describe why the pruning is required to complete the algorithm through the Fig. 2 (b).

There are potential costs of T, α, and v with the corresponding costs of minimum cost paths to destination nodes d_1, d_2 and d_3. $PC(v)$ and $PC(\alpha)$ are 12. And it is certain that $SC(\alpha)$ is smaller than $SC(v)$, since $C^*(VT,\alpha)$ is smaller than $C^*(VT,v)$ as shown in Fig. 2 (b). But the node α cannot be the *intermediate-node*, because $C(\alpha, d_3)$ is larger than $C^*(VT, d_3)$ and the characteristic function $\chi(\alpha)$ is set to ∞. So the v is connected to T as an *intermediate-node* through the $P^*(VT, v)$. By the way, α happens to be the node in $P^*(VT, v)$, and consequently it is connected to T with v. Now the algorithm finds the d_{min} among d_1, d_2 and d_3. Maybe d_1 is to be the d_{min} and connected to T through the $P(\alpha, d_1)$ instead of $P(v, d_1)$. If the next loops of the algorithm to connect the d_2 and d_3 would not use the v as the connection point for spanning the tree any more, then the v remains as a leaf which is both needless for construction of multicast tree and waste of cost. Therefore the algorithm prunes the leaves which are not the member of multicast group at the last step of the tree construction.

3.2 Pseudo-code and Time-Complexity

In this subsection, we present the pseudo code of the new proposed algorithm, and analyze its worst case execution time by asymptotic upper bound, big-oh notation.

Heuristic for constructing the minimum cost multicast tree
Input: Network topology $G = (V, E)$, source node s, set of destination nodes D
Output: Minimum cost multicast tree $T = (VT, ET)$
1. Calculate $C(g,h)$ for each $g \in V$, $h \in D$.
2. Initiate the tree $T = (VT, ET)$, where $VT = \{s\}$ and $ET = \emptyset$.
3. **LOOP** until $D \subset VT$
4.   Calculate $PC_T = \sum_{d \in D \setminus VT} C^*(VT, d)$.
5.   Calculate $PC(i) = \sum_{d \in D \setminus VT} C(i, d)$, for each $i \in V \setminus VT$.
6.   Calculate $C^*(VT, i)$, for each $i \in V \setminus VT$.
7.   Calculate $SC(i) = C^*(VT, i) + PC(i)$, for each $i \in V \setminus VT$.
8.   Find an *intermediate-node* $v \in V \setminus VT$ such that $SC(v) < PC_T$ and
        $f(v) = min\{f(i) = SC(i) \times \chi(i) \mid i \in V \setminus VT\}$
        $\chi(i) = \begin{cases} 1, & \text{if } C(i,d) < C^*(VT, d) \; \forall d \in D \setminus VT \\ \infty, & otherwise \end{cases}$
        If there are several is with minimum $f(i)$ value, select the one with minimum $C^*(VT, i)$.
9.   If found v then,
10.   Add $P^*(VT, v)$ to T.
        i.e., $VT = VT \cup \{$ nodes in $P^*(VT, v)\}$,
        $ET = ET \cup \{$ edges in $P^*(VT, v)\}$.
11.   Calculate $C^*(VT, i)$, for each $i \in V \setminus VT$. //Because VT was changed.
12.   If $v \notin D$ or not found v then,
13.   Find a node d_{min} such that
        $C^*(VT, d_{min}) = min\{C^*(VT, d) \mid d \in D \setminus VT\}$.

14.   Add $P^*(VT, d_{min})$ to T.
         i.e., $VT = VT \cup \{$ nodes in $P^*(VT, d_{min})\}$,
         $ET = ET \cup \{$ edges in $P^*(VT, d_{min})\}$.
15. Prune $T(VT, ET)$, if necessary, so that all leaves in T are the nodes in D.

The time-complexity of the proposed algorithm is evaluated as follows. Step 1 is executed in $O(|D||V|^2)$ time based on Dijkstra's algorithm. Step 2 can be completed in $O(|V|^2)$ time if the data structure for $T = (VT, ET)$ is the adjacency matrix. The loop from Step 3 to 14 is repeated $|D|$ times, since one destination node is connected to T by one loop. Steps 4 and 5 are executed in $O(|D||V|)$ time using the result from Step 1. Each of Steps 6 and 11 is executed in $O(|V|^2)$ time using Dijkstra's algorithm. Step 7 is completed in $O(|V|)$ time using the result from Steps 5 and 6. Since the time-complexity for computing χ of one node in $V \setminus VT$ is $O(|D|)$ using the result from Step 1 and SC is already calculated at Step 7, the time complexity of Step 8 is $O(|D||V|)$. Each of Steps 10 and 14 can be executed in $O(|V|)$ time, since the maximum hop of a minimum cost path is $|V|-1$. Step 13 is executed in $O(|D|)$ time using the result from Step 11 or 6. Step 15 could be done in $O(|V|^2)$ time. Hence the total time-complexity of our entire algorithm is $O(|D||V|^2)$ based on the dominating Steps 6 and 11 in the loop. We know that Step 1 also was the same complexity.

3.3 Case Study

In this subsection, we illustrate the operational mechanism of the proposed algorithm. Fig. 3 (a) shows a sample network topology with link cost specified on the middle of each link, source node 1 and set of destination nodes $\{2, 6, 8, 9\}$. The link cost is symmetric only for the simplicity. Fig. 3 (b) represents the minimum cost multicast tree T_{TM} generated by TM algorithm, whose tree cost is 13. TM has spanned each destination node one by one using $P(1, 2)$, $P(1, 6)$, $P(6, 9)$ and $P(9, 8)$, respectively.

Fig. 3. (c), (d), (e) and (f) describe the way that the proposed algorithm spans each destination node using the Table 1, 2, 3, 4 and 5. First of all, the proposed algorithm calculates $C(g, h)$ for each $g \in V$, $h \in D$, as you see the result in Table 1. There are several information which are needed to select the *intermediate-node* at the first loop of the algorithm in Table 2. The algorithm selects the node 0 as an *intermediate-node* whose f is both minimal($f(0) = 17$) and less than $PC_T = 24$. Then it connects to T through $P(1, 0)$. d_{min} is node 2 and connects to T through $P(0, 2)$. At this step current tree is illustrated in Fig. 3 (c). Each of Table 3, 4 and 5 is matched with Fig. 3 (d), (e) and (f), respectively. There are nodes 4, 7 and 9 with the same value of f in Table 3. In this case, our algorithm selects the node with minimum $C^*(VT, i)$, so node 4 is selected as an *intermediate-node* at the second loop of the algorithm as illustrated in Fig. 3 (d). The *intermediate-node* 7 of the third loop of the algorithm follows the same manner (Table 4 and Fig. 3 (e)). Since $T = (VT, ET)$ in Fig. 3 (f) has no leaf which is not the destination node, the pruning is not executed. So it is the minimum cost multicast tree T_{new} generated by the proposed algorithm.

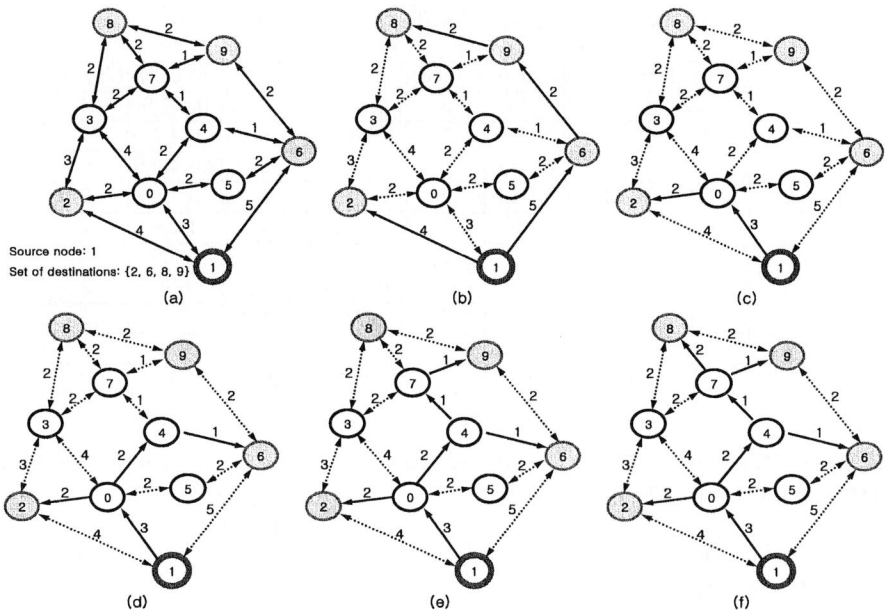

Fig. 3. (a)Sample network topology. (b)T_{TM}, $C_T(T_{TM}) = 13$. (c)$T = (VT, ET)$ after the first loop. The *intermediate-node* is 0 and d_{min} is 2. (d)T after the second loop. The *intermediated-node* is 4 and d_{min} is 6. (e)T after the third loop. The *intermediate-node* is 7 and d_{min} is 9. (f)T after the final loop. The *intermediate-node* is not found and d_{min} is 8. This is the T_{new} and $C_T(T_{new}) = 12$.

4 Performance Evaluation

In order to evaluate the performance of the proposed algorithm, we compare it with the TM algorithm in terms of the tree cost. To generate random topologies, we use an algorithm in [15,16] which generates the random connected graph. First, the algorithm generates a random spanning tree to guarantee a connected graph with $|V|$ nodes. Then, it calculates the adjusted edge probability P_e^a for the given edge probability P_e for each node pair and determines additional edges based on P_e^a.

The routines needed for the simulation including the TM and proposed algorithm are implemented in C++. The following is the simulation routine for the performance evaluation.

    for $P_e = 0.3, 0.4, 0.5, 0.6, 0.7, 0.8$
        for $|V| = 100, 200, 300, 400$
            do generate random graph 40 times
                for $|D| = 5\%, 10\%, 15\%, \cdots, 90\%, 95\%$ of $|V|$
                      do generate a source node, and destination nodes 40 times, randomly
                            run TM algorithm and get $C_T(T_{TM})$
                            run new proposed algorithm and get $C_T(T_{new})$
                            compare $C_T(T_{TM})$ and $C_T(T_{new})$

Table 1. $C(g,h)$ and $P(g,h)$ for each $g \in V$, $h \in D$

$g \in V$	$P(g,2)$	$C(g,2)$	$P(g,6)$	$C(g,6)$	$P(g,8)$	$C(g,8)$	$P(g,9)$	$C(g,9)$
0	0,2	2	0,4,6	3	0,4,7,8	5	0,4,7,9	4
1	1,2	4	1,6	5	1,0,4,7,8	8	1,0,4,7,9	7
2	2	0	2,0,4,6	5	2,3,8	5	2,0,4,7,9	6
3	3,2	3	3,7,4,6	4	3,8	2	3,7,9	3
4	4,0,2	4	4,6	1	4,7,8	3	4,7,9	2
5	5,0,2	4	5,6	2	5,6,4,7,8	6	5,6,9	4
6	6,4,0,2	5	6	0	6,4,7,8	4	6,9	2
7	7,4,0,2	5	7,4,6	2	7,8	2	7,9	1
8	8,3,2	5	8,7,4,6	4	8	0	8,9	2
9	9,7,4,0,2	6	9,6	2	9,8	2	9	0

Table 2. $P^*(VT,i)$, $C^*(VT,i)$, $PC(i)$, $SC(i)$ and $f(i)$ at the first loop of the algorithm with $VT = \{1\}$ and $ET = \emptyset$, $PC_T = 24$

$i \in V \setminus VT$	0	2	3	4	5	6	7	8	9
$P^*(VT,i)$	1,0	1,2	1,0,3	1,0,4	1,0,5	1,6	1,0,4,7	1,0,4,7,8	1,0,4,7,9
$C^*(VT,i)$	3	4	7	5	5	5	6	8	7
$PC(i)$	14	16	12	10	16	11	10	11	10
$SC(i)$	17	20	19	15	21	16	16	19	17
$f(i)$	17	∞	19	∞	∞	∞	∞	∞	∞

Table 3. $P^*(VT,i)$, $C^*(VT,i)$, $PC(i)$, $SC(i)$ and $f(i)$ at the second loop of the algorithm with $VT = \{0,1,2\}$, $PC_T = 12$

$i \in V \setminus VT$	3	4	5	6	7	8	9
$P^*(VT,i)$	2,3	0,4	0,5	0,4,6	0,4,7	0,4,7,8	0,4,7,9
$C^*(VT,i)$	3	2	2	3	3	5	4
$PC(i)$	9	6	12	6	5	6	4
$SC(i)$	12	8	14	9	8	11	8
$f(i)$	∞	8	∞	9	8	∞	8

Table 4. $P^*(VT,i)$, $C^*(VT,i)$, $PC(i)$, $SC(i)$ and $f(i)$ at the third loop of the algorithm with $VT = \{0,1,2,4,6\}$, $PC_T = 5$

$i \in V \setminus VT$	3	5	7	8	9
$P^*(VT,i)$	4,7,3	0,5	4,7	4,7,8	4,7,9
$C^*(VT,i)$	3	2	1	3	2
$PC(i)$	5	10	3	2	2
$SC(i)$	8	12	4	5	4
$f(i)$	∞	∞	4	5	4

Table 5. $P^*(VT,i)$, $C^*(VT,i)$, $PC(i)$, $SC(i)$ and $f(i)$ at the final loop of the algorithm with $VT = \{0,1,2,4,6,7,9\}$, $PC_T = 2$

$i \in V \setminus VT$	3	5	8
$P^*(VT,i)$	7,3	0,5	7,8
$C^*(VT,i)$	2	2	2
$PC(i)$	2	2	0
$SC(i)$	4	4	2
$f(i)$	∞	∞	∞

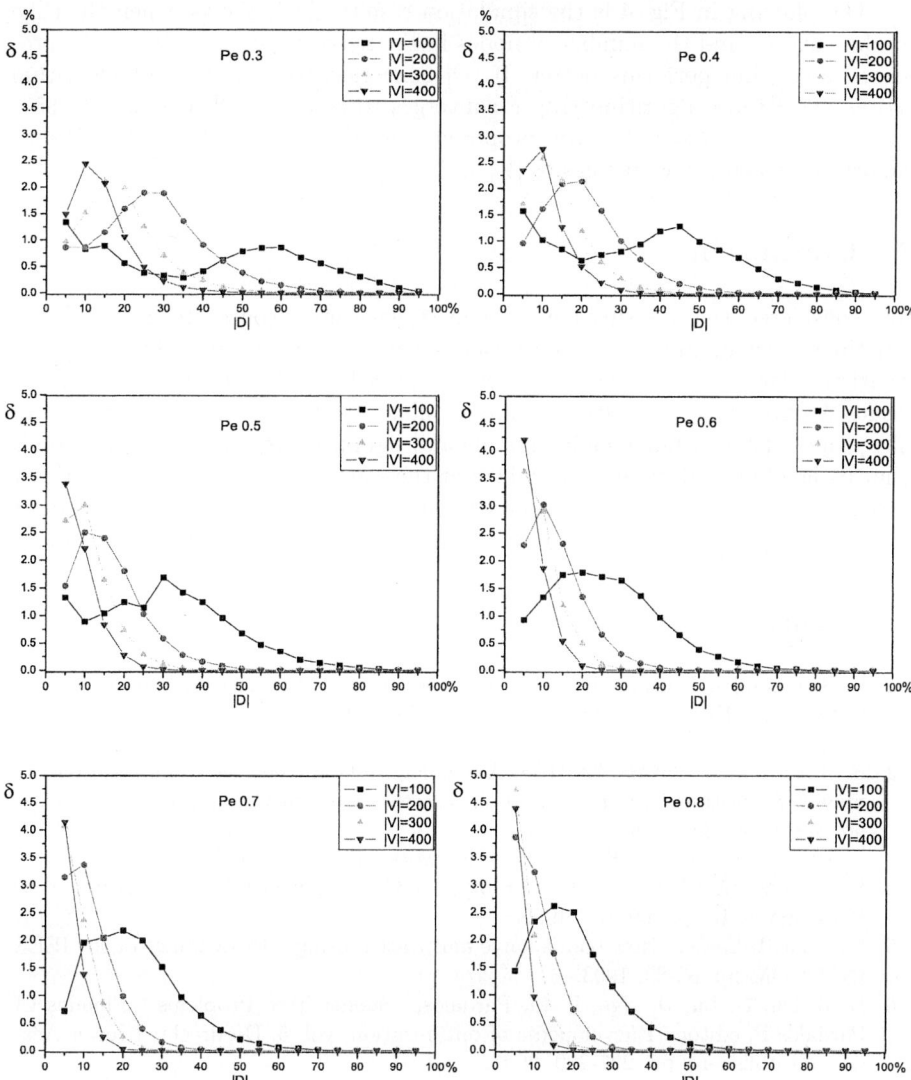

Fig. 4. The simulation results for different number of nodes for network topologies, different number for destination nodes and different edge probability

For the performance comparison, we define the δ as follows:

$$\delta = avg\left(\frac{C_T(T_{TM}) - C_T(T_{new})}{C_T(T_{TM})} \times 100\right)$$

The plotting in Fig. 4 is the simulation results. As it shows, when the edge probability P_e and the number of nodes in the network become larger, the proposed algorithm performs better. If $|D|$ converges to $|V|$, the TM algorithm works like Prim's algorithm [13]. δ converges to zero, as $|D|$ increases to 95% of $|V|$. So we can say that the proposed algorithm also performs like Prim's algorithm, when $|D|$ converges to $|V|$.

5 Conclusion

We considered the transmission of a message from a source to a set of destinations with minimum cost over random network topologies. The proposed heuristic algorithm is based on greedy approach to choose the *intermediate-node*. We presented simulation results to illustrate the relative performance of the proposed algorithm. One interesting and significant result from simulation is that if the global information is known at the source and the size of a multicast group is appropriate, the proposed algorithm outperforms TM which is the most straightforward and efficient minimum cost multicasting method known so far.

References

1. F. Bauer and A. Varma, "Distributed Algorithms for Multicast Path Setup in Data Networks," IEEE/ACM Transactions on Networking, vol. 4, no. 2, pp. 181-191, 1996.
2. F. Bauer and A. Varma, "ARIES: A rearrangeable inexpensive edge-based on-line Steiner Algorithm," IEEE Journal on Selected Areas in Communications, vol 15, no. 3, pp. 382-397, 1997.
3. D. Bertsckas and R. Gallager. "Data Networks. Prentice-Hall," 1992.
4. E. W. Dijkstra, "A Note on Two Problems in Connexion with Graphs," Numerische Mathematik 1, pp. 269-271, 1959.
5. M. Doar, I. Leslie, "How bad is naive multicast routing," Proceedings of the IEEE INFOCOM pp. 82-89, 1993.
6. D. Z. Du, B. Lu, H. Ngo, P. M. Pardalos, "Steiner Tree Problems," Floudas C, Pardalos P, editors. Encyclopedia of optimization, vol. 5, Dordrecht: Kluwer Academic Publishers, pp. 227-290, 2001.
7. M. R. Garey and D. S. Johnson, "Computers and Intractability: A Guide to the Theory of NP-Completeness," W. H. Freeman and Co., San Francisco, 1979.
8. F. K. Hwang, D. Richards, "Steiner Tree Problems," Networks, vol. 22, pp. 55-89, 1992.
9. B. K. Kadaba and J. M. Jaffe, "Routing to Multiple Destinations in Computer Networks," IEEE Transactions on Communications, COM-31, vol. 31, no. 3, pp. 343-351, 1983.
10. R. M. Karp, "Reducibility among combinatorial problems," Complexity of computer computations (R. E. Miller, J. W. Thather eds.), pp. 85-104, Newyork Plenum Press, 1972.
11. V. P. Kompella, J. C. Pasquale, and G. C. Polyzos, "Multicast Routing for Multimedia Communications," IEEE/ACM Transactions on Networking, vol. 1, no. 3, pp. 286-292, 1993.

12. L. Kou, G. Markowsky, and L. Berman, "A fast algorithm for Steiner trees," Acta Informatica, vol. 15, pp. 141-145, 1981.
13. R. C. Prim, "Shortest connection networks and some generalizations," Bell System Tech.J., 36, pp. 1389-1401, 1957.
14. S. Ramanathan, "Multicast Tree Generation in Networks with Asymmetric Links," IEEE/ACM Transactions on Networking, vol. 4, no. 4, pp. 558-568, 1996.
15. A.S. Rodionov and H. Choo, "On generating random network structures: Trees," Springer-Verlag Lecture Notes in Computer Science, vol. 2658, pp. 879-887, June 2003.
16. A.S. Rodionov and H. Choo, "On generating random network structures: Connected Graphs," Lecture Notes in Computer Science, vol. 3090, pp. 483-491, September 2004.
17. V. J. Rayward-Smith, "A Clare, On finding Steiner vertices," Networks 16(3), pp. 283-294, 1986.
18. H. Takahashi and A. Matsuyama, "An Approximate Solution for the Steiner Problem in Graphs," Mathematica Japonica, vol. 24, no. 6, pp. 573-577, 1980.
19. Bin Wang and J. C. Hou, "Multicast Routing and Its QoS Extension: Problems, Algorithms, and Protocols," IEEE Network, vol. 14, no. 1 , pp. 22-36, 2000.
20. B. M. Waxman, "Routing of multipoint connections," IEEE Journal on Selected Areas in Communications, vol. 6, no. 9, pp. 1617-1622, 1988.
21. P. Winter, "Steiner Problem in Networks: A Survey," Networks, vol. 17, pp. 129-167, 1987.

Efficient Active Clustering of Mobile Ad-Hoc Networks

Damianos Gavalas[1], Grammati Pantziou[2],
Charalampos Konstantopoulos[3], and Basilis Mamalis[2]

[1] Department of Cultural Technology and Communication, University of the Aegean,
Arionos & Sapfous Str., 81100, Mytilini, Lesvos Island, Greece
dgavalas@aegean.gr
[2] Department of Informatics, Technological Education Institute of Athens,
Ag. Spyridonos Str., 12210, Egaleo-Athens, Greece
{pantziou, vmamalis}@teiath.gr
[3] Computer Technology Institute, 11 Aktaiou & Poulopoulou Str.,
11851 Thiseio, Athens, Greece
konstant@cti.gr

Abstract. Mobile ad hoc networks comprise a collection of wireless nodes that dynamically create a network among themselves without using any pre-existing infrastructure. Clustering of mobile nodes among separate domains has been proposed as an efficient approach to answer the organization, scalability and routing problems of mobile ad hoc networks. In this work, we propose an efficient distributed clustering algorithm that uses both location and energy metrics for stable cluster formation. Unlike existing active clustering methods, out algorithm relieves the network from the unnecessary burden of control messages broadcasting. This is achieved through adapting broadcast period according to mobile nodes mobility pattern. For relative static network topologies, broadcast period is lengthened. In contrast, broadcast period is shortened to meet the requirements of highly dynamic networks for consistent cluster configurations.

1 Introduction

The field of wireless networking emerges from the integration of personal computing, cellular technology, and the Internet. This is due to the increasing interactions between communication and computing, which is changing information access from "anytime anywhere" into "all the time, everywhere". At present, a large variety of networks exists, ranging from the well-known infrastructure of cellular networks to infrastructureless mobile wireless ad-hoc networks (MANETs).

Unlike fixed wireless networks, MANETs are characterized by the lack of infrastructure offering fixed communication backbone to network users. Mobile Hosts (MHs) are free to move and organize themselves in an arbitrary fashion, while communication between peers is performed through multiple, multi-hop links. In the absence of a wired infrastructure, MHs are required to relay messages to other devices apart from solely transmitting and receiving packets [5].

Routing in ad hoc networks faces extreme challenges from node mobility/dynamics, potentially very large numbers of nodes, and limited communication resources (e.g. bandwidth and energy). The routing protocols for ad hoc wireless networks need to adapt quickly to frequent and unpredictable topology changes and must be parsimonious of communications and processing resources [2].

Several application fields have been identified for MANETs, including collaborative computing in convention centers, conferences, and electronic classrooms, on-the-fly message and file exchanges, crisis management services applications (e.g. disaster recovery); they are also expected to play an important role in the military and law enforcement.

Among the many challenges for ad hoc network designers and users, scalability is a critical issue. In particular, for topologies including large numbers of nodes, control overhead, such as routing packets, requires a large percentage of the limited wireless bandwidth. This problem becomes more emphatic due to the mobility feature of topology nodes and frequent wireless link failures. One promising approach to address the scalability issue is to build hierarchies among the nodes, such that the network topology can be abstracted. This process is commonly referred to as *clustering* and the substructures that are collapsed in higher levels are called *clusters* [1].

The concept of clustering in MANETs is not new, and there have been many algorithms that consider different metrics and focus on diverse objectives. However, existing algorithms fail to guarantee stable cluster formations. More importantly, they are all based on periodic broadcasting of control messages resulting in increased consumption of network traffic and MH energy. In this article, we describe a distributed algorithm for efficient and scalable clustering of MANETs that corrects the two aforementioned weaknesses.

The remainder of the paper is organized as follows: Section 2 provides an overview of clustering concepts and algorithms. Section 3 describes the details of our Adaptive Broadcast Period algorithm. Finally, Section 4 concludes the paper and draws directions for future work.

2 Clustering

In clustering procedure, a representative of each subdomain (cluster) is 'elected' as a *cluster head* (CH) and a node that belongs to more than two clusters at the same time is called a *gateway*. Remaining members are called *ordinary nodes*. A cluster is defined by the transmission area of its CH. With an underlying cluster structure, non-ordinary nodes can be the dominant forwarding nodes, as shown in Fig 1.

CHs hold routing and topology information, relaxing ordinary MHs from such requirement, however they represent network bottleneck points. In clusters without CHs, every MH has to store and exchange more topology information, yet, that eliminates the bottleneck of CHs. Yi et al. identified two approaches for cluster formation, *active* clustering and *passive* clustering [6]. In active clustering, MHs cooperate to elect CHs by periodically exchanging information, regardless of data transmission. On the other hand, passive clustering suspends clustering algorithm until the data traffic commences. It exploits on-going traffic to propagate "cluster-related information" (e.g., the state of a node in a cluster, the IP address of the node) and collects neighbor information through promiscuous packet receptions.

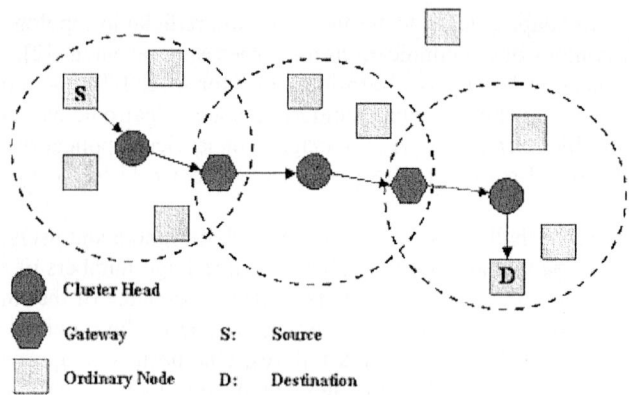

Fig. 1. Cluster heads, gateways and ordinary nodes in mobile ad hoc network clustering; demonstration of message forwarding through cluster heads and gateways

Passive clustering eliminates major control overhead of active clustering, still, it implies larger setup latency which might be important for time critical applications; this latency is experienced whenever data traffic exchange commences. On the other hand, in active clustering scheme, the MANET is flooded by control messages, even while data traffic is not exchanged thereby consuming valuable bandwidth and battery power resources.

A good clustering method should be able to partition a MANET quickly with little control overhead. Due to the dynamic nature of MANETs, optimal cluster formations are not easy to build. To this end, two distributed clustering algorithms have been proposed: Lowest ID algorithm (LID) and Highest Degree algorithm (HD) [6]. Both of them belong to active clustering scheme.

In LID algorithm, each node is assigned a distinct ID. Periodically, nodes broadcast the list of nodes located within their transmission range (including themselves) through a "Hello" control message. The lowest-ID node in a neighborhood is then elected as the CH; nodes which can 'hear' two or more CHs become gateways, while remaining MHs are considered as ordinary nodes. In HD algorithm, the highest degree node in a neighborhood, i.e. the node with the largest number of neighbors is elected as CH. Fig. 2 compares LID vs. HD algorithm approaches.

LID method is a quick clustering method, as it only takes two "Hello" message periods to decide upon cluster structure and also provides a more stable cluster formation than HD. In contrast, HD needs three "Hello" message periods to establish a clustered architecture [3]. In HD method, losing contact of a single node (due to MH movement), may cause failure of the current CH to be re-elected. However, HD method can get fewer clusters than LID, which is more advantageous in large-scale network environments.

In current clustering schemes, stability and cluster size are very important parameters; however, reducing the number of clusters does not necessarily result in more efficient architectures. A CH may end up dominating so many MHs that its computational, bandwidth and battery resources will rapidly exhaust. Therefore, effective control of cluster scale is another crucial factor.

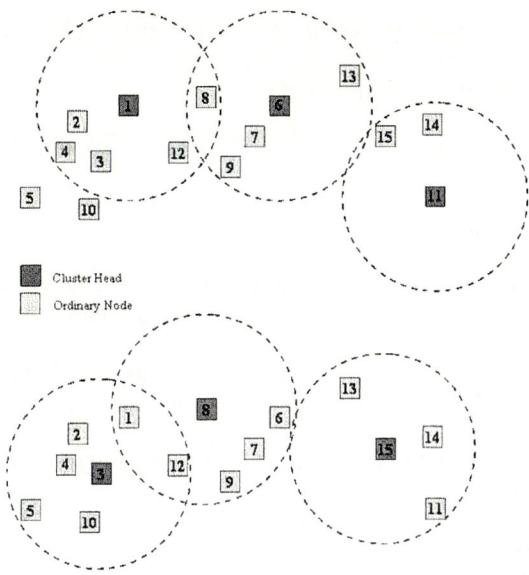

Fig. 2. LID vs. HD algorithms clustering

Summarizing, both LID and HD algorithms use exclusively location information to form clusters and elect CHs. In a more recent approach, Li et al proposed Vote-based Clustering (VC) algorithm, where CH elections are based not purely on location but also on the power level of MHs [3]. In particular, MHs with high degree (large number of neighbors) and sufficient battery power are elected as CHs. However, simulations have shown that the combination of position and power information in clustering procedure results in frequent CH changes, i.e. overall cluster structure instability [3].

In addition, LID, HD and VC algorithms share a common design characteristic which derives from their active clustering origin. Cluster formation is based on the periodic broadcast of 'Hello' signaling messages. In cases where MHs are relatively static (e.g. in collaborative computing, on-the-fly conferencing, etc), periodic 'storms' of control messages only occur to confirm that cluster structure established in previous periods should remain unchanged. These unnecessary message broadcasts not only consume network bandwidth, but valuable battery power as well.

3 Adaptive Broadcast Period (ABP) Algorithm

Our Adaptive Broadcast Period (ABP) algorithm aspires to correct the inefficiencies of existing active clustering algorithms (LID, HD and VC). Emphasis is given on two directions:

- A quick method for cluster formation is needed; required speed though should not be achieved at the expense of instable cluster configurations. To meet this objective, we modify VC algorithm so as to avoid frequent CH 're-elections'.

- Control messages broadcast period should be dynamically adapted in order to avoid unnecessary message exchanges when the mobility pattern of MHs is such that network topology is relatively static.

The methodology chosen to achieve the three aforementioned objectives is detailed in the following sections.

3.1 Cluster Formation

Cluster formation strategy extends the ideas implemented in VC algorithm. Unlike LID and HD protocols, both position and battery power metrics are considered in CH election.

However, emphasis has been given to prevent frequent CH changes and prolong the average lifetime of CH and cluster membership, therefore, meeting the requirement for steadier cluster formations.

We assume that each MH has a unique identifier (MH_ID), which is a positive integer. MHs also hold information about the identity of their assigned CH (CH_ID). CHs are easily identified by their identical MH_ID and CH_ID values.

Control information is communicated through 'Hello' messages, transmitted on the common wireless channel. Every MH acquires topology information from incoming 'Hello' messages. Another attribute of MHs is their battery power level (percentage of remaining over full battery power), which is a positive integer, $0 \leq b \leq 100$, linearly decreased over time; naturally, battery energy of CHs exhausts faster than ordinary MHs as they serve a number of MHs, forwarding messages on their behalf.

Clustering algorithm. Our clustering algorithm considers both location and power information to partition a MANET into separate clusters. In this context, we introduce the concept of "cluster head competence" (CHC) which represents the competence of a MH to undertake the role of a CH.

The format of a typical 'Hello' message is shown in Fig. 3. Each 'Hello' message includes identifications of its sender (MH_ID) and sender's assigned CH (CH_ID). CCH represents a weighted sum of sender's degree (number of valid neighbors) and its battery power level. Finally, the BP field is used to adapt the broadcast period within a particular cluster (see Section 3.2).

MH_ID	CH_ID	CHC	BP
8 bit	8 bit	8 bit	8 bit

Fig. 3. 'Hello' packet format

CHC values are calculated according to the following equation:

$$CHC = (w_1 \times d + w_2 \times b) - p \qquad (1)$$

- c_1, c_2: weighted coefficients of MH degree and battery availability, respectively;
- d: Number of neighbors (degree of MH);
- b: Remaining battery lifetime (percentage of remaining over full battery power);
- p: 'handover' penalty coefficient (explained below).

The algorithm involves the following steps:

1. Each MH sends a 'Hello' message randomly during a 'Hello' cycle. If a MH has just joined the MANET, it sets CH_ID value equal to a negative number. That signifies a MH is not a member of any cluster and has no knowledge of whether it is within transmission radius of another MH.
2. Each MH counts how many 'Hello' messages it received during a 'Hello' period, and considers that number as its own degree (d).
3. Each MH broadcasts another 'Hello' message, setting CHC field value equal to that calculated from Equation (1).
4. Recording received 'Hello' messages during two 'Hello' cycles, each MH identifies the sender with highest CHC value and thereafter considers it as its CH.

In the next 'Hello' cycle, CH_ID value will be set to elected CH's ID value. In the case of two or more MHs having the same lowest CHC value, the one with the lowest ID is 'elected' as CH. Following the aforementioned algorithm steps, clustering procedure is completed within two 'Hello' cycles.

The penalty coefficient p of Equation (1) is introduced to ensure that the algorithm provides stable cluster formations (cluster instability has been identified as the main weakness of HD and VC algorithms [3]), i.e. i.e. clusters insensitivity to hosts mobility. Clusters instability derives from frequent CH re-elections; according to the preceding algorithm description, such re-elections occur when an ordinary MH claims higher CHC value compared to current CH. For instance, when: a new MH moves within a cluster boundary or the current CH presents slightly lower power level than an ordinary MH. CH re-elections typically trigger a global cluster reconfiguration process and massive transfers of routing data among elected CHs.

To correct this inefficiency, we introduce a penalty coefficient p in the calculation of CHC value, as shown in Equation (1). The value of p is set to an integer value ($p > 0$) for ordinary MHs, while $p = 0$ for CHs. Assigning an appropriate value to p, we prevent MHs with slightly higher degree or lower battery power to that of current CHs to take up the role of CH, thereby avoiding unnecessary handovers.

3.2 Dynamically Adaptive Control Messages Broadcast Period

A principal consideration of our Adaptive Broadcast Period (ABP) algorithm is to reduce the number of control messages circulated throughout the ad-hoc network. Minimization of message broadcasts would provide bandwidth savings and conserve computational resources and battery power on both CHs and ordinary nodes.

Ad-hoc networks have been proposed for many applications that do not involve highly mobile structures, e.g. in convention centers, conferences or electronic classrooms. Existing active clustering algorithms involve periodic broadcast of 'Hello' messages to sense potential topological differences between two successive 'Hello' periods. In relatively static MANET topologies though, such differences seldom occur; namely, bandwidth and power resources are unnecessarily consumed.

ABP algorithm corrects this clear inefficiency by adjusting 'Hello' messages broadcast period (BP). For highly mobile MHs, BP is shortened, i.e. message broadcasts are frequent enough to maintain consistent and accurate topology information. However, when mobility rate (MR) is low, i.e., MHs position on the plane does not considerably change over time relatively to their neighbors position, BP is lengthened, relaxing the MANET from unnecessary control message storms.

The main issue to be addressed is to accurately measure mobility pattern of MHs. In order to meet this objective, MR is measured by individual MHs through contrasting the topological information obtained during successive BPs; when MR increases, BP is shortened, otherwise it is prolonged.

In order to measure MR, CHs need to maintain vectors representing the IDs of the MHs dominated by the CH; each vector instance refers to a different 'Hello' BP. Calculated MR value is actually the 'distance' of vectors recorded during the two latest 'Hello' cycles. The latter is an integer value indicating not only the change of CH's degree but also changes in CH's network neighborhood (potential substitutions of its dominated MHs by other MHs). We assume that BP duration always lies between two limits: $BP_{min} \leq BP \leq BP_{max}$; at startup, BP is globally set to BP_{min}. This default value changes over time reflecting different mobility patterns among separate clusters, according to Equation (2):

$$BP_{t+1} = \begin{cases} \max(BP_{min}, BP_t - kMR_t), \text{if } MR_t > T \\ \min(BP_{max}, BP_t + c), \text{if } MR_t = 0 \end{cases} \quad (2)$$

where k is a normalization factor, T is a threshold value, c is a constant and MR_T the mobility rate measured over the last BP. Modifications of BP values are announced by CHs to all their dominated MHs to achieve the required synchronization; this is done through setting appropriately the value of 'BP' field in 'Hello' message (see Fig. 3). Ordinary MHs set 'BP' field value equal to 0. MHs receiving a 'Hello' message from their assigned CH ('Hello' message CH_ID value coincides with their assigned CH's ID) adapt their BP duration accordingly.

An inviting side-effect of ABP algorithm is that it fits well in environments with high 'local' mobility: BP may differ among separate clusters, depending on the mobility pattern of their respective MHs. That way control traffic is localized only where needed, leaving unaffected clusters whose members exhibit low mobility.

4 Conclusions – Future Work

In this paper, we introduced a novel active clustering algorithm; its contributions, compared to existing solutions, are summarized in the following: (a) clustering procedure is completed within two 'Hello' cycles; (b) both location and battery power metrics are taken into account in clustering process; (c) derived cluster formations exhibit enhanced stability by preventing unnecessary CH re-elections; (d) for relatively static network topologies, control traffic volume is minimized; (f) fast packet forwarding and delivery is enabled, as clusters are pro-actively formed. The abovementioned contributions are achieved at the expense of slightly increased control packet sizes.

At the time this article was written, the proposed algorithm was under evaluation through simulations. Apart of our proposed algorithm, LID, HD and VC have also been implemented for demonstration and comparison purposes. Simulation results are evaluated to compare these algorithms in terms of: (a) overall control packet overhead, (b) CH changes, (c) average lifetime of CH and cluster membership. All these parameters are measured as a function of MHs density and mobility pattern.

Acknowledgements

The research work presented herein has been co-funded by 75% from EU and 25% from the Greek government under the framework of the Education and Initial Vocational Training II, Programme Archimedes.

References

1. Y. P. Chen, A. L. Liestman, J. Liu: Clustering Algorithms for Ad Hoc Wireless Networks. In Y. Pan and Y. Xiao (eds): Ad Hoc and Sensor Networks, Nova Science Publishers (2004).
2. X. Hong, K. Xu, M. Gerla: Scalable Routing Protocols for Mobile Ad Hoc Networks. IEEE Network, Vol. 16, No 4 (2002) 11-21.
3. Fei Li, Shile Zhang, Xin Wang, Xiangyang Xue, Hong Shen. Vote-Based Clustering Algorithm in Mobile Ad Hoc Networks. In: Proceedings of International Conference on Networking Technologies for Broadband and Mobile Networks (ICOIN'2004), LNCS vol. 3090. Springer-Verlag (2004), 13 – 23.
4. Li C. R., Gerla Mario. Adaptive Clustering for Mobile Wireless Networks. IEEE Journal of Selected Areas in Communications, Vol. 15, No 7 (1997) 1265-1275.
5. C. Perkins. Ad Hoc Networking. Addison-Wesley (2001).
6. Y. Yi, M. Gerla, T. Kwon. Efficient Flooding in Ad hoc Networks: a Comparative Performance Study. In: Proceedings of the IEEE International Conference on Communications (ICC'2003) (2003).

Evaluation of Audio Streaming in Secure Wireless Access Network[*]

Binod Vaidya[1], JongWoo Kim[2], JaeYoung Pyun[2], JongAn Park[2], and SeungJo Han[2]

[1] Dept. of Electronics & Computer Eng., Tribhuvan Univ., Nepal
bvaidya@ioe.edu.np
[2] Dept. of Information & Communication Eng., Chosun Univ., Korea
mmm@7.co.kr, {jypyun, japark, sjbhan}@chosun.ac.kr

Abstract. Advances in the Internet and multimedia technologies have spurred many research efforts in Internet-based multimedia access systems, which integrate wireline and wireless networks. Internet-based multimedia streaming services are in need of a service creation model. In this paper, we presented such a model and framework for delivering real-time traffics to a wireless access network over public Internet Protocol (IP) backbone network. We have presented a performance analysis of audio streaming when IP tunneling network using Generic Route Encapsulation (GRE) along with Internet Protocol Security (IPSec) is implemented. The impacts on performance, with particular attention to Quality of Service (QoS) characteristics have been evaluated through a series of experiments. In this paper, the effects of a compression scheme based on compressed real-time transport protocol (CRTP) and Resource Reservation protocol (RSVP) are analyzed when delivering real-time traffics to the wireless access network through secured IP Network.

1 Introduction

With the growth of the Internet and high-speed access links, Internet users can enjoy large amounts of web content on the Internet. At the same time, multimedia streaming services are becoming popular over the Internet. Wireless access networks are becoming popular for providing IP-based multimedia streaming services in addition to web access services. Today, with the rise of multimedia and network technologies, multimedia has become an indispensable feature on the Internet. Multimedia networking applications such as Internet telephony and other audio streaming applications have appeared on the market. Streaming services, however, present a lot of challenges for network engineers. Unlike Transmission Control Protocol (TCP) applications, streaming services require a certain amount of bandwidth to ensure the bit-rate needed by each media stream and the strict delay variation (i.e., jitter) needed to avoid buffer underflow at streaming clients.

---

[*] This study was supported (in part) by research funds from Chosun University 2005.

2 Architectural Model

The architectural model for the secure wireless access network is depicted in Fig. 1. In this model, it comprises of a service provider, IP backbone network and wireless access networks. The Service Provider has pool of servers with all necessary communication equipment which are capable of providing audio streaming services. IP Backbone network is public network such as Internet whereas wireless access networks provide access to mobile users. As the service provider provides audio streaming services, the secure channel such as Virtual private network (VPN) is created over public IP network.

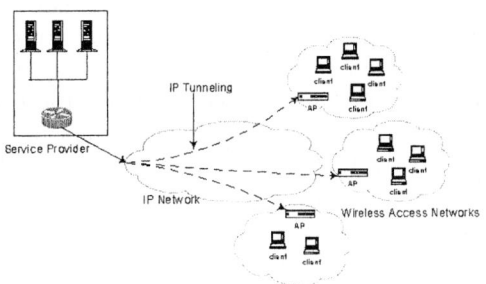

Fig. 1. Architectural Model

3 Security Issues: IP Tunneling

Due to the interest in emerging scenarios such as wireless access networks over public IP environments some tunneling technologies have been introduced. There are currently four primary tunneling protocols relevant to VPNs: Layer 2 Tunneling Protocol (L2TP) [1] Tunnel, Layer 2 Forwarding (L2F) Tunnel [2], IP Security (IPSec) Tunnel, and Generic Route Encapsulation (GRE) Tunnel [3].

3.1 IP Security (IPSec)

IPSec is a suite of protocols "designed to provide interoperable, high quality, cryptographically-based security for IPv4 and IPv6" [4]. IPSec provides security services, such as access control, data integrity, authentication, confidentiality (encryption), and replay protection to the IP layer as well as the layers above.

IPSec could protect one or more paths between two pairs of hosts, between a pair of security gateways (SG) or between a host and a security gateway. The key concept behind this idea is called a Security Association (SA). An SA is uniquely identified by a Security Parameter Index (SPI), an IP destination address, and a security protocol. Authentication Header (AH) [5] and Encapsulating Security Payload (ESP) [6] are secure protocols provided by IPSec to form SAs. The first provides connectionless integrity, data origin authentication, and an optional anti-replay service. The second may provide confidentiality and limited traffic flow confidentiality, as well as all the functionality provided by the AH. Each SA defines the algorithms for encryption, authentication, hash and key exchange (attributes) for protecting a particular path [7].

3.2 Generic Route Encapsulation (GRE)

Generic Route Encapsulation (GRE) [8] is a tunneling protocol that encapsulates traffic with new packet headers to ensure delivery to specific destinations. The network is considered private because traffic normally enters a tunnel only at the beginning and endpoint of the tunnel. Although limiting traffic access in this manner may deem the network private, it does not provide message confidentiality or integrity. Thus GRE tunnel allows any protocol to be tunneled in an IP packet. This feature allows the Type of Service (ToS) bits to be copied to the tunnel header when the router encapsulates the packets using GRE. It allows routers between GRE-based tunnel endpoints to adhere to precedence bits thereby improving the routing of premium service packets.

GRE can be used to encapsulate non-IP traffic in IP packets. The GRE tunnel packet is an IP unicast packet, so the GRE packet can be encrypted using IPSec. In this scenario, GRE does the tunneling work and IPSec does the encryption part of supporting the VPN network.

4 Quality of Service Issues

Since Quality of service (QoS) is a set of techniques to manage network resources to assure that delay-sensitive information travels the network in a timely manner, for multimedia traffic, this means prioritizing real-time packets over the network to avoid maximum delay and packet loss. When delivering real-time applications, QoS protocols must be adopted in order to be able to meet the requirements on transmission parameters such as transmission delay, delay variation (jitter) and buffering delay. It is of paramount importance to audio steaming application that QoS can be guaranteed from end-to-end.

4.1 Real-Time Transport Protocol

Realtime transport protocol (RTP) [9] is an IP-based protocol providing support for the transport of real-time data such as video and audio streams. Thus RTP provides end-to-end delivery services for data with real-time characteristics. The services provided by RTP include time reconstruction, loss detection, security and content identification. It can be used for interactive services such as Internet telephony.

RTP itself however, does not provide all of the functionality required for the transport of data and, therefore, applications usually run it on top of a transport protocol such as UDP. RTP is designed to work in conjunction with the auxiliary control protocol, Real Time Control Protocol (RTCP), to get feedback on quality of data transmission and information about participants in the on-going and to provide minimal control over the delivery of the data.

4.2 Compressed Real-Time Transport Protocol

In many services and applications e.g., Voice over IP (VoIP), messaging etc, the payload of the IP packet is almost of the same size or even smaller than the header. Over the end-to-end connection, comprised of multiple hops, these protocol headers are extremely important but over just one link (hop-to-hop) these headers serve no useful purpose. It is possible to compress those headers, thus save the bandwidth and use the expensive resources efficiently. IP header compression [10] also provides other important benefits, such as reduction in packet loss and improved interactive response time.

RTP header compression (CRTP) [11] was designed to reduce the header overhead of IP/UDP/RTP datagram by compressing the three headers. The IP/UDP/RTP headers are compressed to 2-4 bytes most of the time. CRTP was designed for reliable point to point links with short delays. It does not perform well over links with high rate of packet loss, packet reordering and long delays.

CRTP implementation may not be suitable for the situations, where packet losses, reordering, and long delays are common characteristics. In those cases, Enhanced CRTP [12] can be used, which is the modification and extension to CRTP to increase robustness to both packet loss and misordering between the compressor and the decompressor. Although these new mechanisms impose some additional overhead, the overall compression is still substantial.

4.3 Resource Reservation Protocol

Resource Reservation Protocol (RSVP) [13] allows applications to dynamically reserve network bandwidth and thereby request a specific QoS for a data flow. RSVP provides for an end-to-end guarantee of reserved bandwidth so all devices along the route (hosts and routers) must support RSVP. RSVP treats data flow from receiver to sender as logically independent from the flow from sender to receiver. Accordingly, a reservation for data from sender to receiver is independent from a reservation from receiver to sender. Since RSVP establishes a reservation for simplex flows, reservations for traffic can be made from any or both directions. RSVP is a hop-by-hop QoS signaling protocol. This means that RSVP messages are transmitted from one node to another through all RSVP aware nodes along the data path.

5 Related Works

There have been many studies on impact of CRTP performance over cellular environment using real-time traffic such IP telephony [14]. However, little has been done on studying the network problems such as end-to-end delay, jitter and packet loss that affect audio quality for multimedia access service in IP tunneling implementation.

6 Experimental Validation

In order to validate the conceived architectural model, we have simulated a scenario that includes the real-time application services such as audio streaming to the wireless access network over public IP network using OPNET Modeler, [15] which a discrete event-driven simulator tool capable of modeling both wireless and wireline network.

6.1 Scenarios

Practical applications of multimedia services for mobile users are likely to occur in scenarios where a wireless access network is extended over public IP backbone network (i.e. the Internet). The basic architecture for the audio streaming service in secure wireless access network is shown in Fig. 2.

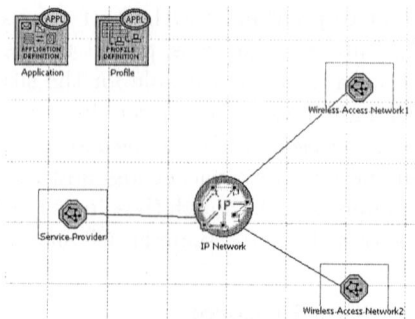

Fig. 2. Experimental Model

In Fig. 3a and Fig. 3b, the service provider and wireless access network are depicted. The service provider consists of a farm of audio streaming servers. And the wireless access network consists of several mobile users using wireless IEEE 802.11b devices.

For the experimental purpose, three scenarios have been designed. The first scenario is audio streaming service to the wireless access network with IP tunneling only. In order to securely deliver the real-time traffics over public IP network, GRE tunnel over IPSec is used. So only designated wireless access network can have access to the Service Provider. The second scenario is audio streaming service to the wireless access network with IP tunneling along with CRTP. In OPNET Modeler, we have modified existing node models of the router and access point with CRTP. The third scenario is audio streaming service to the wireless access network with IP tunneling along with RSVP.

When specifying the QoS, following performance metrics are taken into account: End-to-End Delay (Latency) - The average time it takes for a packet to travel the network from a sending to receiving device.; Delay Variation (Jitter)

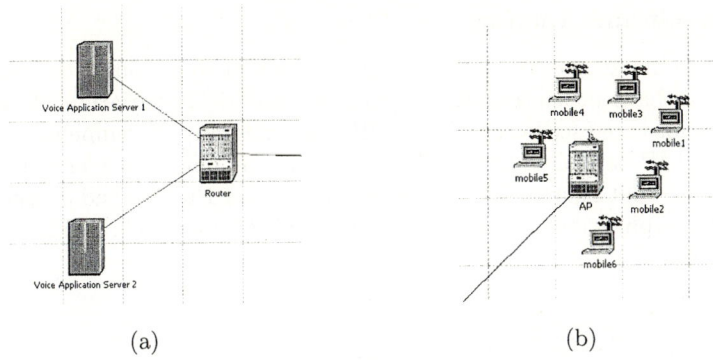

Fig. 3. (a) Service Provider (b) Wireless Access Network

- The variation in end-to-end delay of sequentially transmitted packets.; Packet Loss - The percent of transmitted packets that never reach the intended destination.; and Throughput - The amount of data transferred between two given nodes during a given amount of time. This reflects the bandwidth of the network and is a significant factor to QoS.

6.2 Assumptions

For real-time streaming services, we have selected audio streaming application. In this case, we have considered audio application using G.723.1 codec scheme since it has better jitter resistance.

In selecting the protocol for the IPSec, we have considered the "SA Bundle" [4]. In this case, we have considered GRE tunneling with ESP (transport) for encryption, and AH for integrity and authentication are used to secure channel.

Hashed Message Authentication Codes (HMAC) [3,16] is a secret key authentication algorithm. We have considered the use of HMAC with Secure Hash Algorithm (SHA-1) [17] as a keyed authentication mechanism within the context of the ESP and the AH.

Data Encryption Standard (DES) [18] is a block cipher. In Triple DES (3DES), we apply three stages of DES with a separate key for each stage. So the key length in 3DES is 168 bits. In this experimental model, we have chosen 3DES as the encryption algorithm.

In order to visualize the effect of packet loss and packet latency in IP Network on the real-time traffics, we have assumed two cases: a case "A" is defined as IP Network with 5% packet discard ratio and average packet latency of 0.1 sec whereas case "B" is with 10% packet discard ratio and average packet latency of 0.5 sec.

For the third scenario, in order to envisage the impact of bandwidth on response time between the audio application server and the end-user wireless client, we have conducted several analyses with the various packet loss and latency in the network. We have assumed the different packet loss in percentage such as 0%, 5% and 10% and change in latency be 0ms, 20ms and 50ms.

6.3 Result and Analysis

In order to investigate the performance of the real-time audio streaming applications, we have measured end-to-end delay and delay variation at the mobile end-users for three scenarios, that is, IP tunneling only, IP tunneling along with CRTP and IP tunneling along with RSVP. It has been considered for two different cases, that is, case "A" and case "B". Packet End-to-End delays for voice streaming applications for case "A" and case "B" are shown in Fig. 4 and Fig. 5 respectively.

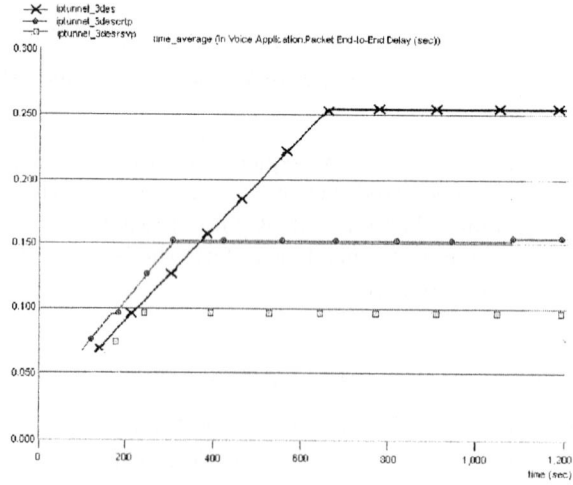

Fig. 4. End-to-end delay for case "A"

It is found that with IP tunneling only, end-to-end delay is relatively high, that is about 250 msec, which is due to the additional delays incorporated with IP tunneling. It can be seen that the packet End-to-End delays have been reduced to 150 msec when implementing IP tunneling along with CRTP. As per our experiment, it is found that better result for packet end-to-end delay (100 msec) was obtained with the network while implementing IP tunneling along with RSVP. It is clearly noticeable that with the increase of packet discard ratio and packet latency in IP network, the End-to-End delays also increase significantly.

Packet Delay variations, or jitter, for voice streaming applications for case "A" and case "B" are shown in Fig. 6 and Fig. 7 respectively. Similarly, it is found that with IP tunneling only, delay variation is relatively high when comparing with the cases of a network implementing the IP tunneling along with CRTP and a network implementing the IP tunneling along with RSVP. It is evident that with the increase of packet discard ratio and packet latency in IP network, the delay variations also increase. As per our experiment, it is found that the delay variation can be minimized with the network while implementing IP tunneling along with RSVP.

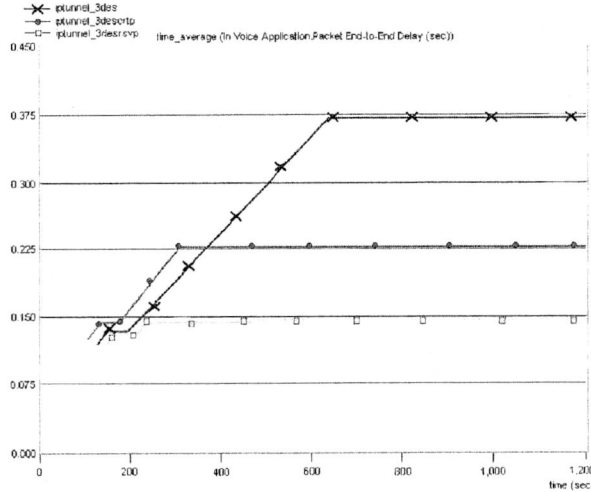

Fig. 5. End-to-end delay for case "B"

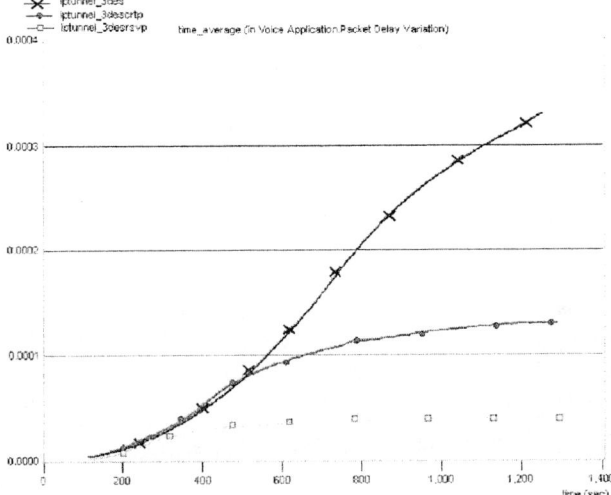

Fig. 6. Delay variation for case "A"

On analyzing the impact of bandwidth on response time, we have found that with the increase in the bandwidth, the response time decreases. The impact of bandwidth on response time for various latencies is shown in Fig. 8. As we have considered changes in latency as 0ms, 20ms, and 50ms, the response time increases with the increase in the latency. It is found that for the latency of 50ms, the response time is highest, ie about 245 sec from bandwidth of 250kbps to 2Mbps.

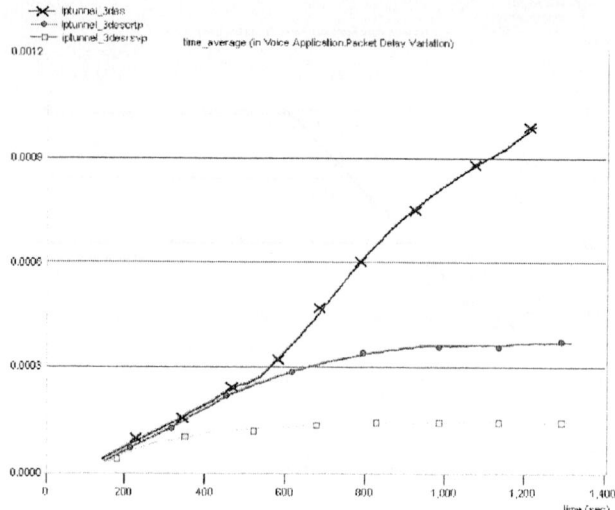

Fig. 7. Delay variation for case "B"

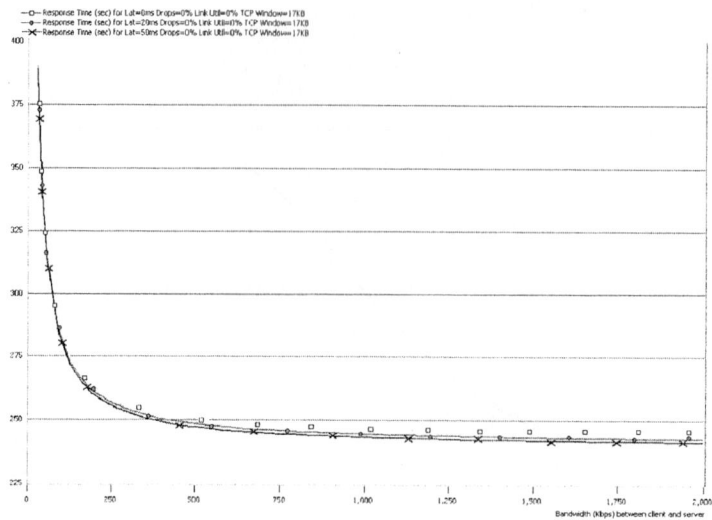

Fig. 8. Response Time vs Bandwidth for various Latencies

The impact of bandwidth on response time for various packet losses is shown in Fig. 9. As we have considered changes in packet drops from 0% to 10% (ie 0%, 5% and 10%), the response time increases with the increase in the packet drops. It is found that the packet drop of 10% has highest response time, ie about 260 sec from bandwidth of 250kbps to 2Mbps.

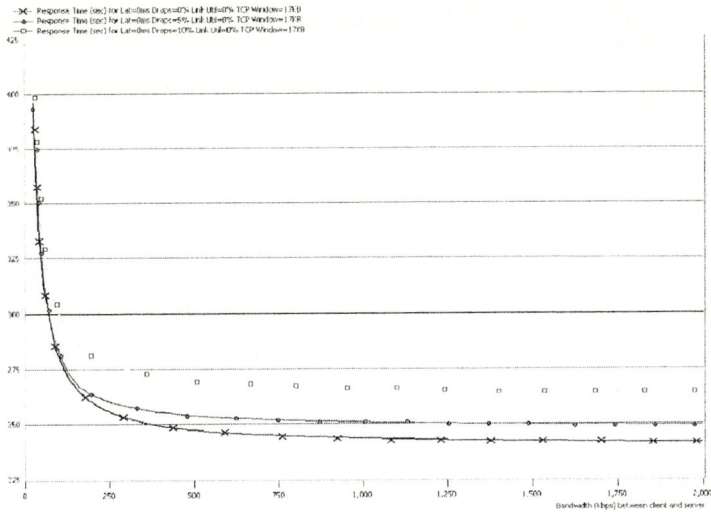

Fig. 9. Response Time vs Bandwidth for various packet drops

7 Conclusion and Future Work

This paper provides a framework for audio streaming application through the public IP backbone network to the wireless access network using IP tunneling. In this paper we present the results of the experimental analysis of real-time application such as audio streaming over secure communication links implementing GRE tunneling over IPsec. Critical parameters characterizing the real-time transmission of voice traffics over a secured IP network are presented. We present two QoS solutions such as CRTP and RSVP for minimizing the end-to-end delay and delay variations of the real-time traffic in IP tunneled network using IPsec. Simulation results show that under IP tunneling over IP network both schemes significantly reduce the QoS characteristics such as the packet end-to-end delays and delay variations. Future work with this model will concentrate on more detailed investigations for the improvement of the network performance while implementing IP tunneling in multimedia service network.

References

1. W. Townsley, A. Valencia, A. Rubens, G. Pall, G. Zorn, B. Palter, "Layer Two Tunneling Protocol (L2TP)", IETF RFC 2661, Aug 1999.
2. A. Valencia, M. Littlewood, T. Kolar, "Cisco Layer Two Forwarding (Protocol) - L2F", IETF RFC 2341, May 1998.
3. G. Schafer, Security in Fixed and Wireless Networks, John Wiley & Sons, 2003.
4. R. Atkinson and S. Kent, "Security Architecture for Internet Protocol," IETF RFC 2401, Nov 1998.
5. R. Atkinson and S. Kent, "IP Authentication Header," IETF RFC 2402, Nov. 1998.

6. R. Atkinson and S. Kent, "IP Encapsulating Security Payload (ESP)," IETF RFC 2406, Nov 1998.
7. W. Stallings, Cryptography and Network Security: Principles and Practices, Prentice Hall, 2003.
8. D. Farinacci, T. Li, S. Hanks, D. Meyer, and P. Traina, "Generic Routing Encapsulation (GRE)" IETF RFC 2784, March 2000.
9. H. Schulzrinne, S. Casner, R. Frederick, and V. Jacobson, "RTP: A Transport Protocol for Real-Time Applications," IETF RFC 1889, Jan 1996.
10. M. Degermark, B. Nordgren, and S. Pink, "IP Header Compression," IETF RFC 2507, Feb. 1999.
11. S. Casner and V. Jacobson, "Compressing IP/UDP/RTP Headers for Low-Speed Serial Links," IETF RFC 2508, Feb. 1999.
12. T. Koren, S. Casner, J. Geevarghese, B. Thompson, and P. Ruddy, "Enhanced Compressed RTP (CRTP) for Links with High Delay, Packet Loss and Reordering" IETF RFC 3545, July 2003.
13. Braden, R., Zhang, L., Berson, S., Herzog, S. and S. Jamin, "Resource Reservation Protocol (RSVP) – Version 1 Functional Specification", RFC 2205, Sept. 1997.
14. M. Degermark, H. Hannu, L. Jonsson, and K. Svanbro, "Evaluation of CRTP Performance over Cellular Radio Links", IEEE Personal Communications, Vol. 7, No. 4, pp. 20-25, August 2000.
15. OPNET Modeler Simulation Software, http://www.opnet.com.
16. A.J. Menezes, P.C. van Oorschot, and S.A. Vanstone, Handbook of Applied Cryptography, CRC Press, 1997.
17. National Institute of Standards and Technology, FIPS PUB 180-2: Secure Hash Standard, http://csrc.nist.gov/publications/fips/fips180-2withchangenotice.pdf
18. National Institute of Standards and Technology, FIPS PUB 46-3: Data Encryption Standard, http://csrc.nist.gov/cryptval/des.htm

Reliable Transmission Using Intermediate Sink or Source Nodes in Sensor Networks*

Bo-Hyung Lee[1], Hyung-Wook Yoon[1], Jongho Park[2],
Min Young Chung[2], and Tae-Jin Lee[2]

[1] Telecommunication Network Business,
Samsung Electronics, Suwon, 440-600, Korea
{bohyeong.lee, hyungwook.yoon}@samsung.com
[2] School of Information and Communication Engineering,
Sungkyunkwan University, Suwon, 442-746, Korea
{tamalove, mychung, tjlee}@ece.skku.ac.kr

Abstract. In some critical applications, in sensor networks the most important issue is to transmit sensing information to the end user (the sink node) with reliability. Reliable information forwarding using multiple paths in sensor networks (ReInForM) can achieve desired reliability in the error-prone channel, but it needs increasing transmission overhead as the channel error rate becomes high and the number of hops between the source node and the sink node increases. In this paper, we propose reliable transmission using intermediate source nodes in sensor networks (ReTrust) to reduce packet overhead while keeping the desired reliability. Intermediate source or sink (IS) nodes are formed between the source node and the sink node. The IS nodes should be determined so that the given transmission reliability is satisfied while reducing the number of packets or multi-paths. ReTrust has been shown to provide desired reliability and reduced overhead via simulations and analysis.

1 Introduction

A sensor network consists of sensor nodes with small size, low cost, low power consumption, and multi-functions to sense, to process and to communicate [1]. Previous researches mainly focus on minimizing power consumption of sensor nodes [2,3]. In general, sensing information at a source node should be transmitted to a sink node. Not all the sensing information needs to be received at the sink node at once as long as the source node transmits the data periodically. However, when a sensor node detects emergency information or generates important data, this must be transmitted with reliability.

Depending on the environment of a sensor network, the channel error rate may be high or fluctuate especially in a hostile terrain. And, if there are many hops from a source node to a sink node, packets may reach the sink with low

---

* This research was supported by University IT Research Center Project. The corresponding author is Tae-Jin Lee.

probability of success. Typical data dissemination protocols do not transmit packets adaptively according to the channel error rate, e.g., intermediate nodes along the path are not adaptively selected. This may incur significant resource leakage to compensate for unreliable transmission.

Reliable information forwarding using multiple paths in sensor networks (ReInForM) is proposed to solve this problem [4]. ReInForM assumes that sensors have very limited memory and do not employ Automatic Repeat reQuest (ARQ), so transmitted packets are not saved once they are transmitted. It achieves reliable transmission by using the multi-path-multi-packet and information-aware forwarding algorithm. It, however, has a problem that the number of required packets and paths increases rapidly as the number of hops between a sink node and a sensor node increases and the channel error rate becomes high.

In this paper, we propose a reliable transmission mechanism using intermediate sink or source nodes in sensor networks (ReTrust) to reduce the overhead of ReInForM while maintaining the required reliability between a source node and a sink node. The rationale is to use proper intermediate source (IS) nodes which can lessen the original source's or the sink's burden to copy and broadcast multiple packets and thus reduce the number of multi-paths than ReInForM. We present two methods of setting IS nodes originating from the source node and from the sink node.

The remainder of this paper is organized as follows. In Section 2, we discuss some of the related works. In Section 3, we review ReInForM and explain our proposed ReTrust. In Section 4, we evaluate performance of our algorithm. In Section 5, analysis and simulation results are presented. Section 6 concludes the paper.

2 Related Works

The concept of the differentiated services for sensor network was proposed in [5], in which level of data packets is prioritized by degree of importance. And, information awareness is used so that nodes forward packets to their corresponding sink nodes adaptively according to the channel error rate and the required reliability.

In conventional networks, the method of guaranteeing reliability is achieved by using hop-by-hop or end-to-end acknowledgments (ACK). In terms of overhead, end-to-end schemes perform poorly in comparison with hop-by-hop schemes in multi-hop wireless networks [6]. However, in wireless sensor networks, both of them may cause frequent retransmissions because sensor networks tend to operate in the harsh environment with the high channel error rate [4]. And it requires additional packet overhead and memory to store data received from other nodes at intermediate nodes. Thus, using acknowledgements is not suitable for sensor networks due to the limited energy and memory of sensor nodes.

The main purpose of multi-paths routing algorithms is to recover a broken path quickly to reduce routing delay and to maintain a robust path [7], [8]. Also, multi-paths schemes can be used to reduce energy consumption by dispersing packets (traffic) which were concentrated on specific nodes or paths in a sensor network. However, it incurs extra overhead of forming multiple paths and maintaining their states in each node. In addition, they are not adaptive to varying local channel error rates and the required reliability of packet transmission.

In [4], ReInForM algorithm can satisfy the desired reliability for the criticality of data by transmitting multiple copies of packets in place of received packets to compensate for limited performance of sensor nodes and high channel error rate. In ReInForM, the total number of packets to transmit is determined by the required reliability between the source and the destination. It causes, however, that the number of multi-paths and the packet overhead increase drastically as the path length increases.

3 Proposed ReTrust

Basically, ReInForM assumes that the memory size of a sensor node is very small and the channel error rate is high. Therefore, the intermediate nodes along the path do not store any transmitted data packets. And, nodes do not use ACK for a reliable data transmission due to high channel error rate. Instead, ReInForM achieves a reliable transmission using multi-packets and multi-paths instead of time consuming retransmission. If a node senses and collects information around its environment, it decides whether the data is important or not. The sensed or generated data receives higher priority in proportion to the degree of criticality or emergency. The node then calculates the number of multi-paths according to the required reliability and the channel error rate. And it writes the determined information in the packet header as dynamic packet state (DPS) [9]. The multi-paths used for data forwarding is set by periodical routing updates of the sink node. The routing packets of the sink node are broadcast to all the nodes of a network, so that they know the shortest paths from the sink node to themselves. The information is then transmitted along the multi-paths. Some nodes may transmit redundant copies of the packet due to multi-paths implemented by TDMA [10] for collision-free transmission. Fig. 1 illustrates that a source node located at (10, 10) transmits 10 packets to the sink node at (90, 90) through multi-paths to achieve the reliability of 70% under the channel error rate of 30%.

We note that the overhead of setting up multi-paths and that of transmitting multiple copies may become large to meet the reliability in ReInForM. So, we propose to set IS nodes between the source node and the sink node in order to reduce the number of multi-paths and transmitted packets (see Fig. 2). We call the mechanism ReTrust. Given the reliability between the source node and the sink node, one can determine IS nodes and find the intermediate reliabilities, i.e, the reliability between the source node and an IS node, that between two IS nodes, and that between an IS node and the sink node. Using such intermediate reliability, the number of multi-paths can be decided.

In our ReTrust, it is important how to determine IS nodes in a sensor network. We propose two mechanisms to set IS nodes from the viewpoint of the source

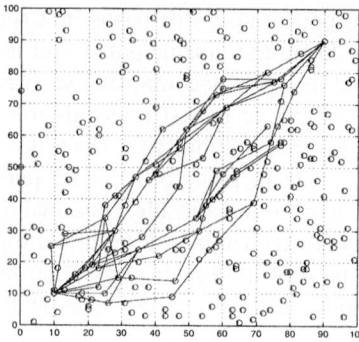 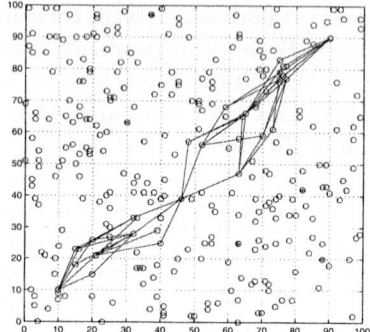

Fig. 1. Illustration of ReInForM   **Fig. 2.** Illustration of proposed ReTrust

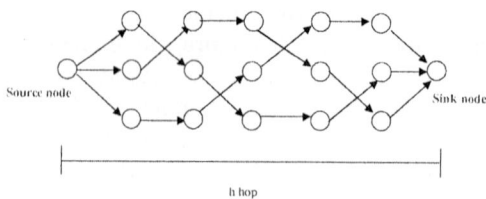

Fig. 3. ReInForM

node and from the sink node. In the following subsection, we present two methods to set up IS nodes in details.

3.1 Setting IS Nodes from the Sink Node

In the first proposed method, the sink node sets an IS node before data transmission through multi-paths. Sensor nodes know the shortest path from the sink node to themselves. We assume that sensor nodes periodically transmit the sensing information to the sink node. This information is transmitted via the shortest path. When the sink node receives this information, it transmits an ACK to the source node. The ACK packet is assumed to include a parameter (required hop count from the sink node for an IS node) to set an intermediate source. When a node receives the ACK, it recognizes the parameter and the node can becomes an IS node if the parameter is the same as the actual number of hops from the sink node. The IS node then broadcasts its role to the other nodes between the source node and the IS node. The source node receiving the IS information computes the required number of multi-paths to the IS node according to the desired intermediate reliability. This method is rather simple, but it requires large overhead to broadcast the IS information if there are many independent source nodes.

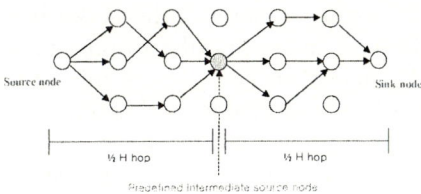

Fig. 4. ReTrust setting up of sink-based IS node

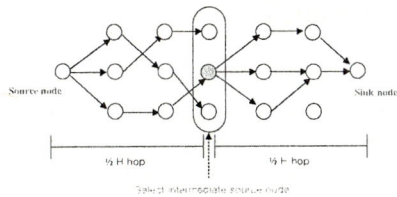

Fig. 5. ReTrust setting up of source-based IS node

To assure less packet overhead when many source nodes want to transmit via multi-paths, we propose another sink-based method, in which the sink node calculates a desired hop distance to set an IS node according to the channel error rate and reliability. This information is broadcast to all the nodes with periodical routing updates to find the shortest paths from the sink node. If the number of hops of a node equals to the desired hops in the packet header, the node becomes an IS node. As soon as a node becomes an IS node, the IS node broadcasts a denial packet to the neighbor nodes within one hop distance so that the neighbor nodes of the IS node do not become another IS node. Then, the IS node broadcasts information to the nodes between the source node and the IS node to inform the shortest paths from the IS node. And the source node having required reliability calculates the number of multi-paths and transmits packets to the IS node along the shortest path from the source. This method should have less overhead than the first method if many source nodes require multi-paths for reliabilities.

3.2 Setting IS Node from the Source Node

In this method, the source node takes control over setting an IS node. If the source node requires reliable transmission, it calculates a proper number of hops to an IS node according to the desired reliability and the channel error rate. And it also computes the required number of multi-paths from the source to the IS node based on the desired intermediate reliability between the source and the IS node. The source node records this desired hop information in the packet header and transmits packets along the multi-paths. If a receiving node has the same actual hop count as the hop count in the packet, it becomes an IS node. Then the IS node broadcasts a deny signal and the nodes receiving the deny signal do not broadcast packets any more in order to prevent setting further IS node in the network. The IS node then also plays a role as an intermediate source node to the sink node. This method does not need to send the routing update information on the shortest paths from the nodes between the source and the IS node to the IS node because IS nodes are determined in the process of actual data transmission. Fig. 3 ~ 5 illustrate transmission of data in ReInForM and two methods in ReTrust.

4 Performance Evaluation

In ReInForM, the expected number of copies of a packet (N_s) to transmit at a node given the desired reliability (R) can be found in a probabilistic way. It is assumed that multiple copies of each data packet flow through the nodes along the single shortest path from a source to a sink.

Let e_p be the packet error rate and h be number of hops along the shortest path from the source node to the sink node. Then, the probability of failure to receive a packet correctly when N_s copies of a packet are transmitted is

$$P_f = (1 - (1 - e_p)^h)^{N_s}. \qquad (1)$$

Since the desired reliability is R, following equation must hold

$$1 - R = P_f \qquad (2)$$

So, N_s can be expressed as

$$N_s = \frac{\log(1 - R)}{\log(1 - (1 - e_p)^h)}. \qquad (3)$$

When a node with i hops from the source node receives a packet correctly, the probability of successfully receiving the packet at the node is $(1 - e_p)^i$. Thus, we can write the total packet overhead (O_s) as

$$O_s = N_s \sum_{i=0}^{h-1}(1 - e_p)^i = \frac{(1 - (1 - e_p)^h)\log(1 - R)}{e_p \log(1 - (1 - e_p)^h)}. \qquad (4)$$

So O_s is the number of successfully received copies of a packet along the path.

Now, let's assume that there exist IS nodes between the source and the sink as in our proposed ReTrust. Let IS_i be ith IS node apart from the source node (IS_0 is the source node) and R_{IS_i} be the required reliability from IS_i to IS_{i+1} and M be the total desired number of IS nodes. The total reliability from the source node to the sink node R_{total} must satisfy

$$R_{total} = \prod_{i=0}^{M} R_{IS_i}. \qquad (5)$$

Let N_{total} be the total number of required multi-paths (or the number of multiple copies of a packet), which is the sum of required multi-paths at each IS node, and N_{IS_i} be the number of required multi-paths at IS_i node from IS_i to IS_{i+1}. We can find N_{IS_i}, which is similar to Eq. (3)

$$N_{IS_i} = \frac{\log(1 - R_{IS_i})}{\log(1 - (1 - e_p)^{h_i})}, \quad 0 \leq i \leq M, \tag{6}$$

where, h_i is the hop count between IS node IS_i and IS node IS_{i+1}. Then, N_{total} can be derived as

$$N_{total} = N_{IS_0} + \sum_{i=0}^{M-1} \left(\prod_{j=0}^{i} R_{IS_j} \right) \times N_{IS_{i+1}}. \tag{7}$$

Similarly, total packet overhead O_{total} is given

$$O_{total} = O_{IS_0} + \sum_{i=0}^{M-1} \left(\prod_{j=0}^{i} R_{IS_j} \right) \times O_{IS_{i+1}}, \tag{8}$$

where O_{IS_i} is the packet overhead to transmit packets from IS_i to IS_{i+1}. And O_{IS_i} is obtained as

$$O_{IS_i} = \frac{(1 - (1 - e_p)^{h_i}) \log(1 - R_{IS_i})}{e_p \log(1 - (1 - e_p)^{h_i})}, \quad 0 \leq i \leq M. \tag{9}$$

Based on this analysis, we evaluate performance of ReInForM and ReTrust. In ReTrust, an IS node is assumed to set at the half of the path from a source to a sink and the total reliability of ReTrust is assumed to be the same as ReInForM. Fig. 6 and 7 show the required number of multi-paths and the overhead for varying hop count from the source node to the sink node. It shows that ReTrust requires less number of multi-paths and overhead than ReInForM does as the distance from the sink node to the source node increases. Especially, our

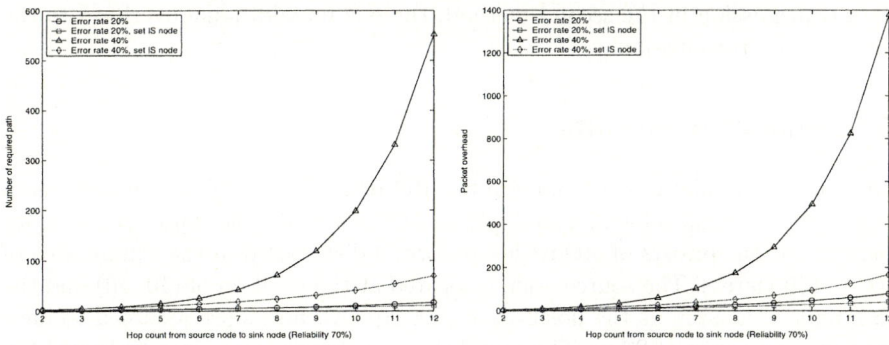

Fig. 6. The number of multi-paths with reliability of 70%

Fig. 7. Total packet overhead with reliability of 70%

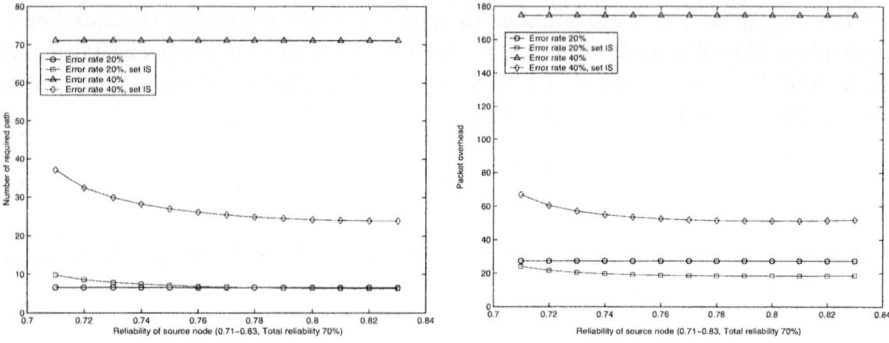

Fig. 8. The number of multi-paths for varying reliability between the source and the IS (total reliability of 70%)

Fig. 9. Total packet overhead for varying reliability between the source and the IS (total reliability of 70%)

algorithm is shown to be more efficient than ReInForM as the channel error rate become large.

In Fig. 8 and Fig. 9 show the required number of multi-paths and the overhead, as the reliability from the source node to the IS node varies while keeping the total reliability to 70%. The hop count between the source node and the sink node is set to 8. Fig. 8 shows that the expected number of paths in ReTrust is less than ReInFroM when the channel error rate is 40%, but it may be larger than ReInFroM when the channel error rate is 20%. However, total packet overhead of ReTrust is always less than ReInForM regardless of the channel error rate as shown in Fig. 9. We also note that the packet overhead becomes the minimum when the source node have and the IS node the same desired reliability.

The slight overhead increase in ReTrust due to setting IS nodes is inevitable, but it is far less than the overhead of increasing number of multi-paths in ReInForM. Especially, if the hop distance from the source to the sink is large, the overhead of selecting the IS node might be negligible than the increasing multiple packet transmission overhead. Since IS nodes are determined in the actual data transmission in the second method, there is no additional overhead to the multi-paths transmission.

5 Simulation Results

We conduct simulations to compare the ReInForM and ReTrust algorithms in terms of the actual reliability and the packet overhead. The sensor network for the simulation consists of 300 nodes uniformly distributed in the square area of 100×100 meters. The source node is located at the position of (10, 10) and the sink node is located at the position of (90, 90). All nodes are assumed to have transmission range of 20 m. The hop distance between the source node and the sink node is assumed to be 7. The number of IS nodes is one (M=1) and IS node is set at 4 hop distance from the sink node. The intermediate reliabilities, R_{IS_0}

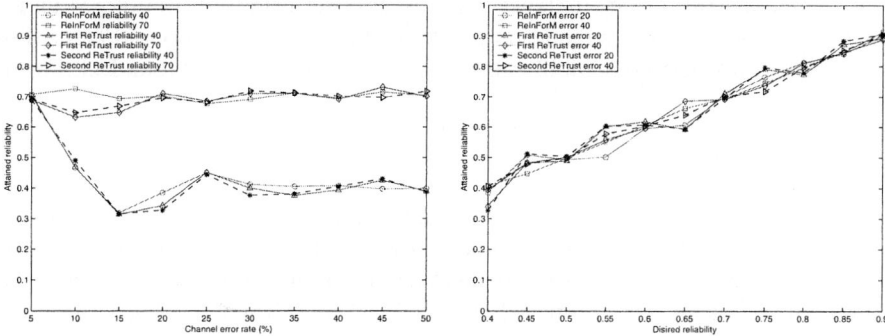

Fig. 10. Attained reliability under increasing channel error rate

Fig. 11. Attained reliability vs. desired reliability

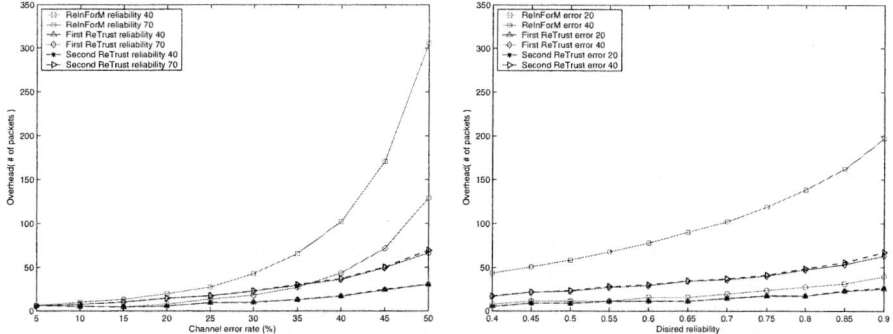

Fig. 12. Packet overhead for increasing channel error rate

Fig. 13. Packet overhead for varying desired reliability

and R_{IS_1}, are assumed to be equal under the given total reliability. The source has 200 packets to send to the sink.

Fig. 10 shows the attained reliability as the channel error rate increases from $5 \sim 50\%$ given the desired reliability of 40 % and 70 %. At the channel error rate of $5 \sim 10\%$ and the reliability of 40 %, the attained reliability is little bit higher than the desired reliability. And, the attained reliability is somewhat lower than the desired reliability at the channel error rate of $15\% \sim 20\%$. The reason is that the reliability is affected by the number of multi-paths at the source node. The less the number of multi-paths, the larger the impact on the reliability is. Both ReInForM and ReTrust show that the attained reliability matches with the desired reliability as shown in Fig. 11. Thus it is verified that our algorithm achieves desired reliability even when IS nodes are utilized. Fig. 12 shows the total packet overhead in ReInForM and ReTrust. Under the same reliability, ReTrust shows less packet overhead than ReInForM. The packet overheads of the first method and the second one in ReTrust are shown to be same. In

Fig. 13 demonstrates that, ReTrust requires less overhead than ReInForM under the same error rate. The simulation results exhibit that our proposed algorithm satisfies not only desired reliability, but also less packet overhead than ReInFroM.

6 Conclusion

In this paper, we proposed the ReTrust algorithm to meet desired reliability in sensor networks. ReTrust reduces packet overhead, *i.e.*, the number of multi-paths by using IS nodes, as well as meeting the desired reliability between the source and the sink. Our proposed two ReTrust algorithms has been shown to exhibit better performance than ReInForM via analysis and simulations, especially if the channel error rate is high and the number of hops from the source node to the sink node become large. These results will also lead to less collision and energy consumption.

References

1. I. F. Akyildiz and W. Su. A survey on sensor network. *IEEE communications Magazine*, volume 40, pages 102–114, Aug. 2002.
2. W. R. Heinzelman, J. Kulik, and H. Balakrishnan. Adaptive protocols for information dissemination in wireless sensor networks. In *Proc. of ACM MobiCom*, pages 174–185, 1999.
3. S. Singh, M. Woo, and C. S. Raghavendra. Power-aware routing in mobile Ad Hoc networks In *Proc. of ACM MobiCom*, pages 181–190, Nov. 1998.
4. B. Deb, S. Bhatnagar and B. Nath. ReInForM: Reliable information forwarding using multiple paths in sensor networks. In *Proc. of LCN03*, pages 406 – 415, Oct. 2003.
5. S. Bhatnagar, B. Deb, and B. Nath. Service differentiation in sensor networks. In *Proc. of Wireless Personal Multimedia Communication*, Sep. 2001.
6. A. Bhargava, J. Kurose, D. Towsley, and G. Vanleemput. Performance comparison of error control schemes in high speed computer communication networks. *IEEE Journal of Selected Areas in Communications*, volume 6, number 9, pages 1565 – 1575, 1988.
7. S. De, C. M. Qiao, and H. Y. Wu, Meshed multipath routing: An efficient strategy in sensor networks. In *Proc. of IEEE WCNC 2003*, volume 3, Pages 1912 – 1917, Mar. 2003.
8. D. Ganesan, R. Govindan, S. Shenker, and D. Estrin. Highly resilient, energy-efficient multipath routing in wireless sensor networks. In *Mobile Computing and Communications Review(MC2R)*, volume 1, number 2, pages 11 – 25, 2002.
9. I. Stoica, S. Shenker, and H. Zhang. Core-stateless fair queueing: Achieving approximately fair bandwidth allocations in high speed networks. In *Proc. of SIGCOMM*, pages 118 – 130, 1998.
10. K. Arisha, M. Youssef, and M. Younis. Energy-aware TDMA based mac for sensor networks. In *Proc. of IEEE IMPACCT 2002, New York City, New York*, 2002.

A Novel Heuristic Routing Algorithm Using Simulated Annealing in Ad Hoc Networks

Lianggui Liu and Guangzeng Feng

Department of Communication Engineering,
Nanjing University of Posts & Telecommunications, 210003, Nanjing, China
liangguiliu@126.com, gzfeng@njupt.edu.cn

Abstract. Multi-constrained quality-of-service routing (QoSR) is to find a feasible path that satisfies multiple constraints simultaneously, as an NPC problem, which is also a big challenge for ad hoc networks. In this paper, we propose a novel heuristic routing algorithm based on Simulated Annealing (SA_HR). This algorithm first uses an energy function to translate multiple QoS weights into a single metric and then seeks to find a feasible path by simulated annealing. The paper outlines simulated annealing algorithm and analyzes the problems met when we apply it to QoSR in ad hoc networks. Theoretical analysis and experiment results demonstrate that the proposed method is an effective approximate algorithms showing good performance in seeking the (approximate) optimal configuration within a period of polynomial time.

1 Introduction

Ad hoc networks are dynamic multihop wireless networks that are established by a group of mobile nodes on a shared wireless channel by virtue of their proximity to each other. Ad hoc wireless networks are self-creating, self-organizing, and self-administering. The attractive infrastructure-less nature of mobile ad hoc networks has gained a lot of attention in the research community. Most applications that attract interest for use in current wired networks (e.g., video conferencing, on-line live movies, and instant messenger with camera enabled) would attract interest for ad hoc networks as well. Numerous challenges must be overcome to realize the practical benefits of ad hoc networking. These include effective routing, medium (or channel) access, mobility management, power management, security, and, of principal interest here, quality of service (QoS) issues. Cost-effective resolution of these issues at appropriate levels is essential for widespread general use of ad hoc networking.

QoS guarantees can be attained only with appropriate resource reservation techniques. The most important element among them is QoSR. The main function of QoSR is to find a feasible path that satisfies multiple constraints for QoS applications (e.g., multimedia transportation and real-time traffic). In wired networks, there are many QoSR methods which has been proposed [1~3]. But they can not been directly applied to ad hoc networks because unlike the wired network, the network topology may change constantly, the available state information for routing is inherently imprecise, and the network itself is noncentralization. QoS for ad hoc networks has been previously explored by [3~8]. Path computation algorithms in these literatures care about only a single metric, such as delay or hop-count, and most of them only deal with the best effort data traffic. SBR [4] fulfills both signal-to-interference (SIR) and bandwidth requirements from different multimedia users in ad hoc mobile networks. In [5], the proposed approach adopts bandwidth as a QoS metric. In CEDAR [7], the bandwidth is used as the only QoS parameter for routing. The proposed algorithm has three key components: a) the establishment and maintenance of the core of the network for performing the route computations; b) propagation and use of bandwidth and stability information of links in the ad hoc network; and c) the QoS route computation algorithm. While the core provides an efficient and low-overhead infrastructure to perform routing and broadcasts in an ad hoc network, the increase/decrease wave-based state propagation mechanism ensures that the core nodes have the important link state they need for route computation, without incurring the high overhead of state maintenance for dynamic links. The QoS routing algorithm is robust and uses only local state for route computation at each core node. In [8], the proposed approach selects a network path with sufficient resources to satisfy a certain delay (or bandwidth) requirement in a dynamic multihop mobile environment while working with imprecise state information. Multiple paths are searched in parallel to find the most qualified one. Fault tolerance techniques are brought in for the maintenance of the routing paths when the nodes move, join, or leave the network. Algorithms proposed there consider not only the QoS requirement, but also the cost optimality of the routing path to improve the overall network performance. There the delay and bandwidth are used for QoS routing but not simultaneously.

More than one QoS constraints often make the QoSR problem NP complete [9]. Approximated solutions and heuristic algorithms have been successfully applied to solve many combinatorial optimization NPC problems. Inspired from this, we propose a novel heuristic routing algorithm based on simulated annealing (SA_HR) for multi-constrained routing in ad hoc networks. Different from the non-linear programming methods, SA_HR is a heuristic method which uses explicit rules to find feasible routes.

In ad hoc networks, finding a loop-free path as a legitimate route between a source-destination pair may become impossible if the changes in network topology occur too frequently. Rapid topology changes militate against QoS guarantees. Let T_u and T_{uc} denote the interval between two consecutive topology change events and the time it takes to complete the calculation and the propagation of the topology updates resulting from the last topology change, respectively. Only the ad hoc network that is combinatorially stable is considered. Here combinatorially stable means $T_{uc} < T_u$. We call QoS in this kind of circumstance Soft QoS [8] which is better than best effort service rather than guaranteed hard QoS. Therefore, combinatorial stability must first be met before we can consider providing QoS service. There are many networks that satisfy this requirement. For example, consider a network made up of students in a class; students may join the lecture late, some may leave the classroom, but most stay in the stationary position. If the just computed feasible route ceases to exist during the corresponding topology update, the QoS guarantee becomes meaningless.

The paper is organized as follows. Section 2 introduces the problem formulation and the basic principle of SA. The novel method based on SA is proposed in Section

3. Section 4 gives the complexity analysis and experiment results. Finally, we draw conclusions in Section 5.

2 Pertinent Information

Above all, Simulated Annealing (SA) algorithm is introduced.

From the viewpoint of statistical mechanics, in temperature T, the probability for a molecule of substance which is keeping its thermal equilibrium stay in the state i satisfies Gibbs canonical distribution [10]:

$$P_T(i) = \frac{1}{Z_T} \exp(\frac{-E_i}{\kappa T}) \qquad (1)$$

where Z_T is the system partition function which is defined as:

$$Z_T = \sum_{i \in S} \exp(\frac{-E_i}{\kappa T}) \qquad (2)$$

where κ is Boltzmann's constant and S is state space. By formula (1), the probability with which the crystal stay in a microscopic state i with energy E_i is given.

Annealing is a *very* slow physical process. After a crystal is heated, when it is cooled slowly, the molecule of the body stays in different states with different probabilities, which satisfies Gibbs canonical distribution. There are usually two necessary conditions to be required:

(1) The initialization temperature is high enough so that the probabilities for a molecule to stay in arbitrary microscopic states are approximately equal, that is, crystal will stay in quasi-equilibrium. It is apparent that

$$\lim_{T \to \infty} P_T(i) = \lim_{T \to \infty} e^{-\frac{E_i}{\kappa T}} / \sum_{j \in S} e^{-\frac{E_j}{\kappa T}} = \frac{1}{|S|} \qquad (3)$$

that is, the probabilities are approximately equal.

(2) When it is cooled down so that temperature becomes 0, all of the molecules will stay in the least energy state with the probability being one, i.e., when t tends to 0 or the cost of the final configuration in a serial group of Markov Chain does not change, the global optimal solution with the least cost will be found with the probability of 1.

In the basic form of SA, it first generates an initial solution as the current feasible solution using Metropolis algorithms [10]. Then another solution is selected in the neighborhood of the current solution and replaces the current solution with the new one with the following transition probability given by Metropolis criterion:

$$P(i \Rightarrow j) = \begin{cases} 1 & \text{if } f(j) \leq f(i) \\ \exp(\frac{f(i)-f(j)}{t}) & \text{otherwise} \end{cases} \qquad (4)$$

where $t \in R^+$ represents the control parameter. $f(i)$ and $f(j)$ are energy functions corresponding to state i and j respectively. The same process continues iteratively for lots of times. Non-optimal configuration with probability $\exp(\frac{f(i)-f(j)}{t})$ is used to avoid being stuck in a local optimization each time, although the goal is to find a global optimal configuration. Obviously, result of one arbitrary taste is only dependent upon the result of the previous taste, thus concepts in a Markov Chain corresponding to a control temperature t can be used. As to SA, one-step transition matrix in a Markov Chain is defined as follows:

$$P_t(i,j) = [s(q+1)=j | s(q)=i] = \begin{cases} 0 & \text{if } j \notin N(i) \text{ and } j \neq i \\ G(i,j)\min\{1, e^{\frac{f(i)-f(j)}{T}}\} & \text{if } j \in N(i) \text{ and } j \neq i \\ 1-\sum_{i \neq i} G(i,i')\min\{1, e^{\frac{f(i)-f(j)}{T}}\} & \text{otherwise} \end{cases} \quad (5)$$

where $G(i,j)$ represent the probability with which configuration j is derived from i, and $N(i) \subseteq S$ is the neighborhood set of i. With the temperature decreasing, only the better deterioration configuration can be accepted. Finally, when $t \to 0$, no deterioration configuration will be accepted, that is, it is guaranteed to find a global optimal configuration.

3 Method Description

Here we firstly give some assumptions as follows:

Assumption 1 The network is homogeneous, i.e., all nodes communicate on the same shared wireless channel, the effective direct communication distance of every node is equal, etc.

Assumption 2 A effective MAC layer protocol exist in order to resolve the media contention, support resource reservation and local multicast [3].

Assumption 3 The topology of network changes not very rapidly and satisfies the constraints mentioned above, that is, the network is combinatorially stable.

A. *Problem representation*

To use SA effectively in ad hoc QoSR, we should adopt some tactics as follows:

(1). The possible configurations space are defined as follows:

$$\Xi(s,d) = \{p_1, p_2, \cdots p_i, p_j, \cdots p_r\} = \{\text{arrangement of all the loop-free paths from source to destination}\}$$

(2). Energy function:

$$E = \frac{\sum_{s=1}^{n} \tau_s}{\prod_{s=1}^{n} \chi_s} \tag{6}$$

where n is the number of wireless links in a path and τ and χ are time delay and transmission success rate both of which will be regarded as QoS parameters by the proposed algorithm SA_HR, respectively.

(3). Here we use a tactics named "plus-minus" as disturbance mechanism. From the configurations space, one configuration constituted by chain of nodes is randomly selected. Then a possible new node joins the chain or a node is deleted from the chain, thus a new possible configuration will be produced.

For example, an ad hoc network with 7 nodes and 8 links is concerned.

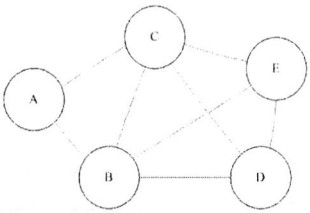

Fig. 1. A given ad hoc topology

Suppose A is source node and E destination node. All loop-free routes are expressed by the network possible spanning tree shown in Fig. 2.

When a source wants to send data packets to a destination node, the network first transformed in a spanning tree rooted with the source node. The source node labels each of them with a series of consecutive natural number, and then constituent elements of a configuration space are all included.

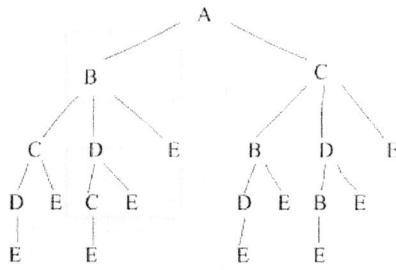

Fig. 2. Possible spanning tree

B. Step of QoSR in ad hoc based on SA

Firstly, a proper initialization temperature T_0 will be selected, either will the termination temperature T_t and the length of the Markov Chain L_m.

Secondly, a function which controls the decrease of temperature should be defined.
Thirdly, a state transference criterion should also be introduced (See formula (4)).
Finally, termination criteria of SA should be given.

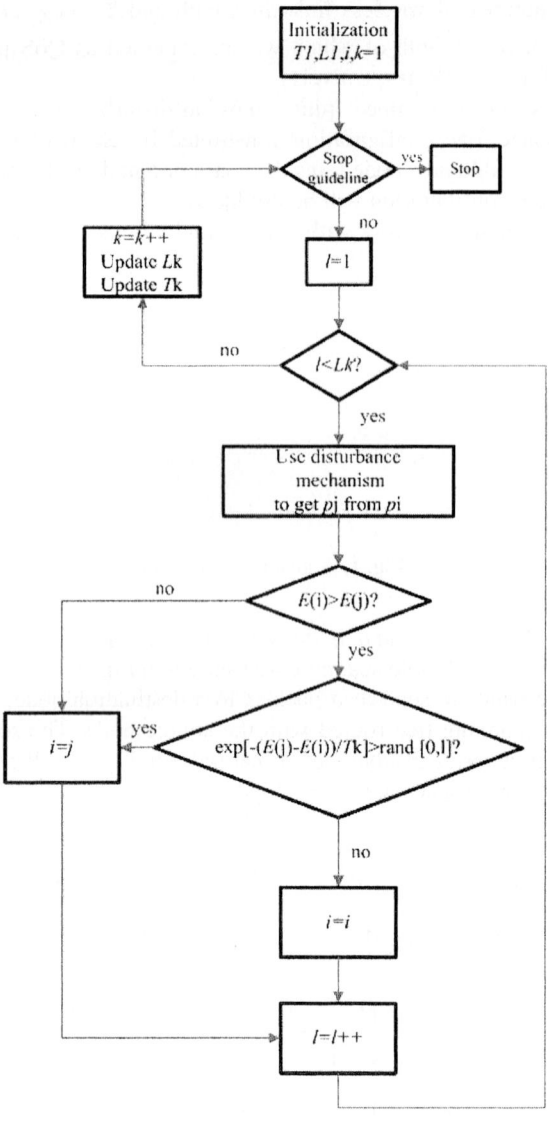

Fig. 3. QoSR in ad hoc networks based on SA

The procedure flow graph is provided as Fig. 3. Algorithms starts from one initialized configuration randomly selected. With the help of the Markov Chain series which are produced during the period while the control parameter T descending, we repeat "create new configuration—calculate the difference of the objective function—judge whether it accept the new configuration or not—accept (or discard) the new configuration" cycle until a satisfactory configuration to the problem is found, or some other termination criteria are met. In Fig. 3., the symbols are listed as follows:

i, j denote the feasible paths; l represents the number of configurations which have been produced in each temperature; k is used to label the temperature; T_k and L_k are the temperature and the permitted length of the k th Markov Chain, respectively. Rand [0,1] is a random value produced by a generator, which is uniformly distributed between 0 and 1. E is used as an energy function to evaluate the selected states (routes). By minimizing the E value, the τ value is minimized and the χ value is maximized. This means that a packet from source to destination is transmitted with a small delay and a high transmission success rate.

4 Performance Evaluation

A. Complexity analysis

We now analyze the computation complexity of SA_HR. In a general way, the hunting coverage of the proposed algorithm here is composed of $\sum_{\lambda=0}^{k} L_\lambda$ configurations which may spread in the neighborhood structure of $1-\sum_{\lambda=0}^{k} L_\lambda$ configuration(s). The iteration degree k and the length of the Markov Chains are given by the cooling schedule which will directly affect the quality of the final configurations. Controlled by the cooling schedule, SA_HR has computation complexity of $O(kL_m t(n))$ where L_m is the length of the longest Markov Chain and $t(n)$ is a polynomial function of the problem scale.

B. experiment results

We have performed SA_HR in different scenarios. Ad hoc networks with different number nodes (routes) are considered. We initialize the delay and transmission success rate of the valid link randomly and then E can be calculated.

Fig. 4. shows the Convergence time (CT) versus the length of Markov Chain. Here we initialize the pertinent parameters as follows: let $T_0=10$, $T_t \to 0$, respectively, and the control function is given as $T_{k+1}=\alpha T_k$ (let $\alpha=0.9$). In the different scenarios where only the numbers of existing nodes (routes) are different, each of the Markov Chains has been initialized the same length for simplification. As this figure shows, with the number of nodes (routes) increasing, the running time increases, but not so rapidly as exponent time. On the other hand, given the number of nodes (routes), we can see that the convergence time is proportional to the length of Markov Chain which chimed in with our analysis mentioned above.

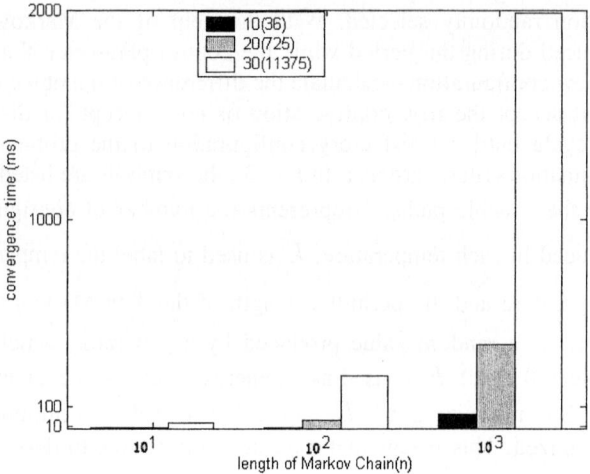

Fig. 4. Convergence time versus the length of Markov Chain

Fig. 5. depicts the convergence time versus the initialization temperature. Correspondingly to each different temperature, there is a different running time, but the relationship between these two parameters are not intimate, that is, it seems that the initialization temperature does not affect the Convergence time greatly.

Concludingly, when the scale of the network is relatively small, these needed timecan be tolerated in practice in order to meet the more rigorous QoS service request. The proposed method is an effective approximate algorithms showing good performance in seeking the (approximate) optimal configuration within a period of polynomial time.

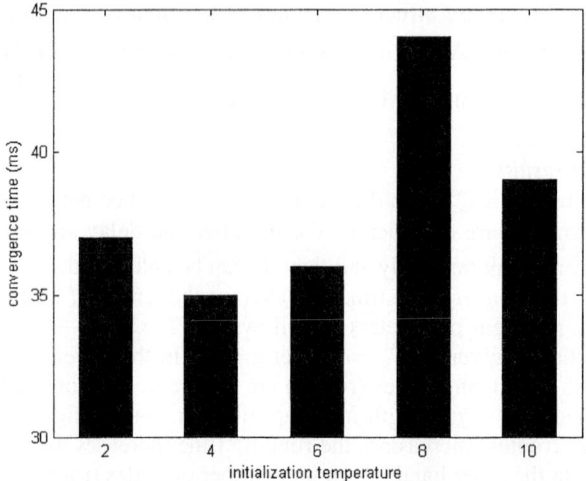

Fig. 5. Convergence time versus the initialization temperature (20 nodes (725 routes))

5 Conclusion

For the NP-completeness of multi-constrained QoSR Problem in networks especially in ad hoc networks, there is no efficient algorithm up to now. Inspired by the successful application of optimization computing methods—Simulated Annealing (SA) in other combinational optimization problems, a novel algorithm based on SA (SA_HR) is proposed to fulfill multi-constraint routing in ad hoc networks. We demonstrate that this novel heuristic routing algorithm is a promising algorithm for QoSR in ad hoc networks by theoretical analysis and experiments. In addition, this proposed algorithm has computation complexity of $O(kL_m t(n))$, which is proportional to the iteration degree k, the length of the longest Markov Chain L_m, and polynomial function of the problem scale $t(n)$, respectively.

Acknowledgement

The authors would like to thank the anonymous reviewers for their helpful comments, which were very helpful to this paper.

References

1. Y. Cui, J. P. Wu, K. Xu, et al.: Research on internetwork QoS routing algorithms: a survey. Chinese Journal of Software, vol. 13, no. 11. (2002) 2065-2075
2. Zheng Wang, jon Crowcroft.: Quality-of-service Routing for Supporting Multimedia Applications. IEEE Journal of Selected Areas in Communications, vol. 14, no. 7. (1996) 1228-1234
3. S. Chen.: Routing Support for Providing Guaranteed End-To-End Quality-Of- Service. Ph.D. thesis, Univ. of IL at Urbana-Champaign, http://cairo.cs.uiuc.edu/ papers/Cthesis. ps, (1999)
4. Dongwoo Kim, Chan-Ho Min, and Sehun Kim.: Routing With Transmit Power Assignment in Ad Hoc Mobile Networks. IEEE transactions on vehicular technology, vol. 53, no. 4. (2004) pp. 1215-1223
5. C. R. Lin and J.-S. Liu.: QoS routing in ad hoc wireless networks. IEEE J. Select. Areas Commun., vol. 17. (1999) pp. 1426–1438
6. C. R. Lin.: On-demand QoS routing in multihop mobile networks. in Proc. IEEE INFOCOM, 2001, pp. 1735–1744.
7. R. Sivakumar, P. Sinha, V. Bharghavan.: CEDAR: a Core-Extraction Distributed Ad-Hoc Routing Algorithm. IEEE Journal of Selected Areas in Communications, Vol.17, No.8. (1999) 1454-1465
8. S. Chen, K. Nahrstedt.: Distributed Quality-of-Service Routing in Ad-Hoc Networks. IEEE Journal of Selected Areas in Communications, Vol.17, No.8. (1999) 1-18
9. K. Wu, J. Harms.: QoS Support in Mobile Ad Hoc Networks. Crossing Boundaries - an interdisciplinary journal, Vol.1, No.1. (2001) 92-106
10. P. J. M. Van Laarhoven, E. H. L. Aarts.: Simulated annealing: Theory and applications. D. Reidel (1987)

Balancing HTTP Traffic Using Dynamically Updated Weights, an Implementation Approach

A. Karakos, D. Patsas, A. Bornea, and S. Kontogiannis

Democritus University of Thrace,
Dept. of Electrical & Computer Engineering, Xanthi, Greece
{karakos, dpats, ancutzab, skontog}@ee.duth.gr

Abstract. In this paper we present a load balancing application for HTTP traffic that uses dynamic weights. We introduce a load balancing policy based on two criteria: *"process time"* and *"network delay"*. The former describes Web servers ability to process a forthcoming request, while the latter tries to estimate network conditions. Calculation of the two criteria is periodically updated. A *Weighted Round Robin* algorithm was implemented using the two aforementioned metrics in order to dynamically estimate the balancing weights.

We confirm that the combination of the two criteria increases sensitivity and responsiveness of the application towards network conditions and therefore the performance of the whole load balancing system. Balancing decisions should not be only "load" or "connection" dependent, but also contention dependent.

1 Introduction

Web system scalability is defined as the ability to support large numbers of accesses and resources, while still providing adequate performance. Taxonomy of scale-up techniques, differentiates in cost effective hardware and software solutions. Furthermore, software scale-up is classified to operating system improvements, building more efficient Web servers and implementing different scheduling policies on requests. For example, to improve performance of the Apache Web server, Nanda et al. [21], have proposed several reduction techniques on the number of system calls in the typical I/O path. Zeus Web server [22] uses a small number of single-threaded I/O processes, that each one can handle many simultaneous connections. Queuing policies like: *Shortest Remaining Processing Time first*, proposed by Bansal et al. [9], improve system performance.

In addition to the previous scalable techniques, a distributed Web system comprised by several server nodes can also present scale-up enhancements. Distributed Web architectures are classified to: *Cluster-based Web systems (or Web-clusters)*, *Virtual Web clusters* and *Distributed Web systems*, as mentioned by Colajanni et al. [15]. Our Web system implementation uses the *Cluster based Web system* architecture and is comprised of the following structural parts; The *routing mechanisms* that redirect clients to appropriate target servers, the *dispatching algorithm* that selects the best suited target servers to respond to requests and the *executor* that supports the routing mechanisms and carries out the dispatching algorithm. From the basic structural parts of our system we focus on the selection process of the dispatching algorithm. We present the estimation criteria and mechanism in detail and evaluate the benefits of our algorithm towards performance and efficiency of the balancing system. This paper structure is as follows: In section 2 we examine several Cluster-based Web system techniques and mechanisms. In section 3 we analyze our implementation, the dispatching algorithm structure and weight calculation. In section 4 we present our scenario and discuss our implementation results.

2 Cluster-Based Web Systems

A cluster-based Web system is a collection of Web server machines, joined together as a single unity. These Web server machines are interconnected through broadband networks and oppose a single system image for the outside world. A cluster-based Web system is advertised with a site name and a virtual IP address (VIP). Figure 1, depicts a clustered Web system. The front end node of such a

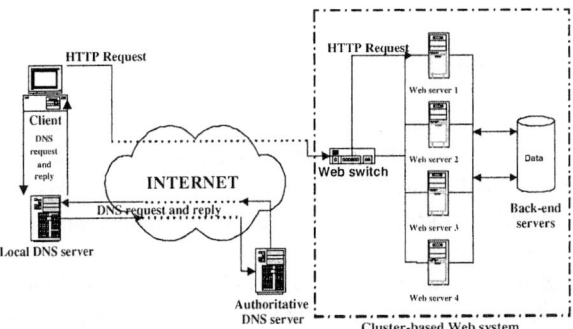

Fig. 1. The architecture of a cluster-based Web system

system, called *"Web switch"*. The Web switch receives all in-bound packets that clients send to the VIP address and routes them equivalently to the Web-server nodes.

2.1 Routing Mechanisms

There are two basic categories of Web switches that differentiate on the usage of "content-aware" (Layer-7 switch) or "content-blind" (Layer-3,4 switch) routing mechanisms.

Content-blind routing process is instantiated upon the arrival of the first "SYN" packet at the Web switch, indicating a new TCP connection. The routing techniques commonly used in a content-blind environment are the following:

1. Packet rewriting based on the IP Network Address Translation approach [10], [11], 2. Packet tunneling and 3. Packet forwarding (also referred as "MAC address translation"). These techniques may apply for both in-bound and out-bound HTTP traffic. De-centralized approaches like DPR [1] that use the aforementioned methods and do not depend on the existence of centralized control may apply. Statefull inspection per connection at the Web switch is also an option, but degrades significantly system performance. Moreover, Content blind load balancing is commonly implemented by providing mappings from a single host name to multiple IP addresses. This prequisites the existence of a DNS authority that will advertise IP addresses in a Round Robin fashion [12].

Content-aware routing examines HTTP requests at the application layer. It is less efficient than *Content-blind* routing, but can support more sophisticated dispatching policies. Some routing methods that are used to such environments are: 1. TCP proxy getaways (transparent or not), 2. TCP splicing [4] and for one way architectures only: 1. TCP connection hop [13] and 2. TCP hand-off [18]. The major advantage of Layer-7 routing mechanisms is the use of content-aware dispatching algorithms at the Web switch. On the other hand Layer-7 routing mechanisms introduce severe processing overhead at the Web switch to the extent of degrading Web cluster scalability, as mentioned by Levy et al. [5].

2.2 Dispatching Algorithms

The dispatching policy used at the Web switch, coordinates the whole clustered Web system. There are several alternatives of dispatching algorithms, such as: connection sharing, load sharing, centralized, distributed, static and dynamic algorithms. Dispatching algorithms are the heart of a load balancing system, but their tendency is not towards absolute stability, especially when we are dealing with a highly dynamic case. Perfect cluster work-balance is not the aim of a load balancing system, but user efficiency is. In this paper we will present a load balancing implementation that uses content blind routing and dynamic dispatching algorithms.

Static dispatching algorithms do not consider any kind of system state information. Typical examples of such algorithms are *Random* and *Round-Robin*. Although the round-robin DNS [12] works this way, it is quite different from *Round-Robin*; Per host DNS caching that usually takes effect, will lead the system to a definite state of load imbalance. In contrast round robin implementation in virtual server [19] is more superior to round-robin DNS due to fine scheduling per connection granularity. Furthermore, the static *Weighted Round Robin* (WRR) can be used as dispatching algorithm on Web servers with different processing capacities in order to introduce fairness. In this case, each server is assigned a static integer weight by the network administrator that corresponds to an index of its own capacity. More specifically: $w_i = \frac{C_i}{min(C)}$, where $min(C)$ is the minimum server capacity. The dispatching Round-Robin sequence will be generated according to the server weights. Moreover, a "fair WRR" implementation was proposed at [19] and implemented by [7], [20].

Dynamic dispatching algorithms take into account client-server state information in order to achieve more efficient load balancing. Client state algorithms categorize clients to client families using administrative criteria or hash functions that are applied to client IP addresses. Server state algorithms take into account information advertised by servers or agent look-ups, in order to investigate several server conditions. These conditions are important for the selection of the appropriate dispatching policy. Some the criteria commonly used are: "number of connections", "server uptime" or "ICMP reply time".

Both Random and Round-Robin policies can easily extend to treat web servers of heterogeneous capacities, as mentioned at [8] and [15]. For example if C_i is an indication of the server capacity, the relative server capacity can be defined as:

$$R_i = \frac{C_i}{max(C_1, ..C_i, ..C_k)}, \ 0 \leq R_i \leq 1 \quad (1)$$

For Random policy, different probabilities can be assigned to heterogeneous capacities. For Round-Robin policy, a random generated number p, where $0 \leq p \leq 1$, can be compared with relative server capacity in order to circulate to another server. That is:

$$S_{i+1} \leftarrow if \ p \leq R_i$$

else:

$$S_{i+2} \leftarrow Next$$

The *Weighted Least Connections* approach [20], [19], that is used also in many commercial systems [3], takes into account current server connections in order to assign new requests to the server with the least number of active connections. Similarly, the *Least Loaded* approach uses the WRR algorithm, with weights depended on the advertised snmp protocol load index. Moreover, the *Fastest Response Time* policy, assigns new connections to the Web servers that respond faster. The basic criteria used is the HTTP response time which equals to the amount of time that is needed for Web servers HTML objects to be downloaded by the Web switch. Finally, the dynamic *Geographically* distributed systems and algorithms place one ore more Web clusters in different strategic Internet regions and use HTTP redirection mechanisms trying to "divide and conquer" clients. Such an approach uses locational information accommodated with periodically updated Web server status advertisements [16].

The term "Load balancing" for Cisco describes also a functionality in a router that distributes packets across multiple links based on Layer-3 routing information. This means that the balancing process is either per destination or per packet and the scheduling policy depends on routing protocols (RIP, IGRP). Cisco's main representative is IGRP routing protocol [2]. IGRP is a protocol that allows balancing switches (getaways) to build up their routing tables based on broadcasting routing updates. It uses the generic Bellman-Ford algorithm, modified in three aspects: First, instead of a simple metric, a vector of metrics is used to characterize paths. Second, instead of picking a single path with the smallest metric, traffic is split among several paths (where metrics fall into a specified range). Third, several features are introduced for stability, like *split horizon*, *hold-down* and fix of *erroneous routes* [2]. Composite metric computation is achieved using the following equation. The best path is selected based on a composite metric:

$$CM = (K_1 \cdot BW + \frac{K_2 \cdot BW}{256 - Load} + K_3 \cdot Dc)(\frac{K_5}{Reliability + K_4}) \qquad (2)$$

where Dc equals to the sum of switching delay between interfaces, circuit delay (propagation delay of 1 bit) and transmission delay (for a 1500 bit broadcast packet). BW is the Bandwidth of the narrowest bandwidth segment (interface) of the path. Reliability is the fraction of packets that arrive undamaged at the destination. IGRP-based load balancers are fast, general purpose load balancers that use at some extent network information n order to score a "correct" balancing decision, but not in thorough extent (queueing delay). From the other hand being fast is not a precondition for efficiency. Being more selective and less fast might be more efficient than being less selective and fast. Summarizing, the drawbacks of Cisco IGRP balancing solutions are: 1) The use of broadcast as updates 2) high cost and 3) the fact that a generic network specific balancing might not be always efficient for specific application needs and from an application-specific load balancer additionally.

2.3 Web-Content Distribution

HTTP content distribution among Web systems is very important in terms of performance. Several techniques have been proposed in order to improve efficiency of the load balancing systems. The use of a distributed file system among the Web servers, like NFS, ensures the consistency of data. The major drawback of a distributed file-system is the multiple I/O requests between Web servers and the remote shared file-system. Multiple I/O requests degrade significantly system performance and constitute the NFS share as the system's weakest point.

Another commonly used technique for Web-content distribution, is the periodic file content replication method. With this technique each cluster node maintains a local copy of the Web documents. During periods of low traffic, replication agents update the contents of Web server nodes, while control agents supervise the replication process. The main drawback of this technique is that it introduces heavy disk and network overheads when data are highly volatile and frequently updated.

Finally, the most promising technique for content distribution is data partitioning. With Web data partitioning, each Web server maintains some part of the Web documents and is responsible only for its replication. Partitioning techniques increase scalability and offer significant reduction of the overhead due to periodic file replication. On the other hand partitioning may eventually lead to uneven distribution of Web document popularity and thus producing load imbalance.

3 Implementation

We implemented a load balancing application that tries to estimate dynamically both network conditions and Web systems capability, in order to make balancing decisions.

3.1 Introduction of the Criteria

Two basic criteria were used in order to calculate and adjust the Web servers weights; These are "*HTTP response time*" and "*network delay*". Criteria calculation is periodically updated. More specifically, the load balancer sends an HTTP request to each server and waits for a reply. The application estimates the time that the request was sent and the time that the reply was received. The time difference between request and reply, corresponds to the *HTTP response time*. If, however, the server does not respond within a fixed "timeout" interval, then the application marks it as being down and excludes it from receiving further requests (for another fixed period).

The *HTTP response time* metric is equal to the sum of the network propagation delay, network queuing delay and Web server processing delay:

$$http\_resp = Q_{Prop} + Q_n + Q_{Proc} \qquad (3)$$

Propagation delay is the time required for a signal to travel from one point to another and it is assumed equally divided among all Web servers. *Queuing delay* in a packet-switched network is the sum of all the delays encountered by a packet from the time of its insertion into the network until the delivery to its destination. *Processing delay* of a Web server is the time needed for a process to perform a request and construct an appropriate reply message.

In order to estimate network delay a "TCP SYN" packet is constructed, with source IP the IP address of the Web switch and destination IP address, each one of the Web servers. An appropriate timeout is set for "SYN" packet transmission, in order to avoid the application to be characterised as a malicious one. The application running at the Web switch, sends the packet and awaits for an acknowledgment. Then it calculates the inter-arrival time between request and reply. This inter-arrival time is an index of the propagation and queuing delay between the Web server and the Web switch; An approximation of the Web server *network delay*:

$$ndelay = Q_{Prop} + Q_n \qquad (4)$$

Network delay metric is a fair estimation of the propagation and queuing delay of the Web server. We assume a constant propagation delay for all Web servers and therefore we extract it from the previous equations. The time difference between *HTTP response time* and *network delay* metrics equals to the processing delay at the Web server. If the Web server does not respond within a "timeout" interval then the application marks the server as being down and excludes it from receiving any further requests (for a period of time). When the application starts, an initial static weight is distributed among the Web servers. This static weight is introduced by the administrator during installation of the application. The value of the initial weight must be analogous to the maximum *HTTP response time* (in seconds), that according to the administrator, satisfies his network perceptive needs.

3.2 Dispatching Algorithm Structure

The dispatching algorithm used by the application is as follows: If all the Web servers have *HTTP response time* greater than the initial criterion, then the weights are calculated using the product of process time for each server with the network delay (propagation plus queuing delay). The reason for using the product instead of the sum is to increase sensitivity of the load balancing system towards network conditions.

3.3 Weight Calculation

When the load balancing application starts, it parses the configuration file in order to collect information about the initial weights. These weights are introduced by the network administrator as a primer estimation of the system's balance point. Then a round-robin database is created where the load balancing criteria will be held. Monitoring pages with "real-time" graphs of Web servers criteria status are also created. The criteria used in the current application are: *HTTP response time*, *network delay* and static weights that were introduced initially by the administrator. At first, the "dynamically updated" criteria are not known and therefore the requests received by the load balancer will be periodically redirected to all servers.

After each time interval (period), defined at the configuration file, the metrics of *HTTP response time* and *network delay* for each server are updated. If the *HTTP response time* of all Web servers takes a value different than zero or at least one Web server has *HTTP response time* less than the initial criteria (introduced by the administrator), then the weights for each Web server are calculated using the following equation:

$$\mathbf{Weight}_i = \frac{\frac{1}{\text{http\_resp}_i}}{\sum_{i=1}^{n} \frac{1}{\text{http\_resp}_i}} \quad (5)$$

where $i = 1..n$ is the number of Web servers that load balance HTTP traffic. If there is at least one Web server with *HTTP response* time less than its initial criterion, then the weight calculation is performed according to equation (5). For those servers that their corresponding *HTTP response time* is greater than their initial criterion their weights are assigned to zero. However if there are no Web servers that have *HTTP response time* less than the static criteria, then the weights of all Web servers that are up and running are estimated based on equation (6):

$$\text{Weight}_i = \frac{\frac{1}{\text{ndelay}_i \cdot (\text{http\_resp}_i - \text{ndelay}_i)}}{\sum_{i=1}^{n} \frac{1}{\text{delay}_i \cdot (\text{http\_resp}_i - \text{ndelay}_i)}} \quad (6)$$

As it can be seen from (6), both *network delay* and *HTTP response time* are used for the weight estimation. In addition, if none of the servers are up for more than three time periods, then the administrator is notified. Based on the weight calculation, the server that will receive the first requests is found and WRR is implemented. Threaded Agents are called to modify the kernel "iptables" and redirect (NAT) the incoming requests.

4 Scenario Results and Discussion

Application output is consisted of two graphs per Web server that plot in "real-time" the variation of *HTTP response time* and *network delay* correspondingly. In an experimental scenario, we implemented the load balancing application on a Web switch that runs a Linux operating system. This Web switch supports two Web servers of equivalent processing power. The first Web server ("*blue-one - black*") sustains twice the number of HTTP requests (HTTP GET 250 Mbyte File) than the second Web server ("*red-one - light gray*"), for a period of twelve(12) hours. We measured both *HTTP response time* and *network delay* metrics (from the application output) and the dynamically updated weights. The time variations of the two metrics (using one minute update interval), are depicted in figure 2.

It is obvious from the graphs that the "*red*" Web server has less processing delay and therefore *HTTP response time*, than the "*blue*" one. This is because

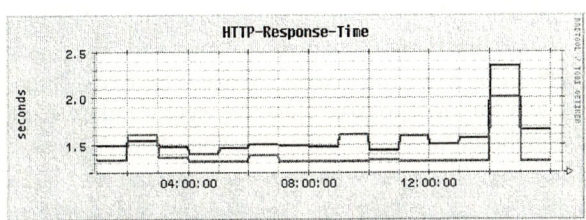

(a) HTTP response time variation over time

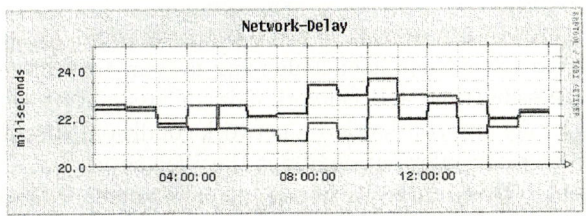

(b) Network delay variation over time

Fig. 2. Output results of our implementation using dynamically updated weights

it serves less requests. So the *"red"* Web server will be selected for handling HTTP traffic for almost the whole duration. What about congestion and network delay [17]? Changing the value of the initial criteria to less than one second, *network delay* metric will be taken into account and will be multiplied to *HTTP response time* metric, for the final weight calculation. This will increase the sensitivity of the dispatching algorithm towards congestive incidents, introducing queuing delay as important factor as the processing delay for the final Web server selection. So when *network delay* metric of the *"red"* Web server overcomes the value of the *"blue-one"* (congestive network conditions [17]), the *"blue"* Web server will also be as applicable as the *"red-one"*, (for handling part of the HTTP traffic), as depicted in figure 2(b) for the time interval 11h-2h. Furthermore, another information that can be extracted from the two figures is that both metrics converge in time, representing the actual meaning of load balancing.

TOS field in the IP header and IEFT differentiating services architecture [14], are commonly used by network administrators in order to provide QoS and traffic classification. This type of provision is mainly application performance dependent. In addition, HTTP traffic alone is in need for further classification so as to meet different application requirements. For instance, someone might be using HTTP protocol in order to download files from an HTTP service while someone else might be using HTTP protocol for an interactive application (like chat) from the same service. Moreover someone might require different types of service for a single HTTP flow. For instance he might need to perform a fast HTTP database query (non-congestive), while the HTTP database reply might not be that fast (congestive). As proposed by the authors of [6] TCP traffic can be differentiated according to the queueing delay that it may cause to a router to: congestive or non-congestive. This differentiation is based on the packet length and can be easily translated by a router without packet rewriting, marking or further calculation delays. In a higher level of abstraction, HTTP traffic can also be classified as congestive or non-congestive and handled appropriately by the Web switch. This can be performed with the use of an NCQ [6] or a *"metric of congestion"* that will be incorporated into the weight calculation formula. This capability will be included in the following version of our Web switch application (dispatcher).

5 Conclusions

It is important for an efficient load balancing system to take decisions both according to processing time and network delay. Classic WRR algorithms and dispatchers don't take into consideration network conditions. Usually, snmp protocol requests that carry information about the Web server's load and network connections are used to dynamically update dispatching algorithms and routing selections. This is a minor, since queueing and therefore network delay does not always follow the processing ability of the Web server.

It should also be taken into consideration that network queues that are responsible for handling in "general" TCP traffic, are not used only by HTTP traffic. Routers that stand in the way of a multi-server load balancing system might get congested by external factors and start dropping HTTP packets. Such congestive situations may cause unpredictable behavior to the performance and scalability of a cluster-based Web system. The introduction of network delay into the selection process of a load balancing system, will lead the system to a more operational equilibrium, improving both its performance and efficiency. Differentiation and classification among HTTP flows according to the application requirements, will take us a step further. Congestive or Non-congestive, hi or low priority HTTP traffic that will experience different types of service, may lead to better and more fair resource sharing.

References

1. A. Bestavros, M. Crovella, J. Liu and D. Martin. "Distributed Packet Rewriting and its Application to Scalable Web Server Architectures". *In Proc. of the 6th International Conference on Network Protocols ICNP*, Octomber 1998.
2. Cisco Company. "Cisco - An introduction to IGRP", 2004.
3. Cisco Inc. "Cisco Distributed Director", http://www.cisco.com/warp/public/cc/pd/cxsr/dd/, 2004.
4. D. Maltz and P. Bhagwat. "Application layer proxy performance using TCP splice". Technical report, IBM T.J. Watson Research Center, 1998.
5. J. Song, E. Levy-Abegnoli and D. Dias. "Design alternatives for scalable Web server accelerators". *In Proc. of the 2000 IEEE International Symposium on Performance Analysis of Systems and Software*, April 2000.
6. L. Mamatas and V. Tsaoussidis. "A new approach to Service Differentiation: Non-Congestive Queueing". Technical report, Democritus University of Thrace, 2004.
7. Linux VS Team. "Linux Virtual Server Implementation", 2002.
8. M. Colajanni, P. Yu and M. D. Dias. "Analysis of task assignment policies in scalable distributed Web-server systems". *IEEE Trans. on Parallel Distributed Systems*, June 1998.
9. N. Bansal and M. Harchol Balter. "Analysis of SRPT scheduling: Investigating unfairness". *In Proc. of the 2001 ACM/IFIP Joint International Conference on Measurement and Modeling of Computer Systems*, March 2001.
10. P. Srisuresh and D. Gan. "Load sharing using IP Network Address Translation", RFC 2391, 1999.
11. P. Srisuresh and K. Egevang. "Traditional IP Network Address Translation", RFC 3022, 2001.
12. R. J. Schemers. "ldnamed: A load Balancing Name Server in Perl". *In Proc. of the 9th Systems Administration Conference*, 1995.
13. RESONATE Team,. "TCP Connection Hop". *White paper*, April 2001.
14. S. Blake, D. Black, M. Carlson, E. Davies et al. "An Architecture for Differentiated Service", RFC 2475, December 1998.
15. V. Cardellini, E. Casalicchio, M. Colajanni and P. Yu. "The State of the Art in Locally Distributed Web-Server Systems". *ACM Computing Surveys*, Vol. 34 No. 2:263–311, June 2002.
16. V. Cardellini, M. Colajanni, P.S. Yu. "Geographic load balancing for scalable distributed Web systems". *In Proc. of the 8th International Symposium on Modeling, Analysis and Simulation of Computer and Telecommunication Systems*, 2000.

17. V. Jacobson. "Congestion Avoidance and Control". *In Proc. of the ACM SIGCOMM '88*, August 1988.
18. V. Pai, M. Aron, G. Banga, M. Svendsen, P. Druschel, W. Zwaenepoel and E Nahum. "Locality-aware request distribution in cluster-based network servers". *In Proc. of the 8th ACM Conference on Architectural Support fro Programming Languages and Operating Systems*, Octomber 1998.
19. W. Zhang. "Linux Server Clusters for Scalable Network Services". *Free Software Symposim, China*, 2002.
20. W. Zhang and W. Zhang. "Linux Virtual Server Clusters". *Linux Magazine*, November 2003.
21. Y. Hu, A. Nanda and Q. Yang. "Measurement, analysis and performance improvement of Apache Web server". *In Proc. of the 18th IEEE International Performance, Computing and Communications Conference*, February 1999.
22. Zeus Development Team. "Zeus Web Server", http://www.zeus.com.uk. Technical report, Zeus Technology, 2002.

A Review of Microsoft Products, Strategy and Technologies[*]

Fotis Draganidis

DPE Group, Microsoft Hellas, Kifisias Ave 221, 151 24 Marousi, Greece
`t-fotisd@microsoft.com`

Abstract. Recent surveys for e-business future in western European countries, show that there is a huge growth potential as the total amount spent on e-business (B2B and B2C) is forecasted to rise from 150BUSD in 2004 to 650BUSD in 2008 and web buyers will rise from 67M in 2004 to 94M in 2008 [source, IDC 2004]. Interestingly, Greece seems to have an even greater potential with a forecast of increasing e-business transactions from 2.861mUSD in 2004 to 13000mUSD in 2008 [source, IDC 2004]. As a result, all major software vendors are working on strategy, products and technologies in order to obtain the pole position in business-to-business and business-to-consumer commerce.

This paper discusses the e-business strategy, products and technologies of a major software vendor, which is expected to have a key role in this area during the next years, Microsoft Corporation. Firstly, an architectural and functions' overview of Microsoft e-business servers, namely "Biztalk Server", "Content Management Server" and "Commerce Server" is provided. Secondly, "Jupiter", the codename for Microsoft's e-business roadmap and vision is presented and discussed. With "Jupiter" Microsoft aims at reducing IT complexity and connect people, processes and information through an integrated, standards-based e-business infrastructure. Finally, the underlying technologies of the abovementioned products and strategy, such as XML, Web services, SOAP, .NET, are presented, together with the latest advancements in e-business facilitator standards, such as web services interoperability standards.

---

[*] Invited paper.

Author Index

Adamou, Christodoulos 641
Akoumianakis, Demosthenes 491
Alexandridis, Georgios C. 651
Alexandridou, Anastasia 426
Alexandrou, D. 469
Ampeliotis, Dimitris 765
Ananiadou, Sophia 382
Anastopoulos, Nikos 600
Antoniou, Grigoris 404
Athanasaki, Evangelia 600
Avaritsiotis, I.N. 611
Azariadis, Philip 296

Bagis, Aytekin 776
Banerjee, A. 36
Bang, Young-Cheol 112
Barrasa, M. Inmaculada 457
Bassiliades, Nick 404
Bekos, M.A. 80
Bellas, Nikolaos 633
Belsis, Meletis A. 684
Berberidis, Christos 426
Berberidis, Kostas 765
Bogárdi-Mészöly, Ágnes 223
Bornea, A. 858
Borotis, Spiros A. 559
Boulougoura, M. 735
Bouras, A. 469

Caballero-Gil, Pino 695
Charaf, Hassan 223, 393
Charalambous, Maria 415
Chatziantoniou, Damianos 672
Chazapis, Antony 234
Choo, Hyunseung 112, 808
Christopoulos, D. 155
Christopoulou, Eleni 256
Christou, K. 735
Chung, Min Young 839
Ciftlikli, Cebrail 776

Dagdilelis, Vassilios 502
Demetriadis, Stavros N. 523
Develi, Ibrahim 776
Dimitriou, G. 611

Dimitriou, Georgios 622
Dimopoulos, Vassilis 661
Diplaris, Sotiris 448
Doukidis, Georgios 571
Draganidis, Fotis 869
Drosos, Nicolas 256
Drossos, Dimitris 278

Economou, Daphne 188
Emiris, Ioannis Z. 90

Feng, Guangzeng 849
Ferri, Fernando 317
Ford, James 437
Fotakis, Dimitris 47
Fotopoulos, V. 705
Fragoudakis, Christodoulos 145
Fúster-Sabater, Amparo 695

Gaitatzes, A. 155
Gavalas, Damianos 820
Giaglis, George M. 199, 278
Gouvas, P. 469
Grifoni, Patrizia 317
Gritzalis, Stefanos 684
Gudas, Saulius 480
Gunopulos, D. 36

Han, SeungJo 828
Hatzakis, A. 469
Hatzigeorgiou, Artemis G. 457
Hong, Kwang-Seok 286
Houstis, Catherine 360
Huang, Heng 437

Ilias, A. 705
Ioannidis, Stratis 57

Jho, Gunu 808

Kagani, Katerina 502
Kalogeraki, V. 36
Kameas, Achilles 256
Karagiannidis, Charalampos 534
Karakos, A. 858
Karanikas, Haralampos 25
Karatza, Helen D. 211

Author Index

Katakis, Ioannis   338
Katsaros, Dimitrios   267
Katsavounidis, Ioannis   633
Katsikas, Sokratis K.   548, 787
Katsikis, Georgios   513
Kaufmann, M.   80
Kikiras, P.K.   611
Kim, Duk-Gyoo   757
Kim, Jin-Dong   382
Kim, JongWoo   828
Kim, Moonseong   112, 808
Kodogiannis, V.S.   735
Konofaos, N.   582
Konstantopoulos, Charalampos   820
Kontogiannis, S.   858
Kontogiannis, Spyros   101
Kontopoulos, Efstratios   404
Kopanakis, Ioannis   25
Kotsiantis, S.B.   328
Kotsifakos, Evangelos   14
Koukopoulos, D.K.   166
Kourtis, Kornilios   600
Kouskouvelis, Ilias   371
Kowalczyk, Wojtek   349
Koziri, Maria   633
Koziris, Nectarios   234, 600

Lee, Bo-Hyung   839
Lee, Seung-Ik   757
Lee, Tae-Jin   839
Lengyel, László   393
Leros, Assimakis K.   787
Levendovszky, Tihamér   223, 393
Liu, Lianggui   849
Lopez, Javier   548

Magiorkinis, G.   469
Makedon, Fillia S.   437
Mamalis, Basilis   820
Manolopoulos, Yannis   1, 267
Margaritis, Konstantinos G.   245
Markou, Euripides   145
Mavromoustakis, Constandinos X.   211
Mavroudkis, Thomas   25
McNaught, John   382
Megraw, Molly   457
Mengoudis, Naoum   513
Mentzas, G.   469
Michailidis, Panagiotis D.   245

Micha, Katy   188
Mitkas, Pericles A.   448
Mitra, A.   36

Najjar, W.   36
Nanopoulos, Alexandros   1, 513
Nikolaidis, Nikos   716
Nikolaou, Christos   545
Nikolopoulos, Stavros D.   68
Nomikos, Christos   57
Ntalaperas, D.   582
Ntoutsi, Irene   14

Ohta, Tomoko   382

Pachoulakis, Ioannis   491
Pagourtzis, Aris   57
Palios, Leonidas   68
Panagis, Y.   134
Pantziou, Grammati   820
Papadopoulos, Apostolos N.   1
Papadopoulos, Giorgos   661
Papadopoulos, Pantelis M.   523
Papaioannou, Georgios   155, 307
Pappas, Stylianos Sp.   787
Paraskevis, D.   469
Park, JongAn   828
Park, Jongho   839
Pateli, Adamantia G.   199
Patsas, D.   858
Pearlman, Justin D.   437
Pehlivanides, George   177
Pelekis, Nikos   25
Pernul, Günther   548
Pintelas, P.E.   328
Pitas, Ioannis   716, 725
Pitikakis, Marios   360
Pitkänen, Esa   123
Pnevmatikatos, Dionisios   661
Polychronopoulos, Constantine   622
Potika, K.   80
Poulymenakou, Angeliki K.   559
Pramatari, Katerina   571
Pyun, JaeYoung   828

Rafanelli, Maurizio   317
Rantanen, Ari   123
Rousu, Juho   123

Sairamesh, Jakka 545
Samoladas, Ioannis 513
Sapidis, Nickolas 296
Sartatzemi, Maya 502
Serpanos, Dimitrios N. 651
Sethupathy, Praveen 457
Sfakianakis, Yiannis 349
Shin, Jeong-Hoon 286
Simitsis, Alkis 684
Sioutas, S. 134
Skersys, Tomas 480
Skodras, A.N. 705
Solachidis, V. 725
Spinellis, Diomidis D. 199, 672
Spirakis, Paul 101
Stamatakis, Alexandros 415
Stamelos, Ioannis 513
Stamoulis, G.I. 611, 633
Stavrou, Kyriakos 589
Stefanidis, Vasilis 245
Stolze, Markus 545
Symvonis A. 80
Szitás, Zoltán 223

Tateishi, Yuka 382
Theodoridis, E. 134
Theodoridis, Yannis 14
Theodoropoulos, K. 582
Titsias, Michalis K. 746
Trancoso, Pedro 415, 589, 641
Tsadiras, Athanasios K. 371
Tsakalidis, A. 134, 582
Tsekouras, G.E. 328

Tsoukalas, Ioannis A. 523
Tsoumakas, Grigorios 338, 448
Tsujii, Jun'ichi 382
Tsuruoka, Yoshimasa 382
Tzanis, George 426

Ukkonen, Esko 123

Vaidya, Binod 828
Vandierendonck, Hans 641
Vasilakis, George 360
Vassiliadis, B. 705
Vavalis, Manolis 360
Vavoula, Giasemi 534
Vlachos, Vasileios 672
Vlahavas, Ioannis 338, 404, 426, 448
Vlassis, Nikos 349
Vouzi, Vassiliki 672
Voyiatzis, Artemios G. 651
Vretos, N. 725

Wadge, E. 735
Williams, Christopher K.I. 746

Xiong, Fei 437

Yoon, Hyung-Wook 839

Zachos, Stathis 57, 145
Zeinalipour-Yazti, D. 36
Zervoudakis, Kyriakos 90
Zhang, Lianyi 798
Zheng, Chongxun 798

Lecture Notes in Computer Science

For information about Vols. 1–3661

please contact your bookseller or Springer

Vol. 3781: S.Z. Li, Z. Sun, T. Tan, S. Pankanti, G. Chollet, D. Zhang (Eds.), Advances in Biometric Person Authentication. XI, 250 pages. 2005.

Vol. 3766: N. Sebe, M.S. Lew, T.S. Huang (Eds.), Computer Vision in Human-Computer Interaction. X, 231 pages. 2005.

Vol. 3765: Y. Liu, T. Jiang, C. Zhang (Eds.), Computer Vision for Biomedical Image Applications. X, 563 pages. 2005.

Vol. 3752: N. Paragios, O. Faugeras, T. Chan, C. Schnoerr (Eds.), Variational, Geometric, and Level Set Methods in Computer Vision. XI, 369 pages. 2005.

Vol. 3751: T. Magedanz, E.R. M. Madeira, P. Dini (Eds.), Operations and Management in IP-Based Networks. X, 213 pages. 2005.

Vol. 3750: J.S. Duncan, G. Gerig (Eds.), Medical Image Computing and Computer-Assisted Intervention – MICCAI 2005, Part II. XL, 1018 pages. 2005.

Vol. 3749: J.S. Duncan, G. Gerig (Eds.), Medical Image Computing and Computer-Assisted Intervention – MICCAI 2005, Part I. XXXIX, 942 pages. 2005.

Vol. 3747: C.A. Maziero, J.G. Silva, A.M.S. Andrade, F.M.d. Assis Silva (Eds.), Dependable Computing. XV, 267 pages. 2005.

Vol. 3746: P. Bozanis, E.N. Houstis (Eds.), Advances in Informatics. XIX, 873 pages. 2005.

Vol. 3744: T. Magedanz, A. Karmouch, S. Pierre, I. Venieris (Eds.), Mobility Aware Technologies and Applications. XIV, 418 pages. 2005.

Vol. 3739: W. Fan, Z. Wu, J. Yang (Eds.), Advances in Web-Age Information Management. XXIV, 930 pages. 2005.

Vol. 3738: V.R. Syrotiuk, E. Chávez (Eds.), Ad-Hoc, Mobile, and Wireless Networks. XI, 360 pages. 2005.

Vol. 3735: A. Hoffmann, H. Motoda, T. Scheffer (Eds.), Discovery Science. XVI, 400 pages. 2005. (Subseries LNAI).

Vol. 3734: S. Jain, H.U. Simon, E. Tomita (Eds.), Algorithmic Learning Theory. XII, 490 pages. 2005. (Subseries LNAI).

Vol. 3733: P. Yolum, T. Güngör, F. Gürgen, C. Özturan (Eds.), Computer and Information Sciences - ISCIS 2005. XXI, 973 pages. 2005.

Vol. 3731: F. Wang (Ed.), Formal Techniques for Networked and Distributed Systems - FORTE 2005. XII, 558 pages. 2005.

Vol. 3728: V. Paliouras, J. Vounckx, D. Verkest (Eds.), Integrated Circuit and System Design. XV, 753 pages. 2005.

Vol. 3726: L.T. Yang, O.F. Rana, B. Di Martino, J. Dongarra (Eds.), High Performance Computing and Communcations. XXVI, 1116 pages. 2005.

Vol. 3725: D. Borrione, W. Paul (Eds.), Correct Hardware Design and Verification Methods. XII, 412 pages. 2005.

Vol. 3724: P. Fraigniaud (Ed.), Distributed Computing. XIV, 520 pages. 2005.

Vol. 3723: W. Zhao, S. Gong, X. Tang (Eds.), Analysis and Modelling of Faces and Gestures. XI, 4234 pages. 2005.

Vol. 3722: D. Van Hung, M. Wirsing (Eds.), Theoretical Aspects of Computing – ICTAC 2005. XIV, 614 pages. 2005.

Vol. 3721: A. Jorge, L. Torgo, P. Brazdil, R. Camacho, J. Gama (Eds.), Knowledge Discovery in Databases: PKDD 2005. XXIII, 719 pages. 2005. (Subseries LNAI).

Vol. 3720: J. Gama, R. Camacho, P. Brazdil, A. Jorge, L. Torgo (Eds.), Machine Learning: ECML 2005. XXIII, 769 pages. 2005. (Subseries LNAI).

Vol. 3719: M. Hobbs, A.M. Goscinski, W. Zhou (Eds.), Distributed and Parallel Computing. XI, 448 pages. 2005.

Vol. 3718: V.G. Ganzha, E.W. Mayr, E.V. Vorozhtsov (Eds.), Computer Algebra in Scientific Computing. XII, 502 pages. 2005.

Vol. 3717: B. Gramlich (Ed.), Frontiers of Combining Systems. X, 321 pages. 2005. (Subseries LNAI).

Vol. 3716: L. Delcambre, C. Kop, H.C. Mayr, J. Mylopoulos, O. Pastor (Eds.), Conceptual Modeling – ER 2005. XVI, 498 pages. 2005.

Vol. 3715: E. Dawson, S. Vaudenay (Eds.), Progress in Cryptology – Mycrypt 2005. XI, 329 pages. 2005.

Vol. 3714: H. Obbink, K. Pohl (Eds.), Software Product Lines. XIII, 235 pages. 2005.

Vol. 3713: L. Briand, C. Williams (Eds.), Model Driven Engineering Languages and Systems. XV, 722 pages. 2005.

Vol. 3712: R. Reussner, J. Mayer, J.A. Stafford, S. Overhage, S. Becker, P.J. Schroeder (Eds.), Quality of Software Architectures and Software Quality. XIII, 289 pages. 2005.

Vol. 3711: F. Kishino, Y. Kitamura, H. Kato, N. Nagata (Eds.), Entertainment Computing - ICEC 2005. XXIV, 540 pages. 2005.

Vol. 3710: M. Barni, I. Cox, T. Kalker, H.J. Kim (Eds.), Digital Watermarking. XII, 485 pages. 2005.

Vol. 3709: P. van Beek (Ed.), Principles and Practice of Constraint Programming - CP 2005. XX, 887 pages. 2005.

Vol. 3708: J. Blanc-Talon, W. Philips, D. Popescu, P. Scheunders (Eds.), Advanced Concepts for Intelligent Vision Systems. XXII, 725 pages. 2005.

Vol. 3707: D.A. Peled, Y.-K. Tsay (Eds.), Automated Technology for Verification and Analysis. XII, 506 pages. 2005.

Vol. 3706: H. Fuks, S. Lukosch, A.C. Salgado (Eds.), Groupware: Design, Implementation, and Use. XII, 378 pages. 2005.

Vol. 3704: M. De Gregorio, V. Di Maio, M. Frucci, C. Musio (Eds.), Brain, Vision, and Artificial Intelligence. XV, 556 pages. 2005.

Vol. 3703: F. Fages, S. Soliman (Eds.), Principles and Practice of Semantic Web Reasoning. VIII, 163 pages. 2005.

Vol. 3702: B. Beckert (Ed.), Automated Reasoning with Analytic Tableaux and Related Methods. XIII, 343 pages. 2005. (Subseries LNAI).

Vol. 3701: M. Coppo, E. Lodi, G. M. Pinna (Eds.), Theoretical Computer Science. XI, 411 pages. 2005.

Vol. 3699: C.S. Calude, M.J. Dinneen, G. Păun, M. J. Pérez-Jiménez, G. Rozenberg (Eds.), Unconventional Computation. XI, 267 pages. 2005.

Vol. 3698: U. Furbach (Ed.), KI 2005: Advances in Artificial Intelligence. XIII, 409 pages. 2005. (Subseries LNAI).

Vol. 3697: W. Duch, J. Kacprzyk, E. Oja, S. Zadrożny (Eds.), Artificial Neural Networks: Formal Models and Their Applications – ICANN 2005, Part II. XXXII, 1045 pages. 2005.

Vol. 3696: W. Duch, J. Kacprzyk, E. Oja, S. Zadrożny (Eds.), Artificial Neural Networks: Biological Inspirations – ICANN 2005, Part I. XXXI, 703 pages. 2005.

Vol. 3695: M.R. Berthold, R. Glen, K. Diederichs, O. Kohlbacher, I. Fischer (Eds.), Computational Life Sciences. XI, 277 pages. 2005. (Subseries LNBI).

Vol. 3694: M. Malek, E. Nett, N. Suri (Eds.), Service Availability. VIII, 213 pages. 2005.

Vol. 3693: A.G. Cohn, D.M. Mark (Eds.), Spatial Information Theory. XII, 493 pages. 2005.

Vol. 3692: R. Casadio, G. Myers (Eds.), Algorithms in Bioinformatics. X, 436 pages. 2005. (Subseries LNBI).

Vol. 3691: A. Gagalowicz, W. Philips (Eds.), Computer Analysis of Images and Patterns. XIX, 865 pages. 2005.

Vol. 3690: M. Pěchouček, P. Petta, L.Z. Varga (Eds.), Multi-Agent Systems and Applications IV. XVII, 667 pages. 2005. (Subseries LNAI).

Vol. 3689: G.G. Lee, A. Yamada, H. Meng, S.H. Myaeng (Eds.), Information Retrieval Technology. XVII, 735 pages. 2005.

Vol. 3688: R. Winther, B.A. Gran, G. Dahll (Eds.), Computer Safety, Reliability, and Security. XI, 405 pages. 2005.

Vol. 3687: S. Singh, M. Singh, C. Apte, P. Perner (Eds.), Pattern Recognition and Image Analysis, Part II. XXV, 809 pages. 2005.

Vol. 3686: S. Singh, M. Singh, C. Apte, P. Perner (Eds.), Pattern Recognition and Data Mining, Part I. XXVI, 689 pages. 2005.

Vol. 3685: V. Gorodetsky, I. Kotenko, V. Skormin (Eds.), Computer Network Security. XIV, 480 pages. 2005.

Vol. 3684: R. Khosla, R.J. Howlett, L.C. Jain (Eds.), Knowledge-Based Intelligent Information and Engineering Systems, Part IV. LXXIX, 933 pages. 2005. (Subseries LNAI).

Vol. 3683: R. Khosla, R.J. Howlett, L.C. Jain (Eds.), Knowledge-Based Intelligent Information and Engineering Systems, Part III. LXXX, 1397 pages. 2005. (Subseries LNAI).

Vol. 3682: R. Khosla, R.J. Howlett, L.C. Jain (Eds.), Knowledge-Based Intelligent Information and Engineering Systems, Part II. LXXIX, 1371 pages. 2005. (Subseries LNAI).

Vol. 3681: R. Khosla, R.J. Howlett, L.C. Jain (Eds.), Knowledge-Based Intelligent Information and Engineering Systems, Part I. LXXX, 1319 pages. 2005. (Subseries LNAI).

Vol. 3680: C. Priami, A. Zelikovsky (Eds.), Transactions on Computational Systems Biology II. IX, 153 pages. 2005. (Subseries LNBI).

Vol. 3679: S.d.C. di Vimercati, P. Syverson, D. Gollmann (Eds.), Computer Security – ESORICS 2005. XI, 509 pages. 2005.

Vol. 3678: A. McLysaght, D.H. Huson (Eds.), Comparative Genomics. VIII, 167 pages. 2005. (Subseries LNBI).

Vol. 3677: J. Dittmann, S. Katzenbeisser, A. Uhl (Eds.), Communications and Multimedia Security. XIII, 360 pages. 2005.

Vol. 3676: R. Glück, M. Lowry (Eds.), Generative Programming and Component Engineering. XI, 448 pages. 2005.

Vol. 3675: Y. Luo (Ed.), Cooperative Design, Visualization, and Engineering. XI, 264 pages. 2005.

Vol. 3674: W. Jonker, M. Petković (Eds.), Secure Data Management. X, 241 pages. 2005.

Vol. 3673: S. Bandini, S. Manzoni (Eds.), AI*IA 2005: Advances in Artificial Intelligence. XIV, 614 pages. 2005. (Subseries LNAI).

Vol. 3672: C. Hankin, I. Siveroni (Eds.), Static Analysis. X, 369 pages. 2005.

Vol. 3671: S. Bressan, S. Ceri, E. Hunt, Z.G. Ives, Z. Bellahsène, M. Rys, R. Unland (Eds.), Database and XML Technologies. X, 239 pages. 2005.

Vol. 3670: M. Bravetti, L. Kloul, G. Zavattaro (Eds.), Formal Techniques for Computer Systems and Business Processes. XIII, 349 pages. 2005.

Vol. 3669: G.S. Brodal, S. Leonardi (Eds.), Algorithms – ESA 2005. XVIII, 901 pages. 2005.

Vol. 3668: M. Gabbrielli, G. Gupta (Eds.), Logic Programming. XIV, 454 pages. 2005.

Vol. 3666: B.D. Martino, D. Kranzlmüller, J. Dongarra (Eds.), Recent Advances in Parallel Virtual Machine and Message Passing Interface. XVII, 546 pages. 2005.

Vol. 3665: K. S. Candan, A. Celentano (Eds.), Advances in Multimedia Information Systems. X, 221 pages. 2005.

Vol. 3664: C. Türker, M. Agosti, H.-J. Schek (Eds.), Peer-to-Peer, Grid, and Service-Orientation in Digital Library Architectures. X, 261 pages. 2005.

Vol. 3663: W.G. Kropatsch, R. Sablatnig, A. Hanbury (Eds.), Pattern Recognition. XIV, 512 pages. 2005.

Vol. 3662: C. Baral, G. Greco, N. Leone, G. Terracina (Eds.), Logic Programming and Nonmonotonic Reasoning. XIII, 454 pages. 2005. (Subseries LNAI).